Access Your Free Subscription to *N.C. Crimes Online*

The purchase of this supplement includes FREE access to the online version of *N.C. Crimes*. The online version offers the following features:

- Updated content through December 2020
- Keyword searching
- Linking to cross-references
- Printable pages
- Accessibility anywhere your electronic device can connect to the Internet
- Collapsible and expandable statutes

First-Time Registrants

Follow the instructions below to begin using the online version of *N.C. Crimes*:

- Visit **bit.ly/nccrimesonline2020**
- Use the registration code **nccrimesonline2021-r95876**
- Enter your information to complete your account profile
- You will receive a confirmation email ensuring your access has been properly authenticated

Returning Users*

Follow the instructions below to update and renew your access to the online version:

- Log into your *N.C. Crimes Online* account
- Go to the "Account Updates" box on the right-hand side of the page
- Click the link at "Start Here" to update your information
- Click "Edit" **above** your profile information
- Replace your current registration code with **nccrimesonline2021-r95876**
- Click "Save" at the bottom of the page

* Users who have not created or renewed an account after March 2018 may need to follow the "First-Time Registrants" steps.

This is a free subscription. You will not be charged.

For questions about your online subscription, contact **sales@sog.unc.edu** or call **919.966-5381**.

For information about other publications and resources from the School of Government, visit **sog.unc.edu**.

2020 Cumulative
Supplement to
NORTH CAROLINA

CRIMES

A Guidebook on the Elements of Crime

Seventh Edition

Jessica Smith
James M. Markham

UNC | SCHOOL OF GOVERNMENT

The School of Government at the University of North Carolina at Chapel Hill works to improve the lives of North Carolinians by engaging in practical scholarship that helps public officials and citizens understand and improve state and local government. Established in 1931 as the Institute of Government, the School provides educational, advisory, and research services for state and local governments. The School of Government is also home to a nationally ranked Master of Public Administration program, the North Carolina Judicial College, and specialized centers focused on community and economic development, information technology, and environmental finance.

As the largest university-based local government training, advisory, and research organization in the United States, the School of Government offers up to 200 courses, webinars, and specialized conferences for more than 12,000 public officials each year. In addition, faculty members annually publish approximately 50 books, manuals, reports, articles, bulletins, and other print and online content related to state and local government. The School also produces the *Daily Bulletin Online* each day the General Assembly is in session, reporting on activities for members of the legislature and others who need to follow the course of legislation.

Operating support for the School of Government's programs and activities comes from many sources, including state appropriations, local government membership dues, private contributions, publication sales, course fees, and service contracts.

Visit sog.unc.edu or call 919.966.5381 for more information on the School's courses, publications, programs, and services.

Printed in the United States of America

27 26 25 24 23 4 5 6 7 8

ISBN 978-1-64238-018-7

Contents

Introduction

This book supplements NORTH CAROLINA CRIMES: A GUIDEBOOK ON THE ELEMENTS OF CRIME (UNC School of Government, 7th ed. 2012). It includes cases decided and legislation enacted through December 31, 2020. Chapter and page numbers used throughout this supplement refer to chapters and pages in the main edition.

Due to the very large body of case law regarding charging language that threatened to overwhelm the book, all notes on that topic have been deleted from this supplement. Please consult the following resources for more information. For a detailed paper on point, see Jessica Smith, *The Criminal Indictment: Fatal Defect, Fatal Variance, and Amendment*, ADMINISTRATION OF JUSTICE BULLETIN NO. 2008/03, www.sog.unc.edu/publications/bulletins/criminal-indictment-fatal-defect-fatal-variance-and-amendment. For all relevant cases decided since 2008, see JESSICA SMITH, SMITH'S CRIMINAL CASE COMPENDIUM, www.sog.unc.edu/sccc (under heading "Criminal Procedure," subheading "Indictment & Pleading Issues").

1
States of Mind

General Intent and Specific Intent (page 4)

Delete the second sentence of the first paragraph of this section and replace it with the following:

> Examples of general intent crimes include assault on a law enforcement officer in violation of G.S. 14-33(c)(4), State v. Mylett, 253 N.C. App. 198, 209 (2017); assault with a firearm on a law enforcement officer, State v. Childers, 154 N.C. App. 375, 382 (2002); and shooting into occupied property, State v. Byrd, 132 N.C. App. 220, 222 (1999); State v. Maldonado, 241 N.C. App. 370, 374 (2015); State v. Bryant, 244 N.C. App. 102, 109 (2015).

Add the following at the end of the third paragraph:

> ; *Maldonado*, 241 N.C. App. at 373–74 (same; shooting into occupied property).

Wantonly (page 7)

> For another case supporting the statement in this section that this mental state is essentially the same as willfully, see *State v. Hunt*, 250 N.C. App. 238, 243 (2016).

Criminal Negligence (page 7)

Add the following at the end of this section:

> In assault cases, the State is required to allege a theory of criminal negligence. State v. Stevens, 228 N.C. App. 352, 357 (2013) (error in an assault on a child under 12 case where criminal negligence was not alleged in the indictment).

Strict Liability (page 9)

As a result of 2015 legislation, S.L. 2015-181, the first three bullets in this section should read as follows:

- G.S. 14-27.24 (first-degree statutory rape). State v. Anthony, 351 N.C. 611, 616 (2000) (noting that first-degree statutory rape is a strict liability crime); State v. Rose, 312 N.C. 441, 445 (1984) (noting that for first-degree statutory rape, mistake regarding the victim's age is no defense); State v. Ainsworth, 109 N.C. App. 136, 145 (1993) ("Criminal mens rea is not an element of statutory rape.").
- G.S. 14-27.29 (first-degree statutory sexual offense). *Anthony*, 351 N.C. at 616–18 (construing former G.S. 14-27.4 and noting that consent is not a defense to statutory sexual offense).
- G.S. 14-27.25, -27.30 (respectively, statutory rape and sexual offense of a person 15 years old or younger). *Anthony*, 351 N.C. at 616–18 (construing former G.S. 14-27.7A (statutory rape or sexual offense of a person who is 13, 14, or 15 years old) and holding that consent is not a defense under that statute); State v. Browning, 177 N.C. App. 487, 491 (2006) ("Statutory rape under [former G.S.] 14-27.7A is a strict liability crime."); State v. Sines, 158 N.C. App. 79, 84 (2003) ("Statutory sexual offense and statutory rape are categorized as strict liability crimes.").

Delete the fourth bullet in this section.

Add the following to the bulleted list in this section:

- G.S. 90-95(d1)(1)c. (possession of pseudoephedrine after methamphetamine conviction). State v. Miller, 246 N.C. App. 330, 335 (2016), *rev'd on other grounds*, 369 N.C. 658 (2017).
- G.S. 113-135(a) (violations of marine fisheries regulations). State v. Waterfield, ___ N.C. App. ___, 850 S.E.2d 609 (2020) (unattended gill nets).

In the sixth paragraph of this section, delete the citation to *State v. Haskins*.

2
Bars and Defenses

Bars to Prosecution (page 13)

Double Jeopardy (page 13)

The sixth paragraph of this section states that even when offenses are not the same, legislative intent controls whether multiple punishments may be imposed at the same trial. It goes on to indicate that some decisions analyze this issue as one of double jeopardy. For another such case, see *State v. Baldwin*, 240 N.C. App. 413, 425 (2015) (because the assault inflicting serious bodily injury statute begins with the language "[u]nless the conduct is covered under some other provision of law providing greater punishment," the trial court erred by sentencing the defendant to this Class F felony when it also sentenced the defendant for assault with a deadly weapon with intent to kill inflicting serious injury, a Class C felony).

Add the following to this section:

For a case where the trial court's erroneous entry of judgment of not guilty by reason of insanity did not create a jeopardy bar to further proceedings, see *State v. Payne*, 256 N.C. App. 572, 589–90 (2017) (the trial court's order dismissing the charges with leave did not constitute an acquittal to which jeopardy attached; the order was more akin to a procedural dismissal than a substantive ruling).

For additional support for the statement in this section that double jeopardy does not prevent a retrial when the first trial ended in a hung jury, see *State v. Allbrooks*, 256 N.C. App. 505, 510 (2017). Jeopardy continues after a hung-jury mistrial such that a voluntary dismissal entered after the mistrial terminates jeopardy in the defendant's favor, and thus bars retrial. State v. Courtney, 372 N.C. 458 (2019).

Delete the last paragraph of this section and replace it with the following:

For a more detailed discussion of double jeopardy, see Robert Farb, *Double Jeopardy and Related Issues, in* NORTH CAROLINA SUPERIOR COURT JUDGES' BENCHBOOK (Oct. 2013), http://benchbook.sog.unc.edu/criminal/double-jeopardy.

Lack of Jurisdiction (page 16)

As a result of 2014 legislation, S.L. 2014-100, sec. 34.30.(b), add the following to the list of statutes in this section:

§ 14-7.45. Crimes committed by use of unmanned aircraft systems.
All crimes committed by use of an unmanned aircraft system, as defined in G.S. 15A-300.1, while in flight over this State shall be governed by the laws of this State, and the question of whether the conduct by an unmanned aircraft system while in flight over this State constitutes a crime by the owner of the unmanned aircraft system shall be determined by the laws of this State.

Expiration of Statute of Limitations (page 17)

The text discusses G.S. 15-1, which contains the two-year statute of limitations for misdemeanors. Effective for offenses committed on or after December 1, 2017, S.L. 2017-212, sec. 5.3 amends G.S. 15-1 to provide that all misdemeanors except malicious misdemeanors must be charged within two years after commission. The statute had provided that the misdemeanor had to "be presented or found by the grand jury" within two years. The amended statute also provides that if any pleading is defective (it had been limited to indictments), another prosecution may be instituted for the same offense within one year after the State abandoned the first prosecution. This legislation was in response to *State v. Turner*, 250 N.C. App. 776 (2016), which held that the statute of limitations barred prosecution in that case, but which later was reversed per curiam by the North Carolina Supreme Court. State v. Turner, 371 N.C. 427 (2018) (reversing for the reasons stated in State v. Curtis, 371 N.C. 355 (2018)). The statute of limitations remains tolled by the filing of a citation, magistrate's order, or misdemeanor statement of charges in district court when a defendant is subsequently charged in superior court by presentment and indictment. State v. Stevens, 266 N.C. App. 233 (2019).

2019 legislation, S.L. 2019-245, effective for offenses committed on or after December 1, 2019, lengthens the statute of limitations applicable to five misdemeanor offenses as follows:

Under G.S. 15-1, the following misdemeanors have a ten-year statute of limitations:

- G.S. 7B-301(b) ("Duty to Report Abuse, Neglect, Dependency, or Death")
- G.S. 14-27.33 ("Sexual Battery")
- G.S. 14-202.2 ("Indecent Liberties Between Children")
- G.S. 14-318.2 ("Child Abuse")
- G.S. 14-318.6 ("Failure to Report Crimes against Juveniles")

Defenses That Justify (page 18)

Self-Defense, Defense of Others, and Defense of Property (page 18)

Add the following at the end of the first paragraph of this section:

A defendant is not entitled to a self-defense instruction when he or she claims the killing was accidental, State v. Harvey, 372 N.C. 304 (2019), or that he or she acted involuntarily or did not recall shooting the victim, State v. Yarborough, ___ N.C. App. ___, 843 S.E.2d 454 (2020).

Add the following at the end of the third paragraph of this section:

; John Rubin, *The Statutory Law of Self-Defense in North Carolina*, N.C. Crim. L.: A UNC Sch. of Gov't Blog (June 4, 2019), https://nccriminallaw.sog.unc.edu/the-statutory-law-of-self-defense-in-north-carolina.

Add the following two paragraphs to the end of this section:

In North Carolina, the right to use deadly force to defend oneself is provided by both statute and case law. By statute, there are two circumstances in which individuals are justified in using deadly force. First, under G.S. 14-51.3, a person is justified in the use of deadly force and does not have a duty to retreat in any place that person has the lawful right to be if he or she reasonably believes that such force is necessary to prevent imminent death or great bodily harm to him- or herself or another. Additionally, the lawful occupant of a home, motor vehicle, or workplace is presumed to have held a reasonable fear of imminent death or serious bodily harm to him- or herself or another when using defensive force intended or likely to cause death or serious bodily harm to another if the person against whom the defensive force was used was in the process of unlawfully and forcefully entering, or had unlawfully and forcibly entered, the property, or if that person had removed or was attempting to remove another against that person's will from the property, and the person who used the defensive force knew or had reason to believe that an unlawful and forcible entry or unlawful and forcible act was occurring or had occurred. G.S. 14-51.2(b); State v. Coley, 375 N.C. 156 (2020) (the defendant was entitled to an instruction on self-defense and the defense of habitation based on the increasingly violent and unpredictable acts of the aggressor, who rushed into the defendant's residence). A person's "home" for the purposes of G.S. 14-51.2(b) includes its curtilage, but the curtilage does not include an area 200 to 250 feet away from the residence, which may not have been on the defendant's property at all. *See* State v. Dilworth, ___ N.C. App. ___, 851 S.E.2d 406 (2020) (no error on those facts to decline the defendant's request for an instruction on defense of habitation). A person does not have a duty to retreat but may stand his ground against an intruder. State v. Lee, 370 N.C. 671 (2018).

A person has the right to resist an unlawful arrest with the use of force reasonably necessary to prevent an unlawful restraint of the person's liberty. State v. Burwell, 256 N.C. App. 722, 730–31 (2017) (the trial court did not err by failing to instruct the jury on the right to resist an unlawful arrest where the arrest was lawful). If an officer uses excessive force to execute a lawful arrest, the person arrested may defend against the excessive force. *Id.* at 736 (the trial court did not err by failing to instruct the jury on the right to defend oneself from excessive force by an officer where the officer's use of force was not excessive).

Necessity and Duress (page 18)

For another case discussing the elements of the defense of necessity and holding that it is a defense to impaired driving, see *State v. Miller*, 258 N.C. App. 325, 327 (2018) (the trial court erred by failing to give a jury instruction on necessity).

For another case supporting the statement in this section that duress is not a defense to any charge of intentional homicide, see *State v. Faulk*, 256 N.C. App. 255, 258–59 (2017) (citing *Cheek* and other precedent to hold that the trial court did not err by failing to instruct the jury on duress as a defense to premeditated and deliberate first-degree murder).

For a case where the defendant was not entitled to a jury instruction on duress, see *State v. Burrow*, 248 N.C. App. 663, 666–67 (2016) (attempted felony breaking or entering case; among other things, the defendant failed to show that his actions were caused by a reasonable fear that he would suffer immediate death or serious bodily injury if he did not act). For a contrasting case holding that the evidence supported an instruction on duress, see *Miller*, 258 N.C. App. at 327 (impaired driving case).

Public Authority (page 19)

The G.S. 20-145 exemption from speed limits does not apply to bail bondsmen. State v. McGee, 234 N.C. App. 285, 288 (2014).

Justification (new note)

Justification is an affirmative defense that serves only as a legal excuse for the criminal act and is based on additional facts and circumstances that are distinct from the conduct constituting the underlying offense. A defendant has the burden to prove his or her justification defense to the satisfaction of the jury. To establish justification as a defense to a criminal charge, a defendant must show that (1) he or she was under unlawful and present, imminent, and impending threat of death or serious bodily injury; (2) the defendant did not negligently or recklessly place him- or herself in a situation where the defendant would be forced to engage in criminal conduct; (3) the defendant had no reasonable legal alternative to violating the law; and (4) there was a direct causal relationship between the criminal action and the avoidance of the threatened harm. State v. Mercer, 373 N.C. 459 (2020) (adopting the four-factor test from *United States v. Deleveaux*, 205 F.3d 1292, 1297–98 (11th Cir. 2000)). The defendant was entitled to an instruction on justification as a defense to possession of a firearm by a felon when he presented evidence that he took possession of a firearm in response to a threat from a large group of people blocking him from entering his house, apparently armed and ready to fight him. *Mercer*, 373 N.C. at 464–66.

Defenses Showing Lack of Blameworthiness (page 20)

Entrapment (page 21)

But see State v. Keller, 374 N.C. 637 (2020) (the evidence in the defendant's solicitation of child by computer trial warranted an entrapment instruction when the Craigslist forum through which the defendant initially communicated with the undercover officer required users to be at least 18 years old; when the detective said he was a 15-year-old child, the defendant said they would have to wait to have sex until he reached the age of consent; and the defendant testified that he agreed to a meeting only out of concern that the supposed child would meet with someone else who could hurt or kill him).

The trial court erred by refusing to instruct on entrapment in a drug delivery case where an undercover officer tricked the defendant into believing that the officer was romantically interested in the defendant to persuade him to obtain cocaine, the defendant had no predisposition to commit the offense, and the criminal design originated solely with the officer. State v. Foster, 235 N.C. App. 365, 374–76 (2014).

Failure of Proof or "Negating" Defenses (page 22)

Accident (page 22)

The trial court did not err by refusing to instruct the jury on the defense of accident in a child sexual offense case where no evidence indicated that the defendant digitally penetrated the victim accidentally. State v. Clapp, 235 N.C. App. 351, 361 (2014).

For another case supporting the statement in this section that the defense of accident is not available if the defendant was engaged in misconduct at the time of the killing, see *State v. Robinson*, 251 N.C. App. 326, 327 (2016) ("A person who, while carrying a loaded firearm, starts a physical fight and discharges the firearm injuring another person, is not entitled to a jury instruction on the defense of accident.").

For a case where the trial court erred by failing to instruct the jury on the defense of accident, see *State v. Bediz,* 269 N.C. App. 39 (2019) (the defendant's testimony in his assault trial that he was trying park his car and did not realize he had hit the victim with his side-view mirror was sufficient evidence from which a jury could have found that he hit the victim unintentionally).

Voluntary Intoxication (page 23)

Add the following at the end of the first paragraph of this section:

For a case where the defendant's evidence—showing that she smelled of alcohol and was behaving somewhat erratically, but not indicating that she was incapable of comprehending her surroundings—was insufficient to support her request for an instruction on voluntary intoxication, see *State v. Meader*, 269 N.C. App. 446, *writ of supersedeas allowed*, 374 N.C. 744 (2020).

3
Participants in Crimes

Principals—Acting in Concert (page 29)

Notes (page 29)

Generally (page 29)

The acting in concert theory generally does not apply to possession offenses, as it tends to become confused with other theories of guilt. State v. Diaz, 155 N.C. App. 307 (2002).

Element (1) (page 29)

The fact that a person helped plan a crime, was available to an accomplice by telephone when it was committed, or was present at the crime scene after the offense occurred does not establish constructive presence. State v. Hardison, 243 N.C. App. 723, 725–26 (2015).

For cases holding that the evidence was insufficient to establish that the defendant was actually or constructively present, see *State v. Greenlee*, 227 N.C. App. 133, 138 (2013) (obtaining property by false pretenses case arising out of sales of stolen goods to a pawn shop); *Hardison*, 243 N.C. App. at 725–26 (contaminating a public water system case where the defendant was never present when the accomplice broke the water lines in question); and *State v. Bradsher*, ___ N.C. App. ___, 852 S.E.2d 716 (2020) (the defendant, an elected district attorney charged with obtaining property by false pretenses for a scheme involving payments to his wife, was not constructively present for the purposes of acting in concert when he was in a different county from the employee who actually submitted fraudulent timesheets for his wife).

For cases holding that the evidence was sufficient to establish that the defendant was actually or constructively present when a crime occurred, see *State v. Guy*, 262 N.C. App. 313 (2018) (although the defendant was not identified as being at the scene of a robbery, a witness saw a fleeing car blow a tire and, less than one minute later and within a quarter-mile of the scene, an officer found the defendant changing a tire on his car; the victim's stolen debit card and a gun matching one described by the victim as having been used during the robbery were found in close proximity to the car); *State v. Johnson*, 251 N.C. App. 260, 272–73 (2016) (among other things, the victim's blood was found on the defendant's pants and after the shooting the defendant aided the shooter in a fight with the victim to gain control of the gun).

Element (2) (page 29)

For a larceny case where the evidence was sufficient as to this Element, see *State v. Glidewell*, 255 N.C. App. 110, 117–18 (2017) (the defendant rode with his accomplice to the store in question and together they entered the store, looked at merchandise, and were seen on surveillance video concealing merchandise; the two left the store within seconds of each other and departed the premises in the same vehicle).

Element (3) (page 30)
The defendant need not expressly vocalize his or her assent to the criminal conduct; all that is required is an implied mutual understanding or agreement. State v. Marion, 233 N.C. App. 195, 204–05 (2014) (evidence was sufficient to support convictions for murder, burglary, and armed robbery on theories of acting in concert and aiding and abetting where, among other things, the defendant was present for discussions and aware of the group's plan to commit a robbery and remained in the vicinity of the crime scene where she helped by telling her accomplices that two of them had fled and encouraging the others to hurry up and leave).

For a larceny case where the evidence was sufficient as to this Element, see *Glidewell*, 255 N.C. App. at 117–18 (the defendant rode with his accomplice to the store in question and together they entered the store, looked at merchandise, and were seen on surveillance video concealing merchandise; the two left the store within seconds of each other and departed the premises in the same vehicle).

For a case where the evidence was insufficient with respect to this Element, see *State v. Holloway*, 250 N.C. App. 674, 684–85 (2016) (the State presented no evidence that the defendant had a common plan or purpose to possess drugs or paraphernalia with his alleged accomplice, McEntire; at most, the evidence showed that the two were acquainted and that the defendant was present when drugs were found at McEntire's home; mere presence at the scene of a crime is insufficient where the State presented no evidence that the two shared any criminal intent).

Extent of criminal liability (page 30)
Although a group initially planned to rob just one person at a residence, their attempted robbery of a second person found there was in pursuit of the group's common purpose. State v. Jastrow, 237 N.C. App. 325, 330 (2014).

Aiding and Abetting (page 31)

Notes (page 31)

Generally (page 31)
For another case supporting the statement in this note that actual or constructive presence is not required to prove a crime under the theory of aiding and abetting, see *State v. Dick*, 370 N.C. 305, 310–11 (2017).

Element (2) (page 32)
For cases where the evidence was sufficient to support convictions on a theory of aiding and abetting, see *State v. Golder*, 374 N.C. 238 (2020) (there was sufficient evidence that the defendant aided and abetted a clerk's scheme involving bond forfeitures when he met with the clerk and agreed to participate in the scheme, sent text messages with instructions specific to the scheme, and paid the clerk for entering fraudulent motions related to the scheme); *State v. Bauguss*, 265 N.C. App. 33 (2019) (sufficient evidence to convict the defendant of statutory sexual offense of a child by an adult on an aiding and abetting theory when he encouraged the victim's mother to perform sex acts on the victim and asked for photos and videos of specific sex acts); *State v. Cannon*, 254 N.C. App. 794, 797 (2017) (the evidence was sufficient as to aiding and abetting a larceny where, among other things, Amanda Eversole was seen trying to leave a Denver, NC, Walmart store without paying for items and her companion William Black was caught on surveillance video taking items from the store; Black was found sitting in a vehicle owned by the defendant, parked in the lot, filled with store goods, and positioned for easy escape; and the defendant, who was at the scene, claimed that he just met Eversole and

Black and was paid $50 to drive to the Denver Walmart from Gastonia), *aff'd per curiam*, 370 N.C. 487 (2018); and *State v. Marion*, 233 N.C. App. 195, 204–05 (2014) (the evidence was sufficient to support convictions for murder, burglary, and armed robbery on theories of acting in concert and aiding and abetting where, among other things, the defendant was present for discussions about and aware of the group's plan to commit a robbery and remained in the vicinity of the crime scene where she helped by telling her accomplices that two of them had fled and encouraging the others to hurry up and leave).

Related Offenses Not in This Chapter (page 34)

Add the following offense to this list:

Bank examiner aiding and abetting by making false or fraudulent report. G.S. 53C-8-7.

Accessory before the Fact to a Felony (page 34)

Punishment (page 34)

Replace the citation at the end of this section with the following:

G.S. 14-5.2; *see* State v. Larrimore, 340 N.C. 119 (1995); State v. Grainger, 367 N.C. 696, 699 (2014) (because the defendant's conviction for first-degree felony murder was not based solely on the uncorroborated testimony of a principal, the exception in G.S. 14-5.2 did not apply). A defendant is convicted of a capital felony when he or she is convicted of first-degree murder, even if the case was tried non-capitally. State v. Grainger, 224 N.C. App. 623, 630–31 (2012), *rev'd on other grounds*, 367 N.C. 696 (2014) (noting that this conclusion was central to the decision of the North Carolina Court of Appeals holding that the G.S. 14-5.2 exception applied; the state supreme court held that the exception did not apply for a separate reason: because the conviction did not rest on uncorroborated testimony of a principal).

4

Punishment under Structured Sentencing

Felonies (page 39)

Prior Record Level (page 40)

Delete the last paragraph of this section.

Aggravating and Mitigating Factors (page 41)

As a result of 2013 legislation, S.L. 2013-284, sec. 2(b); S.L. 2013-368, sec. 14, the first sentence of the fourth paragraph in this section should read as follows:

> G.S. 15A-1340.16(d) sets out more than twenty statutory aggravating factors, including, among others, that the crime was especially heinous, atrocious, or cruel, *id.* § -1340.16(d)(7); that the victim was very young, very old, or mentally or physically infirm or handicapped, *id.* § -1340.16(d)(11); and that the defendant involved a person under the age of 16 in the commission of the crime, *id.* § -1340.16(d)(13).

Sentence Disposition (page 43)

Active punishment (page 43)

As a result of 2017 legislation, S.L. 2017-186, sec. 2(qqq), replace the references to the "Department of Correction" in this section with: Division of Adult Correction and Juvenile Justice.

Intermediate punishment (page 44)

2012 legislation, S.L. 2012-146, amended G.S. 15A-1343(a1), adding the following condition to those listed on page 45:

- Abstain from alcohol consumption and submit to continuous alcohol monitoring when alcohol dependency or chronic abuse has been identified by a substance abuse assessment.

Community punishment (page 45)

2012 legislation, S.L. 2012-39, repealed G.S. 15A-1382.1(b). Thus, the last paragraph of this section (page 46) should be deleted.

Restitution (page 46)

Delete the second sentence of the third paragraph in this section.

2019 legislation, S.L. 2019-216, passed in response to a 2018 constitutional amendment on victims' rights, N.C. CONST. art. I, § 37, makes changes to the offenses covered by the CVRA. Delete the bulleted list in this same paragraph and replace it with the following:

- Any offense against the person, defined as a felony violation of Subchapters III and VII of G.S. Chapter 14; Article 39 of Chapter 14; any offense in Chapter 20 with an element that involves impairment of the defendant or injury or death to the victim; a violation of a valid protective order under G.S. 50B-4.1, including but not limited to G.S. 14-134.3 and -269.8; Article 35 of Chapter 14 if the elements of the offense involve communicating a threat or stalking; any other offense that triggers the enumerated victims' rights, as required by the North Carolina Constitution. G.S. 15A-830(6a).
- Any felony property crime, defined as a felony violation of Subchapter IV or V of G.S. Chapter 14. G.S. 15A-830(3b).

Special Provisions (page 47)

Class A felonies (page 47)

Delete the last sentence of this section and replace it with the following:

For a discussion of capital sentencing issues, see JEFFREY B. WELTY, NORTH CAROLINA CAPITAL CASE LAW HANDBOOK (UNC School of Government, 3d ed. 2013).

Armed habitual felon (new note)

2013 legislation, S.L. 2013-369, sec. 26, created a new armed habitual felon status. Put simply, when a person who has been convicted of one firearm-related felony commits a second such offense, the defendant may, in the discretion of the district attorney, be charged as an armed habitual felon. If convicted, the defendant must be sentenced as a Class C felon with a minimum 120-month prison term. *See generally* G.S. 14-7.35 through -7.41 (enacted by S.L. 2013-369, sec. 26).

Habitual breaking and entering status offender (page 48)

2017 legislation, S.L. 2017-176, sec. 3(a), amended G.S. 14-7.25, adding the following offense to the covered felony breaking and entering offenses included in this section's bulleted list:

- Breaking or entering with intent to terrorize or injure an occupant of the building under G.S. 14-54(a1) (covered in this supplement under "Felony Breaking or Entering of a Building").

Firearm or deadly weapon enhancement (page 48)

2013 legislation, S.L. 2013-369, sec. 5, amended the enhancement described in this section so that punishment applies as follows:

- If the felony is a Class A through E felony, the minimum term of imprisonment is increased by 72 months; the applicable maximum is the maximum that corresponds to the enhanced minimum.
- If the felony is a Class F or G felony, the minimum term of imprisonment is increased by 36 months; the applicable maximum is the maximum that corresponds to the enhanced minimum.
- If the felony is a Class H or I felony, the minimum term of imprisonment is increased by 12 months; the applicable maximum is the maximum that corresponds to the enhanced minimum.

G.S. 15A-1340.16A(c) (as amended by S.L. 2013-369, sec. 5).

Conditional discharge for certain drug offenders (page 49)

Replace this section with the following text:

G.S. 90-96, as amended by S.L. 2017-102, sec. 38, allows for conditional discharge of certain drug convictions in specified circumstances.

Methamphetamine enhancement (page 49)

As a result of 2013 legislation, S.L. 2013-124, sec. 2, the following should be added at the end of this section:

If a defendant is convicted of manufacturing of methamphetamine and a person under 18 years old or a disabled or elder adult

- resided on the property used for the manufacture of methamphetamine or
- was present where methamphetamine was being manufactured,

the defendant's minimum sentence must be increased by 24 months. G.S. 15A-1340.16D(a1). If both a minor and a disabled or elder adult resided on the property or were present, the minimum sentence must be increased by 48 months. *Id.* The maximum sentence is the maximum that corresponds to the enhanced minimum. The terms "disabled adult" and "elder adult" are defined by cross-reference to G.S. 14-32.3(d). *Id.* § (a2). The facts supporting the enhancement must be alleged in an indictment or information and proved to a jury beyond a reasonable doubt, unless the defendant pleads guilty or no contest to the issue. *Id.* §§ (b), (c).

Drug trafficking (page 49)

As a result of 2020 legislation, S.L. 2020-47, the following should be added at the end of this section:

Certain defendants convicted of trafficking by possession or conspiracy to commit trafficking by possession of the lowest trafficking category amount of a controlled substance may receive a reduced fine and a sentence consistent with the ordinary felony sentencing grid for their offense classification and prior record level as provided in G.S. 90-95(h)(5a).

Domestic violence protective order enhancement (page 50)

The G.S. 50B-4.1(d) enhancement does not apply to felony convictions when the defendant also is charged with a Class A or B1 felony or charged under G.S. 50B-4.1(f) or (g). State v. Jacobs, 239 N.C. App. 425, 427 (2015) (trial court erred by enhancing the defendant's conviction for assault with a deadly weapon with intent to kill inflicting serious injury and attempted second-degree kidnapping where the defendant also was charged with a violation of G.S. 50B-4.1(g)).

Criminal gang activity enhancement (new note)

G.S. 15A-1340.16E, enacted by S.L. 2017-194, sec. 5, creates certain sentencing enhancements that apply when the offense is committed as part of criminal gang activity and when the defendant is a criminal gang leader or organizer. The enhancements do not apply to any gang offense included in Article 13A of G.S. Chapter 14 (the North Carolina Criminal Gang Suppression Act). The statute specifies the procedural requirements for application of the enhancements.

Misdemeanors (page 50)

Sentence Disposition (page 52)

Active punishment (page 52)

2014 legislation, S.L. 2014-100, sec. 16C.1, made changes to the place of confinement for misdemeanants.

Special Provisions (page 53)

Infamous or related misdemeanor enhancement (page 53)

The evidence was sufficient to establish that the defendant obstructed justice with deceit and intent to defraud where he gave eight different statements to authorities, providing an array of scenarios surrounding the victim's death and identifying four different individuals as the perpetrator, and admitted that he had been untruthful to investigators. State v. Cousin, 233 N.C. App. 523, 530–31 (2014).

Enhancement for criminal gang activity (page 54)

As a result of 2017 legislation, S.L. 2017-194, sec. 11, the enhancement under G.S. 14-50.22 applies to any misdemeanor committed for the benefit of, at the direction of, or in association with, any "criminal gang." The term "criminal gang" is defined in the statute accompanying "Soliciting Participation in Criminal Gang Activity" in this supplement.

Conditional discharge for certain drug offenders (page 54)

Replace this section with the following text:

G.S. 90-96, as amended by S.L. 2017-102, sec. 38, allows for conditional discharge of certain drug convictions in specified circumstances.

Tables

Table 1 (page 55)

2013 legislation, S.L. 2013-410, sec. 3(a), amended the punishment for a Class A felony from "Life Imprisonment Without Parole or Death" to "Life Imprisonment With Parole or Without Parole, or Death."

Table 2A (page 58)

2013 legislation, S.L. 2013-101, sec. 6, made three changes to the maximum sentences grid, effective October 1, 2013, and applicable to offenses committed on or after that date:

The maximum sentence for a 66-month minimum is 92 months.

The maximum sentence for an 86-month minimum is 116 months.

The maximum sentence for a 216-month minimum is 272 months.

Tables 3 and 3A (pages 60, 62)

These forms have been updated. Revised N.C. AOC forms are available here: www.nccourts.org/Forms/FormSearch.asp.

Table 4 (page 63)

2013 legislation, S.L. 2013-360, sec. 18B.13, amended the misdemeanor sentencing grid shown in this table. Specifically, for misdemeanor offense Class 3 at prior conviction level II, the punishment should read:

1–15 days C if one to three prior convictions

1–15 days C/I if four prior convictions

That same legislation also enacted G.S. 15A-1340.23(d), providing that "[u]nless otherwise provided for a specific offense, the judgment for a person convicted of a Class 3 misdemeanor who has no more than three prior convictions shall consist only of a fine."

5
General Crimes

Attempt (page 67)

Notes (page 67)

Generally (page 67)

For another case on the elements of attempt, see *State v. Floyd*, 369 N.C. 329 (2016).

Evidence that the defendant committed a completed crime is sufficient to support a conviction of an attempt to commit that crime. State v. Baker, 369 N.C. 586, 598 (2017) (evidence that a completed rape occurred was sufficient to support a conviction for attempted rape); State v. Primus, 227 N.C. App. 428, 431–32 (2013) (evidence that a completed larceny occurred was sufficient to support a conviction for attempted larceny).

Element (1) (page 68)

In attempted rape cases, the State need not show that the defendant made an actual physical attempt to have intercourse. State v. Baker, 245 N.C. App. 94, 98–99 (2016), *rev'd on other grounds*, 369 N.C. 586 (2017). Intent is established "if the evidence shows that defendant, at any time during the incident, had an intent to gratify his passion upon the victim, notwithstanding any resistance on her part." *Id.* (internal quotation marks, citations omitted).

For cases where the evidence was sufficient to show an intent to engage in a sexual assault, see *State v. Marshall*, 246 N.C. App. 149, 157 (2016) (the evidence was sufficient to establish attempted sex offense and attempted rape; after isolating the victim from her husband, one of the perpetrators said, "Maybe we should," to which the other responded, "Yeah"; an accomplice then forced the victim to perform fellatio on him; after the defendant touched the victim, saying, "Nice," the victim's husband tried to protect her and was shot; a reasonable jury could infer that the defendant intended to engage in a continuous sexual assault involving both fellatio (like his accomplice) and rape and was thwarted only because of the husband's intervention); *State v. Minyard*, 231 N.C. App. 605, 616–17 (2014) ("The act of placing one's penis on a child's buttocks provides substantive evidence of intent to commit a first degree sexual offense, specifically anal intercourse."); *State v. Miles*, 237 N.C. App. 170, 173–74 (2014) (the defendant's conduct before and after his request that the victim perform fellatio on him sufficiently established that he intended to commit a sexual offense by force and against her will).

For a case where the evidence was insufficient to show an intent to engage in a sexual assault, see *Baker*, 245 N.C. App. at 100 (the defendant sat next to the victim, touched her shoulder and chest, and tried to get her to lie down).

Element (2) (page 68)

Delete the citation to *State v. Lawrence* in this note and replace it with the following:

State v. Bauguss, 265 N.C. App. 33 (2019) (an attempted sexual offense charge was proper based on the defendant's instruction to the victim's mother to dress the victim without panties and other overt actions that were part of the defendant's scheme to groom the victim for sexual activity);

Attempted homicide (page 68)
The crime of attempted first-degree felony murder does not exist under North Carolina law. State v. Marion, 233 N.C. App. 195, 202 (2014).

For another case holding that assault with a deadly weapon with intent to kill inflicting serious injury is not a lesser-included offense of attempted first-degree murder and that a defendant may be convicted of and punished for both offenses, see *State v. Rogers*, 219 N.C. App. 296, 307–08 (2012).

Conspiracy to commit attempted murder is a cognizable offense in North Carolina. State v. Lyons, 268 N.C. App. 603 (2019).

Attempted assault (page 69)

Delete the text of this note and replace it with the following:

In *State v. Floyd*, 369 N.C. 329 (2016), the supreme court held that attempted assault is a crime in North Carolina; it reversed the court of appeals, which had held that attempted assault with a deadly weapon inflicting serious injury is not a recognized crime because it constituted an attempt of an attempt. *Id.* The *Floyd* court concluded that "[a]ttempted assault is not an attempt of an attempt because assault may be defined by the show-of-violence rule," a form of assault that "does not involve an attempt to cause injury to another person, but is based upon a violent act or threat that causes fear in another person." *Id.* at 336.

Conspiracy (page 72)

Notes (page 72)

Element (1) (page 72)
Circumstantial evidence can establish the scope of the agreement. State v. Fish, 229 N.C. App. 584, 591–92 (2013) (evidence that the defendant and an accomplice stole property valued at more than $1,000 established that they had an agreement to do so).

For a case where there was sufficient evidence of a conspiracy to possess a stolen pistol, see *State v. Greene*, 251 N.C. App. 627, 635 (2017) (after the defendant made a phone call from jail to his alleged co-conspirator, the co-conspirator showed up at the residence near where the pistol was found and admitted to "working with" the defendant).

For other cases where there was sufficient evidence of an agreement to commit robbery, see *State v. Stroud*, 259 N.C. App. 411, 419 (2018) (the evidence was sufficient to establish an agreement to commit robbery where the victim identified the defendant, Raborn, and Bowen as the perpetrators and the defendant confirmed to a detective the accuracy of Bowen's statement that the robbery was in retaliation for the victim's robbery of Bowen's cousin); *State v. Young*, 248 N.C. App. 815, 822 (2016) (circumstantial evidence established that the defendant and his accomplices agreed to rob a second victim; the accomplices agreed to take the first victim's car and then commit other unlawful acts, with the defendant wielding a shotgun and another person driving the vehicle; the acts against the second victim occurred within minutes of and very near the acts against the first); *State v. Oliphant*, 228 N.C. App. 692, 704 (2013) (implied agreement to commit armed robbery where the defendants approached the victim from behind and one held a gun while the other reached for the victim's cell phone); and *State v. Rogers*, 227 N.C. App. 617, 623–24 (2013) (conspiracy to commit armed robbery; implied understanding to use a dangerous weapon).

For a case where there was insufficient evidence of an agreement to commit robbery, see *State v. Fleming*, 247 N.C. App. 812, 819 (2016) (the "mere fact that the crime the defendant allegedly conspired with others to commit took place does not, without more, prove the existence of a conspiracy").

For other cases where the evidence was insufficient to establish an agreement to engage in drug offenses, see *State v. Velazquez-Perez*, 233 N.C. App. 585, 593 (2014) (among other things, there was no evidence that the driver of a vehicle owned by an alleged co-conspirator knew about drugs hidden in the vehicle), and *State v. McClaude*, 237 N.C. App. 350, 353–54 (2014) (following *State v. Euceda-Valle*, 182 N.C. App. 268 (2007), where the evidence showed only that drugs were found in a car driven by another person in which the defendant was a passenger).

For cases where the evidence was sufficient to show an agreement to engage in drug offenses, see *State v. Winkler*, 368 N.C. 572, 581–83 (2015) (rejecting the defendant's argument that the evidence showed only "the mere existence of a relationship between the two individuals"); *State v. Glisson*, 251 N.C. App. 844, 848–49 (2017) (sufficient evidence to establish that the defendant conspired with an accomplice to traffic in opium where, among other things, the defendant brought the accomplice to all three controlled buys, the drugs were maintained in the same vehicle as the accomplice, and the defendant exchanged the drugs and counted the money in front of the accomplice); *State v. Garrett*, 246 N.C. App. 651, 656–57 (2016) (sufficient evidence of conspiracy to sell methamphetamine where the incident arose out of a controlled buy involving the defendant and two accomplices); *State v. Torres-Gonzalez*, 227 N.C. App. 188, 195 (2013) (conspiracy to traffic in cocaine by possession where the defendant and an accomplice worked together to complete a drug sale); and *State v. Davis*, 236 N.C. App. 376, 385 (2014) (implied agreement to engage in drug trafficking by manufacture where the defendant was present at the scene and aware that his accomplice was involved in producing methamphetamine and the defendant was involved in the manufacturing process; "Where two subjects are involved together in the manufacture of methamphetamine and the methamphetamine recovered is enough to sustain trafficking charges, we hold the evidence sufficient to infer an implied agreement between the subjects to traffic in methamphetamine by manufacture and withstand a motion to dismiss.").

Multiple convictions and punishments (page 74)

For cases where the evidence supported the existence of multiple conspiracies, see *State v. Stimpson*, 256 N.C. App. 364, 371, 807 S.E.2d 603, 608 (2017) (holding that the evidence supported five separate offenses of conspiracy to commit armed robbery arising from five separate incidents; concluding, in part, that the random nature and happenstance of the robberies did not indicate a single conspiracy and that the victims selected and crimes committed arose at random and by pure opportunity), *aff'd per curiam*, 371 N.C. 470 (2018); *Glisson*, 251 N.C. App. at 849–50 (the evidence supported the existence of multiple separate conspiracies to traffic in controlled substances; noting the time between the transactions and that each was initiated by an informant or a detective).

Relation to other offenses (page 75)

Conspiracy to commit attempted murder is a cognizable offense in North Carolina. State v. Lyons, 268 N.C. App. 603 (2019).

Withdrawal (new note)

Due process is not violated when the trial court puts the burden on the defendant to prove withdrawal from the conspiracy. Smith v. United States, 568 U.S. 106, 110 (2013).

Related Offenses Not in This Chapter (page 75)

As a result of 2015 legislation, S.L. 2015-47, delete the last offense in this list and replace it with the following:

Furnishing poison, controlled substances, deadly weapons, cartridges, ammunition, or alcoholic beverages to inmates; furnishing tobacco products or mobile phones to inmates; furnishing mobile phones to delinquent juveniles. G.S. 14-258.1.

Continuing Criminal Enterprise—Non-Drug Offenses (page 75)

Statute (page 75)

2012 legislation, S.L. 2012-38, amended G.S. 14-7.20, making three changes. First, subsection (a) was amended to read:

> (a) Except as otherwise provided in subsection (a1) of this section, any person who engages in a continuing criminal enterprise shall be punished as a Class H felon and in addition shall be subject to the forfeiture prescribed in subsection (b) of this section.

Second, a new subsection, (a1), was enacted as follows:

> (a1) Any person who engages in a continuing criminal enterprise where the felony violation required by subdivision (c)(1) of this section is a violation of G.S. 14-10.1 shall be punished as a Class D felon and, in addition, shall be subject to the forfeiture prescribed in subsection (b) of this section.

Third, the first sentence of subsection (b) was amended to read:

> (b) Any person who is convicted under subsection (a) or (a1) of this section of engaging in a continuing criminal enterprise shall forfeit to the State of North Carolina:

Punishment (page 76)

Delete the first sentence of this section and replace it with the following:

Class H felony, G.S. 14-7.20(a), except that if the offense constitutes the crime of terrorism under G.S. 14-10.1, it is punished as a Class D felony. G.S. 14-7.20(a1); *see generally* "Terrorism" in Chapter 20 (Bombing, Terrorism, and Related Offenses) in this supplement.

Accessory after the Fact to a Felony (page 76)

Notes (page 77)

Element (2) (page 77)

For an additional case supporting the statement in this note that a person does not become an accessory after the fact simply because he or she knew that a crime was committed and failed to provide information about it, see *State v. Ditenhafer*, 258 N.C. App. 537, 551–52 (2018) (the evidence was insufficient to support a charge of accessory after the fact to sexual activity by a substitute parent based on the allegation that the defendant failed to report her husband's sexual abuse of her daughter; merely failing to report a crime is insufficient evidence of this Element), *aff'd in part*, 373 N.C. 116 (2019).

For a case where the evidence was sufficient as to this Element, see *State v. Cousin*, 233 N.C. App. 523, 532–33 (2014) (there was sufficient evidence of accessory after the fact to murder where the defendant made false statements to the police to shield the perpetrator's identity; the defendant gave eight different written statements to authorities, providing an array of scenarios surrounding the victim's death and identifying four different individuals as the perpetrator; he also admitted that he had been untruthful to investigators).

Element (3) (page 78)
For a case where the evidence was sufficient to show that the defendant knew the identity of the murderer and was protecting that person from apprehension, see *Cousin*, 233 N.C. App. at 532.

For a case where the evidence was sufficient to establish that the defendant knew that a gun he hid previously was used to commit a murder, see *State v. Schiro*, 219 N.C. App. 105, 113–14 (2012).

Multiple convictions and punishments (page 78)
No double jeopardy violation occurred when the trial court sentenced the defendant for felony obstruction of justice and accessory after the fact to murder arising out of the same conduct. *Cousin*, 233 N.C. App. at 537 (reasoning that each offense contains an element not in the other); State v. Cruz, ___ N.C. App. ___, 845 S.E.2d 199 (2020).

6

Homicide

Murder (page 83)

First-Degree Murder (page 83)

Statute (page 83)

Several pieces of legislation, S.L. 2017-94; S.L. 2017-115, sec. 9; S.L. 2013-47; S.L. 2013-410, sec. 3(a); and S.L. 2012-165, amended G.S. 14-17. The amended statute reads:

> **§ 14-17. Murder in the first and second degree defined; punishment.**
>
> (a) A murder which shall be perpetrated by means of a nuclear, biological, or chemical weapon of mass destruction as defined in G.S. 14-288.21, poison, lying in wait, imprisonment, starving, torture, or by any other kind of willful, deliberate, and premeditated killing, or which shall be committed in the perpetration or attempted perpetration of any arson, rape or a sex offense, robbery, kidnapping, burglary, or other felony committed or attempted with the use of a deadly weapon shall be deemed to be murder in the first degree, a Class A felony, and any person who commits such murder shall be punished with death or imprisonment in the State's prison for life without parole as the court shall determine pursuant to G.S. 15A-2000, except that any such person who was under 18 years of age at the time of the murder shall be punished in accordance with Part 2A of Article 81B of Chapter 15A of the General Statutes.
>
> (a1) If a murder was perpetrated with malice as described in subdivision (1) of subsection (b) of this section, and committed against a spouse, former spouse, a person with whom the defendant lives or has lived as if married, a person with whom the defendant is or has been in a dating relationship as defined in G.S. 50B-1(b)(6), or a person with whom the defendant shares a child in common, there shall be a rebuttable presumption that the murder is a "willful, deliberate, and premeditated killing" under subsection (a) of this section and shall be deemed to be murder in the first degree, a Class A felony, if the perpetrator has previously been convicted of one of the following offenses involving the same victim:
>
> (1) An act of domestic violence as defined in G.S. 50B-1(a).
> (2) A violation of a domestic violence protective order under G.S. 50B-4.1(a), (f), (g), or (g1) or G.S. 14-269.8 when the same victim is the subject of the domestic violence protective order.
> (3) Communicating a threat under G.S. 14-277.1.
> (4) Stalking as defined in G.S. 14-277.3A.
> (5) Cyberstalking as defined in G.S. 14-196.3.
> (6) Domestic criminal trespass as defined in G.S. 14-134.3.
>
> (b) A murder other than described in subsection (a) or (a1) of this section or in G.S. 14-23.2 shall be deemed second degree murder. Any person who commits second degree murder shall be punished as a Class B1 felon, except that a person who commits

second degree murder shall be punished as a Class B2 felon in either of the following circumstances:

(1) The malice necessary to prove second degree murder is based on an inherently dangerous act or omission, done in such a reckless and wanton manner as to manifest a mind utterly without regard for human life and social duty and deliberately bent on mischief.

(2) The murder is one that was proximately caused by the unlawful distribution of any opium, opiate, or opioid; any synthetic or natural salt, compound, derivative, or preparation of opium, or opiate, or opioid; cocaine or other substance described in G.S. 90-90(1)d.; methamphetamine; or a depressant described in G.S. 90-92(a)(1), and the ingestion of such substance caused the death of the user.

(c) For the purposes of this section, it shall constitute murder where a child is born alive but dies as a result of injuries inflicted prior to the child being born alive. The degree of murder shall be determined as described in subsections (a) and (b) of this section.

Punishment (page 84)

Replace the last sentence of the second paragraph in this section with the following:

For a discussion of capital law, see Jeffrey B. Welty, North Carolina Capital Case Law Handbook (UNC School of Government, 3d ed. 2013).

Add the following to the end of the third paragraph in this section:

In *Miller v. Alabama*, 567 U.S. 460, 479 (2012), the U.S. Supreme Court held that an automatic sentence of life imprisonment without the possibility of parole for a person under 18 years old who is convicted of murder violates the Eighth Amendment. Because North Carolina law had required such a sentence for a juvenile's conviction for first-degree murder, the General Assembly enacted legislation to bring the state's law in compliance with *Miller*. S.L. 2012-148. That legislation authorizes a sentence of life imprisonment with the possibility of parole after 25 years for defendants convicted of first-degree murder who were under 18 years old at the time of the offense. G.S. 15A-1340.19A. If a conviction is based solely on the felony murder rule, the court must impose this sentence. G.S. 15A-1340.19B(a)(1). In other first-degree murder cases, the court must conduct a hearing to determine whether the defendant should be sentenced to life imprisonment with or without the possibility of parole. *Id.* § (a)(2).

The last paragraph of this section cites G.S. 15A-2005(b). 2015 legislation, S.L. 2015-247, sec. 5, amended that statute to, among other things, replace the term "mentally retarded" with "intellectual disability."

Notes (page 84)

Elements (1) and (2) (page 84)

G.S. 14-17(c) provides that it is murder when a child is born alive but dies as a result of injuries inflicted prior to the child being born alive. *See* State v. Broom, 225 N.C. App. 137, 143–44 (2013) (the trial court did not err by denying the defendant's motion to dismiss first-degree murder charges where the victim was in utero at the time of the incident but was born alive and lived for one month before dying).

Element (3)(a)(i) (page 84)

This note describes three forms of malice. Delete (1) and replace it with the following:

(1) express malice, in the form of hatred, ill will, or spite, State v. Reynolds, 307 N.C. 184, 191 (1982);

Replace the paragraph after the numbered list in this note with the following:

The second form of malice—commission of an inherently dangerous act—sometimes is called "depraved heart malice." State v. Lail, 251 N.C. App. 463, 468 (2016). Although depraved heart malice is frequently used to support second-degree murder convictions based on impaired driving, it is not limited to cases involving impaired driving. *Id.* at 469–70 (citing cases). The second form of malice was found when the defendant, knowing that two people became violently ill after using certain drugs, supplied the same drugs to the victim, who later died. *Liner*, 98 N.C. App. 600.

Element (3)(a)(ii) (page 85)

For additional cases where the evidence was sufficient to establish premeditation and deliberation, see *State v. Yarborough*, ___ N.C. App. ___, 843 S.E.2d 454 (2020) (the defendant said he would kill the victim if she did not obey him, struck her over the head twice with a handgun, and described her as a hostage); *State v. Madonna*, 256 N.C. App. 112, 115–16 (2017) (among other things, the defendant-wife and victim-husband had been arguing about financial matters; the defendant was having a romantic relationship with her therapist and planned to ask the victim for a divorce; Internet searches were done on the home computer for "upon death of a veteran," "can tasers kill people," "can tasers kill people with a heart condition," "what is the best handgun for under $200," "death in absentia USA," and "declare someone dead if missing 3 years"; on the date of death the defendant got a gun and knife from her nephew, telling him that she was concerned about her safety due to break-ins in her neighborhood; she then went on a drive with the victim and used the gun to shoot him and the knife to stab him twelve times; she later messaged her therapist "it's almost done" and "it got ugly"; and after the incident, the defendant disposed of her bloodstained clothing, threw away the victim's medications and identification, and said that he had either gone to Florida or was at a rehabilitation center); *State v. Hicks*, 241 N.C. App. 345, 355–56 (2015) (among other things, there was no provocation by the unarmed victim; the defendant shot the victim at least four times; and after the shooting, the defendant immediately left the scene without aiding the victim); *State v. Mitchell*, 240 N.C. App. 246, 256 (2015) (among other things, there was no provocation by the victim; just before the shooting, the defendant said he was going to shoot a man over a trivial matter; the defendant shot the victim three times; and the victim may have been turning away or trying to escape at the time); *State v. Horskins*, 228 N.C. App. 217, 225–26 (2013) (after exchanging words in a nightclub parking lot, the defendant shot the unarmed victim, who had not reached for a weapon, had not engaged the defendant in a fight, and did not provoke the defendant's violent response; after the victim fell from the defendant's first shot, the defendant shot the victim six more times; and the defendant left the scene and attempted to hide evidence); *State v. Rogers*, 227 N.C. App. 617, 621–22 (2013) (the victim begged for his life and was shot eight times, primarily in the head and chest, and there was a lack of provocation); and *State v. Broom*, 225 N.C. App. 137, 144 (2013) (the defendant was having an affair with another woman and wanted his wife to terminate her pregnancy; he became angry when his wife said that if they divorced she might move out of the state with their children; and before he shot her, the defendant placed his wife's cell phone out of her reach).

2017 legislation added a new subsection, (a1), to the statute, creating a rebuttable presumption that certain domestic violence murders are "willful, deliberate and premeditated" under certain circumstances. G.S. 14-17(a1), *as amended by* S.L. 2017-94. *See* Jeff Welty, *Many Questions and a Few Answers about Britny's Law*, N.C. Crim. L.: A UNC Sch. of Gov't Blog (Aug. 28, 2017), https://nccriminallaw.sog.unc.edu/many-questions-answers-britnys-law/.

Element (3)(b) (page 86)

Add the following at the end of the first paragraph of this note:

; State v. Grullon, 240 N.C. App. 55, 60–61 (2015) (neither specific intent to kill nor deadly purpose to kill is required; the evidence was sufficient where the defendant ambushed the victim for the purpose of committing a robbery).

Add the following at the end of the second paragraph of this note:

For recent cases where the evidence was sufficient to establish lying in wait, see *State v. Cox*, 256 N.C. App. 511 (2017) (rejecting the defendant's argument that the evidence was insufficient because he announced his presence; the evidence showed that the victim exited his residence to speak with the defendant, that the defendant did not threaten or harm the victim during their conversation, and that after waiting for the victim to return inside, the defendant fired into the residence, killing the victim; the victim was taken by surprise and had no opportunity to defend himself); *State v. Gosnell*, 231 N.C. App. 106, 113 (2013); and *Grullon*, 240 N.C. App. at 61–62 (the defendant hid under a darkened staircase for the purpose of robbing the victim).

To starve a victim is to willfully deprive him or her of the food or liquids necessary in the nourishment of the human body to sustain life. The deprivation need not be absolute, but if it is so severe as to cause death, it may be the basis for murder by starving. State v. Cheeks, 267 N.C. App. 579 (2019) (adopting a definition previously set out by the North Carolina Supreme Court in dicta in *State v. Evangelista*, 319 N.C. 152 (1987)). Murder by starving does not require as an element that the defendant have a legal duty (as a parent or formal caregiver, for example) to feed the victim; the victim's situational dependence on the defendant for food or water can suffice. *Id.* at 604–05. Just as with murder by poisoning or torture, murder by starving implies the requisite malice, and a separate showing of malice is not necessary. *Id.* at 605–06.

Element (3)(c) (page 86)

Add the following to the fourth paragraph of this note:

For another case supporting the statement in this note that felonious child abuse can support a felony murder charge, see *State v. Perry*, 229 N.C. App. 304, 318 (2013). For another case supporting the statement in this note that discharging a firearm into occupied property can support a felony murder charge, see *State v. Juarez*, 243 N.C. App. 466, 469 (2015), *rev'd on other grounds*, 369 N.C. 351 (2016). Attempted murder of one person can support a felony murder charge for the death of another person when the defendant's hands, arms, feet, or other appendages constitute a deadly weapon. State v. Steen, ___ N.C. ___, 852 S.E.2d 14 (2020).

The sixth paragraph of this note discusses the continuous transaction doctrine. Add the following to that discussion:

There need not be a causal relationship between the underlying felony and the homicide; all that is required is that the felony and the killing occur in a single transaction. State v. Maldonado, 241 N.C. App. 370, 376 (2015). However, the felony murder rule will not apply where there is a break in the chain of events between the felony and the act causing death. *Id.* For a case where the court rejected the defendant's argument that such a break occurred, see *id.* (in a case where the felony murder charge was based on shooting into occupied property, the court rejected the defendant's argument that the victim's attempt to take his gun after he entered the house constituted a break in the chain of events that led to her later shooting death at the defendant's hand inside the property).

Replace the last sentence of the sixth paragraph of this note with the following:

For a fuller discussion of the continuous transaction doctrine, see JEFFREY B. WELTY, NORTH CAROLINA CAPITAL CASE LAW HANDBOOK 22–23 (UNC School of Government, 3d ed. 2013).

Delete the seventh paragraph and replace it with the following:

Although the felony and the homicide must be part of a continuous transaction, *State v. Jones*, 353 N.C. 159 (2000), suggests that when the underlying offense is an assault on a single victim who dies from injuries inflicted during the assault, the assault cannot be used as an underlying felony for purposes of the felony murder rule. *Id.* at 170 n.3 (reasoning that "[o]therwise, virtually all felonious assaults on a single victim that result in his or her death would be first-degree murders via felony murder, thereby negating lesser homicide charges such as second-degree murder and manslaughter"). However, if the transaction involves multiple assaults, only one of which caused death, the *Jones* rule does not apply. For example, in *State v. Carroll*, 356 N.C. 526 (2002), the defendant committed a nonfatal assault on the victim with a machete and then killed her by strangulation. The state supreme court held that the felony assault with a machete was a separate offense from the strangulation and properly was used as a felony to support felony murder. *Id.* at 535. Additionally, the *Jones* rule applies only when a single victim is involved; cases involving multiple victims fall outside of this rule. *Jones*, 353 N.C. at 170 n.3 (distinguishing the single-victim scenario from one involving a felonious assault on one victim that results in the death of another victim); State v. Jackson, 189 N.C. App. 747, 752 n.3 (2008). The court of appeals has interpreted these cases as "stand[ing] for the limited proposition that a single assault on one victim that leads to that person's death cannot serve as the underlying felony for purposes of the felony murder rule." State v. Spruiell, 252 N.C. App. 486, 496 (2017) (footnote omitted). It has, however, rejected the "far broader proposition that *no* offense—regardless of whether the offense is classified as an assault or as some other crime—can serve as the basis for a felony murder conviction where the crime results from a 'single assaultive act' against one victim." *Id.* at 494–99. And it has held—in the context of an ineffective assistance of counsel claim—that notwithstanding *Jones*, a felony murder conviction can be based on the predicate felony of discharging a weapon into occupied property where a single shot was fired at a single victim. *Id.* at 499–500. *Spruiell* is consistent with pre-*Jones* cases that upheld felony murder convictions based on non-assault offenses that caused death. *See, e.g.*, State v. King, 316 N.C. 78 (1986) (felony murder based on discharging a firearm into occupied property); State v. Pierce, 346 N.C. 471, 493 (1997) (same based on felonious child abuse).

Replace the last sentence of the eleventh paragraph with the following:

For a fuller discussion of the merger rule, see JEFFREY B. WELTY, NORTH CAROLINA CAPITAL CASE LAW HANDBOOK 113–14 (UNC School of Government, 3d ed. 2013).

Proximate cause (page 88)

The defendant's shooting of the victim's mother while the victim was in utero was a proximate cause of the victim's death after being born alive, where the gunshot wound required the child's early delivery, which in turn caused a complicating condition that resulted in death. State v. Broom, 225 N.C. App. 137, 143 (2013).

Greater and lesser-included offenses (page 90)

Replace the first sentence of this note with the following:

Second-degree murder is a lesser-included offense of premeditated and deliberate first-degree murder, State v. Stevenson, 327 N.C. 259, 263 (1990), but not of first-degree felony murder, State v. Frazier, 248 N.C. App. 252, 258 (2016).

Delete the last sentence of this note.

Attempted first-degree murder (page 90)

The crime of attempted first-degree felony murder does not exist under North Carolina law. State v. Marion, 233 N.C. App. 195, 202 (2014).

Related Offenses Not in This Chapter (page 90)

Add the following offenses to this list:

Interfering with gas, water, or electric meters and causing death. G.S. 14-151.
Violation of Chapter 95, Article 15 (Passenger Tramway Safety) causing death. G.S. 95-125.3(g), *as enacted by* S.L. 2017-211, sec. 14(c).

The last listed offense should read:

"Concealing a Death" (Chapter 21).

Second-Degree Murder (page 90)

Punishment (page 91)

As a result of 2012 and 2017 legislation, S.L. 2012-165; S.L. 2017-115, sec. 9, delete the text of this section and replace it with the following:

> Class B1 felony, except that punishment is as a Class B2 felony when (1) the malice necessary to prove second-degree murder is based on an inherently dangerous act or omission, done in such a reckless and wanton manner as to manifest a mind utterly without regard for human life and social duty and deliberately bent on mischief (this is the second form of malice discussed in the note on Element (3)(a)(i) to "First-Degree Murder" (page 84)); or (2) the murder was proximately caused by the unlawful distribution of any opium, opiate, or opioid; any synthetic or natural salt, compound, derivative, or preparation of opium, or opiate, or opioid; cocaine or other substance described in G.S. 90-90(1)d.; methamphetamine; or a depressant described in G.S. 90-92(a)(1), and the ingestion of such substance caused the death of the user. G.S. 14-17(b).

Notes (page 91)

Element (3) (page 91)

For another second-degree murder case involving impaired driving, see *State v. Grooms*, 230 N.C. App. 56, 68–69 (2013) (there was sufficient evidence of malice where the defendant drove impaired and killed two bicyclists; the defendant was warned of the dangers of drinking and driving and his prior incident of doing so on the same road led a passenger to fear for her life; his blood alcohol level was 0.16; the defendant knowingly consumed an illegal controlled substance that caused impairment; the defendant swerved off the road three times before the collision, giving him notice that he was driving dangerously; the defendant failed to watch the road and made a phone call right before the collision; and the defendant failed to apply his brakes before or after the collision, to call 911, or to aid the victims).

Insert the following after the first sentence of the first full paragraph on page 92:

> State v. Schmieder, 265 N.C. App. 95 (2019) (defendant's two-decade-long history of prior driving convictions, including speeding, reckless driving, illegal passing, and failure to reduce speed, coupled with witness testimony about his speeding, close following, and improper passing, was sufficient for a reasonable jury to infer that he acted with malice); State v. Rollins, 220 N.C. App. 443, 453–55 (2012) (the defendant drove without a license after being cited twice for that offense; the defendant took control of the vehicle from another driver by climbing over the back seat while the vehicle was moving; the defendant was evading the police because he had shoplifted items in the vehicle; the defendant drove well in excess of the speed limit, crossed a yellow line to pass, passed vehicles using a turn lane, drove through a corn field and ditch, and again crossed the center line, colliding with another vehicle while traveling 66 mph and without applying his brakes; and to avoid arrest, the defendant repeatedly struck an injured passenger as he tried to exit the vehicle and escape);

Insert the following paragraph at the end of this note:

> For a case where the evidence showed that the death resulted from a mishap with a gun and that there was insufficient evidence of malice, see *State v. Hatcher*, 231 N.C. App. 114, 118–20 (2013).

Death resulting from distribution and ingestion of a controlled substance (page 92)

This note states that if a defendant unlawfully distributes opium, cocaine, or a derivative of either substance, or methamphetamine, and ingestion of that substance causes the user's death, the defendant is guilty of second-degree murder. The statute, however, has been amended; it now applies to any opium, opiate, or opioid; any synthetic or natural salt, compound, derivative, or preparation of opium, opiate, or opioid; cocaine or other substance described in G.S. 90-90(1)d.; methamphetamine; or a depressant described in G.S. 90-92(a)(1). G.S. 14-17(b)(2), *as amended by* S.L. 2017-115, sec. 9.

Add the following to this note:

Where there was no evidence that the defendant intended to kill the victim by selling him methadone, the trial court did not err by instructing the jury on second-degree murder and involuntary manslaughter. State v. Barnes, 226 N.C. App. 318, 329–30 (2013) (rejecting the defendant's argument that under G.S. 14-17 he could have been convicted only of second-degree murder).

Murder of an Unborn Child (page 94)

Related Offenses Not in This Chapter (page 96)

Add the following offense to this list:

Sale of remains of an unborn child. G.S. 14-46.1.

Manslaughter (page 96)

Voluntary Manslaughter (page 96)

Notes (page 96)

Elements (1) and (2) (page 96)

Although no intent to kill is required for this crime, the act that causes death must be intentional. State v. English, 241 N.C. App. 98, 107 (2015) (the evidence was sufficient to show that the defendant intentionally hit the victim with her car).

Element (3) generally (page 96)

No legally adequate provocation existed when the victim insisted, shortly after having sex with the defendant, that he allow her to use his cell phone to text another man saying that she and the defendant were no longer in a relationship, and when the defendant refused, the victim taunted him. State v. Chaves, 246 N.C. App. 100, 105 (2016) (internal quotation marks, citations omitted) (noting that "[m]ere words, however abusive or insulting are not sufficient provocation" and that "this level of provocation must ordinarily amount to an assault or threatened assault by the victim against the perpetrator").

Although evidence that a defendant acted in the heat of passion can negate the malice required for the greater offenses of first- and second-degree murder, the State need not prove that the defendant acted in the heat of passion in order to obtain a conviction for voluntary manslaughter. State v. Coleman, 254 N.C. App. 497 (2017) (rejecting the defendant's argument that the trial court should have granted his motion for a directed verdict on voluntary manslaughter because the State presented no evidence that he acted in the heat of passion).

Multiple convictions and punishments (page 98)

G.S. 20-141.4(c) does not bar simultaneous prosecutions for involuntary manslaughter and death by vehicle; it only bars punishment for both offenses when they arise out of the same death. State v. Elmore, 224 N.C. App. 331, 336 (2012).

Involuntary Manslaughter (page 99)

Notes (page 99)

Element (3)(a) (page 100)

Other acts that fall within this Element include

- misdemeanor improper storage of a firearm, State v. Lewis, 222 N.C. App. 747, 752 (2012);
- supplying alcohol to a person under 21, State v. Noble, 226 N.C. App. 531, 536–37 (2013) (person under 21 died from alcohol poisoning; the defendant aided and abetted the victim in the possession or consumption of alcohol in violation of G.S. 18B-302); and
- affray, State v. Gomola, 257 N.C. App. 816, 818–19 (2018) (also holding that the trial court committed prejudicial error by not giving a jury instruction on defense of others as a defense to affray, the unlawful act underlying the involuntary manslaughter charge; if the jury had been given the instruction, it may have determined that the defendant's involvement in the affray was not unlawful).

Element (3)(b) (page 100)

For another case where the defendant's culpably negligent act was sufficient to support a conviction of this offense, see *State v. Fisher*, 228 N.C. App. 463, 473–75 (2013) (the defendant attacked the victim, leaving him semiconscious; instead of taking the victim to be picked up by his parents as arranged, the defendant drove him to an isolated area and again beat him; the defendant abandoned the victim outside knowing that the temperature was in the 20s and that the victim was injured, intoxicated, and not wearing a shirt; the defendant realized that his actions put the victim in jeopardy; and after being told that the victim was missing and that officers were concerned about him, the defendant lied about the victim's whereabouts, hindering efforts to find and help the victim).

Proximate cause (page 100)

For a case where improper storage of a firearm was the proximate cause of a child's death, see *Lewis*, 222 N.C. App. at 752.

Submitting involuntary manslaughter to the jury as a lesser-included offense of first-degree murder (page 101)

Add the following citation to the first paragraph of this note:

State v. Coleman, 254 N.C. App. 497, 505–06 (2017) (holding that the defendant was not entitled to a jury instruction on involuntary manslaughter; reasoning that in the context of a shooting, for a defendant to be entitled to such an instruction there must be evidence of "the absence of intent to discharge the weapon"; and explaining: "This distinguishes involuntary manslaughter from its voluntary counterpart, which requires proof of intent.").

As a result of 2019 legislation, S.L. 2019-83, add the following new offense, effective for offenses committed on or after December 1, 2019, to this chapter:

Death by Distribution of Certain Controlled Substances (new crime)

Statute

§ 14-18.4. Death by distribution of certain controlled substances; aggravated death by distribution of certain controlled substances; penalties.

(a) Legislative Intent. – The General Assembly recognizes that deaths due to the opioid epidemic are devastating families and communities across North Carolina. The General Assembly finds that the opioid crisis is overwhelming medical providers engaged in the lawful distribution of controlled substances and is straining prevention and treatment efforts. Therefore, the General Assembly enacts this law to encourage effective intervention by the criminal justice system to hold illegal drug dealers accountable for criminal conduct that results in death.

(b) Death by Distribution of Certain Controlled Substances. – A person is guilty of death by distribution of certain controlled substances if all of the following requirements are met:

(1) The person unlawfully sells at least one certain controlled substance.
(2) The ingestion of the certain controlled substance or substances causes the death of the user.
(3) The commission of the offense in subdivision (1) of this subsection was the proximate cause of the victim's death.
(4) The person did not act with malice.

(c) Aggravated Death by Distribution of Certain Controlled Substances. – A person is guilty of aggravated death by distribution of certain controlled substances if all of the following requirements are met:

(1) The person unlawfully sells at least one certain controlled substance.
(2) The ingestion of the certain controlled substance or substances causes the death of the user.
(3) The commission of the offense in subdivision (1) of this subsection was the proximate cause of the victim's death.
(4) The person did not act with malice.
(5) The person has a previous conviction under this section, G.S. 90-95(a)(1), 90-95.1, 90-95.4, 90-95.6, or trafficking in violation of G.S. 90-95(h), or a prior conviction in any federal or state court in the United States that is substantially similar to an offense listed, within seven years of the date of the offense. In calculating the seven-year period under this subdivision, any period of time during which the person was incarcerated in a local, state, or federal detention center, jail, or prison shall be excluded.

(d) Certain Controlled Substance. – For the purposes of this section, the term "certain controlled substance" includes any opium, opiate, or opioid; any synthetic or natural salt, compound, derivative, or preparation of opium, opiate, or opioid; cocaine or any other substance described in G.S. 90-90(1)(d); methamphetamine; a depressant described in G.S. 90-92(a)(1); or a mixture of one or more of these substances.

(e) Lesser Included Offense. – Death by distribution of certain controlled substances constitutes a lesser included offense of aggravated death by distribution of certain controlled substances in violation of this section.

(f) Samaritan Protection. – Nothing in this section shall be construed to restrict or interfere with the rights and immunities provided under G.S. 90-96.2.

(g) Lawful Distribution. – This section shall not apply to any of the following:

(1) Issuing a valid prescription for a controlled substance for a legitimate medical purpose by an individual practitioner acting in the usual course of professional practice.
(2) Dispensing, delivering, or administering a controlled substance pursuant to a prescription, by a pharmacy permitted under G.S. 90-85.21, a pharmacist, or an individual practitioner.

(h) Penalties. – Unless the conduct is covered under some other provision of law providing greater punishment, the following classifications apply to the offenses set forth in this section:

(1) Death by distribution of certain controlled substances is a Class C felony.
(2) Aggravated death by distribution of certain controlled substances is a Class B2 felony.

Elements

A person guilty of this offense

(1) unlawfully
(2) and without malice

(3) sells at least one certain controlled substance, *and*
(4) ingestion of the certain controlled substance or substances causes the user's death, *and*
(5) sale of the certain controlled substance is the proximate cause of the death.

Punishment

Class C felony.

Notes

Element (1)

This offense does not apply to controlled substances issued by prescription for a legitimate medical purpose by a practitioner acting in the usual course of professional practice or to a controlled substance dispensed, delivered, or administered by a pharmacy, pharmacist, or individual practitioner. G.S. 14-18.4(g).

Element (2)

See the discussion of this Element (designated as Element 3) of "Voluntary Manslaughter," above.

Element (3)

For the purposes of this offense, "certain controlled substance" means any opium, opiate, or opioid; any synthetic or natural salt, compound, derivative, or preparation of opium, opiate, or opioid; cocaine or any other substance described in G.S. 90-90(1)d.; methamphetamine; a depressant described in G.S. 90-92(a)(1); or a mixture of one or more of these substances. G.S. 14-18.4(d).

Element (5)

See the note "Proximate cause" under "First-Degree Murder," above.

Multiple convictions and punishments

This offense is a lesser-included offense of "Aggravated Death by Distribution of Certain Controlled Substances." G.S. 14-18.4(e).

Samaritan protection

This offense does not restrict or interfere with the limited immunity from prosecution under G.S. 90-96.2 for persons seeking medical assistance for themselves or others in the event of a drug-related overdose.

As a result of 2019 legislation, S.L. 2019-83, add the following new offense, effective for offenses committed on or after December 1, 2019, to this chapter:

Aggravated Death by Distribution of Certain Controlled Substances (new crime)

Statute

See G.S. 14-18.4(c), reproduced above.

Elements

A person guilty of this offense
(1) unlawfully
(2) and without malice
(3) sells at least one certain controlled substance, *and*
(4) ingestion of the certain controlled substance or substances causes the user's death, *and*

(5) sale of the certain controlled substance is the proximate cause of the death, *and*
(6) the person has a previous conviction within seven years of the date of the offense under G.S. 14-18.4, 90-95(a)(1), 90-95.1, 90-95.4, 90-95.6, 90-95(h), or any state or federal offense that is substantially similar to an offense listed.

Punishment

Class B2 felony.

Notes

Element (1)

See the discussion of this Element of "Death by Distribution of Certain Controlled Substances," above.

Element (2)

See the discussion of this Element (designated as Element 3) of "Voluntary Manslaughter," above.

Element (3)

See the discussion of this Element of "Death by Distribution of Certain Controlled Substances," above.

Element (5)

See the note "Proximate cause" under "First-Degree Murder," above.

Element (6)

In calculating the seven-year lookback period for the prior offenses described in this Element, any period of time during which the person was incarcerated in a local, state, or federal detention center, jail, or prison shall be excluded. G.S. 14-18.4(c)(5).

Samaritan protection

This offense does not restrict or interfere with the limited immunity from prosecution under G.S. 90-96.2 for persons seeking medical assistance for themselves or others in the event of a drug-related overdose.

Death by Vehicle (page 103)

Statute (page 103)

2012 legislation, S.L. 2012-165, amended subsection (a6) of G.S. 20-141.4 by deleting the last sentence of that subsection. That same legislation also amended subsection (b), the punishment provision, to provide:

> (b) Punishments.—Unless the conduct is covered under some other provision of law providing greater punishment, the following classifications apply to the offenses set forth in this section:
>
> (1) Repeat felony death by vehicle is a Class B2 felony.
> (1a) Aggravated felony death by vehicle is a Class D felony. Notwithstanding the provisions of G.S. 15A-1340.17, the court shall sentence the defendant in the aggravated range of the appropriate Prior Record Level.
> (2) Felony death by vehicle is a Class D felony. Notwithstanding the provisions of G.S. 15A-1340.17, intermediate punishment is authorized for a defendant who is a Prior Record Level I offender.
> (3) Aggravated felony serious injury by vehicle is a Class E felony.
> (4) Felony serious injury by vehicle is a Class F felony.
> (5) Misdemeanor death by vehicle is a Class A1 misdemeanor.

Felony Death by Vehicle (page 104)

Punishment (page 104)

As a result of the 2012 legislation noted above, delete the text of this section and replace it with the following:

Class D felony. G.S. 20-141.4(b)(2). Notwithstanding G.S. 15A-1340.17, intermediate punishment is authorized for a defendant who is a Prior Record Level I offender. *Id.*

Notes (page 104)

Element (4) (page 104)

Impairment can be shown by a combination of evidence that a defendant has both ingested an impairing substance and operated a vehicle in a manner showing that he or she was oblivious to a visible risk of harm. State v. Shelton, 263 N.C. App. 681 (2019) (sufficient evidence of impairment where, in addition to blood tests revealing Oxycodone and Tramadol in the defendant's blood in amounts greater than 25 nanograms per milliliter, the defendant did not see the victim standing on the side of the road while other witnesses did, was not aware that he had struck the victim, and drove away from the scene despite knowing that his brakes were inoperable).

Element (5) (page 104)

Impairment can be the proximate cause of death despite the existence of other contributing factors. *Shelton*, 263 N.C. App. at 689–90 (2019) ("[T]he fact that [the defendant's] brakes were in poor condition is not incompatible with the proposition that he was driving while impaired and that his impairment constituted a proximate cause of the death . . . .").

Multiple convictions and punishments (page 104)

Delete the first paragraph of this note and replace it with the following:

G.S. 20-141.4(b), the punishment provision for all death by vehicle offenses, provides, in part, that unless the conduct is covered under some other provision of law providing greater punishment, repeat felony death by vehicle is a Class B2 felony, aggravated felony death by vehicle is a Class D felony, felony death by vehicle is a Class D felony, and misdemeanor death by vehicle is a Class A1 misdemeanor. Thus, a defendant may not be punished for a death by vehicle offense when the defendant is convicted also for an offense carrying a greater punishment and both offenses are based on the same conduct. State v. Davis, 364 N.C. 297, 303 (2010) (the trial court erred by imposing punishment for felony death by vehicle (then a Class E felony) and second-degree murder (Class B2 felony)).

Insert the following at the end of the second paragraph of this note:

G.S. 20-141.4(c) does not bar simultaneous prosecutions for involuntary manslaughter and death by vehicle; it only bars punishment for both offenses when they arise out of the same death. State v. Elmore, 224 N.C. App. 331, 334–36 (2012).

Related Offenses Not in This Chapter (page 105)

Add the following offense to this list:

Death by impaired boating offenses. G.S. 75A-10.3.

Aggravated Felony Death by Vehicle (page 105)

Punishment (page 105)

As a result of the 2012 legislation noted above, delete the text of this section and replace it with the following:

Class D felony. G.S. 20-141.4(b)(1a). Notwithstanding G.S. 15A-1340.17, the defendant must be sentenced in the aggravated range. *Id.*

Repeat Felony Death by Vehicle (page 106)

Punishment (page 106)

As a result of the 2012 legislation noted above, delete the text of this section and replace it with the following:

> Class B2 felony. G.S. 20-141.4(b)(1).

Notes (page 106)

Multiple convictions and punishments (page 107)

Delete the text of this note and replace it with the following:

> See this note to "Felony Death by Vehicle," as amended by this supplement.

7

Assaults

Simple Assault (page 111)

Statute (page 111)

2012 legislation, S.L. 2012-149, enacted a new subsection, (c1), to G.S. 14-33 as follows:

> **(c1) No school personnel as defined in G.S. 14-33(c)(6) who takes reasonable actions in good faith to end a fight or altercation between students shall incur any civil or criminal liability as the result of those actions.**

2015 legislation, S.L. 2015-62, sec. 4(b), amended the definition of "in the presence of a minor" in G.S. 14-33(d)(2) to read as follows:

> **(2) "In the presence of a minor" means that the minor was in a position to see or hear the assault.**

2019 legislation, S.L. 2019-194, effective for offenses committed on or after December 1, 2019, enacted a new subdivision, (c)(9), to G.S. 14-33 as follows, creating a new Class A1 misdemeanor:

> **(9) Assaults a transportation network company (TNC) driver providing a transportation network company (TNC) service. For the purposes of this subdivision, the definitions for "TNC driver" and "TNC service" as defined in G.S. 20-280.1 shall apply.**

Notes (page 113)

Element (1) (page 113)

Add the following citation after the first sentence of this note:

State v. Floyd, 369 N.C. 329 (2016);

Add the following to this note:

For another case defining and explaining the two forms of assault discussed in this note, see *State v. Floyd*, 369 N.C. 329 (2016). In *Floyd* the North Carolina Supreme Court explained that its case law regarding the second form of assault—assault by show of violence—"appears to have evolved from early cases in which a person caused another to flee, leave a place sooner than desired, or otherwise alter course through the threatened use of a weapon." *Id.* at 336 (going on to discuss one of the court's earliest assault by show of violence cases, *State v. Shipman*, 81 N.C. 513 (1879)). Importantly, in *Floyd* the court held that assault by show of violence "does not involve an attempt to cause injury to another person, but is based upon a violent act or threat that causes fear in another person." *Id.* It continued: "Accordingly, although North Carolina law provides one definition of assault that describes the offense in terms of 'an overt act or an attempt, or the unequivocal appearance of an attempt,' our common law also provides a second definition that does not include any reference to attempt." *Id.* The court went on to hold that "[a]ttempted assault is not an attempt of an attempt because assault may be defined by the show-of-violence rule." *Id.* It explained that "there is substantial overlap between the two definitions of assault because an overt act or attempt to do immediate physical injury to another person is likely to constitute a show of violence that causes fear and a change of behavior." *Id.* at 337. "As a result," it concluded, "relying upon the show-of-violence rule to define attempted assault does not create a significant limitation on the conduct covered by this offense." *Id.* Ultimately, the *Floyd* court reversed the court of appeals, which had held that the offense of attempted assault with a deadly weapon inflicting serious injury is not a recognized crime in North Carolina because it constituted an attempt of an attempt. *Id.* In *State v. English*, ___ N.C. App. ___, 845 S.E.2d 901 (2020), there was sufficient evidence of assault with a deadly weapon under both the show of violence theory and as an overt act to physically injure another person with force and violence when the defendant drove a car toward the victim at a high rate of speed after they had been engaged in a violent struggle.

2012 legislation, S.L. 2012-149, enacted G.S. 14-33(c1), providing that no school personnel defined in G.S. 14-33(c)(6) who take reasonable actions in good faith to end a fight or altercation between students shall incur any civil or criminal liability as the result of those actions.

The absence of consent is not an element of assault. State v. Russell, ___ N.C. App. ___, 844 S.E.2d 586 (2020) (the trial court did not err by declining to instruct the jury on consent when one witness said the victim had told the defendant to hit him).

Attempted assault (page 114)

Delete the text of this note and replace it with the following:

In *State v. Floyd*, 369 N.C. 329 (2016), the state supreme court held that attempted assault is a crime in North Carolina; it reversed the court of appeals, which had held that attempted assault with a deadly weapon inflicting serious injury is not a recognized crime because it constituted an attempt of an attempt. *Id.* The *Floyd* court concluded that "[a]ttempted assault is not an attempt of an attempt because assault may be defined by the show-of-violence rule," a form of assault that "does not involve an attempt to cause injury to another person, but is based upon a violent act or threat that causes fear in another person." *Id.* at 336.

District attorney approval required for charging (new note)

As a result of 2012 legislation, S.L. 2012-149, G.S. 15A-301(b1) requires district attorney approval before a magistrate may charge a school employee defined in G.S. 14-33(c)(6) with an offense that occurred while the school employee was in the process of discharging his or her duties of employment. The new statute does not apply to traffic offenses or to offenses that occur in the presence of an officer. Additional procedures are specified if the district attorney declines to accept this authority to approve charges. Although not specifically targeted to assaults, the new statute is most likely to apply with respect to these crimes.

Greater and lesser-included offenses (page 114)

Simple assault is a lesser-included offense of common law robbery. State v. Cromartie, 257 N.C. App. 790, 796 (2018).

Multiple convictions and punishments (page 114)

The State presented substantial evidence supporting two separate assaults where the defendant attacked his wife with his hands and, when his child intervened with a baseball bat to protect his mother, the defendant grabbed the bat and used it to beat his wife; the assaults involved separate thought processes, they were distinct in time, and the victim sustained injuries on different parts of her body as a result of each assault. State v. Wilkes, 367 N.C. 116 (2013) (affirming per curiam 225 N.C. App. 233 (2013)). For a case where the State sufficiently proved two distinct incidents of assault with a deadly weapon inflicting serious injury supporting two convictions, see *State v. Lanford*, 225 N.C. App. 189, 204 (2013) (rejecting the argument that only one offense occurred because the assaults were part of chronic and continual abuse).

A defendant's raising a gun and firing it—two acts that occurred in rapid succession without interruption—cannot support two separate counts of assault (one for assault by pointing a gun and one for assault with a deadly weapon). State v. Jones, 265 N.C. App. 644 (2019).

Assaults Inflicting a Particular Type of Injury (page 115)

Assault Inflicting Serious Injury (page 115)

Notes (page 115)

Element (3) (page 115)

Insert the following after the first sentence of the last paragraph of this note:

State v. Anderson, 222 N.C. App. 138, 145 (2012) (the trial court did not err by instructing the jury that three gunshot wounds to the leg constituted serious injury where the victim was hospitalized for two days, had surgery to remove a bone fragment, and experienced pain at the time of trial);

Multiple convictions and punishments (page 116)

Add the following to the string cite following the fourth sentence of this note:

State v. Fields, 374 N.C. 629 (2020) (based on the "unless covered" language in G.S. 14-33, a defendant may not be convicted and sentenced for both assault inflicting serious bodily injury (Class F felony) and habitual misdemeanor assault (Class H felony)); State v. Perry, 260 N.C. App. 659 (2018) (based on the "unless covered" language in G.S. 14-33, a defendant may not be convicted of assault on a child under G.S. 14-33 (Class A1 misdemeanor) and assault under G.S. 14-32 (felonious assault with a deadly weapon with intent to kill inflicting serious injury (Class C felony)) based on the same conduct); State v. McPhaul, 256 N.C. App. 303, 306 (2017) (based on the "unless covered" language in G.S. 14-32.4 (assault inflicting serious bodily injury, a Class F felony), the defendant could not be convicted of both that offense and assault with a deadly weapon with intent to kill inflicting serious injury, a Class C felony); State v. Baldwin, 240 N.C. App. 413, 425–26 (2015) (same); State v. Coakley, 238 N.C. App. 480, 491–92 (2014) (based on the "unless covered" language in G.S. 14-32.4(a) (assault inflicting serious bodily injury, a Class F felony), the defendant could not be convicted for both that offense and the more serious offense of assault with a deadly weapon inflicting serious injury under G.S. 14-32(b), a Class E felony); State v. Jones, 237 N.C. App. 526, 532–33 (2014) (because of the "unless the conduct is covered" language in the assault on a female statute, the trial court erred by sentencing the defendant to that offense (Class A1 misdemeanor) and habitual misdemeanor assault (Class H felony) when both convictions were based on the same conduct); State v. Jamison, 234 N.C. App. 231, 238–39 (2014) (the defendant could not be convicted and sentenced for both assault inflicting serious bodily injury (Class F felony) and assault on a female (Class A1 misdemeanor) when based on the same conduct; the "unless covered" language in the assault on a female statute reflects a legislative intent to limit a trial court's authority to impose punishment for that offense when punishment also is imposed for higher-class offenses that apply to the same conduct).

The courts have noted that *Hines*, discussed in this note, is distinguishable from this line of cases because the offenses at issue there (aggravated assault on a handicapped person and armed robbery) were based on distinct conduct, not the same act. *Jones*, 237 N.C. App. at 531–32. And the court of appeals has held that the "unless covered" language does not preclude multiple assault convictions when the assault convictions are based on separate and distinct conduct. State v. Harding, 258 N.C. App. 306, 318 (2018) (notwithstanding the "unless covered" language in G.S. 14-33(c) with respect to assault on a female, the defendant was properly convicted of that offense (a Class A1 misdemeanor) and the more serious offense of assault by strangulation (a Class H felony) where the convictions were based on separate conduct; the defendant's act of pinning down the victim and choking her to stop her from screaming supported the assault by strangulation conviction and his separate and distinct acts of grabbing her hair, tossing her down a rocky embankment, and punching her face and head multiple times supported the assault on a female conviction).

Delete the second to last sentence of this note.

Related Offenses Not in This Chapter (page 117)

Add the following offense to this list:

Violation of Chapter 95, Article 15 (Passenger Tramway Safety) causing serious injury. G.S. 95-125.3(g), *as enacted by* S.L. 2017-211, sec. 14(c).

Assault Inflicting Serious Bodily Injury (page 117)

Notes (page 118)

Element (3) (page 118)

Add the following after the last bullet in this note:

- the victim had broken bones in her face, a broken hand, and a cracked knee; she could not see properly out of her eye at the time of trial and she testified that her hand and eye "hurt all of the time," State v. Jamison, 234 N.C. App. 231, 235–36 (2014);
- the defendant's bites to the victim's body caused extreme pain, skin removal, hospitalization, and permanent scarring, State v. Burwell, 256 N.C. App. 722, 727–28 (2017);
- the victim, a transgender woman, suffered a long rip in her genitals that required stitches and pain medication, resulted in time off from work, and caused significant pain for six months, in addition to a jagged scar that the court deemed a serious permanent disfigurement, State v. Fields, 265 N.C. App. 69 (2019);
- the victim had a concussion and severe headaches that continued four years after the attack, State v. Griffin, 264 N.C. App. 490 (2019); and
- the victim's fractured eye socket resulted in the "protracted loss or impairment of the function of a bodily member or organ" when it left her completely blind in one eye for one week and her vision was not fully restored for two full weeks after the assault; she could not drive for one week and was not able to return to work until her vision was completely restored, State v. Rushing, 268 N.C. App. 285 (2019).

Add the following at the end of this note:

For a case where the evidence was insufficient to establish that an officer sustained serious bodily injury from the defendant's bites, see *State v. Williams*, 255 N.C. App. 168, 181–83 (2017) (the injury did not rise to the level of a permanent or protracted condition causing extreme pain where, among other things, upon leaving the hospital the officer returned to the police station to complete paperwork and went to work the following day; also rejecting the argument that the officer suffered serious, permanent disfigurement because a bite mark–shaped discoloration remained on his forearm for approximately two years after the incident, concluding that the presence of a minor scar or other mild disfigurement alone does not constitute serious bodily injury).

For a case involving a charge of child abuse inflicting serious bodily injury under G.S. 14-318.4(a3) where the evidence was insufficient to establish serious bodily injury, see *State v. Dixon*, 258 N.C. App. 78, 85–86 (2018) (scars from surgery to address an injury to the victim's leg did not by themselves constitute serious bodily injury where, by the time of trial, the victim was engaged in unrestricted physical activities and an expert testified that she would have no permanent disfiguration or loss or impairment of function due to the scars; the evidence did not establish that the victim experienced a permanent or protracted condition causing extreme pain where she testified that her leg stopped hurting long before trial and the evidence showed that she was cleared to engage in normal activities within nine months of surgery; no evidence showed that the victim was ever at risk of death due to the injury).

Assault Inflicting Physical Injury by Strangulation (page 119)

Notes (page 119)

Element (3) (page 119)
The evidence was sufficient to establish assault by strangulation where the defendant strangled the victim twice; a medical expert testified that the victim's injuries were consistent with strangulation; and photographic evidence showed bruising, abrasions, and a bite mark on and around the victim's neck. State v. Lowery, 228 N.C. App. 229, 232–33 (2013) (rejecting the defendant's arguments that the statute required "proof of physical injury beyond what is inherently caused by every act of strangulation" or extensive physical injury).

Element (4) (page 119)
The statute does not require a particular method of restricting the victim's airway, such as direct application of force to the trachea. State v. Lanford, 225 N.C. App. 189, 197 (2013). Thus, the evidence is sufficient when it shows that the defendant obstructed the victim's airway by putting his hand over her nose and mouth. *Id.*

Deadly Weapon Assaults (page 120)

Assault with a Deadly Weapon (page 120)

Notes (page 120)

Element (3) (page 120)
For a case where the trial court properly concluded that a knife was not a deadly weapon per se and left that determination to the jury, see *State v. Edgerton*, 234 N.C. App. 412, 419 (2014) (there was conflicting evidence regarding whether or not the knife was capable of producing death or great bodily harm; among other things, a witness testified that the knife was so dull that even though the defendant was "sawing" the victim's neck with it, the knife left only nicks on her neck), *rev'd on other grounds*, 368 N.C. 32 (2015).

Insert the following after the citation to *State v. Ferguson* in the fourth bullet on page 121:

State v. Spencer, 218 N.C. App. 267, 274–75 (2012) (based on a vehicle's high rate of speed and the fact that the victim had to take affirmative action to avoid harm, a car was a deadly weapon as a matter of law);

Insert the following after the eighth bullet on page 121:

- a kitchen table chair, State v. James, 224 N.C. App. 164, 170 (2012);

Insert the following at the end of this note:

Because there was evidence that the defendant assaulted the victim with a lawn chair and not with his fists alone, the State was not required to present evidence as to the defendant's and the victim's size or condition. State v. Mills, 221 N.C. App. 409, 413 (2012).

Greater and lesser-included offenses (page 122)
Assault with a deadly weapon is a lesser-included offense of armed robbery. State v. Hinton, 361 N.C. 207, 210 (2007); State v. Richardson, 279 N.C. 621, 628 (1971).

Multiple convictions and punishments (page 122)
A defendant's raising a gun and firing it—two acts that occurred in rapid succession without interruption—cannot support two separate counts of assault (one for assault by pointing a gun and one for assault with a deadly weapon). State v. Jones, 265 N.C. App. 644 (2019).

Related Offenses Not in This Chapter (page 123)

Remove the following offense from this list:

Transporting dangerous weapon or substance during emergency; possessing off premises; exceptions. G.S. 14-288.7.

Assault with a Deadly Weapon with Intent to Kill (page 123)

Notes (page 124)

Element (1) (page 124)
A concurring opinion in *State v. Floyd*, 369 N.C. 329, 342 (2016), states that the court's decision in *State v. Birchfield*, 235 N.C. 410, 413 (1952), "recognized that the statutory definition of 'assault' under [G.S. 14-32] requires a completed battery."

Element (4) (page 124)
For additional assault cases where the evidence was sufficient to show an intent to kill, see *State v. Cox*, 256 N.C. App. 511, 524–25 (2017) (rejecting the defendant's argument that the State was required to prove that the defendant specifically intended to kill victim Stokes when he fired into a trailer while Stokes and others were inside; the court reasoned that "[i]t is not determinative . . . whether or not Defendant knew Stokes was in the trailer," concluding that there was sufficient evidence that the defendant "intended to kill whoever was inside the trailer" where, among other things, he fired numerous shots into the trailer knowing it was occupied); *State v. Stewart*, 231 N.C. App. 134, 145–46 (2013) (after shooting and killing eight people, the defendant ignored an officer's instruction to drop his shotgun, reloaded it, and fired at the officer); *State v. Stokes*, 225 N.C. App. 483, 485 (2013) (during a robbery the defendant fired a gun beside the victim's head, and the victim thought the defendant was going to kill him); and *State v. Wilkes*, 225 N.C. App. 233, 237 (the defendant hit the victim with a bat and, after she fell to her knees, he repeatedly struck her head until she lost consciousness, she never fought back, and the wounds could have been fatal; the circumstances of the attack, including the parties' conduct, provided additional evidence of intent to kill, including that the two had a volatile relationship and the victim had recently filed for divorce), *aff'd per curiam*, 367 N.C. 116 (2013).

Assault with a Deadly Weapon Inflicting Serious Injury (page 124)

Notes (page 125)

Element (1) (page 125)

A concurring opinion in *State v. Floyd,* 369 N.C. 329, 342 (2016), states that the court's decision in *State v. Birchfield,* 235 N.C. 410, 413 (1952), "recognized that the statutory definition of 'assault' under [G.S. 14-32] requires a completed battery."

Multiple convictions and punishments (page 125)

This offense is not a lesser-included offense of assault by a prisoner with a deadly weapon inflicting bodily injury, and thus a defendant may be convicted of and sentenced for both crimes. State v. Smith, 267 N.C. App. 364 (2019).

Assault with a Deadly Weapon with Intent to Kill Inflicting Serious Injury (page 125)

Notes (page 126)

Element (1) (page 126)

A concurring opinion in *State v. Floyd,* 369 N.C. 329, 342 (2016), states that the court's decision in *State v. Birchfield,* 235 N.C. 410, 413 (1952), "recognized that the statutory definition of 'assault' under [G.S. 14-32] requires a completed battery."

Greater and lesser-included offenses (page 126)

Replace the first sentence of this note with the following:

Because all of the elements of (1) simple assault, (2) assault with a deadly weapon, (3) assault with a deadly weapon with intent to kill, (4) assault inflicting serious injury, and (5) assault with a deadly weapon inflicting serious injury are included in assault with a deadly weapon with intent to kill inflicting serious injury, all of those offenses are lesser-included offenses of this offense.

Multiple convictions and punishments (page 126)

Assault with a deadly weapon with intent to kill inflicting serious injury is not a lesser-included offense of attempted first-degree murder; a defendant may be convicted of and punished for both offenses. State v. Rogers, 219 N.C. App. 296, 307–09 (2012).

Assault by Pointing a Gun (page 126)

Notes (page 127)

Element (2) (page 127)

For a case with multiple victims where the court rejected the defendant's argument that the State's evidence was too vague for the jury to infer that he pointed the gun at any particular person, see *State v. Pender,* 243 N.C. App. 142, 153 (2015) (witnesses testified that the defendant waved the gun "at us" and pointed the gun "toward everybody in one room").

Related Offenses Not in This Chapter (page 127)

Remove the following offense from this list:

Transporting dangerous weapon or substance during emergency. G.S. 14-288.7.

Discharging Barreled Weapons and Firearms (page 128)

Discharging a Barreled Weapon or Firearm into Occupied Property (page 128)

Notes (page 128)

Element (1) (page 128)

Insert the following after the first sentence of this note:

State v. Bryant, 244 N.C. App. 102, 109–10 (2015).

Element (3) (page 128)

Add the following at the end of the second paragraph of this note:

; State v. Hicks, 241 N.C. App. 345, 353 (2015) (same); State v. Mitchell, 240 N.C. App. 246, 257–58 (2015) (same; the evidence was sufficient where the defendant's hips, chest, and head were outside the vehicle and part of his leg and arm were inside it).

Element (4) (page 129)

Replace the second paragraph of this note with the following:

To be guilty of this offense, a defendant must discharge the weapon "with knowledge that the building is then occupied . . . or when he has reasonable grounds to believe that the building might be occupied." State v. James, 342 N.C. 589, 596 (1996) (quoting *State v. Williams*, 284 N.C. 67, 73 (1973), and emphasizing the word "might" in this standard); *see also* State v. Everette, 361 N.C. 646, 650 (2007). For cases where there was sufficient evidence that the defendant had reasonable grounds to believe that property might be occupied, see *State v. Jones*, 265 N.C. App. 644 (2019) (defendant slowly drove by the house a few minutes before shooting into it, and then stepped out of his car and loudly called to people in the house, challenging them to come outside); *Everette*, 361 N.C. at 651 (lights were on in a restaurant in an area known to be crowded in the early morning hours, the surrounding streets were crowded, and nearby establishments remained open until the early morning); *James*, 342 N.C. at 597 (reasonable grounds to believe that cars were occupied when the defendant fired a semiautomatic weapon in a club's parking lot knowing that vehicles were parked there and that people who had left the club were in the parking lot); and *State v. Charleston*, 248 N.C. App. 671, 676 (2016) (a shooting into the victim's residence occurred in a residential neighborhood in the evening while the victim's car was parked outside her home).

Add the following text to this note:

A residence was occupied when the family was on the front porch. State v. Miles, 223 N.C. App. 160, 163–64 (2012).

Multiple convictions and punishments (page 129)

Add the following text to the first paragraph of this note:

If the weapon used requires the defendant to pull and release the trigger each time he or she decides to shoot (that is, it is not a machine gun or other automatic weapon), then each shot can constitute a separate and distinct act, and can therefore support a separate conviction. State v. Morrison, ___ N.C. App. ___, 847 S.E.2d 238 (2020) (the evidence indicated the defendant used a semi-automatic weapon that required a separate trigger pull for each of seven shots). Multiple convictions are also proper when a single shot enters multiple dwellings. State v. Ray, 97 N.C. App. 621 (1990) (two convictions under G.S. 14-34.1 did not violate double jeopardy where the defendant fired a single bullet that entered two apartments). Multiple charges are not proper, however, when a single shot injures multiple occupants of the same dwelling. State v. Miller, 267 N.C. App. 639 (2019) (requiring the court to arrest judgment on one of two convictions under G.S. 14-34.1 resulting from a single shot into a single occupied vehicle).

Discharging a Barreled Weapon or Firearm into an Occupied Dwelling or Occupied Conveyance in Operation (page 130)

Notes (page 130)

Multiple convictions and punishments (page 130)
No violation of double jeopardy occurred when the defendant was sentenced for three counts of discharging a firearm into occupied property where each shot was "distinct in time, and each bullet hit the [house] in a different place." State v. Kirkwood, 229 N.C. App. 656, 667–68 (2013) (internal quotation marks, citations omitted).

Discharging Firearm within Occupied Building, etc. to Incite Fear (new crime)

This offense was enacted by 2013 legislation, S.L. 2013-144.

Statute

§ 14-34.10. Discharge firearm within enclosure to incite fear.
Unless covered under some other provision of law providing greater punishment, any person who willfully or wantonly discharges or attempts to discharge a firearm within any occupied building, structure, motor vehicle, or other conveyance, erection, or enclosure with the intent to incite fear in another shall be punished as a Class F felon.

Elements

A person guilty of this offense

(1) willfully or wantonly
(2) discharges or attempts to discharge a firearm
(3) within any occupied building, structure, motor vehicle, or other conveyance, erection, or enclosure
(4) with the intent to incite fear in another.

Punishment

Class F felony. G.S. 14-34.10.

Notes

Element (1). See this note to "Discharging a Barreled Weapon or Firearm into Occupied Property" in the main volume.

Element (2). See this note to "Discharging a Barreled Weapon or Firearm into Occupied Property" in the main volume. Note that unlike the other "Discharging Barreled Weapons and Firearms" offenses, this one only covers discharge of a firearm, not a barreled weapon.

Element (3). For the meaning of the term "occupied," see the note on Element (4) to "Discharging a Barreled Weapon or Firearm into Occupied Property" in the main volume. Note that this offense covers discharge of a firearm "within" the building, etc. The other "Discharging Barreled Weapons and Firearms" offenses cover discharging "into" the specified location.

Attempt. See this note to "Discharging a Barreled Weapon or Firearm into Occupied Property" in the main volume.

Multiple convictions and punishments. See this note to "Discharging a Barreled Weapon or Firearm into Occupied Property" in the main volume. This statute begins with the language, "Unless covered under some other provision of law providing greater punishment." For a discussion of the meaning of this phrase, see this note on "Assault Inflicting Serious Injury" in the main volume.

Related Offenses Not in This Chapter

See the offenses listed under "Discharging a Barreled Weapon or Firearm into Occupied Property" in the main volume.

Assault on a Female (page 133)

Notes (page 133)

Greater and lesser-included offenses (page 133)

Assault on a female is not a lesser-included offense of first-degree sexual offense. State v. Martin, 222 N.C. App. 213, 221–22 (2012).

Assaults Involving Children (page 133)

Assault in the Presence of a Minor (page 134)

Statute (page 134)

2015 legislation, S.L. 2015-62, sec. 4(b), amended G.S. 14-33(d)(2) as noted under "Simple Assault," above in this supplement.

Notes (page 135)

Element (4) (page 135)

Delete the first sentence of this note and replace it with the following:

"In the presence of a minor" means that the minor was in a position to see or hear the assault. G.S. 14-33(d)(2).

Female Genital Mutilation of a Child (new crime)

This offense was enacted by 2019 legislation, S.L. 2019-183, effective for offenses committed on or after October 1, 2019.

Statute

§ 14-28.1. Female genital mutilation of a child.

(a) Legislative Intent. – The General Assembly finds that female genital mutilation is a crime that causes a long-lasting impact on the victim's quality of life and has been recognized internationally as a violation of the human rights of girls and women. The practice is mostly carried out on girls under the age of 15 years old. The General Assembly also recognizes that the practice includes any procedure that intentionally alters or injures the female genital organs for nonmedical reasons. These procedures can cause severe pain, excessive bleeding, urinary problems, and death. Therefore, the General Assembly enacts this law to protect these vulnerable victims.

(b) Mutilation. – A person who knowingly and unlawfully circumcises, excises, or infibulates the whole or any part of the labia majora, labia minora, or clitoris of a child less than 18 years of age is guilty of a Class C felony.

(c) Consent to Mutilation. – A parent, or a person providing care to or supervision of a child less than 18 years of age, who consents to or permits the unlawful circumcision, excision, or infibulation, in whole or in any part, of the labia majora, labia minora, or clitoris of the child, is guilty of a Class C felony.

(d) Removal for Mutilation. – A parent, or a person providing care to or supervision of a child less than 18 years of age, who knowingly removes or permits the removal of the child from the State for the purpose of having the child's labia majora, labia minora, or clitoris circumcised, excised, or infibulated, is guilty of a Class C felony.

(e) Exceptions. – A surgical operation is not a violation of this section if the operation meets either of the following requirements: (1) The operation is necessary to the health of the person on whom it is performed and is performed by a person licensed in the State as a medical practitioner. (2) The operation is performed on a person in labor who has just given birth and is performed for medical purposes connected with that labor or birth by a person licensed in this State as a medical practitioner or certified nurse midwife, or a person in training to become licensed as a medical practitioner or certified nurse midwife.

(f) No Defense. – It is not a defense to prosecution under this section that the person on whom the circumcision, excision, or infibulation is performed, or any other person, believes that the circumcision, excision, or infibulation is required as a matter of custom or ritual, or that the person on whom the circumcision, excision, or infibulation is performed consented to the circumcision, excision, or infibulation.

Elements

A person guilty of this offense

(1) knowingly and unlawfully
(2) (a) circumcises,
    (b) excises, *or*
    (c) infibulates
(3) the whole or part of the labia majora, labia minora, or clitoris
(4) of a child less than 18 years of age.

Punishment

Class C felony. G.S. 14-28.1(b).

Notes

Element (2). Circumcision, excision, and infibulation describe different procedures falling under the umbrella term of female genital mutilation. The term "circumcision"—though rejected by medical practitioners because it suggests a fallacious analogy to male circumcision—generally refers to a partial removal of the clitoris. In "excision," both the clitoris and labia minora are typically removed. In "infibulation," the clitoris and some or all of the labia minora are removed and the labia majora are cut and stitched, often to cover part of the vaginal opening. MARTHA C. NUSSBAUM, SEX AND SOCIAL JUSTICE 119–20 (1999).

Exceptions. Surgical operations are not a violation of this offense when performed (1) by a licensed medical practitioner for the health of the person on whom the procedure is performed or (2) by a licensed medical practitioner, certified midwife, or person in training to become licensed or certified on a person in labor or a person who has just given birth. G.S. 14-28.1(e). That the procedure is conducted as a matter of custom, ritual, or by consent is no defense to this offense. *Id.* § (f).

Related Offenses Not in This Chapter

Consenting to Genital Mutilation. G.S. 14-28.1(c).
Removal for Genital Mutilation. G.S. 14-28.1(d).
See "Child Abuse" offenses in Chapter 9 (Abuse and Neglect) of the main volume.

Assaults on Persons with Disabilities (page 139) (revised title)

Simple Assault on a Person with a Disability (page 139) (revised title)

Statute

2018 legislation, S.L. 2018-47, sec. 4(m), amended the statute to read as follows:

§ 14-32.1. Assaults on individuals with a disability; punishments.

(a) For purposes of this section, an "individual with a disability" is an individual who has one or more of the following that would substantially impair the ability to defend oneself:

(1) A physical or mental disability, such as a decreased use of arms or legs, blindness, deafness, intellectual disability, or mental illness.

(2) An infirmity.

(b) through (d) Repealed by Session Laws 1993 (Reg. Sess., 1994), c. 767, s. 31, effective October 1, 1994.

(e) Unless the conduct is covered under some other provision of law providing greater punishment, any person who commits any aggravated assault or assault and battery on an individual with a disability is guilty of a Class F felony. A person commits an aggravated assault or assault and battery upon an individual with a disability if, in the course of the assault or assault and battery, that person does any of the following:

(1) Uses a deadly weapon or other means of force likely to inflict serious injury or serious damage to an individual with a disability.

(2) Inflicts serious injury or serious damage to an individual with a disability.

(3) Intends to kill an individual with a disability.

(f) Any person who commits a simple assault or battery upon an individual with a disability is guilty of a Class A1 misdemeanor.

Elements (page 139)

As a result of the 2018 legislation noted above, the elements to this offense should now read:

A person guilty of this offense

(1) commits an assault or battery

(2) on an individual with a disability

(3) knowing or having reason to know that the individual has a disability.

Notes (page 139)

Terminology change (new note)

The 2018 legislation noted above replaced the statutory term "handicapped" with the term "individual with a disability." Except as updated here, the notes in the main volume continue to reference the old statutory term "handicapped" that was interpreted by the relevant case law.

Element (2) (page 139)

As a result of the 2018 legislation noted above, delete the first paragraph of this note and replace it with the following:

The statute defines an "individual with a disability" as a person who has one or both of the following conditions, substantially impairing the ability to defend: (1) a physical or mental disability, such as a decreased use of arms or legs, blindness, deafness, intellectual disability, or mental illness; or (2) an infirmity. G.S. 14-32.1(a).

Add the following to this note:

There was a sufficient factual basis to support a plea where the victim was 80 years old, crippled by arthritis in her knees, and walked with a crutch. State v. Collins, 221 N.C. App. 604, 607–08 (2012).

Aggravated Assault on a Person with a Disability (page 140) (revised title)

Elements (page 140)

As a result of the 2018 legislation noted above, the elements to this offense should now read:

A person guilty of this offense

(1) commits an assault or battery
(2) on an individual with a disability
(3) knowing or having reason to know that the individual has a disability *and*
(4) (a) uses a deadly weapon or other means of force likely to cause serious injury or serious damage to a person with a disability,
    (b) inflicts serious injury on a person with a disability, *or*
    (c) intends to kill a person with a disability.

Notes (page 140)

Terminology change (new note)

The 2018 legislation noted above replaced the statutory term "handicapped" with the term "individual with a disability." Except as updated here, the notes in the main volume continue to reference the old statutory term "handicapped" that was interpreted by the relevant case law and to reference the old name of the related offense "Simple Assault on a Handicapped Person."

Assaults on Government Officers, Employees, and Similar Persons (page 141)

Assault on a Governmental Officer or Employee (page 141)

Notes (page 141)

Element (2) (page 141)

Add the following to the second paragraph of this note:

For a case supporting the statement in this paragraph, see *State v. Mylett*, 253 N.C. App. 198, 209 (2017) (holding that the mens rea element of this offense "is satisfied whenever a defendant while in the course of assaulting another individual instead assaults an individual he knows, or reasonably should know, is a government officer"). *See also* State v. Burwell, 256 N.C. App. 722, 727 (2017) (proving assault inflicting serious bodily injury on an officer under G.S. 14-34.7(a) requires proof that the defendant knew or had reasonable grounds to know that the victim was a law enforcement officer).

The evidence was sufficient to show that the defendant knew or had reasonable grounds to know that the victim was a law enforcement officer where the officer arrived in a marked patrol vehicle, was uniformed, and told the defendant that he was a law enforcement officer. *Burwell*, 256 N.C. App. at 728.

Element (3) (page 141)

Add the following to the first paragraph of this note:

An officer was discharging the duties of his office when (1) after transporting the defendant to the jail and escorting him to a holding cell, the officer remained at the jail, State v. Friend, 237 N.C. App. 490, 495 (2014) (reasoning that by remaining at the jail, the officer was ensuring the safety of other officers), and (2) responding to a report about a trespasser, the officer was conducting investigative work and acting on the results of his investigation. *Burwell*, 256 N.C. App. at 728.

Delete the third paragraph of this note and replace it with the following:

> In *Friend*, the court stated that "unlike the offense of resisting, delaying, or obstructing an officer, criminal liability for the offense of assaulting an officer is not limited to situations where an officer is engaging in lawful conduct in the performance or attempted performance of his or her official duties." *Friend*, 237 N.C. App. at 495 (citation omitted). *See also Burwell*, 256 N.C. App. at 728 (citing *Friend* for this proposition).

Assault with a Firearm on a Law Enforcement Officer, Probation or Parole Officer, Member of the National Guard, or Detention Facility Employee (page 145) (revised title)

Statute (page 145)

2015 legislation, S.L. 2015-74, sec. 2, changed the title of the statute and added a new subsection, (a1), to the statute to read as follows:

> **§ 14-34.5. Assault with a firearm on a law enforcement, probation, or parole officer, or on a member of the North Carolina National Guard, or on a person employed at a State or local detention facility.**
> (a1) Any person who commits an assault with a firearm upon a member of the North Carolina National Guard while the member is in the performance of his or her duties is guilty of a Class E felony.

Elements (page 145)

As a result of the 2015 legislation noted immediately above, Element (3) should read as follows:

(3) on a
 (a) law enforcement officer,
 (b) probation officer,
 (c) parole officer,
 (d) member of the North Carolina National Guard, *or*
 (e) state or local government detention facility employee

Punishment (page 145)

2019 legislation, S.L. 2019-116, increases the punishment for this offense for offenses committed on or after December 1, 2019, when committed against certain victims as follows:

> Class E felony if committed against a member of the North Carolina National Guard. G.S. 14-34.5(a1). Class D felony if committed against a law enforcement officer, probation officer, parole officer, or state or local government detention facility employee. *Id.* §§ (a), (b).

Assault Inflicting Physical Injury on a Law Enforcement Officer, Probation or Parole Officer, Member of the National Guard, or Detention Facility Employee (page 146) (revised title)

Statute (page 146)

2015 legislation, S.L. 2015-74, sec. 1, amended the statute to read as follows:

> **§ 14-34.7. Certain assaults on a law enforcement, probation, or parole officer, or on a member of the North Carolina National Guard, or on a person employed at a State or local detention facility; penalty.**
> (a) Unless covered under some other provision of law providing greater punishment, a person is guilty of a Class F felony if the person assaults a law enforcement officer, probation officer, or parole officer while the officer is discharging or attempting to discharge his or her official duties and inflicts serious bodily injury on the officer.

(a1) Unless covered under some other provision of law providing greater punishment, a person is guilty of a Class F felony if the person assaults a member of the North Carolina National Guard while he or she is discharging or attempting to discharge his or her official duties and inflicts serious bodily injury on the member.

(b) Unless covered under some other provision of law providing greater punishment, a person is guilty of a Class F felony if the person assaults a person who is employed at a detention facility operated under the jurisdiction of the State or a local government while the employee is in the performance of the employee's duties and inflicts serious bodily injury on the employee.

(c) Unless covered under some other provision of law providing greater punishment, a person is guilty of a Class I felony if the person does any of the following:

(1) Assaults a law enforcement officer, probation officer, or parole officer while the officer is discharging or attempting to discharge his or her official duties and inflicts physical injury on the officer.
(2) Assaults a person who is employed at a detention facility operated under the jurisdiction of the State or a local government while the employee is in the performance of the employee's duties and inflicts physical injury on the employee.
(3) Assaults a member of the North Carolina National Guard while he or she is discharging or attempting to discharge his or her official duties and inflicts physical injury on the member.

For the purposes of this subsection, "physical injury" includes cuts, scrapes, bruises, or other physical injury which does not constitute serious injury.

Elements (page 147)

As a result of the 2015 legislation noted immediately above, Element (2) should read as follows:

(2) on a
  (a) law enforcement officer,
  (b) probation officer,
  (c) parole officer,
  (d) member of the North Carolina National Guard, *or*
  (e) state or local government detention facility employee

Assault Inflicting Serious Injury or Serious Bodily Injury on a Law Enforcement Officer, Probation or Parole Officer, Member of the National Guard, or Detention Facility Employee (page 147) (revised title)

Statute (page 147)

As a result of the 2015 legislation noted above, the statutory citation in this section should read as follows:

See G.S. 14-34.7(a), (a1), and (b).

Elements (page 147)

As a result of the 2015 legislation noted above, Element (2) should read as follows:

(2) on a
  (a) law enforcement officer,
  (b) probation officer,
  (c) parole officer,
  (d) member of the North Carolina National Guard, *or*
  (e) state or local government detention facility employee.

Punishment (page 148)

Delete the citation in this section and replace it with the following:

G.S. 14-34.7.

Notes (page 148)

Element (4) (page 148)

2015 legislation, S.L. 2015-74, sec. 1, revised the title of this offense, deleting the words "serious injury" and thus calling into question the reasoning of the *Crawford* case cited in this note. If this statutory change was meant to abrogate *Crawford*, only proof of serious bodily injury would satisfy the statute.

In *State v. Williams*, 255 N.C. App. 168 (2017), the court had to determine whether the evidence was sufficient to show serious bodily injury. The trial court had instructed the jury that "[s]erious bodily injury is an injury that creates or causes serious permanent disfigurement, a permanent or protracted condition that causes extreme pain, or permanent or protracted loss or impairment of the function of any bodily member or organ." *Id.* at 179. The *Williams* court determined that "[b]ecause the trial court limited its instruction concerning serious bodily injury to the above, we do not consider any other potential definitions of 'serious bodily injury.' " *Id.*

Malicious Conduct by a Prisoner (page 148)

Statute (page 148)

2017 legislation, S.L. 2017-186, sec. 2(gg), amended the statute, and 2018 legislation, S.L. 2018-67, sec. 2, substantially rewrote it to read as follows:

§ 14-258.4. Malicious conduct by prisoner.

(a) Any prisoner who knowingly and willfully throws, emits, or causes to be used as a projectile, any bodily fluids, excrement, or unknown substance at an employee, while the employee is in the performance of the employee's duties, is guilty of a Class F felony.

(b) Any prisoner who knowingly and willfully exposes genitalia to an employee while the employee is in the performance of the employee's duties is guilty of a Class I felony.

(c) The provisions of this section apply to violations committed inside or outside of the prison, jail, detention center, or other confinement facility.

(d) Sentences imposed under this Article shall run consecutively to and shall commence at the expiration of any sentence being served by the person sentenced under this section.

Elements (page 148)

As a result of the legislation noted above, the elements of this offense should read as follows:

A person guilty of this offense

(1) while a prisoner
(2) knowingly and willfully
(3) throws, emits, or causes to be used as a projectile, any bodily fluids, excrement, or unknown substance
(4) at an employee, while the employee is in the performance of the employee's duties.

Punishment (page 149)

As a result of the 2018 legislation noted above, add the following to this section:

This offense is in G.S. Chapter 14, Article 33 (Prison Breach and Prisoners). The statute provides that "[s]entences imposed under this Article shall run consecutively to and shall commence at the expiration of any sentence being served by the person sentenced under this section." G.S. 14-258.4(d). This appears to mean that any sentence imposed for an Article 33 offense must run consecutively to a sentence being served for this offense.

Notes (page 149)

Generally (new note)

The 2018 legislation noted above substantially rewrote the statute. The notes in the main volume continue to apply to prosecutions initiated under the old statute and to the new statute to the extent there is overlap.

Element (1) (under amended version of the statute)
Prior to the 2018 amendments, the statute applied to certain persons in the "custody" of specified entities. As amended in 2018, it now applies to any "prisoner," but the definition of that term tracks the old statutory language. Specifically, the term "prisoner" includes any person in the custody of the Division of Adult Correction and Juvenile Justice of the Department of Public Safety, any law enforcement officer, or any local confinement facility as defined in G.S. 153A-217 or -230.1, including persons pending trial, appellate review, or presentence diagnostic evaluation. G.S. 14-254.5(2).

The offense need not occur at a custodial facility; the statute specifies that the offense applies to conduct "committed inside or outside of the prison, jail, detention center, or other confinement facility." G.S. 14-258.4(c).

Element (4) (under amended version of the statute)
An employee is defined to mean any person hired or contracted to work for the State or for a local government. G.S. 14-254.5(1).

Multiple convictions and punishments (page 149)
A defendant may be convicted of two counts of this offense for two acts that occurred during one incident. State v. Heavner, 227 N.C. App. 139, 146 (2013) (the defendant spit on an officer's forehead while the defendant was in a house; five minutes later he spit on the officer's arm after being taken out of the house).

Related Offenses Not in This Chapter (page 149)

Prisoner exposing genitalia to employee. G.S. 14-258.4(b) (enacted by S.L. 2018-67, sec. 2).

Assault on an Executive, Legislative, or Court Officer (page 150)

Statute (page 150)

2014 legislation, S.L. 2014-119, sec. 6(a), amended G.S. 14-16.6(a) to read as follows:

> (a) Any person who assaults any legislative officer, executive officer, or court officer, or assaults another person as retaliation against any legislative officer, executive officer, or court officer because of the exercise of that officer's duties, or any person who makes a violent attack upon the residence, office, temporary accommodation or means of transport of any one of those officers or persons in a manner likely to endanger the officer or person, shall be guilty of a felony and shall be punished as a Class I felon.

2014 legislation, S.L. 2014-100, sec. 17.1(v), amended G.S. 14-19.9 to read as follows:

> Any person who has been elected to any office covered by this Article but has not yet taken the oath of office shall be considered to hold the office for the purpose of this Article and G.S. 143B-919.

Elements (page 150)

As a result of the legislative changes noted above, Element (2) should read as follows:

(2) any
 (a) executive officer,
 (b) legislative officer,
 (c) court officer, *or*
 (d) other person as retaliation against any executive officer, legislative officer, or court officer because of the exercise of that officer's duties.

Notes (page 150)

Additional conduct included within statute (page 151)

As a result of the first legislative change noted above, replace the text of this note with the following:

> The statute also prohibits a violent attack on the residence, office, temporary accommodation, or means of transport of any covered officer in a manner likely to endanger the officer, as well as a similar attack on the residence, office, temporary accommodation, or means of transport of any person as retaliation against any executive officer, legislative officer, or court officer because of the exercise of that officer's duties. G.S. 14-16.6(a).

Assaults on Firefighters and Emergency and Medical Personnel (page 155)

Assault on a Firefighter or Medical Personnel Inflicting Physical Injury (page 155)

(revised title)

Statute (page 155)

2015 legislation, S.L. 2015-97, amended both the title of the statute and subsection (a)(3), as further amended by 2019 legislation, S.L. 2019-228, to read as follows:

> **§ 14-34.6. Assault or affray on a firefighter, an emergency medical technician, medical responder, and hospital personnel.**
>
> (a)(3) Hospital personnel and licensed healthcare providers who are providing or attempting to provide health care services to a patient.

2017 legislation, S.L. 2017-57, sec. 16B.3(a), added a new subsection, (a)(6), as follows:

> (6) Hospital security personnel.

Elements (page 156)

As a result of the 2015, 2017, and 2019 legislation noted above, Elements (2)(d) through new Element (2)(f) should read as follows:

 (d) a medical responder,
 (e) hospital personnel and licensed healthcare providers who are providing or attempting to provide healthcare services to a patient, *or*
 (f) hospital security personnel.

Assault on a Firefighter or Medical Personnel Inflicting Serious Injury or Inflicting Physical Injury and Using a Deadly Weapon Other Than a Firearm (page 157) (revised title)

Elements (page 157)

As a result of the 2015, 2017, and 2019 legislation noted above, Elements (2)(d) through new Element (2)(f) should read as follows:

(d) a medical responder,
(e) hospital personnel and licensed healthcare providers who are providing or attempting to provide healthcare services to a patient, *or*
(f) hospital security personnel.

Element (4)(b) of this offense should read:

causes physical injury and uses a deadly weapon other than a firearm.

Punishment (page 157)

As a result of the 2019 legislation noted above, the punishment for this offense is amended as follows, effective for offenses committed on or after December 1, 2019:

Class G felony. G.S. 14-34.6(b).

Assault on a Firefighter or Medical Personnel Causing Physical Injury and with a Firearm (page 158) (revised title)

Elements (page 158)

As a result of the 2015, 2017, and 2019 legislation noted above, Elements (2)(d) through new Element (2)(f) should read as follows:

(d) a medical responder,
(e) hospital personnel and licensed healthcare providers who are providing or attempting to provide healthcare services to a patient, *or*
(f) hospital security personnel.

Revise Element (4) and add Element (5) as follows:

(4) causes physical injury *and*
(5) uses a firearm.

Punishment (page 158)

As a result of the 2019 legislation noted above, the punishment for this offense is amended as follows, effective for offenses committed on or after December 1, 2019:

Class E felony. G.S. 14-34.6(c).

Habitual Misdemeanor Assault (page 161)

Notes (page 161)

Element (1)(a)(ii) (page 161)

Add the following citations after the first sentence of this note:

G.S. 14-33.2; State v. Garrison, 225 N.C. App. 170, 174 (2013) (trial court erred by failing to instruct the jury that the assault under G.S. 14-33 must have inflicted physical injury).

Multiple convictions and punishments (page 162)

A defendant may not be punished for both habitual misdemeanor assault and assault inflicting serious bodily injury for the same assaultive act. Though the habitual misdemeanor assault statute does not include the prefatory language "unless the conduct is covered under some other provision of law providing greater punishment" that customarily limits a court's authority to impose separate punishments for the same conduct, that language is included in the simple assault statute, which is a necessary prerequisite for the habitual misdemeanor assault conviction. State v. Fields, 374 N.C. 629 (2020).

Malicious Injury by Use of an Explosive or Incendiary (page 164)

Related Offenses Not in This Chapter (page 164)

Remove the following offense from this list:

Transporting dangerous weapon or substance during emergency; possessing off premises; exceptions. G.S. 14-288.7.

8

Threats, Harassment, Stalking, and Violation of Domestic Protective Orders

Communicating Threats (page 167)

Notes (page 167)

Element (4) (page 168)

For a case where the State presented sufficient evidence that a detention officer believed that the defendant—an inmate—would carry out his threats against her, see *State v. Hill*, 227 N.C. App. 371, 378–80 (2013).

Related Offenses Not in This Chapter (page 168)

Add the following offenses to this list:

Cyberbullying of school employee by student. G.S. 14-458.2.
Threat of Mass Violence on Educational Property or Place of Worship. G.S. 14-277.6; -277.7, *as enacted by* S.L. 2018-72, secs. 1–2.

Threat to Kill or Inflict Serious Injury on Executive, Legislative, or Court Officers (page 168)

Statute (page 168)

2014 legislation, S.L. 2014-119, sec. 6(b), amended G.S. 14-16.7 to read as follows:

> (a) Any person who knowingly and willfully makes any threat to inflict serious bodily injury upon or to kill any legislative officer, executive officer, or court officer, or who knowingly and willfully makes any threat to inflict serious bodily injury upon or kill any other person as retaliation against any legislative officer, executive officer, or court officer because of the exercise of that officer's duties, shall be guilty of a felony and shall be punished as a Class I felon.
>
> (b) Any person who knowingly and willfully deposits for conveyance in the mail any letter, writing, or other document containing a threat to commit an offense described in subsection (a) of this section shall be guilty of a felony and shall be punished as a Class I felon.

Elements (page 169)

As a result of the legislative change noted above, Element (5) should read as follows:

(5) any
  (a) executive officer,
  (b) legislative officer,
  (c) court officer, *or*
  (d) any person as retaliation against any executive officer, legislative officer, or court officer because of the exercise of that officer's duties.

In light of *State v. Taylor*, discussed below, add new Element (6) as follows:

(6) specifically intending the statement to be understood as a real threat expressing an intention to carry out the actions threatened.

Notes (page 169)

Element (3) (new note)

For this offense to conform to the First Amendment as interpreted in *Virginia v. Black*, 538 U.S. 343 (2003), a threat must be a "true threat," meaning a statement an ordinary, reasonable person familiar with the context in which the statement was made would interpret as a serious expression of intent to do harm. State v. Taylor, ___ N.C. App. ___, 841 S.E.2d 776, *review allowed*, ___N.C. ___, 847 S.E.2d 412 (2020) (mem.). In *Taylor*, the defendant made a series of Facebook posts threatening the elected district attorney after she declined to prosecute a case involving the death of a child. The court of appeals concluded that the defendant's statements calling for "[mountain] justice," that "[t]hey make new ammo everyday," and that the district attorney would "be the first to go" during a rebellion against the government were too vague to be considered true threats. Additionally, the defendant's statement that "if our head prosecutor won't do anything then the [sic] death to her as well" was not a true threat, as it did not include sufficient detail that would cause a reasonable person to interpret it as an actual plan to kill the district attorney. *Id.* at ___, 841 S.E.2d at 789.

Element (6) (new note)

The defendant must subjectively intend that his or her statements will be understood as a threat by the intended recipient. *Taylor, id.* at ___, 841 S.E.2d at 816. (adopting the Ninth Circuit's subjective-intent standard, drawn from *United States v. Cassel*, 408 F.3d 622 (9th Cir. 2005), for North Carolina's anti-threat statute). In *Taylor*, there was insufficient evidence of the defendant's subjective intent that his Facebook comments would reach the district attorney and that she would believe he was actually planning to kill her when he deleted the posts within hours of having posted them and told investigators he had not intended to make the district attorney feel threatened. *Id.* at 793–94.

Harassing Telephone Calls (page 169)

Using Threatening Language on the Telephone (page 170)

Related Offenses Not in This Chapter (page 171)

Remove the following offense from this list:

False report of emergency. G.S. 14-401.8.

Cyberstalking (page 174)

Statute (page 174)

2015 legislation, S.L. 2015-282, added new subsections (a)(3) and (4) as follows:

(3) Electronic tracking device.—An electronic or mechanical device that permits a person to remotely determine or track the position and movement of another person.

(4) Fleet vehicle.—Any of the following: (i) one or more motor vehicles owned by a single entity and operated by employees or agents of the entity for business or government purposes, (ii) motor vehicles held for lease or rental to the general public, or (iii) motor vehicles held for sale, or used as demonstrators, test vehicles, or loaner vehicles, by motor vehicle dealers.

That same legislation added a new subsection, (b)(5), as follows:

(5) Knowingly install, place, or use an electronic tracking device without consent, or cause an electronic tracking device to be installed, placed, or used without consent, to track the location of any person. The provisions of this subdivision do not apply to the installation, placement, or use of an electronic tracking device by any of the following:

a. A law enforcement officer, judicial officer, probation or parole officer, or employee of the Division of Corrections, Department of Public Safety, when any such person is engaged in the lawful performance of official duties and in accordance with State or federal law.

b. The owner or lessee of any vehicle on which the owner or lessee installs, places, or uses an electronic tracking device, unless the owner or lessee is subject to (i) a domestic violence protective order under Chapter 50B of the General Statutes or (ii) any court order that orders the owner or lessee not to assault, threaten, harass, follow, or contact a driver or occupant of the vehicle.

c. A legal guardian for a disabled adult, as defined in G.S. 108A-101(d), or a legally authorized individual or organization designated to provide protective services to a disabled adult pursuant to G.S. 108A-105(c), when the electronic tracking device is installed, placed, or used to track the location of the disabled adult for which the person is a legal guardian or the individual or organization is designated to provide protective services.

d. The owner of fleet vehicles, when tracking such vehicles.

e. A creditor or other secured party under a retail installment agreement involving the sale of a motor vehicle or the lessor under a retail lease of a motor vehicle, and any assignee or successor in interest to that creditor, secured party, or lessor, when tracking a motor vehicle identified as security under the retail installment sales agreement or leased pursuant to a retail lease agreement, including the installation, placement, or use of an electronic tracking device to locate and remotely disable the motor vehicle, with the express written consent of the purchaser, borrower, or lessee of the motor vehicle.

f. The installation, placement, or use of an electronic tracking device authorized by an order of a State or federal court.

g. A motor vehicle manufacturer, its subsidiary, or its affiliate that installs or uses an electronic tracking device in conjunction with providing a vehicle subscription telematics service, provided that the customer subscribes or consents to that service.

h. A parent or legal guardian of a minor when the electronic tracking device is installed, placed, or used to track the location of that minor unless the parent or legal guardian is subject to a domestic violence protective order under Chapter 50B of the General Statutes or any court order that orders the parent or legal guardian not to assault, threaten, harass, follow, or contact that minor or that minor's parent, legal guardian, custodian, or caretaker as defined in G.S. 7B-101.

i. An employer, when providing a communication device to an employee or contractor for use in connection with his or her work for the employer.

j. A business, if the tracking is incident to the provision of a product or service requested by the person, except as limited in sub-subdivision k. of this subdivision.

k. A private detective or private investigator licensed under Chapter 74C of the General Statutes, provided that (i) the tracking is pursuant to authority under G.S. 74C-3(a)(8), (ii) the tracking is not otherwise contrary to law, and (iii) the person being tracked is not under the protection of a domestic violence protective order under Chapter 50B of the General Statutes or any other court order that protects against assault, threat, harassment, following, or contact.

Unauthorized Use of Electronic Tracking Device (new crime)

This offense was created by the 2015 legislation noted immediately above.

Statute

See G.S. 14-196.3(b)(5), reproduced above in this supplement.

Elements

A person guilty of this offense

(1) knowingly *and*
(2) without consent
(3) (a) installs, places, or uses an electronic tracking device *or*
    (b) causes an electronic tracking device to be installed, placed, or used
(4) to track the location of any person.

Punishment

Class 2 misdemeanor. G.S. 14-196.3(d).

Notes

Element (1). See "Knowingly" in Chapter 1 (States of Mind).

Element (3). An "electronic tracking device" refers to an electronic or mechanical device that permits a person to remotely determine or track the position and movement of another. G.S. 14-196.3(a)(3).

Exceptions. See this note to "Using Electronic Mail or Communication to Threaten or Extort" in the main volume.

G.S. 14-196.3(b)(5), reproduced above, sets out eleven exceptions to this offense, including, among others, exceptions for law enforcement officers engaged in their duties, owners of fleet vehicles, certain creditors, and private detectives and private investigators in certain circumstances.

Related Offenses Not in This Chapter

None.

Cyberbullying (page 179)

Statute (page 179)

2012 legislation, S.L. 2012-149, sec. 3, amended G.S. 14-458.1(a)(3) to read as follows:

> (3) Make any statement, whether true or false, intending to immediately provoke, and that is likely to provoke, any third party to stalk or harass a minor.

That same legislation amended G.S. 14-458.1(a)(5) and (6) to read as follows:

> (5) Sign up a minor for a pornographic Internet site with the intent to intimidate or torment the minor.
> (6) Without authorization of the minor or the minor's parent or guardian, sign up a minor for electronic mailing lists or to receive junk electronic messages and instant messages, with the intent to intimidate or torment the minor.

Elements (page 180)

Elements (2)(c), (e), and (f) should be revised to conform to the legislative changes noted above. Element 2(c) should be revised to read:

> (c) to make any statement intending to immediately provoke, and that is likely to provoke, any third party to stalk or harass a minor,

Elements (2)(e) and (f) should be revised to read:

> (e) sign up a minor for a pornographic Internet site with the intent to intimidate or torment the minor, *or*
> (f) without authorization of the minor or the minor's parent or guardian, sign up a minor for electronic mailing lists or to receive junk electronic messages and instant messages, with the intent to intimidate or torment the minor.

Notes (page 181)

Element (2)(a) (page 181)

2012 legislation, S.L. 2012-149, sec. 2, amended G.S. 14-453(7c) to include within the meaning of the term "profile" "a Web site user's personal page or section of a page made up of data, in text or graphical form, which displays significant, unique, or identifying information, including, but not limited to, listing acquaintances, interests, associations, activities, or personal statements."

Constitutionality (new note)

In *State v. Bishop*, 368 N.C. 869 (2016), the state supreme court held that G.S. 14-458.1(a)(1)d. is unconstitutional; that portion of the cyberbullying statute criminalizes use of a computer or computer network, with the intent to intimidate or torment a minor, to post or encourage others to post on the Internet private, personal, or sexual information pertaining to a minor and is listed as Element (2)(a)(iv) in the main volume of this book. The court found that the provision restricts speech; the restriction is content based; and the statute is not narrowly tailored to the State's asserted interest in protecting children from the harms of online bullying; it thus concluded that the provision violates the First Amendment to the U.S. Constitution. *Id.* at 872–80.

Related Offenses Not in This Chapter (page 181)

Add the following offense to this list:

> Cyberbullying of school employee by student. G.S. 14-458.2.

Stalking (page 182)

Misdemeanor Stalking (page 183)

Notes (page 183)

Constitutionality (page 184)
As applied to a defendant who posted unwelcome comments about a victim on social media, the court of appeals deemed North Carolina's stalking statute a content-based restriction on speech that violates the First Amendment to the U.S. Constitution. Other non-expressive conduct by the defendant, including delivering gifts to the victim's workplace or emailing the victim's friend, were not constitutionally protected. State v. Shackelford, 264 N.C. App. 542 (2019). A prior version of the stalking statute was upheld in the face of a challenge that it was unconstitutionally vague. State v. Watson, 169 N.C. App. 331 (2005).

Jury instructions (new note)
When the charged conduct encompasses conduct occurring both before and after statutory amendments that changed the elements of this offense, the trial court must submit a special verdict form to the jury. State v. Williams, 226 N.C. App. 393, 401 (2013) (plain error to fail to do so).

Stalking When a Court Order Is in Place (page 186)

Notes (page 186)

Element (5) (page 186)
This Element is satisfied when the order is a pretrial release order specifying that the defendant have no contact with the victim. State v. Mitchell, 259 N.C. App. 866 (2018) (rejecting the defendant's argument that he was not subject to pretrial release orders because he never posted bond and remained in jail when he contacted the victim).

Violation of a Domestic Violence Protective Order (page 186)

Misdemeanor Violation of a Domestic Violence Protective Order (page 187)

Notes (page 187)

Element (1) (page 187)
For a case where the evidence was insufficient to establish that the defendant knowingly violated a domestic violence protective order (DVPO), see *State v. Williams*, 226 N.C. App. 393, 406 (2013) (DVPO required the defendant to "stay away from" the victim's place of work without identifying her workplace; there was no evidence that the defendant was aware that the victim worked at the location he visited). *See also* State v. Tucker, ___ N.C. App. ___, 848 S.E.2d 265 (insufficient evidence that the defendant knew a second DVPO—the one allegedly violated—had been entered against him when he was not present for the hearing at which it was issued), *temp. stay allowed*, 375 N.C. 499, 846 S.E.2d 748 (2020).

Element (2) (new note)
The evidence was insufficient to establish that the defendant violated a DVPO provision that he "stay away from" the victim's workplace when he was seen at a mall parking lot when the victim

was working at a salon in the mall. *Williams*, 226 N.C. App. at 410 (the defendant was not in a location that would permit him to harass, communicate with, follow, or even observe the victim).

Element (2)(a) (page 187)

Add the following at the end of the first paragraph on page 188:

The statute and recent cases appear to make this law applicable to same-sex relationships. For example, if the parties are current or former spouses or are current or former household members, they fall within the definition of "personal relationship" regardless of their sex, and the law therefore applies to them. G.S. 50B-1(b). The portion of the statute covering those in a present or former dating relationship limits the law's coverage to "persons of the opposite sex." However, in the context of an appeal where the trial judge denied a plaintiff's complaint seeking a domestic violence protective order against a same-sex defendant with whom she had been in a dating relationship, the Court of Appeals concluded that limiting the statute's coverage to "persons of the opposite sex" would violate the plaintiff's state and federal constitutional rights to due process and equal protection of the laws. The appellate court therefore instructed the trial court to apply G.S. 50B-1(b)(6) as though it states "[a]re persons who are in a dating relationship or have been in a dating relationship," excising the language regarding "persons of the opposite sex." M.E. v. T.J., ___ N.C. App. ___, ___ S.E.2d ___ (2020), *review allowed*, ___ N.C.___, ___ S.E.2d ___ (2021).

Add the following citation at the end of the last paragraph of this note:

State v. Poole, 228 N.C. App. 248, 259 (2013) (pursuant to legislative amendments to the statute, an ex parte DVPO is valid).

Add the following text to the end of this note:

Although a 2012 case held that a consent DVPO that lacks a finding that the defendant committed an act of domestic violence is void *ab initio*, Kenton v. Kenton, 218 N.C. App. 603 (2012), and cannot support a charge under this statute, 2013 legislation changed that rule. Specifically, S.L. 2013-237 amended G.S. 50B-3 to provide that a consent protective order may be entered without findings of fact and conclusions of law if the parties agree in writing. The statute further provides that such a consent protective order is valid and enforceable.

Repeat Violation of a Domestic Violence Protective Order (page 188)

Notes (page 189)

Multiple convictions and punishments (page 189)

Delete all text after the first sentence of this note and replace it with the following:

Thus, a defendant may not be convicted of this offense and another that is sentenced more severely when the convictions are based on the same conduct. State v. Jones, 237 N.C. App. 526, 530–32 (2014) (trial court erred by sentencing the defendant for felony violation of a domestic violence protective order (Class H felony) and interfering with a witness (Class G felony) based on the same conduct).. For a discussion of this issue in the assault context, see this note under "Assault Inflicting Serious Injury" in Chapter 7 (Assaults).

Violation of a Domestic Violence Protective Order with a Deadly Weapon (page 189)

Related Offenses Not in This Chapter (page 190)

Add the following offense to this list:

Purchase or possession of firearms by person subject to domestic violence order prohibited. G.S. 14-269.8; 50B-3.1(j).

Entering Domestic Violence Safe House or Haven (page 190)

Notes (page 190)

Element (3) (page 190)

For a defendant to be guilty of this offense, the State need not show that the defendant actually entered the building housing the safe house or haven; it need only prove that the defendant entered the real property on which the building was located. State v. Williams, 247 N.C. App. 239, 242 (2016).

9

Abuse and Neglect

Child Abuse (page 193)

Misdemeanor Child Abuse (page 193)

Notes (page 193)

Element (2) (page 194)

For cases where the evidence was sufficient as to this Element, see *State v. Reed*, 371 N.C. App. 106 (2018) (per curiam) (the state supreme court reversed the court of appeals for the reasons stated in the dissent; the evidence showed that while the defendant used the bathroom in her home for a few minutes, her toddler fell into an outdoor pool and drowned; in the opinion below, the dissenting judge concluded that the State presented sufficient evidence of the defendant's failure to supervise the child); *State v. Watkins*, 247 N.C. App. 391, 395–96 (2016) (the defendant left a 2-year-old alone in a vehicle and out of her sight line for more than six minutes; one of the vehicle's windows was open, the outside temperature was 18 degrees, and weather included sleet, snow, and wind; the court relied on the harsh weather conditions, the child's young age, and the danger of him being abducted or subjected to physical harm).

Child abuse reporting (page 194)

As a result of 2013 legislation, S.L. 2013-52, sec. 7, delete the text of this note and replace it with the following:

G.S. 7B-301(a) requires any person or institution suspecting that a child has been abused to report the incident to the local director of the local social services department. Any person or institution that knowingly or wantonly fails to make the required report or that knowingly or wantonly prevents another person from making a report is guilty of a Class 1 misdemeanor. G.S. 7B-301(b). Additionally, any director of social services who receives a report of a juvenile's sexual abuse in a child care facility and who knowingly fails to notify the State Bureau of Investigation is guilty of a Class 1 misdemeanor. *Id.* § (c).

Multiple convictions and punishments (page 195)

For a case where the State sufficiently proved three instances of felony child abuse, see *State v. Lanford*, 225 N.C. App. 189, 204 (2013) (rejecting the argument that the fact that the assaults were part of chronic and continual abuse precluded such a holding).

Related Offenses Not in This Chapter (page 195)

Add the following offenses to this list:

"Sale, Surrender, or Purchase of a Minor," in Chapter 12 (Kidnapping and Related Offenses) of this supplement.

Unlawful transfer of custody of minor child. G.S. 14-321.2.

Replace the last offense in this list with the following:

Unlawful payments related to adoption. G.S. 48-10-102.

Child Abuse—Inflicting Serious Mental or Physical Injury (page 195)

Statute (page 195)

2013 legislation, S.L. 2013-35, modified the punishments set out in G.S. 14-318.4 for felony child abuse as described below.

Another piece of 2013 legislation, S.L. 2013-52, sec. 3, added a new subsection, (a6), as follows:

> (a6) For purposes of this section, a "grossly negligent omission" in providing care to or supervision of a child includes the failure to report a child as missing to law enforcement as provided in G.S. 14-318.5(b).

Punishment (page 196)

2013 legislation, S.L. 2013-35, increased the punishment for this offense from a Class E to a Class D felony.

Notes (page 196)

Element (2) (page 196)
For another case holding that when the State proceeds under Element (2)(b), it need not prove that the defendant intended to inflict serious injury, see *State v. Frazier*, 248 N.C. App. 252, 260–61 (2016) (the State need only prove that the assault was intentional and that it resulted in serious injury).

Child Abuse—Willful Act or Omission Causing Serious Mental or Physical Injury (page 197)

Punishment (page 198)

2013 legislation, S.L. 2013-35, increased the punishment for this offense from a Class H to a Class G felony.

Notes (page 198)

Element (2)(b) (new note)
Failing to report the disappearance of a child as required by G.S. 14-318.5(b) constitutes a grossly negligent omission. G.S. 14-318.4(a6); see "Failure to Report the Disappearance of a Child" (new crime), below in this supplement.

Child Abuse—Inflicting Serious Bodily Injury or Mental or Emotional Injury (page 198)

Punishment (page 199)

The 2013 legislation cited immediately above increased the punishment for this offense from a Class C to a Class B2 felony.

Notes (page 199)

Element (3)(a) (page 199)
There was sufficient evidence of serious bodily injury where the victim experienced subarachnoid hemorrhaging. State v. Bohannon, 247 N.C. App. 756, 763 (2016).

Child Abuse—Willful Act or Omission Causing Serious Bodily Injury (page 200)

Notes (page 200)

Element (2)(b) (new note)

Failing to report the disappearance of a child as required by G.S. 14-318.5(b) constitutes a grossly negligent omission. G.S. 14-318.4(a6); see "Failure to Report the Disappearance of a Child" (new crime), below in this supplement.

Child Abuse—Prostitution (page 201)

Punishment (page 201)

The 2013 legislation cited above increased the punishment for this offense from a Class E to a Class D felony.

Related Offenses Not in This Chapter (page 201)

Add the following offense to this list:

"Sale, Surrender, or Purchase of a Minor," in Chapter 12 (Kidnapping and Related Offenses) of this supplement.

Replace the last offense in this list with the following:

Unlawful payments related to adoption. G.S. 48-10-102.

Child Abuse—Sexual Act (page 202)

Punishment (page 202)

The 2013 legislation cited above increased the punishment for this offense from a Class E to a Class D felony.

Notes (page 202)

Element (2)(a) (page 202)

The text of this note discusses whether the definition of "sexual act" in G.S. 14-27.1(4), recodified by 2015 legislation, S.L. 2015-181, sec. 2, as G.S. 14-27.20(4), applies to this offense. Delete the text of this note and replace it with the following:

In *State v. Alonzo*, 373 N.C. 437 (2020), the state supreme court held that the definition of "sexual act" in G.S. 14-27.20(4), which defines a sexual act to include cunnilingus, fellatio, anilingus, anal intercourse, or the penetration by any object into the genital or anal opening of another person's body, but not vaginal intercourse, does not apply to a prosecution under G.S. 14-318.4(a2). To the contrary, that definition is limited to its own statutory article, Article 7B of Chapter 14. Applying *Alonzo*, the court of appeals concluded in *State v. Wohlers*, ___ N.C. App. ___, 847 S.E.2d 781 (2020), that the trial court did not err by instructing the jury based on N.C.P.J.I.—Crim. 239.55B that a sexual act is "an immoral, improper or indecent touching or act by the defendant upon the child." In *State v. Gonzales*, 263 N.C. App. 527 (2019) the court deemed its prior precedent in *State v. McClamb*, 234 N.C. App. 753 (2014), controlling and held that vaginal intercourse is included within the definition of sexual act as it is used in G.S. 14-318.4(a2).

Failure to Report Crimes against Juveniles (new crime)

Statute

§ 14-318.6. Failure to report crimes against juveniles; penalty.

(a) Definitions. – As used in this section, the following definitions apply:

(1) Juvenile. – As defined in G.S. 7B-101. For the purposes of this section, the age of the juvenile at the time of the abuse or offense governs.

(2) Serious bodily injury. – As defined in G.S. 14-318.4(d).

(3) Serious physical injury. – As defined in G.S. 14-318.4(d).

(4) Sexually violent offense. – An offense committed against a juvenile that is a sexually violent offense as defined in G.S. 14-208.6(5). This term also includes the following: an attempt, solicitation, or conspiracy to commit any of these offenses; aiding and abetting any of these offenses.

(5) Violent offense. – Any offense that inflicts upon the juvenile serious bodily injury or serious physical injury by other than accidental means. This term also includes the following: an attempt, solicitation, or conspiracy to commit any of these offenses; aiding and abetting any of these offenses.

(b) Requirement. – Any person 18 years of age or older who knows or should have reasonably known that a juvenile has been or is the victim of a violent offense, sexual offense, or misdemeanor child abuse under G.S. 14-318.2 shall immediately report the case of that juvenile to the appropriate local law enforcement agency in the county where the juvenile resides or is found. The report may be made orally or by telephone. The report shall include information as is known to the person making it, including the name, address, and age of the juvenile; the name and address of the juvenile's parent, guardian, custodian, or caretaker; the name, address, and age of the person who committed the offense against the juvenile; the location where the offense was committed; the names and ages of other juveniles present or in danger; the present whereabouts of the juvenile, if not at the home address; the nature and extent of any injury or condition resulting from the offense or abuse; and any other information which the person making the report believes might be helpful in establishing the need for law enforcement involvement. The person making the report shall give his or her name, address, and telephone number.

(c) Penalty. – Any person 18 years of age or older, who knows or should have reasonably known that a juvenile was the victim of a violent offense, sexual offense, or misdemeanor child abuse under G.S. 14-318.2, and knowingly or willfully fails to report as required by subsection (b) of this section, or who knowingly or willfully prevents another person from reporting as required by subsection (b) of this section, is guilty of a Class 1 misdemeanor.

(d) Construction. – Nothing in this section shall be construed as relieving a person subject to the requirement set forth in subsection (b) of this section from any other duty to report required by law.

(e) Protection. – The identity of a person making a report pursuant to this section must be protected and only revealed as provided in G.S. 132-1.4(c)(4).

(f) Good-Faith Immunity. – A person who makes a report in good faith under this Article, cooperates with law enforcement in an investigation, or testifies in any judicial proceeding resulting from a law enforcement report or investigation is immune from any civil or criminal liability that might otherwise be incurred or imposed for that action, provided that person was acting in good faith.

(g) Law Enforcement Duty to Report Evidence to the Department of Social Services. – If any law enforcement officer, as the result of a report, finds evidence that a juvenile may be abused, neglected, or dependent as defined in G.S. 7B-101, the law enforcement officer shall make an oral report as soon as practicable and make a subsequent written report of the findings to the director of the department of social services within 48 hours after discovery of the evidence. When a report of abuse, neglect, or dependency is received, the director of the department of social services shall make a prompt and thorough assessment, in accordance with G.S. 7B-302, to determine whether protective services should be provided or the complaint filed as a petition.

(h) Nothing in this section shall be construed as to require a person with a privilege under G.S. 8-53.3, 8-53.7, 8-53.8, or 8-53.12 or with attorney-client privilege to report pursuant to this section if that privilege would prevent them from doing so.

Elements

A person guilty of this offense

(1) is any person
(2) 18 years of age or older
(3) who
  (a) knows *or*
  (b) should have reasonably known
(4) that a juvenile has been or is the victim of
  (a) a violent offense,
  (b) a sexual offense, *or*
  (c) misdemeanor child abuse under G.S. 14-318.2, *and*
(5) knowingly or willfully
(6) (a) fails to report as required by G.S. 14-318.6(b) *or*
  (b) prevents another person from reporting as required by G.S. 14-318.6(b).

Punishment

Class 1 misdemeanor. G.S. 14-318.6(c).

Notes

Element (1). This offense can apply to any person over the age of 18; no special relationship with the victim is required.

Element (4). "Juvenile" is a person who is younger than 18 years of age and is not married, emancipated, or a member of the United States Armed Forces. G.S. 7B-101(14). The person's age at the time of the enumerated offenses applies. *Id.* § 14-318.6(a)(1).

Element (4)(a). "Violent offense" is defined in G.S. 14-318.6(a)(5) as "[a]ny offense that inflicts upon the juvenile serious bodily injury or serious physical injury by other than accidental means," and an attempt, solicitation, or conspiracy to commit any such offense or aiding and abetting such an offense. "Serious physical injury" and "serious bodily injury" are defined in G.S. 14-318.4(d). See the notes on Element (3) to "Child Abuse—Inflicting Serious Mental or Physical Injury" and on Element (3)(a) to "Child Abuse—Inflicting Serious Bodily Injury or Mental or Emotional Injury," above.

Element 4(b). "Sexual offense" is not a defined term for this crime. It may have been intended to refer to "sexually violent offense," as defined in G.S. 14-318.6(a)(4) by reference to G.S. 14-208.6(5), or to sexual offense crimes, such as "First-Degree Forcible Sexual Offense" under G.S. 14-27.4.

Element 4(c). Only "Misdemeanor Child Abuse" (Chapter 9) is covered under this Element. Other child abuse crimes may be covered under Element (4)(a) to the extent they meet the definition of a violent offense.

Element (6). Under G.S. 14-318.6(b), a person who knows or should have reasonably known about covered offenses against a juvenile must immediately report the case, orally or by telephone, to the appropriate local law enforcement agency in the county where the juvenile resides or is found. The report shall include information as is known to the person making it, including listed information about the victim; the victim's parent, guardian, custodian, or caretaker; the person who allegedly committed the offense; and other listed information. The person making the report must give his or her name, address, and telephone number; however, his or her identity must be protected and only revealed as provided in G.S. 132-1.4(c)(4).

Good-faith immunity. A person who, in good faith, makes a report under this law, cooperates with law enforcement in an investigation, or testifies in any judicial proceeding resulting from a law enforcement report or investigation is immune from any civil or criminal liability that might otherwise be incurred or imposed for that action. G.S. 14-318.6(f).

Exceptions. A person with a privilege under G.S. 8-53.3 (psychologist-patient), 8-53.7 (social worker), 8-53.8 (counselor), 8-53.12 (agents of rape crisis centers and domestic violence programs), or an attorney-client privilege is not required to report if that privilege would prevent him or her from doing so. G.S. 14-318.6(h).

Related Offenses Not in This Chapter

"Concealing a Death" (Chapter 21)
Failure to report abuse, neglect, dependency, or death of a juvenile. G.S. 7B-301(b).
Misdemeanor failure to report the disappearance of a child who might be in danger. G.S. 14-318.5(c).

Failure to Report the Disappearance of a Child (new crime)

Statute

§ 14-318.5. Failure to report the disappearance of a child to law enforcement; immunity of person reporting in good faith.

(a) The following definitions apply in this section:

(1) Child.—Any person who is less than 16 years of age.

(2) Disappearance of a child.—When the parent or other person providing supervision of a child does not know the location of the child and has not had contact with the child for a 24-hour period.

(b) A parent or any other person providing care to or supervision of a child who knowingly or wantonly fails to report the disappearance of a child to law enforcement is in violation of this subsection. Unless the conduct is covered under some other provision of law providing greater punishment, a violation of this subsection is punishable as a Class I felony.

(c) Any person who reasonably suspects the disappearance of a child and who reasonably suspects that the child may be in danger shall report those suspicions to law enforcement within a reasonable time. Unless the conduct is covered under some other provision of law providing greater punishment, a violation of this subsection is punishable as a Class 1 misdemeanor.

(d) This section does not apply if G.S. 110-102.1 is applicable.

(e) Notwithstanding subsection (b) or (c) of this section, if a child is absent from school, a teacher is not required to report the child's absence to law enforcement officers under this section, provided the teacher reports the child's absence from school pursuant to Article 26 of Chapter 115C of the General Statutes.

(f) The felony of failure to report the disappearance of a child as required by subsection (b) of this section is an offense additional to other civil and criminal provisions and is not intended to repeal or preclude any other sanctions or remedies.

(g) Any person who reports the disappearance of a child as required by this section is immune from any civil or criminal liability that might otherwise be incurred or imposed for that action, provided that the person was acting in good faith. In any proceeding involving liability, good faith is presumed.

Elements

A person guilty of this offense

(1) is a parent or any other person providing care to or supervision of a child *and*
(2) knowingly or wantonly
(3) fails to report
(4) the disappearance of a child
(5) to law enforcement.

Punishment

Class I felony. G.S. 14-318.5(b).

Notes

Element (1). A child is a person less than 16 years of age. G.S. 14-318.5(a)(1).

Element (4). The disappearance of a child occurs "[w]hen the parent or other person providing supervision of a child does not know the location of the child and has not had contact with the child for a 24-hour period." G.S. 14-318.5(a)(2).

Exceptions and immunity. This offense "does not apply if G.S. 110-102.1 is applicable." G.S. 14-318.5(d). G.S. 110-102.1 pertains to reports of missing or deceased children by child care providers.

If a child is absent from school, a teacher is not required to report the absence to law enforcement officers, provided the teacher reports the child's absence from school pursuant to Article 26 of G.S. Chapter 115C. G.S. 14-318.5(e).

Any person who reports the disappearance of a child as required is immune from any civil or criminal liability that might result from that action, so long as the person acted in good faith, which is presumed. G.S. 14-318.5(g).

Multiple convictions and punishments. The statute provides that "[u]nless the conduct is covered under some other provision of law providing greater punishment," a violation is a Class I felony. G.S. 14-318.5(b). This may suggest that a defendant cannot be convicted of this offense and another offense providing greater punishment. See the note on this Element to "Assault Inflicting Serious Injury" in the main volume. However, this conclusion is unclear given that the statute also provides that the crime "is an offense additional to other civil and criminal provisions and is not intended to repeal or preclude any other sanctions or remedies." G.S. 14-318.5(f).

Related Offenses Not in This Chapter

"Concealing a Death" (Chapter 21)

Misdemeanor failure to report the disappearance of a child who might be in danger. G.S. 14-318.5(c).

Contributing to a Juvenile's Being Delinquent, Undisciplined, Abused, or Neglected (page 203)

Statute (page 203)

Effective December 1, 2019, the 2017 Juvenile Justice Reinvestment Act, S.L. 2017-57, sec. 16D.4, amends the statute to make it apply to persons who are at least 18 years old. *Id.* sec. 16D.4(p). After that Act takes effect, the first sentence of the statute should read as follows:

> **Any person who is at least 18 years old who knowingly or willfully causes, encourages, or aids any juvenile within the jurisdiction of the court to be in a place or condition, or to commit an act whereby the juvenile could be adjudicated delinquent, undisciplined, abused, or neglected as defined by G.S. 7B-101 and G.S. 7B-1501 shall be guilty of a Class 1 misdemeanor.**

As a result of 2017 legislation, S.L. 2017-186, sec. 2(ii), replace the reference to the Department of Juvenile Justice with the Juvenile Justice Section of the Division of Adult Correction and Juvenile Justice of the Department of Public Safety.

Elements (page 203)

As a result of the 2017 legislation noted above, effective December 1, 2019, Element (1) should read as follows:

(1) is at least 18 years old *and*

The statutory reference in Element (6)(d) should read:

G.S. 7B-101(15).

Notes (page 203)

Generally (new note)

This offense does not require the defendant to be the juvenile's parent, guardian, custodian, or caretaker. State v. Stevens, 228 N.C. App. 352, 355 (2013); State v. Harris, 236 N.C. App. 388, 394 (2014) (following *Stevens*).

Element (4) (page 203)

Effective December 1, 2019, the 2017 Juvenile Justice Reinvestment Act, S.L. 2017-57, sec. 16D.4, raises the age of juvenile jurisdiction to 18 and extends the court's jurisdiction over juveniles. As a result, when that Act takes effect, the second sentence of this note should read as follows:

> Although a delinquent juvenile is within the court's jurisdiction when the juvenile is at least 6 years old and less than 20 years old, G.S. 7B-1501(7) (defining a delinquent juvenile), *as amended by* S.L. 2017-57, sec. 16D.4(a); *id.* § -1601 (specifying the court's jurisdiction over delinquent juveniles), *as amended by* S.L. 2017-57, sec. 16D.4(b), because only a juvenile under 18 can be adjudicated delinquent, see the note on Element (6)(a), immediately below, for purposes of this Element, 18 rather than 20 years old constitutes the upper age limit for delinquent juveniles to be within the jurisdiction of the court.

Element (6)(a) (page 204)

Effective December 1, 2019, the 2017 Juvenile Justice Reinvestment Act, S.L. 2017-57, sec. 16D.4, amends the definition of delinquent juvenile. *Id.* sec. 16D.4(a). After that Act becomes effective, this note should read as follows:

> A delinquent juvenile is
>
> - any juvenile who, while less than 16 years old but at least 6 years old, commits a crime or infraction under state law or under a local government ordinance, including violation of the motor vehicle laws, or who commits indirect contempt by a juvenile as defined in G.S. 5A-31 and
> - any juvenile who, while less than 18 years old but at least 16 years old, commits a crime or an infraction under state law or under a local government ordinance, excluding violation of the motor vehicle laws, or who commits indirect contempt by a juvenile as defined in G.S. 5A-31.
>
> G.S. 7B-1501(7), *as amended by* S.L. 2017-57, sec. 16D.4(a).

Element (6)(c) (page 204)

2018 legislation, S.L. 2018-68, amended the definition of "abused juvenile" to include juveniles less than 18 years old who are victims of human trafficking, involuntary servitude, or sexual servitude.

Element (6)(d) (page 204)

2018 legislation, S.L. 2018-68, sec. 8.1(b), amended the definition of "neglected juvenile" to include juveniles less than 18 years old who are victims of human trafficking, involuntary servitude, or sexual servitude.

Add the following to this note:

The State presented sufficient evidence of this Element where (1) the defendant failed to supervise her child, who fell into an outdoor pool and drowned while the defendant was in the bathroom, State v. Reed, 371 N.C. 106 (2018), (2) the defendant took the juvenile away from the area near the juvenile's home, ignored the juvenile after he was injured, and abandoned the sleeping juvenile in a parking lot, State v. Stevens, 228 N.C. App. 352, 357 (2013), and (3) the defendant entered the child's bedroom, tried to get her to drink liquor, squeezed her buttocks, and asked to suck on her chest, State v. Harris, 236 N.C. App. 388, 395 (2014) (the child "was clearly placed in a location in which and subject to conditions under which she could not and did not receive proper care from her caretakers").

Jury instructions (new note)

The jury instructions should define the statutory terms "delinquent," "undisciplined," "abused," and "neglected." *Harris*, 236 N.C. App. at 397 n.4.

Related Offenses Not in This Chapter (page 204)

Add the following offenses to this list:

"Sale, Surrender, or Purchase of a Minor," in Chapter 12 (Kidnapping and Related Offenses) of this supplement.

Unlawful transfer of custody of minor child. G.S. 14-321.2.

The offense listed as "Selling cigarettes to minors. G.S. 14-313" should read as follows:

Youth access to tobacco products, tobacco-derived products, vapor products, and cigarette wrapping papers. G.S. 14-313.

Replace the second to last offense in this list with the following:

Unlawful payments related to adoption. G.S. 48-10-102.

Abuse or Neglect of a Disabled or Elder Adult (page 210)

Abuse of a Disabled or Elder Adult Causing Mental or Physical Injury (page 210)

Notes (page 211)

Element (1) (page 211)

There was sufficient evidence that a defendant voluntarily assumed responsibility for the care of a victim when the defendant had a close relationship with the victim, was around the victim's home with increasing frequency, performed odd jobs for the victim, wrote checks for him, took him to buy a headstone and dentures, helped him renovate his home, and cut his toenails at least once. State v. Forte, 206 N.C. App. 699 (2010). Even in the absence of a close relationship between the defendant and the victim, there was sufficient evidence that the defendant was the victim's caretaker when she helped the victim bathe, purchased food and supplies for her, helped pay her bills, and purchased life insurance for the victim at her request. State v. Stubbs, ___ N.C. App. ___, 845 S.E.2d 125, *temp. stay allowed*, 374 N.C. 749 (2020).

10
Sexual Assaults

2012 legislation, S.L. 2012-40, amended G.S. 7B-1111(a) to provide that a court may terminate parental rights upon a finding that the parent "has been convicted of a sexually related offense under Chapter 14 of the General Statutes that resulted in the conception of the juvenile." All of the offenses covered in this chapter fall within Chapter 14 of the General Statutes.

2014 legislation, S.L. 2014-100, sec. 17.1(r), amended various sex offender statutes, substituting the words "Department of Public Safety" for the term "Division" in all instances except where the relevant statute refers to the Division of Adult Correction.

2015 legislation substantially reorganized and revised the rape and sex offense statutes. S.L. 2015-181. Specific changes are noted in the sections that follow.

Rape (page 217)

First-Degree Forcible Rape (page 217)

Statute (page 217)

2015 legislation, S.L. 2015-181, secs. 3(a) and (b), recodified and amended the statute. 2017 legislation, S.L. 2017-30, sec. 1, further amended the statute. The amended statute provides:

> **§ 14-27.21. First-degree forcible rape.**
>
> (a) A person is guilty of first-degree forcible rape if the person engages in vaginal intercourse with another person by force and against the will of the other person, and does any of the following:
>
> (1) Uses, threatens to use, or displays a dangerous or deadly weapon or an article which the other person reasonably believes to be a dangerous or deadly weapon.
>
> (2) Inflicts serious personal injury upon the victim or another person.
>
> (3) The person commits the offense aided and abetted by one or more other persons.
>
> (b) Any person who commits an offense defined in this section is guilty of a Class B1 felony.
>
> (c) Upon conviction, a person convicted under this section has no rights to custody of or rights of inheritance from any child born as a result of the commission of the rape, nor shall the person have any rights related to the child under Chapter 48 or Subchapter 1 of Chapter 7B of the General Statutes.

2019 legislation, S.L. 2019-245, effective for offenses committed on or after December 1, 2019, adds new G.S. 14-27.20(1a).

> **§ 14-27.20. Definitions.**
>
> (1a) Against the will of the other person. – Either of the following:
>
> a. Without consent of the other person.
>
> b. After consent is revoked by the other person, in a manner that would cause a reasonable person to believe consent is revoked.

Elements (page 217)

As a result of the 2017 legislation noted above, Element (5)(a) should read as follows:

(a) uses, threatens to use, or displays a dangerous or deadly weapon (or what reasonably appears to be a dangerous or deadly weapon),

Punishment (page 218)

As a result of the 2015 legislative change noted above, the statutory citation in this section should be to G.S. 14-27.21(b).

Notes (page 218)

Element (1) (page 218)

As a result of 2015 legislation, S.L. 2015-181, sec. 15, the statutory citation included in the first paragraph of this note should be to G.S. 14-27.36.

Add the following to this note:

For a case where there was sufficient evidence of vaginal intercourse notwithstanding the child victim's use of ambiguous terms, see *State v. Combs*, 226 N.C. App. 87, 90–91 (2013) (the child used terms such as "manhood" and "middle hole" but went on to explain what these terms meant).

For a case where there was sufficient evidence of penetration even though the victim did not remember the incident, see *State v. White*, 261 N.C. App. 506 (2018) (bystanders responding to the victim's screams found the defendant straddling her in an alley in a "missionary position"; when the defendant was pushed away, his pants were down and he had an erection and the victim's underwear and pants were at her ankles; and a nurse found debris and a small black hair most consistent with a pubic hair inside the victim's vagina, the victim did not have pubic hair, and the nurse testified that debris cannot enter the vaginal walls in their normal collapsed state and that "they only open up if something is introduced inside of them").

Element (2) (page 218)

As a result of 2015 legislation, S.L. 2015-181, sec. 15, the statutory citation included in this note should be to G.S. 14-27.34.

Element (3) (page 218)

The evidence sufficiently established use of force when, after the victim repeatedly declined the defendant's advances, the defendant pushed her to the ground and got on top of her. State v. Norman, 227 N.C. App. 162, 167–68 (2013) (rape and sexual offense case).

In a second-degree sexual offense case, the court held that the touching was by force and against the victim's will when the defendant surprised a store shopper by putting his hand up her skirt and penetrating her vagina; the court rejected the defendant's argument that because his action surprised the victim, she did not have the opportunity to consent or resist and that therefore he did not act by force and against the victim's will. State v. Henderson, 233 N.C. App. 538, 540–41 (2014).

Evidence (1) that a juvenile threatened the minor victims he had met at a school for special needs with exposing their secrets and their participation with him in sexual activities and (2) of a power differential between the juvenile and the victims was insufficient to establish constructive force; for constructive force to apply, threats resulting in fear, fright, or coercion must be threats of physical harm. *In re* T.W., 221 N.C. App. 193, 199 (2012).

Although constructive force can be inferred from a special relationship, such as between a parent and a child, such an inference is inappropriate where the relationship between a juvenile defendant and the victims was one of "leader to . . . follower[s] among children in school" and did "not involve the same wielding of authority, disparity of power, and degree of fear that occurs between an abusive parent and a child." *Id.* at 200.

Element (4) (page 218)

As a result of 2019 legislation, S.L. 2019-245, delete the note to Element (4) and replace it with the following text:

Under G.S. 14-27.20(1a), an offense is against the will of the other person if it is either without the consent of the other person or after consent is revoked by the other person in a manner that would cause a reasonable person to believe that consent is revoked. That statutory provision was intended to supersede *State v. Way*, 297 N.C. 293 (1979), in which the state supreme court held under a prior North Carolina rape statute that if penetration initially occurred with a victim's consent, no rape occurs despite the victim's withdrawal of consent during the same act of intercourse. Evidence of physical resistance is not necessary to prove a lack of consent. State v. Hall, 293 N.C. 559 (1977).

Element (5)(a) (page 218)

As a result of the 2015 legislation noted above, the statutory citation in the first paragraph of this note should be to G.S. 14-27.21(a)(1).

Element (5)(b) (page 219)

There was sufficient evidence that the victim suffered serious personal injury where the victim had blood on her lip and bruises on her ribs, arms, and face and was in pain for four or five days after the incident; because she felt unsafe, the victim left her boyfriend, terminated her lease, and moved in with her family; and at the time of trial, roughly a year later, the victim still felt unsafe being alone, State v. Gates, 245 N.C. App. 525, 528 (2016); the victim, who was seven months pregnant, struggled to protect her stomach while the defendant dragged her down thirty-three concrete stairs and into nearby woods; a nurse compared the victim's injuries to "road rash" that one might suffer after falling off a motorcycle traveling at 55 mph; and the victim testified that her injuries were painful and that at the time of trial she still had extensive scars, State v. Gentle, 260 N.C. App. 269 (2018); and the defendant was a 43-year-old male approximately 5'10" tall with a medium build and the victim was a 22-year-old female, approximately 5'1" tall and weighing 96 pounds; the defendant unexpectedly grabbed the victim and threw her down a steep, rocky embankment, punched her face and head, straddled her, pinned her down, and strangled her; the victim suffered a head injury; experienced pain for days; had two black eyes, body bruises, and hoarseness in her voice; had difficulty concentrating and remembering; experienced short-term memory loss from the attacks; and testified that she continued to have trouble trusting people, opening up to others, and maintaining friendships, State v. Harding, 258 N.C. App. 306, 319–20 (2018).

Element (5)(d) (page 220)

For a case applying the general rule that actual or constructive presence is not required for aiding and abetting to this Element in a first-degree sexual offense case and finding that the evidence was sufficient, see *State v. Dick*, 370 N.C. 305, 312 (2017) (although the defendant was alone in a room with the victim when the sexual offense occurred, the defendant, together with his accomplices, taped the victim's mouth and taped her hands behind her back, moved her into the bedroom where the sexual offense occurred, removed her clothes, and touched her inappropriately).

Jury instructions (new note)

When the evidence of penetration is clear and positive, the trial court does not err by failing to instruct the jury on attempt. State v. Matsoake, 243 N.C. App. 651, 658–59 (2015) (rape case); State v. Norman, 227 N.C. App. 162, 168 (2013) (same). However, when the evidence of penetration is conflicting, the trial court should instruct on attempt, though it may not be plain error to fail to do so. State v. Carter, 366 N.C. 496, 500–01 (2013) (no plain error; sex offense); State v. Boyett, 229 N.C. App. 576, 578, 741 (2013) (no plain error; rape and incest case).

Defendant under 14 (page 221)

As a result of 2015 legislation, S.L. 2015-181, sec. 15, the statutory citation included in this note should be to G.S. 14-27.35.

Greater and lesser-included offenses (page 221)

For another case holding that assault on a female is not a lesser-included offense of first-degree sexual offense, see *State v. Martin*, 222 N.C. App. 213, 221–22 (2012).

In a 2012 case, the state court of appeals held that a defendant cannot be convicted of second-degree sexual offense (mentally disabled victim) and crime against nature (where lack of consent was based on the fact that the victim was mentally disabled, incapacitated, or physically helpless) based on the same conduct (fellatio). State v. Hunt, 221 N.C. App. 489, 495–97 (2012), *aff'd on other grounds*, 367 N.C. 700 (2014) (per curiam). The court found that "on the . . . facts of [the] case," crime against nature was a lesser-included offense of second-degree sexual offense and that conviction of both offenses violated double jeopardy. *Id.* However, the North Carolina Supreme Court previously held that crime against nature is not a lesser-included offense of forcible sexual offense, State v. Etheridge, 319 N.C. 34, 50–51 (1987); State v. Warren, 309 N.C. 224, 230–31 (1983), and that a definitional test—not a factual test—applies when determining whether offenses are lesser-included offenses. State v. Nickerson, 365 N.C. 279, 280 (2011); *Warren*, 309 N.C. at 230–31; *see also* State v. Robinson, 368 N.C. 402, 407–08 (2015) (applying a definitional test to the analysis).

As a result of the 2015 legislation noted above, (1) the penultimate sentence of the fifth paragraph in this note should read as follows:

But when a short-form rape indictment is not used and the indictment charges the crime using the language in the rape statute, assault on a female may not be submitted to the jury unless it has been separately charged. *State v. Hedgepeth*, 165 N.C. App. 321 (2004) (decided under former G.S. 14-27.2).

As a result of that same legislation, the citations in the last paragraph of this note should read as follows:

G.S. 14-27.23(e); -27.28(d).

Multiple convictions and punishments (page 222)

A defendant may be sentenced for statutory rape and incest arising out of the same transaction. State v. Marlow, 229 N.C. App. 593, 599–600 (2013) (reasoning that the offenses are not the same under the *Blockburger* test (referencing Blockburger v. United States, 284 U.S. 299 (1932)).

A defendant may be convicted and sentenced for both statutory rape of a 13-, 14-, or 15-year-old and second-degree rape of a mentally disabled person when the convictions are based on a single act of sexual intercourse. State v. Banks, 367 N.C. 652, 658–59 (2014).

Convicted defendant has no rights to custody or inheritance (page 223)

As a result of the 2015 legislation noted above, the text of this note should begin as follows: "G.S. 14-27.21(c) provides."

Related Offenses Not in This Chapter (page 223)

Add the following offense to this list:

Committing or attempting to commit sexual penetration on human remains. G.S. 14-401.22(c).
Sexual contact or penetration under pretext of medical treatment. G.S. 14-27.33A.

Second-Degree Forcible Rape (page 223)

Statute (page 223)

As a result of 2015 legislation, S.L. 2015-181, secs. 4(a) and (b), recodifying and amending the statute, and 2018 legislation, S.L. 2018-47, sec. 4(b), further amending it, the statute now reads as follows:

> **§ 14-27.22. Second-degree forcible rape.**
> (a) A person is guilty of second-degree forcible rape if the person engages in vaginal intercourse with another person:
> (1) By force and against the will of the other person; or
> (2) Who has a mental disability or who is mentally incapacitated or physically helpless, and the person performing the act knows or should reasonably know the other person has a mental disability or is mentally incapacitated or physically helpless.
> (b) Any person who commits the offense defined in this section is guilty of a Class C felony.
> (c) Upon conviction, a person convicted under this section has no rights to custody of or rights of inheritance from any child conceived during the commission of the rape, nor does the person have any rights related to the child under Chapter 48 of the General Statutes or Subchapter 1 of Chapter 7B of the General Statutes.

Elements (page 223)

As a result of 2018 legislation, S.L. 2018-47, sec. 4(a), and to correct a typographical error in the main volume, the elements of this offense should read as follows:

> A person guilty of this offense
> (1) has vaginal intercourse
> (2) with a person
> (3) and the intercourse is
> (a) by force and against the person's will *or*
> (b) with a person
> (i) who has a mental disability,
> (ii) is mentally incapacitated, *or*
> (iii) is physically helpless *and*
>
> the defendant knew or should have known that the victim has a mental disability, is mentally incapacitated, or is physically helpless.

Punishment (page 224)

As a result of the 2015 legislation noted above, the statutory citation in this note should be to G.S. 14-27.22(b).

Notes (page 224)

Elements (3)(b)(i), (ii), and (iii) (page 224)

These notes cite G.S. 14-27.1. That statute was recodified as G.S. 14-27.20 by 2015 legislation. S.L. 2015-181, sec. 2.

Element (3)(b)(i) (page 224)

As a result of 2018 legislation, S.L. 2018-47, sec. 4(a), delete the first paragraph of this note and replace it with the following:

> A person who has a mental disability is one "who has an intellectual disability or a mental disorder that temporarily or permanently renders the victim substantially incapable of appraising the nature of his or her conduct, or of resisting the act of vaginal intercourse or a sexual act, or of communicating unwillingness to submit to the act of vaginal intercourse or a sexual act." G.S. 14-27.20(2a).

As a result of that same legislation, replace the term "mentally disabled" as used in the second paragraph of this note with "mentally disabled, as that term was used in a prior version of the statute."

Reversing a case cited in this note, *State v. Hunt*, 211 N.C. App. 452 (2011), the North Carolina Supreme Court held that expert testimony is not required for the State to establish that the victim had a mental disability, as that term was used in a prior version of the statute, for purposes of second-degree sexual offense. State v. Hunt, 365 N.C. 432, 441 (2012).

Element (3)(b)(ii) (page 224)

As a result of 2018 legislation, S.L. 2018-47, sec. 4(a), further amended by 2019 legislation, S.L. 2019-245, sec. 6.(c), delete the first sentence of this note and replace it with the following:

> "Mentally incapacitated" means that any act has rendered the victim substantially incapable of either appraising the nature of his or her conduct or resisting the act. G.S. 14-27.20(2).

Element (3)(b)(iii) (page 224)

Add the following citation at the end of the first paragraph of this note:

> State v. Lopez, 264 N.C. App. 496 (2019) (a victim, who had no prior sexual relationship with the defendant and who consumed sizable portions of alcohol, was physically ill at a club, was unable to remember anything after leaving the club, was physically unable to resist the defendant, and was, therefore, physically helpless).

Convicted defendant has no rights to custody or inheritance (page 225)

As a result of the 2015 legislation noted above, the statutory citation in this note should be to G.S. 14-27.22(c).

First-Degree Statutory Rape (page 225)

Statute (page 225)

> **§ 14-27.24. First-degree statutory rape.**
>
> (a) A person is guilty of first-degree statutory rape if the person engages in vaginal intercourse with a victim who is a child under the age of 13 years and the defendant is at least 12 years old and is at least four years older than the victim.
>
> (b) Any person who commits an offense defined in this section is guilty of a Class B1 felony.
>
> (c) Upon conviction, a person convicted under this section has no rights to custody of or rights of inheritance from any child born as a result of the commission of the rape, nor shall the person have any rights related to the child under Chapter 48 or Subchapter 1 of Chapter 7B of the General Statutes.

No substantive changes were made to the elements of the offense.

Punishment (page 226)

As a result of the 2015 legislation noted above, the statutory citation in this section should read: G.S. 14-27.24(b).

Notes (page 226)

Element (2) (page 226)

For another case supporting the statement in this note that mistake of age is no defense to this crime, see *State v. Ward*, 250 N.C. App. 254, 263 (2016).

Add the following citation to the third sentence of the first paragraph of this note regarding the lack of a requirement for certified copies of birth records:

> ; State v. DeJesus, 265 N.C. App. 279 (2019) (a non-original copy of the victim's Honduran birth certificate, obtained through her school records, properly established her age).

Consent (page 226)

For another case supporting the statement in this note that consent is no defense to this crime, see *Ward*, 250 N.C. App. at 263.

Sex offender registration (page 227)

Add the following citation at the end of this note:

> , *as amended by* S.L. 2017-102, sec. 5.

Statutory Rape by an Adult (page 227)

Statute (page 227)

Legislation, S.L. 2015-181, secs. 5(a) and (b), recodified and amended the statute. The new title of the statute is:

> **§ 14-27.23. Statutory rape of a child by an adult.**

A conforming change was made to subsection (a) so that it reads:

> **(a) A person is guilty of statutory rape of a child by an adult if the person is at least 18 years of age and engages in vaginal intercourse with a victim who is a child under the age of 13 years.**

Due to other recodifications made in that same legislation, conforming changes were made to subsection (e) so that it reads:

> **(e) The offense under G.S. 14-27.24 is a lesser included offense of the offense in this section.**

Punishment (page 228)

As a result of the 2015 legislation noted above, the statutes referenced in this section should be to the same subsections in new G.S. 14-27.23.

Add the following to this section:

> The trial court has no discretion to sentence the defendant to less than 300 months for this offense. State v. Agustin, 229 N.C. App. 240, 246 (2013).

This section indicates that the statutory provision providing that a defendant may be sentenced to an active term above that normally provided for a Class B1 felony if the judge finds egregious aggravation appears to run afoul of the United States Supreme Court decision in *Blakely v. Washington*, 542 U.S. 296 (2004) (holding that any factor, other than a prior conviction, that increases punishment beyond the prescribed statutory maximum must be submitted to the jury and proved beyond a reasonable doubt). In *State v. Singletary*, 247 N.C. App. 368, 384–85 (2016), the North Carolina Court of Appeals so held as to the parallel punishment provision for Statutory Sexual Offense by an Adult; that holding almost certainly applies to this offense as well.

Notes (page 228)

Lifetime satellite-based monitoring (page 228)

As a result of the 2015 legislation noted above, the statutory citation in this note should be to G.S. 14-27.23(b).

Convicted defendant has no rights of custody or inheritance (page 228)

As a result of the 2015 legislation noted above, the statutory citation in this note should be to G.S. 14-27.23(d).

Statutory Rape of a Person 15 or Younger by a Defendant Who Is at Least 12 Years Old and at Least Six Years Older Than the Victim (page 229) (revised title)

Statute (page 229)

2015 legislation both amended and recodified the statute. S.L. 2015-62, sec. 1(a); S.L. 2015-181, secs. 7(a) and (b). As amended, the statute reads as follows:

> **§ 14-27.25. Statutory rape of person who is 15 years of age or younger.**
>
> **(a) A defendant is guilty of a Class B1 felony if the defendant engages in vaginal intercourse with another person who is 15 years of age or younger and the defendant is at**

least 12 years old and at least six years older than the person, except when the defendant is lawfully married to the person.

(b) Unless the conduct is covered under some other provision of law providing greater punishment, a defendant is guilty of a Class C felony if the defendant engages in vaginal intercourse with another person who is 15 years of age or younger and the defendant is at least 12 years old and more than four but less than six years older than the person, except when the defendant is lawfully married to the person.

Elements (page 229)

As a result of the statutory changes noted above, elements (2) and (3) should read as follows:

(2) with a child who is 15 years old or younger *and*
(3) the defendant is
  (a) at least 12 years old *and*
  (b) at least six years older than the child.

Punishment (page 229)

As a result of the 2015 legislative changes noted above, the statutory citation in this section should be to G.S. 14-27.25(a).

Notes (page 229)

Element (2) (page 229)

As a result of the statutory changes noted above, the crime now applies whenever the victim is 15 years of age or younger.

Exceptions (page 230)

As a result of the 2015 legislation noted above, the statutory citation in this note should be to G.S. 14-27.25(a).

Statutory Rape of a Person 15 or Younger by a Defendant Who Is at Least 12 Years Old and Is More Than Four but Less Than Six Years Older Than the Victim (page 231) (revised title)

Statute (page 231)

2015 legislation both amended and recodified the statute. S.L. 2015-62, sec. 1(a); S.L. 2015-181, secs. 7(a) and (b). The amended statute is reproduced in this supplement under "Statutory Rape of a Person 15 or Younger by a Defendant Who Is at Least 12 Years Old and at Least Six Years Older Than the Victim."

Elements (page 231)

As a result of the statutory changes noted above, elements (2) and (3) should read as follows:

(2) with a child who is 15 years old or younger *and*
(3) the defendant is
  (a) at least 12 years old *and*
  (b) more than four but less than six years older than the child.

Punishment (page 231)

As a result of the 2015 legislation noted above, the statutory citation in this section should be to G.S. 14-27.25(b).

Notes (page 231)

Multiple convictions and punishments (new note)

2015 legislation amended the statute to provide that punishment is as a Class C felony "[u]nless the conduct is covered under some other provision of law providing greater punishment." G.S. 14-27.25(b), *as amended by* S.L. 2015-62, sec. 1(a); S.L. 2015-181, secs. 7(a) and (b). This means that a defendant cannot be punished for this offense and one that provides for harsher punishment.

Sexual Offenses (page 231)

First-Degree Forcible Sexual Offense (page 231)

Statute (page 231)

2015 legislation, S.L. 2015-181, secs. 8(a) and (b), recodified and amended statute. 2017 legislation, S.L. 2017-30, sec. 2, further amended the statute. The amended statute reads as follows:

> **§ 14-27.26. First-degree forcible sexual offense.**
>
> (a) A person is guilty of a first degree forcible sexual offense if the person engages in a sexual act with another person by force and against the will of the other person, and does any of the following:
>
> (1) Uses, threatens to use, or displays a dangerous or deadly weapon or an article which the other person reasonably believes to be a dangerous or deadly weapon.
>
> (2) Inflicts serious personal injury upon the victim or another person.
>
> (3) The person commits the offense aided and abetted by one or more other persons.
>
> (b) Any person who commits an offense defined in this section is guilty of a Class B1 felony.

Elements (page 232)

As a result of the 2017 legislation noted above, Element (5)(a) should read as follows:

> (a) uses, threatens to use, or displays a dangerous or deadly weapon (or what reasonably appears to be a dangerous or deadly weapon),

Punishment (page 232)

As a result of the 2015 legislation noted above, the statutory citation in this section should be to G.S. 14-27.26(b).

Notes (page 232)

Element (1) (page 232)

This note cites G.S. 14-27.1 and -27.10. Those statutes were recodified as G.S. 14-27.20 and -27.36, respectively, by 2015 legislation. S.L. 2015-181, secs. 2, 15.

Add the following to this note:

> The defendant's act of forcing the victim at gunpoint to penetrate her vagina with her own fingers constitutes a sexual act. State v. Green, 229 N.C. App. 121, 128 (2013).
>
> Proof of vaginal penetration cannot support a sexual offense conviction; a sexual act other than vaginal intercourse is required. State v. Spence, 237 N.C. App. 367, 378–79 (2014).
>
> When the sex act is fellatio, proof of penetration is not required. *In re* J.F., 237 N.C. App. 218, 225–26 (2014).
>
> The prosecution need not show that the defendant performed a sexual act on the victim; the State need only prove that the defendant engaged in a sexual act with the victim. *Id.* (victim performed fellatio on the juvenile).
>
> For other cases where the evidence was sufficient to establish penetration with an object, see *State v. Phachoumphone*, 257 N.C. App. 848, 862 (2018) (the evidence was sufficient to show digital penetration where the 6-year-old victim demonstrated that the defendant digitally penetrated her vagina by inserting her finger into a hole which the interpreter created with her hand, and confirmed that her demonstration showed "what [defendant] did with his finger in [her] body"; a doctor testified that the victim's hymen was substantially missing, an irregular finding which could only have been caused by a penetrating injury; and the doctor observed

redness in the vaginal area behind where the hymen was, indicating a penetrating injury within the last forty-eight hours), and *State v. Wilson*, 260 N.C. App. 698 (2018) (in this sex offense by a substitute parent case, the evidence was sufficient to establish digital penetration where an officer testified to the defendant's confession that he put his hands "in [the victim's] genital area," causing her to become sexually aroused and "wet"; from this description a jury could infer that the defendant at least penetrated the victim's labia).

Sexual purpose (new note)
Proof of this crime does not require evidence that the defendant acted with a sexual purpose. *J.F.*, 237 N.C. App. at 224–25.

Defenses (page 233)

This note cites G.S. 14-27.1. That statute was recodified as G.S. 14-27.20 by 2015 legislation. S.L. 2015-181, sec. 2.

Add the following at the end of this note:

For the defendant to be entitled to a jury instruction on this affirmative defense, there must be direct testimony that the conduct was for a medically accepted purpose. State v. Stepp, 367 N.C. 772 (2015) (per curiam opinion reversing *State v. Stepp*, 232 N.C. App. 132 (2014), for reasons stated in the dissenting opinion below; the defendant admitted penetrating the victim's genital opening with his finger but claimed it was for an accepted medical purpose; noting the absence of any direct testimony that this was done for an accepted medical purpose, the dissenting judge found that the defendant was not entitled to a jury instruction on the defense).

Second-Degree Forcible Sexual Offense (page 234)

Statute (page 234)

As a result of 2015 legislation, S.L. 2015-181, secs. 4(a) and (b), recodifying and amending the statute, and 2018 legislation, S.L. 2018-47, sec. 4(c), further amending it, the statute now reads as follows:

§ 14-27.27. Second-degree forcible sexual offense.

(a) A person is guilty of second degree forcible sexual offense if the person engages in a sexual act with another person:

(1) By force and against the will of the other person; or
(2) Who has a mental disability or who is mentally incapacitated or physically helpless, and the person performing the act knows or should reasonably know that the other person has a mental disability or is mentally incapacitated or physically helpless.

(b) Any person who commits the offense defined in this section is guilty of a Class C felony.

Elements (page 234)

As a result of 2018 legislation, S.L. 2018-47, sec. 4(c), and to correct a typographical error in the main volume, the elements of this offense should read as follows:

A person guilty of this offense

(1) engages in a sexual act other than vaginal intercourse
(2) with a person
(3) and the act is
    (a) by force and against the person's will *or*
    (b) with a person
        (i) who has a mental disability
        (ii) is mentally incapacitated, *or*
        (iii) is physically helpless *and*
(4) the defendant knew or should have known that the victim has a mental disability, is mentally incapacitated, or is physically helpless.

Punishment (page 234)

As a result of the 2015 legislation noted above, the statutory citation in this section should be to G.S. 14-27.27(b).

First-Degree Statutory Sexual Offense (page 235)

Statute (page 235)

2015, S.L. 2015-181, secs. 8(b) and 11, removed first-degree statutory sexual offense from old G.S. 14-27.4 (recodified by the same legislation as G.S. 14-27.26), recodifying it as follows:

> **§ 14-27.29. First-degree statutory sexual offense.**
> (a) A person is guilty of first-degree statutory sexual offense if the person engages in a sexual act with a victim who is a child under the age of 13 years and the defendant is at least 12 years old and is at least four years older than the victim.
> (b) Any person who commits an offense defined in this section is guilty of a Class B1 felony.

No substantive changes were made to the elements of the offense.

Punishment (page 235)

As a result of the 2015 legislation noted above, the statutory citation in this section should be to G.S. 14-27.29(b).

Statutory Sexual Offense by an Adult (page 236)

Statute (page 236)

2015, S.L. 2015-181, secs. 10(a) and (b), recodified and amended the statute. The new title of the statute is:

> **§ 14-27.28. Statutory sexual offense with a child by an adult.**

A conforming change was made to subsection (a) so that it reads:

> (a) A person is guilty of statutory sexual offense with a child by an adult if the person is at least 18 years of age and engages in a sexual act with a victim who is a child under the age of 13 years.

Due to other recodifications made in that same legislation, conforming changes were made to subsection (d) so that it reads:

> (d) The offense under G.S. 14-27.29 is a lesser included offense of the offense in this section.

Punishment (page 237)

As a result of the 2015 legislation noted above, the first two sentences of this section should read as follows:

> Class B1 felony, except that the offense is subject to a mandatory minimum of 300 months of active time. G.S. 14-27.28(b). G.S. 14-27.28(c) provides that a defendant may be sentenced to an active term above that normally provided for a Class B1 felony if the judge finds egregious aggravation.

This section indicates that the statutory provision providing that a defendant may be sentenced to an active term above that normally provided for a Class B1 felony if the judge finds egregious aggravation runs afoul of the United States Supreme Court decision in *Blakely v. Washington*, 542 U.S. 296 (2004) (holding that any factor, other than a prior conviction, that increases punishment beyond the prescribed statutory maximum must be submitted to the jury and proved beyond a reasonable doubt). *State v. Singletary*, 247 N.C. App. 368, 384–85 (2016).

Notes (page 237)

Lifetime satellite-based monitoring required (page 238)

As a result of the 2015 legislation noted above, the statutory citation in this note should be to G.S. 14-27.28(b).

Statutory Sexual Offense of a Person 15 or Younger by a Defendant Who Is at Least 12 Years Old and Is at Least Six Years Older Than the Victim (page 238) (revised title)

Statute (page 238)

2015 legislation, S.L. 2015-181, secs. 7(a), 7(b), and 12, removed this offense from G.S. 14-27.7A (which was recodified as G.S. 14-27.25), recodifying it as follows:

> **§ 14-27.30. Statutory sexual offense with a person who is 15 years of age or younger.**
> (a) A defendant is guilty of a Class B1 felony if the defendant engages in a sexual act with another person who is 15 years of age or younger and the defendant is at least 12 years old and at least six years older than the person, except when the defendant is lawfully married to the person.
> (b) Unless the conduct is covered under some other provision of law providing greater punishment, a defendant is guilty of a Class C felony if the defendant engages in a sexual act with another person who is 15 years of age or younger and the defendant is at least 12 years old and more than four but less than six years older than the person, except when the defendant is lawfully married to the person.

Elements (page 238)

As a result of the statutory changes noted above, elements (2) and (3) should read as follows:

(2) with a child who is 15 years old or younger *and*
(3) the defendant is
  (a) at least 12 years old *and*
  (b) at least six years older than the child.

Punishment (page 238)

As a result of the 2015 legislation noted above, the statutory citation in this section should be to G.S. 14-27.30(a).

Notes (page 238)

Element (2) (page 238)

As a result of the statutory changes noted above, the crime now applies whenever the victim is 15 years of age or younger.

Statutory Sexual Offense of a Person 15 or Younger by a Defendant Who Is at Least 12 Years Old and Is More Than Four but Less Than Six Years Older Than the Victim (page 239) (revised title)

Statute (page 239)

2015 legislation, S.L. 2015-181, secs. 7(a), 7(b), and 12, removed this offense from G.S. 14-27.7A (which was recodified as G.S. 14-27.25), putting it in a new statutory section, G.S. 14-27.30, reproduced in this supplement under "Statutory Sexual Offense of a Person 15 or Younger by a Defendant Who Is at Least 12 Years Old and Is at Least Six Years Older Than the Victim."

Elements (page 239)

As a result of the statutory changes noted above, elements (2) and (3) should read as follows:

(2) with a child who is 15 years old or younger *and*
(3) the defendant is
  (a) at least 12 years old *and*
  (b) more than four but less than six years older than the child.

Punishment (page 239)

As a result of the 2015 legislation noted above, the statutory citation in this section should be to G.S. 14-27.30(b).

Notes (page 240)

Multiple convictions and punishments (new note)

2015 legislation, S.L. 2015-181, sec. 12, amended the recodified statute to provide that punishment is as a Class C felony "[u]nless the conduct is covered under some other provision of law providing greater punishment." G.S. 14-27.30(b). This means that a defendant cannot be punished for this offense and one that provides for harsher punishment.

Sexual Activity by a Substitute Parent (page 240)

Statute (page 240)

2015 legislation, S.L. 2015-181, secs. 13(a) and (b), amended and recodified the statute to read as follows:

> **§ 14-27.31. Sexual activity by a substitute parent or custodian.**
>
> (a) If a defendant who has assumed the position of a parent in the home of a minor victim engages in vaginal intercourse or a sexual act with a victim who is a minor residing in the home, the defendant is guilty of a Class E felony.
>
> (b) If a person having custody of a victim of any age or a person who is an agent or employee of any person, or institution, whether such institution is private, charitable, or governmental, having custody of a victim of any age engages in vaginal intercourse or a sexual act with such victim, the defendant is guilty of a Class E felony.
>
> (c) Consent is not a defense to a charge under this section.

The statutory amendments did not make any substantive changes to this offense.

Punishment (page 241)

As a result of 2015 legislation noted above, the statutory citation in this section should be to G.S. 14-27.31(a).

Notes (page 241)

Element (1) (page 241)

Add the following to the end of the first paragraph of this note:

It is not necessary for the defendant to have maintained a romantic relationship with the victim's parent or to exercise any legal rights over the child in order to be prosecuted under this offense. *Bailey*, 163 N.C. App. at 94. A defendant was deemed to have assumed the position of a parent of a victim when he paid for the victim's care and support, referred to himself as her "godfather" and told others she was his daughter, and tried to get her enrolled in school. State v. Sheridan, 263 N.C. App. 697 (2019). A 16-year-old minor can be a victim of this offense. State v. Oakley, 167 N.C. App. 318 (2004).

Consent (page 241)

As a result of the 2015 legislation noted above, the statutory citation in this note should be to G.S. 14-27.31(c).

Sexual Activity by a Custodian (page 242)

Statute (page 242)

2015 legislation amended and recodified the statute. S.L. 2015-181, secs. 13(a) and (b). The amended statute is reproduced in this supplement under "Sexual Activity by a Substitute Parent." The statutory amendments did not make any substantive changes to this offense.

Punishment (page 242)

As a result of the 2015 legislation noted above, the statutory citation in this section should be to G.S. 14-27.31(b).

Notes (page 242)

Element (1) (page 242)

As a result of the 2015 legislation noted above, the statutory citation in this note should be to G.S. 14-27.31(b).

Consent (page 243)

As a result of the 2015 legislation noted above, the statutory citation in this note should be to G.S. 14-27.31(c).

Sexual Activity with a Student (page 243)

Sexual Activity with a Student by a Teacher, School Administrator, Student Teacher, Coach, or School Safety Officer (page 243)

Statute (page 243)

2015 legislation, S.L. 2015-181, secs. 14(a) and (b); S.L. 2015-44, sec. 2, amended and recodified the statute to read as follows:

§ 14-27.32. Sexual activity with a student.

(a) If a defendant, who is a teacher, school administrator, student teacher, school safety officer, or coach, at any age, or who is other school personnel, and who is at least four years older than the victim engages in vaginal intercourse or a sexual act with a victim who is a student, at any time during or after the time the defendant and victim were present together in the same school, but before the victim ceases to be a student, the defendant is guilty of a Class G felony, except when the defendant is lawfully married to the student. The term "same school" means a school at which the student is enrolled and the defendant is employed, assigned, or volunteers.

(b) A defendant who is school personnel, other than a teacher, school administrator, student teacher, school safety officer, or coach, and is less than four years older than the victim and engages in vaginal intercourse or a sexual act with a victim who is a student, is guilty of a Class I felony.

(c) This section shall apply unless the conduct is covered under some other provision of law providing for greater punishment.

(d) Consent is not a defense to a charge under this section.

(e) For purposes of this section, the terms "school", "school personnel", and "student" shall have the same meaning as in G.S. 14-202.4(d). For purposes of this section, the term "school safety officer" shall include a school resource officer or any other person who is regularly present in a school for the purpose of promoting and maintaining safe and orderly schools.

The statutory amendments did not make any substantive changes to this offense.

Punishment (page 243)

As a result of the 2015 legislation noted above, the statutory citation in this section should be to G.S. 14-27.32(a).

Notes (page 243)

Element (1) (page 243)

As a result of the 2015 legislation noted above, the statutory citation in this note should be to G.S. 14-27.32(e).

Whether a defendant is a "teacher" within the meaning of this statute is determined through a case-by-case functional analysis, not merely by looking at the defendant's job title. That analysis requires evaluation of whether the defendant works part time or full time and whether he or she teaches students on a regular basis. *See* State v. Smith, 375 N.C. 224 (2020) (despite his lack of certification, a substitute teacher on long-term assignment who taught students daily, had a planning period, and had full access to students was a "teacher" within the meaning of this law).

Element (3) (page 244)

As a result of the 2015 legislation noted above, replace the statutory citations in this note to G.S. 14-27.7(b) with G.S. 14-27.32(e).

Element (4) (page 244)

As a result of the 2015 legislation noted above, the statutory citation in this note should be to G.S. 14-27.32(a).

Exceptions (page 244)

As a result of the 2015 legislation noted above, the statutory citation in this note should be to G.S. 14-27.32(a).

Multiple convictions and punishments (page 244)

As a result of the 2015 legislation noted above, the statutory citation in this note should be to G.S. 14-27.32(c).

Sexual Activity with a Student by School Personnel Other Than a Teacher, School Administrator, Student Teacher, Coach, or School Safety Officer Who Is at Least Four Years Older Than the Student (page 244) (revised title)

Statute (page 244)

2015 legislation amended and recodified the statute. S.L. 2015-181, secs. 14(a) and (b). The new statute is reproduced in this supplement under "Sexual Activity with a Student by a Teacher, School Administrator, Student Teacher, Coach, or School Safety Officer." The statutory amendments did not make any substantive changes to this offense.

Punishment (page 245)

As a result of the 2015 legislation noted above, the statutory citation in this section should be to G.S. 14-27.32(a).

Notes (page 245)

Element (1) (page 245)

As a result of the 2015 legislation noted above, replace the citation to G.S. 14-27.7(b) in this note with G.S. 14-27.32(e).

Sexual Activity with a Student by School Personnel Other Than a Teacher, School Administrator, Student Teacher, Coach, or School Safety Officer Who Is Less Than Four Years Older Than the Student (page 245) (revised title)

Statute (page 245)

2015 legislation amended and recodified the statute. S.L. 2015-181, secs. 14(a) and (b); S.L. 2015-44, sec. 2. The new statute is reproduced in this supplement under "Sexual Activity with a Student by a Teacher, School Administrator, Student Teacher, Coach, or School Safety Officer."

Punishment (page 246)

As a result of the 2015 legislation noted above, delete the text of this section and replace it with the following:

Class I felony. G.S. 14-27.32(b).

Indecent Liberties (page 246)

Indecent Liberties with a Child (page 246)

Notes (page 246)

General discussion of Elements (2)(a) and (2)(b) (page 247)
There was sufficient evidence of an indecent liberty where the defendant digitally penetrated the child's vagina. State v. Phachoumphone, 257 N.C. App. 848, 863–64 (2018).

Element (2)(a)(i) (page 248)
The defendant's purpose may be inferred from his or her actions. State v. Godley, 234 N.C. App. 562, 569 (2014); State v. Minyard, 231 N.C. App. 605, 621 (2014). For example, there was sufficient evidence of the required purpose when the defendant kissed the victim on the mouth, fondled her under her clothing, touched her breasts and vagina, and engaged in conduct giving rise to first-degree rape charges. *Godley*, 234 N.C. App. at 569.

There was sufficient proof that the defendant's purpose was to arouse or gratify sexual desire where he repeatedly raped the victim while she was living in his home. State v. Kpaeyeh, 246 N.C. App. 694, 700–01 (2016) (rejecting the defendant's argument that evidence of vaginal penetration is insufficient by itself to prove that a rape was committed for the purpose of arousing or gratifying sexual desire).

Element (3) (new note)
An actual child victim is not required to sustain a conviction for attempted taking indecent liberties. State v. Heelan, 263 N.C. App. 275 (2018) (although the person the defendant communicated with and sexually pursued was actually an undercover police officer, the defendant believed that he was communicating with and pursuing a child).

Attempts (page 249)
A defendant attempted to take an indecent liberty with a child when he wrote a letter asking her to have sex with him and gave it to the victim's grandmother, asking her to deliver it to the child, regardless of the fact that the victim never received the letter or otherwise saw or communicated with the defendant. State v. Southerland, 266 N.C. App. 217 (2019).

Jury instructions (page 249)
Because indecent liberties is a single offense that may be proved by evidence of any one of a number of acts, the trial court did not err by declining to instruct the jury according to a bill of particulars. State v. Stephens, 234 N.C. App. 292, 295–96 (2014) (the trial court properly instructed the jury that it could find the defendant guilty if it found that the defendant willfully took "any immoral, improper, or indecent liberties" with the child; the actual act committed for the purposes of arousing himself or gratifying his sexual desire was immaterial).

In a case involving five counts of indecent liberties, no unanimity issue arose where the trial court framed the jury instructions in terms of the statutory requirements and referenced the indictments, each of which specified a different, non-overlapping time frame; the instructions distinguished the five charges and directed the jurors to find the defendant guilty only if they found that he committed the requisite acts within the designated time period and each verdict sheet was paired with an indictment. State v. Comeaux, 224 N.C. App. 595, 605 (2012).

The trial judge properly instructed the jury in a case where the indictment tracked the statute and did not allege an evidentiary basis for the charge and the instructions identified the defendant's conduct as placing his penis between the child's feet. State v. Carter, 210 N.C. App. 156, 168–69 (2011) (the instruction was a clarification of the evidence for the jury).

Multiple convictions and punishments (page 249)

Add the following to the second paragraph of this note:

In *State v. Minyard*, 231 N.C. App. 605, 620–21 (2014), the court held that the victim's testimony that the defendant touched the victim's buttocks with his penis "four or five times" supported five indecent liberties convictions. Distinguishing *Laney* and finding the case similar to *James*, the court concluded that the State need not prove that the conduct occurred in discrete, separate settings when it involved acts "more explicit than mere touching." *Id.* at 620.

In *State v. Pierce*, 238 N.C. App. 537, 549–50 (2014), the court, citing *James*, held that the defendant properly was convicted of two counts of indecent liberties when the evidence showed that he had sex with his girlfriend in the presence of the victim, performed oral sex on the victim, and then forced his girlfriend to perform oral sex on the victim while he watched.

Indecent Liberties between Children (page 250)

Notes (page 250)

Element (2) (page 250)

For cases where the evidence was insufficient to establish a juvenile's sexual purpose with respect to the crime of Sexual Battery, see the note on Element (1) to that offense in this supplement.

Taking Indecent Liberties with a Student by a Teacher, School Administrator, Student Teacher, School Safety Officer, or Coach (page 251) (revised title)

Statute (page 251)

2015 legislation, S.L. 2015-44, sec. 3, amended G.S. 14-202.4(b) to read as follows:

> (b) If a defendant, who is school personnel, other than a teacher, school administrator, student teacher, school safety officer, or coach, and who is less than four years older than the victim, takes indecent liberties with a student as provided in subsection (a) of this section, the defendant is guilty of a Class I felony.

That same legislation amended the definition of "school personnel" in G.S. 14-202.4(d)(3) to read as follows:

> (3) "School personnel" means any person included in the definition contained in G.S. 115C-332(a)(2), including those employed by a nonpublic, charter, or regional school, and any person who volunteers at a school or a school-sponsored activity.

2015 legislation, S.L. 2015-181, sec. 16, made a conforming change to the last sentence of subsection (d) of the statute to read as follows:

> For purposes of this section, the term indecent liberties does not include vaginal intercourse or a sexual act as defined by G.S. 14-27.20.

Notes (page 252)

Element (2) (page 252)

This note cites G.S. 14-27.1. That statute was recodified as G.S. 14-27.20 by 2015 legislation. S.L. 2015-181, sec. 2.

Element (3) (page 252)

If the victim is enrolled in kindergarten or grade 1 through 12, the victim is a student within the meaning of the statute, even if the incident occurs during a school break. State v. Stephens, 234 N.C. App. 292, 296–97 (2014) (incident occurred during summer vacation).

Taking Indecent Liberties with a Student by School Personnel Other Than a Teacher, School Administrator, Student Teacher, School Safety Officer, or Coach Who Is at Least Four Years Older Than the Student (page 253) (revised title)

Statute (page 253)

As noted above under "Taking Indecent Liberties with a Student by a Teacher, School Administrator, Student Teacher, School Safety Officer, or Coach," 2015 legislation amended the statute.

Notes (page 253)

Element (1) (page 253)

As a result of 2015 legislation, S.L. 2015-44, sec. 3, delete the first sentence of this note and replace it with the following:

> "School personnel" means any person included in the definition contained in G.S. 115C-332(a)(2), including those employed by a nonpublic, charter, or regional school, and any person who volunteers at a school or a school-sponsored activity. G.S. 14-202.4(d)(3).

Taking Indecent Liberties with a Student by School Personnel Other Than a Teacher, School Administrator, Student Teacher, School Safety Officer, or Coach Who Is Less Than Four Years Older Than the Student (page 253) (revised title)

Statute (page 253)

As noted above under "Taking Indecent Liberties with a Student by a Teacher, School Administrator, Student Teacher, School Safety Officer, or Coach," 2015 legislation amended the statute.

Punishment (page 254)

As a result of the 2015 legislation noted above under "Taking Indecent Liberties with a Student by a Teacher, School Administrator, Student Teacher, School Safety Officer, or Coach," delete the text of this section and replace it with the following:

> Class I felony. G.S. 14-202.4(b).

Sexual Battery (page 254)

Statute (page 254)

2015 legislation, S.L. 2015-181, sec. 15, recodified the statute as G.S. 14-27.33; 2018 legislation, S.L. 2018-47, sec. 4(d), amended it. As a result of these changes, the statute reads as follows:

> **§ 14-27.33. Sexual battery.**
>
> (a) A person is guilty of sexual battery if the person, for the purpose of sexual arousal, sexual gratification, or sexual abuse, engages in sexual contact with another person:
>
> (1) By force and against the will of the other person; or
>
> (2) Who has a mental disability or who is mentally incapacitated or physically helpless, and the person performing the act knows or should reasonably know that the other person has a mental disability or is mentally incapacitated or physically helpless.
>
> (b) Any person who commits the offense defined in this section is guilty of a Class A1 misdemeanor.

Elements (page 254)

As a result of the 2018 legislation noted above, Element 3(b) should read as follows:

(3)(b) who has a mental disability or who is mentally incapacitated or physically helpless, and the person knows or should reasonably know that the other person has a mental disability or is mentally incapacitated or physically helpless.

Punishment (page 254)

As a result of the 2015 legislation noted above, the statutory citation in this section should be to G.S. 14-27.33(b).

Notes (page 255)

Element (1) (page 255)

The court of appeals has noted that in cases involving adult defendants, "the element of acting for the purpose of sexual arousal, sexual gratification, or sexual abuse may be inferred from the very act itself." *In re* S.A.A., 251 N.C. App. 131, 135 (2016) (internal quotation marks omitted). However, that rule does not apply with respect to juveniles. *Id.*; *In re* K.C., 226 N.C. App. 452, 457 (2013). For a juvenile, there must be "evidence of the child's maturity, intent, experience, or other factor indicating his purpose in acting." *S.A.A.*, 251 N.C. App. at 135 (quoting *K.C.*, 226 N.C. App. at 457). For cases where the evidence was held to be insufficient to establish a juvenile's sexual purpose required for this crime, see *K.C.*, 226 N.C. App. at 457–58 (evidence of sexual purpose was insufficient where, among other things, the juvenile and the victim were the same age; there was no evidence that the juvenile exercised control over the situation; and the incident occurred in a public school room during the day), and *S.A.A.*, 251 N.C. App. at 137 (evidence of sexual purpose was insufficient where, among other things, the juvenile and the girls in question were middle school students; neither the location nor the alleged manner of the touching was secretive in nature; nothing about the juvenile's attitude suggested a sexual motivation; the juvenile made no sexual remarks to the girls; and the juvenile did not attempt to exert any control over the girls). For a case where the evidence was sufficient to establish a juvenile's sexual purpose with respect to the crime of Indecent Liberties between Children, see the note on Element (2) to that crime in the main volume.

Element (2) (page 255)

This note cites G.S. 14-27.1. That statute was recodified as G.S. 14-27.20 by 2015 legislation.

Solicitation of a Child by Computer or Other Electronic Device (page 255)

Solicitation of a Child by Computer or Other Electronic Device to Commit an Unlawful Sex Act (page 255)

Notes (page 256)

Element (5)(b) (new note)

For a case where the evidence was sufficient to establish that the defendant believed the victim to be a child, see *State v. Heelan*, 263 N.C. App. 275 (2018) (although the person the defendant communicated with and sexually pursued was actually an undercover police officer, the defendant believed that he was communicating with and pursuing a child).

Sex Offender Crimes (page 258)

Statute (page 258)

G.S. 14-208.6 has been amended, *see* S.L. 2012-153, sec. 3; S.L. 2012-194, sec. 4(a); S.L. 2015-181, sec. 32; S.L. 2017-102, sec. 5; S.L. 2017-186, sec. 2(q); S.L. 2018-47, sec. 4(h), to read as follows:

§ 14-208.6. Definitions.

The following definitions apply in this Article:

(1a) Aggravated offense.—Any criminal offense that includes either of the following: (i) engaging in a sexual act involving vaginal, anal, or oral penetration with a victim of any age through the use of force or the threat of serious violence; or (ii) engaging in a sexual act involving vaginal, anal, or oral penetration with a victim who is less than 12 years old.

(1b) County registry.—The information compiled by the sheriff of a county in compliance with this Article.

(1c) Department.—The Department of Public Safety.

(1d) Electronic mail.—The transmission of information or communication by the use of the Internet, a computer, a facsimile machine, a pager, a cellular telephone, a video recorder, or other electronic means sent to a person identified by a unique address or address number and received by that person.

(1e) Employed.—Includes employment that is full-time or part-time for a period of time exceeding 14 days or for an aggregate period of time exceeding 30 days during any calendar year, whether financially compensated, volunteered, or for the purpose of government or educational benefit.

(1f) Entity.—A business or organization that provides Internet service, electronic communications service, remote computing service, online service, electronic mail service, or electronic instant message or chat services whether the business or organization is inside or outside the State.

(1g) Instant Message.—A form of real-time text communication between two or more people. The communication is conveyed via computers connected over a network such as the Internet.

(1h) Institution of higher education.—Any postsecondary public or private educational institution, including any trade or professional institution, college, or university.

(1i) Internet.—The global information system that is logically linked together by a globally unique address space based on the Internet Protocol or its subsequent extensions; that is able to support communications using the Transmission Control Protocol/Internet Protocol suite, its subsequent extensions, or other Internet Protocol compatible protocols; and that provides, uses, or makes accessible, either publicly or privately, high-level services layered on the communications and related infrastructure described in this subdivision.

(1j) Mental abnormality.—A congenital or acquired condition of a person that affects the emotional or volitional capacity of the person in a manner that predisposes that person to the commission of criminal sexual acts to a degree that makes the person a menace to the health and safety of others.

(1k) Nonresident student.—A person who is not a resident of North Carolina but who is enrolled in any type of school in the State on a part-time or full-time basis.

(1l) Nonresident worker.—A person who is not a resident of North Carolina but who has employment or carries on a vocation in the State, on a part-time or full-time basis, with or without compensation or government or educational benefit, for more than 14 days, or for an aggregate period exceeding 30 days in a calendar year.

(1m) Offense against a minor.—Any of the following offenses if the offense is committed against a minor, and the person committing the offense is not the minor's parent: G.S. 14-39 (kidnapping), G.S. 14-41 (abduction of children), and G.S. 14-43.3 (felonious restraint). The term also includes the following if the person convicted of the following is not the minor's parent: a solicitation or conspiracy to commit any of these offenses; aiding and abetting any of these offenses.

(1n) Online identifier.—Electronic mail address, instant message screen name, user ID, chat or other Internet communication name, but it does not mean social security number, date of birth, or pin number.

(2) Penal institution.—Any of the following:
   a. A detention facility operated under the jurisdiction of the Section of Prisons of the Division of Adult Correction and Juvenile Justice of the Department of Public Safety.
   b. A detention facility operated under the jurisdiction of another state or the federal government.
   c. A detention facility operated by a local government in this State or another state.

(2a) Personality disorder.—An enduring pattern of inner experience and behavior that deviates markedly from the expectations of the individual's culture, is pervasive and inflexible, has an onset in adolescence or early adulthood, is stable over time, and leads to distress or impairment.

(2b) Recidivist.—A person who has a prior conviction for an offense that is described in G.S. 14-208.6(4).

(3) Release.—Discharged or paroled.

(4) Reportable conviction.—Any of the following:
   a. A final conviction for an offense against a minor, a sexually violent offense, or an attempt to commit any of those offenses unless the conviction is for aiding and abetting. A final conviction for aiding and abetting is a reportable conviction only if the court sentencing the individual finds that the registration of that individual under this Article furthers the purposes of this Article as stated in G.S. 14-208.5.
   b. A final conviction in another state of an offense, which if committed in this State, is substantially similar to an offense against a minor or a sexually violent offense as defined by this section, or a final conviction in another state of an offense that requires registration under the sex offender registration statutes of that state.
   c. A final conviction in a federal jurisdiction (including a court martial) of an offense, which is substantially similar to an offense against a minor or a sexually violent offense as defined by this section.
   d. A final conviction for a violation of G.S. 14-202(d), (e), (f), (g), or (h), or a second or subsequent conviction for a violation of G.S. 14-202(a), (a1), or (c), only if the court sentencing the individual issues an order pursuant to G.S. 14-202(l) requiring the individual to register.
   e. A final conviction for a violation of G.S. 14-43.14, only if the court sentencing the individual issues an order pursuant to G.S. 14-43.14(e) requiring the individual to register.

(5) Sexually violent offense.—A violation of former G.S. 14-27.6 (attempted rape or sexual offense), G.S. 14-27.21 (first-degree forcible rape), G.S. 14-27.22 (second-degree forcible rape), G.S. 14-27.23 (statutory rape of a child by an adult), G.S. 14-27.24 (first-degree statutory rape), G.S. 14-27.25(a) (statutory rape of a person who is 15 years of age or younger and where the defendant is at least six years older), G.S. 14-27.26 (first-degree forcible sexual offense), G.S. 14-27.27 (second-degree forcible sexual offense), G.S. 14-27.28 (statutory sexual offense with a child by an adult), G.S. 14-27.29 (first-degree statutory sexual offense), G.S. 14-27.30(a) (statutory sexual offense with a person who is 15 years of age or younger and where the defendant is at least six years older), G.S. 14-27.31 (sexual activity by a substitute parent or custodian), G.S. 14-27.32 (sexual activity with a student), G.S. 14-27.33 (sexual battery),

G.S. 14-43.11 (human trafficking) if (i) the offense is committed against a minor who is less than 18 years of age or (ii) the offense is committed against any person with the intent that they be held in sexual servitude, G.S. 14-43.13 (subjecting or maintaining a person for sexual servitude), G.S. 14-178 (incest between near relatives), G.S. 14-190.6 (employing or permitting minor to assist in offenses against public morality and decency), G.S. 14-190.9(a1) (felonious indecent exposure), G.S. 14-190.16 (first degree sexual exploitation of a minor), G.S. 14-190.17 (second degree sexual exploitation of a minor), G.S. 14-190.17A (third degree sexual exploitation of a minor), G.S. 14-202.1 (taking indecent liberties with children), G.S. 14-202.3 (Solicitation of child by computer or certain other electronic devices to commit an unlawful sex act), G.S. 14-202.4(a) (taking indecent liberties with a student), G.S. 14-205.2(c) or (d) (patronizing a prostitute who is a minor or has a mental disability), G.S. 14-205.3(b) (promoting prostitution of a minor or person who has a mental disability), G.S. 14-318.4(a1) (parent or caretaker commit or permit act of prostitution with or by a juvenile), or G.S. 14-318.4(a2) (commission or allowing of sexual act upon a juvenile by parent or guardian). The term also includes the following: a solicitation or conspiracy to commit any of these offenses; aiding and abetting any of these offenses.

(6) Sexually violent predator.—A person who has been convicted of a sexually violent offense and who suffers from a mental abnormality or personality disorder that makes the person likely to engage in sexually violent offenses directed at strangers or at a person with whom a relationship has been established or promoted for the primary purpose of victimization.

(7) Sheriff.—The sheriff of a county in this State.

(8) Statewide registry.—The central registry compiled by the Department in accordance with G.S. 14-208.14.

(9) Student.—A person who is enrolled on a full-time or part-time basis, in any postsecondary public or private educational institution, including any trade or professional institution, or other institution of higher education.

2013 legislation, S.L. 2013-205, amended G.S. 14-208.11(a)(1) to read as follows:

(1) Fails to register as required by this Article, including failure to register with the sheriff in the county designated by the person, pursuant to G.S. 14-208.8, as their expected county of residence.

That same legislation enacted a new subsection, (a2), to G.S. 14-208.11 as follows:

(a2) A person arrested pursuant to subsection (a1) of this section shall be subject to the jurisdiction of the prosecutorial and judicial district that includes the sheriff's office in the county where the person failed to register, pursuant to this Article. If the arrest is made outside of the applicable prosecutorial district, the person shall be transferred to the custody of the sheriff of the county where the person failed to register and all further criminal and judicial proceedings shall be held in that county.

2013 legislation, S.L. 2013-28, amended G.S. 14-208.16(a) to read as follows:

(a) A registrant under this Article shall not knowingly reside within 1,000 feet of the property on which any public or nonpublic school or child care center is located. This subsection applies to any registrant who did not establish his or her residence, in accordance with subsection (d) of this section, prior to August 16, 2006.

2016 legislation, S.L. 2016-102, sec. 1, amended G.S. 14-208.18(a) so that subsection (3) and new subsection (4) read as follows:

(3) At any place where minors frequently congregate, including, but not limited to, libraries, arcades, amusement parks, recreation parks, and swimming pools, when minors are present.

(4) On the State Fairgrounds during the period of time each year that the State Fair is conducted, on the Western North Carolina Agricultural Center grounds during the period of time each year that the North Carolina Mountain State

Fair is conducted, and on any other fairgrounds during the period of time that an agricultural fair is being conducted.

2015 and 2016 legislation, S.L. 2015-62, sec. 5(a); S.L. 2016-102, sec. 1, amended G.S. 14-208.18(c) to read as follows:

(c) The subdivisions of subsection (a) of this section are applicable as follows:

(1) Subdivisions (1), (3), and (4) of subsection (a) of this section apply to persons required to register under this Article who have committed any of the following offenses:

a. Any offense in Article 7A of this Chapter or any federal offense or offense committed in another state, which if committed in this State, is substantially similar to an offense in Article 7A of this Chapter.

b. Any offense where the victim of the offense was under the age of 18 years at the time of the offense.

(2) Subdivision (2) of subsection (a) of this section applies to persons required to register under this Article if either of the following applies:

a. The person has committed any offense in Article 7B of this Chapter or any federal offense or offense committed in another state, which if committed in this State is substantially similar to an offense in Article 7B of this Chapter, and a finding has been made in any criminal or civil proceeding that the person presents, or may present, a danger to minors under the age of 18.

b. The person has committed any offense where the victim of the offense was under the age of 18 years at the time of the offense.

2017 legislation, S.L. 2017-186, sec. 2(aa), amended G.S. 14-208.44(c) and (d) to read as follows:

(c) Any person required to enroll in a satellite-based monitoring program who fails to provide necessary information to the Division of Adult Correction and Juvenile Justice or fails to cooperate with the Division of Adult Correction and Juvenile Justice's guidelines and regulations for the program shall be guilty of a Class 1 misdemeanor.

(d) For purposes of this section, "enroll" shall include appearing, as directed by the Division of Adult Correction and Juvenile Justice to receive the necessary equipment.

Failure to Register, etc. as a Sex Offender (page 268)

Notes (page 269)

Element (1) (page 269)

Registration requirements that became effective on January 1, 1996, and applied to offenders then serving a sentence for a reportable offense applied to the defendant and made him a person required to register where he was convicted in 1994 of indecent liberties and his prison release date for that conviction was September 24, 1995, but he was not actually released until January 24, 1999, because he was serving a consecutive term for crime against nature. State v. Surratt, 241 N.C. App. 380, 385–86 (2015) (concluding that the defendant's actual release date, January 24, 1999, governs; also concluding that because he was required to register when the 2008 amendments to the registration statutes took effect, the 2008 amendments applied to the defendant as well).

Element (3)(a) (page 269)

2013 legislation, S.L. 2013-205, amended the statute to clarify that failure to register includes failure to register with the sheriff in the county designated by the person as his or her expected county of residence.

Element (3)(b) (page 269)

Add the following to this note:

This prong of the statute applies to a sex offender who has already complied with the initial registration requirements and is later incarcerated and then released. State v. Crockett,

368 N.C. 717, 722 (2016); State v. Barnett, 368 N.C. 710, 714 (2016) (holding that this provision applied where the defendant failed to change his address after being released from a term of incarceration imposed after his initial registration).

The evidence was sufficient to establish this Element where (1) after previously registering as required under the statute, the defendant failed to register a change of address after being released from one month's incarceration after a parole violation, State v. Reynolds, 253 N.C. App. 359, 364–66 (2017); (2) after initially registering, the defendant was incarcerated in the county jail and upon his release did not provide notice that he had changed his address from the county jail, *Crockett*, 368 N.C. at 724–25; (3) the defendant moved from North Carolina to South Carolina without providing written notice to the sheriff, *id.* at 725–26; (4) the defendant was not residing at his registered address, State v. McFarland, 234 N.C. App. 274, 280–81 (2014) (the State need not present evidence of the defendant's new address, only that he or she failed to register a change of address); and (5) the defendant may have maintained a permanent residence in one county, but he also established a temporary home address at his ex-wife's residence in another county. State v. Pierce, 238 N.C. App. 141, 148–49 (2014).

Element (3)(c) (page 270)

Delete the second sentence of this note and replace it with the following:

To obtain a conviction under this prong of the statute, the State must prove five things: (1) the defendant is required to register, (2) law enforcement mailed a non-forwardable verification form to the defendant's last reported address, (3) the defendant actually received the verification form, (4) law enforcement made a reasonable attempt to verify that the defendant was residing at the registered address, and (5) the defendant willfully failed to return the verification form to the sheriff within three business days. State v. Moore, 240 N.C. App. 465, 473 (2015) (stating these requirements and holding that the State failed to prove that the defendant actually received the verification form, that the sheriff's office made a reasonable attempt to verify that the defendant was still residing at his last reported address, or that the defendant acted willfully); State v. Braswell, 203 N.C. App. 736, 739 (2010) (the State failed to prove that the defendant actually received the verification form). A "business day" is any calendar day except Saturday, Sunday, or any legal holiday declared in G.S. 103-4. State v. Patterson, 266 N.C. App. 567 (2019) (concluding that Columbus Day is a legal holiday under G.S. 103-4, and therefore not a business day within the meaning of G.S. 14-208.9A—regardless of whether the sheriff's office was actually open for business).

Element (3)(d) (page 270)

Falsely stating information on any forms submitted pursuant to the sex offender registration program supports a conviction. State v. Pressley, 235 N.C. App. 613, 617 (2014) (in a case where the defendant listed a false address, the court rejected the defendant's argument that the only verification forms that count are the initial verification form and those required to be filed every six months thereafter; the court concluded that the statute criminalizes providing false or misleading information on forms submitted pursuant to the act, regardless of when the forms are submitted). However, the statute only applies to providing false or misleading information on an executed verification form required by the statute; the statute does not apply to oral verifications to a law enforcement officer. State v. Surratt, 241 N.C. App. 380, 387 (2015).

Constitutionality (new note)

Requiring a person adjudicated as an incompetent to notify a sheriff of a change of address is unconstitutional. State v. Young, 140 N.C. App. 1 (2000).

The court of appeals has rejected the argument that the statute's change of address requirement was void for vagueness because it failed to define the term "address." State v. McFarland, 234 N.C. App. at 274, 277–79 (2014) (the homeless defendant unsuccessfully argued that a person of ordinary intelligence would not know what "address" meant in his case).

Jurisdiction (new note)
2013 legislation, S.L. 2013-205, amended G.S. 14-208.11 to provide that a person arrested for a failure-to-register violation must be prosecuted in the prosecutorial district that includes the sheriff's office in the county where the defendant failed to register. G.S. 14-208.11(a2). If the arrest is made outside of the applicable prosecutorial district, the defendant must be transferred to the custody of the sheriff of the county where the defendant failed to register. *Id.*

Multiple convictions and punishments (page 271)
For a case holding that double jeopardy prohibits a defendant from being punished for failing to register a change of address under both G.S. 14-208.11(a)(2) (failing to notify the last registering sheriff of a change of address) and -208.11(a)(7) (failing to report in person to the sheriff) based on the same failure to report, see *State v. Reynolds*, 253 N.C. App. 359, 362–64 (2017).

Falsely reporting an address on verification forms submitted on two separate occasions supports two convictions. State v. Pressley, 235 N.C. App. 613, 619 (2014) (rejecting the defendant's argument that this constituted a continuing offense and could support only one conviction; submission of each form was a distinct offense).

Knowingly Residing Near a School or Child Care Center (page 272)

Notes (page 272)

Element (5) (page 272)

As a result of 2019 legislation, S.L. 2019-245, sec. 8.(a), add the following sentence at the end of the first paragraph of this note:

However, for the purposes of this offense, the term "school" shall also include any construction project designated for use as a public school, if the governing body has notified the sheriff with jurisdiction within 1,000 feet of the construction project of the construction of the public school. G.S. 14-208.16(b).

As a result of 2014 legislation, S.L. 2014-21, add the following sentence at the end of the second paragraph of this note:

However, a "child care center" does include the permanent locations of organized clubs of Boys and Girls Clubs of America. G.S. 14-208.16(b).

Exceptions (page 272)

As a result of 2013 legislation, S.L. 2013-28, delete the last paragraph of this note and replace it with the following:

Additionally, this offense does not apply to a person who established his or her residence before August 16, 2006. G.S. 14-208.16(a).

Being Present at a Location Used by Minors (page 274)

Statute (page 274)

As noted in this supplement, 2015 and 2016 legislation, S.L. 2015-62, sec. 5(a); S.L. 2016-102, sec.1, amended the statute.

Elements (page 274)

As a result of the 2015 and 2016 legislation noted above, delete the text of this section and replace it with the following:

A person guilty of this offense

(1) is required to register as a sex offender
(2) because of a conviction for any
  (a) rape, sexual offense, sexual battery, or related offense in G.S. Chapter 14, Article 7B or substantially similar offense under federal law or the laws of another state *or*
  (b) offense in which the victim was less than 18 years old *and*

(3) knowingly
(4) is present
   (a) on the premises of any place intended primarily for the use, care, or supervision of minors, including, but not limited to, schools, children's museums, child care centers, nurseries, and playgrounds;
   (b) within 300 feet of any location intended primarily for the use, care, or supervision of minors when the place is located on premises that are not intended primarily for the use, care, or supervision of minors, including malls, shopping centers, or other property open to the general public and, if the person is required to register because of a rape, sexual offense, sexual battery, or related offense in G.S. Chapter 14, Article 7B or substantially similar offense under federal law or the laws of another state, a finding has been made in any criminal or civil proceeding that the person presents, or may present, a danger to minors under the age of 18;
   (c) at any place where minors frequently congregate, including, but not limited to, libraries, arcades, amusement parks, recreation parks, and swimming pools, when minors are present; *or*
   (d) on the State Fairgrounds when the State Fair is conducted, on the Western North Carolina Agricultural Center grounds when the North Carolina Mountain State Fair is conducted, or on any other fairgrounds when an agricultural fair is being conducted.

Notes (page 274)

Element (2)(b) (new note)
If the prior offense does not include an element as to the victim's age, the State must prove that the victim was younger than the statutory age at the time of the offense. State v. Fryou, 244 N.C. App. 112, 121–22 (2015).

Element (3) (page 274)
For a case where the evidence was sufficient as to this Element, see *Fryou*, 244 N.C. App. at 122–23 (church widely advertised its preschool and posted a sign at the church entrance indicating that a "nursery" was held on the premises).

Element (4) (page 274)
The evidence was insufficient to support a conviction for being a sex offender on the premises of a daycare when the defendant was seen in a parking lot of a strip mall containing the daycare center, other businesses, and a restaurant. State v. Anderson, 254 N.C. App. 765, 776 (2017) (none of the spaces in the parking lot were specifically reserved or marked for the daycare and the daycare center, which was, including its playground, surrounded by a chain-link fence).

To satisfy Element (4)(b), the State must prove that the location is intended primarily for the use of minors; evidence that minors sometimes use the location is insufficient. State v. Simpson, 235 N.C. App. 398, 403–05 (2014) (the evidence was insufficient where the defendant sat on a park bench in close proximity to one of the park's batting cages and ball fields and the State failed to present evidence that the batting cages and ball fields were intended primarily for use by minors).

Although *Fryou*, 244 N.C. App. at 123, held that the State need not prove that minors were actually present at the location at the time of the offense, 2016 legislative changes provided that the ban on being present at any place where minors frequently congregate (Element (4)(c) of this offense) applies only when "minors are present." S.L. 2016-102, sec. 1.

Multiple convictions and punishments (new note)
In *State v. Daniels*, 224 N.C. App. 608, 612 (2012), the court held that elements (4)(a) through (c) constitute three separate and distinct criminal offenses. This holding likely would apply to Element (4)(d) as well.

Constitutionality (new note)

2016 legislation, S.L. 2016-102, sec. 1, amended the statute in response to determinations in a federal district court case that (1) the prior statutory provision banning sex offenders from any place where minors gather for regularly scheduled educational, recreational, or social programs was unconstitutionally vague, Does v. Cooper, 148 F. Supp. 3d 477, 494 (M.D.N.C. 2015); and (2) the "300-foot rule" ban was unconstitutionally overbroad under the First Amendment. Does v. Cooper, No. 1:13CV711, 2016 WL 1629282 (M.D.N.C. Apr. 22, 2016). The General Assembly responded by revising the "any place where minors gather" provision and by adding to the 300-foot rule a requirement that a finding has been made in any criminal or civil proceeding that the person presents, or may present, a danger to minors under the age of 18. S.L. 2016-102, sec. 1. Lawmakers also provided that these changes are repealed if the federal district court's determinations are stayed or overturned. *Id.* sec. 2. The Fourth Circuit affirmed the lower court's rulings in *Does v. Cooper*, 842 F.3d 833 (4th Cir. 2016).

In *Daniels*, 224 N.C. App. at 621, the court held that the previous version of G.S. 14-208.18(a)(3), which prohibited a sex offender from being "at any place" where minors gather for regularly scheduled programs, was unconstitutionally vague as applied to the defendant. The defendant's two charges arose from his presence at two public parks. The State alleged that on one occasion the defendant was "out kind of close to the parking lot area or that little dirt road area[,]" between the ballpark and the road and that on the second occasion he was at an "adult softball field" adjacent to a "tee ball" field. The court found that on these facts, the portion of G.S. 14-208.18(a)(3) prohibiting presence "at any place" was unconstitutionally vague as applied to the defendant because it fails to give the person of ordinary intelligence a reasonable opportunity to know what is prohibited and it fails to provide explicit standards for those who apply the law. *Id.* at 622. By contrast, the court rejected an as-applied vagueness challenge to G.S. 14-208.18(a)(2) in a case involving the defendant's presence at a church that operated a preschool on the premises. State v. Fryou, 244 N.C. App. 112, 127–28 (2015). As noted in this supplement, 2016 legislation amended the prohibitions in G.S. 14-208.18(a)(2) and (3).

Accessing a Social Networking Site (page 274)

Notes (page 275)

Constitutionality (new note)

In *Packingham v. North Carolina*, ___ U.S. ___, 137 S. Ct. 1730 (2017), the United States Supreme Court struck down G.S. 14-202.5 on grounds that it violates the First Amendment.

Online Conduct by High-Risk Sex Offenders (new crime)

After *Packingham*, G.S. 14-202.5 was substantially amended by 2019 legislation, S.L. 2019-245, effective for offenses committed on or after December 1, 2019.

Statute

§ 14-202.5. Ban online conduct by high-risk sex offenders that endangers children.

(a) Offense. – It is unlawful for a high-risk sex offender to do any of the following online:

(1) To communicate with a person that the offender believes is under 16 years of age.

(2) To contact a person that the offender believes is under 16 years of age.

(3) To pose falsely as a person under 16 years of age with the intent to commit an unlawful sex act with a person the offender believes is under 16 years of age.

(4) To use a Web site to gather information about a person that the offender believes is under 16 years of age.

(5) To use a commercial social networking Web site in violation of a policy, posted in a manner reasonably likely to come to the attention of users, prohibiting convicted sex offenders from using the site.

(b) Definition of Commercial Social Networking Web Site. – For the purposes of this section, a "commercial social networking Web site" includes any Web site, application, portal, or other means of accessing the Internet that meets all of the following requirements:

(1) Is operated by a person who derives revenue from membership fees, advertising, or other sources related to the operation of the Web site.

[The session law strikes through subdivision (b)(2) but does not replace it.]

(3) Allows users to create personal Web pages or profiles that contain information such as the user's name or nickname, photographs of the user, and other personal information.

(4) Provides users or visitors a mechanism to communicate with others, such as a message board, chat room, or instant messenger.

(c) Exclusions from Commercial Social Networking Web Site Definition. – A commercial social networking Web site does not include a Web site that meets either of the following requirements:

[The session law strikes through subdivision (c)(1) but does not replace it.]

(2) Has as its primary purpose the facilitation of commercial transactions, the dissemination of news, the discussion of political or social issues, or professional networking.

(3) Is a Web site owned or operated by a local, State, or federal governmental entity.

(c1) Definition of High-Risk Sex Offender. – For purposes of this section, the term "high-risk sex offender" means any person registered in accordance with Article 27A of Chapter 14 of the General Statutes that meets any of the following requirements:

(1) Was convicted of an aggravated offense, as that term is defined in G.S. 14-208.6, against a person under 18 years of age.

(2) Is a recidivist, as that term is defined in G.S. 14-208.6, and one offense is against a person under 18 years of age.

(3) Was convicted of an offense against a minor, as that term is defined in G.S. 14-208.6.

(4) Was convicted of a sexually violent offense, as that term is defined in G.S. 14-208.6, against a person under 18 years of age.

(5) Was found by a court to be a sexually violent predator, as that term is defined in G.S. 14-208.6, based on a conviction of a sexually violent offense committed against a minor.

(d) Jurisdiction. – The offense is committed in the State for purposes of determining jurisdiction, if the transmission that constitutes the offense either originates in the State or is received in the State.

(e) Punishment. – A violation of this section is a Class H felony.

(f) Severability. – If any provision of this section or its application is held invalid, the invalidity does not affect other provisions or applications of this section that can be given effect without the invalid provisions or applications, and, to this end, the provisions of this section are severable.

Elements

A person guilty of this offense

(1) is a high-risk sex offender *and*

(2) does any of the following online

(a) communicates with a person that the offender believes is under 16 years of age,

(b) contacts a person that the offender believes is under 16 years of age,

(c) poses falsely as a person under 16 years of age with the intent to commit an unlawful sex act with a person the offender believes is under 16 years of age,

(d) uses a website to gather information about a person that the offender believes is under 16 years of age, *or*

(e) uses a commercial social networking website in violation of a policy, posted in a manner reasonably likely to come to the attention of users, prohibiting convicted sex offenders from using the site.

Punishment

Class H felony. G.S. 14-202.5.

Notes

Element (1). A high-risk sex offender is any person registered as a sex offender in North Carolina who is a recidivist; was convicted of an aggravated offense, an offense against a minor, or a sexually violent offense; or was found to be a sexually violent predator, as those terms are defined in G.S. 14-208.6.

Element (4)(e). A commercial social networking website is any website, application, portal, or other means of accessing the Internet that is operated by a person who derives revenue through fees, advertising, or other sources by allowing users to create personal webpages and providing a mechanism to communicate with others. G.S. 14-202.5(b). The definition of a commercial social networking website excludes sites that have as their primary purpose the facilitation of commercial transactions, the dissemination of news, the discussion of political or social issues, or professional networking. *Id.* § -202.5(c).

Jurisdiction. The offense is committed in North Carolina if the transmission at issue either originates or is received in North Carolina. G.S. 14-202.5(d).

Related Offenses Not in This Chapter

See "Child Abuse" offenses and "Contributing to a Juvenile's Being Delinquent, Undisciplined, Abused, or Neglected" in Chapter 9 (Abuse and Neglect) of the main volume.

See "Failure to Report the Disappearance of a Child" (new crime) in Chapter 9 (Abuse and Neglect) of this supplement.

Unlawful payments related to adoption. G.S. 48-10-102.

11
Crime against Nature, Incest, Indecent Exposure, and Related Offenses

Crime against Nature (page 281)

Notes (page 281)

Constitutionality (page 282)
For an additional case supporting the statement in this note that the statute may be used to prosecute conduct involving a minor, non-consensual or coercive sexual acts, conduct occurring in a public place, or conduct involving prostitution or solicitation, see *State v. Gentle*, 260 N.C. App. 269 (2018).

For a case where the evidence established that the conduct occurred in a public place, see *Gentle*, 260 N.C. App. at 275–76 (the conduct occurred near a parking lot; the court rejected the defendant's argument that the conduct also must occur in public view).

Consent (page 282)
Reversing a case cited in this note, *State v. Hunt*, 211 N.C. App. 452 (2011), the North Carolina Supreme Court held that there was sufficient evidence that the victim's conditions rendered her substantially incapable of resisting the defendant's advances and that expert testimony is not required to prove the extent of a victim's mental capacity to consent to sexual acts. State v. Hunt, 365 N.C. 432, 441 (2012).

Penetration required (page 282)
For another case supporting the statement in this note that penetration of or by a sexual organ is required for this offense, see *In re* J.F., 237 N.C. App. 218, 225–27 (2014) (distinguishing *Heil* and finding the evidence insufficient to establish penetration).

Sexual purpose (new note)
Proof of this crime does not require evidence that the defendant acted with a sexual purpose. *Id.* at 224–25.

Greater and lesser-included offenses (page 283)
The court of appeals has held that a defendant cannot be convicted of second-degree sexual offense (mentally disabled victim) and crime against nature (where lack of consent was based on the fact that the victim was mentally disabled, incapacitated, or physically helpless) based on the same conduct (fellatio). State v. Hunt, 221 N.C. App. 489, 496–97 (2012), *aff'd on other grounds*, 367 N.C. 700 (2014) (per curiam). The court found that on the facts of the case, crime against nature was a lesser-included offense of second-degree sexual offense and that conviction of both violated double jeopardy. *Id.* However, the North Carolina Supreme Court previously held that crime against nature is not a lesser-included offense of forcible sexual

offense, State v. Etheridge, 319 N.C. 34, 50–51 (1987); State v. Warren, 309 N.C. 224, 230–31 (1983), and that a definitional test—not a factual test—applies when determining whether offenses are lesser-included offenses. State v. Nickerson, 365 N.C. 279, 280 (2011); *Warren*, 309 N.C. at 230–31; *see also* State v. Robinson, 368 N.C. 402, 406–08 (2015) (applying a definitional test to the analysis).

Incest Offenses (page 284)

Incest (page 284)

Notes (page 284)

Jury instructions (new note)

For a discussion of this issue with respect to rape, see this note on "First-Degree Forcible Rape" above in this supplement.

Multiple convictions and punishments (page 285)

A defendant may be sentenced for both statutory rape and incest arising out of the same transaction. State v. Marlow, 229 N.C. App. 593, 599–601 (2013) (reasoning that the offenses are not the same under the *Blockburger* test (referencing Blockburger v. United States, 284 U.S. 299 (1932)).

Indecent Exposure (page 289)

Statute (page 289)

2015 legislation, S.L. 2015-250, secs. 2–2.3, amended the statute, adding new subsections as follows:

> (a2) Unless the conduct is prohibited by another law providing greater punishment, any person who shall willfully expose the private parts of his or her person in the presence of anyone other than a consenting adult on the private premises of another or so near thereto as to be seen from such private premises for the purpose of arousing or gratifying sexual desire is guilty of a Class 2 misdemeanor.
>
> . . .
>
> (a4) Unless the conduct is punishable by another law providing greater punishment, any person at least 18 years of age who shall willfully expose the private parts of his or her person in a private residence of which they are not a resident and in the presence of any other person less than 16 years of age who is a resident of that private residence shall be guilty of a Class 2 misdemeanor.
>
> (a5) Unless the conduct is prohibited by another law providing greater punishment, any person located in a private place who shall willfully expose the private parts of his or her person with the knowing intent to be seen by a person in a public place shall be guilty of a Class 2 misdemeanor.

Misdemeanor Indecent Exposure (page 289)

Notes (page 290)

Element (4) (page 290)

Add the following at the end of the second paragraph of this note:

The defendant masturbated in a public place when he did so on his own property in front of his garage; the garage was directly off a public road and was in full view from the street and a neighbor's house. State v. Pugh, 244 N.C. App. 326 (2015).

The 2015 legislation noted above created three new Class 2 misdemeanor versions of this offense, all of which apply when the exposure occurs on or near a private place.

Element (5) (page 290)

To satisfy this Element, it is not necessary that a defendant expose himself "to" a person; all that is required is that a defendant expose himself "in the presence of" a person. The test for presence is not whether the victim saw the exposure or could have seen it had he or she looked, but rather whether the defendant has positioned him- or herself so he or she is sufficiently close to the victim. State v. Hoyle, 373 N.C. 454 (2020). In *Hoyle,* there was sufficient evidence that the defendant's exposure was in the presence of a child within the meaning of this offense when the defendant exposed himself while sitting in his car in front of the victim's house, about twenty feet from the child, notwithstanding the fact that the child did not see the exposure and could not have seen it without being positioned differently. *Id.* at 458.

Multiple convictions and punishments (page 290)

Add the following at the end of this note:

; *see also* State v. Hayes, 248 N.C. App. 414 (2016) (citing the statute and holding that where the defendant simultaneously exposed himself to a minor and an adult, he could not be convicted of both misdemeanor indecent exposure under G.S. 14-190.9(a) (for the exposure to the adult) and felonious indecent exposure under G.S. 14-190.9(a1) (for the exposure to the minor)).

Related Offenses Not in This Chapter (page 291)

Add the following offense to this list:

Indecent exposure in a private place. G.S. 14-190.9(a2), (a4), (a5).
Prisoner exposing genitalia to employee. G.S. 14-258.4(b) (enacted by S.L. 2018-67, sec. 2).

Felony Indecent Exposure (page 291)

Notes (page 291)

Element (5) (new note)

For the misdemeanor version of this offense, the exposure must occur in the presence of another person; for the felony version, it must occur in the presence of a person less than 16 years old. For a discussion of the term "in the presence of," see the note on Element (5) to "Misdemeanor Indecent Exposure" in the main volume and above in this supplement.

Multiple convictions and punishments (page 292)

Insert the following at the beginning of this note:

See this note to "Misdemeanor Indecent Exposure."

Peeping (page 292)

Statute (page 292)

2012 legislation, S.L. 2012-183, sec. 1, and 2017 legislation, S.L. 2017-186, sec. 2(p), amended G.S. 14-202(m)(2) to read:

> (2) Personnel of the Division of Adult Correction and Juvenile Justice of the Department of Public Safety, or of a local confinement facility for security purposes or during investigation of alleged misconduct by a person in the custody of the Division or the local confinement facility.

Peeping into a Room Occupied by Another (page 293)

Related Offenses Not in This Chapter (page 294)

Add the following offense to this list:

Unlawful distribution of images obtained through the use of an unmanned aircraft device. G.S. 14-401.25.

Peeping while Possessing a Device Capable of Creating a Photographic Image (page 295) (revised title)

Related Offenses Not in This Chapter (page 296)

Add the following offense to this list:

Unlawful distribution of images obtained through the use of an unmanned aircraft device. G.S. 14-401.25.

Disseminating Images Obtained in Violation of the Peeping Statute (page 299)

Related Offenses Not in This Chapter (page 299)

Add the following offense to this list:

Unlawful distribution of images obtained through the use of an unmanned aircraft device. G.S. 14-401.25.

12
Kidnapping and Related Offenses

First-Degree Kidnapping (page 303)

Notes (page 304)

Element (1)(a) (page 304)

There was sufficient evidence that the defendant confined a child when, while threatening the child and his mother with a gun, the defendant told the mother to put her son in his room and she complied; whenever her son called out, the mother told him to stay in his bedroom. State v. Bell, 221 N.C. App. 535, 547–48 (2012).

Element (1)(b) (page 305)

For a felonious restraint case where the evidence was sufficient to show that the defendant restrained the victim by defrauding her into entering his car and driving to Florida with him, see *State v. Lalinde*, 231 N.C. App. 308, 315–16 (2013).

Element (1)(c) (page 305)

Add the following at the end of the first paragraph of this note:

There was sufficient evidence of asportation when the defendant began his sexual assault of the victim by a water fountain and then took her to a secluded place, the men's restroom, to complete his sexual acts outside of the presence of potential witnesses. State v. Coffey, ___ N.C. App. ___, ___ S.E.2d ___ (2020).

Element (3)(b) (page 305)

The plain language of G.S. 14-39(a) does not permit prosecution of a parent for kidnapping, at least when that parent has custodial rights with respect to the child or children. State v. Pender, 243 N.C. App. 142 (2015). The court of appeals has not decided "whether a parent without custodial rights may be held criminally liable for kidnapping." *Id.* at 155, n.2.

Element (4)(g) (page 307)

For another case supporting the definition of "terrorizing" described in this note and the point that the relevant fact is not whether the victim was in fact terrorized but, rather, whether the defendant intended to terrorize the victim, see *Pender*, 243 N.C. App. 142.

The evidence was sufficient for the jury to infer an intent to terrorize where the defendant shot victim Nancy's truck parked outside her mother's house in a manner such that everyone inside the house could hear, cut the telephone line to the house at night, shot through the windows multiple times to break into the house, yelled repeatedly upon entering the house that he was going to kill Nancy, corralled the occupants of the house into a single room and demanded to know where Nancy was, stated that he was going to kill her, and pointed his shotgun at the occupants; *id.*; the defendant threatened to kill the victim and assaulted her, placed her in headlock, and choked her; the victim was in a state of intense fright and apprehension; and witnesses heard the victim yelling for help and saw the defendant punch and choke her, rendering her unconscious, and then drag her across the street. State v. James, 248 N.C. App. 751, 758–59 (2016). *See also* State v. English, ___ N.C. App. ___, 845 S.E.2d 901 (2020) (sufficient evidence that the defendant acted with the purpose of terrorizing the victim when he hid in the back seat of her car with a knife, applied choking force to her neck, and hit her on the top of the head with enough force to cause her to be lightheaded and so afraid that she frantically exited the car screaming).

Element (5)(a) (page 308)

Add the following to the bulleted list in this note:

- the defendant dragged the victim to the middle of a gravel driveway and left her there, unconscious and injured; rather than leaving her in the care of nearby witnesses, the defendant ran away after seeing those persons; and the defendant took one of the victim's cell phones, perhaps not realizing that she had a second phone, *James*, 248 N.C. App. at 760–61;
- the defendant left the traumatized victim in a clearing in the woods near, but not easily visible from, a service road that extended off an interstate exit ramp; the area was very remote and secluded and almost impossible to see from the highway, State v. Gordon, 248 N.C. App. 403, 408–09 (2016).

Add the following to the bullet in this note stating that "the victim escaped":

State v. Massey, 265 N.C. App. 301 (2019) (the victim fled when the defendant turned away for a moment; the defendant never told or otherwise indicated to the victim that he was free to leave);

Element (5)(b) (page 308)

For a case where the evidence was sufficient to establish this Element, see *James*, 248 N.C. App. at 760–61 (the victim suffered cuts, bruises, abrasions, and scratches requiring emergency room treatment, and serious emotional trauma requiring therapy for many months continuing through the time of trial).

Multiple convictions and punishments (page 309)

For other cases supporting the proposition in this note that a defendant cannot be convicted of both first-degree kidnapping and a sexual assault if the sexual assault is the factor in Element (5) that elevates kidnapping from second-degree to first-degree, see *State v. Barksdale*, 237 N.C. App. 464, 473–74 (2014), and *State v. Holloman*, 231 N.C. App. 426, 432 (2013).

Add the following after the citation to *State v. Belton*:

; State v. Pabon, ___ N.C. App. ___, 850 S.E.2d 512 (2020) (a sexual battery committed in one room and a rape committed in another room were separate and distinct offenses, only one of which was used to elevate the kidnapping to first-degree; the defendant could therefore also be punished for the other sexual assault).

In the first bulleted list of this note, insert the following in the first bulleted paragraph (cases holding that the evidence supported kidnapping and robbery convictions):

, *State v. Stokes*, 367 N.C. 474, 482 (2014) (attempted kidnapping and robbery convictions were proper; after the robbery was completed, the defendant ordered the victim at gunpoint to the back of the store and then into a vehicle outside the store, but the victim refused to comply with both commands); *State v. Curtis*, 369 N.C. 310 (2016) (per curiam) (after robbing or attempting to rob two victims in a home invasion, the perpetrators moved the victims upstairs, where they restrained them while assaulting a third resident and searching for items that were later stolen); *State v. Thomas*, 268 N.C. App. 121 (2019) (the defendant's act of removing the victim from the bedroom to the living room after stealing her car keys was restraint and removal not inherent and integral to the underlying armed robbery); *State v. Bell*, 221 N.C. App. 535, 546–47 (2012).

In the first bulleted list of this note, insert the following in the second bulleted paragraph (cases holding that the evidence was sufficient to sustain kidnapping and sexual assault convictions):

, *State v. China*, 370 N.C. 627, 635–36 (2018) (after the sexual offense was completed, the defendant pulled the victim off the bed, causing his head to hit the floor, and called to an accomplice who, with the defendant, kicked and stomped the victim; these additional actions increased the victim's helplessness and vulnerability beyond the initial attack that enabled the defendant to commit the sexual offense and constituted an additional restraint, which exposed the victim to greater danger than that inherent in the sexual offense), *State v. King*, 249 N.C. App. 440, 444 (2016) (the defendant forced the victim into his car after sexually assaulting her), *State v. Knight*, 245 N.C. App. 532, 552–53 (2016) (commission of the rape did not require the defendant to seize and restrain the victim and to carry her from her living room couch to her bedroom), *aff'd as modified*, 369 N.C. 640 (2017), *Bell*, 221 N.C. App. at 547.

In the first bulleted list of this note, insert the following in the fourth bulleted paragraph (cases holding that the evidence was sufficient to sustain kidnapping and assault convictions):

, *State v. James*, 248 N.C. App. 751, 758 (2016) (finding two separate, distinct restraints sufficient to support convictions for both kidnapping and assault by strangulation).

In the second bulleted list of this note, insert the following in the second bulleted paragraph (cases holding that the evidence was insufficient to sustain kidnapping and sexual assault convictions):

, *State v. Parker*, 237 N.C. App. 546, 549–50 (2014) (restraint supporting the kidnapping charge was inherent in the charged rapes and sexual assault), *State v. Martin*, 222 N.C. App. 213, 219–21 (2012).

In the second bulleted list of this note, insert the following new bulleted paragraph:

- The defendant's restraint of the victim was inherent in an assault by strangulation of the victim, and thus the kidnapping conviction was improper. *Martin*, 222 N.C. App. at 221.

Abduction of a Child (page 315)

Notes (page 315)

Element (1) (page 315)

Notwithstanding the statutory language saying the crime must be committed "without legal justification or defense," this is a general intent crime, requiring only a showing that it has been committed knowingly, not willfully. State v. French, ___ N.C. App. ___, 849 S.E.2d 360 (2020) (concluding that child abduction is neither a strict liability nor a specific intent crime). There was substantial evidence that the defendant knowingly abducted a child when he continued to lead police on a chase for at least fifteen minutes after discovering the child in his truck. *Id.*

Element (2) (new note)

For a case where the evidence was sufficient to show that the defendant induced the child to leave, see *State v. Diaz*, 256 N.C. App. 528, 537–38 (2017) (rejecting an argument by the defendant, who had a sexual relationship with the child victim, that the evidence was insufficient because it showed that the child voluntarily left her home; the defendant induced the child to leave by telling her that if she did not come with him she would never see him again).

Related Offenses Not in This Chapter (page 316)

Add the following offense to this list:

Unlawful transfer of custody of minor child. G.S. 14-321.2.

Human Trafficking, Involuntary Servitude, and Sexual Servitude (page 316)

Statute (page 316)

2018 legislation, S.L. 2018-75, sec. 1, enacted a new subsection, (a)(6), to G.S. 14-43.10 (Definitions) as follows:

> (6) Victim.—Unless the context requires otherwise, a person subjected to the practices set forth in G.S. 14-43.11, 14-43.12, or 14-43.13.

G.S. 14-43.11 has been amended, *see* S.L. 2013-368, sec. 1; S.L. 2017-151, sec. 1, to read as follows:

> **§ 14-43.11. Human trafficking.**
>
> (a) A person commits the offense of human trafficking when that person (i) knowingly or in reckless disregard of the consequences of the action recruits, entices, harbors, transports, provides, or obtains by any means another person with the intent that the other person be held in involuntary servitude or sexual servitude or (ii) willfully or in reckless disregard of the consequences of the action causes a minor to be held in involuntary servitude or sexual servitude.
>
> (b) A person who violates this section is guilty of a Class C felony if the victim of the offense is an adult. A person who violates this section is guilty of a Class B2 felony if the victim of the offense is a minor.
>
> (c) Each violation of this section constitutes a separate offense and shall not merge with any other offense. Evidence of failure to deliver benefits or perform services standing alone shall not be sufficient to authorize a conviction under this section.
>
> (c1) Mistake of age is not a defense to prosecution under this section. Consent of a minor is not a defense to prosecution under this section.
>
> (d) A person who is not a legal resident of North Carolina, and would consequently be ineligible for State public benefits or services, shall be eligible for the public benefits and services of any State agency if the person is otherwise eligible for the public benefit and is a victim of an offense charged under this section. Eligibility for public benefits and services shall terminate at such time as the victim's eligibility to remain in the United States is terminated under federal law.

S.L. 2013-368, sec. 2, amended subsection (a) of G.S. 14-43.12, the involuntary servitude statute, to read as follows:

> (a) A person commits the offense of involuntary servitude when that person knowingly and willfully or in reckless disregard of the consequences of the action holds another in involuntary servitude.

That same law also enacted a new subsection, (c1), to G.S. 14-43.12 as follows:

> (c1) Mistake of age is not a defense to prosecution under this section. Consent of a minor is not a defense to prosecution under this section.

S.L. 2013-368, sec. 3, amended subsection (a) of G.S. 14-43.13, the sexual servitude statute, to read as follows:

> (a) A person commits the offense of sexual servitude when that person knowingly or in reckless disregard of the consequences of the action subjects or maintains another in sexual servitude.

That same law also increased the punishment for this offense to a Class D felony and enacted a new subsection, (b1), to G.S. 14-43.13 as follows:

> (b1) Mistake of age is not a defense to prosecution under this section. Consent of a minor is not a defense to prosecution under this section.

2018 legislation, S.L. 2018-75, sec. 2, enacted a new section in G.S. Chapter 14, Article 10A (Human Trafficking) as follows:

> **§ 14-43.15. Affirmative defense.**
>
> (a) Affirmative Defense.—It is an affirmative defense to a prosecution under this Article that the person charged with the offense was a victim at the time of the offense and was coerced or deceived into committing the offense as a direct result of the person's status as a victim.

(b) Construction.—Nothing in this section shall be construed to limit or abrogate any other affirmative defense to a prosecution under this Article available to a person by statute or common law.

Human Trafficking (page 318)

Elements (page 318)

As a result of 2013 legislation, S.L. 2013-368, sec. 1, the elements of this offense should read as follows:

A person guilty of this offense

(1) (a) knowingly or in reckless disregard of the consequences
    (b) recruits, entices, harbors, transports, provides, or obtains
    (c) another person
    (d) with the intent that the other person be held in involuntary or sexual servitude *or*
(2) (a) willfully or in reckless disregard of the consequences
    (b) causes a minor to be held in involuntary or sexual servitude.

Punishment (page 318)

As result of 2017 legislation, S.L. 2017-151, sec. 1, delete this paragraph and replace it with the following:

Class C felony if the victim is an adult. G.S. 14-43.11(b). Class B2 felony if the victim is less than 18 years old. *Id.*, *id.* § -43.10(a)(4). If the Class B2 version of this offense is charged, the relevant fact elevating punishment must be alleged in the charging instrument and proved at trial.

Notes (page 318)

Element (4) (page 318)

Retitle this note to read:

Elements (1)(d) and (2)(b).

Mistake of age and consent (new note)
Neither mistake of age nor consent by a minor is a defense to prosecution. G.S. 14-43.11(c1).

Greater and lesser-included offenses (new note)
"Sale, Surrender, or Purchase of a Minor" (new crime), discussed below in this supplement, is a lesser-included offense of this crime. G.S. 14-43.14(d).

Sex offender registration (new note)
2013 legislation, S.L. 2013-33, provides that human trafficking is a sexually violent offense under G.S. 14-208.6(5) requiring sex offender registration if the offense is committed against

- a minor who is less than 18 years of age or
- any person with the intent that the person be held in sexual servitude.

Affirmative defense (new note)
2018 legislation, S.L. 2018-75, sec. 2, provides that it is an affirmative defense to a prosecution "that the person charged with the offense was a victim at the time of the offense and was coerced or deceived into committing the offense as a direct result of the person's status as a victim." The term "victim" is defined in new G.S. 14-43.10(a)(6), reproduced above.

Related Offenses Not in This Chapter (page 318)

Violating confidentiality of victim, alleged victim, or family member of a victim of human trafficking and related offenses. G.S. 14-43.16 (enacted by S.L. 2018-75, sec. 3(a)).

Involuntary Servitude (page 318)

Elements (page 318)

As a result of 2013 legislation, S.L. 2013-368, sec. 2, Element (1) of this offense should read as follows:

A person guilty of this offense

(1) (a) knowingly and willfully *or*
(b) in reckless disregard of the consequences

Notes (page 319)

Mistake of age and consent (new note)
Neither mistake of age nor consent by a minor is a defense to prosecution. G.S. 14-43.12(c1).

Affirmative defense (new note)
See this note under "Human Trafficking," above in this supplement.

Related Offenses Not in This Chapter (page 319)

Delete the first line of this section and replace it with the following:

See the offenses listed under "First-Degree Kidnapping" and "Human Trafficking."

Sexual Servitude (page 319)

Elements (page 319)

As a result of 2013 legislation, S.L. 2013-368, sec. 3, Element (1) of this offense should read as follows:

A person guilty of this offense

(1) (a) knowingly *or*
(b) in reckless disregard of the consequences

As a result of 2019 legislation, S.L. 2019-158, sec. 1, elements (2) and (3) of this offense should read as follows:

(2) subjects, maintains, or obtains another
(3) for the purposes of sexual servitude.

Punishment (page 319)

As a result of 2013 legislation, S.L. 2013-368, sec. 3, delete the first sentence of this section and replace it with the following:

Class D felony if the victim is an adult.

Notes (page 319)

Mistake of age and consent (new note)
Neither mistake of age nor consent by a minor is a defense to prosecution. G.S. 14-43.13(b1).

Affirmative defense (new note)
See this note under "Human Trafficking," above in this supplement.

Related Offenses Not in This Chapter (page 320)

Delete the first line of this section and replace it with the following:

See the offenses listed under "First-Degree Kidnapping" and "Human Trafficking."

Sale, Surrender, or Purchase of a Minor (new crime)

This offense was enacted by 2012 legislation. S.L. 2012-153, sec. 1.

Statute

§ 14-43.14. Unlawful sale, surrender, or purchase of a minor.

(a) A person commits the offense of unlawful sale, surrender, or purchase of a minor when that person, acting with willful or reckless disregard for the life or safety of a minor, participates in any of the following: the acceptance, solicitation, offer, payment, or transfer of any compensation, in money, property, or other thing of value, at any time, by any person in connection with the unlawful acquisition or transfer of the physical custody of a minor, except as ordered by the court. This section does not apply to actions that are ordered by a court, authorized by statute, or otherwise lawful.

(b) A person who violates this section is guilty of a Class F felony and shall pay a minimum fine of five thousand dollars ($5,000). For each subsequent violation, a person is guilty of a Class F felony and shall pay a minimum fine of ten thousand dollars ($10,000).

(c) A minor whose parent, guardian, or custodian has sold or attempted to sell a minor in violation of this Article is an abused juvenile as defined by G.S. 7B-101(1). The court may place the minor in the custody of the Department of Social Services or with such other person as is in the best interest of the minor.

(d) A violation of this section is a lesser included offense of G.S. 14-43.11.

(e) When a person is convicted of a violation of this section, the sentencing court shall consider whether the person is a danger to the community and whether requiring the person to register as a sex offender pursuant to Article 27A of this Chapter would further the purposes of that Article as stated in G.S. 14-208.5. If the sentencing court rules that the person is a danger to the community and that the person shall register, then an order shall be entered requiring the person to register.

Elements

A person guilty of this offense

(1) (a) willfully *or*
  (b) with reckless disregard for the life or safety of a minor
(2) participates in any acceptance, solicitation, offer, payment, or transfer of any compensation, in money, property, or other thing of value, by any person
(3) in connection with the unlawful acquisition or transfer of the physical custody of a minor.

Punishment

Class F felony. G.S. 14-43.14(b). For a first offense, the defendant must pay a minimum fine of $5,000; for subsequent violations, the defendant must pay a minimum fine of $10,000. *Id.*

Notes

Element (1)(a). See "Willfully" in Chapter 1 (States of Mind) of the main volume.

Exceptions. The statute does not apply to actions that are ordered by a court, are authorized by statute, or are otherwise lawful. G.S. 14-43.14(a). A parent may not be prosecuted for this offense when the parent abandons an infant less than seven days of age by voluntarily delivering the infant in compliance with the provisions of G.S. 7B-500(b) or (d) and does not express an intention to return for the infant. G.S. 14-322.3.

Minor declared abused. A minor whose parent, guardian, or custodian has sold or attempted to sell the minor in violation of the statute is an abused juvenile and may be placed in appropriate custody. G.S. 14-43.14(c).

Greater and lesser-included offenses. This offense is a lesser-included offense of human trafficking. G.S. 14-43.14(d).

Sex offender registration. The sentencing judge must require registration if he or she finds that a person convicted of this crime is a danger to the community and that requiring the person to register as a sex offender would further the purpose of the sex offender statute. G.S. 14-43.14(e).

Affirmative defense (new note)
See this note under "Human Trafficking," above in this supplement.

Related Offenses Not in This Chapter

See "Child Abuse" offenses and "Contributing to a Juvenile's Being Delinquent, Undisciplined, Abused, or Neglected" in Chapter 9 (Abuse and Neglect) of the main volume.
See "Failure to Report the Disappearance of a Child" (new crime) in Chapter 9 (Abuse and Neglect) of this supplement.
Unlawful payments related to adoption. G.S. 48-10-102.

Promoting Travel for Unlawful Sexual Conduct (new crime)

This offense was enacted by 2019 legislation. S.L. 2019-158, sec. 2.(a), effective for offenses committed on or after December 1, 2019.

Statute

§ 14-208.1. Promoting travel for unlawful sexual conduct.

(a) Definition. – For purposes of this section, the term "travel services" means transportation by air, sea, or ground; hotel or other lodging accommodations; package tours, or the provision of vouchers or coupons to be redeemed for future travel; or accommodations for a fee, commission, or other valuable consideration.

(b) Offense. – A person commits the offense of promoting travel for unlawful sexual conduct if the person sells or offers to sell travel services that the person knows to include travel for the purpose of committing any of the following offenses in this State or for the purpose of engaging in conduct that would constitute any one of the following offenses if occurring within this State:

(1) An offense under Article 7B of Chapter 14 of the General Statutes.
(2) Any of the following offenses involving the sexual exploitation of a minor:
  a. G.S. 14-190.16.
  b. G.S. 14-190.17.
  c. G.S. 14-190.17A.
(3) Any of the following offenses involving indecent liberties with a minor:
  a. G.S. 14-202.1.
  b. G.S. 14-202.4.
(4) Any of the following prostitution offenses:
  a. G.S. 14-204.
  b. G.S. 14-205.1.
  c. G.S. 14-205.2.
  d. G.S. 14-205.3.

(c) Punishment. – A violation of this section is a Class G felony.

Elements

A person guilty of this offense

(1) (a) sells *or*
  (b) offers to sell
(2) travel services as defined in G.S. 14-208.1(a)
(3) (a) the person knows to include travel for the purpose of committing any of the listed offenses, *or*
  (b) for the purpose of engaging in conduct that would constitute any one of the listed offenses if occurring within North Carolina.

Punishment

Class G felony. G.S. 14-208.1(c).

Notes

Element (2)

"Travel services" means transportation by air, sea, or ground; hotel or other lodging accommodations; package tours; or the provision of vouchers or coupons to be redeemed for future travel; or accommodations for a fee, commission, or other valuable consideration. G.S. 14-208.1(a).

Elements (3)(a) and (b)

Travel for the purposes of committing or engaging in conduct that would constitute any of the following offenses is covered under this Element: First-Degree Sexual Exploitation of a Minor, Second-Degree Sexual Exploitation of a Minor, Third-Degree Sexual Exploitation of a Minor, Indecent Liberties with a Child, Indecent Liberties with a Student, Prostitution, Solicitation of Prostitution, Patronizing a Prostitute, Promoting Prostitution, or any offense included in Article 7B of G.S. Chapter 14 (Rape and Other Sex Offenses). G.S. 14-208.1(b).

13

Larceny, Possession of Stolen Goods, Embezzlement, and Related Offenses

Larceny (page 323)

Misdemeanor Larceny (page 323)

Statute (page 323)

2012 legislation, S.L. 2012-154, enacted G.S. 14-72(b)(6), proscribing the crime of "Habitual Misdemeanor Larceny," discussed below in this supplement.

(6) Committed after the defendant has been convicted in this State or in another jurisdiction for any offense of larceny under this section, or any offense deemed or punishable as larceny under this section, or of any substantially similar offense in any other jurisdiction, regardless of whether the prior convictions were misdemeanors, felonies, or a combination thereof, at least four times. A conviction shall not be included in the four prior convictions required under this subdivision unless the defendant was represented by counsel or waived counsel at first appearance or otherwise prior to trial or plea. If a person is convicted of more than one offense of misdemeanor larceny in a single session of district court, or in a single week of superior court or of a court in another jurisdiction, only one of the convictions may be used as a prior conviction under this subdivision; except that convictions based upon offenses which occurred in separate counties shall each count as a separate prior conviction under this subdivision.

Elements (page 324)

The first line of this section should read:

A person guilty of this offense

Notes (page 324)

Element (1) (page 324)

A taking occurred (1) in a larceny case when the defendant wrongfully removed an overpayment from his bank account through transfers and withdrawals, State v. Jones, 369 N.C. 631, 637 (2017), (2) in a robbery case when the defendant grabbed the victim's cell phone and threw it away, State v. Mason, 222 N.C. App. 223, 228 (2012) (noting that the brevity of the taking is irrelevant), and (3) in another robbery case when the defendant forced the victim at gunpoint to take the defendant as a passenger in the victim's car; the fact that the victim was physically present in the car did not negate the inference that the defendant had sole control of the car. State v. Watkins, 218 N.C. App. 94, 103–04 (2012).

Element (3) (page 325)
The victim's possession of the property can be actual or constructive. *Jones*, 369 N.C. at 634 (adopting for larceny cases the analysis used to determine constructive possession in drug and other cases). Because a depositor retained the ability to affect a reversal of an erroneous deposit into the defendant's bank account, the depositor had constructive possession of the funds when the defendant later learned of the erroneous deposit but withdrew the funds anyhow. *Id.* at 635 (also concluding that the fact that the depositor's reversal order was not successful does not negate the depositor's constructive possession).

For a case where the evidence sufficiently established that the victim was in possession of a company checkbook at the time it was stolen, see *State v. Forte*, 260 N.C. App. 245 (2018), *vacated in part on other grounds*, 263 N.C. App. 710 (2019) (unpublished).

A defendant cannot be convicted of larceny with respect to property that is in his or her lawful possession. State v. Bradsher, 255 N.C. App. 625, 631 (2017) (as conceded by the State, the defendant was in lawful possession of appliances installed in her rented home). Similarly, a defendant cannot be convicted of larceny if he or she had possession of the property simultaneously with the victim. *Jones*, 369 N.C. at 636. A defendant does not have possession of funds when the defendant passively but knowingly receives a direct deposit overpayment into his or her bank account and then proceeds to withdraw the excess funds against the wishes of the rightful possessor. *Id.* (reasoning that the defendant had mere custody of the funds and not possession of them).

In a case involving felony larceny charges, the state supreme court held that a person who has mere custody of property may be convicted of larceny when he or she appropriates the property to his or her own use with felonious intent. *Id.* (stating: "The moment that the person in custody of the property wrongfully interferes with the rightful possessor's possessory interest is the moment that he takes that property.").

Element (5) (page 325)
To constitute a larceny, a taking must be wrongful; in other words, the taking must be by an act of trespass. *Jones*, 369 N.C. at 634. The trespass can be actual or constructive. *Id.* A constructive trespass occurs "when possession of the property is fraudulently obtained by some trick or artifice." *Id.* (internal quotation omitted). An actual trespass occurs when the taking is without the consent of the owner. *Id.*

Element (6) (page 325)
As a general rule, when a defendant takes property from its owner and keeps it until the defendant is apprehended, the element of intent to permanently deprive the owner is established. State v. Rogers, 255 N.C. App. 413, 415–16 (2017) (holding that the evidence was sufficient to establish this Element where the stolen pistol was found hidden in the spare tire well of the defendant's vehicle when he was apprehended).

Greater and lesser-included offenses (page 326)

Include the following after the citation to *State v. Watson* in the first paragraph of this note:

State v. Hole, 240 N.C. App. 537, 540 (2015) (same but concluding that no plain error occurred when the trial court failed to instruct on the lesser-included offense);

Add the following to this note:

Misdemeanor larceny is a lesser-included offense of common law robbery. State v. Cromartie, 257 N.C. App. 790, 796 (2018).

Multiple convictions and punishments (page 326)
For another case supporting the statement in this note that a defendant may be convicted for only one larceny if several pieces of property are taken during one continuous act or transaction, see *State v. Forte*, 260 N.C. App. 245 (2018) (the trial court erred by entering judgment for eight counts of felony larceny where all of the property was stolen in a single transaction), *vacated in part on other grounds*, 263 N.C. App. 710 (2019) (unpublished).

However, the court of appeals has held that when a defendant takes property from two different victims during one incident, the defendant may be convicted and punished for two larceny offenses. State v. Greene, 251 N.C. App. 627, 638 (2017).

Doctrine of recent possession (page 327)
"Exclusive possession" within the meaning of the doctrine of recent possession can include joint possession of co-conspirators or persons acting in concert. State v. McDaniel, 372 N.C. 594 (2019) (doctrine properly applied to a woman who had been in control of the stolen items for two weeks, regardless of whether she was acting at the direction of a co-defendant).

The jury may be instructed on the doctrine even if the defendant is not charged with taking the property that he or she is alleged to have recently possessed. State v. Street, 254 N.C. App. 214, 219 (2017) (the doctrine applied where the defendant was charged with obtaining property by false pretenses for selling a pair of hedge trimmers to a pawn shop less than two hours after the trimmers were stolen).

Related Offenses Not in This Chapter (page 329)

Add the following offenses to this list:

Theft of waste kitchen grease. G.S. 14-79.2.
Taking, etc., of certain wild plants from land of another. G.S. 14-129.
Felony taking of Venus flytrap. G.S. 14-129.3.
Injuring, tampering with, removing, etc. firefighting or emergency medical services machinery or equipment. G.S. 14-160.3, *as enacted by* S.L. 2017-89.

Habitual Misdemeanor Larceny (new crime)

Statute

2012 legislation, S.L. 2012-154, enacted G.S. 14-72(b)(6), reproduced above under "Misdemeanor Larceny."

Elements

A person guilty of this offense

(1) commits a larceny *and*
(2) has four prior larceny convictions.

Punishment

Class H felony. G.S. 14-72(a).

Notes

Element (1). See "Misdemeanor Larceny" in the main volume.

Element (2). The prior offense can be

- a North Carolina conviction under G.S. 14-72 or
- a substantially similar offense in any other jurisdiction.

G.S. 14-72(b)(6). The prior offenses can be misdemeanors, felonies, or a combination of the two. *Id.* A prior conviction cannot be counted unless the defendant was represented by or waived counsel. *Id.* However, the defendant's representation by or waiver of counsel for his or her prior convictions is not an essential element of this offense that must be alleged in the charging instrument. State v. Edgerton, 266 N.C. App. 521 (2019). If a person is convicted of more than one offense of misdemeanor larceny in a single session of district court or in a single week of superior court or a court in another jurisdiction, only one of the convictions may be used as a prior conviction, except that convictions based on offenses that occurred in separate counties each count as a separate prior conviction. *Id.*

Related Offenses Not in This Chapter

See the offenses listed under "Misdemeanor Larceny" in the main volume.

Felony Larceny (page 330)

Notes (page 330)

Element (8)(a) (page 331)

For another case holding that fair market value is the relevant measure, see *State v. Redman*, 224 N.C. App. 363, 366 (2012). A witness need not be an expert to give an opinion as to value; one who has knowledge of value gained from experience, information, and observation may give his or her opinion of the value of the stolen item. *Id.* Where a vehicle owner testified to a vehicle's value, there was sufficient evidence of this Element. *Id.* at 367. For a case where the State presented sufficient evidence that the fair market value of stolen boat batteries was more than $1,000, see *State v. Fish*, 229 N.C. App. 584, 587–89 (2013).

For a case holding that it is error to allow the jury to estimate the value of an item without any evidence to establish a basis for that estimation, see *State v. Bacon*, 254 N.C. App. 463, 473 (2017) (although "certain property may, by its very nature, be of value obviously greater than $1000.00," the television and the earrings in this case "are not such items").

Element (8)(b) (page 331)

A larceny was from the person when the defendant (1) stole the victim's purse from the child's seat of her grocery cart; at the time, the victim was looking at a store product and was within hand's reach of her cart and realized that the larceny was occurring as it happened, State v. Sheppard, 228 N.C. App. 266, 269–70 (2013); and (2) stole the victim's laptop from an apartment; the victim had taken a momentary break from doing her homework on the laptop and was about three feet away from it. State v. Hull, 236 N.C. App. 415, 418–19 (2014).

For a case where the evidence was insufficient to establish that the property was taken from the victim's person or was within the victim's protection, see *State v. Greene*, 251 N.C. App. 627, 629–35 (2017) (the defendant stole items from purses that were next to (but not touching) the victims while they slept in a medical waiting room; rejecting the State's argument that the property was within the victims' protection because the medical room was under video surveillance).

Multiple convictions and punishments (page 332)

A defendant may not be sentenced for both larceny from the person and larceny of goods worth more than $1,000 based on a single larceny. *Sheppard*, 228 N.C. App. at 270–71 (the crimes are not separate offenses but, rather, alternative ways to establish a felony larceny; while it is proper to indict on alternative theories of felony larceny and allow the jury to determine guilt as to each theory, where there is only one larceny, judgment may only be entered for one larceny).

Larceny of a Chose in Action (page 333)

Notes (page 333)

Element (2) (page 333)
A blank check is not a chose in action. State v. Grier, 224 N.C. App. 150, 155 (2012).

Relation to other offenses (new note)
Forgery and larceny of a chose in action are not mutually exclusive offenses. *Grier*, 224 N.C. App. at 153.

Unauthorized Use of a Motor-Propelled Conveyance (page 334)

Notes (page 334)

Element (5) generally (new note)
For a case where the evidence was insufficient on the issue of lack of consent, see *In re A.N.C.*, 225 N.C. App. 315, 325 (2013).

Greater and lesser-included offenses (page 335)

Delete the first paragraph of this note and replace it with the following:

North Carolina courts have held that unauthorized use of a motor-propelled conveyance is not a lesser-included offense of possession of stolen goods, *see* State v. Nickerson, 365 N.C. 279, 281–83 (2011) (applying the definitional test and concluding that unauthorized use of a motor-propelled conveyance contains at least one element not present in possession of stolen goods), nor is it a lesser-included offense of possession of a stolen vehicle. State v. Robinson, 368 N.C. 402, 406–08 (2015) (applying a definitional analysis).

Replace the first sentence of the second paragraph of this note with the following:

Notwithstanding *Nickerson* and *Robinson*, the court of appeals has held that, depending on the evidence, unauthorized use of a motor-propelled conveyance can be a lesser-included offense of larceny of a motor vehicle, discussed below.

Insert the following after the citation to *State v. Watson* in the second paragraph of this note:

State v. Hole, 240 N.C. App. 537, 540 (2015) (same but concluding that no plain error occurred when the trial court failed to instruct on the lesser-included offense);

Possession of Stolen Goods (page 335)

Misdemeanor Possession of Stolen Goods (page 335)

Notes (page 336)

Element (1) (page 336)
Evidence that a defendant is operating a stolen vehicle is sufficient to establish possession. State v. Quinones, 258 N.C. App. 559, 561 (2018). However, merely being present in a stolen vehicle is insufficient by itself to establish possession. *Id.* at 562–63 (going on to hold that the evidence was sufficient to establish that the defendant operated the stolen vehicle and was not

merely a passenger; specifically, an individual in a white shirt fled from the driver's side of the car after it was abandoned and the driver's door was the only door left open; officers maintained almost constant visual contact with the defendant as he fled, the defendant was arrested wearing a white t-shirt, and he never denied being inside the automobile).

For other cases where the evidence was sufficient to establish constructive possession of stolen goods, see *State v. Guy*, 262 N.C. App. 313 (2018) (a robbery victim's debit card was found near a gun in close proximity to the defendant and his vehicle; the gun matched one described by the victim as having been used in the robbery, and an officer located the defendant's car less than a quarter-mile from the victim's residence and about one minute after receiving information about the incident), and *State v. Rice*, 252 N.C. App. 480, 482–86 (2017) (although the defendant did not have exclusive possession of the rented van in which the goods were found, other incriminating circumstances existed to establish constructive possession, including, among other things, that the defendant was nervous and admitted ownership of another item found near the stolen property).

The evidence was insufficient to establish that the defendant constructively possessed jewelry when it showed only that the defendant was a high-ranking member of a gang to which others involved in a robbery and subsequent transfer of stolen goods belonged; the defendant accompanied a person in possession of stolen property to an enterprise at which a legitimate transaction occurred; the defendant made ambiguous references to "more scrap gold" and "rings" unaccompanied by any indication that these items were stolen. State v. Privette, 218 N.C. App. 459, 472–73 (2012).

Element (3) (page 336)
For a case where the evidence was sufficient to establish that the defendant knew or had reasonable grounds to believe that items were stolen, see *State v. Jester*, 249 N.C. App. 101, 114 (2016) (although the property was valued at more than $1,000, the defendant sold it for $114, told a detective that he obtained it from a "white man" but could not give the man's name, did not state that he had purchased the items, and did not produce a receipt for them).

Greater and lesser-included offenses (page 337)

Delete the citation to *Oliver* in this note.

Multiple convictions and punishments (page 338)
The text of this note states that "[a] defendant may not be sentenced for both robbery and possession of stolen property taken during the robbery." For another case supporting that principle, see *State v. Guy*, 262 N.C. App. 313 (2018). However, that principle only applies "for possession during the course of the same conduct, and where the property is the 'same property.' " State v. Hendricksen, 257 N.C. App. 345, 352 (2018) (holding that the defendant's conviction after a guilty plea in Harnett County to two counts of misdemeanor possession of stolen goods involving two lottery tickets did not preclude his later trial and conviction in Johnston County for an armed robbery of a convenience store during which he obtained approximately $1,900 in cash and approximately 800 lottery tickets, including the two that were the subject of the Harnett County charges).

Related Offenses Not in This Chapter (page 338)

Add the following offense to this list:

Secondary metals recycler purchase violations. G.S. 66-424; -429.

As a result of 2019 legislation, S.L. 2019-40, add the following new offense, effective for offenses committed on or after December 1, 2019:

Possession of a Stolen Controlled Substance (new crime)

Statute

See G.S. 14-54.2, reproduced under "Breaking or Entering a Pharmacy," in Chapter 15 of this supplement.

Elements

A person guilty of this offense

(1) possesses
(2) any controlled substance
(3) stolen in violation of G.S. 14-54.2(b), "Breaking or Entering a Pharmacy,"
(4) knowing or having reasonable grounds to believe that the controlled substance was stolen.

Punishment

Class F felony. G.S. 14-54.2(c). Any interest a person acquires or maintains in property obtained in violation of this section is subject to forfeiture as set forth in G.S. 90-112. *Id.* § -54.2(d).

Notes

Generally. Relevant notes to "Misdemeanor Possession of Stolen Goods" apply to this offense as well.

Element (2)
A "controlled substance" is any drug, substance, or immediate precursor included in Schedules I through VI of the Controlled Substances Act. G.S. 90-87(5).

Element (3)
The named offense, "Breaking or Entering a Pharmacy," is discussed in Chapter 15 of this supplement.

Related Offenses Not in This Chapter

See the offenses listed under "Misdemeanor Possession of Stolen Goods," above.
Breaking or Entering a Pharmacy (Chapter 15).

Receiving Stolen Goods (page 342)

As a result of 2019 legislation, S.L. 2019-40, add the following new offense, effective for offenses committed on or after December 1, 2019:

Receiving a Stolen Controlled Substance (new crime)

Statute

See G.S. 14-54.2, reproduced under "Breaking or Entering a Pharmacy," in Chapter 15 of this supplement.

Elements

A person guilty of this offense

(1) receives
(2) any controlled substance

(3) stolen in violation of G.S. 14-54.2(b), "Breaking or Entering a Pharmacy,"
(4) knowing or having reasonable grounds to believe that the controlled substance was stolen.

Punishment

Class F felony. G.S. 14-54.2(c). Any interest a person acquires or maintains in property obtained in violation of this section is subject to forfeiture as set forth in G.S. 90-112. *Id.* § -54.2(d).

Notes

Generally. Relevant notes to "Misdemeanor Receiving of Stolen Goods" apply to this offense as well.

Element (2)
A "controlled substance" is any drug, substance, or immediate precursor included in Schedules I through VI of the Controlled Substances Act. G.S. 90-87(5).

Element (3)
The named offense, "Breaking or Entering a Pharmacy," is discussed in Chapter 15 of this supplement.

Related Offenses Not in This Chapter

See the offenses listed under "Misdemeanor Receiving of Stolen Goods," above.
Breaking or Entering a Pharmacy (Chapter 15).

Vehicle and Vehicle Part Offenses (page 345)

The following offense, enacted by 2012 legislation, S.L. 2012-46, should be added as a related offense to the vehicle and vehicle part offenses covered here:

Secondary metals recycler purchase of catalytic converters in certain circumstances. G.S. 66-424.

Possession of a Stolen Vehicle (page 345)

Statute (page 345)

2019 legislation, S.L. 2019-186, section 1.(c), recodified this offense as G.S. 14-71.2, effective for offenses committed on or after December 1, 2019.

Notes (page 345)

Greater and lesser-included offenses (new note)
Unauthorized use is not a lesser-included offense of possession of a stolen vehicle. State v. Robinson, 368 N.C. 402, 406–08 (2015).

Altering, Destroying, etc. any Stolen Motor Vehicle or Part (page 347)

Statute (page 347)

2013 legislation, S.L. 2013-323, amended subsection (a) of G.S. 14-72.7 to read as follows:

> (a) A person is guilty of a Class G felony if that person engages in any of the following activities, without regard to the value of the property in question:
>
> (1) Altering, destroying, disassembling, dismantling, reassembling, or storing any motor vehicle or motor vehicle part the person knows or has reasonable grounds to believe has been illegally obtained by theft, fraud, or other illegal means.
>
> (2) Permitting a place to be used for any activity prohibited by this section, where the person either owns or has legal possession of the place, and knows or has reasonable grounds to believe that the place is being used for any activity prohibited by this section.
>
> (3) Purchasing, disposing of, selling, transferring, receiving, or possessing a motor vehicle or motor vehicle part either knowing or having reasonable grounds to believe that the vehicle identification number of the motor vehicle, or vehicle part identification number of the vehicle part, has been altered, counterfeited, defaced, destroyed, disguised, falsified, forged, obliterated, or removed.
>
> (4) Purchasing, disposing of, selling, transferring, receiving, or possessing a motor vehicle or motor vehicle part to or from a person engaged in any activity prohibited by this section, knowing or having reasonable grounds to believe that the person is engaging in that activity.

Elements (page 348)

As a result of that same 2013 legislation, the elements for this offense should read as follows:

A person guilty of this offense

(1) (a) alters,
    (b) destroys,
    (c) disassembles,
    (d) dismantles,
    (e) reassembles, *or*
    (f) stores
(2) any
    (a) motor vehicle *or*
    (b) motor vehicle part
(3) knowing or having reasonable grounds to believe that it was illegally obtained.

Punishment (page 348)

As a result of the 2013 legislation noted above, delete the text in this section and replace it with the following:

Class G felony. G.S. 14-72.7(a).

Notes (page 348)

Element (1) (page 348)

As a result of the 2013 legislation noted above, delete this note.

Element (3) (page 348)

This note should be titled Element (2).

Element (4) (page 348)

As a result of the 2013 legislation noted above, delete this note.

Related Offenses Not in This Chapter (page 349)

Add the following offenses to this list:

Purchase of vehicles for purposes of scrap or parts only. G.S. 20-62.1.
Secondary metals recycler purchase of catalytic converters in certain circumstances. G.S. 66-424.

Permitting a Place to Be Used to Violate the Chop Shop Laws (page 349)

Elements (page 349)

As a result of 2013 legislation, S.L. 2013-323, the elements for this offense should read as follows:

A person guilty of this offense

(1) permits
(2) a place that the person owns or has legal possession of
(3) to be used for any activity prohibited by G.S. 14-72.7 *and*
(4) knows or has reasonable grounds to believe that the place is being used for the prohibited activity.

Punishment (page 349)

As a result of the 2013 legislation noted above, delete the text in this section and replace it with the following:

Class G felony. G.S. 14-72.7(a).

Notes (page 349)

Element (1) (page 349)

As a result of the 2013 legislation noted above, delete this note.

Related Offenses Not in This Chapter (page 349)

Add the following offenses to this list:

Purchase of vehicles for purposes of scrap or parts only. G.S. 20-62.1.
Secondary metals recycler purchase of catalytic converters in certain circumstances. G.S. 66-424.

Purchasing, Selling, etc. of a Motor Vehicle or Part with an Altered Identification Number (page 349)

Elements (page 349)

As a result of 2013 legislation, S.L. 2013-323, the elements for this offense should read as follows:

A person guilty of this offense

(1) (a) purchases,
(b) disposes of,
(c) sells,
(d) transfers,
(e) receives, *or*
(f) possesses
(2) (a) a motor vehicle *or*
(b) motor vehicle part

(3) knowing or having reasonable grounds to believe that the vehicle identification number has been altered, counterfeited, defaced, destroyed, disguised, falsified, forged, obliterated, or removed.

Punishment (page 350)

As a result of the 2013 legislation noted above, delete the text in this section and replace it with the following:

Class G felony. G.S. 14-72.7(a).

Notes (page 350)

As a result of the 2013 legislation noted above, which caused a renumbering and revision of the elements of this offense, delete the text in this section and replace it with the following:

Element (1)(c). For an explanation of the term "sells" in the context of drug offenses, see the note on Element (2)(a) to "Sale or Delivery of a Controlled Substance" in Chapter 27 (Drug Offenses) of the main volume.

Element (1)(e). For a discussion of the term "receives," see the note on Element (1) to "Misdemeanor Receiving of Stolen Goods" in the main volume.

Element (1)(f). For a discussion of the term "possesses," see the note on Element (1) to "Misdemeanor Possession of Stolen Goods" in the main volume.

Element (2). For a definition of the term "motor vehicle" as used in the context of motor vehicle offenses, see the note on Element (2) to "Driving While License Revoked" in Chapter 28 (Motor Vehicle Offenses) of the main volume.

Element (3). For definitions of the terms "vehicle identification number" and "vehicle part identification number," see G.S. 14-72.7(f)(2) and (3).

Exceptions. See this note to "Altering, Destroying, etc. Any Stolen Motor Vehicle or Part" in the main volume.

Seizure and forfeiture. See this note to "Altering, Destroying, etc. Any Stolen Motor Vehicle or Part" in the main volume.

Related Offenses Not in This Chapter (page 350)

Add the following offenses to this list:

Purchase of vehicles for purposes of scrap or parts only. G.S. 20-62.1.
Secondary metals recycler purchase of catalytic converters in certain circumstances. G.S. 66-424.

Purchasing, Disposing of, etc. a Motor Vehicle or Part in Connection with a Chop Shop Violation (page 350)

Elements (page 350)

As a result of 2013 legislation, S.L. 2013-323, the elements for this offense should read as follows:

A person guilty of this offense

(1) (a) purchases,
(b) disposes of,
(c) sells,
(d) transfers,
(e) receives, *or*
(f) possesses

(2) (a) a motor vehicle *or*
    (b) motor vehicle part
(3) to or from a person
(4) engaged in any activity prohibited by G.S. 14-72.7
(5) knowing or having reasonable grounds to believe that the person is engaging in that activity.

Punishment (page 351)

As a result of the 2013 legislation noted above, delete the text in this section and replace it with the following:

Class G felony. G.S. 14-72.7(a).

Notes (page 351)

As a result of the 2013 legislation noted above, which caused a renumbering and revision of the elements of this offense, delete the text in this section and replace it with the following:

Element (1)(c). For an explanation of the term "sells" in the context of drug offenses, see the note on Element (2)(a) to "Sale or Delivery of a Controlled Substance" in Chapter 27 (Drug Offenses) of the main volume.

Element (1)(e). For a discussion of the term "receives," see the note on Element (1) to "Misdemeanor Receiving of Stolen Goods" in the main volume.

Element (1)(f). For a discussion of the term "possesses," see the note on Element (1) to "Misdemeanor Possession of Stolen Goods" in the main volume.

Element (2). For a definition of the term "motor vehicle" as used in the context of motor vehicle offenses, see the note on Element (2) to "Driving While License Revoked" in Chapter 28 (Motor Vehicle Offenses) of the main volume.

Exceptions. See this note to "Altering, Destroying, etc. Any Stolen Motor Vehicle or Part" in the main volume.

Seizure and forfeiture. See this note to "Altering, Destroying, etc. Any Stolen Motor Vehicle or Part" in the main volume.

Related Offenses Not in This Chapter (page 351)

Add the following offenses to this list:

Purchase of vehicles for purposes of scrap or parts only. G.S. 20-62.1.
Secondary metals recycler purchase of catalytic converters in certain circumstances. G.S. 66-424.

Larceny of a Motor Vehicle Part (page 351)

Notes (page 352)

Element (3)

Add the following text at the end of this note:

The statute's requirement of $1,000 in repair costs refers to the cost to repair a single vehicle, not to (1) the cost to repair multiple vehicles in the aggregate or (2) the value of car parts stolen where no vehicle is involved. State v. Stephenson, 267 N.C. App. 475 (2019).

Related Offenses Not in This Chapter (page 352)

Add the following offense to this list:

Secondary metals recycler purchase of catalytic converters in certain circumstances. G.S. 66-424.

Stealing from Merchants and Retail Establishments (page 352)

Larceny from a Merchant (page 352)

Statute (page 352)

2017 legislation, S.L. 2017-162, sec. 1, amended the statute to read as follows:

§ 14-72.11. Larceny from a merchant.

A person is guilty of a Class H felony if the person commits larceny against a merchant under any of the following circumstances:

(1) By taking property that has a value of more than two hundred dollars ($200.00), using an exit door erected and maintained to comply with the requirements of 29 C.F.R. § 1910.36 and 29 C.F.R. § 1910.37, to exit the premises of a store.

(2) By removing, destroying, or deactivating a component of an antishoplifting or inventory control device to prevent the activation of any antishoplifting or inventory control device.

(3) By affixing a product code created for the purpose of fraudulently obtaining goods or merchandise from a merchant at less than its actual sale price.

(4) When the property is infant formula valued in excess of one hundred dollars ($100.00). As used in this subsection, the term "infant formula," has the same meaning as found in 21 U.S.C. § 321(z).

(5) By exchanging property for cash, a gift card, a merchandise card, or some other item of value, knowing or having reasonable grounds to believe the property is stolen.

Elements (page 353)

As a result of the 2017 legislation noted above, Element (3) should read as follows:

(3) (a) takes property valued at more than $200 using a specified exit door to leave the premises;

(b) removes, destroys, or deactivates a component of an anti-shoplifting or inventory control device to prevent the activation of any such device;

(c) affixes a product code created to fraudulently obtain goods or merchandise at less than actual sale price;

(d) the property is infant formula valued at more than $100; *or*

(e) exchanges property for cash, a gift card, a merchandise card, or another item of value, knowing or having reasonable grounds to believe that the property is stolen.

Notes (page 353)

Element (3)(a) (page 353)

As a result of the 2017 legislation noted above, delete the text of this note and replace it with the following:

The exit door must be erected and maintained to comply with the requirements of 29 C.F.R. § 1910.36 (a federal regulation dealing with design and construction requirements for exit routes) and § 1910.37 (a federal regulation dealing with maintenance, safeguards, and operational features for exit routes).

Organized Retail Theft (new crime)

As a result of 2017 legislation, S.L. 2017-162, sec. 2, this new crime replaces two crimes covered in the main volume: "Conspiracy to Commit Retail Theft" and "Receiving or Possessing Stolen Retail Property."

Statute (page 353)

§ 14-86.6. Organized retail theft.

(a) A person is guilty of a Class H felony if the person does either of the following:

(1) Conspires with another person to commit theft of retail property from retail establishments, with a value exceeding one thousand five hundred dollars ($1,500) aggregated over a 90-day period, with the intent to sell that retail property for monetary or other gain, and who takes or causes that retail property to be placed in the control of a retail property fence or other person in exchange for consideration.

(2) Receives or possesses any retail property that has been taken or stolen in violation of subdivision (1) of this subsection while knowing or having reasonable grounds to believe the property is stolen.

(a1) A person is guilty of a Class G felony if the person does either of the following:

(1) Conspires with another person to commit theft of retail property from one or more retail establishments, with a value exceeding twenty thousand dollars ($20,000) aggregated over a 90-day period, with the intent to sell that retail property for monetary or other gain, and who takes or causes that retail property to be placed in the control of a retail property fence or other person in exchange for consideration.

(2) Conspires with two or more other persons as an organizer, supervisor, financier, leader, or manager to engage for profit in a scheme or course of conduct to effectuate the transfer or sale of property stolen from a merchant in violation of this section.

(b) Any interest a person has acquired or maintained in violation of this section shall be subject to forfeiture pursuant to the procedures for forfeiture set out in G.S. 18B-504.

(c) Thefts of retail property occurring in more than one county may be aggregated into an alleged violation of this section. Each county where a part of the charged offense occurs has concurrent venue as described in G.S. 15A-132.

Elements

A person guilty of this offense:

(1) (a) conspires with another
 (b) to commit theft
 (c) of retail property
 (d) valued at either
  (i) more than $1,500 aggregated over a 90-day period *or*
  (ii) more than $20,000 aggregated over a 90-day period
 (e) from retail establishments
 (f) with the intent to sell the property for gain *and*
 (g) takes or causes the property to be placed in the control of a retail property fence or other person in exchange for consideration,

(2) (a) receives or possesses
 (b) retail property
 (c) that has been taken or stolen as provided in the Element (1)(d)(i) version of this offense
 (d) knowing or having reasonable grounds to believe that the property is stolen, *or*

(3) (a) conspires with two or more persons
 (b) as an organizer, supervisor, financier, leader, or manager

(c) to engage for profit in a scheme or course of conduct to effectuate the transfer or sale of property
(d) stolen from a merchant in violation of the statute.

Punishment

For violations of the Element (1) version of this offense where the property is valued at more than $1,500 under Element (1)(d)(i), the offense is a Class H felony, G.S. 14-86.6(a)(1); where the property is valued at more than $20,000 under Element (1)(d)(ii), the offense is a Class G felony. *Id.* § (a1)(1). A violation of the Element (2) version of this offense is a Class H felony. *Id.* § (a)(2). A violation of the Element (3) version of this offense is a Class G felony. *Id.* § (a1)(2).

Notes

Elements (1)(a) and (3)(a). See "Conspiracy" in Chapter 5 (General Crimes) of the main volume. Normally a conspiracy requires that the defendant enter into an agreement with at least one other person. *Id.* The Element (1) version of this offense follows that general rule. However, the Element (3) version of this offense requires the defendant to conspire with two or more people.

Element (1)(b). "Theft" is defined as follows: "[t]o take possession of, carry away, transfer, or cause to be carried away the retail property of another with the intent to steal the retail property." G.S. 14-86.5(3).

Elements (1)(c) and (2)(b). "Retail property" is defined as "[a]ny new article, product, commodity, item, or component intended to be sold in retail commerce." G.S. 14-86.5(1).

Element (1)(d). The value of an item is defined as the "retail value of an item as advertised by the affected retail establishment, to include all applicable taxes." G.S. 14-86.5(4). Retail property thefts occurring in more than one county may be aggregated "into an alleged violation of this section." *Id.* § -86.6(c).

Element (1)(g). A "retail property fence" is "[a] person or business that buys retail property knowing or believing that retail property is stolen." G.S. 14-86.5(2).

Element (2)(a). For a discussion of the term "receives," see the note on Element (1) to "Misdemeanor Receiving of Stolen Goods" in the main volume. For a discussion of the term "possesses," see the note on Element (1) to "Misdemeanor Possession of Stolen Goods" in the main volume.

Element (2)(d). See the note on Element (3) to "Misdemeanor Possession of Stolen Goods" in the main volume.

Element (3)(d). The statute provides that this version of the offense occurs when the accomplices conspire to "effectuate the transfer or sale of property stolen from a merchant in violation of this section." G.S. 14-86.6(a1)(2). While another provision of the statute expressly refers to a specific "subdivision" of the statute, see *id.* § (a)(2), this provision uses the word "section," suggesting that any violation of the statute might satisfy this Element. That is, however, unclear. For example, the Element (2) version of the offense applies to receiving or possessing property, not stealing.

Forfeiture. Any interest a person acquires or maintains in violation of G.S. 14-86.6 is subject to forfeiture under G.S. 18B-504. G.S. 14-86.6(b).

Venue. Each county where a part of the charged offense occurs has concurrent venue as described in G.S. 15A-132. G.S. 14-86.6(c).

Related Offenses Not in This Chapter

"Conspiracy" (Chapter 5)

Conspiracy to Commit Retail Theft (page 353)

For the reasons discussed above under "Organized Retail Theft," delete this offense.

Receiving or Possessing Stolen Retail Property (page 354)

For the reasons discussed above under "Organized Retail Theft," delete this offense.

Financial Transaction Card Theft (page 359)

Taking or Withholding a Card (page 360)

Notes (page 360)

Element (5) (page 360)

For a case where the evidence was sufficient to establish this Element, see *State v. Sellers*, 248 N.C. App. 293, 299 (2016) (someone other than the victim used the card at two stores on the day it was stolen; surveillance video showed the defendant at one of the stores when the card was swiped, and an employee testified that the defendant tried to use a card issued in another person's name).

Embezzlement Offenses (page 364)

Embezzlement by Employee (page 364)

Notes (page 365)

Element (3) (page 365)

Cash paid by a customer to the defendant shop manager for services was entrusted to the defendant for use by the employer. State v. Fink, 252 N.C. App. 379, 384–86 (2017) (rejecting the defendant's argument that the cash remained the customer's property until the work was completed; concluding that as soon as the customer tendered payment to the defendant, the funds became the property of the shop).

Related Offenses Not in This Chapter (page 366)

Delete the text of this section and replace it with the following:

See the offenses listed under "Embezzlement" in this supplement and in the main volume.

Embezzlement (page 366)

Elements (page 366)

To correct a typographical error in the main volume, Element (1) should read as follows:

(1) fraudulently or knowingly and willfully

Notes (page 367)

Element (1) (page 367)

The State need not prove that the defendant acted fraudulently, knowingly, and willfully; it need only prove that the defendant acted fraudulently *or* knowingly and willfully. State v. Booker, 262 N.C. App. 290 (2018).

The State can establish the requisite intent by direct or circumstantial evidence. State v. Parker, 233 N.C. App. 577, 580 (2014) (evidence was sufficient where the defendant used school system funds for improper purchases).

Element (2) (page 367)

For other cases supporting the proposition in this note that the person entrusted with the property need not convert it to his or her own use, see *Parker*, 233 N.C. App. at 580, and *Booker*, 262 N.C. App. 290 (quoting *Parker*).

Element (4) (page 367)

For a case where there was sufficient evidence that the defendant was an agent of a corporation and not an independent contractor, see *State v. Smalley*, 220 N.C. App. 142, 144–45 (2012) (the defendant was alleged to have improperly written company checks to herself).

There was sufficient evidence that the defendant had constructive possession of the corporation's money when she was given complete access to the corporation's accounts and could write checks on behalf of the corporation and delegate where the corporation's money went. *Id.*

There was sufficient evidence of embezzlement in another case where the defendant, a bookkeeper controller for the victim company, was instructed to close the company's credit cards but failed to do so, instead incurring personal charges on the cards and paying the card bills from company funds. State v. Renkosiak, 226 N.C. App. 377, 378–79 (2013).

For another case where the evidence was sufficient to establish that the defendant was entrusted with the property in question, see *State v. Grandy*, 261 N.C. App. 691 (2018) (the defendant, a foundation's director of accounting, was entrusted with funds that she transferred from the foundation's account to her personal account; to access the funds, the foundation's bank required her to use two security devices, referred to as "key fobs," both of which her employer entrusted to her even though the bank intended for two separate employees to participate in each transaction as a security measure).

Related Offenses Not in This Chapter (page 369)

Add the following offense to this list:

Embezzlement from a bank. G.S. 53C-8-11.

14
Robbery, Extortion, and Blackmail

Common Law Robbery (page 379)

Notes (page 379)

Element (2) (page 379)

Add the following at the end of the first paragraph of this note:

; and (3) personal property from a victim who was forced by intruders to lie on the ground, State v. McLean, 251 N.C. App. 850, 856 (2017).

Element (3) (page 380)

In a multi-count robbery case, there was sufficient evidence that victim Adrienne relinquished her property because of violence or intimidation; although Adrienne herself did not testify, evidence showed that she was a resident of premises where the robbery occurred, another victim heard her screaming during the intrusion, her face was injured, two witnesses testified that she had been beaten, and her personal belongings were taken. State v. Jones, 241 N.C. App. 132, 141 (2015).

Add the following at the end of this note:

; State v. Young-Kirkpatrick, ___ N.C. App. ___, 846 S.E.2d 525 (2020) (citing *State v. Tuck*, 173 N.C. App. 61 (2005), and concluding that defendant's earlier assault on the victim caused her to flee from her car to the house, making it possible for the defendant to take her keys, wallet, and car title).

Multiple convictions and punishments (page 381)

Where the defendant attempted to rob two victims inside a residence, two charges were proper; the fact that only one residence was involved was irrelevant where the defendant demanded that each victim turn over his personal property. State v. Jastrow, 237 N.C. App. 325, 329–30 (2014).

The second paragraph of this notes states that "[a] defendant may not be sentenced for both robbery and possession of stolen property taken during the robbery." For another case supporting that principle, see *State v. Guy*, 262 N.C. App. 313 (2018). However, that principle only applies "for possession during the course of the same conduct, and where the property is the 'same property.'" State v. Hendricksen, 257 N.C. App. 345, 352 (2018) (holding that the defendant's conviction after a guilty plea in Harnett County to two counts of misdemeanor possession of stolen goods involving two lottery tickets did not preclude his later trial and conviction in Johnston County for an armed robbery of a convenience store during which he obtained approximately $1,900 in cash and approximately 800 lottery tickets, including the two that were the subject of the Harnett County charges).

Armed Robbery (page 381)

Statute (page 381)

2017 legislation, S.L. 2017-31, amended the statute, adding a new subsection, (a1), as follows:

> **(a1) Attempted robbery with a dangerous weapon shall constitute a lesser included offense of robbery with a dangerous weapon, and evidence sufficient to prove robbery with a dangerous weapon shall be sufficient to support a conviction of attempted robbery with a dangerous weapon.**

Notes (page 382)

Element (3) (page 382)

For a case where the evidence was sufficient to show that either the defendant or his accomplice used a firearm to induce the victim to part with her purse, see *State v. James*, 226 N.C. App. 120, 125 (2013).

For a case where there was sufficient evidence that a lawn chair was a dangerous weapon, see *State v. Mills*, 221 N.C. App. 409, 413 (2012).

An unopened knife wielded by the defendant can be a dangerous weapon. State v. Whisenant, 249 N.C. App. 456, 459 (2016) (in a case where the defendant yelled, "I will kill you" while brandishing the knife, the court held that "the unopened knife was a dangerous weapon when Defendant threatened to use it to cause great bodily harm or death").

A box cutter with the blade exposed is a dangerous weapon as a matter of law. State v. Redmond, 266 N.C. App. 580 (2019) (citing State v. Wiggins, 78 N.C. App. 405 (1985)).

Element (4) (page 383)

The evidence was sufficient to establish that the defendant's gun threatened or endangered the life of a person, even though the defendant did not point it at the victims. State v. Wright, 252 N.C. App. 501, 505–09 (2017) (distinguishing cases where victims and bystanders did not see the defendant's weapon; here, the defendant was seen holding the gun in his hand during the robberies).

For another case supporting the statement in this note that it is not necessary to prove that the victim feared for his or her life, see *Wright*, *id.* at 509–10 (the victim testified that she was not scared during the incident).

The evidence was sufficient to establish that an unopened knife endangered or threatened the victim's life where, while the victim attempted to disarm the defendant, the defendant threatened, "I will kill you," and the victim felt afraid. *Whisenant*, 249 N.C. App. at 458–59.

Timing of elements (page 384)

There was sufficient evidence that a theft and the use of force were part of a continuous transaction where the defendant went to the victim's home with the intent to rob him, shot and killed the victim, and left with money and drugs. State v. Rogers, 227 N.C. App. 617, 622–23 (2013). Even when there is some attenuation between the use of force and the taking, the action can still amount to a continuous transaction sufficient to constitute a robbery. State v. Young-Kirkpatrick, ___ N.C. App. ___, 846 S.E.2d 525 (2020) (taking the victim's keys, car title, and wallet within 20 minutes of an argument and assault related to the victim's car was a continuous transaction).

Jury instructions (new note)

Where the evidence showed that the defendant displayed and threatened to use a weapon by pointing it at the victim, the trial court was not required to give the mere possession instruction in footnote 6 to element seven of N.C.P.I.—Crim. 217.20. State v. Bell, 227 N.C. App. 339, 345 (2013).

Attempt (page 384)
For cases where the evidence was sufficient to prove an attempted armed robbery, see *State v. Calderon*, 242 N.C. App. 125, 137–38 (2015) (the defendant did not consummate the offense because the victim was passed out or asleep and, therefore, could not be induced to give up his money due to the threat that the accomplices' weapons presented and because no one saw the defendant take anything from the victim's pockets), and *State v. Evans*, 228 N.C. App. 454, 461–62 (2013) (the defendant planned a robbery with an accomplice, waited in a vehicle until the accomplice went into the residence and sent a message with the location of each individual inside, entered the residence and went directly to the victim's bedroom, and proceeded to wield his firearm in a threatening manner toward the victim; the evidence was sufficient even though the defendant did not make a specific demand for money).

Even though assault with a deadly weapon is a lesser-included offense of armed robbery, a defendant may be convicted for that assault and armed robbery when each conviction arises from discrete conduct. State v. Ortiz, 238 N.C. App. 508, 515 (2014).

Evidence that is sufficient to prove armed robbery is sufficient to prove attempted armed robbery. G.S. 14-87, *as amended by* S.L. 2017-31.

Greater and lesser-included offenses (page 385)
Attempted armed robbery is a lesser-included offense of armed robbery. G.S. 14-87, *as amended by* S.L. 2017-31.

Extortion is not a lesser-included offense of armed robbery. State v. Wright, 240 N.C. App. 270, 273 (2015) (applying a definitional rather than a factual test).

For another case supporting the statements in this note that larceny and assault are lesser-included offenses of robbery, see *State v. Cromartie*, 257 N.C. App. 790, 796–97 (2018) (misdemeanor larceny and simple assault are lesser-included offenses of common law robbery).

"Presumption" of the use of a dangerous weapon (page 385)
The trial court did not err by failing to instruct the jury on common law robbery and by denying the defendant's motion to dismiss armed robbery charges where there was no evidence that the gun was inoperable or unloaded and thus no evidence to rebut the presumption that the firearm was functioning properly. State v. Williamson, 220 N.C. App. 512, 515–16 (2012). Alternatively, the trial court erred in denying the defendant's motion to dismiss when the State presented no evidence that an air pistol and a pellet rifle were capable of inflicting death or serious bodily injury. State v. Williamson, ___ N.C. App. ___, 845 S.E.2d 876 (2020).

Although a defendant's testimony that a gun was unloaded extinguished the presumption that a dangerous weapon was used, a permissive inference remained and supported denial of a motion to dismiss. State v. Bell, 227 N.C. App. 339, 342–44 (2013) (in addition to the victim's testimony that the defendant entered her business, pointed a gun at her, and demanded money, evidence showed that upon leaving, the defendant saw the police and ran into the woods, where he left his hoodie and gun and jumped off of an embankment).

Although the fact that a BB pistol and a pellet gun were found outside the residence where the robbery occurred extinguished the presumption that a dangerous weapon was used, in light of the victim's testimony that the defendant used handguns, a permissive inference remained and supported denial of a motion to dismiss. State v. Holt, 241 N.C. App. 577, 585 (2015) (noting that no evidence conclusively connected a BB pistol or pellet gun to the robbery).

Claim of right defense (new note)
A defendant is not guilty of robbery if he or she can show that property was taken from another under a bona fide claim of right or title to the property. State v. Spratt, 265 N.C. 524 (1965). However, a defendant may not lawfully engage in "self-help" by virtue of a bona fide claim of right or title to property that is the subject of an illegal transaction. State v. Cox, 375 N.C. 165 (2020) (the defendant had the requisite felonious intent when he conspired to use violence to collect on a perceived debt for illegal drugs).

Extortion (page 386)

Notes (page 386)

Element (2) (page 386)

The statute requires proof that the defendant intentionally utilized unjust or unlawful means in attempting to obtain the property or other acquittance, advantage, or immunity; it does not require proof that the defendant sought to achieve an end to which he or she had no entitlement. State v. Privette, 218 N.C. App. 459, 477 (2012).

Jury instructions (new note)

The trial judge properly instructed the jury on extortion using the pattern jury instruction. *Id.*

Greater and lesser-included offenses (new note)

Extortion is not a lesser-included offense of armed robbery. State v. Wright, 240 N.C. App. 270, 273 (2015) (applying a definitional rather than a factual test).

Defenses (new note)

North Carolina does not recognize a "claim of right" defense to extortion. *Id.*; *Privette,* 218 N.C. App. at 477.

15
Burglary, Breaking or Entering, and Related Offenses

First-Degree Burglary (page 391)

Notes (page 392)

Element (2) (page 393)

An entering did not occur when (1) the defendant used a shotgun to break a window and the end of the shotgun entered the premises, State v. Watkins, 218 N.C. App. 94, 100–01 (2012), and (2) the defendants used landscaping bricks and a fire pit bowl to break a home's window, but there was no evidence that they entered the premises. State v. Lucas, 234 N.C. App. 247, 251–54 (2014) (following *Watkins* and distinguishing *State v. Salters*, 137 N.C. App. 553 (2000) (evidence of a splintered door frame and broken lock, along with evidence that a suitcase missing from inside the residence was seen in the defendant's possession, was sufficient to establish an entering)).

Element (7) (page 394)

There was sufficient evidence that a burglary occurred at nighttime when the defendant left his girlfriend's apartment after 10 p.m. and did not return until 6 a.m. the next day; the burglary occurred during that time period; after taking judicial notice of the time of civil twilight (5:47 a.m.) and the driving distance between the victim's residence and the girlfriend's apartment, the court concluded that it would have been impossible for the defendant to commit the crime after 5:47 a.m. and be back at the apartment by 6 a.m. State v. Brown, 221 N.C. App. 383, 387–88 (2012).

Element (8) (page 395)

For another case supporting the statement in the first paragraph of this note that the defendant must intend to commit the required crime inside the dwelling, see *State v. Allah*, 231 N.C. App. 88, 93–95 (2013) (insufficient evidence that the defendant intended to commit a felonious restraint inside the building; that offense requires that the defendant transport the victim by motor vehicle or other conveyance, and the car the defendant was driving was left running outside).

Evidence that items were missing after a breaking or entering can be sufficient to prove the defendant's intent to commit a larceny inside the premises. State v. Northington, 230 N.C. App. 575, 579 (2013).

The evidence was sufficient to establish the requisite intent when (1) the defendants were walking from house to house in a neighborhood to determine whether the houses were occupied and were trying to open doors of parked cars, State v. Lucas, 234 N.C. App. 247, 254–55 (2014); (2) the defendant unlawfully broke and entered a church late at night; he did not have permission to be there and could not remember what he did there; and the defendant's wallet was found near where missing items had been stored, State v. Campbell, 368 N.C. 83 (2015); and (3) responding officers determined that a building broken into was in disarray and appeared to have been rummaged through, with certain items that had been inside the building earlier that day having been removed and placed in a fenced-in area surrounding the building, State v. McNair, 253 N.C. App. 178, 186 (2017).

The sixth paragraph of this note states that the fact that an intruder broke and entered a dwelling at nighttime is sufficient, in the absence of contrary evidence, to support a finding that the intruder intended to steal. This inference is sometimes called the *McBryde* inference, after the seminal case *State v. McBryde*, 97 N.C. 393 (1887). For another case applying the *McBryde* inference, see *State v. Mims*, 241 N.C. App. 611, 615–17 (2015). Additionally, in *Mims* the court applied the *McBryde* inference to an attempted breaking or entering that occurred during daylight hours.

Doctrine of recent possession (page 396)
When the victim's laptop and other items were found in the defendant's possession hours after the burglary, the doctrine of recent possession provided sufficient evidence that the defendant was the perpetrator. State v. Brown, 221 N.C. App. 383, 388 (2012).

Felony Breaking or Entering of a Building (page 398)

Statute (page 398)

2013 legislation, S.L. 2013-95, added subsection (a1) to G.S. 14-54 as follows:

> (a1) Any person who breaks or enters any building with intent to terrorize or injure an occupant of the building is guilty of a Class H felony.

Elements (page 398)

As a result of that same legislation, Element (5) should be revised as follows:

(5) with the intent to
  (a) commit any felony or larceny therein *or*
  (b) terrorize or injure an occupant of the building.

Notes (page 399)

Element (3) (page 399)
Distinguishing *Boone* (discussed in the first paragraph of this note in the main volume as holding that a defendant who entered a clothing store during business hours and stole two sweaters entered with the owner's consent), the court of appeals held that a defendant's entry into a store is without consent when the defendant has received notice from the store prohibiting his or her entry onto the premises. State v. Allen, 258 N.C. App. 285, 290 (2018) (after receiving a Notice of Prohibited Entry banning him from Belk stores for fifty years, the defendant entered a Belk store).

For purposes of breaking or entering, a person can have consent to enter a portion but not all of a building. State v. Vetter, 257 N.C. App. 915, 923 (2018). Thus, a defendant who had permission to access a garage to collect his belongings but lacked permission to enter the residence itself was properly convicted of this offense when he kicked in a door connecting the residence and garage and entered the residence. *Id.*

Element (5) (page 400)

The 2013 statute does not define the term "terrorize." That term is, however, used in the context of kidnapping, where it has been defined by case law. See the note on Element (4)(g) to "First-Degree Kidnapping" in Chapter 12 (Kidnapping and Related Offenses) of the main volume.

In *State v. Griffin*, 264 N.C. App. 490 (2019), the court applied the definition used for kidnapping (putting a person in some high degree of fear, a state of intense fright, or apprehension) and concluded that the defendant's uninvited entry, without announcing himself, into the victim's home and violent attack of the victim supported the conclusion that the defendant entered the home with the intent to terrorize the victim within the meaning of this offense.

Greater and lesser-included offenses (page 400)
For another case supporting the statement in this note that first-degree trespass is a lesser-included offense of this one, see *State v. Lucas*, 234 N.C. App. 247, 256 (2014).

Breaking or Entering a Place of Worship (page 401)

Notes (page 401)

Element (4) (page 401)
This Element was not satisfied when the defendant broke into a small barn located approximately fifty feet behind a building that was being rented by a church for holding religious services. State v. McNair, 253 N.C. App. 178, 182 (2017) (although the owner of the building allowed the church to store equipment in the barn, the barn was not used for religious worship; the court rejected the State's argument that because the barn was within the curtilage of the chapel it should be deemed an extension of it; the specific building broken into must be one regularly used and clearly identifiable as a place of religious worship).

As a result of 2019 legislation, S.L. 2019-40, add the following new offense, effective for offenses committed on or after December 1, 2019:

Breaking or Entering a Pharmacy (new crime)

Statute

§ 14-54.2. Breaking or entering a pharmacy.

(a) Definition. – The following definitions apply to this section:

(1) Pharmacy. – A business that has a pharmacy permit under G.S. 90-85.21.

(2) Controlled substance. – As defined in G.S. 90-87(5).

(b) Offense. – A person who breaks or enters a pharmacy with the intent to commit a larceny of a controlled substance is guilty of a Class E felony.

(c) Additional Offense. – Unless the conduct is covered under some other provision of law providing greater punishment, a person who receives or possesses any controlled substance stolen in violation of subsection (b) of this section, knowing or having reasonable grounds to believe the controlled substance was stolen, is guilty of a Class F felony.

(d) Forfeiture. – Any interest a person has acquired or maintained in property obtained in violation of this section shall be subject to forfeiture pursuant to the procedures for forfeiture as set forth in G.S. 90-112.

Elements

A person guilty of this offense

(1) breaks *or* enters
(2) without consent
(3) a pharmacy
(4) with the intent to commit a larceny of a controlled substance.

Punishment

Class E felony. G.S. 14-54.2(b). Any interest a person acquires or maintains in property obtained in violation of this section is subject to forfeiture as set forth in G.S. 90-112. *Id.* § -54.2(d).

Notes

Generally. Relevant notes to "Felony Breaking or Entering of a Building" apply to this offense as well.

Element (3)
A "pharmacy" is defined as a business that has a pharmacy permit under G.S. 90-85.21.

Element (4)
Unlike the similar element of "Felony Breaking or Entering of a Building," which covers the intent to commit any felony or larceny in the building, this Element of this offense requires that the defendant intend to commit a larceny of a controlled substance. A "controlled substance" is any drug, substance, or immediate precursor included in Schedules I through VI of the Controlled Substances Act. G.S. 90-87(5).

Related Offenses Not in This Chapter

See the offenses listed under "First-Degree Burglary," above.

Possession of Burglar's Tools (page 401)

Notes (page 402)

Element (1) (new note)
For a case where the evidence was sufficient to show that the defendant had constructive possession of burglar's tools found at the scene of a breaking or entering, see *State v. McNair*, 253 N.C. App. 178, 187–88 (2017) (the defendant was found alone inside a privately owned, fenced-in area at 1 a.m.; officers saw him scaling a 10-foot wall in an attempt to avoid apprehension and determined that someone had broken into the building; padlocks were found on the ground; and several pieces of property that had been stored inside the building were found in the fenced-in area).

Breaking or Entering a Vehicle (page 402)

Statute (page 402)

2015 legislation, S.L. 2015-286, sec. 3.3(a), amended the statute, putting the existing text in subsection (a) and creating a new subsection (b), as follows:

> (b) It shall not be a violation of this section for any person to break or enter any railroad car, motor vehicle, trailer, aircraft, boat, or other watercraft of any kind to provide assistance to a person inside the railroad car, motor vehicle, trailer, aircraft, boat, or watercraft of any kind if one or more of the following circumstances exist:
>
> (1) The person acts in good faith to access the person inside the railroad car, motor vehicle, trailer, aircraft, boat, or watercraft of any kind in order to provide first aid or emergency health care treatment or because the person inside is, or is in imminent danger of becoming unconscious, ill, or injured.
>
> (2) It is reasonably apparent that the circumstances require prompt decisions and actions in medical, other health care, or other assistance for the person inside the railroad car, motor vehicle, trailer, aircraft, boat, or watercraft of any kind.
>
> (3) The necessity of immediate health care treatment or removal of the person from the railroad car, motor vehicle, trailer, aircraft, boat, or other watercraft of any kind is so reasonably apparent that any delay in the rendering of treatment or removal would seriously worsen the physical condition or endanger the life of the person.

Notes (page 403)

Element (5) (page 403)

For a case where the State failed to present evidence that the boats in question contained items of value, see *State v. Fish*, 229 N.C. App. 584, 590 (2013) (rejecting the State's argument that boat batteries constituted items of value, reasoning that they were part of the boats themselves).

Element (6) (page 403)

For another case supporting the statement in this note that the intended felony or larceny may be a theft of the motor vehicle that is the subject of the breaking or entering, see *State v. Mitchell*, 234 N.C. App. 423, 428 (2014) (citing *Clark*).

Jury instructions (new note)

When an indictment alleges that the defendant broke *and* entered a vehicle, the trial court does not err by instructing the jury that the defendant can be found guilty if he or she broke *or* entered the vehicle. *Id.* at 428–29 (citing similar case law regarding breaking or entering a building).

Good Samaritan exception (new note)

The offense does not occur if a person breaks or enters to assist someone inside if the requirements of G.S. 14-56(b) are satisfied.

16

Fraud, Forgery, False Pretenses, and Related Offenses

Worthless Checks (page 411)

Worthless Checks—Making or Uttering (page 411)

Statute (page 411)

2013 legislation, S.L. 2013-244, sec. 4, amended the title of G.S. 14-107 and subsections (a) and (b) to read as follows:

§ 14-107. Worthless checks; multiple presentation of checks.

(a) It is unlawful for any person, firm or corporation, to draw, make, utter or issue and deliver to another, any check or draft on any bank or depository, for the payment of money or its equivalent, knowing at the time of the making, drawing, uttering, issuing and delivering the check or draft, that the maker or drawer of it:

(1) Has not sufficient funds on deposit in or credit with the bank or depository with which to pay the check or draft upon presentation, or

(2) Has previously presented the check or draft for the payment of money or its equivalent.

(b) It is unlawful for any person, firm or corporation to solicit or to aid and abet any other person, firm or corporation to draw, make, utter or issue and deliver to any person, firm or corporation, any check or draft on any bank or depository for the payment of money or its equivalent, being informed, knowing or having reasonable grounds for believing at the time of the soliciting or the aiding and abetting that the maker or the drawer of the check or draft:

(1) Has not sufficient funds on deposit in, or credit with, the bank or depository with which to pay the check or draft upon presentation, or

(2) Has previously presented the check or draft for the payment of money or its equivalent.

Another piece of 2013 legislation, S.L. 2013-360, sec. 18B.14(b), amended subsection (d)(1) to read as follows:

(1) Except as provided in subdivision (3) or (4) of this subsection, the person is guilty of a Class 3 misdemeanor.

Elements (page 412)

As a result of 2013 legislation, S.L. 2013-244, sec. 4, Element (4) should be revised as follows:

(4) knowing that
  (a) there are insufficient funds or credit available for the payment *or*
  (b) the maker or drawer has previously presented the check or draft for the payment.

Punishment (page 412)

As a result of 2013 legislation, S.L. 2013-360, sec. 18B.14(b), the first three words of this section should read:

Class 3 misdemeanor

Notes (page 412)

Elements (3) and (4) (page 413)

In the note on Element (3), delete the second sentence of the second paragraph. Add the following text at the end of the first paragraph of the note on Element (4):

A postdated check implies no more than that on its date the drawer will have or expects to have funds or credit in the bank to insure its payment at that time. State v. Crawford, 198 N.C. 522 (1930); State v. Byrd, 204 N.C. 162 (1933).

Obtaining Property for a Worthless Check (page 416)

Statute (page 416)

2013 legislation, S.L. 2013-360, sec. 18B.14(a), amended the statute to lower the punishment for this offense to a Class 3 misdemeanor.

Punishment (page 416)

As a result of the 2013 legislation noted above, delete the text of this section and replace it with the following:

Class 3 misdemeanor. G.S. 14-106.

Obtaining Property by False Pretenses (page 417)

Notes (page 417)

Element (1) (page 417)

The evidence was sufficient to establish this Element where the defendant (1) uttered a forged check, State v. Conley, 220 N.C. App. 50, 60–61 (2012); (2) approached two elderly women, falsely told them that their roofs needed repair, took payment for the work, and then performed shoddy work or failed to complete the job, State v. Barker, 240 N.C. App. 224, 231 (2015); and (3) submitted false invoices for moving expenses from companies that did not exist in North Carolina, State v. Holanek, 242 N.C. App. 633, 643 (2015).

Element (2) (page 418)

For cases where the evidence was sufficient to establish a false representation regarding pawned items, see *State v. Mostafavi*, 370 N.C. 681, 687 (2018) (the defendant falsely represented that he owned the property where the pawn tickets described the conveyed items; contained the defendant's name, address, driver's license number, and date of birth; and included language explicitly stating that the defendant was "giving a security interest in the . . . described goods"), and *State v. Greenlee*, 227 N.C. App. 133, 137–38 (2013) (the defendant falsely represented to a pawn shop that items were not stolen).

The State failed to offer sufficient evidence to establish that the defendant made a false representation with the intent to deceive when he told the victims that he intended to invest money they had loaned him in legitimate institutions and would repay it with interest at a specified time; the evidence showed only that the defendant, "after seriously overestimating his investing skills, made a promise that he was unable to keep." State v. Braswell, 225 N.C. App. 734, 742 (2013).

Element (3) (page 418)
The State failed to offer sufficient evidence to establish that the defendant made a false representation with the intent to deceive when he told the victims that he intended to invest the money they loaned him in legitimate institutions and would repay it with interest at a specified time; the evidence showed only that the defendant, "after seriously overestimating his investing skills, made a promise that he was unable to keep." *Braswell*, 225 N.C. App. at 742.

For cases where the evidence was sufficient to prove an intent to deceive, see *State v. Phillips*, 252 N.C. App. 194, 199 (2017) (the defendant advertised "Michael Kors" bags for sale for $45, knowing they were counterfeit), and *State v. Pendergraft*, 238 N.C. App. 516, 527 (2014) (rejecting the defendant's argument that his honest but mistaken belief that he could obtain title to a property by adverse possession precluded a finding that he had the required intent to deceive), *aff'd per curiam by an equally divided court*, 368 N.C. 314 (2015) (noting that the decision below is left undisturbed and stands without precedential value).

Element (4) (page 418)
In a case where the defendant obtained money by selling to company BIMCO electrical wire falsely represented as not having been stolen, there was sufficient evidence that his false representation in fact deceived BIMCO; the court rejected the defendant's argument that BIMCO was indifferent to legal ownership and employed a "nod and wink system" in which no actual deception occurred, noting evidence that the defendant represented himself as the lawful owner of the material and that BIMCO paid him for it. State v. Hallum, 246 N.C. App. 658 (2016).

When a defendant is charged with a completed offense, proof that the victim was deceived is required. *Phillips*, 252 N.C. App. at 199. However, when the defendant is charged with attempting to obtain property by false pretenses, which (as discussed in the note to this offense entitled "Attempt") is punished at the same level as the completed offense, the State need not prove that the victim was in fact deceived. *Id.*

Element (5) (page 418)

Delete the first sentence of the second paragraph of this note and replace it with the following:

> For the completed version of this crime, the defendant must gain possession of the property but need not gain title to or an ownership interest in it.

Add the following to this note:

> Like a loan, a provisional credit of $600 placed in the defendant's bank account after he falsely told the bank that his girlfriend had fraudulently signed and cashed checks drawn on his account was a thing of value. State v. Buchanan, 253 N.C. App. 783, 786 (2017) (the credit was the equivalent of money being placed in his account, to which the defendant had access, at least temporarily; access to money for a period of time, even if it eventually has to be paid back, is a thing of value).
>
> For a case where the evidence was insufficient to establish that the defendant obtained a thing of value, see *State v. Mathis*, 261 N.C. App. 263 (2018) (in a case arising out of false information submitted in connection with the defendant's work as a bail bondsman, the indictment alleged the thing of value obtained to be a professional bail bondsman's license; the defendant already had a bail bondsman license and the State asserted that his false representations allowed him to retain his license; the court disagreed, concluding that retaining is not the same as obtaining).

Attempt (page 420)
This offense was committed even though the defendant returned the victim's payment; the defendant's actions were sufficient to constitute an attempt. State v. Seelig, 226 N.C. App. 147, 162 (2013). A scheme between a clerk and bail bondsman to alter bail bond forfeiture notations in court files involved a "thing of value" to the extent that it was an attempt to reduce the bail bond company's liability as a surety. State v. Golder, 374 N.C. 238 (2020).

Multiple convictions and punishments (page 420)
When a defendant obtains multiple items in a single transaction, only one conviction can result. *Buchanan*, 253 N.C. App. at 787 (where the defendant attempted to collect the value of three checks he falsely claimed to be fraudulent but was successful only with respect to one of them, only a single offense occurred; however, the defendant waived the double jeopardy issue by failing to raise it at trial).

Relation to other offenses (page 420)
A defendant may be sentenced for both this offense and insurance fraud arising from the same alleged misrepresentation; each offense requires an element not required by the other, and they punish conduct that is violative of two separate and distinct social norms. State v. Ray, ___ N.C. App. ___, 851 S.E.2d 653 (2020).

Doctrine of recent possession (new note)
The doctrine of recent possession applies to obtaining property by false pretenses. State v. Street, 254 N.C. App. 214, 219 (2017) (concluding that the jury may be instructed on the doctrine even if the defendant is not charged with taking the property that he or she is alleged to have recently possessed; here, the defendant was charged with obtaining property by false pretenses for selling a pair of hedge trimmers to a pawn shop less than two hours after the trimmers were stolen). See generally this note to "Misdemeanor Larceny" in the main volume.

As a result of 2019 legislation, S.L. 2019-193, add the following note to this offense, effective for offenses committed on or after December 1, 2019:

Venue (new note)
The State is not required to establish that all of the acts constituting this offense occurred in North Carolina or within a single city, county, or local jurisdiction of this state, and it is no defense that not all of the acts constituting this offense occurred in North Carolina or within a single local jurisdiction. G.S. 14-100(b1).

Related Offenses Not in This Chapter (page 420)

Add the following offenses to this list:

Hiring with intent to defraud. G.S. 14-168.
Unemployment insurance fraud. G.S. 96-18.

The offense listed in this section as "Improper receipt of decedent's retirement allowance. G.S. 135-18.11, 128-38.5, 135-75.2, and 120-4.34" should read:

Improper receipt of decedent's retirement allowance or monthly benefit under the Disability Income Plan. G.S. 135-18.11, 128-38.5, 135-75.2, and 120-4.34.

Exploitation of a Disabled or Elder Adult (page 421)

Exploitation of a Disabled or Older Adult through a Position of Trust or Business Relationship (page 421) (revised title)

Statute (page 421)

2013 legislation, S.L. 2013-337, replaced the term "elder adult" with "older adult" throughout G.S. 14-112.2. It also amended subsection (a)(2) to read as follows:

(2) Older adult.—A person 65 years of age or older.

That same legislation also amended subsection (c) to read as follows:

> (c) It is unlawful for a person to knowingly, by deception or intimidation, obtain or use, endeavor to obtain or use, or conspire with another to obtain or use an older adult's or disabled adult's funds, assets, or property with the intent to temporarily or permanently deprive the older adult or disabled adult of the use, benefit, or possession of the funds, assets, or property, or benefit someone other than the older adult or disabled adult. This subsection shall not apply to a person acting within the scope of that person's lawful authority as the agent for the older adult or disabled adult.

Another 2013 law, S.L. 2013-203, amended the statute, adding a new subsection, (f), as follows:

> (f) If a person is charged with a violation of this section that involves funds, assets, or property valued at more than five thousand dollars ($5,000), the district attorney may file a petition in the pending criminal proceeding before the court with jurisdiction over the pending charges to freeze the funds, assets, or property of the defendant in an amount up to one hundred fifty percent (150%) of the alleged value of funds, assets, or property in the defendant's pending criminal proceeding for purposes of restitution to the victim. The standard of proof required to freeze the defendant's funds, assets, or property shall be by clear and convincing evidence. The procedure for petitioning the court under this subsection shall be governed by G.S. 14-112.3.

Elements (page 422)

As a result of the 2013 legislation noted above, replace the term "elder adult" with "older adult" throughout this section.

Notes (page 423)

Element (2) (page 423)

As a result of 2013 legislation, S.L. 2013-337, delete the second paragraph of this note and replace it with the following:

An "older adult" is a person 65 years old or older. G.S. 14-112.2(a)(2). Prior to 2013 legislative changes, the statute applied to an "elder adult." Interpreting the latter provision, one case held that there was sufficient evidence that the victim was an elder adult when the victim was at least 99 years old and received help to pay his bills, cash his checks, and perform personal hygiene tasks, among other things. State v. Forte, 206 N.C. App. 699, 704–05 (2010).

Asset freeze (new note)

If the offense involves funds, assets, or property valued at more than $5,000, new G.S. 14-112.2(f) allows the district attorney to file a petition to freeze the defendant's funds, assets, or property for purposes of restitution. New G.S. 14-112.3 sets out the relevant procedure.

Exploitation of a Disabled or Older Adult Lacking Capacity (page 423) (revised title)

Elements (page 423)

As a result of 2013 legislation, S.L. 2013-337, the elements of this offense are revised to read:

A person guilty of this offense

(1) knowingly *and*
(2) by deception or intimidation
(3) obtains, uses, endeavors to obtain or use, or conspires with another to obtain or use a disabled or older adult's funds, assets, or property
(4) with the intent to
   (a) temporarily or permanently deprive the disabled or older adult of the use, benefit, or possession of the funds, assets, or property *or*
   (b) benefit someone other than the disabled or older adult.

Notes (page 423)

Element (1) (new note)
See "Knowingly" in Chapter 1 (States of Mind) of the main volume.

Element (2) (page 423)

Delete the text of this note and replace it with the following:

For definitions of "disabled adult" and "older adult," see the note on Element (2) to "Exploitation of a Disabled or Older Adult through a Position of Trust or Business Relationship" (revised title), above in this supplement and in the main volume.

Asset freeze (new note)
See this note to "Exploitation of a Disabled or Older Adult through a Position of Trust or Business Relationship" (revised title), above in this supplement.

Identity Theft and Frauds (page 424)

Identity Theft (page 426)

Notes (page 427)

Element (2)(b) (page 427)
The evidence was sufficient to establish that the defendant "used" or "possessed" another person's Social Security number to avoid legal consequences when, after being detained and questioned for shoplifting, the defendant falsely gave the officer his name as Roy Lamar Ward and provided the officer with the name of an employer, date of birth, and possible address; the officer then obtained Ward's Social Security number, wrote it on the citation, and issued the citation to the defendant, but the defendant neither signed the citation nor confirmed the listed Social Security number. State v. Sexton, 223 N.C. App. 341, 345 (2012).

Element (2)(c) (page 427)
See the discussion of *Sexton*, 223 N.C. App. 341, immediately above.

Element (3) (page 427)
"Identifying information" is not limited to the fourteen examples listed in G.S. 14-113.20(b). State v. Miles, 267 N.C. App. 78 (2019) (holding that another person's name, date of birth, and address are identifying information when used to escape arrest and possibly receive hospital services).

Element (4) (new note)
Where the evidence showed that the defendant had used other individuals' credit card numbers, it was sufficient to show that he possessed the victims' credit cards with the intent to fraudulently represent that he was those individuals for the purpose of making financial transactions in their names. State v. Jones, 367 N.C. 299, 305 (2014). The fact that the defendant used false names not matching those on the victims' credit cards did not negate the defendant's intent to fraudulently represent that he was the cardholder. *Id.* at 306.

Related Offenses Not in This Chapter (page 428)

Add the following offense to this list:

Identity theft in connection with tax submission. G.S. 105-236(a)(9b), *as enacted by* S.L. 2017-204, sec. 3.1(a).

Impersonating a Transportation Network Company Driver (new crime)

This offense was enacted in 2019, S.L. 2019-194, effective for offenses committed on or after December 1, 2019, to read as follows:

Statute

§ 14-401.27. Impersonation of a transportation network company driver.

It shall be unlawful for any person to impersonate a transportation network company (TNC) driver, as defined in G.S. 20-280.1, by a false statement, false display of distinctive signage or emblems known as a trade dress, trademark, branding, or logo of the TNC, or any other act which falsely represents that the person has a current connection with a transportation network company or falsely represents that the person is responding to a passenger ride request for a transportation network company. A violation of this section is a Class H felony if the person impersonates a TNC driver during the commission of a separate felony offense. Any other violation of this section is a Class 2 misdemeanor.

Elements

A person guilty of this offense

(1) impersonates
(2) a transportation network company (TNC) driver, as defined in G.S. 20-280.1
(3) by
  (a) a false statement;
  (b) a false display of distinctive signage or emblems known as a trade dress, trademark, branding, or logo of the TNC; *or*
  (c) any other act which falsely represents that the person has a current connection with a TNC or is responding to a passenger ride request for a TNC.

Punishment

Class 2 misdemeanor. G.S. 14-401.27. This offense is a Class H felony if the person impersonates a TNC driver during the commission of a separate felony offense. *Id.*

Notes

Element (2). A TNC driver is an individual who uses a passenger vehicle in connection with a TNC's online-enabled application or platform to connect with passengers in exchange for payment of a fee to the TNC. G.S. 20-280.1.

Crimes Involving Security Interests (page 430)

Fraudulent Filings (page 431)

Statute (page 431)

2012 legislation, S.L. 2012-150, sec. 6, amended the statute, making the crime a Class I felony.

Punishment (page 432)

As a result of the 2012 legislation noted above, delete the text of this section and replace it with the following:

Class I felony. G.S. 14-401.19.

Related Offenses Not in This Chapter (page 432)

Add the following offense to this list:

Simulation of court process in connection with collection of claim, demand or account. G.S. 14-118.1.

False Liens (new crime)

This offense was enacted in 2012, S.L. 2012-150. It was amended in 2013, S.L. 2013-170; S.L. 2013-410, sec. 27.8; in 2015, S.L. 2015-87; in 2017, S.L. 2017-102, sec. 3; and in 2019, S.L. 2019-117, sec. 3; S.L. 2019-243, sec. 29.(a), to read as follows:

Statute

§ 14-118.6. Filing false lien or encumbrance.

(a) It shall be unlawful for any person to present for filing or recording in a public record or a private record generally available to the public a false lien or encumbrance against the real or personal property of an owner or beneficial interest holder, knowing or having reason to know that the lien or encumbrance is false or contains a materially false, fictitious, or fraudulent statement or representation. Any person who violates this subsection shall be guilty of a Class I felony.

(b) When presented to the register of deeds for recording, if a register of deeds has a reasonable suspicion that an instrument purporting to be a lien or encumbrance is materially false, fictitious, or fraudulent, the register of deeds may refuse to record the purported lien or encumbrance. Neither the register of deeds nor any other entity shall be liable for recording or the refusal to record a purported lien or encumbrance as described in this section. If the recording of the purported lien or encumbrance is denied, the register of deeds shall allow the recording of a Notice of Denied Lien or Encumbrance Filing on a form adopted by the Secretary of State, for which no filing fee shall be collected. The Notice of Denied Lien or Encumbrance Filing shall not itself constitute a lien or encumbrance. When recording is denied, any interested person may initiate a special proceeding in the county where the recording was denied within ten (10) business days of the filing of the Notice of Denied Lien or Encumbrance Filing asking the superior court of the respective county to find that the proposed recording has a statutory or contractual basis and to order that the document be recorded. If, after hearing, upon a minimum of five (5) days' notice as provided in Rule 5 of the Rules of Civil Procedure and opportunity to be heard to all interested persons and all persons claiming an ownership interest in the property, the court finds that there is a statutory or contractual basis for the proposed recording, the court shall order the document recorded, and the party submitting the instrument shall pay the filing fee in accordance with G.S. 161-10. A lien or encumbrance recorded upon order of the court under this subsection shall have a priority interest as of the time of the filing of the Notice of Denied Lien or Encumbrance Filing. If the court finds that there is no statutory or contractual basis for the proposed recording, the court shall enter an order finding that the proposed recording is null and void and that it shall not be filed, indexed, or recorded and a certified copy of that order shall be recorded by the register of deeds that originally denied the recording, for which the party who submitted the instrument shall pay the filing fee in accordance with G.S. 161-10. The review by the judge under this subsection shall not be deemed a finding as to any underlying claim of the parties involved. If a special proceeding is not initiated under this subsection within ten (10) business days of the filing of the Notice of Denied Lien or Encumbrance Filing, the purported lien or encumbrance is deemed null and void as a matter of law.

(b1) When a purported lien or encumbrance is presented to a clerk of superior court for filing and the clerk of court has a reasonable suspicion that the purported lien or encumbrance is materially false, fictitious, or fraudulent, the clerk of court may refuse to file the purported lien or encumbrance. Neither the clerk of court nor the clerk's staff shall be liable for filing or the refusal to file a purported lien or encumbrance under this subsection. The clerk of superior court shall not file, index, or docket the document against the property until that document is approved by any judge of the judicial district having subject matter jurisdiction for filing by the clerk of superior court. If the judge determines that the filing is not false, the clerk shall index the claim of lien. A lien or encumbrance filed upon order of the court under this subsection shall have a priority interest as of the date and time of indexing by the clerk of superior court. If the court finds that there is no statutory or contractual basis for the proposed filing, the court shall enter an order that the proposed filing is null and void as a matter of law, and that it shall not be filed or indexed. The clerk of superior court shall serve the order and return the original denied filing to the person or entity that presented it. The person or entity shall have 30 days from the entry of the order to appeal the order. If the order is not appealed within the applicable time period, the clerk may destroy the filing.

(c) Upon being presented with an order duly issued by a court of competent jurisdiction of this State declaring that a lien or encumbrance already recorded or filed is false, and therefore null and void as a matter of law, the register of deeds or clerk of court that received the recording or filing, in addition to recording or filing the court's order finding the lien or encumbrance to be false, shall conspicuously mark on the first page of the original record previously filed the following statement: "THE CLAIM ASSERTED IN THIS DOCUMENT IS FALSE AND IS NOT PROVIDED FOR BY THE GENERAL LAWS OF THIS STATE."

(d) In addition to any criminal penalties provided for in this section, the presentation of an instrument for recording or filing with a register of deeds or clerk of superior court that purports to be a lien or encumbrance that is determined to be materially false, fictitious, or fraudulent shall constitute a violation of G.S. 75-1.1.

(e) Subsections (b), (b1), and (c) of this section shall not apply to filings under Article 9 of Chapter 25 of the General Statutes or under Chapter 44A of the General Statutes.

Elements

As a result of the 2019 legislative changes noted above, the elements of this offense should read as follows:

A person guilty of this offense

(1) presents for filing in a public record or a private record generally available to the public
(2) a false lien or encumbrance
(3) against the real or personal property of an owner or beneficial interest holder
(4) knowing or having reason to know that the lien or encumbrance is false or contains a materially false, fictitious, or fraudulent statement or representation.

Punishment

Class I felony. G.S. 14-118.6(a).

Notes

Element (3) generally. For the definition of the term "real property," see the note on Element (3) to "Injury to Real Property" in Chapter 18 (Trespass, Property Damage, and Littering) of the main volume. For the definition of the term "personal property," see the note on Element (3) to "Injury to Personal Property," also in Chapter 18 of the main volume.

Element (3)(b). The term "immediate family member" means a spouse or child. G.S. 14-118.6(a).

Related Offenses Not in This Chapter

No docketing of lien unless authorized by statute. G.S. 44A-12.1.

Residential Mortgage Fraud (page 433)

Statute (page 433)

2012 legislation, S.L. 2012-150, sec. 5, amended G.S. 14-118.12, adding a new subsection, (a)(5), as follows:

> (5) Knowingly files in a public record or a private record generally available to the public a document falsely claiming that a mortgage loan has been satisfied, discharged, released, revoked, or terminated or is invalid.

Elements (page 434)

As a result of the 2012 legislation noted above, a new Element, (3)(d), should be added to this offense as follows:

> (d) knowingly files in a public or private record generally available to the public a document falsely claiming that a mortgage loan has been satisfied, discharged, released, revoked, or terminated or is invalid.

Related Offenses Not in This Chapter (page 435)

Add the following offenses to this list:

Simulation of court process in connection with collection of claim, demand or account. G.S. 14-118.1.
Bank fraud. G.S. 53C-8-11.

Forgery and Related Offenses (page 435)

Forgery and Counterfeiting of Instruments (page 437)

Notes (page 438)

Relation to other offenses (new note)
Forgery and larceny of a chose in action are not mutually exclusive offenses. State v. Grier, 224 N.C. App. 150, 153 (2012).

Uttering Forged Instruments or Instruments with False Endorsements (page 439)

Notes (page 440)

Element (3) (page 440)
For a case where there was sufficient evidence that a check was falsely made, see *State v. Conley*, 220 N.C. App. 50, 60–61 (2012).

Electronic Food and Nutrition Benefits Fraud (page 456)

Fraudulently Obtaining or Transferring Electronic Food and Nutrition Benefits (page 456)

Notes (page 456)

Element (3) (new note)
The trial court did not err by denying the defendant's motion to dismiss where the evidence showed that the defendant knowingly submitted a fraudulent wage verification form to obtain food benefits to which he was not entitled. State v. Davis, 230 N.C. App. 50, 53–54 (2013).

Computer Fraud (page 461)

Accessing a Government Computer to Defraud or Obtain Property (page 465)

Elements (page 465)

In light of the *Mathis* case discussed in the note on Element (1) immediately below in this supplement, Element (1) should read as follows:

(1) willfully and without authorization

Notes (page 465)

Element (1) (page 465)
G.S. 14-454.1(a) states that the defendant must act willfully. Case law, however, has interpreted the statute to require that the defendant act both willfully and without authorization. State v. Mathis, 261 N.C. App. 263 (2018). G.S. 14-453(1a) defines "authorization" for purposes of computer-related crime to mean "having the consent or permission of the owner, or of the person licensed or authorized by the owner to grant consent or permission to access a computer, computer system, or computer network in a manner not exceeding the consent or permission."

For cases where this Element was satisfied, see *Mathis*, 261 N.C. App. at 278–79 (although the defendant had authorization to use the computer system, he exceeded that authorization by inputting fraudulent information), and *State v. Barr*, 218 N.C. App. 329, 336–40 (2012) (involving transfers of title by the defendant's license plate agency for an unlicensed company).

Element (2) (page 465)
For a case where the evidence was sufficient to establish that the defendant accessed or caused another to access a government computer, see *Mathis*, 261 N.C. App. at 278 (the defendant's unique user name and password were used to access the database and his email was used to submit reports; even if the defendant only transmitted information that was then uploaded by government personnel, the evidence was sufficient because the statute covers causing a government computer to be accessed).

Element (4)(b) (new note)
The evidence was sufficient to sustain a conviction under G.S. 14-454.1(a)(2) where the State alleged that the defendant, who worked for a private license plate agency, submitted false information into the State Title and Registration System (STARS) so that a car dealer whose dealer number was invalid could transfer title. The defendant admitted that she personally accessed STARS to make three transfers for the dealer, that she told a co-worker to run a fourth transaction in a similar fashion, and that she received payment for doing so. *Barr*, 218 N.C. App. at 334–35.

Accessing a Government Computer without Authorization (page 466)

Notes (page 466)

Element (2) (new note)

For a definition of the term "authorization," see the note on Element (1) to "Accessing a Government Computer to Defraud or Obtain Property," above in this supplement.

Accessing Testing Material in a Government Computer (page 467)

Notes (page 467)

Element (2) (new note)

For a definition of the term "authorization," see the note on Element (1) to "Accessing a Government Computer to Defraud or Obtain Property," above in this supplement.

Willful Failure to File a State Tax Return, Supply State Tax Information, or Pay State Tax (page 467)

Related Offenses Not in This Chapter (page 468)

Add the following offense to this list:

Possession, transfer, or use of automated sales suppression device. G.S. 14-118.7.

17

Arson and Burning Offenses

Arson Offenses (page 471)

First-Degree Arson (page 471)

Notes (page 471)

Element (1) (page 471)

Delete the second sentence of this note and replace it with the following:

As used for arson, these terms mean that the act was done "voluntarily and without excuse or justification and without any bona fide claim of right." State v. White, 288 N.C. 44, 50 (1975); State v. Eubanks, 83 N.C. App. 338, 339 (1986). An intent or animus against either the property or its owner is not required. *White*, 288 N.C. at 50; *Eubanks*, 83 N.C. App. at 339.

Add the following at the end of this note:

The evidence was sufficient to establish malice where, among other things, the defendant was enraged at the property owner for evicting him. State v. Burton, 224 N.C. App. 120, 126 (2012).

Burning Offenses (page 474)

Burning during Commission of Felony (new crime)

2018 legislation, S.L. 2018-31, sec. 1, enacted this new crime.

Statute

§ 14-67.2. Burning caused during commission of another felony.

(a) If any person, during the commission of a felony, knowingly damages any dwelling, structure, building, or conveyance referenced in this Article by means of fire or explosive that results in damages valued at ten thousand dollars ($10,000) or more, the person shall be punished as a Class D felon unless the person's conduct is covered under some other provision of law providing greater punishment.

(b) If any person, during the commission of a felony, knowingly causes, aids, abets, advises, encourages, hires, counsels, or procures another person to damage any dwelling, structure, building, or conveyance referenced in this Article by means of fire or explosive that results in damages valued at ten thousand dollars ($10,000) or more, the person shall be punished as a Class D felon unless the person's conduct is covered under some other provision of law providing greater punishment.

Elements

A person guilty of this offense

(1) during the commission of a felony
(2) knowingly
(3) damages any dwelling, structure, building, or conveyance
(4) by means of fire or explosive *and*
(5) causes damages of $10,000 or more.

Punishment

Class D felony. G.S. 14-67.2(a).

Notes

Element (2)

See "Knowingly" in Chapter 1 (States of Mind) of the main volume.

Aiding and abetting, soliciting, etc.

The statute includes a special offense for aiders and abettors, those who solicit this activity, etc. Specifically, it provides that any person who, during the commission of a felony, knowingly causes, aids, abets, advises, encourages, hires, counsels, or procures another person to damage any dwelling, structure, building, or conveyance by means of fire or explosive that results in damages of $10,000 or more shall be punished as a Class D felon unless the person's conduct is covered under some other provision of law providing greater punishment. G.S. 14-67.2(b). This provision duplicates the general rule that those who aid and abet a crime are punished as if they committed that crime, see "Aiding and Abetting" in Chapter 3 (Participants in Crime) of the main volume, and overrides the general rule that solicitation is punished two classes lower than the felony solicited. See "Solicitation" in Chapter 5 (General Crimes) in the main volume.

Multiple convictions and punishments

A person may not be punished for this offense if the conduct is covered by another crime that carries a more severe punishment. G.S. 14-67.2(a). See this note to "Assault Inflicting Serious Injury" (Chapter 7) in the main volume.

Arson or Burning Causing Serious Bodily Injury to Firefighter, Law Enforcement Officer, Fire Investigator, or EMT (page 482) (revised title)

2018 legislation, S.L. 2018-31, sec. 2, amended the statute as described here.

Statute (page 482)

The 2018 legislation noted above amended the statute to read as follows:

§ 14-69.3. Arson or other unlawful burning that results in serious bodily injury to a firefighter, law enforcement officer, fire investigator, or emergency medical technician.

(a) The following definitions apply in this section:

(1) Emergency medical technician.—The term includes an emergency medical technician, an emergency medical technician-intermediate, and an emergency medical technician-paramedic, as those terms are defined in G.S. 131E-155.

(2) Fire investigator.—The term includes any person who, individually or as part of an investigative team, has the responsibility and authority to determine the origin, cause, or development of a fire or explosion.

(b) A person is guilty of a Class E felony if the person commits a felony under Article 15 of Chapter 14 of the General Statutes and a firefighter, law enforcement officer, fire investigator, or emergency medical technician suffers serious bodily injury while discharging or attempting to discharge official duties on the property, or proximate to the property, that is the subject of the firefighter's, law enforcement officer's, fire investigator's, or emergency medical technician's discharge or attempt to discharge his or her respective duties.

Elements (page 482)

As a result of the 2018 legislation noted above, elements (2) and (4) should read as follows:

(2) a firefighter, law enforcement officer, fire investigator, or emergency medical technician

. . .

(4) while discharging or attempting to discharge his or her official duties

Notes (page 482)

Element (2) (page 482)

As a result of the 2018 legislation noted above, the citation listed in this note should read as follows:

G.S. 14-69.3(a)(1).

As a result of the 2018 legislation noted above, add the following to this note:

The term "fire investigator" means any person who, individually or as part of an investigative team, has the responsibility and authority to determine the origin, cause, or development of a fire or explosion. G.S. 14-69.3(a)(2).

Setting Fire Offenses (page 483)

Setting Fire to Woods and Fields (page 483)

Statute (page 483)

2015 legislation, S.L. 2015-263, sec. 36(a), amended the statute, replacing "Department of Environmental Quality" with "Department of Agriculture and Consumer Services."

Elements (page 483)

As a result of the 2015 legislative change noted above, Element (4) should read as follows:

(4) in any county that is under the protection of the Department of Agriculture and Consumer Services in its work of forest fire control.

18

Trespass, Property Damage, and Littering

Trespass Offenses (page 489)

First-Degree Trespass (page 489)

Statute (page 489)

G.S. 14-159.12 has been amended, see S.L. 2012-168, sec. 1; S.L. 2014-103, sec. 10(a); S.L. 2016-26, sec. 1; S.L. 2018-66, to read as follows:

§ 14-159.12. First degree trespass.

(a) Offense.—A person commits the offense of first degree trespass if, without authorization, he enters or remains:

(1) On premises of another so enclosed or secured as to demonstrate clearly an intent to keep out intruders;

(2) In a building of another; or

(3) On the lands of the Eastern Band of Cherokee Indians after the person has been excluded by a resolution passed by the Eastern Band of Cherokee Indian Tribal Council.

(b) Except as otherwise provided in subsection (c), (d), or (f) of this section, first degree trespass is a Class 2 misdemeanor.

(c) Except as otherwise provided in subsection (d) of this section, a violation of subsection (a) of this section is a Class A1 misdemeanor if all of the following circumstances exist:

(1) The offense is committed on the premises of any of the following:

a. A facility that is owned or operated by an electric power supplier as defined in G.S. 62-133.8(a)(3) and that is either an electric generation facility, a transmission substation, a transmission switching station, a transmission switching structure, or a control center used to manage transmission operations or electrical power generating at multiple plant locations.

b. Any facility used or available for use in the collection, treatment, testing, storing, pumping, or distribution of water for a public water system.

c. Any facility, including any liquefied natural gas storage facility or propane air facility, that is owned or operated by a natural gas local distribution company, natural gas pipeline carrier operating under a certificate of public convenience and necessity from the Utilities Commission, municipal corporation operating a municipally owned gas distribution system, or regional natural gas district organized and operated pursuant to Article 28 of Chapter 160A of the General Statutes used for transmission, distribution, measurement, testing, regulating, compression, control, or storage of natural gas.

d. Any facility used or operated for agricultural activities, as that term is defined in G.S. 106-581.1.

(2) The person actually entered a building, or it was necessary for the person to climb over, go under, or otherwise surmount a fence or other barrier to reach the facility.

(d) If, in addition to the circumstances set out in subsection (c) of this section, the violation also includes any of the following elements, then the offense is a Class H felony:

(1) The offense is committed with the intent to disrupt the normal operation of any of the facilities described in subdivision (1) of subsection (c) of this section.

(2) The offense involves an act that places either the offender or others on the premises at risk of serious bodily injury.

(e) As used in subsections (c) and (d) of this section, the term "facility" shall mean a building or other infrastructure.

(f) A violation of subsection (a) of this section is a Class I felony and shall include a fine of not less than one thousand dollars ($1,000) for each violation, if any of the following circumstances exist:

(1) The offense occurs on real property where the person has reentered after having previously been removed pursuant to the execution of a valid order or writ for possession.

(2) The offense occurs under color of title where the person has knowingly created or provided materially false evidence of an ownership or possessory interest.

(3) The offense is the person's second or subsequent violation of subdivision (a) (3) of this section.

Elements (page 489)

As a result of 2018 legislation, S.L. 2018-66, Element (3) should read as follows:

(3) (a) on premises of another so enclosed or secured as to demonstrate clearly an intent to keep out intruders,

(b) in a building of another, *or*

(c) on the lands of the Eastern Band of Cherokee Indians.

Punishment (page 489)

The offense is elevated to a Class A1 misdemeanor if (1) it is committed on the premises of certain electric power supplier facilities, public water system facilities, liquefied natural gas storage or propane air facilities, or agricultural facilities and (2) the defendant entered a building or it was necessary to climb over, go under, or surmount a fence or barrier to reach the facility. G.S. 14-159.12(c).

The offense is elevated to a Class H felony if, in addition to the circumstances required for the Class A1 misdemeanor version of the offense, it is committed with the intent to disrupt the normal operation of the facility or involves an act that puts either the offender or those on the premises at risk of serious bodily injury. G.S. 14-159.12(d).

The offense is elevated to a Class I felony, with a mandatory fine of not less than $1,000 for each violation, if it occurs on real property where the defendant has reentered after having previously been removed pursuant to the execution of a valid order or writ for possession; occurs under color of title where the defendant has knowingly created or provided materially false evidence of an ownership or possessory interest; or is a second or subsequent trespass by the defendant on lands of the Eastern Band of Cherokee Indians after having previously been excluded from those lands. G.S. 14-159.12(f).

Whenever the elevated version of this offense is charged, the relevant facts must be alleged in the charging instrument and proved to the jury beyond a reasonable doubt.

Notes (page 489)

Element (1) (page 489)
For the Element (3)(c) version of this offense, the entity withdrawing authorization is very specific; the statute provides that the person must have been excluded from the lands by a resolution passed by the Eastern Band of Cherokee Indian Tribal Council. G.S. 14-159.12(a)(3).

Element (2) (page 490)
As a general rule, a person who enters premises open to the public has implied consent to remain there. State v. Nickens, 262 N.C. App. 353 (2018). However, that implied consent is revoked if the person does some act rendering the implied consent void or if someone with authority asks the person to leave. *Id.* (implied consent to remain was revoked when the defendant was told to leave a DMV office).

Greater and lesser-included offenses (page 490)
For another case supporting the statement in this note that first-degree trespass is a lesser-included offense of felony breaking or entering, see *State v. Lucas*, 234 N.C. App. 247, 256 (2014).

Related Offenses Not in This Chapter (page 490)

Add the following offenses to this list:

Felony taking of Venus flytrap. G.S. 14-129.3.
Trespass on utility facility. G.S. 14-159.12(c), (d).
Unlawful distribution of images taken through use of unmanned aircraft system. G.S. 14-401.25.
Use of an unmanned aircraft system near a confinement or correctional facility. G.S. 15A-300.3, *as enacted by* S.L. 2017-179.

Domestic Criminal Trespass (page 492)

Notes (page 493)

Element (1) (new note)
For a case where the evidence was sufficient to establish that the defendant was forbidden to enter the victim's residence, see *State v. Vetter*, 257 N.C. App. 915, 924 (2018) (the victim ended her relationship with the defendant and ordered him to leave her residence; two months later, she discovered the defendant in her driveway and reaffirmed that he was not allowed inside the house by locking the door and activating the alarm system; this conduct served to prevent the defendant from entering the residence and functioned as a prohibition against him doing so; the court rejected the defendant's argument that he was never forbidden from entering the residence because the victim "never expressly prohibited him from doing so"; the court also rejected the defendant's argument that by giving him permission to enter the garage to collect his belongings, the victim consented to his entry into the entire premises, including the interior of the residence; the court noted that although the victim gave the defendant limited permission to enter the garage to collect his things, her consent never extended to the inside of the residence).

Element (4) (page 493)
The victim need not be physically present at the premises when the conduct occurs. *Vetter*, 257 N.C. App. at 926 (rejecting the defendant's argument that because the victim was not physically present when he entered her home the premises were not "occupied").

Related Offenses Not in This Chapter (page 493)

The citation to the last item in this list should read as follows:

G.S. 14-269.8; 50B-3.1(j).

Injury to Property Offenses (page 495)

Injury to Real Property (page 495)

Notes (page 495)

Element (3) (page 495)

An air conditioning unit attached to the exterior of a mobile home was real property where it was affixed in a manner such that it "became an irremovable part of" the home and attached to the home for the use and enjoyment of the home's renter. State v. Hardy, 242 N.C. App. 146, 157 (2015).

Related Offenses Not in This Chapter (page 495)

Add the following offenses to this list:

Graffiti vandalism. G.S. 14-127.1.
Felony taking of Venus flytrap. G.S. 14-129.3.
Cutting, mutilating, defacing, or injuring property to obtain nonferrous metals. G.S. 14-159.4.

Defacing a Public Building, Statue, or Monument (page 496)

Statute (page 496)

2014 legislation, S.L. 2014-100, sec. 17.1(w), amended G.S. 14-132(c)(3) to read as follows:

(3) Designated by the Director of the State Bureau of Investigation in accordance with G.S. 143B-987.

2015 legislation, S.L. 2015-72, sec. 2, amended G.S. 14-132(d) to read as follows:

(d) Unless the conduct is covered under some other provision of law providing greater punishment, any person who violates any provision of this section is guilty of a Class 2 misdemeanor.

Notes (page 497)

Multiple convictions and punishments (new note)

The "[u]nless the conduct is covered" language added to the punishment provision in 2015 means that a defendant may not be punished for this offense and one that carries a more severe punishment.

Related Offenses Not in This Chapter (page 497)

Add the following offenses to this list:

Graffiti vandalism. G.S. 14-127.1.
Interfering with gas, water, or electric meters. G.S. 14-151.
Cutting, mutilating, defacing, or injuring property to obtain nonferrous metals. G.S. 14-159.4.

Injury to Personal Property (page 497)

Notes (page 497)

Element (1) (page 497)

For a case where the evidence was insufficient with respect to this Element, see *State v. Bradsher*, 255 N.C. App. 625, 633 (2017) (the property in question was appliances, owned by the defendant's landlord, that the defendant was alleged to have damaged while moving them from one home to another).

Related Offenses Not in This Chapter (page 498)

Add the following offenses to this list:

Damaging or contaminating waste kitchen grease or container. G.S. 14-79.2.
Cutting, mutilating, defacing, or injuring property to obtain nonferrous metals. G.S. 14-159.4.
Injuring, tampering with, removing, etc. firefighting or emergency medical services machinery or equipment. G.S. 14-160.3, *as enacted by* S.L. 2017-89.

Littering (page 500)

Elements (page 503)

As a result of *State v. Rankin*, 371 N.C. 885 (2018), Element (6) should read as follows:

(6) the property has not been designated by the state or a political subdivision for the disposal of garbage and refuse, and the person is not authorized to use the property for this purpose.

Notes (page 503)

Element (6) (page 504)

The text of this note opines that the provision in G.S. 14-399(a)(1)—that the property has not been designated for the disposal of garbage and refuse by the state or a political subdivision—is likely to be deemed an element of the offense and not an exception. The state supreme court has now held that to be so. *Rankin*, 371 N.C. 885.

19

Disorderly Conduct, Riot, and Gang Offenses

Drunk and Disruptive (page 507)

Statute (page 507)

2015 legislation, S.L. 2015-247, sec. 3(c), amended subsection (b) of the statute to read as follows:

> (b) Any person who violates this section shall be guilty of a Class 3 misdemeanor.

Notes (page 508)

Guilty pleas (page 508)

As a result of the 2015 legislation noted above, delete this note.

Disorderly Conduct (page 508)

Statute (page 508)

2012 legislation, S.L. 2012-12, sec. 2(b), amended G.S. 14-288.4(a)(4)c. to read as follows:

> c. If an emergency is occurring or is imminent within the institution, an order given by any law-enforcement officer acting within the scope of the officer's authority.

2013 legislation, S.L. 2013-6, sec. 1, amended G.S. 14-288.4(a)(8) to read as follows:

> (8) Engages in conduct with the intent to impede, disrupt, disturb, or interfere with the orderly administration of any funeral, memorial service, or family processional to the funeral or memorial service, including a military funeral, service, or family processional, or with the normal activities and functions occurring in the facilities or buildings where a funeral or memorial service, including a military funeral or memorial service, is taking place. Any of the following conduct that occurs within two hours preceding, during, or within two hours after a funeral or memorial service shall constitute disorderly conduct under this subdivision:
>
> a. Displaying, within 500 feet of the ceremonial site, location being used for the funeral or memorial, or the family's processional route to the funeral or memorial service, any visual image that conveys fighting

words or actual or imminent threats of harm directed to any person or property associated with the funeral, memorial service, or processional route.

b. Uttering, within 500 feet of the ceremonial site, location being used for the funeral or memorial service, or the family's processional route to the funeral or memorial service, loud, threatening, or abusive language or singing, chanting, whistling, or yelling with or without noise amplification in a manner that would tend to impede, disrupt, disturb, or interfere with a funeral, memorial service, or processional route.

c. Attempting to block or blocking pedestrian or vehicular access to the ceremonial site or location being used for a funeral or memorial.

That same legislation also amended G.S. 14-288.4(c), the punishment provision of the statute, to make a first offense a Class 1 misdemeanor, a second offense a Class I felony, and a third or subsequent offense a Class H felony.

Disorderly Conduct by Fighting (page 510)

Notes (page 510)

Element (3) (new note)

For a case where the evidence was sufficient as to this Element, see *In re T.T.E.*, 372 N.C. 413 (2019) (a juvenile threw a chair at his brother in the school cafeteria where other students were present).

Related Offenses Not in This Chapter (page 510)

Add the following offenses to this list:

Violating Governor's order during a state of emergency. G.S. 166A-19.30(d); 14-288.20A(2).
Violating county or municipality's ordinance during a state of emergency. G.S. 166A-19.31(h); 14-288.20A(1).
Willfully refusing to leave a public building as directed under a Governor's order. G.S. 14-288.20A(3).

Remove the following offenses from this list:

Violation of state of emergency ordinance. G.S. 14-288.12 through -288.15.
Governor's power to order evacuation of public building. G.S. 14-288.19.
Using profane or indecent language on public highways. G.S. 14-197.

Disorderly Conduct by Disrupting Students (page 513)

Notes (page 513)

Element (1) (new note)

The evidence was sufficient to show that a juvenile acted intentionally where he was described as "very defiant" and he could have avoided the physical contact at issue. *In re* M.J.G., 234 N.C. App. 350, 357–58 (2014).

Element (3) (page 513)

To satisfy this Element the defendant's conduct must constitute "substantial interference" with the teaching of students. *In re* Eller, 331 N.C. 714 (1992). A defendant's conduct was not a substantial interference of the operation of a school when her profanity was overheard by only a small group of students as they walked to class, did not disrupt classroom instruction, and was not accompanied by aggressive or violent behavior. State v. Humphreys, ___ N.C. App. ___, ___ S.E.2d ___ (2020).

For additional cases where the evidence was sufficient as to this Element, see *In re I.W.P.*, 259 N.C. App. 254, 258 (2018) (after repeated encouragement from the juvenile, another student pulled the fire alarm, resulting in chaos on school grounds; the juvenile's actions disrupted, disturbed, and interfered with the teaching of students and disturbed the peace, order, or discipline at the school), and *M.J.G.*, 234 N.C. App. at 360–61 (the juvenile's conduct substantially interfered with the operation of the school where it required intervention by several teachers, the assistant principal, and the school resource officer, and a group of special needs students missed their buses because of the disturbance).

Disorderly Conduct by Disrupting a Funeral (page 515)

Punishment (page 515)

2013 legislation, S.L. 2013-6, changed the punishments for this offense. As a result, delete the text in this section and replace it with the following:

Class 1 misdemeanor for a first offense, Class I felony for a second offense, and Class H felony for a third or subsequent offense. G.S. 14-288.4(c). If an elevated version of this offense is charged, the fact elevating punishment must be alleged in a charging instrument and proved at trial, unless the defendant pleads guilty or no contest to the issue. *See* G.S. 15A-928 (alleging and proving prior convictions).

Notes (page 515)

Element (3) (page 515)

As a result of the 2013 legislation noted above, delete the text of this note and replace it with the following:

The statute expressly includes military funerals and services. G.S. 14-288.4(a)(8). It also provides that any of the following conduct occurring within the time period beginning two hours before the service and ending two hours after the service constitutes disorderly conduct:

- displaying, within 500 feet of the ceremonial site or processional route, any visual image that conveys fighting words or actual or imminent threats of harm directed to any person or property associated with the event or processional route;
- uttering, within 500 feet of the ceremonial site or processional route, loud, threatening, or abusive language or singing, chanting, whistling, or yelling with or without noise amplification in a manner that would tend to impede, disrupt, disturb, or interfere with a funeral, memorial service, or processional route; or
- attempting to block or blocking pedestrian or vehicular access to the ceremonial site or location being used for a funeral or memorial.

Id.

Disorderly Conduct in a Public Building (page 516)

Statute (page 516)

2014 legislation, S.L. 2014-100, sec. 17.1(w), amended G.S. 14-132(c)(3) to read as follows:

(3) Designated by the Director of the State Bureau of Investigation in accordance with G.S. 143B-987.

Notes (page 517)

Constitutionality (new note)

In *State v. Dale*, 245 N.C. App. 497, 508–09 (2016), the court rejected the defendant's void-for-vagueness and as-applied constitutional challenges to a conviction for this offense.

Failure to Disperse on Command (page 526)

Related Offenses Not in This Chapter (page 527)

Add the following offenses to this list:

Violating Governor's order during a state of emergency. G.S. 166A-19.30(d); 14-288.20A(2).
Violating county or municipality's ordinance during a state of emergency. G.S. 166A-19.31(h); 14-288.20A(1).
Willfully refusing to leave a public building as directed under a Governor's order. G.S. 14-288.20A(3).

Remove the following offense from this list:

Transporting dangerous weapon or substance during emergency; possessing off premises. G.S. 14-288.7.

Gang-Related Crimes (page 527)

Statute (page 527)

Because 2017 legislation, S.L. 2017-194, sec. 1, repealed G.S. 14-50.16, delete the statute that is reproduced in this section.

Street Gang Activity (page 528)

Because 2017 legislation, S.L. 2017-194, sec. 1, repealed G.S. 14-50.16, delete this crime.

Organizer of Street Gang Activity (page 529)

Because 2017 legislation, S.L. 2017-194, sec. 1, repealed G.S. 14-50.16, delete this crime.

Soliciting Participation in Criminal Gang Activity (page 530) (revised title)

Statute (page 530)

As a result of 2017 legislation, S.L. 2017-194, secs. 7–8, G.S. 14-50.17 and -50.18 were revised to replace the term "criminal street gang activity" with the term "criminal gang activity."

As a result of that same legislation, S.L. 2017-194, sec. 4, add the following new statute to this section:

§ 14-50.16A. Criminal gang activity.

Definitions.—The following definitions apply in this Article:

(1) Criminal gang.—Any ongoing organization, association, or group of three or more persons, whether formal or informal, that (i) has as one of its primary activities the commission of criminal or delinquent acts and (ii) shares a common name, identification, signs, symbols, tattoos, graffiti, attire, or other distinguishing characteristics, including common activities, customs, or behaviors. The term shall not include three or more persons associated in fact, whether formal or informal, who are not engaged in criminal gang activity.

(2) Criminal gang activity.—The commission of, attempted commission of, or solicitation, coercion, or intimidation of another person to commit (i) any offense under Article 5 of Chapter 90 of the General Statutes or (ii) any

offense under Chapter 14 of the General Statutes except Article 9, 22A, 40, 46, or 59 thereof, and further excepting G.S. 14-82, 14-145, 14-183, 14-184, 14-186, 14-190.9, 14-247, 14-248, or 14-313 thereof, and either of the following conditions is met:

a. The offense is committed with the intent to benefit, promote, or further the interests of a criminal gang or for the purposes of increasing a person's own standing or position within a criminal gang.
b. The participants in the offense are identified as criminal gang members acting individually or collectively to further any criminal purpose of a criminal gang.

[*Subsection (3), defining the term "criminal gang leader or organizer," is not reproduced here.*]

(4) Criminal gang member.—Any person who meets three or more of the following criteria:

a. The person admits to being a member of a criminal gang.
b. The person is identified as a criminal gang member by a reliable source, including a parent or a guardian.
c. The person has been previously involved in criminal gang activity.
d. The person has adopted symbols, hand signs, or graffiti associated with a criminal gang.
e. The person has adopted the display of colors or the style of dress associated with a criminal gang.
f. The person is in possession of or linked to a criminal gang by physical evidence, including photographs, ledgers, rosters, written or electronic communications, or membership documents.
g. The person has tattoos or markings associated with a criminal gang.
h. The person has adopted language or terminology associated with a criminal gang.
i. The person appears in any form of social media to promote a criminal gang.

Elements (page 530)

As a result of the 2017 legislation noted above, Element (3) of this offense should be revised to read as follows:

(3) to participate in criminal gang activity.

Notes (page 530)

As a result of the 2017 legislation noted above, delete the notes included in this section and replace them with the following:

Element (3). The term "criminal gang activity" is defined in G.S. 14-50.16A(2), reproduced above.

Exception for certain juveniles. G.S. 14-50.28 provides that the criminal gang offenses do not apply to juveniles under the age of 16.

Multiple convictions and punishments. G.S. 14-50.21 provides that every violation of the criminal gang statutes in G.S. 14-50.16 through -50.20 constitutes a separate offense.

Forfeiture. G.S. 14-50.23 provides for seizure and forfeiture of property associated with criminal gang activity.

Public nuisance. G.S. 14-50.42 provides that real property associated with criminal gang activity constitutes a public nuisance and may be abated as provided for in the General Statutes. G.S. 14-50.43 provides that criminal gangs constitute a public nuisance.

Related Offenses Not in This Chapter (page 531)

As a result of the 2017 legislation noted above, delete the first sentence of this section and add the following two offenses to the list:

"Continuing Criminal Enterprise—Non-Drug Offenses" (Chapter 5)
"Continuing Criminal Enterprise—Drug Offenses" (Chapter 27)

Intimidation to Deter or Retaliation for Gang Withdrawal (page 531) (revised title)

Statute (page 531)

2017 legislation, S.L. 2017-194, secs. 9–10, revised the statutes to read as follows:

§ 14-50.19. Intimidation to deter from gang withdrawal.

(a) It is unlawful for any person to communicate a threat of injury to a person, or to damage the property of another, with the intent to deter a person from assisting another to withdraw from membership in a criminal gang.

(a1) It is unlawful for any person to injure a person with the intent to deter a person from assisting another to withdraw from membership in a criminal gang.

(b) A violation of subsection (a) of this section is a Class G felony. A violation of subsection (a1) of this section is a Class F felony.

§ 14-50.20. Punishment or retaliation for gang withdrawal.

(a) It is unlawful for any person to communicate a threat of injury to a person, or to damage the property of another, as punishment or retaliation against a person for having withdrawn from a criminal gang.

(a1) It is unlawful for any person to injure a person as punishment or retaliation against a person for having withdrawn from a criminal gang.

(b) A violation of subsection (a) of this section is a Class G felony. A violation of subsection (a1) of this section is a Class F felony.

Elements (page 531)

As a result of the 2017 legislation noted above, the elements of this offense should read as follows:

A person guilty of this offense

(1) (a) communicates
  (b) a threat of injury to a person or of damage to the property of another
  (c) (i) with the intent to deter a person from assisting another to withdraw from membership in a criminal gang, *or*
    (ii) as punishment or retaliation against a person for having withdrawn from a criminal gang, *or*

(2) (a) injures a person
  (b) (i) with the intent to deter a person from assisting another to withdraw from membership in a criminal gang
    (ii) as punishment or retaliation against a person for having withdrawn from a criminal gang.

Punishment (page 531)

As a result of the 2017 legislation noted above, delete the text of this section and replace it with the following:

A violation of the Element (1) version of this offense is a Class G felony; a violation of the Element (2) version of this offense is a Class F felony. G.S. 14-50.19(b); -50.20(b).

Notes (page 531)

As a result of the 2017 legislation noted above, delete the notes listed for this offense and replace them with the following:

Definition of the term "criminal gang". The term "criminal gang" is defined in new G.S. 14-50.16A(1), reproduced above in this supplement.

Exception for certain juveniles. See this note to "Soliciting Participation in Criminal Gang Activity," above in this supplement.

Multiple convictions and punishments. See this note to "Soliciting Participation in Criminal Gang Activity," above in this supplement.

Forfeiture. See this note to "Soliciting Participation in Criminal Gang Activity," above in this supplement.

Public nuisance. See this note to "Soliciting Participation in Criminal Gang Activity," above in this supplement.

Related Offenses Not in this Chapter (page 531)

As a result of the 2017 legislation noted above, delete the first sentence of this section and replace it with the following:

See the offenses listed under "Soliciting Participation in Criminal Gang Activity," above in this supplement.

Discharging a Firearm as a Part of Criminal Gang Activity (page 532) (revised title)

Statute (page 532)

2017 legislation, S.L. 2017-194, sec. 6, amended the statute to read as follows:

§ 14-34.9. Discharging a firearm from within an enclosure.

Unless covered under some other provision of law providing greater punishment, any person who willfully or wantonly discharges or attempts to discharge a firearm, as a part of criminal gang activity, from within any building, structure, motor vehicle, or other conveyance, erection, or enclosure toward a person or persons not within that enclosure shall be punished as a Class E felon.

Elements (page 532)

As a result of the 2017 legislation noted above, Element (6) of this offense should read as follows:

(6) as a part of criminal gang activity.

Notes (page 532)

Element (6) (page 532)

As a result of the 2017 legislation noted above, delete the text of this note and replace it with the following:

The term "criminal gang activity" and related terms are defined in new G.S. 14-50.16A(2), reproduced under "Soliciting Participation in Criminal Gang Activity," above in this supplement.

Related Offenses Not in This Chapter (page 533)

As a result of the 2017 legislation noted above, delete the first sentence of this section and replace it with the following:

See the offenses listed under "Soliciting Participation in Criminal Gang Activity," above in this supplement.

20 Bombing, Terrorism, and Related Offenses

Terrorism (new crime)

This offense was enacted by 2012 legislation. S.L. 2012-38.

Statute

§ 14-10.1. Terrorism.

(a) As used in this section, the term "act of violence" means a violation of G.S. 14-17; a felony punishable pursuant to G.S. 14-18; any felony offense in this Chapter that includes an assault, or use of violence or force against a person; any felony offense that includes either the threat or use of any explosive or incendiary device; or any offense that includes the threat or use of a nuclear, biological, or chemical weapon of mass destruction.

(b) A person is guilty of the separate offense of terrorism if the person commits an act of violence with the intent to do either of the following:

(1) Intimidate the civilian population at large, or an identifiable group of the civilian population.

(2) Influence, through intimidation, the conduct or activities of the government of the United States, a state, or any unit of local government.

(c) A violation of this section is a felony that is one class higher than the offense which is the underlying act of violence, except that a violation is a Class B1 felony if the underlying act of violence is a Class A or Class B1 felony offense. A violation of this section is a separate offense from the underlying offense and shall not merge with other offenses.

(d) All real and personal property of every kind used or intended for use in the course of, derived from, or realized through an offense punishable pursuant to this Article shall be subject to lawful seizure and forfeiture to the State as set forth in G.S. 14-2.3 and G.S. 14-7.20. However, the forfeiture of any real or personal property shall be subordinate to any security interest in the property taken by a lender in good faith as collateral for the extension of credit and recorded as provided by law, and no real or personal property shall be forfeited under this section against an owner who made a bona fide purchase of the property, or a person with rightful possession of the property, without knowledge of a violation of this Article.

Elements

A person guilty of this offense

(1) commits an act of violence
(2) with the intent to
  (a) intimidate the civilian population, or an identifiable group of the civilian population, *or*
  (b) influence, through intimidation, a government's conduct or activities.

Punishment

This offense is punished as a felony that is one class higher than the offense that constitutes the underlying act of violence, except that a violation is a Class B1 felony if the underlying act of violence is a Class A or B1 felony. G.S. 14-10.1(c).

Notes

Element (1). G.S. 14-10.1(a) defines the term "act of violence" to include

- murder under G.S. 14-17;
- manslaughter under G.S. 14-18;
- any G.S. Chapter 14 felony that includes an assault or use of violence or force against a person;
- any felony that includes either the threat or use of any explosive or incendiary device; and
- any offense that includes the threat or use of a nuclear, biological, or chemical weapon of mass destruction.

The statute does not define the phrase "explosive or incendiary device". That term is defined in two other statutory provisions, but it is not clear which of these definitions is meant to apply to this offense. Specifically, G.S. 14-50.1 defines an "explosive or incendiary device or material" as including "nitroglycerine, dynamite, gunpowder, other high explosive, incendiary bomb or grenade, other destructive incendiary device, or any other destructive incendiary or explosive device, compound, or formulation; any instrument or substance capable of being used for destructive explosive or incendiary purposes against persons or property, when the circumstances indicate some probability that such instrument or substance will be so used; or any explosive or incendiary part or ingredient in any instrument or substance included above, when the circumstances indicate some probability that such part or ingredient will be so used." G.S. 14-72(b)(3) defines an "explosive or incendiary device or substance" as "any explosive or incendiary grenade or bomb; any dynamite, blasting powder, nitroglycerin, TNT, or other high explosive; or any device, ingredient for such device, or type or quantity of substance primarily useful for large-scale destruction of property by explosive or incendiary action or lethal injury to persons by explosive or incendiary action." That section further provides that the definition does not include "fireworks; or any form, type, or quantity of gasoline, butane gas, natural gas, or any other substance having explosive or incendiary properties but serving a legitimate non-destructive or nonlethal use in the form, type, or quantity stolen." G.S. 14-72(b)(3).

Presumably the phrase "any offense that includes the threat or use of a nuclear, biological, or chemical weapon of mass destruction" refers to the nuclear, biological, or chemical weapon of mass destruction offenses in G.S. 14-288.21 through -288.24.

Element (2)(b). The governments covered include the federal government, any state government, and any unit of local government. G.S. 14-10.1(b)(2).

Multiple convictions and punishments. A defendant may be convicted and punished for both this offense and the underlying offense that constitutes the act of violence. G.S. 14-10.1(c).

Seizure and forfeiture of property. All real and personal property used or intended for use in the course of, derived from, or realized through this offense is subject to seizure and forfeiture pursuant to G.S. 14-2.3 and 14-7.20. G.S. 14-10.1(d). However, the forfeiture is subordinate to any security interest in the property taken by a lender in good faith as collateral for the extension of credit and recorded as provided by law. *Id.* Also, no property may be forfeited against an owner who made a bona fide purchase of it, or against a person with rightful possession of the property, without knowledge of the criminal violation. *Id.*

Related Offenses Not in This Chapter

"Riot" (Chapter 19)
"Gang-Related Crimes" (Chapter 19)

Malicious Damage by Use of Explosives or Incendiaries (page 537)

Malicious Damage to Occupied Property by Use of an Explosive or Incendiary (page 537)

Related Offenses Not in This Chapter (page 538)

Add the following offenses to this list:

Interference with manned aircraft by unmanned aircraft systems. G.S. 14-280.3.
Transporting dangerous weapon or substance during emergency; possessing off premises. G.S. 14-288.7.
Unlawful possession and use of unmanned aircraft systems. G.S. 14-401.24.

Perpetrating a Hoax by Use of a False Bomb or Other Device (page 543)

Perpetrating a Hoax in or at a Public Building (page 543)

Notes (page 543)

Element (1) (new note)
For a case where there was sufficient evidence that the defendant intended to perpetrate a hoax with a false bomb, see *State v. Golden*, 224 N.C. App. 136, 147 (2012).

Element (2) (new note)
For a case where there was sufficient evidence that the defendant placed or concealed a false bomb in his vehicle, see *Golden*, 224 N.C. App. at 146.

Making a False Report Concerning Mass Violence on Educational Property (page 544)

Notes (page 545)

Element (1) (page 545)
Mere uttering or writing a statement is not necessarily a report. A message not directed to or seen by anyone in particular is not a report within the meaning of this offense. Only credible reports—those that a reasonable person would believe could represent a threat—are covered. *In re* D.W.L.B., 267 N.C. App. 392 (2019) (offense not committed based on school bathroom graffiti because "no one would reasonably believe that the words 'BOMB INCOMING,' written in a bathroom at some unknown time in the past and obviously by an elementary-school-aged student, represented a report of an actual threat that a bomb was incoming to the school").

Element (3) (page 545)
The words "bomb incoming" could reasonably be construed as something that could cause mass violence. *D.W.L.B.*, 267 N.C. App. at 392.

Threat of Mass Violence on Educational Property or Place of Worship (new crime)

2018 legislation, S.L. 2018-72, secs. 1, 2, enacted this new crime.

Statute

§ 14-277.6. Communicating a threat of mass violence on educational property.

(a) A person who, by any means of communication to any person or groups of persons, threatens to commit an act of mass violence on educational property or at a curricular or extracurricular activity sponsored by a school is guilty of a Class H felony.

(b) The definitions in G.S. 14-277.5 apply to this section.

§ 14-277.7. Communicating a threat of mass violence at a place of religious worship.

(a) A person who, by any means of communication to any person or groups of persons, threatens to commit an act of mass violence at a place of religious worship is guilty of a Class H felony.

(b) The following definitions apply to this section:

(1) Mass violence.—As defined in G.S. 14-277.5(a)(2).

(2) Place of religious worship.—Any church, chapel, meetinghouse, synagogue, temple, longhouse, or mosque, or other building that is regularly used, and clearly identifiable, as a place for religious worship.

Elements

A person guilty of this offense

(1) communicates

(2) to any person or groups of persons

(3) a threat to commit an act of mass violence

(4) (a) on educational property or at a school-sponsored activity *or*

(b) at a place of religious worship.

Punishment

Class H felony. G.S. 14-277.6; -277.7.

Notes

Element (1)

The threat may be communicated "by any means." G.S. 14-277.6(a); -277.7(a).

Element (3)

Because the statutes define "mass violence" by cross-reference to G.S. 14-277.5, see the note on Element (3) to "Making a False Report Concerning Mass Violence on Educational Property" in Chapter 20 (Bombing, Terrorism, and Related Offenses) of the main volume for a definition of that term. The words "bomb incoming" could reasonably be construed as something that could cause mass violence. *In re* D.W.L.B., 267 N.C. App. 392 (2019).

Element (4)(a)

The school-sponsored activity may be a curricular or extracurricular activity. G.S. 14-277.6(a).

Because the statute defines the terms "educational property" and "school" by cross-reference to G.S. 14-277.5, see the note on Element (5) to "Making a False Report Concerning Mass Violence on Educational Property" in Chapter 20 of the main volume for definitions of those terms.

Element (4)(b)

The term "place of religious worship" means any church, chapel, meetinghouse, synagogue, temple, longhouse, mosque, or other building regularly used and clearly identifiable as a place for religious worship. G.S. 14-277.7(b)(2).

Related Offenses Not in This Chapter

"Assault on a Child under 12" in Chapter 7 (Assaults)
"Assault on School Personnel" in Chapter 7 (Assaults)
"Ethnic Intimidation" in Chapter 7 (Assaults)
"Communicating Threats" in Chapter 8 (Threats, Harassment, Stalking, and Violation of Domestic Protective Orders)
"Breaking or Entering a Place of Worship" in Chapter 15 (Burglary, Breaking or Entering, and Related Offenses)
"Burning a Schoolhouse" in Chapter 17 (Arson and Burning Offenses)
"Burning a Church or Other Religious Building" in Chapter 17 (Arson and Burning Offenses)
Various disorderly conduct offenses involving schools, students, religious services and assemblies, and funerals in Chapter 19 (Disorderly Conduct, Riot, and Gang Offenses)
Various offenses involving possession of weapons or explosives on school grounds in Chapter 22 (Weapons Offenses)
"Discharging a Firearm on School Grounds" in Chapter 22 (Weapons Offenses)

Manufacture, Possession, etc. of a Machine Gun, Sawed-Off Shotgun, or Weapon of Mass Destruction (page 550)

Notes (page 552)

Element (2) (page 552)

A flash-bang grenade is a weapon of mass death and destruction within the meaning of this offense. State v. Carey, 373 N.C. 445 (2020).

Exceptions (page 553)

For example, the law exempts "[p]ersons under contract with the United States, the State of North Carolina, or any agency of either government, with respect to any activities lawfully engaged in under their contracts." G.S. 14-288.8(b)(3). A trial court erred by not giving a jury instruction on that exception for a defendant who presented evidence that he was on active duty in the Marine Corps and possessed and transported flash-bang grenades with his command's knowledge and consent. State v. Carey, ___ N.C. App. ___, 849 S.E.2d 111 (2020).

21
Perjury, Bribery, Obstruction, Resisting, and Related Crimes

Obstruction of Justice (page 557)

Punishment (page 557)

For an additional case supporting the statement in this note that the offense is a Class H felony if done with deceit and intent to defraud, see *State v. Mitchell*, 259 N.C. App. 866 (2018). *See also* State v. Ditenhafer, ___ N.C. App. ___, 840 S.E.2d 850 (2020) (the defendant acted with deceit and intent to defraud when she encouraged her daughter to lie to investigators about sexual abuse committed by the defendant's husband and took other steps to frustrate the investigation into the abuse).

Notes (page 557)

Element (2) (page 557)

Add the following at the end of the bulleted list in this note:

- making false statements to law enforcement officers about a crime under investigation. State v. Cousin, 233 N.C. App. 523, 530–31 (2014) (the defendant gave eight different written statements to authorities, providing a wide array of scenarios surrounding the victim's death and identifying four different individuals as being the perpetrator; he also admitted that he had been untruthful to investigators).
- pressuring a victim to recant. *State v. Ditenhafer*, 258 N.C. App. 537, 548–49 (2018) (the defendant pressured her daughter to recant statements regarding sexual abuse where, among other things, the defendant directed her daughter to recant and, when she refused, the defendant punished her, verbally abused her, and turned immediate family members against her, even after admitting to others that she believed the abuse occurred; and the defendant coached her daughter on what to say in person, on the telephone, and in emails in order to recant), *aff'd in part and rev'd in part on other grounds*, 373 N.C. 116 (2019).
- a parent denying authorities access to a child to investigate crimes committed against the child. *Ditenhafer*, 373 N.C. at 128 (the defendant was present and "talked over" her daughter in interviews and generally "successfully induced [the daughter] to refuse to speak with investigating officers and social workers").

There was insufficient evidence that the defendant obstructed justice when one of his statements to the SBI was "at most misleading, and not false," and another of his statements, while false, did not actually impede the course of the investigation. State v. Bradsher, ___ N.C. App. ___, 852 S.E.2d 716 (2020).

Relation to other offenses (page 558)

Add the following to the last paragraph of this note:

Likewise, the codification of the offense of accessory after the fact to a felony did not abrogate this common law offense. State v. Cruz, ___ N.C. App. ___, 845 S.E.2d 199 (2020).

Multiple convictions and punishments (new note)

No double jeopardy violation occurred when the trial court sentenced the defendant for felony obstruction of justice and accessory after the fact to murder arising out of the same conduct. *Cousin*, 233 N.C. App. at 535–37 (reasoning that each offense contains an element not in the other); *Cruz*, ___ N.C. App. ___, 845 S.E.2d 199 (same).

Interfering with Witnesses (page 558)

Intimidating a Witness (page 559)

Notes (page 559)

Element (1) (page 559)

For a case where there was sufficient evidence that a defendant charged with rape threatened the victim, see *State v. Barnett*, 245 N.C. App. 101, 106–07 (among other things, on the day of the incident the defendant threatened to kill the victim if she called the police and subsequently sent her a letter stating, "What did I tell you, [*sic*] would happen, if you took charges; [*sic*] out on me? You remember what I told you. And I'ma [*sic*] stand by my word. Because you knew not to press charges or go to the hospital. You knew better then [*sic*] that."), *rev'd in part on other grounds*, 369 N.C. 298 (2016).

Element (2) (page 559)

In *State v. Shannon*, 230 N.C. App. 583, 586 (2013), the court of appeals held that the statute applied to a person who is a prospective witness but who has not been formally summoned. *See also* State v. Jones, 237 N.C. App. 526, 533–35 (2014) (trial court did not err by instructing the jury that "it is immaterial that the victim was regularly summoned or legally bound to attend").

The State need not prove the specific court proceeding that the defendant intended to deter the witness from attending. *Barnett*, 245 N.C. App. at 107 (the State need only prove that the witness had been summoned or was acting as a witness in a state court proceeding).

Because the statute covers attempts to intimidate a witness, a defendant may be convicted of this offense even if the victim did not receive the defendant's threatening letters. *Id.* at 108.

Perjury Offenses (page 562)

Perjury (page 562)

Statute (page 562)

2019 legislation, S.L. 2019-243, sec. 3.(c), amended G.S. 14-209 to read as follows, effective for offenses committed on or after December 1, 2019:

§ 14-209. Punishment for perjury.

If any person knowingly and intentionally makes a false statement under oath or affirmation in any suit, controversy, matter or cause, depending in any of the courts of the

State; in any deposition or affidavit taken pursuant to law; in any oath or affirmation duly administered of or concerning any matter or thing where such person is lawfully required to be sworn or affirmed, that person is guilty of perjury, and punished as a Class F felon.

Elements (page 562)

As a result of the 2019 legislation noted above, the elements for this offense should read as follows:

A person guilty of this offense

(1) knowingly and intentionally
(2) while under oath or affirmation
(3) makes a statement
(4) that is false *and*
(5) that is material.

Notes

Element (1) (page 562)

As a result of the 2019 legislation noted above, delete the first sentence of this note and replace it with the following:

Before the statute for this offense was amended in 2019, its reference to perjury committed "willfully and corruptly" was understood to mean knowingly, purposefully, and designedly. N.C. Pattern Jury Instructions—Crim. 228.10.

Element (2) (page 562)

As a result of the 2019 legislation noted above, delete the first sentence of this note and replace it with the following:

The statement may be made "in any suit, controversy, matter or cause, depending in any of the courts of the State; in any deposition or affidavit taken pursuant to law; in any oath or affirmation duly administered of or concerning any matter or thing where such person is lawfully required to be sworn or affirmed." G.S. 14-209.

Related Offenses Not in This Chapter (page 563)

Add the following offenses to this list:

False or fraudulent report by bank examiner. G.S. 53C-8-7.
False reports and statements regarding a bank. G.S. 53C-8-11(a)(5).

Delete the offense listed as "False swearing in fire investigation by Attorney General. G.S. 58-79-10" and replace it with the following:

False swearing in fire investigation by Director of the State Bureau of Investigation. G.S. 58-79-10.

Bribery Offenses (page 564)

Taking or Agreeing to Take a Bribe (page 564)

Related Offenses Not in This Chapter (page 566)

Add the following offense to this list:

Keeping or accepting a bribe by bank examiner. G.S. 53C-8-7.

Resisting, Delaying, or Obstructing an Officer (page 567)

Notes (page 567)

Element (1) (page 567)

For cases where there was sufficient evidence of willfulness, see *State v. Peters*, 255 N.C. App. 382, 388 (2017), *State v. Smith*, 225 N.C. App. 471, 478 (2013), and *State v. Cornell*, 222 N.C. App. 184, 189 (2012).

For a case where the evidence was insufficient as to this Element, see *In re T.T.E.*, 260 N.C. App. 378 (2018) (after a juvenile threw a chair in a school cafeteria and ran out of the room, a school resource officer, without telling the juvenile to stop, snuck up on the juvenile and grabbed him from behind; the juvenile's action in yelling "no" and cursing when the officer grabbed him does not constitute conduct that is willful, unlawful, and without justification or excuse; "[m]ost people would probably have some sort of similar reaction if grabbed from behind without knowing who was grabbing them"), *rev'd in part on other grounds*, 372 N.C. 413 (2019). A defendant did not act willfully and unlawfully within the meaning of this Element when she stood near her car to observe an officer's search of it, saying that she was "breaking no law" by doing so. State v. Humphreys, ___ N.C. App. ___, ___ S.E.2d ___ (2020).

Element (2) (page 567)

Add the following at the end of the first full paragraph on page 568:

A defendant's actions did not exceed mere remonstration, and therefore did not satisfy this Element, when she stayed in view of the investigating officer as instructed and her actions, though loud, were not aggressive or suggestive of violence. State v. Humphreys, ___ N.C. App. ___, ___ S.E.2d ___ (2020).

Add the following at the end of the second full paragraph on page 568:

The evidence also was sufficient to sustain a conviction when (6) during a ten- to fifteen-second incident, the defendant stepped between an officer and gang members and refused the officer's instructions to step away, *Cornell*, 222 N.C. App. at 189; (7) the defendant refused to provide the officer with his identification so that the officer could issue the defendant a citation for a seatbelt violation, State v. Friend, 237 N.C. App. 490, 493–94 (2014); (8) the defendant, who had been detained by a store loss-prevention officer for theft, provided the responding officer with an identification card containing an altered identification number and, upon being asked whether the listed identification number was accurate, the defendant falsely stated that it was, *Peters*, 255 N.C. App. at 388; and (9) a defendant resisted officers in the discharge of their investigative duties when he refused to roll down his car window when asked, repeatedly tried to start his car after being commanded to stop, refused a breath test at least ten times, and repeatedly put his hands in his pockets during nystagmus testing after being instructed not to. State v. Hoque, 269 N.C. App. 347 (2020).

Add the following as the last two paragraphs of this note:

In *Friend*, 237 N.C. App. at 493–94, the North Carolina Court of Appeals stated that "failure to provide information about one's identity during a lawful stop can constitute resistance, delay, or obstruction within the meaning of [the statute]." Note that *Friend* requires that the defendant's failure to identify actually delay the officer in completing a lawful task, there, issuing a seatbelt citation to the defendant-passenger. *Id.*

Note also that the *Friend* court qualified its ruling, stating, "There are, of course, circumstances where one would be excused from providing his or her identity to an officer," such as when doing so would violate the Fifth Amendment's protection against compelled self-incrimination. 237 N.C. App. at 493–94. *See also* State v. Ellis, 374 N.C. App. 340 (2020) (noting that refusing to identify oneself to an officer during a valid traffic stop may be a violation of this offense, but concluding that the defendant's act of gesturing with his middle finger was not likely to cause a breach of the peace, and therefore did not give the officer reasonable suspicion to justify the stop).

Element (5) (page 569)
Because G.S. 20-49.1 delegates to North Carolina Division of Motor Vehicles (NCDMV) officers the authority to enforce criminal laws under specified circumstances, an inspector with the NCDMV License and Theft Bureau was acting within the scope of his duties when he ordered the defendant to leave a NCDMV driver's license office where the inspector worked and arrested her when she failed to comply with that order. State v. Nickens, 262 N.C. App. 353 (2018).

Because the officer did not read or produce a copy of the search warrant as required by G.S. 15A-252 before seeking to search the defendant, the officer was not engaged in lawful conduct and the evidence was insufficient to support a conviction based on the defendant's refusal to allow the officer to search him pursuant to the warrant. State v. Carter, 237 N.C. App. 274, 279–80 (2014).

Defenses (new note)
For a case where the court rejected the defendant's argument that his conduct was justified on grounds that he acted out of concern for a minor in his care, see *State v. Cornell*, 222 N.C. App. 184, 189 (2012).

Related Offenses Not in This Chapter (page 570)

Add the following offenses to this list:

Violating Governor's order during a state of emergency. G.S. 166A-19.30(d); 14-288.20A(2).
Violating county or municipality's ordinance during a state of emergency. G.S. 166A-19.31(h); 14-288.20A(1).
Willfully refusing to leave a public building as directed under a Governor's order. G.S. 14-288.20A(3).

Remove the following offenses from this list:

Violation of state of emergency ordinance. G.S. 14-288.12 through -288.14.
Violating a provision of a proclamation of the Governor in an emergency. G.S. 14-288.15.
Failure to evacuate on Governor's command. G.S. 14-288.19.

False Report to Law Enforcement Agencies or Officers (page 571)

Statute (page 571)

2013 legislation, S.L. 2013-52, sec. 6, amended the statute to read as follows:

§ 14-225. False reports to law enforcement agencies or officers.

(a) Except as provided in subsection (b) of this section, any person who shall willfully make or cause to be made to a law enforcement agency or officer any false, deliberately misleading or unfounded report, for the purpose of interfering with the operation of a law enforcement agency, or to hinder or obstruct any law enforcement officer in the performance of his duty, shall be guilty of a Class 2 misdemeanor.

(b) A violation of subsection (a) of this section is punishable as a Class H felony if the false, deliberately misleading, or unfounded report relates to a law enforcement investigation involving the disappearance of a child as that term is defined in G.S. 14-318.5 or child victim of a Class A, B1, B2, or C felony offense. For purposes of this subsection, a child is any person who is less than 16 years of age.

Elements (page 571)

As a result of the 2013 legislation noted above, Element (4) should read as follows:

(4) a false or deliberately misleading or unfounded report

Punishment (page 571)

As a result of the 2013 legislation noted above, this section should read as follows:

Class 2 misdemeanor. G.S. 14-225(a). Class H felony if the report relates to a law enforcement investigation involving

- the disappearance of a child (as defined by G.S. 14-318.5) or
- a child victim of a Class A through C felony.

G.S. 14-225(b). A child is a person less than 16 years of age. *Id.* Any fact elevating punishment must be alleged in the charging instrument and proved to a jury, unless the defendant pleads guilty or no contest to the issue.

As a result of 2019 legislation, S.L. 2019-134, effective for offenses committed on or after December 1, 2019, add the following new offense:

Giving False Fire Alarms in a Prison or Local Confinement Facility (new crime)

Statute

§ 14-286. Giving false fire alarms; molesting fire-alarm, fire-detection or fire-extinguishing system.

(a) Offense. – It shall be unlawful for any person or persons to wantonly and willfully give or cause to be given, or to advise, counsel, or aid and abet anyone in giving, a false alarm of fire, or to break the glass key protector, or to pull the slide, arm, or lever of any station or signal box of any fire-alarm system, except in case of fire, or willfully misuse or damage a portable fire extinguisher, or in any way to willfully interfere with, damage, deface, molest, or injure any part or portion of any fire-alarm, fire-detection, smoke-detection or fire-extinguishing system.

(b) Penalty. – Any person who willfully interferes with, damages, defaces, molests, or injures any part or portion of a fire-alarm, fire-detection, smoke-detection, or fire-extinguishing system in a prison or local confinement facility is guilty of a Class H felony. Any person violating any of the provisions who commits any other violation of this section is guilty of a Class 2 misdemeanor. For purposes of this subsection, the term "local confinement facility" means a county or city jail, a local lockup, or a detention facility for adults operated by a local government.

Elements

A person guilty of this offense

(1) willfully
(2) (a) interferes with,
    (b) damages,
    (c) defaces,
    (d) molests, *or*
    (e) injures
(3) any part or portion of any fire-alarm, fire-detection, smoke-detection, or fire-extinguishing system
(4) in a prison or local confinement facility.

Punishment

Class H felony. G.S. 14-286(b). A violation of this statute in a location other than a prison or local confinement facility is a Class 2 misdemeanor.

Notes

Element (4)

The term "local confinement facility" means a county or city jail, a local lockup, or a detention facility for adults operated by a local government. G.S. 153A-217(5).

Interfering with Emergency Communication (page 571)

Related Offenses Not in This Chapter (page 573)

Add the following offense to this list:

Injuring, tampering with, removing, etc. firefighting or emergency medical services machinery or equipment. G.S. 14-160.3, *as enacted by* S.L. 2017-89.

Concealing a Death (page 573)

Statute (page 573)

As a result of 2013 legislation, S.L. 2013-52, sec. 5, G.S. 14-401.22 has been revised to read:

> (a) Except as provided in subsection (a1) of this section, any person who, with the intent to conceal the death of a person, fails to notify a law enforcement authority of the death or secretly buries or otherwise secretly disposes of a dead human body is guilty of a Class I felony.
>
> (a1) Any person who, with the intent to conceal the death of a child, fails to notify a law enforcement authority of the death or secretly buries or otherwise secretly disposes of a dead child's body is guilty of a Class H felony. For purposes of this subsection, a child is any person who is less than 16 years of age.
>
> [*To save space, subsections (b) through (f) are not reproduced here.*]

Punishment (page 573)

As a result of the 2013 legislation noted above, this section should be revised to read as follows:

Class I felony. G.S. 14-401.22(a). If the body is of a child less than 16 years old, the offense is a Class H felony. *Id.* § (a1). If the defendant knew or had reason to know that the person did not die of natural causes, the offense is a Class D felony. *Id.* § (e). All facts elevating punishment must be alleged in the charging instrument and proved to the jury, unless the defendant pleads guilty or no contest to the issue.

Related Offenses Not in This Chapter (page 573)

Add the following offense to this list:

Disturbing, vandalizing, or desecrating human remains; committing sexual penetration on human remains. G.S. 14-401.22(c).

Prison and Other Escapes (page 574)

Prison Breach and Escape from County or Municipal Confinement Facilities or Officers (page 574)

Statute (page 574)

2013 legislation, S.L. 2013-389, sec. 3, amended subsection (1) to read as follows:

(1) He has been charged with or convicted of a felony and has been committed to the facility pending trial or transfer to the State prison system; or

Punishment (page 574)

As a result of the 2013 legislation noted above, the second sentence of this note should read as follows:

Class H felony if the defendant

- has been charged with or convicted of a felony and has been committed to the facility pending trial or transfer to the state prison system or
- is serving a sentence imposed on conviction of a felony.

Related Offenses Not in This Chapter (page 574)

Add the following offense to this list:

Use of an unmanned aircraft system near a confinement or correctional facility. G.S. 15A-300.3, *as enacted by* S.L. 2017-179.

As a result of 2018 legislation, S.L. 2018-67, sec. 3, delete the sixth entry in this list and replace it with the following:

Providing articles forbidden by prison rules or items for prison escape, assault, or insurrection; possessing items for prison escape, assault, or insurrection. G.S. 14-258.

Delete the seventh entry in this list and replace it with the following:

Furnishing poison, controlled substances, deadly weapons, cartridges, ammunition, or alcoholic beverages to inmates; furnishing tobacco or mobile phones to inmates; furnishing mobile phones to delinquent juveniles. G.S. 14-258.1.

Escape from the State Prison System (page 575)

Statute (page 575)

As a result of 2017 legislation, S.L. 2017-186, sec. 2.(eeeeeeee), replace the term "Division of Adult Correction," as used in the statute, with Division of Adult Correction and Juvenile Justice.

Notes (page 576)

Aiders and assisters (page 577)

As a result of 2018 legislation, S.L. 2018-67, sec. 3, delete the last parenthetical in this note and replace it with the following:

(providing articles forbidden by prison rules or items for prison escape, assault, or insurrection; possessing items for prison escape, assault, or insurrection).

22
Weapons Offenses

Possession of a Firearm by a Felon (page 581)

Notes (page 582)

Element (2)(c) (page 582)

There was sufficient evidence of actual possession of a firearm when officers found the weapon between the seat and the passenger side door of the defendant's vehicle, near where the defendant's hand had been immediately before the officers opened the car door. State v. Chevallier, 264 N.C. App. 204 (2019).

For a discussion of recent case law modifying the text in the second paragraph of this note regarding the necessary proof to establish constructive possession when the defendant does not have exclusive control over the place where contraband is found, see the note on Element (2) to "Possession of a Controlled Substance," below in this supplement.

There was insufficient evidence of constructive possession where (1) the only evidence connecting the defendant to a rifle recovered in a wooded area 75 to 100 yards away from the defendant was canine tracking evidence, State v. Battle, 253 N.C. App. 141, 147 (2017) (the court distinguished other cases upholding convictions where the defendant was identified as the perpetrator by a tracking canine, noting that here the canine's tracking behavior was the *only* evidence of guilt; the canine was not tracking a known scent; the canine lost the track at one point; another man was found in the woods; and no other evidence, such as fingerprints, DNA, or ownership, linked the defendant to the rifle or the site where it was found); (2) the defendant did not have exclusive control of the apartment in which guns were found and the State failed to present evidence of other incriminating circumstances, State v. Perry, 222 N.C. App. 813, 819 (2012); and (3) the defendant did not have exclusive control of the car that he owned but in which he was a passenger when a rifle was found; the rifle was registered to the defendant's girlfriend, who was driving; the defendant and his girlfriend had equal access to the location where the weapon was found; and there was no physical evidence, such as fingerprints, tying the defendant to the rifle. State v. Bailey, 233 N.C. App. 688, 692–93 (2014).

The fact that a person is aware of a weapon does not, by itself, establish constructive possession. *Id.* at 693.

There was sufficient evidence (1) that the defendant constructively possessed drugs and a firearm found in a vehicle where, notwithstanding the defendant's nonexclusive possession of the vehicle, his control as its driver was sufficient to give rise to an inference of constructive possession, and other incriminating circumstances supported that inference, State v. Wirt, 263 N.C. App. 370 (2018); (2) that the defendant constructively possessed drugs and a rifle found in a bedroom that was not under his exclusive control; among other things, photographs, a Father's Day card, a cable bill, a cable installation receipt, and a pay stub found in the bedroom linked him to the contraband and placed him in the room within two days of when the contraband was found, State v. Bradshaw, 366 N.C. 90, 96–97 (2012); (3) that the defendant constructively possessed a firearm when he was driving a rental vehicle, had a female passenger, and the gun was found in a purse in the car's glove container; the court reasoned that the defendant was driving the car, and his interactions with the police showed that he was aware of the vehicle's contents, State v. Mitchell, 224 N.C. App. 171, 178 (2012); and (4) that the defendant constructively possessed a gun where an anonymous 911 caller reported seeing a man wearing a plaid shirt holding a gun near a black car beside a field; someone saw the man drop the gun; an officer saw the defendant standing near a black car wearing a plaid shirt; the defendant later returned to the scene claiming ownership of the car; and officers found a firearm in a vacant lot approximately ten feet from the car. State v. McKiver, 247 N.C. App. 614, 619–20 (2016) (noting that additional incriminating circumstances existed, beyond the defendant's mere presence at the scene and proximity to the firearm, to infer that he constructively possessed the firearm), *rev'd on other grounds*, 369 N.C. 652 (2017).

Exceptions (page 584)

Add the following at the end of the first paragraph of this note:

See Booth v. State, 227 N.C. App. 484 (2013) (offense does not apply to a person who has received a Pardon of Forgiveness for his or her prior felony).

Constitutionality (page 584)

This note cites *Baysden v. North Carolina*, 217 N.C. App. 20 (2011), as holding that the statute was unconstitutional as applied to the plaintiff. With one justice taking no part in consideration of the case, an equally divided North Carolina Supreme Court left undisturbed that opinion, which stands without precedential value. Baysden v. State, 366 N.C. 370 (2013). Because of that decision, and to incorporate additional new case law, delete all text in this paragraph from the words "Post-*Britt* North Carolina Court of Appeals cases" onward and replace it with the following:

Post-*Britt* North Carolina Court of Appeals cases involving as-applied state constitutional challenges include *State v. Fernandez*, 256 N.C. App. 539, 547–48 (2017) (rejecting the defendant's as-applied challenge); *State v. Whitaker*, 201 N.C. App. 190, 202–07 (2009) (same), *aff'd*, 364 N.C. 404 (2010); *State v. Price*, 233 N.C. App. 386, 397–98 (2014) (same); and *State v. Bonetsky*, 246 N.C. App. 640, 643–50 (2016) (same).

For a case rejecting a defendant's as-applied federal constitutional challenge, see *Fernandez*, 256 N.C. App. at 545–47.

Add the following to this note:

In *Johnston v. State*, 367 N.C. 164 (2013), the court per curiam affirmed the decision below, *Johnston v. State*, 224 N.C. App. 282 (2012), which reversed the trial court's ruling that G.S. 14-415.1 violated the plaintiff's substantive due process rights under the U.S. and N.C. constitutions and remanded to the trial court for additional proceedings; the court of appeals also reversed the trial court's ruling that the statute was facially invalid on procedural due process grounds, under both the U.S. and N.C. constitutions.

Defenses (page 586)

In narrow and extraordinary circumstances, the common law defense of justification may be an affirmative defense to a charge for this crime. State v. Mercer, 373 N.C. 459 (2020). In *Mercer*, the court adopted the formulation of the defense articulated in *United States v. Deleveaux*, 205 F.3d 1292, 1297 (11th Cir. 2000), which requires the defendant to show four elements: that the defendant was under unlawful and present, imminent, and impending threat of death or serious bodily injury; that the defendant did not negligently or recklessly place himself or herself in a situation where he or she would be forced to engage in criminal conduct; that the defendant had no reasonable legal alternative to violating the law; and that there was a direct causal relationship between the criminal action and the avoidance of the threatened harm. *Id.* at 464. The court further held that because there was substantial evidence of each element of the defense, the trial court's failure to give a justification defense jury instruction constituted prejudicial error. *Id.* at 466.

Add the following after the second sentence of this note:

State v. Monroe, 367 N.C. 771 (2015) (per curiam); State v. Edwards, 239 N.C. App. 391, 393–94 (2015);

Multiple convictions and punishments (page 586)

There is a typographical error in the parenthetical to *State v. Wiggins*, a case included in this note; specifically, the word "commission" is misspelled.

Related Offenses Not in This Chapter (page 586)

As a result of 2018 legislation, S.L. 2018-67, sec. 3, delete the third entry in this list and replace it with the following:

Providing articles forbidden by prison rules or items for prison escape, assault, or insurrection; possessing items for prison escape, assault, or insurrection. G.S. 14-258.

As a result of 2015 legislation, S.L. 2015-47, delete the fourth entry in this list and replace it with the following:

Furnishing poison, controlled substances, deadly weapons, cartridges, ammunition or alcoholic beverages to inmates; furnishing tobacco products or mobile phones to inmates; furnishing mobile phones to delinquent juveniles. G.S. 14-258.1.

Remove the following offense from this list:

Transporting dangerous weapon or substance during emergency. G.S. 14-288.7.

Add the following offense to this list:

Unlawful possession and use of unmanned aircraft systems with weapon attached. G.S. 14-401.24.

The citation for the listed offense "Purchase or possession of firearms by person subject to domestic violation order prohibited" should read:

G.S. 14-269.8; 50B-3.1(j).

Carrying a Concealed Weapon (page 587)

Statute (page 587)

2015 legislation, S.L. 2015-264, sec. 3, amended subsection (a), replacing the word "shurikin" with "shuriken." That same legislation also amended subsections (a), (a1), and (b1), making them gender-neutral.

2013 legislation, S.L. 2013-369, sec.1, enacted subsection (a2) of G.S. 14-269 as follows:

(a2) This prohibition does not apply to a person who has a concealed handgun permit issued in accordance with Article 54B of this Chapter, has a concealed handgun permit considered valid under G.S. 14-415.24, or is exempt from obtaining a permit pursuant to G.S. 14-415.25, provided the weapon is a handgun, is in a closed compartment or container within the person's locked vehicle, and the vehicle is in a parking area that is owned or leased by State government. A person may unlock the vehicle to enter or exit the vehicle, provided the handgun remains in the closed compartment at all times and the vehicle is locked immediately following the entrance or exit.

2015 legislation, S.L. 2015-215, sec. 2.5, enacted a new subsection, (b)(3a), as follows:

(3a) A member of the North Carolina National Guard who has been designated in writing by the Adjutant General, State of North Carolina, who has a concealed handgun permit issued in accordance with Article 54B of this Chapter or considered valid under G.S. 14-415.24, and is acting in the discharge of his or her official duties, provided that the member does not carry a concealed weapon while consuming alcohol or an unlawful controlled substance or while alcohol or an unlawful controlled substance remains in the member's body.

2015 legislation, S.L. 2015-195, sec. 1(a), amended subsection (b)(4a) to read as follows:

(4a) Any person who is a district attorney, an assistant district attorney, or an investigator employed by the office of a district attorney and who has a concealed handgun permit issued in accordance with Article 54B of this Chapter or considered valid under G.S. 14-415.24; provided that the person shall not carry a concealed weapon at any time while in a courtroom or while consuming alcohol or an unlawful controlled substance or while alcohol or an unlawful controlled substance remains in the person's body. The district attorney, assistant district attorney, or investigator shall secure the weapon in a locked compartment when the weapon is not on the person of the district attorney, assistant district attorney, or investigator. Notwithstanding the provisions of this subsection, a district attorney may carry a concealed weapon while in a courtroom;

2013 legislation, S.L. 2013-369, sec. 25, amended subsection (b)(4b) to read as follows:

(4b) Any person who is a qualified retired law enforcement officer as defined in G.S. 14-415.10 and meets any one of the following conditions:

a. Is the holder of a concealed handgun permit in accordance with Article 54B of this Chapter.
b. Is exempt from obtaining a permit pursuant to G.S. 14-415.25.
c. Is certified by the North Carolina Criminal Justice Education and Training Standards Commission pursuant to G.S. 14-415.26;

Section 21 of that same law enacted subsections (b)(4d) and (4e) as follows:

(4d) Any person who is a North Carolina district court judge, North Carolina superior court judge, or a North Carolina magistrate and who has a concealed handgun permit issued in accordance with Article 54B of this Chapter or considered valid under G.S. 14-415.24; provided that the person shall not carry a concealed weapon at any time while consuming alcohol or an unlawful controlled substance or while alcohol or an unlawful controlled substance remains in the person's body. The judge or magistrate shall secure the weapon in a locked compartment when the weapon is not on the person of the judge or magistrate;

(4e) Any person who is serving as a clerk of court or as a register of deeds and who has a concealed handgun permit issued in accordance with Article 54B of this Chapter or considered valid under G.S. 14-415.24; provided that the person shall not carry a concealed weapon at any time while consuming alcohol or an unlawful controlled substance or while alcohol or an unlawful controlled substance remains in the person's body. The clerk of court or register of deeds shall secure the weapon in a locked compartment when the weapon is not on the person of the clerk of court or register of deeds. This subdivision does not apply to assistants, deputies, or other employees of the clerk of court or register of deeds;

2015 legislation, S.L. 2015-5; S.L. 2015-195, sec. 1(a), as modified by the codifier, enacted subsections (b)(7), (8), and (9). 2017 legislation, S.L. 2017-186, sec. 2(hh), amended subsection (b)(9). Those provisions read as follows:

(7) A person employed by the Department of Public Safety who has been designated in writing by the Secretary of the Department, who has a concealed handgun permit issued in accordance with Article 54B of this Chapter or considered valid under G.S. 14-415.24, and has in the person's possession written proof of the designation by the Secretary of the Department, provided that the person shall not carry a concealed weapon at any time while consuming alcohol or an unlawful controlled substance or while alcohol or an unlawful controlled substance remains in the person's body.

(8) Any person who is an administrative law judge described in Article 60 of Chapter 7A of the General Statutes and who has a concealed handgun permit issued in accordance with Article 54B of this Chapter or considered valid under G.S. 14-415.24, provided that the person shall not carry a concealed weapon at any time while consuming alcohol or an unlawful controlled substance or while alcohol or an unlawful controlled substance remains in the person's body.

(9) State correctional officers, when off-duty, provided that an officer does not carry a concealed weapon while consuming alcohol or an unlawful controlled substance or while alcohol or an unlawful controlled substance remains in the officer's body. If the concealed weapon is a handgun, the correctional officer must meet the firearms training standards of the Division of Adult Correction and Juvenile Justice of the Department of Public Safety.

2014 legislation, S.L. 2014-119, sec. 12(a), amended subsection (c) of the statute to read:

> (c) Any person violating the provisions of subsection (a) of this section shall be guilty of a Class 2 misdemeanor. Any person violating the provisions of subsection (a1) of this section shall be guilty of a Class 2 misdemeanor for the first offense and a Class H felony for a second or subsequent offense. A violation of subsection (a1) of this section punishable under G.S. 14-415.21(a) is not punishable under this section.

Carrying a Concealed Pistol or Gun (page 589)

Elements (page 589)

The North Carolina Court of Appeals has held that the exception in G.S. 14-269(a1)(2) (having a permit) is a defense to, not an element of, this offense. State v. Mather, 221 N.C. App. 593, 602 (2012). This exception is listed as Element (5)(b). If this holding applies to the other (a1) exceptions, Element (5) in its entirety would be deleted and elements (5)(a) through (c) would constitute defenses as well.

Punishment (page 589)

As a result of 2014 legislation, S.L. 2014-119, sec. 12(a), punishment for a second or subsequent offense has been elevated to a Class H felony.

Notes (page 589)

Element (3) (page 589)

There was sufficient evidence that a weapon was concealed about the defendant's person where officers found one razor blade under a table in a room adjoining the defendant's cell and where the defendant had been seated earlier in the day; they found another on a ledge below the window in the defendant's cell, moments after he held such a blade in his hand while threatening an officer. State v. Hill, 227 N.C. App. 371, 380–82 (2013).

Element (5) generally (page 589)

The exception in G.S. 14-269(a1)(2) (having a permit) is a defense to, not an essential element of, this offense. *Mather*, 221 N.C. App. at 602. This holding is likely to apply to the (a1)(1) and (a1)(3) exceptions as well.

Element 5(b) (page 590)

This note mentions and cites G.S. 14-415.27 as exempting district attorneys and related individuals from the limitations in G.S. 14-415.11(c), provided the exemption is consistent with federal law. 2013 legislation, S.L. 2013-269, sec. 22, expanded the scope of G.S. 14-415.27 to also include judges, magistrates, clerks of court, and registers of deeds. 2015 legislation further expanded the scope of that provision. S.L. 2015-195, sec. 1(c).

As a result of 2013 and 2015 legislation, S.L. 2013-369, sec. 16; S.L. 2015-195, sec. 9, add the following to the end of the second paragraph of this note:

Additionally, a person who has a valid permit but carries a concealed handgun in violation of G.S. 14-415.11(c2) is guilty of a Class 1 misdemeanor. G.S. 14-415.21(a1).

Constitutionality (page 591)

G.S. 14-415.12 (criteria to qualify for a concealed handgun permit) was not unconstitutional as applied to the petitioner because the petitioner's right to carry a concealed handgun did not fall within the scope of the Second Amendment. Kelly v. Riley, 223 N.C. App. 261, 268 (2012).

Defenses (page 591)

The exception in G.S. 14-269(a1)(2) (having a permit) is a defense to, not an element of, this offense. *Mather*, 221 N.C. App. at 602. The State has no initial burden of producing evidence to show that the defendant's carrying a concealed weapon does not fall within the (a1) exception. *Id.* However, once the defendant puts forth evidence showing that his or her conduct falls within an exception, the burden of persuasion to show that the defendant's action was outside the exception falls on the prosecution. *Id.* These rules are likely to apply to the (a1)(1) and (a1)(3) exceptions as well.

Exceptions (page 591)

With respect to the fifth bullet in this list, 2015 legislation, S.L. 2015-195, sec. 1(a), amended the exception in G.S. 14-269(b)(4a) to provide, in relevant part, "Notwithstanding the provisions of this subsection, a district attorney may carry a concealed weapon while in a courtroom."

As a result of 2013 legislation, S.L. 2013-269, sec. 25, the sixth bullet in this note should be modified to read:

- qualified retired law enforcement officers, as defined in G.S. 14-415.10, who have concealed handgun permits in accordance with G.S. Chapter 14, Article 54B, who are exempt from obtaining permits under G.S. 14-415.25, or who are certified by the North Carolina Criminal Justice Education and Training Standards Commission under G.S. 14-415.26;

2013 legislation, S.L. 2013-269, secs. 1 and 21, enacted new exceptions to this crime. First, new G.S. 14-269(a2) provides that this offense does not apply to a person who has or is exempted from obtaining a concealed handgun permit when the weapon is a handgun, it is in a closed compartment or container in the person's locked vehicle, and the vehicle is in a parking area that is owned or leased by state government. Second, new G.S. 14-269(b)(4d) and (4e) provide exceptions for certain judges, magistrates, clerks, or registers of deeds in certain circumstances.

2015 legislation added additional exceptions. S.L. 2015-215, sec. 2.5, added an exception in new G.S. 14-269(b)(3a) pertaining to members of the North Carolina National Guard. S.L. 2015-5 added an exception in new G.S. 14-269(b)(7) pertaining to off-duty state correctional officers. S.L. 2015-195, sec. 1(a), added exceptions for certain persons employed by the Department of Public Safety and certain administrative law judges.

Multiple convictions and punishments (new note)

2014 legislation, S.L. 2014-119, sec. 12(a), amended G.S. 14-269(c) to provide that a violation of G.S. 14-269(a1) that is punishable under G.S. 14-415.21(a) (person with a valid permit who is found to be carrying a concealed handgun without the permit or who fails to disclose to any officer that the person holds a valid permit and is carrying a concealed handgun) is not punishable under G.S. 14-269.

Carrying a Concealed Weapon Other Than a Pistol or Gun (page 592)

Elements (page 592)

As a result of 2015 legislation, S.L. 2015-264, sec. 3, Element (4)(h) should read as follows:

(h) shuriken

Possession of Weapons on School Grounds (page 594)

Statute (page 594)

2013 legislation, S.L. 2013-360, sec. 8.45(a), added a new subsection, (3a), to G.S. 14-269.2(a) as follows:

(3a) Volunteer school safety resource officer.—A person who volunteers as a school safety resource officer as provided by G.S. 162-26 or G.S. 160A-288.4.

As a result of 2013 and 2014 legislation, S.L. 2013-360, sec. 8.45(b); S.L. 2014-119, sec. 9(a), G.S. 14-269.2(g) reads as follows:

(g) This section shall not apply to any of the following:

(1) A weapon used solely for educational or school-sanctioned ceremonial purposes, or used in a school-approved program conducted under the supervision of an adult whose supervision has been approved by the school authority.

(1a) A person exempted by the provisions of G.S. 14-269(b).

(2) Firefighters, emergency service personnel, North Carolina Forest Service personnel, detention officers employed by and authorized by the sheriff to carry firearms, and any private police employed by a school, when acting in the discharge of their official duties.

(3) Home schools as defined in G.S. 115C-563(a).

(4) Weapons used for hunting purposes on the Howell Woods Nature Center property in Johnston County owned by Johnston Community College when used with the written permission of Johnston Community College or for hunting purposes on other educational property when used with the written permission of the governing body of the school that controls the educational property.

(5) A person registered under Chapter 74C of the General Statutes as an armed armored car service guard or an armed courier service guard when acting in the discharge of the guard's duties and with the permission of the college or university.

(6) A person registered under Chapter 74C of the General Statutes as an armed security guard while on the premises of a hospital or health care facility located on educational property when acting in the discharge of the guard's duties with the permission of the college or university.

(7) A volunteer school safety resource officer providing security at a school pursuant to an agreement as provided in G.S. 115C-47(61) and either G.S. 162-26 or G.S. 160A-288.4, provided that the volunteer school safety resource officer is acting in the discharge of the person's official duties and is on the educational property of the school that the officer was assigned to by the head of the appropriate local law enforcement agency.

2013 legislation, S.L. 2013-369, sec. 2, added new subsections (i), (j), and (k) to the statute. 2015 legislation, S.L. 2015-195, sec. 2, amended subsection (k). These subsections read as follows:

(i) The provisions of this section shall not apply to an employee of an institution of higher education as defined in G.S. 116-143.1 or a nonpublic post-secondary educational institution who resides on the campus of the institution at which the person is employed when all of the following criteria are met:

(1) The employee's residence is a detached, single-family dwelling in which only the employee and the employee's immediate family reside.

(2) The institution is either:

a. An institution of higher education as defined by G.S. 116-143.1.

b. A nonpublic post-secondary educational institution that has not specifically prohibited the possession of a handgun pursuant to this subsection.

(3) The weapon is a handgun.

(4) The handgun is possessed in one of the following manners as appropriate:
a. If the employee has a concealed handgun permit that is valid under Article 54B of this Chapter, or who is exempt from obtaining a permit pursuant to that Article, the handgun may be on the premises of the employee's residence or in a closed compartment or container within the employee's locked vehicle that is located in a parking area of the educational property of the institution at which the person is employed and resides. Except for direct transfer between the residence and the vehicle, the handgun must remain at all times either on the premises of the employee's residence or in the closed compartment of the employee's locked vehicle. The employee may unlock the vehicle to enter or exit, but must lock the vehicle immediately following the entrance or exit if the handgun is in the vehicle.
b. If the employee is not authorized to carry a concealed handgun pursuant to Article 54B of this Chapter, the handgun may be on the premises of the employee's residence, and may only be in the employee's vehicle when the vehicle is occupied by the employee and the employee is immediately leaving the campus or is driving directly to their residence from off campus. The employee may possess the handgun on the employee's person outside the premises of the employee's residence when making a direct transfer of the handgun from the residence to the employee's vehicle when the employee is immediately leaving the campus or from the employee's vehicle to the residence when the employee is arriving at the residence from off campus.

(j) The provisions of this section shall not apply to an employee of a public or nonpublic school who resides on the campus of the school at which the person is employed when all of the following criteria are met:

(1) The employee's residence is a detached, single-family dwelling in which only the employee and the employee's immediate family reside.
(2) The school is either:
a. A public school which provides residential housing for enrolled students.
b. A nonpublic school which provides residential housing for enrolled students and has not specifically prohibited the possession of a handgun pursuant to this subsection.
(3) The weapon is a handgun.
(4) The handgun is possessed in one of the following manners as appropriate:
a. If the employee has a concealed handgun permit that is valid under Article 54B of this Chapter, or who is exempt from obtaining a permit pursuant to that Article, the handgun may be on the premises of the employee's residence or in a closed compartment or container within the employee's locked vehicle that is located in a parking area of the educational property of the school at which the person is employed and resides. Except for direct transfer between the residence and the vehicle, the handgun must remain at all times either on the premises of the employee's residence or in the closed compartment of the employee's locked vehicle. The employee may unlock the vehicle to enter or exit, but must lock the vehicle immediately following the entrance or exit if the handgun is in the vehicle.
b. If the employee is not authorized to carry a concealed handgun pursuant to Article 54B of this Chapter, the handgun may be on the premises of the employee's residence, and may only be in the employee's vehicle when the vehicle is occupied by the employee and the employee is immediately leaving the campus or is driving directly to their residence from off campus. The employee may possess the handgun on the employee's person outside the premises of the employee's residence

when making a direct transfer of the handgun from the residence to the employee's vehicle when the employee is immediately leaving the campus or from the employee's vehicle to the residence when the employee is arriving at the residence from off campus.

(k) The provisions of this section shall not apply to a person who has a concealed handgun permit that is valid under Article 54B of this Chapter, or who is exempt from obtaining a permit pursuant to that Article, if any of the following conditions are met:

(1) The person has a handgun in a closed compartment or container within the person's locked vehicle or in a locked container securely affixed to the person's vehicle and only unlocks the vehicle to enter or exit the vehicle while the firearm remains in the closed compartment at all times and immediately locks the vehicle following the entrance or exit.

(2) The person has a handgun concealed on the person and the person remains in the locked vehicle and only unlocks the vehicle to allow the entrance or exit of another person.

(3) The person is within a locked vehicle and removes the handgun from concealment only for the amount of time reasonably necessary to do either of the following:

a. Move the handgun from concealment on the person to a closed compartment or container within the vehicle.

b. Move the handgun from within a closed compartment or container within the vehicle to concealment on the person.

2015 legislation, S.L. 2015-195, sec. 3, added a new subsection, (l), as follows:

(l) It is an affirmative defense to a prosecution under subsection (b) or (f) of this section that the person was authorized to have a concealed handgun in a locked vehicle pursuant to subsection (k) of this section and removed the handgun from the vehicle only in response to a threatening situation in which deadly force was justified pursuant to G.S. 14-51.3.

Possession of Firearms on School Grounds (page 596)

Notes (page 596)

Element (1) (page 596)

Although the court of appeals held that the State must prove that the defendant both knowingly possessed or carried a prohibited weapon and knowingly entered educational property with that weapon, State v. Huckelba, 240 N.C. App. 544, 558 (2015), that decision was reversed by the state supreme court on grounds that even if the trial court erred in its jury instructions, the error did not rise to the level of plain error. State v. Huckelba, 368 N.C. 569 (2015).

No criminal intent required (page 597)

Delete this note. Although *Haskins* held that no criminal intent was required, the statute subsequently was amended to add the element that the defendant acts knowingly.

Exceptions (page 597)

Several new exceptions have been added to this offense:

- G.S. 14-269.2(g)(2) was amended to create an exception for detention officers employed by and authorized by a sheriff to carry firearms. S.L. 2014-119, sec. 9(a).
- A new subsection, G.S. 14-269.2(g)(7), creates an exception for certain volunteer school safety resource officers when acting in the discharge of their official duties on educational property. S.L. 2013-360, sec. 8.45(b).

- Two new subsections, G.S. 14-269.2(i) and (j), provide that the offense does not apply to certain school employees who reside at educational institutions and schools. S.L. 2013-369, sec. 2.
- A new subsection, G.S. 14-269.2(k), provides that the offense does not apply to individuals who either have a valid concealed handgun permit or are exempt from obtaining a permit and have a handgun in a locked vehicle under circumstances specified in the statute. S.L. 2013-369, sec. 2, S.L. 2015-195, sec. 2.

Affirmative defense (new note)

It is an affirmative defense to a prosecution under subsection G.S. 14-269.2(b) or (f) that the person was authorized to have a concealed handgun in a locked vehicle pursuant to G.S. 14-269.2(k) and removed the handgun from the vehicle only in response to a threatening situation in which deadly force was justified pursuant to G.S. 14-51.3. G.S. 14-269.2(l).

Multiple convictions and punishments (new note)

A defendant may lawfully be convicted of only one count of this offense for the simultaneous possession of multiple firearms on educational property. State v. Conley, 374 N.C. 209 (2020).

Storing a Firearm in a Manner Accessible to a Minor (page 601)

Notes (page 602)

Element (5) (new note)

For a case where there was sufficient circumstantial evidence that the defendant stored or left a gun in a condition and manner accessible to a minor, see *State v. Lewis*, 222 N.C. App. 747, 750–51 (2012).

Carrying a Gun into an Assembly or Establishment Where Alcoholic Beverages Are Sold and Consumed (page 602)

Statute (page 602)

2013 legislation, S.L. 2013-369, sec. 3, amended subsection (b) of G.S. 14-269.3 to read as follows:

(b) This section shall not apply to any of the following:

(1) A person exempted from the provisions of G.S. 14-269.

(2) The owner or lessee of the premises or business establishment.

(3) A person participating in the event, if the person is carrying a gun, rifle, or pistol with the permission of the owner, lessee, or person or organization sponsoring the event.

(4) A person registered or hired as a security guard by the owner, lessee, or person or organization sponsoring the event.

(5) A person carrying a handgun if the person has a valid concealed handgun permit issued in accordance with Article 54B of this Chapter, has a concealed handgun permit considered valid under G.S. 14-415.24, or is exempt from obtaining a permit pursuant to G.S. 14-415.25. This subdivision shall not be construed to permit a person to carry a handgun on any premises where the person in legal possession or control of the premises has posted a conspicuous notice prohibiting the carrying of a concealed handgun on the premises in accordance with G.S. 14-415.11(c).

Notes (page 603)

Exceptions (page 603)

As a result of that same legislation, add the following text at the end of this section:

- a person carrying a handgun who has a valid concealed handgun permit, who has a permit considered valid under G.S. 14-415.24, or who is exempt from obtaining a permit.

G.S. 14-269.3(b)(5). However, this last exception does not apply if the person in legal possession or control of the premises has posted a conspicuous notice prohibiting the carrying of a concealed handgun on the premises in accordance with G.S. 14-415.11(c). *Id.*

Weapons at Parades, etc. (page 604)

Statute (page 604)

2013 legislation, S.L. 2013-369, sec. 15, amended G.S. 14-277.2, adding a new subsection, (d), as follows:

> (d) The provisions of this section shall not apply to concealed carry of a handgun at a parade or funeral procession by a person with a valid permit issued in accordance with Article 54B of this Chapter, with a permit considered valid under G.S. 14-415.24, or who is exempt from obtaining a permit pursuant to G.S. 14-415.25. This subsection shall not be construed to permit a person to carry a concealed handgun on any premises where the person in legal possession or control of the premises has posted a conspicuous notice prohibiting the carrying of a concealed handgun on the premises in accordance with G.S. 14-415.11(c).

Notes (page 604)

Exceptions (page 604)

Pursuant to 2013 legislation, S.L. 2013-369, sec. 15, this offense does not apply to the concealed carry of a handgun at a parade or funeral procession by a person with a valid permit, with a permit considered valid under G.S. 14-415.24, or with an exemption from getting a permit under G.S. 14-415.25. G.S. 14-277.2(d). However, this exception does not allow a person to carry a concealed handgun on premises where the person in legal possession or control of the premises has posted a conspicuous notice prohibiting the carrying of a concealed handgun in accordance with G.S. 14-415.11(c). *Id.*

Going Armed to the Terror of the People

This is not a new crime. It was deleted from the 7th edition of North Carolina Crimes but appears here again in response to requests for its inclusion.

Statute

This is a common law offense. State v. Dawson, 272 N.C. 535, 541–42 (1968); State v. Huntly, 25 N.C. 418, 418 (1843); State v. Staten, 32 N.C. App. 495, 496–97 (1977) (citing *Dawson*).

Elements

A person guilty of this offense

(1) arms himself or herself with an unusual and dangerous weapon
(2) for the purpose of terrifying others *and*
(3) goes about on public highways
(4) in a manner to cause terror to the people.

Punishment

Class 1 misdemeanor. G.S. 14-3(a); *Dawson*, 272 N.C. at 549 (offense is a misdemeanor).

Notes

Generally. For the elements of this offense, see *Dawson*, 272 N.C. at 549, and *Staten*, 32 N.C. App. at 497.

For a case where the evidence was sufficient to establish this offense, see, for example, *Dawson*, 272 N.C. at 549 (armed with a carbine and four pistols, the defendant and three others drove on the public highways at night, firing bullets into a store and two homes).

Element (1). In *Huntly*, the court held that any gun is an unusual and dangerous weapon for purposes of this offense. 25 N.C. at 422. In that case it was argued that a gun cannot constitute an unusual weapon, "for there is scarcely a man in the community who does not own and occasionally use a gun of some sort." *Id.* The court rejected that argument, concluding: "A gun is an 'unusual weapon,' wherewith to be armed and clad. No man amongst us carries it about with him, as one of his every day accoutrements—as a part of his dress—and never we trust will the day come when any deadly weapon will be worn or wielded in our peace loving and law-abiding State, as an appendage of manly equipment." *Id.*; *see also* State v. Toler, 716 S.E.2d 875, *6 (2011) (unpublished) (gun was an unusual and dangerous weapon).

In *State v. Lanier*, 71 N.C. 288, 289 (1874), the defendant was charged with going armed to the terror of the people after riding a horse, at a canter, through a courthouse after court had adjourned. Witnesses saw no arms of any kind. The North Carolina Supreme Court "attach[ed] no importance to the fact that the defendant had no arms," stating, "we think it may be conceded that the driving or riding without arms through a court house or a crowded street at such a rate or in such a manner as to endanger the safety of the inhabitants amounts to a breach of the peace and is an indictable offence at common law." *Id.* at 290 (but going on to conclude that the trial court erred by instructing the jury that if they believed either one of the two witnesses, they must find the defendant guilty; the court determined that the circumstances of the defendant's act were relevant and created a jury issue, stating: "We conceive that the riding through a court house or a street at 12 o'clock at night, when no one is present, is a very different thing from riding through at 12 o'clock in the day, when the court house or street is full of people. The same act may be criminal or innocent, according to the surrounding circumstances." *Id.*).

Element (2). The crime requires that the defendant act for the purpose of terrifying others. *See, e.g., Toler*, 716 S.E.2d 875, at *6 (the evidence was sufficient to establish that the defendant acted with the required purpose when he shot his gun on a public highway while driving closely behind another vehicle with his high beams on).

Element (3). It appears that the offense would not occur if the defendant remained on private property.

Element (4). In an unpublished case involving a charge of going armed to the terror of the people, the North Carolina Court of Appeals found this Element satisfied where the defendant shot his gun while driving closely behind another vehicle on a public highway with his high beams on. *Toler*, 716 S.E.2d 875, at *6 (rejecting the defendant's argument that his actions were not "to the terror of the people" where the only people involved were those in the victim's car).

The offense of affray involves fighting in public to the terror of the people. For purposes of that offense, cases hold that if members of the public experience fear, the "to the terror of the people" element is satisfied. *In re* May, 357 N.C. 423, 428 (2003).

Relation to open carry. Because of the elements noted above, this offense would not apply to mere open carry. State v. Huntly, 25 N.C. 418, 422–23 (1843) ("[I]t is to be remembered that the carrying of a gun per se constitutes no offence. For any lawful purpose—either of business or amusement—the citizen is at perfect liberty to carry his gun. It is the wicked purpose—and the mischievous result—which essentially constitute the crime. He shall not carry about this or any other weapon of death to terrify and alarm, and in such manner as naturally will terrify and alarm, a peaceful people.").

23
Prostitution

2013 legislation, S.L. 2013-368, rewrote the state's prostitution offenses. As a result, delete the text of this chapter and replace it with the content that follows. Any additional legislative changes made after 2013 are noted in the text below.

Prostitution

Statute

2015 legislation, S.L. 2015-181, sec. 17, made conforming changes to G.S. 14-203(5). The amended statute reads as follows:

§ 14-203. Definition of terms.

The following definitions apply in this Article:

(1) Advance prostitution.—The term includes all of the following:

a. Soliciting for a prostitute by performing any of the following acts when acting as other than a prostitute or a patron of a prostitute:

1. Soliciting another for the purpose of prostitution.
2. Arranging or offering to arrange a meeting of persons for the purpose of prostitution.
3. Directing another to a place knowing the direction is for the purpose of prostitution.
4. Using the Internet, including any social media Web site, to solicit another for the purpose of prostitution.

b. Keeping a place of prostitution by controlling or exercising control over the use of any place that could offer seclusion or shelter for the practice of prostitution and performing any of the following acts when acting as other than a prostitute or a patron of a prostitute:

1. Knowingly granting or permitting the use of the place for the purpose of prostitution.
2. Granting or permitting the use of the place under circumstances from which the person should reasonably know that the place is used or is to be used for purposes of prostitution.
3. Permitting the continued use of the place after becoming aware of facts or circumstances from which the person should know that the place is being used for the purpose of prostitution.

(2) Minor.—Any person who is less than 18 years of age.

(3) Profit from prostitution.—When acting as other than a prostitute, to receive anything of value for personally rendered prostitution services or to receive anything of value from a prostitute, if the thing received is not for lawful consideration and the person knows it was earned in whole or in part from the practice of prostitution.

(4) Prostitute.—A person who engages in prostitution.

(5) Prostitution.—The performance of, offer of, or agreement to perform vaginal intercourse, any sexual act as defined in G.S. 14-27.20, or any sexual contact as defined in G.S. 14-27.20, for the purpose of sexual arousal or gratification for any money or other consideration.

§ 14-204. Prostitution.

(a) Offense.—Any person who willfully engages in prostitution is guilty of a Class 1 misdemeanor.

(b) First Offender; Conditional Discharge.

(1) Whenever any person who has not previously been convicted of or placed on probation for a violation of this section pleads guilty to or is found guilty of a violation of this section, the court, without entering a judgment and with the consent of such person, shall place the person on probation pursuant to this subsection.

(2) When a person is placed on probation, the court shall enter an order specifying a period of probation of 12 months and shall defer further proceedings in the case until the conclusion of the period of probation or until the filing of a petition alleging violation of a term or condition of probation.

(3) The conditions of probation shall be that the person (i) not violate any criminal statute of any jurisdiction, (ii) refrain from possessing a firearm or other dangerous weapon, (iii) submit to periodic drug testing at a time and in a manner as ordered by the court, but no less than three times during the period of the probation, with the cost of the testing to be paid by the probationer, (iv) obtain a vocational assessment administered by a program approved by the court, and (v) attend no fewer than 10 counseling sessions administered by a program approved by the court.

(4) The court may, in addition to other conditions, require that the person do any of the following:

a. Make a report to and appear in person before or participate with the court or such courts, person, or social service agency as directed by the court in the order of probation.

b. Pay a fine and costs.

c. Attend or reside in a facility established for the instruction or residence of defendants on probation.

d. Support the person's dependents.

e. Refrain from having in the person's body the presence of any illicit drug prohibited by the North Carolina Controlled Substances Act, unless prescribed by a physician, and submit samples of the person's blood or urine or both for tests to determine the presence of any illicit drug.

(5) Upon violation of a term or condition of probation, the court may enter a judgment on its original finding of guilt and proceed as otherwise provided.

(6) Upon fulfillment of the terms and conditions of probation, the court shall discharge the person and dismiss the proceedings against the person. Upon the discharge of the person and dismissal of the proceedings against the person under this subsection, the person is eligible to apply for expunction of records pursuant to G.S. 15A-145.6.

(7) Discharge and dismissal under this subsection shall not be deemed a conviction for purposes of structured sentencing or for purposes of disqualifications or disabilities imposed by law upon conviction of a crime.

(8) There may be only one discharge and dismissal under this section.

(c) Immunity From Prosecution for Minors.—Notwithstanding any other provision of this section, if it is determined, after a reasonable detention for investigative purposes, that a person suspected of or charged with a violation of this section is a minor, that person shall be immune from prosecution under this section and instead shall be taken into temporary protective custody as an undisciplined juvenile pursuant to Article 19 of Chapter 7B of the General Statutes. Pursuant to the provisions of G.S. 7B-301, a law enforcement officer who takes a minor into custody under this section shall immediately report an allegation of a violation of G.S. 14-43.11 and G.S. 14-43.13 to the director of the department of social services in the county where the minor resides or is found, as appropriate, which shall commence an initial investigation into child abuse or child neglect within 24 hours pursuant to G.S. 7B-301 and G.S. 7B-302.

Elements

A person guilty of this offense

(1) willfully

(2) engages in prostitution.

Punishment

Class 1 misdemeanor. G.S. 14-204(a). For conditional discharge, see G.S. 14-204(b). For special probation conditions, see G.S. 14-205.4.

Notes

Element (1). See "Willfully" in Chapter 1 (States of Mind) of the main volume.

Element (2). "Prostitution" is the performance of, offer of, or agreement to perform vaginal intercourse, a sexual act, or sexual contact for the purpose of sexual arousal or gratification and for money or other consideration. G.S. 14-203(5).

"Sexual act" includes cunnilingus, fellatio, analingus, anal intercourse, and the penetration by any object into the genital or anal opening of another person's body, except when done for accepted medical purposes. G.S. 14-203(5); 14-27.1(4) (this statute was recodified as G.S. 14-27.20 by 2015 legislation, S.L. 2015-181, sec. 2).

"Sexual contact" includes touching the sexual organ, anus, breast, groin, or buttocks of another; touching another with one's own sexual organ, anus, breast, groin, or buttocks; and ejaculating, emitting, or placing semen, urine, or feces on another. G.S. 14-203(5); 14-27.1(5) (this statute was recodified as G.S. 14-27.20 by 2015 legislation, S.L. 2015-181, sec. 2). "Touching" means physical contact, including through clothing. G.S. 14-27.1(6) (this statute was recodified as G.S. 14-27.20 by 2015 legislation, S.L. 2015-181, sec. 2).

Evidence issues. G.S. 14-206 provides that "testimony of a prior conviction, or testimony concerning the reputation of any place, structure, or building, and of the person or persons who reside in or frequent the same, and of the defendant" is admissible to prove this offense.

Immunity for minors. The law provides for immunity from prosecution for persons less than 18 years of age. G.S. 14-204(c); 14-203(2) (defining a "minor").

Related Offenses Not in This Chapter

"Crime against Nature" (Chapter 11)

"Fornication and Adultery" (Chapter 11)

Opposite sexes occupying same bedroom at hotel for immoral purposes; falsely registering as husband and wife. G.S. 14-186.

Keeping bawdy house. G.S. 14-188.

Solicitation of Prostitution

2015 legislation, S.L. 2015-183, and 2018 legislation, S.L. 2018-47, sec. 4(e), amended the statute to read as follows:

Statute

§ 14-205.1. Solicitation of prostitution.

(a) Except as otherwise provided in this section, any person who solicits another for the purpose of prostitution is guilty of a Class 1 misdemeanor for a first offense and a Class H felony for a second or subsequent offense. Any person 18 years of age or older who willfully solicits a minor for the purpose of prostitution is guilty of a Class G felony. Any person who willfully solicits a person who has a severe or profound mental disability for the purpose of prostitution is guilty of a Class E felony. Punishment under this section may include participation in a program devised for the education and prevention of sexual exploitation (i.e. "John School"), where available. A person who violates this subsection is not eligible for a disposition of prayer for judgment continued under any circumstances.

(b) Immunity From Prosecution for Minors.—Notwithstanding any other provision of this section, if it is determined, after a reasonable detention for investigative purposes, that a person suspected of or charged with a violation of this section is a minor who is soliciting as a prostitute, that person shall be immune from prosecution under this section and instead shall be taken into temporary protective custody as an undisciplined juvenile pursuant to Article 19 of Chapter 7B of the General Statutes. Pursuant to G.S. 7B-301, a law enforcement officer who takes a minor into custody under this section shall immediately report an allegation of a violation of G.S. 14-43.11 and G.S. 14-43.13 to the director of the department of social services in the county where the minor resides or is found, as appropriate, which shall commence an initial investigation into child abuse or child neglect within 24 hours pursuant to G.S. 7B-301 and G.S. 7B-302.

Elements

A person guilty of this offense

(1) solicits another

(2) for prostitution.

Punishment

Class 1 misdemeanor for a first offense; Class H felony for a second or subsequent offense. G.S. 14-205.1(a). The statute provides for two enhanced versions of this offense. First, a person 18 years or older who willfully solicits a minor under 18 years old is guilty of a Class G felony. *Id.*; G.S. 14-203(2). Second, a person who willfully solicits a person who has a severe or profound mental disability is guilty of a Class E felony. G.S. 14-205.1(a). The term "severe or profound mental disability" is not defined. For a definition of the term "mental disability" as that term is used in G.S. Chapter 14, Article 7B (Rape and Other Sex Offenses), see the note on Element (3)(b)(i) to "Second-Degree Forcible Rape," above in this supplement. The term "severely or profoundly mentally disabled" is not defined. The additional facts enhancing punishment must be alleged in the charging instrument and found by a jury, unless the defendant pleads guilty or no contest to the issue. For all versions of the offense, punishment may include participation in a "John School." G.S. 14-205.1(a). A prayer for judgment continued (PJC) is not allowed. *Id.* For special probation conditions, see G.S. 14-205.4.

Notes

Element (2). See "Prostitution," above in this supplement.

Evidence issues. See this note to "Prostitution," above in this supplement.

Immunity from prosecution (new note)
The statute provides for immunity from prosecution for minors who solicit as prostitutes. G.S. 14-205.1(b).

Related Offenses Not in This Chapter

See the offenses listed under "Prostitution," above in this supplement.

Patronizing a Prostitute

Statute

2015 legislation, S.L. 2015-181, sec. 18, and 2018 legislation, S.L. 2018-47, sec. 4(f), amended the statute to read as follows:

§ 14-205.2. Patronizing a prostitute.

(a) Any person who willfully performs any of the following acts with a person not his or her spouse commits the offense of patronizing a prostitute:

(1) Engages in vaginal intercourse, any sexual act as defined in G.S. 14-27.20, or any sexual contact as defined in G.S. 14-27.20, for the purpose of sexual arousal or gratification with a prostitute.

(2) Enters or remains in a place of prostitution with intent to engage in vaginal intercourse, any sexual act as defined in G.S. 14-27.20, or any sexual contact as defined in G.S. 14-27.20, for the purpose of sexual arousal or gratification.

(b) Except as provided in subsections (c) and (d) of this section, a first violation of this section is a Class A1 misdemeanor. Unless a higher penalty applies, a second or subsequent violation of this section is a Class G felony.

(c) A violation of this section is a Class F felony if the defendant is 18 years of age or older and the prostitute is a minor.

(d) A violation of this section is a Class D felony if the prostitute has a severe or profound mental disability.

Elements

A person guilty of this offense

(1) willfully

(2) (a) (i) engages in vaginal intercourse, a sexual act, or a sexual contact

(ii) for the purpose of sexual arousal or gratification

(iii) with a prostitute *or*

(b) (i) enters or remains

(ii) in a place of prostitution

(iii) with intent to engage in vaginal intercourse, a sexual act, or a sexual contact

(iv) for the purpose of sexual arousal or gratification *and*

(3) the acts are done with a person who is not the defendant's spouse.

Punishment

A first offense is a Class A1 misdemeanor; a second or subsequent offense is a Class G felony. G.S. 14-205.2(b). There are two enhanced versions of this offense. First, a violation is a Class F felony if the defendant is 18 years old or older and the prostitute is less than 18 years old. *Id.* § (c); 14-203(2). Second, a violation is a Class D felony if the prostitute has a severe or profound mental disability. G.S. 14-205.2(d). The additional facts enhancing punishment must be alleged in the charging instrument and found by a jury, unless the defendant pleads guilty or no contest to the issue. The term "severe or profound mental disability" is not defined. For a definition of the term "mental disability" as that term is used in G.S. Chapter 14, Article 7B (Rape and Other Sex Offenses), see the note on Element (3)(b)(i) to "Second-Degree Forcible Rape," above in this supplement. Both elevated versions of this offense qualify as sexually violent offenses for the purposes of the sex offender registration statutes. G.S. 14-190.13(5). For special probation conditions, see G.S. 14-205.4.

Notes

Element (1). See "Willfully" in Chapter 1 (States of Mind) of the main volume.

Element (2). The terms "sexual act" and "sexual contact" are defined in the note on Element (2) to "Prostitution," above in this supplement. A prostitute is "a person who engages in prostitution." G.S. 14-203(4).

Element (3). It is not clear if this provision is an element of the offense or a defense to it.

Evidence issues. See this note to "Prostitution," above in this supplement.

Related Offenses Not in This Chapter

See the offenses listed under "Prostitution," above in this supplement.

Promoting Prostitution

2018 legislation, S.L. 2018-47, sec. 4(g), amended the statute to read as follows:

Statute

§ 14-205.3. Promoting prostitution.

(a) Any person who willfully performs any of the following acts commits promoting prostitution:

(1) Advances prostitution as defined in G.S. 14-203.

(2) Profits from prostitution by doing any of the following:

a. Compelling a person to become a prostitute.

b. Receiving a portion of the earnings from a prostitute for arranging or offering to arrange a situation in which the person may practice prostitution.

c. Any means other than those described in sub-subdivisions a. and b. of this subdivision, including from a person who patronizes a prostitute. This sub-subdivision does not apply to a person engaged in prostitution who is a minor. A person cannot be convicted of promoting prostitution under this sub-subdivision if the practice of prostitution underlying the offense consists exclusively of the accused's own acts of prostitution under G.S. 14-204.

(b) Any person who willfully performs any of the following acts commits the offense of promoting prostitution of a minor or person who has a mental disability:

(1) Advances prostitution as defined in G.S. 14-203, where a minor or person who has a severe or profound mental disability engaged in prostitution, or any person engaged in prostitution in the place of prostitution is a minor or has a severe or profound mental disability at the time of the offense.

(2) Profits from prostitution by any means where the prostitute is a minor or has a severe or profound mental disability at the time of the offense.

(3) Confines a minor or person who has a severe or profound mental disability against the person's will by the infliction or threat of imminent infliction of great bodily harm, permanent disability, or disfigurement or by administering to the minor or person who has a severe or profound mental disability, without the person's consent or by threat or deception and for other than medical purposes, any alcoholic intoxicant or a drug as defined in Article 5 of Chapter 90 of the General Statutes (North Carolina Controlled Substances Act) and does any of the following:

a. Compels the minor or person who has a severe or profound mental disability to engage in prostitution.

b. Arranges a situation in which the minor or person who has a severe or profound mental disability may practice prostitution.

c. Profits from prostitution by the minor or person who has a severe or profound mental disability.

For purposes of this subsection, administering drugs or an alcoholic intoxicant to a minor or a person who has a severe or profound mental disability, as described in subdivision (3) of this subsection, shall be deemed to be without consent if the administering is done without the consent of the parents or legal guardian or if the administering is performed or permitted by the parents or legal guardian for other than medical purposes. Mistake of age is not a defense to a prosecution under this subsection.

(c) Unless a higher penalty applies, a violation of subsection (a) of this section is a Class F felony. A violation of subsection (a) of this section by a person with a prior conviction for a violation of this section or a violation of G.S. 14-204 (prostitution), G.S. 14-204.1 (solicitation of prostitution), or G.S. 14-204.2 (patronizing a prostitute) is a Class E felony.

(d) Unless a higher penalty applies, a violation of subdivision (1) or (2) of subsection (b) of this section is a Class D felony. A violation of subdivision (3) of subsection (b) of this section is a Class C felony. Any violation of subsection (b) of this section by a person with a prior conviction for a violation of this section or a violation of G.S. 14-204 (prostitution), G.S. 14-204.1 (solicitation of prostitution), G.S. 14-204.2 (patronizing a prostitute) is a Class C felony.

Elements

A person guilty of this offense

(1) willfully
(2) (a) advances prostitution *or*
    (b) profits from prostitution.

Punishment

Class F felony. G.S. 14-205.3(c). Class E felony if the defendant has a prior conviction for this offense, for prostitution (G.S. 14-204), for solicitation of prostitution (G.S. 14-204.1), or for patronizing a prostitute (G.S. 14-204.2). *Id.* For special probation conditions, see G.S. 14-205.4.

Notes

Element (1). See "Willfully" in Chapter 1 (States of Mind) of the main volume.

Element (2)(a). A person advances prostitution when, acting as other than a prostitute or a patron of a prostitute, he or she

- solicits another for prostitution;
- arranges or offers to arrange a meeting of people for prostitution;
- directs another to a place knowing the direction is for prostitution; or
- uses the Internet, including social media, to solicit another for prostitution.

G.S. 14-203(1)(a).

A person also advances prostitution by keeping a place of prostitution. This means controlling or exercising control over the use of a place that could offer seclusion or shelter for prostitution and performing any of the following acts, when acting as other than a prostitute or a prostitute's patron:

- knowingly granting or permitting the use of the place for prostitution,
- granting or permitting the use of the place under circumstances from which the person should reasonably know that the place is used or is to be used for prostitution, or
- permitting the continued use of the place when the person should know that the place is being used for prostitution.

G.S. 14-203(1)(b).

Element (2)(b). To profit from prostitution means "[w]hen acting as other than a prostitute, to receive anything of value for personally rendered prostitution services or to receive anything of value from a prostitute, if the thing received is not for lawful consideration and the person knows it was earned in whole or in part from the practice of prostitution." G.S. 14-203(3). The profiting may occur by compelling a person to become a prostitute, by receiving a portion of the earnings from a prostitute for arranging or offering to arrange a situation in which the person may practice prostitution, or by any other means. G.S. 14-205.3(a)(2). However, profiting from prostitution "by any other means" does not apply to a minor engaged in prostitution or when the practice of prostitution underlying the offense consists exclusively of the defendant's own acts of prostitution under G.S. 14-204. *Id.* § (a)(2)c.

Evidence issues. See this note to "Prostitution," above in this supplement.

Related Offenses Not in This Chapter

See the offenses listed under "Prostitution," above in this supplement.

Promoting Prostitution of a Minor or Person Who Has a Mental Disability (revised title)

Statute

See G.S. 14-205.3(b), reproduced above in this supplement under "Promoting Prostitution."

Elements

A person guilty of this offense

(1) willfully
(2) (a) (i) advances prostitution *and*
(ii) a minor or person who has a severe or profound mental disability engaged in prostitution, *or*
(iii) any person engaged in prostitution in the place of prostitution is a minor or has a severe or profound mental disability, *or*
(b) (i) profits from prostitution *and*
(ii) the prostitute is
1. a minor *or*
2. has a severe or profound mental disability, *or*
(c) (i) confines
(ii) a minor or person who has a severe or profound mental disability
(iii) against the person's will
(iv) by
1. the infliction or threat of imminent infliction of great bodily harm, permanent disability, or disfigurement *or*
2. administering an alcoholic intoxicant or controlled substance, without consent or by threat or deception and for non-medical purposes, *and*
(v) does any of the following:
1. compels the minor or person who has a severe or profound mental disability to engage in prostitution,
2. arranges a situation for the minor or person who has a severe or profound mental disability to practice prostitution, *or*
3. profits from prostitution by the minor or person who has a severe or profound mental disability.

Punishment

If elements (2)(a) or (b) are involved, Class D felony. G.S. 14-205.3(d). If Element (2)(c) is involved, Class C felony. *Id.* Additionally, if the person has a prior conviction for violating this statute, G.S. 14-204 (prostitution), G.S. 14-204.1 (solicitation of prostitution), or G.S. 14-204.2 (patronizing a prostitute), punishment is as a Class C felony. *Id.* For special probation conditions, see G.S. 14-205.4.

Notes

Element (1). See "Willfully" in Chapter 1 (States of Mind) of the main volume.

Element (2) generally. A minor is a person under 18 years old. G.S. 14-203(2). The statute does not define the term "severe or profound mental disability." For a definition of the term "mental disability" as that term is used in G.S. Chapter 14, Article 7B (Rape and Other Sex Offenses), see the note on Element (3)(b)(i) to "Second-Degree Forcible Rape," above in this supplement.

Element (2)(a). "Advances prostitution" is defined under "Promoting Prostitution," above in this supplement.

Element (2)(c)(iii). Administering drugs or alcoholic intoxicants is deemed to be without consent if it is done without the consent of the parents or legal guardian of a minor or person with a severe or profound mental disability or if it is performed or permitted by the parents or legal guardian for non-medical purposes. G.S. 14-205.3(b).

Mistake of age. Mistake of age is not a defense. G.S. 14-205.3(b).

Evidence issues. See this note to "Prostitution," above in this supplement.

Sex offender registration. A conviction of this offense triggers sex offender registration requirements. G.S. 14-190.13(5).

Related Offenses Not in This Chapter

See the offenses listed under "Prostitution," above in this supplement.

24

Obscenity, Exploitation of a Minor, and Adult Establishment Offenses

Obscenity Offenses (page 621)

Disseminating Obscenity (page 621)

Notes (page 622)

Element (3) (page 622)

Replace the last paragraph of this note with the following:

Nothing in G.S. 14-190.1 requires the State to produce the precise material alleged to be obscene. State v. Wilson, 263 N.C. App. 567 (2019) (rejecting the defendant's argument that contemporary community standards must take into account what can be seen on premium cable channels like Showtime and HBO, and concluding that evidence of the defendant's large collection of pornographic DVDs allowed the jury to reasonably infer that the material shown to the victim was obscene under contemporary community standards); State v. Mueller, 184 N.C. App. 553, 564–67 (2007) (a witness's testimony describing the material alleged to be obscene was sufficient to sustain a conviction without introduction of the material itself).

Disseminating and Exhibiting Material Harmful to Minors (page 628)

Displaying Material Harmful to Minors (page 628)

Notes (page 630)

Element (3) (page 630)

Add the following to the portion of this note discussing the definition of "sexual activity":

Although proving vaginal intercourse and anal intercourse under G.S. 14-190.13(5)(b) requires proof of penetration, proving oral intercourse under that provision does not. State v. Fletcher, 370 N.C. 313, 329–30 (2017). The term "oral intercourse" is a "gender-neutral reference to cunnilingus and fellatio," neither of which requires penetration. *Id.*

Sexual Exploitation of a Minor (page 633)

First-Degree Sexual Exploitation of a Minor (page 633)

Notes (page 634)

Element (2) (page 634)
In a case prosecuted under the Element (2)(a) version of this offense, the court of appeals held that "the minor in question is required to have engaged in sexual activity" and that when a minor is merely depicted as being engaged in sexual activity as the result of digital manipulation, this offense has not occurred. *Fletcher*, 370 N.C. at 329–30.

Second-Degree Sexual Exploitation of a Minor (page 635)

Notes (page 636)

Element (1) (new note)
There was sufficient evidence that the defendant was aware of the contents of pornographic files found on his computer where, among other things, the files' titles clearly indicated that they contained pornographic images of children. State v. Jones, 248 N.C. App. 418, 428–29 (2016).

Element (2) (new note)
A defendant's act of downloading images from the Internet onto his computer constituted a "duplication" within the meaning of the statute. State v. Williams, 232 N.C. App. 152, 157–58 (2014) (deciding this issue of first impression).

Element (4) (page 636)
A photograph depicting a minor standing naked except for her socks in her father's bedroom meets the definition of lascivious under this offense, and the minor's pubic area was "exhibited" despite her hands partially blocking view of her genital area. State v. Corbett, 264 N.C. App. 93 (2019).

Multiple convictions and punishments (page 636)
In *Williams*, 232 N.C. App. at 158–60, the court rejected the defendant's argument that the General Assembly did not intend to punish defendants for both receiving and possessing the same images.

Disclosure of Private Images (new crime)

This offense was enacted in 2015. S.L. 2015-250.

Statute

2017 legislation, S.L. 2017-93, amended the statute to provide as follows:

§ 14-190.5A. Disclosure of private images.

(a) Definitions.—The following definitions apply in this section:

(1) Disclose.—Transfer, publish, distribute, or reproduce.

(2) Image.—A photograph, film, videotape, recording, live transmission, digital or computer-generated visual depiction, or any other reproduction that is made by electronic, mechanical, or other means.

(3) Intimate parts.—Any of the following naked human parts: (i) male or female genitals, (ii) male or female pubic area, (iii) male or female anus, or (iv) the nipple of a female over the age of 12.
(4) [repealed]
(5) [repealed]
(6) Sexual conduct.—Includes any of the following:
a. Vaginal, anal, or oral intercourse, whether actual or simulated, normal or perverted.
b. Masturbation, excretory functions, or lewd exhibition of uncovered genitals.
c. An act or condition that depicts torture, physical restraint by being fettered or bound, or flagellation of or by a nude person or a person clad in undergarments or in revealing or bizarre costume.

(b) Offense.—A person is guilty of disclosure of private images if all of the following apply:
(1) The person knowingly discloses an image of another person with the intent to do either of the following:
a. Coerce, harass, intimidate, demean, humiliate, or cause financial loss to the depicted person.
b. Cause others to coerce, harass, intimidate, demean, humiliate, or cause financial loss to the depicted person.
(2) The depicted person is identifiable from the disclosed image itself or information offered in connection with the image.
(3) The depicted person's intimate parts are exposed or the depicted person is engaged in sexual conduct in the disclosed image.
(4) The person discloses the image without the affirmative consent of the depicted person.
(5) The person obtained the image without consent of the depicted person or under circumstances such that the person knew or should have known that the depicted person expected the images to remain private.

(c) Penalty.—A violation of this section shall be punishable as follows:
(1) For an offense by a person who is 18 years of age or older at the time of the offense, the violation is a Class H felony.
(2) For a first offense by a person who is under 18 years of age at the time of the offense, the violation is a Class 1 misdemeanor.
(3) For a second or subsequent offense by a person who is under the age of 18 at the time of the offense, the violation is a Class H felony.

(d) Exceptions.—This section does not apply to any of the following:
(1) Images involving voluntary exposure in public or commercial settings.
(2) Disclosures made in the public interest, including, but not limited to, the reporting of unlawful conduct or the lawful and common practices of law enforcement, criminal reporting, legal proceedings, medical treatment, or scientific or educational activities.
(3) Providers of an interactive computer service, as defined in 47 U.S.C. § 230(f), for images provided by another person.

(e) Destruction of Image.—In addition to any penalty or other damages, the court may award the destruction of any image made in violation of this section.

(f) Other Sanctions or Remedies Not Precluded.—A violation of this section is an offense additional to other civil and criminal provisions and is not intended to repeal or preclude any other sanctions or remedies.

(g) Civil Action.—In addition to any other remedies at law or in equity, including an order by the court to destroy any image disclosed in violation of this section, any person whose image is disclosed, or used, as described in subsection (b) of this section, has a civil cause of action against any person who discloses or uses the image and is entitled to recover from the other person any of the following:

(1) Actual damages, but not less than liquidated damages, to be computed at the rate of one thousand dollars ($1,000) per day for each day of the violation or in the amount of ten thousand dollars ($10,000), whichever is higher.
(2) Punitive damages.
(3) A reasonable attorneys' fee and other litigation costs reasonably incurred.

The civil cause of action may be brought no more than one year after the initial discovery of the disclosure, but in no event may the action be commenced more than seven years from the most recent disclosure of the private image.

Elements

A person guilty of this offense:

(1) knowingly
(2) discloses an image of another person
(3) with the intent to
  (a) coerce, harass, intimidate, demean, humiliate, or cause financial loss to the depicted person, *or*
  (b) cause others to coerce, harass, intimidate, demean, humiliate, or cause financial loss to the depicted person, *and*
(4) the depicted person is identifiable from the disclosed image or from information offered in connection with it,
(5) the depicted person's intimate parts are exposed or the depicted person is engaged in sexual conduct in the disclosed image,
(6) the person discloses the image without the affirmative consent of the depicted person, *and*
(7) the person obtained the image without the consent of the depicted person or under circumstances such that the person knew or should have known that the depicted person expected the images to remain private.

Punishment

If the defendant is 18 or older at the time of the offense, Class H felony. G.S. 14-190.5A(c)(1). If the defendant is less than 18 years old at the time of the offense, a first offense is a Class 1 misdemeanor and a second or subsequent offense is a Class H felony. *Id.* §§ (c)(2), (3).

Notes

Element (1). See "Knowingly" in Chapter 1 (States of Mind) of the main volume.

Element (2). To "disclose" means to transfer, publish, distribute, or reproduce. G.S. 14-190.5A(a)(1). The term "image" includes a photograph, film, videotape, recording, live transmission, digital or computer-generated visual depiction, or any other reproduction that is made by electronic, mechanical, or other means. *Id.* § (a)(2).

Element (5). The term "intimate parts" means any of the following naked human parts: genitals, pubic area, anus, or the nipple of a female over the age of 12. G.S. 14-190.5A(a)(3). The term "sexual conduct" means any of the following:

- vaginal, anal, or oral intercourse, whether actual or simulated, normal or perverted;
- masturbation, excretory functions, or lewd exhibition of uncovered genitals;
- an act or condition that depicts torture, physical restraint by being fettered or bound, or flagellation of or by a nude person or a person clad in undergarments or in revealing or bizarre costume.

G.S. 14-190.5A(a)(6). This is the same definition of sexual conduct that applies with respect to obscenity. G.S. 14-190.1(c).

Exceptions. The statute carves out exceptions for

- images involving voluntary exposure in public or commercial settings and
- disclosures made in the public interest, including, but not limited to, the reporting of unlawful conduct or the lawful and common practices of law enforcement, criminal reporting, legal proceedings, medical treatment, or scientific or educational activities.

G.S. 14-190.5A(d)(1), (2). The statute also provides an exception for "[p]roviders of an interactive computer service, as defined in 47 U.S.C. § 230(f), for images provided by another person." *Id.* § (d)(3).

Destruction of images. The court may order the destruction of images made in violation of the statute. G.S. 14-190.5A(e).

Multiple convictions and punishments. Punishment for this offense does not preclude punishment for some other criminal offense that might apply to the conduct at issue. G.S. 14-190.5A(f).

Civil action. Prosecution for this offense does not preclude civil sanctions or remedies. *Id.* In fact, the statute sets out a civil cause of action. *Id.* § (g).

Adult Establishment Offenses (page 638)

Statute (page 638)

2017 legislation, S.L. 2017-151, secs. 2(a) and (b), amended G.S. 14-202.10, repealing subsections (7) and (8) and amending subsection (2) to read as follows:

> (2) "Adult establishment" means an adult bookstore, adult motion picture theatre, adult mini motion picture theatre, or adult live entertainment business as defined in this section.

2017 legislation, S.L. 2017-151, sec. 2(c), amended G.S. 20-202.11, adding a new subsection, (a1), as follows:

> (a1) No person shall permit the practice of massage and bodywork therapy, as defined in Article 36 of Chapter 90 of the General Statutes, in an adult establishment.

Permitting a Facility to Contain Multiple Adult Establishments (page 639)

Notes (page 640)

Element (3) (page 640)

As a result of 2017 legislation, S.L. 2017-151, sec. 2(a), delete the first sentence of this note and replace it with the following:

G.S. 14-202.10(2) defines an "adult establishment" as an adult bookstore, adult motion picture theatre, adult mini motion picture theatre, or adult live entertainment business.

Related Offenses Not in This Chapter (page 640)

Add the following offense to this list:

Permitting the practice of massage and bodywork therapy in an adult establishment. G.S. 14-202.11(a1).

25

Lotteries, Gambling, and Related Offenses

Lottery Offenses (page 645)

Advertising a Lottery (page 645)

Related Offenses Not in This Chapter (page 646)

Replace the related offense that reads "Unlawful bingo. G.S. 14-309.5; 14-309.12." with the following:

Unlawful bingo. G.S. 14-309.5; 14-309.12; 14-309.14.

Gambling (page 650)

Notes (page 651)

Exceptions (page 651)
2012 legislation, S.L. 2012-6, enacted G.S. 14-292.2, making lawful certain Class III gaming on Indian lands. A 2019 amendment, S.L. 2019-163, added sports and horse-race wagering to the list of lawful Class III games. G.S. 14-292.2(b)(5). Under legislation effective June 1, 2019, it is lawful for certain exempt organizations and employers to conduct "game nights" pursuant to the rules and permitting requirements described in G.S. 14-309.25 through -309.37. S.L. 2019-13.

Possession of a Slot Machine (page 651)

Notes (page 653)

Exceptions (page 653)
2012 legislation, S.L. 2012-6, enacted G.S. 14-292.2, making lawful certain Class III gaming on Indian lands.

Operation, etc. of a Video Gaming Machine (page 654)

Statute (page 654)

G.S. 14-306.1A(e) was repealed by 2012 legislation, S.L. 2012-6, sec. 3.

Notes (page 655)

Exceptions (page 655)

Delete the first sentence (and related citations) of this note and replace it with the following:

2012 legislation, S.L. 2012-6, enacted G.S. 14-292.2, making lawful certain Class III gaming on Indian lands.

Electronic Sweepstakes (page 657)

Notes (page 659)

Element (3) (page 659)

A sweepstakes can be conducted through the use of an entertaining display even if the prize is revealed to the patron before he or she plays the game. State v. Spruill, 237 N.C. App. 383, 386–87 (2014). A sweepstakes game run through a kiosk displaying a video game resembling a reel-spinning slot machine, which involved spinning the wheel on the display and nudging virtual reels, was an "entertaining display" regardless of whether skill or chance predominated over the game and was, therefore, a violation of this offense. Gift Surplus, LLC v. State *ex rel.* Cooper, 268 N.C. App. 1 (2019), *review allowed sub nom.* Sandhill Amusements, Inc. v. State *ex rel.* Cooper, 373 N.C. 587 (2020).

Constitutionality (new note)

In *Hest Technologies, Inc. v. North Carolina,* 366 N.C. 289 (2012), the court held that G.S. 14-306.4 does not violate the First Amendment.

26
Abandonment and Nonsupport

Abandonment and Nonsupport—Children (page 666)

Nonsupport of an Illegitimate Child (page 667)

2013 legislation, S.L. 2013-198, sec. 17, amended G.S. 49-2 to substitute the term "child born out of wedlock" for the term "illegitimate child."

27
Drug Offenses

Statute (page 673)

As a result of 2017 legislation, S.L. 2017-115, sec. 2, G.S. 90-87(14a) reads:

> **(14a) The term "isomer" means any type of isomer, including structural, geometric, or optical isomers, and stereoisomers.**

As a result of 2015 and 2016 legislation, S.L. 2015-299, sec. 2; S.L. 2016-93, sec. 6, add the following sentence at the end of subsection G.S. 90-87(16):

> **The term does not include industrial hemp as defined in G.S. 106-568.51, when the industrial hemp is produced and used in compliance with rules issued by the North Carolina Industrial Hemp Commission.**

As a result of 2017 legislation, S.L. 2017-115, sec. 2, G.S. 90-87(17)a. reads:

> **a. Opium, opiate and opioid, and any salt, compound, derivative, or preparation of opium, opiate, or opioid.**

This same 2017 legislation created a new subsection, G.S. 90-87(18a), as follows:

> **(18a) "Opioid" means any synthetic narcotic drug having opiate like activities but is not derived from opium.**

2017 legislation, S.L. 2017-74, sec. 3, created a new subsection, G.S. 90-87(26a), as follows:

> **(26a) "Targeted controlled substance" means any controlled substance included in G.S. 90-90(1) or (2) or G.S. 90-91(d).**

2015 legislation, S.L. 2015-162, sec. 1, 2017 legislation, S.L. 2017-115, sec. 3, and 2018 legislation, S.L. 2018-44, secs. 2–3, amended G.S. 90-89 (Schedule I) so that it reads as follows:

> **§ 90-89. Schedule I controlled substances.**
>
> **This schedule includes the controlled substances listed or to be listed by whatever official name, common or usual name, chemical name, or trade name designated. In determining that a substance comes within this schedule, the Commission shall find: a high potential for abuse, no currently accepted medical use in the United States, or a lack of accepted safety for use in treatment under medical supervision. The following controlled substances are included in this schedule:**
>
> **(1) Opiates.—Any of the following opiates or opioids, including the isomers, esters, ethers, salts and salts of isomers, esters, and ethers, unless specifically excepted, or listed in another schedule, whenever the existence of such isomers, esters, ethers, and salts is possible within the specific chemical designation:**
>
> **a. Acetyl-alpha-methylfentanyl (N[1-(1-methyl-2-phenethyl)-4/y-piperidinyl]-N-phenylacet amide).**
>
> **b. Acetylmethadol.**
>
> **c. Repealed by Session Laws 1987, c. 412, s. 2.**
>
> **d. Alpha-methylthiofentanyl (N-[1-methyl-2-(2-thienyl)ethyl/y-4/y-piperidinyl]-N-phenylpropanamide).**
>
> **e. Allylprodine.**
>
> **f. Alphacetylmethadol (except levo-alphacetylmethadol, also known as levomethadyl acetate and LAAM).**
>
> **g. Alphameprodine.**

h. Alphamethadol.
i. Alpha-methylfentanyl (N-(1-(alpha-methyl-beta-phenyl) ethyl-4-piperidyl) propionalilide; 1(1-methyl-2-phenyl-ethyl)-4-(N-propanilido) piperidine).
j. Benzethidine.
k. Betacetylmethadol.
l. Beta-hydroxfentanyl (N-[1-(2-hydroxy-2-phenethyl)-4-piperidinyl]-N-phenylpropanamide).
m. Beta-hydroxy-3-methylfentanyl (N-[1-(2-hydroxy-2-phenethyl)-3-methyl-4-piperidinyl]-N-pheny lpropanamide).
n. Betameprodine.
o. Betamethadol.
p. Betaprodine.
q. Clonitazene.
r. Dextromoramide.
s. Diampromide.
t. Diethylthiambutene.
u. Difenoxin.
v. Dimenoxadol.
w. Dimepheptanol.
x. Dimethylthiambutene.
y. Dioxaphetyl butyrate.
z. Dipipanone.
aa. Ethylmethylthiambutene.
bb. Etonitazene.
cc. Etoxeridine.
dd. Furethidine.
ee. Hydroxypethidine.
ff. Ketobemidone.
gg. Levomoramide.
hh. Levophenacylmorphan.
ii. 1-methyl-4-phenyl-4-propionoxypiperidine (MPPP).
jj. 3-Methylfentanyl (N-[3-methyl-1-(2-Phenylethyl)-4-Pi- peridyl]-N-Phenylpropanamide).
kk. 3-Methylthiofentanyl (N-[(3-methyl-1-(2-thienyl)ethyl/y-4-piperidinyl]-N-phenylpropanamide).
ll. Morpheridine.
mm. Noracymethadol.
nn. Norlevorphanol.
oo. Normethadone.
pp. Norpipanone.
qq. Para-fluorofentanyl (N-(4-fluorophenyl)-N-[1-(2-phen-ethyl)-4-piperidinyl]-propanamide.
rr. Phenadoxone.
ss. Phenampromide.
tt. 1-(2-phenethyl)-4-phenyl-4-acetoxypiperidine (PEPAP).
uu. Phenomorphan.
vv. Phenoperidine.
ww. Piritramide.
xx. Proheptazine.
yy. Properidine.
zz. Propiram.
aaa. Racemoramide.
bbb. Thiofentanyl (N-phenyl-N-[1-(2-thienyl)ethyl-4-piperidinyl]-propanamide.
ccc. Tilidine.

ddd. Trimeperidine.
eee. Acetyl Fentanyl.
fff. Trans-3,4-dichloro-N-(2(dimethylamino)cyclohexyl)-N-methyl-benzamide (U47700).
ggg. 3,4-dichloro-N([1(dimethylamino)cyclohexyl]methyl)benzamide; 1-(3,4-dichlorobenzamidomethyl)cyclohexyldimethylamine) (also known as AH-7921).
hhh. 3,4-dichloro-N-([diethylamino)cyclohexyl]-N-methylbenzamide (also known as U-49900).
iii. U-77891.
jjj. 1-phenylethylpiperidylidene-2-(4-chlorphenyl)sulfonamide; 1-(4-nitro-phenylethyl)piperidylidene-2-(4-chlorophenyl)sulfonamide; 4-chloro-N-[1-[2-(4-nitrophenyl)ethyl]-2-piperidinylidene]-benzenesulfonamide (also known as W-18).
kkk. 1-phenylethylpiperidylidene-2-(4-chlorophenyl)sulfonamide; 4-chloro-N-[1-(2-phenylethyl)-2-piperidinylidene]-benzenesulfonamide (also known as W-15).
lll. 1-cyclohexyl-4-(1,2-diphenylethyl)piperazine (also known as MT-45).

(1a) Fentanyl derivatives.—Any compounds structurally derived from N-[1-(2-phenylethyl)-4-piperidinyl]-N-phenylpropanamide (Fentanyl) by any substitution on or replacement of the phenethyl group, any substitution on the piperidine ring, any substitution on or replacement of the propanamide group, any substitution on the anilido phenyl group, or any combination of the above unless specifically excepted or listed in another schedule to include their salts, isomers, and salts of isomers. Fentanyl derivatives include, but are not limited to, the following:
a. N-(1-phenylethylpiperidin-4-yl)-N-phenylfuran-2-carboxamide (also known as Furanyl Fentanyl).
b. N-(1-phenethylpiperidin-4-yl)-N-phenylbutyramide; N-(1-phenethylpiperidin-4-yl)-N-phenylbutanamide (also known as Butyryl Fentanyl).
c. N-[1-[2-hydroxy-2-(thiophen-2-yl)ethyl]piperidin-4-yl]-N-phenylpropionamide; N-[1-[2-hydroxy-2-(2-thienyl)ethyl]-4-piperidinyl]-N-phenyl-propanamide (also known as Beta-Hydroxythiofentanyl).
d. N-phenyl-N-[1-(2-phenylethyl)piperidin-4-yl]-2propenamide (also known as Acrylfentanyl).
e. N-phenyl-N-[1-(2-phenylethyl)-4-piperidinyl]-pentanamide (also known as Valeryl Fentanyl).
f. N-(2-fluorophenyl)-N-[1-(2-phenylethyl)-4-piperidinyl]-propanamide (also known as 2-fluorofentanyl).
g. N-(3-fluorophenyl)-N-[1-(2-phenylethyl)-4-piperidinyl]-propanamide (also known as 3-fluorofentanyl).
h. N-(1-phenethylpiperidin-4-yl)-N-phenyltetrahydrofuran-2-carboxamide (also known as tetrahydrofuran fentanyl).
i. N-(4-fluorophenyl)-2-methyl-N-[1-(2-phenylethyl)-4-piperidinyl]-propanamide (also known as 4-fluoroisobutyryl fentanyl, 4-FIBF).
j. N-(4-fluorophenyl)-N-[1-(2-phenylethyl)-4-piperidinyl]-butanamide (also known as 4-fluorobutyryl fentanyl, 4-FBF).

(2) Opium derivatives.—Any of the following opium derivatives, including their salts, isomers, and salts of isomers, unless specifically excepted, or listed in another schedule, whenever the existence of such salts, isomers, and salts of isomers is possible within the specific chemical designation:
a. Acetorphine.
b. Acetyldihydrocodeine.
c. Benzylmorphine.
d. Codeine methylbromide.
e. Codeine-N-Oxide.

f. Cyprenorphine.
g. Desomorphine.
h. Dihydromorphine.
i. Etorphine (except hydrochloride salt).
j. Heroin.
k. Hydromorphinol.
l. Methyldesorphine.
m. Methyldihydromorphine.
n. Morphine methylbromide.
o. Morphine methylsulfonate.
p. Morphine-N-Oxide.
q. Myrophine.
r. Nicocodeine.
s. Nicomorphine.
t. Normorphine.
u. Pholcodine.
v. Thebacon.
w. Drotebanol.

(3) Hallucinogenic substances.—Any material, compound, mixture, or preparation which contains any quantity of the following hallucinogenic substances, including their salts, isomers, and salts of isomers, unless specifically excepted, or listed in another schedule, whenever the existence of such salts, isomers, and salts of isomers is possible within the specific chemical designation:

a. 3, 4-methylenedioxyamphetamine.
b. 5-methoxy-3, 4-methylenedioxyamphetamine.
c. 3, 4-Methylenedioxymethamphetamine (MDMA).
d. 3,4-methylenedioxy-N-ethylamphetamine (also known as N-ethyl-alpha-methyl-3,4-(methylenedioxy) phenethylamine, N-ethyl MDA, MDE, and MDEA).
e. N-hydroxy-3,4-methylenedioxyamphetamine (also known as N-hydroxy/y-alpha-methyl-3,4-(methylenedioxy) phenethylamine, and N-hydroxy MDA).
f. 3, 4, 5-trimethoxyamphetamine.
g. Alpha-ethyltryptamine. Some trade or other names: etryptamine, Monase, alpha-ethyl-1H-indole-3-ethanamine, 3-(2-aminobutyl) indole, alpha-ET, and AET.
h. Bufotenine.
i. Diethyltryptamine.
j. Dimethyltryptamine.
k. 4-methyl-2, 5-dimethoxyamphetamine.
l. Ibogaine.
m. Lysergic acid diethylamide.
n. Mescaline.
o. Peyote, meaning all parts of the plant presently classified botanically as Lophophora Williamsii Lemaire, whether growing or not; the seeds thereof; any extract from any part of such plant; and every compound, manufacture, salt, derivative, mixture or preparation of such plant, its seed or extracts.
p. N-ethyl-3-piperidyl benzilate.
q. N-methyl-3-piperidyl benzilate.
r. Psilocybin.
s. Psilocin.
t. 2, 5-dimethoxyamphetamine.
u. 2, 5-dimethoxy-4-ethylamphetamine. Some trade or other names: DOET.

v. 4-bromo-2, 5-dimethoxyamphetamine.
w. 4-methoxyamphetamine.
x. Ethylamine analog of phencyclidine. Some trade or other names: N-ethyl-1-phenylcyclohexylamine, (1-phenylcyclohexyl) ethylamine, N-(1-phenylcyclohexyl) ethylamine, cyclohexamine, PCE.
y. Pyrrolidine analog of phencyclidine. Some trade or other names: 1-(1-phenylcyclohexyl)-pyrrolidine, PCPy, PHP.
z. Thiophene analog of phencyclidine. Some trade or other names: 1-[1-(2-thienyl)-cyclohexyl]-piperidine, 2-thienyl analog of phencyclidine, TPCP, TCP.
aa. 1-[1-(2-thienyl)cyclohexyl]pyrrolidine; Some other names: TCPy.
bb. Parahexyl.
cc. 4-Bromo-2, 5-Dimethoxyphenethylamine.
dd. Alpha-Methyltryptamine.
ee. 5-Methoxy-N,N-diisopropyltryptamine.
ff. Methoxetamine (other names: MXE, 3-MeO-2-Oxo-PCE).
gg. BTCP (Benzothiophenylcyclohexylpiperidine).
hh. Deschloroketamine.
jj. 3-MeO-PCP (3-methoxyphencyclidine).
kk. 4-hydroxy-MET.
ll. 4-OH-MiPT (4-hydroxy-N-methyl-N-isopropyltryptamine).
mm. 5-methoxy-N-methyl-N-propyltryptamine (5-MeO-MiPT).

(4) Systemic depressants.—Any material compound, mixture, or preparation which contains any quantity of the following substances having a depressant effect on the central nervous system, including its salts, isomers, and salts of isomers whenever the existence of such salts, isomers, and salts of isomers is possible within the specific chemical designation, unless specifically excepted or unless listed in another schedule:
a. Mecloqualone.
b. Methaqualone.
c. Gamma hydroxybutyric acid; Some other names: GHB, gamma-hydroxybutyrate, 4-hydroxybutyrate, 4-hydroxybutanoic acid; sodium oxybate; sodium oxybutyrate.
d. Etizolam.
e. Flubromazepam.
f. Phenazepam.

(5) Stimulants.—Unless specifically excepted or unless listed in another schedule, any material, compound, mixture, or preparation that contains any quantity of the following substances having a stimulant effect on the central nervous system, including its salts, isomers, and salts of isomers:
a. Aminorex. Some trade or other names: aminoxaphen; 2-amino-5-phenyl-2-oxazoline; or 4,5-dihydro-5-phenyl-2-oxazolamine.
b. Cathinone. Some trade or other names: 2-amino-1-phenyl-1-propanone, alpha-aminopropiophenone, 2-aminopropiophenone, and norephedrone.
c. Fenethylline.
d. Methcathinone. Some trade or other names: 2-(methylamino)- propiophenone, alpha-(methylamino)propiophenone, 2-(methy- lamino)-1-phenylpropan-1-one, alpha-N-methylamino- propiophenone, monomethylproprion, ephedrone, N-methylcathinone, methylcathinone, AL-464, AL-422, AL-463, and UR1432.
e. (+-)cis-4-methylaminorex [(+-)cis-4,5-dihydro-4-methyl-5-phenyl-2-oxazolamine] (also known as 2-amino-4-methyl-5-phenyl-2-oxazoline).
f. N,N-dimethylamphetamine. Some other names: N,N,alpha-trimethylbenzeneethaneamine; N,N,alpha-trimethylphenethylamine.

g. N-ethylamphetamine.
h. 4-methylmethcathinone (also known as mephedrone).
i. 3,4-Methylenedioxypyrovalerone (also known as MDPV).
j. Substituted cathinones. A compound, other than bupropion, that is structurally derived from 2-amino-1-phenyl-1-propanone by modification in any of the following ways: (i) by substitution in the phenyl ring to any extent with alkyl, alkoxy, alkylenedioxy, haloalkyl, or halide substituents, whether or not further substituted in the phenyl ring by one or more other univalent substituents; (ii) by substitution at the 3-position to any extent; or (iii) by substitution at the nitrogen atom with alkyl, dialkyl, benzyl, or methoxybenzyl groups or by inclusion of the nitrogen atom in a cyclic structure.
k. N-Benzylpiperazine.
l. 2,5—Dimethoxy-4-(n)-propylthiophenethylamine.

(6) NBOMe compounds.—Any material compound, mixture, or preparation which contains any quantity of the following substances, including its salts, isomers, and salts of isomers whenever the existence of such salts, isomers, and salts of isomers is possible within the specific chemical designation unless specifically excepted or unless listed in another schedule:
a. 25B-NBOMe (2C-B-NBOMe) 2-(4-Bromo-2,5-dimethoxyphenyl)-N-(2-methoxybenzyl)ethanamine.
b. 25C-NBOMe (2C-C-NBOMe) 2-(4-Chloro-2,5-dimethoxyphenyl)-N-(2-methoxybenzyl)ethanamine.
c. 25D-NBOMe (2C-D-NBOMe) 2-(2,5-dimethoxy-4-methylphenyl)-N-(2-methoxybenzyl)ethanamine.
d. 25E-NBOMe (2C-E-NBOMe) 2-(4-Ethyl-2,5-dimethoxyphenyl)-N-(2-methoxybenzyl)ethanamine.
e. 25G-NBOMe (2C-G-NBOMe) 2-(2,5-dimethoxy-3,4-dimethylphenyl)-N-(2-methoxybenzyl)ethanamine.
f. 25H-NBOMe (2C-H-NBOMe) 2-(2,5-dimethoxyphenyl)-N-(2-methoxybenzyl) ethanamine.
g. 25I-NBOMe (2C-I-NBOMe) 2-(4-Iodo-2,5-dimethoxyphenyl)-N-(2-methoxybenzyl)ethanamine.
h. 25N-NBOMe (2C-N-NBOMe) 2-(2,5-dimethoxy-4-nitrophenyl)-N-(2-methoxybenzyl)ethanamine.
i. 25P-NBOMe (2C-P-NBOMe) 2-(4-Propyl-2,5-dimethoxyphenyl)-N-(2-methoxybenzyl)ethanamine.
j. 25T2-NBOMe (2C-T2-NBOMe) 2,5-dimethoxy-N-[(2-methoxyphenyl) methyl]-4-(methylthio)-benzeneethanamine.
k. 25T2-NBOMe (2C-T2-NBOMe) 2,5-dimethoxy-N-[(2-methoxyphenyl) methyl]-4-(methylthio)-benzeneethanamine.
l. 25T7-NBOMe (2C-T7-NBOMe) 2,5-dimethoxy-N-[(2-methoxyphenyl) methyl]-4-(propylthio)-benzeneethanamine.

(7) Synthetic cannabinoids.—Any quantity of any synthetic chemical compound that (i) is a cannabinoid receptor agonist and mimics the pharmacological effect of naturally occurring substances or (ii) has a stimulant, depressant, or hallucinogenic effect on the central nervous system that is not listed as a controlled substance in Schedules I through V, and is not an FDA-approved drug. Synthetic cannabinoids include, but are not limited to, the substances listed in sub-subdivisions a. through p. of this subdivision and any substance that contains any quantity of their salts, isomers (whether optical, positional, or geometric), homologues, and salts of isomers and homologues, unless specifically excepted, whenever the existence of these salts, isomers, homologues, and salts of isomers and homologues is possible within the specific chemical designation. The following substances are

examples of synthetic cannabinoids and are not intended to be inclusive of the substances included in this Schedule:

a. Naphthoylindoles. Any compound containing a 3-(1-naphthoyl)indole structure with substitution at the nitrogen atom of the indole ring by an alkyl, haloalkyl, alkenyl, cycloalkylmethyl, cycloalkylethyl, 1-(N-methyl-2-piperidinyl)methyl, or 2-(4-morpholinyl)ethyl group, whether or not further substituted in the indole ring to any extent and whether or not substituted in the naphthyl ring to any extent. Some trade or other names: JWH-015, JWH-018, JWH-019, JWH-073, JWH-081, JWH-122, JWH-200, JWH-210, JWH-398, AM-2201, and WIN 55-212.
b. Naphthylmethylindoles. Any compound containing a 1H-indol-3-yl-(1-naphthyl)methane structure with substitution at the nitrogen atom of the indole ring by an alkyl, haloalkyl, alkenyl, cycloalkylmethyl, cycloalkylethyl, 1-(N-methyl-2-piperidinyl)methyl, or 2-(4-morpholinyl) ethyl group, whether or not further substituted in the indole ring to any extent and whether or not substituted in the naphthyl ring to any extent.
c. Naphthoylpyrroles. Any compound containing a 3-(1-naphthoyl) pyrrole structure with substitution at the nitrogen atom of the pyrrole ring by an alkyl, haloalkyl, alkenyl, cycloalkylmethyl, cycloalkylethyl, 1-(N-methyl-2-piperidinyl)methyl, or 2-(4-morpholinyl)ethyl group, whether or not further substituted in the pyrrole ring to any extent and whether or not substituted in the naphthyl ring to any extent. Another name: JWH-307.
d. Naphthylmethylindenes. Any compound containing a naphthylideneindene structure with substitution at the 3-position of the indene ring by an alkyl, haloalkyl, alkenyl, cycloalkylmethyl, cycloalkylethyl, 1-(N-methyl-2-piperidinyl)methyl, or 2-(4-morpholinyl)ethyl group, whether or not further substituted in the indene ring to any extent and whether or not substituted in the naphthyl ring to any extent.
e. Phenylacetylindoles. Any compound containing a 3-phenylacetylindole structure with substitution at the nitrogen atom of the indole ring by an alkyl, haloalkyl, alkenyl, cycloalkylmethyl, cycloalkylethyl, 1-(N-methyl-2-piperidinyl)methyl, or 2-(4-morpholinyl)ethyl group, whether or not further substituted in the indole ring to any extent and whether or not substituted in the phenyl ring to any extent. Some trade or other names: SR-18, RCS-8, JWH-250, and JWH-203.
f. Cyclohexylphenols. Any compound containing a 2-(3-hydroxycyclohexyl)phenol structure with substitution at the 5-position of the phenolic ring by an alkyl, haloalkyl, alkenyl, cycloalkylmethyl, cycloalkylethyl, 1-(N-methyl-2-piperidinyl)methyl, or 2-(4-morpholinyl)ethyl group, whether or not substituted in the cyclohexyl ring to any extent. Some trade or other names: CP 47,497 (and homologues), cannabicyclohexanol.
g. Benzoylindoles. Any compound containing a 3-(benzoyl)indole structure with substitution at the nitrogen atom of the indole ring by an alkyl, haloalkyl, alkenyl, cycloalkylmethyl, cycloalkylethyl, 1-(N-methyl-2-piperidinyl)methyl, or 2-(4-morpholinyl)ethyl group, whether or not further substituted in the indole ring to any extent and whether or not substituted in the phenyl ring to any extent. Some trade or other names: AM-694, Pravadoline (WIN 48,098), and RCS-4.
h. 2,3-Dihydro-5-methyl-3-(4-morpholinylmethyl)pyrrolo[1,2,3-de]-1, 4-benzoxazin-6-yl]-1-napthalenylmethanone. Some trade or other name: WIN 55,212-2.

i. (6aR,10aR)-9-(hydroxymethyl)-6, 6-dimethyl-3-(2-methyloctan-2-yl)—6a,7,10,10a-tetrahydrobenzo[c]chromen-1-ol 7370. Some trade or other name: HU-210.

j. 3-(cyclopropylmethanone) indole or 3-(cyclobutylmethanone) indole or 3-(cyclopentylmethanone) indole by substitution at the nitrogen atom of the indole ring, whether or not further substituted in the indole ring to any extent, whether or not further substituted on the cyclopropyl, cyclobutyl, or cyclopentyl rings to any extent. Substances in this class include, but are not limited to: UR-144, fluoro-UR-144, XLR-11, A-796,260, and A-834,735.

k. Indole carboxaldehydes. Any compound structurally derived from 1H-indole-3-carboxaldehyde or 1H-indole-2-carboxaldehyde substituted in both of the following ways:
   1. At the nitrogen atom of the indole ring by an alkyl, haloalkyl, cyanoalkyl, alkenyl, cycloalkylmethyl, cycloalkylethyl, 1-(N-methyl-2-piperidinyl)methyl, 2-(4-morpholinyl)ethyl, 1-(N-methyl-2-pyrrolidinyl)methyl, 1-(N-methyl-3-morpholinyl)methyl, tetrahydropyranylmethyl, benzyl, or halo benzyl group; and
   2. At the carbon of the carboxaldehyde by a phenyl, benzyl, naphthyl, adamantyl, cyclopropyl, or propionaldehyde group; whether or not the compound is further modified to any extent in the following ways: (i) substitution to the indole ring to any extent, (ii) substitution to the phenyl, benzyl, naphthyl, adamantyl, cyclopropyl, or propionaldehyde group to any extent, (iii) a nitrogen heterocyclic analog of the indole ring, or (iv) anitrogen heterocyclic analog of the phenyl, benzyl, naphthyl, adamantyl, or cyclopropyl ring. Substances in this class include, but are not limited to: AB-001.

l. Indole carboxamides. Any compound structurally derived from 1H-indole-3-carboxamide or 1H-indole-2-carboxamide substituted in both of the following ways:
   1. At the nitrogen atom of the indole ring by an alkyl, haloalkyl, cyanoalkyl, alkenyl, cycloalkylmethyl, cycloalkylethyl, 1-(N-methyl-2-piperidinyl)methyl, 2-(4-morpholinyl)ethyl, 1-(N-methyl-2-pyrrolidinyl)methyl, 1-(N-methyl-3-morpholinyl)methyl, tetrahydropyranylmethyl, benzyl, or halo benzyl group; and
   2. At the nitrogen of the carboxamide by a phenyl, benzyl, naphthyl, adamantyl, cyclopropyl, or propionaldehyde group; whether or not the compound is further modified to any extent in the following ways: (i) substitution to the indole ring to any extent, (ii) substitution to the phenyl, benzyl, naphthyl, adamantyl, cyclopropyl, or propionaldehyde group to any extent, (iii) a nitrogen heterocyclic analog of the indole ring, or (iv) a nitrogen heterocyclic analog of the phenyl, benzyl, naphthyl, adamantyl, or cyclopropyl ring. Substances in this class include, but are not limited to: SDB-001 and STS-135.

m. Indole carboxylic acids. Any compound structurally derived from 1H-indole-3-carboxylic acid or 1H-indole-2-carboxylic acid substituted in both of the following ways:
   1. At the nitrogen atom of the indole ring by an alkyl, haloalkyl, cyanoalkyl, alkenyl, cycloalkylmethyl, cycloalkylethyl, 1-(N-methyl-2-piperidinyl)methyl, 2-(4-morpholinyl)ethyl, 1-(N-methyl-2-pyrrolidinyl)methyl, 1-(N-methyl-3-morpholinyl)methyl, tetrahydropyranylmethyl, benzyl, or halo benzyl group; and
   2. At the nitrogen of the carboxamide by a phenyl, benzyl, naphthyl, adamantyl, cyclopropyl, or propionaldehyde group; whether or not the compound is further modified to any extent in the following ways: (i) substitution to the indole ring to any extent, (ii) substitu-

tion to the phenyl, benzyl, naphthyl, adamantyl, cyclopropyl, or propionaldehyde group to any extent, (iii) a nitrogen heterocyclic analog of the indole ring, or (iv) a nitrogen heterocyclic analog of the phenyl, benzyl, naphthyl, adamantyl, or cyclopropyl ring. Substances in this class include, but are not limited to: SDB-001 and STS-135; whether or not the compound is further modified to any extent in the following ways: (i) substitution to the indole ring to any extent, (ii) substitution to the phenyl, benzyl, naphthyl, adamantyl, cyclopropyl, or propionaldehyde group to any extent, (iii) a nitrogen heterocyclic analog of the indole ring, or (iv) a nitrogen heterocyclic analog of the phenyl, benzyl, naphthyl, adamantyl, or cyclopropyl ring. Substances in this class include, but are not limited to: PB-22 and fluoro-PB-22.

n. Indazole carboxaldehydes. Any compound structurally derived from 1H-indazole-3-carboxaldehyde or 1H-indazole-2-carboxaldehyde substituted in both of the following ways:
   1. At the nitrogen atom of the indazole ring by an alkyl, haloalkyl, cyanoalkyl, alkenyl, cycloalkylmethyl, cycloalkylethyl, 1-(N-methyl-2-piperidinyl)methyl, 2-(4-morpholinyl)ethyl, 1-(N-methyl-2-pyrrolidinyl)methyl, 1-(N-methyl-3-morpholinyl)methyl, tetrahydropyranylmethyl, benzyl, or halo benzyl group; and
   2. At the carbon of the carboxaldehyde by a phenyl, benzyl, whether or not the compound is further modified to any extent in the following ways: (i) substitution to the indazole ring to any extent, (ii) substitution to the phenyl, benzyl, naphthyl, adamantyl, cyclopropyl, or propionaldehyde group to any extent, (iii) a nitrogen heterocyclic analog of the indazole ring, or (iv) a nitrogen heterocyclic analog of the phenyl, benzyl, naphthyl, adamantyl, or cyclopropyl ring.

o. Indazole carboxamides. Any compound structurally derived from 1H-indazole-3-carboxamide or 1H-indazole-2-carboxamide substituted in both of the following ways:
   1. At the nitrogen atom of the indazole ring by an alkyl, haloalkyl, cyanoalkyl, alkenyl, cycloalkylmethyl, cycloalkylethyl, 1-(N-methyl-2-piperidinyl)methyl, 2-(4-morpholinyl)ethyl, 1-(N-methyl-2-pyrrolidinyl)methyl, 1-(N-methyl-3-morpholinyl)methyl, tetrahydropyranylmethyl, benzyl, or halo benzyl group; and
   2. At the nitrogen of the carboxamide by a phenyl, benzyl, naphthyl, adamantyl, cyclopropyl, or propionaldehyde group; whether or not the compound is further modified to any extent in the following ways: (i) substitution to the indazole ring to any extent, (ii) substitution to the phenyl, benzyl, naphthyl, adamantyl, cyclopropyl, or propionaldehyde group to any extent, (iii) a nitrogen heterocyclic analog of the indazole ring, or (iv) a nitrogen heterocyclic analog of the phenyl, benzyl, naphthyl, adamantyl, or cyclopropyl ring. Substances in this class include, but are not limited to: AKB-48, fluoro-AKB-48, APINCACA, AB-PINACA, AB-FUBINACA, ADB-FUBINACA, and ADB-PINACA.

p. Indazole carboxylic acids. Any compound structurally derived from 1H-indazole-3-carboxylic acid or 1H-indazole-2-carboxylic acid substituted in both of the following ways:
   1. At the nitrogen atom of the indazole ring by an alkyl, haloalkyl, cyanoalkyl, alkenyl, cycloalkylmethyl, cycloalkylethyl, 1-(N-methyl-2-piperidinyl)methyl, 2-(4-morpholinyl)ethyl, 1-(N-methyl-2-pyrrolidinyl)methyl, 1-(N-methyl-3-morpholinyl)methyl, tetrahydropyranylmethyl, benzyl, or halo benzyl group; and

2. At the hydroxyl group of the carboxylic acid by a phenyl, benzyl, naphthyl, adamantyl, cyclopropyl, or propionaldehyde group; whether or not the compound is further modified to any extent in the following ways: (i) substitution to the indazole ring to any extent, (ii) substitution to the phenyl, benzyl, naphthyl, adamantyl, cyclopropyl, or propionaldehyde group to any extent, (iii) a nitrogen heterocyclic analog of the indazole ring, or (iv) a nitrogen heterocyclic analog of the phenyl, benzyl, naphthyl, adamantyl, or cyclopropyl ring.

q. Carbazoles. Any compound containing a carbazole ring system with a substituent on the nitrogen atom and bearing an additional substituent at the 1, 2, or 3 position of the carbazole ring system, with a linkage connecting the ring system to the substituent:
  1. Where the linkage connecting the carbazole ring system to the substituent if its 1, 2, or 3 position is any of the following: Alkyl, Carbonyl, Ester, Thione, Thioester, Amino, Alkylamino, Amido, or Alkylamido.
  2. Where the substituent at the 1, 2, or 3 position of the carbazole ring system, disregarding the linkage, is any of the following groups: Naphthyl, Quinolinyl, Adamantyl, Phenyl, Cycloalkyl (limited to cyclopropyl, cyclobutyl, cyclopentyl, or cyclohexyl), Biphenyl, Alkylamido (limited to ethylamido, propylamido, butanamido, pentamido), Benzyl, Carboxylic acid, Ester, Ether, Phenylpropylamido, or Phenylpropylamino; whether or not further substituted in either of the following ways: (i) the substituent at the 1, 2, or 3 position of the carbazole ring system, disregarding the linkage, is further substituted to any extent (ii) further substitution on the carbazole ring system to any extent. This class includes, but is not limited to, the following: MDMB CHMCZCA, EG-018, and EG-2201.

r. Naphthoylnaphthalenes. Any compound structurally derived from naphthalene-1-yl-(naphthalene-1-yl) methanone with substitutions on either of the naphthalene rings to any extent. Substances in this class include, but are not limited to: CB-1313.

2017 legislation, S.L. 2017-115, sec. 4, and 2018 legislation, S.L. 2018-44, sec. 4, amended G.S. 90-90(1) and (2) to read as follows:

(1) Any of the following substances whether produced directly or indirectly by extraction from substances of vegetable origin, or independently by means of chemical synthesis, or by a combination of extraction and chemical synthesis, unless specifically excepted or unless listed in another schedule:

a. Opium, opiate, or opioid and any salt, compound, derivative, or preparation of opium and opiate, excluding apomorphine, nalbuphine, dextrorphan, naloxone, naltrexone and nalmefene, and their respective salts, but including the following:
  1. Raw opium.
  2. Opium extracts.
  3. Opium fluid extracts.
  4. Powdered opium.
  5. Granulated opium.
  6. Tincture of opium.
  7. Codeine.
  8. Ethylmorphine.
  9. Etorphine hydrochloride.
  10. Any material, compound, mixture, or preparation which contains any quantity of hydrocodone.
  11. Hydromorphone.
  12. Metopon.

13. Morphine.
14. Oxycodone.
15. Oxymorphone.
16. Thebaine.
17. Dihydroetorphine.

b. Any salt, compound, derivative, or preparation thereof which is chemically equivalent or identical with any of the substances referred to in paragraph 1 of this subdivision, except that these substances shall not include the isoquinoline alkaloids of opium.
c. Opium poppy and poppy straw.
d. Cocaine and any salt, isomer, salts of isomers, compound, derivative, or preparation thereof, or coca leaves and any salt, isomer, salts of isomers, compound, derivative, or preparation of coca leaves, or any salt, isomer, salts of isomers, compound, derivative, or preparation thereof which is chemically equivalent or identical with any of these substances, except that the substances shall not include decocanized coca leaves or extraction of coca leaves, which extractions do not contain cocaine or ecgonine.
e. Concentrate of poppy straw (the crude extract of poppy straw in either liquid, solid or powder form which contains the phenanthrine alkaloids of the opium poppy).

(2) Any of the following opiates or opioids, including their isomers, esters, ethers, salts, and salts of isomers, whenever the existence of such isomers, esters, ethers, and salts is possible within the specific chemical designation unless specifically exempted or listed in other schedules:

a. Alfentanil.
b. Alphaprodine.
c. Anileridine.
d. Bezitramide.
e. Carfentanil.
f. Dihydrocodeine.
g. Diphenoxylate.
h. Fentanyl.
h1. Fentanyl immediate precursor chemical, 4-anilino-N-phenethyl-4-piperidine (ANPP).
i. Isomethadone.
j. Levo-alphacetylmethadol. Some trade or other names: levo-alpha-acetylmethadol, levomethadyl acetate, or LAAM.
k. Levomethorphan.
l. Levorphanol.
m. Metazocine.
n. Methadone.
o. Methadone—Intermediate, 4-cyano-2-dimethylamino-4, 4/y-diphenyl butane.
p. Moramide—Intermediate, 2-methyl-3-morpholino-1, 1-diphenyl-propane-carboxylic acid.
q. Pethidine.
r. Pethidine—Intermediate—A, 4-cyano-1-methyl-4/y-phenylpiperidine.
s. Pethidine—Intermediate—B, ethyl-4-phenylpiperidine-4-carboxylate.
t. Pethidine—Intermediate—C, 1-methyl-4-phenylpiperidine-4-carboxylic acid.
u. Phenazocine.
v. Piminodine.
w. Racemethorphan.
x. Racemorphan.
y. Remifentanil.

z. Sufentanil.
aa. Tapentadol.

2015 legislation, S.L. 2015-162, sec. 2, amended G.S. 90-90(3)d. to read as follows:

d. **Methylphenidate, including its salts, isomers, and salts of its isomers.**

2017 legislation, S.L. 2017-115, sec. 5, amended G.S. 90-91(d), repealing subsections (d)3. and (d)4. and adding a new subsection, (d)9., as follows:

9. **Buprenorphine.**

2016 and 2017 legislation, S.L. 2016-113, sec. 9; S.L. 2017-115, sec. 5, amended G.S. 90-91(k) so that it reads as follows:

(k) Anabolic steroids. The term "anabolic steroid" means any drug or hormonal substance, chemically and pharmacologically related to testosterone (other than estrogens, progestins, and corticosteroids) that promotes muscle growth, including, but not limited to, the following:
1. Methandrostenolone,
2. Stanozolol,
3. Ethylestrenol,
4. Nandrolone phenpropionate,
5. Nandrolone decanoate,
6. Testosterone propionate,
7. Chorionic gonadotropin,
8. Boldenone,
8a. Boldione,
9. Chlorotestosterone (4-chlorotestosterone),
10. Clostebol,
11. Dehydrochlormethyltestosterone,
11a. Desoxymethyltesterone (17[alpha]-methyl-5[alpha]-androst-2-en-17[beta]-ol) (also known as madol),
12. Dibydrostestosterone (4-dihydrotestosterone),
13. Drostanolone,
14. Fluoxymesterone,
15. Formebulone (formebolone),
16. Mesterolene,
17. Methandienone,
18. Methandranone,
19. Methandriol,
19a. Methasterone,
20. Methenolene,
21. Methyltestosterone,
22. Mibolerone,
23. Nandrolene,
24. Norethandrolene,
25. Oxandrolone,
26. Oxymesterone,
27. Oxymetholone,
28. Stanolone,
29. Testolactone,
30. Testosterone,
31. Trenbolone,
31a. 19-nor-4,9(10)-androstadienedione (estra-4,9(10)-diene-3,17-dione), and
32. Any salt, ester, or isomer of a drug or substance described or listed in this subsection, if that salt, ester, or isomer promotes muscle growth. Except such term does not include (i) an anabolic steroid which is expressly intended for administration through implants to cattle or other nonhuman species and which has been approved

by the Secretary of Health and Human Services for such administration or (ii) chorionic gonadotropin when administered by injection for veterinary use by a licensed veterinarian or the veterinarian's designated agent. If any person prescribes, dispenses, or distributes such steroid for human use, such person shall be considered to have prescribed, dispensed, or distributed an anabolic steroid within the meaning of this subsection.

2017 legislation, S.L. 2017-115, sec. 6, amended the list of depressants in G.S. 90-92(a)(1) to include the following additional substances:

d1. Carisoprodol.
n1. Dichloralphenazone.
u1. Fospropol.
yy. Zopiclone.

2017 legislation, S.L. 2017-115, sec. 6; S.L. 2017-212, sec. 8.8(a), amended G.S. 90-92(a)(5) to read as follows:

(5) Narcotic Drugs.—Unless specifically excepted or unless listed in another schedule, any material, compound, mixture, or preparation containing limited quantities of any of the following narcotic drugs, or any salts thereof:
a. Not more than 1 milligram of difenoxin and not less than 25 micrograms of atropine sulfate per dosage unit.
[b. Repealed]
c. 2-[(dimethylamino)methyl]-1-(3-methoxyphenyl)cyclohexanol, its salts, optical and geometric isomers, and salts of these isomers (including tramadol).

Note that while S.L. 2017-212, sec. 8.8(a) appears to retain 90-92(a)(5)b., listing buprenorphine, S.L. 2017-115 repealed that provision and moved buprenorphine to G.S. 90-91(d).

2017 legislation, S.L. 2017-115, sec. 7, amended G.S. 90-93, adding a new subsection, (a)(4), as follows:

(4) Anticonvulsants.—Unless specifically exempted or excluded or unless listed in another schedule, any material, compound, mixture, or preparation which contains any quantity of the following substances having a stimulant effect on the central nervous system, including its salts, isomers, and salts of isomers:
a. Ezogabine.
b. Lacosamide.
c. Brivaracetam.
d. Pregabalin

2017 legislation, S.L. 2017-115, sec. 8, repealed G.S. 90-94(3).

As a result of 2017 legislation, S.L. 2017-115, sec. 11, G.S. 90-95(b)(2) reads as follows:

(2) A controlled substance classified in Schedule III, IV, V, or VI shall be punished as a Class I felon, except that the sale of a controlled substance classified in Schedule III, IV, V, or VI shall be punished as a Class H felon. The transfer of less than 5 grams of marijuana for no remuneration shall not constitute a delivery in violation of G.S. 90-95(a)(1).

As a result of that same 2017 legislation, G.S. 90-95(d)(4) reads as follows:

(4) A controlled substance classified in Schedule VI shall be guilty of a Class 3 misdemeanor, but any sentence of imprisonment imposed must be suspended and the judge may not require at the time of sentencing that the defendant serve a period of imprisonment as a special condition of probation. If the quantity of the controlled substance exceeds one-half of an ounce (avoirdupois) of marijuana or one-twentieth of an ounce (avoirdupois) of the extracted resin of marijuana, commonly known as hashish, the violation shall be punishable as a Class 1 misdemeanor. If the quantity of the controlled substance exceeds one and one-half ounces (avoirdupois)

of marijuana, or three-twentieths of an ounce (avoirdupois) of the extracted resin of marijuana, commonly known as hashish, or if the controlled substance consists of any quantity of synthetic tetrahydrocannabinols or tetrahydrocannabinols isolated from the resin of marijuana, the violation shall be punishable as a Class I felony.

As a result of S.L. 2013-124; S.L. 2014-115, sec. 41(a); and S.L. 2015-32, sec. 1, G.S. 90-95(d1) reads as follows:

(d1) (1) Except as authorized by this Article, it is unlawful for any person to:

a. Possess an immediate precursor chemical with intent to manufacture a controlled substance; or

b. Possess or distribute an immediate precursor chemical knowing, or having reasonable cause to believe, that the immediate precursor chemical will be used to manufacture a controlled substance; or

c. Possess a pseudoephedrine product if the person has a prior conviction for the possession of methamphetamine, possession with the intent to sell or deliver methamphetamine, sell or deliver methamphetamine, trafficking methamphetamine, possession of an immediate precursor chemical, or manufacture of methamphetamine. The prior conviction may be from any jurisdiction within the United States.

Except where the conduct is covered under subdivision (2) of this subsection, any person who violates this subdivision shall be punished as a Class H felon.

As a result of 2015 legislation, S.L. 2015-32, sec. 1, and 2018 legislation, S.L. 2018-44, secs. 5–6, G.S. 90-95(d2) reads as follows:

(d2) The immediate precursor chemicals to which subsection (d1) of this section applies are those immediate precursor chemicals designated by the Commission pursuant to its authority under G.S. 90-88, and the following (until otherwise specified by the Commission):

(1) Acetic anhydride.
(2) Acetone.
(2a) Ammonium nitrate.
(2b) Ammonium sulfate.
(3) Anhydrous ammonia.
(4) Anthranilic acid.
(5) Benzyl chloride.
(6) Benzyl cyanide.
(7) 2 Butanone (Methyl Ethyl Ketone).
(8) Chloroephedrine.
(9) Chloropseudoephedrine.
(10) D lysergic acid.
(11) Ephedrine.
(12) Ergonovine maleate.
(13) Ergotamine tartrate.
(13a) Ether based starting fluids.
(14) Ethyl ether.
(15) Ethyl Malonate.
(16) Ethylamine.
(17) Gamma butyrolactone.
(18) Hydrochloric Acid. (Muriatic Acid).
(19) Iodine.
(20) Isosafrole.
(21) Sources of lithium metal.
(22) Malonic acid.
(23) Methylamine.
(24) Methyl Isobutyl Ketone.
(25) N acetylanthranilic acid.

(26) N ethylephedrine.
(27) N ethylepseudoephedrine.
(28) N methylephedrine.
(29) N methylpseudoephedrine.
(29a) N-phenethyl-4-piperidinone (NPP).
(30) Norpseudoephedrine.
(30a) Petroleum based organic solvents such as camping fuels and lighter fluids.
(31) Phenyl 2 propanone.
(32) Phenylacetic acid.
(33) Phenylpropanolamine.
(34) Piperidine.
(35) Piperonal.
(36) Propionic anhydride.
(37) Pseudoephedrine.
(38) Pyrrolidine.
(39) Red phosphorous.
(40) Safrole.
(40a) Sodium hydroxide (Lye).
(41) Sources of sodium metal.
(42) Sulfuric Acid.
(43) Tetrachloroethylene.
(44) Thionylchloride.
(45) Toluene.

Sale or Delivery and Related Offenses (page 694)

Sale or Delivery of a Controlled Substance (page 694)

Punishment (page 694)

Delete the third paragraph of this section and replace it with the following:

> The delivery of a Schedule III, IV, V, or VI substance is a Class I felony; the sale of a Schedule III, IV, V, or VI substance is a Class H felony. G.S. 90-95(b)(2).

Notes (page 694)

Element (2)(b) (page 694)

As a result of 2017 legislation, S.L. 2017-115, sec. 11, delete the second sentence of this note and replace it with the following:

> It is not a delivery to transfer for no remuneration less than 5 grams of marijuana, G.S. 90-95(b)(2); such activity could be punished only as possession of a controlled substance.

Add the following text to this note:

> The State need not show that the defendant personally received compensation in exchange for the delivery. State v. Land, 223 N.C. App. 305, 313 (2012), *aff'd per curiam*, 366 N.C. 550 (2013).

Attempt and conspiracy (page 695)

Insert the following after the second sentence of this note:

> *See also* State v. Warren, 244 N.C. App. 134, 150–51 (2015) (applying G.S. 90-98 and holding that conspiracy to manufacture methamphetamine was properly punished as a Class C felony).

Jury instructions (new note)

Where the evidence showed that the defendant transferred less than 5 grams of marijuana, the trial court erred by not instructing the jury that in order to prove delivery, the State was required to prove that the defendant transferred the marijuana for remuneration. *Land*, 223 N.C. App. at 315.

Defenses (page 695)

For a case where the trial court did not err by declining to instruct the jury that the defendant would be exempt from prosecution if he was an "ultimate user" pursuant to G.S. 90-101(c), see *State v. Bice*, 261 N.C. App. 664 (2018) (the evidence did not support the defense).

Multiple convictions and punishments (page 696)

For another case standing for the proposition stated in this note that a defendant may not be separately convicted of both the sale and delivery of a controlled substance arising from a single transaction, see *State v. Fleig*, 232 N.C. App. 647, 650–51 (2014) (purchaser gave the defendant $20 for a bag of marijuana; purchaser then asked for another bag in light of the payment made and the defendant provided it).

Related Offenses Not in This Chapter (page 696)

Add the following offense to this list:

Distributing, dispensing, delivering, or purchasing marijuana on property used for industrial hemp production or in a manner intended to disguise the marijuana due to its proximity to industrial hemp. G.S. 106-568.57(a).

Furnishing a Controlled Substance to an Inmate (page 697)

Related Offenses Not in This Chapter (page 698)

Add the following offense to this list:

Use of an unmanned aircraft system near a confinement or correctional facility. G.S. 15A-300.3, *as enacted by* S.L. 2017-179.

As a result of 2018 legislation, S.L. 2018-67, sec. 3, delete the first item in this list and replace it with the following:

Providing articles forbidden by prison rules or items for prison escape, assault, or insurrection; possessing items for prison escape, assault, or insurrection. G.S. 14-258.

Delete the third offense in the list and replace it with the following:

Furnishing alcoholic beverages, tobacco products, or mobile phones to an inmate or a delinquent juvenile. G.S. 14-258.1(b)–(d).

Delete the last offense in this list and replace it with the following:

Inmate's possession of a tobacco product. G.S. 14-258.1(e).

Inmate's possession of a mobile phone or wireless communication device or component. G.S. 14-258.1(g).

Manufacture of a Controlled Substance (page 698)

Notes (page 699)

Element (2) (page 699)

Where officers find a controlled substance and an array of items used to package and distribute that substance, the evidence suffices to support a manufacturing conviction. State v. Miranda, 235 N.C. App. 601, 612 (2014) (evidence was sufficient where more than 28 grams of cocaine and several items that are commonly used to weigh, separate, and package cocaine for sale were seized from the defendant's bedroom).

There was sufficient evidence of manufacturing methamphetamine where an officer observed the defendant and another person at the scene for approximately forty minutes and among the items recovered there were a handbag containing a syringe and methamphetamine; a duffle bag containing a clear, two-liter bottle containing methamphetamine; empty boxes and blister packs of pseudoephedrine; a full pseudoephedrine blister pack; an empty pack of lithium batteries; a lithium battery from which the lithium had been removed; iodized salt; sodium hydroxide; drain opener; funnels; tubing; coffee filters; syringes; various items of clothing; and a plastic bottle containing white and pink granular material; the defendant's presence at the scene, the evidence recovered, the officer's testimony that the defendant and his accomplice were going back and forth in the area moving bottles, and testimony that the defendant gave instructions to his accomplice to keep the smoke out of her eyes was sufficient evidence of manufacturing. State v. Davis, 236 N.C. App. 376, 382–83 (2014).

Element (4) (page 699)

For additional cases supporting the proposition that in a manufacturing case based on preparing or compounding the State must prove intent to distribute, see *Miranda*, 235 N.C. App. at 610 (stating this requirement but finding no plain error where the trial court allowed the jury to find the defendant guilty of manufacturing by packaging as well as compounding and the undisputed evidence showed that he packed the controlled substance), and *State v. Simpson*, 230 N.C. App. 119, 124–25 (2013) (reiterating this requirement but finding no plain error where a jury instruction on this issue was lacking).

Multiple convictions and punishments (new note)

Where a defendant engages in manufacturing of methamphetamine in two separate distinct locations, two convictions for manufacturing may obtain. State v. Maloney, 253 N.C. App. 563, 572 (2017) (rejecting the defendant's argument that his conduct constituted a single continuing offense; two separate methamphetamine labs were discovered: one in the trunk of a car and one in a storage unit).

No double jeopardy violation occurs when a defendant is convicted of trafficking in methamphetamine, manufacturing methamphetamine, and possession of methamphetamine based on the same illegal substance. *Simpson*, 230 N.C. App. at 126–27.

Related Offenses Not in This Chapter (page 700)

Add the following offense to this list:

Manufacture of marijuana on property used for industrial hemp production or in a manner intended to disguise the marijuana due to its proximity to industrial hemp. G.S. 106-568.57(a).

Possession Offenses (page 700)

Possession of a Controlled Substance (page 700)

Punishment (page 701)

In the first bulleted list in this section, replace the word "cocoa" with "coca."

As a result of 2017 legislation, S.L. 2017-115, sec. 11, delete the fourth paragraph of this note and replace it with the following:

Except as discussed immediately below, for a Schedule VI controlled substance, the offense is a Class 3 misdemeanor for which a sentence of imprisonment must be suspended and the judge may not require that the defendant serve a period of imprisonment as a special condition of probation. G.S. 90-95(d)(4). There are two exceptions to this punishment level for Schedule VI controlled substances. First, if the defendant possessed

- more than ½ ounce of marijuana and up to 1½ ounces of marijuana or
- more than 1/20 of an ounce and up to 3/20 of an ounce of hashish,

the offense is a Class 1 misdemeanor. Second, if the defendant possessed

- more than 1½ ounces of marijuana,
- more than 3/20 of an ounce of hashish, or
- any quantity of synthetic tetrahydrocannabinols or tetrahydrocannabinols isolated from the resin of marijuana,

the offense is a Class I felony. G.S. 90-95(d)(4).

This section states that for all misdemeanor controlled substance offenses, several provisions—including G.S. 90-95(e)(3)—elevate punishment based on the defendant's prior conviction record. Because G.S. 90-95(e)(3) establishes a separate felony offense rather than merely a sentence enhancement of the underlying misdemeanor, an offense punished under this provision may be subject to habitual felon status. State v. Howell, 370 N.C. 647, 654 (2018).

Notes (page 702)

Element (1) (page 702)

A presumption that the defendant has the required guilty knowledge is created when the State makes a prima facie case that the defendant has committed a crime, such as possession of a controlled substance, trafficking by possession, or trafficking by transportation, that lacks a specific intent element. State v. Galaviz-Torres, 368 N.C. 44 (2015). However, when the defendant denies or contests having knowledge of the specific controlled substance that he or she has been charged with possessing or transporting, the existence of the requisite guilty knowledge becomes an issue of fact that must be decided by the jury. *Id.*; State v. Coleman, 227 N.C. App. 354, 359–60 (2013) (trafficking by possession case; the trial court committed plain error by failing to instruct on this Element; although the defendant did not testify or present evidence to raise the issue of knowledge as a disputed fact, the State presented evidence that the defendant told a detective that he did not know the container contained heroin; this constituted a contention that the defendant did not know the true identity of what he possessed). For example, when a defendant admits having possession of a box stored in his or her car but denies knowing that the box contained the controlled substance at issue, whether the defendant knowingly possessed the controlled substance is an issue for the jury. *Coleman*, 227 N.C. App. at 359. By contrast, a defendant's denial of any knowledge of having possessed any container or controlled substance does not defeat the presumption and likewise does not create an issue on which the jury must be instructed. *Galaviz-Torres*, 368 N.C. 44 (in this trafficking case the defendant did not deny knowledge of the contents of a gift bag in which cocaine was found or admit that he possessed a particular substance while denying any knowledge of the substance's identity; rather, the defendant denied having had any knowledge that the van he was driving contained either the gift bag or cocaine). A defendant's denial of any knowledge about the existence of a substance or claim that it belonged to someone else similarly does not defeat the presumption of guilty knowledge. State v. Stallings, ___ N.C. App. ___, 843 S.E.2d 310 (2020).

For a trafficking and possession with intent case where the evidence was insufficient to establish that the defendant knowingly possessed or transported the controlled substance, see *State v. Velazquez-Perez*, 233 N.C. App. 585, 588–93 (2014) (drugs were found in secret compartments of a truck driven by the defendant Villalvavo but owned by a passenger, Velazquez-Perez, who hired Villalvavo to drive the truck; while evidence regarding the truck's log books may have been incriminating as to Velazquez-Perez, it did not apply to Villalvavo, who had not been working for Velazquez-Perez long and had no stake in the company or control over Velazquez-Perez; Villalvavo's nervousness during the stop did not constitute adequate incriminating circumstances).

Element (2) (page 702)

The following content modifies the text in the second and third paragraphs of this note regarding the necessary proof to establish constructive possession when the defendant does not have exclusive control over the place where contraband is found.

In *State v. Chekanow*, 370 N.C. 488, 494–95 (2018), the court stated that "for evidence of constructive possession to be sufficient, if the defendant owns the premises on which the contraband is found, (1) he must also have exclusive possession of the premises on which the contraband is found, or (2) the State must show additional incriminating circumstances demonstrating the defendant has dominion or control over the contraband." However, in *State v. Wirt*, 263 N.C. App. 370 (2018), the court of appeals distinguished *Chekanow*, holding that evidence of a defendant's power as the driver to control an automobile in which contraband is found (in that case, drugs and a firearm) is sufficient, *in and of itself*, to give rise to an inference of constructive possession, even if the defendant's possession of the vehicle is nonexclusive. In *Wirt*, the court expressly rejected the defendant's argument that because he did not have exclusive possession of the vehicle, the State was required to show other incriminating circumstances. Quoting from *State v. Mitchell*, 224 N.C. App. 171, 177 (2012), the court noted that "the courts in this State have held consistently that the driver of a borrowed car, like the owner of the car, has the power to control the contents of the car. Moreover, power to control the automobile where [contraband] was found *is sufficient, in and of itself*, to give rise to the inference of knowledge and possession sufficient to go to the jury." Although the defendant in *Wirt* was the driver of the vehicle, the court clearly seems to view ownership of a vehicle in the same way.

For additional cases holding that the evidence was sufficient to establish constructive possession, see *Chekanow*, 370 N.C. at 496 (the evidence was sufficient to establish constructive possession of marijuana plants found on property the defendants owned but did not exclusively possess; additional incriminating circumstances included, among other things, that the plants were in close proximity to an area maintained by the defendants, the defendants' residence was in "reasonably close proximity" to the plants, the plants were surrounded by a fence that was not easily surmountable, the defendants had the ability to control who entered this portion of the property by establishing the sole entry point in the front yard next to their home, other items belonging to the defendants were in the same location as the plants, and one defendant appeared to flee the premises as a helicopter hovered to investigate the plants); *State v. Lindsey*, 366 N.C. 325 (2012) (reversing 219 N.C. App. 249 (2012) for the reasons stated in the dissenting opinion, which found sufficient evidence of constructive possession where, after the defendant fled from his crashed van, officers found a bag containing marijuana near trash receptacles in the parking lot where the crash occurred; detailed evidence concerning the distance of the bag from the defendant's van, the condition of the bag, and the fact that the van's passenger window was open supported the inference that the defendant discarded the bag while fleeing); *State v. Bradshaw*, 366 N.C. 90, 96–97 (2012) (sufficient evidence of constructive possession of drugs and a rifle when those items were found in a bedroom that was not under the defendant's exclusive control but several documents linked him to the contraband and placed him in the room within two days of when the contraband was found); *State v. Wirt*, 263 N.C. App. 370 (2018) (notwithstanding his nonexclusive possession of a vehicle, the defendant's control as its driver was sufficient to give rise to an inference of constructive possession of drugs and a firearm in the vehicle; moreover, the State presented evidence of additional incriminating circumstances to support that inference); *State v. Guy*, 262 N.C. App. 313 (2018) (marijuana and a robbery victim's debit card were found near a gun in close proximity to the defendant and his vehicle; the gun matched one described by the victim as having been used in the robbery, and an officer located the defendant's car less than a quarter-mile from the victim's residence and about one minute after receiving information about the incident); *State v. Steele*, 260 N.C. App. 315 (2018) (in this trafficking case there was sufficient evidence that the defendant constructively possessed cocaine found in a bedroom dresser drawer where, among other things, the defendant and another person shared the bedroom, which was padlocked from the outside to prevent entry; the two had the only keys to the lock and the other person stated that she did not put the cocaine in the dresser and that it was not hers; and the defendant's own statements established that he knew the weight of the cocaine); *State v. Davis*, 236 N.C. App. 376, 383–84 (2014) (there was sufficient evidence that the defendant constructively possessed methamphetamine found in a duffle bag where, among other things, the defendant and his accomplice were the only people at the scene of the "one pot" outdoor meth lab and for approximately forty minutes both moved freely about the site where all of the items were laid out on a blanket); *State v. Rodelo*, 231 N.C. App. 660, 665–66 (2014) (in a trafficking by possession case there was sufficient evidence of constructive possession where the defendant was found hiding alone in a tractor-trailer where money was secreted; cocaine was found in a car parked, with its doors open, in close proximity to the tractor-trailer; the cash and the cocaine were packaged similarly; wrappings were all over the tractor-trailer and in the open area of a car parked close by; the defendant admitted knowing where the money was hidden; and the entire warehouse in which the vehicles were located had a chemical smell of cocaine); *State v. Torres-Gonzalez*, 227 N.C. App. 188, 195 (2013) (sufficient evidence in a trafficking by possession case involving an undercover sale); *State v. Hazel*, 226 N.C. App. 336, 344 (2013) (sufficient evidence that the defendant constructively possessed heroin found in an apartment that was not owned or rented by him); *State v. Chisholm*, 225 N.C. App. 592, 597 (2013) (sufficient evidence of constructive possession even though the defendant did not have exclusive possession of the bedroom where the drugs were found); *State v. Huerta*, 221 N.C. App. 436, 448–49 (2012) (sufficient evidence of constructive possession where the defendant admitted living for three years at the home where the drugs were found; where an illegally purchased pistol, ammunition, and more than $9,000 in cash were in his closet; and where he had more than $2,000 in cash on his person); and *State v. Adams*, 218 N.C. App. 589, 594–95 (2012) (sufficient evidence of constructive possession where the defendant drove a drug provider to a location that the defendant had arranged for a drug sale, knowing that the provider had the drugs).

For cases where there was insufficient evidence of constructive possession, see *State v. Royster*, 262 N.C. App. 701 (2018) (after the defendant produced a black box in exchange for his kidnapped father, a shooting broke out and one of the kidnappers ran into the woods while holding the box; approximately eighteen hours later, officers found a black box containing cocaine fifty–seventy-five yards into the woods; the box was dry, despite heavy rain, and a dry mason jar containing additional cocaine was found nearby), *aff'd*, 373 N.C. 157 (2019); *State v. Holloway*, 250 N.C. App. 674, 681 (2016) (the only evidence tying the defendant to a residence or to contraband was his presence at the residence on the afternoon in question and a single photograph of him found face down in a plastic storage bin in a bedroom of the residence); *State v. Dulin*, 247 N.C. App. 799, 809–10 (2016) (there was insufficient evidence that the defendant constructively possessed marijuana found in an uncovered fishing boat located in the yard of a home occupied by multiple people, including the defendant; the boat was roughly seventy feet from the house in an unfenced area, there was no evidence that the defendant had any ownership interest in or possession of the boat, and the defendant was never seen near the boat); and *State v. Garrett*, 246 N.C. App. 651, 655–56 (2016) (there was insufficient evidence of constructive possession of methamphetamine in a case that arose out of a controlled drug buy where, although the defendant led individuals to a trailer to buy drugs and entered the trailer with their money, the other individuals were the only ones who actually possessed the drugs).

Exceptions (new note)
Before searching a person or his or her premises or vehicle, an officer may ask the person whether a hypodermic needle or other sharp object that may cut or puncture the officer is on the defendant's person or in the premises or vehicle to be searched. If such an object is present and the person alerts the officer of that fact before the search, the person may not be charged with or prosecuted for possession of drug paraphernalia for the needle or sharp object or for possession of residual amounts of a controlled substance contained in the needle or sharp object. G.S. 90-113.22(c).

Greater and lesser-included offenses (page 706)
Simple possession is a lesser-included offense of possession of a controlled substance on the premises of a local confinement facility, and a defendant may not be convicted of both when they stem from the same act of possession. State v. Barnes, 229 N.C. App. 556, 568–69 (2013), *aff'd*, 367 N.C. 453 (2014) (per curiam).

Multiple convictions and punishments (page 706)
Where the defendant was in possession of a bag containing a mixture of two separate Schedule I controlled substances, two convictions were proper. State v. Williams, 252 N.C. App. 231, 234 (2017).

No double jeopardy violation occurs when a defendant is convicted of trafficking in methamphetamine, manufacturing methamphetamine, and possession of methamphetamine based on the same illegal substance. State v. Simpson, 230 N.C. App. 119, 126–27 (2013).

Limited immunity from prosecution (new note)
A 2013 law, S.L. 2013-23, provides limited immunity from prosecution for persons seeking medical assistance for themselves or others in the event of a drug-related overdose. The law enacts G.S. 90-96.2, providing that a person who experiences a drug-related overdose or who seeks medical assistance for someone experiencing a drug-related overdose shall not be prosecuted for

- a misdemeanor offense under G.S. 90-95(a)(3) or
- a felony offense under G.S. 90-95(a)(3) involving less than 1 gram of cocaine or heroin

if the evidence of the crime was obtained as a result of the person seeking medical assistance. G.S. 90-96.2(b), (c). The term "drug-related overdose" means "an acute condition, including mania, hysteria, extreme physical illness, coma, or death resulting from the consumption or use of a controlled substance, or another substance with which a controlled substance was combined, and that a layperson would reasonably believe to be a drug overdose that requires medical assistance." *Id.* § (a). This "Good Samaritan" provision creates an immunity from prosecution that is waived if not asserted by the defendant; it is not a matter of subject matter jurisdiction. State v. Osborne, ___ N.C. App. ___, ___ S.E.2d ___ (2020).

2016 legislation, S.L. 2016-88, sec. 4, enacted G.S. 90-113.27(c), providing limited immunity for employees, volunteers, and participants in authorized needle and hypodermic syringe exchange programs when those persons possess residual amounts of a controlled substance contained in a used needle, hypodermic syringe, or injection supplies obtained from or returned to a program.

Possession of a Controlled Substance at a Prison or Local Confinement Facility (page 707)

Notes (page 707)

Element (1) (new note)
This offense is a general intent crime, and there is no requirement that a defendant specifically intended to possess the controlled substance on the premises of a local confinement facility. State v. Barnes, 229 N.C. App. 556, 561–66 (2013) (rejecting the defendant's argument that he did not voluntarily enter the premises but was brought to the facility by officers against his wishes; the fact that the officers failed to warn the defendant that taking a controlled substance into the jail would constitute a separate offense was of no consequence), *aff'd*, 367 N.C. 453 (2014) (per curiam).

Element (2) (new note)
The defendant's own testimony that he had a "piece of dope . . . in the jail" was sufficient evidence that he possessed a controlled substance on the premises. State v. Poole, 223 N.C. App. 185, 194 (2012). The State is not required to prove unlawful possession as an element of this offense; under G.S. 90-113.1(a), the burden is on the defendant to claim an exception, such as possession under a valid prescription. State v. Palmer, ___ N.C. App. ___, 847 S.E.2d 449 (2020).

Greater and lesser-included offenses (new note)
Simple possession is a lesser-included offense of possession of a controlled substance on the premises of a local confinement facility, and a defendant may not be convicted of both when they stem from the same act of possession. *Barnes*, 229 N.C. App. at 568–69.

Possession of a Controlled Substance with Intent to Manufacture, Sell, or Deliver (page 708)

Notes (page 708)

Element (4) (page 708)
For cases where there was sufficient evidence of the requisite intent, see *State v. Coley*, 257 N.C. App. 780, 788–89 (2018) (although the defendant's vehicle contained only 11.5 grams of marijuana, it was packaged in two sandwich bags and a digital scale and twenty-three additional loose sandwich bags were found in the vehicle), *State v. Yisrael*, 255 N.C. App. 184, 193 (2017) (although only 10.88 grams of marijuana was found, its packaging was suggestive of the requisite intent and the 20-year-old defendant was carrying a large amount of cash on the grounds of a high school where he was not a student and a stolen, loaded handgun was found inside the vehicle), *aff'd per curiam*, 371 N.C. 108 (2018), *State v. Blakney*, 233 N.C. App. 516, 520 (2014) (84.8 grams of marijuana was found in the defendant's car in multiple containers, including four dime bags, along with a box of sandwich bags, digital scales, and a large quantity of cash in small denominations), and *State v. Wilson*, 269 N.C. App. 648 (2020) (defendant's possession of .34 grams of cocaine in a corner bag and 11.19 grams in a package, in conjunction with his evasive actions, constituted sufficient evidence of intent, despite the absence of cash or paraphernalia).

Related Offenses Not in This Chapter (page 710)

Add the following offense to this list:

Possession with intent to manufacture, distribute, dispense, deliver, or purchase marijuana on property used for industrial hemp production or in a manner intended to disguise the marijuana due to its proximity to industrial hemp. G.S. 106-568.57(a).

Possession of an Immediate Precursor with Intent to Manufacture a Controlled Substance (page 710)

Statute (page 710)

As noted above in this supplement, the list of immediate precursor chemicals in G.S. 90-95(d2) was amended by 2015 legislation. S.L. 2015-32, sec.1.

Notes (page 711)

Element (3) (page 711)

As noted above in this supplement, the list of immediate precursor chemicals in G.S. 90-95(d2) was amended by 2015 legislation. S.L. 2015-32, sec.1.

Add the following to this note:

In a case involving possession of pseudoephedrine with intent to manufacture methamphetamine, the court held that the evidence was sufficient even though the pseudoephedrine had not been identified through a chemical analysis. State v. Hooks, 243 N.C. App. 435, 445–46 (2015) (reasoning that chemical analysis is required only for a "controlled substance" and that pseudoephedrine is not such a substance).

Possession of Pseudoephedrine after Methamphetamine Conviction (new crime)

This offense was enacted by 2013 legislation, S.L. 2013-124, sec. 1, and amended by S.L. 2015-32, sec.1.

Statute

See G.S. 90-95(d1)(1)c., reproduced above in this supplement.

Elements

A person guilty of this offense

(1) possesses
(2) a pseudoephedrine product *and*
(3) has a prior conviction for
 (a) possession of methamphetamine,
 (b) possession with the intent to sell or deliver methamphetamine,
 (c) sale or delivery of methamphetamine,
 (d) trafficking in methamphetamine,
 (e) possession of an immediate precursor chemical, *or*
 (f) manufacture of methamphetamine.

Punishment

Class H felony. G.S. 90-95(d1).

Notes

Element (1). See the note on Element (2) to "Possession of a Controlled Substance" in the main volume.

Element (3). The prior conviction may be from any jurisdiction within the United States. G.S. 90-95(d1)(1)c.

Strict liability. This is a strict liability offense. State v. Miller, 246 N.C. App. 330, 336–38 (2016), *rev'd on other grounds*, 369 N.C. 658 (2017).

Constitutionality. For a case where the North Carolina Supreme Court rejected an as-applied constitutional challenge to the statute, see *Miller*, 369 N.C. 658 (rejecting the notion that the defendant's conviction rested on wholly passive conduct and concluding that it rested on his own active conduct).

Related Offenses Not in This Chapter

See the offenses listed under "Possession of an Immediate Precursor with Intent to Manufacture a Controlled Substance" in the main volume.

Counterfeit Controlled Substance Offenses (page 711)

Creating a Counterfeit Controlled Substance (page 711)

Notes (page 712)

Element (3) (page 712)

For another case supporting the statement in this note that the State need not prove all of the factors in G.S. 90-87(6)b. to prove that the substance was intentionally misrepresented, see *State v. Chisholm*, 225 N.C. App. 592, 595 (2013).

Sale or Delivery of a Counterfeit Controlled Substance (page 713)

Notes (page 713)

Multiple convictions and punishments (new note)

A defendant may not be separately convicted of both the sale and delivery of a counterfeit controlled substance arising from a single transfer. State v. Chevallier, 264 N.C. App. 204 (2019) (citing State v. Moore, 327 N.C. 378 (1990)).

Drug Offenses Involving Minors (page 714)

Manufacture, Sale, Delivery, or Possession of a Controlled Substance with Intent to Manufacture, Sell, or Deliver at or Near a School, Child Care Center, or Public Park (page 719)

Notes (page 720)

Element (5)(b) (page 720)

For a case where the evidence was insufficient to establish that the property was used for a child care center, see *State v. Piland*, 263 N.C. App. 323 (2018).

Trafficking (page 721)

Statute (page 721)

2012 legislation, S.L. 2012-188, sec. 5, amended G.S. 90-95(h), adding time to the maximum sentences for drug trafficking to cover early release onto post-release supervision. The act adds three months to the maximum sentences for Class C, D, and E trafficking and nine months to the maximum sentences for Class F, G, and H trafficking.

2018 legislation, S.L. 2018-44, sec. 7, amended G.S. 90-95(h)(3d), changing its coverage from MDPV to substituted cathinones as follows:

> (3d) Any person who sells, manufactures, delivers, transports, or possesses 28 grams or more of any substituted cathinone, as defined in G.S. 90-89(5)(j), or any mixture containing such substance shall be guilty of a felony, which felony shall be known as "trafficking in substituted cathinones," and if the quantity of such substance or mixture involved:
>
> a. Is 28 grams or more, but less than 200 grams, such person shall be punished as a Class F felon and shall be sentenced to a minimum term of 70 months and a maximum term of 93 months in the State's prison and shall be fined not less than fifty thousand dollars ($50,000);
>
> b. Is 200 grams or more, but less than 400 grams, such person shall be punished as a Class E felon and shall be sentenced to a minimum term of 90 months and a maximum term of 120 months in the State's prison and shall be fined not less than one hundred thousand dollars ($100,000);
>
> c. Is 400 grams or more, such person shall be punished as a Class C felon and shall be sentenced to a minimum term of 225 months and a maximum term of 282 months in the State's prison and shall be fined at least two hundred fifty thousand dollars ($250,000).

That same 2018 legislation repealed G.S. 90-95(h)(3e).

That same 2018 legislation also amended G.S. 90-95(h)(4), replacing the terms "opium or opiate" with "opium, opiate, or opioid." The revised subsection now reads as follows:

> (4) Any person who sells, manufactures, delivers, transports, or possesses four grams or more of opium, opiate, or opioid, or any salt, compound, derivative, or preparation of opium, opiate, or opioid (except apomorphine, nalbuphine, analoxone and naltrexone and their respective salts), including heroin, or any mixture containing such substance, shall be guilty of a felony which felony shall be known as "trafficking in opium, opiate, opioid, or heroin" and if the quantity of such controlled substance or mixture involved:
>
> a. Is four grams or more, but less than 14 grams, such person shall be punished as a Class F felon and shall be sentenced to a minimum term of 70 months and a maximum term of 93 months in the State's prison and shall be fined not less than fifty thousand dollars ($50,000);
>
> b. Is 14 grams or more, but less than 28 grams, such person shall be punished as a Class E felon and shall be sentenced to a minimum term of 90 months and a maximum term of 120 months in the State's prison and shall be fined not less than one hundred thousand dollars ($100,000);
>
> c. Is 28 grams or more, such person shall be punished as a Class C felon and shall be sentenced to a minimum term of 225 months and a maximum term of 282 months in the State's prison and shall be fined not less than five hundred thousand dollars ($500,000).

That same 2018 legislation also amended G.S. 90-95(h)(4b) to correct a typographical error in the statute. It had stated that the proscribed offense shall be known as "trafficking in MDADMA." The 2018 amendment clarifies that the proscribed offense is "trafficking in MDA/MDMA."

Trafficking in Marijuana (page 725)

Punishment (page 725)

For 2012 legislative changes to the punishment provision, see "Statute," above in this supplement under "Trafficking."

Notes (page 726)

Element (1) (page 726)

See this note to "Possession of a Controlled Substance," above.

Handling a drug solely for inspection purposes, standing alone, does not constitute possession. State v. Moose, 101 N.C. App. 59 (1990). For example, when a defendant tasted a substance to test its quality and then gave it back to back to the undercover officer, he did not knowingly possess the substance within the meaning of this offense. State v. Wheeler, 138 N.C. App. 163 (2000). Likewise, there was not substantial evidence of possession when a defendant identified a substance as "re-rock" (that is, fake) methamphetamine and declined to complete a purchase, even when the substance included a mixture of actual methamphetamine. State v. Campbell, ___ N.C. App. ___, 845 S.E.2d 119 (2020).

In a trafficking by possession and transportation case there was sufficient evidence of knowing possession and transportation where the defendant drove the vehicle that contained the cocaine. State v. Lopez, 219 N.C. App. 139, 149–50 (2012).

For a case where the evidence was insufficient to establish that the defendant knowingly possessed or transported the controlled substance, see *State v. Velazquez-Perez*, 233 N.C. App. 585, 588–93 (2014) (drugs were found in secret compartments of a truck driven by the defendant Villalvavo but owned by a passenger, Velazquez-Perez, who hired Villalvavo to drive the truck; while evidence regarding the truck's log books may have been incriminating as to Velazquez-Perez, it did not apply to Villalvavo, who had not been working for Velazquez-Perez long and had no stake in the company or control over Velazquez-Perez; Villalvavo's nervousness during the stop did not constitute adequate incriminating circumstances).

Element (3) (page 727)

As a result of 2015 and 2016 legislation, S.L. 2015-299, sec. 2; S.L. 2016-93, sec. 6, add the following at the end of this note, before the ending quotation mark:

The term does not include industrial hemp as defined in G.S. 106-568.51, when the industrial hemp is produced and used in compliance with rules issued by the North Carolina Industrial Hemp Commission.

Element (5) (page 727)

When a defendant simultaneously possesses more than one cache of controlled substances, the amounts of each cache may—in certain circumstances—be combined to reach the trafficking amount. State v. Hazel, 226 N.C. App. 336, 347 (2013) (trafficking in heroin by possession case; amount of heroin recovered from the defendant's person outside an apartment was combined with heroin recovered from the apartment).

Greater and lesser-included offenses (page 728)

Conspiracy to traffic in cocaine is not a lesser-included offense of trafficking in cocaine. State v. Rodelo, 231 N.C. App. 660, 667 (2014).

Multiple convictions and punishments (page 728)

No double jeopardy violation occurs when a defendant is convicted of trafficking in methamphetamine, manufacturing methamphetamine, and possession of methamphetamine based on the same illegal substance. State v. Simpson, 230 N.C. App. 119, 126–27 (2013).

Relation to other offenses (page 729)

Delete this note.

Trafficking in Synthetic Cannabinoids (page 729)

Punishment (page 729)

For 2012 legislative changes to the punishment provision, see "Statute," above in this supplement under "Trafficking."

Notes (page 730)

Elements (3) and (5) (new note)
A synthetic cannabinoid is defined in G.S. 90-89(7), reproduced at the beginning of this chapter in this supplement.

Element (5) (page 730)
When a defendant simultaneously possesses more than one cache of controlled substances, the amounts of each cache may—in certain circumstances—be combined to reach the trafficking amount. State v. Hazel, 226 N.C. App. 336, 347 (2013) (trafficking in heroin by possession case; amount of heroin recovered from the defendant's person outside an apartment was combined with heroin recovered from the apartment).

The entire weight of a mixture containing a controlled substance covered by the trafficking statutes can be used to support trafficking charges; the fact that the mixture is at an intermediate stage in the manufacturing process and is not ingestible, is unstable, and is not ready for distribution is irrelevant. State v. Davis, 236 N.C. App. 376, 386–87 (2014).

For purposes of the trafficking statutes, a mixture includes a combination of a controlled substance and rice, added to remove moisture. State v. Miranda, 235 N.C. App. 601, 608–09 (2014) (rejecting the defendant's argument that a combination of cocaine and rice did not constitute a mixture within the meaning of the trafficking statute).

Constitutionality (new note)
This trafficking offense and the ones listed below cover trafficking in the specified controlled substance and in mixtures containing that substance. The North Carolina Court of Appeals has rejected constitutional challenges grounded in the statute's coverage of mixtures. State v. Ellison, 213 N.C. App. 300, 309–12 (2011) (rejecting the defendant's due process and cruel and unusual punishment arguments in a trafficking in opium case), *aff'd on other grounds*, 366 N.C. 439 (2013).

Relation to other offenses (new note)
The listing of a particular controlled substance on the drug schedules does not limit the State's ability to prosecute a defendant for trafficking in a substance when a trafficking statute otherwise applies. *Ellison*, 213 N.C. App. at 323 ("the controlled substance schedule to which a particular opiate derivative is assigned has nothing to do with the extent to which activities involving that substance are subject to punishment under the trafficking statutes").

Trafficking in Methaqualone (page 730)

The section on "Punishment" and the new notes listed above in this supplement under "Trafficking in Synthetic Cannabinoids" apply to this offense as well.

Trafficking in Cocaine (page 731)

The section on "Punishment" and the new notes listed above in this supplement under "Trafficking in Synthetic Cannabinoids" apply to this offense as well.

Trafficking in Methamphetamine (page 732)

The section on "Punishment" and the new notes listed above in this supplement under "Trafficking in Synthetic Cannabinoids" apply to this offense as well.

Trafficking in Amphetamine (page 733)

The section on "Punishment" and the new notes listed above in this supplement under "Trafficking in Synthetic Cannabinoids" apply to this offense as well.

Trafficking in Substituted Cathinones (page 734) (revised title)

The section on "Punishment" and the new notes listed above in this supplement under "Trafficking in Synthetic Cannabinoids" apply to this offense as well.

2018 legislation, S.L. 2018-44, sec. 7, amended this offense so that it now applies to substituted cathinones, as defined in G.S. 90-89(5)(j), instead of MDPV.

Elements (page 734)

As a result of the 2018 legislation noted above, the elements of this offense should read as follows:

A person guilty of this offense

(1) knowingly
(2) (a) sells, manufactures, delivers, transports, or possesses *or*
    (b) conspires to sell, manufacture, deliver, transport, or possess
(3) substituted cathinones or any mixture containing substituted cathinones
(4) to another person (if the person sells or delivers) *and*
(5) the quantity of substituted cathinones or any mixture containing substituted cathinones is
    (a) 28 grams or more but less than 200 grams,
    (b) 200 grams or more but less than 400 grams, *or*
    (c) 400 grams or more.

Notes (page 735)

Elements (3) and (5) (new note)
A substituted cathinone is defined in G.S. 90-89(5)(j). G.S. 90-95(h)(3d).

Trafficking in Mephedrone (page 735)

2018 legislation, S.L. 2018-44, sec. 7, repealed the statute proscribing trafficking in mephedrone.

Trafficking in Opium, Opiate, Opioid, or Heroin (page 736) (revised title)

The section on "Punishment" and the new notes listed above in this supplement under "Trafficking in Synthetic Cannabinoids" apply to this offense as well.

Elements (page 736)

As a result of 2018 legislation, S.L. 2018-44, sec. 7, when stating the covered controlled substances the elements should refer to opium, opiate, opioid, or heroin.

Notes (page 736)

Element (3) (page 736)

As a result of that same 2018 legislation, delete the first paragraph of this note and replace it with the following:

> The statute prohibits trafficking in the following substances: "opium, opiate, or opioid, or any salt, compound, derivative, or preparation of opium, opiate, or opioid (except apomorphine, nalbuphine, analoxone and naltrexone and their respective salts), including heroin, or any mixture containing such substance." G.S. 90-95(h)(4).

Add the following to this note:

> This trafficking offense bases criminal liability on the total weight of the mixture involved; tablets and pills are mixtures covered by that provision, including prescription pharmaceuticals. State v. Ellison, 366 N.C. 439, 443–44 (2013).

Immunity for treatment with opioid antagonist (new note)
G.S. 90-12.7, as amended by S.L. 2017-74, sec. 2, provides immunity, in certain circumstances, for treating an overdose with the opioid antagonist naloxone hydrochloride.

Trafficking in LSD (page 737)

The section on "Punishment" and the new notes listed above in this supplement under "Trafficking in Synthetic Cannabinoids" apply to this offense as well.

Trafficking in MDA and MDMA (page 738)

The section on "Punishment" and the new notes listed above in this supplement under "Trafficking in Synthetic Cannabinoids" apply to this offense as well.

Controlled Substance Offenses Involving Fraud, Misrepresentation, or Similar Activities (page 740)

Obtaining a Controlled Substance by Misrepresenting Oneself as a Licensed Practitioner (page 740)

Statute (page 740)

Replace the statute reproduced in the main volume with the following:

§ 90-108. Prohibited acts; penalties.

(a) It shall be unlawful for any person:

(1) Other than practitioners licensed under Articles 1, 2, 4, 6, 11, 12A of this Chapter to represent to any registrant or practitioner who manufactures, distributes, or dispenses a controlled substance under the provision of this Article that he or she is a licensed practitioner in order to secure or attempt to secure any controlled substance as defined in this Article or to in any way impersonate a practitioner for the purpose of securing or attempting to secure any drug requiring a prescription from a practitioner as listed above and who is licensed by this State.

[*Subsections (2) through (15) are not reproduced here.*]

(b) Any person who violates this section shall be guilty of a Class 1 misdemeanor. Provided, that if the criminal pleading alleges that the violation was committed intentionally, and upon trial it is specifically found that the violation was committed intentionally, such violations shall be a Class I felony . . . .

[*Subsections (1) through (3) are not reproduced here.*]

Related Offenses Not in This Chapter (page 742)

As a result of 2018 legislation, S.L. 2018-44, sec. 9, add the following to this section:

Embezzle, misapply, divert, etc., a controlled substance prescribed to another by one providing medical care or related services. G.S. 14-108(a)(15).

Maintaining a Store, Dwelling, Vehicle, Boat, or Other Place for Use, Storage, or Sale of Controlled Substances (page 743)

Notes (page 744)

Element (1) (page 744)
For a case where this Element was satisfied, see *State v. Huerta*, 221 N.C. App. 436, 450 (2012).

Element (2) (page 744)
As used in this Element, the term "keeps" "refers to possessing something for at least a short period of time—or intending to retain possession of something in the future—for a certain use." State v. Rogers, 371 N.C. 397, 402 (2018).

For cases where the evidence was sufficient to establish this Element, see *Rogers*, *id.* at 401–02 (the evidence was sufficient to establish this Element with respect to a vehicle where, during ninety minutes of police surveillance, the defendant was the only person who used the car and a service receipt dated two and one-half months earlier and containing his name was found in it); *State v. Alvarez*, 260 N.C. App. 571 (2018), *aff'd*, 372 N.C. 303 (2019) (per curiam) (although the vehicle alleged to have been used in the offense was registered in his wife's name, the defendant described it as "[his] truck" and acknowledged that no one else used it); *State v. Williams*, 242 N.C. App. 361, 371 (2015) (the defendant received mail addressed to him at the residence alleged to have been used in the offense; his probation officer visited him there to conduct routine home contacts; the defendant's personal effects were at the residence, including a pay stub and work gear; and he identified the house to a third party as being his; the court rejected the defendant's argument that the evidence was insufficient because it failed to show that he was financially or otherwise responsible for the dwelling or its upkeep, noting that residency standing alone can establish this Element).

For another case where the evidence was insufficient to establish this Element, see *State v. Holloway*, 250 N.C. App. 674, 683–84 (2016) (there was no evidence that the defendant was the owner or lessee of the residence alleged to have been involved in the offense, paid for its utilities or upkeep, had been seen in or around the dwelling, or lived there).

Element (4)(a) (new note)

A defendant cannot be convicted under this prong on the basis of his or her own use of drugs in his or her vehicle. State v. Simpson, 230 N.C. App. 119, 121–22 (2013).

Element (4)(b) (page 745)

Delete the fourth and fifth sentences of this note and replace them with the following:

As used in Element (2), the term "keeps" "refers to possessing something for at least a short period of time—or intending to retain possession of something in the future—for a certain use." *Rogers*, 371 N.C. at 402. As used in Element (4)(b), the term "keeping" has a different meaning.

The second paragraph of this note states: "As used in Element (4)(b), the term 'keeping' 'denotes not just possession, but possession that occurs over a duration of time.' State v. Dickerson, 152 N.C. App. 714, 716 (2002) (quoting State v. Mitchell, 336 N.C. 22, 32 (1994))." The North Carolina Supreme Court's decision in *Rogers*, 371 N.C. at 406, disavows the quoted language from *Mitchell*. As a result, delete all text in the second paragraph of this note suggesting that keeping denotes possession over time and replace it with the following:

In *Rogers*, 371 N.C. at 403, the North Carolina Supreme Court held that as used in this Element, the term "keeping" refers to the storing of drugs. In so holding, the court specifically rejected any language in *Mitchell*, 336 N.C. at 32, that has been read as requiring that the "keeping" of drugs requires possession that occurs over a duration of time. *Id.* The supreme court explained:

> [T]he statutory text does not require that drugs be kept for "a duration of time." . . . [T]he linchpin of the inquiry . . . is whether the defendant was using th[e] vehicle, building, or other place for the storing of drugs. So, for instance, when the evidence indicates that a defendant has possessed a car for at least a short period of time, but that he had just begun storing drugs inside his car at the time of his arrest, that defendant has still violated [the statute]—even if, arguably, he has not stored the drugs for any appreciable "duration of time." The critical question is *whether* a defendant's car is used to store drugs, not *how long* the defendant's car has been used to store drugs for. As a result, we reject any notion that [the statute] requires that a car kept or maintained by a defendant be used to store drugs for a certain minimum period of time—or that evidence of drugs must be found in the vehicle, building, or other place on more than one occasion—for a defendant to have violated [the statute]. But again, merely having drugs in a car (or other place) is not enough to justify a conviction . . . . The evidence and all reasonable inferences drawn from the evidence must indicate, based "on the totality of the circumstances," that the drugs are also being stored there. To the extent that Mitchell's "duration of time" requirement conflicts with the text of [the statute], therefore, this aspect of *Mitchell* is disavowed.

> *Rogers*, 371 N.C. at 406 (citation omitted). In *Rogers*, the supreme court went on to hold that the evidence in the case before it was sufficient to establish that the defendant was using the vehicle in question for the keeping of controlled substances. *Id.* (the court noted that cocaine was found in the gas-cap compartment and that no one else was seen using the vehicle; because neither the defendant nor anyone else accessed the gas-cap compartment, it can be inferred that the cocaine was placed there before police surveillance began; the defendant's actions—arriving at a hotel, remaining for forty-five minutes with the drugs in the compartment, and then leaving in the vehicle—indicate that he was not using the car only to transport drugs; additionally, the court noted, a person who wants to store contraband will prefer to do so in a hidden place, "which is exactly what putting the cocaine in the gas-cap compartment would accomplish," *id.* at 404; the court further noted that putting the drugs in a place that is hard to access suggests storage rather than mere transportation; this evidence, the court concluded, indicates that the defendant was using the vehicle to store cocaine; moreover, other evidence in the case suggesting that the defendant was selling drugs supports an inference that the defendant was using the vehicle to store cocaine).

The second paragraph of this note also states that "when the allegation is that the property is being used for the selling of controlled substances, evidence of more than one sale is required." As a preliminary matter, based on pre-*Rogers* case law, it is more accurate to state that while evidence of one sale of a controlled substance does not by itself demonstrate that the property was kept or maintained for selling controlled substances, the court may look at the totality of the circumstances. State v. Dunston, 256 N.C. App. 103, 106 (2017), *aff'd per curiam*, 371 N.C. 76 (2018). Additionally, based on *Rogers* and its rejection of the notion that the term "keeping" requires possession that occurs over a duration of time, it is not clear that the term "selling" requires more than one sale.

Because cases holding that the evidence was sufficient to establish this Element under the stricter pre-*Rogers* standard are likely to remain good law under the more permissive *Rogers* test, add the following to this note:

> For additional cases where the evidence was sufficient to establish this Element, see *State v. Alvarez*, 260 N.C. App. 571 (2018) (under a totality of the circumstances the evidence was sufficient where, among other things, a trafficking amount of cocaine was found in a false-bottomed compartment in a truck-bed floor that was constructed by the defendant; the cocaine was wrapped in plastic and oil to evade detection by canine units; and the defendant was involved in a drug-related transaction immediately before his arrest), *aff'd*, 372 N.C. 303 (2019) (per curiam); *State v. Dunston*, 256 N.C. App. 103, 106 (2017) (the defendant was in the vehicle alleged to have been used in the offense at a known drug location; he unwrapped and rerolled cigars after manipulating them, activity an officer thought was consistent with distributing marijuana; the driver engaged in a hand-to-hand exchange of cash with another person and was discovered to be in possession of marijuana; and a search found that the defendant no longer had possession of the "cigars" but possessed a trafficking quantity of heroin along with plastic bags, two sets of digital scales, three cell phones, and $155 in cash), *aff'd per curiam*, 371 N.C. 76 (2018); *State v. Rousseau*, 250 N.C. App. 825, *3 (2016) (unpublished) (rejecting the defendant's argument that the evidence was insufficient to show that a vehicle was used for the selling or keeping of a controlled substance; officers found marijuana remnants throughout the vehicle's interior space as well as a sock containing 29.927 grams of marijuana in the vehicle's engine compartment), *aff'd per curiam*, 370 N.C. 268 (2017); *State v. Alston*, 254 N.C. App. 90, 94 (2017) (controlled substances and drug paraphernalia were found in a residence; a security camera set up in the living room of that residence observed the front yard; the defendant, a convicted felon, had constructive possession of a handgun; an officer observed traffic at the residence over several days consistent with drug transactions; and a confidential source bought a controlled substance from the residence); and *State v. Williams*, 242 N.C. App. 361, 373 (2015) (officers found a bag containing 39.7 grams of 4-methylethcathinone and methylone, a plastic bag containing "numerous little corner baggies," a set of digital scales, and $460 in twenty dollar bills).

For a post-*Rogers* case where the evidence of this Element was insufficient, see *State v. Miller*, 264 N.C. App. 517 (2019) (merely having drugs in a car does not justify a conviction under this offense when, under the totality of the circumstances, there was no other evidence of drugs, drug paraphernalia, cash, weapons, or other implements of the drug trade).

Drug Paraphernalia Offenses (revised title)

Possession of Drug Paraphernalia (page 747)

Statute (page 747)

2014 legislation, S.L. 2014-119, sec. 3(a), amended G.S. 90-113.22(a) to read as follows:

> (a) It is unlawful for any person to knowingly use, or to possess with intent to use, drug paraphernalia to plant, propagate, cultivate, grow, harvest, manufacture, compound, convert, produce, process, prepare, test, analyze, package, repackage, store, contain, or conceal a controlled substance other than marijuana which it would be unlawful to possess, or to inject, ingest, inhale, or otherwise introduce into the body a controlled substance other than marijuana which it would be unlawful to possess.

2013 legislation, S.L. 2013-147, added a new subsection, (c), to the statute, which subsequently was amended by 2015 legislation, S.L. 2015-284, sec. 2, to read as follows:

> (c) Prior to searching a person, a person's premises, or a person's vehicle, an officer may ask the person whether the person is in possession of a hypodermic needle or other sharp object that may cut or puncture the officer or whether such a hypodermic needle or other sharp object is on the premises or in the vehicle to be searched. If there is a hypodermic needle or other sharp object on the person, on the person's premises, or in the person's vehicle and the person alerts the officer of that fact prior to the search, the person shall not be charged with or prosecuted for possession of drug paraphernalia for the needle or sharp object, or for residual amounts of a controlled substance contained in the needle or sharp object. The exemption under this subsection does not apply to any other drug paraphernalia that may be present and found during the search. For purposes of this subsection, the term "officer" includes "criminal justice officers" as defined in G.S. 17C-2(3) and a "justice officer" as defined in G.S. 17E-2(3).

2019 legislation, S.L. 2019-159, added a new subsection, (d), to the statute, effective July 11, 2019, to read as follows:

> (d) Notwithstanding the provisions of subsection (a) of this section, it is not unlawful for (i) a person who introduces a controlled substance into his or her body, or intends to introduce a controlled substance into his or her body, to knowingly use, or to possess with intent to use, testing equipment for identifying or analyzing the strength, effectiveness, or purity of that controlled substance or (ii) a governmental or nongovernmental organization that promotes scientifically proven ways of mitigating health risks associated with drug use and other high-risk behaviors to possess such testing equipment or distribute such testing equipment to a person who intends to introduce a controlled substance into his or her body.

Notes (page 749)

Element (2) (new note)

For a discussion of actual and constructive possession in the context of drug possession offenses, see the note on Element (2) to "Possession of a Controlled Substance."

For cases where the evidence was sufficient to establish that the defendant possessed drug paraphernalia, see *State v. Sawyers*, 256 N.C. App. 339, 345–46 (2017) (the marijuana pipe in question was found in a crashed vehicle; although the defendant did not have exclusive possession of the vehicle, sufficient incriminating circumstances established constructive possession, including that the defendant was driving the vehicle, the pipe was found on the driver's side floorboard, and the defendant admitted ownership of a small amount of marijuana found on his person); *State v. Dulin*, 247 N.C. App. 799, 804–06 (2016) (paraphernalia (including, among other items, a digital scale and a marijuana grinder) was in plain view in a common living area of a home over which the defendant exercised nonexclusive control; the defendant spent hours at the house on the day in question and admitted that a blunt was in his truck parked out front; police found marijuana in the truck's console and in the house behind a photograph of the defendant; and several people visited the house while the defendant was there, including a man who shook hands with the defendant as if they were passing an item back and forth).

Element (5) (new note)
As a result of 2014 legislation, this offense pertains to controlled substances other than marijuana. G.S. 90-113.22(a) (as amended by S.L. 2014-119, sec. 3(a)). If the controlled substance is marijuana, "Possession of Marijuana Paraphernalia," below, applies.

Exceptions (new note)
Before searching a person or his or her premises or vehicle, an officer may ask the person whether a hypodermic needle or other sharp object that may cut or puncture the officer is on the defendant's person or in the premises or vehicle to be searched. If such an object is present and the person alerts the officer of that fact before the search, the person may not be charged with or prosecuted for possession of drug paraphernalia for the needle or sharp object or for possession of residual amounts of a controlled substance contained in the needle or sharp object. G.S. 90-113.22(c). The exception does not apply to any other drug paraphernalia found during the search. *Id.*

A person who introduces or intends to introduce a controlled substance into his or her body may use or possess testing equipment for identifying or analyzing the strength, effectiveness, or purity of that controlled substance. A governmental or nongovernmental organization that promotes scientifically proven ways of mitigating health risks associated with drug use and other high-risk behaviors may also possess such testing equipment or distribute it to potential controlled substance users. G.S. 90-113.22(d).

Greater and lesser-included offenses (new note)
"Possession of Marijuana Paraphernalia," below, is a lesser-included offense of this one. G.S. 90-113.22A.

Limited immunity from prosecution (new note)
A 2013 law, S.L. 2013-23, provides limited immunity from prosecution for persons seeking medical assistance for themselves or others in the event of a drug-related overdose. The law enacts G.S. 90-96.2, providing that a person who experiences a drug-related overdose or who seeks medical assistance for someone experiencing a drug-related overdose shall not be prosecuted for this offense if the evidence of the crime was obtained as a result of the person seeking medical assistance. G.S. 90-96.2(b), (c). The term "drug-related overdose" means "an acute condition, including mania, hysteria, extreme physical illness, coma, or death resulting from the consumption or use of a controlled substance, or another substance with which a controlled substance was combined, and that a layperson would reasonably believe to be a drug overdose that requires medical assistance." G.S. 90-96.2(a).

2016 legislation, S.L. 2016-88, sec. 4, enacted G.S. 90-113.27(c), providing limited immunity for employees, volunteers, and participants in authorized needle and hypodermic syringe exchange programs when those persons possess needles, hypodermic syringes, or other injection supplies obtained from or returned to an exchange program.

Possession of Marijuana Paraphernalia (new crime)

Statute

See G.S. 90-113.21, reproduced in the main volume under "Possession of Drug Paraphernalia."

§ 90-113.22A. Possession of marijuana drug paraphernalia.

(a) It is unlawful for any person to knowingly use, or to possess with intent to use, drug paraphernalia to plant, propagate, cultivate, grow, harvest, manufacture, compound, convert, produce, process, prepare, test, analyze, package, repackage, store, contain, or conceal marijuana or to inject, ingest, inhale, or otherwise introduce marijuana into the body.

(b) A violation of this section is a Class 3 misdemeanor. A violation of this section shall be a lesser included offense of G.S. 90-113.22.

2019 legislation, S.L. 2019-159, added a new subsection, (c), to the statute, effective July 11, 2019, to read as follows:

(c) Notwithstanding the provisions of subsection (a) of this section, it is not unlawful for (i) a person who introduces a controlled substance into his or her body, or intends to introduce a controlled substance into his or her body, to knowingly use, or to possess with intent to use, testing equipment for identifying or analyzing the strength, effectiveness, or purity of that controlled substance or (ii) a governmental or nongovernmental organization that promotes scientifically proven ways of mitigating health risks associated with drug use and other high-risk behaviors to possess such testing equipment or distribute such testing equipment to a person who intends to introduce a controlled substance into his or her body.

Elements

A person guilty of this offense

(1) knowingly
(2) uses or possesses with the intent to use
(3) drug paraphernalia
(4) for any of the following purposes:
   (a) to plant, propagate, cultivate, grow, harvest, manufacture, compound, convert, produce, process, prepare, test, analyze, package, repackage, store, contain, or conceal *or*
   (b) to inject, ingest, inhale, or otherwise introduce into the body
(5) marijuana.

Punishment

Class 3 misdemeanor. G.S. 90-113.22A(b).

Notes

Generally. This offense was enacted in 2014. S.L. 2014-119, sec. 3(b). In terms of elements, it is the same as "Possession of Drug Paraphernalia" except that this offense pertains only to marijuana paraphernalia. Thus, the relevant notes to that offense apply here as well.

Greater and lesser-included offenses. This offense is a lesser-included offense of "Possession of Drug Paraphernalia." G.S. 90-113.22A(b).

Exceptions (new note)
A person who introduces or intends to introduce a controlled substance into his or her body may use or possess testing equipment for identifying or analyzing the strength, effectiveness, or purity of that controlled substance. A governmental or nongovernmental organization that promotes scientifically proven ways of mitigating health risks associated with drug use and other high-risk behaviors may also possess such testing equipment or distribute it to potential controlled substance users. G.S. 90-113.22A(c).

Related Offenses Not in This Chapter

See the offenses listed under "Possession of Drug Paraphernalia."

28

Motor Vehicle Offenses

Driving While License Revoked or Disqualified (page 755)

Statute (page 755)

Several pieces of legislation, S.L. 2012-146, sec. 8; S.L. 2013-360, sec. 18B.14(f); S.L. 2015-186, sec. 2; S.L. 2015-264, sec. 38(a); S.L. 2017-186, sec. 2(kkkk), have amended the statute so that subsections (a), (a1), (a2), and (a3) read as follows:

> (a) Driving While License Revoked.—Except as provided in subsections (a1) or (a2) of this section, any person whose drivers license has been revoked who drives any motor vehicle upon the highways of the State while the license is revoked is guilty of a Class 3 misdemeanor.
>
> (a1) Driving While License Revoked for Impaired Driving.—Any person whose drivers license has been revoked for an impaired driving revocation as defined in G.S. 20-28.2(a) and who drives any motor vehicle upon the highways of the State is guilty of a Class 1 misdemeanor. Upon conviction, the person's license shall be revoked for an additional period of one year for the first offense, two years for the second offense, and permanently for a third or subsequent offense.
>
> If the person's license was originally revoked for an impaired driving revocation, the court may order as a condition of probation that the offender abstain from alcohol consumption and verify compliance by use of a continuous alcohol monitoring system, of a type approved by the Division of Adult Correction and Juvenile Justice of the Department of Public Safety, for a minimum period of 90 days.
>
> The restoree of a revoked drivers license who operates a motor vehicle upon the highways of the State without maintaining financial responsibility as provided by law shall be punished as for driving without a license.
>
> (a2) Driving Without Reclaiming License.—A person convicted under subsection (a) or (a1) of this section shall be punished as if the person had been convicted of driving without a license under G.S. 20-35 if the person demonstrates to the court that either of the following is true:
>
> (1) At the time of the offense, the person's license was revoked solely under G.S. 20-16.5 and one of the following applies:
>
> a. The offense occurred more than 45 days after the effective date of a revocation order issued under G.S. 20-16.5(f) and the period of revocation was 45 days as provided under subdivision (3) of that subsection; or
>
> b. The offense occurred more than 30 days after the effective date of the revocation order issued under any other provision of G.S. 20-16.5.
>
> (2) At the time of the offense the person had met the requirements of G.S. 50-13.12, or G.S. 110-142.2 and was eligible for reinstatement of the person's drivers license privilege as provided therein.
>
> In addition, a person punished under this subsection shall be treated for drivers license and insurance rating purposes as if the person had been convicted of driving

without a license under G.S. 20-35, and the conviction report sent to the Division must indicate that the person is to be so treated.

(a3) Driving After Notification or Failure to Appear.—A person shall be guilty of a Class 1 misdemeanor if:

(1) The person operates a motor vehicle upon a highway while that person's license is revoked for an impaired drivers license revocation after the Division has sent notification in accordance with G.S. 20-48; or

(2) The person fails to appear for two years from the date of the charge after being charged with an implied consent offense.

Upon conviction, the person's drivers license shall be revoked for an additional period of one year for the first offense, two years for the second offense, and permanently for a third or subsequent offense. The restoree of a revoked drivers license who operates a motor vehicle upon the highways of the State without maintaining financial responsibility as provided by law shall be punished as for driving without a license.

2015 legislation, S.L. 2015-186, sec. 2, amended subsection (d) so that the first sentence of that subsection reads as follows:

A person who was convicted of a violation that disqualified the person and required the person's drivers license to be revoked who drives a motor vehicle during the revocation period is punishable as provided in subsection (a1) of this section.

Driving While License Revoked (page 756)

Punishment (page 756)

As a result of the legislation noted above, delete the text of this section and replace it with the following:

Class 3 misdemeanor, except that if the circumstances listed in G.S. 20-28(a2) apply, the person will be punished as if he or she had been convicted of driving without a license under G.S. 20-35. G.S. 20-28(a2).

Notes (page 757)

Element (2) (page 757)

As a result of 2016 legislation, S.L. 2016-90, sec. 13(a), delete the text after the first sentence of this note and replace it with the following:

Neither mopeds nor electric assisted bicycles are motor vehicles. G.S. 20-4.01(7a) (definition of electric assisted bicycle); -4.01(23) (definition of motor vehicle); -4.01(27)(d1) (definition of moped).

Element (4) (page 757)

2016 legislation, S.L. 2016-90, sec. 10(c), amended G.S. 20-48, allowing the DMV to give notice by email or other electronic means under certain circumstances.

For another case stating that the defendant must have actual or constructive knowledge of the revocation, see *State v. Green*, 258 N.C. App. 87, 91 (2018) (trial court committed prejudicial error by failing to instruct the jury on this issue where the defendant testified that he did not receive the DMV's notice and offered evidence to explain why the mailed notification might not have reached him).

Related Offenses Not in This Chapter (page 758)

The statutory citation for the second offense in this list should be to G.S. 20-28.

Driving While License Revoked for an Impaired Driving Revocation (page 758)

Statute (page 758)

As a result of the 2015 legislation noted above, the statutory citation in this section should read as follows:

G.S. 20-28(a1).

Punishment (page 758)

As a result of the 2015 legislation noted above, delete the text of this section and replace it with the following:

Class 1 misdemeanor, G.S. 20-28(a1), except that if the circumstances listed in G.S. 20-28(a2) apply, the person will be punished as if he or she had been convicted of driving without a license under G.S. 20-35. G.S. 20-28(a2).

Failure to Appear after an Implied Consent Offense Charge (page 760)

Statute (page 760)

As a result of the 2015 legislation noted above, the statutory citation in this section should read as follows:

G.S. 20-28(a3).

Impaired Driving and Related Offenses (page 762)

Impaired Driving (page 762)

Punishment (page 762)

2012 legislation, S.L. 2012-146, sec. 9, amended G.S. 20-179(g) (Level One punishment) to provide that a judge may reduce the minimum term of imprisonment to a term of not less than 10 days if a condition of special probation is imposed requiring the defendant to abstain from alcohol consumption and be monitored by a continuous alcohol monitoring (CAM) system for a period of not less than 120 days. Pretrial CAM monitoring may be credited against the 120-day monitoring period, up to 60 days.

S.L. 2012-146 also amended G.S. 20-179(h) (Level Two punishment) to now provide that the term of imprisonment may be suspended only if a condition of special probation is imposed to require the defendant to serve a term of imprisonment of at least 7 days or to abstain from consuming alcohol for at least 90 consecutive days, as verified by a CAM system. Up to 60 days of pretrial CAM monitoring may be credited against the 90-day monitoring period. 2013 legislation, S.L. 2013-348, made additional changes to G.S. 20-179(h), requiring the completion of 240 hours of community service in certain circumstances.

As amended by S.L. 2012-194, S.L. 2012-146 also added new subsections, (k2) and (k3), to G.S. 20-179 providing as follows:

- The judge may order as a condition of special probation for any level of offense under G.S. 20-179 that the defendant abstain from alcohol consumption as verified by a CAM system. G.S. 20-179(k2).
- The court may authorize probation officers to require defendants to submit to CAM for assessment purposes if the defendant has been required to abstain from alcohol

consumption during the term of probation and the probation officer believes the defendant is consuming alcohol. G.S. 20-179(k3). The defendant bears the cost of the CAM in these circumstances. *Id.*

Notes (page 764)

Element (1) (page 764)

A person who is asleep behind the wheel of a car with the engine running is driving the car within the meaning of this offense. State v. Mabe, 85 N.C. App. 500 (1987); State v. Hoque, 269 N.C. App. 347 (2020) (a defendant in the driver's seat of a vehicle with the engine running who revved the engine when an officer asked him to pull forward drove within the meaning of the statute).

Although the vehicle's engine was not running when the officer approached, the evidence was sufficient to establish that the defendant was driving the vehicle when it was parked by the front door of a hotel where guests typically stop to check in, the defendant was sitting in the driver's seat, the vehicle was registered to the defendant, and the defendant admitted that he had been driving. State v. Burris, 253 N.C. App. 525 (2017).

There was sufficient evidence, apart from the defendant's extrajudicial confession that he was driving the vehicle, to establish that the defendant was in fact the driver when the defendant was the only person in the vehicle and he was sitting in the driver's seat. State v. Reeves, 218 N.C. App. 570, 573–74 (2012).

Element (2) (page 765)

As a result of 2016 legislation, S.L. 2016-90, sec. 13(a), delete the last sentence of the first paragraph of this note and replace it with the following:

Mopeds and electric assisted bicycles are vehicles but are not motor vehicles. G.S. 20-4.01(7a) (definition of electric assisted bicycle), -4.01(23) (definition of motor vehicle), and -4.01(27)(d1) (definition of moped). *See* State v. Boykin, ___ N.C. App. ___, ___ S.E.2d ___ (2020) (despite the parties' repeated use of the word "moped" at trial, the evidence showed that the defendant's vehicle was actually a "motor vehicle" within the meaning of the definitional statute).

Element (3) (page 765)

In *State v. Ricks*, 237 N.C. App. 359, 364–66 (2014), the court held that a cut-through on a vacant lot was not a "public vehicular area" and that when instructing the jury on this Element, the court should give the entire statutory definition of that term.

Element (4)(a) (page 765)

In a felony death by vehicle case, the evidence was sufficient to establish that the defendant was impaired even without evidence of the defendant's blood-alcohol level where the defendant admitted to drinking "at least a 12-pack" to an officer and admitted at trial that she drank at least seven or eight beers; a responding officer noticed the strong odor of alcohol and that the defendant slurred her words and opined that she seemed intoxicated; and a doctor who treated the defendant at the hospital diagnosed her with alcohol intoxication, largely based on her behavior. State v. Hawk, 236 N.C. App. 177, 180–81 (2014).

For other cases where the evidence was sufficient as to this Element, see *State v. Hoque*, 269 N.C. App. 347 (2020) (sufficient evidence of impairment notwithstanding the defendant's refusal to submit to an intoxilyzer test when the defendant was slumped over and apparently asleep in the driver's seat; the officer detected a strong odor of alcohol; the defendant's speech was slurred and his eyes were glassy and bloodshot; the defendant failed the horizontal and vertical nystagmus tests; the defendant admitted he had consumed alcohol; and chemical analysis of the defendant's blood showed alcohol, THC, THCA, amphetamine, and methamphetamine); and *State v. Fincher*, 259 N.C. App. 159, 162–63 (2018) (the evidence was sufficient to establish that the defendant was under the influence of alprazolam when she hit another vehicle; responding officers noted that her eyes were red and glassy and her speech was slurred; the defendant admitted that she had consumed alprazolam that morning; the defendant presented six of six clues indicating impairment on an HGN test; and after performing a twelve-step DRE evaluation, an officer determined that she was impaired by a central nervous system depressant).

For cases where the evidence was insufficient to establish this Element, see *State v. Eldred*, 259 N.C. App. 345, 349 (2018) (the defendant's admission to being "on meth" when found by an officer walking along a road two to three miles from an accident scene and his later admission to wrecking his vehicle a couple of hours earlier was insufficient to establish that he was impaired while driving); and *State v. Nazzal*, ___ N.C. App. ___, 840 S.E.2d 881 (2020) (the only evidence of impairment came from the officer's passive observations of the defendant five hours after the collision occurred, and the officer did not perform any field sobriety tests or ask the defendant if or when he had ingested any impairing substances).

Defenses (page 767)

Necessity is a defense to driving while impaired. State v. Miller, 258 N.C. App. 325, 327 (2018) (the trial court erred by failing to give a jury instruction on this defense). See "Necessity and Duress" in Chapter 2 of the main volume.

Related Offenses Not in This Chapter (page 768)

Add the following offense to this list:

Impaired boating offenses. G.S. 75A-10.3.

Operating a School Bus, School Activity Bus, Child Care Vehicle, Ambulance, Other EMS Vehicle, Firefighting Vehicle, or Law Enforcement Vehicle after Consuming Alcohol (page 772) (revised title)

Statute (page 772)

2013 legislation, S.L. 2013-105, amended subsection (a) of G.S. 20-138.2B to read as follows:

> (a) Offense.—A person commits the offense of operating a school bus, school activity bus, child care vehicle, ambulance, other emergency medical services vehicle, firefighting vehicle, or law enforcement vehicle after consuming alcohol if the person drives a school bus, school activity bus, child care vehicle, ambulance, other emergency medical services vehicle, firefighting vehicle, or law enforcement vehicle upon any highway, any street, or any public vehicular area within the State while consuming alcohol or while alcohol remains in the person's body. This section does not apply to law enforcement officers acting in the course of, and within the scope of, their official duties.

Elements (page 772)

As a result of 2013 legislation, S.L. 2013-105, Element (2) should read as follows:

(2) a school bus, school activity bus, child care vehicle, ambulance, other emergency medical services vehicle, firefighting vehicle, or law enforcement vehicle

Notes (page 773)

Exception (new note)

This offense does not apply to law enforcement officers acting in the course and scope of their official duties. G.S. 20-138.2B(a) (as amended by S.L. 2013-105).

Habitual Impaired Driving (page 773)

Notes (page 774)

Element (5) (page 774)
The three prior convictions need not be from different court dates. State v. Mayo, 256 N.C. App. 298, 300–01 (2017) (a case where two of the three prior convictions were obtained on the same date in Wake County District Court).

Serious Injury by a Vehicle (page 777)

Felony Serious Injury by a Vehicle (page 778)

Notes (page 778)

Element (6) (page 778)
For a case following *Leonard* (discussed in this note in the main volume) and rejecting the defendant's argument that the statutory proximate cause language forecloses the possibility of the State proving proximate cause in conjunction with some other concurrent cause, see *State v. Cox*, 253 N.C. App. 306, 319 (2017).

Related Offenses Not in This Chapter (page 779)

Add the following offense to this list:

Injury by impaired boating offenses. G.S. 75A-10.3.

Reckless Driving (page 781)

Reckless Driving: Carelessly and Heedlessly (page 781)

Notes (page 781)

Multiple convictions and punishments (page 782)
Double jeopardy bars convicting a defendant of speeding and reckless driving when the defendant also is convicted of felony speeding to elude arrest, which was raised from a misdemeanor to a felony based on the aggravating factors of speeding and driving recklessly. State v. Mulder, 233 N.C. App. 82, 89–94 (2014) (going on to conclude that, additionally, the legislature did not intend for multiple punishments in this context).

Reckless Driving: Endangering Persons or Property (page 782)

Notes (page 783)

Generally (new note)
There was sufficient evidence of reckless driving where the defendant was intoxicated, all four tires of her vehicle went off the road, road marks indicated that she lost control of her vehicle, and the vehicle overturned twice and traveled 131 feet from where it went off the road before it

flipped and another 108 feet after it flipped. State v. Geisslercrain, 233 N.C. App. 186, 189–90 (2014).

The mere fact that an unlicensed driver ran off the road and collided with a utility pole is insufficient to sustain a conviction. *In re* A.N.C., 225 N.C. App. 315, 325–26 (2013) (evidence showed only that the juvenile's vehicle collided with a utility pole; there was no evidence that the collision resulted from careless or reckless driving).

Hit and Run and Related Offenses (page 785)

2017 legislation, S.L. 2017-166, enacted a new G.S. 20-401(f), creating special rules regarding the duty of fully autonomous vehicles to stop in the event of a crash. These rules apply the provisions in G.S. 20-166(a) through (c2), 20-166(e), and 20-166.1(a) and (c).

Driver's Failure to Stop or Remain at the Scene When Serious Bodily Injury or Death Occurs (page 785)

Notes (page 787)

Element (6) (page 787)

For a case confirming that the statute penalizes only willful violations, see *State v. Scaturro*, 253 N.C. App. 828, 829 (2017).

There was sufficient evidence upon which a jury could conclude that the defendant did not act willfully when he left the scene of a crash to take the victim to the nearest hospital for medical assistance. *Id.* (holding that the trial court's failure to provide an instruction on willfulness constituted plain error).

Exceptions (page 787)

Taking a seriously injured individual to the hospital to receive medical treatment is not prohibited by the statute if such assistance is reasonable under the circumstances. *Id.*

Greater and lesser-included offenses (new note)

Hit and run resulting in injury is a lesser-included offense of hit and run resulting in death. State v. Malloy, 257 N.C. App. 191, 193–94 (2017).

School Bus Offenses (page 796)

Statute (page 796)

As a result of 2013 legislation, S.L. 2013-293, subsection (e) of G.S. 20-217 is amended to read as follows:

> (e) Except as provided in subsection (g) of this section, any person violating this section shall be guilty of a Class 1 misdemeanor and shall pay a minimum fine of five hundred dollars ($500.00). A person who violates subsection (a) of this section shall not receive a prayer for judgment continued under any circumstances.

That legislation also amended subsection (g) and enacted subsections (g1) and (g2) to read as follows:

> (g) Any person who willfully violates subsection (a) of this section and strikes any person shall be guilty of a Class I felony and shall pay a minimum fine of one thousand

two hundred fifty dollars ($1,250). Any person who willfully violates subsection (a) of this section and strikes any person, resulting in the death of that person, shall be guilty of a Class H felony and shall pay a minimum fine of two thousand five hundred dollars ($2,500).

(g1) The Division shall revoke, for a period of one year, the drivers license of a person convicted of a second misdemeanor violation under this section within a three-year period. The Division shall revoke, for a period of two years, the drivers license of a person convicted of a Class I felony violation under this section. The Division shall revoke, for a period of three years, the drivers license of a person convicted of a Class H felony violation under this section. The Division shall permanently revoke the drivers license of (i) a person convicted of a second felony violation under this section within any period of time and (ii) a person convicted of a third misdemeanor violation under this section within any period of time.

In the case of a first felony conviction under this section, the licensee may apply to the sentencing court for a limited driving privilege after a period of six months of revocation, provided the person's drivers license has not also been revoked or suspended under any other provision of law. A limited driving privilege issued under this subsection shall be valid for the period of revocation remaining in the same manner and under the terms and conditions prescribed in G.S. 20-16.1(b). If the person's drivers license is revoked or suspended under any other statute, the limited driving privilege issued pursuant to this subsection is invalid.

In the case of a permanent revocation of a person's drivers license for committing a third misdemeanor violation under this section within any period of time, the person may apply for a drivers license after two years. The Division may, with or without a hearing, issue a new drivers license upon satisfactory proof that the former licensee has not been convicted of a moving violation under this Chapter or the laws of another state. The Division may impose any restrictions or conditions on the new drivers license that the Division considers appropriate. Any conditions or restrictions imposed by the Division shall not exceed two years.

In the case of a permanent revocation of a person's drivers license for committing a second Class I felony violation under this section within any period of time, the person may apply for a drivers license after three years. The Division may, with or without a hearing, issue a new drivers license upon satisfactory proof that the former licensee has not been convicted of a moving violation under this Chapter or the laws of another state. The Division may impose any restrictions or conditions on the new drivers license that the Division considers appropriate. Any conditions or restrictions imposed by the Division shall not exceed three years.

Any person whose drivers license is revoked under this section is disqualified pursuant to G.S. 20-17.4 from driving a commercial motor vehicle for the period of time in which the person's drivers license remains revoked under this section.

(g2) Pursuant to G.S. 20-54, failure of a person to pay any fine or costs imposed pursuant to this section shall result in the Division withholding the registration renewal of a motor vehicle registered in that person's name. The clerk of superior court in the county in which the case was disposed shall notify the Division of any person who fails to pay a fine or costs imposed pursuant to this section within 20 days of the date specified in the court's judgment, as required by G.S. 20-24.2(a)(2). The Division shall continue to withhold the registration renewal of a motor vehicle until the clerk of superior court notifies the Division that the person has satisfied the conditions of G.S. 20-24.1(b) applicable to the person's case. The provisions of this subsection shall be in addition to any other actions the Division may take to enforce the payment of any fine imposed pursuant to this section.

2017 legislation, S.L. 2017-188, sec. 4, amended subsection (h) to read as follows:

(h) Automated school bus safety cameras, as defined in G.S. 115C-242.1, may be used to detect and prosecute violations of this section. Any photograph or video recorded by an automated school bus safety camera shall, if consistent with the North Carolina Rules of Evidence, be admissible as evidence in any proceeding alleging a violation of subsection (a) of this section. Failure to produce a photograph or video recorded by an automated school bus safety camera shall not preclude prosecution under this section.

Passing or Failing to Stop for a Stopped School Bus (page 796)

Punishment (page 797)

As a result of 2013 legislation, S.L. 2013-293, delete the text of this section and replace it with the following:

Class 1 misdemeanor and mandatory minimum fine of $500. G.S. 20-217(e). A defendant may not receive a prayer for judgment continued for this offense. *Id.*

Notes (page 797)

Evidence issues (new note)
Any photograph or video recorded by an automated school bus safety camera (defined in G.S. 115C-242.1) is, if consistent with the Evidence Rules, admissible as evidence in any prosecution for this offense. G.S. 20-217(h). Failure to produce a photograph or video recorded by an automated school bus safety camera does not preclude prosecution. *Id.*

License revocations and consequences for failure to pay fines (new note)
2013 legislation, S.L. 2013-293, enacted G.S. 20-217(g1) and (g2) pertaining to license revocations and consequences for failing to pay fines imposed upon conviction.

Felony Passing or Failing to Stop for a School Bus (page 797)

Punishment (page 798)

As a result of the 2013 legislation noted above, delete the text of this section and replace it with the following:

If Element (3)(a) is present, the offense is a Class I felony with a mandatory minimum fine of $1,250. G.S. 20-217(g). If Element (3)(b) is present, the offense is a Class H felony with a mandatory minimum fine of $2,500. *Id.*

Notes (page 798)

Evidence issues (page 798)

Delete the text of this note and replace it with the following:

See this note to "Passing or Failing to Stop for a Stopped School Bus," above in this supplement.

License revocations and consequences for failure to pay fines (new note)
See this note under "Passing or Failing to Stop for a Stopped School Bus," above in this supplement.

Failure to Stop, Move Over, or Slow Down for an Emergency Vehicle (page 801)

Statute (page 801)

2013 legislation, S.L. 2013-415, sec. 1(e), amended subsection (a) of G.S. 20-157 to read as follows:

(a) Upon the approach of any law enforcement or fire department vehicle or public or private ambulance or rescue squad emergency service vehicle, or a vehicle operated by the Division of Marine Fisheries, or the Division of Parks and Recreation of the Department of Environment and Natural Resources, or the North Carolina Forest Service of the Department of Agriculture and Consumer Services when traveling in response to a fire alarm or other emergency response purpose, giving warning signal by appropriate light and by audible bell, siren or exhaust whistle, audible under normal conditions from a distance not less than 1000 feet, the driver of every other vehicle shall immediately drive the same to a position as near as possible and parallel to the right-hand edge or curb, clear of any

> intersection of streets or highways, and shall stop and remain in such position unless otherwise directed by a law enforcement or traffic officer until the law enforcement or fire department vehicle, or the vehicle operated by the Division of Marine Fisheries, or the Division of Parks and Recreation of the Department of Environment and Natural Resources, or the North Carolina Forest Service of the Department of Agriculture and Consumer Services, or the public or private ambulance or rescue squad emergency service vehicle shall have passed. Provided, however, this subsection shall not apply to vehicles traveling in the opposite direction of the vehicles herein enumerated when traveling on a four lane limited access highway with a median divider dividing the highway for vehicles traveling in opposite directions, and provided further that the violation of this subsection shall be negligence per se. Violation of this subsection is a Class 2 misdemeanor.

2012 legislation, S.L. 2012-14, and 2015 legislation, S.L. 2015-26, sec. 3, amended the definition of the term "public service vehicle" in G.S. 20-157(f). That term now includes:

> a vehicle that (i) is being used to assist motorists or law enforcement officers with wrecked or disabled vehicles, (ii) is being used to install, maintain, or restore utility service, including electric, cable, telephone, communications, and gas, (iii) is being used in the collection of refuse, solid waste, or recycling, or (iv) is a highway maintenance vehicle owned and operated by or contracted by the State or a local government and is operating an amber colored flashing light authorized by G.S. 20-130.2.

Failure to Stop for an Emergency Vehicle (page 802)

Elements (page 802)

As a result of the 2013 legislation noted above, Element (3) should read as follows:

(3) upon the approach of a
- (a) law enforcement or fire department vehicle, ambulance, rescue squad vehicle, *or*
- (b) vehicle operated by the Division of Marine Fisheries, the Division of Parks and Recreation, or the North Carolina Forest Service when traveling in response to a fire alarm or other emergency response purpose

---

Aggravated Failure to Stop for an Emergency Vehicle (page 803)

Elements (page 803)

As a result of the 2013 legislation noted above, sec. 1(e), Element (3) should read as follows:

(3) upon the approach of a
- (a) law enforcement or fire department vehicle, ambulance, rescue squad vehicle, *or*
- (b) vehicle operated by the Division of Marine Fisheries, the Division of Parks and Recreation, or the North Carolina Forest Service when traveling in response to a fire alarm or other emergency response purpose

Punishment (page 803)

2019 legislation, S.L. 2019-157, effective for offenses committed on or after December 1, 2019, increases the punishment for this offense as follows:

> A violation involving Element (6)(c) is a Class F felony.

Notes (page 804)

Element (6) (page 804)

Delete the second paragraph of this note and replace it with the following:

The term "public service vehicle" means a vehicle that

- is being used to assist motorists or law enforcement officers with wrecked or disabled vehicles;
- is being used to install, maintain, or restore utility service, including electric, cable, telephone, communications, and gas;
- is being used in the collection of refuse, solid waste, or recycling; or
- is a highway maintenance vehicle owned and operated by or contracted by the State or a local government and is operating an amber-colored flashing light authorized by G.S. 20-130.2.

G.S. 20-130.2. G.S. 20-157(f), *as amended by* S.L. 2012-14 *and* S.L. 2015-26, sec. 3.

Failure to Move Over or Slow Down for a Stopped Emergency or Public Service Vehicle (page 804)

Elements (page 804)

As a result of the 2013 legislation noted above, Element (4)(a) should read as follows:

(4) (a) (i) law enforcement or fire department vehicle, ambulance, rescue squad vehicle, or public service vehicle, *or*
(ii) vehicle operated by the Division of Marine Fisheries, the Division of Parks and Recreation, or the North Carolina Forest Service when traveling in response to a fire alarm or other emergency response purpose

---

Speeding to Elude Arrest (page 806)

Statute (page 806)

As a result of 2013 legislation, S.L. 2013-243, secs. 6–7, the italicized note after G.S. 20-141.5 should read:

[*Subsections (d) through (k) are not reproduced here.*]

Felony Speeding to Elude Arrest (page 806)

Notes (page 807)

Element (1) (page 807)

For a case where there was sufficient evidence, even though the officer lost sight of the vehicle for a period of time, that the defendant was the driver of the vehicle, see *State v. Lindsey*, 366 N.C. 325 (2012) (per curiam) (reversing 219 N.C. App. 249 (2012) for the reasons stated in the dissenting opinion).

Element (7)(d) (new note)

For a case where the evidence was sufficient to establish that the defendant caused property damage in excess of $1,000, see *State v. Gorham*, 262 N.C. App. 483 (2018) (where the defendant drove *through* a house, jurors could use "common sense" to determine that the damages to the house would exceed $1,000).

State of mind (new note)

The evidence established that the defendant intended to elude an officer notwithstanding her assertion that she drove away because she preferred to be arrested by a female officer rather than the male officer who stopped her; the defendant's preference was irrelevant to whether she intended to elude the officer. State v. Cameron, 223 N.C. App. 72, 74–75 (2012).

Multiple convictions and punishments (new note)
Double jeopardy bars convicting a defendant of speeding and reckless driving when the defendant also is convicted of felony speeding to elude arrest, which was raised from a misdemeanor to a felony based on the aggravating factors of speeding and driving recklessly. State v. Mulder, 233 N.C. App. 82, 89–94 (2014) (going on to conclude that, additionally, the legislature did not intend for multiple punishments in this context).

Forfeiture (new note)
2013 legislation, S.L. 2013-243, sec. 6, repealed existing forfeiture provisions and enacted G.S. 20-141.5(k), S.L. 2013-243, sec. 7, providing that if a person is convicted of felony speeding to elude arrest, the motor vehicle used is subject to forfeiture in accordance with the procedure set out in G.S. 20-28.2, -28.3, -28.4, and -28.5.

Aggravated Felony Speeding to Elude Arrest (page 808)

Notes (page 809)

Forfeiture (new note)
See this note under "Felony Speeding to Elude Arrest," above in this supplement.

Aggravated Misdemeanor Speeding to Elude Arrest (page 810)

Notes (page 810)

Forfeiture (new note)
See this note under "Felony Speeding to Elude Arrest," above in this supplement.

Case Index

U

V

Table of Statutes

North Carolina General Statutes

North Carolina Session Laws

United States Code

Code of Federal Regulations

Access Your Free Subscription to *N.C. Crimes Online*

The purchase of this supplement includes FREE access to the online version of *N.C. Crimes*. The online version offers the following features:

- Updated content through December 2020
- Keyword searching
- Linking to cross-references
- Printable pages
- Accessibility anywhere your electronic device can connect to the Internet
- Collapsible and expandable statutes

First-Time Registrants

Follow the instructions below to begin using the online version of *N.C. Crimes*:

- Visit **bit.ly/nccrimesonline2020**
- Use the registration code **nccrimesonline2021-r95876**
- Enter your information to complete your account profile
- You will receive a confirmation email ensuring your access has been properly authenticated

Returning Users*

Follow the instructions below to update and renew your access to the online version:

- Log into your *N.C. Crimes Online* account
- Go to the "Account Updates" box on the right-hand side of the page
- Click the link at "Start Here" to update your information
- Click "Edit" **above** your profile information
- Replace your current registration code with **nccrimesonline2021-r95876**
- Click "Save" at the bottom of the page

* Users who have not created or renewed an account after March 2018 may need to follow the "First-Time Registrants" steps.

This is a free subscription. You will not be charged.

For questions about your online subscription, contact **sales@sog.unc.edu** or call **919.966-5381**.

For information about other publications and resources from the School of Government, visit **sog.unc.edu**.

NORTH CAROLINA

CRIMES

A Guidebook on the Elements of Crime

Seventh Edition • 2012

Jessica Smith

UNC
SCHOOL OF
GOVERNMENT

The School of Government at the University of North Carolina at Chapel Hill works to improve the lives of North Carolinians by engaging in practical scholarship that helps public officials and citizens understand and improve state and local government. Established in 1931 as the Institute of Government, the School provides educational, advisory, and research services for state and local governments. The School of Government is also home to a nationally ranked graduate program in public administration and specialized centers focused on information technology, environmental finance, and civic education for youth.

As the largest university-based local government training, advisory, and research organization in the United States, the School of Government offers up to 200 courses, seminars, and specialized conferences for more than 12,000 public officials each year. In addition, faculty members annually publish approximately fifty books, book chapters, bulletins, and other reference works related to state and local government. Each day that the General Assembly is in session, the School produces the *Daily Bulletin*, which reports on the day's activities for members of the legislature and others who need to follow the course of legislation.

The Master of Public Administration Program is a full-time, two-year program that serves up to sixty students annually. It consistently ranks among the best public administration graduate programs in the country, particularly in city management. With courses ranging from public policy analysis to ethics and management, the program educates leaders for local, state, and federal governments and nonprofit organizations.

Operating support for the School of Government's programs and activities comes from many sources, including state appropriations, local government membership dues, private contributions, publication sales, course fees, and service contracts. Visit www.sog.unc.edu or call 919.966.5381 for more information on the School's courses, publications, programs, and services.

First edition 1977. Seventh edition 2012.

Printed in the United States of America

27 26 25 24 23 17 18 19 20 21

ISBN 978-1-56011-682-0

This publication is printed on permanent, acid-free paper in compliance with the North Carolina General Statutes.

Printed on recycled paper

Contents

16
Fraud, Forgery, False Pretenses, and Related Offenses 409

Preface

This is the seventh edition of a book first published in 1977. This edition updates the sixth edition with new offenses, legislative changes, and case law. Also, in response to reader requests I replaced the old shortened case citations with full case citations, including case names. Other new features include a case index and simplified table of statutes and many new additional notes, including those regarding charging issues, multiple convictions and punishments, defenses, and exceptions. Finally, our design team improved the layout of the book, making it even easier to use and ensuring that you will be able to quickly find what you need.

North Carolina Crimes embodies the work of many School of Government faculty and staff over thirty-five years. This edition builds on all of the great work that came before. For this edition, I thank School of Government faculty members Robert Farb, John Rubin, Jeff Welty, Jamie Markham, and Shea Denning, all of whom reviewed drafts of chapters. Thanks also to my law student research assistants William Biggers and Jason McGuirt and lawyer Stefanie Rodriguez. William, Jason, and Stefanie performed much of the tedious cite checking that ensures the accuracy of the book. However, I am responsible for any errors that remain. Thanks to the School of Government staff members who contributed to editing and production, especially editor Melissa Twomey for her precision and keen eye and Katrina Hunt who kept the whole train rolling. And finally, thanks to Chris, Ariel, and Zoe for putting up with my high stress levels and sub-par dinner offerings for well over a year as I juggled writing this book and all of my other work. Your unwavering confidence in me sealed my success.

I welcome comments about this book. You can reach me by email at smithj@sog.unc.edu or by regular mail at the School of Government, CB # 3330, Knapp Building, The University of North Carolina at Chapel Hill, Chapel Hill, NC 27599-3330.

Jessica Smith
Chapel Hill
December 2011

Introduction

Purpose of This Book

North Carolina Crimes is a treatise on North Carolina substantive criminal law. Originally it was designed primarily to help law enforcement officers decide which offenses to charge, if any, and what evidence should be gathered to prepare a case for trial. The book has evolved from its original purpose and now serves as an important secondary reference source on substantive criminal law for law enforcement officers, magistrates, prosecutors, public defenders, defense lawyers, and judges, as well as for those studying criminal law in the academic setting.

Two core principles guide all School of Government work: nonpartisanship and non-advocacy. Thus, this book is designed to be neutral; it presents the law and leaves it to the advocates to make the best arguments possible for their clients based on that law.

Readers should not rely on the book for charging language. Another School of Government publication, Arrest Warrant and Indictment Forms, 6th edition (2010), by Jeff Welty, provides sample charging language for a wide variety of crimes.

This edition incorporates statutory changes made through the 2011 session of the General Assembly and case law through December 31, 2011. It supersedes all earlier editions and supplements.

Coverage of This Book

This book attempts to cover all criminal offenses except those that are charged only rarely in the North Carolina criminal justice system. Also, while it covers some motor vehicle offenses, it does not attempt to comprehensively cover motor vehicle law. Nor does it attempt to cover other special subjects such as alcoholic beverage control law and fish and game law.

How to Find Offenses in This Book

Readers can find a particular offense in this book by consulting

(1) the detailed table of contents at the beginning of the book, which lists all covered offenses;
(2) the table of statutes at the back of the book; or
(3) the subject index, also at the back of the book.

Contents of This Book

The book has introductory chapters on states of mind, defenses, participants in crimes, and punishment under Structured Sentencing and separate chapters on various major categories of offenses, such as homicide and assaults. For each substantive offense covered, the book contains five sections:

Statute. In this section, the relevant statute is reproduced. If the offense is a common law offense, this section will indicate that fact.

Elements. In this section, the book sets out the elements of the offense. Usually an offense is broken down into elements according to the pattern established by a North Carolina appellate case or by the North Carolina Pattern Jury Instructions. In some cases, the breakdown of elements appearing here is original. There is no single "right" way to list elements. One person might regard one element of the crime of misdemeanor larceny as being "takes personal property belonging to another," while another person might break that phrase down into three elements: "(1) takes (2) personal property (3) belonging to another."

Punishment. In this section, the book sets out the punishment for the offense. See Chapter 4 (Punishment under Structured Sentencing) for a detailed discussion of punishment under Structured Sentencing.

Notes. The notes section contains explanatory points regarding the offense. Some of the notes will be keyed to the elements—for example, there may be a note about Element (1) of an offense. However, many elements do not have notes; this merely means that nothing needs to be said about a given element that is not obvious or that there is no interpreting case law for that element. Other notes will address common issues that arise regarding the offense, such as charging issues and multiple convictions and punishments.

Related Offenses Not in This Chapter. In this section, the book lists related offenses not covered in the particular chapter. Thus, a reader looking under "Common Law Robbery" will not find armed robbery listed as a related offense because armed robbery is dealt with in the same chapter as common law robbery. On the other hand, felonious larceny is listed as a related offense because it appears in another chapter. When the related offense is included in another chapter, the reader will be directed to the relevant chapter.

This section also lists related crimes that did not seem sufficiently important or frequent to be included in the book. When such an offense is listed, it appears without enclosing quotation marks and with a citation to the relevant provision in the North Carolina General Statutes. For example, in this section under "Misdemeanor Child Abuse" in Chapter 9 (Abuse and Neglect) the following offense appears: Exposing child to fire. G.S. 14-318.

Citations to Legal Authority

This book does not attempt to give complete legal authority for every point made. For most issues, it gives at least some legal authorities to be used as starting points for those who might want to look further. In other instances, the citations might be fairly comprehensive. The later history of a case, such as the fact that it was affirmed by a higher court, often is not included. Obviously, cases should be checked before being cited as authority.

This book uses standard case citation form. However, because most North Carolina judicial officials do not use the South Eastern Reporter, parallel citations are included only for newer cases for which the North Carolina citations are not yet available. Because the North Carolina General Statutes are cited so frequently, this book employs the shorthand form "G.S." to refer to the General Statutes. Thus, a citation to G.S. 14-318.4 refers to section 318.4 of

Chapter 14 of the North Carolina General Statutes. The short form "S.L." refers to a North Carolina session law. Session laws are available on the North Carolina General Assembly's web page (www.ncga.state.nc.us/).

Miscellaneous Points of Interpretation

"He". Many North Carolina criminal statutes employ the word "he". Under rules of statutory construction, words in the masculine gender, such as "he", should be read as referring to females as well as males unless the context clearly shows to the contrary. G.S. 12-3(1). Thus, unless otherwise specified, a crime may be committed by either a male or a female.

"Person" includes corporation. The word "person" in a criminal statute (and the word "person" used in the descriptions of the elements of offenses in this book) includes a corporation. G.S. 12-3(6). Thus, a corporation may be convicted of a crime and may be a victim of a crime, just like a natural person. However, a corporation is charged and served with criminal process in a different manner than a natural person. G.S. 15A-773.

1

States of Mind

1
States of Mind

Generally

As a general rule, a criminal offense consists of both an act (or omission) and a criminal state of mind. The criminal state of mind sometimes is called a "guilty mind" or "mens rea." The necessary state of mind varies from offense to offense. For example, one crime may require that the defendant act willfully and another may require that the defendant act maliciously. For a some crimes, no guilty mind is required; as discussed below, these crimes are called strict liability crimes. Defining the various states of mind is difficult. In addition to a lack of precision in the case law, the states of mind overlap, as for example when intent is implied by culpable negligence.

The notes that follow describe the various states of mind that are required for many of the crimes included in this book. These notes will be referred to later in this book when the necessary state of mind for a particular criminal offense is discussed. Other states of mind that occur less frequently will be explained in connection with the crimes to which they apply. Additional notes on states of mind will be included in connection with specific crimes, as necessary to explain their application to the particular elements of the offense. For example, sale of a counterfeit controlled substance requires that a person knowingly sell a counterfeit controlled substance to another. But what must the defendant know? That he or she is selling a substance? That it is a counterfeit controlled substance? Both? A note accompanying this crime will provide the necessary explanation.

Intentionally

Some crimes require that the defendant act intentionally. Typically, this mental state is required as to an act, such as the act of striking someone or the act of firing a gun. For example, one version of "Child Abuse—Inflicting Serious Mental or Physical Injury" (in Chapter 9 (Abuse and Neglect)) occurs when the defendant intentionally assaults a child and the assault results in serious injury. In this example, the act—the assault—must be intentional. Sometimes, however, this mental state is required as to a result. For example, the same child abuse offense also can occur when the defendant intentionally inflicts serious injury on a child. In this example, the result—the serious injury—must be intentionally inflicted.

The traditional view of intent is that a person intends certain consequences when the person desires that his or her acts (or omissions) cause those consequences or knows that those consequences are substantially certain to result from his or her acts (or omissions). 1 W. LaFave & A. Scott Jr., Substantive Criminal Law 340 (2d ed. 2003). Except when specific intent is required (see "General Intent and Specific Intent," below, for a discussion of specific intent), a person is presumed to intend the natural and probable consequences of his or her act. State v. Ferguson, 261 N.C. 558, 561 (1964).

As a practical matter, intent ordinarily must be proved circumstantially, by proving facts from which the intent may be inferred. State v. Cauley, 244 N.C. 701, 708 (1956). For example: An intent to kill may be inferred from the nature of the assault, the manner in which it was made, the conduct of the parties, and other relevant circumstances. *Id.* at 708 (evidence sufficient when, among other things, the defendant, an adult male, beat a three-year-old for hours with a belt with a metal buckle); State v. Liggons, 194 N.C. App. 734, 739–40 (2009) (evidence sufficient when the defendant and his accomplice discussed intentionally forcing motorists off the highway to rob them; they deliberately threw a very large rock or concrete chunk through the driver's side windshield of the victim's vehicle as it was approaching at approximately 55 or 60 mph; and it was easily foreseeable that such action could result in death, either from the impact of the rock or from the victim losing control of her vehicle).

A defendant's intent at the time of a breaking and entering can be inferred from what the defendant did after he or she broke and entered. State v. Clagon, ___ N.C. App. ___, 700 S.E.2d 89, 92 (2010) (upon entering a residence carrying an axe, the defendant asked where the victim was and upon locating her, began swinging the axe at her; this was sufficient evidence that the defendant intended to commit a felony in the residence).

An intent to sell or distribute a controlled substance may be inferred from the packaging, labelling and storage of the controlled substance, the defendant's activities, the quantity of controlled substance found, and the presence of cash or drug paraphernalia. *In re* D.L.D., ___ N.C. App. ___, 694 S.E.2d 395, 405 (2010) (evidence sufficient; noting that "Even where the amount of drugs involved is small, the surrounding circumstances may allow the jury to find an intent to distribute.").

Circumstantial evidence of intent to embezzle can include receiving money under an agency relationship and failing to transmit it to the party to whom it is due as well as personal financial problems. State v. Newell, 189 N.C. App. 138, 142–43 (2008) (evidence sufficient on these facts).

General Intent and Specific Intent

General intent crimes require only the intent to do an act, such as fire a gun or strike another. State v. Oakman, 191 N.C. App. 796, 800 (2008). Examples of general intent crimes are assault with a firearm on a law enforcement officer, State v. Childers, 154 N.C. App. 375, 382 (2002), and shooting into occupied property, State v. Byrd, 132 N.C. App. 220, 222 (1999).

A specific intent crime is one that includes a special mental element above and beyond the general intent to do an act. 1 LaFave & Scott, cited in full *supra,* at 354. For example, assault is a general intent crime that may be proved by showing that the defendant intentionally hit the victim. In contrast, assault with a deadly weapon with intent to kill is a specific intent crime that requires proof of a special mental element: the specific intent to kill.

Whether a crime is a general or specific intent crime can be important. For example, certain defenses apply only to specific intent crimes. State v. Harris, 171 N.C. App. 127, 131 (2005) (defense of voluntary intoxication does not apply to general intent crimes); *Childers,* 154 N.C. App. at 382 (diminished capacity does not apply to general intent crimes).

Transferred Intent

The doctrine of transferred intent provides that when a defendant intends to harm victim A but ends up harming victim B, the defendant's criminal liability is determined with respect to his or her intent toward A. State v. Davis, 349 N.C. 1, 37 (1998) (quoting State v. Wynn, 278 N.C. 513, 519 (1971)). If B is killed, the defendant is guilty or innocent exactly as if the fatal act had killed A. *Id.* (quoting *Wynn,* 278 N.C. at 519). As it is sometimes said, "intent follows the bullet." *Id.* (quoting *Wynn,* 278 N.C. at 519). Thus, under the doctrine of transferred intent, it does not matter whether the defendant intended to injure B; the defendant need only act with the required intent toward someone (here A). *Id.* at 38. There are a number of North Carolina cases on point, including *State v. Locklear*, 331 N.C. 239, 244–46 (1992) (doctrine applied as to charge of assault with intent to kill B, who was shot by the defendant while he was shooting to kill B's mother), *Davis*, 349 N.C. at 37–39 (an instruction on transferred intent was proper when the defendant engaged in a shooting spree, intending to harm company management but harming another person who happened to be present in the office at the time), *State v. Crandell*, ___ N.C. App. ___, 702 S.E.2d 352 (2010) (there was sufficient evidence of premeditation and deliberation when, after having a confrontation with an individual named Thomas, the defendant began firing at Thomas, resulting in the death of an innocent bystander), and *State v. Goode*, 197 N.C. App. 543, 550–51 (2009) (instruction on transferred intent was proper as to a charge of attempted murder of B when the defendant drove a car into A and B, intending to kill A). Also, there is a pattern jury instruction on point. N.C. PATTERN JURY INSTRUCTIONS—CRIM. 104.13 ("If the defendant intended to harm one person but actually harmed a different person, the legal effect would be the same as if the defendant had harmed the intended victim."); *see also Davis*, 349 N.C. at 38 (it is not necessary that the person the defendant intended to harm be named in the jury instructions).

In North Carolina, the doctrine of transferred intent is not limited to situations where an unintended victim suffers harm. Under North Carolina law, the doctrine also permits a conviction when the defendant intended one type of harm but caused another type of harm. Specifically, cases have held that under this doctrine, a defendant may be convicted of discharging a firearm into occupied property when the defendant intended to shoot a person but ended up shooting into property that he or she knew was occupied. State v. Small, ___ N.C. App. ___, 689 S.E.2d 444 (2009); State v. Fletcher, 125 N.C. App. 505, 512–13 (1997). However, application of the doctrine in this context is not without controversy. As a general rule, an intention to cause one type of harm cannot serve as a substitute for a requirement of intention as to another type of harm. 1 LAFAVE & SCOTT, cited in full *supra*, at 350, 458–60. Under this general rule, for example, if a defendant intentionally steals a gas meter out of a house, and as a result a woman is made ill by the escaping gas, the defendant's intent to steal does not suffice to establish an intent to injure another. *Id.* at 458–59 (but going on to note that the defendant might be guilty of injuring another in these circumstances if the injury to another offense requires only recklessness or criminal negligence). Of course, exceptions exist, most notably, the felony murder rule. If, while robbing a store with a firearm, the defendant's firearm goes off, killing bystander A, the felony murder doctrine allows the defendant to be convicted for A's murder. See the note on Element (3)(c) to "First-Degree Murder" in Chapter 6 (Homicide). The felony murder rule, however, derives from a statutory definition of murder. *See* G.S. 14-17 (defining murder).

Some North Carolina cases suggest that the doctrine of transferred intent may be applicable to other states of mind. State v. Crandell, ___ N.C. App. ___, 702 S.E.2d 352 (2010) (applying the doctrine to premeditation and deliberation and stating the traditional rule as "*malice* or intent follows the bullet") (emphasis added).

Knowingly

Subjective Knowledge

Some North Carolina crimes are defined with a subjective mental state. For example, a person is guilty of making a worthless check if he or she makes and delivers a check without having sufficient funds or credit with the bank for the check to be paid, knowing that there are insufficient funds or credit available for the payment. See "Worthless Checks—Making or Uttering" in Chapter 16 (Fraud, Forgery, False Pretenses, and Related Offenses). This crime includes a subjective mental state—the defendant must know in his or her own mind that there are insufficient funds or credit for the payment.

When a crime is defined to include subjective knowledge, the law states that a person acts (or fails to act) "knowingly" when the person is aware or conscious of what he or she is doing. Underwood v. Bd. of Alcoholic Control, 278 N.C. 623, 631 (1971); State v. Stephenson, 218 N.C. 258 (1940). For example, a person has knowledge of a condition—such as that an insurance claim is false—when he or she has actual information concerning the condition. *Stephenson,* 218 N.C. 258. The fact that the circumstances would cause a reasonable person to believe a fact is insufficient to establish that the defendant acted knowingly; to establish this mental state, the person must actually have knowledge of the fact. State v. Miller, 212 N.C. 361 (1937) (decided before G.S. 14-71 was amended to allow for conviction when the defendant had objective knowledge, discussed below).

Like intent, knowledge may be inferred by circumstantial evidence, such as the defendant's conduct and statements, statements made to the defendant by others, and by evidence of reputation that may be inferred to have come to the defendant's attention. State v. Bogle, 324 N.C. 190, 195 (1989).

Objective Knowledge

Some North Carolina crimes are defined to include both a subjective and objective mental state. For example, second-degree rape occurs when a person has vaginal intercourse with someone who is mentally disabled and the defendant knows or reasonably should have known of the victim's condition. See "Second-Degree Forcible Rape" in Chapter 10 (Sexual Assaults). The "should have known" aspect of the required mental state is referred to as objective knowledge, and it can be established with evidence that a reasonable person would have known the relevant fact. State v. Williams, ___ N.C. App. ___, 698 S.E.2d 542, 546–47 (2010) (in a sexual offense case, sufficient evidence was presented that the defendant reasonably should have known that the victim was mentally disabled). Thus, a defendant may be convicted of this offense if he or she actually knew that the victim was mentally disabled (subjective knowledge) or if a reasonable person would have known that the victim was mentally disabled (objective knowledge). *Id.* at 547.

Willful Blindness

Some jurisdictions have adopted a doctrine of willful blindness. This doctrine permits a finding that a person has knowledge when he or she deliberately chooses to remain ignorant of illegal activity that would have been disclosed by further investigation. *Bogle,* 324 N.C. at 194 (describing the doctrine as applied in other jurisdictions). In *Bogle,* 324 N.C. at 194, the North Carolina Supreme Court held that this doctrine is inconsistent with North Carolina law. However, the *Bogle* court noted that North Carolina law allows knowledge to be inferred and that North Carolina's concept of inferred knowledge is broader than the limited doctrine of willful blindness. *Id.* at 195.

Willfully

"Willfully" means the wrongful doing of an act without legal excuse or justification, or the commission of an act purposely and deliberately in violation of law. State v. Brackett, 306 N.C. 138 (1982); State v. Arnold, 264 N.C. 348 (1965). An example of justification may be found in a case involving a charge of willful cruelty to an animal where it was held that punishment of an animal in a good faith effort to train it is not without justification and thus not willful. State v. Fowler, 22 N.C. App. 144 (1974).

Maliciously

North Carolina courts have recognized three meanings of "malice." In homicide cases, it is said that a killing is done maliciously when

(1) it is done with ill will, hatred, or spite (sometimes called actual, express, or particular malice);
(2) the act that causes death is inherently dangerous to human life and is done so recklessly and wantonly that it reflects disregard of life and social duty; or
(3) it is done intentionally and without just cause, excuse, or justification (in a murder case, this third type of malice may be inferred from the intentional infliction of a wound with a deadly weapon).

State v. Snyder, 311 N.C. 391 (1984); State v. Reynolds, 307 N.C. 184 (1982). For a more detailed discussion of this state of mind as it applies to homicide crimes, see the note on Element (3)(a)(i) to "First-Degree Murder" and on Element (3) to "Second-Degree Murder," both in Chapter 6 (Homicide). The three-pronged formulation of malice described above has been applied outside of the homicide context—for example, in a case involving malicious damage to an occupied real property by use of an incendiary device. State v. Sexton, 357 N.C. 235 (2003).

Wantonly

Although the North Carolina Supreme Court has stated that an act is done "wantonly" when it is done with conscious and intentional disregard of and indifference to the rights and safety of others, it also has stated that this mental state is essentially the same as willfully. State v. Brackett, 306 N.C. 138 (1982); State v. Williams, 284 N.C. 67 (1973).

Criminal Negligence

Criminal negligence (sometimes called culpable negligence) means recklessness or carelessness that shows a thoughtless disregard of consequences or a heedless indifference to the safety and rights of others. State v. Jones, 353 N.C. 159 (2000); State v. Early, 232 N.C. 717, 720 (1950). The showing required to establish criminal negligence is less than the level of recklessness required to show malice for purposes of second-degree murder. State v. Mack, ___ N.C. App. ___, 697 S.E.2d 490, 494 (2010) (comparing culpable negligence to malice for purposes of second-degree murder). It is, however, more than the deviation from reasonable conduct required for civil tort liability. State v. Everhart, 291 N.C. 700, 702 (1977); State v. McAdams, 51 N.C. App. 140 (1981).

Examples of cases in which the evidence was sufficient to establish culpable negligence include those where:

- a juvenile failed to render aid with due caution to a victim, who became sick after ingesting a drug provided by the juvenile and after the juvenile undertook some efforts to provide help, *In re* Z.A.K., 189 N.C. App. 354, 359–60 (2008);
- a gun went off, fatally shooting another person in the room while the defendant attempted to unload the gun, State v. Replogle, 181 N.C. App. 579 (2007); *see also McAdams*, 51 N.C. App. at 142 (with a loaded rifle pointing at his wife, the defendant attempted to force the rifle's bolt forward by slamming it, causing the weapon to fire and killing the wife);

- after being ordered by an officer to exit his truck, the defendant continued driving while the officer held on to the truck door; the defendant hit the officer, attempting to knock him off the truck, and the officer ultimately was struck by the truck, State v. Spellman, 167 N.C. App. 374 (2004); *see also* State v. Kaley, 343 N.C. 107, 110 (1997) (culpable negligence occurred when an accomplice drove a vehicle while the victim was outside the car but being held by the defendant, a front seat passenger); and
- the defendant attempted to knock a loaded and cocked gun from another's hand and scuffled for control of the gun, at which time the gun went off, killing the other person, State v. Reynolds, 160 N.C. App. 579 (2003).

In contrast to these cases are others in which the evidence was insufficient to establish culpable negligence. *See, e.g., Everhart*, 291 N.C. 700 (no evidence of culpable negligence when the defendant, a young girl with a 72 I.Q., gave birth to a baby unassisted and while lying on the floor and then dropped the baby while trying to put him on a bed; thinking the baby was dead, the defendant wrapped the baby in a blanket; a medical expert concluded that the baby was accidentally smothered or died of neonatal respiratory failure).

Criminal negligence also may be established by an intentional, willful, or wanton violation of a statute designed for the protection of human life or limb. *Jones*, 353 N.C. at 165. For example, in *State v. Powell*, 336 N.C. 762 (1994), the defendant left his dogs unattended and not restrained and restricted to his property by fence, in violation of Section 3-18 of the Winston-Salem Code, and the violation was intentional, willful, or wanton. This was sufficient evidence of culpable negligence in an involuntary manslaughter prosecution brought after the dogs killed a jogger. *Id.* at 771–73.

The issue of whether culpable negligence is established by a safety statute violation arises most frequently in impaired driving cases. In that regard, the courts have repeatedly held that G.S. 20-138.1, the statute prohibiting drivers from operating motor vehicles while under the influence of impairing substances, is a safety statute designed for the protection of human life and limb and that its violation constitutes culpable negligence as a matter of law. *Jones*, 353 N.C. at 165. Other motor vehicle safety statutes that can give rise to culpable negligence include G.S. 20-141 (speed restrictions) and G.S. 20-146 (drive on right side of highway). *Jones*, 353 N.C. at 165.

When a safety statute is unintentionally violated, culpable negligence exists if the violation is "accompanied by recklessness of probable consequences of a dangerous nature, when tested by the rule of reasonable [foreseeability], amounting altogether to a thoughtless disregard of consequences or of a heedless indifference to the safety of others." *Id.* (quotation omitted).

Culpable negligence sometimes is stated as an element of an offense. *See* State v. Replogle, 181 N.C. App. 579, 581 (2007) (defining involuntary manslaughter to include culpable negligence); G.S. 14-32.2 (defining patient abuse to include certain culpably negligent conduct). For other offenses, the courts have held that the requisite intent can be implied from culpable negligence. *Jones*, 353 N.C. at 166 (so noting as to assault with a deadly weapon inflicting serious injury and assault with a deadly weapon with intent to kill); State v. Oakman, 191 N.C. App. 796 (2008) (same as to felonious child abuse); State v. Spellman, 167 N.C. App. 374, 384 (2004) (so noting as to assaults and so holding as to assault with a deadly weapon on a government official). However, culpable negligence cannot be used to imply the necessary intent for first-degree felony murder. *Jones*, 353 N.C. 159 (explaining that for felony murder, an actual intent to commit the underlying felony is required).

Negligence

A small number of North Carolina crimes require only negligence, not criminal negligence. Although there are no cases on point, these statutes presumably incorporate the civil law negligence standard of failure to use due care. They include:

- G.S. 14-137 (setting fire to woods and fields)
- G.S. 14-157 (felling trees on telephone and electric power wires)
- G.S. 14-241 (disposing of public documents)
- G.S. 14-359 (tenant neglecting crop)
- G.S. 14-418 (prohibited handling of reptiles)

Strict Liability

Strict liability crimes are crimes that do not include a mental state (such as intentionally, knowingly, or maliciously) as an element of the offense. To obtain a conviction for a strict liability crime, the State need only prove that the defendant committed the prohibited act. Also, certain defenses are unavailable for strict liability offenses. *See, e.g.*, State v. Harris, 171 N.C. App. 127, 131 (2005) (voluntary intoxication is not a defense to a strict liability crime).

Identifying strict liability statutory offenses would be easy if the General Assembly expressly identified crimes as strict liability offenses. However, that does not happen. When a statutory offense is enacted and omits a mental state as an element, the courts must determine whether the legislative intent was to create a strict liability crime. State v. Watterson, 198 N.C. App. 500 (2009) ("Whether a criminal intent is a necessary element of a statutory offense is a matter of construction to be determined from the language of the statute in view of its manifest purpose and design."). The North Carolina courts have had several occasions to undertake such an analysis. Among the crimes that our courts have identified as strict liability offenses are:

- G.S. 14-27.2 (first-degree statutory rape). State v. Anthony, 351 N.C. 611, 616 (2000) (noting that first-degree statutory rape is a strict liability crime); State v. Rose, 312 N.C. 441, 445 (1984) (noting that under G.S. 14-27.2, mistake regarding the victim's age is no defense); State v. Ainsworth, 109 N.C. App. 136, 145 (1993) ("Criminal mens rea is not an element of statutory rape.").
- G.S. 14-27.4 (first-degree statutory sexual offense). *Anthony*, 351 N.C. at 616–18 (noting that consent is not a defense to statutory sexual offense).
- G.S. 14-27.7A (statutory rape or sexual offense of a person who is 13, 14, or 15 years old). *Anthony*, 351 N.C. at 616–18 (consent is not a defense under this statute); State v. Browning, 177 N.C. App. 487, 491 (2006) ("Statutory rape under [G.S.] 14-27.7A is a strict liability crime."); State v. Sines, 158 N.C. App. 79, 84 (2003) ("Statutory sexual offense and statutory rape are categorized as strict liability crimes.").
- G.S. 14-269.2 (possess or carry weapons on campus or other educational property). State v. Haskins, 160 N.C. App. 349 (2003).
- G.S. 14-288.8 (possession, etc., of a weapon of mass death and destruction). *Watterson*, 198 N.C. App. at 503–12 (the State was not required to prove that the defendant knew the physical characteristics of the shotguns that made them unlawful (barrels of less than eighteen inches)).

Although failure to comply with sex offender registration requirements under G.S. 14-208.11 was at one time interpreted as a strict liability crime, State v. Bryant, 359 N.C. 554, 562 (2005), the statute has been amended, S.L. 2006-247, sec. 8(a), and now requires that the defendant act willfully.

Although statutory rape and sex offenses are included in the list above of strict liability crimes, it is worth noting that the North Carolina Court of Appeals appears to have somewhat eroded the strict liability status of these crimes by recognizing automatism as a defense to them. *See, e.g.*, State v. Bush, 164 N.C. App. 254 (2004); see generally "Unconsciousness or Automatism" in Chapter 2 (Bars and Defenses).

Strict liability crimes often are thought of as minor offenses with relatively light punishment in the area of public health, safety and welfare. However, as the above list indicates, North Carolina's strict liability crimes include felonies that carry significant punishment. *See Watterson*, 198 N.C. App. at 510 (noting that the General Assembly has imposed "fairly harsh" punishments for strict liability offenses). The courts have rejected policy arguments that strict liability should not attach for serious crimes, indicating that such arguments more appropriately are addressed to the General Assembly. State v. Anthony, 351 N.C. 611, 618 (2000); State v. Browning, 177 N.C. App. 487, 493–94 (2006) .

The United States Supreme Court has recognized that legislatures may enact strict liability crimes. Lambert v. California, 355 U.S. 225, 228 (1957) ("conduct alone without regard to the intent of the doer is often sufficient" for criminal liability; "[t]here is wide latitude in the lawmakers to declare an offense and to exclude elements of knowledge and diligence from its definition"). In North Carolina, constitutional challenges to the imposition of strict liability have failed. State v. Haskins, 160 N.C. App. 349, 353 (2003) (rejecting the defendant's argument that without a mens rea element, G.S. 14-269.2 (weapons on campus or educational property) violates equal protection); State v. Ainsworth, 109 N.C. App. 136, 145 (1993) (rejecting the defendant's argument that the constitution requires that statutory rape include some mens rea). However, when the strict liability crime involves wholly passive conduct, due process may require that the defendant have notice of the criminality of his or her conduct. State v. Bryant, 359 N.C. 554, 562 (2005) (regarding G.S. 14-208.11 (failure to register, etc. by a sex offender), which at one point was a strict liability crime).

If a defendant is prosecuted as an aider and abettor to a strict liability crime, a mental state is required. Put another way, "North Carolina case law does not support a theory of vicarious strict liability." State v. Bowman, 188 N.C. App. 635, 650 (2008) ("[a]lthough statutory rape is a strict liability crime, aiding and abetting statutory rape is not"). Thus, in *Bowman*, 188 N.C. App. 635, the court of appeals held that the trial court erred by denying the defendant's request for an instruction that the defendant had to know the age of the victims in order to be convicted of aiding and abetting statutory rape.

If the defendant is prosecuted for an attempt to commit a strict liability crime, the elements of attempt require intent. State v. Sines, 158 N.C. App. 79, 85 (2003). However, the intent element for an attempted strict liability crime appears to be less stringent than the intent element for aiding and abetting a strict liability crime. In *Sines*, 158 N.C. App. 79, for example, the court of appeals held that attempted statutory sexual offense does not require that the defendant intended to commit a sexual act with an underage person, only that the defendant intended to commit a sexual act with the victim; thus, a defendant's knowledge of the victim's age or the victim's consent are not defenses to the crime of attempted statutory sexual offense. *Id.* at 85.

2
Bars and Defenses

2

Bars and Defenses

Bars to Prosecution

Generally

A defendant charged with an offense sometimes may prevent successful prosecution by demonstrating facts, unrelated to guilt or innocence, that cut off—or "bar"—prosecution. Among these bars are double jeopardy, ex post facto, lack of jurisdiction, expiration of the statute of limitations, and state-granted immunity. Each of these bars is discussed briefly below.

Double Jeopardy

The Double Jeopardy Clause of the Fifth Amendment to the United States Constitution provides that no person shall "be subject for the same offense to be twice put in jeopardy of life or limb." U.S. CONST. amend V. This provision has been interpreted to protect against

(1) a second prosecution for the same offense after acquittal,
(2) a second prosecution for the same offense after conviction (by trial or plea), and
(3) multiple punishments for the same offense.

North Carolina v. Pearce, 395 U.S. 711, 717 (1969). Article I, Section 19, of the North Carolina Constitution also has been interpreted to protect against double jeopardy. State v. Rambert, 341 N.C. 173, 175 (1995) (the defendant's conviction and sentences for three counts of discharging a firearm into occupied property did not offend double jeopardy as each shot was a separate event).

Offenses are not the same for double jeopardy purposes if each contains an element that is not in the other. United States v. Dixon, 509 U.S. 688, 696 (1993). This principle, known as the *Blockburger* test, comes from the United States Supreme Court's decision in *Blockburger v. United States*, 284 U.S. 299, 304 (1932). Under the *Blockburger* test, armed robbery and assault with a deadly weapon with intent to kill are not the same offense because each has an element that is not in the other: armed robbery requires that the person commit or attempt to commit a larceny and the assault requires an intent to kill. By contrast, misdemeanor larceny and felony larceny are the same offense for double jeopardy purposes; although felony larceny has an element that is not included in misdemeanor larceny, all of the elements of misdemeanor larceny are included in felony larceny. In double jeopardy analysis, a lesser-included offense always is treated as the same offense as the greater. State v. Corbett, 196 N.C. App. 508, 510–11 (2009) (assault is not a lesser-included offense of sexual battery).

The first double jeopardy protection noted above—the protection against a second prosecution for the same offense after acquittal—protects against successive prosecutions. For example, once a jury finds a defendant not guilty of murder, the State may not bring the defendant into court for a second trial on the same offense; the not guilty verdict constitutes an acquittal barring a successive prosecution. The second protection noted above—the protection against a second prosecution after conviction—also protects against successive prosecutions.

It prohibits, for example, the State from prosecuting a defendant for felony larceny after the defendant was tried and convicted of misdemeanor larceny of the same goods; because the offenses are the same under the *Blockburger* test, the defendant's conviction for the misdemeanor bars a successive prosecution for the felony.

While the first two double jeopardy protections prevent successive prosecutions and can bar a second trial on the same offense, the clause's final protection prohibits multiple punishment for the same conduct. It does not operate to bar a prosecution; rather, it bars double punishment. State v. Gardner, 315 N.C. 444, 451–52 (1986) (clarifying the protections of double jeopardy with respect to single and successive prosecutions). Criminal punishments are covered by the Double Jeopardy Clause, as are civil remedies that courts have found in limited circumstances to constitute punishment. Hudson v. United States, 522 U.S. 93 (1997); *see also* State v. Hinchman, 192 N.C. App. 657, 665–66 (2008) (civil license revocation under G.S. 20-16.5 is not punishment for purposes of double jeopardy).

With respect to imposition of multiple punishments at the same trial—as opposed to in successive trials—the Double Jeopardy Clause only bars the sentencing court from prescribing greater punishments than the legislature intended. *Gardner*, 315 N.C. at 452–55. It does not prohibit multiple punishment for two offenses that are the same if they are tried at the same time and the legislature intended for both offenses to be separately punished. *Id.* at 455; State v. Ezell, 159 N.C. App. 103, 107 (2003). To determine the legislature's intent, the court must examine the subject, language, and history of the statutes at issue. *Gardner*, 315 N.C. at 461. Applying this analysis, the North Carolina Supreme Court held that the legislature intended that the crime of breaking or entering and the crime of felony larceny pursuant to that breaking or entering be separately punished and that therefore a defendant may be punished for both crimes when the convictions are obtained in a single trial. *Id.* at 463. Similarly, in *State v. Pipkins*, 337 N.C. 431, 434–35 (1994), the court held that although felony possession of cocaine and trafficking in cocaine by possession are the same offense, because the legislature intended to proscribe and punish the same conduct under two separate statutes, a trial court could, in a single trial, impose punishments for both offenses. *See also* State v. Springs, 200 N.C. App. 288, 294–95 (2009) (following *Pipkins* and holding that no double jeopardy violation occurs when the defendant is sentenced for felony possession of marijuana and possession of marijuana with intent to sell and deliver).

Even if offenses are not the same, legislative intent controls whether multiple punishment may be imposed at the same trial. State v. Davis, 364 N.C. 297 (2010) (concluding that the defendant failed to preserve his double jeopardy claim but agreeing with his assertion that G.S. 20-141.4(b) reflects a legislative intent to prohibit punishment for death by vehicle and serious injury by vehicle when the defendant is punished for the same conduct under another offense carrying a higher punishment). Some decisions analyze this issue as one of double jeopardy. *See, e.g.,* State v. Fulcher, 294 N.C. 503, 523 (1978) ("[C]ertain felonies (e.g., forcible rape and armed robbery) cannot be committed without some restraint of the victim . . . . G.S. 14-39 was not intended . . . to make a restraint, which is an inherent, inevitable feature of such other felony, also kidnapping so as to permit the conviction and punishment . . . for both crimes. To hold otherwise would violate . . . double jeopardy."); State v. Moses, ___ N.C. App. ___, 698 S.E.2d 688 (2010) (because the legislature did not intend to punish a defendant for both robbery and possession of stolen goods that were the proceeds of the same robbery, the defendant's right to be free from double jeopardy was violated); State v. Williams, 201 N.C. App. 161, 172–74 (2009) (even though assault inflicting serious bodily injury and assault by strangulation require proof of different elements, double jeopardy prohibited punishment for both because the legislature intended that a defendant only be sentenced for the higher of the two offenses); State v. Ezell, 159 N.C. App. 103, 111 (2003) (double jeopardy was violated when the defendant was punished, at the same trial, for assault with a deadly weapon with intent to kill inflicting serious injury and assault inflicting serious bodily injury; G.S. 32.4, criminalizing assault inflicting serious bodily injury, provides that the offense is punished as a Class F felony "[u]nless the conduct is covered under some other provision of law providing greater punishment"). However, in this situation double jeopardy is not at issue because the offenses are not the same. *See Davis*, 364 N.C. 297 (addressing the issue as one of legislative intent not double jeopardy); State v. Beatty, 347 N.C. 555, 558–60 (1998) (in response to the State's argument that *Fulcher*, 294 N.C. 503, was based on an outmoded view of double jeopardy, the court concluded that *Fulcher* did not rest solely on constitutional grounds but also relied on an interpretation of legislative intent; going on to decide the issue as one of legislative intent); State v. Fernandez, 346 N.C. 1, 18–20 (1997) (because first-degree murder and first-degree kidnapping elevated because of the murders were not the same under *Blockburger*, an analysis of legislative intent was not necessary to resolve the defendant's double jeopardy claim); State v. Martin, 195 N.C. App. 43, 54–55 (2009) (because indecent liberties with a child and using a minor in obscenity are different offenses, a defendant may be convicted of both, even when the convictions are based on the same evidence); State v. Garris, 191 N.C. App. 276, 286–87 (2008) (because attempted murder and assault with a deadly weapon with intent to kill are not the same offenses, a defendant may be convicted of both without violating double jeopardy).

Law enforcement officers and magistrates never can create a double jeopardy bar by making an arrest, issuing an arrest warrant, or charging a crime. This is because jeopardy does not attach until trial. More specifically, jeopardy attaches in a jury trial when the jury is empaneled and sworn; in a non-jury trial, it attaches when the court begins to hear evidence or testimony. Serfass v. United States, 420 U.S. 377, 389 (1975); State v. Brunson, 327 N.C. 244, 245–50 (1990). For guilty pleas, jeopardy attaches when the court accepts the plea. State v. Wallace, 345 N.C. 462, 467 (1997); State v. Ross, 173 N.C. App. 569, 573 (2005). Thus, while a defendant later may assert a double jeopardy bar to a criminal prosecution, jeopardy does not attach because of the mere fact of arrest or charging.

Notwithstanding the double jeopardy bar, a defendant can, in certain circumstances, be retried after jeopardy attached in a first trial. This can occur, for example, when the first trial had to be called off midstream (a "mistrial") for manifest necessity, such as when the jury could not reach a unanimous verdict (a "hung jury"). Richardson v. United States, 468 U.S. 317, 323–26 (1984). It also can occur when the defendant is convicted in the first trial but then obtains a reversal on appeal for a reason other than insufficiency of the evidence. United States v. Scott, 437 U.S. 82, 90–91 (1978).

For a more detailed discussion of double jeopardy, see Robert L. Farb, Double Jeopardy, Ex Post Facto, and Related Issues (Jan. 2007), UNC School of Government faculty paper (online at www.sog.unc.edu/sites/www.sog.unc.edu/files/djoverview.pdf).

Ex Post Facto

Both the United States and North Carolina Constitutions preserve the right of the people to be free from ex post facto laws. The United States Constitution provides that "[n]o State shall . . . pass any . . . ex post facto Law." U.S. Const. art. I, § 10, cl. 1. The North Carolina Constitution states that "Retrospective laws, punishing acts committed before the existence of such laws and by them only declared criminal, are oppressive, unjust, and incompatible with liberty, and therefore no ex post facto law shall be enacted." N.C. Const. art. I § 16. These two provisions "are evaluated under the same definition." State v. Whitaker, 364 N.C. 404, 406 (2010) (quotation omitted). They prohibit:

(1) the enactment of a statute that creates a new crime and applies it retroactively to conduct not criminal at the time committed;
(2) eliminating an element of an offense;
(3) taking away a defense formerly available;
(4) increasing the punishment for a crime after the act constituting the crime was committed; and

(5) altering the rules of evidence to allow less or different testimony than the law required when the crime was committed, in order to convict.

1 W. LaFave & A. Scott Jr., Substantive Criminal Law 154–61 (2d ed. 2003).

Ex post facto challenges arise in a number of procedural contexts, such as sex offender satellite-based monitoring, *see, e.g.,* State v. Bowditch, 364 N.C. 335 (2010) (subjecting defendants to satellite-based monitoring does not violate the constitutional prohibition against ex post facto laws), sentencing, *see, e.g.,* State v. Watkins, 195 N.C. App. 215 (2009) (application of prior record level for purposes of felony sentencing did not violate the ex post facto prohibition), and corrections, *see, e.g.,* Jones v. Keller, 364 N.C. 249 (2010) (interpretation by Department of Correction of its good time, gain time, and merit time regulations did not constitute an ex post facto violation). This book, however, is concerned with substantive rather than procedural law. Although ex post facto challenges are less common with respect to substantive law, they do arise. *See, e.g., Whitaker,* 364 N.C. 404 (2010) (G.S. 14-415.1 (proscribing the crime of felon in possession of a firearm) was not an impermissible ex post facto law or bill of attainder).

For more information about ex post facto issues, see Robert L. Farb, Double Jeopardy, Ex Post Facto, and Related Issues (Jan. 2007), UNC School of Government faculty paper (online at www.sog.unc.edu/sites/www.sog.unc.edu/files/djoverview.pdf).

Lack of Jurisdiction

When the State lacks jurisdiction to try a person for an offense, it means that the State has no power or authority to try a person for that offense. North Carolina has territorial jurisdiction to try a person for an offense if any of the essential acts forming the crime take place in the state. State v. Rick, 342 N.C. 91, 98–99 (1995); State v. Vines, 317 N.C. 242, 250–51 (1986); State v. Darroch, 305 N.C. 196, 201 (1982); State v. First Resort Props., 81 N.C. App. 499, 500–01 (1986). For example, in *State v. White,* 134 N.C. App. 338 (1999), North Carolina had jurisdiction to try a defendant for trafficking in heroin when a witness testified that he saw the defendant cut, bag, and sell heroin in North Carolina; the fact that the defendant was arrested with the heroin in New York did not defeat jurisdiction. However, in *State v. Williams,* 74 N.C. App. 131 (1985), North Carolina did not have jurisdiction when the defendant, who was charged with felony larceny of an automobile and felonious possession of stolen property, was found with the car in the District of Columbia a few hours after it was stolen; the defendant claimed that he did not know of the theft and that he received the car from a friend, and there was no evidence that the defendant possessed the car in North Carolina.

When a defendant challenges jurisdiction, the State must prove, beyond a reasonable doubt, that the crime occurred in North Carolina. State v. Harris, 361 N.C. 400, 405 n.2 (2007).

The following statutes deal with the problem of deciding whether an act occurred in North Carolina:

§15-131. Assault in this State, death in another.
In all cases of felonious homicide, when the assault has been made within this State, and the person assaulted dies without the limits thereof, the offender shall be indicted and punished for the crime in the county where the assault was made, in the same manner, to all intents and purposes, as if the person assaulted had died within the limits of this State.

§15-132. Person in this State injuring one in another.
If any person, being in this State, unlawfully and willfully puts in motion a force from the effect of which any person is injured while in another state, the person so setting such force in motion shall be guilty of the same offense in this State as he would be if the effect had taken place within this State.

§15-133. In county where death occurs.
If a mortal wound is given or other violence or injury inflicted or poison is administered on

the high seas or land, either within or without the limits of this State, by means whereof death ensues in any county thereof, the offense may be prosecuted and punished in the county where the death happens.

§15A-134. Offense occurring in part outside North Carolina.
If a charged offense occurred in part in North Carolina and in part outside North Carolina, a person charged with that offense may be tried in this State if he has not been placed in jeopardy for the identical offense in another state.

For a more detailed discussion of territorial jurisdiction, see 1 NORTH CAROLINA DEFENDER MANUAL Chapter 10 at 4–7 (UNC School of Government rev. Oct. 2010) (online at www.ncids.org/Def%20Manual%20Info/Defender_Manual/DefManChpt10.pdf).

Expiration of Statute of Limitations

A statute of limitations provides that if a criminal charge is not brought against a defendant within a certain time, it may not be prosecuted at all. North Carolina has no statute of limitations for felonies. State v. Hefler, 310 N.C. 135, 142 (1984); State v. Johnson, 275 N.C. 264, 271 (1969). G.S. 15-1 provides a two-year statute of limitations for misdemeanors. Malicious misdemeanors are excepted from this rule. G.S. 15-1. The two-year period begins to run when the final act that is part of the offense is completed. State v. Brewer, 258 N.C. 533, 538–44 (1963). Some offenses, such as failure to support a child, are statutorily defined as continuing offenses for purposes of the statute of limitations. G.S. 14-322 (failure to support a child is a continuing offense "and shall not be barred by any statute of limitations until the . . . child . . . shall reach the age of 18 years").

In order to comply with the misdemeanor statute of limitations, the State must issue a valid criminal process before the two years expire. When an indictment or presentment is required, issuance of either document tolls the statute of limitations. State v. Underwood, 244 N.C. 68, 70 (1956); State v. Whittle, 118 N.C. App. 130, 134 (1995) (either an indictment or presentment arrests the statute of limitations). However, if the defendant may be tried in superior court on a warrant, issuance of the warrant will suffice. *Underwood,* 244 N.C. at 70. Issuance of a void criminal process does not satisfy the statute. State v. Hundley, 272 N.C. 491, 494 (1968). Mitigating this rule is G.S. 15-1, which provides that if a timely indictment is found to be defective, another prosecution may be instituted for the same offense within one year of dismissal; this exception is limited to indictments and does not apply to warrants. State v. Madry, 140 N.C. App. 600, 603 (2000).

The statute of limitations applicable to misdemeanor offenses does not apply when the issue of a defendant's guilt of a misdemeanor offense is submitted to the jury as a lesser-included offense of a properly charged felony. State v. Taylor, ___ N.C. App. ___, 713 S.E.2d 82 (2011) (applying this rule, the court held that the two-year misdemeanor statute of limitations does not bar conviction for misdemeanor common law obstruction of justice when the misdemeanor was submitted to the jury as a lesser-included offense of felonious obstruction of justice, the crime charged in the indictment).

The defense is waived if the defendant fails to plead it or request jury instructions, State v. Holder, 133 N.C. 710 (1903), pleads guilty, State v. Brinkley, 193 N.C. 747 (1927), or fails to introduce evidence that the time limit has expired, State v. Colson, 222 N.C. 28 (1942).

State-Granted Immunity

G.S. 15A-1051 through 15A-1054 make it possible for the court or prosecutor to give a person immunity from prosecution for a certain offense in exchange for that person's agreement to plead guilty to another offense or to provide testimony against another defendant. When this kind of immunity has been granted, the person may not be prosecuted for that offense, regardless of the evidence against him or her.

Defenses That Justify

Generally

A person may not be guilty of a crime, even if the person did the act charged and knew what he or she was doing, if there was a reason for committing the act that the law recognizes as a valid justification. Examples of defenses based on such justification are discussed briefly below.

Self-Defense, Defense of Others, and Defense of Property

Self-defense, defense of others, and defense of property have been called "defensive-force defenses." When these defenses apply, they justify conduct that otherwise would be criminal. Thus, for example, the law of self-defense provides, in part, that a person may kill an attacker if he or she reasonably believes that his or her acts are necessary in order to keep the attacker from killing him or her or doing him or her great bodily harm. Also, a person may, as a general rule, use force against another when the amount of force is reasonably necessary to protect himself or herself from the other person's assault, even when the other person's assault is not deadly. The law relating to defense of others tracks, for the most part, the rules regarding self-defense.

Defense of property can, under appropriate circumstances, justify the use of nondeadly force. By contrast, defense of one's home, workplace, or motor vehicle allows, in certain circumstances, for the use of deadly force.

For a more comprehensive discussion of these defensive-force defenses, see JOHN RUBIN, THE LAW OF SELF-DEFENSE IN NORTH CAROLINA (UNC Institute of Government, 1996). For a discussion of significant 2011 legislation addressing these defenses, see the blog post John Rubin, *The New Law of Self-Defense?* (online at http://sogweb.sog.unc.edu/blogs/ncclaw/?p=2798).

Necessity and Duress

If a person, under the pressure of circumstances, commits an act that would otherwise be a crime, that person may be justified by "necessity" and not guilty of the crime in question. 2 W. LAFAVE & A. SCOTT JR., SUBSTANTIVE CRIMINAL LAW 116 (2d ed. 2003). In essence, the defense justifies action when the person chooses the lesser of two evils. 2 *id.* at 124; State v. Thomas, 103 N.C. App. 264, 265 (1991). Traditionally, it was thought that for an act to be justified by necessity, the pressure must come from physical forces, such as a storm. 2 LAFAVE & SCOTT at 116. An example of necessity caused by physical forces would be when, in order to save passengers from certain death in a violent storm, a captain moors a boat at a private dock and trespasses on property to bring the passengers to safety. Another example would be when, in order to prevent a driverless truck from rolling down a hill and harming someone, a person under the influence of an impairing substance jumps into the truck and steers it to safety. State v. Hudgins, 167 N.C. App. 705 (2005). When the pressure came from human beings, the defense was called "duress." 2 LAFAVE & SCOTT at 116–17. An example of pressure from a human being is when one person holds a gun in another's side while forcing that person to steal from a store. In modern times, however, the distinction between the two defenses is sometimes blurred. 2 *id.* at 117. These defenses are sometimes classified as "excuse" defenses, rather than "justification" defenses; in this context, that debate is an academic one, with no impact on the legal rules discussed.

In North Carolina, the defense of necessity applies when a person acts under force of circumstances to protect life, limb, or health in a reasonable manner and with no other acceptable choice. *Hudgins*, 167 N.C. App. at 710–11; State v. Haskins, 160 N.C. App. 349, 356 (2003). It is limited to situations where a person is saved from death or peril or relieved from severe suffering. *Hudgins*, 167 N.C. App. at 710. Necessity is not available as a defense for attempts to prevent "serious events" or property damage. *Id.*

The defense was held not to be available to a licensed bail runner who, while in pursuit of a fugitive, carried a weapon on educational property, because several alternatives were available to the bondsman, including leaving his weapon off campus and notifying the school principal. *Haskins*, 160 N.C. App. at 355–56.

Necessity is not intended to excuse criminal activity by those who disagree with decisions and policies of the lawmaking branches of government. State v. Thomas, 103 N.C. App. 264, 265 (1991). Thus, this defense could not be claimed by anti-abortion protesters who trespassed onto an abortion clinic's property in an effort to save fetuses from abortion, because the General Assembly had made a clear choice to make abortions performed in accordance with G.S. 14-45.1 lawful. *Id.* at 267.

To invoke the duress defense, a defendant must show that his or her actions were caused by a reasonable fear that he or she would suffer immediate death or serious bodily injury if he or she failed to act. State v. Cheek, 351 N.C. 48, 61–62 (1991); State v. Sanders, ___ N.C. App. ___, 687 S.E.2d 531 (2010) (the trial court did not err by denying the defendant's request for a jury instruction on duress when the defendant voluntarily joined with accomplices to commit an armed robbery, did not object or attempt to exit the vehicle as an accomplice forced the victims into the car, and took jewelry from one victim while an accomplice pointed a gun at her; there was no evidence that any coercive measures were directed toward the defendant prior to the crimes being committed); State v. Smarr, 146 N.C. App. 44, 54 (2001). Duress will not apply if the defendant had a reasonable opportunity to avoid doing the act in question without undue exposure to death or serious bodily harm. State v. Brock, 305 N.C. 532, 541 (1982) (the defendant had the opportunity to run away without undue exposure to death or serious bodily harm); *Sanders*, ___ N.C. App. ___, 687 S.E.2d at 535; State v. Smith, 152 N.C. App. 29 (2002); *Smarr*, 146 N.C. App. at 55 (the defendant had an opportunity to leave the scene without undue exposure to death or serious bodily harm); State v. Cooke, 94 N.C. App. 386 (1989). Courts have found a "break in the continuity of the coercion" fatal to the defense because such a break affords a reasonable opportunity to avoid the act. State v. Henderson, 64 N.C. App. 536, 540 (1983). The defense is not available unless the defendant surrendered himself or herself to the police once he or she was "out from under [the] coercive influence." *Smith*, 152 N.C. App. at 40–41; *Henderson*, 64 N.C. App. at 540. It is not available to any charge of intentional homicide, *Cheek*, 351 N.C. at 61; State v. Strickland, 307 N.C. 274, 295–96 (1983); *Brock*, 305 N.C. at 540–41, and probably is not available to any charge of homicide except possibly a felony murder when the defendant did not actually do the killing, State v. Brower, 289 N.C. 644, 657 (1976).

One traditional form of duress was coercion of a wife by her husband. Under common law, a wife who committed a criminal act in the presence of her husband and at his command was presumed to have committed the act under duress from him. State v. Cauley, 244 N.C. 701, 709 (1956). Although the doctrine has not been abolished in North Carolina, courts have recognized that it is outdated. State v. Owen, 133 N.C. App. 543, 547–48 (1999); State v. Smith, 33 N.C. App. 511, 517–20 (1977) .

There is a special five-factor test to prove the defense of duress to a charge of escape from a prison or jail. State v. Watts, 60 N.C. App. 191, 193 (1982).

Public Authority

Certain actions taken by public officers—such as using reasonable force against another, taking another's property, or entering onto private property—are justified if the officer is acting pursuant to law or court order or process. 2 LaFave & Scott, cited in full *supra*, at 133. Thus, an officer is not guilty of trespass for entering a home pursuant to a valid search warrant. Nor is a law enforcement officer guilty of assault for handcuffing an unruly arrestee. State v. Sigman, 106 N.C. 728 (1890). However, the officer loses this defense by going beyond his or her authority. State v. Mincher, 172 N.C. 895 (1916). G.S. 15A-401(d) and (e) describe the limits of authority in using force to arrest. G.S. 20-145 exempts from speed limits ambulances and fire trucks in emergencies, law enforcement officers who are pursuing violators, and a few others. There also may be a public authority defense for a person who acts at the behest of a law enforcement officer. JOHN RUBIN, THE ENTRAPMENT DEFENSE IN NORTH CAROLINA 39 (UNC Institute of Government, 2001). For a discussion of the related issue of an individual's ability to defend against action taken by law enforcement officers, see JOHN RUBIN, THE LAW OF SELF-DEFENSE IN NORTH CAROLINA § 5.5 (UNC Institute of Government, 1996).

Domestic Authority

In some instances people without public authority also claim authority, by virtue of their private position, to do acts that would otherwise be crimes. A parent and a teacher who stands in the parent's place are the primary examples of people with this domestic authority. For a discussion of when a parent or teacher may impose moderate punishment to correct a child without criminal liability, see the note on Element (1) to "Assault on a Child Under 12" in Chapter 7 (Assaults).

For a discussion of other situations in which persons may discipline others without criminal liability, see 2 LAFAVE & SCOTT, cited in full *supra,* at 140–42.

Crime Prevention

Common law permits a citizen to use reasonable force to prevent or terminate a felony or a misdemeanor amounting to a breach of the peace, 2 LAFAVE & SCOTT at 183, although this defense is infrequently applied in North Carolina. Older law provided that deadly force was justifiable to prevent a felony. State v. Roane, 13 N.C. 58 (1828); State v. Rutherford, 8 N.C. 457 (1821). The modern rule, however, limits deadly force to felonies involving substantial risk of death or serious bodily harm. 2 LAFAVE & SCOTT at 183. In addition, a citizen is authorized to detain, and then turn over to law enforcement officers, anyone the citizen has probable cause to believe has committed in his or her presence a felony, a breach of the peace, a crime involving physical injury to another, or theft or destruction of property. G.S. 15A-404; State v. Ataei-Kachuei, 68 N.C. App. 209, 212–14 (1984). The detention must be reasonable and the suspect must be surrendered to a law enforcement officer as early as possible unless he or she has been released. G.S. 15A-404. G.S. 15A-405 allows private persons to assist law enforcement officers in effectuating arrests and preventing escape from custody upon request and limits their criminal liability when providing such assistance.

Defenses Showing Lack of Blameworthiness

Generally

Sometimes a defendant charged with an offense may show his or her innocence, even though the defendant did the illegal act and the act is not justified, by establishing that the circumstances were such that he or she should not be blamed for the act. These are "excuse" defenses—that is, defenses showing that a person was not responsible for what he or she did. Several excuse defenses are described briefly below.

Insanity

In order for a defendant to be excused from criminal responsibility by reason of insanity, the defendant must prove that at the time of the act, he or she was laboring under such a defect of reason caused by disease or a deficiency of the mind that he or she was incapable of knowing the nature and quality of his or her act or, if he or she did know the nature and quality of the act, that he or she was incapable of distinguishing between right and wrong in relation to the act. State v. Ingle, 336 N.C. 617, 630 (1994); State v. Jones, 293 N.C. 413, 425 (1977).

A person is presumed to be sane, State v. Thompson, 328 N.C. 477, 484 (1991); State v. Staten, 172 N.C. App. 673, 684 (2005), and the defendant has the burden of proving insanity to the satisfaction of the jury, State v. Spangler, 314 N.C. 374, 378 (1985). When no evidence tends to rebut this presumption, the State is not required to offer evidence of sanity. *Jones*, 293 N.C. at 426. However, the presumption of sanity does not relieve the State of its burden of proving all of the essential elements of each charged crime. *Thompson*, 328 N.C. at 484. Uncontradicted evidence of a defendant's insanity does not entitle the defendant to a directed verdict of not guilty by reason of insanity; the credibility of the defendant's evidence is for the jury to determine and precludes entry of a directed verdict. State v. Leonard, 300 N.C. 223, 235 (1980); *Thompson*, 328 N.C. 477. A defendant found not guilty by reason of insanity is subject to civil commitment proceedings. G.S. 15A-1321.

Immaturity

In North Carolina, a person under 16 who commits a crime generally is not subject to trial in adult courts; instead, the person is under the jurisdiction of the juvenile court. G.S. 7B-1501(7) & -1601. But if a juvenile was 13 years of age or older when he or she committed a Class A felony, the juvenile must be tried as an adult. G.S. 7B-2200. Also, a juvenile 13 years of age or older at the time any other felony offense is committed may be tried as an adult. *Id.* In addition, a child under six may not even be brought before the juvenile court as a delinquent. G.S. 7B-1501(7). Immaturity as a defense to sexual offenses is discussed in Chapter 10 (Sexual Assaults).

Unconsciousness or Automatism

A person charged with a crime may establish his or her innocence by showing that he or she committed the acts at issue while unconscious. State v. Jerrett, 309 N.C. 239, 264 (1983); State v. Caddell, 287 N.C. 266, 284–85 (1975). Automatism has been defined as "the state of a person who, though capable of action, is not conscious of what he is doing." State v. Boggess, 195 N.C. App. 770, 772 (2009) (quoting State v. Fields, 324 N.C. 204, 208 (1989)). It is a complete defense because absence of consciousness not only precludes any specific mental state but also excludes the possibility of a voluntary act. *Boggess*, 195 N.C. App. at 772; State v. Bush, 164 N.C. App. 254, 265 (2004). Automatism is a separate defense from insanity, *Jerrett*, 309 N.C. at 264; it is an affirmative defense and the defendant bears the burden of proving its existence to the satisfaction of the jury, State v. Boyd, 343 N.C. 699, 714 (1996).

The case law suggests that the following causes of unconsciousness can support the defense: epilepsy, a blow to the head, fever, sleepwalking, being asleep, involuntary intoxication, or involuntary use of drugs. State v. Williams, 296 N.C. 693, 699 (1979); *see also* State v. Connell, 127 N.C. App. 685, 692 (1997) (instruction proper on the basis that the defendant was asleep at the time of the alleged indecent liberty). Unconsciousness as a result of voluntary ingestion of alcohol or drugs does not qualify for this defense. State v. Morganherring, 350 N.C. 701, 733 (1999); State v. Fisher, 336 N.C. 684, 705 (1994).

Entrapment

If a person was entrapped into committing an offense by a law enforcement officer or some other person acting on behalf of a public agency, the person is not guilty of that crime. As discussed in more detail in JOHN RUBIN, THE ENTRAPMENT DEFENSE IN NORTH CAROLINA (UNC Institute of Government, 2001), in order to succeed on a claim of entrapment, a defendant must show that (1) law enforcement officers or their agents, by trickery, fraud, or persuasion, induced the defendant to commit the charged offense and (2) the defendant was not predisposed to commit the offense. *See, e.g.,* State v. Morse, 194 N.C. App. 685-86, 694–95 (2009) (the trial judge did not err by refusing to instruct on entrapment in a case involving a charge of soliciting a person believed to be a child by computer with intent to commit an unlawful sex act; although the child was a law enforcement officer pretending to be a 14-year-old in an adults-only Yahoo chat room, there was no credible evidence that the criminal design originated in the minds of the government officials, rather than the defendant; undercover deputies merely provided the opportunity for the defendant and, when presented with that opportunity, the defendant pursued it with little hesitance).

Failure of Proof or "Negating" Defenses

Generally

When a defendant introduces evidence at trial showing that some element of the crime has not been proved, the strategy is sometimes described as a failure of proof or a "negating" defense. 2 W. LaFave & A. Scott Jr., Substantive Criminal Law 5 (2d ed. 2003). The sections below explore some of the more common failures of proof or negating defenses.

Accident

When a killing or other injury is unintentional, occurs during the course of lawful conduct, and does not involve culpable negligence, accident may be a defense to the crime charged. N.C. Pattern Jury Instructions—Crim. 307.10 (accident as a defense to homicides other than felony murder); 307.11 (accident in cases other than homicide). In homicide cases, the defense of accident is triggered when the defendant, without premeditation, intent, or culpable negligence, commits acts that bring about the victim's death. State v. Turner, 330 N.C. 249, 262 (1991); State v. Yarborough, 198 N.C. App. 22, 33 (2009). Accident is not an affirmative defense, rather it negates the mens rea element of homicide. *Turner,* 330 N.C. at 262; *Yarborough,* 198 N.C. App. at 33.

The defense of accident is not available if the defendant was engaged in misconduct at the time of the killing. State v. Riddick, 340 N.C. 338, 342 (1995) (although the defendant claimed his gun went off accidentally, the trial court did not err by refusing to instruct on accident when the defendant sought out the victim, intentionally confronted the victim with a loaded firearm, assaulted the victim, and held the gun when two bullets were fired); *Yarborough,* 198 N.C. App. at 33–34 (the trial court did not commit plain error by failing to instruct on accident when the defendant was engaged in misconduct at the time of the killing; the defendant broke into a home with the intent to commit robbery; the killing occurred during a struggle over the defendant's gun); State v. Vincent, 195 N.C. App. 761, 764–65 (2009) (an instruction on accident was not required when the defendant was engaged in unlawful conduct; the defendant followed a vehicle driven by the victim's parents and when it pulled over, argued with the victim's father, obtained a gun from his truck, and fired a shot that killed the victim); State v. Gattis, 166 N.C. App. 1, 11 (2004) (in a homicide case, accident was not available as a defense when the defendant unlawfully entered the victim's home with a loaded gun, threatened the victim with the gun, unlawfully fired the gun and reloaded, and struck the victim in the head with the gun before the fatal bullet was fired).

Mistake of Fact

Ignorance or mistake as to a matter of fact is a defense if it negates a mental state required to establish an element of the crime. State v. Breathette, ___ N.C. App. ___, 690 S.E.2d 1, 4 (2010). For example, this defense would apply when a person charged with larceny of property asserts that he or she took the property under a reasonable but mistaken belief that he or she was the lawful possessor of the property. *See* State v. Lamson, 75 N.C. App. 132, 135–36 (1985) (error not to give an instruction on mistake of fact when there was evidence that the defendant thought he was entering a house where his friend was visiting); State v. Walker, 35 N.C. App. 182, 186–87 (1978) (the trial court erred by not giving an instruction on mistake of fact when the defendant and his son mistakenly abducted a child believed to be the defendant's granddaughter and his son's child).

When the elements of the crime do not require the defendant to know the fact at issue, mistake of fact is no defense. For example, because a defendant need not know the victim's age for statutory rape, mistake as to age is no defense to this crime. State v. Browning, 177 N.C. App. 487, 492–94 (2006). The same is true for indecent liberties with a child. *Breathette*, ___ N.C. App. ___, 690 S.E.2d at 4–6. However, if the defendant is charged with aiding and abetting statutory rape (or, presumably, indecent liberties), mistake of fact is a defense because aiding and abetting requires that the defendant knowingly aid the perpetrator in committing the offense. State v. Bowman, 188 N.C. App. 635, 647–50 (2008) (in an aiding and abetting statutory rape case, the trial court erred by failing to instruct as to mistake of fact; North Carolina does not recognize vicarious strict liability). Also, if the defendant argues that the touching was accidental, mistake of fact may be a defense to a sexual assault on a child. State v. Connell, 127 N.C. App. 685, 690–91 (1997) (in an indecent liberties case in which the State presented only circumstantial evidence that the defendant was awake and intended to touch the child and the defendant's evidence indicated that he thought he was touching the child's mother, the trial court should have instructed the jury as to the mistake of fact).

Mistake of fact should not be confused with ignorance of the law, which, as a general rule, is no excuse. State v. Howard, 158 N.C. App. 226, 233 (2003); State v. Rogers, 68 N.C. App. 358, 385 (1984).

Voluntary Intoxication

The fact that the defendant was voluntarily intoxicated from alcohol or drugs when he or she committed an offense is not a complete defense. However, voluntary intoxication can prevent the formation of the requisite mental state for specific intent crimes. State v. Kyle, 333 N.C. 687 (1993); State v. Gerald, 304 N.C. 511, 521 (1981); *see generally* the note on "General intent and specific intent" to "Intentionally" in Chapter 1 (States of Mind). In order for the jury to be instructed on voluntary intoxication, the evidence must show that at the time of the incident, "the defendant's mind and reason were so completely intoxicated and overthrown that [the defendant] could not form [the requisite] specific intent." *Gerald*, 304 N.C. at 521. When voluntary intoxication negates the required intent, the defendant cannot be found guilty of the specific intent offense but may be found guilty of a lesser-included offense. State v. Howie, 116 N.C. App. 609, 613 (1994).

Examples of specific intent crimes for which voluntary intoxication may be a defense include premeditated and deliberate first-degree murder, State v. Mash, 323 N.C. 339, 343–47 (1988), common law robbery, State v. Golden, 143 N.C. App. 426, 430–33 (2001), attempted rape (note: specific intent is an essential element of any attempt), State v. Boone, 307 N.C. 198, 210 (1982), and burglary, State v. Keitt, 153 N.C. App. 671, 676–77 (2002). Voluntary intoxication is not a defense to offenses that do not include a specific intent element, such as a first-degree murder based on the theory of lying in wait. State v. Baldwin, 330 N.C. 446, 461–62 (1992); State v. Leroux, 326 N.C. 368, 377–78 (1990).

A more detailed discussion of this defense is provided in John Rubin, *The Voluntary Intoxication Defense*, ADMIN. OF JUST. MEMORANDUM NO. 93/01 (UNC Institute of Government, May 1993) (online at www.sog.unc.edu/sites/www.sog.unc.edu/files/aojm9301_0.pdf).

Diminished Capacity

A defendant whose mental condition is diminished at the time of an alleged offense but who cannot establish the insanity defense still may have a partial defense to some crimes. The diminished capacity defense allows a defendant to introduce evidence of mental or emotional conditions negating the defendant's ability to form a specific intent. For example, a defendant may present evidence that a diminished capacity, although not rising to the level of insanity, negates his or her ability to form the specific intent to kill required for a first-degree murder conviction on the basis of premeditation and deliberation. State v. Page, 346 N.C. 689, 698 (1997). Like voluntary intoxication, diminished capacity is available as a defense to specific intent offenses, such as premeditated and deliberate first-degree murder, *id.*, and indecent liberties with a child, State v. Connell, 127 N.C. App. 685, 692 (1997), but not for general intent crimes, *Page*, 346 N.C. at 700.

For a comprehensive discussion of this defense, see John Rubin, *The Diminished Capacity Defense*, ADMIN. OF JUST. MEMORANDUM NO. 92/01 (UNC Institute of Government, Sept. 1992) (online at www.sog.unc.edu/sites/www.sog.unc.edu/files/aojm9301_0.pdf).

3

Participants in Crimes

3

Participants in Crimes

Crimes often are committed by only one person. Sometimes, however, two or more people participate in committing a crime. In such a case, the participants might play similar or different roles in carrying out the offense. This chapter explains basic doctrines that categorize the various roles a person can play in committing a crime. These doctrines do not establish separate offenses; rather, they merely describe the nature of a person's participation in a given offense. State v. Small, 301 N.C. 407 (1980).

Principals—Committing the Entire Crime

Statute

This is a common law concept.

Elements

A person is a principal to a crime based on this concept when

(1) with the required state of mind

(2) he or she commits all of the acts necessary to constitute the crime.

Punishment

A person who is a principal to a crime is guilty of that crime and is punishable as provided for that crime.

Notes

Generally. The term "principal" is used to describe a person who participates in committing a crime. The most important way of being a principal is by personally committing a crime. State v. Williams, 299 N.C. 652 (1980). One also can be a principal, however, by committing part of a crime that others complete or by helping someone else commit a crime. *Id.* These other ways of being a principal are discussed on the following pages.

The law divides principals into two types: principals in the first degree and principals in the second degree. *Id.* A principal in the first degree is one who commits an entire crime, who acts indirectly to cause a crime, or who acts in concert with others to commit a crime. A principal in the second degree is one who aids and abets in the commission of a crime. *Small,* 301 N.C. 407. However, principals in the first degree and in the second degree are equally guilty of the offense and are punished the same. *Id.*

Element (1). Typically, a person is guilty of a crime only if he or she has a certain state of mind (for example, a crime may require that the defendant act intentionally or recklessly). See Chapter 1 (States of Mind) (describing these and other criminal states of mind). In some cases, a person may be found guilty without regard to his or her state of mind. See "Strict Liability" in Chapter 1 (States of Mind).

Element (2). This element requires that the defendant do all of the acts necessary for the crime. For example, in a possession of controlled substance case, it requires that the defendant personally possess (actually or constructively) the controlled substance. See "Possession of a Controlled Substance" in Chapter 27 (Drug Offenses).

Actual presence not required. Actual presence is not required to be a principal under this concept. Thus, one who leaves poison for another to drink but is not present when the poison is consumed may be liable as a principal. 2 W. LAFAVE & A. SCOTT JR., SUBSTANTIVE CRIMINAL LAW 329 (2d ed. 2003).

Related Offenses Not in This Chapter

None

Principals—Acting Indirectly

Statute

This is a common law concept.

Elements

A person is a principal to a crime based on this concept when

(1) with the required state of mind
(2) he or she causes the occurrence that constitutes the crime
(3) by using another who is not himself or herself guilty but brings about the occurrence in the person's absence.

Punishment

A person who is a principal to a crime is guilty of that crime and is punishable as provided for that crime.

Notes

Generally. As explained above, the type of principal participation does not establish a separate crime; it merely describes a person's participation in a crime. *Small,* 301 N.C. 407; see also this note to "Principals—Committing the Entire Crime," above.

Element (1). See this note to "Principals—Committing the Entire Crime."

Element (3). If the defendant employs another to commit the act and the other person cannot be found guilty because of insanity, immaturity, or absence of knowledge of what he or she was doing, then the defendant is guilty as a principal. State v. Benton, 276 N.C. 641 (1970); 2 LAFAVE & SCOTT at 327. If the other person is not innocent, the defendant may be an accessory before the fact, *Benton,* 276 N.C. 641, or an aider and abettor. See "Aiding and Abetting" and "Accessory before the Fact to a Felony," below.

Related Offenses Not in This Chapter

"Attempt" (Chapter 5)
"Conspiracy" (Chapter 5)
"Solicitation" (Chapter 5)

Principals—Acting in Concert

Statute

This is a common law concept.

Elements

A person is a principal to a crime based on this concept when he or she

(1) is actually or constructively present at the scene when a crime is committed *and*
(2) acts together with another who does acts necessary to constitute the crime
(3) pursuant to a common plan or purpose.

Punishment

A person who is a principal to a crime is guilty of that crime and is punishable as provided for that crime.

Notes

Generally. As explained above, being a principal by acting in concert is not a separate crime; it merely describes a person's participation in a crime. See this note to "Principals—Committing the Entire Crime." The doctrine of acting in concert provides that if two persons join in a purpose to commit a crime, each of them, if actually or constructively present, is not only guilty as a principal if the other commits the particular crime but also is guilty of any other crime committed by the other in pursuance of the common purpose or as a natural or probable consequence of it. State v. Barnes, 345 N.C. 184 (1997); N.C. PATTERN JURY INSTRUCTIONS—CRIM. 202.10. Typically, acting in concert becomes an issue when the defendant was an actual participant in the crime but did not personally do all of the necessary acts constituting the crime. N.C. PATTERN JURY INSTRUCTIONS—CRIM. 202.10.

Element (1). Actual presence is established when the person was physically there when the crime occurred. State v. Gilmore, 330 N.C. 167 (1991). A person is constructively present when he or she is close enough to be able to render assistance if needed and to encourage the actual perpetration of the crime. State v. Mann, 355 N.C. 294 (2002); State v. Combs, 182 N.C. App. 365, 370 (2007). Thus, a "get-away" driver may be constructively present at the crime scene if stationed a convenient distance away. *Combs*, 182 N.C. App. at 370 (a defendant who participated in two crimes with an accomplice, remained in a truck during a third crime (a store robbery), and then drove away with the accomplice was constructively present during the store robbery).

Element (2). A defendant can be a principal by acting in concert with another person if the defendant commits an act that satisfies one or more elements of a crime. For example, if a defendant threatened a victim with violence, and an accomplice took personal property from the victim, the defendant would be a principal in the first degree with respect to the robbery. However, even if the defendant's conduct does not constitute an element of a crime, the doctrine of acting in concert can apply if the defendant is present when the offense is committed and the defendant's conduct indicates a shared or common purpose with a co-participant whose actions constitute the elements of the offense. State v. Abraham, 338 N.C. 315 (1994); State v. Williams, 299 N.C. 652 (1980); State v. Joyner, 297 N.C. 349 (1979).

For a case in which the evidence was insufficient on this element, see *State v. Bowden*, ___ N.C. App. ___, ___ S.E.2d ___ (Oct. 4, 2011) (in a felony breaking or entering and larceny case, an unknown man, who appeared to be concealing his identity, was seen walking around the victim's yard carrying property later determined to have been stolen from the home; the man fled when he saw officers and was never apprehended or identified; the defendant also was seen in the yard and fled from officers but was never seen entering or leaving the home or carrying any stolen property and no evidence linked him to the unknown man).

Element (3). The required common purpose for acting in concert is not necessarily the intent to commit the crime charged; rather, it is sufficient if the crime charged is a natural occurrence of, or flows from, a common criminal purpose. State v. Herring, 176 N.C. App. 395 (2006). Thus, in a felony murder case based on acting in concert and on an underlying felony of trafficking in cocaine by possession with a deadly weapon, it was sufficient that the defendant acted with a common purpose of possession or attempted possession of cocaine, even if the defendant did not know that his accomplice had a gun. *Id.*

For cases in which the evidence supported a common purpose, see *State v. Parker*, 187 N.C. App. 131 (2007) (the defendant, a county jail shift supervisor, shared a common purpose with another during a beating of a prisoner), *State v. Sloan*, 180 N.C. App. 527 (2006) (common purpose of forcibly confronting the victim with a weapon), *State v. Perkins*, 181 N.C. App. 209 (2007) (common purpose to commit larceny), *State v. Hill*, 182 N.C. App. 88 (2007) (common purpose to commit armed robbery), *State v. Bagley*, 183 N.C. App. 514 (2007) (same), *State v. Pope*, 163 N.C. App. 486 (2004) (first-degree murder), *State v. Lewis*, 162 N.C. App. 277 (2004) (possession with the intent to sell or deliver cocaine and the sale or delivery of cocaine), and *State v. Poag*, 159 N.C. App. 312 (2003) (second-degree murder, attempted first-degree murder, and robbery with a firearm).

Required state of mind. Under current law, if two people join in a purpose to commit a crime, and the crime has as an element a specific intent to do something (for example, the specific intent to kill as an element of first-degree murder committed by premeditation and deliberation), proof of each person's specific intent is not required; all that needs to be established is that one of the principals had that specific intent. State v. Barnes, 345 N.C. 184 (1997); *see also* State v. Clagon, ___ N.C. App. ___, 700 S.E.2d 89 (2010) (rejecting the defendant's argument that to convict him of burglary on a theory of acting in concert, the State had to show that the defendant specifically intended that an accomplice assault the victim; the evidence was sufficient to establish that the assault was in pursuance of a common purpose when the defendant forcibly entered the residence accompanied by two men carrying guns and by another person, armed with an ax, who immediately asked where the victim was located and then attacked her).

The diminished capacity defense does not negate the general intent necessary for acting in concert. State v. Roache, 358 N.C. 243 (2004).

Extent of criminal liability. If two people join in a purpose to commit a crime, each of them—if actually or constructively present during the commission of the crime—not only is guilty as a principal if the other commits that particular crime but also is guilty of any other crime committed by the other in pursuing the common purpose or as a natural or probable consequence thereof. *Barnes*, 345 N.C. 184; *State v. Jackson*, ___ N.C. App. ___, 716 S.E.2d 61, 66–67 (2011) (affirming an armed robbery conviction obtained under a theory of acting in concert even though the record did not reveal whether the defendant shared the intent or purpose to use a dangerous weapon during the robbery). In *State v. Bellamy*, 172 N.C. App. 649, 669 (2005), the court held that while a murder committed during an armed robbery is normally a natural or probable consequence of the robbery, a sexual assault may or may not be, and the determination must be made on a case-by-case basis. Distinguishing *Bellamy*, *State v. Sapp*, 190 N.C. App. 698 (2008), held that a rape by an accomplice in the course of a residential robbery was a natural and probable consequence of the intended robbery. In that case, the defendant twice raped the victim in the presence of the accomplice to induce her boyfriend to turn over cash and drugs and then told her to wash up in a bathroom, where she was raped by the accomplice. *Sapp*, 190 N.C. App. 698.

Acquittal of other principal. A defendant can be convicted of acting in concert even if the person he or she allegedly was acting in concert with is acquitted in the same trial. State v. Reid, 335 N.C. 647 (1994).

Withdrawal. One who acts in concert cannot escape liability by quietly withdrawing from the scene. The influence of his or her acting in concert continues until that person renounces the common purpose and makes it plain to the others that he or she has done so and does not intend to participate further. State v. Wilson, 354 N.C. 493 (2001).

Charging issues. In charging a substantive offense (such as murder), it is unnecessary to allege the theory of acting in concert. State v. Westbrooks, 345 N.C. 43 (1996).

Jury instructions. The trial court did not err by instructing the jury that it could find the defendant guilty of second-degree burglary under a theory of accessory before the fact, aiding and abetting, or acting in concert; the separate theories were not separate offenses but, rather, merely different methods by which the jury could find the defendant guilty. State v. Surrett, ___ N.C. App. ___, ___ S.E.2d ___ (Nov. 15, 2011); *see also* State v. Pridgen, 313 N.C. 80, 95 (1985) (the judge properly instructed the jury on acting in concert and aiding and abetting when the facts support both theories).

Related Offenses Not in This Chapter

"Conspiracy" (Chapter 5)
"Misdemeanor Inciting to Riot" (Chapter 19)
"Felony Inciting to Riot" (Chapter 19)
"Subornation of Perjury" (Chapter 21)

Aiding and Abetting

Statute

This is a common law concept. Some statutes include aiding and abetting as a form of the offense, *see, e.g.,* G.S. 14-190.9(a) (aiding and abetting indecent exposure); G.S. 14-107(b) (aiding and abetting worthless check); G.S. 14-46 (aiding and abetting concealing birth of child), although that is not required to obtain a conviction on this theory.

Elements

A person is a principal to a crime based on this concept when

(1) a crime is committed by another person,
(2) he or she knowingly advises, instigates, encourages, procures, or helps the other person commit the crime, *and*
(3) his or her actions or statements caused or contributed to the commission of the crime by the other person.

Punishment

As a general rule, a person who aids or abets a crime is guilty of that crime and is punishable as provided for that crime. A few criminal statutes punish aiding and abetting the crime at a lower level, *see, e.g.,* G.S. 14-46 (providing that the main crime (concealing birth of child) is punished as a Class I felony, while aiding and abetting the crime is a Class 1 misdemeanor), or at a specific level, *see, e.g.,* G.S. 20-179(f1) (aiding and abetting impaired driving is subject to Level Five punishment).

Notes

Generally. Aiding and abetting is not a separate crime; it merely describes a person's participation in a crime. See this note to "Principals—Committing the Entire Crime," above. As a general rule, aiding and abetting arises in cases in which it is not clear whether the defendant personally committed any part of the crime.

For the elements of aiding and abetting, see *State v. Goode*, 350 N.C. 247 (1999), and N.C. PATTERN JURY INSTRUCTIONS—CRIM. 202.20.

Although older case law required actual or constructive presence in order to prove a crime under the theory of aiding and abetting, that is no longer required. State v. Bond, 345 N.C. 1 (1996). By enacting G.S. 14-5.2, the General Assembly abolished all distinctions between accessories before the fact and principals in the commission of felonies. Thus, accessories before the fact, who did not actually commit the crime and were not present when it was committed, now can be convicted as principals under an aiding and abetting theory. *Id.* However, because the concept of accessory before the fact remains relevant to capital cases, it is discussed below. See "Accessory before the Fact to a Felony," below. The concept of aiding and abetting applies equally to felonies and misdemeanors.

Element (1). The principal in the first degree need not be convicted before a person can be found guilty of aiding and abetting that principal. State v. Beach, 283 N.C. 261, 269 (1973) (citing State v. Jarrell, 141 N.C. 722 (1906)); State v. Williams, 28 N.C. App. 320, 323 (1976). However, the State must establish that the crime in fact was committed. *Beach,* 283 N.C. at 269; State v. Cassell, 24 N.C. App. 717, 722 (1975).

Element (2). The defendant must know that the other person is committing a crime. State v. Bowman, 188 N.C. App. 635 (2008); *see also* State v. Estes, 186 N.C. App. 364, 370 (2007) (evidence that the defendant knowingly and willingly laundered nearly $500,000 through his personal and business banking accounts was sufficient to establish that he aided and abetted others in obtaining property by false pretenses). As discussed in more detail under "Strict Liability" in Chapter 1 (States of Mind), because aiding and abetting requires that the defendant act knowingly, when the defendant is prosecuted as an aider and abetter to a strict liability crime, a mental state is required. *See, e.g., Bowman,* 188 N.C. App. at 650 ("[a]lthough statutory rape is a strict liability crime, aiding and abetting statutory rape is not"; the trial court erred by denying the defendant's request for an instruction that the defendant had to know the age of the victims in order to be convicted of aiding and abetting statutory rape).

Even if the defendant is not immediately present, he or she can satisfy this element by standing by in a position in which he or she can help and the principal in the first degree knows that. State v. McKinnon, 306 N.C. 288 (1982). However, mere presence does not make the defendant an aider or abettor, even if the defendant has an intent to assist; to be guilty, the defendant must aid or actively encourage the person committing the crime or communicate to that person in some way his or her intention to assist. State v. Lucas, 353 N.C. 568 (2001); State v. Goode, 350 N.C. 247 (1999). The communication or intent to aid does not have to be shown by express words and may be inferred from the defendant's actions and from his or her relation to the perpetrator. *Goode,* 350 N.C. 247. One exception to the rule that mere presence does not make the defendant an aider and abettor is when the bystander is a friend of the perpetrator and knows that his or her presence will be regarded by the perpetrator as encouragement and protection. *Lucas,* 353 N.C. 568; *Goode,* 350 N.C. 247.

The failure of a parent who is present to take all steps reasonably possible to protect his or her child from attack or sexual assault by another person constitutes an act of omission by the parent showing the parent's consent and contribution to the crime and thus is sufficient to support a conviction based on aiding and abetting. State v. Walden, 306 N.C. 466 (1982); State v. Ainsworth, 109 N.C. App. 136 (1993).

Effect of acquittal of the principal. North Carolina law is not entirely clear as to the effect of an acquittal of the principal on an aider and abettor's conviction. Some case law suggests that if the principal and the aider and abettor are tried *separately,* the defendant may be convicted of aiding and abetting even if a principal in the first degree is acquitted. State v. Beach, 283 N.C. 261, 268–69 (1973) (the defendant's conviction as an aider and abetter was valid when the indictment alleged that the defendant aided and abetted "an unknown party" and the principal was acquitted in a separate trial); State v. Witt, 113 N.C. 716 (1893) (in a murder case, rejecting the defendant's argument that the trial judge improperly instructed the jury that the principal's prior acquittal should not affect its determination as to the defendant's guilt or innocence of aiding and abetting). Distinguishing this law, however, at least one case has held that if the indictment names a principal, the defendant may not be convicted of aiding and abetting if the named principal is acquitted in a separate trial. State v. Byrd, 122 N.C. App. 497, 498–99 (1996).

If the principal and the aider and abettor are tried *jointly*, at least one court of appeals case suggests that acquittal of the principal does not bar a conviction of the aider and abettor. *Byrd*, 122 N.C. App. at 498. Other decisions, however, including those of the North Carolina Supreme Court, hold that an aider and abettor's conviction is improper in these circumstances. *See* State v. Spruill, 214 N.C. 123, 125 (1938) (a theory of aiding and abetting could not support the defendant's manslaughter conviction arising out of a vehicle accident; the vehicle was owned by the defendant but driven by the principal, who was acquitted in a joint trial); State v. Gainey, 273 N.C. 620, 623 (1968) (citing *Spruill* and holding that because the evidence was insufficient to support the principal's conviction for carrying a concealed weapon, the conviction of two others for aiding and abetting also must fail); State v. Austin, 31 N.C. App. 20, 24 (1976) ("Where there is insufficient evidence to convict a specifically named principal defendant of the crime charged, another person may not be convicted of aiding and abetting him."); State v. Spencer, 18 N.C. App. 499, 499 (1973) (in a case in which the principal and the aider and abettor were tried jointly but appealed separately, the court noted that a new trial had been ordered on the principal's conviction; citing *Gainey*, it went on to indicate that if the principal is not convicted in the new trial, the aider and abettor's conviction cannot stand).

Effect of the principal's plea to a lesser offense. In *State v. Cassell*, 24 N.C. App. 717 (1975), the court held that a principal's guilty plea to voluntary manslaughter did not invalidate the defendant's conviction in a separate trial as an aider and abettor to second-degree murder. The court reasoned that although the State allowed the principal to plead guilty to voluntary manslaughter before the defendant's trial, the plea "did not . . . determine that the crime of second[-]degree murder had not been committed." *Id.* at 722.

Withdrawal before completion of offense. If a person who would otherwise be guilty as an aider and abettor withdraws before the offense is completed, the person may avoid guilt as a principal, but only if the withdrawal is communicated to the other participant(s) at the time, so as to remove any encouragement. State v. Spears, 268 N.C. 303 (1966).

Charging issues. In charging a substantive offense, it is not necessary to allege the theory of aiding and abetting. State v. Lancaster, 37 N.C. App. 528 (1978); State v. Ainsworth, 109 N.C. App. 136 (1993); State v. Estes, 186 N.C. App. 364 (2007) (a trial judge can instruct the jury on aiding and abetting even though the indictment alleges acting in concert; both theories are surplusage). An aiding and abetting indictment is valid if it does not name the principal and alleges simply aiding and abetting an unknown party. State v. Beach, 283 N.C. 261, 69 (1973) (the indictment alleged that the defendant aided and abetted "an unknown party"); State v. Williams, 28 N.C. App. 320, 323 (1976) ("it is not necessary that the actual perpetrators of the crime be . . . named in the indictment").

Jury instructions. The trial court did not err by instructing the jury that it could find the defendant guilty of second-degree burglary under a theory of accessory before the fact, aiding and abetting, or acting in concert; the separate theories were not separate offenses but, rather, merely different methods by which the jury could find the defendant guilty. State v. Surrett, ___ N.C. App. ___, ___ S.E.2d ___ (Nov. 15, 2011); *see also* State v. Pridgen, 313 N.C. 80, 95 (1985) (the judge properly instructed the jury on acting in concert and aiding and abetting when the facts support both theories).

Aiding and abetting voluntary manslaughter. Aiding and abetting voluntary manslaughter is a crime. State v. Shaw, 164 N.C. App. 723 (2004).

Related Offenses Not in This Chapter

"Accessory after the Fact to a Felony" (Chapter 5)
"Conspiracy" (Chapter 5)
"Solicitation" (Chapter 5)

Accessory before the Fact to a Felony

Statute

§14-5.2. Accessory before fact punishable as principal felon.

All distinctions between accessories before the fact and principals to the commission of a felony are abolished. Every person who heretofore would have been guilty as an accessory before the fact to any felony shall be guilty and punishable as a principal to that felony. However, if a person who heretofore would have been guilty and punishable as an accessory before the fact is convicted of a capital felony, and the jury finds that his conviction was based solely on the uncorroborated testimony of one or more principals, coconspirators, or accessories to the crime, he shall be guilty of a Class B2 felony.

Elements

A person is a principal to a crime based on this concept when

(1) before a felony is committed by another person, he or she counsels, procures, commands, or knowingly aids the other person to commit the felony,
(2) the felony is committed by the other person,
(3) he or she is not present when the other person commits the felony, *and*
(4) his or her actions or statements caused or contributed to the commission of the crime by the other person.

Punishment

Under G.S. 14-5.2, an accessory before the fact to a felony is guilty as a principal to the felony and is punishable as provided for that felony. The only exception to this rule is a defendant who is guilty as an accessory before the fact to a capital felony who a jury finds was convicted solely on the uncorroborated testimony of another principal, co-conspirator, or accessory; such a defendant is guilty of a Class B2 felony. *See* State v. Larrimore, 340 N.C. 119 (1995).

Notes

Generally. G.S. 14-5.2 abolished all distinctions between an accessory before the fact to a felony and a principal, with the exception of a limited circumstance in capital cases discussed in the section above on "Punishment." Thus, but for this one exception, the conduct that used to be covered by accessory before the fact to a felony is now covered by aiding and abetting, discussed above. *Bond,* 345 N.C. 1; *see also* State v. Surrett, ___ N.C. App. ___, ___ S.E.2d ___ (Nov. 15, 2011) (by enacting G.S. 14-5.2 the General Assembly did not abolish the theory of accessory before the fact; the statute merely abolished the distinction between an accessory before the fact and a principal). Because the concept remains relevant for capital cases, it is discussed here. For the elements to accessory before the fact, see *State v. Davis,* 319 N.C. 620 (1987).

Element (1). A defendant is an accessory before the fact only if assistance occurs *before* the crime. As such, this offense is aimed at the person who is not actually or constructively present when the crime is committed.

Element (4). The State must prove that the defendant's actions somehow caused or contributed to the principal's commission of the crime. In other words, there must be a causal connection between the defendant's actions and the principal's commission of the crime. *Davis,* 319 N.C. 620.

Effect of principal's acquittal or plea to a lesser offense. A defendant may not be convicted on a theory of accessory before the fact if *all* of the principals are completely acquitted. State v. Wilson, 338 N.C. 244, 254 (1994); State v. Robey, 91 N.C. App. 198 (1988). In this situation, the accessory before the fact must be acquitted because there is no proof of commission of the crime. Shortridge v. Macon, 61 N.C. 400 (1867); State v. Suites, 109 N.C. App. 373 (1993). This rule applies even if the principal is acquitted after the accessory before the fact has pled guilty. *Suites,* 109 N.C. App. 373 (plea to accessory before the fact must be set aside).

When all principals are acquitted of a greater offense but convicted of a lesser one, a defendant may be found guilty of nothing higher than being an accessory before the fact to the lesser offense. *Wilson,* 338 N.C. at 254 ("[I]f the only principal is 'acquitted' of first-degree murder but is found guilty of second-degree murder, the most an accessory before the fact could be convicted of is second-degree murder."). However, in this respect, a guilty plea is not the same as an acquittal. Thus, if the principals plead guilty to a lesser offense, a defendant still may be convicted of being an accessory before the fact to the greater offense. *Id.* (rejecting the defendant's argument that because all of the people who perpetrated the killing pled guilty to second-degree murder, he could not be convicted of being an accessory before the fact to first-degree murder); State v. Larrimore, 340 N.C. 119 (1995).

Jury instructions. The trial court did not err by instructing the jury that it could find the defendant guilty of second-degree burglary under a theory of accessory before the fact, aiding and abetting, or acting in concert; the separate theories were not separate offenses but, rather, merely different methods by which the jury could find the defendant guilty. State v. Surrett, ___ N.C. App. ___, ___ S.E.2d ___ (Nov. 15, 2011).

Guilt for crimes other than those counseled, procured, or planned. If the principal who is counseled or assisted by the defendant to commit a crime commits a different crime from the one counseled by the defendant, or additional crimes, the defendant still is guilty as an accessory before the fact if the other principal's criminal act is a natural and probable consequence of the crime counseled by the defendant. State v. Ruffin, 90 N.C. App. 705 (1988).

Greater and lesser-included offenses. Solicitation to commit murder is a lesser-included offense of murder that is committed as an accessory before the fact. State v. Westbrooks, 345 N.C. 43 (1996). Thus, a conviction of solicitation to commit murder is not permitted when a murder conviction is obtained under the theory of accessory before the fact.

Multiple convictions and punishments. A defendant may be convicted of accessory before the fact to a crime and of conspiracy to commit the same crime. State v. Wilson, 338 N.C. 244, 260–61 (1994). See the note entitled "Greater and lesser-included offenses," above.

Relation to other offenses. If the defendant counseled, procured, commanded, or knowingly helped the principal commit the felony and then was present when the felony was committed or stood by with intent to render assistance, he or she would be guilty under the aiding and abetting principle. State v. Bass, 255 N.C. 42 (1961); State v. Wiggins, 16 N.C. App. 527 (1972); see "Aiding and Abetting," above.

Related Offenses Not in This Chapter

"Accessory after the Fact to a Felony" (Chapter 5)
"Conspiracy" (Chapter 5)
"Solicitation" (Chapter 5)
See inciting to riot (various offenses) in Chapter 19 (Disorderly Conduct, Riot, and Gang Offenses).
"Subornation of Perjury" (Chapter 21)

4

Punishment under Structured Sentencing

4

Punishment under Structured Sentencing

Generally

This chapter briefly describes the sentencing law that applies to felonies and misdemeanors. The sentencing scheme currently in place in North Carolina is called Structured Sentencing. Structured Sentencing became effective for offenses committed on or after October 1, 1994. G.S. 15A-1340.10; S.L. 1994-22 Ex. Sess. It applies to all offenses except:

- first-degree murder, G.S. 15A-2000;
- impaired driving, G.S. 15A-1340.10; G.S. 20-138.1(d);
- commercial impaired driving, G.S. 20-138.2(e);
- a second or subsequent conviction of a zero tolerance offense by a commercial driver or a school bus or child care vehicle driver, G.S. 20-138.2A(c); G.S. 20-138.2B(c);
- violation of health control measures under G.S. 130A-25, G.S. 15A-1340.10; and
- drug trafficking, G.S. 90-95.

The punishment scheme for the listed motor vehicle offenses is provided in G.S. 20-179 and is discussed in more detail in the section entitled "Punishment" to those offenses, all of which are discussed in Chapter 28 (Motor Vehicle Offenses). Also exempt from Structured Sentencing are felony convictions in which defendants are sentenced as violent habitual felons under G.S. 14-7.12. Such defendants are sentenced to life without parole. *Id.*

Felonies

The centerpiece of Structured Sentencing for felonies is the statutory table of punishments, commonly referred to as the sentencing grid, in G.S. 15A-1340.17(c) and included as Table 1 at the end of this chapter. Four other tables necessary to determine the appropriate sentence for a felony also are included: Tables 2 and 2A, dealing with maximum sentences, and Tables 3 and 3A, dealing with prior record levels.

A sentencing court must take seven steps to determine the appropriate sentence for felonies under Structured Sentencing. These steps are:

(1) Determine the offense class for the felony conviction (listed under each offense in this book under the heading "Punishment").
(2) Determine the defendant's prior record level. See Tables 3 and 3A.
(3) Consider aggravating and mitigating factors and decide whether to sentence in the mitigated, presumptive, or aggravated range. G.S. 15A-1340.16(b).
(4) Select a minimum sentence from the applicable minimum sentence range. See Table 1.
(5) Select the corresponding maximum sentence. See Tables 2 and 2A.
(6) Select a sentence disposition (active, intermediate, or community). See Table 1.
(7) Consider restitution (discussed later in this chapter).

Each of these steps is summarized below. The main exceptions also are noted, under the heading "Special Provisions."

Offense Class

The first step in determining the appropriate sentence for a felony is to identify the class of the felony. There are ten classes of felonies under Structured Sentencing: A, B1, B2, C, D, E, F, G, H, and I. Punishments increase in severity as you move from Class I to Class A. For each felony listed in this book, the class of the offense is indicated under the heading "Punishment." For example, a violation of G.S. 14-32(c) ("Assault with a Deadly Weapon with Intent to Kill," discussed in Chapter 7 (Assaults)) is a Class E felony. Typically, the statute creating the offense sets out the offense class. When no offense class is specified, the felony is classified as a Class I felony. G.S. 15A-1340.17(a). As as a general rule, conspiracies and attempts are punished one class below the main offense (for example, an attempt to commit a Class E felony is punished as a Class F felony) and solicitations are punished two offense classes below the main offense. See "Attempt," "Solicitation," and "Conspiracy" in Chapter 5 (General Crimes). However, some statutes punish these versions of the crimes at the same level as the main offense. See "Armed Robbery" in Chapter 14 (Robbery, Extortion, and Blackmail) (statute specifies that attempts are punished like the completed offense) and "Indecent Liberties with a Child" in Chapter 10 (Sexual Assaults) (same).

Prior Record Level

The second step in felony sentencing is to determine the defendant's prior record level. Under G.S. 15A-1340.14(c), a defendant is assigned to one of six prior record levels (I through VI) based on the number of points he or she receives under Structured Sentencing. For example, a defendant with six to nine points is assigned to prior record level III. Punishments increase in severity as you move from prior record level I to VI. The six prior record levels, and the point ranges for each level, are indicated in the prior record level worksheet, Form AOC-CR-600 (online at www.nccourts.org/Forms/Documents/145.pdf) and Form AOC-CR-600A (online at www.nccourts.org/Forms/Documents/1255.pdf), which appear as Tables 3 and 3A at the end of this chapter. The felony portion of AOC-CR-600 is derived from G.S. 15A-1340.14, while the misdemeanor portion is from G.S. 15A-1340.21. These forms will be used by the prosecutor and the judge to make a record of a defendant's criminal history. Readers should check for updated versions of these forms before using the versions reproduced in this book.

Under G.S. 15A-1340.14(b), a defendant is assigned prior record level points in one of three ways. First, if a defendant has any prior convictions, points are assigned to each conviction based on the offense class of the prior conviction. For example, a prior conviction for a Class H felony is assigned two points. The point values for each offense class are indicated in Table 3. In calculating points for prior convictions, the following rules must be kept in mind.

Prior misdemeanors. In determining a defendant's prior record level for the purpose of felony sentencing, prior convictions of Class 2 and 3 misdemeanors do not count, nor do prior misdemeanor offenses of any class under Chapter 20 of the General Statutes, except

- misdemeanor death by vehicle under G.S. 20-141.4(a2),
- impaired driving under G.S. 20-138.1, and
- commercial impaired driving under G.S. 20-138.2.

G.S. 15A-1340.14(b).

Current classification of prior conviction. Under the Structured Sentencing rules for felonies, the classification of the prior offense is the classification assigned to that offense at the time the current offense was committed. For example, if the defendant has a prior conviction for second-degree burglary, the points assigned to the conviction depend on the current classification of the offense (now Class G), not the classification in effect at the time the conviction occurred. G.S. 15A-1340.14(c).

Multiple prior convictions. If the defendant was convicted of more than one offense in a single superior court during one calendar week, only the conviction with the highest point total is counted. If the defendant was convicted of more than one offense during a single session (typically a day) of district court, only the most serious conviction is counted. G.S. 15A-1340.14(d).

Convictions from other jurisdictions. Unless the prosecution or defendant proves otherwise, a conviction from another jurisdiction is classified as a Class I felony if that jurisdiction classifies the offense as a felony. Similarly, unless the prosecution proves otherwise, a conviction from another jurisdiction is classified as a Class 3 misdemeanor (and thus does not count) if the other jurisdiction classifies the offense as a misdemeanor. G.S. 15A-1340.14(e). The default classifications do not apply when the defendant or the State proves, by a preponderance of the evidence, that the out-of-state conviction is substantially similar to a North Carolina crime. *Id.* When this showing is made, the out-of-state crime is classified like the substantially similar North Carolina crime. *Id.* The question of whether an out-of-state conviction is substantially similar to a North Carolina crime is a question of law which must be determined by a judge; although a defendant may stipulate to the existence of an out-of-state conviction, a stipulation that such a conviction is substantially similar to a North Carolina conviction is ineffective. State v. Bohler, 198 N.C. App. 631, 635–38 (2009). The United States Supreme Court's decision in *Blakely v. Washington,* 542 U.S. 296 (2004) (holding that any fact other than a prior conviction that increases the statutory maximum punishment must be submitted to a jury and found beyond a reasonable doubt), does not change the rule that "substantial similarity" is determined by a judge. State v. Hanton, 175 N.C. App. 250, 252–55 (2006); State v. Hadden, 175 N.C. App. 492, 500 (2006).

The second way a defendant is assigned prior record level points is if all the elements of the present offense are included in a prior offense. In essence, the current offense must be the same as or a lesser-included offense of a prior offense committed by the defendant. This fact adds one point, and the additional point may be counted whether or not the prior offense was used in determining the prior record level. G.S. 15A-1340.14(b)(6). Whether a point is assigned on this basis is a question of law; as such, a stipulation to this point is ineffective. State v. Prush, 185 N.C. App. 472, 479–80 (2007). This prior record level point is not affected by the United States Supreme Court's decision in *Blakely,* 542 U.S. 296, and thus may be determined by a judge. State v. Poore, 172 N.C. App. 839, 843 (2005).

Third, one point is added if the defendant was on probation, parole, or post-release supervision, was serving a sentence of imprisonment, or was an escapee when the current offense was committed. G.S. 15A-1340.14(b)(7). Unless admitted to by the defendant, this prior record level point must be submitted to the jury and proved beyond a reasonable doubt. G.S. 15A-1340.16(a5).

For a more detailed discussion of prior record level points, see Jamie Markham, *Sentencing: Prior Record Level, in* The Survival Guide: Superior Court Judges' Trial Notebook (UNC School of Government, May 2009) (online at www.sog.unc.edu/sites/www.sog.unc.edu/files/SentencingPriorRecordLevel.pdf).

Aggravating and Mitigating Factors

Table 1, the sentencing grid, contains three ranges of punishment for all but one of the ten felony classes. The exception is Class A, for which punishment is death or life imprisonment without parole. The three ranges of punishment for all of the other felony classes are mitigated, presumptive, and aggravated.

Mitigated terms are at the low end, aggravated terms are at the high end, and presumptive sentences fall in the middle. G.S. 15A-1340.17(c)(2)–(4). The presumptive range is the default sentencing range, and the judge does not need to make any special findings to impose a sentence in this range. G.S. 15A-1340.16(c); 15A-1340.17(c)(2). A judge may deviate upward from the presumptive range and sentence in the aggravated range if he or she determines that aggravating factors are sufficient to outweigh any mitigating factors. G.S. 15A-1340.16(b). Similarly, a judge may sentence in the mitigated range if he or she determines that mitigating factors are present and are sufficient to outweigh any aggravating factors. G.S. 15A-1340.16(b). Although the sentencing judge is required to consider evidence of aggravating and mitigating factors, the decision to sentence in the mitigated or aggravated range is discretionary. State v. Bivens, 155 N.C. App. 645, 648 (2002). If the judge exercises this discretionary authority, then he or she must make written findings as to the aggravating and/or mitigating factors, even if the defendant is being sentenced after a plea with stipulations. State v. Bright, 135 N.C. App. 381, 382–83 (1999). Form AOC-CR-605 (online at www.nccourts.org/Forms/Documents/1097.pdf) should be used to record all findings of aggravating and mitigating factors.

As a general rule, aggravating factors must be submitted to the jury and proved beyond a reasonable doubt, unless admitted to by the defendant. G.S. 15A-1340.16(a)–(a1). G.S. 15A-1340.16(b) sets out an exception to this rule, providing that the statutory aggravating factor in G.S. 15A-1340.16(d)(12a) (the defendant has, during the ten-year period prior to the commission of the offense, been found in willful violation of the conditions of probation imposed pursuant to a suspended sentence or of a condition of parole or post-release supervision imposed pursuant to release from incarceration) may be found by a judge. Although the same subsection also provides that the G.S. 15A-1340.16(d)(18a) statutory aggravating factor (previously adjudicated delinquent for an offense that would be a Class A, B1, B2, C, D, or E felony if committed by an adult) also may be found by a judge, there are conflicting court of appeals opinions on whether this factor must be submitted to the jury and proved beyond a reasonable doubt. *Compare* State v. Yarrell, 172 N.C. App. 135, 141–43 (2005) (must be submitted to the jury), *with* State v. Boyce, 175 N.C. App. 663, 669 (2006) (need not be submitted to the jury).

G.S. 15A-1340.16(d) sets out twenty-five statutory aggravating factors, including, among other things, that the crime was especially heinous, atrocious, or cruel, *id.* at -1340.16(d)(7); that the victim was very young, very old, or mentally or physically infirm or handicapped, *id.* at -1340.16(d)(11); and that the defendant involved a person under the age of 16 in the commission of the crime, *id.* at -1340.16(d)(13). In addition to the statutory aggravating factors, non-statutory aggravating factors can affect a defendant's sentence. G.S. 15A-1340.16(d)(20). A non-statutory aggravating factor must be "reasonably related to the purposes of sentencing." *Id.* Examples include leaving a badly injured victim without offering aid, State v. Applewhite, 127 N.C. App. 677, 683 (1997), and causing the victim to incur excessive medical expenses, State v. Pender, 176 N.C. App. 688, 695–97 (2006).

The defendant bears the burden of proving, by a preponderance of the evidence, that a mitigating factor exists. G.S. 15A-1340.16(a). G.S. 15A-1340.16(e) sets out twenty statutory mitigating factors, including, among other things, that the defendant has made substantial or full restitution to the victim, *id.* at -1340.16(e)(5), reasonably believed his or her conduct was legal, *id.* at -1340.16(e)(10), and has a positive employment history or is gainfully employed, *id.* at -1340.16(e)(19). In addition to the statutory mitigating factors, non-statutory mitigating factors can affect a defendant's sentence. *Id.* at -1340.16(e)(21). Non-statutory mitigating factors must be "reasonably related to the purposes of sentences." *Id.* Examples include that the defendant had no prior criminal record, State v. Pender, 176 N.C. App. 688, 691 (2006), or that the defendant identified a co-defendant at an early stage of the prosecution, State v. Easterling, 119 N.C. App. 22, 35 (1995).

Minimum Sentence

Once the sentencing court determines the class of felony, prior record level, and whether to sentence in the aggravated, mitigated, or presumptive range, the court must select a minimum term of imprisonment from Table 1. G.S. 15A-1340.13(c). To determine the minimum term, the court must locate the class of felony at issue along the left-hand side of the grid and the prior record level along the top of the grid. The cell in which the felony class and prior record level intersect shows the range of permissible minimum sentences that the court may impose. Having determined whether to impose a term of imprisonment from the presumptive, aggravated, or mitigated ranges (expressed in months) shown in the particular cell, the court must select a minimum term of imprisonment from within the applicable range.

Maximum Sentence

The judgment of the court also must contain a maximum term of imprisonment. G.S. 15A-1340.13(c). The maximum term is set by statute based on the minimum term imposed by the court. For Class B1 through E felonies committed before December 1, 2011, the maximum term of imprisonment is 120 percent of the minimum term rounded to the next highest month, plus nine months to allow time for post-release supervision. For Class F through I felonies committed before December 1, 2011, the maximum term of imprisonment is 120 percent of the minimum term rounded to the next highest month. G.S. 15A-1340.17(d), (e), (e1).

A minimum/maximum table containing these calculations is shown as Table 2. The numbers in the table to the left of the dash represent the minimum term of imprisonment imposed by the court, expressed in months. The numbers to the right of the dash represent the corresponding maximum term required by statute. The table is in two parts—the first part lists maximum sentences for Class B1 through E felonies, and the second lists the maximum sentences for Class F through I felonies.

For felonies committed on or after December 1, 2011, all defendants who serve a period of imprisonment will be released into post-release supervision. S.L. 2011-192. The maximum sentences for those crimes were increased accordingly. For Class B1 through E felonies, the maximum term of imprisonment is 120 percent of the minimum term rounded to the next highest month, plus 12 months. For Class F through I felonies, the maximum term of imprisonment is 120 percent of the minimum term rounded to the next highest month, plus nine months. A minimum/maximum table containing these calculations is shown as Table 2A, which is the same as Table 2, described above, except for the listed maximums.

For new special maximum terms that apply to certain sex offenders, see "Sex offenders" under "Special Provisions," below.

Sentence Disposition

The next step in felony sentencing is to determine the sentence disposition, which is prescribed in Table 1. Each cell in the grid contains a sentence disposition, signified by the letter "A," "I," or "C," or a combination of these letters. "A" represents active punishment; "I" represents intermediate punishment; and "C" represents community punishment. G.S. 15A-1340.17(c)(1). All of these terms are described below. The court must impose a sentence disposition indicated in the applicable cell. Some cells in the grid prescribe two or three possible dispositions, separated by a slash (for example, "I/A"). In those cases, the court can impose either disposition.

Active punishment. Active punishment is an unsuspended term of imprisonment. G.S. 15A-1340.11(1). If the court imposes an active punishment, the minimum and maximum term of imprisonment previously determined by the court may not be suspended. The maximum term may be reduced by earned-time credit (awarded by the Department of Correction or local jail), but the term of imprisonment may not be reduced (except for credit for time served awaiting trial) below the minimum term imposed by the court. G.S. 15A-1340.13(d).[1]

Ordinarily, if the only disposition prescribed in a particular cell is "A," the court must impose active imprisonment. Upon a finding of extraordinary mitigation, however, the court may impose an intermediate punishment even when only an active punishment is prescribed. See "Extraordinary mitigation," discussed below under "Special Provisions." In drug-trafficking cases, the court is not required to impose an active punishment (regardless of the class of offense or the defendant's prior record level) if it finds that the defendant provided "substantial assistance" within the meaning of G.S. 90-95(h)(5). Drug trafficking is discussed further below, under the heading "Special Provisions."

When sentencing a defendant for multiple offenses, the court may consolidate sentences, run them concurrently, or run them consecutively. G.S. 15A-1340.15; 15A-1354. Unless otherwise specified by the court, sentences run concurrently. G.S. 15A-1340.15(a); 15A-1354(a). If the court consolidates offenses for sentencing, the most serious offense is controlling—the sentence disposition and the minimum and maximum terms of imprisonment must conform to the Structured Sentencing rules for that offense. G.S. 15A-1340.15(b). If the court imposes consecutive sentences, the minimum term of imprisonment is the sum of the minimum terms imposed for the offenses, and the maximum term is the sum of the maximum terms for the offenses. G.S. 15A-1354(b).[2]

A defendant sentenced to active punishment for a felony is committed to the custody of the Department of Correction. G.S. 15A-1352(b).

Intermediate punishment. For defendants placed on probation based on offenses that occurred before December 1, 2011, intermediate punishment is supervised probation involving at least one of the following:

- special probation,
- assignment to a residential program,
- house arrest with electronic monitoring,
- intensive probation,
- assignment to a day-reporting center, or
- assignment to a drug treatment court program.

G.S. 15A-1340.11(6).

For these defendants, if the court imposes an intermediate punishment, it must suspend the minimum and maximum term of imprisonment and impose a period of supervised probation with at least one of the six conditions listed above.

---

1. Defendants who receive post-release supervision are automatically released from prison a set period before the end of their maximum terms of imprisonment. For offenses committed before December 1, 2011, Class B1 through E felons are released from prison into post-release supervision nine months before the end of their maximum imposed sentences. For offenses committed on or after December 1, 2011, Class B1 through E felons are released from prison into post-release supervision twelve months before the end of their maximum imposed sentences, and Class F through I felons are released nine months before attaining their maximums. In every case, the defendant may be released sooner if his or her maximum sentence has been reduced through earned time credit awarded by the Department of Correction, G.S. 15A-1368.2, but a defendant may never be released before serving the minimum term of imprisonment imposed by the court. G.S. 15A-1340.13(d). If the defendant violates a condition of post-release supervision during that period, he or she can be returned to prison as provided in G.S. 15A-1368.3. For special post-release supervision provisions related to sex offenders, see "Sex offenders" under "Special Provisions," below.

2. For offenses committed before December 1, 2011, if the court imposes consecutive terms of imprisonment for more than one Class B1 through E felony, the maximum term for each second and subsequent Class B1 through E felony is reduced by nine months. G.S. 15A-1354(b)(1). For offenses committed on or after December 1, 2011, if the court imposes consecutive terms of imprisonment for more than one Class B1 through E felony, the maximum term for each second and subsequent B1 through E felony is reduced by twelve months (or sixty months if the defendant has multiple convictions sentenced under G.S. 15A-1340.17(f), see "Sex offenders" under "Special Provisions," below); for Class F through Class I felonies, the same rule applies but the reduction is nine months. G.S. 15A-1354(b)(1) (as amended by S.L. 2011-192). For certain offenders, advanced supervised release may be available. G.S. 15A-1340.18.

2011 legislation changed the nature of intermediate punishment. S.L. 2011-192, sec. 1(b). As a result of that legislation and for defendants placed on probation based on offenses that occur on or after December 1, 2011, intermediate punishment consists of supervised probation. G.S. 15A-1340.11(6) (as amended by S.L. 2011-192). It may include drug treatment court, special probation as defined in G.S. 15A-1351(a), and one or more of the conditions set forth in new G.S. 15A-1343(a1). *Id.* The conditions in new G.S. 15A-1343(a1), which are in addition to any conditions authorized by G.S. 15A-1343(b1), include:

- House arrest with electronic monitoring.
- Perform community service.
- Submission to a period or periods of confinement in a local confinement facility for a total of no more than six days per month during any three separate months during the period of probation. The six days per month confinement may only be imposed as two-day or three-day consecutive periods. When a defendant is on probation for multiple judgments, confinement periods must run concurrently and may total no more than six days per month.
- Substance abuse assessment, monitoring, or treatment.
- Participation in an educational or vocational skills development program, including an evidence-based program.
- Submission to satellite-based monitoring in certain circumstances.

G.S. 15A-1343(a1). For intermediate punishments for felonies under both the old and new statutes, the court is authorized to impose a period of probation ranging from eighteen to thirty-six months. G.S. 15A-1343.2(d)(4). The court may depart from this range upon finding that a longer or shorter period is necessary, but that period may not exceed five years. G.S. 15A-1343.2(d).

As a condition of intermediate punishment under both the old and new statutes, the court is authorized to impose special probation, also known as a split sentence. Under special probation, the court suspends the term of imprisonment, places the defendant on probation, and requires the defendant to submit to a period of imprisonment as a condition of probation. G.S. 15A-1351(a). The period of imprisonment pursuant to special probation may not exceed one-fourth of the maximum term of imprisonment imposed. *Id.* Periods of incarceration under special probation may be continuous or non-continuous, but all incarceration must be served within two years of the conviction. G.S. 15A-1351(a).

Community punishment. For defendants placed on probation based on offenses that occurred before December 1, 2011, community punishment is any sentence that does not include an active or intermediate punishment. G.S. 15A-1340.11(2). The court must suspend any term of imprisonment; it may not impose an active term of imprisonment or special probation requiring a period of imprisonment.

For these defendants, a community punishment may include unsupervised probation or supervised probation with any authorized condition other than one defined as an intermediate punishment. G.S. 15A-1340.11(2); 15A-1340.11(6).

2011 legislation changed the nature of community punishment. S.L. 2011-192, sec. 1(a). As a result of that legislation and for defendants placed on probation based on offenses that occur on or after December 1, 2011, community punishment consists of a sentence that includes supervised or unsupervised probation and any condition of probation except drug treatment court or special probation. G.S. 15A-1340.11(2) (as amended by S.L. 2011-192). Community punishment may include any one or more of the conditions set forth in new G.S. 15A-1343(a1). *Id.* The conditions in new G.S. 15A-1343(a1) are set out under "Immediate punishment," above.

For community punishments for felonies under both the old and new statutes, the court is authorized to impose a period of probation ranging from twelve to thirty months. G.S. 15A-1343.2(d)(3). The court may depart from this range upon finding that a longer or shorter period is necessary, but that period may not exceed five years. G.S. 15A-1343.2(d). A community punishment also may consist of a fine only, without probation. G.S. 15A-1340.17(b).

G.S. 15A-1382.1(b) provides that if the court finds that there was a personal relationship, as defined in G.S. 50B-1(b), between the defendant and the victim and imposes a sentence of community punishment, the court must determine whether the defendant must comply with any of the special conditions of probation in G.S. 15A-1343(b1). G.S. 15A-1382.1(b) also provides that the court may impose house arrest under G.S. 15A-1343(b1)(3c). It is not clear whether this subsection is meant to apply to any case in which the court finds that there was a personal relationship or whether it is limited to the offenses mentioned in G.S. 15A-1382.1(a), which include assault and communicating a threat.

Fines. The court may impose a fine as part of any disposition, whether active, intermediate, or community. Unless otherwise provided by statute, the amount of the fine is in the court's discretion. G.S. 15A-1340.17(b); 15A-1343(b)(9).

Restitution

The last step in felony sentencing is for the judge to consider whether the defendant should be required to pay restitution. G.S. 15A-1340.34 (this step is mandatory). For a detailed discussion of restitution, see Jamie Markham, *Restitution, in* SUPERIOR COURT JUDGES' TRIAL NOTEBOOK (UNC School of Government, Apr. 2009) (online at www.sog.unc.edu/sites/www.sog.unc.edu/files/Restitution.pdf), from which much of the discussion here is drawn directly.

Restitution can be ordered in addition to any other punishment that is imposed, including an active sentence. G.S. 15A-1340.34(c). Article 81C of G.S. Chapter 15A, G.S. 15A-1340.34 through 15A-1340.38, governs restitution in all criminal cases.

If the offense is subject to the Crime Victims' Rights Act (CVRA), G.S. 15A-830 through 15A-841, restitution is mandatory. Offenses covered by the CVRA include:

- any Class A, B1, B2, C, D, or E felony;
- the following Class F felonies: G.S. 14-16.6(b); 14-16.6(c); 14-18; 14-32.1(e); 14-32.2(b)(3); 14-32.3(a); 14-32.4; 14-34.2; 14-34.6(c); 14-41; 14-43.3; 14-43.11; 14-190.17; 14-190.19; 14-202.1; former 14-277.3; 14-277.3A; 14-288.9; and 20-138.5;
- the following Class G felonies: G.S. 14-32.3(b); 14-51; 14-58; 14-87.1; and 20-141.4;
- the following Class H felonies: G.S. 14-32.3(a); 14-32.3(c); 14-33.2; former 14-277.3; and 14-277.3A;
- the following Class I felonies: G.S. 14-32.3(b); 14-34.6(b); and 14-190.17A;
- an attempt to do one of the listed felonies if the attempt is punishable as a felony;
- any of the following misdemeanor offenses when the offense is committed between persons who have a personal relationship as defined in G.S. 50B-1(b): G.S. 14-33(c)(1); 14-33(c)(2); 14-33(a); 14-34; 14-134.3; former 14-277.3; and 14-277.3A and
- any violation of a valid protective order under G.S. 50B-4.1.

G.S. 15A-830(7).

The amount of restitution must be supported by evidence presented at trial or sentencing. *See, e.g.,* State v. Replogle, 181 N.C. App. 579 (2007). The court may delegate to a probation officer the authority to determine a restitution payment schedule and may authorize the probation officer to transfer the defendant to unsupervised probation after all moneys are paid. G.S. 15A-1343(g).

G.S. 15A-1340.35 specifies the factors that a judge must consider when determining restitution. For example, for offenses resulting in bodily injury to the victim, the judge must consider: the cost of medical and related professional services, including physical, psychiatric, and psychological care; the cost of necessary physical and occupational therapy and rehabilitation; and lost income. Restitution may not be ordered for a victim's pain and suffering. State v. Wilson, 158 N.C. App. 235, 241 (2003).

When determining restitution, the court must consider the defendant's ability to pay but is not required to make findings as to this determination. G.S. 15A-1340.36(b).

The court may order partial restitution; if it does so, it must state on the record the reasons for doing so. G.S. 15A-1340.36. A court can order restitution in addition to any penalty authorized by law, including an active sentence. *Id.* The court may require restitution to be paid by a certain date or in installments over a specified time period. G.S. 15A-1340.36(b).

When an active sentence is imposed, the court must consider whether to recommend that restitution be made out of any earnings gained by the defendant if he or she is granted work release privileges. G.S. 15A-1340.36(c).

The judge generally may not order a criminal defendant to pay money to a victim as a "civil judgment." State v. Clemmons, 111 N.C. App. 569 (1993). However, restitution for offenses covered by the CVRA and exceeding $250 may be enforced like a civil judgment. G.S. 15A-1340.38(a). Such judgments may be collected in the same manner as a civil judgment, unless the restitution is ordered as a condition of probation. In probation cases, the judgment may not be executed upon the defendant's property until the clerk is notified that the defendant's probation has been terminated or revoked and the judge has made a finding that restitution in a sum certain remains owed. G.S. 15A-1340.38(c). The court can use Form AOC-CR-612 to document that finding (online at www.nccourts.org/Forms/Documents/158.pdf).

Special Provisions

A number of provisions depart from the basic Structured Sentencing scheme for felonies, described above. The principal exceptions are as follows:

Class A felonies. Class A felonies are punishable by death or life without parole, regardless of the defendant's prior record level. The only Class A felonies are first-degree murder under G.S. 14-17 and injuring another by use of a nuclear, biological, or chemical weapon of mass destruction under G.S. 14-288.22. For a discussion of capital sentencing issues, see ROBERT L. FARB, NORTH CAROLINA CAPITAL CASE LAW HANDBOOK (UNC School of Government, 2d ed. 2004).

Habitual felon. A person becomes a habitual felon when he or she has been convicted of three felony offenses as set out in G.S. 14-7.1. When a defendant is convicted of a felony that was committed before December 1, 2011, after having achieved the status of habitual felon, the punishment for that offense is elevated to a Class C felony (unless the offense for which he or she was convicted is a Class A, B1, or B2 felony). G.S. 14-7.6. For example, a defendant found to be a habitual felon after being convicted of felonious breaking or entering under G.S. 14-54, ordinarily a Class H felony, is sentenced as though he or she was convicted of a Class C felony.

2011 legislation changed the sentencing of habitual felons. S.L. 2011-192. Under the new legislation, if the principal felony occurred on or after December 1, 2011, a habitual felon is punished four classes higher than the principal felony for which the person was convicted, up to a maximum of Class C. G.S. 14-7.6 (as amended by S.L. 2011-192). Thus, a defendant who is determined to be a habitual felon after being convicted of a Class H felony will be sentenced as a Class D felon. But a defendant who is determined to be a habitual felon after being convicted of a Class D felony will be sentenced as a Class C felon.

Under both the old and new law, a defendant's status as a habitual felon is determined by a jury at a hearing held after a conviction, unless the defendant admits to being a habitual felon. G.S. 14-7.5. Prior convictions used to establish habitual felon status cannot be used in determining the prior record level in sentencing for the Class C felony. G.S. 14-7.6.

Violent habitual felon. A person becomes a violent habitual felon when he or she has been convicted of two violent felony offenses as set out in G.S. 14-7.7. When a defendant is convicted of a violent felony after having achieved the status of violent habitual felon, the punishment for that offense (except when the death penalty has been imposed) is life imprisonment without parole. G.S. 14-7.12.

Habitual breaking and entering status offender. Under 2011 legislation, S.L. 2011-192, a person becomes a habitual breaking and entering status offender when he or she has been convicted of or pled guilty to one or more prior felony offenses of breaking and entering in any federal or state court. G.S. 14-7.26. When a habitual breaking and entering status offender commits a felony breaking and entering offense, the offender must be sentenced as a Class E felon. G.S. 14-7.31(a). The covered felony breaking and entering offenses include:

- "First-Degree Burglary," discussed in Chapter 15 (Burglary, Breaking or Entering, and Related Offenses);
- "Second-Degree Burglary," discussed in Chapter 15 (Burglary, Breaking or Entering, and Related Offenses);
- "Felony Breaking or Entering of a Building," discussed in Chapter 15 (Burglary, Breaking or Entering, and Related Offenses);
- "Breaking or Entering a Place of Worship," discussed in Chapter 15 (Burglary, Breaking or Entering, and Related Offenses);
- Breaking out of dwelling house as proscribed by G.S. 14-53;
- Any repealed or superseded offense substantially equivalent to any of the offenses listed above; and
- Any offense committed in another jurisdiction substantially similar to any of the offenses listed above.

G.S. 14-7.25.

As with habitual felon and violent habitual felon status, described above, a defendant's status as a habitual breaking and entering offender is determined by a jury at a hearing held after conviction. G.S. 14-7.30. A prior conviction used to establish a person's status as a habitual breaking and entering offender cannot be used to determine the prior record level in sentencing for the Class E felony. G.S. 14-7.31(b). For more detail on this status offense, see G.S. 14-7.25 through -7.31.

Although this status offense appears to elevate punishment for such offenders, it may operate to lower punishment in some instances. Two of the covered offenses, "First-Degree Burglary" and breaking out of a dwelling house already are classified as Class D felonies. See the section entitled "Punishment" under "First-Degree Burglary" in Chapter 15 (Burglary, Breaking or Entering, and Related Offenses); G.S. 14-53 (breaking out of a dwelling house). If a defendant who committed either of those offenses was prosecuted for this status offense, his or her punishment would be reduced from a Class D felony to a Class E felony. It is thus unlikely that prosecutors will indict such a defendant for this status offense. For all of the other covered offenses, the new status offense increases punishment.

Habitual impaired driving. As discussed in the note on "Punishment" under "Habitual Impaired Driving" in Chapter 28 (Motor Vehicle Offenses), a defendant convicted of this Class F felony must, under G.S. 20-138.5, be sentenced to an active term of imprisonment of at least twelve months, which may not be suspended.

Firearm or deadly weapon enhancement. Subject to certain exceptions, a defendant who, during the commission of a Class A through E felony, (1) used, displayed, or threatened to use or display a firearm or deadly weapon and (2) actually possessed the firearm or deadly weapon about his or her person must be sentenced to an additional sixty months imprisonment. G.S. 15A-1340.16A(c). The sixty-month enhancement attaches to the minimum term of imprisonment; the applicable maximum term is calculated using the enhanced minimum. *Id.* The facts supporting the enhancement must be alleged in an indictment or information and proved to a jury beyond a reasonable doubt, unless the defendant pleads guilty or no contest to the issue. G.S. 15A-1340.16A(d), (e).

Sex offenders. Certain Class B1 through E felonies committed on or after December 1, 2011, that are reportable convictions under the sexual offender registration program are subject to higher statutory maximum sentences than those reflected in Tables 2 and 2A. Specifically, unless otherwise provided in a statute setting out the punishment for a specific crime, for defendants sentenced for Class B1 through E felonies that are reportable convictions, the maximum term of imprisonment is 120 percent of the minimum term of imprisonment rounded to the next highest month, plus sixty additional months. G.S. 15A-1340.17(f). The additional sixty months corresponds to the five-year period of post-release supervision applicable to sex offenders under G.S. 15A-1368.2(c). A defendant with the extended maximum sentence will be released from prison sixty months before the end of his or her maximum imposed sentence, less earned time. G.S. 15A-1368.2(a) (as amended by S.L. 2011-307). Offenders who violate a condition of post-release supervision can be returned to prison to serve the time remaining on their maximum imposed terms. G.S. 1368.3(c). For other Class B1 through E felonies, the "plus" is nine months (for offenses occurring before December 1, 2011) or twelve months (for offenses occurring on or after that date). For a discussion of the sex offender registration program, see the note entitled "Generally" to "Failure to Register, etc. as a Sex Offender" in Chapter 9 (Sexual Assaults).

B1 felonies against young victims. Subject to an exception, a person who commits a Class B1 felony—such as first-degree rape or sex offense—against a victim who was 13 years old or younger and who has a prior Class B1 felony conviction will be sentenced to life imprisonment without parole. G.S. 15A-1340.16B(a). The facts supporting the enhancement must be alleged in an indictment or information and proved to a jury beyond a reasonable doubt, unless the defendant pleads guilty or no contest to the issue. G.S. 15A-1340.16B(d), (e). The enhancement does not apply if there are any mitigating factors present under G.S. 15A-1340.16(e). G.S. 15A-1340.16B(f).

Bullet-proof vest enhancement. Subject to certain exceptions, a person who commits a felony while wearing or having in his or her immediate possession a bullet-proof vest will be punished one class higher than the underlying felony. G.S. 15A-1340.16C(a). Thus, if the felony is punishable as a Class D felony, the person will be sentenced as a Class C felon. The facts supporting the enhancement must be alleged in an indictment or information and proved to a jury beyond a reasonable doubt, unless the defendant pleads guilty or no contest to the issue. G.S. 15A-1340.16C(c), (d). For the relevant exceptions, see G.S. 15A-1340.16C(b1), (e).

Conditional discharge for certain drug offenders. Under G.S. 90-96, as amended by 2011 legislation, S.L. 2011-192, for certain offenders convicted of a misdemeanor under the North Carolina Controlled Substances Act or a felony possession of a controlled substance offense under G.S. 90-95(a)(3), see "Possession of a Controlled Substance" and other drug crimes in Chapter 27 (Drug Offenses), conditional discharge is mandatory.

Methamphetamine enhancement. Unless an exception applies, if a person is convicted of manufacturing methamphetamine and a law enforcement, probation, or parole officer, an emergency medical services employee, or a firefighter suffered serious injury caused by the hazards associated with the manufacture of methamphetamine, then that person's minimum term of imprisonment is enhanced by twenty-four months. G.S. 15A-1340.16D(a). The facts supporting the enhancement must be alleged in an indictment or information and proved to a jury beyond a reasonable doubt, unless the defendant pleads guilty or no contest to the issue. G.S. 15A-1340.16D(b), (c). The enhancement does not apply if the offense is packaging or repackaging methamphetamine, or labeling or relabeling the methamphetamine container. G.S. 15A-1340.16D(d).

Drug trafficking. Drug trafficking is punished according to a separate table of punishments, containing minimum and maximum terms of imprisonment that depart from the sentencing grid. Minimum fines also are prescribed for drug-trafficking offenses. *See* G.S. 90-95(h); Chapter 27 (Drug Offenses). The sentencing court can deviate from the prescribed sentences for drug trafficking if the defendant is determined to have provided "substantial assistance in the identification, arrest, or conviction of any accomplices, accessories, co-conspirators, or principals." G.S. 90-95(h)(5).

Domestic violence protective order enhancement. G.S. 50B-4.1(d) provides that, unless covered under some other provision of law providing greater punishment, when a person commits a felony knowing that the behavior is prohibited by a valid protective order as provided in G.S. 50B-4.1(a), punishment for the felony is elevated by one class. This provision does not apply to a person:

- charged with or convicted of a Class A or B1 felony;
- charged with an offense under G.S. 50B-4.1(f) (knowingly violating a valid protective order after having been previously convicted of two 50B offenses); or
- charged with an offense under G.S. 50B-4.1(g) (knowingly violating a valid protective order by failing to stay away from a place or a person while possessing a deadly weapon).

G.S. 50B-4.1(d). The enhancement must be alleged in the charging instrument and there must be a finding that the person knowingly violated the protective order while committing the underlying felony. G.S. 50B-4.1(e).

Extraordinary mitigation. G.S. 15A-1340.13(g) provides that a court may impose an intermediate punishment for a class of offense and prior record level that ordinarily requires the imposition of an active punishment if it finds, in writing, that

- extraordinary mitigating factors of a kind significantly greater than in the normal case are present;
- those factors substantially outweigh any factors in aggravation; and
- it would be a manifest injustice to impose an active punishment in the case.

The sentencing court must consider evidence of extraordinary mitigating factors, but the decision to find any such factors, or to impose an intermediate punishment, is in the court's discretion. G.S. 15A-1340.13(g). Any extraordinary mitigating factors found by the court must be specified in the judgment. *Id.* Extraordinary mitigation may not be applied if:

- the offense is a Class A or Class B1 felony,
- is a drug-trafficking offense under G.S. 90-95(h) or drug-trafficking conspiracy offense under G.S. 90-95(i), or
- if the defendant has five or more prior record points as determined by G.S. 15A-1340.14.

G.S. 15A-1340.16(h). Extraordinary mitigation does not allow a sentencing judge to deviate from the applicable sentencing range. State v. Messer, 142 N.C. App. 515 (2001). Form AOC-CR-606 should be used in connection with extraordinary mitigation (online at www.nccourts.org/Forms/Documents/152.pdf).

Misdemeanors

The focus of Structured Sentencing for misdemeanors is the statutory table of punishments in G.S. 15A-1340.23 (see Table 4 at the end of this chapter). All misdemeanors, except those mentioned at the beginning of this chapter, are subject to Structured Sentencing. G.S. 15A-1340.10.

A sentencing court must take five steps to determine the appropriate sentence for a misdemeanor:

(1) Determine the offense class for each misdemeanor conviction (listed under each offense in this book as "Punishment")

(2) Determine the defendant's prior conviction level (Table 3)
(3) Select a sentence length from the appropriate sentence range (Table 4)
(4) Select a sentence disposition (active, intermediate, or community) (Table 4)
(5) Consider the appropriateness of restitution (discussed earlier in this chapter)

Except for the special provisions discussed below, the *Blakely* decision discussed above has no impact on Structured Sentencing for misdemeanors. Under Structured Sentencing, the only enhancing factors that apply in misdemeanor sentencing are prior convictions—factors specifically excluded from *Blakely*.

Offense Class

The first step in determining the appropriate sentence for a misdemeanor is to identify the misdemeanor's offense class. There are four classes of misdemeanors under Structured Sentencing: A1, 1, 2, and 3. Punishments increase in severity as you move from a Class 3 misdemeanor up to a Class A1 misdemeanor. For each misdemeanor listed in this book, the class of the offense is indicated under the "Punishment" section of the discussion. For example, "Assault by Pointing a Gun," discussed in Chapter 7 (Assaults), is a Class A1 misdemeanor.

Some misdemeanor offenses have no classification and no punishment listed in the General Statutes. Under G.S. 14-3(a), those offenses generally are considered Class 1 misdemeanors. Other misdemeanor offenses have a punishment but no classification listed. Under G.S. 14-3(a), those offenses are classified as follows: as a Class 1 misdemeanor if punishable by more than six months imprisonment; as a Class 2 misdemeanor if punishable by more than thirty days but not more than six months imprisonment; and as a Class 3 misdemeanor if punishable by imprisonment of thirty days or less or by a fine only.

As a general rule, conspiracies and attempts are punished one class below the main offense (for example, an attempt to commit a Class 1 misdemeanor is punished as a Class 2 misdemeanor). Solicitation to commit a misdemeanor is a Class 3 misdemeanor. G.S. 14-2.6(b); see "Attempt," "Solicitation," and "Conspiracy" in Chapter 5 (General Crimes).

Other provisions increase punishment for misdemeanors. Specifically, unclassified misdemeanors that are infamous, done in secrecy and malice, or done with deceit and intent to defraud are punished as Class H felonies pursuant to G.S. 14-3(b), see "Committing an Infamous or Related Misdemeanor" in Chapter 5 (General Crimes), and misdemeanors committed because of the victim's race, color, religion, nationality, or country or origin are punished as either Class 1 misdemeanors or Class H felonies under G.S. 14-3(c), see "Committing Misdemeanor Because of Prejudice" in Chapter 5 (General Crimes).

Prior Conviction Level

The second step in determining the appropriate sentence for a misdemeanor is to determine the defendant's prior conviction level. A defendant is assigned to one of three prior conviction levels (I through III) based on his or her total number of prior felony and misdemeanor convictions. G.S. 15A-1340.21(b). The three prior conviction levels, and the number of convictions applicable to each level, are indicated in Table 4.

Any conviction, whether a felony or misdemeanor (including driving while impaired and other misdemeanors under Chapter 20 of the North Carolina General Statutes), counts as one conviction. G.S. 15A-1340.21(b). If the defendant was convicted of more than one offense in a single week of superior court or a single session (typically, a day) of district court, only one of the convictions counts. G.S. 15A-1340.21(d). Neither infractions nor juvenile adjudications count.

A prior offense may be counted as a conviction only if the offense is classified as a felony or misdemeanor at the time the defendant committed the current offense. G.S. 15A-1340.21(b). Thus, if an offense had been changed from a misdemeanor to an infraction (for example, speeding 50 mph in a 35 mph zone) when a defendant committed a new misdemeanor, a prior conviction for that offense would not count in misdemeanor sentencing.

Sentence Length

Once the class of misdemeanor and prior conviction level are determined, the court must determine the length of any term of imprisonment. (If the court selects a community punishment as the sentence disposition, discussed under the next heading, it may impose a judgment consisting of a fine only; in those circumstances, it would be unnecessary for the court to specify any term of imprisonment.) To determine the length of any term of imprisonment, the court must locate the class of misdemeanor at issue along the left-hand side of Table 4 and the prior conviction level along the top of Table 4. The cell in which the misdemeanor class and prior conviction level intersect shows the possible terms of imprisonment (expressed in days) that the court may impose. The court must select a single term of imprisonment from the range shown in the applicable cell; there are no minimum and maximum terms of imprisonment, as in felony sentencing.

Sentence Disposition

The next step in misdemeanor sentencing is to determine the sentence disposition, which is prescribed in Table 4. Each cell in Table 4 contains a sentence disposition, signified by the letter "A," "I," or "C," or a combination of these letters. See this note under "Felonies," above, for a discussion of sentence disposition.

Active punishment. If the court imposes an active punishment, the term of imprisonment previously determined by the court must be activated. A defendant's term of imprisonment may be reduced by earned-time credit up to four days per month of incarceration (awarded by the Department of Correction or the local jail). G.S. 15A-1340.20(d).

When sentencing a defendant for multiple offenses, the court may consolidate sentences or run them concurrently. Subject to certain limitations, the court also may impose consecutive sentences. Unless otherwise specified by the court, sentences run concurrently. If the court consolidates offenses for sentencing, the most serious offense is controlling—the sentence disposition and the term of imprisonment must conform to the Structured Sentencing rules for that offense. G.S. 15A-1340.22(b). If the court imposes consecutive sentences, the length of imprisonment cannot exceed twice the longest term of imprisonment authorized for the class and prior conviction level of the most serious misdemeanor conviction. G.S. 15A-1340.22(a). Consecutive sentences cannot be imposed, however, if all of the convictions are for Class 3 misdemeanors. G.S. 15A-1340.22(a).

A defendant sentenced for a misdemeanor to active punishment of ninety days or less must be committed to a local jail facility, except as provided in G.S. 148-32.1(b). G.S. 15A-1352(a). For sentences imposed on or after January 1, 2012, a defendant sentenced for a misdemeanor (other than impaired driving) that requires confinement of 91 to 180 days shall be committed to confinement pursuant to the Statewide Misdemeanant Confinement program described in G.S. 148-32.1. G.S. 15A-1352(e); S.L. 2011-192. If a misdemeanor sentence or sentences require confinement for more than 180 days, the defendant must be committed to the Department of Correction. G.S. 15A-1352(e).

An active sentence may be imposed for any misdemeanor, even if an active sentence would not otherwise be authorized, if the sentence does not exceed the total amount of time that the defendant has spent in pretrial confinement awaiting trial for that misdemeanor. In effect, a sentence of "credit for time served" may be imposed for any misdemeanor. G.S. 15A-1340.20(c1).

Intermediate punishment. Intermediate punishment for misdemeanors is the same as intermediate punishment for felonies, except for the period of probation. For misdemeanor intermediate punishment, the court is authorized to impose a period of probation ranging from twelve to twenty-four months. G.S. 15A-1343.2(d)(2). The court may depart from this range upon finding that a longer or shorter period is necessary; however, the maximum period may not exceed five years. G.S. 15A-1343.2(d).

Community punishment. Community punishment for misdemeanors is the same as community punishment for felonies, except for the period of probation. For misdemeanor community punishment, the court is authorized to impose a period of probation ranging from six to eighteen months. G.S. 15A-1343.2(d)(1) The court may depart from this range upon finding that a longer or shorter period is necessary, but the maximum period may not exceed five years. G.S. 15A-1343.2(d). A community punishment also may consist of a fine only, without probation. G.S. 15A-1340.23(b).

Fines. The court may impose a fine as part of any disposition, whether active, intermediate, or community. G.S. 15A-1340.23(b). Unless otherwise provided by statute, the maximum fine for each class of misdemeanor is as indicated in Table 4.

Restitution

The last step in misdemeanor sentencing is to determine the appropriateness of restitution. The restitution requirements in G.S. 15A-1340.34 through 15A-1340.38, discussed earlier in this chapter in connection with felonies, apply equally to misdemeanors.

The main difference with restitution in misdemeanor versus felony cases is that far fewer misdemeanors are subject to the Crime Victims' Rights Act (CVRA). Only the following misdemeanors are covered:

(1) assault with a deadly weapon,
(2) assault inflicting serious injury,
(3) assault on a female,
(4) simple assault,
(5) assault by pointing a gun,
(6) domestic criminal trespass, and
(7) stalking.

G.S. 15A-830(7)(g). Further, the CVRA applies to the above misdemeanors only if the defendant and victim were in one of six different "personal relationships" described in G.S. 50B-1(b) (for example, as current or former spouses). G.S. 15A-830(7)(g).

Special Provisions

Infamous or related misdemeanor enhancement. G.S. 14-3(b) provides that if a person commits a misdemeanor for which no specific punishment is prescribed and the misdemeanor is infamous, done in secrecy and malice, or done with deceit and intent to defraud, punishment is elevated to a Class H felony. The applicable factors that elevate punishment (infamous, done in secrecy and malice, or done with deceit and intent to defraud) must be alleged in the criminal pleading, State v. Bell, 121 N.C. App. 700, 702 (1996); State v. Rambert, 116 N.C. App. 89, 93 (1994), submitted to the jury, and proved beyond a reasonable doubt, unless properly admitted by the defendant, Blakely v. Washington, 542 U.S. 296 (2004).

The group of misdemeanors to which this provision may apply was reduced by implementation of Structured Sentencing. Structured Sentencing provides specific statutory punishments for most offenses, including attempts and solicitations (see the discussion of those offenses in Chapter 5 (General Crimes)). For example, attempted common law robbery (discussed in Chapter 14 (Robbery, Extortion, and Blackmail)) was formerly punished under this statute because it was an infamous misdemeanor, but now that offense is specifically punished as a Class H felony pursuant to G.S. 14-2.5. After Structured Sentencing, this provision applies only to a misdemeanor offense "as to which no specific punishment is prescribed." This provision would apply only to misdemeanors such as common law obstruction of justice and common law forgery, which have no punishment prescribed by a specific statute. The statute specifically excludes from its coverage conspiracy to commit a misdemeanor. See G.S. 14-3(a) to determine how to classify misdemeanors that were not assigned a classification under Structured Sentencing. See G.S. 14-2.4, 14-2.5, and 14-2.6 for classifications of conspiracies, attempts, and solicitations (all of these offenses are discussed in Chapter 5 (General Crimes)).

The factor that elevates punishment (infamous, done in secrecy and malice, or done with deceit and intent to defraud) must be a necessary element of the underlying offense, rather than a particular circumstance of the individual case. State v. Glidden, 317 N.C. 557 (1986); State v. Hageman, 307 N.C. 1 (1982). An offense is "infamous" if it is an act of depravity, involves moral turpitude, and reveals a heart devoid of social duty and a mind fatally bent on mischief. *Glidden*, 317 N.C. at 560.

An obstruction of justice indictment properly charged a felony elevated by G.S. 14-3(b) when it alleged that the act was done "with deceit and intent to interfere with justice." State v. Blount, ___ N.C. App. ___, 703 S.E.2d 921 (2011) (the language "deceit and intent to interfere with justice" adequately put the defendant on notice that the State intended to seek a felony conviction; additionally, the indictment alleged that the defendant acted "feloniously").

Prejudice enhancement. G.S. 14-3(c) provides that a punishment for a misdemeanor may be increased when the misdemeanor is committed because of the victim's race, color, religion, nationality, or country of origin. If the underlying offense is a Class 2 or Class 3 misdemeanor, the offense is punishable as a Class 1 misdemeanor. G.S. 14-3(c). If the underlying offense is a Class A1 or Class 1 misdemeanor, the offense is punishable as a Class H felony. *Id.*

If the applicable factor of prejudice that elevates the punishment elevates punishment from a misdemeanor to a felony, it must be proved to a jury beyond a reasonable doubt, unless properly admitted by the defendant. Blakely v. Washington, 542 U.S. 296 (2004). Note that by statute and case law, similar provisions that elevate punishment for misdemeanors and felonies must be alleged in the criminal pleading. See "Infamous or related misdemeanor enhancement," immediately above; "Felonies," "Special Provisions," above.

Any Class A1, 1, 2, or 3 misdemeanor may be enhanced under this statute. Generally, however, assaults, property offenses, and trespass offenses are likely to be the underlying misdemeanors. A felony offense is not eligible for this kind of enhancement.

To qualify for this enhancement, an offense must be committed because of the *victim's* race, color, religion, nationality, or country of origin. The statute applies even if the defendant and the victim are the same race. State v. Brown, ___ N.C. App. ___, 689 S.E.2d 210 (2010) (the defendant, a white male, shot the victim, also a white male, because the victim was in a relationship with an African-American female). "Ethnic Intimidation," in Chapter 7 (Assaults), applies to assaultive and property damage offenses committed because of the personal characteristics of the victim *or* another person.

Enhancement for criminal gang activity. G.S. 14-50.22 provides that a person age 15 or older who is convicted of a misdemeanor committed for the benefit of, at the direction of, or in association with any criminal street gang is guilty of an offense that is one class higher than the offense committed. A Class A1 misdemeanor is enhanced to a Class I felony. G.S. 14-50.22. G.S. 14-50.29 provides for a conditional discharge for first offenders under the age of 18 sentenced under the criminal street gang enhancement. For a definition of the term "criminal street gang," see the note on Element (2) to "Street Gang Activity" in Chapter 19 (Disorderly Conduct, Riot, and Gang Offenses).

Conditional discharge for certain drug offenders. Under G.S. 90-96, as amended by 2011 legislation, S.L. 2011-192, for certain offenders convicted of a misdemeanor under the North Carolina Controlled Substances Act or a felony possession of a controlled substance offense under G.S. 90-95(a)(3), see "Possession of a Controlled Substance" and other drug crimes in Chapter 27 (Drug Offenses), conditional discharge is mandatory.

Table 1
Felony Sentence Dispositions and Minimum Prison Term Ranges (shown in months) for Offenses Committed on or after December, 1, 2009

A = active punishment **I** = intermediate punishment **C** = community punishment

	Prior Record Level						
	I	II	III	IV	V	VI	
	0–1 Pts	**2–5 Pts**	**6–9 Pts**	**10–13 Pts**	**14–17 Pts**	**18+ Pts**	
Felony Class A	Death or life without parole						
	A	A	A	A	A	A	**Disposition**
	240–300	276–345	317–397	365–456	Life without parole	Life without parole	*Aggravated Range*
B1	**192–240**	**221–276**	**254–317**	**292–365**	**336–420**	**386–483**	**Presumptive Range**
	144–192	166–221	190–254	219–292	252–336	290–386	*Mitigated Range*
	A	A	A	A	A	A	
	157–196	180–225	207–258	238–297	273–342	314–393	*Aggravated Range*
B2	**125–157**	**144–180**	**165–207**	**190–238**	**219–273**	**251–314**	**Presumptive Range**
	94–125	108–144	124–165	143–190	164–219	189–251	*Mitigated Range*
	A	A	A	A	A	A	
	73–92	83–104	96–120	110–138	127–159	146–182	*Aggravated Range*
C	**58–73**	**67–83**	**77–96**	**88–110**	**101–127**	**117–146**	**Presumptive Range**
	44–58	50–67	58–77	66–88	76–101	87–117	*Mitigated Range*
	A	A	A	A	A	A	
	64–80	73–92	84–105	97–121	111–139	128–160	*Aggravated Range*
D	**51–64**	**59–73**	**67–84**	**78–97**	**89–111**	**103–128**	**Presumptive Range**
	38–51	44–59	51–67	58–78	67–89	77–103	*Mitigated Range*
	I/A	I/A	A	A	A	A	
	25–31	29–36	33–41	38–48	44–55	50–63	*Aggravated Range*
E	**20–25**	**23–29**	**26–33**	**30–38**	**35–44**	**40–50**	**Presumptive Range**
	15–20	17–23	20–26	23–30	26–35	30–40	*Mitigated Range*
	I/A	I/A	I/A	A	A	A	
	16–20	19–23	21–27	25–31	28–36	33–41	*Aggravated Range*
F	**13–16**	**15–19**	**17–21**	**20–25**	**23–28**	**26–33**	**Presumptive Range**
	10–13	11–15	13–17	15–20	17–23	20–26	*Mitigated Range*
	I/A	I/A	I/A	I/A	A	A	
	13–16	14–18	17–21	19–24	22–27	25–31	*Aggravated Range*
G	**10–13**	**12–14**	**13–17**	**15–19**	**17–22**	**20–25**	**Presumptive Range**
	8–10	9–12	10–13	11–15	13–17	15–20	*Mitigated Range*
	C/I/A	I/A	I/A	I/A	I/A	A	
	6–8	8–10	10–12	11–14	15–19	20–25	*Aggravated Range*
H	**5–6**	**6–8**	**8–10**	**9–11**	**12–15**	**16–20**	**Presumptive Range**
	4–5	4–6	6–8	7–9	9–12	12–16	*Mitigated Range*
	C	C/I	I	I/A	I/A	I/A	
	6–8	6–8	6–8	8–10	9–11	10–12	*Aggravated Range*
I	**4–6**	**4–6**	**5–6**	**6–8**	**7–9**	**8–10**	**Presumptive Range**
	3–4	3–4	4–5	4–6	5–7	6–8	*Mitigated Range*

Source: G.S. 15A-1340.17(c).

Table 2
Felony Minimum and Maximum Prison Terms (shown in months)
for Offenses Committed on or after December 1, 2009, but before December 1, 2011

Felony Classes B1, B2, C, D, and E

15–27	56–77	97–126	138–175	179–224	220–273	261–323	302–372
16–29	57–78	98–127	139–176	180–225	221–275	262–324	303–373
17–30	58–79	99–128	140–177	181–227	222–276	263–325	304–374
18–31	59–80	100–129	141–179	182–228	223–277	264–326	305–375
19–32	60–81	101–131	142–180	183–229	224–278	265–327	306–377
20–33	61–83	102–132	143–181	184–230	225–279	266–329	307–378
21–35	62–84	103–133	144–182	185–231	226–281	267–330	308–379
22–36	63–85	104–134	145–183	186–233	227–282	268–331	309–380
23–37	64–86	105–135	146–185	187–234	228–283	269–332	310–381
24–38	65–87	106–137	147–186	188–235	229–284	270–333	311–383
25–39	66–89	107–138	148–187	189–236	230–285	271–335	312–384
26–41	67–90	108–139	149–188	190–237	231–287	272–336	313–385
27–42	68–91	109–140	150–189	191–239	232–288	273–337	314–386
28–43	69–92	110–141	151–191	192–240	233–289	274–338	315–387
29–44	70–93	111–143	152–192	193–241	234–290	275–339	316–389
30–45	71–95	112–144	153–193	194–242	235–291	276–341	317–390
31–47	72–96	113–145	154–194	195–243	236–293	277–342	318–391
32–48	73–97	114–146	155–195	196–245	237–294	278–343	319–392
33–49	74–98	115–147	156–197	197–246	238–295	279–344	320–393
34–50	75–99	116–149	157–198	198–247	239–296	280–345	321–395
35–51	76–101	117–150	158–199	199–248	240–297	281–347	322–396
36–53	77–102	118–151	159–200	200–249	241–299	282–348	323–397
37–54	78–103	119–152	160–201	201–251	242–300	283–349	324–398
38–55	79–104	120–153	161–203	202–252	243–301	284–350	325–399
39–56	80–105	121–155	162–204	203–253	244–302	285–351	326–401
40–57	81–107	122–156	163–205	204–254	245–303	286–353	327–402
41–59	82–108	123–157	164–206	205–255	246–305	287–354	328–403
42–60	83–109	124–158	165–207	206–257	247–306	288–355	329–404
43–61	84–110	125–159	166–209	207–258	248–307	289–356	330–405
44–62	85–111	126–161	167–210	208–259	249–308	290–357	331–407
45–63	86–113	127–162	168–211	209–260	250–309	291–359	332–408
46–65	87–114	128–163	169–212	210–261	251–311	292–360	333–409
47–66	88–115	129–164	170–213	211–263	252–312	293–361	334–410
48–67	89–116	130–165	171–215	212–264	253–313	294–362	335–411
49–68	90–117	131–167	172–216	213–265	254–314	295–363	336–413
50–69	91–119	132–168	173–217	214–266	255–315	296–365	337–414
51–71	92–120	133–169	174–218	215–267	256–317	297–366	338–415
52–72	93–121	134–170	175–219	216–269	257–318	298–367	339–416
53–73	94–122	135–171	176–221	217–270	258–319	299–368	340 or more*
54–74	95–123	136–173	177–222	218–271	259–320	300–369	
55–75	96–125	137–174	178–223	219–272	260–321	301–371	

Table 2 (*continued*)
Felony Minimum and Maximum Prison Terms (shown in months)
for Offenses Committed on or after December 1, 2009, but before December 1, 2011

Felony Classes F, G, H, and I

3–4	9–11	15–18	21–26	27–33	33–40	39–47
4–5	10–12	16–20	22–27	28–34	34–41	40–48
5–6	11–14	17–21	23–28	29–35	35–42	41–50
6–8	12–15	18–22	24–29	30–36	36–44	
7–9	13–16	19–23	25–30	31–38	37–45	
8–10	14–17	20–24	26–32	32–39	38–46	

*For offenses committed on or after December 1, 2009, but before December 1, 2011, where the minimum term is 340 months or more, the maximum is 120% of the minimum rounded to the next highest month, plus 9 months. G.S. 15A-1340.17(e1).

Note: This table is to be used in conjunction with Table 1. For an explanation of the steps used in determining the appropriate sentence, see the section entitled "Felonies" in the text above.

Table 2A
Felony Minimum and Maximum Prison Terms (shown in months) for Offenses Committed on or after December 1, 2011

Felony Classes B1, B2, C, D, and E

15–30	56–80	97–129	138–178	179–227	220–276	261–326	302–375
16–32	57–81	98–130	139–179	180–228	221–278	262–327	303–376
17–33	58–82	99–131	140–180	181–230	222–279	263–328	304–377
18–34	59–83	100–132	141–182	182–231	223–280	264–329	305–378
19–35	60–84	101–134	142–183	183–232	224–281	265–330	306–380
20–36	61–86	102–135	143–184	184–233	225–282	266–332	307–381
21–38	62–87	103–136	144–185	185–234	226–284	267–333	308–382
22–39	63–88	104–137	145–186	186–236	227–285	268–334	309–383
23–40	64–89	105–138	146–188	187–237	228–286	269–335	310–384
24–41	65–90	106–140	147–189	188–238	229–287	270–336	311–386
25–42	66–91	107–141	148–190	189–239	230–288	271–338	312–387
26–44	67–93	108–142	149–191	190–240	231–290	272–339	313–388
27–45	68–94	109–143	150–192	191–242	232–291	273–340	314–389
28–46	69–95	110–144	151–194	192–243	233–292	274–341	315–390
29–47	70–96	111–146	152–195	193–244	234–293	275–342	316–392
30–48	71–98	112–147	153–196	194–245	235–294	276–344	317–393
31–50	72–99	113–148	154–197	195–246	236–296	277–345	318–394
32–51	73–100	114–149	155–198	196–248	237–297	278–346	319–395
33–52	74–101	115–150	156–200	197–249	238–298	279–347	320–396
34–53	75–102	116–152	157–201	198–250	239–299	280–348	321–398
35–54	76–104	117–153	158–202	199–251	240–300	281–350	322–399
36–56	77–105	118–154	159–203	200–252	241–302	282–351	323–400
37–57	78–106	119–155	160–204	201–254	242–303	283–352	324–401
38–58	79–107	120–156	161–206	202–255	243–304	284–353	325–402
39–59	80–108	121–158	162–207	203–256	244–305	285–354	326–404
40–60	81–110	122–159	163–208	204–257	245–306	286–356	327–405
41–62	82–111	123–160	164–209	205–258	246–308	287–357	328–406
42–63	83–112	124–161	165–210	206–260	247–309	288–358	329–407
43–64	84–113	125–162	166–212	207–261	248–310	289–359	330–408
44–65	85–114	126–164	167–213	208–262	249–311	290–360	331–410
45–66	86–115	127–165	168–214	209–263	250–312	291–362	332–411
46–68	87–117	128–166	169–215	210–264	251–314	292–363	333–412
47–69	88–118	129–167	170–216	211–266	252–315	293–364	334–413
48–70	89–119	130–168	171–218	212–267	253–316	294–365	335–414
49–71	90–120	131–170	172–219	213–268	254–317	295–366	336–416
50–72	91–122	132–171	173–220	214–269	255–318	296–368	337–417
51–74	92–123	133–172	174–221	215–270	256–320	297–369	338–418
52–75	93–124	134–173	175–222	216–271	257–321	298–370	339–419
53–76	94–125	135–174	176–224	217–273	258–322	299–371	
54–77	95–126	136–176	177–225	218–274	259–323	300–372	
55–78	96–128	137–177	178–226	219–275	260–324	301–374	

Table 2A (*continued*)
Felony Minimum and Maximum Prison Terms (shown in months) for Offenses Committed on or after December 1, 2011

Felony Classes F, G, H, and I

3–13	9–20	15–27	21–35	27–42	33–49	39–56
4–14	10–21	16–29	22–36	28–43	34–50	40–57
5–15	11–23	17–30	23–37	29–44	35–51	41–59
6–17	12–24	18–31	24–38	30–45	36–53	
7–18	13–25	19–32	25–39	31–47	37–54	
8–19	14–26	20–33	26–41	32–48	38–55	

*For offenses committed on or after December 1, 2011, where the minimum term is 340 months or more, the maximum is 120% of the minimum rounded to the next highest month, plus 12 months. G.S. 15A-1340.17(e1) (as amended by S.L. 2011-192).

Note: This table is to be used in conjunction with Table 1. For an explanation of the steps used in determining the appropriate sentence, see the section entitled "Felonies" in the text above.

Table 3
Prior Record Level Worksheet: AOC-CR-600

STATE OF NORTH CAROLINA

File No.

_______________ County

In The General Court Of Justice
☐ District ☐ Superior Court Division

STATE VERSUS

Name And Address Of Defendant

Social Security No.	SID No.

Race	Sex	DOB

WORKSHEET PRIOR RECORD LEVEL FOR FELONY SENTENCING AND PRIOR CONVICTION LEVEL FOR MISDEMEANOR SENTENCING (STRUCTURED SENTENCING)

(For Offenses Committed On Or After Dec. 1, 2009)

G.S. 15A-1340.14, 15A-1340.21

I. SCORING PRIOR RECORD/FELONY SENTENCING

NUMBER	TYPE	FACTORS	POINTS
	Prior Felony Class A Conviction	X10	
	Prior Felony Class B1 Conviction	X 9	
	Prior Felony Class B2 or C or D Conviction	X 6	
	Prior Felony Class E or F or G Conviction	X 4	
	Prior Felony Class H or I Conviction	X 2	
	Prior Class A1 or 1 Misdemeanor Conviction *(see note on reverse)*	X 1	
		SUBTOTAL	

Defendant's Current Charge(s):

If all the elements of the present offense are included in any prior offense whether or not the prior offenses were used in determining prior record level.	+ 1	
If the offense was committed: (a) while on supervised or unsupervised probation, parole, or post-release supervision; or (b) while serving a sentence of imprisonment; or (c) while on escape.	+ 1	
	TOTAL	

II. CLASSIFYING PRIOR RECORD/CONVICTION LEVEL

MISDEMEANOR

NOTE: *If sentencing for a misdemeanor, total the number of prior conviction(s) listed on the reverse and select the corresponding prior conviction level.*

No. Of Prior Convictions	Level
0	I
1 - 4	II
5+	III

PRIOR CONVICTION LEVEL ☐

☐ The Court has determined the number of prior convictions to be ___________ and the level to be as shown above.

☐ In making this determination, the Court has relied upon the State's evidence of the defendant's prior convictions from a computer printout of DCI-CCH.

FELONY

NOTE: *If sentencing for a felony, locate the prior record level which corresponds to the total points determined in Section I above.*

Points	Level
0 - 1	I
2 - 5	II
6 - 9	III
10 - 13	IV
14 - 17	V
18+	VI

PRIOR RECORD LEVEL ☐

☐ The Court finds the prior convictions, prior record points and the prior record level of the defendant to be as shown herein.

☐ In making this determination, the Court has relied upon the State's evidence of the defendant's prior convictions from a computer printout of DCI-CCH.

☐ In finding a prior record level point under G.S. 15A-1340.14(b)(7), the Court has relied on the jury's determination of this issue beyond a reasonable doubt or the defendant's admission to this issue.

☐ The Court finds that all of the elements of the present offense are included in a prior offense.

☐ For each out-of-state conviction listed in Section V on the reverse, the Court finds by a preponderance of the evidence that the offense is substantially similar to a North Carolina offense and that the North Carolina classification assigned to this offense in Section V is correct.

☐ The Court finds that the State and the defendant have stipulated in open court to the prior convictions, points and record level.

Date	Name Of Presiding Judge (Type Or Print)	Signature Of Presiding Judge

AOC-CR-600, Rev. 4/11

(Over)

Table 3 (*continued*)
Prior Record Level Worksheet: AOC-CR-600

III. STIPULATION

The prosecutor and defense counsel, or the defendant, if not represented by counsel, stipulate to the information set out in Sections I and V of this form, and agree with the defendant's prior record level or prior conviction level as set out in Section II based on the information herein.

Date	Signature Of Prosecutor	Date	Signature Of Defense Counsel Or Defendant

IV. DNA CERTIFICATION (For Offenses Committed On Or After Feb. 1, 2011)

A review of the case record (the form required by G.S. 15A-266.3A(c)) and the records of the State Bureau of Investigation (the DCI-CCH rap sheet) indicates that *(check one):*

☐ 1. The defendant is **NOT** required to provide a DNA sample for this conviction because (i) the offense is not covered by G.S. 15A-266.4 or (ii) a sample of the defendant's DNA has previously been obtained and the defendant's DNA record is currently stored in the State DNA database.

☐ 2. The defendant **IS** required to provide a DNA sample for this conviction because (i) the offense is covered by G.S. 15A-266.4 and (ii) a sample of the defendant's DNA has not previously been obtained and the defendant's DNA record has not previously been stored in the State DNA Database, or if previously obtained and stored, the defendant's DNA sample and record have been expunged.

Date	Name Of Prosecutor (Type Or Print)	Signature Of Prosecutor

V. PRIOR CONVICTION

NOTE: *Federal law precludes making computer printout of DCI-CCH (rap sheet) part of permanent public court record.*

NOTE: *The only misdemeanor offenses under Chapter 20 that are assigned points for determining prior record level for felony sentencing are misdemeanor death by vehicle [G.S. 20-141.4(a2)] and, for sentencing for felony offenses committed on or after December 1, 1997, impaired driving [G.S. 20-138.1] and commercial impaired driving [G.S. 20-138.2]. First Degree Rape and First Degree Sexual Offense convictions prior to October 1, 1994, are Class B1 convictions.*

Source Code	Offenses	File No.	Date Of Conviction	County (Name of State if not NC)	Class

☐ See AOC-CR-600A for additional prior convictions.

Source Code: **1 - DCI** **2 - NCIC** **3 - AOC/Local** **4 - AOC/Statewide** **5 - ID Bureau** **6 - Other**

Date Prepared: ____________________

Prepared By: ____________________

AOC-CR-600, Side Two, Rev. 4/11

Table 3A
Prior Record Level Worksheet Continuation Page: AOC-CR-600A

STATE VERSUS | *File No.*

Name Of Defendant

V. PRIOR CONVICTIONS (continued)

Source Code	Offenses	File No.	Date Of Conviction	County (*Name of State if not NC*)	Class

Source Code: **1 - DCI** **2 - NCIC** **3 - AOC/Local** **4 - AOC/Statewide** **5 - ID Bureau** **6 - Other**

Date Prepared: ____________

Prepared By: ____________

AOC-CR-600A, New 4/11

Table 4
Misdemeanor Sentence Dispositions and Prison/Jail Term Ranges

A = active punishment **I** = intermediate punishment **C** = community punishment

	Level I: No Prior Convictions	Level II: 1 to 4 Prior Convictions	Level III: 5 or More Prior Convictions
Misdemeanor Class A1 (fine discretionary)	C/I/A 1–60 days	C/I/A 1–75 days	C/I/A 1–150 days
Misdemeanor Class 1 (fine discretionary)	C 1–45 days	C/I/A 1–45 days	C/I/A 1–120 days
Misdemeanor Class 2 (maximum fine $1,000)	C 1–30 days	C/I 1–45 days	C/I/A 1–60 days
Misdemeanor Class 3 (maximum fine $200)	C 1–10 days	C/I 1–15 days	C/I/A 1–20 days

Source: G.S. 15A-1340.23(b), (c).

5
General Crimes

5
General Crimes

Attempt

Statute

This is a common law offense. Some statutes specifying particular offenses include attempt as a form of the offense (see the note on "Punishment," below). Thus, before charging an attempt, one should check the appropriate offense that has been attempted to determine whether attempt is included as a form of the offense.

Elements

A person guilty of attempt to commit a crime,

(1) while specifically intending to do something that is a crime,
(2) performs an overt act calculated and designed to bring about the crime *and*
(3) the act falls short of the completed offense.

Punishment

Unless a different classification is specifically provided by statute, an attempt to commit a felony or misdemeanor is punishable under the next lower classification as the offense attempted, except that an attempt to commit a Class A or B1 felony is a Class B2 felony; an attempt to commit a Class B2 felony is a Class C felony; an attempt to commit a Class I felony is a Class 1 misdemeanor; and an attempt to commit a Class 3 misdemeanor is also a Class 3 misdemeanor. G.S. 14-2.5. For example, an attempt to commit a Class G felony is punishable as a Class H felony, and an attempt to commit a Class 1 misdemeanor is punishable as a Class 2 misdemeanor. An example of a statute providing a different classification for attempt is G.S. 14-288.22, punishing an attempt to injure another by the use of a nuclear, biological, or chemical weapon of mass destruction as a Class B1 felony when the completed offense is a Class A felony.

For a few offenses, the relevant statute provides that an attempt is punished as if the offense had actually been committed. When that is the case for an offense covered by this book, this issue will be specifically discussed. For example, G.S. 14-87 provides that attempted armed robbery is a Class D felony, like the completed offense, see "Armed Robbery" in Chapter 14 (Robbery, Extortion, and Blackmail), and G.S. 14-202.1 provides that an attempted indecent liberty is a Class F felony, like the completed offense, see "Indecent Liberties with a Child" in Chapter 10 (Sexual Assaults).

Notes

Generally. For the elements of attempt, see, for example, *State v. Coble*, 351 N.C. 448, 449 (2000), and *State v. Mueller*, 184 N.C. App. 553, 563 (2007).

Element (1). A defendant may attempt to commit either a felony or a misdemeanor. *See, e.g.,* State v. Batson, 220 N.C. 411 (1941). In both situations, the defendant must have the specific intent to commit the crime that is attempted. Thus, if the charge is attempted rape, the defendant must have the specific intent to commit rape. State v. Farmer, 158 N.C. App. 699 (2003). The intent may be inferred from evidence of previous commissions of the crime attempted, State v. Edwards, 224 N.C. 527 (1944), or from the facts and surrounding circumstances, State v. Edwards, 174 N.C. App. 490 (2005) (sufficient evidence of intent to kill a child in an attempted murder case); State v. Owen, 159 N.C. App. 204 (2003) (in an attempted rape case, intent to commit rape properly inferred from the defendant's actions); *Farmer*, 158 N.C. App. 699 (same).

For cases in which the evidence was sufficient to establish the requisite intent, see *State v. Simpson*, 187 N.C. App. 424 (2007) (intent to commit rape; the defendant, whose pants were unzipped, straddled the victim and tried to pull up her shirt), *State v. Mueller*, 184 N.C. App. 553 (2007) (intent to engage in vaginal intercourse; the defendant repeatedly asked the victim to have sex with him, told her that he wanted to be "inside [her]" and be "[her] first," and performed sexual acts on her), and *State v. Legins*, 184 N.C. App. 156 (2007) (intent to commit robbery).

The precise nature of the intended crime need not be proved; for example, it is not necessary to prove the particular object a person charged with attempted larceny intended to take. State v. Utley, 82 N.C. 556 (1880).

An attempt charge cannot be based on an "attempt to attempt" or on an attempt to commit some other crime that is itself a form of attempt, State v. Hewett, 158 N.C. 627 (1912), such as assault, State v. Hefner, 199 N.C. 778 (1930); see also "Attempted assault," below.

Element (2). In addition to the requisite intent, the person must commit an overt act toward commission of the offense. State v. Addor, 183 N.C. 687, 689 (1922). For example, in *State v. Farrar*, 179 N.C. App. 561 (2006), the court held that there was sufficient evidence of an overt act in an attempted armed robbery case. In that case, three men entered a house, one of them with a gun drawn. One of the men grabbed the victim's pocketbook, asked if it contained any money, and dropped it only when he was told it contained none. *Id.* The court held that the grabbing of the pocketbook was an overt act. *Id.* For other cases in which there was sufficient evidence of an overt act, see *State v. Lawrence*, ___ N.C. App. ___, 706 S.E.2d 822 (2011) (the evidence was sufficient to prove attempted kidnapping and attempted robbery; to prove an overt act for these crimes, the State need not prove that the defendant was in the presence of his intended victim; the defendant and his accomplices stole get-away cars and acquired cell phones, jump suits, masks, zip ties, gasoline, and guns; additionally, the defendant hid in the woods behind the home of his intended victim, waiting for her to appear, fleeing only upon the arrival of officers and armed neighbors), *review allowed*, 710 S.E.2d 6 (N.C. 2011); *State v. Legins*, 184 N.C. App. 156 (2007) (attempted robbery), and *State v. Henderson*, 182 N.C. App. 406 (2007) (attempted first-degree sexual offense; the defendant removed his pants, walked into a room where the child victim was seated, stood in front of her, and asked her to put his penis in her mouth).

Element (3). To be sufficient to establish an attempt, the act must amount to the "commencement of the consummation" of the attempted crime; the act must be more than mere preparation. State v. Collins, 334 N.C. 54 (1993); State v. Addor, 183 N.C. 687 (1922); *Legins*, 184 N.C. App. at 159 (act need not be the last proximate act to the consummation of the offense but must go beyond mere preparation) (quotation omitted).

Attempted homicide. A person commits the crime of attempted first-degree murder if the person (1) specifically intends to kill another person unlawfully; (2) commits an overt act calculated to carry out that intent, beyond mere preparation; (3) acts with malice, premeditation, and deliberation; and (4) falls short of committing the murder. State v. Cozart, 131 N.C. App. 199 (1998). Neither assault with a deadly weapon inflicting serious injury, State v. Rainey,

154 N.C. App. 282 (2002), nor assault with a deadly weapon with intent to kill inflicting serious injury, State v. Peoples, 141 N.C. App. 115 (2000), is a lesser-included offense of attempted first-degree murder. A defendant may be convicted and punished for both attempted first-degree murder and an assault based on the same conduct. State v. Haynesworth, 146 N.C. App. 523 (2001) (attempted first-degree murder and assault with a firearm on a law enforcement officer); State v. Wright, ___ N.C. App. ___, 711 S.E.2d 797 (2011) (the defendant properly was convicted of attempted murder and assault as to each victim).

Although the crime of attempted second-degree murder does not exist, State v. Coble, 351 N.C. 448 (2000), attempted voluntary manslaughter is a recognized crime, *Rainey*, 154 N.C. App. at 289; State v. Bullock, 154 N.C. App. 234 (2002).

Attempted assault. Attempted assault is not a crime; because an assault includes an overt act or attempt, or the unequivocal appearance of an attempt, an attempted assault would be an attempt to attempt. State v. Barkdale, 181 N.C. App. 302 (2007); *see also* the note on Element (1), above.

Attempted statutory sexual offense. Attempted statutory sexual offense is a crime. State v. Sines, 158 N.C. App. 79 (2003).

Charging issues. An indictment charging a completed offense is sufficient to support a conviction for an attempt to commit the offense. *See* G.S. 15-170; State v. Slade, 81 N.C. App. 303, 306 (1986); State v. Gray, 58 N.C. App. 102, 106 (1982). This is true even if the completed crime and the attempt are not in the same statute. *See Slade*, 81 N.C. App. at 306 (discussing *State v. Arnold*, 285 N.C. 751, 755 (1974), and describing it as a case in which the defendant was indicted for the common law felony of arson but was convicted of the statutory felony of attempted arson). G.S. 15-144, authorizing the use of a short-form indictment for homicide, permits the use of the short-form indictment to charge attempted first-degree murder. State v. Jones, 359 N.C. 832, 834–38 (2005) (it is sufficient for the State to insert the words "attempt to" into the short-form language); State v. Reid, 175 N.C. App. 613, 617–18 (2006) (following *Jones*). The statutory short-form indictments for rape, G.S. 15-144.1, and sex offense, G.S. 15-144.2, expressly state that they cover certain attempts.

Impossibility. As a general rule, the fact that the defendant's acts would not have constituted a crime even if they had been fully carried out does not prevent a conviction for attempt, provided that the defendant specifically intended to commit the crime and did all the acts necessary to commit an attempt. State v. Hageman, 307 N.C. 1 (1982); State v. Addor, 183 N.C. 687 (1922). For example, a defendant may be convicted of attempting to possess cocaine when the defendant intends to possess cocaine, drives to an area known for drug sales, approaches people believed to be cocaine dealers, and provides money for what the defendant thinks is cocaine but in fact are pieces of Brazil nut. State v. Gunnings, 122 N.C. App. 294 (1996). Also, the evidence can be sufficient to sustain a conviction on child sex charges even when the victim was actually an adult law enforcement officer, not a child. *See* State v. Ellis, 188 N.C. App. 820 (2008) (attempted indecent liberties where the defendant had the specific intent to take indecent liberties with a child he believed to be 12 years old but who was in fact a law enforcement officer; attempted solicitation of a child by computer to commit an unlawful sexual act where the person solicited was an undercover officer (note that G.S. 14-202.3 was later amended, making it possible to commit the substantive crime if the defendant solicited someone whom the defendant believed to be a child under 16)).

Related Offenses Not in This Chapter

"Discharging a Barreled Weapon or Firearm into Occupied Property" (attempt) (Chapter 7)
"Simple Assault" and other assault crimes (Chapter 7)
"Indecent Liberties with a Child" (attempt) (Chapter 10)
"Armed Robbery" (attempt) (Chapter 14)

"Safecracking" (attempt) (Chapter 15)
"Obtaining Property by False Pretenses" (attempt) (Chapter 16)
"Subornation of Perjury" (Chapter 21)
Drugs (various offenses) (some of which cover attempts) (Chapter 27)
See discussion of attempt under specific offenses throughout this book.
Being found in a building with intent to commit any felony or larceny. G.S. 14-55.

Solicitation

Statute

This is a common law offense.

Elements

A person guilty of this offense

(1) entices, advises, counsels, incites, induces, orders, or commands another to commit a crime
(2) with the specific intent that the other person commit the crime.

Punishment

Unless a different classification is specifically stated in a statute, solicitation to commit a felony is punishable two classes lower than the felony solicited, except that solicitation to commit a Class A or B1 felony is a Class C felony; solicitation to commit a Class B2 felony is a Class D felony; solicitation to commit a Class H felony is a Class 1 misdemeanor; solicitation to commit a Class I felony is a Class 2 misdemeanor; and solicitation to commit any misdemeanor is punishable as a Class 3 misdemeanor. G.S. 14-2.6. For example, solicitation to commit a Class G felony would be a Class I felony. An example of a statute providing for different punishment for solicitation is G.S. 14-288.22, punishing solicitation to injure to another by the use of a nuclear, biological, or chemical weapon of mass destruction as a Class B1 felony when the main offense is a Class A felony.

For some crimes, the relevant statute provides that a solicitation is punished just like the completed crime. *See, e.g.,* G.S. 14-118.12 (solicitation of residential mortgage fraud is punished like the main offense).

Notes

Element (1). A solicitation has occurred even if the person solicited is a law enforcement officer who has no intention of carrying out the crime. State v. Keen, 25 N.C. App. 567 (1975). However, the defendant must entice, advise, counsel, incite, induce, order, or command someone to commit the crime. Thus, the evidence was insufficient to establish solicitation to commit murder when it showed only that the defendant had a "plan" to have the victim killed, had an agreement with the killer about when he should arrive at the scene to kill the victim, and twice stated that she wanted the victim "gone," but there was no evidence that the defendant counseled, enticed, or induced the killer to murder the victim. State v. Crowe, 188 N.C. App. 765 (2008).

Element (2). A solicitation is committed even if the crime solicited is not carried out; the solicitation itself is the offense. State v. Hampton, 210 N.C. 283 (1936).

Charging issues. In solicitation indictments, it is not necessary to allege the nature of the solicitation "with technical precision." State v. Furr, 292 N.C. 711, 722 (1977).

Greater and lesser-included offenses. Solicitation to commit murder is a lesser-included offense of murder that is committed as an accessory before the fact. State v. Westbrooks, 345 N.C. 43 (1996). Solicitation to commit murder is not a lesser-included offense of murder that is committed based on the theory of acting in concert. State v. Kemmerlin, 356 N.C. 446 (2002). Solicitation is not a lesser-included offense of conspiracy. State v. Richardson, 100 N.C. App. 240 (1990); see also the note entitled "Relation to other offenses," below.

Multiple convictions and punishments. A single solicitation may continue over a period of time and involve several contacts when the person solicited gives no definite refusal to the solicitor's request. But a definite refusal coupled with a lapse of some time may end the transaction so that a new request upon another occasion may constitute a new offense. *Furr*, 292 N.C. 711. In such a case, a defendant may be charged with more than one solicitation.

Because the offenses are separate and distinct, a defendant may be punished for both solicitation and an attempt to commit the same offense. State v. Clemmons, 100 N.C. App. 286, 290 (1990).

Relation to other offenses. A solicitation could make the defendant an accessory before the fact and, therefore, a principal to the crime, if the offense solicited is carried out. In this case, the solicitation is a lesser-included offense of the accessory before the fact offense. See the note entitled "Greater and lesser-included offenses," above (discussing this rule as to solication to commit murder and accessory before the fact to murder).

A solicitation is complete when the request to commit the crime is made. State v. Benardello, 164 N.C. App. 708 (2004). Conspiracy, however, requires an agreement to do an unlawful act. *Id.*; see "Conspiracy," below. It is possible to solicit someone to commit a crime without the agreement required for a conspiracy ever being reached, *Benardello*, 164 N.C. App. at 711; in such a case, solicitation and not conspiracy is the proper charge.

Solicitation to commit a misdemeanor. North Carolina case law has recognized the offenses of solicitation to commit misdemeanor assault, State v. Suggs, 117 N.C. App. 654 (1995), and solicitation to commit common law obstruction of justice, *Clemmons*, 100 N.C. App. 286. It is unclear whether solicitation to commit other kinds of misdemeanors would be recognized. 2 W. LaFave & A. Scott Jr., Substantive Criminal Law 4, 4–5 (2d ed. 2003).

Related Offenses Not in This Chapter

"Solicitation of a Child by a Computer or Other Electronic Device to Commit an Unlawful Sex Act" (Chapter 10)
"Soliciting Participation in Street Gang Activity" (Chapter 19)
"Misdemeanor Inciting to Riot" (Chapter 19)
"Felony Inciting to Riot" (Chapter 19)
"Offering a Bribe" (Chapter 21)
"Subornation of Perjury" (Chapter 21)
"Procuring for Prostitution" (Chapter 23)
See sexual exploitation of a minor (various offenses) in Chapter 24 (Obscenity, Exploitation of a Minor, and Adult Establishment Offenses).
"Employing or Intentionally Using a Minor to Commit a Controlled Substance Offense" (Chapter 27)
"Promoting Drug Sales by a Minor" (Chapter 27)
Enticing minors out of the State for the purpose of employment. G.S. 14-40.
Soliciting charitable contributions by telephone. G.S. 14-401.12.

Conspiracy

Statute

This is a common law offense.

Elements

A person guilty of this offense

(1) enters into an agreement with at least one other person
(2) to commit an unlawful act
(3) with intent that the agreement be carried out.

Punishment

Unless a different classification is stated in a statute, conspiracy to commit a crime is punishable one class lower than the crime the defendant conspired to commit, except that conspiracy to commit a Class A or B1 felony is a Class B2 felony; conspiracy to commit a Class B2 felony is a Class C felony; conspiracy to commit a Class I felony is a Class 1 misdemeanor; and conspiracy to commit a Class 3 misdemeanor is a Class 3 misdemeanor. G.S. 14-2.4. An example of a statute providing for different punishment for conspiracy is G.S. 14-288.22, punishing conspiracy to commit injury to another by the use of a nuclear, biological, or chemical weapon of mass destruction as a Class B1 felony when the main offense is a Class A felony.

Some statutes provide that a conspiracy to commit a particular crime is punished like the main offense. See "Trafficking" in Chapter 27 (Drug Offenses) (conspiracy to commit drug trafficking is punished the same as the completed drug-trafficking offense); G.S. 14-118.12 (conspiracy to commit residential mortgage fraud is punished like the main offense).

Notes

Element (1). For a conspiracy to occur, there must be an agreement between the defendant and at least one other person. If the only other person involved is pretending to enter the agreement but has no intent to carry it out (such as an undercover officer), there is no conspiracy. State v. Horton, 275 N.C. 651 (1969) (in such a case, a solicitation may have occurred). The court of appeals has rejected the common law view that a husband and wife are one entity, holding instead that a criminal conspiracy can exist between them. State v. Stroud, 147 N.C. App. 549 (2001).

An agreement may take the form of written or spoken words, a mutual understanding, State v. Lyons, 102 N.C. App. 174 (1991), or a nonverbal act (for example, handing a knife to a co-conspirator in an assault would be a nonverbal act sufficient to show agreement), *see* State v. Brown, 67 N.C. App. 223 (1984). An agreement may be established by circumstantial evidence. State v. Brewton, 173 N.C. App. 323 (2005). However, a conspiracy may not be established by a mere suspicion or a mere relationship or association between the parties. *Id.*; State v. Benardello, 164 N.C. App. 708 (2004).

For cases in which there was sufficient evidence of an agreement, see *State v. Boyd*, ___ N.C. App. ___, 705 S.E.2d 774 (2011) (in a conspiracy to commit robbery case, the evidence was sufficient to establish a mutual, implied understanding between the defendant and another man to rob the victim; the other man drove the defendant to intercept the victim; the defendant wore a ski mask and had a gun; after the defendant hesitated to act, the other person assaulted the victim and took his money; and the two got into a car and departed); *State v. Dubose*, ___ N.C. App. ___, 702 S.E.2d 330 (2010) (the evidence was sufficient to show an agreement to discharge a firearm into occupied property; the defendant and his accomplices understood and impliedly agreed that the defendant would shoot the victim as they drove by, the victim was standing by the doors of a gym, and there was a substantial likelihood that bullets would enter or hit the gym); *State v. Sanders*, ___ N.C. App. ___, 701 S.E.2d 380 (2010) (words and actions of the defendant and others provided sufficient evidence of an implied agreement to assault the victim; the spontaneity of the plan did not defeat the conspiracy;

a meeting of the minds can occur when a party accepts an offer by actions); *State v. Crowe*, 188 N.C. App. 765 (2008) (conspiracy to commit murder); *State v. Robledo*, 193 N.C. App. 521 (2008) (conspiracy to traffic in marijuana by possession); *State v. Shelly*, 181 N.C. App. 196 (2007) (conspiracy to commit first-degree murder); *State v. Wiggins*, 185 N.C. App. 376 (2007) (conspiracy to traffic in cocaine by possession); *State v. Brewton*, 173 N.C. App. 323 (2005) (conspiracy to commit murder); *State v. Howell*, 169 N.C. App. 741 (2005) (drug-trafficking conspiracy); *State v. Baldwin*, 161 N.C. App. 382 (2003) (same); *State v. Batchelor*, 157 N.C. App. 421 (2003) (same).

For a case in which the evidence was insufficient to establish an agreement to traffic in cocaine by transportation, see *State v. Euceda-Valle*, 182 N.C. App. 268 (2007) (the defendant was stopped while driving a vehicle with one passenger, cocaine was found in the vehicle's trunk, both men were nervous, and the vehicle smelled of air freshener; there was no evidence of conversation between the two, no unusual movements or actions, no large amounts of cash, no possession of weapons, or anything else suggesting an agreement).

Element (2). The agreement must be to do something unlawful. State v. Wilson, 106 N.C. App. 342 (1992). Some old cases suggest that it could be something that is unlawful but not criminal (such as noncriminal fraud), R. PERKINS & R. BOYCE, CRIMINAL LAW 696 (3d ed. 1982), but conspiracy charges probably should be brought only against those who agree to commit criminal acts.

Element (3). Even if one of several parties to the agreement has no intent to carry out the crime, it is a conspiracy if at least two parties have the required intent. State v. Horton, 275 N.C. 651 (1969). If the State is able to identify and charge only one conspirator, trial and conviction of that single conspirator is not precluded; trial may proceed if the State can prove the existence of other conspirators. State v. Graham, 24 N.C. App. 591 (1975).

Charging issues. For a discussion of charging issues in connection with conspiracy offenses, see Jessica Smith, *The Criminal Indictment: Fatal Defect, Fatal Variance, and Amendment*, ADMIN. OF JUST. BULL. NO. 2008/03 (UNC School of Government, July 2008) (online at www.sog.unc.edu/pubs/electronicversions/pdfs/aojb0803.pdf).

A conspiracy indictment must allege an agreement to do the unlawful act. *State v. Billinger*, ___ N.C. App. ___, 714 S.E.2d 201 (2011).

A conspiracy indictment need not specifically identify the defendant's conspirator(s). State v. Gallimore, 272 N.C. 528, 533–35 (1968) (indictment was not defective for alleging merely that the defendant conspired with "others"; noting, however, that the better practice is to name the conspirators if their identities are known). However, if the conspiracy indictment does name specific individuals with whom the defendant is alleged to have conspired and the evidence shows that the defendant may have conspired with others, it is error for the trial court to instruct the jury that it may find the defendant guilty based upon an agreement with persons not named in the indictment. State v. Pringle, ___ N.C. App. ___, 694 S.E.2d 505 (2010). One twist on this rule is that the jury instruction need not specifically name the individuals with whom the defendant was alleged to have conspired provided that the instruction comports with the material allegations in the indictment and the evidence at trial. *Id.* (the indictment alleged that the defendant conspired with Jimon Dollard and an unidentified male; the evidence showed that the defendant and two other men conspired to commit robbery; one of the other men was identified by testifying officers as Jimon Dollard; the third man evaded capture and was never identified; the trial court instructed the jury that it could find the defendant guilty if he conspired with "at least one other person;" although the instruction did not limit the conspiracy to those named in the indictment, it was in accord with the material allegations in the indictment and the evidence presented at trial, and thus there was no error).

Although indictments charging sale or delivery of a controlled substance must allege the name of the person to whom the sale or delivery was made when that person's name is known or allege that the person's name was unknown, when the charge is conspiracy to sell or deliver, the person with whom the defendant conspired to sell and deliver need not be named. State v. Lorenzo, 147 N.C. App. 728, 734–35 (2001) (conspiracy to traffic in marijuana by delivery).

Greater and lesser-included offenses. Conspiracy to possess heroin is a lesser-included offense of conspiracy to possess heroin with intent to sell and deliver. State v. Overton, 60 N.C. App. 1, 26 (1982).

Multiple convictions and punishments. A defendant who enters into a single agreement to commit multiple offenses may be convicted of only one count of conspiracy (of course, the defendant still may be convicted of any offenses actually committed pursuant to the conspiracy). State v. Wilson, 106 N.C. App. 342 (1992). Separate agreements to commit separate offenses may be prosecuted as separate conspiracy offenses, even if the crimes were committed together. State v. Gay, 334 N.C. 467 (1993); State v. Gibbs, 335 N.C. 1 (1993). The number of separate agreements, not the number of offenses the conspirators agree to commit, determines the number of conspiracy charges. *Gibbs*, 335 N.C. 1; State v. McLamb, 313 N.C. 572 (1985); State v. Dalton, 122 N.C. App. 666 (1996); State v. Smallwood, 112 N.C. App. 83 (1993); State v. Worthington, 84 N.C. App. 150 (1987). Factors such as time intervals between discussions, participants, objectives, and number of meetings also help determine the number of conspiracies. State v. Tirado, 358 N.C. 551 (2004); State v. Howell, 169 N.C. App. 741 (2005); State v. Brunson, 165 N.C. App. 667 (2004); *Wilson,* 106 N.C. App. 342. For sample cases on point, compare *State v. Lawrence*, ___ N.C. App. ___, 706 S.E.2d 822 (2011) (the evidence was insufficient to support two charges of conspiracy to commit armed robbery when, having failed to achieve the objective of the conspiracy on their first attempt, co-conspirators returned the next day to try again; only one agreement existed: in both attempts, the intended victim and participants were the same; the time interval between the two attempts was approximately thirty-six hours; on the second attempt the group did not agree to a new plan; and while the co-conspirators considered robbing a different victim, that only was a back-up plan; the court rejected the State's argument that because the co-conspirators met after the first attempt, acquired additional materials, made slight modifications on how to execute their plan, and briefly considered robbing a different victim, they abandoned their first conspiracy and formed a second one), *review allowed,* 710 S.E.2d 6 (N.C. 2011); *Brunson*, 165 N.C. App. 667 (drug transactions were part of a single conspiracy); *Howell*, 169 N.C. App. 741 (only one conspiracy existed and it encompassed trafficking in heroin by transportation and trafficking in heroin by possession); *State v. Tabron*, 147 N.C. App. 303 (2001) (evidence was insufficient to support two convictions for conspiracy to commit robbery); and *State v. Shelly*, 176 N.C. App. 575 (2006) (in a double homicide case, the evidence supported only one conspiracy to commit murder), with *Tirado*, 358 N.C. 551 (evidence supported multiple separate conspiracies to commit several crimes against different victims); *State v. Choppy*, 141 N.C. App. 32 (2000) (evidence supported two convictions for conspiracy to commit first-degree murder, involving different victims); and *State v. Roberts*, 176 N.C. App. 159 (2006) (evidence supported two separate convictions for conspiracy to commit burglary and armed robbery, where crimes occurred on two sequential nights; there was no evidence that the first agreement encompassed the crimes that occurred on the second night).

Evidence of a conspiracy may be used to establish that a conspirator aided and abetted or acted in concert or to show that an absent conspirator was an accessory before the fact. State v. Small, 301 N.C. 407 (1980). Because the agreement necessary for a conspiracy is not an element of accessory before the fact to a felony, a defendant may be convicted of both conspiracy and the principal offense as an accessory before the fact if the defendant's conduct satisfies the elements of both offenses. State v. Gallagher, 313 N.C. 132 (1985); State v. Looney, 294 N.C. 1 (1978). For a more detailed discussion of acting in concert, aiding and abetting, and accessory before the fact, see Chapter 3 (Participants in Crimes).

Relation to other offenses. A solicitation is complete when the request to commit the crime is made. State v. Benardello, 164 N.C. App. 708 (2004). Conspiracy, however, requires an agreement to do an unlawful act. *Id.* It is possible to solicit someone to commit a crime without the agreement required for a conspiracy ever being reached. *Id.* This would be the case, for example, when the defendant asks another to commit a crime but that person refuses to do so. In such a case, solicitation—not conspiracy—is the proper charge.

No need for an overt act. A conspiracy is complete once the agreement is made. Therefore, it is irrelevant whether the substantive crime ever is committed, State v. Morgan, 329 N.C. 654, 658 (1991), or whether an overt act occurred, State v. Gallimore, 272 N.C. 528, 532 (1968).

Jurisdiction. A person may be charged with this offense if any co-conspirator commits within the state an overt act in furtherance of the unlawful agreement, even if the conspiracy was entered into outside the state. State v. Goldberg, 261 N.C. 181, 203 (1964); State v. Drakeford, 104 N.C. App. 298 (1991). See generally "Lack of Jurisdiction" in Chapter 2 (Bars and Defenses).

Acquittal of co-conspirators. Generally, if all of the other alleged co-conspirators are acquitted, then the sole remaining defendant may not be convicted. State v. Littlejohn, 264 N.C. 571 (1965); State v. Raper, 204 N.C. 503 (1933). However, a defendant's conspiracy conviction remains valid even if all alleged co-conspirators are found not guilty at a *later* trial. State v. Soles, 119 N.C. App. 375, 379–80 (1995) (distinguishing *Raper*, 204 N.C. 503). Additionally, a voluntary dismissal by the State is not the equivalent of an acquittal. State v. Robledo, 193 N.C. App. 521 (2008) (upholding conspiracy to traffic in marijuana by possession when the State took a voluntary dismissal of the conspiracy charge against the co-conspirator).

When one of the co-conspirators could not be convicted if acting alone. A person may be convicted of a conspiracy to commit a crime even though he or she could not be convicted of the crime if acting alone. For example, a person may be convicted of conspiracy to commit the crime of larceny by employee even though the person could not be convicted of that crime if acting alone because he or she is not an employee. State v. Saunders, 126 N.C. App. 524 (1997).

Related Offenses Not in This Chapter

"Exploitation of a Disabled or Elder Adult" (Chapter 16)
See the various drug offenses in Chapter 27 (Drug Offenses).
Forgery of deeds, wills and certain instruments. G.S. 14-122.
Conspiracy to break or enter jail with intent to injure prisoner. G.S. 14-221.
Furnishing poison, deadly weapons, cartridges, ammunition or alcoholic beverages to inmates of charitable, mental or penal institutions or local confinement facilities; furnishing tobacco products or mobile phones to inmates. G.S. 14-258.1.

Continuing Criminal Enterprise—Non-Drug Offenses

Statute

§14-7.20. Continuing criminal enterprise.

(a) Any person who engages in a continuing criminal enterprise shall be punished as a Class H felon and in addition shall be subject to the forfeiture prescribed in subsection (b) of this section.

(b) Any person who is convicted under subsection (a) of this section of engaging in a continuing criminal enterprise shall forfeit to the State of North Carolina:

(1) The profits obtained by the person in the enterprise, and
(2) Any of the person's interest in, claim against, or property or contractual rights of any kind affording a source of influence over, such enterprise.

(c) For purposes of this section, a person is engaged in a continuing criminal enterprise if:
(1) The person violates any provision of this Chapter, the punishment of which is a felony; and
(2) The violation is a part of a continuing series of violations of this Chapter:
a. Which are undertaken by the person in concert with five or more other persons with respect to whom the person occupies a position of organizer, a supervisory position, or any other position of management; and
b. From which the person obtains substantial income or resources.

Elements

A person guilty of this offense

(1) commits any felony in Chapter 14 (Criminal Law) of the North Carolina General Statutes
(2) that is part of a continuing series of violations of Chapter 14
(3) that are undertaken in concert with five or more other persons
(4) over whom the person occupies a position of organizer, supervisor, or other position of management, *and*
(5) the person obtains substantial income or resources from the continuing violations.

Punishment

Class H felony. G.S. 14-7.20(a). Additionally, property set out in G.S. 14-7.20(b) must be forfeited.

Notes

Generally. This offense is very similar to "Continuing Criminal Enterprise—Drug Offenses" in Chapter 27 (Drug Offenses).

Element (1). This offense is limited to felonies defined by Chapter 14. Therefore, drug offenses (in G.S. Ch. 90), motor vehicle offenses (in G.S. Ch. 20), and offenses defined in other chapters of the General Statutes are not covered by this offense.

Related Offenses Not in This Chapter

"Gang-Related Crimes" (Chapter 19)
"Continuing Criminal Enterprise—Drug Offenses" (Chapter 27)

Accessory after the Fact to a Felony

Statute

§14-7. Accessories after the fact; trial and punishment.

If any person shall become an accessory after the fact to any felony, whether the same be a felony at common law or by virtue of any statute made, or to be made, such person shall be guilty of a crime, and may be indicted and convicted together with the principal felon, or after the conviction of the principal felon, or may be indicted and convicted for such crime whether the principal felon shall or shall not have been previously convicted, or shall or shall not be amenable to justice. Unless a different classification is expressly stated, that person shall be punished for an offense that is two classes lower than the felony the principal felon committed, except that an accessory after the fact to a Class A or Class B1 felony is a Class C felony, an accessory after the fact to a Class B2 felony is a Class D felony, an accessory after the fact to a Class H felony is a Class 1 misdemeanor, and an accessory after the fact to a Class I felony is a Class 2 misdemeanor. The offense of such person may be inquired of, tried, determined and punished by any court which shall have jurisdiction of the principal felon, in the same manner as if the act, by reason whereof such person shall have become an accessory, had been committed at the same place as the principal felony, although such act may have been committed without the limits of the State; and in case the principal felony shall have been committed within the body of any county, and the act by reason whereof any person shall have become accessory shall have been committed within the body of any other county, the offense of such person guilty of a felony as aforesaid may be inquired of, tried, determined, and punished in either of said counties: Provided, that no person who shall be once duly tried for such felony shall be again indicted or tried for the same offense.

Elements

A person is guilty of this offense

(1) when a felony was committed by another person (the principal) *and*
(2) after the felony was committed, the person knowingly gave the principal personal assistance in escaping or attempting to escape detection, arrest, or punishment
(3) knowing that the principal committed the crime.

Punishment

Unless a different classification is expressly stated by statute, this offense is punishable two classes lower than the felony committed by the principal felon, except that accessory after the fact to a Class A or B1 felony is a Class C felony, accessory after the fact to a Class B2 felony is a Class D felony, accessory after the fact to a Class H felony is a Class 1 misdemeanor, and accessory after the fact to a Class I felony is a Class 2 misdemeanor. G.S. 14-7.

Notes

Generally. Accessory before the fact is not a separate crime; rather, it is a doctrine under which one can be determined to be a principal (see "Accessory before the Fact to a Felony" in Chapter 3 (Participants in Crimes)). By contrast, this crime is a separate "stand alone" crime.

Element (1). There can be no conviction of this offense if the named principal is acquitted. State v. Robey, 91 N.C. App. 198 (1988).

Element (2). The offense can occur only *after* the principal offense has been completed, State v. McIntosh, 260 N.C. 749 (1963); a defendant cannot be convicted of accessory after the fact if the assistance is rendered *before* the offense has been committed.

The case law is inconsistent on whether a defendant may be convicted of accessory after the fact to murder when the defendant provides assistance after the victim is wounded but before the victim dies. At least one older North Carolina Supreme Court case held that a conviction could not stand on these facts. State v. Williams, 229 N.C. 348 (1948). However, a more recent North Carolina Court of Appeals case suggests otherwise. State v. Cole, ___ N.C. App. ___, 703 S.E.2d 842 (2011) (the State presented sufficient evidence of accessory after the fact to a second-degree murder perpetrated by Stevons; after Stevons shot the victim, the defendant drove Stevons away from the scene and the victim later died; the court rejected the defendant's argument that because he gave aid to Stevons after the victim had been wounded but before the victim died, he did not know that Stevons had committed murder, concluding that because the defendant knew that Stevons shot the victim at close range, a jury could reasonably infer that the defendant knew that the shot was fatal).

The court of appeals has rejected the argument that a robbery is not complete until the defendant reaches a place of safety. *Id.* at 848 (sufficient evidence of accessory after the fact to armed robbery; the court rejected the defendant's argument that the robbery was not complete until the defendant arrived at a safe place, concluding that a taking is complete once the thief succeeds in removing the stolen property from the victim's possession).

A person does not become an accessory after the fact simply because he or she knew that a crime was committed and failed to provide information about it or committed the act of "falsifying concerning his [or her] knowledge." State v. Potter, 221 N.C. 153 (1942). However, a person does become an accessory after the fact when he or she gives false testimony regarding the crime in order to advantage the perpetrator. *Id.*

Element (3). To be guilty of this offense the defendant must have known that the person aided committed a felony. *Id.*; State v. Earnhardt, 307 N.C. 62 (1982).

Charging issues. Accessory after the fact to a felony is not a lesser-included offense of the principal felony. See "Greater and lesser-included offenses," below. Thus, an indictment charging only the principal felony will be insufficient to support a conviction for accessory after the fact.

An indictment charging accessory after the fact to first-degree murder is sufficient to support a conviction of accessory after the fact to second-degree murder. *Cole*, ___ N.C. App. ___, 703 S.E.2d 842, 846–47.

Charge against or conviction of principal. G.S. 14-7 provides that an accessory after the fact may be indicted and convicted (1) together with the principal, (2) after conviction of the principal, (3) regardless of whether the principal previously has been convicted, and (4) regardless of whether the principal is amenable to justice. A conviction for accessory after the fact to a felony can stand even if the principal pleads guilty to a lesser-included offense of that felony. State v. McGee, 197 N.C. App. 366 (2009). However, as noted in the note on Element (1), above, a conviction cannot stand if the named principal is acquitted.

Greater and lesser-included offenses. Accessory after the fact to a felony is not a lesser-included offense of the principal felony. State v. Jones, 254 N.C. 450 (1961); State v. McIntosh, 260 N.C. 749, 753 (1963).

Multiple convictions and punishments. A defendant may be charged with and tried for both being a participant in a felony (such as an aider and abettor) and being an accessory after the fact to that felony. State v. Jewell, 104 N.C. App. 350, 353–54 (1991). However, a defendant may not be convicted of both of those offenses. *McIntosh*, 260 N.C. at 752–53 (robbery); State v. Surrett, ___ N.C. App. ___, ___ S.E.2d ___ (Nov. 15, 2011) (the trial court erred by failing to arrest judgment on the defendant's conviction for accessory after the fact to second-degree burglary where the defendant also was convicted as a principal to that crime); State v. Keller, 198 N.C. App. 639, 643 (2009) (a defendant may not be convicted of second-degree murder and accessory after the fact to first-degree murder of the same victim).

A defendant may not be convicted of accessory after the fact to first-degree murder and accessory after the fact to first-degree kidnapping when the verdict did not indicate whether the jury found the defendant guilty of accessory after the fact to first-degree murder because of premeditation and deliberation or because of felony murder with kidnapping as the underlying felony. State v. Best, 196 N.C. App. 220, 229–30 (2009).

Jurisdiction and venue. G.S. 14-7 provides that an accessory may be tried by any court with jurisdiction over the principal felon, even if the accessory's acts occurred outside of the State. It also provides that if the principal's acts occurred in one county and the accessory's in another, the accessory may be tried in either county but not both. See generally "Lack of Jurisdiction" in Chapter 2 (Bars and Defenses).

Related Offenses Not in This Chapter

"Aiding and Abetting" (Chapter 3)
"Assisting a Violator of Registration Obligations in Eluding Arrest" (Chapter 10)
"Altering or Removing a Serial Number" (Chapter 13)
"Buying, Selling, or Possessing Property with an Altered Serial Number" (Chapter 13)
"Felony Possession of Stolen Goods" (Chapter 13)
"Misdemeanor Possession of Stolen Goods" (Chapter 13)
"Felony Receiving Stolen Goods" (Chapter 13)
"Misdemeanor Receiving Stolen Goods" (Chapter 13)
Misprision of felony (common law); R. Perkins & R. Boyce, Criminal Law 572 (3d ed. 1982)
Harboring or aiding certain persons. G.S. 14-259.

Compounding a Felony

Statute

This is a common law offense.

Elements

A person is guilty of this offense

(1) when another person (the principal) has committed a felony *and*
(2) the person knows that the principal has committed a crime *and*
(3) agrees
  (a) not to prosecute,
  (b) not to inform, *or*
  (c) to dismiss the prosecution
(4) in exchange for something of value.

Punishment

Class 1 misdemeanor

Notes

Generally. Few published North Carolina cases discuss this crime, and none of the cases are very recent. For a more detailed discussion, see 2 W. LAFAVE & A. SCOTT JR., SUBSTANTIVE CRIMINAL LAW 4, 410–13 (2d ed. 2003).

Element (1). It must be proved that the person with whom the corrupt agreement was made actually committed a felony. State v. Hodge, 142 N.C. 665 (1906). This offense seems to occur only when the offense compounded is a felony, but there is some indication that it could apply as well to a misdemeanor. 2 LAFAVE & SCOTT at 412.

Element (2). This element requires that the felon is known to the defendant. *Hodge*, 142 N.C. 665 (1906). It probably is satisfied even when the defendant does not specifically know of the felony, if the defendant has inferred it, and the fact that he or she agreed not to proceed against the felony should be sufficient evidence of knowledge. PERKINS & BOYCE at 580.

Element (3). An agreement is the heart of this offense. 2 LAFAVE & SCOTT at 410. The offense has not been committed if a person merely refrains from proceeding against the felony in the hope of receiving a reward but without an agreement. *Id.* It appears that the agreement need not be with the one who committed the felony.

Element (4). Mere failure to proceed against a person does not constitute compounding; compounding must be done in exchange for something of value. *Id.* That consideration could be for the benefit of either the defendant or someone else. And the consideration can include return of the victim's own property. That is, compounding could include an agreement by the victim not to press charges or not to testify if the offender will pay restitution.

Application to public officials. A public official, just like a private citizen, can be guilty of compounding. State v. Furr, 121 N.C. 606 (1897).

Related Offenses Not in This Chapter

"Offering a Bribe" (Chapter 21)
Misprision of felony (common law); PERKINS & BOYCE at 572
Willfully failing to discharge duties. G.S. 14-230.

6
Homicide

6
Homicide

Murder

First-Degree Murder

Statute

§14-17. Murder in the first and second degree defined; punishment.

A murder which shall be perpetrated by means of a nuclear, biological, or chemical weapon of mass destruction as defined in G.S. 14-288.21, poison, lying in wait, imprisonment, starving, torture, or by any other kind of willful, deliberate, and premeditated killing, or which shall be committed in the perpetration or attempted perpetration of any arson, rape or a sex offense, robbery, kidnapping, burglary, or other felony committed or attempted with the use of a deadly weapon shall be deemed to be murder in the first degree, a Class A felony, and any person who commits such murder shall be punished with death or imprisonment in the State's prison for life without parole as the court shall determine pursuant to G.S. 15A-2000, except that any such person who was under 18 years of age at the time of the murder shall be punished with imprisonment in the State's prison for life without parole. All other kinds of murder, including that which shall be proximately caused by the unlawful distribution of opium or any synthetic or natural salt, compound, derivative, or preparation of opium, or cocaine or other substance described in G.S. 90-90(1)d., or methamphetamine when the ingestion of such substance causes the death of the user, shall be deemed murder in the second degree, and any person who commits such murder shall be punished as a Class B2 felon.

Elements

A person guilty of this offense

(1) kills
(2) another living human being
(3) (a) (i) with malice *and*
 (ii) with a specific intent to kill formed after premeditation and deliberation,
 (b) by poisoning, lying in wait, imprisonment, starvation, or torture,
 (c) while committing or attempting arson, rape, sex offense, robbery, burglary, kidnapping, or any felony in which a deadly weapon is used, *or*
 (d) by means of a nuclear, biological, or chemical weapon of mass destruction as defined in G.S. 14-288.21.

Punishment

Class A felony punishable by death or imprisonment for life without possibility of parole. G.S. 14-17.

Before the jury may impose the death penalty, it must find beyond a reasonable doubt that one or more of the aggravating circumstances listed in G.S. 15A-2000 (for example, that the murder was heinous, atrocious, or cruel or was committed during a robbery) exist and that the aggravating circumstance or circumstances outweigh any mitigating circumstance or circumstances (for example, the defendant's age or lack of significant prior criminal history). This determination of the sentence takes place in a separate hearing after the defendant is found guilty of first-degree murder. For a discussion of capital law, see ROBERT L. FARB, NORTH CAROLINA CAPITAL CASE LAW HANDBOOK (UNC School of Government, 2d ed. 2004).

G.S. 14-17 provides that if a defendant under age 18 is convicted of first-degree murder, the mandatory sentence is life imprisonment without parole. This provision is consistent with *Roper v. Simmons*, 543 U.S. 551 (2005), which held that the Eighth Amendment prohibits a death sentence for a defendant who is convicted of a capital offense committed before his or her 18th birthday.

No person who is mentally retarded may be sentenced to death. Atkins v. Virginia, 536 U.S. 304 (2002); G.S. 15A-2005(b). If convicted of first-degree murder, such a person receives a punishment of life imprisonment without parole. G.S. 15A-2005(h).

Notes

Elements (1) and (2). To kill oneself is suicide, which is not a crime in North Carolina. G.S. 14-17.1. To shoot someone who is already dead is not murder; the victim must be living in order for the act to be murder. 2 W. LAFAVE & A. SCOTT JR. , SUBSTANTIVE CRIMINAL LAW 419 (2d ed. 2003).

Under the doctrine of transferred intent, a defendant who intended to kill one person but mistakenly killed another is still guilty of murder. See "Transferred intent" in Chapter 1 (States of Mind.)

Element (3)(a)(i). The law of homicide recognizes three forms of malice:

(1) the express emotions of hatred, ill will, and spite, State v. Stinson, 297 N.C. 168 (1979);
(2) the commission of an inherently dangerous act (or omission to act when there is a legal duty to do so) in such a reckless and wanton manner "as to manifest a mind utterly without regard for human life and social duty and deliberately bent on mischief," State v. Rich, 351 N.C. 386 (2000); State v. Snyder, 311 N.C. 391 (1984); State v. Trott, 190 N.C. 674 (1925); State v. Liner, 98 N.C. App. 600 (1990); State v. Byers, 105 N.C. App. 377 (1992); and
(3) a condition of the mind which prompts a person to take the life of another intentionally, or to intentionally inflict serious bodily injury which proximately results in death, without just cause, excuse, or justification, State v. Reynolds, 307 N.C. 184 (1982); see "Maliciously" in Chapter 1 (States of Mind).

The second form of malice—commission of an inherently dangerous act—was found when the defendant, knowing that two people became violently ill after using certain drugs, supplied the same drugs to the victim, who later died. *Liner*, 98 N.C. App. 600.

The third form of malice can be inferred from the intentional infliction of a wound with a deadly weapon. State v. Patterson, 297 N.C. 247 (1979); *Reynolds*, 307 N.C. 184; State v. Bondurant, 309 N.C. 674 (1983); State v. Hunter, ___ N.C. App. ___, 703 S.E.2d 776 (2010) (sufficient evidence of malice when the victim was stabbed in the torso with a golf club shaft; shaft entered her back near the neck and was moved downward and forward toward her chest to a depth of 8 inches, where it perforated her aorta, causing death). This is the case even if the alleged homicide involved a mercy killing. State v. Forrest, 321 N.C. 186 (1987). Malice also may be inferred from the use of hands alone to inflict a fatal injury when an adult assaults an infant. State v. Perdue, 320 N.C. 51 (1987). See the discussion of what constitutes a deadly weapon under the offense "Assault with a Deadly Weapon" in Chapter 7 (Assaults).

For an extensive discussion of the term "malice" as used in second-degree murder, see the note on Element (3) to "Second-Degree Murder," below.

Element (3)(a)(ii). "Specific intent to kill" means that the defendant intended his or her actions to result in the victim's death; the fact that the defendant committed an intentional act that resulted in the victim's death is not enough to satisfy this element. State v. Keel, 333 N.C. 52 (1992); State v. Pittman, 174 N.C. App. 745, 750 (2005). For cases in which there was sufficient evidence of a specific intent to kill, see, for example, *State v. Teague*, ___ N.C. App. ___, 715 S.E.2d 919, 924–25 (2011) (the defendant attacked the sleeping victims, stabbing them in their throats); *Pittman*, 174 N.C. App. at 750–51 (in order to avoid paying child support, the defendant abandoned an infant in 30-degree weather in a remote, dilapidated shed where she would not likely be found), and *State v. Kirby*, 187 N.C. App. 367 (2007) (the defendant, who had a history of beating the victim, hit the victim without provocation on the day of the killing, told others to tell him good-bye, and told the victim to say his prayers; the cause of death was strangulation and blunt trauma; and the defendant attempted to conceal the body and evidence).

"Premeditation" means thinking about something beforehand, for some length of time, however short; "deliberation" refers to an intention to kill formed while defendant was in a "cool state of blood." State v. Bullock, 326 N.C. 253 (1990); State v. Ruof, 296 N.C. 623 (1979); State v. Blue, ___ N.C. App. ___, 699 S.E.2d 661, 665–66 (2010) (the defendant's statement that he formed the intent to kill and contemplated whether he would be caught before he began the attack was sufficient evidence that he formed the intent to kill in a cool state of blood). A cool state of blood does not mean absence of passion and emotion; a person may be capable of forming murderous intent, premeditating and deliberating, yet be prompted and to a large extent controlled by passion at the time of the offense. State v. Vause, 328 N.C. 231 (1991). Rather, it means that a killing was committed with a fixed design to kill, regardless of whether the defendant was angry or gripped with passion at the time of the act. *Bullock*, 326 N.C. 253; *Ruof*, 296 N.C. 623. It also means that the defendant's anger or emotion was not so strong as to overcome his or her reason. State v. Hunt, 330 N.C. 425 (1991). Premeditation and deliberation need not last for any perceptible length of time. State v. Walters, 275 N.C. 615 (1969); State v. Bynum, 175 N.C. 777 (1918).

Circumstantial evidence, rather than direct evidence, generally proves premeditation and deliberation. State v. Bell, 338 N.C. 363 (1994). Circumstances showing premeditation and deliberation include:

- lack of provocation, State v. Corn, 303 N.C. 293 (1981),
- the defendant's conduct before and after killing, State v. Walker, 332 N.C. 520 (1992); State v. Lane, 328 N.C. 598 (1991); State v. Freeman, 326 N.C. 40 (1990),
- the defendant's statements of ill will toward the victim, State v. Gallagher, 313 N.C. 132 (1985),
- the defendant's previous assault of the victim, State v. Simpson, 327 N.C. 178 (1990),
- previous difficulties between the defendant and the victim, State v. Bullock, 326 N.C. 253, 258 (1990),
- threats before and during the killing, *id.*,
- the brutal nature of the killing (such as by strangulation), State v. Richardson, 328 N.C. 505 (1991); State v. Greene, 332 N.C. 565 (1992),
- blows dealt after the victim is helpless, *Bullock*, 326 N.C. at 258, and
- the nature and number of the victim's wounds, State v. Watson, 338 N.C. 168 (1994); State v. Montgomery, 331 N.C. 559 (1992); State v. Vause, 328 N.C. 231 (1991).

For general lists and discussions of these circumstances, see *State v. Smith,* 357 N.C. 604 (2003), *State v. Sweatt,* 333 N.C. 407 (1993), *State v. Small,* 328 N.C. 175 (1991), and *State v. Myers,* 309 N.C. 78 (1983). For cases in which the evidence sufficiently established premeditation and deliberation, see *State v. Bonilla,* ___ N.C. App. ___, 706 S.E.2d 288 (2011) (in a first-degree murder case, there was sufficient evidence of premeditation, deliberation, and intent to kill; after the defendant and an accomplice beat and kicked the victim, they hog-tied him so severely that his spine was fractured and put tissue in his mouth; due to the severe arching of his back, the victim suffered a fracture in his thoracic spine and died from a combination of suffocation and strangulation); *State v. Bass,* 190 N.C. App. 339, 345 (2008) (the defendant had time to contemplate his actions, threatened the victim, was not provoked, shot the victim in the back, and did not surrender), *State v. Forrest,* 168 N.C. App. 614, 626 (2005) (the defendant attacked an unsuspecting victim and made statements suggesting an intent to kill), and *State v. Dennison,* 171 N.C. App. 504, 509–10 (2005) (the wounds were brutal, the blows multiple, the victim had harassed the defendant, and the defendant left the crime scene).

For cases in which the evidence was insufficient to establish premeditation and deliberation, see *State v. Corn,* 303 N.C. 293, 297–98 (1981) (the victim entered the defendant's home while highly intoxicated, approached the sofa on which the defendant was lying, and insulted the defendant; the defendant immediately jumped up, grabbed a nearby rifle, and shot the victim several times in the chest; the incident lasted only a few moments; there was no evidence that the defendant acted with a fixed design, had sufficient time to weigh the consequences of his actions, previously threatened the victim, or exhibited conduct indicating that he formed any intent to kill before to the incident; there was no significant history of arguments or ill will between the parties and although the defendant fired several shots, there was no evidence that he shot or hit the victim once the victim fell), and *State v. Williams,* 144 N.C. App. 526, 531 (2001) (there was no evidence of animosity, that the defendant and the victim knew each other before incident, or that defendant threatened the victim; when the victim provoked the defendant by assaulting him, the defendant immediately retaliated by firing one shot; the defendant's actions did not show planning or forethought; although the defendant left the scene, he turned himself in the next day).

For a discussion of when accident, voluntary intoxication, and other failure of proof defenses can negate the specific intent to kill required for first-degree murder, see "Failure of Proof or 'Negating' Defenses" in Chapter 2 (Bars and Defenses).

Element (3)(b). If the defendant killed the victim by poison, lying in wait, imprisonment, starving, or torture, and if the defendant's act was the proximate cause of death, the crime of first-degree murder has occurred. Neither specific intent to kill nor premeditation and deliberation are elements of this category of first-degree murder. State v. Roper, 328 N.C. 368 (1991); State v. Brown, 320 N.C. 179 (1987); State v. Johnson, 317 N.C. 193 (1986). Nor is malice an element of this kind of first degree murder. State v. Smith, 351 N.C. 251 (2000); State v. Phillips, 328 N.C. 1 (1991); State v. Crawford, 329 N.C. 466 (1991).

Lying in wait requires ambush and surprise of the victim. State v. Lynch, 327 N.C. 210 (1990). It may mean stationing oneself in advance or lying in ambush to attack a victim, but a defendant can be lying in wait even though not concealed. State v. Allison, 298 N.C. 135 (1979). A victim may even be aware of the attacker's presence; there would be adequate surprise in such a circumstance if the victim does not expect to be attacked. State v. Leroux, 326 N.C. 368 (1990). Lying in wait does not require that an attacker wait at the site of the killing for some period of time; "a moment's deliberate pause" before killing a victim unaware of the impending assault, and consequently without an opportunity for self-defense, satisfies the definition of murder by lying in wait. *Id.*

Torture is the act or process of inflicting great, severe, or extreme pain, usually by more than a single act. State v. Lee, 348 N.C. 474 (1998); State v. Phillips, 328 N.C. 1 (1991).

Element (3)(c). Murder perpetrated under this prong is referred to as felony murder. Evidence of this type of first-degree murder consists of evidence of commission or attempt of one of the listed felony offenses and an act that was the proximate cause of the victim's death. This prong does not require proof of premeditation or deliberation, State v. Mays, 225 N.C. 486 (1945), or proof that the killing was intentional, State v. Streeton, 231 N.C. 301 (1949). Additionally, the State is not required to prove malice under the felony murder theory because malice is implied from the underlying felony or the use of a deadly weapon. State v. Crawford, 329 N.C. 466 (1991); State v. Gardner, 315 N.C. 444 (1986); State v. Womble, 292 N.C. 455 (1977).

The fact that the killing was accidental is no defense if it was committed in the course of one of the named felonies. State v. Phillips, 264 N.C. 508 (1965).

Self-defense is a defense to felony murder only if it is a defense to the underlying felony supporting the felony murder charge. State v. Jacobs, 363 N.C. 815, 822 (2010).

In addition to listing specific crimes that can qualify as the underlying felony for felony murder (arson, rape, sex offense, robbery, burglary, and kidnapping), the statute includes a catch-all category covering any "other felony committed or attempted with the use of a deadly weapon." G.S. 14-17. Crimes that have qualified under this catch-all category include discharging a firearm into an occupied vehicle or structure, felonious escape, armed felonious breaking and entering and larceny, sodomy under threat of deadly weapon, assault with a deadly weapon with intent to kill or with intent to inflict serious injury, felonious child abuse, State v. Jones, 353 N.C. 159 (2000) (citing cases), and sale or attempted sale of a controlled substance, State v. Squires, 357 N.C. 529 (2003); State v. Freeman, ___ N.C. App. ___, 690 S.E.2d 17, 20–21 (2010) (attempted sale). Felonious child abuse can support a felony murder charge when the defendant's hands constitute the deadly weapon. State v. Pierce, 346 N.C. 471 (1997); State v. Krider, 145 N.C. App. 711 (2001).

A defendant may not be convicted of first-degree felony murder when the underlying felonies (in this case, felonious assaults of the surviving occupants in a vehicle struck by the impaired defendant's vehicle) are committed through culpable negligence only. *Jones*, 353 N.C. 159. A defendant may not be convicted of first-degree felony murder involving vehicular homicide when the underlying felony is operating a motor vehicle to elude arrest. State v. Woodard, 146 N.C. App. 75 (2001).

The continuous transaction doctrine applies to felony murder. Under this doctrine, a person may commit felony murder when the felony (a sexual assault or arson, for example) occurs before, during, or soon after the victim's death, as long as the felony and the murder form one continuous transaction. State v. Campbell, 332 N.C. 116 (1992); State v. Thomas, 329 N.C. 423 (1991); State v. Hutchins, 303 N.C. 321 (1981); *Freeman*, ___ N.C. App. ___, 690 S.E.2d 17, 20–21 (one week after the defendant delivered cocaine to the victim, he went to the victim's residence to collect payment; the attempted sale of the controlled substance and the murder were part of a continuous transaction); State v. Lowry, 198 N.C. App. 457, 470–71 (2009) (evidence that a murder victim's pocketbook was missing, her credit card bills and statements were strewn about, a person matching the defendant's description tried to use her ATM card, and her credit cards were found near a house frequented by the defendant was sufficient to show that a robbery occurred at the same time as a murder). Thus, a defendant may be convicted under the felony murder theory when the death occurs during the defendant's escape or flight from the scene of the felony. State v. Doyle, 161 N.C. App. 247 (2003). A defendant also may be convicted under the felony murder theory when the underlying felony is armed robbery and the defendant used the object of the robbery as the murder weapon. State v. McMillan, ___ N.C. App. ___, ___ S.E.2d ___ (Aug. 2, 2011) (the underlying felony was armed robbery and the defendant used the stolen item—a .357 Glock handgun—to commit the murder; the two crimes occurred during a continuous transaction). A time interval of three-and-one-half hours between a murder and an arson of the murder victim's dwelling did not defeat application of the continuous transaction doctrine. State v. Jaynes, 342 N.C. 249 (1995). For a fuller discussion of the continuous transaction doctrine, see FARB, NORTH CAROLINA CAPITAL CASE LAW HANDBOOK, cited in full *supra*, at 17–18 & 149–52.

Although the felony and the homicide must be part of a continuous transaction, they cannot be the same offense. The underlying felony must be a separate offense from the act that causes death. In a case where the defendant committed a nonfatal assault on the victim with a machete and then killed her by strangulation, the felony assault with a machete was held to be a separate offense from the strangulation and was properly used as a felony to support felony murder. State v. Carroll, 356 N.C. 526 (2002).

The prosecution need not elect for submission to a jury between theories of felony murder and murder with specific intent formed after premeditation and deliberation if its proof supports both types of murder. State v. Greene, 314 N.C. 649 (1985).

One who aids and abets another in the commission of felony murder is guilty as a principal. State v. Lane, 328 N.C. 598, 610 (1991). For a more detailed discussion of aiding and abetting and related doctrines, see Chapter 3 (Participants in Crimes).

The prosecution may attempt to prove first-degree murder by felony murder based on the commission of more than one felony. For example, a jury may find a defendant guilty of first-degree murder based on predicate felonies of both armed robbery and felonious breaking and entering. However, if an appellate court finds insufficient evidence to support one of the felonies on which felony murder was based and it is impossible to determine if the jury convicted the person based on the erroneously submitted felony, a new trial may be ordered. State v. Pakulski, 326 N.C. 434 (1990). *But see* State v. Oglesby, 174 N.C. App. 658 (2005). This problem can be solved with a special verdict sheet on which the jury indicates its verdict as to each of the underlying felonies.

Under the "merger rule," a defendant convicted of first-degree murder based only on the felony murder theory may not also be sentenced for a conviction on the underlying felony. State v. Barlowe, 337 N.C. 371 (1994). Exceptions to the rule exist. For example, in *State v. Cunningham*, 140 N.C. App. 315 (2000), the court held that an attempted armed robbery conviction did not merge with first-degree felony murder when the underlying felony was first-degree burglary and attempted armed robbery was the intended felony of first-degree burglary. For a fuller discussion of the merger rule, see FARB, NORTH CAROLINA CAPITAL CASE LAW HANDBOOK, cited in full *supra*, at 17–18 & 149–52.

For felony murder to apply, the defendant, co-conspirators, aiders, or others acting in concert with the defendant must have committed the homicide. A defendant may not be held responsible on this theory for a homicide committed by an adversary (a law enforcement officer, for example) or a victim. State v. Bonner, 330 N.C. 536 (1992); State v. Williams, 185 N.C. App. 318, 331 (2007). However, a defendant may be convicted of first-degree felony murder for shooting and killing an accomplice during the commission of the crime. State v. Torres, 171 N.C. App. 419 (2005).

Proximate cause. To constitute this offense (and, indeed, to constitute any form of homicide), the defendant's act must be the proximate cause of the death. Proximate cause does not require the State to prove that a defendant's act was the sole or immediate cause of death. Rather, the act need only be a contributing cause of death if the direct cause is "a natural result of the criminal act." State v. Cummings, 301 N.C. 374 (1980); State v. Jones, 290 N.C. 292 (1976); State v. Minton, 234 N.C. 716, 722 (1952) ("An accused who wounds another with intent to kill him and leaves him lying out of doors in a helpless condition on a frigid night is guilty of homicide if his disabled victim dies as the result of exposure to the cold. This is true because the act of the accused need not be the immediate cause of the death. He is legally accountable if the direct cause is the natural result of his criminal act."). Thus, if the defendant inflicts a dangerous wound that is a contributing cause of death, he or she is liable for murder. *Minton*, 234 N.C. at 722. Proximate cause exists even if a victim died from negligent medical treatment after an assault, unless the negligent treatment was the sole cause of death. *Jones*, 290 N.C. at 298–99 (1976); State v. Lane, 115 N.C. App. 25 (1994). Proximate cause also exists when the defendant's criminal act was a contributing cause of the victim's death, even if a victim chose surgery against medical advice and died, State v. Gilreath, 118 N.C. App. 200 (1995), refused on religious grounds to accept blood transfusions and died, State v. Welch, 135 N.C. App. 499 (1991), or there was a voluntary decision by family members to remove the victim from life support systems, State v. Garcia-Lorenzo, 110 N.C. App. 319 (1993). For acts of others to insulate the defendant from criminal liability, those acts must "break the causal chain" and constitute the sole proximate cause of death. State v. Hollingsworth, 77 N.C. App. 36, 39–40 (1985); State v. Tioran, 65 N.C. App. 122, 123–25 (1983); *see also* State v. Pierce, ___ N.C. App. ___, ___ S.E.2d ___ (Oct. 18, 2011) (in a case in which a second officer got into a vehicular accident and died while responding to a first officer's communication about the defendant's flight from a lawful stop, the defendant's flight from the first officer was the proximate cause of the second officer's death; the evidence was sufficient to allow a reasonable jury to conclude that the second officer's death would not have occurred had the defendant not fled and that the second officer's death was reasonably foreseeable; the court rejected the defendant's argument that the second officer's contributory negligence broke the causal chain); State v. Norman, ___ N.C. App. ___, 711 S.E.2d 849 (2011) (there was sufficient evidence that the defendant's actions were the proximate cause of death in a homicide case arising out of a vehicle accident; the defendant argued that two unforeseeable events proximately caused the victims' deaths: a third-party's turn onto the road and the victims' failure to yield the right-of-way; the court found that the first event was foreseeable; as to the second, it noted that the defendant's speeding and driving while impaired were concurrent proximate causes).

For cases involving a death caused by ingestion of a controlled substance and issues of proximate cause, see *In re Z.A.K.*, 189 N.C. App. 354, 358–60 (2008) (the defendant's failure to aid the victim after giving her a drug that made her ill and failure to act appropriately after undertaking aid was a proximate cause of the victim's death), and *State v. Parlee*, ___ N.C. App. ___, 703 S.E.2d 866 (2011) (the defendant was charged with second-degree murder for having proximately caused a death by the unlawful distribution and ingestion of Oxymorphone; there was sufficient evidence that the defendant's sale of the pill was a proximate cause of death where the defendant unlawfully sold the pill to the two friends, who split it in half and consumed it; the victim was pronounced dead the next morning, and cause of death was acute Oxymorphone overdose).

It is not a defense that a victim's pre-existing physical condition (for example, alcoholism) made the victim peculiarly vulnerable to an assault; the defendant's assault is considered to be the proximate cause of death, even if the assault would not have been fatal without the pre-existing condition. State v. Atkinson, 298 N.C. 673 (1979); State v. Hargett, 255 N.C. 412 (1961).

Although some cases reject the notion that forseeability of death is a component of proximate cause, State v. Woods, 278 N.C. 210, 219 (1971) ("The crucial question is whether a wound inflicted by an unlawful assault proximately caused the death—not whether death was a natural and probable result of such a wound and should have been foreseen. Foreseeability is not an element of proximate cause in a homicide case where an intentionally inflicted wound caused the victim's death."); State v. Lane, 115 N.C. App. 25, 29–30 (1994) (rejecting the defendant's argument that he was not the proximate cause of the victim's death due to the unforeseeable consequences of the assault; "[r]esponsibility cannot be avoided due to a preexisting condition of a decedent [here, chronic alcoholism that made the victim more susceptible to brain swelling and subdural hematomas] which renders him less able to withstand an assault"), as discussed below, at least one case holds that forseeability is required for involuntary manslaughter; see "Proximate cause" under "Involuntary Manslaughter," below.

The common law rule that a person could not be convicted of murder if the victim died more than a year and a day after the criminal act has been abolished. State v. Vance, 328 N.C. 613 (1991).

Charging issues. G.S. 15-144 prescribes a short-form indictment for murder and manslaughter. The United States Supreme Court's ruling in *Ring v. Arizona*, 536 U.S. 584 (2002), did not render the short-form murder indictment under G.S. 15-144 unconstitutional. State v. Hunt, 357 N.C. 257 (2003). For a more detailed discussion of charging issues in connection with homicide offenses, see Jessica Smith, *The Criminal Indictment: Fatal Defect, Fatal Variance,* *and Amendment,* ADMIN. OF JUST. BULL. NO. 2008/03 (UNC School of Government, July 2008) (online at www.sog.unc.edu/pubs/electronicversions/pdfs/aojb0803.pdf).

Greater and lesser-included offenses. Second-degree murder is a lesser-included offense of premeditated and deliberate first-degree murder. State v. Stevenson, 327 N.C. 259, 263 (1990). Voluntary manslaughter is a lesser-included of first-degree murder. State v. Simonovich, ___ N.C. App. ___, 688 S.E.2d 67, 71 (2010). Involuntary manslaughter is a lesser-included offense of first- and second-degree murder and voluntary manslaughter. State v. Shook, 327 N.C. 74, 81 (1990); State v. Greene, 314 N.C. 649 (1985). Misdemeanor and felony assaults are not lesser-included offenses of murder involving assault when the short-form murder indictment is used. State v. Collins, 334 N.C. 54 (1993). For a more detailed discussion of the lesser-included offenses of first-degree murder, see FARB, NORTH CAROLINA CAPITAL CASE LAW HANDBOOK, cited in full *supra,* at 139–43.

Multiple convictions and punishments. When a defendant is convicted of first-degree murder under the felony murder theory only, the merger rule prevents punishment for the first-degree murder and the underlying felony supporting the felony murder charge; in this instance, the proper procedure is to arrest judgment on the underlying felony. See the discussion of the "merger rule" in the note on Element (3)(c), above.

For a discussion of when a defendant may be convicted of attempted murder and other crimes, see the note entitled "Attempted homicide" under "Attempt" in Chapter 5 (General Crimes).

Attempted first-degree murder. An attempt to commit this offense is a Class B2 offense. G.S. 14-2.5. Neither assault with a deadly weapon inflicting serious injury, State v. Rainey, 154 N.C. App. 282 (2002), nor assault with a deadly weapon with intent to kill inflicting serious injury, State v. Tirado, 358 N.C. 551 (2004); State v. Bethea, 173 N.C. App. 43 (2005); State v. Peoples, 141 N.C. App. 115 (2000), are lesser-included offenses of attempted first-degree murder. A defendant may be convicted and punished for both attempted first-degree murder and assault with a firearm on a law enforcement officer based on the same conduct. State v. Haynesworth, 146 N.C. App. 523 (2001).

Constitutionality. The murder by torture provision is not unconstitutionally vague. State v. Crawford, 329 N.C. 466 (1991).

Related Offenses Not in This Chapter

See patient abuse (various offenses) in Chapter 9 (Abuse and Neglect).
Producing miscarriage. G.S. 14-45 and 14-45.1
Concealment of death; disturbing human remains; dismembering human remains. G.S. 14-401.22.

Second-Degree Murder

Statute

See G.S. 14-17, reproduced under "First-Degree Murder," above.

Elements

A person guilty of this offense

(1) kills
(2) another living human being
(3) with malice.

Punishment

Class B2 felony. G.S. 14-17.

Notes

Elements (1) and (2). See the notes on these elements to "First-Degree Murder," above.

Element (3). See the note on Element (3)(a)(i) to "First-Degree Murder," above, for a general discussion of malice in connection with homicide offenses.

Because malice can be inferred from the intentional use of a deadly weapon to inflict harm, this offense can be established by showing a voluntary unlawful killing committed with a deadly weapon. State v. Mercer, 275 N.C. 108 (1969). The deadly weapon whose use gives rise to the inference of malice may be a weapon that is deadly by its very nature, such as a gun, State v. Benson, 183 N.C. 795 (1922), or because of the way it is used, such as hands and feet used against an infant or a disabled or feeble person, State v. Lang, 309 N.C. 512 (1983); State v. Jones, 35 N.C. App. 48 (1978); State v. Sallie, 13 N.C. App. 499 (1972). For a more detailed discussion of deadly weapons, see "Assault with a Deadly Weapon" in Chapter 7 (Assaults).

Reckless use of an automobile may establish malice for second-degree murder. However, the recklessness required to show malice for second-degree murder is greater than that required to show culpable negligence, which would support involuntary manslaughter. State v. Mack, ___ N.C. App. ___, 697 S.E.2d 490, 494 (2010); see "Criminal Negligence" in Chapter 1 (States of Mind). Often, these types of vehicle cases involve impaired driving. State v. Rich, 351 N.C. 386 (2000); State v. Snyder, 311 N.C. 391 (1984); State v. Trott, 190 N.C. 674 (1925); State v. Westbrook, 175 N.C. App. 128 (2005); State v. Grice, 131 N.C. App. 48 (1998); State v. McBride, 109 N.C. App. 64 (1993); State v. Byers, 105 N.C. App. 377 (1992). Prior impaired driving convictions or pending charges can, under certain circumstances, be admitted under North Carolina Evidence Rule 404(b) as evidence of malice. *Compare* State v. Jones, 353 N.C. 159, 173 (2000) (evidence of defendant speeding, driving on the wrong side of the road, and running other motorists off the road while impaired was properly admitted to show malice because the evidence demonstrated that defendant was aware that his conduct was reckless and dangerous to human life), *and* State v. Locklear, 159 N.C. App. 588 (2003) (the trial court properly allowed the State to introduce evidence of the facts and circumstances surrounding the defendant's prior arrest and conviction of driving while impaired to prove malice), *with* State v. Davis, ___ N.C. App. ___, 702 S.E.2d 507 (2010) (the trial court committed prejudicial error by admitting the defendant's prior impaired driving convictions to show malice; three of the defendant's four prior convictions occurred eighteen or nineteen years before the accident at issue and one occurred two years prior; given the sixteen-year gap between the older convictions and the more recent one, there was no clear and consistent pattern of criminality and the older convictions were too remote to be admissible). For vehicle cases involving alcohol in which there was sufficient evidence of malice, see *State v. Norman* ___ N.C. App. ___, 711 S.E.2d 849 (2011) (the defendant admitted that he drank beer prior to driving; the State's expert calculated his blood alcohol level to be 0.08 at the time of the collision and other witnesses testified that he was impaired; evidence showed that he ingested cocaine and that the effects of cocaine are correlated with high-risk driving; the defendant admitted that he was speeding, and experts calculated his speed to be approximately 15 mph over the posted limit; the State also introduced evidence of prior driving while impaired convictions); *State v. Patterson*, ___ N.C. App. ___, 708 S.E.2d 133 (2011) (a chemical analysis of blood taken from the defendant after the accident showed a blood alcohol content (BAC) of 0.14, and the State's expert estimated that his BAC was 0.19 at the time of the accident; the defendant admitted having consumed five or six beers that day; witnesses testified that they detected a strong odor of alcohol emanating from the defendant immediately after the accident; the defendant had bloodshot eyes and was combative with emergency personnel; the defendant's speed exceeded 100 mph and he failed to use his brakes or make any attempt to avoid the collision); *State v. Tellez*, 200 N.C. App. 517 (2009) (the defendant drove recklessly, drank alcohol before and while operating a motor vehicle, had prior convictions for impaired driving and driving while license revoked, and fled and engaged in elusive behavior after the accident); and *State v. Davis*, 197 N.C. App. 738, 742–43 (2009) (the defendant consumed nine to twelve beers in two hours, had a blood-alcohol level of 0.13, and drove his truck on a busy highway; the defendant continued driving after running over a sign, weaved in the road, ran off the road without braking or attempting to avoid a collision, and hit the victims' truck, knocking it into the air).

Malice can be found in vehicle cases in the absence of impairment. State v. Pierce, ___ N.C. App. ___, ___ S.E.2d ___ (Oct. 18, 2011) (in a case in which a second officer got into a vehicular accident and died while responding to a first officer's communication about the defendant's flight from a lawful stop, the evidence was sufficient to establish malice for purposes of second-degree murder; the defendant intentionally fled from the first officer, driving 65 mph in 25 mph zone, and threw bags of marijuana out of the vehicle while driving); State v. Mack, ___ N.C. App. ___, 697 S.E.2d 490, 493–95 (2010) (the defendant, whose license was revoked, drove extremely dangerously to evade arrest, including driving more than 90 mph, running a red light, and traveling the wrong way on a highway); State v. Neville, ___ N.C. App. ___, 688 S.E.2d 76, 79 (2010) (the defendant ran over a child; was angry, out of control, and had an "evil look;" her vehicle created acceleration marks but was functioning properly; and the yard was dark, several small children were present, and the defendant did not know where the children were when she started her car); State v. Lloyd, 187 N.C. App. 174, 179–80 (2007) (the defendant drove knowing that his license was revoked, took the vehicle without permission, and fled from police); State v. Bethea, 167 N.C. App. 215, 219–20 (2004) (the defendant drove with a revoked license, fled to elude officers, sped through a red light and stop signs, drove as fast as 100 mph, crossed into the oncoming traffic lane several times, and turned his car lights off on dark rural roads, decreasing his own visibility and making his car difficult to see, while traveling at speeds between 90–95 mph).

Cruel and reckless acts that indicate a total disregard for human life, such as extreme and brutal child abuse, are sufficient to supply the malice necessary for second-degree murder. State v. Wilkerson, 295 N.C. 559 (1978). For a case in which the defendant's shaking of an infant victim was insufficient to support a finding that the defendant acted with malice, see *State v. Blue*, 138 N.C. App. 404 (2000). For a case in which the evidence was sufficient, see *State v. Trogdon*, ___ N.C. App. ___, 715 S.E.2d 635 (2011) (in a case involving the death of a 16-month-old child, there was sufficient evidence of malice when the jury could find that while the victim was in the defendant's sole custody, he suffered non-accidental injuries to the head with acute brain injury due to blunt force trauma of the head with at least four impacts, most likely due to his head being slammed into a soft object; combined with evidence that the defendant bit the victim, was upset about the victim's mother's relationship with the victim's father, and that the defendant resented the victim, the jury could find that the defendant intentionally attacked the child, resulting in his death).

Death resulting from distribution and ingestion of a controlled substance. If a defendant unlawfully distributes opium, cocaine, or a derivative of either substance, or methamphetamine, and ingestion of that substance causes the user's death, the defendant is guilty of second-degree murder. G.S. 14-17. If the drugs are not included in this list, supplying them and causing the user's death still may constitute this crime. See the note on Element (3)(a)(i) to "First-Degree Murder," above.

State v. Parlee, ___ N.C. App. ___, 703 S.E.2d 866 (2011), is a relatively recent case on point. In that case, the defendant was charged with second-degree murder for having proximately caused a murder by the unlawful distribution and ingestion of Oxymorphone. On appeal, the court held that there was sufficient evidence of malice where the victim and a friend approached the defendant to purchase prescription medication, the defendant sold them an Oxymorphone pill for $20.00, telling them that it was "pretty strong pain medication" and not to take a whole pill or "do anything destructive with it." *Id.* at 870. The defendant also told a friend that he liked Oxymorphone because it "messe[d]" him up. *Id.* The court reasoned that the jury could have reasonably inferred that the defendant knew Oxymorphone was an inherently dangerous drug and that he acted with malice when he supplied the pill. *Id.; see also* State v. Liner, 98 N.C. App. 600 (1990) (there was sufficient evidence of second-degree murder when a defendant supplied illegal drugs to a victim with knowledge that the drugs were inherently dangerous; the defendant witnessed two other people become violently ill after using the drugs in the defendant's presence).

Possible charges and convictions in a homicide involving impaired driving. When a defendant willfully violates the impaired driving laws and that violation is a proximate cause of death, at least three different homicide charges are possible, depending on the defendant's state of mind. The possible charges are: second-degree murder, involuntary manslaughter, and felony death by vehicle. As indicated in the notes on Element (3)(a)(i) to "First-Degree Murder," above, and on Element (3), above, second-degree murder is a possible charge only if evidence shows recklessness amounting to malice. To convict a defendant of involuntary manslaughter, there must be evidence that the defendant committed an unlawful act that does not amount to a felony and is not ordinarily dangerous to life or engaged in a culpably negligent act or omission. See "Involuntary Manslaughter," below, As discussed under "Criminal Negligence" in Chapter 1 (States of Mind), the violation of the impaired driving laws constitutes culpable negligence. The final possible charge, felony death by vehicle, is described below in this chapter. In this context, felony death by vehicle overlaps with involuntary manslaughter, allowing for conviction if the defendant's impaired driving proximately caused death. However, punishment for felony death by vehicle is a Class E felony whereas punishment for involuntary manslaughter is a Class F felony. As explained in the note below entitled "Multiple convictions and punishments," a defendant may not be convicted of both of those offenses.

Charging issues. See this note to "First-Degree Murder," above.

Greater and lesser-included offenses. See this note to "First-Degree Murder." Felony death by vehicle is not a lesser-included offense of second-degree murder based on a vehicular homicide. State v. Grice, 131 N.C. App. 48 (1998).

Multiple convictions and punishments. For purposes of double jeopardy, a second-degree murder conviction based on unlawful distribution of and ingestion of a controlled substance is not the same offense as sale or delivery of a controlled substance to a juvenile or possession with intent to sell or deliver a controlled substance, and thus a defendant may be convicted of both. State v. Parlee, ___ N.C. App. ___, 703 S.E.2d 866 (2011).

A defendant may be convicted and punished for both impaired driving and second-degree murder based on a vehicular homicide committed while driving while impaired. State v. Armstrong, ___ N.C. App. ___, 691 S.E.2d 433 (2010) (evidence of malice included the fact that the defendant drove with a revoked license and that he drove impaired after being convicted of impaired driving), *review allowed*, 364 N.C. 328 (2010); State v. McAllister, 138 N.C. App. 252 (2000). A defendant may not be sentenced for both involuntary manslaughter and felony death by vehicle arising out of the same death. State v. Davis, 198 N.C. App. 443, 452 (2009).

Proximate cause. See this note to "First-Degree Murder," above.

Attempted second-degree murder is not a crime. The crime of attempted second-degree murder does not exist. State v. Coble, 351 N.C. 448 (2000) (attempt requires that the defendant specifically intend to commit the underlying offense; it is logically impossible for a person to specifically intend to commit a form of murder which does not have as an element the specific intent to kill).

Defenses. Because specific intent to kill is not an element of this offense, voluntary intoxication is not a defense to this crime. State v. Harvell, 334 N.C. 356 (1993); State v. Bunn, 283 N.C. 444

(1973). See "Voluntary Intoxication" under "Failure of Proof or 'Negating' Defenses" in Chapter 2 (Bars and Defenses).

Related Offenses Not in This Chapter

See the offenses listed under "First-Degree Murder," above.

Murder of an Unborn Child

Statute

§ 14-23.1. Definition.

As used in this Article only, "unborn child" means a member of the species homo sapiens, at any stage of development, who is carried in the womb.

§ 14-23.2. Murder of an unborn child; penalty.

(a) A person who unlawfully causes the death of an unborn child is guilty of the separate offense of murder of an unborn child if the person does any one of the following:

(1) Willfully and maliciously commits an act with the intent to cause the death of the unborn child.

(2) Causes the death of the unborn child in perpetration or attempted perpetration of any of the criminal offenses set forth under G.S. 14-17.

(3) Commits an act causing the death of the unborn child that is inherently dangerous to human life and is done so recklessly and wantonly that it reflects disregard of life.

(b) Penalty.—An offense under:

(1) Subdivision (a)(1) or (a)(2) of this section shall be a Class A felony, and any person who commits such offense shall be punished with imprisonment in the State's prison for life without parole.

(2) Subdivision (a)(3) of this section shall be subject to the same sentence as if the person had been convicted of second degree murder pursuant to G.S. 14-17.

§ 14-23.7. Exceptions.

Nothing in this Article shall be construed to permit the prosecution under this Article of any of the following:

(1) Acts which cause the death of an unborn child if those acts were lawful, pursuant to the provisions of G.S. 14-45.1.

(2) Acts which are committed pursuant to usual and customary standards of medical practice during diagnostic testing or therapeutic treatment.

(3) Acts committed by a pregnant woman with respect to her own unborn child, including, but not limited to, acts which result in miscarriage or stillbirth by the woman. The following definitions shall apply in this section:

a. Miscarriage.—The interruption of the normal development of an unborn child, other than by a live birth, and which is not an induced abortion permitted under G.S. 14-45.1, resulting in the complete expulsion or extraction from a pregnant woman of the unborn child.

b. Stillbirth.—The death of an unborn child prior to the complete expulsion or extraction from a woman, irrespective of the duration of pregnancy and which is not an induced abortion permitted under G.S. 14-45.1.

§ 14-23.8. Knowledge not required.

Except for an offense under G.S. 14-23.2(a)(1), an offense under this Article does not require proof of either of the following:

(1) The person engaging in the conduct had knowledge or should have had knowledge that the victim of the underlying offense was pregnant.

(2) The defendant intended to cause the death of, or bodily injury to, the unborn child.

Elements

A person guilty of this offense

(1) unlawfully
(2) causes the death of an unborn child
(3) (a) by willfully and maliciously committing an act with the intent to cause the death of the unborn child,
  (b) in perpetration or attempted perpetration of any of the criminal offenses set forth under G.S. 14-17, *or*
  (c) commits an act causing the death of the unborn child that is inherently dangerous to human life and is done so recklessly and wantonly that it reflects disregard of life.

Punishment

If Elements (3)(a) or (b) are present, the offense is a Class A felony punished with life in prison without parole. G.S. 14-23.2(b). If Element (3)(c) is present, the offense is punished as a Class B2 felony. *Id.*

Notes

Generally. This crime was enacted in 2011 and applies to offenses committed on or after December 1, 2011. S.L. 2011-60, sec. 8.

Element (2). The term "unborn child" means "a member of the species homo sapiens, at any stage of development, who is carried in the womb." G.S. 14-23.1. For a discussion of causation as it generally applies in homicide law, see the note entitled, "Proximate cause" to "First-Degree Murder," above.

Element (3) generally. Elements (3)(a) through (c) are alternate ways to commit this offense. G.S. 14-23.8 provides that except for the Element (3)(a) version of this offense, this offense does not require proof that the person engaging in the conduct knew or should have known that the woman was pregnant or that the defendant intended to cause the death of the unborn child.

Element (3)(a). See "Willfully" and "Maliciously" in Chapter 1 (States of Mind).

Element (3)(b). It is not clear whether this element is meant to refer only to first- and second-degree murder as described in G.S. 14-17, only to the felonies identified in G.S. 14-17 that support first-degree felony murder, or both. For a discussion for first- and second-degree murder, see "First-Degree Murder" and "Second-Degree Murder," above. For a discussion of the felonies that support first-degree felony murder, see the note on Element (3)(c) to "First-Degree Murder," above.

Element (3)(c). This element seems to be similar to one of the forms of malice recognized by the homicide law and discussed in the note on Element (3)(a)(i) to "First-Degree Murder," above (discussing the three forms of malice recognized by homicide law). Because the statute only mentions "acts," it is not clear whether omissions are covered.

Criminal liability of the pregnant woman. The Session Law enacting this offense provides that it may not be used to impose criminal liability on an expectant mother who is the victim of acts of domestic violence which cause injury or death to her unborn child. S.L. 2011-60, sec. 4. The term "domestic violence" is defined by cross-reference to G.S. Chapter 50B. *Id.* See also the note entitled "Exceptions," immediately below.

Exceptions. The following acts are excluded from coverage by this offense:

- causing the death of an unborn child if the acts were lawful pursuant to G.S. 14-45.1 (when abortion is not unlawful);

- acts committed pursuant to usual and customary standards of medical practice during diagnostic testing or therapeutic treatment, or
- acts committed by a pregnant woman with respect to her own unborn child, including, but not limited to, acts which result in miscarriage or stillbirth.

G.S. 14-23.7. "Miscarriage" means the "interruption of the normal development of an unborn child, other than by a live birth, and which is not an induced abortion permitted under G.S. 14-45.1, resulting in the complete expulsion or extraction from a pregnant woman of the unborn child." G.S. 14-23.7. "Stillbirth" means the "death of an unborn child prior to the complete expulsion or extraction from a woman, irrespective of the duration of pregnancy and which is not an induced abortion permitted under G.S. 14-45.1." *Id.*

Multiple convictions and punishments. G.S. 14-23.2(a) states that murder of an unborn child is a "separate offense." This indicates a legislative intent that a defendant may be convicted of this offense and any other offense (such as a felonious assault on the woman) when based on the same conduct. This reading is confirmed by the Session Law, which states: "A prosecution for or conviction under this act is not a bar to conviction of or punishment for any other crime committed by the defendant as part of the same conduct." S.L. 2011-60, sec. 7.

Related Offenses Not in This Chapter

"Battery on an Unborn Child" (Chapter 7)
"Assault Inflicting Serious Bodily Injury on an Unborn Child" (Chapter 7)
"Sale or Delivery of a Controlled Substance to a Pregnant Female" (Chapter 27)
G.S. 14-44. Using drugs or instruments to destroy unborn child.
G.S. 14-45. Using drugs or instruments to produce miscarriage or injure pregnant woman.
G.S. 14-46. Concealing birth of a child.

Manslaughter

Voluntary Manslaughter

Statute

Voluntary manslaughter is a common law offense, *see* State v. Rainey, 154 N.C. App. 282, 288 (2002), for which punishment is prescribed by statute, G.S. 14-18.

Elements

A person guilty of this offense

(1) kills
(2) another living human being
(3) without malice.

Punishment

Class D felony. G.S. 14-18.

Notes

Elements (1) and (2). See the discussion of these elements to "First-Degree Murder," above.

Element (3) generally. Unlike second-degree murder, voluntary manslaughter is a killing without malice. For a discussion of malice, see the note on Element (3)(a)(i) to "First-Degree Murder" and the note on Element (3) to "Second-Degree Murder," both above. The law recognizes two types of unlawful killings that result from intentional conduct but might not involve malice:

(1) a killing committed in the sudden heat of passion caused by adequate provocation that would arouse an ordinary person beyond his or her power of control, State v. McLawhorn, 270 N.C. 622 (1967), and
(2) a killing committed during the exercise of an "imperfect" right of self-defense, State v. Norris, 303 N.C. 526 (1981); State v. Wilkerson, 295 N.C. 559, 579 (1978).

These circumstances do not completely justify or excuse a killing. Rather, they displace the element of malice, reducing the offense from second-degree murder to voluntary manslaughter. Classic examples of voluntary manslaughter are a killing committed by a defendant who discovers his or her spouse in an act of adultery and a killing caused by the use of excessive force in self-defense.

"Sudden heat of passion" means emotions such as "rage, anger, hatred, furious resentment, or terror, rendering the mind incapable of cool reflection." State v. Huggins, 338 N.C. 494 (1994). A killing is done in the sudden heat of passion only if it is done before the defendant has had time to cool down. For example, a killing committed in anger aroused during a sudden, mutual fight will reduce a homicide to voluntary manslaughter. State v. Rummage, 280 N.C. 51 (1971); State v. Baldwin, 152 N.C. 822 (1910). But if a person arms himself or herself in expectation of being assaulted and then kills during the assault, the person has not killed in the sudden heat of passion. State v. Hogue, 51 N.C. 381 (1859). A killing committed when the defendant finds his or her spouse in an act of adultery is manslaughter if done at the time the act is discovered in progress or immediately thereafter, but not when there has been time for the defendant's passion to cool. State v. Ward, 286 N.C. 304 (1974); State v. Samuel, 48 N.C. 74 (1855); State v. Collins, 64 N.C. App. 656 (1983). While finding one's spouse in an act of adultery is adequate provocation, mere discovery of the fact of adultery is not. State v. John, 30 N.C. 330 (1848); State v. Simonovich, ___ N.C. App. ___, 688 S.E.2d 67, 70–72 (2010) (an instruction on voluntary manslaughter was not required when, although the defendant knew his wife was having sex with other men and she threatened to continue this behavior, he did not find her in the act of intercourse or in circumstances clearly indicating that intercourse had just occurred; additionally, the defendant testified that he strangled his wife to quiet her).

An assault against a defendant or a close relative of the defendant is recognized as adequate provocation. State v. Jones, 299 N.C. 103 (1979). Mere words or insulting gestures—such as throwing a cigarette butt at a defendant—that are not accompanied by threatening conduct are not adequate provocation to reduce murder to manslaughter. State v. Watson, 287 N.C. 147 (1975); State v. Hightower, 226 N.C. 62 (1946); State v. Owens, 65 N.C. App. 107 (1983). Trespass is not by itself adequate provocation for a killing, and the killing of a mere trespasser is murder rather than manslaughter. State v. Brandon, 53 N.C. 463 (1862).

The distress that prompts a person to commit a mercy killing to end an ill relative's extreme physical suffering does not constitute adequate provocation; thus a mercy killing is properly categorized as first-degree murder rather than voluntary manslaughter. State v. Forrest, 321 N.C. 186 (1987).

Voluntary manslaughter is committed in the exercise of imperfect self-defense when a person uses excessive force in self-defense or is an aggressor, without murderous intent, in bringing on a fight or difficulty. State v. Norris, 303 N.C. 526 (1981); State v. Wilkerson, 295 N.C. 559 (1978); State v. Rummage, 280 N.C. 51 (1971). See the discussion of self-defense in Chapter 2 (Bars and Defenses).

Proximate cause. See this note to "First-Degree Murder," above.

Attempted voluntary manslaughter. Attempted voluntary manslaughter is a crime and is a lesser-included offense of attempted first-degree murder. State v. Hames, 170 N.C. App. 312 (2005).

At least two North Carolina Court of Appeals cases have held that a jury's conclusion that a defendant did not act with intent to kill in connection with an assault charge precludes a conviction of attempted voluntary manslaughter. *Id.* at 323 (a defendant charged with assault with a deadly weapon with intent to kill inflicting serious injury and attempted voluntary manslaughter of the same victim may not be convicted of attempted manslaughter and assault with a deadly weapon inflicting serious injury; having found that the defendant did not have the intent to kill for the charged felonious assault, a guilty verdict on the lesser assault is inconsistent with a guilty verdict on attempted voluntary manslaughter); State v. Chang Yang, 174 N.C. App. 755, 761–62 (2005) (guilty verdicts for assault with a deadly weapon inflicting serious injury and attempted voluntary manslaughter concerning the same victim are mutually exclusive when the jury rejected a felonious assault charge involving an intent to kill). However, these decisions are questionable in light of *State v. Mumford*, 364 N.C. 394 (2010) (holding that because a not guilty verdict under G.S. 20-138.1 (impaired driving) and a guilty verdict under G.S. 20-141.4(a3) (felony serious injury by vehicle) were merely inconsistent, the trial court did not err by accepting the verdict where it was supported with sufficient evidence; to require reversal, the verdicts would have to be both inconsistent and legally contradictory, also referred to as mutually exclusive verdicts (for example, guilty verdicts of embezzlement and obtaining property by false pretenses; the verdicts are mutually exclusive because property cannot be obtained simultaneously pursuant to both lawful and unlawful means)).

Aiding and abetting voluntary manslaughter. *State v. Coble*, 351 N.C. 448 (2000) (attempted second-degree murder is not a crime), does not change the rule that a defendant may be convicted of aiding and abetting voluntary manslaughter. State v. Shaw, 164 N.C. App. 723 (2004).

Charging issues. See this note to "First-Degree Murder," above.

Multiple convictions and punishments. Attempted voluntary manslaughter is a lesser-included offense of a felonious assault offense that includes an element of intent to kill, and the defendant may not be convicted of both. *Chang Yang*, 174 N.C. App. at 762–63.

Relation to other offenses. See the discussion in the note entitled "Greater and lesser-included offenses" under "First-Degree Murder," above.

Related Offenses Not in This Chapter

See the offenses listed under "First-Degree Murder," above.

Voluntary Manslaughter of an Unborn Child

Statute

See G.S. 14-23.1, reproduced under "Murder of an Unborn Child," above.

§ 14-23.3. Voluntary manslaughter of an unborn child; penalty.

(a) A person is guilty of the separate offense of voluntary manslaughter of an unborn child if the person unlawfully causes the death of an unborn child by an act that would be voluntary manslaughter if it resulted in the death of the mother.

(b) Penalty.—Any person who commits an offense under this section shall be guilty of a Class D felony.

See G.S. 14-23.7 and 14-23.8, reproduced under "Murder of an Unborn Child," above.

Elements

A person guilty of this offense

(1) unlawfully
(2) causes the death of an unborn child

(3) by an act that would be voluntary manslaughter if it resulted in the death of the mother.

Punishment

Class D felony. G.S. 14-23.3(b).

Notes

Generally. This crime was enacted in 2011 and applies to offenses committed on or after December 1, 2011. S.L. 2011-60, sec. 8.

Element (2). See this note to "Murder of an Unborn Child," above.

Element (3). For a discussion of what constitutes voluntary manslaughter, see "Voluntary Manslaughter," above. G.S. 14-23.8 provides that this offense does not require proof that the person engaging in the conduct knew or should have known that the woman was pregnant or that the defendant intended to cause the death of the unborn child.

Criminal liability of the pregnant woman. See this note to "Murder of an Unborn Child."

Exceptions. See this note to "Murder of an Unborn Child," above.

Multiple convictions and punishments. G.S. 14-23.3(a) states that voluntary manslaughter of an unborn child is a "separate offense." This indicates a legislative intent that a defendant may be convicted of this offense and any other offense (such as a felonious assault on the woman) when based on the same conduct. This reading is confirmed by the Session Law, which states: "A prosecution for or conviction under this act is not a bar to conviction of or punishment for any other crime committed by the defendant as part of the same conduct." S.L. 2011-60, sec. 7.

Related Offenses Not in This Chapter

See the offenses listed under "Murder of an Unborn Child," above.

Involuntary Manslaughter

Statute

Involuntary manslaughter is a common law offense, State v. Davis, 198 N.C. App. 443, 446 (2009), the punishment for which is prescribed by statute, G.S. 14-18.

Elements

A person guilty of this offense

(1) kills
(2) another living human being
(3) (a) by an unlawful act that does not amount to a felony and is not ordinarily dangerous to life *or*
    (b) by a culpably negligent act or omission.

Punishment

Class F felony. G.S. 14-18.

Notes

Generally. The key feature of involuntary manslaughter is that it involves an unintentional killing. State v. Fritsch, 351 N.C. 373, 380 (2000); State v. Greene, 314 N.C. 649, 651 (1985); N.C. PATTERN JURY INSTRUCTIONS—CRIM. 206.50. It has been defined as an unlawful killing without malice, without premeditation and deliberation, and without an intent to kill or inflict serious bodily injury. *See, e.g.,* State v. Powell, 336 N.C. 762, 767(1994); *Greene,* 314 N.C. at 651.

For the elements of involuntary manslaughter, see, for example, *State v. Hudson*, 345 N.C. 729, 733 (1997), and *Greene*, 314 N.C. at 651.

Elements (1) and (2). See the notes on these elements to "First-Degree Murder," above.

Element (3) generally. The killing must be unlawful; Elements (3)(a) and (b) are alternative grounds on which the prosecution may allege and prove unlawfulness. *Greene*, 314 N.C. at 651.

Element (3)(a). An example of an act that would fall within this element is a slap to the head (simple assault, a misdemeanor) of a victim who dies as a result of the contact.

Element (3)(b). For a detailed discussion of culpable negligence, see "Criminal Negligence" in Chapter 1 (States of Mind). As discussed there, criminal negligence means a carelessness or recklessness that shows a thoughtless disregard of consequences or a heedless indifference to the safety and rights of others. By contrast, the malice required for second-degree murder includes commission of an inherently dangerous act in such a reckless and wanton manner as to manifest a mind utterly without regard for human life and social duty and deliberately bent on mischief. *See* the note on Element (3)(a)(i) to "First-Degree Murder" (defining malice for homicide crimes), above. Thus, courts have stated that "[t]he difference between involuntary manslaughter and second-degree murder is one of the degree of risk and recklessness involved." State v. Ray, 149 N.C. App. 137, 148 (2002); *see also* State v. Rich, 351 N.C. 386, 395 (2000).

This element includes both culpably negligent acts and culpably negligent omissions. *See, e.g.,* State v. Phillips, 328 N.C. 1, 19–20 (1991); N.C. PATTERN JURY INSTRUCTIONS—CRIM. 206.50, nn. 1–2. To be liable for involuntary manslaughter for failing to act to prevent harm to a victim, a defendant must have a legal duty to protect the victim. Thus, a parent who fails to feed a child is guilty of involuntary manslaughter if the child dies of starvation, because the law imposes a duty on parents to care for their children. State v. Fritsch, 351 N.C. 373, 380–82 (2000) (evidence was sufficient to establish involuntary manslaughter for failure to feed child); State v. Mason, 18 N.C. App. 433 (1973). However, if the parent intentionally fails to feed the child, the crime is first-degree murder by starvation. See "First-Degree Murder," above.

Proximate cause. See this note under "First-Degree Murder," above, for a discussion of proximate cause. For involuntary manslaughter, as with all homicides, the defendant's act must proximately cause the victim's death. State v. Bruton, 344 N.C. 381, 393 (1996) (even if the defendant was culpably negligent in discharging his weapon, he was not entitled to a jury instruction on involuntary manslaughter because his act did not proximately cause the victim's death; rather, the evidence showed that a co-defendant intentionally fired the shot which killed the victim). As discussed in the note mentioned above, a proximate cause is a cause without which the victim's death would not have occurred; it need not have been the only cause, nor the last or nearest cause of death. Although some cases suggest that forseeability is not an essential part of proximate cause when a homicide results from an intentional assault, see the note on "Proximate cause" under "First-Degree Murder," above, at least one case holds that it is an essential part of proximate cause in an involuntary manslaughter case. However, the requirement of forseeability articulated by that case, *State v. Cole*, 343 N.C. 399, 416 (1996), is not very stringent. It does not require that the defendant must have foreseen the exact injury incurred; rather, it means that in the exercise of reasonable care, the defendant might have foreseen that some injury would result from his or her act or omission, or that consequences of a generally injurious nature might have been expected. *Id.* In *Cole*, the defendant was convicted of involuntary manslaughter in connection with having stabbed a victim twice. On appeal, he argued that the victim's death was not foreseeable. The court disagreed, concluding that it was not necessary that the defendant foresee that the victim would die from the assault, only that he foresee some serious injury. *Id.* Because the defendant was aware of the victim's health (she had coronary atherosclerosis; cause of death was cardiac arrhythmia precipitated by stress from the defendant's attack), it was reasonable that he would have foreseen that two stab wounds would be injurious to her. *Id.*

Possible charges in homicide involving impaired driving offense. See this note to "Second-Degree Murder," above.

Charging issues. See this note to "First-Degree Murder," above.

Greater and lesser-included offenses. Neither felony death by vehicle nor impaired driving are lesser-included offenses of involuntary manslaughter. State v. Lovett, 119 N.C. App. 689, 694 (1995) (felony death by vehicle); State v. Davis, 198 N.C. App. 443 (2009) (a defendant may be sentenced for both involuntary manslaughter and impaired driving arising out of the same incident); State v. Hudson, 345 N.C. 729, 733 (1997) (impaired boating includes an element not included in involuntary manslaughter and therefore is not a lesser-included offense of involuntary manslaughter).

Multiple convictions and punishments. G.S. 20-141.4(c) provides that (1) no person who has been placed in jeopardy for death by vehicle may be prosecuted for manslaughter arising out of the same death and (2) no person who has been placed in jeopardy for manslaughter may be prosecuted for death by vehicle arising out of the same death. *See also Davis*, 198 N.C. App. 443 (a defendant may not be sentenced for both involuntary manslaughter and felony death by vehicle arising out of the same death).

A defendant may be sentenced for both involuntary manslaughter and impaired driving arising out of the same incident. *Id; see also Hudson*, 345 N.C. at 734 (impaired boating includes an element not included in involuntary manslaughter and therefore is not a lesser-included offense of involuntary manslaughter).

Submitting involuntary manslaughter to the jury as a lesser-included offense of first-degree murder. Many defendants charged with first-degree murder ask for a jury instruction on the lesser-included offense of involuntary manslaughter. When there is no evidence that the killing was unintentional, such an instruction is not proper. State v. Smith, 351 N.C. 251, 268 (2000) (the defendant was not entitled to an instruction on involuntary manslaughter; the defendant had knowledge of and experience with farm pesticides, obtained the deadly pesticide, made up a story as to why he needed it, showed it to others, put it in his children's Kool-Aid, and as his children lay dying or ill, failed to say anything about why they were sick); State v. Eubanks, 151 N.C. App. 499, 503–04 (2002) (the trial court did not err by failing to submit involuntary manslaughter; although the gun was old and might have been prone to accidental discharge, there was no evidence that killing was unintentional); State v. Stafford, 150 N.C. App. 566, 572 (2002) (notwithstanding the defendant's evidence that he did not fire or possess the gun, an instruction on involuntary manslaughter was not required when the State's evidence showed that the defendant intentionally shot the victim); State v. Evans, 149 N.C. App. 767, 775–76 (2002) (instruction not warranted when the defendant's evidence—that he shot because he "was scared because of the alcohol"—indicated that the shooting was deliberate, not accidental); see also the note "Generally," above.

An instruction on involuntary manslaughter as a lesser-included offense of murder is not proper when the evidence shows that the victim was killed in the course of a felony supporting a theory of felony murder. State v. Ray, 149 N.C. App. 137, 148 (2002); State v. Cunningham, 140 N.C. App. 315, 326 (2000) (the victim was killed during a felonious breaking or entering; even if the defendant did not intend to kill the victim or the gun went off accidentally, this is irrelevant to felony murder; accordingly, the trial court was not required to submit involuntary manslaughter); see also Element (3)(a) above. But when the evidence is conflicting as to the underlying felony, an instruction on involuntary manslaughter may be required. State v. Thomas, 325 N.C. 583 (1989) (instruction required).

Related Offenses Not in This Chapter

See the offenses listed under "First-Degree Murder," above.

Involuntary Manslaughter of an Unborn Child

Statute

See G.S. 14-23.1, reproduced under "Murder of an Unborn Child," above.

> **§ 14-23.4. Involuntary manslaughter of an unborn child; penalty.**
>
> (a) A person is guilty of the separate offense of involuntary manslaughter of an unborn child if the person unlawfully causes the death of an unborn child by an act that would be involuntary manslaughter if it resulted in the death of the mother.
>
> (b) Penalty.—Any person who commits an offense under this section shall be guilty of a Class F felony.

See G.S. 14-23.7 and 14-23.8, reproduced under "Murder of an Unborn Child," above.

Elements

A person guilty of this offense

(1) unlawfully
(2) causes the death of an unborn child
(3) by an act that would be involuntary manslaughter if it resulted in the death of the mother.

Punishment

Class F felony. G.S. 14-23.4(b).

Notes

Generally. This crime was enacted in 2011 and applies to offenses committed on or after December 1, 2011. S.L. 2011-60, sec. 8.

Element (2). See this note to "Murder of an Unborn Child," above.

Element (3). For a discussion of what constitutes involuntary manslaughter, see "Involuntary Manslaughter," above. G.S. 14-23.8 provides that this offense does not require proof that the person engaging in the conduct knew or should have known that the woman was pregnant or that the defendant intended to cause the death of the unborn child.

Criminal liability of the pregnant woman. See this note to "Murder of an Unborn Child," above.

Exceptions. See this note to "Murder of an Unborn Child," above.

Multiple convictions and punishments. G.S. 14-23.4(a) states that voluntary manslaughter of an unborn child is a "separate offense." This indicates a legislative intent that a defendant may be convicted of this offense and any other offense (such as a felonious assault on the woman) when based on the same conduct. This reading is confirmed by the Session Law, which states: "A prosecution for or conviction under this act is not a bar to conviction of or punishment for any other crime committed by the defendant as part of the same conduct." S.L. 2011-60, sec. 7.

Related Offenses Not in This Chapter

See the offenses listed under "Murder of an Unborn Child," above.

Death by Vehicle

Statute

§20-141.4. Felony and misdemeanor death by vehicle; felony serious injury by vehicle; aggravated offenses; repeat felony death by vehicle.

(a) Repealed by Session Laws 1983, c. 435, s. 27.

(a1) Felony Death by Vehicle.—A person commits the offense of felony death by vehicle if:

(1) The person unintentionally causes the death of another person,
(2) The person was engaged in the offense of impaired driving under G.S. 20-138.1 or G.S. 20-138.2, and
(3) The commission of the offense in subdivision (2) of this subsection is the proximate cause of the death.

(a2) Misdemeanor Death by Vehicle.—A person commits the offense of misdemeanor death by vehicle if:

(1) The person unintentionally causes the death of another person,
(2) The person was engaged in the violation of any State law or local ordinance applying to the operation or use of a vehicle or to the regulation of traffic, other than impaired driving under G.S. 20-138.1, and
(3) The commission of the offense in subdivision (2) of this subsection is the proximate cause of the death.

Subsections (a3) and (a4) are not reproduced here.

(a5) Aggravated Felony Death by Vehicle.—A person commits the offense of aggravated felony death by vehicle if:

(1) The person unintentionally causes the death of another person,
(2) The person was engaged in the offense of impaired driving under G.S. 20-138.1 or G.S. 20-138.2,
(3) The commission of the offense in subdivision (2) of this subsection is the proximate cause of the death, and
(4) The person has a previous conviction involving impaired driving, as defined in G.S. 20-4.01(24a), within seven years of the date of the offense.

(a6) Repeat Felony Death by Vehicle Offender.—A person commits the offense of repeat felony death by vehicle if:

(1) The person commits an offense under subsection (a1) or subsection (a5) of this section; and
(2) The person has a previous conviction under:
   a. Subsection (a1) of this section;
   b. Subsection (a5) of this section; or
   c. G.S. 14-17 or G.S. 14-18, and the basis of the conviction was the unintentional death of another person while engaged in the offense of impaired driving under G.S. 20-138.1 or G.S. 20-138.2.

   The pleading and proof of previous convictions shall be in accordance with the provisions of G.S. 15A-928.

   A person convicted under this subsection shall be subject to the same sentence as if the person had been convicted of second degree murder.

(b) Punishments.—Unless the conduct is covered under some other provision of law providing greater punishment, the following classifications apply to the offenses set forth in this section:

(1) Aggravated felony death by vehicle is a Class D felony.
(2) Felony death by vehicle is a Class E felony.
(3) Aggravated felony serious injury by vehicle is a Class E felony.
(4) Felony serious injury by vehicle is a Class F felony.
(5) Misdemeanor death by vehicle is a Class A1 misdemeanor.

(c) No Double Prosecutions.—No person who has been placed in jeopardy upon a charge of death by vehicle may be prosecuted for the offense of manslaughter arising out of the same death; and no person who has been placed in jeopardy upon a charge of manslaughter may be prosecuted for death by vehicle arising out of the same death.

Felony Death by Vehicle

Statute

See G.S. 20-141.4(a1), reproduced above.

Elements

A person guilty of this offense

(1) kills
(2) another living human being
(3) unintentionally,
(4) while engaged in the offense of
  (a) impaired driving under G.S. 20-138.1 *or*
  (b) impaired driving in a commercial vehicle under G.S. 20-138.2, *and*
(5) commission of the impaired driving offense is the proximate cause of death.

Punishment

Class E felony. G.S. 20-141.4(b)(2).

Notes

Generally. The statute covers unintentional killings committed when the defendant drives a vehicle while impaired. To convict on this charge, it is not necessary to prove reckless or careless driving or malice.

Elements (1) and (2). See the notes to these elements to "First-Degree Murder," above.

Element (4). See "Impaired Driving" and "Impaired Driving in a Commercial Vehicle" in Chapter 28 (Motor Vehicle Offenses).

Element (5). As in manslaughter and murder, a defendant is guilty of death by vehicle only if the defendant's act—in this case, impaired driving—is the proximate cause of death. See the note "Proximate cause" under "First-Degree Murder," above, for an explanation of proximate cause.

Possible charges in homicide involving impaired driving offense. See this note to "Second-Degree Murder," above.

Charging issues. See this note to "First-Degree Murder," above.

Greater and lesser-included offenses. This offense is not a lesser-included offense of involuntary manslaughter, State v. Lovett, 119 N.C. App. 689, 694 (1995); State v. Williams, 90 N.C. App. 614, 621 (1988), or second-degree murder, State v. Grice, 131 N.C. App. 48, 52 (1998). Because misdemeanor death by vehicle involves death resulting from a violation other than impaired driving, it is not a lesser-included offense of felony death by vehicle. See "Misdemeanor Death by Vehicle," below.

Multiple convictions and punishments. G.S. 20-141.4(b), the punishment provision for all death by vehicle offenses except repeat felony death by vehicle, provides, in part, that unless the conduct is covered under some other provision of law providing greater punishment, aggravated felony death by vehicle is a Class D felony, felony death by vehicle is a Class E felony, and misdemeanor death by vehicle is a Class A1 misdemeanor. Thus, a defendant may not be punished for one of these death by vehicle offense when the defendant also is convicted for an offense carrying a greater punishment and both offenses are based on the same conduct. State v. Davis, 364 N.C. 297, 303 (2010) (the trial court erred by imposing punishment for felony death by vehicle (Class E felony) and second-degree murder (Class B2 felony)).

G.S. 20-141.4(c) provides that (1) no person who has been placed in jeopardy for death by vehicle may be prosecuted for manslaughter arising out of the same death and (2) no person who has been placed in jeopardy for manslaughter may be prosecuted for death by vehicle arising out of the same death. *See also* State v. Davis, 198 N.C. App. 443 (2009) (a defendant may not be sentenced for both involuntary manslaughter and felony death by vehicle arising out of the same death).

Because driving while impaired is a lesser-included offense of felony death by vehicle, a defendant may not be sentenced for both felony death by vehicle and driving while impaired. *Id.*

Relation to other offenses. While an unintentional killing of a human being proximately caused by impaired driving in violation of G.S. 20-138.1 may be both involuntary manslaughter and felony death by vehicle, involuntary manslaughter is a broader offense; felony death by vehicle is restricted to deaths proximately caused by driving while impaired. By contrast, the culpable negligence element of involuntary manslaughter need not consist of driving while impaired. *Davis,* 198 N.C. App. at 446. However, felony death by vehicle is punished as a Class E felony and involuntary manslaughter is punished as a Class F felony.

Related Offenses Not in This Chapter

"Felony Serious Injury by a Vehicle" (Chapter 28)
"Aggravated Felony Serious Injury by a Vehicle" (Chapter 28)
"Felony Speeding to Elude Arrest" (Chapter 28)
"Impaired Driving" (Chapter 28)
"Impaired Driving in a Commercial Vehicle" (Chapter 28)
"Misdemeanor Speeding to Elude Arrest" (Chapter 28)

Aggravated Felony Death by Vehicle

Statute

See G.S. 20-141.4(a5), reproduced above.

Elements

A person guilty of this offense

(1) kills
(2) another living human being
(3) unintentionally,
(4) while engaged in the offense of
    (a) impaired driving under G.S. 20-138.1 *or*
    (b) impaired driving in a commercial vehicle under G.S. 20-138.2, *and*
(5) commission of the impaired driving offense is the proximate cause of death *and*
(6) the person has a previous conviction involving impaired driving within seven years of the date of the offense.

Punishment

Class D felony. G.S. 20-141.4(b)(1).

Notes

Generally. This offense is the same as "Felony Death by Vehicle" except that this offense includes a sixth element requiring that the person have a specified prior conviction. Thus, the notes to that offense apply here as well.

Element (6). G.S. 20-4.01(24a) defines offenses involving impaired driving. They include:

- impaired driving;
- habitual impaired driving;
- impaired driving in commercial vehicle;
- death by vehicle under G.S. 20-141.4 based on impaired driving;
- first-degree or second-degree murder under G.S. 14-17 based on impaired driving;
- involuntary manslaughter under G.S. 14-18 based on impaired driving; and
- substantially similar offenses committed in another state or jurisdiction.

For more information, see the note on Element (5) to "Habitual Impaired Driving" in Chapter 28 (Motor Vehicle Offenses).

Related Offenses Not in This Chapter

See the offenses listed under "Felony Death by Vehicle," above.

Repeat Felony Death by Vehicle

Statute

See G.S. 20-141.4(a6), reproduced above.

Elements

A person guilty of this offense

(1) commits the offense of
  (a) felony death by vehicle *or*
  (b) aggravated felony death by vehicle *and*
(2) has a previous conviction for
  (a) felony death by vehicle,
  (b) aggravated felony death by vehicle,
  (c) first- or second-degree murder, when the basis of the murder conviction was the unintentional death of another person while engaged in the offense of impaired driving under G.S. 20-138.1 or impaired driving in commercial vehicle under G.S. 20-138.2, *or*
  (d) voluntary or involuntary manslaughter, when the basis of the manslaughter conviction was the unintentional death of another person while engaged in the offense of impaired driving under G.S. 20-138.1 or impaired driving in commercial vehicle under G.S. 20-138.2.

Punishment

Class B2 felony. G.S. 20-141(a6); G.S. 14-17.

Notes

Element (2) generally. It appears that a prior conviction will satisfy this element, no matter when the conviction occurred. G.S. 20-141.4(a6) provides that the pleading and proof of previous convictions must be in accordance with the provisions of G.S. 15A-928.

Element (2)(a). See "Felony Death by Vehicle," above.

Element (2)(b). See "Aggravated Felony Death by Vehicle," above.

Elements (2)(c) and (d). See "First-Degree Murder," "Second-Degree Murder," "Voluntary Manslaughter," and "Involuntary Manslaughter," above. See the note on Element (4) to "Felony Death by Vehicle," above.

Charging issues. See this note to "First-Degree Murder," above.

Multiple convictions and punishments. Unlike the other offenses in G.S. 20-141.4, the punishment provision for repeat felony death by vehicle is in G.S. 20-141.4(a6), not G.S. 20-141.4(b). Thus, the limitation on multiple convictions imposed in subsection (b) and discussed in this note to "Felony Death by Vehicle" does not appear to apply to repeat felony death by vehicle.

Related Offenses Not in This Chapter

See the offenses listed under "Felony Death by Vehicle," above.

Misdemeanor Death by Vehicle

Statute

See G.S. 20-141.4(a2), reproduced above.

Elements

A person guilty of this offense

(1) kills
(2) another living human being
(3) unintentionally,
(4) while committing a violation of any state law or local ordinance applying to the operation and use of a vehicle or to the regulation of traffic, other than impaired driving under G.S. 20-138.1, *and*
(5) commission of that offense is the proximate cause of death.

Punishment

Class A1 misdemeanor. G.S. 20-141.4(b)(5).

Notes

Generally. This statute covers unintentional killings committed while the defendant operates a vehicle in violation of either state law or local ordinance. To convict for this crime, it is not necessary to prove reckless or careless driving or malice.

Elements (1) and (2). See the notes on these elements to "First-Degree Murder," above.

Element (5). See the note "Proximate cause" to "First-Degree Murder," above.

Proving violation of local ordinances. See the provisions of G.S. 160A-79 and G.S. 153A-50 on pleading and proving a city or county ordinance.

Charging issues. See this note to "First-Degree Murder," above.

Greater and lesser-included offenses. This offense is a lesser-included offense of involuntary manslaughter but not of felony death by vehicle. See the note "Greater and lesser-included offenses" under "Felony Death by Vehicle," above.

Multiple convictions and punishments. See this note to "Felony Death by Vehicle," above.

Related Offenses Not in This Chapter

See the offenses in Chapter 28 (Motor Vehicle Offenses).

7

Assaults

7 Assaults

Simple Assault

Statute

§14-33. Misdemeanor assaults, batteries, and affrays, simple and aggravated; punishments.

(a) Any person who commits a simple assault or a simple assault and battery or participates in a simple affray is guilty of a Class 2 misdemeanor.

(b) Unless his conduct is covered under some other provision of law providing greater punishment, any person who commits any assault, assault and battery, or affray is guilty of a Class 1 misdemeanor if, in the course of the assault, assault and battery, or affray, he:

(1) through (3) Repealed by Session Laws 1995, c. 507, s. 19.5(b);
(4) through (7) Repealed by Session Laws 1991, c. 525, s. 1;
(8) Repealed by Session Laws 1995, c. 507, s. 19.5(b);
(9) Commits an assault and battery against a sports official when the sports official is discharging or attempting to discharge official duties at a sports event, or immediately after the sports event at which the sports official discharged official duties. A "sports official" is a person at a sports event who enforces the rules of the event, such as an umpire or referee, or a person who supervises the participants, such as a coach. A "sports event" includes any interscholastic or intramural athletic activity in a primary, middle, junior high, or high school, college, or university, any organized athletic activity sponsored by a community, business, or nonprofit organization, any athletic activity that is a professional or semiprofessional event, and any other organized athletic activity in the State.

(c) Unless the conduct is covered under some other provision of law providing greater punishment, any person who commits any assault, assault and battery, or affray is guilty of a Class A1 misdemeanor if, in the course of the assault, assault and battery, or affray, he or she:

(1) Inflicts serious injury upon another person or uses a deadly weapon;
(2) Assaults a female, he being a male person at least 18 years of age;
(3) Assaults a child under the age of 12 years;
(4) Assaults an officer or employee of the State or any political subdivision of the State, when the officer or employee is discharging or attempting to discharge his official duties;
(5) Repealed by Session Laws 1999-105, s. 1, effective December 1, 1999; or
(6) Assaults a school employee or school volunteer when the employee or volunteer is discharging or attempting to discharge his or her duties as an employee or volunteer, or assaults a school employee or school volunteer as a result of the discharge or attempt to discharge that individual's duties as a

school employee or school volunteer. For purposes of this subdivision, the following definitions shall apply:

a. "Duties" means:
   1. All activities on school property;
   2. All activities, wherever occurring, during a school authorized event or the accompanying of students to or from that event; and
   3. All activities relating to the operation of school transportation.

b. "Employee" or "volunteer" means:
   1. An employee of a local board of education; or a charter school authorized under G.S. 115C-238.29D, or a nonpublic school which has filed intent to operate under Part 1 or Part 2 of Article 39 of Chapter 115C of the General Statutes;
   2. An independent contractor or an employee of an independent contractor of a local board of education, charter school authorized under G.S. 115C-238.29D, or a nonpublic school which has filed intent to operate under Part 1 or Part 2 of Article 39 of Chapter 115C of the General Statutes, if the independent contractor carries out duties customarily performed by employees of the school; and
   3. An adult who volunteers his or her services or presence at any school activity and is under the supervision of an individual listed in sub-sub-subdivision 1. or 2. of this sub-subdivision.

(7) Assaults a public transit operator, including a public employee or a private contractor employed as a public transit operator, when the operator is discharging or attempting to discharge his or her duties.

(8) Assaults a company police officer certified pursuant to the provisions of Chapter 74E of the General Statutes or a campus police officer certified pursuant to the provisions of Chapter 74G, Chapter 17C, or Chapter 116 of the General Statutes in the performance of that person's duties.

(d) Any person who, in the course of an assault, assault and battery, or affray, inflicts serious injury upon another person, or uses a deadly weapon, in violation of subdivision (c)(1) of this section, on a person with whom the person has a personal relationship, and in the presence of a minor, is guilty of a Class A1 misdemeanor. A person convicted under this subsection, who is sentenced to a community punishment, shall be placed on supervised probation in addition to any other punishment imposed by the court.

A person committing a second or subsequent violation of this subsection shall be sentenced to an active punishment of no less than 30 days in addition to any other punishment imposed by the court.

The following definitions apply to this subsection:

(1) "Personal relationship" is as defined in G.S. 50B-1(b).

(2) "In the presence of a minor" means that the minor was in a position to have observed the assault.

(3) "Minor" is any person under the age of 18 years who is residing with or is under the care and supervision of, and who has a personal relationship with, the person assaulted or the person committing the assault.

Elements

A person guilty of this offense

(1) commits an assault

(2) on another.

Punishment

Class 2 misdemeanor. G.S. 14-33(a).

Notes

Generally. Although this offense is commonly known as "assault" it actually includes both assaults and batteries, both of which are discussed below. See the note on Element (1) and the note entitled "Battery," both below.

Element (1). Assault is not defined by statute; instead, it is defined by common law. State v. Roberts, 270 N.C. 655, 658 (1967); State v. Corbett, 196 N.C. App. 508, 511 (2009). North Carolina recognizes two forms of assault. The first form is an overt act or attempt or the unequivocal appearance of attempt, with force and violence, to immediately physically injure another person, with the show of force or menace of violence being sufficient to put a reasonable person in fear of immediate physical injury. *Roberts*, 270 N.C. at 658 (insufficient evidence of assault); State v. Spellman, 167 N.C. App. 374, 384 (2004); N.C. PATTERN JURY INSTRUCTIONS—CRIM. 208.40. To constitute an assault, it is not necessary that the victim be placed in fear; it is enough if the act was sufficient to put a reasonable person in fear of immediate bodily harm. State v. Starr, ___ N.C. App. ___, 703 S.E.2d 876 (2011). This definition places emphasis on the intent or state of mind of the accused. *Roberts*, 270 N.C. at 658; State v. McDaniel, 111 N.C. App. 888, 890 (1993). While intent is an essential element of this form of assault, it may be implied from criminal negligence (also called culpable negligence) if the injury or fear caused is the direct result of intentional acts done under circumstances showing a reckless disregard for the safety of others and a willingness to inflict injury. State v. Jones, 353 N.C. 159, 165 (2000); *Spellman*, 167 N.C. App. at 384. Committing the offense of impaired driving constitutes criminal negligence as a matter of law. State v. Davis, ___ N.C. App. ___, 678 S.E.2d 385, 390 (2009). Criminal negligence has been found in assault cases involving vehicles used as deadly weapons even in the absence of impaired driving. *Spellman*, 167 N.C. App. 374 (sufficient evidence to support conviction for assault with a deadly weapon inflicting serious injury when evidence showed that the defendant continued to drive a truck while an officer held onto the driver's side door of the truck and the defendant repeatedly struck the officer while the officer was hanging onto the truck door); State v. Wade, 161 N.C. App. 686 (2003) (sufficient evidence to support conviction for assault with a deadly weapon inflicting serious injury when evidence showed that the defendant drove his vehicle over a double yellow line in an attempt to pass two vehicles as he approached a sharp curve and the defendant had no visibility around the curve). For a more detailed discussion of criminal negligence, see "Criminal Negligence" in Chapter 1 (States of Mind).

The second form of assault recognized in North Carolina is assault by show of violence. This form occurs when (1) the defendant shows an apparent ability to inflict injury (even if there is no actual ability); (2) the act is such that a reasonable person would fear harm from it; and (3) the act causes the victim to do something the victim would not have done or to not do something he or she would have done, such as leaving a place or taking a different route. State v. Roberts, 270 N.C. 655, 658 (1967); State v. Allen, 245 N.C. 185, 189 (1956); State v. McIver, 231 N.C. 313 (1949); State v. McDaniel, 111 N.C. App. 888 (1993). The difference between the two forms of assault is that the first focuses on the intent of the defendant while the second places emphasis on the reasonable apprehension of the victim. *Roberts*, 270 N.C. at 658; *McDaniel*, 111 N.C. App. at 890–91.

Battery. A battery is an assault whereby any force, however slight, is applied, directly or indirectly, to another. State v. West, 146 N.C. App. 741, 744 (2001); N.C. PATTERN JURY INSTRUCTIONS—CRIM. 208.41. For example, a battery occurs when the defendant punches the victim. If the defendant only threatens to punch the victim but does so in a way that would put a reasonable person in fear of immediate physical injury, there would be no battery but there would be an assault.

When a battery is committed, the State is not required to show that the victim was placed in fear. State v. Lassiter, 18 N.C. App. 208, 212 (1973); State v. Thompson, 27 N.C. App. 576, 578 (1975) (citing *Lassiter*); State v. Hill, 266 N.C. 103 (1965).

As a general rule, the statutes use the terms "assault" and "battery" interchangeably, often using "assault" for acts that involve a striking (such as assault inflicting serious injury). For simplicity, "assault," as used in this book, includes battery. Note, however, that some crimes require both an assault and a battery as elements, see, for example, "Secret Assault," below, and that for others only a battery will suffice, see, for example, "Battery on An Unborn Child," below. When this is the case, special note will be made.

Aiding and abetting by failure to defend. A parent may be convicted of aiding and abetting an assault on his or her child if the parent was present when the child was assaulted and did not take reasonable steps to prevent the assault. See the note on Element (2) to "Aiding and Abetting" in Chapter 3 (Participants in Crimes).

Attempted assault. Attempted assault is not a crime; because an assault includes an overt act or attempt, or the unequivocal appearance of an attempt, an attempted assault would be an attempt to attempt. State v. Barksdale, 181 N.C. App. 302, 308 (2007).

Charging issues. For a discussion of charging issues regarding assault and the related offenses covered in this chapter, see Jessica Smith, *The Criminal Indictment: Fatal Defect, Fatal Variance, and Amendment*, ADMIN. OF JUST. BULLETIN 2008/03 (UNC School of Government, July 2008) (online at www.sogpubs.unc.edu/electronicversions/pdfs/aojb0803.pdf). For an additional case on point decided after publication of that bulletin, see *In re D.S.*, 197 N.C. App. 598 (2009) (no fatal variance when a juvenile petition alleged that the juvenile assaulted the victim with his hands and the evidence established that he touched her with an object).

Greater and lesser-included offenses. Simple assault is not a lesser-included offense of attempted second-degree rape, State v. Robinson, 97 N.C. App. 597, 604 (1990), or sexual battery, State v. Corbett, 196 N.C. App. 508, 511 (2009) (assault contains elements that are not in sexual battery).

Multiple convictions and punishments. To find a defendant guilty of two separate assaults on the same victim, there must be a distinct interruption in the original assault followed by a second assault. For example, only one conviction was proper when (1) the evidence was insufficient to show a distinct interruption between two assaults done with a deadly weapon and inflicting serious injury, State v. Brooks, 138 N.C. App. 185, 189–90 (2000); and (2) five shots were fired at the victim in rapid succession with a semiautomatic handgun, State v. Maddox, 159 N.C. App. 127, 131–32 (1993). By comparison, the evidence supported two assault convictions when (1) the defendant drove his vehicle over the victim's leg and then later reentered his vehicle and drove it toward the victim, placing him in fear of injury, State v. Spellman, 167 N.C. App. 374 (2004); (2) the victim was stabbed multiple times, stopped struggling, and fell to the ground and then was shot twice in the leg by a handgun; each assault was temporally distinct and the wounds were inflicted in different locations on the victim's body, State v. Littlejohn, 158 N.C. App. 628, 636–37 (2003); and (3) the defendant fired three distinct shots from a pistol at a vehicle, State v. Rambert, 341 N.C. 173, 177 (1995) ("Each shot, fired from a pistol, as opposed to a machine gun or other automatic weapon, required that defendant employ his thought processes each time he fired the weapon. Each act was distinct in time, and each bullet hit the vehicle in a different place.").

For a discussion of when a defendant may be convicted of attempted murder and an assault based on the same conduct, see the note entitled "Attempted homicide" to "Attempt" in Chapter 5 (General Crimes).

Related Offenses Not in This Chapter

"Simple Affray" (Chapter 19)
"Disorderly Conduct" (Chapter 19)
Hazing of student. G.S. 14-35.

Assaults Inflicting a Particular Type of Injury

Assault Inflicting Serious Injury

Statute

See G.S. 14-33(c)(1), reproduced under "Simple Assault," above.

Elements

A person guilty of this offense
(1) commits an assault
(2) on another *and*
(3) inflicts serious injury.

Punishment

Class A1 misdemeanor. G.S. 14-33(c).

Notes

Element (1). See this note to "Simple Assault," above.

Element (3). The serious injury may be physical or mental. State v. Everhardt, 326 N.C. 777, 781 (1990). Whether an injury is serious is a question of fact. *Id.* at 781; State v. Ferguson, 261 N.C. 558, 560 (1964). Relevant factors in determining whether an injury is serious include but are not limited to pain and suffering; loss of blood; hospitalization; and time lost from work. State v. Tice, 191 N.C. App. 506, 509 (2008); State v. Morgan, 164 N.C. App. 298, 303 (2004).

The following have been found to be serious injuries:

- gunshot wounds, State v. Shankle, 7 N.C. App. 564 (1970) (to the wrist); State v. Bagley, 183 N.C. App. 514, 526–27 (2007) (bullet wound went through the victim's leg; the victim was unable to drive to the hospital, was treated there, and suffered pain for two or three weeks); State v. Tice, 191 N.C. App. 506, 510 (2008) (a gunshot wound to the knee; the victim received hospital treatment, took prescribed pain medication for two weeks, had a limp for one to two weeks, and required one month to heal; so holding even though the victim drove himself to the hospital); State v. McLean, ___ N.C. App. ___, 712 S.E.2d 271 (2011) (there was sufficient evidence that the victim suffered serious injury when, among other things, the defendant shot the victim with a shotgun, causing injuries to the victim's calf and causing eighteen to twenty pellets to lodge in his leg, which did not fully work themselves out for six months);
- head injuries, State v. Smith, 5 N.C. App. 635 (1969) (swelling on the skull); State v. Allen, 193 N.C. App. 375 (2008) (traumatic head injuries, extreme facial bruising and swelling, bleeding from the ear and nose, an eye swollen shut for over one month, damage to the inside of the ear and mouth, and a loss of consciousness);
- cuts, punctures, and stab wounds, *Morgan*, 164 N.C. App. 298 (multiple lacerations to the forearm, small stab wounds to the leg, a deep laceration to the thumb, bruising to the back, and a puncture wound to the right orbital rim, causing a bone fracture, with both eye and thumb wounds requiring treatment by specialists); State v. Walker, ___ N.C. App. ___, 694 S.E.2d 484, 495 (2010) (the victim lost "a lot" of blood, was stabbed or cut eight or nine times, and had wounds on his lip, back, and arm; he was removed by stretcher to the emergency room, where he remained for twelve hours, receiving a chest tube to drain blood and stitches; he was put on a ventilator because of a lung puncture; he received pain medication for approximately one week; and at trial had visible scars on his lip, arm, and back);
- a nostril that has caved in and knocked-out teeth, State v. Lane, 1 N.C. App. 539 (1968);

- shards of glass in the arm and shoulder of drive-by shooting victim, coupled with an officer's observation that the victim was shaken, State v. Alexander, 337 N.C. 182 (1994); and
- a badly bruised shoulder, an inability to move the arm properly for three days, and pain and suffering, State v. Ramseur, 338 N.C. 502 (1994).

Mental injury amounting to serious injury was properly found when a victim was sexually assaulted for several days with devices used to degrade and dehumanize and the victim required hospital admission and treatment for severe depression, suicidal tendencies, anorexia, insomnia, and feelings of hopelessness and helplessness. State v. Everhardt, 326 N.C. 777 (1990).

Proving serious injury requires less evidence than proving serious bodily injury for "Assault Inflicting Serious Bodily Injury," below. State v. Hannah, 149 N.C. App. 713 (2002); State v. Williams, 150 N.C. App. 497 (2002).

When the evidence is not conflicting and is such that reasonable minds could not differ as to the serious nature of the injuries, the trial court may give the jury a peremptory instruction on the issue. State v. Pettiford, 60 N.C. App. 92, 97–98 (1982) (peremptory proper where bullet was lodged in the victim's head). However, if reasonable minds could differ as to whether the injury was serious, it is error to give a peremptory instruction. State v. Bagley, 183 N.C. App. 514, 527 (2007) (error to give peremptory instruction as to gunshot wound to a leg).

Charging issues. See this note to "Simple Assault," above.

Greater and lesser-included offenses. Because all of the elements of simple assault are included in assault inflicting serious injury, simple assault is a lesser-included offense of this crime. State v. Tillery, 186 N.C. App. 447, 449 (2007).

Multiple convictions and punishments. See this note to "Simple Assault," above.

This statute, like a number of assault statutes, begins with or contains the following language: "Unless the conduct is covered under some other provision of law providing greater punishment." G.S. 14-33(c). For example, G.S. 14-32.4(b) provides that "Unless the conduct is covered under some other provision of law providing greater punishment, any person who assaults another person and inflicts physical injury by strangulation is guilty of a Class H felony." A plain reading suggests that this means, in the case of G.S. 14-32.4(b), for example, that the defendant may not be punished for assault by strangulation when the conduct is covered by another crime that carries a more severe punishment. Several cases are consistent with that reading. *See* State v. Williams, 201 N.C. App. 161 (2009) (even though assault by strangulation (Class H felony) and assault inflicting serious bodily injury (Class F felony) require proof of different elements so as to be distinct crimes for purposes of double jeopardy, the statutory language reflects a legislative intent that a defendant only be sentenced for the higher of the two offenses); State v. Ezell, 159 N.C. App. 103 (2003) (the defendant could not be convicted of assault inflicting serious bodily injury and assault with a deadly weapon inflicting serious injury under G.S. 14-32(b) (Class E felony) when G.S. 14-32.4(a) includes the "unless covered" language); State v. McCoy, 174 N.C. App. 105 (2005) (following *Ezell* with respect to convictions for (1) assault inflicting serious bodily injury and assault with a deadly weapon inflicting serious injury; and (2) assault with a deadly weapon inflicting serious injury and assault inflicting serious injury under G.S. 14-33(c)(1)). However, other cases create confusion on the issue. *See* State v. Coria, 131 N.C. App. 449 (1998) (the defendant was properly convicted of assault with a deadly weapon on a law enforcement officer under G.S. 14-34.2 (Class F felony) and assault with a deadly weapon with intent to kill under G.S. 14-32(c) (Class E felony) even though G.S. 14-34.2 contains the statutory "unless covered" language; holding that because each offense had an element not in the other, there was no double jeopardy violation but not mentioning the "unless covered" language); State v. Chambers, 152 N.C. App. 478 (2002) (unpublished) (following *Coria* and holding that the defendant was properly convicted of assault with a deadly weapon on a law enforcement officer and assault with a deadly weapon with intent to kill inflicting serious injury under G.S. 14-32(a) (Class C felony) even though G.S. 14-34.2 contains the "unless covered" language; concluding that the purpose of G.S. 14-34.2 is to impose greater punishment for knowing assaults on law enforcement officers and the purpose of G.S. 14-32(a) is to protect life and limb). Adding to the complexity is *State v. Hines*, 166 N.C. App. 202, 208 (2004), in which the defendant was convicted of aggravated assault on a handicapped person under G.S. 14-32.1 (Class F felony) and armed robbery (Class D felony). Citing the "unless covered" language in G.S. 14-32.1, the defendant argued that the trial court erred by sentencing her for the assault and the more serious robbery offense. The court rejected this argument, distinguishing *Ezell* on grounds that it dealt with two assault convictions. The *Hines* court concluded that the statutory language barred punishment for aggravated assault on a handicapped person and another assault offense, not armed robbery. It is unclear whether this distinction would hold up if presented to the North Carolina Supreme Court. *See* State v. Davis, 364 N.C. 297 (2010) (holding, based on identical statutory language, that a defendant may not be convicted of (1) felony death by vehicle under G.S. 20-141.4 (Class E felony) and second-degree murder (Class B2 felony); or (2) felony serious injury by vehicle under G.S. 20-141.4 (Class F felony) and assault with a deadly weapon inflicting serious injury (Class E felony).

Related Offenses Not in This Chapter

"Aggravated Misdemeanor Affray" (Chapter 19)
See disorderly conduct (various offenses) in Chapter 19 (Disorderly Conduct, Riot, and Gang Offenses).
See inciting to riot (various offenses) in Chapter 19 (Disorderly Conduct, Riot, and Gang Offenses).
"Injuring Another with a Nuclear, Biological, or Chemical Weapon of Mass Destruction" (Chapter 20)
"Resisting, Delaying, or Obstructing an Officer" (Chapter 21)
Malicious castration. G.S. 14-28.
Castration or other maiming without malice aforethought. G.S. 14-29.
Malicious maiming. G.S. 14-30.
Malicious throwing of corrosive acid or alkal. G.S. 14-30.1.
Hazing of students. G.S. 14-35.

Assault Inflicting Serious Bodily Injury

Statute

§14-32.4. Assault inflicting serious bodily injury; strangulation; penalties.

(a) Unless the conduct is covered under some other provision of law providing greater punishment, any person who assaults another person and inflicts serious bodily injury is guilty of a Class F felony. "Serious bodily injury" is defined as bodily injury that creates a substantial risk of death, or that causes serious permanent disfigurement, coma, a permanent or protracted condition that causes extreme pain, or permanent or protracted loss or impairment of the function of any bodily member or organ, or that results in prolonged hospitalization.

(b) Unless the conduct is covered under some other provision of law providing greater punishment, any person who assaults another person and inflicts physical injury by strangulation is guilty of a Class H felony.

Elements

A person guilty of this offense

(1) commits an assault

(2) on another *and*
(3) inflicts serious bodily injury.

Punishment

Class F felony. G.S. 14-32.4(a).

Notes

Element (1). See the note on Element (1) to "Simple Assault," above.

Element (3). G.S. 14-32.4(a) defines serious bodily injury as "bodily injury that creates a substantial risk of death, or that causes serious permanent disfigurement, coma, a permanent or protracted condition that causes extreme pain, or permanent or protracted loss or impairment of the function of any bodily member or organ, or that results in prolonged hospitalization." This definition requires proof of a more severe injury than is required for the crime of assault inflicting serious injury, discussed above. State v. Rouse, 198 N.C. App. 378, 382 (2009). There was sufficient evidence of serious bodily injury when:

- the victim had a broken jaw that was wired shut for two months causing him to lose thirty pounds and he incurred $6,000 in dental costs, suffered broken ribs, and twice suffered back spasms requiring trips to the emergency room; the back spasms continued until trial, and a doctor said that the broken jaw would cause "quite a bit" of pain and discomfort, State v. Williams, 150 N.C. App. 497, 503–04 (2002);
- the victim lost a natural tooth; even though a dental implant could address the injury, the damage constituted a serious permanent disfigurement, State v. Downs, 179 N.C. App. 860, 862 (2006);
- a 70-year-old female victim had dried blood on her lips and in her nostrils, abdominal pain, a broken collarbone, cuts in her hand requiring stitches, received morphine immediately and was prescribed additional pain medicine, had to return to the emergency room due to an infection in the sutured hand requiring re-stitching and antibiotics, and was in so much pain that a nurse was unable to use a speculum while gathering a rape kit, *Rouse*, 198 N.C. App. at 383;
- the victim suffered a cracked pelvic bone, a broken rib, torn ligaments in her back, a deep cut over her left eye, and was unable to have sex for seven months; the eye injury developed an infection that lasted months and was never completely cured and the incident left a scar, State v. Williams, 201 N.C. App. 161, 169–70 (2009); and
- the victim sustained a puncture wound to the back of her scalp and a parietal scalp hematoma and went into premature labor as a result of the attack, *id.* at 187.

There was insufficient evidence of serious bodily injury when the victim received a vicious beating but there was no substantial risk of death; although the victim was sore five months later, there was no evidence of extreme pain. *Id.* at 425.

Charging issues. See this note to "Simple Assault," above.

Greater and lesser-included offenses. Because all of the elements of simple assault are included in assault inflicting serious bodily injury, simple assault is a lesser-included offense of this offense.

Assault inflicting serious bodily injury is not a lesser-included offense of assault with a deadly weapon with intent to kill inflicting serious injury. State v. Hannah, 149 N.C. App. 713, 717 (2002).

Multiple convictions and punishments. See this note to "Simple Assault" and "Assault Inflicting Serious Injury," both above.

Related Offenses Not in This Chapter

See the offenses listed under "Assault Inflicting Serious Injury," above.

Assault Inflicting Physical Injury by Strangulation

Statute

See G.S. 14-32.4(b), reproduced under "Assault Inflicting Serious Bodily Injury," above.

Elements

A person guilty of this offense

(1) commits an assault
(2) on another *and*
(3) inflicts physical injury
(4) by strangulation.

Punishment

Class H felony. G.S. 14-32.4(b).

Notes

Element (1). See the note on Element (1) to "Simple Assault," above.

Element (3). The statute does not define the term "physical injury." Although this term is also used in habitual misdemeanor assault, it is not defined there either. It appears to require something more than mere physical contact. In *State v. Little*, 188 N.C. App. 152, 157 (2008), the court held that the evidence was sufficient to establish physical injury when the victim testified that she received cuts and bruises on her neck as a result of being strangled. Note that in 2011, the General Assembly amended a different assault statute creating a new crime, "Assault Inflicting Physical Injury on a Law Enforcement Officer, Probation or Parole Officer, or Detention Facility Employee," discussed below. S.L. 2011-356, sec. 1. For purposes of that new crime, the General Assembly defined the term "physical injury" to include cuts, scrapes, bruises, or other physical injury which does not constitute serious injury. *Id.*; G.S. 34.7(c).

Element (4). The statute does not define the term "strangulation," and that term is not used in any other assault offenses. One case held that "wrapping one's hands around another's throat and applying pressure until the person loses consciousness" constitutes strangulation. *Little*, 188 N.C. App. at 157. Other cases have held that the evidence was sufficient when the defendant (1) grabbed the victim by the throat, causing her to have difficulty breathing, State v. Braxton, 183 N.C. App. 36, 42–43 (2007) (the State need not prove that the victim had a complete inability to breathe); and (2) pushed down on the victim's neck with his foot, and the victim thought he was trying to "chok[e] her out" or render her unconscious and that she was going to die, State v. Williams, 201 N.C. App. 161, 170–71 (2009). The North Carolina Criminal Pattern Jury Instructions define "strangulation" as "a form of asphyxia characterized by closure of the blood vessels and/or air passages of the neck as a result of external pressure on the neck brought about by hanging, ligature, or the manual assertion of pressure." N.C. PATTERN JURY INSTRUCTIONS—CRIM. 208.61 n.1.

Charging issues. See this note to "Simple Assault," above. For an additional case on point decided after publication of the bulletin cited in that note, see *State v. Williams*, 201 N.C. App. 161 (2009) (even if there was a fatal variance between the indictment, which alleged that the defendant accomplished the strangulation by placing his hands on the victim's neck, and the evidence at trial, the variance was immaterial because the allegation regarding the method of strangulation was surplusage).

Greater and lesser-included offenses. Because all of the elements of simple assault are included in assault inflicting serious injury by strangulation, simple assault is a lesser-included offense of this offense.

Assault on a female is not a lesser-included offense of assault inflicting physical injury by strangulation. State v. Brunson, 187 N.C. App. 472, 478 (2007).

Multiple convictions and punishments. See this note to "Simple Assault" and "Assault Inflicting Serious Injury," both above.

Related Offenses Not in this Chapter

None

Deadly Weapon Assaults

Assault with a Deadly Weapon

Statute

See G.S. 14-33(c)(1), reproduced under "Simple Assault," above.

Elements

A person guilty of this offense

(1) commits an assault
(2) on another
(3) with a deadly weapon.

Punishment

Class A1 misdemeanor. G.S. 14-33(c).

Notes

Element (1). See this note to "Simple Assault," above.

The State must prove either that the defendant had the actual intent to strike the victim with the deadly weapon or that the defendant acted with culpable negligence from which intent may be implied. State v. Maready, ___ N.C. App. ___, 695 S.E.2d 771 (2010). For a discussion of culpable negligence, see "Criminal Negligence" in Chapter 1 (States of Mind).

There was sufficient evidence of assault with a firearm when the defendant reached for but did not touch a weapon that was inches away from his hand. State v. Barksdale, 181 N.C. App. 302, 307 (2007).

Element (3). A "deadly weapon" is any instrument that under the circumstances of its use is likely to cause death or serious bodily injury. State v. Walker, ___ N.C. App. ___, 694 S.E.2d 484, 493 (2010); State v. Lane, 1 N.C. App. 539, 541 (1968). Whether a weapon is deadly may depend on its nature and size, how it is used—for example, whether it left cut marks, State v. Randolph, 228 N.C. 228 (1947)—and the strength of the defendant compared to the victim, State v. Shubert, 102 N.C. App. 419 (1991).

Some weapons, such as guns, are deadly by their very nature. State v. Torain, 316 N.C. 111 (1986) (utility knife is a dangerous or deadly weapon). When that is the case, the judge should so instruct the jury. State v. Flaugher, ___ N.C. App. ___, 713 S.E.2d 576 (2011) (the trial court did not err by instructing the jury that a pickaxe was a deadly weapon; the pickaxe handle was about three feet long and the pickaxe weighed nine to ten pounds; the defendant swung the pickaxe approximately eight times, causing cuts to the victim's head that required fifty-three staples and slashed his middle finger, leaving it hanging only by a piece of skin); State v. Graham, 186 N.C. App. 182, 194–95 (2007) (the trial court did not err by instructing the jury that a knife is a deadly weapon). In all other circumstances, the jury decides whether the weapon is deadly. State v. Sinclair, 120 N.C. 603 (1897). When there is a factual issue about whether a weapon is deadly, the trial judge must instruct on a lesser non–deadly weapon assault offense.

State v. Clark, ___ N.C. App. ___, 689 S.E.2d 553, 557–58 (2009); State v. Tillery, 186 N.C. App. 447, 449–51 (2007); State v. Smith, 186 N.C. App. 57, 65–66 (2007). However, the weapon need not be produced in court to obtain a conviction. State v. Walker, ___ N.C. App. ___, 694 S.E.2d 484, 494 (2010); *Graham*, 186 N.C. App. at 194–95 (the trial court did not err by instructing the jury that a knife is a deadly weapon where the victim suffered life-threatening injuries but the knife was not introduced or described in detail at trial). Examples of deadly weapons include:

- a pistol used to fire a bullet, State v. Benson, 183 N.C. 795 (1922), or to strike, State v. Bell, 87 N.C. App. 626 (1987);
- a knife, *Walker*, ___ N.C. App. ___, 694 S.E.2d at 494 (knife was three inches long and victim sustained significant injuries); State v. Caudle, 172 N.C. App. 261 (2005);
- a belt with a metal buckle, State v. Cauley, 244 N.C. 701 (1956);
- an automobile, State v. Jones, 353 N.C. 159, 165 (2000); State v. Ferguson, 261 N.C. 558, 560 (1964); State v. Batchelor, 167 N.C. App. 797 (2005). *But see* State v. Clark, ___ N.C. App. ___, 689 S.E.2d 553, 559 (2009) (vehicle was not a deadly weapon as a matter of law when there was no evidence that it was moving at a high speed; given the victim's lack of significant injury and the lack of damage to the other vehicle, a jury could conclude that the vehicle was not aimed directly at the victim and that the impact was more of a glancing contact);
- a firebomb, State v. Avery, 315 N.C. 1 (1985);
- a fire used to burn a house and harm a person inside, State v. Riddick, 315 N.C. 749 (1986);
- a dog, State v. Cook, 164 N.C. App. 139;
- a box cutter, State v. Doisey, 162 N.C. App. 447 (2004);
- a broken wine bottle, State v. Morgan, 156 N.C. App. 523 (2003); and
- a rock, State v. Liggons, 194 N.C. App. 734, 742-43 (2009) (deadly weapon as a matter of law when deliberately thrown through the driver's side windshield of a vehicle traveling at 55–60 mph).

For assaults, hands and feet may be considered deadly weapons depending on the manner in which they were used and the relative size and condition of the parties involved. State v. Harris, 189 N.C. App. 49, 59 n.1 (2008) (distinguishing State v. Hinton, 361 N.C. 207 (2007) (hands and feet are not deadly weapons for purposes of armed robbery)); State v. Allen, 193 N.C. App. 375, 378 (2008) (same). For example, the evidence was sufficient to establish that hands and/or feet were deadly weapons when:

- the defendant outweighed the victim by 65 pounds; the victim had a shoe print on her back and handprint bruises on her arms, thighs, and buttocks; and handprints consistent with a neck choke hold may have caused swelling in her mouth, tongue, and throat, *Harris*, 189 N.C. App. at 60;
- the defendant was 13 years younger, 7 inches taller, and 40 pounds heavier than the victim; he repeatedly struck the victim, causing traumatic head injuries, extreme facial bruising and swelling, bleeding from the ear and nose, an eye that was swollen shut for over one month, damage to the inside of the ear and mouth, and a loss of consciousness, *Allen*, 193 N.C. App. at 378–79;
- the defendant was a 40-year-old female, 5 feet 2 inches tall and weighing 125 pounds, and the victim was a 79-year-old male, 6 feet tall and weighing 165 pounds but with a heart condition and polyneuropathy; the defendant and her accomplice outweighed the victim by 72 pounds, State v. Wallace, 197 N.C. App. 339, 345–46 (2009);
- the defendant was a big, stocky man, probably larger than the victim, who was a female and likely a user of crack cocaine, and the victim sustained serious injuries, State v. Williams, ___ N.C. App. ___, 689 S.E.2d 412, 422 (2009);

- the defendant used his hands to throw the victim, a small-framed, pregnant woman with a cocaine addiction, onto a concrete floor, cracking her head open, and he put his hands around her neck, *id.* at 427;
- the defendant, a 39-year-old male weighing 210 pounds, hit the victim, a 60-year-old woman, in the head and stomach; brain hemorrhages and other injuries resulted from the beating, causing the victim to be unable to care for herself, State v. Jacobs, 61 N.C. App. 610 (1983);
- the defendant weighed approximately 175 pounds and the victim weighed approximately 107 pounds; the defendant beat the victim about the head with his fists, breaking her jaw and causing her to require extensive hospitalization, and choked her three separate times, leaving marks around her neck, State v. Grumbles, 104 N.C. App. 766 (1991);
- the defendant hit the victim, causing a cracked cheekbone, broken nose, and broken jaw requiring surgery; the defendant choked the victim, leaving marks on her neck; and the defendant was a 6-foot-2-inch-tall male who weighed 165 pounds while the victim was a female who was approximately five foot three and weighed 99 pounds, State v. Rogers, 153 N.C. App. 203 (2002); and
- the male defendant weighed 230 pounds and the pregnant, female victim weighed 190 pounds; the defendant beat the victim with his hands and feet so severely that she had to be flown to a special hospital for treatment, admitted to intensive care, and placed on a ventilator; and her injuries included fractures of the left orbit and the left maxillary and swelling and contusions about her face, neck, and upper chest, State v. Hunt, 153 N.C. App. 316 (2002).

Although one case reached the same conclusion without analyzing the relative size of the defendant and the victims, State v. Yarrell, 172 N.C. App. 135 (2005), another, decided one month later, struck down a conviction on grounds that the State did not present sufficient evidence as to the defendant's size or condition compared to that of the victim, State v. Lawson, 173 N.C. App. 270 (2005). In the later case, the court rejected the State's argument that the jury had an opportunity to observe the defendant and victim at trial, concluding that mere observation at trial was not sufficient evidence. *Id.* In an even more recent case, the court of appeals found the evidence sufficient to sustain a motion to dismiss when it showed a great disparity in height between the defendant (six feet five inches) and the victim (four feet eleven inches) but no evidence was presented as to their respective weights. State v. Brunson, 180 N.C. App. 188 (2006). A defendant's act of holding the victim's head under water constituted use of a deadly weapon; because the defendant did not use his hands alone, the State was not required to present evidence as to the size or condition of the victim and the defendant. State v. Smith, 186 N.C. App. 57, 6364 (2007).

Charging issues. See this note to "Simple Assault," above.

Greater and lesser-included offenses. Because all of the elements of simple assault are included in assault with a deadly weapon, it is a lesser-included offense of that offense.

This offense is not a lesser-included offense of discharging a barreled weapon or firearm into occupied property, discussed below, State v. Turner, 330 N.C. 249 (1991), or attempted armed robbery, State v. Rowland, 89 N.C. App. 372, 374–77 (1988). But it is a lesser-included offense of assault with a firearm on a law enforcement officer, probation or parole officer, or detention facility employee, discussed below. State v. Dickens, 162 N.C. App. 632, 638 (2004).

Multiple convictions and punishments. See this note to "Simple Assault" and "Assault Inflicting Serious Injury," both above.

A defendant may be convicted of assault with a deadly weapon and assault with a firearm or other deadly weapon on a governmental officer or employee or company or campus police officer when the convictions are based on distinct conduct. State v. Spellman, 167 N.C. App. 374, 379–84 (2004) (an assault with a deadly weapon on a law enforcement officer occurred when the defendant ran over the officer's leg with his vehicle; the assault with a deadly weapon occurred after the defendant re-entered the vehicle and drove it toward the officer, thereby placing him in fear of injury).

Relation to other offenses. This offense is different from assault by pointing a gun because (1) to prove this offense in a case involving a gun, the State need not prove that the defendant pointed the gun at the victim, *Dickens*, 162 N.C. App. at 636; and (2) this offense may be committed with weapons other than guns.

For assaults with deadly weapons against employees and security officers, see "Assault with a Firearm or Other Deadly Weapon on a Governmental Officer or Employee or Company or Campus Police Officer;" "Assault with a Firearm on a Law Enforcement Officer, Probation or Parole Officer, or Detention Facility Employee;" "Assault on an Executive, Legislative, or Court Officer Using a Deadly Weapon or Inflicting Serious Injury;" "Assault on a Firefighter or Medical Personnel Inflicting Serious Injury or Using a Deadly Weapon Other Than a Firearm;" and "Assault on a Firefighter or Medical Personnel with a Firearm," all below.

Related Offenses Not in This Chapter

"Armed Robbery" (Chapter 14)
"Aggravated Misdemeanor Affray" (Chapter 19)
"Disorderly Conduct" (Chapter 19)
See riot (various offenses) in Chapter 19 (Disorderly Conduct, Riot, and Gang Offenses).
"Manufacture, Possession, etc. of a Machine Gun, Sawed-Off Shotgun, or Weapon of Mass Destruction" (Chapter 20)
"Possession of a Firearm by a Felon" (Chapter 22)
"Carrying a Concealed Weapon" (Chapter 22)
"Carrying a Gun into an Assembly or Establishment Where Alcoholic Beverages Are Sold and Consumed" (Chapter 22)
See possession of weapons on school grounds (various offenses) in Chapter 22 (Weapons Offenses).
Criminal use of laser device. G.S. 14-34.8.
Transporting dangerous weapon or substance during emergency; possession off premises; exceptions. G.S. 14-288.7.
Use of dangerous weapon by prisoner in assault. G.S. 14-258.2.

Assault with a Deadly Weapon with Intent to Kill

Statute

§14-32. Felonious assault with deadly weapon with intent to kill or inflicting serious injury; punishments.

(a) Any person who assaults another person with a deadly weapon with intent to kill and inflicts serious injury shall be punished as a Class C felon.

(b) Any person who assaults another person with a deadly weapon and inflicts serious injury shall be punished as a Class E felon.

(c) Any person who assaults another person with a deadly weapon with intent to kill shall be punished as a Class E felon.

Elements

A person guilty of this offense

(1) commits an assault
(2) on another
(3) with a deadly weapon
(4) with intent to kill.

Punishment

Class E felony. G.S. 14-32(c).

Notes

Element (1). See this note to "Simple Assault," above.

Element (3). See the note on Element (3) to "Assault with a Deadly Weapon," above.

Element (4). Intent to kill may be inferred from the circumstances of the assault, including the use of a deadly weapon, the manner in which the assault was carried out, and the degree of injury. State v. Thacker, 281 N.C. 447 (1972); State v. Ferguson, 261 N.C. 558 (1964); State v. Revels, 227 N.C. 34 (1946); State v. Peoples, 141 N.C. App. 115 (2000). For a more detailed discussion of intent to kill, see the note on Element (3)(a)(ii) to "First-Degree Murder" in Chapter 6 (Homicide).

For assault cases in which the evidence was sufficient to show an intent to kill, see *State v. Wright*, ___ N.C. App. ___, 708 S.E.2d 112 (2011) (the trial court did not err by failing to instruct the jury on a lesser-included assault not including an intent to kill when the defendant broke into a trailer in the middle of the night and used an iron pipe to repeatedly beat in the head an unarmed, naked victim who had just woken up); *State v. Liggons*, 194 N.C. App. 734 (2009) (there was sufficient evidence of an intent to kill when the defendant and his accomplice discussed intentionally forcing drivers off the road in order to rob them and one of the two then deliberately threw a very large rock or concrete chunk through the driver's side windshield of the victim's automobile as it was approaching at approximately 55 or 60 mph); *State v. Pointer*, 181 N.C. App. 93, 96–97 (2007) (even though the defense offered unrebutted expert testimony that the defendant could not form an intent to kill due to mental disorders and excessive medication, there was sufficient evidence of that intent given the number of stab wounds inflicted on the victims and the manner in which the stabbings took place (the defendant stabbed one victim twenty-two times, knocked her to the ground, got on top of her, and continued stabbing her, and he stabbed another victim five times, inflicting serious injuries), as well as the defendant's statement that he attacked one of the victims), *State v. Cromartie*, 177 N.C. App. 73 (2006), *State v. Nicholson*, 169 N.C. App. 390 (2005), *State v. Duff*, 171 N.C. App. 662 (2005), *State v. Maddox*, 159 N.C. App. 127 (2003), and *State v. Scott*, 161 N.C. App. 104 (2003).

Charging issues. See this note to "Simple Assault," above.

Greater and lesser-included offenses. Because all of the elements of (1) simple assault; and (2) assault with a deadly weapon are included in assault with a deadly weapon with intent to kill, both are lesser-included offenses of assault with a deadly weapon with intent to kill.

Assault with a deadly weapon with intent to kill is not a lesser-included offense of attempted first-degree murder. State v. Garris, 191 N.C. App. 276, 285–87 (2008).

Multiple convictions and punishments. See this note to "Simple Assault" and "Assault Inflicting Serious Injury," both above.

Related Offenses Not in This Chapter

"Aggravated Misdemeanor Affray" (Chapter 19)
See riot (various offenses) in Chapter 19 (Disorderly Conduct, Riot, and Gang Offenses).
See the offenses in Chapter 22 (Weapons Offenses).

Assault with a Deadly Weapon Inflicting Serious Injury

Statute

See G.S. 14-32(b), reproduced under "Assault with a Deadly Weapon with Intent to Kill," above.

Elements

A person guilty of this offense

(1) commits an assault
(2) on another
(3) with a deadly weapon *and*
(4) inflicts serious injury.

Punishment

Class E felony. G.S. 14-32(b).

Notes

Element (1). See this note to "Simple Assault," above.

Element (3). See the note on Element (3) to "Assault with a Deadly Weapon," above.

Element (4). See the note on Element (4) to "Assault Inflicting Serious Injury," above.

Charging issues. See this note to "Simple Assault," above.

Greater and lesser-included offenses. Because all of the elements of (1) simple assault; (2) assault with a deadly weapon; and (3) assault inflicting serious injury are included in assault with a deadly weapon inflicting serious injury, all three of those offenses are lesser-included offenses of this one. State v. Tillery, 186 N.C. App. 447, 449 (2007) (assault inflicting serious injury is a lesser-included offense of assault with a deadly weapon inflicting serious injury).

This offense is not a lesser-included offense of attempted first-degree murder. State v. Rainey, 154 N.C. App. 282 (2002).

Multiple convictions and punishments. See this note to "Simple Assault" and "Assault Inflicting Serious Injury," above.

A defendant was properly convicted of three counts of this offense when he drove while impaired and crashed his vehicle into the victims' vehicle, seriously injuring three occupants. State v. Jones, 353 N.C. 159, 165 (2000).

A defendant may be convicted and punished for this offense and felony child abuse based on the same conduct. State v. Carter, 153 N.C. App. 756 (2002).

Related Offenses Not in This Chapter

See the offenses listed under "Assault with a Deadly Weapon with Intent to Kill," above.

Assault with a Deadly Weapon with Intent to Kill Inflicting Serious Injury

Statute

See G.S. 14-32(a), reproduced under "Assault with a Deadly Weapon with Intent to Kill," above.

Elements

A person guilty of this offense

(1) commits an assault
(2) on another
(3) with a deadly weapon *and*
(4) with intent to kill *and*
(5) inflicts serious injury.

Punishment

Class C felony. G.S. 14-32(a).

Notes

Element (1). See this note to "Simple Assault," above.

Element (3). See the note on Element (3) to "Assault with a Deadly Weapon," above.

Element (4). See this note to "Assault with a Deadly Weapon With Intent to Kill," above.

Element (5). See the note on Element (3) to "Assault Inflicting Serious Injury," above.

Charging issues. See this note to "Simple Assault," above.

Greater and lesser-included offenses. Because all of the elements of (1) simple assault; (2) assault with a deadly weapon; (3) assault with a deadly weapon with intent to kill; and (4) assault inflicting serious injury are included in assault with a deadly weapon with intent to kill inflicting serious injury, all four of those offenses are lesser-included offenses of this one. However, assault inflicting serious bodily injury is not a lesser-included offense. State v. Hannah, 149 N.C. App. 713, 717–19 (2002).

Multiple convictions and punishments. See this note to "Simple Assault," above.

Because each offense includes an element that is not included in the other, double jeopardy does not bar convicting and sentencing a defendant for assault with a deadly weapon with intent to kill inflicting serious injury and the following offenses, when based on the same conduct:

- attempted first-degree murder, State v. Tirado, 358 N.C. 551, 578–79 (2004); State v. Bethea, 173 N.C. App. 43, 58–59 (2005) (following *Tirado*);
- secret assault, State v. Woodberry, 126 N.C. App. 78, 80–81 (1997);
- discharging a firearm into occupied property, State v. Allah, 168 N.C. App. 190, 196–97 (2005); and
- first-degree kidnapping, State v. Smith, 160 N.C. App. 107, 119 (2003).

Verdict. The court of appeals has held that if a defendant is charged with assault with a deadly weapon with intent to kill inflicting serious injury and attempted voluntary manslaughter and is convicted of attempted voluntary manslaughter and assault with a deadly weapon inflicting serious injury, the convictions cannot stand; the court reasoned that the jury's determination that the defendant did not commit assault with a deadly weapon with intent to kill inflicting serious injury excludes the possibility that the defendant committed attempted voluntary manslaughter, which requires an intent to kill. State v. Hames, 170 N.C. App. 312 (2005); State v. Chang Yang, 174 N.C. App. 755, 761–62 (2005) (following *Hames*). However, a subsequent supreme court case calls those decisions into question. State v. Mumford, 364 N.C. 394 (2010).

Related Offenses Not in This Chapter

See the offenses listed under "Assault with a Deadly Weapon with Intent to Kill," above.

Assault by Pointing a Gun

Statute

§14-34. Assaulting by pointing gun.

If any person shall point any gun or pistol at any person, either in fun or otherwise, whether such gun or pistol be loaded or not loaded, he shall be guilty of a Class A1 misdemeanor.

Elements

A person guilty of this offense

(1) intentionally
(2) points a gun
(3) at another.

Punishment

Class A1 misdemeanor. G.S. 14-34.

Notes

Element (1). Even though the defendant might actually have pointed a gun at someone, the offense has not occurred unless the defendant intended to do so. State v. Kluckhohn, 243 N.C. 306 (1956). If the defendant intends to point the gun at one person and mistakenly points it at someone else, he or she has committed this offense. State v. Thornton, 43 N.C. App. 564 (1979). See "Transferred Intent" in Chapter 1 (States of Mind).

If a person points a gun at another with legal justification, then this offense has not occurred. Lowe v. Dep't of Motor Vehicles, 244 N.C. 353 (1956); *In re* J.A., 103 N.C. App. 720 (1991). For example, if a law enforcement officer points a gun at a person in the good faith discharge of the officer's official duties, then this offense has not been committed. See generally "Public Authority" in Chapter 2 (Bars and Defenses). The absence of legal justification is not an element of the offense; instead, a defendant must raise the issue as a defense. State v. Gullie, 96 N.C. App. 366 (1989). *But see* State v. Dickens, 162 N.C. App. 632 (2004) (describing the elements of the offense as (1) pointing a gun (2) without justification).

Element (2). The statute provides that this offense occurs regardless of the defendant's purpose in pointing the gun ("in fun or otherwise") and regardless of whether the gun was loaded. G.S. 14-34.

The evidence was insufficient to support an adjudication of delinquency based on assault by pointing a gun when the weapon was an airsoft gun from which plastic pellets were fired using a "pump action" mechanism. *In re* N.T., ___ N.C. App. ___, ___ S.E.2d ___ (Aug. 2, 2011). The court reasoned that for purposes of this statute, the term "gun" "encompasses devices ordinarily understood to be 'firearms' and not other devices that fall outside that category," such as imitation firearms. *Id.*

Charging issues. See this note to "Simple Assault," above.

Greater and lesser included offenses. Assault by pointing a gun is not a lesser-included offense of assault with a firearm on a law enforcement officer, probation or parole officer, or detention facility employee. *Dickens*, 162 N.C. App. at 638 .

Multiple convictions and punishments. See this note to "Simple Assault" and "Assault Inflicting Serious Injury," both above.

Relation to other offenses. An assault by pointing a gun also could be an assault with a deadly weapon if the pointing amounts to an assault, such as when the defendant points a gun at someone and threatens to shoot. See the note on Element (1) to "Simple Assault," above. However, this offense applies even if the pointing does not amount to an assault.

If a person dies as a result of this offense, the assault may constitute criminal negligence supporting a charge of involuntary manslaughter. See "Criminal Negligence" in Chapter 1 (States of Mind) for a detailed discussion of criminal negligence, including when gun mishaps constitute criminal negligence.

Related Offenses Not in This Chapter

See the offenses in Chapter 22 (Weapons Offenses).
Criminal use of laser device. G.S. 14-34.8.
Transporting dangerous weapon or substance during emergency. G.S. 14-288.7.

Discharging Barreled Weapons and Firearms

Discharging a Barreled Weapon or Firearm into Occupied Property

Statute

§14-34.1. Discharging certain barreled weapons or a firearm into occupied property.

(a) Any person who willfully or wantonly discharges or attempts to discharge any firearm or barreled weapon capable of discharging shot, bullets, pellets, or other missiles at a muzzle velocity of at least 600 feet per second into any building, structure, vehicle, aircraft, watercraft, or other conveyance, device, equipment, erection, or enclosure while it is occupied is guilty of a Class E felony.

(b) A person who willfully or wantonly discharges a weapon described in subsection (a) of this section into an occupied dwelling or into any occupied vehicle, aircraft, watercraft, or other conveyance that is in operation is guilty of a Class D felony.

(c) If a person violates this section and the violation results in serious bodily injury to any person, the person is guilty of a Class C felony.

Elements

A person guilty of this offense

(1) willfully or wantonly
(2) discharges or attempts to discharge a firearm or a barreled weapon
(3) into property
(4) that is occupied when the weapon is discharged.

Punishment

Class E felony. G.S. 14-34.1(a).

Notes

Generally. Although this crime is covered in the chapter on assaults, it does not require proof of an assault.

Element (1). The State is not required to prove that the defendant intentionally discharged the firearm at a victim or at the occupied property; this is a general intent crime and the intent element applies to the discharging of the firearm, not the eventual destination of the bullet. State v. Canady, 191 N.C. App. 680, 685–86 (2008); State v. McLean, ___ N.C. App. ___, 712 S.E.2d 271 (2011) (as a general intent crime, this offense does not require the State to prove any specific intent to shoot into the vehicle; rather, the State need only show that the defendant intentionally fired a weapon under circumstances where he or she had reason to believe the conveyance that ended up being shot was occupied). For a more detailed discussion of the required state of mind, see "Willfully" and "Wantonly," both in Chapter 1 (States of Mind).

Element (2). A "firearm" is a weapon that propels shot, shell, or bullets by the action of an explosive within it, BLACK'S LAW DICTIONARY 648 (7th ed. 1999); it includes a handgun, shotgun, or rifle which expels a projectile by action of an explosive. State v. Small, ___ N.C. App. ___, 689 S.E.2d 444, 450 (2009). G.S. 14-34.1(a) provides that a "barreled weapon" includes only weapons capable of discharging shot, bullets, pellets, or other missiles at a muzzle velocity of at least 600 feet per second. Thus, any air rifle or air pistol with the required muzzle velocity would be covered. Only a barreled weapon must meet the velocity requirements of G.S. 14-34.1(a); a firearm need not meet these requirements. *Small*, ___ N.C. App. at ___, 689 S.E.2d at 450–51.

Element (3). The statute specifies the property as "any building, structure, vehicle, aircraft, watercraft, or other conveyance, device, equipment, erection, or enclosure."

A firearm is discharged "into" occupied property even if the firearm is inside the property, provided that the defendant is outside the property. For example, a person who, while standing outside a car, puts a pistol into an open window and fires the pistol into the car has discharged a firearm into property. State v. Mancuso, 321 N.C. 464, 468 (1988); State v. Bray, 321 N.C. 663, 670 (1988) (citing *Mancuso*).

Striking an exterior wall of an apartment building constitutes shooting "into" an apartment. *Canady*, 191 N.C. App. at 686–88.

Sufficient evidence supported a conviction when the defendant, while in his apartment, discharged a shotgun and a shotgun round went through the apartment's common wall and into another occupied apartment. State v. Cockerham, 155 N.C. App. 729 (2003).

Element (4). For other crimes, it has been held that property is "occupied" if someone actually is present there. State v. Tippett, 270 N.C. 588 (1967) (burglary).

A person is guilty of this offense only if he or she knows or has reasonable grounds to believe that the property is occupied. State v. Everette, 361 N.C. 646, 650 (2007); State v. Williams, 284 N.C. 67 (1973); State v. James, 342 N.C. 589, 596 (1996) (following *Williams*). For cases in which there was sufficient evidence that the defendant had reasonable grounds to believe that property was occupied, see *Everette*, 361 N.C. at 651 (lights were on in a restaurant located in an area known to be crowded in the early morning hours, the surrounding streets were crowded, and nearby establishments stayed open until the early morning); *James*, 342 N.C. at 597 (reasonable grounds to believe that cars were occupied when the defendant fired a semiautomatic weapon in a club's parking lot knowing that parked vehicles were there and that people had left the club and were present in the parking lot).

Attempt. The statute attaches the same punishment to an attempt to commit this offense as to the completed offense. This is an exception to the general rule that an attempt to commit a crime is punished one level below the completed offense. *See* "Attempt" in Chapter 5 (General Crimes).

Felony murder. This offense can constitute a felony supporting a conviction of first-degree murder under the felony murder theory. State v. Wall, 304 N.C. 609, 612–13 (1982); see also the note on Element (3)(c) to "First-Degree Murder" in Chapter 6 (Homicide).

Charging issues. See this note to "Simple Assault," above.

Multiple convictions and punishments. Each separate shot from a pistol supports a separate conviction. State v. Rambert, 341 N.C. 173, 176–77 (1995) (three distinct shots from a pistol fired into an occupied car supported three convictions and punishments; distinguishing the use of a pistol from a machine gun or other automatic weapon because the firing of a pistol requires the defendant to "employ his thought processes each time he fire[s] the weapon"); State v. Hagans, 188 N.C. App. 799, 805 (2008) (following *Rambert*).

Even when based on the same conduct, a defendant may be convicted and punished for both discharging a barreled weapon or firearm into occupied property and:

- assault with a deadly weapon, discussed above, State v. Messick, 88 N.C. App. 428, 436–37 (1988);
- assault with a deadly weapon with intent to kill inflicting serious injury, discussed above, State v. Allah, 168 N.C. App. 190, 196–97 (2005); and
- assault with a firearm on a law enforcement officer, probation or parole officer, or detention facility employee, discussed below, State v. Sellers, 155 N.C. App. 51, 59–60 (2002) (the defendant shot into a vehicle occupied by the officer).

Related Offenses Not in This Chapter

"Discharging a Firearm in Connection with a Pattern of Street Gang Activity" (Chapter 19)
"Malicious Damage to Occupied Property by Use of an Explosive or Incendiary" (Chapter 20)

"Manufacture, Possession, etc. of a Machine Gun, Sawed-Off Shotgun, or Weapon of Mass Destruction" (Chapter 20)
"Possession of a Firearm by a Felon" (Chapter 22)

Discharging a Barreled Weapon or Firearm into an Occupied Dwelling or Occupied Conveyance in Operation

Statute

See G.S. 14-34.1(b), reproduced under "Discharging a Barreled Weapon or Firearm into Occupied Property," above.

Elements

A person guilty of this offense

(1) willfully or wantonly
(2) discharges a firearm or barreled weapon
(3) (a) into an occupied dwelling *or*
    (b) into an occupied vehicle, aircraft, watercraft, or other conveyance that is in operation.

Punishment

Class D felony. G.S. 14-34.1(b).

Notes

Element (1). See this note to "Discharging a Barreled Weapon or Firearm into Occupied Property," above.

Element (2). See this note to "Discharging a Barreled Weapon or Firearm into Occupied Property," above.

Element (3)(a). For the meaning of the term "occupied," see the note on Element (3) to "Discharging a Barreled Weapon or Firearm into Occupied Property," above. The statute does not define the term "dwelling." For an explanation of that term as used in burglary, see the note on Element (4) to "First-Degree Burglary" in Chapter 15 (Burglary, Breaking or Entering, and Related Offenses).

Element (3)(b). For the meaning of the term "occupied," see the note on Element (3) to "Discharging a Barreled Weapon or Firearm into Occupied Property," above. The statute does not define the term "in operation." For an explanation of that term as used in the motor vehicle statutes, see the note on Element (1) to "Driving While License Revoked" in Chapter 28 (Motor Vehicle Offenses).

Charging issues. See this note to "Simple Assault," above. For an additional case on point decided after publication of the bulletin cited in that note, see *State v. Curry*, ___ N.C. App. ___, 692 S.E.2d 129 (2010) (fact that indictment charging discharging a barreled weapon into an occupied dwelling used the term "residence" instead of the statutory term "dwelling" did not result in a lack of notice as to the relevant charge).

Multiple convictions and punishments. See this note to "Discharging a Barreled Weapon or Firearm into Occupied Property," above.

Related Offenses Not in This Chapter

See the offenses listed under "Discharging a Barreled Weapon or Firearm into Occupied Property," above.

Discharging a Barreled Weapon or Firearm into Occupied Property Causing Serious Bodily Injury

Statute

See G.S. 14-34.1(c), reproduced under "Discharging a Barreled Weapon or Firearm into Occupied Property," above.

Elements

A person guilty of this offense

(1) (a) violates G.S. 14-34.1(a) (see "Discharging a Barreled Weapon or Firearm into Occupied Property," above) *or*
(b) violates G.S. 14-34.1(b) (see "Discharging a Barreled Weapon or Firearm into an Occupied Dwelling or Occupied Conveyance in Operation," above) *and*
(2) causes serious bodily injury.

Punishment

Class C felony. G.S. 14-34.1(c)

Notes

Element (1)(a). See the notes to "Discharging a Barreled Weapon or Firearm into Occupied Property," above.

Element (1)(b). See the notes to "Discharging a Barreled Weapon or Firearm into an Occupied Dwelling or Occupied Conveyance in Operation," above.

Element (2). The statute does not define the term "serious bodily injury." It is likely that a court would use the definition of "serious bodily injury" in G.S. 14-32.4. See "Assault Inflicting Serious Bodily Injury," above.

Charging issues. See this note to "Simple Assault," above.

Multiple convictions and punishments. See this note to "Discharging a Barreled Weapon or Firearm into Occupied Property," above.

Related Offenses Not in This Chapter

See the offenses listed under "Discharging a Barreled Weapon or Firearm into Occupied Property," above.

Secret Assault

Statute

§14-31. Maliciously assaulting in a secret manner.

If any person shall in a secret manner maliciously commit an assault and battery with any deadly weapon upon another by waylaying or otherwise, with intent to kill such other person, notwithstanding the person so assaulted may have been conscious of the presence of his adversary, he shall be punished as a Class E felon.

Elements

A person guilty of this offense

(1) commits an assault and battery
(2) on another
(3) with a deadly weapon

(4) in a secret manner
(5) with intent to kill *and*
(6) with malice.

Punishment

Class E felony. G.S. 14-31.

Notes

Element (1). The statute specifies that both an assault and a battery must occur. For a discussion of what constitutes a battery, see the note entitled "Battery" to "Simple Assault," above. For a discussion of what constitutes an assault, see the note on Element (1) to "Simple Assault," above.

Element (2). The State must prove that the assault and battery was committed against a particular individual. State v. Lyons, 330 N.C. 298 (1991) (jury instruction allowing conviction if the defendant assaulted one, two, or both victims was improper).

Element (3). See the note on Element (3) to "Assault with a Deadly Weapon," above.

Element (4). An assault is secret if the victim is (1) unaware of the defendant's presence; or (2) aware of the defendant's presence but unaware of the defendant's purpose to commit the assault. State v. Holcombe, ___ N.C. App. ___, 691 S.E.2d 740, 744 (2010) (insufficient evidence of this element). Examples of assaults that are secret include:

- a sudden shooting through a window, State v. McLamb, 203 N.C. 442 (1932);
- a sudden attack on the driver from a concealed position in a car's back seat, State v. Kline, 190 N.C. 177 (1925); and
- a shooting from ambush, State v. Miller, 189 N.C. 695 (1925).

For an example of a case in which the evidence was insufficient to establish a secret assault, see *State v. Wright*, ___ N.C. App. ___, 708 S.E.2d 112 (2011) (in the middle of the night, the victim heard a noise and looked up to see someone standing in the bedroom doorway; the victim jumped on the person and hit him with a chair; the victim was aware of the defendant's presence and purpose before the assault began; in fact, the victim started defending himself before the defendant's assault was initiated).

Element (5). See the note on Element (4) to "Assault with a Deadly Weapon with Intent to Kill," above.

Element (6). For a detailed discussion of the meaning of the term "malice," see "Maliciously" in Chapter 1 (States of Mind) and the notes on Element (3)(a)(i) to "First-Degree Murder" and on Element (3) to "Second-Degree Murder," both in Chapter 6 (Homicide).

Charging issues. See this note to "Simple Assault," above.

Greater and lesser-included offenses. Because all of the elements of simple assault are included in secret assault, simple assault is a lesser-included offense of secret assault.

Multiple convictions and punishments. See this note to "Simple Assault," above.

Because each offense contains an element that is not in the other, double jeopardy is not violated when a defendant is convicted and punished for this offense and assault with a deadly weapon with intent to kill inflicting serious injury, even when both offenses are based on the same assault. State v. Woodberry, 126 N.C. App. 78, 80–81 (2007).

Related Offenses Not in This Chapter

See the offenses in Chapter 22 (Weapons Offenses).
Use of dangerous weapon by prisoner in assault. G.S. 14-258.2.

Assault on a Female

Statute

See G.S. 14-33(c)(2), reproduced under "Simple Assault," above.

Elements

A person guilty of this offense

(1) is a male
(2) at least 18 years old *and*
(3) commits an assault
(4) on a female.

Punishment

Class A1 misdemeanor. G.S. 14-33(c).

Notes

Element (2). The jury may estimate a defendant's age solely by observing his appearance in court, without relying on any additional evidence of age. State v. Evans, 298 N.C. 263 (1979). Circumstantial evidence may be adequate for a jury's decision. State v. Barnes, 324 N.C. 539 (1989); State v. Ackerman, 144 N.C. App. 452 (2001).

The age requirement for this offense pertains only to the defendant; there is no age requirement for the victim. State v. Mueller, 184 N.C. App. 553, 570–71 (2007).

Element (3). See the note on Element (1) to "Simple Assault," above.

Constitutionality. This offense does not violate the Equal Protection Clause of the Fourteenth Amendment to the U.S. Constitution even though a male defendant is subject to a greater penalty than a female who commits the same act. State v. Gurganus, 39 N.C. App. 395 (1979).

Charging issues. See this note to"Simple Assault," above.

Greater and lesser-included offenses. Because all of the elements of simple assault are included in this offense, simple assault is a lesser-included offense of assault on a female.

This offense is not a lesser-included offense of (1) first-degree statutory rape, State v. Weaver, 306 N.C. 629 (1982); or (2) attempted second-degree rape, State v. Wortham, 318 N.C. 669 (1987); State v. Herring, 322 N.C. 733 (1988).

Multiple convictions and punishments. See this note to "Simple Assault" and "Assault Inflicting Serious Injury," both above.

Related Offenses Not in This Chapter

See the offenses in Chapter 10 (Sexual Assaults).
"Aggravated Misdemeanor Affray" (Chapter 19)

Assaults Involving Children

Assault on a Child under 12

Statute

See G.S. 14-33(c)(3), reproduced under "Simple Assault," above.

Elements

A person guilty of this offense

(1) commits an assault
(2) on a child under the age of 12 years.

Punishment

Class A1 misdemeanor. G.S. 14-33(c).

Notes

Element (1). See the note on Element (1) to "Simple Assault," above. As a general rule, the person who is in charge of a child (a parent or school teacher, for example) is not criminally liable for inflicting moderate punishment to correct the child. "Moderate punishment" is punishment that does not cause lasting injury. State v. Alford, 68 N.C. 322 (1873). See G.S. 115C-390.3 for the authority of school personnel to use reasonable force. See G.S. 115C-390.4 regarding corporal punishment in schools. See generally "Domestic Authority" in Chapter 2 (Bars and Defenses).

Element (2). If the child actually is under the age of 12, it is immaterial whether the defendant believed that the child was 12 or over. See the note on Element (2) to "First-Degree Statutory Rape" in Chapter 10 (Sexual Assaults).

Charging issues. See this note to "Simple Assault," above.

Greater and lesser-included offenses. Because all of the elements of simple assault are included in this offense, simple assault is a lesser-included offense of assault on a child.

This offense is not a lesser-included offense of first-degree statutory rape. State v. Weaver, 306 N.C. 629 (1982).

Multiple convictions and punishments. See this note to "Simple Assault" and "Assault Inflicting Serious Injury," both above.

Relation to other offenses. If the victim is 12 or older but under 16 and the defendant is the child's parent or guardian, child abuse might be charged. See the various child abuse offenses in Chapter 9 (Abuse and Neglect).

Related Offenses Not in This Chapter

"Indecent Liberties with a Child" (Chapter 10)
"Aggravated Misdemeanor Affray" (Chapter 19)

Assault in the Presence of a Minor

Statute

See G.S. 14-33(d), reproduced under "Simple Assault," above.

Elements

A person guilty of this offense

(1) in the course of an assault, assault and battery, or affray
(2) (a) inflicts serious injury *or*
    (b) uses a deadly weapon
(3) on a person with whom the defendant has a personal relationship *and*
(4) in the presence of a minor.

Punishment

Class A1 misdemeanor. G.S. 14-33(d). If convicted and sentenced to a community punishment, the defendant must be placed on supervised probation in addition to any other punishment imposed. *Id.* Second or subsequent convictions must receive active punishment of no less than thirty days, in addition to any other punishment imposed. *Id.*

Notes

Element (1). For a discussion of the terms "assault" and "battery," see the note on Element (1) and the note entitled "Battery" to "Simple Assault," above. For a discussion of the term "affray," see "Simple Affray" in Chapter 19 (Disorderly Conduct, Riot, and Gang Offenses).

Element (2)(a). For an explanation of the term "serious injury," see the note on Element (3) to "Assault Inflicting Serious Injury," above.

Element (2)(b). For an explanation of the term "deadly weapon," see the note on Element (3) to "Assault with a Deadly Weapon," above.

Element (3). The term "personal relationship" means relationships in which the parties:

- are current or former spouses;
- are persons of opposite sex who live or have lived together;
- are related as parents and children (including others acting in loco parentis to a minor child or as grandparents and grandchildren);
- have a child in common;
- are current or former household members; or
- are persons of the opposite sex who are or have been in a dating relationship.

G.S. 14-33(d); G.S. 50B-1(b). A "dating relationship" is one in which the parties are romantically involved over time and on a continuous basis during the course of the relationship. G.S. 50B-1(b). A casual acquaintance or ordinary fraternization between persons in a business or social context is not a dating relationship. *Id.*

Element (4). "In the presence of a minor" means that the minor was in a position to have observed the assault. G.S. 14-33(d). A "minor" is any person under the age of 18 years who is residing with or is under the care and supervision of, and who has a personal relationship with, the person assaulted or the person committing the assault. *Id.*

Charging issues. See this note to "Simple Assault," above.

Greater and lesser-included offenses. Because all of the elements of simple assault are included in this offense, simple assault is a lesser-included offense of assault in the presence of a minor.

Multiple convictions and punishments. See this note to "Simple Assault," above.

Related Offenses Not in This Chapter

"Violation of Domestic Violence Protective Order" (Chapter 8)
"Aggravated Misdemeanor Affray" (Chapter 19)
"Simple Affray" (Chapter 19)

Battery on an Unborn Child

Statute

§14-23.1. Definition.

As used in this Article only, "unborn child" means a member of the species homo sapiens, at any stage of development, who is carried in the womb.

§14-23.6. Battery on an unborn child.

(a) A person is guilty of the separate offense of battery on an unborn child if the person commits a battery on a pregnant woman. This offense is a lesser included offense of G.S. 14 23.5.

(b) Penalty. – Any person who commits an offense under this section is guilty of a Class A1 misdemeanor.

§14-23.7. Exceptions.

Nothing in this Article shall be construed to permit the prosecution under this Article of any of the following:

(1) Acts which cause the death of an unborn child if those acts were lawful, pursuant to the provisions of G.S. 14 45.1.
(2) Acts which are committed pursuant to usual and customary standards of medical practice during diagnostic testing or therapeutic treatment.
(3) Acts committed by a pregnant woman with respect to her own unborn child, including, but not limited to, acts which result in miscarriage or stillbirth by the woman. The following definitions shall apply in this section:
    a. Miscarriage. – The interruption of the normal development of an unborn child, other than by a live birth, and which is not an induced abortion permitted under G.S. 14 45.1, resulting in the complete expulsion or extraction from a pregnant woman of the unborn child.
    b. Stillbirth. – The death of an unborn child prior to the complete expulsion or extraction from a woman, irrespective of the duration of pregnancy and which is not an induced abortion permitted under G.S. 14 45.1.

§14-23.8. Knowledge not required.

Except for an offense under G.S. 14 23.2(a)(1), an offense under this Article does not require proof of either of the following:

(1) The person engaging in the conduct had knowledge or should have had knowledge that the victim of the underlying offense was pregnant.
(2) The defendant intended to cause the death of, or bodily injury to, the unborn child.

Elements

A person guilty of this offense

(1) commits a battery
(2) on a pregnant woman.

Punishment

Class A1 misdemeanor. G.S. 14-23.6(b).

Notes

Generally. This crime was enacted in 2011 and applies to offenses committed on or after December 1, 2011. S.L. 2011-60, sec. 8.

Element (1). This offense only applies to a battery—that is, the actual striking. For a discussion of the difference between an assault and a battery, see the note entitled "Battery" to "Simple Assault," above.

Element (2). G.S. 14-23.8 provides that this offense does not require proof that the person engaging in the conduct knew or should have known that the woman was pregnant or that the defendant intended to cause the death of or bodily injury to the unborn child.

Criminal liability of the pregnant woman. The session law enacting this offense provides that it may not be used to impose criminal liability on an expectant mother who is the victim of acts of domestic violence that cause injury or death to her unborn child. S.L. 2011-60, sec. 4.

The term "domestic violence" is defined by cross-reference to G.S. Chapter 50B. *Id.* See also the note entitled "Exceptions," immediately below.

Exceptions. The following acts are excluded from coverage by this offense:

- causing the death of an unborn child if the acts were lawful pursuant to G.S. 14-45.1 (when abortion is not unlawful);
- acts committed pursuant to usual and customary standards of medical practice during diagnostic testing or therapeutic treatment; or
- acts committed by a pregnant woman with respect to her own unborn child, including, but not limited to, acts which result in miscarriage or stillbirth by the woman.

G.S. 14-23.7. "Miscarriage" means the "interruption of the normal development of an unborn child, other than by a live birth, and which is not an induced abortion permitted under G.S. 14-45.1, resulting in the complete expulsion or extraction from a pregnant woman of the unborn child." G.S. 14-23.7. "Stillbirth" means the "death of an unborn child prior to the complete expulsion or extraction from a woman, irrespective of the duration of pregnancy and which is not an induced abortion permitted under G.S. 14-45.1." *Id.*

Greater and lesser-included offenses. This offense is a lesser-included offense of "Assault Inflicting Serious Bodily Injury on an Unborn Child," below. G.S. 14-23.6(a).

Multiple convictions and punishments. G.S. 14-23.6(a) states that battery on an unborn child is a "separate offense." This indicates a legislative intent that a defendant may be convicted of this offense and any other offense (such as a felonious assault on the woman) when based on the same conduct. This reading is confirmed by the session law, which states: "A prosecution for or conviction under this act is not a bar to conviction of or punishment for any other crime committed by the defendant as part of the same conduct." S.L. 2011-60, sec. 7.

Related Offenses Not in This Chapter

"Murder of an Unborn Child" (Chapter 6)
"Voluntary Manslaughter of an Unborn Child" (Chapter 6)
"Involuntary Manslaughter of an Unborn Child" (Chapter 6)
"Sale or Delivery of a Controlled Substance to a Pregnant Female" (Chapter 27)
Using drugs or instruments to destroy unborn child. G.S. 14-44.
Using drugs or instruments to produce miscarriage or injure pregnant woman. G.S. 14-45.
Concealing birth of a child. G.S. 14-46.

Assault Inflicting Serious Bodily Injury on an Unborn Child

Statute

See G.S. 14-23.1, reproduced under "Battery on an Unborn Child," above.

§14-23.5. Assault inflicting serious bodily injury on an unborn child; penalty.

(a) A person is guilty of the separate offense of assault inflicting serious bodily injury on an unborn child if the person commits a battery on the mother of the unborn child and the child is subsequently born alive and suffered serious bodily harm as a result of the battery.

(b) For purposes of this section, "serious bodily harm" is defined as bodily injury that creates a substantial risk of death, or that causes serious permanent disfigurement, coma, a permanent or protracted condition that causes extreme pain, or permanent or protracted loss or impairment of the function of any bodily member or organ, or that results in prolonged hospitalization, or causes the birth of the unborn child prior to 37-weeks gestation, if the child weighs 2,500 grams or less at the time of birth.

(c) Penalty. – Any person who commits an offense under this section shall be guilty of a Class F felony.

See G.S. 14-23.7 and 14-23.8, reproduced under "Battery on an Unborn Child," above.

Elements

A person guilty of this offense

(1) commits a battery
(2) on the mother of an unborn child *and*
(3) the child is subsequently born alive *and*
(4) suffered serious bodily harm as a result of the battery.

Punishment

Class F felony. G.S. 14-23.5(c).

Notes

Generally. This crime was enacted in 2011 and applies to offenses committed on or after December 1, 2011. S.L. 2011-60, sec. 8.

Element (1). See the note on Element (1) to "Battery on an Unborn Child," above.

Element (2). The term "unborn child" means "a member of the species homo sapiens, at any stage of development, who is carried in the womb." G.S. 14-23.1.

Element (3). The statute does not define the term "born alive." In the context of homicide law nationally, the term has come to mean that the fetus is "fully brought forth" and "established an 'independent circulation.'" 2 W. LaFave & A. Scott Jr., Substantive Criminal Law 419–20 (2d ed. 2003).

Element (4). The term "serious bodily harm" means "bodily injury that creates a substantial risk of death, or that causes serious permanent disfigurement, coma, a permanent or protracted condition that causes extreme pain, or permanent or protracted loss or impairment of the function of any bodily member or organ, or that results in prolonged hospitalization, or causes the birth of the unborn child prior to 37-weeks gestation, if the child weighs 2,500 grams or less at the time of birth." G.S. 14-23.5(b).

G.S. 14-23.8 provides that this offense does not require proof that the person engaging in the conduct knew or should have known that the woman was pregnant or that the defendant intended to cause the death of or bodily injury to the unborn child.

Criminal liability of the pregnant woman. See this note to "Battery on an Unborn Child," above.

Exceptions. See this note to "Battery on an Unborn Child," above.

Multiple convictions and punishments. G.S. 14-23.5(a) states that assault inflicting serious bodily injury on an unborn child is a "separate offense." This indicates a legislative intent that a defendant may be convicted of this offense and any other offense (such as a felonious assault on the woman) when based on the same conduct. This reading is confirmed by the session law, which states: "A prosecution for or conviction under this act is not a bar to conviction of or punishment for any other crime committed by the defendant as part of the same conduct." S.L. 2011-60, sec. 7.

Related Offenses Not in This Chapter

See the offenses listed under "Battery on an Unborn Child," above.

Assaults on Handicapped Persons

Simple Assault on a Handicapped Person

Statute

§14-32.1. Assaults on handicapped persons; punishments.

(a) For purposes of this section, a "handicapped person" is a person who has:

(1) A physical or mental disability, such as decreased use of arms or legs, blindness, deafness, mental retardation or mental illness; or

(2) Infirmity which would substantially impair that person's ability to defend himself.

(b) through (d) Repealed by Session Laws 1993 (Reg. Sess., 1994), c. 767, s. 31.

(e) Unless his conduct is covered under some other provision of law providing greater punishment, any person who commits any aggravated assault or assault and battery on a handicapped person is guilty of a Class F felony. A person commits an aggravated assault or assault and battery upon a handicapped person if, in the course of the assault or assault and battery, that person:

(1) Uses a deadly weapon or other means of force likely to inflict serious injury or serious damage to a handicapped person; or

(2) Inflicts serious injury or serious damage to a handicapped person; or

(3) Intends to kill a handicapped person.

(f) Any person who commits a simple assault or battery upon a handicapped person is guilty of a Class A1 misdemeanor.

Elements

A person guilty of this offense

(1) commits an assault or battery

(2) on a handicapped person

(3) knowing or having reason to know that the person is handicapped.

Punishment

Class A1 misdemeanor. G.S. 14-32.1(f).

Notes

Element (1). See the note on Element (1) and the note entitled "Battery" to "Simple Assault," both above.

Element (2). A "handicapped person" is someone who has a physical or mental disability (such as decreased use of arms or legs, blindness, deafness, mental retardation, or mental illness) or an infirmity that substantially impairs that person's ability to defend himself or herself. G.S. 14-32.1(a).

Sufficient evidence of the victim's handicap was presented when the victim testified that she would not be able to hear someone come up behind her unless the person was making "a lot of noise" and that being out on the street where the incident occurred reduced her ability to hear. State v. Hines, 166 N.C. App. 202 (2004).

Element (3). The State must prove that the defendant knew or had reasonable grounds to know that the victim was handicapped. State v. Singletary, 163 N.C. App. 449 (2004); N.C. PATTERN JURY INSTRUCTIONS—CRIM. 208.40A. For a case holding that the evidence was sufficient to allow a reasonable juror to find that the defendant knew or should have known of the victim's handicap, see *Singletary*, 163 N.C. App. 449.

Charging issues. See this note to "Simple Assault," above.

Greater and lesser-included offenses. Because all of the elements of simple assault are included in this offense, simple assault is a lesser-included offense.

Multiple convictions and punishments. See this note to "Simple Assault," above.

Related Offenses Not in This Chapter

Injuring or killing law enforcement agency animal or an assistance animal. G.S. 14-163.1.

Aggravated Assault on a Handicapped Person

Statute

See G.S. 14-32.1(e), reproduced under "Simple Assault on a Handicapped Person," above.

Elements

A person guilty of this offense

(1) commits an assault or battery
(2) on a handicapped person
(3) knowing or having reason to know that the person is handicapped *and*
(4) (a) uses a deadly weapon or other means of force likely to cause serious injury or serious damage to a handicapped person,
    (b) inflicts serious injury on a handicapped person, *or*
    (c) intends to kill a handicapped person.

Punishment

Class F felony. G.S. 14-32.1(e).

Notes

Generally. This offense is the same as "Simple Assault on a Handicapped Person," above, except that this offense requires proof of the additional Element (4). Thus, the notes on Elements (1) through (3) to "Simple Assault on a Handicapped Person" apply here as well.

Element (4)(a). For an explanation of the term "deadly weapon," see the note on Element (3) to "Assault with a Deadly Weapon," above. For an explanation of the term "serious injury," see the note on Element (3) to "Assault Inflicting Serious Injury," above.

Element (4)(b). See the note on Element (3) to "Assault Inflicting Serious Injury," above.

Element (4)(c). See the note on Element (4) to "Assault with a Deadly Weapon with Intent to Kill," above.

Charging issues. See this note to "Simple Assault," above.

Greater and lesser-included offenses. Because all of the elements of (1) simple assault; and (2) simple assault on a handicapped person are included in this offense, both are lesser-included offenses of this crime.

Multiple convictions and punishment. See this note to "Simple Assault" and "Assault Inflicting Serious Injury," both above.

Related Offenses Not in This Chapter

See the offenses listed under "Simple Assault on a Handicapped Person," above.

Assaults on Government Officers, Employees, and Similar Persons

Assault on a Governmental Officer or Employee

Statute

See G.S. 14-33(c)(4), reproduced under "Simple Assault," above.

Elements

A person guilty of this offense

(1) commits an assault
(2) on an officer or employee of the state or any political subdivision of the state
(3) who is discharging or attempting to discharge his or her official duties.

Punishment

Class A1 misdemeanor. G.S. 14-33(c).

Notes

Element (1). See the note on Element (1) to "Simple Assault," above.

Element (2). This statute protects law enforcement officers and other government officers and employees.

It seems that the defendant must know or have reasonable grounds to know that the person he or she assaults is a state officer or employee. In interpreting a similarly written statute concerning assault on law enforcement officers, the North Carolina Supreme Court ruled that the State must prove that the defendant knew that the person he or she assaulted was a law enforcement officer. State v. Avery, 315 N.C. 1 (1985); *see also* N.C. PATTERN JURY INSTRUCTIONS—CRIM. 208.82 (requiring that the defendant knew or had reasonable grounds to believe the person was an officer).

It is not clear whether company police and campus police are covered by this offense. However, in 2005, the General Assembly enacted legislation covering assault on these individuals. See "Assault on a Company or Campus Police Officer," below.

When off-duty members of a city police force were assaulted while working as security guards for a restaurant, charges of assault on a law enforcement officer under former G.S. 14-33(b)(4) (now repealed) were proper. State v. Lightner, 108 N.C. App. 349 (1992) (the officers were working in police uniform and were carrying sidearms, the officers' employment with the restaurant was arranged through the city police department, the officers were required to follow police department rules and guidelines, and the officers were attempting to place the defendant under arrest—an official duty of office while working for the city—when they were assaulted); *see also* State v. Gaines, 332 N.C. 461 (1992). In similar circumstances, there also might be a violation of this statute, which covers assaults on law enforcement officers.

Element (3). The statute specifies that the assault may occur either while an officer or employee is discharging a duty of his or her office or while he or she is attempting to discharge such a duty. For example, an assault that occurs while an officer is executing or attempting to execute a search warrant would be covered. It is not clear that the defendant must know that the officer or employee is discharging, or attempting to discharge, a duty of his or her office.

Assaults committed because of a duty previously discharged by the officer or employee are not covered. For example, assaulting a police officer in the grocery store because of an arrest made a week ago would not be covered.

The duty being discharged must be a lawful duty. If, for example, the officer or employee was making an illegal arrest, then this element would not be satisfied. See the note on Element (2) to "Resisting, Delaying, or Obstructing an Officer" in Chapter 21 (Perjury, Bribery, Obstruction, Resisting, and Related Crimes).

Charging issues. See this note to "Simple Assault," above. For additional cases on point decided after publication of the bulletin cited in that note, see *State v. Noel*, ___ N.C. App. ___, 690 S.E.2d 10 (2010) (an indictment charging assault on a governmental officer under G.S. 14-33(c)(4) need not allege the specific duty the officer was performing; if it does, it is surplusage); *State v. Roman*, ___ N.C. App. ___, 692 S.E.2d 431 (2010) (there was no fatal variance between a warrant charging assault on a governmental officer under G.S. 14-33(c)(4) and the evidence at trial; the warrant charged that the assault occurred while the officer was discharging the duty of arresting the defendant for communicating threats, but at trial the officer testified that the assault occurred when he was arresting the defendant for being intoxicated and disruptive in public; the pivotal element was whether the assault occurred while the officer was discharging his duties; what crime the arrest was for is immaterial).

Greater and lesser-included offenses. Because all of the elements of simple assault are included in this offense, simple assault is a lesser-included offense of this crime.

Multiple convictions and punishments. See this note to "Simple Assault" and "Assault Inflicting Serious Injury," both above.

Even though assault on a governmental officer or employee and resist, delay, and obstruct an officer each contain elements not in the other and therefore are not the "same" for purposes of double jeopardy, the North Carolina courts have held that double jeopardy prohibits a defendant from being convicted and punished for both offenses when based on the same conduct. State v. Summrell, 282 N.C. 157, 173 (1972); State v. Hardy, 298 N.C. 191, 197–98 (1979) (citing *Summrell*); State v. Raynor, 33 N.C. App. 698, 701 (1977). The cases also hold that a defendant may be convicted of both of these crimes when different conduct supports each conviction, even if all of the conduct occurred during the same incident. State v. Newman, 186 N.C. App. 382, 386–89 (2007) (no double jeopardy violation when different conduct supported each charge). These cases are not in accord with the great majority of double jeopardy decisions. *See, e.g.*, State v. Martin, 47 N.C. App. 223, 231 (1980) ("If . . . a single act constitutes an offense against two statutes and each statute requires proof of an additional fact which the other does not, the offenses are not the same in law and a defendant may be convicted and punished for both."); State v. Martin, 195 N.C. App. 43, 54–55 (2009) ("'[D]ouble jeopardy is not violated merely because the same evidence is relevant to show both crimes.'" (quoting State v. Cumber, 32 N.C. App. 329, 337 (1977)); see also "Double Jeopardy" in Chapter 2 (Bars and Defenses) and the notes entitled "Multiple convictions and punishments," throughout this book.

Related Offenses Not in This Chapter

"Threat to Kill or Inflict Serious Injury on Executive, Legislative, or Court Officers" (Chapter 8)
"Aggravated Misdemeanor Affray" (Chapter 19)
"Resisting, Delaying, or Obstructing an Officer" (Chapter 21)
Injuring or killing law-enforcement agency animal or an assistance animal. G.S. 14-163.1.
Use of dangerous weapon by prisoner in assault. G.S. 14-258.2.

Assault on a Company or Campus Police Officer

Statute

See G.S. 14-33(c)(8), reproduced under "Simple Assault," above.

Elements

A person guilty of this offense

(1) commits an assault

(2) on a certified company police officer or a certified campus police officer
(3) who is performing his or her duties.

Punishment

Class A1 misdemeanor. G.S. 14-33(c).

Notes

Element (1). See the note on Element (1) to "Simple Assault," above.

Element (2). The company police officer must have been certified pursuant to G.S. Chapter 74E. The campus police officer must have been certified pursuant to G.S. Chapter 74G, Chapter 17C, or Chapter 116.

Charging issues. See this note to "Simple Assault," above.

Greater and lesser-included offenses. Because all of the elements of simple assault are included in this crime, simple assault is a lesser-included offense.

Multiple convictions and punishments. See this note to "Simple Assault" and "Assault Inflicting Serious Injury," both above.

Relation to other offenses. To the extent that the campus police officer is employed by a unit of state or local government, such as an officer employed by a state university, this offense overlaps with assault on a governmental officer or employee.

Related Offenses Not in This Chapter

None

Assault with a Firearm or Other Deadly Weapon on a Governmental Officer or Employee or Company or Campus Police Officer

Statute

§14-34.2. Assault with a firearm or other deadly weapon upon governmental officers or employees, company police officers, or campus police officers.

Unless a person's conduct is covered under some other provision of law providing greater punishment, any person who commits an assault with a firearm or any other deadly weapon upon an officer or employee of the State or of any political subdivision of the State, a company police officer certified pursuant to the provisions of Chapter 74E of the General Statutes, or a campus police officer certified pursuant to the provisions of Chapter 74G, Chapter 17C, or Chapter 116 of the General Statutes, in the performance of his duties shall be guilty of a Class F felony.

Elements

A person guilty of this offense

(1) commits an assault
(2) with
  (a) a firearm *or*
  (b) any other deadly weapon
(3) (a) on an officer or employee of the state or any political subdivision of the state,
  (b) a certified company police officer, *or*
  (c) a certified campus police officer
(4) who is performing a duty of his or her office.

Punishment

Class F felony. G.S. 14-34.2.

Notes

Element (1). See the note on Element (1) to "Simple Assault," above. An assault with a firearm or other deadly weapon upon governmental officers or employees, company police officers, or campus police officers occurred when the defendant reached for but did not touch a weapon that was inches away from his hand. State v. Barksdale, 181 N.C. App. 302, 307 (2007) (concluding that the defendant's conduct constituted an unequivocal appearance of an attempt to harm the officers with the gun).

Element (2)(a). See the note on Element (2) to "Discharging a Barreled Weapon or Firearm into Occupied Property," above.

Element (2)(b). For a definition of "deadly weapon," see the note on Element (3) to "Assault with a Deadly Weapon," above.

Element (3). See the note on Element (2) to "Assault on a Governmental Officer or Employee," above.

Company and campus police officers are explicitly covered by this offense, while their inclusion as possible victims of assault on a governmental officer or employee is not always clear.

In interpreting a previous version of this G.S. 14-34.2, the courts ruled that the defendant must know that the victim is one of the designated kinds of officers or employees. State v. Avery, 315 N.C. 1 (1985); State v. Mayberry, 38 N.C. App. 509 (1978). This statute is likely to be interpreted similarly.

For a case holding that there was substantial evidence to show that the defendant knew or had reason to know the officers were law enforcement officers and, therefore, government officials, see *State v. Batchelor*, 167 N.C. App. 797 (2005).

Element (4). This offense is committed only if the officer or employee assaulted is engaged in a lawful duty. However, to be covered by this statute, the duty performed need not be a duty required by law; it need only be a duty permitted by law. For example, a law enforcement officer investigating a minor traffic accident that the officer has no statutory duty to investigate still is discharging a duty of his or her office. State v. Adams, 88 N.C. App. 139 (1987).

When the victim is a law enforcement officer, the duty need not be making an arrest; the officer could be patrolling, checking licenses, or engaged in any other official task. See the note on Element (4) to "Resisting, Delaying, or Obstructing an Officer" in Chapter 21 (Perjury, Bribery, Obstruction, Resisting, and Related Crimes). When an officer fired his pistol at the defendant in attempting to make an arrest, the officer was performing a duty of his office for purposes of this statute, and it was a violation of this statute for the defendant to return fire with a firearm. State v. Irick, 291 N.C. 480 (1977). However, if an officer uses excessive force in making an arrest, the person the officer is attempting to arrest can use reasonable force in self-defense. State v. Mensch, 34 N.C. App. 572 (1977).

Charging issues. See this note to "Simple Assault," above.

Greater and lesser-included offenses. Because all of the elements of (1) simple assault; (2) assault with a deadly weapon; (3) assault on a governmental officer or employee; and (4) assault on a company or campus police officer are included in this offense, all four of those offenses are lesser-included offenses of this crime.

Multiple convictions and punishments. See this note to "Simple Assault" and "Assault Inflicting Serious Injury," both above.

Relation to other offenses. Previous versions of this statute made it a crime to commit these kinds of assaults against firefighters, emergency medical services personnel, ambulance attendants, and paramedics, among others. To the extent that such officials are public employees, company police, or campus police, assaults on them will come under this statute. They also may be covered under "Assaults on Firefighters and Emergency or Medical Personnel," below.

Related Offenses Not in This Chapter

See the offenses listed under "Assault on a Governmental Officer or Employee," above.
See the offenses in Chapter 22 (Weapons Offenses).
Interference with firefighters. G.S. 58-82-1.

Assault with a Firearm on a Law Enforcement Officer, Probation or Parole Officer, or Detention Facility Employee

Statute

§14-34.5. Assault with a firearm on a law enforcement, probation, or parole officer or on a person employed at a State or local detention facility.

(a) Any person who commits an assault with a firearm upon a law enforcement officer, probation officer, or parole officer while the officer is in the performance of his or her duties is guilty of a Class E felony.

(b) Anyone who commits an assault with a firearm upon a person who is employed at a detention facility operated under the jurisdiction of the State or a local government while the employee is in the performance of the employee's duties is guilty of a Class E felony.

Elements

A person guilty of this offense

(1) commits an assault
(2) with a firearm
(3) on a
  (a) law enforcement officer,
  (b) probation officer,
  (c) parole officer, *or*
  (d) state or local government detention facility employee
(4) who is performing his or her duties.

Punishment

Class E felony. G.S. 14-34.5.

Notes

Element (1). See the note on Element (1) to "Simple Assault," above.

Element (4). See the note on Element (2) to "Discharging a Barreled Weapon or Firearm into Occupied Property," above.

The State does not need to prove that the defendant pointed a firearm at the covered officer or employee. Rather, it need only prove that the defendant put on a show of force or violence sufficient to put an officer of reasonable firmness in fear of immediate physical injury, State v. Dickens, 162 N.C. App. 632 (2004); State v. Childers, 154 N.C. App. 375 (2002), such as where the defendant slammed a gun down on a counter and then waved it around as he interacted with officers, *Childers*, 154 N.C. App. 375.

Element (3). To be guilty of this offense, the defendant must have known or had reasonable grounds to know that the victim was a law enforcement officer. *Dickens*, 162 N.C. App. 632. For a case in which the evidence was sufficient to show that the defendant knew or had reasonable grounds to know that the victim was a law enforcement officer, see *Dickens*, 162 N.C. App. 632.

Element (3)(a). Although G.S. 14-34.5 does not define "law enforcement officer," another statute and certain court decisions suggest that company police officers are covered by the term under some circumstances. "Company police officers" is a statutory term that includes most campus police officers at public and private colleges and universities, railroad police officers, and any other privately employed law enforcement officer. G.S. 74E-6(b). G.S. 74E-6(c) authorizes company police officers to make arrests and to charge infractions on specified types of property, so they appear to fit the definition of "law enforcement officer" in G.S. 14-288.1(5), which includes any "person authorized under the laws of North Carolina to make arrests and . . . acting within his territorial jurisdiction." Also, the North Carolina Court of Appeals has characterized company police officers as "public, although limited police officer[s]" in contrasting them with private detectives. N.C. Ass'n of Licensed Detectives v. Morgan, 17 N.C. App. 701 (1973). They probably would be considered law enforcement officers when enforcing state law but not when acting solely to protect private interests of their employers. Tate v. S. Ry. Co., 205 N.C. 51 (1933). They would be considered law enforcement officers when they both enforce state law and protect their employer's private interests at the same time. See the note on Element (2) to "Assault on a Governmental Officer or Employee," above.

Element (4). See the note on Element (4) to "Assault with a Firearm or Other Deadly Weapon on a Governmental Officer or Employee or Company or Campus Police Officer," above.

Charging issues. See this note to "Simple Assault," above.

Greater and lesser-included offenses. Because all of the elements of (1) simple assault; and (2) assault with a deadly weapon are included in this offense, both offenses are lesser-included offenses of this one. *Dickens*, 162 N.C. App. at 638.

Multiple convictions and punishments. See this note to "Simple Assault," above.

Even if based on the same conduct, a defendant may be convicted and punished for assault with a firearm on a law enforcement officer, probation or parole officer, or detention facility employee and (1) attempted first-degree murder, State v. Haynesworth, 146 N.C. App. 523, 531 (2001); and (2) discharging a barreled weapon or firearm into occupied property. State v. Sellers, 155 N.C. App. 51 (2002).

Related Offenses Not in This Chapter

See the offenses listed under "Assault on a Governmental Officer or Employee," above.

Assault Inflicting Physical Injury on a Law Enforcement Officer, Probation or Parole Officer, or Detention Facility Employee

Statute

§14-34.7. Assault inflicting serious injury on a law enforcement, probation, or parole officer or on a person employed at a State or local detention facility.

(a) Unless covered under some other provision of law providing greater punishment, a person is guilty of a Class F felony if the person assaults a law enforcement officer, probation officer, or parole officer while the officer is discharging or attempting to discharge his or her official duties and inflicts serious bodily injury on the officer.

(b) Anyone who assaults a person who is employed at a detention facility operated under the jurisdiction of the State or a local government while the employee is in the performance of the employee's duties and inflicts serious bodily injury on the employee is guilty of a Class F felony, unless the person's conduct is covered under some other provision of law providing greater punishment.

(c) Unless covered under some other provision of law providing greater punishment, a person is guilty of a Class I felony if the person does either of the following:

(1) Assaults a law enforcement officer, probation officer, or parole officer while the officer is discharging or attempting to discharge his or her official duties and inflicts physical injury on the officer.

(2) Assaults a person who is employed at a detention facility operated under the jurisdiction of the State or a local government while the employee is in

> the performance of the employee's duties and inflicts physical injury on the employee.
>
> For the purposes of this subsection, "physical injury" includes cuts, scrapes, bruises, or other physical injury which does not constitute serious injury.

Elements

A person guilty of this offense

(1) commits an assault
(2) on a
  (a) law enforcement officer,
  (b) probation officer,
  (c) parole officer, *or*
  (d) state or local government detention facility employee
(3) who is discharging or attempting to discharge his or her official duties *and*
(4) inflicts physical injury on the officer or employee.

Punishment

Class I felony. G.S. 14-34.7(c).

Notes

Element (1). See the note on Element (1) to "Simple Assault," above.

Element (2). See the note on Element (3) to "Assault with a Firearm on a Law Enforcement Officer, Probation or Parole Officer, or Detention Facility Employee," above.

Element (2)(a). For a discussion of the term "law enforcement officer" as used in a related offense, see the note on Element (2)(a) to "Assault with a Firearm on a Law Enforcement Officer, Probation or Parole Officer, or Detention Facility Employee," above.

Element (3). See the note on Element (4) to "Assault with a Firearm or Other Deadly Weapon on a Governmental Officer or Employee or Company or Campus Police Officer," above.

Element (4). The term "physical injury" includes "cuts, scrapes, bruises, or other physical injury which does not constitute serious injury." G.S. 14-34.7(c).

Charging issues. See this note to "Simple Assault," above.

Multiple convictions and punishments. See this note to "Simple Assault" and "Assault Inflicting Serious Injury," both above.

Related Offenses Not in This Chapter

See the offenses listed under "Assault on a Governmental Officer or Employee," above.

Assault Inflicting Serious Injury or Serious Bodily Injury on a Law Enforcement Officer, Probation or Parole Officer, or Detention Facility Employee

Statute

See G.S. 14-34.7(a) & (b), reproduced under "Assault Inflicting Physical Injury on a Law Enforcement Officer, Probation or Parole Officer, or Detention Facility Employee," above.

Elements

A person guilty of this offense

(1) commits an assault
(2) on a
  (a) law enforcement officer,

(b) probation officer,
(c) parole officer, *or*
(d) state or local government detention facility employee
(3) who is discharging or attempting to discharge his or her official duties *and*
(4) inflicts serious injury or serious bodily injury on the officer or employee.

Punishment

Class F felony. G.S. 13-34.7.

Notes

Generally. This offense is the same as "Assault Inflicting Physical Injury on a Law Enforcement Officer, Probation or Parole Officer, or Dentention Facility Employee," above, except with respect to Element (4) pertaining to the injury inflicted. Thus, the relevant notes to that offense apply here as well.

Element (4). Notwithstanding the statutory language requiring serious bodily injury, the North Carolina Court of Appeals has ruled that the statute can be satisfied with proof of either serious injury or serious bodily injury. State v. Crawford, 167 N.C. App. 777 (2005). For a definition of "serious injury," see the note on Element (3) to "Assault Inflicting Serious Injury," above. Although the term "serious bodily injury" is not defined, a court would likely use the definition of that term in G.S. 14-32.4. For a discussion of that statutory definition, see the note on Element (3) to "Assault Inflicting Serious Bodily Injury," above.

Greater and lesser-included offenses. Because all of the elements of (1) simple assault; (2) assault inflicting serious injury; and (3) assault inflicting serious bodily injury are included in this offense, all three of those offenses are lesser-included offenses of this crime.

Multiple convictions and punishments. See this note to "Simple Assault" and "Assault Inflicting Serious Injury," both above.

Related Offenses Not in This Chapter

See the offenses listed under "Assault on a Governmental Officer or Employee," above.

Malicious Conduct by a Prisoner

Statute

§14-258.4. Malicious conduct by prisoner.

(a) Any person in the custody of the Department of Correction, the Department of Juvenile Justice and Delinquency Prevention, any law enforcement officer, or any local confinement facility (as defined in G.S. 153A-217, or G.S. 153A-230.1), including persons pending trial, appellate review, or presentence diagnostic evaluation, who knowingly and willfully throws, emits, or causes to be used as a projectile, bodily fluids or excrement at a person who is an employee of the State or a local government while the employee is in the performance of the employee's duties is guilty of a Class F felony. The provisions of this section apply to violations committed inside or outside of the prison, jail, detention center, or other confinement facility.

(b) Reserved.

Elements

A person guilty of this offense

(1) while in the custody of
(a) the Department of Correction,
(b) the Department of Juvenile Justice and Delinquency Prevention,

(c) any law enforcement officer, *or*
(d) any local confinement facility
(2) knowingly and willfully
(3) throws, emits, or causes to be used as a projectile
(4) bodily fluids or excrement
(5) at a person who is a state or local government employee
(6) while the employee is in the performance of his or her duties.

Punishment

Class F felony. G.S. 14-258.4.

Notes

Element (1). Proof of a defendant's being in "custody" is satisfied by showing that a reasonable person in the defendant's position would have believed he or she was not free to leave. State v. Ellis, 168 N.C. App. 651 (2005); State v. Noel, ___ N.C. App. ___, 690 S.E.2d 10, 16 (2010) (quoting *Ellis*). For example, the defendant was in custody when he was handcuffed, seated on a curb, and told that he was not free to leave. *Noel,* ___ N.C. App. ___, 690 S.E.2d at 16.

This offense applies to violations committed inside or outside of a prison, jail, or other confinement facility as long as the person is in custody at the time of the incident. G.S. 14-258.4(a).

Element (1)(d). G.S. 153A-217 defines a "local confinement facility" to include a county or city jail, a local lockup, a regional or district jail, a juvenile detention facility, a detention facility for adults operated by a local government, and any other facility operated by a local government for confinement of persons awaiting trial or serving sentences. It further provides that the term does not include a "county satellite jail/work release unit." G.S. 153A-217(5). A "satellite jail/work release unit" means a building or designated portion of a building primarily designed, staffed, and used for the housing of misdemeanants participating in a work release program; the units may house misdemeanants only, except that the Sheriff may accept responsibility from the Department of Correction for the housing of certain felons. G.S. 153A-230.1

Element (2). See "Knowingly" and "Willfully" in Chapter 1 (States of Mind). Inadvertent conduct is not covered because the prisoner must act knowingly and willfully. G.S. 14-258.4(a). The evidence was sufficient to establish this element when the defendant was uncooperative with and belligerent toward officers and immediately before the incident said to an approaching officer, "F--k you, n----r. I ain't got nothing. You ain't got nothing on me." *Noel,* ___ N.C. App. ___, 690 S.E.2d at 16.

Element (4). Spitting is covered by the statute. *Noel,* ___ N.C. App. ___, 690 S.E.2d 10.

Element (5). Intentional conduct by a prisoner toward another prisoner or a visitor is not covered; the statute requires that the conduct be directed at a state or local government employee.

Charging issues. See this note to "Simple Assault," above. For an additional case on point decided after publication of the bulletin cited in that note, see *State v. Noel,* ___ N.C. App. ___, 690 S.E.2d 10 (2010) (indictment charging malicious conduct by prisoner under G.S. 14-258.4 need not allege the specific duty the officer was performing; if it does, it is surplusage).

Greater and lesser-included offenses. Assault on a governmental officer is not a lesser-included offense of malicious conduct by a prisoner. State v. Crouse, 169 N.C. App. 382, 386 (2005).

Multiple convictions and punishments. See this note to "Simple Assault," above.

Related Offenses Not in This Chapter

"Resisting, Delaying, or Obstructing an Officer" (Chapter 21)

Assault on an Executive, Legislative, or Court Officer

Statute

§14-16.6. Assault on executive, legislative, or court officer.

(a) Any person who assaults any legislative officer, executive officer, or court officer, or any person who makes a violent attack upon the residence, office, temporary accommodation or means of transport of any one of those officers in a manner likely to endanger the officer, shall be guilty of a felony and shall be punished as a Class I felon.

(b) Any person who commits an offense under subsection (a) and uses a deadly weapon in the commission of that offense shall be punished as a Class F felon.

(c) Any person who commits an offense under subsection (a) and inflicts serious bodily injury to any legislative officer, executive officer, or court officer, shall be punished as a Class F felon.

§14-16.9. Officers-elect to be covered.

Any person who has been elected to any office covered by this Article but has not yet taken the oath of office shall be considered to hold the office for the purpose of this Article and G.S. 114-15.

§14-16.10. Definitions.

The following definitions apply in this Article:

(1) Court officer.—Magistrate, clerk of superior court, acting clerk, assistant or deputy clerk, judge, or justice of the General Court of Justice; district attorney, assistant district attorney, or any other attorney designated by the district attorney to act for the State or on behalf of the district attorney; public defender or assistant defender; court reporter; juvenile court counselor as defined in G.S. 7B-1501(18a); any attorney or other individual employed by or acting on behalf of the department of social services in proceedings pursuant to Subchapter I of Chapter 7B of the General Statutes; any attorney or other individual appointed pursuant to G.S. 7B-601 or G.S. 7B-1108 or employed by the Guardian ad Litem Services Division of the Administrative Office of the Courts.

(2) Executive officer.—A person named in G.S. 147-3(c).

(3) Legislative officer.—A person named in G.S. 147-2(1), (2), or (3).

Elements

A person guilty of this offense

(1) assaults
(2) any
  (a) executive officer,
  (b) legislative officer, *or*
  (c) court officer.

Punishment

Class I felony. G.S. 14-16.6(a).

Notes

Element (1). See the note on Element (1) to "Simple Assault," above.

Element (2) generally. It is not clear whether the defendant must know or have reasonable grounds to believe that the victim was a covered officer. Compare, e.g., "Assault on a Child under 12," discussed above (for this offense it is immaterial whether the defendant believed that the child was over 12), with "Simple Assault on a Handicapped Person," also discussed above (for this offense the defendant must know or have reasonable grounds to believe that the victim is handicapped). The N.C. Pattern Jury Committee determined that such knowledge is required. N.C. PATTERN JURY INSTRUCTIONS—CRIM. 208.01.

Element (2)(a). The term "executive officer" includes:

- the Governor,
- the Lieutenant Governor,
- the private secretary for the Governor,
- the Secretary of State,
- the Auditor,
- the Treasurer,
- the Attorney General,
- the Superintendent of Public Instruction,
- members of the Governor's Council,
- the Commissioner of Agriculture,
- the Commissioner of Labor, and
- the Commissioner of Insurance.

G.S. 14-16.10(2) (incorporating G.S. 147-3(c)). Individuals who have been elected to a covered office but not yet taken the oath are covered as well. G.S. 14-16.9.

Element (2)(b). "Legislative officers" include:

- senators,
- members of the House of Representatives, and
- the House Speaker.

G.S. 14-16.10(3) (incorporating G.S. 147-2(1) through (3)). Individuals who have been elected to a covered office but not yet taken the oath are covered as well. G.S. 14-16.9.

Element (2)(c). A "court officer" is defined in G.S. 14-16.10(1) as a:

- magistrate;
- clerk or acting clerk of superior court;
- assistant or deputy clerk;
- judge or justice of the General Court of Justice;
- district attorney, assistant district attorney, or any other attorney designated by the district attorney to act for the State or on behalf of the district attorney;
- public defender or assistant defender;
- court reporter;
- juvenile court counselor as defined in G.S. 7B-1501(18a);
- any attorney or other individual employed by or acting on behalf of the department of social services in proceedings pursuant to Subchapter I of Chapter 7B of the General Statutes; and
- any attorney or other individual appointed pursuant to G.S. 7B-601 or G.S. 7B-1108 or employed by the Guardian ad Litem Services Division of the Administrative Office of the Courts.

Individuals who have been elected to a covered office but not yet taken the oath are covered as well. G.S. 14-16.9.

Unlike other assaults on public officials discussed in this chapter, this offense does not require that a court officer be performing a duty of office when assaulted.

Additional conduct included within statute. The statute also prohibits a violent attack upon the residence, office, temporary accommodation, or means of transport of any covered officer in a manner likely to endanger the officer. G.S. 14-16.6(a).

Charging issues. See this note to "Simple Assault," above.

Greater and lesser-included offenses. Because all of the elements of simple assault are included in this offense, simple assault is a lesser-included offense.

Multiple convictions and punishments. See this note to "Simple Assault," above.

Related Offenses Not in This Chapter

"Threat to Kill or Inflict Serious Injury on Executive, Legislative, or Court Officers" (Chapter 8)

Assault on an Executive, Legislative, or Court Officer Using a Deadly Weapon or Inflicting Serious Injury

Statute

See G.S. 14-16.6(b) and (c), reproduced under "Assault on an Executive, Legislative, or Court Officer," above.

Elements

A person guilty of this offense

(1) assaults
(2) any
  (a) executive officer,
  (b) legislative officer, *or*
  (c) court officer *and*
(3) (a) uses a deadly weapon *or*
  (b) inflicts serious bodily injury.

Punishment

Class F felony. G.S. 14-16.6(b) and (c).

Notes

Generally. This offense is the same as "Assault on an Executive, Legislative, or Court Officer," above, except that this offense contains an additional element—Element (3). Thus, the relevant notes to that offense apply here as well.

Element (3). For a definition of "deadly weapon," see the note on Element (3) to "Assault with a Deadly Weapon," above. The statute does not define the term "serious bodily injury." For a definition of "serious bodily injury" that applies in another assault offense, see the note on Element (3) to "Assault Inflicting Serious Bodily Injury," above.

Greater and lesser-included offenses. Because all of the elements of (1) simple assault; and (2) assault on an executive, legislative, or court officer are included in this offense, both are lesser-included offenses of this crime.

Related Offenses Not in This Chapter

"Threat to Kill or Inflict Serious Injury on Executive, Legislative, or Court Officers" (Chapter 8)

Assault on School Personnel

Statute

See G.S. 14-33(c)(6), reproduced under "Simple Assault," above.

Elements

A person guilty of this offense

(1) commits an assault
(2) on a school employee or school volunteer
(3) (a) who is discharging or attempting to discharge his or her duties *or*
(b) as a result of the employee's or volunteer's discharge or attempt to discharge his or her duties.

Punishment

Class A1 misdemeanor. G.S. 14-33(c).

Notes

Element (1). See the note on Element (1) to "Simple Assault," above.

Element (2). The terms "employee" and "volunteer" mean:

- an employee of a local board of education, a charter school authorized under G.S. 115C-238.29D, or a nonpublic school which has filed intent to operate under Part 1 or Part 2 of Article 39 of G.S. Chapter 115C;
- an independent contractor or an employee of an independent contractor of a local board of education, charter school authorized under G.S. 115C-238.29D, or a nonpublic school which has filed intent to operate under Part 1 or Part 2 of Article 39 of G.S. Chapter 115C, if the independent contractor carries out duties customarily performed by employees of the school; and
- an adult who volunteers his or her services or presence at any school activity and is under the supervision of an individual listed under (1) or (2) above.

G.S. 14-33(c)(6)b.

Element (3). The term "duties" means all activities:

- on school property;
- wherever occurring, during a school authorized event or the accompanying of students to or from that event; and
- relating to the operation of school transportation.

G.S. 14-33(c)(6)a. An assault committed because of a duty discharged by the employee or volunteer is covered by this offense.

Charging issues. See this note to "Simple Assault," above.

Greater and lesser-included offenses. Because all of the elements of simple assault are included in this offense, simple assault is a lesser-included offense of this crime.

Multiple convictions and punishments. See this note to "Simple Assault" and "Assault Inflicting Serious Injury," both above.

Relation to other offenses. This offense, to the extent it includes governmental employees such as teachers, overlaps with "Assault on a Governmental Officer or Employee," above. However, that offense, unlike this one, does not cover an assault on a teacher committed as a result of the discharge of his or her duties (for example, a parent assaulting a teacher at a shopping mall because the teacher had disciplined his child at school). See Element (3)(b), above.

Related Offenses Not in This Chapter

None

Assault and Battery on a Sports Official

Statute

See G.S. 14-33(b)(9), reproduced under "Simple Assault," above.

Elements

A person guilty of this offense

(1) commits an assault and battery
(2) against a sports official
(3) when the sports official is discharging or attempting to discharge official duties
(4) at a sports event or immediately after a sports event at which the sports official discharged official duties.

Punishment

Class 1 misdemeanor. G.S. 14-33(b).

Notes

Element (1). This offense requires an assault and a battery. For an explanation of those terms, see the note on Element (1) and the note entitled "Battery" to "Simple Assault," above.

Element (2). A "sports official" is "a person at a sports event who enforces the rules of the event, such as an umpire or referee, or a person who supervises the participants, such as a coach." G.S. 14-33(b)(9).

Element (4). A "sports event" includes

- any interscholastic or intramural athletic activity in a primary, middle, junior high, or high school, college, or university;
- any organized athletic activity sponsored by a community, business, or nonprofit organization;
- any athletic activity that is a professional or semiprofessional event; and
- any other organized athletic activity in the State.

G.S. 14-33(b)(9).

Charging issues. See this note to "Simple Assault," above.

Greater and lesser-included offenses. Because all of the elements of simple assault are included in this offense, simple assault is a lesser-included offense of this crime.

Multiple convictions and punishments. See this note to "Simple Assault" and "Assault Inflicting Serious Injury," both above.

Related Offenses Not in This Chapter

"Throwing Objects at Sporting Events" (Chapter 19)

Assault on a Public Transit Operator

Statute

See G.S. 14-33(c)(7), reproduced under "Simple Assault," above.

Elements

A person guilty of this offense

(1) assaults a public transit operator
(2) when the operator is discharging or attempting to discharge his or her duties.

Punishment

Class A1 misdemeanor. G.S. 14-33(b).

Notes

Element (1). A "public transit operator" includes a "public employee or a private contractor employed as a public transit operator, when the operator is discharging or attempting to discharge his or her duties". G.S. 14-33(c)(7).

Charging issues. See this note to "Simple Assault," above.

Greater and lesser-included offenses. Because all of the elements of simple assault are included in this offense, simple assault is a lesser-included offense of this crime.

Multiple convictions and punishments. See this note to "Simple Assault" and "Assault Inflicting Serious Injury," both above.

Relation to other offenses. When the public transit officer is a public employee, the defendant could be charged with this offense or, alternatively, with "Assault on a Governmental Officer or Employee," above, another Class A1 misdemeanor.

Related Offenses Not in This Chapter

None

Assaults on Firefighters and Emergency and Medical Personnel

Assault on a Firefighter or Medical Personnel

Statute

§14-34.6. Assault or affray on a firefighter, an emergency medical technician, medical responder, and emergency department personnel.

(a) A person is guilty of a Class I felony if the person commits an assault or an affray causing physical injury on any of the following persons who are discharging or attempting to discharge their official duties:

(1) An emergency medical technician or other emergency health care provider.
(2) A medical responder.
(3) The following emergency department personnel: physicians, physicians assistants, nurses, and licensed nurse practitioners.
(5) A firefighter.

(b) Unless a person's conduct is covered under some other provision of law providing greater punishment, a person is guilty of a Class H felony if the person violates subsection (a) of this section and (i) inflicts serious bodily injury or (ii) uses a deadly weapon other than a firearm.

(c) Unless a person's conduct is covered under some other provision of law providing greater punishment, a person is guilty of a Class F felony if the person violates subsection (a) of this section and uses a firearm.

Note: 2011 legislation, S.L. 2011-356, amended G.S. 34.6(a), deleting subsection (4). However, that legislation did not renumber subsection (5). Presumably, this issue will be remedied by the codifier of statutes but has not been resolved as of the writing of this book.

Elements

A person guilty of this offense

(1) commits an assault or affray
(2) on
   (a) a firefighter,
   (b) an emergency medical technician,
   (c) any other emergency health care provider,
   (d) a medical responder, *or*
   (e) an emergency department physician, physician's assistant, nurse, or licensed nurse practitioner
(3) who is discharging or attempting to discharge an official duty *and*
(4) inflicts physical injury.

Punishment

Class I felony. G.S. 14-34.6(a).

Notes

Element (1). See the note on Element (1) to "Simple Assault," above, and the discussion of "Simple Affray" in Chapter 19 (Disorderly Conduct, Riot, and Gang Offenses).

Element (2)(a). The statute does not define the term "firefighter."

Element (2)(b). The statute does not define the term "emergency medical technician." However, it is defined in G.S. 131E-155(10) as "an individual who has completed an educational program in emergency medical care approved by the Department and has been credentialed as an emergency medical technician by the Department."

Element (2)(d). The statute does not define the term "medical responder." However, it is defined in G.S. 131E-155(14a) as "an individual who has completed an educational program in emergency medical care and first aid approved by the Department and has been credentialed as a medical responder by the Department."

Element (4). The statute does not define the term "physical injury." Although that term is used in other assault offenses, see "Assault Inflicting Physical Injury by Strangulation," above, and "Habitual Misdemeanor Assault," below, it is not defined in those offenses either. Note that in 2011, the General Assembly amended a different assault statute creating a new crime, "Assault Inflicting Physical Injury on a Law Enforcement Officer, Probation or Parole Officer, or Detention Facility Employee," discussed above. S.L. 2011-356, sec. 1. For purposes of that new crime, the General Assembly defined the term "physical injury" to include cuts, scrapes, bruises, or other physical injury which does not constitute serious injury. *Id.*; G.S. 14-34.7(c).

Charging issues. See this note to "Simple Assault," above.

Greater and lesser-included offenses. Because all of the elements of simple assault are included in this offense, simple assault is a lesser-included offense of this crime.

Multiple convictions and punishments. See this note to "Simple Assault," above.

Related Offenses Not in This Chapter

"Aggravated Misdemeanor Affray" (Chapter 19)
"Simple Affray" (Chapter 19)

Assault on a Firefighter or Medical Personnel Inflicting Serious Injury or Using a Deadly Weapon Other Than a Firearm

Statute

See G.S. 14-34.6(a) and (b), reproduced under "Assault on a Firefighter or Medical Personnel," above.

Elements

A person guilty of this offense

(1) commits an assault or affray
(2) on
  (a) a firefighter,
  (b) an emergency medical technician,
  (c) any other emergency health care provider,
  (d) a medical responder, *or*
  (e) an emergency department physician, physician's assistant, nurse, or licensed nurse practitioner
(3) who is discharging or attempting to discharge an official duty *and*
(4) (a) inflicts serious bodily injury *or*
  (b) uses a deadly weapon.

Punishment

Class H felony. G.S. 14-34.6(a) and (b).

Notes

Generally. This offense is the same as "Assault on a Firefighter or Medical Personnel," above, except for Element (4). Thus, the relevant notes to that offense apply here as well.

Element (4)(a). Although "serious bodily injury" is not defined, a court would likely use the definition of that term in G.S. 14-32.4(a). For a discussion of that statute, see the note on Element (3) to "Assault Inflicting Serious Bodily Injury," above.

Element (4)(b). For a discussion of the meaning of the term "deadly weapon," see the note on Element (3) to "Assault with a Deadly Weapon," above. Note that G.S. 14-34.6 does not cover firearms. G.S. 14-34.6(b).

Greater and lesser-included offenses. Because all of the elements of (1) simple assault; (2) assault on a firefighter or medical personnel; (3) assault inflicting serious injury; and (4) assault with a deadly weapon are included in this offense, all four of those offenses are lesser-included offenses of this crime.

Multiple convictions and punishments. See this note to "Simple Assault" and "Assault Inflicting Serious Injury," both above.

Related Offenses Not in This Chapter

"Aggravated Misdemeanor Affray" (Chapter 19)
"Simple Affray" (Chapter 19)

Assault on a Firefighter or Medical Personnel with a Firearm

Statute

See G.S. 14-34.6(a) and (c), reproduced under "Assault on a Firefighter or Medical Personnel," above.

Elements

A person guilty of this offense

(1) commits an assault or affray
(2) on
  (a) a firefighter,
  (b) an emergency medical technician,
  (c) any other emergency health care provider,
  (d) a medical responder, *or*
  (e) an emergency department physician, physician's assistant, nurse, or licensed nurse practitioner
(3) who is discharging or attempting to discharge an official duty *and*
(4) uses a firearm.

Punishment

Class F felony. G.S. 14-34.6(c).

Notes

Generally. This offense is the same as "Assault on a Firefighter or Medical Personnel," above, excpet for Element (4). Thus, the relevant notes to that offense apply here as well.

Element (4). See the note on Element (2) to "Discharging a Barreled Weapon or Firearm into Occupied Property," above.

Greater and lesser-included offenses. Because all of the elements of simple assault are included in this offense, simple assault is a lesser-included offense of this crime.

Multiple convictions and punishments. See this note to "Simple Assault" and "Assault Inflicting Serious Injury," both above.

Related Offenses Not in This Chapter

"Aggravated Misdemeanor Affray" (Chapter 19)
"Simple Affray" (Chapter 19)

Assault on Emergency Personnel Inflicting Physical Injury

Statute

§14-288.9. Assault on emergency personnel; punishments.

(a) An assault upon emergency personnel is an assault upon any person coming within the definition of "emergency personnel" which is committed in an area:

(1) In which a declared state of emergency exists; or
(2) Within the immediate vicinity of which a riot is occurring or is imminent.

(b) The term "emergency personnel" includes law-enforcement officers, firemen, ambulance attendants, utility workers, doctors, nurses, and other persons lawfully engaged in providing essential services during the emergency.

(c) Any person who commits an assault causing physical injury upon emergency personnel is guilty of a Class I felony. Any person who commits an assault upon emergency personnel with or through the use of any dangerous weapon or substance shall be punished as a Class F felon.

Elements

A person guilty of this offense

(1) commits an assault

(2) on

(a) a law enforcement officer,

(b) a firefighter,

(c) a doctor,

(d) a utility worker, *or*

(e) any other person providing essential services

(3) (a) in an area in which a state of emergency has been declared *or*

(b) within the immediate vicinity of a riot or an imminent riot *and*

(4) the assault causes physical injury on the emergency personnel.

Punishment

Class I felony. G.S. 14-288.9(c).

Notes

Element (1). See the note on Element (1) to "Simple Assault," above.

Element (2). For a discussion of the term "law enforcement officer," see the note on Element (3)(a) to "Assault with a Firearm on a Law Enforcement Officer, Probation or Parole Officer, or Detention Facility Employee," above. "Emergency personnel" has generally meant paramedics and officials who respond to accidents, fires, and other life-threatening events in everyday life. That, however, is not the group of people covered by this statute. To be covered by this statute, the person who is assaulted must be providing service during a declared state of public emergency. The statute covers assaults on any person providing essential services during the emergency; thus it may include persons such as utility workers or Red Cross workers. It is not clear whether the defendant must know that the victim is a designated kind of emergency worker to commit this offense. *See generally* State v. Avery, 315 N.C. 1 (1985) (interpreting a statute concerning assault on law enforcement officers, the court ruled that the State must prove that the defendant knew that the person assaulted was a law enforcement officer); State v. Singletary, 163 N.C. App. 449 (2004) (for assault on a handicapped person, the State must prove that the defendant knew or had reasonable grounds to know that the victim was handicapped).

Element (3). A state of emergency may be declared by certain city and county officials and by the governor under the authority of the Riot and Civil Disorder Act, G.S. Ch. 14, Art. 36A, when an emergency exists because of civil disorder or natural disaster. See the notes under "Misdemeanor Riot" in Chapter 19 (Disorderly Conduct, Riot, and Gang Offenses) for the elements of the offense of riot.

Element (4). The statute does not define the term "physical injury." Although that term is used in other assault offenses, see "Assault Inflicting Physical Injury by Strangulation," above, and "Habitual Misdemeanor Assault," below, it is not defined in those offenses either. Note that in 2011, the General Assembly amended a different assault statute creating a new crime, "Assault Inflicting Physical Injury on a Law Enforcement Officer, Probation or Parole Officer, or Detention Facility Employee," discussed above. S.L. 2011-356, sec. 1. For purposes of that new crime, the General Assembly defined the term "physical injury" to include cuts, scrapes, bruises, or other physical injury which does not constitute serious injury. *Id.*; G.S. 14-34.7(c).

Charging issues. See this note to "Simple Assault," above.

Greater and lesser-included offenses. Because all of the elements of simple assault are included in this offense, simple assault is a lesser-included offense of this crime.

Multiple convictions and punishments. See this note to "Simple Assault," above.

Relation to other offenses. For possible offenses involving emergency personnel acting outside of a state of emergency, see "Assault on a Firefighter or Medical Personnel," "Assault on a Firefighter or Medical Personnel Inflicting Serious Injury or Using a Deadly Weapon Other than Firearm," and "Assault on a Firefighter or Medical Personnel with a Firearm," all above.

Related Offenses Not in This Chapter

"Disorderly Conduct" (Chapter 19)
See riot (various offenses) in Chapter 19 (Disorderly Conduct, Riot, and Gang Offenses).
"Aggravated Misdemeanor Affray" (Chapter 19)
"Resisting, Delaying, or Obstructing an Officer" (Chapter 21)
Interference with firefighters. G.S. 58-82-1.

Assault on Emergency Personnel with a Dangerous Weapon

Statute

See G.S. 14-288.9, reproduced under "Assault on Emergency Personnel," above.

Elements

A person guilty of this offense

(1) commits an assault
(2) on a
  (a) law enforcement officer,
  (b) firefighter,
  (c) doctor,
  (d) utility worker, *or*
  (e) other person who is providing essential services
(3) (a) in an area where a state of emergency has been declared *or*
  (b) within the immediate vicinity of a riot or an imminent riot *and*
(4) uses a dangerous weapon or substance to commit the assault.

Punishment

Class F felony. G.S. 14-288.9(c).

Notes

Generally. This offense is the same as "Assault on Emergency Personnel Inflicting Physical Injury," above, except for Element (4). Thus, the relevant notes to that offense apply here as well.

Element (4). G.S. 14-288.1(2) defines "dangerous weapon or substance" to include "any deadly weapon, ammunition, explosive, incendiary device, radioactive material . . . or any instrument or substance designed for a use that carries a threat of serious bodily injury or destruction of property; or any instrument or substance . . . capable of being used to inflict serious bodily injury, when the circumstances indicate a probability [that it] will be so used; or any part or ingredient in any instrument or substance . . . when the circumstances indicate a probability that such part or ingredient will be so used."

Related Offenses Not in This Chapter

See the offenses listed under "Assault on Emergency Personnel Inflicting Physical Injury," above.

Habitual Misdemeanor Assault

Statute

§14-33.2. Habitual misdemeanor assault.

A person commits the offense of habitual misdemeanor assault if that person violates any of the provisions of G.S. 14-33 and causes physical injury, or G.S. 14-34, and has two or more prior convictions for either misdemeanor or felony assault, with the earlier of the two prior convictions occurring no more than 15 years prior to the date of the current violation. A conviction under this section shall not be used as a prior conviction for any other habitual offense statute. A person convicted of violating this section is guilty of a Class H felony.

Elements

A person guilty of this offense

(1) (a) (i) violates G.S. 14-33 and
(ii) causes physical injury *or*
(b) violates G.S. 14-34 *and*
(2) has two or more prior felony or misdemeanor assault convictions *and*
(3) the earlier of the convictions occurred no more than fifteen years before the date of the offense in Element (1).

Punishment

Class H felony. G.S. 14-33.2.

Notes

Element (1)(a)(i). The following offenses (all of which are discussed above) are included in G.S. 14-33:

- "Simple Assault," G.S. 14-33(a),
- "Assault and Battery on a Sports Official," G.S. 14-33(b)(9),
- "Assault Inflicting Serious Injury," G.S. 14-33(c)(1),
- "Assault with a Deadly Weapon," *id.*,
- "Assault on a Female," G.S. 14-33(c)(2),
- "Assault on a Child under 12," G.S. 14-33(c)(3),
- "Assault on a Governmental Officer or Employee," G.S. 14-33(c)(4),
- "Assault on School Personnel," G.S. 14-33(c)(6),
- "Assault on a Public Transit Operator," G.S. 14-33(c)(7),
- "Assault on a Company or Campus Police Officer," G.S. 14-33(c)(8), and
- "Assault in the Presence of a Minor," G.S. 14-33(d).

Element (1)(a)(ii). It is not enough that the defendant violates G.S. 14-33; the violation also must cause physical injury. The statute, however, does not define the term "physical injury." Although this term also is used in the offense of "Assault Inflicting Physical Injury by Strangulation," discussed above, it is not defined there either. Physical injury would appear to require more proof than mere physical contact. Note that in 2011, the General Assembly amended a different assault statute creating a new crime, "Assault Inflicting Physical Injury on a Law Enforcement Officer, Probation or Parole Officer, or Detention Facility Employee," discussed above. S.L. 2011-356, sec. 1. For purposes of that new crime, the General Assembly defined the term "physical injury" to include cuts, scrapes, bruises, or other physical injury which does not constitute serious injury. *Id.*; G.S. 14- 34.7(c).

Element (1)(b). G.S. 14-34 is "Assault by Pointing a Gun," discussed above.

Element (2). This element requires that the person have at least two prior assault convictions. The convictions may be felony or misdemeanor convictions. G.S. 14-33.2.

Under the previous version of the law, it was permissible to count as separate convictions prior convictions that occurred on the same date. State v. Forrest, 168 N.C. App. 614 (2005).

Element (3). This element prohibits the use of a prior conviction that occurred more than fifteen years before the current offense.

Relation to habitual felon status. The offense of habitual misdemeanor assault constitutes a separate substantive felony offense, unlike being a habitual felon, G.S. 14-7.1, which is a status, not a crime.

Constitutional issues. The use of a prior conviction that occurred before the date of the enactment of G.S. 14-33.2 to prove the offense of habitual misdemeanor assault is not an ex post facto violation. State v. Smith, 139 N.C. App. 209 (2000); State v. McCree, 160 N.C. App. 200 (2003).

The habitual misdemeanor assault statute does not violate double jeopardy; the statute punishes the defendant for the current offense and does not impose a second punishment for the prior convictions that are elements of the crime. State v. Carpenter, 155 N.C. App. 35 (2002). Neither *Apprendi v. New Jersey,* 530 U.S. 466 (2000), nor *Blakely v. Washington,* 542 U.S. 296 (2004), affect this ruling. State v. Massey, 179 N.C. App. 803 (2006).

Limitation on later use of conviction of habitual misdemeanor assault. A conviction of habitual misdemeanor assault for conduct committed on or after December 1, 2004, may not be used for any other habitual offense statute, such as habitual felon. G.S. 14-33.2. The statute contains no prohibition, however, on the prosecution of a person as a habitual felon when the current felony is habitual misdemeanor assault.

Charging issues. See this note to "Simple Assault," above.

Multiple convictions and punishments. See this note to "Simple Assault," above.

A person may be convicted and punished for habitual misdemeanor assault and malicious conduct by a prisoner based on the same assault of an officer. State v. Artis, 174 N.C. App. 668 (2005).

Related Offenses Not in This Chapter

None

Ethnic Intimidation

Statute

§14-401.14. Ethnic intimidation; teaching any technique to be used for ethnic intimidation.

(a) If a person shall, because of race, color, religion, nationality, or country of origin, assault another person, or damage or deface the property of another person, or threaten to do any such act, he shall be guilty of a Class 1 misdemeanor.

(b) A person who assembles with one or more persons to teach any technique or means to be used to commit any act in violation of subsection (a) of this section is guilty of a Class 1 misdemeanor.

Elements

A person guilty of this offense

(1) because of race, color, religion, nationality, or country of origin
(2) (a) assaults another person,
  (b) damages property of another,
  (c) defaces property of another, *or*
  (d) threatens to do (a), (b), or (c).

Punishment

Class 1 misdemeanor. G.S. 14-401.14(a).

Notes

Element (1). The statutory language supports charging this offense when the underlying assault or property damage offense is done because of (1) the victim's race, color, religion, or country of origin; or (2) the race, color, religion, or country of origin of a person other than the victim of the underlying offense.

An e-mail message sent to an African-American school administrator in protest of her alleged differing treatment of the defendant as compared to others who were African American was sent for a racially motivated purpose; the message contained a racial epithet and stated that the KKK would retaliate against the victim if she continued her course of action. *In re* B.C.D., 177 N.C. App. 555 (2006).

Element (2)(d). An e-mail message sent to an African-American school administrator and signed "KKK" communicated an intent to inflict harm on the victim; the sender promised to show up on the victim's doorstep unless the victim stopped suspending students who used a particular racial slur. *Id.*

Teaching ethnic intimidation made an offense. Subsection (b) of the statute provides that it is a Class 1 misdemeanor for a person to "assemble" with one or more people to "teach any technique or means to be used to commit any act" of ethnic intimidation.

Sentencing enhancement for ethnic animosity. G.S. 14-3(c) creates a sentencing enhancement that applies to misdemeanors committed because of the victim's race, color, religion, nationality, or country of origin. For a discussion of that statute, see "Prejudice Enhancement" under special misdemeanor sentencing provisions in Chapter 4 (Punishment under Structured Sentencing). The G.S. 14-3(c) sentencing enhancement is limited to situations in which a crime is committed because of the victim's personal characteristics. Ethnic intimidation, however, can be committed because of the race, color, religion, nationality, or country of origin of a person other than the victim of the crime (for example, if an offender committed simple assault against a person because of the race of that person's spouse, this sentencing enhancement would not apply).

Constitutional issues. This statute raises issues of First Amendment rights of free speech and assembly that have not yet been tested in North Carolina's courts. However, the United States Supreme Court has found a similar statute in Wisconsin to be constitutional. Wisconsin v. Mitchell, 508 U.S. 476 (1993).

Related Offenses Not in This Chapter

See the offenses in Chapter 18 (Trespass, Property Damage, and Littering).
See the offenses in Chapter 8 (Threats, Harassment, Stalking, and Violation of Domestic Violence Protective Orders).
Prohibited Secret Societies and Activities. G.S. Ch. 14, Art. 4A.

Malicious Injury by Use of an Explosive or Incendiary

Statute

§14-49. Malicious use of explosive or incendiary; punishment.

(a) Any person who willfully and maliciously injures another by the use of any explosive or incendiary device or material is guilty of a Class D felony.

Subsections (b), (b1), (b2), and (c) are not reproduced here.

Elements

A person guilty of this offense

(1) willfully and maliciously
(2) injures another
(3) by use of an explosive or incendiary device or material.

Punishment

Class D felony. G.S. 14-49.

Notes

Element (1). See "Willfully" and "Maliciously" in Chapter 1 (States of Mind).

Element (2). This offense apparently can be charged even when the injury is not serious.

Element (3). G.S. 14-50.1 defines "explosive or incendiary device or material" as "nitroglycerine, dynamite, gunpowder, other high explosive, incendiary bomb or grenade, other destructive incendiary device, or any other destructive incendiary or explosive device, compound, or formulation; any instrument or substance capable of being used for destructive explosive or incendiary purposes against persons or property, when the circumstances indicate some probability that such instrument or substance will be so used; or any explosive or incendiary part or ingredient in any instrument or substance included above, when the circumstances indicate some probability that such part or ingredient will be so used."

Related Offenses Not in This Chapter

"Burglary with Explosives" (Chapter 15)
"Making a False Bomb Report" (Chapter 20)
Malicious damage (various offenses) (Chapter 20)
"Manufacture, Possession, etc. of a Machine Gun, Sawed-Off Shotgun, or Weapon of Mass Destruction" (Chapter 20)
Malicious castration. G.S. 14-28.
Malicious maiming. G.S. 14-30.
Malicious throwing of corrosive acid or alkali. G.S. 14-30.1.
Transporting dangerous weapon or substance during emergency; possession off premises; exceptions. G.S. 14-288.7.

8

Threats, Harassment, Stalking, and Violation of Domestic Protective Orders

8

Threats, Harassment, Stalking, and Violation of Domestic Protective Orders

Communicating Threats

Statute

§14-277.1. Communicating threats.

(a) A person is guilty of a Class 1 misdemeanor if without lawful authority:

(1) He willfully threatens to physically injure the person or that person's child, sibling, spouse, or dependent or willfully threatens to damage the property of another;

(2) The threat is communicated to the other person, orally, in writing, or by any other means;

(3) The threat is made in a manner and under circumstances which would cause a reasonable person to believe that the threat is likely to be carried out; and

(4) The person threatened believes that the threat will be carried out.

(b) A violation of this section is a Class 1 misdemeanor.

Elements

A person guilty of this offense

(1) without lawful authority
  (a) willfully threatens to physically injure
    (i) another person *or*
    (ii) that person's child, sibling, spouse, or dependent *or*
  (b) willfully threatens to damage another's property *and*
(2) communicates that threat to the other person
(3) in a manner that would make a reasonable person believe it is likely to be carried out *and*
(4) the threat is believed by the threatened person.

Punishment

Class 1 misdemeanor. G.S. 14-277.1(a) & (b).

Notes

Element (1). See "Willfully" in Chapter 1 (States of Mind).

The message "The End is Near" on the screen saver of a high school computer was insufficient to constitute a threat. State v. Mortimer, 142 N.C. App. 321 (2001).

A conditional threat is covered by this statute if the defendant has no right to impose the condition. For example, a defendant who threatens to hit the victim if the victim comes any closer has committed this offense if the defendant had no right to impose the condition. State v. Roberson, 37 N.C. App. 714 (1978).

Element (2). The threat must be communicated to the victim. The communication may be made orally, in writing, or by any other means. G.S. 14-277.1(a)(2). If the threat is communicated only to a third person and never to the victim, this offense ordinarily has not occurred. However, this offense probably would occur if the defendant communicated the threat to a third person intending that the third person convey it to the victim and the third person actually conveyed the threat to the victim. In *State v. Thompson*, 157 N.C. App. 638 (2003), for example, the defendant told a third party that he was going to shoot the victim and other people, the third party then communicated this threat to the victim and other people, and the victim took the threat seriously. The court held that the evidence was sufficient even though the defendant did not directly communicate the threat to the victim.

Element (3). If the threat is clearly a joke or an exaggeration, the offense does not occur because a reasonable person would not believe that it will be carried out. G.S. 14-277.1(a)(3).

Element (4). The person threatened must actually believe that the defendant will carry out the threat. Thus, this element incorporates a subjective test, State v. Love, 156 N.C. App. 309 (2003), whereas Element (3) incorporates an objective test ("a reasonable person"). See generally "Objective knowledge" and "Subjective knowledge" in Chapter 1 (States of Mind).

Multiple convictions and punishments. A defendant can be charged with and convicted of both communicating threats and assault by pointing a gun, even if both offenses arose from the same incident. State v. Evans, 40 N.C. App. 730 (1979).

Related Offenses Not in This Chapter

"Ethnic Intimidation" (Chapter 7)
"Extortion" (Chapter 14)
"Threat Regarding Gang Withdrawal" (Chapter 19)
"Threat after Gang Withdrawal" (Chapter 19)
"Picketing a Courthouse" (Chapter 21)
Harassment of participant in neighborhood crime watch program. G.S. 14-226.2.
Prohibited Secret Societies and Activities. G.S. Ch. 14, Art. 4A.
Targeted picketing. G.S. 14-277.4A.
Threatening letters. G.S. 14-394.

Threat to Kill or Inflict Serious Injury on Executive, Legislative, or Court Officers

Statute

§14-16.7. Threats against executive, legislative, or court officers.

(a) Any person who knowingly and willfully makes any threat to inflict serious bodily injury upon or to kill any legislative officer, executive officer, or court officer, shall be guilty of a felony and shall be punished as a Class I felon.

(b) Any person who knowingly and willfully deposits for conveyance in the mail any letter, writing, or other document containing a threat to inflict serious bodily injury upon or to kill any legislative officer, executive officer, or court officer, shall be guilty of a felony and shall be punished as a Class I felon.

§14-16.8. No requirement of receipt of the threat.

In prosecutions under G.S. 14-16.7 of this Article it shall not be necessary to prove that any legislative officer, executive officer, or court officer actually received the threatening communication or actually believed the threat.

Elements

A person guilty of this offense

(1) knowingly *and*
(2) willfully
(3) threatens to
(4) (a) inflict serious bodily injury *or*
 (b) kill
(5) any
 (a) executive officer,
 (b) legislative officer, *or*
 (c) court officer.

Punishment

Class I felony. G.S. 14-16.7(a).

Notes

Element (1). See "Knowingly" in Chapter 1 (States of Mind).

Element (2). See "Willfully" in Chapter 1 (States of Mind).

Element (4)(a). The statute does not define the term "serious bodily injury." For a discussion of that term as it applies in the assault context, see the note on Element (3) to "Assault Inflicting Serious Bodily Injury" in Chapter 7 (Assaults).

Elements (5)(a), (b), and (c). For definitions of the terms "executive officer," "legislative officer," and "court officer," see the notes on Elements (2)(a), (b), and (c) to "Assault on Executive, Legislative, and Court Officers" in Chapter 7 (Assaults).

Additional conduct prohibited. G.S. 14-16.7(b) also prohibits making a similar threat by mail.

No requirement of receiving or believing threat. G.S. 14-16.8 provides that it is unnecessary to prove that the victim received or actually believed the threat. In this respect, this offense differs from communicating threats. See the notes on Elements (2) and (4) to "Communicating Threats," above.

Related Offenses Not in This Chapter

"Assault on an Executive, Legislative, or Court Officer" (Chapter 7)
Threatening letters. G.S. 14-394.

Harassing Telephone Calls

Statute

§14-196. Using profane, indecent or threatening language to any person over telephone; annoying or harassing by repeated telephoning or making false statements over telephone.

(a) It shall be unlawful for any person:

(1) To use in telephonic communications any words or language of a profane, vulgar, lewd, lascivious or indecent character, nature or connotation;

(2) To use in telephonic communications any words or language threatening to inflict bodily harm to any person or to that person's child, sibling, spouse, or dependent or physical injury to the property of any person, or for the purpose of extorting money or other things of value from any person;
(3) To telephone another repeatedly, whether or not conversation ensues, for the purpose of abusing, annoying, threatening, terrifying, harassing or embarrassing any person at the called number;
(4) To make a telephone call and fail to hang up or disengage the connection with the intent to disrupt the service of another;
(5) To telephone another and to knowingly make any false statement concerning death, injury, illness, disfigurement, indecent conduct or criminal conduct of the person telephoned or of any member of his family or household with the intent to abuse, annoy, threaten, terrify, harass, or embarrass;
(6) To knowingly permit any telephone under his control to be used for any purpose prohibited by this section.

(b) Any of the above offenses may be deemed to have been committed at either the place at which the telephone call or calls were made or at the place where the telephone call or calls were received. For purposes of this section, the term "telephonic communica-0tions" shall include communications made or received by way of a telephone answering machine or recorder, telefacsimile machine, or computer modem.

(c) Anyone violating the provisions of this section shall be guilty of a Class 2 misdemeanor.

Using Threatening Language on the Telephone

Statute

See G.S. 14-196(a)(2), reproduced above.

Elements

A person guilty of this offense

(1) in a telephonic communication
(2) uses words or language
(3) (a) threatening to inflict bodily harm to any person,
    (b) threatening physical injury to another's property, *or*
    (c) for the purpose of extorting something of value from another.

Punishment

Class 2 misdemeanor. G.S. 14-196(c).

Notes

Element (1). G.S. 14-196(b) provides that the term "telephonic communications" includes communications made or received by way of a telephone answering machine or recorder, telefacsimile machine, or computer modem.

Element (3). The statute does not define the term "bodily harm." Although the terms "serious bodily injury," "serious injury," and "physical injury" are used in connection with assault offenses, see generally the offenses in Chapter 7 (Assaults), the term "bodily harm" is not. The term "serious bodily harm" is used and defined in the kidnapping context. See the note on Element (4)(f) to "First-Degree Kidnapping" in Chapter 12 (Kidnapping and Related Offenses).

For a discussion of the crime of extortion, see "Extortion" in Chapter 14 (Robbery, Extortion, and Blackmail).

Constitutionality. G.S. 14-196(a)(1), which forbids using "indecent" language on the telephone, has been held invalid because it may include speech that is protected by the First Amendment to the federal Constitution. Radford v. Webb, 446 F. Supp. 608 (1978), *aff'd*, 596 F.2d 1205 (4th Cir. 1979). However, G.S. 14-196(a)(3) has been upheld as constitutional. State v. Camp, 59 N.C. App. 38 (1982).

Victim. The victim may be an organization, such as a sheriff's department, as well as a person. *Id.*

Jurisdiction and venue. G.S. 14-196(b) provides that all of the offenses in G.S. 14-196(a) may be deemed to have been committed either where the call was made or received. This is relevant for purposes of jurisdiction and venue. See generally "Lack of Jurisdiction" in Chapter 2 (Bars and Defenses).

Relation to other offenses. G.S. 14-196(b) provides that the statute applies to communications made or received by a telephone answering machine or recorder, telefacsimile machine, or computer modem. Thus, some communications may violate both this statute and "Cyberstalking," discussed below.

Because "Stalking" includes certain communications by telephone, there is some overlap between this offense and that one, discussed below.

Related Offenses Not in This Chapter

"Extortion" (Chapter 14)
"False Bomb Report Offenses" (Chapter 20)
"False Report to Law Enforcement Agencies or Officers" (Chapter 21)
"Picketing a Courthouse" (Chapter 21)
False ambulance request. G.S. 14-286.1, 14-111.1, and 14-111.2.
False fire alarm. G.S. 14-286.
Threatening letters. G.S. 14-394.
False report of emergency. G.S. 14-401.8.

Repeated Telephone Calls to Harass, etc.

Statute

See G.S. 14-196(a)(3), reproduced above.

Elements

A person guilty of this offense

(1) telephones
(2) another
(3) repeatedly
(4) for the purpose of
  (a) abusing,
  (b) annoying,
  (c) threatening,
  (d) terrifying,
  (e) harassing, *or*
  (f) embarrassing
(5) a person at the called number.

Punishment

Class 2 misdemeanor. G.S. 14-196(c).

Notes

Element (1). By its terms, G.S. 14-196(a)(3) applies whether or not a conversation actually occurs. *See also* State v. Van Pelt, ___ N.C. App. ___, 698 S.E.2d 504 (2010) (when the evidence established that the defendant repeatedly called the victim, it was unnecessary for the State to show the two actually spoke).

Element (4). The statute does not define the terms "abusing," "annoying," "threatening," "terrifying," "harassing," or "embarrassing." However, the stalking statute defines the terms "harasses" and "harassment" as knowing conduct directed at a specific person that torments, terrorizes, or terrifies that person and that serves no legitimate purpose. G.S. 14-277.3A(b)(2).

Constitutionality. See this note to "Using Threatening Language on the Telephone," above.

Victim. See this note to "Using Threatening Language on the Telephone," above.

Jurisdiction and venue. See this note to "Using Threatening Language on the Telephone," above.

Relation to other offenses. See this note to "Using Threatening Language on the Telephone," above.

Related Offenses Not in This Chapter

See the offenses listed under "Using Threatening Language on the Telephone," above.

Failing to Hang Up for Purpose of Disrupting Service

Statute

See G.S. 14-196(a)(4), reproduced above.

Elements

A person guilty of this offense

(1) makes a telephone call *and*
(2) fails to hang up or disengage the connection
(3) with the intent to disrupt the service of another.

Punishment

Class 2 misdemeanor. G.S. 14-196(c).

Notes

Constitutionality. See this note to "Using Threatening Language on the Telephone," above.

Victim. See this note to "Using Threatening Language on the Telephone," above.

Jurisdiction and venue. See this note to "Using Threatening Language on the Telephone," above.

Recorded conversation as evidence. See this note to "Using Threatening Language on the Telephone," above.

Relation to other offenses. See this note to "Using Threatening Language on the Telephone," above.

Related Offenses Not in This Chapter

See the offenses listed under "Using Threatening Language on the Telephone," above.

Making False Statements by Telephone to Harass, etc.

Statute

See G.S. 14-196(a)(5), reproduced above.

Elements

A person guilty of this offense

(1) telephones
(2) another *and*
(3) knowingly
(4) makes any false statement
(5) concerning
  (a) death,
  (b) injury,
  (c) illness,
  (d) disfigurement,
  (e) indecent conduct, *or*
  (f) criminal conduct
(6) (a) of the person telephoned *or*
  (b) of any member of the person's family or household
(7) with the intent to
  (a) abuse,
  (b) annoy,
  (c) threaten,
  (d) terrify,
  (e) harass, *or*
  (f) embarrass.

Punishment

Class 2 misdemeanor. G.S. 14-196(c).

Notes

Element (3). See "Knowingly" in Chapter 1 (States of Mind).

Element (7). See the note on Element (4) to "Repeated Telephone Calls to Harrass, etc.," above.

Constitutionality. See this note to "Using Threatening Language on the Telephone," above.

Victim. See this note to "Using Threatening Language on the Telephone," above.

Jurisdiction and venue. See this note to "Using Threatening Language on the Telephone," above.

Relation to other offenses. See this note to "Using Threatening Language on the Telephone," above.

Related Offenses Not in This Chapter

See the offenses listed under "Using Threatening Language on the Telephone," above.

Permitting Use of Telephone for Harassment

Statute

See G.S. 14-196(a)(6), reproduced above.

Elements

A person guilty of this offense

(1) knowingly
(2) permits any telephone under his or her control
(3) to be used for a purpose prohibited by
    (a) "Using Threatening Language on the Telephone,"
    (b) "Repeated Telephone Calls to Harass, etc."
    (c) "Failing to Hang Up for Purpose of Disrupting Service," *or*
    (d) "Making False Statements by Telephone to Harass."

Punishment

Class 2 misdemeanor. G.S. 14-196(c).

Notes

Element (1). See "Knowingly" in Chapter 1 (States of Mind).

Element (3). See "Using Threatening Language on the Telephone," "Repeated Telephone Calls to Harass, etc.," "Failing to Hang Up for Purpose of Disrupting Service," and "Making False Statements by Telephone to Harass," all above.

Constitutionality. See this note to "Using Threatening Language on the Telephone," above.

Victim. See this note to "Using Threatening Language on the Telephone," above.

Jurisdiction and venue. See this note to "Using Threatening Language on the Telephone," above.

Relation to other offenses. See this note to "Using Threatening Language on the Telephone," above.

Related Offenses Not in This Chapter

See the offenses listed under "Using Threatening Language on the Telephone," above.
"Conspiracy" (Chapter 5)

Cyberstalking

Statute

§14-196.3. Cyberstalking.

(a) The following definitions apply in this section:

(1) Electronic communication.—Any transfer of signs, signals, writing, images, sounds, data, or intelligence of any nature, transmitted in whole or in part by a wire, radio, computer, electromagnetic, photoelectric, or photo-optical system.

(2) Electronic mail.—The transmission of information or communication by the use of the Internet, a computer, a facsimile machine, a pager, a cellular telephone, a video recorder, or other electronic means sent to a person identified by a unique address or address number and received by that person.

(b) It is unlawful for a person to:

(1) Use in electronic mail or electronic communication any words or language threatening to inflict bodily harm to any person or to that person's child, sibling, spouse, or dependent, or physical injury to the property of any person, or for the purpose of extorting money or other things of value from any person.

(2) Electronically mail or electronically communicate to another repeatedly, whether or not conversation ensues, for the purpose of abusing, annoying, threatening, terrifying, harassing, or embarrassing any person.
(3) Electronically mail or electronically communicate to another and to knowingly make any false statement concerning death, injury, illness, disfigurement, indecent conduct, or criminal conduct of the person electronically mailed or of any member of the person's family or household with the intent to abuse, annoy, threaten, terrify, harass, or embarrass.
(4) Knowingly permit an electronic communication device under the person's control to be used for any purpose prohibited by this section.

(c) Any offense under this section committed by the use of electronic mail or electronic communication may be deemed to have been committed where the electronic mail or electronic communication was originally sent, originally received in this State, or first viewed by any person in this State.

(d) Any person violating the provisions of this section shall be guilty of a Class 2 misdemeanor.

(e) This section does not apply to any peaceable, nonviolent, or nonthreatening activity intended to express political views or to provide lawful information to others. This section shall not be construed to impair any constitutionally protected activity, including speech, protest, or assembly.

Using Electronic Mail or Communication to Threaten or Extort

Statute

See G.S. 14-196.3(b)(1), reproduced above.

Elements

A person guilty of this offense

(1) uses in
  (a) electronic mail *or*
  (b) electronic communication
(2) words or language
(3) (a) threatening to inflict bodily harm to any person,
  (b) threatening physical injury to the property of another, *or*
  (c) for the purpose of extorting money or other things of value from any person.

Punishment

Class 2 misdemeanor. G.S. 14-196.3(d).

Notes

Element (1)(a). G.S. 14-196.3(a)(2) defines "electronic mail" as the transmission of information or communication by the use of the Internet, a computer, a facsimile machine, a pager, a cellular telephone, a video recorder, or other electronic means sent to a person identified by a unique address or address number and received by that person.

Element (1)(b). G.S. 14-196.3(a)(1) defines an "electronic communication" as any transfer of signs, signals, writing, images, sounds, data, or intelligence of any nature, transmitted in whole or in part by a wire, radio, computer, electromagnetic, photoelectric, or photo-optical system.

Element (3)(a). The statute does not define the term "bodily harm." Although the terms "serious bodily injury," "serious injury," and "physical injury" are used in connection with assault offenses, see generally the offenses in Chapter 7 (Assaults), the term "bodily harm" is not. The term "serious bodily harm" is used and defined in the kidnapping context. See the note on Element (4)(f) to "First-Degree Kidnapping" in Chapter 12 (Kidnapping and Related Offenses).

Element (3)(b). The statute does not define the term "physical injury." Note that in 2011, the General Assembly created a new crime called "Assault Inflicting Physical Injury on a Law Enforcement Officer, Probation or Parole Officer, or Detention Facility Employee," discussed in Chapter 7 (Assaults). For purposes of that new crime, the General Assembly defined the term "physical injury" to include cuts, scrapes, bruises, or other physical injury that does not constitute serious injury. S.L. 2011-356, sec. 1; G.S. 34.7(c).

Element (3)(c). For a discussion of the crime of extortion, see "Extortion" in Chapter 14 (Robbery, Extortion, and Blackmail).

Exceptions. This offense does not apply to any peaceable, nonviolent, or nonthreatening activity intended to express political views or to provide lawful information to others. G.S. 14-196.3(e). Also, this offense may not be construed to impair any constitutionally protected activity, including speech, protest, or assembly. *Id.*

Relation to other offenses. To the extent a person commits this crime by making threats, there is some overlap between this crime and "Communicating Threats," above.

If the person commits this offense and extorts money or other things of value, there is some overlap between this offense and "Extortion," discussed in Chapter 14 (Robbery, Extortion, and Blackmail), a Class F felony.

Because "Harassing Telephone Calls," discussed above, applies to communications received through a telefacsimile machine or computer modem, some communications may violate both that offense and this one.

Finally, there appears to be some overlap between this offense and "Stalking," discussed below.

Jurisdiction and venue. G.S. 14-196.3(c) provides that any cyberstalking offense is considered to have been committed where the electronic mail or electronic communication was originally sent, originally received in North Carolina, or first viewed by a person in North Carolina. This provision is relevant to both jurisdiction and venue. See generally "Lack of Jurisdiction" in Chapter 2 (Bars and Defenses).

Related Offenses Not in This Chapter

"Extortion" (Chapter 14)

Repeated Use of Electronic Mail or Communication to Harass, etc.

Statute

See G.S. 14-196.3(b)(2), reproduced above.

Elements

A person guilty of this offense

(1) (a) electronically mails *or*
    (b) electronically communicates to
(2) another
(3) repeatedly
(4) for the purpose of
    (a) abusing,
    (b) annoying,
    (c) threatening,
    (d) terrifying,
    (e) harassing, *or*
    (f) embarrassing any person.

Punishment

Class 2 misdemeanor. G.S. 14-196.3(d).

Notes

Elements (1)(a) and (b). See the notes on Elements (1)(a) and (b) to "Using Electronic Mail or Communication to Threaten or Extort," above. G.S. 14-196.3(b)(2) provides that this offense occurs whether or not conversation ensues.

Element (4). The statute does not define the terms "abusing," "annoying," "threatening," "terrifying," "harassing," or "embarrassing." However, the stalking statute defines the terms "harasses" and "harassment" as knowing conduct directed at a specific person that torments, terrorizes, or terrifies that person and that serves no legitimate purpose. G.S. 14-277.3A(b)(2).

Apparently, the person the defendant seeks to abuse, annoy, etc., need not be the person to whom the defendant directs the electronic mail or communication. *See* G.S. 14-196.3(b)(2) (to annoy, abuse, etc., "any person").

Exceptions. See this note to "Using Electronic Mail or Communication to Threaten or Extort," above.

Relation to other offenses. See this note to "Using Electronic Mail or Communication to Threaten or Extort," above.

Jurisdiction and venue. See this note to "Using Electronic Mail or Communication to Threaten or Extort," above.

Related Offenses Not in This Chapter

None

Using Electronic Mail or Communication to Send a False Statement

Statute

See G.S. 14-196.3(b)(3), reproduced above.

Elements

A person guilty of this offense

(1) (a) electronically mails to *or*
 (b) electronically communicates with
(2) another *and*
(3) knowingly
(4) makes a false statement
(5) concerning
 (a) death,
 (b) injury,
 (c) illness,
 (d) disfigurement,
 (e) indecent conduct, *or*
 (f) criminal conduct
(6) (a) of the person electronically mailed *or*
 (b) any member of the person's family or household
(7) with the intent to
 (a) abuse,
 (b) annoy,

(c) threaten,
(d) terrify,
(e) harass, *or*
(f) embarrass.

Punishment

Class 2 misdemeanor. G.S. 14-196.3(d).

Notes

Elements (1)(a) and (b). See the notes on these elements to "Using Electronic Mail or Communication to Threaten or Extort," above.

Element (7). See the note on Element (4) to "Repeated Use of Electronic Mail or Communication to Harass, etc.," above.

Exceptions. See this note to "Using Electronic Mail or Communication to Threaten or Extort," above.

Relation to other offenses. See this note to "Using Electronic Mail or Communication to Threaten or Extort," above.

Jurisdiction and venue. See this note to "Using Electronic Mail or Communication to Threaten or Extort," above.

Related Offenses Not in This Chapter

None

Permitting Cyberstalking

Statute

G.S. 14-196.3(b)(4), reproduced above.

Elements

A person guilty of this offense

(1) knowingly
(2) permits an electronic communication device under his or her control
(3) to be used for a purpose prohibited by
  (a) "Using Electronic Mail or Communication to Threaten or Extort,"
  (b) "Repeated Use of Electronic Mail or Communication to Harass, etc.," *or*
  (c) "Using Electronic Mail or Communication to Send a False Statement."

Punishment

Class 2 misdemeanor. G.S. 14-196.3(d).

Notes

Element (1). See "Knowingly" in Chapter 1 (States of Mind).

Element (2). For the definition of "electronic communication," see the note on Element (1)(b) to "Using Electronic Mail or Communication to Threaten or Extort," above.

Element (3). See "Using Electronic Mail or Communication to Threaten or Extort," "Repeated Use of Electronic Mail or Communication to Harass, etc.," and "Using Electronic Mail or Communication to Send a False Statement," all above.

Exceptions. See this note to "Using Electronic Mail or Communication to Threaten or Extort," above.

Relation to other offenses. See this note to "Using Electronic Mail or Communication to Threaten or Extort," above.

Jurisdiction and venue. See this note to "Using Electronic Mail or Communication to Threaten or Extort," above.

Related Offenses Not in This Chapter

"Conspiracy" (Chapter 5)

Cyberbullying

Statute

§14-458.1. Cyber-bullying; penalty.

(a) Except as otherwise made unlawful by this Article, it shall be unlawful for any person to use a computer or computer network to do any of the following:

(1) With the intent to intimidate or torment a minor:

a. Build a fake profile or Web site;

b. Pose as a minor in:

1. An Internet chat room;

2. An electronic mail message; or

3. An instant message;

c. Follow a minor online or into an Internet chat room; or

d. Post or encourage others to post on the Internet private, personal, or sexual information pertaining to a minor.

(2) With the intent to intimidate or torment a minor or the minor's parent or guardian:

a. Post a real or doctored image of a minor on the Internet;

b. Access, alter, or erase any computer network, computer data, computer program, or computer software, including breaking into a password protected account or stealing or otherwise accessing passwords; or

c. Use a computer system for repeated, continuing, or sustained electronic communications, including electronic mail or other transmissions, to a minor.

(3) Plant any statement, whether true or false, tending to provoke or that actually provokes any third party to stalk or harass a minor.

(4) Copy and disseminate, or cause to be made, an unauthorized copy of any data pertaining to a minor for the purpose of intimidating or tormenting that minor (in any form, including, but not limited to, any printed or electronic form of computer data, computer programs, or computer software residing in, communicated by, or produced by a computer or computer network).

(5) Sign up a minor for a pornographic Internet site.

(6) Without authorization of the minor or the minor's parent or guardian, sign up a minor for electronic mailing lists or to receive junk electronic messages and instant messages, resulting in intimidation or torment of the minor.

(b) Any person who violates this section shall be guilty of cyber-bullying, which offense shall be punishable as a Class 1 misdemeanor if the defendant is 18 years of age or older at the time the offense is committed. If the defendant is under the age of 18 at the time the offense is committed, the offense shall be punishable as a Class 2 misdemeanor.

(c) Whenever any person pleads guilty to or is guilty of an offense under this section, and the offense was committed before the person attained the age of 18 years, the court may, without entering a judgment of guilt and with the consent of the defendant, defer further proceedings and place the defendant on probation upon such reasonable terms and conditions as the court may require. Upon fulfillment of the terms and conditions of the probation provided for in this subsection, the court shall discharge the defendant and dismiss the proceedings against the defendant. Discharge and dismissal under this subsection shall be without court adjudication of guilt and shall not be deemed a conviction for purposes of this section or for purposes of disqualifications or disabilities imposed by law upon conviction of a crime. Upon discharge and dismissal pursuant to this subsection, the person may apply for an order to expunge the complete record of the proceedings resulting in the dismissal and discharge, pursuant to the procedures and requirements set forth in G.S. 15A-146.

Elements

A person guilty of this offense

(1) uses a
  (a) computer *or*
  (b) computer network
(2) (a) with the intent to intimidate or torment a minor to
    (i) build a fake profile or Web site,
    (ii) pose as a minor in an Internet chat room or electronic mail or instant message,
    (iii) follow a minor online or into an Internet chat room, *or*
    (iv) post or encourage others to post on the Internet private, personal, or sexual information pertaining to a minor,
  (b) with the intent to intimidate or torment a minor or the minor's parent or guardian to
    (i) post a real or doctored image of a minor on the Internet,
    (ii) access, alter, or erase any computer network, computer data, computer program, or computer software, including breaking into a password protected account or stealing or otherwise accessing passwords, *or*
    (iii) use a computer system for repeated, continuing, or sustained electronic communications, including electronic mail or other transmissions, to a minor,
  (c) to plant any statement, whether true or false, tending to provoke or that actually provokes any third party to stalk or harass a minor,
  (d) to copy and disseminate, or cause to be made, an unauthorized copy of any data pertaining to a minor for the purpose of intimidating or tormenting that minor (in any form, including any printed or electronic form of computer data, computer programs, or computer software residing in, communicated by, or produced by a computer or computer network),
  (e) to sign up a minor for a pornographic Internet site, *or*
  (f) without authorization of the minor or the minor's parent or guardian to sign up a minor for electronic mailing lists or to receive junk electronic messages and instant messages, resulting in intimidation or torment of the minor.

Punishment

Class 1 misdemeanor if the defendant is 18 or older at the time of the offense. G.S. 14-458.1(b). If the defendant is under 18, it is a Class 2 misdemeanor. *Id.* The statute provides for discharge and dismissal of charges against defendants under 18, in certain circumstances, and for expunging the record if discharge and dismissal is ordered. G.S. 14-458.1(c).

Notes

Element (1)(a). The term "computer" means an internally programmed, automatic device that performs data processing or telephone switching. G.S. 14-453(2).

Element (1)(b). The term "computer network" means the interconnection of communication systems with a computer through remote terminals or a complex consisting of two or more interconnected computers or telephone switching equipment. G.S. 14-453(3).

Element (2)(a). The term "profile" means a configuration of user data required by a computer so that the user may access programs or services and have the desired functionality on that computer. G.S. 14-453(7c). The term "electronic mail" means the transmission of information or communication by the use of the Internet, a computer, a facsimile machine, a pager, a cellular telephone, a video recorder, or other electronic means sent to a person identified by a unique address or address number and received by that person. G.S. 14-453(6b); 14-196.3(a)(2). The term "Internet chat room" means a computer service allowing two or more users to communicate with each other in real time. G.S. 14-453(7b).

Element (2)(b). See the note on Element (1)(b) for the definition of the term "computer network." The term "data" means a representation of information, facts, knowledge, concepts, or instructions prepared in a formalized or other manner and intended for use in a computer, computer system, or computer network. G.S. 14-453(6a). Data may be embodied in any form, including computer printouts, magnetic storage media, optical storage media, and punch cards, or may be stored internally in the memory of a computer. *Id.* The term "computer program" means an ordered set of data that are coded instructions or statements that when executed by a computer cause the computer to process data. G.S. 14-453(4). The term "computer software" means a set of computer programs, procedures, and associated documentation concerned with the operation of a computer, computer system, or computer network. G.S. 14-453(5). See the note on Element (2)(a) for the definition of the term "electronic mail."

Element (2)(c). See "Stalking," below, for the meaning of the term "stalk." The statute does not define the term "harass." However, the stalking statute defines the terms "harasses" and "harassment" as knowing conduct directed at a specific person that torments, terrorizes, or terrifies that person and that serves no legitimate purpose. G.S. 14-277.3A(b)(2).

Element (2)(d). See the note to Element (2)(b) for the definitions of the terms "data," "computer program," and "computer software." See the note to Element (1)(b) for the definition of "computer network."

Exceptions. This offense does not apply to or prohibit: (1) any terms or conditions in a contract or license related to a computer, computer network, software, computer system, database, or telecommunication device; or (2) any software or hardware designed to allow a computer, computer network, software, computer system, database, information, or telecommunication service to operate in the ordinary course of a lawful business or designed to allow an owner or authorized holder of information to protect data, information, or rights in it. G.S. 14-453.1.

Jurisdiction and venue. G.S. 14-453.2 provides that when this offense is committed by the use of electronic communication, it may be deemed to have been committed where the electronic communication was originally sent or where it was originally received. See the note on Element (1)(b) to "Using Electronic Mail or Communication to Threaten or Extort," above, for the meaning of the term "electronic communication."

Relation to other offenses. There is some overlap between this offense and "Stalking," below, and "Harassing Telephone Calls," above.

Related Offenses Not in This Chapter

"Ethnic Intimidation" (Chapter 7)
"Extortion" (Chapter 14)

See computer fraud (various offenses) in Chapter 16 (Fraud, Forgery, False Pretenses, and Related Offenses).
See damage to computer offenses (various offenses) in Chapter 18 (Trespass, Property Damage, and Littering).
Threatening letters. G.S. 14-394.

Stalking

Statute

§14-277.3A. Stalking.

(a) Legislative Intent.—The General Assembly finds that stalking is a serious problem in this State and nationwide. Stalking involves severe intrusions on the victim's personal privacy and autonomy. It is a crime that causes a long-lasting impact on the victim's quality of life and creates risks to the security and safety of the victim and others, even in the absence of express threats of physical harm. Stalking conduct often becomes increasingly violent over time.

The General Assembly recognizes the dangerous nature of stalking as well as the strong connections between stalking and domestic violence and between stalking and sexual assault. Therefore, the General Assembly enacts this law to encourage effective intervention by the criminal justice system before stalking escalates into behavior that has serious or lethal consequences. The General Assembly intends to enact a stalking statute that permits the criminal justice system to hold stalkers accountable for a wide range of acts, communications, and conduct. The General Assembly recognizes that stalking includes, but is not limited to, a pattern of following, observing, or monitoring the victim, or committing violent or intimidating acts against the victim, regardless of the means.

(b) Definitions.—The following definitions apply in this section:

(1) Course of conduct.—Two or more acts, including, but not limited to, acts in which the stalker directly, indirectly, or through third parties, by any action, method, device, or means, is in the presence of, or follows, monitors, observes, surveils, threatens, or communicates to or about a person, or interferes with a person's property.

(2) Harasses or harassment.—Knowing conduct, including written or printed communication or transmission, telephone, cellular, or other wireless telephonic communication, facsimile transmission, pager messages or transmissions, answering machine or voice mail messages or transmissions, and electronic mail messages or other computerized or electronic transmissions directed at a specific person that torments, terrorizes, or terrifies that person and that serves no legitimate purpose.

(3) Reasonable person.—A reasonable person in the victim's circumstances.

(4) Substantial emotional distress.—Significant mental suffering or distress that may, but does not necessarily, require medical or other professional treatment or counseling.

(c) Offense.—A defendant is guilty of stalking if the defendant willfully on more than one occasion harasses another person without legal purpose or willfully engages in a course of conduct directed at a specific person without legal purpose and the defendant knows or should know that the harassment or the course of conduct would cause a reasonable person to do any of the following:

(1) Fear for the person's safety or the safety of the person's immediate family or close personal associates.

(2) Suffer substantial emotional distress by placing that person in fear of death, bodily injury, or continued harassment.

(d) Classification.—A violation of this section is a Class A1 misdemeanor. A defendant convicted of a Class A1 misdemeanor under this section, who is sentenced to a community punishment, shall be placed on supervised probation in addition to any other punishment imposed by the court. A defendant who commits the offense of stalking after having been previously convicted of a stalking offense is guilty of a Class F felony. A defendant who commits the offense of stalking when there is a court order in effect prohibiting the conduct described under this section by the defendant against the victim is guilty of a Class H felony.

(e) Jurisdiction.—Pursuant to G.S. 15A-134, if any part of the offense occurred within North Carolina, including the defendant's course of conduct or the effect on the victim, then the defendant may be prosecuted in this State.

Misdemeanor Stalking

Statute

See G.S. 14-277.3A(c), reproduced above.

Elements

A person guilty of this offense

(1) willfully *and*
(2) without legal purpose,
(3) (a) harasses another person on more than one occasion *or*
 (b) engages in a course of conduct directed at a specific person
(4) when the person knows or should know that the harassment or course of conduct would cause a reasonable person to
 (a) fear for the safety of
  (i) him or herself,
  (ii) his or her immediate family, *or*
  (iii) his or her close personal associates *or*
 (b) suffer substantial emotional distress by placing that person in fear of
  (i) death,
  (ii) bodily injury, *or*
  (iii) continued harassment.

Punishment

Class A1 misdemeanor. G.S. 14-277.3A(d). A defendant who is sentenced to community punishment must be placed on supervised probation in addition to any other punishment imposed. *Id.*

Notes

Element (1). See "Willfully" in Chapter 1 (States of Mind).

Element (3)(a). G.S. 14-277.3A(b)(2) defines the terms "harasses" and "harassment" as knowing conduct directed at a specific person that torments, terrorizes, or terrifies that person and that serves no legitimate purpose. It can occur through written or printed communication or transmission; telephone, cellular, or other wireless telephonic communication; facsimile transmission; pager messages or transmissions; answering machine or voice mail messages or transmissions; and electronic mail messages or other computerized or electronic transmissions. *Id.*

Element (3)(b). G.S. 14-277.3A(b)(1) defines "course of conduct" as two or more acts, including, but not limited to, those where the stalker (directly, indirectly, or through third parties) is in any way in the presence of, or follows, monitors, observes, surveils, threatens, or communicates to or about a person, or interferes with a person's property.

Element (4). The term "reasonable person" means a reasonable person in the victim's circumstances. G.S. 14-277.3A(b)(3). "Substantial emotional distress" means significant mental suffering or distress that may or may not require medical or other professional treatment or counseling. G.S. 14-277.3A(b)(4).

Sufficiency of evidence to support stalking conviction. The following cases were decided under a prior version of the stalking statute. There was sufficient evidence of stalking when (1) the defendant assaulted the victim while they were both students at medical school and the defendant was told not to contact the victim; the defendant later traveled to the victim's home three times, hid in the woods, and watched her home; and when the victim saw the defendant at the local library, she reported the incident to the sheriff's department, expressing concern for her safety, State v. Borkar, 173 N.C. App. 162 (2005); (2) during an altercation with the victim, the defendant told her she would "be sorry" and the next day told her she would live to regret her conduct; knowing he was not welcome, the defendant drove up and down an isolated road leading to the victim's house and told her neighbors that he had better not catch them coming from or going to her house; the defendant violated a restraining order by appearing near the victim's workplace; the defendant told an officer he was engaged in psychological warfare against the victim; and the defendant told a third party he intended to engage in violence, State v. Thompson, 157 N.C. App. 638 (2003); (3) although a court order prohibited the defendant from contacting the victim, during a nine-month period he followed her about fifty times; one night he approached her with a knife, causing her to fear for her life, State v. Snipes, 168 N.C. App. 525 (2005) (felony stalking); (4) the defendant sent five facsimile messages to the victim's workplace, only one of which contained a direct threat; among other things, the faxes called the victim, Danny Keel, "Mr. Keel-a-Nigger," referenced the defendant having purchased a shotgun, and mentioned the victim's family; the court noted that the case "diverges from those instances in which our courts historically have applied the stalking statute," State v. Wooten, ___ N.C. App. ___, 696 S.E.2d 570 (2010); and (5) the defendant harassed the victim by written communications, pager, and phone with no legitimate purpose; the communications were directed to the victim, including those to his office staff, made with the request that they be conveyed to the victim; the communication put the victim in fear, and his fear was reasonable given the defendant's behavior exhibiting a pattern of escalation, State v. Van Pelt, ___ N.C. App. ___, 698 S.E.2d 504 (2010).

Constitutionality. A prior version of the stalking statute was upheld in the face of a challenge that it was unconstitutionally vague. State v. Watson, 169 N.C. App. 331 (2005).

Jurisdiction. If any part of the offense occurred within North Carolina, including the defendant's course of conduct or the effect on the victim, then the defendant may be prosecuted in North Carolina. G.S. 14-277.3A(e). See generally "Lack of Jurisdiction" in Chapter 2 (Bars and Defenses).

Multiple convictions and punishments. The defendant's double jeopardy rights were violated when, in separate trials, he was twice convicted of stalking and the time periods for the "course of conduct" alleged in both indictments overlapped. State v. Fox, ___ N.C. App. ___, ___ S.E.2d ___ (Oct. 4, 2011) (reasoning that the same acts could result in a conviction under either indictment and noting that in the second trial the State introduced evidence that would have established stalking during the overlapping time period).

Relation to other offenses. There is some overlap between this offense and "Harassing Telephone Calls" and "Cyberstalking," both above.

Related Offenses Not in This Chapter

See the offenses in Chapter 18 (Trespass, Property Damage, and Littering).

Repeat Stalking

Statute

See G.S. 14-277.3A(c) and (d), reproduced above.

Elements

A person guilty of this offense

(1) willfully,
(2) without legal purpose,
(3) (a) harasses another person on more than one occasion *or*
    (b) engages in a course of conduct directed at a specific person
(4) when the person knows or should know that the harassment or course of conduct would cause a reasonable person to
    (a) fear for the safety of
        (i) him or herself,
        (ii) his or her immediate family, *or*
        (iii) his or her close personal associates *or*
    (b) suffer substantial emotional distress by placing that person in fear of
        (i) death,
        (ii) bodily injury, *or*
        (iii) continued harassment *and*
(5) the person previously has been convicted of a stalking offense.

Punishment

Class F felony. G.S. 14-277.3A(d).

Notes

Generally. This offense is the same as "Misdemeanor Stalking," above, except that for this offense Element (5) requires that the defendant have a prior stalking offense. Thus, the notes to "Misdemeanor Stalking" apply here as well.

Element (5). Some offenses require that the prior conviction occur within a certain period of the new offense. See, for example, "Habitual Impaired Driving" in Chapter 28 (Motor Vehicle Offenses) (requiring that the prior convictions occur within ten years of the new offense). That period is sometimes referred to as a "look back period." For this offense, there is no look back period; put another way, any prior stalking conviction is covered, no matter how old it is.

The statute requires that the defendant have "been previously convicted of a stalking offense." G.S. 14-277.3A(d). It does not limit the prior stalking offense to North Carolina offenses.

Charging issues. The prior convictions must be alleged pursuant to G.S. 15A-928. *Cf.* State v. Stephens, 188 N.C. App. 286 (2008) (the trial court did not err by allowing an amendment of a stalking indictment; the amendment did not change the language of the indictment, but rather separated out the allegation regarding the prior conviction that elevated punishment to a felony, as required by G.S. 15A-928).

Related Offenses Not in This Chapter

See the offenses in Chapter 18 (Trespass, Property Damage, and Littering).

Stalking When a Court Order Is in Place

Statute

See G.S. 14-277.3A(c) and (d), reproduced above.

Elements

A person guilty of this offense

(1) willfully,
(2) without legal purpose,
(3) (a) harasses another person on more than one occasion *or*
    (b) engages in a course of conduct directed at a specific person
(4) when the person knows or should know that the harassment or course of conduct would cause a reasonable person to
    (a) fear for the safety of
        (i) him or herself,
        (ii) his or her immediate family, *or*
        (iii) his or her close personal associates *or*
    (b) suffer substantial emotional distress by placing that person in fear of
        (i) death,
        (ii) bodily injury, *or*
        (iii) continued harassment *and*
(5) there is a court order in effect prohibiting the defendant from engaging in this conduct.

Punishment

Class H felony. G.S. 14-277.3A(d).

Notes

Generally. This offense is the same as "Misdemeanor Stalking," above, except that for this offense Element (5) requires that a court order be in place prohibiting the conduct. Thus, the notes to "Misdemeanor Stalking" apply here as well.

Element (5). G.S. 14-277.3A(d) specifies that there be a "court order in effect prohibiting the conduct described under this section by the defendant against the victim."

Related Offenses Not in This Chapter

See the offenses in Chapter 18 (Trespass, Property Damage, and Littering).

Violation of a Domestic Violence Protective Order

Statute

§50B-4.1. Violation of valid protective order.

(a) Except as otherwise provided by law, a person who knowingly violates a valid protective order entered pursuant to this Chapter or who knowingly violates a valid protective order entered by the courts of another state or the courts of an Indian tribe shall be guilty of a Class A1 misdemeanor.

Subsections (b), (c), (d), and (e) are not reproduced here.

(f) Unless covered under some other provision of law providing greater punishment, any person who knowingly violates a valid protective order as provided in subsection (a) of this section, after having been previously convicted of two offenses under this Chapter, shall be guilty of a Class H felony.

(g) Unless covered under some other provision of law providing greater punishment, any person who, while in possession of a deadly weapon on or about his or her person or within close proximity to his or her person, knowingly violates a valid protective order as provided in subsection (a) of this section by failing to stay away from a place, or a person, as so directed under the terms of the order, shall be guilty of a Class H felony.

(g1) Unless covered under some other provision of law providing greater punishment, any person who is subject to a valid protective order, as provided in subsection (a) of this section, who enters property operated as a safe house or haven for victims of domestic violence, where a person protected under the order is residing, shall be guilty of a Class H felony. A person violates this subsection regardless of whether the person protected under the order is present on the property.

(h) For the purposes of this section, the term "valid protective order" shall include an emergency or ex parte order entered under this Chapter.

Misdemeanor Violation of a Domestic Violence Protective Order

Statute

See G.S. 50B-4.1(a), reproduced above.

Elements

A person guilty of this offense

(1) knowingly
(2) violates a valid protective order entered pursuant to
 (a) Chapter 50B of the General Statutes,
 (b) a court of another state, *or*
 (c) a court of an Indian tribe.

Punishment

Class A1 misdemeanor. G.S. 50B-4.1(a).

Notes

Element (1). See "Knowingly" in Chapter 1 (States of Mind).

Element (2)(a). Chapter 50B of the General Statutes allows a person (hereinafter, plaintiff) who has a "personal relationship" with another person (hereinafter, defendant) to bring a civil action against the defendant for acts of domestic violence committed against the plaintiff or a minor child who resides with the plaintiff or is in the plaintiff's custody. The term "personal relationship" includes

- current or former spouses;
- people of the opposite sex who live together or have lived together;
- parent and child (however, an aggrieved party may not obtain an order of protection against a child under 16);
- a person acting in loco parentis to a minor child (however, an aggrieved party may not obtain an order of protection against a child under 16);
- grandparent and grandchild (however, an aggrieved party may not obtain an order of protection against a grandchild under 16);
- current or former household members;

- people who have a child in common; and
- people of the opposite sex who are or have been in a dating relationship.

G.S. 50B-1(b). The statute defines a dating relationship as one in which the parties are romantically involved over time and on a continuous basis; a casual acquaintance or ordinary fraternization in a business or social context is not a dating relationship. G.S. 50B-1(b)(6).

Acts of "domestic violence" include, among other things, attempting to cause bodily injury; intentionally causing bodily injury; and placing the plaintiff or member of the plaintiff's family or household in fear of imminent serious bodily injury. G.S. 50B-1(a).

The plaintiff may obtain a domestic violence protective order from a district court judge or, under certain circumstances, a designated magistrate. The order may prohibit the defendant from doing a wide variety of things, including assaulting, threatening, abusing, or harassing the plaintiff or the plaintiff's children (residing with the plaintiff or in the plaintiff's custody) or going near the plaintiff's residence or place of work. In addition, the order may give the plaintiff exclusive possession of a residence or vehicle. For a complete list of possible relief, see G.S. 50B-3(a).

A temporary restraining order entered pursuant to Rule 65(b) of the N.C. Rules of Civil Procedure on a motion alleging acts of domestic violence in a divorce action was not a valid domestic violence protective order as defined by G.S. Chapter 50B, was not entered after a hearing by the court or with consent of the parties, and could not support imposition of the punishment enhancement prescribed by G.S. 50B-4.1(d). State v. Byrd, 363 N.C. 214 (2009) (as discussed in the paper available at www.sog.unc.edu/sites/www.sog.unc.edu/files/Byrd2.pdf, other aspects of the *Byrd* decision were reversed by subsequently enacted North Carolina legislation).

Emergency or ex parte orders entered under G.S. Chapter 50B constitute valid protective orders. G.S. 50B-4.1(h).

Related punishment enhancement. As discussed in Chapter 4 (Punishment under Structured Sentencing), G.S. 50B-4.1(d) provides for a special punishment enhancement when a person commits a felony knowing that the conduct is prohibited by a protective order.

Making a false statement regarding a protective order. G.S. 50B-4.2 provides that a person who knowingly makes a false statement to a law enforcement agency or officer that a protective order remains in effect is guilty of a Class 2 misdemeanor.

Related Offenses Not in This Chapter

See the various offenses in Chapter 18 (Trespass, Property Damage, and Littering).
Interfering with emergency communication. G.S. 14-286.2.

Repeat Violation of a Domestic Violence Protective Order

Statute

G.S. 50B-4.1(f), reproduced above.

Elements

A person guilty of this offense

(1) knowingly
(2) violates a valid protective order entered pursuant to
  (a) Chapter 50B of the General Statutes,
  (b) a court of another state, *or*
  (c) a court of an Indian tribe *and*
(3) has previously been convicted of two offenses under Chapter 50B.

Punishment

Class H felony. G.S. 50B-4.1(f).

Notes

Generally. This offense is the same as "Misdemeanor Violation of a Domestic Violence Protective Order," above, except that this offense includes the additional Element (3) pertaining to prior convictions. Thus, the notes to "Misdemeanor Violation of a Domestic Violence Protective Order" apply here as well.

Element (3). Some offenses require that the prior conviction occur within a certain period of the new offense. See, for example, "Habitual Impaired Driving" in Chapter 28 (Motor Vehicle Offenses) (requiring that the prior convictions occur within ten years of the new offense). That period is sometimes referred to as a "look back period." For this offense, there is no look back period; put another way, any prior Chapter 50B conviction is covered, no matter how old it is.

Multiple convictions and punishments. The statute provides that this felony applies "[u]nless covered under some other provision of law providing greater punishment." G.S. 50B-4.1(f). This language may mean that a defendant may not be convicted of both this offense and another one providing for greater punishment if both convictions are based on the same conduct. For a more detailed discussion of this issue in the assault context, see this note under "Assault Inflicting Serious Injury" in Chapter 7 (Assaults).

Related Offenses Not in This Chapter

See the offenses listed under "Misdemeanor Violation of a Domestic Violence Protective Order," above.

Violation of a Domestic Violence Protective Order with a Deadly Weapon

Statute

G.S. 50B-4.1(g), reproduced above.

Elements

A person guilty of this offense

(1) knowingly
(2) violates a valid protective order entered pursuant to
  (a) Chapter 50B of the General Statutes,
  (b) a court of another state, *or*
  (c) a court of an Indian tribe
(3) by failing to stay away from a place or a person, as directed by the order,
(4) while in possession of a deadly weapon.

Punishment

Class H felony. G.S. 50B-4.1(g).

Notes

Generally. This offense is the same as "Misdemeanor Violation of a Domestic Violence Protective Order," above, except that this offense includes the additional Elements (3) and (4). Thus, the notes to "Misdemeanor Violation of a Domestic Violence Protective Order" apply here as well.

Element (4). The statute applies when the person is in possession of a deadly weapon "on or about his or her person or within close proximity to his or her person." G.S. 50B-4.1(g).

For a discussion of the meaning of the term "deadly weapon," see the note on Element (3) to "Assault With a Deadly Weapon" in Chapter 7 (Assaults).

Multiple convictions and punishments. See this note to "Repeat Violation of a Domestic Violence Protective Order," above.

Related Offenses Not in This Chapter

See the offenses listed under "Misdemeanor Violation of a Domestic Violence Protective Order," above.

See the various assault with a deadly weapon offenses in Chapter 7 (Assaults).

Entering Domestic Violence Safe House or Haven

Statute

G.S. 50B-4.1(g1), reproduced above.

Elements

A person guilty of this offense

(1) is subject to a valid protective order entered pursuant to
  (a) Chapter 50B of the General Statutes,
  (b) a court of another state, *or*
  (c) a court of an Indian tribe *and*
(2) enters property operated as a safe house or haven for victims of domestic violence
(3) where a person protected under the order is residing.

Punishment

Class H felony. G.S. 50B-4.1(g1).

Notes

Element (1). See the note to Element(2)(a) to "Misdemeanor Violation of a Domestic Violence Protective Order," above. Apparently the conduct discussed in Elements (2) and (3) need not constitute a violation of the relevant protective order. *See* G.S. 50B-4.1(g1) ("subject to" not "violates").

Element (3). This offense occurs regardless of whether the person protected by the order is present on the property at the time of the offense. G.S. 50B-4.1(g1).

Multiple convictions and punishments. See this note to "Repeat Violation of a Domestic Violence Protective Order," above.

Related Offenses Not in This Chapter

See the offenses listed under "Misdemeanor Violation of a Domestic Violence Protective Order," above.

See the various trespass offenses in Chapter 18 (Trespass, Property Damage, and Littering).

9

Abuse and Neglect

9

Abuse and Neglect

Child Abuse

Misdemeanor Child Abuse

Statute

§14-318.2. Child abuse a misdemeanor.

(a) Any parent of a child less than 16 years of age, or any other person providing care to or supervision of such child, who inflicts physical injury, or who allows physical injury to be inflicted, or who creates or allows to be created a substantial risk of physical injury, upon or to such child by other than accidental means is guilty of the Class A1 misdemeanor of child abuse.

(b) The Class A1 misdemeanor of child abuse is an offense additional to other civil and criminal provisions and is not intended to repeal or preclude any other sanctions or remedies.

(c) A parent who abandons an infant less than seven days of age pursuant to G.S. 14-322.3 shall not be prosecuted under this section for any acts or omissions related to the care of that infant.

Elements

A person guilty of this offense

(1) (a) is a parent of a child less than 16 years of age *or*
    (b) is a person providing care to or supervision of a child less than 16 years of age *and*
(2) (a) inflicts physical injury on,
    (b) allows physical injury to be inflicted on, *or*
    (c) creates or allows to be created a substantial risk of physical injury to
(3) the child
(4) other than by accident.

Punishment

Class A1 misdemeanor. G.S. 14-318.2(a).

Notes

Element (1). The statute applies only to the child's parent or someone who is providing care for or supervision of the child (such as a babysitter). A defendant provided care to or supervision of a child when he resided with the child and the child's mother for two months before the child's murder, he shared a bedroom with them, and the child's mother left the child in the defendant's care for short periods of time. State v. Carrilo, 149 N.C. App. 543 (2002).

Element (2). The statute does not define the term "physical injury." For an explanation of that term as used in a new assault offense, see the note on Element (4) to "Assault Inflicting Physical Injury on a Law Enforcement Officer, Probation or Parole Officer, or Detention Facility Employee" in Chapter 7 (Assaults). It seems that "physical injury" would require less than serious injury, as used in some abuse and neglect of a disabled or elder adult offenses (covered below), serious physical injury, as used in some child abuse offenses, see "Child Abuse—Inflicting Serious Mental or Physical Injury" and "Child Abuse—Willful Act or Omission Causing Serious Mental or Physical Injury," both below, and serious bodily injury, as used in some child abuse, patient abuse, and assault offenses, see "Child Abuse—Inflicting Serious Bodily Injury," "Child Abuse—Willful Act or Omission Causing Serious Bodily Injury," "Patient Abuse—Willful or Culpably Negligent Pattern of Conduct Causing Serious Bodily Injury," all below, and "Assault Inflicting Serious Bodily Injury" in Chapter 7 (Assaults).

Other abuse offenses cover physical or mental injury. See "Child Abuse—Inflicting Serious Mental or Physical Injury," "Child Abuse—Willful Act or Omission Causing Serious Mental or Physical Injury," "Abuse of a Disabled or Elder Adult Causing Mental or Physical Injury," and "Neglect of a Disabled or Elder Adult Causing Mental or Physical Injury," all below. This offense, however, covers only physical injury.

Physical injury does not need to actually occur; it is sufficient if the defendant leaves the child in circumstances in which physical injury is likely to occur. See Element (2)(c), above.

Element (4). This offense does not apply if the injury was inflicted accidentally. G.S. 14-318.2(a) ("by other than accidental means"). "Battered child syndrome" is a circumstance of continuous injury to a child that permits the inference that the injury did not occur by accident but that someone caring for the child was responsible for it. State v. Wilkerson, 295 N.C. 559 (1978); State v. Byrd, 309 N.C. 132 (1983).

Abandonment pursuant to G.S.14-322.3. G.S. 14-318.2(c) provides that a parent who abandons an infant less than seven days old pursuant to G.S. 14-322.3 may not be prosecuted for child abuse for any acts or omissions related to the care of that infant. G.S. 14-322.3 in turn provides that a parent may not be prosecuted for nonsupport of a child when the parent abandons an infant less than seven days old by voluntarily delivering the infant in compliance with the provisions of G.S. 7B-500(b) or 7B-500(d) and does not express an intent to return for the infant.

Predicate for homicide. A violation of this statute that results in death to the child can support a conviction for involuntary manslaughter or second-degree murder. *Wilkerson*, 295 N.C. 559; see generally "Involuntary Manslaughter" and "Second-Degree Murder," both in Chapter 6 (Homicide).

Moderate punishment to correct. As a general rule, a person who is in charge of a child (a parent or schoolteacher, for example) is not criminally liable for inflicting moderate punishment to correct the child. For a discussion of this rule, see the note on Element (1) to "Assault on a Child Under 12" in Chapter 7 (Assaults).

Child abuse reporting. G.S. 7B-301 requires any person or institution suspecting that a child has been abused to report the incident to the local director of the local social services department, but it does not impose a criminal penalty for failure to report. An argument can be made that violation of G.S. 7B-301 is a misdemeanor. Such an argument would rely on the common law rule that if a statute either prohibits or commands the performance of an act and does not impose a sanction for violations, then a violation of the statute is a general misdemeanor. State v. McNeill, 75 N.C. 15 (1876); State v. Bloodworth, 94 N.C. 918 (1886); State v. Bishop, 228 N.C. 371 (1947). If this rule applies to a failure to report, the offense would be a Class 1 misdemeanor under Structured Sentencing. See "Misdemeanors" in Chapter 4 (Punishment under Structured Sentencing).

Multiple convictions and punishments. G.S. 14-318.2(b) provides that this offense "is an offense additional to other . . . criminal provisions and is not intended to repeal or preclude any other sanctions or remedies." This language may mean that a defendant may be convicted of this offense and another offense that is the "same" for purposes of double jeopardy. See "Double Jeopardy" in Chapter 2 (Bars and Defenses) (discussing that under double jeopardy, a defendant may be convicted, in a single trial, of offenses that are the same if the legislature intended that result).

Related Offenses Not in This Chapter

"Assault in the Presence of a Minor" (Chapter 7)
"Assault on a Child under 12" (Chapter 7)
See the offenses in Chapter 10 (Sexual Assaults).
"Abduction of a Child" (Chapter 12)
See the offenses involving minors in Chapter 22 (Weapons Offenses).
See the offenses involving minors in Chapter 23 (Prostitution).
See the offenses involving children in Chapter 26 (Abandonment and Nonsupport).
See the offenses involving minors in Chapter 27 (Drug Offenses).
Permitting child to use firearm. G.S. 14-316.
Exposing child to fire. G.S. 14-318.
Rebirthing. G.S. 14-401.21.
Illegally receiving or giving compensation for placing child for adoption. G.S. 48-37.

Child Abuse—Inflicting Serious Mental or Physical Injury

Statute

§14-318.4. Child abuse a felony.

(a) A parent or any other person providing care to or supervision of a child less than 16 years of age who intentionally inflicts any serious physical injury upon or to the child or who intentionally commits an assault upon the child which results in any serious physical injury to the child is guilty of a Class E felony, except as otherwise provided in subsection (a3) of this section.

(a1) Any parent of a child less than 16 years of age, or any other person providing care to or supervision of the child, who commits, permits, or encourages any act of prostitution with or by the child is guilty of child abuse and shall be punished as a Class E felon.

(a2) Any parent or legal guardian of a child less than 16 years of age who commits or allows the commission of any sexual act upon the child is guilty of a Class E felony.

(a3) A parent or any other person providing care to or supervision of a child less than 16 years of age who intentionally inflicts any serious bodily injury to the child or who intentionally commits an assault upon the child which results in any serious bodily injury to the child, or which results in permanent or protracted loss or impairment of any mental or emotional function of the child, is guilty of a Class C felony.

(a4) A parent or any other person providing care to or supervision of a child less than 16 years of age whose willful act or grossly negligent omission in the care of the child shows a reckless disregard for human life is guilty of a Class E felony if the act or omission results in serious bodily injury to the child.

(a5) A parent or any other person providing care to or supervision of a child less than 16 years of age whose willful act or grossly negligent omission in the care of the child shows a reckless disregard for human life is guilty of a Class H felony if the act or omission results in serious physical injury to the child.

(b) The felony of child abuse is an offense additional to other civil and criminal provisions and is not intended to repeal or preclude any other sanctions or remedies.

(c) Abandonment of an infant less than seven days of age pursuant to G.S. 14-322.3 may be treated as a mitigating factor in sentencing for a conviction under this section involving that infant.

(d) The following definitions apply in this section:

(1) Serious bodily injury. – Bodily injury that creates a substantial risk of death or that causes serious permanent disfigurement, coma, a permanent or protracted condition that causes extreme pain, or permanent or protracted loss or impairment of the function of any bodily member or organ, or that results in prolonged hospitalization.

(2) Serious physical injury. – Physical injury that causes great pain and suffering. The term includes serious mental injury.

Elements

A person guilty of this offense

(1) (a) is a parent of a child less than 16 years of age *or*
(b) is a person providing care to or supervision of a child less than 16 years of age *and*
(2) (a) intentionally inflicts on or to the child *or*
(b) intentionally commits an assault on the child which results in
(3) serious mental or physical injury.

Punishment

Class E felony. G.S. 14-318.4(a). G.S. 14-318.4(c) provides that abandonment of an infant less than seven days old pursuant to G.S. 14-322.3 may be treated as a mitigating factor in sentencing for a conviction involving that infant. G.S. 14-322.3 provides that a parent may not be prosecuted for nonsupport of a child when the parent abandons an infant less than seven days of age by voluntarily delivering the infant in compliance with the provisions of G.S. 7B-500(b) or 7B-500(d) and does not express an intent to return for the infant.

Notes

Element (1). See the note on Element (1) to "Misdemeanor Child Abuse," above.

Element (2). See "Intentionally," in Chapter 1 (States of Mind). The State can prove its case by showing that the defendant intentionally inflicted serious injury on the child. See Elements (2)(a) and (3), above. However, the State also can establish its case by proving that the defendant intentionally inflicted an assault on the child that resulted in serious injury. See Elements (2)(b) and (3), above. The significant difference between this proof is that if the State proceeds on the second prong, it need not prove that the defendant intended to inflict serious injury. State v. Williams, 184 N.C. App. 351, 356–57 (2007); *see also* State v. Oakman, 191 N.C. App. 796, 799 (2008) (in a case in which the defendant was charged under G.S. 14-318.4(a3), the court held: "Whether the defendant intended the assault and not the serious bodily injury is immaterial."). Under either prong, culpable or criminal negligence can provide the requisite intent. *Oakman*, 191 N.C. App. at 801. See generally "Criminal Negligence" in Chapter 1 (States of Mind).

The evidence was sufficient to show that the defendant acted intentionally when he beat the victim with a belt for 40 to 100 minutes; the victim bled, was short of breath due to asthma, and vomited; the victim's arms were covered in bruises, his legs were swollen, and his buttocks were black and blue; the victim was hospitalized after the incident and was in pain for two weeks; and a medical expert testified that the victim's injuries were moderately to seriously severe, could have resulted in complications, and were nonaccidental. *Williams*, 184 N.C. App. at 356–57.

See the note on Element (4) to "Misdemeanor Child Abuse," above, for a discussion of battered child syndrome.

When an adult has exclusive custody of a child for a period of time and that child suffers injuries that are neither self-inflicted nor accidental, the evidence is sufficient to support an inference that the adult inflicted the injuries. State v. Campbell, 316 N.C. 168 (1986); State v. Perdue, 320 N.C. 51 (1987); State v. Riggsbee, 72 N.C. App. 167 (1984).

Element (3). G.S. 14-318.4(d)(2) defines the term "serious physical injury" as physical injury that causes great pain and suffering, including serious mental injury. Presumably this element requires more than "physical or mental injury," as that term is used in certain crimes covering abuse or neglect of a disabled or elder adult, discussed below.

Facts relevant to the determination of whether the injury is serious include: hospitalization, pain, loss of blood, and whether the child was unable to attend school or other activities. State v. Williams, 184 N.C. App. 351, 356 (2007).

There was sufficient evidence of serious physical injury when the defendant (1) hit his one-year-old child at least once with a belt, the child cried after being hit, and suffered a visible bruise to his head as a result of the assault, State v. Romero, 164 N.C. App. 169 (2004); and (2) beat the victim with a belt for 40 to 100 minutes; the victim bled, was short of breath due to asthma, and vomited; the victim's arms were covered in bruises, his legs were swollen, and his buttocks were black and blue; the victim was hospitalized after the incident and was in pain for two weeks; and a medical expert testified that the victim's injuries were moderately to seriously severe and could have resulted in complications, *Williams,* 184 N.C. App. at 356.

Child abuse reporting. See this note to "Misdemeanor Child Abuse," above.

Felony murder. The commission of felony child abuse may support a conviction of first-degree felony murder. See the note on Element (3)(c) to "First-Degree Murder" in Chapter 6 (Homicide).

Charging issues. For a discussion of charging issues related to this crime, see Jessica Smith, *The Criminal Indictment: Fatal Defect, Fatal Variance, and Amendment,* ADMIN. OF JUST. BULL. No. 2008/03 29 (UNC School of Government, July 2008) (online at www.sog.unc.edu/pubs/electronicversions/pdfs/aojb0803.pdf).

Multiple convictions and punishments. G.S. 318.4(b) provides that this offense "is an offense additional to other . . . criminal provisions and is not intended to repeal or preclude any other sanctions or remedies." This language may mean that a defendant may be convicted of this crime and another offense that is the "same" for purposes of double jeopardy. See "Double Jeopardy" in Chapter 2 (Bars and Defenses) (discussing that under double jeopardy, a defendant may be convicted, in a single trial, of offenses that are the same if the legislature intended that result). However, it appears that a defendant may not be convicted of this offense and "Child Abuse—Inflicting Serious Bodily Injury or Mental or Emotional Injury," below. *See* G.S. 14-318.4(a) (a defendant who commits this offense "is guilty of a Class E felony, except as provided in subsection (a3) of this section").

Related Offenses Not in This Chapter

See the offenses listed under "Misdemeanor Child Abuse," above.
"Assault Inflicting Serious Injury" (Chapter 7)

Child Abuse—Willful Act or Omission Causing Serious Mental or Physical Injury

Statute

See G.S. 14-318.4(a5), reproduced under "Child Abuse—Inflicting Serious Mental or Physical Injury," above.

Elements

A person guilty of this offense

(1) (a) is a parent of a child less than 16 years of age *or*
(b) is a person providing care to or supervision of a child less than 16 years of age *and*
(2) whose
(a) willful act *or*
(b) grossly negligent omission in the care of a child
(3) shows a reckless disregard for human life *and*
(4) results in serious mental or physical injury to the child.

Punishment

Class H felony. G.S. 14-318.4(a5). G.S. 14-318.4(c) provides that abandonment of an infant less than seven days of age pursuant to G.S. 14-322.3 may be treated as a mitigating factor in sentencing for a conviction involving that infant. G.S. 14-322.3 in turn provides that a parent may not be prosecuted for nonsupport of a child when the parent abandons an infant less than seven days of age by voluntarily delivering the infant in compliance with the provisions of G.S. 7B-500(b) or 7B-500(d) and does not express an intent to return for the infant.

Notes

Generally. This offense is the same as "Child Abuse—Willful Act or Omission Showing Reckless Disregard and Causing Serious Bodily Injury," below, except for the nature of the injury sustained. For that offense, the injury must be serious bodily injury. For this one, it must be serious mental or physical injury.

Element (1). See the note on Element (1) to "Misdemeanor Child Abuse," above.

Element (4). For a discussion of the injury required, see the note on Element (3) to "Child Abuse—Inflicting Serious Mental or Physical Injury," above.

Charging issues. See this note to "Child Abuse—Inflicting Serious Mental or Physical Injury," above.

Child abuse reporting. See this note to "Misdemeanor Child Abuse," above.

Multiple convictions and punishments. G.S. 14-318.4(b) provides that this offense "is an offense additional to other . . . criminal provisions and is not intended to repeal or preclude any other sanctions or remedies." This language may mean that a defendant may be convicted of this crime and another offense that is the "same" for purposes of double jeopardy. See "Double Jeopardy" in Chapter 2 (Bars and Defenses) (discussing that under double jeopardy, a defendant may be convicted, in a single trial, of offenses that are the same if the legislature intended that result).

Related Offenses Not in This Chapter

See the offenses listed under "Misdemeanor Child Abuse," above.
"Assault Inflicting Serious Injury" (Chapter 7)

Child Abuse—Inflicting Serious Bodily Injury or Mental or Emotional Injury

Statute

See G.S. 14-318.4(a3), reproduced under "Child Abuse—Inflicting Serious Mental or Physical Injury," above.

Elements

A person guilty of this offense

(1) (a) is a parent of a child less than 16 years of age *or*
(b) is a person providing care to or supervision of a child less than 16 years of age *and*
(2) (a) intentionally inflicts on or to the child *or*
(b) intentionally commits an assault on the child which results in
(3) (a) serious bodily injury *or*
(b) permanent or protracted loss or impairment of any mental or emotional function.

Punishment

Class C felony. G.S. 14-318.4(a3). G.S. 14-318.4(c) provides that abandonment of an infant less than seven days of age pursuant to G.S. 14-322.3 may be treated as a mitigating factor in sentencing for a conviction involving that infant. G.S. 14-322.3 in turn provides that a parent may not be prosecuted for nonsupport of a child when the parent abandons an infant less than seven days of age by voluntarily delivering the infant in compliance with the provisions of G.S. 7B-500(b) or 7B-500(d) and does not express an intent to return for the infant.

Notes

Element (1). See the note on Element (1) to "Misdemeanor Child Abuse," above.

Element (2). See the note on Element (2) to "Child Abuse—Inflicting Serious Mental or Physical Injury," above.

Element (3)(a). G.S. 14-318.4(d)(1) defines "serious bodily injury" as "[b]odily injury that creates a substantial risk of death or that causes serious permanent disfigurement, coma, a permanent or protracted condition that causes extreme pain, or permanent or protracted loss or impairment of the function of any bodily member or organ, or that results in prolonged hospitalization." This definition tracks, word for word, the definition of "serious bodily injury" for purposes of assault. See the note on Element (3) to "Assault Inflicting Serious Bodily Injury" in Chapter 7 (Assaults). However, this offense appears to be broader than assault inflicting serious bodily injury in that Element (3)(b) also covers permanent or protracted loss or impairment of any mental or emotional function.

Charging issues. See this note under "Child Abuse—Inflicting Serious Mental or Physical Injury," above. *See also* State v. Oakman, 191 N.C. App. 796 (2008) (no fatal variance when indictment charged that the defendant intentionally inflicted serious bodily injury to his child and the jury instructions stated that he could be found guilty if he intentionally inflicted serious bodily injury to the child or intentionally assaulted the child and such action proximately resulted in serious bodily injury).

Child abuse reporting. See this note under "Misdemeanor Child Abuse," above.

Multiple convictions and punishments. See this note under "Child Abuse—Inflicting Serious Mental or Physical Injury," above.

A defendant may be convicted and sentenced for child abuse—inflicting serious bodily injury and assault with a deadly weapon inflicting serious injury. State v. Carter, 153 N.C. App. 756 (2002) (reasoning that each offense requires proof of elements not included in other).

Related Offenses Not in This Chapter

See the offenses listed under "Misdemeanor Child Abuse," above.
"Assault Inflicting Serious Bodily Injury" (Chapter 7)

Child Abuse—Willful Act or Omission Causing Serious Bodily Injury

Statute

See G.S. 14-318.4(a4) reproduced under "Child Abuse—Inflicting Serious Mental or Physical Injury," above.

Elements

A person guilty of this offense

(1) (a) is a parent of a child less than 16 years of age *or*
(b) is a person providing care to or supervision of a child less than 16 years of age *and*
(2) whose
(a) willful act *or*
(b) grossly negligent omission in the care of the child
(3) shows a reckless disregard for human life *and*
(4) results in serious bodily injury to the child.

Punishment

Class E felony. G.S. 14-318.4(a4). G.S. 14-318.4(c) provides that abandonment of an infant less than seven days of age pursuant to G.S. 14-322.3 may be treated as a mitigating factor in sentencing for a conviction involving that infant. G.S. 14-322.3 in turn provides that a parent may not be prosecuted for nonsupport of a child when the parent abandons an infant less than seven days of age by voluntarily delivering the infant in compliance with the provisions of G.S. 7B-500(b) or 7B-500(d) and does not express an intent to return for the infant.

Notes

Generally. This offense is the same as "Child Abuse—Willful Act or Omission Showing Reckless Disregard and Causing Serious Mental or Physical Injury," above, except for the nature of the injury sustained. For that offense, the injury must be serious mental or physical injury. For this one, it must be serious bodily injury.

Element (1). See the note on Element (1) to "Misdemeanor Child Abuse," above.

Element (4). For the definition of "serious bodily injury," see the note on Element (3)(a) to "Child Abuse—Inflicting Serious Bodily Injury or Mental or Emotional Injury," above.

Charging issues. See this note to "Child Abuse—Inflicting Serious Mental or Physical Injury."

Child abuse reporting. See this note to "Misdemeanor Child Abuse," above.

Multiple convictions and punishments. G.S. 14-318.4(b) provides that this offense "is an offense additional to other . . . criminal provisions and is not intended to repeal or preclude any other sanctions or remedies." This language may mean that a defendant may be convicted of this crime and another offense that is the "same" for purposes of double jeopardy. See "Double Jeopardy" in Chapter 2 (Bars and Defenses) (discussing that under double jeopardy, a defendant may be convicted, in a single trial, of offenses that are the same if the legislature intended that result).

Related Offenses Not in This Chapter

See the offenses listed under "Misdemeanor Child Abuse," above.
"Assault Inflicting Serious Bodily Injury" (Chapter 7)

Child Abuse—Prostitution

Statute

See G.S. 14-318.4(a1), reproduced under "Child Abuse Inflicting Serious Mental or Physical Injury," above.

Elements

A person guilty of this offense

(1) (a) is a parent of a child less than 16 years of age *or*
    (b) is a person providing care to or supervision of a child less than 16 years of age *and*
(2) (a) commits,
    (b) permits, *or*
    (c) encourages
(3) an act of prostitution
(4) with or by the child.

Punishment

Class E felony. G.S. 14-318.4(a1). For special maximums that apply to defendants convicted of Class B1 through E felonies that are reportable convictions under the sex offender registration program, see "Sex offenders" under "Special Provisions" in the discussion of felony sentencing in Chapter 4 (Punishment under Structured Sentencing).

G.S. 14-318.4(c) provides that abandonment of an infant less than seven days of age pursuant to G.S. 14-322.3 may be treated as a mitigating factor in sentencing for a conviction under this section involving that infant. It is not clear whether this provision would ever apply to this offense.

Notes

Element (1). See the note on Element (1) to "Misdemeanor Child Abuse," above.

Element (3). See the definition of "prostitution" in the note on Element (2)(a) to "Engaging in Prostitution" in Chapter 23 (Prostitution).

Child abuse reporting. See this note to "Misdemeanor Child Abuse," above.

Multiple convictions and punishments. G.S. 14-318.4(b) provides that this offense "is an offense additional to other . . . criminal provisions and is not intended to repeal or preclude any other sanctions or remedies." This language may mean that a defendant may be convicted of this crime and another offense that is the "same" for purposes of double jeopardy. See "Double Jeopardy" in Chapter 2 (Bars and Defenses) (discussing that under double jeopardy, a defendant may be convicted, in a single trial, of offenses that are the same if the legislature intended that result).

Sex offender registration. This offense is a "sexually violent offense" requiring registration as a sex offender. G.S. 14-208.6(5).

Related Offenses Not in This Chapter

"Solicitation" (Chapter 5)
"Indecent Liberties with a Child" (Chapter 10)
"Sexual Activity by a Custodian" (Chapter 10)
"Sexual Activity by a Substitute Parent" (Chapter 10)
"Crime against Nature" (Chapter 11)
"Abduction of a Child" (Chapter 12)
"Human Trafficking, Involuntary Servitude, and Sexual Servitude" (Chapter 12)
See the offenses in Chapter 23 (Prostitution).
Illegally receiving or giving compensation for placing child for adoption. G.S. 48-37.

Child Abuse—Sexual Act

Statute

See G.S. 14-318.4(a2), reproduced under "Child Abuse—Inflicting Serious Mental or Physical Injury," above.

Elements

A person guilty of this offense

(1) (a) is a parent of a child less than 16 years of age *or*
(b) is a legal guardian of a child less than 16 years of age *and*
(2) (a) commits a sexual act upon the child *or*
(b) allows another to commit a sexual act upon the child.

Punishment

Class E felony. G.S. 14-318.4(a2). See the additional discussion in "Punishment" under "Child Abuse—Prostitution," above.

Notes

Element (1). Only an actual parent or legal guardian may commit this offense. Thus, a schoolteacher or a babysitter could not be charged with this crime. It is not clear whether this offense applies to a stepparent who has not adopted the child.

Element (2)(a). Although the statute does not define the term "sexual act," it includes digital penetration. State v. Stokes, ___ N.C. App. ___, ___ S.E.2d ___ (Nov. 1, 2011) (digital penetration of the vagina). It also probably includes cunnilingus, analingus, fellatio, anal intercourse, vaginal intercourse, and insertion of other objects in the vagina or anus. G.S. 14-27.1 contains definitions that apply to the offenses in G.S. Chapter 14, Article 7A (Rape and Other Sex offenses). Subsection(4) of that provision excludes vaginal intercourse from the definition of sexual act. Child abuse—sexual act, however, is not included in Article 7A, and thus G.S. 14-27.1 does not apply to this offense. The term "sexual activity" is defined in G.S. 14-190.13(5), but that section limits its applicability to a list of offenses that does not include this one.

Charging issues. The State need not allege the particular sexual act that a defendant committed. State v. Lark, 198 N.C. App. 82 (2009). Any additional language specifying the sexual act, e.g., "anal intercourse," ordinarily is surplusage. *Id.*

Child abuse reporting. See this note to "Misdemeanor Child Abuse," above.

Multiple convictions and punishments. G.S. 14-318.4(b) provides that this offense "is an offense additional to other . . . criminal provisions and is not intended to repeal or preclude any other sanctions or remedies." This language may mean that a defendant may be convicted of this crime and another offense that is the "same" for purposes of double jeopardy. See "Double Jeopardy" in Chapter 2 (Bars and Defenses) (discussing that under double jeopardy, a defendant may be convicted, in a single trial, of offenses that are the same if the legislature intended that result).

Sex offender registration. This offense is defined as a "sexually violent offense" requiring registration as a sex offender. G.S. 14-208.6(5).

Related Offenses Not in This Chapter

See the offenses listed under "Child Abuse—Prostitution," above.

See the offenses in Chapter 24 (Obscenity, Exploitation of a Minor, and Adult Establishment Offenses).

Contributing to a Juvenile's Being Delinquent, Undisciplined, Abused, or Neglected

Statute

§14-316.1. Contributing to delinquency and neglect by parents and others.

Any person who is at least 16 years old who knowingly or willfully causes, encourages, or aids any juvenile within the jurisdiction of the court to be in a place or condition, or to commit an act whereby the juvenile could be adjudicated delinquent, undisciplined, abused, or neglected as defined by G.S. 7B-101 and G.S. 7B-1501 shall be guilty of a Class 1 misdemeanor.

It is not necessary for the district court exercising juvenile jurisdiction to make an adjudication that any juvenile is delinquent, undisciplined, abused, or neglected in order to prosecute a parent or any person, including an employee of the Department of Juvenile Justice and Delinquency Prevention under this section. An adjudication that a juvenile is delinquent, undisciplined, abused, or neglected shall not preclude a subsequent prosecution of a parent or any other person including an employee of the Department of Juvenile Justice and Delinquency Prevention, who contributes to the delinquent, undisciplined, abused, or neglected condition of any juvenile.

Elements

A person guilty of this offense

(1) is at least 16 years old *and*
(2) knowingly or willfully
(3) (a) causes,
    (b) encourages, *or*
    (c) aids
(4) a juvenile within the jurisdiction of the court
(5) (a) to be in a place or condition *or*
    (b) to commit an act
(6) whereby the juvenile could be adjudicated
    (a) delinquent as defined in G.S. 7B-1501(7),
    (b) undisciplined as defined in G.S. 7B-1501(27),
    (c) abused as defined in G.S. 7B-101(1), *or*
    (d) neglected as defined in G.S. 7B-101(5).

Punishment

Class 1 misdemeanor. G.S. 14-316.1.

Notes

Element (2). See "Knowingly" and "Willfully" in Chapter 1 (States of Mind).

Element (4). "Juvenile" is defined generally in G.S. 7B-101(14) in the article concerning abused and neglected juveniles and in G.S. 7B-1501(17) in the article concerning delinquent and undisciplined juveniles. A delinquent juvenile is generally within the court's jurisdiction when the juvenile is at least 6 years old and less than 16 years old. G.S. 7B-1501(7); 7B-1601. An undisciplined juvenile is generally within the court's jurisdiction when the juvenile is at least 6 years old and less than 18 years old. G.S. 7B-1501(27); 7B-1600. An abused or neglected juvenile is generally within the court's jurisdiction when the juvenile is less than 18 years old. G.S. 7B-101(1), (14) & (15); 7B-200.

Element (6). The statute expressly provides that it is unnecessary to prove that the child actually was adjudicated delinquent, undisciplined, abused, or neglected; such an adjudication only must be possible. G.S. 14-316.1.

Element (6)(a). A delinquent juvenile is a juvenile at least 6 years old and less than 16 years old who commits a crime or infraction under state law or under a local government ordinance, including a violation of the motor vehicle laws, or who commits indirect contempt by a juvenile as defined in G.S. 5A-31. G.S. 7B-1501(7).

Element (6)(b). An undisciplined juvenile is (1) a juvenile at least 6 years old and less than 16 years old who is unlawfully absent from school; is regularly disobedient to and beyond the disciplinary control of the juvenile's parent, guardian, or custodian; is regularly found in places where it is unlawful for a juvenile to be; or has run away from home for a period of more than 24 hours; or (2) a juvenile 16 or 17 years old who is regularly disobedient to and beyond the disciplinary control of the juvenile's parent, guardian, or custodian; is regularly found in places where it is unlawful for a juvenile to be; or has run away from home for a period of more than 24 hours. G.S. 7B-1501(27).

Element (6)(c). The definition of an "abused juvenile" under the North Carolina Juvenile Code (G.S. 7B-101(1)) is not identical to the definition of "child abuse" under the criminal child abuse statutes, G.S. 14-318.2 and 14-318.4, although there are substantial similarities between the terms. See the various child abuse offenses covered above. In determining whether a charge for this particular offense is appropriate, the definition of "abuse" under the Juvenile Code should be consulted. G.S. 7B-101(1) defines an abused juvenile, in part, as a juvenile younger than age 18 whose parent or other person responsible for the juvenile's care inflicts or allows to be inflicted on the juvenile serious, nonaccidental physical injury; creates or allows to be created a substantial risk of such injury; uses or allows to be used cruel or grossly inappropriate procedures or devices to modify behavior; commits, permits, or encourages the commission of a variety of listed sexual assaults, acts of prostitution, and obscenity offenses by, with, or upon the juvenile; creates or allows to be created serious emotional damage to the juvenile; or encourages, directs, or approves of delinquent acts involving moral turpitude committed by the juvenile.

Element (6)(d). A neglected juvenile is a juvenile under age 18 "who does not receive proper care, supervision, or discipline from the juvenile's parent, guardian, custodian, or caretaker; or who has been abandoned; or who is not provided necessary medical care; or who is not provided necessary remedial care; or who lives in an environment injurious to the juvenile's welfare; or who has been placed for care or adoption in violation of law." G.S. 7B-101(15).

Constitutionality. This statute is not unconstitutionally vague. State v. Sparrow, 276 N.C. 499 (1970).

Greater and lesser-included offenses. Contributing to the delinquency of a minor is not a lesser-included offense of second-degree rape. State v. Cronan, 100 N.C. App. 641 (1990).

Multiple convictions and punishments. Convictions for both contributing to the delinquency of a minor and second-degree rape occurring during the same transaction are not barred by double jeopardy. *Id.*

Relation to other offenses. Culpable negligence by a parent resulting in the death of a child may constitute involuntary manslaughter. State v. Mason, 18 N.C. App. 433 (1973); see generally "Involuntary Manslaughter" in Chapter 6 (Homicide).

Related Offenses Not in This Chapter

"Involuntary Manslaughter" (Chapter 6)
See the offenses in Chapter 10 (Sexual Assaults).
See the offenses in Chapter 11 (Crime against Nature, Incest, Indecent Exposure, and Related Offenses).
"Possession of a Handgun by a Minor" (Chapter 22)
See the offenses in Chapter 23 (Prostitution).

See the offenses in Chapter 24 (Obscenity, Exploitation of a Minor, and Adult Establishment Offenses).
See the offenses in Chapter 26 (Abandonment and Nonsupport).
See the offenses involving minors in Chapter 27 (Drug Offenses).
Selling cigarettes to minors. G.S. 14-313.
Selling or giving weapons to minors. G.S. 14-315.
Permitting young children to use dangerous firearms. G.S. 14-316.
Permitting minors to enter barrooms or billiard rooms. G.S. 14-317.
Exposing children to fire. G.S. 14-318.
Discarding or abandoning iceboxes. G.S. 14-318.1.
Selling alcohol to underage person. G.S. 18B-302(a).
Giving alcohol to underage person. G.S. 18B-302(a1).
Illegally receiving or giving compensation for placing child for adoption. G.S. 48-37.
Aid or abet student's unlawful absence from a regional school. G.S. 115C-238.56G(3).

Patient Abuse

Patient Abuse—Willful or Culpably Negligent Pattern of Conduct Causing Bodily Injury

Statute

§14-32.2. Patient abuse and neglect; punishments.

(a) It shall be unlawful for any person to physically abuse a patient of a health care facility or a resident of a residential care facility, when the abuse results in death or bodily injury.

(b) Unless the conduct is prohibited by some other provision of law providing for greater punishment:

(1) A violation of subsection (a) above is a Class C felony where intentional conduct proximately causes the death of the patient or resident;

(2) A violation of subsection (a) above is a Class E felony where culpably negligent conduct proximately causes the death of the patient or resident;

(3) A violation of subsection (a) above is a Class F felony where such conduct is willful or culpably negligent and proximately causes serious bodily injury to the patient or resident;

(4) A violation of subsection (a) is a Class H felony where such conduct evinces a pattern of conduct and the conduct is willful or culpably negligent and proximately causes bodily injury to a patient or resident.

(c) "Health Care Facility" shall include hospitals, skilled nursing facilities, intermediate care facilities, intermediate care facilities for the mentally retarded, psychiatric facilities, rehabilitation facilities, kidney disease treatment centers, home health agencies, ambulatory surgical facilities, and any other health care related facility whether publicly or privately owned.

(c1) "Residential Care Facility" shall include adult care homes and any other residential care related facility whether publicly or privately owned.

(d) "Person" shall include any natural person, association, corporation, partnership, or other individual or entity.

(e) "Culpably negligent" shall mean conduct of a willful, gross and flagrant character, evincing reckless disregard of human life.

(e1) "Abuse" means the willful or culpably negligent infliction of physical injury or the willful or culpably negligent violation of any law designed for the health or welfare of a patient or resident.

(f) Any defense which may arise under G.S. 90-321(h) or G.S. 90-322(d) pursuant to compliance with Article 23 of Chapter 90 shall be fully applicable to any prosecution initiated under this section.

(g) Criminal process for a violation of this section may be issued only upon the request of a District Attorney.

(h) The provisions of this section shall not supersede any other applicable statutory or common law offenses.

Elements

A person guilty of this offense

(1) physically abuses
(2) (a) a patient of a health care facility *or*
    (b) a resident of a residential care facility *and*
(3) the abuse evinces a pattern of conduct
(4) that is
    (a) willful *or*
    (b) culpably negligent *and*
(5) proximately causes
(6) bodily injury to a patient or resident.

Punishment

Class H felony. G.S. 14-32.2(b)(4).

Notes

Element (1). G.S. 14-32.2(e1) defines the term "abuse" to mean "the willful or culpably negligent infliction of physical injury or the willful or culpably negligent violation of any law designed for the health or welfare of a patient or resident." G.S. 14-32.2(e) defines the term "culpably negligent" as "conduct of a willful, gross and flagrant character, evincing reckless disregard of human life." For a discussion of the term as it is used in the criminal law more generally, see "Criminal Negligence" in Chapter 1 (States of Mind). The statute does not define the term "physical injury." For a discussion of that term as it is used in the assault context, see the note on Element (4) to "Assault Inflicting Physical Injury on a Law Enforcement Officer, Probation or Parole Officer, or Detention Facility Employee" in Chapter 7 (Assaults). For a discussion of that term as it is used in the context of child abuse, see "Misdemeanor Child Abuse," above.

Element (2). G.S. 14-32.2(c) defines the term "health care facility" to "include hospitals, skilled nursing facilities, intermediate care facilities, intermediate care facilities for the mentally retarded, psychiatric facilities, rehabilitation facilities, kidney disease treatment centers, home health agencies, ambulatory surgical facilities, and any other health care related facility whether publicly or privately owned." G.S. 14-32.3(c1) defines the term "residential care facility" to "include adult care homes and any other residential care related facility whether publicly or privately owned."

Element (3). The statute does not define the term "pattern of conduct," and no other provision in G.S. Chapter 14 uses that term. The related term "course of conduct" is used in the stalking statute and is statutorily defined. See the note on Element (3)(b) to "Misdemeanor Stalking" in Chapter 8 (Threats, Harassment, Stalking, and Violation of Domestic Violence Protective Orders).

Element (4). See "Willfully" in Chapter 1 (States of Mind). G.S. 14-32.2(e) defines the term "culpably negligent" to mean "conduct of a willful, gross and flagrant character, evincing reckless disregard of human life." For a discussion of that term as it is used in the criminal law generally, see "Criminal Negligence" in Chapter 1 (States of Mind).

Element (5). For a discussion of proximate cause, see the note "Proximate cause" to "First-Degree Murder" in Chapter 6 (Homicide).

Element (6). The statute does not define the term "bodily injury." Presumably it means less than "serious bodily injury," a term that applies in the assault context, see the note on Element (3) to "Assault Inflicting Serious Bodily Injury" in Chapter 7 (Assaults), for some child abuse crimes, see "Child Abuse—Inflicting Serious Bodily Injury or Mental or Emotional Injury," above, and for patient abuse crimes, see "Patient Abuse—Willful or Culpably Negligent Conduct Causing Serious Bodily Injury," below.

Persons who can be charged. G.S. 14-32.2(d) provides that the term "person" means "any natural person, association, corporation, partnership, or other individual or entity," thus contemplating that businesses may face criminal liability under this provision. As discussed in the note " 'Person' includes corporations" in the Introduction to this book, the term "person" in a criminal statute always includes a corporation.

District Attorney must request criminal process. G.S. 14-32.2(g) provides that criminal process charging this offense may be issued only on the request of a district attorney.

Defenses. G.S. 14-32.2(f) provides that any defense that may arise under G.S. 90-321(h) or 90-322(d) pursuant to compliance with Article 23 of Chapter 90 is fully applicable to any prosecution initiated under this section.

Multiple convictions and punishments. G.S. 14-32.2(b) begins with the following language: "Unless the conduct is prohibited by some other provision of law providing greater punishment." This language may mean that a defendant cannot be punished for this offense and another offense that provides for harsher punishment when the charges arise out of the same conduct. For a discussion of this issue in the assault context, see this note to "Assault Inflicting Serious Injury" in Chapter 7 (Assaults).

Related Offenses Not in This Chapter

"Assault Inflicting Serious Injury" (Chapter 7)
"Exploitation of an Elder or Disabled Adult" (Chapter 16)

Patient Abuse—Willful or Culpably Negligent Pattern of Conduct Causing Serious Bodily Injury

Statute

See G.S. 14-13.2(b)(3), reproduced under "Patient Abuse—Willful or Culpably Negligent Pattern of Conduct Causing Bodily Injury," above.

Elements

A person guilty of this offense

(1) physically abuses
(2) (a) a patient of a health care facility *or*
  (b) a resident of a residential care facility *and*
(3) the abuse is
  (a) willful *or*
  (b) culpably negligent *and*
(4) proximately causes
(5) serious bodily injury to a patient or resident.

Punishment

Class F felony. G.S. 14-32.2(b)(3).

Notes

Generally. This offense is the same as "Patient Abuse—Willful or Culpably Negligent Pattern of Conduct Causing Bodily Injury," above, except that this offense (1) does not require a pattern of conduct and (2) requires more serious injury. For "Patient Abuse—Willful or Culpably Negligent Pattern of Conduct Causing Bodily Injury," the injury must be bodily injury; for this offense, there must be serious bodily injury.

Element (1). See the note on Element (1) to "Patient Abuse—Willful or Culpably Negligent Pattern of Conduct Causing Bodily Injury," above.

Element (2). See the note on Element (2) to "Patient Abuse—Willful or Culpably Negligent Pattern of Conduct Causing Bodily Injury," above.

Element (3). See the note on Element (4) to "Patient Abuse—Willful or Culpably Negligent Pattern of Conduct Causing Bodily Injury," above.

Element (4). See the note "Proximate cause" to "First-Degree Murder" in Chapter 6 (Homicide).

Element (6). The statute does not define the term "serious bodily injury." For a discussion of that term as it is used in the context of child abuse and assault, see the note on Element (3)(a) to "Child Abuse—Inflicting Serious Bodily Injury or Mental or Emotional Injury," above, and the note on Element (3) to "Assault Inflicting Serious Bodily Injury" in Chapter 7 (Assaults).

Persons who can be charged. See this note to "Patient Abuse—Willful or Culpably Negligent Pattern of Conduct Causing Bodily Injury," above.

District Attorney must request criminal process. See this note to "Patient Abuse—Willful or Culpably Negligent Pattern of Conduct Causing Bodily Injury," above.

Defenses. See this note to "Patient Abuse—Willful or Culpably Negligent Pattern of Conduct Causing Bodily Injury," above.

Multiple convictions and punishments. See this note to "Patient Abuse—Willful or Culpably Negligent Pattern of Conduct Causing Bodily Injury," above.

Related Offenses Not in This Chapter

"Assault Inflicting Serious Bodily Injury" (Chapter 7)
See exploitation of a disabled or elder adult (various offenses) in Chapter 16 (Fraud, Forgery, False Pretenses, and Related Offenses).

Patient Abuse—Culpably Negligent Conduct Causing Death

Statute

See G.S. 14-32.2(b)(2), reproduced under "Patient Abuse—Willful or Culpably Negligent Pattern of Conduct Causing Bodily Injury," above.

Elements

A person guilty of this offense

(1) physically abuses
(2) (a) a patient of a health care facility *or*
 (b) a resident of a residential care facility *and*
(3) the abuse constitutes culpably negligent conduct

(4) that proximately causes
(5) death of the patient or resident.

Punishment

Class E felony. G.S. 14-32.2(b)(2).

Notes

Generally. This offense is the same as "Patient Abuse—Intentional Conduct Causing Death," below, except that for that offense the defendant's conduct must be intentional and for this one, culpably negligent conduct will suffice.

Element (1). See this note to "Patient Abuse—Willful or Culpably Negligent Pattern of Conduct Causing Bodily Injury," above.

Element (2). See this note to "Patient Abuse—Willful or Culpably Negligent Pattern of Conduct Causing Bodily Injury," above.

Element (3). G.S. 14-32.3(e) defines the term "culpably negligent" to mean "conduct of a willful, gross and flagrant character, evincing reckless disregard of human life." For a discussion of that term as it is used in the criminal law generally, see "Criminal Negligence" in Chapter 1 (States of Mind).

Element (4). For a discussion of proximate cause, see the note "Proximate cause" to "First-Degree Murder" in Chapter 6 (Homicide).

Persons who can be charged. See this note to "Patient Abuse—Willful or Culpably Negligent Pattern of Conduct Causing Bodily Injury," above.

District Attorney must request criminal process. See this note to "Patient Abuse—Willful or Culpably Negligent Pattern of Conduct Causing Bodily Injury," above.

Defenses. See this note to "Patient Abuse—Willful or Culpably Negligent Pattern of Conduct Causing Bodily Injury," above.

Multiple convictions and punishments. See this note to "Patient Abuse—Willful or Culpably Negligent Pattern of Conduct Causing Bodily Injury," above.

Related Offenses Not in This Chapter

See the offenses in Chapter 6 (Homicide).
See exploitation of an elder or disabled adult (various offenses) in Chapter 16 (Fraud, Forgery, False Pretenses, and Related Offenses).

Patient Abuse—Intentional Conduct Causing Death

Statute

See G.S. 14-32.2(b)(1), reproduced under "Patient Abuse—Willful or Culpably Negligent Pattern of Conduct Causing Bodily Injury," above.

Elements

A person guilty of this offense

(1) physically abuses
(2) (a) a patient of a health care facility *or*
 (b) a resident of a residential care facility *and*
(3) the abuse constitutes intentional conduct
(4) that proximately causes
(5) death of the patient or resident.

Punishment

Class C felony. G.S. 14-32.2(b)(1).

Notes

Generally. See this note to "Patient Abuse—Culpably Negligent Conduct Causing Death," above.

Element (1). See this note to "Patient Abuse—Willful or Culpably Negligent Pattern of Conduct Causing Bodily Injury," above.

Element (2). See this note to "Patient Abuse—Willful or Culpably Negligent Pattern of Conduct Causing Bodily Injury," above.

Element (3). See "Intentionally" in Chapter 1 (States of Mind).

Element (4). For a discussion of proximate cause, see the note "Proximate cause" to "First-Degree Murder" in Chapter 6 (Homicide).

Persons who can be charged. See this note to "Patient Abuse—Willful or Culpably Negligent Pattern of Conduct Causing Bodily Injury," above.

District Attorney must request criminal process. See this note to "Patient Abuse—Willful or Culpably Negligent Pattern of Conduct Causing Bodily Injury," above.

Defenses. See this note to "Patient Abuse—Willful or Culpably Negligent Pattern of Conduct Causing Bodily Injury," above.

Multiple convictions and punishments. See this note to "Patient Abuse—Willful or Culpably Negligent Pattern of Conduct Causing Bodily Injury," above.

Related Offenses Not in This Chapter

See the offenses in Chapter 6 (Homicide).

See exploitation of an elder or disabled adult (various offenses) in Chapter 16 (Fraud, Forgery, False Pretenses, and Related Offenses).

Abuse or Neglect of a Disabled or Elder Adult

Abuse of a Disabled or Elder Adult Causing Mental or Physical Injury

Statute

§14-32.3. Domestic abuse, neglect, and exploitation of disabled or elder adults.

(a) Abuse.—A person is guilty of abuse if that person is a caretaker of a disabled or elder adult who is residing in a domestic setting and, with malice aforethought, knowingly and willfully: (i) assaults, (ii) fails to provide medical or hygienic care, or (iii) confines or restrains the disabled or elder adult in a place or under a condition that is cruel or unsafe, and as a result of the act or failure to act the disabled or elder adult suffers mental or physical injury.

If the disabled or elder adult suffers serious injury from the abuse, the caretaker is guilty of a Class F felony. If the disabled or elder adult suffers injury from the abuse, the caretaker is guilty of a Class H felony.

A person is not guilty of an offense under this subsection if the act or failure to act is in accordance with G.S. 90-321 or G.S. 90-322.

(b) Neglect.—A person is guilty of neglect if that person is a caretaker of a disabled or elder adult who is residing in a domestic setting and, wantonly, recklessly, or with gross carelessness: (i) fails to provide medical or hygienic care, or (ii) confines or restrains the disabled or elder adult in a place or under a condition that is unsafe, and as a result of the act or failure to act the disabled or elder adult suffers mental or physical injury.

If the disabled or elder adult suffers serious injury from the neglect, the caretaker is guilty of a Class G felony. If the disabled or elder adult suffers injury from the neglect, the caretaker is guilty of a Class I felony.

A person is not guilty of an offense under this subsection if the act or failure to act is in accordance with G.S. 90-321 or G.S. 90-322.

(c) Repealed by Session Laws 2005-272, s.1, effective December 1, 2005, and applicable to offenses committed on or after that date.

(d) Definitions.—The following definitions apply in this section:

(1) Caretaker.—A person who has the responsibility for the care of a disabled or elder adult as a result of family relationship or who has assumed the responsibility for the care of a disabled or elder adult voluntarily or by contract.
(2) Disabled adult.—A person 18 years of age or older or a lawfully emancipated minor who is present in the State of North Carolina and who is physically or mentally incapacitated as defined in G.S. 108A-101(d).
(3) Domestic setting.—Residence in any residential setting except for a health care facility or residential care facility as these terms are defined in G.S. 14-32.2.
(4) Elder adult.—A person 60 years of age or older who is not able to provide for the social, medical, psychiatric, psychological, financial, or legal services necessary to safeguard the person's rights and resources and to maintain the person's physical and mental well-being.

Elements

A person guilty of this offense

(1) is a caretaker of
(2) (a) a disabled adult *or*
    (b) an elder adult
(3) who is residing in a domestic setting *and,*
(4) with malice, knowingly and willfully
(5) (a) assaults the adult,
    (b) fails to provide medical care or hygienic care to the adult, *or*
    (c) confines or restrains the adult in a place or under a condition that is cruel or unsafe *and*
(6) as a result the adult suffers mental or physical injury.

Punishment

Class H felony. G.S. 14-32.3(a).

Notes

Element (1). The term "caretaker" means "[a] person who has the responsibility for the care of a disabled or elder adult as a result of family relationship or who has assumed the responsibility for the care of a disabled or elder adult voluntarily or by contract." G.S. 14-32.3(d)(1).

Element (2)(a). The term "disabled adult" is defined by G.S. 14-32.3(d)(2) to mean "[a] person 18 years of age or older or a lawfully emancipated minor who is present in the State of North Carolina and who is physically or mentally incapacitated as defined in G.S. 108A-101(d)."

Element (2)(b). An "elder adult" means a person aged 60 years or older who is not able to provide for the social, medical, psychiatric, psychological, financial, or legal services necessary to safeguard his or her rights and resources and to maintain his or her physical and mental well-being. G.S. 14-32.3(d)(4).

Element (3). G.S. 14-32.3(d)(3) defines the term "domestic setting" as a residence in any residential setting except for a health care facility or residential care facility, as defined in G.S. 14-32.2. See the note on Element (2) to "Patient Abuse—Willful or Culpably Negligent Pattern of Conduct Causing Bodily Injury," above, for the meaning of the terms "health care facility" and "residential care facility," as defined by G.S. 14-32.2.

Element (4). See "Knowingly" and "Willfully" in Chapter 1 (States of Mind). The statutory words "malice aforethought" do not require proof of premeditation and deliberation because those words mean the same as malice under the common law. See "Maliciously" in Chapter 1 (States of Mind).

Element (6). The statute expressly covers mental and physical injury. G.S. 14-32.3(a).

Defenses. G.S. 14-32.3(a) provides that a person is not guilty of this offense if the act or failure to act is in accordance with G.S. 90-321 or G.S. 90-322.

Related Offenses Not in This Chapter

See the offenses in Chapter 7 (Assaults).
See the offenses in Chapter 12 (Kidnapping and Related Offenses).
See exploitation of an elder or disabled adult (various offenses) in Chapter 16 (Fraud, Forgery, False Pretenses, and Related Offenses).

Abuse of a Disabled or Elder Adult Causing Serious Mental or Physical Injury

Statute

See G.S. 14-32.3(a), reproduced under "Abuse of a Disabled or Elder Adult Causing Mental or Physical Injury," above.

Elements

A person guilty of this offense

(1) is a caretaker of
(2) (a) a disabled adult *or*
  (b) an elder adult
(3) who is residing in a domestic setting *and,*
(4) with malice, knowingly and willfully
(5) (a) assaults the adult,
  (b) fails to provide medical care or hygienic care to the adult, *or*
  (c) confines or restrains the adult in a place or under a condition that is cruel or unsafe *and*
(6) as a result the adult suffers serious mental or physical injury.

Punishment

Class F felony. G.S. 14-32.3(a).

Notes

Generally. This offense is the same as "Abuse of a Disabled or Elder Adult Causing Mental or Physical Injury," above, except for the injury inflicted. For "Abuse of a Disabled or Elder Adult Causing Mental or Physical Injury," the defendant need only inflict mental or physical injury. For this offense, the mental or physical injury must be serious. Thus, the relevant notes to that offense apply here as well.

Element (6). For a discussion of the term "serious injury" as it applies in the assault context, see the note on Element (3) to "Assault Inflicting Serious Injury" in Chapter 7 (Assaults).

Related Offenses Not in This Chapter

See the offenses listed under "Abuse of a Disabled or Elder Adult Causing Mental or Physical Injury," above.

Neglect of a Disabled or Elder Adult Causing Mental or Physical Injury

Statute

See G.S. 14-32.3(b), reproduced under "Abuse of Disabled or Elder Adult Causing Mental or Physical Injury," above.

Elements

A person guilty of this offense

(1) is a caretaker of
(2) (a) a disabled adult *or*
 (b) an elder adult
(3) who is residing in a domestic setting *and*
(4) wantonly, recklessly, or with gross carelessness
(5) (a) fails to provide medical or hygienic care to the adult *or*
 (b) confines or restrains the adult in a place or under a condition that is unsafe *and*
(6) as a result the adult suffers mental or physical injury.

Punishment

Class I felony. G.S. 14-32.3(b).

Notes

Element (1). See the note on Element (1) to "Abuse of Disabled or Elder Adult Causing Mental or Physical Injury," above.

Element (2). See the note on Element (2) to "Abuse of Disabled or Elder Adult Causing Mental or Physical Injury," above.

Element (3). See the note on Element (3) to "Abuse of Disabled or Elder Adult Causing Mental or Physical Injury," above.

Element (4). See "Wantonly" and "Recklessly" in Chapter 1 (States of Mind).

Element (6). See the note on Element (6) to "Abuse of a Disabled or Elder Adult Causing Mental or Physical Injury," above.

Related Offenses Not in This Chapter

See the offenses listed under "Abuse of a Disabled or Elder Adult Causing Mental or Physical Injury," above.

Neglect of a Disabled or Elder Adult Causing Serious Mental or Physical Injury

Statute

See G.S. 14-32.3(b), reproduced under "Abuse of Disabled or Elder Adult Causing Mental or Physical Injury," above.

Elements

A person guilty of this offense

(1) is a caretaker of
(2) (a) a disabled adult *or*
    (b) an elder adult
(3) who is residing in a domestic setting *and*
(4) wantonly, recklessly, or with gross carelessness
(5) (a) fails to provide medical care or hygienic care to the adult *or*
    (b) confines or restrains the adult in a place or under a condition that is unsafe *and*
(6) as a result the adult suffers serious mental or physical injury.

Punishment

Class G felony. G.S. 14-32.3(b).

Notes

Generally. This offense is the same as "Neglect of a Disabled or Elder Adult Causing Mental or Physical Injury," above, except for the injury caused. For "Neglect of a Disabled or Elder Adult Causing Mental or Physical Injury," the defendant need only inflict injury. For this offense, the injury must be serious. Thus, the relevant notes to that offense apply here as well.

Element (6). The statute covers mental and physical injury. G.S. 14-32.3(b). For a discussion of the term "serious injury" as it applies in the assault context, see the note on Element (3) to "Assault Inflicting Serious Injury" in Chapter 7 (Assaults).

Related Offenses Not in This Chapter

See the offenses listed under "Abuse of a Disabled or Elder Adult Causing Mental or Physical Injury," above.

10

Sexual Assaults

10
Sexual Assaults

Rape

First-Degree Forcible Rape

Statute

§14-27.2. First-degree rape.

(a) A person is guilty of rape in the first degree if the person engages in vaginal intercourse:

(1) With a victim who is a child under the age of 13 years and the defendant is at least 12 years old and is at least four years older than the victim; or

(2) With another person by force and against the will of the other person, and:

a. Employs or displays a dangerous or deadly weapon or an article which the other person reasonably believes to be a dangerous or deadly weapon; or

b. Inflicts serious personal injury upon the victim or another person; or

c. The person commits the offense aided and abetted by one or more other persons.

(b) Any person who commits an offense defined in this section is guilty of a Class B1 felony.

(c) Upon conviction, a person convicted under this section has no rights to custody of or rights of inheritance from any child born as a result of the commission of the rape, nor shall the person have any rights related to the child under Chapter 48 or Subchapter 1 of Chapter 7B of the General Statutes.

Elements

A person guilty of this offense

(1) has vaginal intercourse
(2) with a person
(3) by force *and*
(4) against that person's will *and*
(5) the defendant
 (a) uses or displays a dangerous or deadly weapon (or what reasonably appears to be a dangerous or deadly weapon),
 (b) inflicts serious personal injury on the victim,
 (c) inflicts serious personal injury on another person, *or*
 (d) is aided and abetted by one or more other persons.

Punishment

Class B1 felony. G.S. 14-27.2(b). G.S. 15A-1340.16B provides that certain defendants convicted of Class B1 felonies must be sentenced to life imprisonment without parole. For a discussion of this statute, see "B1 felonies against young victims" under "Felonies," "Special Provisions," in Chapter 4 (Punishment under Structured Sentencing); see also "Sex offenders" in that same section for special maximums that apply to those convicted of Class B1–E felonies that are reportable convictions under the sex offender registration program.

Notes

Generally. This offense is the same as "First-Degree Forcible Sexual Offense," below, except for the sexual conduct involved. For this offense, vaginal intercourse is required. For first-degree forcible sexual offense, a sexual act other than vaginal intercourse is required.

Element (1). "Vaginal intercourse," like the older terms "carnal knowledge" and "sexual intercourse," means the penetration of the female sexual organ by the male sexual organ. State v. Johnson, 317 N.C. 417 (1986). The slightest penetration is sufficient, G.S. 14-27.10; State v. Murry, 277 N.C. 197 (1970); State v. Bell, 159 N.C. App. 151 (2003); neither proof of erection, State v. Williams, 314 N.C. 337 (1985), nor emission of semen is required, G.S. 14-27.10; State v. Bowman, 232 N.C. 374 (1950); *Johnson*, 317 N.C. 417. Penetration of the vulva or labia is sufficient; penetration of the vagina is not required. *Johnson*, 317 N.C. 417.

The victim's testimony that the defendant had sexual intercourse with her is sufficient to establish penetration. State v. Ashford, 301 N.C. 512 (1980); State v. Kitchengs, 183 N.C. App. 369 (2007) (the victim answered in the affirmative when asked if the defendant "had sex" with her).

Element (2). A person may be prosecuted for rape or sexual offense against his or her spouse. G.S. 14-27.8. Put another way, there is no "spousal defense" to rape and sexual offense.

Element (3). Proof of actual force (such as a beating) is not required; constructive force by threat, fear, or duress is sufficient. State v. Locklear, 172 N.C. App. 249 (2005); State v. Lawrence, 165 N.C. App. 548 (2004); State v. Scercy, 159 N.C. App. 344 (2003). Threatened use of force can be holding a gun or knife on the victim to procure submission, State v. Overman, 269 N.C. 453 (1967), or threatening serious bodily harm that reasonably induces fear, State v. Roberts, 293 N.C. 1 (1977); State v. Berkley, 56 N.C. App. 163 (1982). The force does not include the conduct that constitutes the sexual act itself. State v. Raines, 72 N.C. App. 300 (1985). *But see* State v. Brown, 332 N.C. 262 (1992) (where court reserved ruling on this issue). However, at least one case suggests that force is inherent in sex acts with a person who is unable to consent, such as one who is mentally disabled. State v. Washington, 131 N.C. App. 156 (1998) (upholding trial court's denial of motion to dismiss "by force" count on this basis).

Constructive force can be inferred from a parent-child relationship between the defendant and the victim. State v. Etheridge, 319 N.C. 34 (1987); State v. Mueller, 184 N.C. App. 553, 567–69 (2007) (the defendant was the victim's father); *Locklear*, 172 N.C. App. 249; State v. Corbett, 154 N.C. App. 713 (2002); State v. Hardy, 104 N.C. App. 226 (1991).

Element (4). Evidence of physical resistance is not necessary to prove lack of consent. State v. Hall, 293 N.C. 559 (1977). If penetration occurs with the victim's consent, no rape has occurred, even if the victim later withdraws consent during the same act of intercourse. State v. Way, 297 N.C. 293 (1979).

Element (5)(a). Although use or threatened use of the weapon is sufficient, State v. Whittington, 318 N.C. 114 (1986), it is not required. The fact that the defendant displayed the weapon is enough. G.S. 14-27.2(a); State v. Roberts, 310 N.C. 428 (1984); State v. Powell, 306 N.C. 718 (1982); State v. Sturdivant, 304 N.C. 293 (1981).

Use of the weapon need not continue throughout the crime, State v. Dull, 289 N.C. 55 (1975); the evidence is sufficient if it establishes that the defendant used or displayed the weapon (or what reasonably appeared to be a dangerous or deadly weapon) in the course of a continuous transaction that included penetration. State v. Lawrence, 191 N.C. App. 422, 434–37 (2008), *aff'd,* 363 N.C. 118 (2009) (per curiam) (citing other cases on point).

A "deadly weapon" is any instrument which by its nature or under the circumstances of its use is likely to cause death or serious bodily injury. See the note on Element (3) to "Assault with a Deadly Weapon" in Chapter 7 (Assaults); *see also* State v. Bonilla, ___ N.C. App. ___, 706 S.E.2d 288 (2011) (the trial court did not commit plain error by instructing the jury that it could consider whether or not the use of a bottle constituted a deadly weapon during a sexual offense; the defendant and his accomplice, after tying the victim's hands and feet, shoved a rag into his mouth, pulled his pants down, and inserted a bottle into his rectum; the victim thought that he was going to die and an emergency room nurse found a tear in the victim's anal wall accompanied by "serious drainage").

The term "dangerous weapon" is not defined by the rape statute but is used elsewhere in Chapter 14 of the General Statutes. *See, e.g.,* G.S. 14-87 (robbery); G.S. 14-288.9 (assault on emergency personnel); G.S. 14-288.2 (riot). For some of these statutes, it is interpreted as having the same meaning as the term "deadly weapon." See the note on Element (3) to "Armed Robbery" in Chapter 14 (Robbery, Extortion, and Blackmail). For other offenses, a specific definition applies. *See, e.g.,* G.S. 14-288.1(2) (defining the term for the Article in G.S. Chapter 14 on Riots and Civil Disorders). In any event, while hands may constitute deadly weapons for other offenses, see the note on Element (3) to "Assault With a Deadly Weapon" in Chapter 7 (Assaults), a defendant's hands are not dangerous or deadly weapons for purposes of first-degree rape or first-degree sexual offense; for these offenses, an "external" weapon must be used. State v. Adams, 187 N.C. App. 676, 681–83 (2007).

This element is satisfied if the weapon reasonably appeared to the victim to be dangerous or deadly even though it in fact was not—for example, when the defendant uses a toy pistol. State v. McKinnon, 306 N.C. 288 (1982); State v. Lawrence, 191 N.C. App. 422, 433–34 (2008). The evidence was sufficient to prove that the defendant displayed an object that reasonably appeared to be a dangerous or deadly weapon when the defendant held a long, cold metallic object against the victim's head that she thought was a knife, though it could have been a screwdriver, State v. Joyner, 301 N.C. 18 (1980); and grabbed the victim, told her he would kill her, and reached into his pocket to get something; although the victim did not see the object, she said that it was shiny and silver and that she thought it was a knife, *Lawrence,* 191 N.C. App. at 433–34.

When the State alleges that use or display of a dangerous or deadly weapon elevates a rape or sexual offense to a first-degree offense and the jury is not instructed on the theory of acting in concert or aiding and abetting, the evidence must support a finding that the defendant personally used or displayed the weapon. State v. Person, 187 N.C. App. 512, 518–20 (2007).

Element (5)(b). "Serious personal injury" may be proved by showing mental injury or bodily injury, State v. Baker, 336 N.C. 58 (1994); State v. Boone, 307 N.C. 198 (1982); State v. Davis, 101 N.C. App. 12 (1990); State v. Mayse, 97 N.C. App. 559 (1990), a combination of physical and mental injuries, State v. Ackerman, 144 N.C. App. 452 (2001), or death, State v. Richmond, 347 N.C. 412 (1998). Whether the injury is serious is a question of fact. State v. Ferguson, 261 N.C. 558 (1964); *Ackerman,* 144 N.C. App. at 460.

Examples of injuries that constitute "serious personal injury" include:

- a bruised and swollen cheek, a cut lip, and two broken teeth;
- bruises to a victim's rectal area;
- a whiplash injury resulting in leg cramps and requiring two visits to a doctor; and
- blows resulting in five teeth being knocked out of alignment and a broken tooth root.

Ackerman, 144 N.C. App. at 460–61 (citing cases holding that evidence of such injuries was sufficient).

Mental injury must extend for some appreciable time beyond the crime itself and must be an injury beyond that normally experienced in every forcible rape or sexual offense. *Baker*, 336 N.C. 58; State v. Finney, 358 N.C. 79 (2004) (citing *Baker*); State v. Blizzard, 169 N.C. App. 285 (2005). Hysteria and crying for only a relatively short time after the crime are not sufficient to establish mental injury. State v. Boone, 307 N.C. 198 (1982). However, serious mental injury was established when (1) the victim continued to have appetite loss, severe headaches, nightmares, and difficulty sleeping months after being raped, State v. Davis, 101 N.C. App. 12 (1990); and (2) after being sexually assaulted in her home, an elderly victim was too frightened to return home, moved to her niece's residence, and was still there nine months later at the time of trial, State v. Lilly, 342 N.C. 409 (1995) (per curiam), *aff'g* 117 N.C. App. 192 (1994).

Serious personal injury was shown by a combination of physical and mental injuries in a case involving the following facts: the victim suffered three bite marks, a thumb print, a scab, and swelling on the neck as a result of being choked and bruises and swelling about the face, head, neck, chest, and knees resulting from blows from a full beer bottle and the defendant's hands; the defendant's bites to the victim's arm left scars; a blow to the victim's ear caused lasting hearing damage; and some fifteen months after the incident, the victim thought about it every day, dreamed about it every night, and was receiving therapy as a result of the incident. *Ackerman*, 144 N.C. App. at 460–61.

The statute does not require that the injury be inflicted to procure the victim's submission; rather, this element is satisfied if the injury is inflicted at any time during the incident. State v. Thomas, 332 N.C. 544 (1992). The injury can even be inflicted after the sexual act, so long as it is so related to the sexual act that the infliction of injury and the sexual act form a continuous transaction. State v. Blackstock, 314 N.C. 232 (1985). For a discussion of the continuous transaction doctrine as it applies to felony murder, see the note on Element (3)(c) to "First-Degree Murder" in Chapter 6 (Homicide); for a discussion of that doctrine as it applies in robbery cases, see the note entitled "Timing of elements" to "Armed Robbery" in Chapter 14 (Robbery, Extortion, and Blackmail).

Element (5)(c). See the discussion immediately above on the meaning of "serious personal injury." There is no requirement that the other person actually be present during the rape or attempted rape. State v. Rogers, 153 N.C. App. 203 (2002). The element of infliction of serious personal injury is satisfied when there is a series of incidents forming one continuous transaction between the rape or sexual offense and the infliction of the serious personal injury on the other person. *Id.* There was sufficient evidence of this element in a case where the defendant discontinued his attempt to rape victim Prevette when victim Hadley came into the house and then attacked Hadley, hitting her in the face and choking her; a jury could have reasonably inferred that the defendant attacked Hadley to conceal the attempted rape or aid in his escape and that the attempted rape of Prevette and the attack on Hadley were part of one continuous transaction. *Id.* For discussions of the continuous transaction doctrine in other contexts, see the note on Element (5)(b), above.

Element (5)(d). See "Aiding and Abetting" in Chapter 3 (Participants in Crimes) for a discussion of what acts constitute aiding and abetting, including cases involving aiding and abetting by a failure to defend a child from sexual assault. Note that the aider and abettor need not actually have sexual intercourse with the victim during the rape; the evidence is sufficient if he or she simply assists another or stands by to assist if needed. State v. McKinnon, 306 N.C. 288 (1982); State v. Ainsworth, 109 N.C. App. 136 (1993). In this situation, the aider and abettor also would be guilty of first-degree forcible rape. State v. Whitfield, 310 N.C. 608 (1984); *Ainsworth*, 109 N.C. App. 136.

Statute gender-neutral. The defendant may be male or female. Thus, a female would be guilty if she forced a male at gunpoint to have sexual intercourse with her. This offense, however, involves only vaginal intercourse. Thus, a male could not be prosecuted under this offense for having sex with another male, and a female could not be prosecuted under this offense for having sex with another female. Depending on the circumstances, such activity may be prosecuted under other offenses.

Attempt. An attempt to commit this crime is a Class B2 felony. G.S. 14-2.5. See "Attempt" in Chapter 5 (General Crimes) for a discussion of what constitutes an attempt. If the defendant did not achieve penetration, the crime would be attempted first-degree rape. The intent required for attempted rape is established if the evidence shows that the defendant had an intent to gratify his passion upon the victim. State v. Owen, 159 N.C. App. 204 (2003). A defendant's repeated insistence that the victim remove her clothes and come toward him and his attempt to stab her with a knife were overt acts manifesting a sexual purpose or motivation sufficient to establish intent, even though he never removed any of his clothing or said anything to the victim about sexually assaulting her. *Id.* For another case in which there was sufficient evidence of intent in an attempted first-degree rape, see *State v. Garcia*, 358 N.C. 382 (2004). For a case in which the evidence was not sufficiently conflicting on penetration as to require an instruction on attempted rape, see *State v. Thomas*, 187 N.C. App. 140, 144–46 (2007).

Victim's virginity. Virginity is not an element of any rape or sex offense crimes.

Defendant under 14. Old case law held that there was a rebuttable presumption that a male under 14 was incapable of sexual intercourse and could not be convicted of offenses involving sexual intercourse. State v. Rogers, 275 N.C. 411 (1969); State v. Sam, 60 N.C. 293 (1864). That presumption, however, has been removed by statute. G.S. 14-27.9.

Charging issues. For a discussion of charging issues related to sexual assaults, see Jessica Smith, *The Criminal Indictment: Fatal Defect, Fatal Variance, and Amendment*, ADMIN. OF JUST. BULL. NO. 2008/03 (UNC School of Government, July 2008) (online at www.sog.unc.edu/pubs/electronicversions/pdfs/aojb0803.pdf).

Greater and lesser-included offenses. Because so many of the sexual assaults covered in this chapter are closely related, this note outlines the key case law and statutes regarding the greater and lesser-included offenses for many of the crimes included in this chapter, not just first-degree forcible rape.

A second-degree forcible rape committed by force and against the victim's will is a lesser-included offense of first-degree forcible rape. State v. Adams, 187 N.C. App. 676, 683 (2007); State v. Mustafa, 113 N.C. App. 240, 245 (1994). The same rule applies to first- and second-degree forcible sexual offense. *Adams*, 187 N.C. App. at 683.

Simple assault is not a lesser-included offense of attempted rape, State v. Robinson, 97 N.C. App. 597, 603–04 (1990). The relevant case law suggests that the same rule would apply to attempted sexual offense. Also, simple assault is not a lesser-included offense of sexual battery. State v. Corbett, 196 N.C. App. 508, 511 (2009).

Because sexual battery includes an element regarding the defendant's purpose that is not included in rape, it is not a lesser-included offense of that offense. State v. Kelso, 187 N.C. App. 718, 721–22 (2007); State v. Pettis, 186 N.C. App. 116, 119–20 (2007). That same reasoning suggests that it also is not a lesser-included offense of sexual offense.

Because assault on a female contains elements not included in rape, it is not a lesser-included offense of forcible or statutory rape or an attempted version of those crimes. State v. Herring, 322 N.C. 733, 742–43 (1988); State v. Wortham, 318 N.C. 669, 671–72 (1987) (not a lesser-included offense of attempted rape); State v. Weaver, 306 N.C. 629, 638 (1982) (not a lesser-included offense of statutory rape); State v. Thomas, 196 N.C. App. 523, 527 (2009); *Pettis*, 186 N.C. App. at 120–21 (not a lesser-included offense of statutory rape); State v. Hedgepeth, 165 N.C. App. 321, 324 (2004). That reasoning suggests it also is not a lesser-included offense of sexual offense. However, when rape is charged using the short-form indictment prescribed by G.S. 15-144.1, assault on a female may be submitted to the jury. G.S. 15-144.1(a); State v. Hatcher, 117 N.C. App. 78 (1994). When a short-form rape indictment is not used and the indictment charges the crime using the language in G.S. 14-27.2, assault on a female may not be submitted to the jury unless it has been separately charged. *Hedgepeth*, 165 N.C. App. 321. Assault on a female is not a lesser-included offense of indecent liberties. State v. Love, 127 N.C. App. 437, 438–39 (1997).

Assault on a child is not a lesser-included offense of statutory rape. *Weaver*, 306 N.C. at 637–38. The same reasoning would appear to apply to sexual offense.

Indecent liberties is not a lesser-included offense of forcible or statutory rape or sexual offense, crime against nature, or incest. State v. Etheridge, 319 N.C. 34, 50–51 (1987); *Weaver*, 306 N.C. at 637–38 (not a lesser-included offense of statutory rape); State v. Williams, 303 N.C. 507 (1981); State v. Manly, 95 N.C. App. 213, 216–17 (1989) (since a "lewd or lascivious act" is not necessarily a sexual act, indecent liberties is not a lesser-included offense of sexual offense).

Incest is not a lesser-included offense of statutory rape. *Etheridge*, 319 N.C. at 51; State v. Goforth, 67 N.C. App. 537, 539 (1984) (not a lesser-included offense of attempted rape). Similar reasoning would appear to apply to sexual offense.

Crime against nature is not a lesser-included offense of forcible or statutory rape or sexual offense. *Etheridge*, 319 N.C. at 50–51 (not a lesser-included offense of sexual offense); State v. Warren, 309 N.C. 224 (1983).

Because all of the elements of contributing to the delinquency of a minor are not included in rape, it is not a lesser-included offense of that offense. State v. Cronan, 100 N.C. App. 641, 645–46 (1990). The same reasoning would appear to apply to sexual offense.

"First-Degree Statutory Rape" is a lesser-included offense of "Statutory Rape by an Adult," and "First-Degree Statutory Sexual Offense" is a lesser-included offense of "Statutory Sexual Offense by an Adult." G.S. 14-27.2A(e); G.S. 14-27.4A(d).

Multiple convictions and punishments. Each separate act of vaginal intercourse that constitutes rape is a separate, punishable offense. State v. Dudley, 319 N.C. 656, 658–59 (1987); State v. Key, 180 N.C. App. 286 (2006); State v. Owen, 133 N.C. App. 543 (1999); State v. Midyette, 87 N.C. App. 199 (1987); State v. Small, 31 N.C. App. 556 (1976). Thus, a defendant was properly convicted of two counts of rape when he penetrated the victim on a couch, withdrew, and penetrated her again on the floor. State v. Sapp, 190 N.C. App. 698, 703–05 (2008).

A defendant was properly convicted and punished for two separate counts of first-degree rape when he was guilty as the principal by committing forcible sexual intercourse (aided and abetted by another) and as an aider and abettor to another who also committed forcible sexual intercourse. State v. Whitfield, 310 N.C. 608 (1984).

Because forcible rape and statutory rape are two theories for finding a defendant guilty of first-degree rape, a defendant may not be convicted for both forcible and statutory rape when the convictions are based on the same act; the same rule applies to sexual offenses. State v. Ridgeway, 185 N.C. App. 423, 434–35 (2007). However, double jeopardy does not preclude simultaneous convictions for rape or sexual offense (forcible or statutory), indecent liberties with a child, crime against nature, and incest arising out of the same incident. State v. Etheridge, 319 N.C. 34, 50–51 (1987) (rape, incest, and indecent liberties against one victim; sexual offense, indecent liberties, and crime against nature as to another victim); State v. Fletcher, 322 N.C. 415, 419 (1988) (rape, incest, and indecent liberties).

Sex offender registration. This offense is a sexually violent offense triggering registration requirements under the sex offender registration statutes. G.S. 14-208.6(5).

Doctrine of recent possession. If a larceny and a rape occur about the same time as part of a criminal enterprise committed by the same person, the doctrine of recent possession raises a permissible inference that the jury may consider in determining whether a defendant who possesses recently stolen property also may have committed the rape. State v. Joyner, 301 N.C. 18 (1980). For a discussion of that doctrine, see the note entitled "Doctrine of recent possession" to "Misdemeanor Larceny" in Chapter 13 (Larceny, Possession of Stolen Goods, Embezzlement, and Related Offenses).

Rape shield rule. North Carolina Evidence Rule 412, G.S. 8C-1, Rule 412, applies to all rape and sexual offense cases (and their lesser-included offenses) and prohibits, in certain circumstances, inquiry into the victim's past sexual behavior. It does not appear to apply, however, to all of the sexual assaults discussed in this chapter. For a discussion of the rule and its applicability, see Jeff Welty, *Special Evidentiary Issues in Sexual Assault Cases: The Rape Shield Law and Evidence of Prior Sexual Misconduct by the Defendant*, ADMIN. OF JUST. BULLETIN 2009/04 (UNC School of Government, Aug. 2009) (online at http://shopping.netsuite.com/s.nl/c.433425/it.I/id.407/.f).

Convicted defendant has no rights to custody or inheritance. G.S. 14-27.2(c) provides that a person convicted of this offense has no rights to custody of or inheritance from a child born as a result of commission of the rape and has no rights under the adoption or abuse, neglect, and dependency statutes.

Related Offenses Not in This Chapter

"Assault on a Female" (Chapter 7)
"Crime against Nature" (Chapter 11)
"Fornication and Adultery" (Chapter 11)
See incest (various offenses) in Chapter 11 (Crime against Nature, Incest, Indecent Exposure, and Related Offenses).
See kidnapping (various offenses) in Chapter 12 (Kidnapping and Related Offenses).
See prostitution (various offenses) in Chapter 23 (Prostitution).
Contaminating food or drink with intent to commit rape. G.S. 14-401.16(c).

Second-Degree Forcible Rape

Statute

§14-27.3. Second-degree rape.

(a) A person is guilty of rape in the second degree if the person engages in vaginal intercourse with another person:

(1) By force and against the will of the other person; or
(2) Who is mentally disabled, mentally incapacitated, or physically helpless, and the person performing the act knows or should reasonably know the other person is mentally disabled, mentally incapacitated, or physically helpless.

(b) Any person who commits the offense defined in this section is guilty of a Class C felony.

(c) Upon conviction, a person convicted under this section has no rights to custody of or rights of inheritance from any child conceived during the commission of the rape, nor shall the person have any rights related to the child under Chapter 48 or Subchapter 1 of Chapter 7B of the General Statutes.

Elements

A person guilty of this offense

(1) has vaginal intercourse
(2) with a person
(3) and the intercourse is
  (a) by force and against the person's will *or*
  (b) with someone who is
    (i) mentally disabled,
    (ii) mentally incapacitated, *or*
    (iii) physically helpless *and*
(4) the defendant knew or should have known that the victim was mentally disabled, mentally incapacitated, or physically helpless.

Punishment

Class C felony. G.S. 14-27.3(b). See the additional discussion in "Punishment" under "First-Degree Forcible Rape," above.

Notes

Generally. This offense is the same as "Second-Degree Forcible Sexual Offense," below, except for the sexual conduct involved. For second-degree forcible sexual offense, a sexual act other than vaginal intercourse is required. For this offense, vaginal intercourse is required.

Elements (1) and (2). See the notes on Elements (1) and (2) to "First-Degree Forcible Rape," above.

Element (3)(a). See the notes on Elements (3) and (4) to "First-Degree Forcible Rape," above.

Element (3)(b)(i). "Mentally disabled" means that the victim is mentally retarded or has a mental disorder, either of which condition leaves the victim incapable of appraising the conduct or resisting or communicating an unwillingness to submit. G.S. 14-27.1(1).

For a sexual offense case where the evidence was sufficient to establish that the victim was mentally disabled, see *State v. Williams*, ___ N.C. App. ___, 698 S.E.2d 542, 545–46 (2010) (the victim, who had an IQ of 58 and was mildly mentally retarded, was not capable of resisting a sexual act; the victim had difficulty expressing himself verbally and had difficulty answering questions about social abilities; he needed daily assistance with cooking and personal hygiene; notwithstanding the victim's communication of his unwillingness to receive oral sex, the defendant completed the sexual act, allowing an inference that the victim was unable to resist). For a contrasting sexual assault case in which the evidence was insufficient to establish that the victim was mentally disabled, see *State v. Hunt*, ___ N.C. App. ___, 710 S.E.2d 339 (2011) (even if the State presented sufficient evidence of mental retardation, it did not present sufficient evidence that the condition rendered the victim incapable of resistance; the victim was in the top range of achievement in high school, she babysat, she planned to get her driver's license and attend community college, at the time of trial she was living with her boyfriend and his mother, and there was some indication that she was pregnant but there had been no DSS intervention or charges filed against the boyfriend; on the other hand, the victim was described as "childlike," she attended classes for children with learning disabilities and was classified as intellectually disabled in the mild category, with an I.Q. of 61, DSS paid her bills, and it would be difficult for her to get a community college associate's degree; the court held that "where the victim's IQ falls within the range considered to be 'mental retardation[,]' but wh[ere the victim] is highly functional in her daily activities and communication, the State must present expert testimony as to the extent of the victim's mental disability"), *temp. stay allowed*, 708 S.E.2d 717 (2011).

Element (3)(b)(ii). "Mentally incapacitated" means that some act has been committed on the victim that leaves the victim incapable of appraising the nature of the conduct or resisting the act. G.S. 14-27.1(2). A person is not mentally incapacitated when he or she is responsible for the incapacitation (for example, by voluntarily ingesting alcohol). State v. Haddock, 191 N.C. App. 474, 481–84 (2008).

Element (3)(b)(iii). "Physically helpless" means that the victim is unconscious or physically unable to resist the act or to communicate an unwillingness to submit. G.S. 14-27.1(3). A sleeping victim is "physically helpless." State v. Moorman, 320 N.C. 387 (1987). A victim so intoxicated as to be unable to resist also may be "physically helpless." State v. Aiken, 73 N.C. App. 487 (1985); *see also Haddock*, 191 N.C. App. at 481–84. The statute does not require that the defendant be the one who rendered the victim mentally incapacitated or physically helpless. A person is not mentally incapacitated when he or she is responsible for the incapacitation (for example, by voluntarily ingesting alcohol); however, such a victim might be physically helpless. *Haddock*, 191 N.C. App. at 481–84.

There was sufficient evidence that the victim was physically helpless when she was 83 years old, suffered from severe arthritis, used a walker, needed assistance with everyday household chores, and could go down steps or do daily errands only with assistance. State v. Atkins, 193 N.C. App. 200, 205–06 (2008).

Element (4). The defendant knew or should have known that the victim was mentally disabled when an officer testified that within three minutes of talking with the victim it was obvious that the victim had some deficits; the victim could not drive, never held a regular job, could cook only in a microwave, had to be reminded to brush his teeth, did not know how to connect a VCR, and could not read; the defendant had sufficient knowledge about the victim, having dated the victim's mother for thirteen years and having spent many nights at the mother's house, where the victim lived. State v. Williams, ___ N.C. App. ___, 698 S.E.2d 542, 546–47 (2010).

Statute gender-neutral. See this note to "First-Degree Forcible Rape," above.

Attempt. An attempt to commit this offense is a Class D felony. G.S. 14-2.5. See this note to "First-Degree Forcible Rape," above.

Victim's virginity. See this note to "First-Degree Forcible Rape," above.

Defendant under 14. See this note to "First-Degree Forcible Rape," above.

Charging issues. See this note to "First-Degree Forcible Rape," above.

Greater and lesser-included offenses. See this note to "First-Degree Forcible Rape," above.

Multiple convictions and punishments. See this note to "First-Degree Forcible Rape," above.

Sex offender registration. This offense is a sexually violent offense triggering registration requirements under the sex offender registration statutes. G.S. 14-208.6(5).

Doctrine of recent possession. See this note to "First-Degree Forcible Rape," above.

Rape Shield Rule. See this note to "First-Degree Forcible Rape," above.

Convicted defendant has no rights to custody or inheritance. G.S. 14-27.3(c) provides that upon conviction, a person convicted of this offense has no rights to custody of or inheritance from a child born as a result of commission of the rape and has no rights under the adoption or abuse, neglect, and dependency statutes.

Related Offenses Not in This Chapter

See the offenses listed under "First-Degree Forcible Rape," above.

First-Degree Statutory Rape

Statute

See G.S. 14-27.2(a)(1), reproduced above under "First-Degree Forcible Rape."

Elements

A person guilty of this offense

(1) has vaginal intercourse
(2) with a child under the age of 13 years
(3) who is at least four years younger than the defendant *and*
(4) the defendant is at least 12 years old.

Punishment

Class B1 felony. G.S. 14-27.2(b). See the additional discussion in "Punishment" under "First-Degree Forcible Rape," above.

Notes

Generally. This offense is the same as "First-Degree Statutory Sexual Offense," below, except for the sexual conduct involved. For first-degree statutory sexual offense, a sexual act other than vaginal intercourse is required. For this offense, vaginal intercourse is required.

Element (1). See the note on Element (1) to "First-Degree Forcible Rape," above.

Element (2). A child is under the age of 13 years until the day of his or her thirteenth birthday. The defendant is not excused by being misled or mistaken about the victim's age. State v. Wade, 224 N.C. 760 (1944). Birth certificates or certified copies of birth records are not necessary to establish the age elements of this offense; the relevant ages may be established by the victim's or defendant's own testimony. State v. Cortes-Serrano, 195 N.C. App. 644, 652–53 (2009). See also the note on Element (2) to "Statutory Rape of a Person Who Is 13, 14, or 15 Years Old by a Defendant Who Is at Least Six Years Older Than the Victim," below.

If the child is 13 or older, the defendant might be guilty of "Statutory Rape of a Person Who Is 13, 14, or 15 Years Old" or "Indecent Liberties with a Child," both discussed below.

Element (3). The age difference must be measured from the defendant's birthday to the victim's birthday. Thus, if the defendant was born on February 1, 1998, and the victim was born on January 10, 2002, there is not a difference of four full years in age. If the victim had been born a month later, the age difference element would be satisfied. See the note on Element (3) to "Statutory Rape of a Person Who Is 13, 14, or 15 Years Old by a Defendant Who Is at Least Six Years Older Than the Victim," below.

Element (4). Birth certificates or certified copies of birth records are not necessary to establish the required ages; the ages may be established by the victim's or defendant's own testimony. *Cortes-Serrano*, 195 N.C. App. at 652–53.

Some decisions can be read as holding that a jury may determine a defendant's age based on its own observations of the defendant at trial. State v. Samuels, 298 N.C. 783 (1979); State v. Bynum, 111 N.C. App. 845 (1993). However, a more recent court of appeals decision distinguished those cases and held that this element is not sufficiently proved when there is no direct or circumstantial evidence of the defendant's age; the court concluded that the jury's observation of the defendant in the courtroom was insufficient to establish this element. *In re* Jones, 135 N.C. App. 400 (1999).

Statute gender-neutral. See this note to "First-Degree Forcible Rape," above. An adult woman who has consensual vaginal intercourse with a 12-year-old boy is guilty of this offense. State v. Ainsworth, 109 N.C. App. 136, 143–45 (1993).

Consent. Consent is not a defense to this offense. State v. Temple, 269 N.C. 57 (1967); *Ainsworth*, 109 N.C. App. at 145.

Force. To establish this crime, it is not necessary to prove that the intercourse was by force or against the victim's will. State v. Johnson, 226 N.C. 266 (1946).

Attempt. An attempt to commit this crime is a Class B2 felony. G.S. 14-2.5. See this note to "First-Degree Forcible Rape, " above.

Victim's virginity. See this note to "First-Degree Forcible Rape," above.

Defendant under 14. See this note to "First-Degree Forcible Rape," above.

Charging issues. See this note to "First-Degree Forcible Rape," above.

Greater and lesser-included offenses. See this note to "First-Degree Forcible Rape," above.

Multiple convictions and punishments. See this note to "First-Degree Forcible Rape," above.

Sex offender registration. This offense is a sexually violent offense triggering registration requirements under the sex offender registration statutes. G.S. 14-208.6(5).

Doctrine of recent possession. See this note to "First-Degree Forcible Rape," above.

Rape shield rule. See this note to "First-Degree Forcible Rape," above.

Convicted defendant has no rights to custody or inheritance. See this note to "First-Degree Forcible Rape," above.

Related Offenses Not in This Chapter

See the offenses listed under "First-Degree Forcible Rape," above.
"Assault on a Child under 12" (Chapter 7)
See child abuse (various offenses) in Chapter 9 (Abuse and Neglect).
See various offenses involving minors in Chapter 23 (Prostitution).
See various offenses involving minors in Chapter 24 (Obscenity, Exploitation of a Minor, and Adult Establishment Offenses).

Statutory Rape by an Adult

Statute

§14-27.2A. Rape of a child; adult offender.

(a) A person is guilty of rape of a child if the person is at least 18 years of age and engages in vaginal intercourse with a victim who is a child under the age of 13 years.

(b) A person convicted of violating this section is guilty of a Class B1 felony and shall be sentenced pursuant to Article 81B of Chapter 15A of the General Statutes, except that in no case shall the person receive an active punishment of less than 300 months, and except as provided in subsection (c) of this section. Following the termination of active punishment, the person shall be enrolled in satellite-based monitoring for life pursuant to Part 5 of Article 27A of Chapter 14 of the General Statutes.

(c) Notwithstanding the provisions of Article 81B of Chapter 15A of the General Statutes, the court may sentence the defendant to active punishment for a term of months greater than that authorized pursuant to G.S. 15A-1340.17, up to and including life imprisonment without parole, if the court finds that the nature of the offense and the harm inflicted are of such brutality, duration, severity, degree, or scope beyond that normally committed in such crimes, or considered in basic aggravation of these crimes, so as to require a sentence to active punishment in excess of that authorized pursuant to G.S. 15A-1340.17. If the court sentences the defendant pursuant to this subsection, it shall make findings of fact supporting its decision, to include matters it considered as egregious aggravation. Egregious aggravation can include further consideration of existing aggravating factors where the conduct of the defendant falls outside the heartland of cases even the aggravating factors were designed to cover. Egregious aggravation may also be considered based on the extraordinarily young age of the victim, or the depraved torture or mutilation of the victim, or extraordinary physical pain inflicted on the victim.

(d) Upon conviction, a person convicted under this section has no rights to custody of or rights of inheritance from any child born as a result of the commission of the rape, nor shall the person have any rights related to the child under Chapter 48 or Subchapter 1 of Chapter 7B of the General Statutes.

(e) The offense under G.S. 14-27.2(a)(1) is a lesser included offense of the offense in this section.

Elements

A person guilty of this offense

(1) has vaginal intercourse
(2) with a child under the age of 13 years *and*
(3) the defendant is at least 18 years old.

Punishment

Class B1 felony, except that the offense is subject to a mandatory minimum of at least 300 months of active time. G.S. 14-27.2A(b). G.S. 14-27.2A(c) provides that a defendant may be sentenced to an active term above that normally provided for a Class B1 felony if the judge finds egregious aggravation. However, this procedure appears to run afoul of the United States Supreme Court decision in *Blakely v. Washington,* 542 U.S. 296 (2004) (holding that any factor, other than a prior conviction, that increases punishment beyond the prescribed statutory maximum must be submitted to the jury and proved beyond a reasonable doubt). See the additional discussion in "Punishment" under "First-Degree Forcible Rape," above.

Notes

Generally. This offense is the same as "Statutory Sexual Offense by an Adult," below, except for the sexual conduct involved. For statutory sexual offense by an adult, a sexual act other than vaginal intercourse is required. For this offense, vaginal intercourse is required.

Element (1). See the note on Element (1) to "First-Degree Forcible Rape," above.

Element (2). See the note on Element (2) to "First-Degree Statutory Rape," above.

Element (3). See the note on Element (4) to "First-Degree Statutory Rape," above.

Statute gender-neutral. See this note to "First-Degree Forcible Rape," above.

Consent. See this note to "First-Degree Statutory Rape," above.

Force. See this note to "First-Degree Statutory Rape," above.

Attempt. An attempt to commit this crime is a Class B2 felony. G.S. 14-2.5. See this note to "First-Degree Forcible Rape," above.

Victim's virginity. See this note to "First-Degree Forcible Rape," above.

Charging issues. See this note to "First-Degree Forcible Rape," above.

Greater and lesser-included offenses. See this note to "First-Degree Forcible Rape," above.

Multiple convictions and punishment. See this note to "First-Degree Forcible Rape," above.

Sex offender registration. This crime is a sexually violent offense requiring registration as a sex offender. G.S. 14-208.6(5).

Lifetime satellite-based monitoring. Following the termination of active punishment, a person convicted of this offense must submit to satellite-based monitoring for life under the sex offender monitoring statutes. G.S. 14-27.2A(b).

Convicted defendant has no rights of custody or inheritance. A person convicted of this crime loses all custody and inheritance rights from any child born as a result of the commission of the rape and has no rights under the adoption or abuse, neglect, and dependency statutes. G.S. 14-27.2A(d).

Related Offenses Not in This Chapter

See the offenses listed under "First-Degree Forcible Rape" and "First-Degree Statutory Rape," both above.

Statutory Rape of a Person Who Is 13, 14, or 15 Years Old by a Defendant Who Is at Least Six Years Older Than the Victim

Statute

§14-27.7A. Statutory rape or sexual offense of person who is 13, 14, or 15 years old.

(a) A defendant is guilty of a Class B1 felony if the defendant engages in vaginal intercourse or a sexual act with another person who is 13, 14, or 15 years old and the defendant is at least six years older than the person, except when the defendant is lawfully married to the person.

(b) A defendant is guilty of a Class C felony if the defendant engages in vaginal intercourse or a sexual act with another person who is 13, 14, or 15 years old and the defendant is more than four but less than six years older than the person, except when the defendant is lawfully married to the person.

Elements

A person guilty of this offense

(1) has vaginal intercourse
(2) with a child who is 13, 14, or 15 years old *and*
(3) the defendant is at least six years older than the child.

Punishment

Class B1 felony. G.S. 14-27.7A(a). See the additional discussion in "Punishment" under "First-Degree Forcible Rape," above.

Notes

Generally. This offense is the same as "Statutory Sexual Offense against a Person Who Is 13, 14, or 15 Years Old by a Defendant Who Is At Least Six Years Older Than the Victim," discussed below, except for the sexual conduct involved. For the statutory sexual offense version of this offense, a sexual act other than vaginal intercourse is required. For this offense, vaginal intercourse is required.

Element (1). See the note on Element (1) to "First-Degree Forcible Rape," above.

Element (2). In determining whether the victim is 13, 14, or 15 years old, the "birthday rule" applies. Under the birthday rule, a person reaches a certain age on his or her birthday and remains that age until his or her next birthday. State v. Roberts, 166 N.C. App. 649 (2004); State v. Moore, 167 N.C. App. 495 (2004) (citing *Roberts*). Thus, a rape victim who was 15 years, 11 months of age when the offense occurred was 15 years old, *Roberts*, 166 N.C. App. 649, and a rape victim who had sexual intercourse with the defendant two days after her 15th birthday was 15 when the offense occurred, *Moore*, 167 N.C. App. 495.

As with first-degree statutory rape, discussed above, a defendant is not excused by being misled or mistaken about the victim's age. State v. Sines, 158 N.C. App. 79 (2003). If the victim is not one of the ages covered here or under "First-Degree Statutory Rape," the defendant still might be guilty of "Indecent Liberties with a Child" or other sexual assault offenses involving minors discussed later in this chapter.

Element (3). This element differentiates this offense from "Statutory Rape of a Person Who Is 13, 14, or 15 Years Old by a Defendant Who is More Than Four But Less Than Six Years Older than the Victim," below. For this offense, the defendant must be at least six years older than the alleged victim. For the other offense, the defendant must be more than four but less than six years older than the alleged victim. For both offenses, the age difference is measured from the defendant's birthday to the victim's birthday. Thus, if the defendant was born on February 10, 1991, the victim was born on January 10, 1996, and the required sexual conduct occurred in 2010, the offense that occurred is "Statutory Rape of a Person Who Is 13, 14, or 15 Years Old by a Defendant Who is More Than Four But Less Than Six Years Older than the Victim."

In this example, the defendant is 4 years and 11 months older than the victim. The defendant was more than four years older than the victim when, on the date of the offense, the defendant was 19 years, 7 months, and 5 days old and the victim was 15 years, 2 months, and 8 days old; the statutory element of more than 4 years but less than 6 years means 4 years 0 days to 6 years 0 days, "or anywhere in the range of 1460 days to 2190 days." State v. Faulk, 200 N.C. App. 118, 118–20 (2009).

See the note on Element (4) to "First-Degree Statutory Rape," above, concerning proof of a defendant's age.

There was sufficient evidence that the defendant was more than six years older than the victim when the victim testified that the defendant was her biological father and it was biologically impossible for the defendant to be less than six years older than the victim and be her biological father. State v. Ware, 188 N.C. App. 790, 794 (2008); State v. Wiggins, 161 N.C. App. 583 (2003).

Statute gender-neutral. See this note to "First-Degree Forcible Rape," above.

Exceptions. The statute specifically provides that this offense does not apply if the defendant and the alleged victim are lawfully married. G.S. 14-27.7A. The exemption for married couples does not violate equal protection. State v. Clark, 161 N.C. App. 316 (2003). Note that other offenses may apply to conduct between married persons.

Consent. As with first-degree statutory rape, above, consent is not a defense to this crime. State v. Anthony, 351 N.C. 611 (2000).

Force. To establish this crime, it is not necessary to prove that the intercourse was by force or against the victim's will.

Attempt. See this note to "First-Degree Statutory Rape" and "First-Degree Forcible Rape," both above.

Victim's virginity. See this note to "First-Degree Forcible Rape," above.

Charging issues. See this note to "First-Degree Forcible Rape," above.

Greater and lesser-included offenses. See this note to "First-Degree Forcible Rape," above.

Multiple convictions and punishments. See this note to "First-Degree Forcible Rape," above.

Sex offender registration. This offense is a sexually violent offense triggering registration requirements under the sex offender registration statutes. G.S. 14-208.6(5).

Constitutionality. The United States Supreme Court's decision in *Lawrence v. Texas*, 539 U.S. 558 (2003), does not bar a prosecution under this statute. *Clark*, 161 N.C. App. 316. Nor does that decision support a mistake of age defense to this crime. State v. Browning, 177 N.C. App. 487 (2006). See the note entitled "Constitutionality" to "Crime against Nature" in Chapter 11 (Crime against Nature, Indecent Exposure, and Related Offenses).

Doctrine of recent possession. See this note to "First-Degree Forcible Rape," above.

Rape shield rule. See this note to "First-Degree Forcible Rape," above.

Related Offenses Not in This Chapter

See the offenses listed under "First-Degree Forcible Rape" and "First-Degree Statutory Rape," both above.

Statutory Rape of a Person Who Is 13, 14, or 15 Years Old by a Defendant Who Is More Than Four but Less Than Six Years Older Than the Victim

Statute

See G.S. 14-27.7A(b), reproduced under "Statutory Rape of a Person Who Is 13, 14, or 15 Years Old by a Defendant Who Is at Least Six Years Older Than the Victim," above.

Elements

A person guilty of this offense

(1) has vaginal intercourse
(2) with a child who is 13, 14, or 15 years old *and*
(3) the defendant is more than four but less than six years older than the child.

Punishment

Class C felony. G.S. 14-27A(b). See the additional discussion in "Punishment" under "First-Degree Forcible Rape," above.

Notes

Generally. This offense is the same as "Statutory Sexual Offense Against a Person Who Is 13, 14, or 15 Years Old by a Defendant Who Is More Than Four But Less Than Six Years Older Than the Victim," below, except for the conduct involved. For this offense, vaginal intercourse is required. For the sexual offense version, a sexual act other than vaginal intercourse is required. This offense also is the same as "Statutory Rape of a Person Who Is 13, 14, or 15 Years Old by a Defendant Who Is at Least Six Years Older Than the Victim," above, except for the element regarding the defendant's age. Thus, the notes to that offense apply here as well.

Sex offender registration. This offense is not defined as a sexually violent offense and therefore does not require sex offender registration.

Related Offenses Not in This Chapter

See the offenses listed under "First-Degree Forcible Rape" and "First-Degree Statutory Rape," both above.

Sexual Offenses

First-Degree Forcible Sexual Offense

Statute

§14-27.4. First-degree sexual offense.

(a) A person is guilty of a sexual offense in the first degree if the person engages in a sexual act:

(1) With a victim who is a child under the age of 13 years and the defendant is at least 12 years old and is at least four years older than the victim; or

(2) With another person by force and against the will of the other person, and:

a. Employs or displays a dangerous or deadly weapon or an article which the other person reasonably believes to be a dangerous or deadly weapon; or

b. Inflicts serious personal injury upon the victim or another person; or

c. The person commits the offense aided and abetted by one or more other persons.

(b) Any person who commits an offense defined in this section is guilty of a Class B1 felony.

Elements

A person guilty of this offense

(1) engages in a sexual act other than vaginal intercourse
(2) with a person
(3) by force *and*
(4) against that person's will *and*
(5) the defendant
  (a) uses or displays a dangerous or deadly weapon (or what reasonably appears to be a dangerous or deadly weapon),
  (b) inflicts serious personal injury on the victim,
  (c) inflicts serious personal injury on another person, *or*
  (d) is aided and abetted by one or more other persons.

Punishment

Class B1 felony. G.S. 14-27.4(b). See the additional discussion in "Punishment" under "First-Degree Forcible Rape," above.

Notes

Generally. This offense is the same as "First-Degree Forcible Rape," above, except for the sexual conduct involved. For first-degree forcible rape, vaginal intercourse is required. For this offense, a sexual act other than vaginal intercourse is required.

Element (1). "Sexual act" includes cunnilingus, analingus, fellatio, and anal intercourse but not vaginal intercourse, which is the act required for rape. G.S. 14-27.1(4). "Cunnilingus" means the stimulation by tongue or lips of any part of the woman's genitalia; penetration is not required under this statute, although penetration is required as a separate element of the offense of crime against nature. State v. Ludlum, 303 N.C. 666 (1981). "Analingus" means stimulation of a person's anal opening by tongue or lips. State v. White, 101 N.C. App. 593 (1991). As with cunnilingus, penetration by the tongue or lips into the anus is not required. State v. Sloan, 316 N.C. 714 (1986). "Fellatio" is any touching of the male sexual organ by the lips, tongue, or mouth of another person. State v. Hewett, 93 N.C. App. 1 (1989). When the sexual act is anal intercourse, proof of the emission of semen is not necessary; all that is required is penetration, however slight. G.S. 14-27.10. For cases in which the evidence was sufficient to establish penetration in connection with anal intercourse, see *State v. Sprouse*, ___ N.C. App. ___, ___ S.E.2d ___ (Dec. 6, 2011) (the victim testified that the defendant "inserted his penis . . . into [her] butt," that the incident was painful, and that she wiped blood from the area immediately after the incident), and *State v. Carter*, ___ N.C. App. ___, ___ S.E.2d ___ (Nov. 1, 2011) (although the evidence was conflicting, the child victim stated that the defendant's penis penetrated her anus; additionally, a sexual assault nurse examiner testified that the victim's anal fissure could have resulted from trauma to the anal area).

"Sexual act" also includes insertion of "any object" into another's genital or anal opening. The slightest penetration is sufficient. G.S. 14-27.1(4). "Object" means an inanimate object (such as a curtain rod) or animate object (such as a hand or finger). State v. Noble, 326 N.C. 581 (1990); State v. Lucas, 302 N.C. 342 (1981). The evidence was sufficient to establish penetration with an object when (1) the defendant used a gun to spread the victim's labia, State v. Bellamy, 172 N.C. App. 649 (2005); and (2) the child victim testified that the defendant reached under her shorts and touched between "the skin type area" where "you pee out of" and that he rubbed against a pressure point, causing her pain and making her feel faint; a medical expert testified that the victim's description was "more suggestive of touching . . . on the inside," State v. Crocker, 197 N.C. App. 358, 363–64 (2009).

Elements (2), (3), (4), and (5). See the notes on these elements to "First-Degree Forcible Rape," above.

Statute gender-neutral. The wording of this statute means that the defendant may be male or female and the victim may be male or female, depending on the kind of sexual act on which the charge is based.

Attempt. An attempt to commit this crime is a Class B2 felony. G.S. 14-2.5. See "Attempt" in Chapter 5 (General Crimes) for a discussion of what constitutes an attempt. If penetration is a required element of a particular sexual act and the defendant did not achieve penetration, the charge should be attempted sexual offense. For a case in which the evidence on penetration was not conflicting and did not require an instruction on attempted anal intercourse, see *State v. Person,* 187 N.C. App. 512, 524–25 (2007). For a case in which the evidence on penetration was conflicting, requiring an instruction on attempted sexual offense, see *State v. Carter,* ___ N.C. App. ___, ___ S.E.2d ___ (Nov. 1, 2011) (trial court committed plain error by failing to instruct on attempted sexual offense).

Victim's virginity. See this note to "First-Degree Forcible Rape," above.

Defendant under 14. See this note to "First-Degree Forcible Rape," above.

Charging issues. See this note to "First-Degree Forcible Rape," above.

Defenses. If the charge involves penetration with an object, it is an affirmative defense that the penetration was for accepted medical purposes. G.S. 14-27.1(4).

Jury instructions. In one case, the court of appeals held, over a dissent, that the trial court did not err by instructing the jury that it could find the defendant guilty of sexual offense if it found that he engaged in either anal intercourse or fellatio with the victim. State v. Sweat, ___ N.C. App. ___, ___ S.E.2d ___ (Oct. 18, 2011) (reasoning that the jury was not required to agree as to which act occurred), *temp. stay allowed,* ___ N.C. ___, ___ S.E.2d ___ (Nov. 7, 2011).

Greater and lesser-included offenses. See this note to "First-Degree Forcible Rape," above.

Multiple convictions and punishments. See this note to "First-Degree Forcible Rape," above.

In cases of first- and second-degree sexual offense, each unlawful sexual act committed by a defendant against a single victim during a continuous transaction constitutes a separate crime for which the defendant may be separately charged and convicted. State v. Dudley, 319 N.C. 656, 659 (1987); State v. Cortes-Serrano, 195 N.C. App. 644, 653–54 (2009); State v. Midyette, 87 N.C. App. 199 (1987). For example, if a defendant engaged in cunnilingus and anal intercourse with the female victim in a continuous transaction, two separate counts of sexual offense may be charged. This rule applies even if the two sexual acts occur simultaneously. State v. Williams, ___ N.C. App. ___, 689 S.E.2d 412, 425–26 (2009) (the defendant put his hands in the victim's vagina and rectum at the same time). *State v. Petty,* 132 N.C. App. 453 (1999) (when both cunnilingus and inserting object into minor's genital area occurred during single transaction, only one conviction allowed), does not undercut this rule. State v. Gobal, 186 N.C. App. 308, 320 n.5 (2007) (noting that *Petty* dealt with the separate issue of unanimity of the jury verdict and holding that by sentencing the defendant to consecutive terms of imprisonment for two counts of sexual offense, the trial court did not violate the defendant's double jeopardy rights).

Relation to other offenses. Cunnilingus, fellatio, analingus, and anal intercourse—all of which constitute sexual acts for this offense—are also forms of "Crime against Nature," discussed in Chapter 11 (Crime against Nature, Incest, Indecent Exposure, and Related Offenses). Crime against nature does not require that the act be committed without consent. If cunnilingus, fellatio, analingus, or anal intercourse was committed by force, the defendant could be charged either with forcible sexual offense (first- or second-degree, depending on whether a deadly weapon was used, etc.) or with crime against nature, or with both. If the act was done with consent, possible charges would be crime against nature and, if the victim and defendant fall into applicable age groups, one of the statutory sexual offenses described in this chapter. Many sexual offense crimes carry a greater punishment than crime against nature, which is a Class I felony.

Sex offender registration. This offense is a sexually violent offense triggering registration requirements under the sex offender registration statutes. G.S. 14-208.6(5).

Doctrine of recent possession. See this note to "First-Degree Forcible Rape," above.

Rape shield rule. See this note to "First-Degree Forcible Rape," above.

Related Offenses Not in This Chapter

See the offenses listed under "First-Degree Forcible Rape," above.

Second-Degree Forcible Sexual Offense

Statute

§14-27.5. Second-degree sexual offense.

(a) A person is guilty of a sexual offense in the second degree if the person engages in a sexual act with another person:

(1) By force and against the will of the other person; or

(2) Who is mentally disabled, mentally incapacitated, or physically helpless, and the person performing the act knows or should reasonably know that the other person is mentally disabled, mentally incapacitated, or physically helpless.

(b) Any person who commits the offense defined in this section is guilty of a Class C felony.

Elements

A person guilty of this offense

(1) engages in a sexual act other than vaginal intercourse
(2) with a person *and*
(3) the act is
  (a) by force and against the person's will *or*
  (b) with someone who is
    (i) mentally disabled,
    (ii) mentally incapacitated, *or*
    (iii) physically helpless *and*
(4) the defendant knew or should have known that the victim was mentally disabled, mentally incapacitated, or physically helpless.

Punishment

Class C felony. G.S. 14-27.5(b). See the additional discussion in "Punishment" under "First-Degree Forcible Rape," both above.

Notes

Generally. This offense is the same as "Second-Degree Forcible Rape," above, except for the sexual conduct involved. For second-degree forcible rape, vaginal intercourse is required. For this offense, a sexual act other than vaginal intercourse is required.

Element (1). See this note to "First-Degree Forcible Sexual Offense," above.

Element (2). See this note to "First-Degree Forcible Rape," above.

Element (3)(a). See the notes on Elements (3) and (4) to "First-Degree Forcible Rape," above.

Element (3)(b). See the note on Element (3)(b) to "Second-Degree Forcible Rape," above.

Statute gender-neutral. See this note to "First-Degree Forcible Sexual Offense," above.

Attempt. An attempt to commit this crime is a Class D felony. G.S. 14-2.5. See this note to "First-Degree Forcible Sexual Offense," above.

Victim's virginity. See this note to "First-Degree Forcible Rape," above.

Defendant under 14. See this note to "First-Degree Forcible Rape," above.

Charging issues. See this note to "First-Degree Forcible Rape," above.

Defenses. See this note to "First-Degree Forcible Sexual Offense," above.

Greater and lesser-included offenses. See this note to "First-Degree Forcible Rape," above.

Multiple convictions and punishments. See this note to "First-Degree Forcible Rape" and "First-Degree Forcible Sexual Offense," both above.

Relation to other offenses. See this note to "First-Degree Forcible Sexual Offense," above.

Sex offender registration. This offense is a sexually violent offense triggering registration requirements under the sex offender registration statutes. G.S. 14-208.6(5).

Doctrine of recent possession. See this note to "First-Degree Forcible Rape," above.

Rape shield rule. See this note to "First-Degree Forcible Rape," above.

Related Offenses Not in This Chapter

See the offenses listed under "First-Degree Forcible Rape," above.

First-Degree Statutory Sexual Offense

Statute

See G.S. 14-27.4(a)(1), reproduced under "First-Degree Forcible Sexual Offense," above.

Elements

A person guilty of this offense

(1) engages in a sexual act other than vaginal intercourse
(2) with a child under the age of 13 years
(3) who is at least four years younger than the defendant *and*
(4) the defendant is at least 12 years old.

Punishment

Class B1 felony. G.S. 14-27.4(b). See the additional discussion in "Punishment" under "First-Degree Forcible Rape," above.

Notes

Generally. This offense is the same as "First-Degree Statutory Rape," above, except for the sexual conduct involved. For first-degree statutory rape, vaginal intercourse is required. For this offense, a sexual act other than vaginal intercourse is required.

Element (1). See the note on Element (1) to "First-Degree Forcible Sexual Offense," above.

Element (2). See the note on Element (2) to "First-Degree Statutory Rape" and "Statutory Rape of a Person Who Is 13, 14, or 15 Years Old by a Defendant Who Is at Least Six Years Older Than the Victim," both above. If the victim is 13 or older, the defendant might still be guilty of "Statutory Sexual Offense against a Person Who Is 13, 14, or 15 Years Old," "Indecent Liberties with a Child," both discussed below, or "Crime against Nature," discussed in Chapter 11 (Crime against Nature, Incest, Indecent Exposure, and Related Offenses).

Element (3). See the note on Element (3) to "First-Degree Statutory Rape" and "Statutory Rape of a Person Who Is 13, 14, or 15 Years Old by a Defendant Who Is at Least Six Years Older Than the Victim," both above.

Element (4). See the note on this element to "First-Degree Statutory Rape," above.

Statute gender-neutral. See this note to "First-Degree Forcible Sexual Offense," above.

Consent. Consent is not a defense to a statutory sex offense charge. State v. Temple, 269 N.C. 57 (1967).

Force. It is not necessary to show that the act was by force and against the victim's will. State v. Johnson, 226 N.C. 266 (1946).

Attempt. An attempt to commit this crime is a Class B2 felony. See this note to "First-Degree Forcible Sexual Offense," above.

Victim's virginity. See this note to "First-Degree Forcible Rape," above.

Defendant under 14. See this note to "First-Degree Forcible Rape," above.

Charging issues. See this note to "First-Degree Forcible Rape," above.

Greater and lesser-included offenses. See this note to "First-Degree Forcible Rape," above.

Multiple convictions and punishments. See this note to "First-Degree Forcible Rape" and "First-Degree Forcible Sexual Offense," both above.

Relation to other offenses. See this note to "First-Degree Forcible Sexual Offense," above.

Sex offender registration. This offense is a sexually violent offense triggering registration requirements under the sex offender registration statutes. G.S. 14-208.6(5).

Doctrine of recent possession. See this note to "First-Degree Forcible Rape," above.

Rape shield rule. See this note to "First-Degree Forcible Rape," above.

Related Offenses Not in This Chapter

See the offenses listed under "First-Degree Forcible Rape" and "First-Degree Statutory Sexual Offense," both above.

Statutory Sexual Offense by an Adult

Statute

§14-27.4A. Sexual offense with a child; adult offender.

(a) A person is guilty of sexual offense with a child if the person is at least 18 years of age and engages in a sexual act with a victim who is a child under the age of 13 years.

(b) A person convicted of violating this section is guilty of a Class B1 felony and shall be sentenced pursuant to Article 81B of Chapter 15A of the General Statutes, except that in no case shall the person receive an active punishment of less than 300 months, and except as provided in subsection (c) of this section. Following the termination of active punishment, the person shall be enrolled in satellite-based monitoring for life pursuant to Part 5 of Article 27A of Chapter 14 of the General Statutes.

(c) Notwithstanding the provisions of Article 81B of Chapter 15A of the General Statutes, the court may sentence the defendant to active punishment for a term of months greater than that authorized pursuant to G.S. 15A-1340.17, up to and including life imprisonment without parole, if the court finds that the nature of the offense and the harm inflicted are of such brutality, duration, severity, degree, or scope beyond that normally committed in such crimes, or considered in basic aggravation of these crimes, so as to require a sentence to active punishment in excess of that authorized pursuant to G.S. 15A-1340.17. If the court sentences the defendant pursuant to this subsection, it shall make findings of fact supporting its decision, to include matters it considered as egregious aggravation. Egregious aggravation can include further consideration of existing aggravating factors where the conduct of the defendant falls outside the heartland of cases even the aggravating factors were designed to cover. Egregious aggravation may also be considered based on the extraordinarily young age of the victim, or the depraved torture or mutilation of the victim, or extraordinary physical pain inflicted on the victim.

(d) The offense under G.S. 14-27.4(a)(1) is a lesser included offense of the offense in this section.

Elements

A person guilty of this offense

(1) engages in a sexual act other than vaginal intercourse
(2) with a child under the age of 13 years *and*
(3) the defendant is at least 18 years old.

Punishment

Class B1 felony, except that the offense is subject to a mandatory minimum of 300 months of active time. G.S. 14-27.4A(b). G.S. 14-27.4A(c) provides that a defendant may be sentenced to an active term above that normally provided for a Class B1 felony if the judge finds egregious aggravation. However, this procedure appears to run afoul of the United States Supreme Court decision in *Blakely v. Washington,* 542 U.S. 296 (2004) (holding that any factor, other than a prior conviction, that increases punishment beyond the prescribed statutory maximum must be submitted to the jury and proved beyond a reasonable doubt). See the additional discussion in "Punishment" under "First-Degree Forcible Rape," above.

Notes

Generally. This offense is the same as "Statutory Rape by an Adult," above, except for the sexual conduct involved. For statutory rape by an adult, vaginal intercourse is required. For this offense, a sexual act other than vaginal intercourse is required.

Element (1). See the note on Element (1) to "First-Degree Forcible Sexual Offense," above.

Element (2). See the note on Element (2) to "First-Degree Statutory Rape" and "Statutory Rape of a Person Who Is 13, 14, or 15 Years Old by a Defendant Who Is at Least Six Years Older Than the Victim," both above.

Element (3). See the note on Element (4) to "First-Degree Statutory Rape," above.

Consent. See this note to "First-Degree Statutory Sexual Offense," above.

Force. See this note to "First-Degree Statutory Sexual Offense," above.

Victim's virginity. See this note to "First-Degree Statutory Rape," above.

Defendant under 14. See this note to "First-Degree Forcible Rape," above.

Charging issues. See this note to "First-Degree Forcible Rape," above.

Greater and lesser-included offenses. See this note to "First-Degree Forcible Rape," above.

Multiple convictions and punishments. See this note to "First-Degree Forcible Rape" and "First-Degree Forcible Sexual Offense," both above.

Relation to other offenses. See this note to "First-Degree Forcible Sexual Offense," above.

Sex offender registration. This crime is a sexually violent offense requiring registration as a sex offender. G.S. 14-208.6(5).

Lifetime satellite-based monitoring required. Following the termination of active punishment, a person convicted of this offense must submit to satellite-based monitoring for life under the sex offender monitoring statutes. G.S. 14-27.4A(b).

Doctrine of recent possession. See this note to "First-Degree Forcible Rape," above.

Rape shield rule. See this note to "First-Degree Forcible Rape," above.

Related Offenses Not in This Chapter

See the offenses listed under "First-Degree Forcible Rape" and "First-Degree Statutory Rape," both above.

Statutory Sexual Offense against a Person Who Is 13, 14, or 15 Years Old by a Defendant Who Is at Least Six Years Older Than the Victim

Statute

See G.S. 14-27.7A(a), reproduced under "Statutory Rape of a Person Who Is 13, 14, or 15 Years Old by a Defendant Who Is at Least Six Years Older Than the Victim," above.

Elements

A person guilty of this offense

(1) engages in a sexual act other than vaginal intercourse
(2) with a child who is 13, 14, or 15 years old *and*
(3) the defendant is at least six years older than the child.

Punishment

Class B1 felony. G.S. 14-27.7A(a). See the additional discussion in "Punishment" under "First-Degree Forcible Rape," above.

Notes

Generally. Statutory sexual offense against a person who is 13, 14, or 15 years old is the same as "Statutory Rape of a Person Who Is 13, 14, or 15 Years Old," above, except for the sexual conduct involved. For statutory rape, vaginal intercourse is required. For statutory sexual offense, a sexual act other than vaginal intercourse is required.

Element (1). See this note to "First-Degree Forcible Sexual Offense," above.

Element (2). See the note on Element (2) to "First-Degree Statutory Rape" and "Statutory Rape of a Person Who Is 13, 14, or 15 Years Old by a Defendant Who Is at Least Six Years Older Than the Victim," both above. If the victim is not one of the ages covered here or under "First-Degree Statutory Sexual Offense," the defendant might still be guilty of "Indecent Liberties with a Child," other offenses discussed in this chapter, or "Crime against Nature," discussed in Chapter 11 (Crime against Nature, Indecent Exposure, and Related Offenses).

Element (3). See the note on Element (3) to "First-Degree Statutory Rape" and "Statutory Rape of a Person Who Is 13, 14, or 15 Years Old by a Defendant Who Is at Least Six Years Older Than the Victim," both above.

Statute gender-neutral. See this note to "First-Degree Forcible Sexual Offense," above.

Exceptions. See this note to "Statutory Rape of a Person Who Is 13, 14, or 15 Years Old by a Defendant Who Is at Least Six Years Older Than the Victim," above.

Consent. See this note to "Statutory Rape of a Person Who Is 13, 14, or 15 Years Old by a Defendant Who Is at Least Six Years Older Than the Victim," above.

Force. See this note to "Statutory Rape of a Person Who Is 13, 14, or 15 Years Old by a Defendant Who Is at Least Six Years Older Than the Victim," above.

Attempt. The North Carolina Court of Appeals has rejected the argument that attempted statutory sex offense is a logical impossibility and has upheld the offense as a crime. State v. Sines, 158 N.C. App. 79 (2003). See "Attempt" in Chapter 5 (General Crimes) for a discussion of what constitutes an attempt and how it should be punished. If penetration is a requirement of a particular sexual offense, and if the defendant did not achieve penetration, the crime would be attempted sexual offense.

Victim's virginity. See this note to "First-Degree Forcible Rape," above.

Charging issues. See this note to "First-Degree Forcible Rape," above.

Greater and lesser-included offenses. See this note to "First-Degree Forcible Rape," above.

Multiple convictions and punishments. See this note to "First-Degree Forcible Rape" and "First-Degree Forcible Sexual Offense," both above.

Relation to other offenses. See this note to "First-Degree Forcible Sexual Offense," above.

Sex offender registration. This crime is a sexually violent offense requiring registration as a sex offender. G.S. 14-208.6(5).

Doctrine of recent possession. See this note to "First-Degree Forcible Rape," above.

Rape shield rule. See this note to "First-Degree Forcible Rape," above.

Related Offenses Not in This Chapter

See the offenses listed under "First-Degree Forcible Rape" and "First-Degree Statutory Rape," both above.

Statutory Sexual Offense against a Person Who Is 13, 14, or 15 Years Old by a Defendant Who Is More Than Four but Less Than Six Years Older Than the Victim

Statute

See G.S. 14-27.7A(b), reproduced under "Statutory Rape of a Person Who Is 13, 14, or 15 Years Old by a Defendant Who Is at Least Six Years Older Than the Victim," above.

Elements

A person guilty of this offense

(1) engages in a sexual act other than vaginal intercourse
(2) with a child who is 13, 14, or 15 years old *and*
(3) the defendant is more than four but less than six years older than the child.

Punishment

Class C felony. G.S. 14-27.7A(b). See the additional discussion in "Punishment" under "First-Degree Forcible Rape," above.

Notes

Generally. This offense is the same as "Statutory Rape of a Person Who Is 13, 14, or 15 Years Old by a Defendant Who Is More than Four but Less Than Six Years Older Than the Victim," except for the conduct involved. For this offense, a sexual act other than vaginal intercourse is required. For the rape version, vaginal intercourse is required. This offense is the same as "Statutory Sexual Offense against a Person Who Is 13, 14, or 15 Years Old by a Defendant Who Is at Least Six Years Older Than the Victim," except for the element regarding the defendant's age. Thus, the relevant notes to those offenses apply here as well.

Sex offender registration. This offense does not require sex offender registration.

Related Offenses Not in This Chapter

See the offenses listed under "First-Degee Forcible Rape" and "First-Degree Statutory Rape," both above.

Sexual Activity by a Substitute Parent

Statute

§14-27.7 Intercourse and sexual offenses with certain victims; consent no defense.

(a) If a defendant who has assumed the position of a parent in the home of a minor victim engages in vaginal intercourse or a sexual act with a victim who is a minor residing in the home, or if a person having custody of a victim of any age or a person who is an agent or employee of any person, or institution, whether such institution is private, charitable, or governmental, having custody of a victim of any age engages in vaginal intercourse or a sexual act with such victim, the defendant is guilty of a Class E felony. Consent is not a defense to a charge under this section.

(b) If a defendant, who is a teacher, school administrator, student teacher, school safety officer, or coach, at any age, or who is other school personnel, and who is at least four years older than the victim engages in vaginal intercourse or a sexual act with a victim who is a student, at any time during or after the time the defendant and victim were present together in the same school, but before the victim ceases to be a student, the defendant is guilty of a Class G felony, except when the defendant is lawfully married to the student. The term "same school" means a school at which the student is enrolled and the defendant is employed, assigned, or volunteers. A defendant who is school personnel, other than a teacher, school administrator, student teacher, school safety officer, or coach, and is less than four years older than the victim and engages in vaginal intercourse or a sexual act with a victim who is a student, is guilty of a Class A1 misdemeanor. This subsection shall apply unless the conduct is covered under some other provision of law providing for greater punishment. Consent is not a defense to a charge under this section. For purposes of this subsection, the terms "school", "school personnel", and "student" shall have the same meaning as in G.S. 14-202.4(d). For purposes of this subsection, the term "school safety officer" shall include a school resource officer or any other person who is regularly present in a school for the purpose of promoting and maintaining safe and orderly schools.

Elements

A person guilty of this offense

(1) assumes the position of a parent in the home of a person less than 18 years old *and*
(2) has vaginal intercourse or engages in a sexual act
(3) with a person less than 18 years old residing in the home.

Punishment

Class E felony. G.S. 14-27.7(a). See the additional discussion in "Punishment" under "First-Degree Forcible Rape," above.

Notes

Element (1). Apparently an actual parent could not be convicted under this statute, since a parent is not someone who "has assumed the position of a parent." However, the actual parent might be guilty of incest, discussed in Chapter 11 (Crime against Nature, Incest, Indecent Exposure, and Related Offenses), and one of the statutory rape or sexual offense crimes discussed in this chapter, depending on the victim's age. The kinds of persons covered by this phrase include stepparents, State v. Bailey, 163 N.C. App. 84 (2004), and possibly live-in boyfriends and girlfriends, guardians, and others who function in a parental role. *Id.* Such a parental role generally will include evidence of emotional trust, disciplinary authority, and supervisory responsibility. *Id.* The statute does not require that the sexual activity take place in the home.

There was insufficient evidence to prove that the defendant assumed the position of a parent in the home of the alleged minor victim when the mother allowed the defendant to sleep in her apartment in return for babysitting her children while she worked. *Id.* In contrast, there was sufficient evidence to prove that the defendant assumed the position of a parent of the minor victim when the victim lived with the defendant and the defendant represented himself as the victim's temporary custodian. State v. Oakley, 167 N.C. App. 318 (2004).

Element (2). See the note on Element (1) to "First-Degree Forcible Rape," above, discussing "vaginal intercourse." See the note on Element (1) to "First-Degree Forcible Sexual Offense," above, defining "sexual act."

Element (3). Presumably the same rule applies here as in statutory rape—that the defendant is not excused by being misled or mistaken as to the victim's age. State v. Wade, 224 N.C. 760 (1944).

Statute gender-neutral. The wording of the statute means that both the defendant and the victim may be male or female, depending on the kind of sexual activity on which the charge is based.

Consent. The statute specifies that consent is not a defense to this charge. G.S. 14-27.7(a).

Force. The statute does not require force.

Victim's virginity. Virginity is not an element of this offense.

Charging issues. See this note to "First-Degree Forcible Rape," above.

Multiple convictions and punishments. See this note to "First-Degree Forcible Rape" and "First-Degree Forcible Sexual Offense," both above.

Relation to other offenses. Cunnilingus, fellatio, analingus, and anal intercourse—all of which are sexual acts for purposes of this offense—are also forms of "Crime against Nature," discussed in Chapter 11 (Crime against Nature, Incest, Indecent Exposure, and Related Offenses). Whether the victim consents is not an element of this offense or of crime against nature. Thus, for these specified sexual acts, the prosecutor could proceed under either this statute (Class E felony) or crime against nature (Class I felony), or both. Unlike a charge of crime against nature, however, cunnilingus or analingus would not require proof of penetration to prove sexual activity by a substitute parent. See this note to "First-Degree Forcible Sexual Offense," above.

Sex offender registration. This offense is a sexually violent offense triggering registration requirements under the sex offender registration statutes. G.S. 14-208.6(5).

Related Offenses Not in This Chapter

See the offenses listed under "First-Degree Forcible Rape" and "First-Degree Statutory Rape," both above.

Sexual Activity by a Custodian

Statute

See G.S. 14-27.7(a), reproduced under "Sexual Activity by a Substitute Parent," above.

Elements

A person guilty of this offense

(1) has custody of the victim or is an agent or employee of a person or institution having custody of the victim *and*
(2) has vaginal intercourse or engages in a sexual act
(3) with the victim.

Punishment

Class E felony. G.S. 14-27.7(a). See the additional discussion in "Punishment" under "First-Degree Forcible Rape," above.

Notes

Element (1). The defendant can be a police officer, jailer, prison guard, employee of a hospital or nursing home, or someone else in a similar position. The agency that employs the defendant can be either public or private, charitable or not, as long as it has custody of the victim. G.S. 14-27.7(a). If the defendant is an employee of such an institution, it is not necessary that he or she have anything in particular to do with maintaining custody of the victim. *Id.* The cases have involved the following types of custodians:

- a nurse, State v. Raines, 319 N.C. 258 (1987) (a nurse was properly convicted of this offense when he had sexual intercourse with a patient who was voluntarily in a hospital);
- an employee of a youth home that provided food, shelter, and adult supervision to abused and neglected juveniles, State v. Crockett, 138 N.C. App. 109 (2000);
- a person employed by a corporation at its boys' group home location, State v. Coleman, 200 N.C. App. 696 (2009) (the defendant was a custodian of the victim, who lived at the corporation's girls' group home location);
- a recreational assistant with the Job Corps program, State v. Jones, 143 N.C. App. 514 (2001) (the assistant had consensual sexual relations with an unemancipated minor enrolled in the program); and
- a mental health clinician employed by an independent contractor who provided services to prisoners in a local jail, State v. Wilson, 362 N.C. 162, 163–66 (2008) (the clinician was an agent of the sheriff).

The State need not prove that the defendant knew that he or she was the victim's custodian. *Coleman*, 200 N.C. App. at 701.

Element (2). See the note on Element (1) to "First-Degree Forcible Rape," above, discussing "vaginal intercourse." See the note on Element (1) to "First-Degree Forcible Sexual Offense," above, defining "sexual act."

Element (3). The victim's age is irrelevant. Also, the statute does not require that sexual activity take place in the institution where the victim is kept in custody. *See Coleman*, 200 N.C. App. 696 (the defendant worked in a boys' home location and the victim, from a girls' home location, snuck into the boys' home to engage in the sexual activity).

Statute gender-neutral. See this note to "Sexual Activity by a Substitute Parent," above.

Consent. The statute specifies that consent is not a defense to this charge. G.S. 14-27.7(a); *see also Wilson*, 362 N.C. at 166.

Force. No force is required for this offense.

Victim's virginity. Virginity is not an element of this offense.

Charging issues. See this note to "First-Degree Forcible Rape," above.

Relation to other offenses. See this note to "Sexual Activity by a Substitute Parent," above.

Sex offender registration. This offense is a sexually violent offense triggering registration requirements under the sex offender registration statutes. G.S. 14-208.6(5).

Related Offenses Not in This Chapter

See the offenses listed under "First-Degree Forcible Rape" and "First-Degree Statutory Rape," both above.

See patient abuse (various offenses) in Chapter 9 (Abuse and Neglect).

Sexual Activity with a Student

Sexual Activity with a Student by a Teacher, School Administrator, Student Teacher, Coach, or School Safety Officer

Statute

See G.S. 14-27.7(b), reproduced under "Sexual Activity by a Substitute Parent," above.

Elements

A person guilty of this offense

(1) is a teacher, school administrator, student teacher, coach, or school safety officer *and*
(2) engages in vaginal intercourse or a sexual act
(3) with a student
(4) at any time during or after the period when the student and person were present together in the same school but before the victim stops being a student.

Punishment

Class G felony. G.S. 14-27.7(b).

Notes

Element (1). The term "school safety officer" includes a school resource officer or any other person who is regularly present in a school for the purpose of promoting and maintaining safe and orderly schools. G.S. 14-27.7(b).

Element (2). The sexual conduct need not occur at a school.

See the note on Element (1) to "First-Degree Forcible Rape," above, discussing "vaginal intercourse." See the note on Element (1) to "First-Degree Forcible Sexual Offense," above, defining "sexual act."

Element (3). "Student" is defined as a person enrolled in kindergarten or grades 1 through 12 in any school. G.S. 14-27.7(b); G.S. 14-202.4(d)(4). "School" is defined as any public school, charter school, or nonpublic school under Parts 1 and 2, G.S. 115C-547 through 562, of Article 39 of Chapter 115C of the General Statutes. G.S. 14-27.7(b); G.S. 14-202.4(d)(2).

Element (4). The term "same school" means a school at which the student is enrolled and the defendant is employed, assigned, or volunteers. G.S. 14-27.7(b). The conduct can occur while the victim and the perpetrator are at the same school. It also can occur after the student leaves that school, provided that it occurs before the victim ceases to be a student. *Id.* For example, this offense is committed if a student and teacher were present together at a middle school and they engage in a sex act together when the student is later in high school and the teacher is still at the middle school.

Statute gender-neutral. See this note to "Sexual Activity by a Substitute Parent," above.

Exceptions. This offense does not occur when the defendant is lawfully married to the student. G.S. 14-27.7(b).

Consent. Consent is not a defense to this crime. *Id.*

Force. Force is not required for this offense.

Victim's virginity. Virginity is not an element of this offense.

Charging issues. See this note to "First-Degree Forcible Rape," above.

Multiple convictions and punishments. See this note to "First-Degree Forcible Rape" and "First-Degree Forcible Sexual Offense," both above. G.S. 14-27.7(b) states that this subsection "shall apply unless the conduct is covered under some other provision of law providing for greater punishment." This provision appears to bar a conviction and punishment for this offense and a more serious one, such as second-degree rape, if the offenses arise from the same conduct. However, it does not appear to bar a trial for both charges, just a conviction and punishment for both. For a discussion of similar language in the assault context, see this note to "Assault Inflicting Serious Injury" in Chapter 7 (Assaults).

Relation to other offenses. See this note to "Sexual Activity by a Substitute Parent," above.

Sex offender registration. This offense is a sexually violent offense triggering registration requirements under the sex offender registration statutes. G.S. 14-208.6(5).

Related Offenses Not in This Chapter

See the offenses listed under "First-Degree Forcible Rape" and "First-Degree Statutory Rape," both above.

Felony Sexual Activity with a Student by School Personnel Other Than a Teacher, School Administrator, Student Teacher, Coach, or School Safety Officer

Statute

See G.S. 14-27.7(b), reproduced under "Sexual Activity by a Substitute Parent," above.

Elements

A person guilty of this offense

(1) is included in the definition of "school personnel" and is not a teacher, school administrator, student teacher, coach, or school safety officer *and*
(2) engages in vaginal intercourse or a sexual act
(3) with a student
(4) at any time during or after the period when the student and the person were present together in the same school but before the victim stops being a student *and*
(5) the person is at least four years older than the student.

Punishment

Class G felony. G.S. 14-27.7(b).

Notes

Generally. This offense is the same as "Sexual Activity with a Student by a Teacher, School Administrator, Student Teacher, Coach, or School Safety Officer," above, except that this offense (1) applies only to other school personnel; and (2) includes an age requirement for the defendant. Thus, the relevant notes to "Sexual Activity with a Student by a Teacher, School Administrator, Student Teacher, Coach, or School Safety Officer" apply here as well.

Element (1). "School personnel" means any person included in the definition contained in G.S. 115C-332(a)(2) and any person who volunteers at a school or a school-sponsored activity. G.S. 14-27.7(b); G.S. 14-202.4(d)(3). Under G.S. 115C-332(a)(2), "school personnel" means (1) any employee of a local school board, whether full-time or part-time, or (2) any independent contractor or employee of an independent contractor of a local school board—if the independent contractor carries out duties customarily performed by school personnel, whether paid with federal, state, local, or other funds—who has significant access to students. School personnel includes bus drivers, clerical staff, and custodians.

Element (5). The age difference must be measured from the defendant's birthday to the victim's birthday. See the note on Element (3) to "First-Degree Statutory Rape" and "Statutory Rape of a Person Who Is 13, 14, or 15 Years Old by a Defendant Who Is at Least Six Years Older Than the Victim," both above.

Sex offender registration. This offense is a sexually violent offense triggering registration requirements under the sex offender registration statutes. G.S. 14-208.6(5).

Related Offenses Not in This Chapter

See the offenses listed under "First-Degree Forcible Rape" and "First-Degree Statutory Rape," both above.

Misdemeanor Sexual Activity with a Student by School Personnel Other Than a Teacher, School Administrator, Student Teacher, Coach, or School Safety Officer

Statute

See G.S. 14-27.7(b), reproduced under "Sexual Activity by a Substitute Parent," above.

Elements

A person guilty of this offense

(1) is included in the definition of "school personnel" and is not a teacher, school administrator, student teacher, coach, or school safety officer *and*
(2) engages in vaginal intercourse or a sexual act

(3) with a student
(4) at any time during or after the period when the student and the person were present together in the same school but before the victim stops being a student *and*
(5) the person is less than four years older than the student.

Punishment

Class A1 misdemeanor. G.S. 14-27.7(b).

Notes

Generally. This offense is the same as "Felony Sexual Activity with a Student by School Personnel Other Than a Teacher, School Administrator, Student Teacher, Coach, or School Safety Officer" except for the age of the defendant. Thus, the relevant notes to that offense apply here as well.

Sex offender registration. This offense is a sexually violent offense triggering registration requirements under the sex offender registration statutes. G.S. 14-208.6(5).

Related Offenses Not in This Chapter

See the offenses listed under "First-Degree Forcible Rape" and "First-Degree Statutory Rape," both above.

Indecent Liberties

Indecent Liberties with a Child

Statute

§14-202.1. Taking indecent liberties with children.

(a) A person is guilty of taking indecent liberties with children if, being 16 years of age or more and at least five years older than the child in question, he either:

(1) Willfully takes or attempts to take any immoral, improper, or indecent liberties with any child of either sex under the age of 16 years for the purpose of arousing or gratifying sexual desire; or
(2) Willfully commits or attempts to commit any lewd or lascivious act upon or with the body or any part or member of the body of any child of either sex under the age of 16 years.

(b) Taking indecent liberties with children is punishable as a Class F felony.

Elements

A person guilty of this offense

(1) is at least 16 years old *and*
(2) (a) (i) for the purpose of arousing or gratifying sexual desire
(ii) willfully takes or attempts to take an indecent liberty with *or*
(b) willfully commits or attempts to commit a lewd or lascivious act upon the body of
(3) a child under the age of 16 years *and*
(4) the child is five or more years younger than the defendant.

Punishment

Class F felony. G.S. 14-202.1(b).

Notes

Element (1). See the note on Element (4) to "First-Degree Statutory Rape," above.

General discussion of Elements (2)(a) and (2)(b). The terms "immoral, improper and indecent liberties" and "lewd or lascivious act" both deal with improper sexual conduct with a child. State v. Elam, 302 N.C. 157, 162 (1981). "Indecent liberties" are understood to mean acts that society would regard as indecent or improper. State v. McClary, 198 N.C. App. 169, 173 (2009); State v. Hammett, 182 N.C. App. 316, 322 (2007); State v. Every, 157 N.C. App. 200, 205 (2003); N.C. Pattern Jury Instructions—Crim. 226.85. "Lewd" has been defined to mean "inciting to sensual desire or imagination" while "lascivious" means "tending to arouse sexual desire." *Hammett*, 182 N.C. App. at 322 (quotations omitted). The statute is not limited to acts that reflect an unnatural sexual nature. State v. Banks, 322 N.C. 753, 765–67 (1988) (rejecting the defendant's argument that kissing a child is not covered).

An indecent liberty occurred, for example, when the defendant (1) repeatedly engaged the child in sexually graphic and explicit conversations by telephone, told the child that he was masturbating and invited the child to do the same, and the defendant's conversations were punctuated by heavy breathing and groaning, *Every*, 157 N.C. App. at 206; and (2) gave a child a sexually explicit letter designed to solicit sexual intercourse and oral sex for money, *McClary*, 198 N.C. App. at 174.

A "lewd or lascivious act" includes, for example, sexual intercourse with a child, State v. Stell, 39 N.C. App. 75 (1978), pulling down a child's pants and saying, "Let me play with you," State v. Byrd, 67 N.C. App. 168 (1984) (attempt to commit a lewd and lascivious act); and telling the child to "kiss me like you love me" and then "french kissing" the child, State v. Hammett, 182 N.C. App. 316, 322–23 (2007).

A defendant's acts of inserting his tongue in the mouths of two children while kissing them and inserting his tongue in their eyes and noses after getting in bed with them constituted both an indecent liberty and a lewd and lascivious act. State v. Banks, 322 N.C. 753, 765–67 (1988).

For examples of cases in which the evidence was insufficient to support a conviction, see *State v. Brown*, 162 N.C. App. 333 (2004) (conversations between the defendant and the child were neither sexually graphic nor explicit nor accompanied by other actions tending to show that the defendant's purpose was sexually motivated); *State v. Shue*, 163 N.C. App. 58 (2004) (the defendant attempted to grab a child's arm in a bathroom stall); and *State v. Mueller*, 184 N.C. App. 553 (2007) (the victim provided no testimony in support of this charge; the only evidence supporting the charge was a doctor's testimony that the victim "described that [the defendant] wanted her to perform fellatio, or put his penis in her mouth, but that she didn't want to do that"; the doctor's testimony raised only a suspicion or conjecture).

An indecent liberty or lewd or lascivious act may occur even if the defendant does not touch the child. State v. Etheridge, 319 N.C. 34 (1987); State v. McClary, 198 N.C. App. 169, 173 (2009); State v. Every, 157 N.C. App. 200, 206 (2003). Examples of fact patterns where convictions were upheld in these circumstances include when the defendant:

- masturbated in a child's presence, State v. Turman, 52 N.C. App. 376 (1981); State v. Nesbitt, 133 N.C. App. 420 (1999); State v. Hammett, 182 N.C. App. 316, 323 (2007) (masturbation while watching a pornographic movie with the victim);
- photographed a nude child in a clearly sexually suggestive position, State v. Kistle, 59 N.C. App. 724 (1982);
- secretly videotaped a female teenager trying on clothes, State v. McClees, 108 N.C. App. 648 (1993);
- wrote and delivered to a child a letter containing sexually graphic language designed to solicit sexual acts for money, *McClary*, 198 N.C. App. at 174;
- engaged in sex acts with others in the presence of a child, State v. Ainsworth, 109 N.C. App. 136 (1993); and
- watched and facilitated the child's sexual activity with another person, State v. Coleman, 200 N.C. App. 696, 705–06 (2009).

In many cases, the defendant is in the actual presence of the victim. However, actual presence is not required when there is constructive presence, as when the defendant sets up a camera to secretly film the victim or uses a telephone to call the victim and engage in sexually explicit conversations. State v. Every, 157 N.C. App. 200 (2003). When the use of electronic technology enables the defendant to engage in conduct that would constitute an indecent liberty if done in the victim's actual presence, without being actually present, the defendant may be found to be constructively present. *Id.*

Finally, both prongs of this offense require that the defendant act willfully. For a general discussion of this term, see "Willfully" in Chapter 1 (States of Mind); *see also* State v. Breathette, ___ N.C. App. ___, 690 S.E.2d 1, 6 (2010) (the trial court did not err by instructing the jury that the term "willfully" meant that the act was done purposefully and without justification or excuse; this instruction "largely mirrors" the North Carolina Supreme Court's definition of "willfully," which is "the wrongful doing of an act without justification or excuse, or the commission of an act purposely and deliberately in violation of law").

Element (2)(a)(i). Unlike Element (2)(b), Element (2)(a) requires proof that the indecent liberty was taken or attempted for the purpose of arousing or gratifying sexual desire. In many cases, the underlying conduct itself indicates the required purpose because the defendant's motivation is obvious, as for example, when the defendant exposed himself and placed his hand on his penis within several feet of a child. State v. Brown, 162 N.C. App. 333 (2004).

There was sufficient evidence of the defendant's purpose of arousing or gratifying his sexual desire when (1) the defendant touched the victim inappropriately in her private area on the pretext of tickling her, State v. Verrier, 173 N.C. App. 123 (2005); (2) the defendant lifted the child's shirt and kissed her breasts, kissed her "private" area, and penetrated her vagina with his fingers; following these acts, the defendant used a washcloth to "wipe[] something off the bed," State v. Fuller, 166 N.C. App. 548 (2004); (3) the defendant wrote and delivered to a child a letter containing sexually graphic language designed to solicit sexual acts for money, State v. McClary, 198 N.C. App. 169, 174 (2009); (4) the victim had bite marks all over her body and trauma to her vagina and rectum and the defendant admitted that he had bitten another woman while "making love" to her, State v. Ridgeway, 185 N.C. App. 423, 435 (2007); (5) in a prosecution under G.S. 14-202.2 for indecent liberties between children, the 13-year-old juvenile told the victim (who was ten years younger) that the juvenile's privates "taste like candy" and had the victim lick his penis; approximately eleven months prior, the juvenile admitted to having performed fellatio on a four-year-old male relative; the juvenile's age and maturity, the age disparity between him and the victim, coupled with the inducement he employed to convince the victim to perform the act and the suggestion of his prior sexual activity before this event, was sufficient evidence of maturity and intent to show the required element of "for the purpose of arousing or gratifying sexual desire," *In re* A.W., ___ N.C. App. ___, 706 S.E.2d 305 (2011); and (6) while at a store, the defendant crouched down to look at the victim's legs, "fell into" the victim, wrapping his hands around her, and kneeled down, six to eight inches away from her legs; other evidence showed that the defendant had asked another person if he could hug her legs and that he admitted to being obsessed with women's legs, State v. Sims, ___ N.C. App. ___, ___ S.E.2d ___ (Oct. 4, 2011).

In contrast, there was insufficient evidence that the defendant committed an act for the purpose of sexual desire when his hand brushed against the victim's breast for only a couple of seconds and he apologized. State v. Stanford, 169 N.C. App. 214 (2005).

Element (4). The age difference must be measured from the defendant's birthday to the victim's birthday. See the note on Element (3) to "First-Degree Statutory Rape" and "Statutory Rape of a Person Who Is 13, 14, or 15 Years Old by a Defendant Who Is at Least Six Years Older Than the Victim," both above.

Consent. Consent by a victim is no defense to this crime.

Force. The State need not prove force by the defendant.

Constitutionality. This statute is not unconstitutionally vague, its age classification is not a denial of equal protection, and the statute does not unconstitutionally restrict protected sexual activity. State v. Elam, 302 N.C. 157 (1981).

Attempts. Attempts are punished at the same level as the completed crime. G.S. 14-202.1(a)(1)–(2). This is an exception to the general rule that an attempt to commit a crime is punished one level below the completed offense. See "Attempt" in Chapter 5 (General Crimes).

Charging issues. See this note under "First-Degree Forcible Rape," above. *See also* State v. Carter, ___ N.C. App. ___, 707 S.E.2d 700, 709 (2011) (the trial judge's jury instructions were supported by the indictment; the indictment tracked the statute and did not allege an evidentiary basis for the charge; the jury instruction, which identified the defendant's conduct as placing his penis between the child's feet, was a clarification of the evidence for the jury).

Defenses. Mistake of age is not a defense to this crime. State v. Breathette, ___ N.C. App. ___, 690 S.E.2d 1, 3–6 (2010).

Jury instructions. When instructing on indecent liberties, the trial judge is not required to specifically identify the acts that constitute the charge. State v. Smith, 362 N.C. 583, 596–97 (2008).

Greater and lesser-included offenses. See this note to "First-Degree Forcible Rape," above.

Multiple convictions and punishments. Two convictions for the same act are not permitted under both subdivisions (a)(1) and (a)(2) of the indecent liberties statute. State v. Jones, 172 N.C. App. 308, 314–16 (2005).

Whether the defendant's separate conduct during a continuous transaction supports multiple convictions seems to depend on whether the defendant's separate acts involve the same or a different type of sexual contact. For example, in *State v. Laney,* 178 N.C. App. 337, 339–41 (2006), the court held that a number of acts involving the same sexual conduct (touching) committed during a single and continuous transaction constitute only one offense of indecent liberties. However, in *State v. James,* 182 N.C. App. 698, 703–05 (2007), the court held that the defendant's conduct of engaging in three distinct sexual acts on the victim in one transaction—fondling her breasts, performing oral sex on her, and having sexual intercourse with her—supported three separate indecent liberties convictions. *James* distinguished *Laney* on grounds that in *Laney* the defendant's actions all involved the same sexual contact—touching—whereas the case before it involved three distinct sexual acts. *Id.* at 704–05; *see also* State v. Coleman, 200 N.C. App. 696, 705–06 (2009) (the defendant's two acts—touching the child's breasts and watching and facilitating her sexual encounter with another person—supported two convictions).

No double jeopardy violation occurred when the defendant was convicted and punished for indecent liberties and using a minor in obscenity based on the same photograph. State v. Martin, 195 N.C. App. 43, 54–55 (2009).

Sex offender registration. This offense is a sexually violent offense triggering registration requirements under the sex offender registration statutes. G.S. 14-208.6(5).

Related Offenses Not in This Chapter

See the offenses listed under "First-Degree Forcible Rape" and "First-Degree Statutory Rape," both above.

Indecent Liberties between Children

Statute

§14-202.2. Indecent liberties between children.

(a) A person who is under the age of 16 years is guilty of taking indecent liberties with children if the person either:

(1) Willfully takes or attempts to take any immoral, improper, or indecent liberties with any child of either sex who is at least three years younger than the defendant for the purpose of arousing or gratifying sexual desire; or

(2) Willfully commits or attempts to commit any lewd or lascivious act upon or with the body or any part or member of the body of any child of either sex who is at least three years younger than the defendant for the purpose of arousing or gratifying sexual desire.

(b) A violation of this section is punishable as a Class 1 misdemeanor.

Elements

A person guilty of this offense

(1) is less than 16 years old *and*
(2) for the purpose of arousing or gratifying sexual desire
(3) (a) willfully takes or attempts to take any immoral, improper, or indecent liberties with *or*
(b) willfully commits or attempts to commit any lewd or lascivious act upon or with the body or any part or member of the body of
(4) a child
(5) who is at least three years younger than the defendant.

Punishment

Class 1 misdemeanor. G.S. 14-202.2(b).

Notes

Generally. This offense is similar to "Indecent Liberties with a Child," above, except for the victim's age and the age differential between the defendant and the victim. Thus, the relevant notes to "Indecent Liberties with a Child" apply to this offense as well. This offense differs from "Indecent Liberties With a Child" in another respect. Unlike Element (2)(b) of "Indecent Liberties with a Child," Element (3)(b) of this offense requires proof of a purpose of arousing or gratifying sexual desire. *See In re* T.S., 133 N.C. App. 272 (1999) (evidence was insufficient).

Element (1). A juvenile less than 16 years of age may not be prosecuted as an adult for this misdemeanor offense. Instead, a juvenile petition alleging delinquency may be issued.

Element (2). In a prosecution for this offense, the purpose of arousing or gratifying sexual desire may not be inferred from the act alone. *In re* T.C.S., 148 N.C. App. 297 (2002). In child cases, there must be a showing of the child's sexual intent in committing the act; the State must show some evidence of the child's maturity, intent, experience, or other factor indicating his or her purpose before imputing sexual ambitions to the child. *Id.*

There was sufficient evidence of this element when (1) the 5-year-old victim took off her clothes at the 12-year-old juvenile's insistence; the juvenile appeared to have his hands on his private parts while the victim removed her clothes; and the juvenile "smarted off" to a witness when she asked what the children had been doing, saying that it was "none of your business," *id.* at 302–03; and (2) the 13-year-old juvenile told the victim (who was ten years younger) that the juvenile's privates "taste like candy" and had the victim lick his penis; approximately eleven months prior, the juvenile admitted to having performed fellatio on a four-year-old male relative; the juvenile's age and maturity, the age disparity between him and the victim, coupled with the inducement he employed to convince the victim to perform the act and the suggestion of his prior sexual activity before this event, was sufficient evidence of maturity and intent to show the required element of "for the purpose of arousing or gratifying sexual desire," *In re* A.W., ___ N.C. App. ___, 706 S.E.2d 305, 308–09 (2011).

Sex offender registration. This offense does not require sex offender registration.

Related Offenses Not in This Chapter

See the offenses listed under "First-Degree Forcible Rape" and "First-Degree Statutory Rape," both above.

Felony Taking Indecent Liberties with a Student by a Teacher, School Administrator, Student Teacher, School Safety Officer, or Coach

Statute

§14-202.4. Taking indecent liberties with a student.

(a) If a defendant, who is a teacher, school administrator, student teacher, school safety officer, or coach, at any age, or who is other school personnel and is at least four years older than the victim, takes indecent liberties with a victim who is a student, at any time during or after the time the defendant and victim were present together in the same school but before the victim ceases to be a student, the defendant is guilty of a Class I felony, unless the conduct is covered under some other provision of law providing for greater punishment. A person is not guilty of taking indecent liberties with a student if the person is lawfully married to the student.

(b) If a defendant, who is school personnel, other than a teacher, school administrator, student teacher, school safety officer, or coach, and who is less than four years older than the victim, takes indecent liberties with a student as provided in subsection (a) of this section, the defendant is guilty of a Class A1 misdemeanor.

(c) Consent is not a defense to a charge under this section.

(d) For purposes of this section, the following definitions apply:

(1) "Indecent liberties" means:

a. Willfully taking or attempting to take any immoral, improper, or indecent liberties with a student for the purpose of arousing or gratifying sexual desire; or

b. Willfully committing or attempting to commit any lewd or lascivious act upon or with the body or any part or member of the body of a student.

For purposes of this section, the term indecent liberties does not include vaginal intercourse or a sexual act as defined by G.S. 14-27.1.

(1a) "Same school" means a school at which (i) the student is enrolled or is present for a school-sponsored or school-related activity and (ii) the school personnel is employed, volunteers, or is present for a school-sponsored or school-related activity.

(2) "School" means any public school, charter school, or nonpublic school under Parts 1 and 2 of Article 39 of Chapter 115C of the General Statutes.

(3) "School personnel" means any person included in the definition contained in G.S. 115C-332(a)(2), and any person who volunteers at a school or a school-sponsored activity.

(3a) "School safety officer" means any other person who is regularly present in a school for the purpose of promoting and maintaining safe and orderly schools and includes a school resource officer.

(4) "Student" means a person enrolled in kindergarten, or in grade one through grade 12 in any school.

Elements

A person guilty of this offense

(1) is a teacher, school administrator, student teacher, school safety officer, or coach *and*
(2) takes indecent liberties
(3) with a student
(4) at any time during or after the period when the student and the person were present together in the same school but before the victim stops being a student.

Punishment

Class I felony. G.S. 14-202.4(a).

Notes

Element (1). "School safety officer" means any other person who is regularly present in a school for the purpose of promoting and maintaining safe and orderly schools and includes a school resource officer. G.S. 14-202.4(d)(3a).

Element (2). The sexual conduct need not occur at a school. The statute defines indecent liberties in G.S. 14-202.4(d)(1) to encompass the same conduct covered by "Indecent Liberties with a Child," above, except that this offense does not cover vaginal intercourse or a sexual act defined by G.S. 14-27.1. G.S. 14-202.4(d)(1)b. See the note "General Discussion of Elements (2)(a) and (2)(b)" and the note on Element (2)(a)(i) to "Indecent Liberties with a Child," above. Although vaginal intercourse and a sexual act are excluded from this statute, these kinds of sexual activity are prohibited by "Sexual Activity with a Student," above.

Element (3). "Student" is defined as a person enrolled in kindergarten or in grade 1 through grade 12 in any school. G.S. 14-202.4(d)(4). "School," in turn, is defined as any public school, charter school, or nonpublic school under Parts 1 and 2 of Article 39 of Chapter 115C of the General Statutes. G.S. 14-202.4(d)(2).

Element (4). See the note on this element to "Sexual Activity with a Student by a Teacher, School Administrator, Student Teacher, Coach, or School Safety Officer," above. For this offense, the term "same school" means a school at which (1) the student is enrolled or is present for a school-sponsored or school-related activity; and (2) the school personnel is employed, volunteers, or is present for a school-sponsored or school-related activity. G.S. 14-202.4(d)(1a). Note that the term "same school" is defined differently for offenses under "Sexual Activity with a Student," above.

Consent. Consent is not a defense to this offense. G.S. 14-202.4(c).

Exceptions. This offense does not occur if the student and the person are lawfully married. G.S. 14-202.4(a).

Multiple convictions and punishments. See this note to "Indecent Liberties with a Child," above. G.S. 14-202.4(a) states that a violation is a Class I felony "unless the conduct is covered under some other provision of law providing for greater punishment." This provision appears to bar a conviction and punishment for this offense and a more serious offense arising from the same conduct. However, it does not appear to bar a trial for both charges, just a conviction and punishment for both. For a discussion of similar language in the assault context, see this note to "Assault Inflicting Serious Injury" in Chapter 7 (Assaults).

Sex offender registration. This offense is a sexually violent offense triggering registration requirements under the sex offender registration statutes. G.S. 14-208.6(5).

Related Offenses Not in This Chapter

See the offenses listed under "First-Degree Forcible Rape" and "First-Degree Statutory Rape," both above.

Felony Taking Indecent Liberties with a Student by School Personnel Other Than a Teacher, School Administrator, Student Teacher, School Safety Officer, or Coach

Statute

See G.S. 14-202.4(a), reproduced under "Felony Taking Indecent Liberties with a Student by a Teacher, School Administrator, Student Teacher, School Safety Officer, or Coach," above.

Elements

A person guilty of this offense

(1) is included in the definition of "school personnel" and is not a teacher, school administrator, student teacher, school safety officer, or coach *and*
(2) takes indecent liberties
(3) with a student
(4) at any time during or after the period when the student and the person were present together in the same school but before the victim stops being a student *and*
(5) the person is at least four years older than the student.

Punishment

Class I felony. G.S. 14-202.4(a).

Notes

Generally. This offense is the same as "Felony Taking Indecent Liberties with a Student by a Teacher, School Administrator, Student Teacher, School Safety Officer, or Coach," above, except that for this offense (1) the defendant must fall in the category of other school personnel; and (2) there is an age requirement for the defendant. Thus, the relevant notes to that offense apply here as well.

Element (1). "School personnel" means any person included in the definition contained in G.S. 115C-332(a)(2) and any person who volunteers at a school or a school-sponsored activity. G.S. 14-202.4(d)(3). For a discussion of the meaning of the term "school personnel" under G.S. 115C-332(a)(2), see the note on Element (1) to "Sexual Activity with a Student by School Personnel Other Than a Teacher, School Administrator, Student Teacher, Coach, or School Safety Officer," above.

Element (4). The age difference must be measured from the defendant's birthday to the victim's birthday. See the note on Element (3) to "First-Degree Statutory Rape" and "Statutory Rape of a Person Who Is 13, 14, or 15 Years Old by a Defendant Who Is at Least Six Years Older Than the Victim," both above.

Sex offender registration. This offense is a sexually violent offense triggering registration requirements under the sex offender registration statutes. G.S. 14-208.6(5).

Related Offenses Not in This Chapter

See the offenses listed under "First-Degree Forcible Rape" and "First-Degree Statutory Rape," both above.

Misdemeanor Taking Indecent Liberties with a Student by School Personnel Other Than a Teacher, School Administrator, Student Teacher, School Safety Officer, or Coach

Statute

See G.S. 14-202.4(b), reproduced under "Felony Taking Indecent Liberties with a Student by a Teacher, School Administrator, Student Teacher, School Safety Officer, or Coach," above.

Elements

A person guilty of this offense

(1) is included in the definition of "school personnel" and is not a teacher, school administrator, student teacher, school safety officer, or coach *and*
(2) takes indecent liberties
(3) with a student
(4) at any time during or after the period when the student and the person were present together in the same school but before the victim stops being a student *and*
(5) is less than four years older than the student.

Punishment

Class A1 misdemeanor. G.S. 14-202.4(b).

Notes

Generally. This offense is the same as "Felony Taking Indecent Liberties with a Student by School Personnel Other Than a Teacher, School Administrator, Student Teacher, School Safety Officer, or Coach," above, except for the element pertaining to the defendant's age. Thus, the relevant notes to that offense apply here as well.

Sex offender registration. This offense does not require sex offender registration.

Related Offenses Not in This Chapter

See the offenses listed under "First-Degree Forcible Rape" and "First-Degree Statutory Rape," both above.

Sexual Battery

Statute

§14-27.5A. Sexual Battery.

(a) A person is guilty of sexual battery if the person, for the purpose of sexual arousal, sexual gratification, or sexual abuse, engages in sexual contact with another person:

(1) By force and against the will of the other person; or
(2) Who is mentally disabled, mentally incapacitated, or physically helpless, and the person performing the act knows or should reasonably know that the other person is mentally disabled, mentally incapacitated, or physically helpless.

(b) Any person who commits the offense defined in this section is guilty of a Class A1 misdemeanor.

Elements

A person guilty of this offense

(1) for the purpose of sexual arousal, sexual gratification, or sexual abuse
(2) engages in sexual contact with another person
(3) (a) by force and against the will of the other person *or*
 (b) who is mentally disabled, mentally incapacitated, or physically helpless and the person knows or should reasonably know that the other person is mentally disabled, mentally incapacitated, or physically helpless.

Punishment

Class A1 misdemeanor. G.S. 14-27.5A(b).

Notes

Element (1). The evidence was sufficient to establish that the defendant grabbed the victim's crotch for the purpose of sexual arousal, sexual gratification, or sexual abuse when the defendant previously asked the victim, a nurse, for her phone number and for a date and had brushed against her thigh in such a manner that the victim reported the incident to her supervisor and was instructed not to be alone with the defendant. State v. Patino, ___ N.C. App. ___, 699 S.E.2d 678, 683 (2010).

Element (2). "Sexual contact" is defined in G.S. 14-27.1(5) as

- touching the sexual organ, anus, breast, groin, or buttocks of any person,
- touching another person with one's own sexual organ, anus, breast, groin, or buttocks, and
- ejaculating, emitting, or placing semen, urine, or feces on another person.

"Touching" is defined in G.S. 14-27.1(6) as physical contact with another person, whether directly, through the clothing of the person committing the offense, or through the clothing of the victim.

For this offense, neither a sexual act nor penetration is required. State v. Viera, 189 N.C. App. 514, 517 (2008).

Element (3)(a). See the notes on Elements (3) and (4) to "First-Degree Forcible Rape," above. There was constructive force sufficient to sustain a conviction when the defendant, a massage therapist, engaged in sexual contact with a client; an "implicit threat" was delivered through the defendant's abuse of his position of trust and relative authority as a professional massage therapist. *Viera*, 189 N.C. App. at 517–18.

Element (3)(b). See the note on Element (3)(b) to "Second-Degree Forcible Rape," above.

Greater and lesser-included offenses. See this note to "First-Degree Forcible Rape," above.

Sex offender registration. This offense constitutes a "sexually violent offense" within the meaning of G.S. 14-208.6(5), subjecting the defendant to sex offender registration.

Related Offenses Not in This Chapter

Assaults (various offenses) in Chapter 7 (Assaults)

Solicitation of a Child by Computer or Other Electronic Device

Solicitation of a Child by a Computer or Other Electronic Device to Commit an Unlawful Sex Act

Statute

§14-202.3. Solicitation of child by computer or certain other electronic devices to commit an unlawful sex act.

(a) Offense. – A person is guilty of solicitation of a child by a computer if the person is 16 years of age or older and the person knowingly, with the intent to commit an unlawful sex act, entices, advises, coerces, orders, or commands, by means of a computer or any other device capable of electronic data storage or transmission, a child who is less than 16 years of age and at least five years younger than the defendant, or a person the defendant believes to be a child who is less than 16 years of age and who the defendant believes to be at least five years younger than the defendant, to meet with the defendant or any other person for the purpose of committing an unlawful sex act. Consent is not a defense to a charge under this section.

(b) Jurisdiction. – The offense is committed in the State for purposes of determining jurisdiction, if the transmission that constitutes the offense either originates in the State or is received in the State.

(c) Punishment. – A violation of this section is punishable as follows:

(1) A violation is a Class H felony except as provided by subdivision (2) of this subsection.

(2) If either the defendant, or any other person for whom the defendant was arranging the meeting in violation of this section, actually appears at the meeting location, then the violation is a Class G felony.

Elements

A person guilty of this offense

(1) is 16 years of age or older *and*
(2) knowingly, with the intent to commit an unlawful sex act,
(3) (a) entices,
 (b) advises,
 (c) coerces,
 (d) orders, *or*
 (e) commands
(4) by means of
 (a) a computer *or*
 (b) any other device capable of electronic data storage or transmission
(5) (a) a child less than 16 years of age and at least five years younger than the person *or*
 (b) a person the defendant believes to be a child who is less than 16 years of age and who the defendant believes to be at least five years younger than the defendant
(6) to meet any person
(7) for the purpose of committing an unlawful sex act.

Punishment

Class H felony. G.S. 14-202.3(c)(1).

Notes

Element (2). See "Knowingly" in Chapter 1 (States of Mind). An "unlawful sex act" includes, among others, such criminal offenses as rape, sexual offense, indecent liberties, and crime against nature.

Element (3). For a case in which the evidence was sufficient to establish that the defendant advised or enticed an officer posing as a child to meet the defendant, see *State v. Fraley*, ___ N.C. App. ___, 688 S.E.2d 778, 784–85 (2010).

Element (5). The age difference must be measured from the defendant's birthday to the victim's birthday. See the note on Element (3) to "First-Degree Statutory Rape" and "Statutory Rape of a Person Who is 13, 14, or 15 Years Old by a Defendant Who Is at Least Six Years Older Than the Victim," both above.

Jurisdiction. G.S. 14-202.3(b) provides that the offense may be charged if the transmission either originates or is received in North Carolina. See generally "Lack of Jurisdiction" in Chapter 2 (Bars and Defenses).

Consent. Consent is not a defense to this offense. G.S. 14-202.3(a).

Sex offender registration. A violation of this statute is a "sexually violent offense" within the meaning of G.S. 14-208.6(5), triggering registration requirements under the sex offender registration statutes.

Related Offenses Not in This Chapter

"Child Abuse—Prostitution" (Chapter 9)
"Child Abuse—Sexual Act" (Chapter 9)
"Abduction of a Child" (Chapter 12)
See the various offenses involving children in Chapter 23 (Prostitution).
See the various offenses involving children in Chapter 24 (Obscenity, Exploitation of a Minor, and Adult Establishment Offenses).

Solicitation of a Child by a Computer or Other Electronic Device to Commit an Unlawful Sex Act Resulting in Appearance at Meeting Location

Statute

See G.S. 14-202.3(a) and (c)(2), reproduced under "Solicitation of a Child by a Computer or Other Electronic Device to Commit an Unlawful Sex Act," above.

Elements

A person guilty of this offense

(1) is 16 years of age or older *and*
(2) knowingly, with the intent to commit an unlawful sex act,
(3) (a) entices,
(b) advises,
(c) coerces,
(d) orders, *or*
(e) commands
(4) by means of
(a) a computer *or*
(b) any other device capable of electronic data storage or transmission
(5) (a) a child less than 16 years of age and at least five years younger than the person *or*
(b) a person the defendant believes to be a child who is less than 16 years of age and who the defendant believes to be at least five years younger than the defendant
(6) to meet any person
(7) for the purpose of committing an unlawful sex act *and*
(8) either the defendant or any other person for whom the defendant was arranging the meeting actually appears at the meeting location.

Punishment

Class G felony. G.S. 14-202.3(c)(2).

Notes

Generally. This offense is exactly the same as "Solicitation of a Child by a Computer or Other Electronic Device to Commit an Unlawful Sex Act" except that this offense contains the additional Element (8), requiring that someone shows up at the meeting location. Thus, all of the notes to that offense apply here as well.

Related Offenses Not In This Chapter

See the offenses listed under "Solicitation of a Child by a Computer or Other Electronic Device to Commit an Unlawful Sex Act," above.

Sex Offender Crimes

Statute

Part 1. Registration Programs, Purpose and Definitions Generally.

G.S. 14-208.5 (Purpose) is not set forth here.

§14-208.6. Definitions.

The following definitions apply in this Article:

(1a) "Aggravated offense" means any criminal offense that includes either of the following: (i) engaging in a sexual act involving vaginal, anal, or oral penetration with a victim of any age through the use of force or the threat of serious violence; or (ii) engaging in a sexual act involving vaginal, anal, or oral penetration with a victim who is less than 12 years old.

(1b) "County registry" means the information compiled by the sheriff of a county in compliance with this Article.

(1c) "Division" means the Division of Criminal Information of the Department of Justice.

(1d) "Electronic mail" means the transmission of information or communication by the use of the Internet, a computer, a facsimile machine, a pager, a cellular telephone, a video recorder, or other electronic means sent to a person identified by a unique address or address number and received by that person.

(1e) "Employed" includes employment that is full-time or part-time for a period of time exceeding 14 days or for an aggregate period of time exceeding 30 days during any calendar year, whether financially compensated, volunteered, or for the purpose of government or educational benefit.

(1f) "Entity" means a business or organization that provides Internet service, electronic communications service, remote computing service, online service, electronic mail service, or electronic instant message or chat services whether the business or organization is within or outside the State.

(1g) "Instant Message" means a form of real-time text communication between two or more people. The communication is conveyed via computers connected over a network such as the Internet.

(1h) "Institution of higher education" means any postsecondary public or private educational institution, including any trade or professional institution, college, or university.

(1i) "Internet" means the global information system that is logically linked together by a globally unique address space based on the Internet Protocol or its subsequent extensions; that is able to support communications using the Transmission Control Protocol/Internet Protocol suite, its subsequent extensions, or other Internet Protocol compatible protocols; and that provides, uses, or makes accessible, either publicly or privately, high-level services layered on the communications and related infrastructure described in this subdivision.

(1j) "Mental abnormality" means a congenital or acquired condition of a person that affects the emotional or volitional capacity of the person in a manner that predisposes that person to the commission of criminal sexual acts to a degree that makes the person a menace to the health and safety of others.

(1k) "Nonresident student" means a person who is not a resident of North Carolina but who is enrolled in any type of school in the State on a part-time or full-time basis.

(1l) "Nonresident worker" means a person who is not a resident of North Carolina but who has employment or carries on a vocation in the State, on a part-time or full-time basis, with or without compensation or government or educational benefit, for more than 14 days, or for an aggregate period exceeding 30 days in a calendar year.

(1m) "Offense against a minor" means any of the following offenses if the offense is committed against a minor, and the person committing the offense is not the minor's parent: G.S. 14-39 (kidnapping), G.S. 14-41 (abduction of children), and G.S. 14-43.3 (felonious restraint). The term also includes the following if the person convicted of the following is not the minor's parent: a solicitation or conspiracy to commit any of these offenses; aiding and abetting any of these offenses.

(1n) "Online identifier" means electronic mail address, instant message screen name, user ID, chat or other Internet communication name, but it does not mean social security number, date of birth, or pin number.

(2) "Penal institution" means:

a. A detention facility operated under the jurisdiction of the Division of Prisons of the Department of Correction;

b. A detention facility operated under the jurisdiction of another state or the federal government; or

c. A detention facility operated by a local government in this State or another state.

(2a) "Personality disorder" means an enduring pattern of inner experience and behavior that deviates markedly from the expectations of the individual's culture, is pervasive and inflexible, has an onset in adolescence or early adulthood, is stable over time, and leads to distress or impairment.

(2b) "Recidivist" means a person who has a prior conviction for an offense that is described in G.S. 14-208.6(4).

(3) "Release" means discharged or paroled.

(4) "Reportable conviction" means:

a. A final conviction for an offense against a minor, a sexually violent offense, or an attempt to commit any of those offenses unless the conviction is for aiding and abetting. A final conviction for aiding and abetting is a reportable conviction only if the court sentencing the individual finds that the registration of that individual under this Article furthers the purposes of this Article as stated in G.S. 14-208.5.

b. A final conviction in another state of an offense, which if committed in this State, is substantially similar to an offense against a minor or a sexually violent offense as defined by this section, or a final conviction in another state of an offense that requires registration under the sex offender registration statutes of that state.

c. A final conviction in a federal jurisdiction (including a court martial) of an offense, which is substantially similar to an offense against a minor or a sexually violent offense as defined by this section.

d. A final conviction for a violation of G.S. 14-202(d), (e), (f), (g), or (h), or a second or subsequent conviction for a violation of G.S. 14-202(a), (a1), or (c), only if the court sentencing the individual issues an order pursuant to G.S. 14-202(l) requiring the individual to register.

(5) "Sexually violent offense" means a violation of G.S. 14-27.2 (first degree rape), G.S. 14-27.2A (rape of a child; adult offender), G.S. 14-27.3 (second degree rape), G.S. 14-27.4 (first degree sexual offense), G.S. 14-27.4A (sex offense with a child; adult offender), G.S. 14-27.5 (second degree sexual offense), G.S. 14-27.5A (sexual battery), G.S. 14-27.6 (attempted rape or sexual offense), G.S. 14-27.7 (intercourse and sexual offense with certain victims), G.S. 14-27.7A(a) (statutory rape or sexual offense of person who is 13-, 14-, or 15-years-old where the defendant is at least six years older), G.S. 14-43.13 (subjecting or maintaining a person for sexual servitude), G.S. 14-178 (incest between near relatives), G.S. 14-190.6 (employing or permitting minor to assist in offenses against public morality and decency), G.S.

14-190.9(a1) (felonious indecent exposure), G.S. 14-190.16 (first degree sexual exploitation of a minor), G.S. 14-190.17 (second degree sexual exploitation of a minor), G.S. 14-190.17A (third degree sexual exploitation of a minor), G.S. 14-190.18 (promoting prostitution of a minor), G.S. 14-190.19 (participating in the prostitution of a minor), G.S. 14-202.1 (taking indecent liberties with children), G.S. 14-202.3 (Solicitation of child by computer or certain other electronic devices to commit an unlawful sex act), G.S. 14-202.4(a) (taking indecent liberties with a student), G.S. 14-318.4(a1) (parent or caretaker commit or permit act of prostitution with or by a juvenile), or G.S. 14-318.4(a2) (commission or allowing of sexual act upon a juvenile by parent or guardian). The term also includes the following: a solicitation or conspiracy to commit any of these offenses; aiding and abetting any of these offenses.

(6) "Sexually violent predator" means a person who has been convicted of a sexually violent offense and who suffers from a mental abnormality or personality disorder that makes the person likely to engage in sexually violent offenses directed at strangers or at a person with whom a relationship has been established or promoted for the primary purpose of victimization.

(7) "Sheriff" means the sheriff of a county in this State.

(8) "Statewide registry" means the central registry compiled by the Division in accordance with G.S. 14-208.14.

(9) "Student" means a person who is enrolled on a full-time or part-time basis, in any postsecondary public or private educational institution, including any trade or professional institution, or other institution of higher education.

§14-208.6A. Lifetime registration requirements for criminal offenders.
It is the objective of the General Assembly to establish a 30-year registration requirement for persons convicted of certain offenses against minors or sexually violent offenses with an opportunity for those persons to petition in superior court to shorten their registration time period after 10 years of registration. It is the further objective of the General Assembly to establish a more stringent set of registration requirements for recidivists, persons who commit aggravated offenses, and for a subclass of highly dangerous sex offenders who are determined by a sentencing court with the assistance of a board of experts to be sexually violent predators.

To accomplish this objective, there are established two registration programs: the Sex Offender and Public Protection Registration Program and the Sexually Violent Predator Registration Program. Any person convicted of an offense against a minor or of a sexually violent offense as defined by this Article shall register in person as an offender in accordance with Part 2 of this Article. Any person who is a recidivist, who commits an aggravated offense, or who is determined to be a sexually violent predator shall register in person as such in accordance with Part 3 of this Article.

The information obtained under these programs shall be immediately shared with the appropriate local, State, federal, and out-of-state law enforcement officials and penal institutions. In addition, the information designated under G.S. 14-208.10(a) as public record shall be readily available to and accessible by the public. However, the identity of the victim is not public record and shall not be released as a public record.

G.S. 14-208.6B (Registration requirements for juveniles transferred to and convicted in superior court) and G.S. 14-208.6C (Discontinuation of registration requirement) are not reproduced here.

Part 2. Sex Offender and Public Protection Registration Program.

§14-208.7. Registration.

(a) A person who is a State resident and who has a reportable conviction shall be required to maintain registration with the sheriff of the county where the person resides. If the person moves to North Carolina from outside this State, the person shall register within three business days of establishing residence in this State, or whenever the person has been present in the State for 15 days, whichever comes first. If the person is a current resident of North Carolina, the person shall register:

(1) Within three business days of release from a penal institution or arrival in a county to live outside a penal institution; or

(2) Immediately upon conviction for a reportable offense where an active term of imprisonment was not imposed.

Registration shall be maintained for a period of at least 30 years following the date of initial county registration unless the person, after 10 years of registration, successfully petitions the superior court to shorten his or her registration time period under G.S. 14-208.12A.

(a1) A person who is a nonresident student or a nonresident worker and who has a reportable conviction, or is required to register in the person's state of residency, is required to maintain registration with the sheriff of the county where the person works or attends school. In addition to the information required under subsection (b) of this section, the person shall also provide information regarding the person's school or place of employment as appropriate and the person's address in his or her state of residence.

(b) The Division shall provide each sheriff with forms for registering persons as required by this Article. The registration form shall require all of the following:

(1) The person's full name, each alias, date of birth, sex, race, height, weight, eye color, hair color, drivers license number, and home address.

(1a) A statement indicating what the person's name was at the time of the conviction for the offense that requires registration; what alias, if any, the person was using at the time of the conviction of that offense; and the name of the person as it appears on the judgment imposing the sentence on the person for the conviction of the offense.

(2) The type of offense for which the person was convicted, the date of conviction, and the sentence imposed.

(3) A current photograph taken by the sheriff, without charge, at the time of registration.

(4) The person's fingerprints taken by the sheriff, without charge, at the time of registration.

(5) A statement indicating whether the person is a student or expects to enroll as a student within a year of registering. If the person is a student or expects to enroll as a student within a year of registration, then the registration form shall also require the name and address of the educational institution at which the person is a student or expects to enroll as a student.

(6) A statement indicating whether the person is employed or expects to be employed at an institution of higher education within a year of registering. If the person is employed or expects to be employed at an institution of higher education within a year of registration, then the registration form shall also require the name and address of the educational institution at which the person is or expects to be employed.

(7) Any online identifier that the person uses or intends to use.

(c) When a person registers, the sheriff with whom the person registered shall immediately send the registration information to the Division in a manner determined by the Division. The sheriff shall retain the original registration form and other information collected and shall compile the information that is a public record under this Part into a county registry.

(d) Any person required to register under this section shall report in person at the appropriate sheriff's office to comply with the registration requirements set out in this section. The sheriff shall provide the registrant with written proof of registration at the time of registration.

§14-208.8. Prerelease notification.

(a) At least 10 days, but not earlier than 30 days, before a person who will be subject to registration under this Article is due to be released from a penal institution, an official of the penal institution shall do all of the following:

(1) Inform the person of the person's duty to register under this Article and require the person to sign a written statement that the person was so informed or, if the person refuses to sign the statement, certify that the person was so informed.

(2) Obtain the registration information required under G.S. 14-208.7(b)(1), (2), (5), (6), and (7), as well as the address where the person expects to reside upon the person's release.

(3) Send the Division and the sheriff of the county in which the person expects to reside the information collected in accordance with subdivision (2) of this subsection.

(b) If a person who is subject to registration under this Article does not receive an active term of imprisonment, the court pronouncing sentence shall conduct, at the time of sentencing, the notification procedures specified in subsection (a) of this section.

§14-208.8A. Notification requirement for out-of-county employment if temporary residence established.

(a) Notice Required. – A person required to register under G.S. 14-208.7 shall notify the sheriff of the county with whom the person is registered of the person's place of employment and temporary residence, which includes a hotel, motel, or other transient lodging place, if the person meets both of the following conditions:

(1) Is employed or carries on a vocation in a county in the State other than the county in which the person is registered for more than 10 business days within a 30-day period, or for an aggregate period exceeding 30 days in a calendar year, on a part-time or full-time basis, with or without compensation or government or educational benefit.

(2) Maintains a temporary residence in that county for more than 10 business days within a 30-day period, or for an aggregate period exceeding 30 days in a calendar year.

(b) Time Period. – The notice required by subsection (a) of this section shall be provided within 72 hours after the person knows or should know that he or she will be working and maintaining a temporary residence in a county other than the county in which the person resides for more than 10 business days within a 30-day period, or within 10 days after the person knows or should know that he or she will be working and maintaining a temporary residence in a county other than the county in which the person resides for an aggregate period exceeding 30 days in a calendar year.

(c) Notice to Division. – Upon receiving the notice required under subsection (a) of this section, the sheriff shall immediately forward the information to the Division. The Division shall notify the sheriff of the county where the person is working and maintaining a temporary residence of the person's place of employment and temporary address in that county.

§14-208.9. Change of address; change of academic status or educational employment status; change of online identifier; change of name.

(a) If a person required to register changes address, the person shall report in person and provide written notice of the new address not later than the third business day after the change to the sheriff of the county with whom the person had last registered. If the person moves to another county, the person shall also report in person to the sheriff of the new county and provide written notice of the person's address not later than the tenth day after the change of address. Upon receipt of the notice, the sheriff shall immediately forward this information to the Division. When the Division receives notice from a sheriff that a person required to register is moving to another county in the State, the Division shall inform the sheriff of the new county of the person's new residence.

(b) If a person required to register intends to move to another state, the person shall report in person to the sheriff of the county of current residence at least three business days before the date the person intends to leave this State to establish residence in another state or jurisdiction. The person shall provide to the sheriff a written notification that includes all of the following information: the address, municipality, county, and state of intended residence.

(1) If it appears to the sheriff that the record photograph of the sex offender no longer provides a true and accurate likeness of the sex offender, then the sheriff shall take a photograph of the offender to update the registration.

(2) The sheriff shall inform the person that the person must comply with the registration requirements in the new state of residence. The sheriff shall also immediately forward the information included in the notification to the Division, and the Division shall inform the appropriate state official in the state to which the registrant moves of the person's notification and new address.

(b1) A person who indicates his or her intent to reside in another state or jurisdiction and later decides to remain in this State shall, within three business days after the date upon which the person indicated he or she would leave this State, report in person to the sheriff's office to which the person reported the intended change of residence, of his or her intent to remain in this State. If the sheriff is notified by the sexual offender that he or she intends to remain in this State, the sheriff shall promptly report this information to the Division.

(c) If a person required to register changes his or her academic status either by enrolling as a student or by terminating enrollment as a student, then the person shall, within three business days, report in person to the sheriff of the county with whom the person registered and provide written notice of the person's new status. The written notice shall include the name and address of the institution of higher education at which the student is or was enrolled. The sheriff shall immediately forward this information to the Division.

(d) If a person required to register changes his or her employment status either by obtaining employment at an institution of higher education or by terminating employment at an institution of higher education, then the person shall, within three business days, report in person to the sheriff of the county with whom the person registered and provide written notice of the person's new status not later than the tenth day after the change to the sheriff of the county with whom the person registered. The written notice shall include the name and address of the institution of higher education at which the person is or was employed. The sheriff shall immediately forward this information to the Division.

(e) If a person required to register changes an online identifier, or obtains a new online identifier, then the person shall, within 10 days, report in person to the sheriff of the county with whom the person registered to provide the new or changed online identifier information to the sheriff. The sheriff shall immediately forward this information to the Division.

(f) If a person required to register changes his or her name pursuant to Chapter 101 of the General Statutes or by any other method, then the person shall, within three business days, report in person to the sheriff of the county with whom the person registered to provide the name change to the sheriff. The sheriff shall immediately forward this information to the Division.

§14-208.9A. Verification of registration information.

(a) The information in the county registry shall be verified semiannually for each registrant as follows:

(1) Every year on the anniversary of a person's initial registration date, and again six months after that date, the Division shall mail a nonforwardable verification form to the last reported address of the person.

(2) The person shall return the verification form in person to the sheriff within three business days after the receipt of the form.

(3) The verification form shall be signed by the person and shall indicate the following:

a. Whether the person still resides at the address last reported to the sheriff. If the person has a different address, then the person shall indicate that fact and the new address.

b. Whether the person still uses or intends to use any online identifiers last reported to the sheriff. If the person has any new or different online identifiers, then the person shall provide those online identifiers to the sheriff.

c. Whether the person still uses or intends to use the name under which the person registered and last reported to the sheriff. If the person has any new or different name, then the person shall provide that name to the sheriff.

(3a) If it appears to the sheriff that the record photograph of the sex offender no longer provides a true and accurate likeness of the sex offender, then the sheriff shall take a photograph of the offender to include with the verification form.

(4) If the person fails to return the verification form in person to the sheriff within three business days after receipt of the form, the person is subject to the penalties provided in G.S. 14-208.11. If the person fails to report in person and provide the written verification as provided by this section, the sheriff shall make a reasonable attempt to verify that the person is residing at the registered address. If the person cannot be found at the registered address and has failed to report a change of address, the person is subject to the penalties provided in G.S. 14-208.11, unless the person reports in person to the sheriff and proves that the person has not changed his or her residential address.

(b) Additional Verification May Be Required. – During the period that an offender is required to be registered under this Article, the sheriff is authorized to attempt to verify that the offender continues to reside at the address last registered by the offender.

(c) Additional Photograph May Be Required. – If it appears to the sheriff that the current photograph of the sex offender no longer provides a true and accurate likeness of the sex offender, upon in-person notice from the sheriff, the sex offender shall allow the sheriff to take another photograph of the sex offender at the time of the sheriff's request. If requested by the sheriff, the sex offender shall appear in person at the sheriff's office during normal business hours within three business days of being requested to do so and shall allow the sheriff to take another photograph of the sex offender. A person who willfully fails to comply with this subsection is guilty of a Class 1 misdemeanor.

G.S. 14-208.10 (Registration information is public record; access to registration information) is not set forth here.

§14-208.11. Failure to register; falsification of verification notice; failure to return verification form; order for arrest.

(a) A person required by this Article to register who willfully does any of the following is guilty of a Class F felony:

(1) Fails to register as required by this Article.
(2) Fails to notify the last registering sheriff of a change of address as required by this Article.
(3) Fails to return a verification notice as required under G.S. 14-208.9A.
(4) Forges or submits under false pretenses the information or verification notices required under this Article.
(5) Fails to inform the registering sheriff of enrollment or termination of enrollment as a student.
(6) Fails to inform the registering sheriff of employment at an institution of higher education or termination of employment at an institution of higher education.
(7) Fails to report in person to the sheriff's office as required by G.S. 14-208.7, 14-208.9, and 14-208.9A.
(8) Reports his or her intent to reside in another state or jurisdiction but remains in this State without reporting to the sheriff in the manner required by G.S. 14-208.9.
(9) Fails to notify the registering sheriff of out-of-county employment if temporary residence is established as required under G.S. 14-208.8A.
(10) Fails to inform the registering sheriff of any new or changes to existing online identifiers that the person uses or intends to use.

(a1) If a person commits a violation of subsection (a) of this section, the probation officer, parole officer, or any other law enforcement officer who is aware of the violation shall immediately arrest the person in accordance with G.S. 15A-401, or seek an order for the person's arrest in accordance with G.S. 15A-305.

(b) Before a person convicted of a violation of this Article is due to be released from a penal institution, an official of the penal institution shall conduct the prerelease notification procedures specified under G.S. 14-208.8(a)(2) and (3). If upon a conviction for a violation of this Article, no active term of imprisonment is imposed, the court pronouncing sentence shall, at the time of sentencing, conduct the notification procedures specified under G.S. 14-208.8(a)(2) and (3).

(c) A person who is unable to meet the registration or verification requirements of this Article shall be deemed to have complied with its requirements if:

(1) The person is incarcerated in, or is in the custody of, a local, State, private, or federal correctional facility,

(2) The person notifies the official in charge of the facility of their status as a person with a legal obligation or requirement under this Article and

(3) The person meets the registration or verification requirements of this Article no later than 10 days after release from confinement or custody.

§14-208.11A. Duty to report noncompliance of a sex offender; penalty for failure to report in certain circumstances.

(a) It shall be unlawful and a Class H felony for any person who has reason to believe that an offender is in violation of the requirements of this Article, and who has the intent to assist the offender in eluding arrest, to do any of the following:

(1) Withhold information from, or fail to notify, a law enforcement agency about the offender's noncompliance with the requirements of this Article, and, if known, the whereabouts of the offender.

(2) Harbor, attempt to harbor, or assist another person in harboring or attempting to harbor, the offender.

(3) Conceal, or attempt to conceal, or assist another person in concealing or attempting to conceal, the offender.

(4) Provide information to a law enforcement agency regarding the offender that the person knows to be false information.

(b) This section does not apply if the offender is incarcerated in or is in the custody of a local, State, private, or federal correctional facility.

G.S. 14-208.12A (Request for termination of registration requirement), G.S. 14-208.13 (File with Police Information Network), G.S. 14-208.14 (Statewide registry; Division of Criminal Statistics designated custodian of statewide registry), G.S. 14-208.15 (Certain statewide registry information is public record; access to statewide registry), and G.S. 14-208.15A (Release of online identifiers to entity; fee) are not set forth here.

§14-208.16. Residential restrictions.

(a) A registrant under this Article shall not knowingly reside within 1,000 feet of the property on which any public or nonpublic school or child care center is located.

(b) As used in this section, "school" does not include home schools as defined in G.S. 115C-563 or institutions of higher education, and the term "child care center" is defined by G.S. 110-86(3). The term "registrant" means a person who is registered, or is required to register, under this Article.

(c) This section does not apply to child care centers that are located on or within 1,000 feet of the property of an institution of higher education where the registrant is a student or is employed.

(d) Changes in the ownership of or use of property within 1,000 feet of a registrant's registered address that occur after a registrant establishes residency at the registered address shall not form the basis for finding that an offender is in violation of this section. For purposes of this subsection, a residence is established when the registrant does any of the following:

(1) Purchases the residence or enters into a specifically enforceable contract to purchase the residence.
(2) Enters into a written lease contract for the residence and for as long as the person is lawfully entitled to remain on the premises.
(3) Resides with an immediate family member who established residence in accordance with this subsection. For purposes of this subsection, "immediate family member" means a child or sibling who is 18 years of age or older, or a parent, grandparent, legal guardian, or spouse of the registrant.

(e) Nothing in this section shall be construed as creating a private cause of action against a real estate agent or landlord for any act or omission arising out of the residential restriction in this section.

(f) A violation of this section is a Class G felony.

§14-208.17. Sexual predator prohibited from working or volunteering for child-involved activities; limitation on residential use.

(a) It shall be unlawful for any person required to register under this Article to work for any person or as a sole proprietor, with or without compensation, at any place where a minor is present and the person's responsibilities or activities would include instruction, supervision, or care of a minor or minors.

(b) It shall be unlawful for any person to conduct any activity at his or her residence where the person:
(1) Accepts a minor or minors into his or her care or custody from another, and
(2) Knows that a person who resides at that same location is required to register under this Article.

(c) A violation of this section is a Class F felony.

§14-208.18. Sex offender unlawfully on premises.

(a) It shall be unlawful for any person required to register under this Article, if the offense requiring registration is described in subsection (c) of this section, to knowingly be at any of the following locations:
(1) On the premises of any place intended primarily for the use, care, or supervision of minors, including, but not limited to, schools, children's museums, child care centers, nurseries, and playgrounds.
(2) Within 300 feet of any location intended primarily for the use, care, or supervision of minors when the place is located on premises that are not intended primarily for the use, care, or supervision of minors, including, but not limited to, places described in subdivision (1) of this subsection that are located in malls, shopping centers, or other property open to the general public.
(3) At any place where minors gather for regularly scheduled educational, recreational, or social programs.

(b) Notwithstanding any provision of this section, a person subject to subsection (a) of this section who is the parent or guardian of a minor may take the minor to any location that can provide emergency medical care treatment if the minor is in need of emergency medical care.

(c) Subsection (a) of this section is applicable only to persons required to register under this Article who have committed any of the following offenses:
(1) Any offense in Article 7A of this Chapter.
(2) Any offense where the victim of the offense was under the age of 16 years at the time of the offense.

(d) A person subject to subsection (a) of this section who is a parent or guardian of a student enrolled in a school may be present on school property if all of the following conditions are met:
(1) The parent or guardian is on school property for the purpose for one of the following:
a. To attend a conference at the school with school personnel to discuss the academic or social progress of the parents' or guardians' child; or

b. The presence of the parent or guardian has been requested by the principal or his or her designee for any other reason relating to the welfare or transportation of the child.

(2) The parent or guardian complies with all of the following:

a. Notice: The parent or guardian shall notify the principal of the school of the parents' or guardians' registration under this Article and of his or her presence at the school unless the parent or guardian has permission to be present from the superintendent or the local board of education, or the principal has granted ongoing permission for regular visits of a routine nature. If permission is granted by the superintendent or the local board of education, the superintendent or chairman of the local board of education shall inform the principal of the school where the parents' or guardians' will be present. Notification includes the nature of the parents' or guardians' visit and the hours when the parent or guardian will be present at the school. The parent or guardian is responsible for notifying the principal's office upon arrival and upon departure. Any permission granted under this sub-subdivision shall be in writing.

b. Supervision: At all times that a parent or guardian is on school property, the parent or guardian shall remain under the direct supervision of school personnel. A parent or guardian shall not be on school property even if the parent or guardian has ongoing permission for regular visits of a routine nature if no school personnel are reasonably available to supervise the parent or guardian on that occasion.

(e) A person subject to subsection (a) of this section who is eligible to vote may be present at a location described in subsection (a) used as a voting place as defined by G.S. 163-165 only for the purposes of voting and shall not be outside the voting enclosure other than for the purpose of entering and exiting the voting place. If the voting place is a school, then the person subject to subsection (a) shall notify the principal of the school that he or she is registered under this Article.

(f) A person subject to subsection (a) of this section who is eligible under G.S. 115C-378 to attend public school may be present on school property if permitted by the local board of education pursuant to G.S. 115C-391(d)(2).

(g) A juvenile subject to subsection (a) of this section may be present at a location described in that subsection if the juvenile is at the location to receive medical treatment or mental health services and remains under the direct supervision of an employee of the treating institution at all times.

(g1) Notwithstanding any provision of this section, a person subject to subsection (a) of this section who is required to wear an electronic monitoring device shall wear an electronic monitoring device that provides exclusion zones around the premises of all elementary and secondary schools in North Carolina.

(h) A violation of this section is a Class H felony.

G.S. 14-208.19 (Community and public notification) is not reproduced here.

§14-208.19A. Commercial drivers license restrictions.

(a) The Division of Motor Vehicles, in compliance with G.S. 20-37.14A, shall not issue or renew a commercial drivers license with a P or S endorsement to any person required to register under this Article.

(b) The Division of Motor Vehicles, in compliance with G.S. 20-37.13(f) shall not issue a commercial driver learner's permit with a P or S endorsement to any person required to register under this Article.

(c) A person who is convicted of a violation that requires registration under Article 27A of Chapter 14 of the General Statutes is disqualified under G.S. 20-17.4 from driving a commercial motor vehicle that requires a commercial drivers license with a P or S endorsement for the period of time during which the person is required to maintain registration under Article 27A of Chapter 14 of the General Statutes.

(d) A person who drives a commercial passenger vehicle or a school bus and who does not have a commercial drivers license with a P or S endorsement because the person was convicted of a violation that requires registration under Article 27A of Chapter 14 of the General Statutes shall be punished as provided by G.S. 20-27.1.

Part 3. Sexually Violent Predator Registration Program

This Part is not reproduced here.

Part 4. Registration of Certain Juveniles Adjudicated for Committing Certain Offenses

This Part is not reproduced here.

Part 5. Sex Offender Monitoring

G.S. 14-208.40 (Establishment of program; creation of guidelines; duties), G.S. 14-208.40A (Determination of satellite-based monitoring requirement by court), G.S. 14-208.40B (Determination of satellite-based monitoring requirement in certain circumstances), G.S. 14-208.40C (Requirements of enrollment), G.S. 14-208.41 (Enrollment in satellite-based monitoring programs mandatory; length of enrollment); G.S. 14-208.42 (Offenders required to submit to satellite-based monitoring required to cooperate with Department upon completion of sentence); and G.S. 14-208.43 (Request for termination of satellite-based monitoring requirement) are not reproduced here.

§14-208.44. Failure to enroll; tampering with device.

(a) Any person required to enroll in a satellite-based monitoring program who fails to enroll shall be guilty of a Class F felony.

(b) Any person who intentionally tampers with, removes, vandalizes, or otherwise interferes with the proper functioning of a device issued pursuant to a satellite-based monitoring program to a person duly enrolled in the program shall be guilty of a Class E felony.

(c) Any person required to enroll in a satellite-based monitoring program who fails to provide necessary information to the Department, or fails to cooperate with the Department's guidelines and regulations for the program shall be guilty of a Class 1 misdemeanor.

(d) For purposes of this section, "enroll" shall include appearing, as directed by the Department, to receive the necessary equipment.

G.S. 14-208.45 (Fees) is not reproduced here.

Failure to Register, etc. as a Sex Offender

Statute

See G.S. 14-208.11(a), reproduced above.

Elements

A person guilty of this offense

(1) is a sex offender who is required to register *and*
(2) willfully
(3) (a) fails to register,
(b) fails to notify the last registering sheriff of a change of address,
(c) fails to return a verification notice as required under G.S. 14-208.9A,
(d) forges or submits under false pretenses the information or verification notices required,
(e) fails to inform the registering sheriff of enrollment or termination of enrollment as a student,
(f) fails to inform the registering sheriff of employment at an institution of higher education or termination of employment at an institution of higher education,

(g) fails to report in person to the sheriff's office as required by G.S. 14-208.7, 14-208.9, and 14-208.9A,
(h) reports his or her intent to reside in another state or jurisdiction but remains in this State without reporting to the sheriff in the manner required by G.S. 14-208.9,
(i) fails to notify the registering sheriff of out-of-county employment if temporary residence is established as required under G.S. 14-208.8A, *or*
(j) fails to inform the registering sheriff of any new or changes to existing online identifiers that the person uses or intended to use.

Punishment

Class F felony. G.S. 14-208.11(a).

Notes

Generally. The sex offender registration program is a complex set of statutes designed to assist law enforcement agencies and the public in knowing the whereabouts of sex offenders and locating them when necessary. State v. Abshire, 363 N.C. 322, 330 (2009). The twin aims of the program are public safety and protection. *Id.* Although a detailed discussion of the program is beyond the scope of this book, in a nutshell, it requires certain offenders with "reportable convictions" to register on the sex offender registry for thirty years. In some instances lifetime registration and satellite-based monitoring are required. In addition, the law restricts certain conduct by registered sex offenders, and a violation of these restrictions may be a crime. This book covers the main criminal offenses related to the sex offender registration program. For a more detailed discussion of the program, see *The North Carolina Sex Offender and Public Protection Registration Programs* (a publication by the N.C. Attorney General, Jan. 2011) (online at http://ncdoj.gov/Protect-Yourself/Find-Sex-Offenders/SexOffenderRegPrograms.aspx) (hereinafter *N.C. Sex Offender Programs*).

Element (1). This offense applies to any individual who is required to register. For a discussion of who is required to register, see *N.C. Sex Offender Programs* at 2–8 (outlining the categories of persons required to register and the offenses triggering the registration requirement).

A defendant convicted of first-degree kidnapping of a child was properly ordered to register as a sex offender. State v. Sakobie, 165 N.C. App. 447 (2004).

A defendant who resided outside of North Carolina when he committed an offense in North Carolina was a resident required to register when he was released from prison in North Carolina. State v. Williams, 190 N.C. App. 173, 176–77 (2008).

The North Carolina Department of Correction's untimely notification to the defendant of the duty to register as a sex offender (notification was given five days before release instead of at least ten days before release) was not a bar to conviction. State v. Harris, 171 N.C. App. 127 (2005).

Element (2). Although case law had held that this offense is a strict liability offense, State v. White, 162 N.C. App. 183 (2004); see "Strict Liability" in Chapter 1 (States of Mind), 2006 legislation, S.L. 2006-247, added the element of willfulness. See generally "Willfully" in Chapter 1 (States of Mind).

Element (3)(a). G.S. 14-208.7 and G.S. 14-208.22 (lifetime registrants) contain the registration requirements.

Element (3)(b). The requirement to notify the appropriate sheriff of a change of address is set out in G.S. 14-208.9. Requiring a person adjudicated as an incompetent to notify a sheriff of a change of address is unconstitutional. State v. Young, 140 N.C. App. 1 (2000). A conviction was upheld when the State produced substantial evidence that a defendant failed to provide the sheriff with written notice, within ten days of moving, of two changes of address; the defendant signed a verification for the first move over two months late, and he failed to sign a verification for the second move. State v. Holmes, 149 N.C. App. 572 (2002).

As used in the sex offender registration law, "address" means "residence," the "actual place of abode where [the registrant] lives, whether permanent or temporary" where "certain activities of life occur." State v. Abshire, 363 N.C. 322 (2009); *see also* State v. Worley, 198 N.C. App. 329 (2009) (a registrant cannot avoid the obligation to register by "drifting" or by being homeless; for purposes of the sex offender registration statutes, everyone, at all times, has an address of some sort, even if it is a "homeless shelter, a location under a bridge or some similar place").

The evidence was sufficient to establish that the defendant changed his address when, among other things, a neighbor at the new address testified that the defendant stayed in an upstairs apartment every day and evening and although the defendant claimed that he had not moved from his father's address, his father told an officer that the defendant had moved. State v. Fox, ___ N.C. App. ___, 716 S.E.2d 261 (2011).

If a person fails to report in person and provide a written verification indicating whether he or she still resides at the last reported address or has a new address, the sheriff must make a reasonable attempt to verify that the person is residing at the registration address. If the person cannot be found at the registered address, he or she is subject to the penalties in the failure to register statute, unless he or she reports in person to the sheriff and proves that he or she has not moved. G.S. 14-208.9A(a)(4).

Element (3)(c). G.S. 14-208.9A is reproduced above. In order to be convicted for failure to return the verification form, a defendant must actually have received the form. State v. Braswell, ___ N.C. App. ___, 692 S.E.2d 435, 437 (2010).

Element (3)(d). The verification requirements are in G.S. 14-208.9A, reproduced above.

Element (3)(e). The notification requirements for changes in academic status are set forth in G.S. 14-208.9(c), reproduced above.

Element (3)(f). The notification requirements for changes in employment at an institution of higher education are set forth in G.S. 14-208.9(d), reproduced above.

Element (3)(g). G.S. 14-208.7, -208.9, and -208.9A are reproduced above.

Element (3)(h). G.S. 14-208.9 is reproduced above.

Element (3)(i). G.S. 14-208.8A is reproduced above.

Element (3)(j). See G.S. 14-208.7(b)(7) and -208.9(e), reproduced above, for the requirements of providing online identifier information. "Online identifier" means an electronic mail address, instant message screen name, user ID, or chat or other Internet communication name. G.S. 14-208.6(1n). It does not include Social Security number, date of birth, or pin number. *Id.* G.S. 14-208.6, reproduced above, contains definitions of the terms "electronic mail," "instant message," and "Internet."

Constitutionality. Requiring a person adjudicated as an incompetent to notify a sheriff of a change of address is unconstitutional. State v. Young, 140 N.C. App. 1 (2000). A defendant's conviction for failing to register as a sex offender when he moved from South Carolina (where he was registered as a sex offender) to North Carolina did not violate the Due Process Clause of the federal Constitution because a defendant need not be provided with actual notice of the duty to register under these circumstances. State v. Bryant, 359 N.C. 554 (2005). The fact that the defendant's duty to register was based on a conviction of an offense that occurred before the enactment of the sex offender registration law does not violate the ex post facto provisions of the federal and state constitutions. State v. White, 162 N.C. App. 183 (2004). Article 27A of the North Carolina General Statutes does not violate Article XI, Section 1, of the North Carolina Constitution. State v. Sakobie, 165 N.C. App. 447 (2004).

Incarcerated defendants. G.S. 14-208.11(c) provides that a person who is unable to meet the registration or verification requirements shall be deemed to have complied with its requirements if (1) the person is incarcerated in, or is in the custody of, a local, state, private, or federal correctional facility; (2) the person notifies the official in charge of the facility of his or her status as a person with a legal obligation or requirement under the Article; and (3) the person meets the registration or verification requirements of G.S. 14-208.11(c) no later than ten days after release from confinement or custody.

Charging issues. See this note to "First-Degree Forcible Rape," above. *See also* State v. Abshire, 192 N.C. App. 594 (2008) (indictment charging failure to give notice of change of address was not deficient when it alleged "on or about" a four-day period).

Multiple convictions and punishments. Double jeopardy does not bar a prosecution under G.S. 14-208.11 for failing to notify the sheriff of a change in address when the defendant already has had his or her post-release supervision revoked for the same conduct. State v. Sparks, 362 N.C. 181 (2008).

Related Offenses Not in This Chapter

Name change by sex offender. G.S. 14-202.6.
Prohibit baby sitting service by sex offender or in the home of a sex offender. G.S. 14-321.1.
Sex offender's failure to appear for additional photograph. G.S. 14-208.9A(c).

Assisting a Violator of Registration Obligations in Eluding Arrest

Statute

See G.S. 14-208.11A(a), reproduced above.

Elements

A person guilty of this offense

(1) has reason to believe that an offender is in violation of the sex offender registration laws *and*
(2) intends to assist the offender in eluding arrest *and*
(3) (a) withholds information from or fails to notify a law enforcement agency about the offender's noncompliance and, if known, the offender's whereabouts,
(b) harbors, attempts to harbor, or assists another person in harboring or attempting to harbor the offender,
(c) conceals, or attempts to conceal, or assists another person in concealing or attempting to conceal the offender, *or*
(d) provides information to a law enforcement agency regarding the offender that the person knows to be false.

Punishment

Class H felony. G.S. 14-208.11A(a).

Notes

Element (1). See the note entitled "Generally" and the note on Element (1) to "Failure to Register, etc. as a Sex Offender," above.

Attempt. Elements (3)(a) and (b) include attempts to do the listed conduct, making an attempt to do the act punishable like the completed offense as opposed to at a lower level, as is generally the case for attempt. See "Attempt" in Chapter 5 (General Crimes).

Incarcerated defendants. This offense does not apply if the offender is incarcerated in or is in the custody of a local, state, private, or federal correctional facility. G.S. 14-208.11A(b).

Related Offenses Not in This Chapter

"Accessory after the Fact to a Felony" (Chapter 5)

"Compounding a Felony" (Chapter 5)
"Obstruction of Justice" (Chapter 21)
"False Report to Law Enforcement Agencies or Officers" (Chapter 21)
"Resisting, Delaying, or Obstructing an Officer" (Chapter 21)

Knowingly Residing Near a School or Child Care Center

Statute

See G.S. 14-208.16(a), reproduced above.

Elements

A person guilty of this offense

(1) is required to register as a sex offender *and*
(2) knowingly
(3) resides
(4) within 1,000 feet of the property
(5) on which any school or child care center is located.

Punishment

Class G felony. G.S. 14-208.16(f).

Notes

Element (1). See the note entitled "Generally" and the note on Element (1) to "Failure to Register, etc. as a Sex Offender," above.

Element (2). See "Knowingly" in Chapter 1 (States of Mind).

Element (5). The statute covers public and nonpublic schools. G.S. 14-208.16(a). The term "school" does not include home schools or institutions of higher education. G.S. 14-208.16(b).

The term "child care center" is defined by G.S. 110-86(3) as "an arrangement where, at any one time, there are three or more preschool-age children or nine or more school-age children receiving child care." The term "child care" is defined in G.S. 110-86(2). As used in this statute, the term "child care center" does not include child care centers located on or within 1,000 feet of an institution of higher education where the registrant is a student or is employed. G.S. 14-208.16(c).

Exceptions. Charges cannot be based on changes in the ownership of or use of property that occur after the person establishes residency. G.S. 14-208.16(d). Residency is established when the person required to register does any of the following:

- purchases the residence or enters into a specifically enforceable contract to purchase the residence;
- enters into a written lease contract for the residence and for as long as the person is lawfully entitled to remain on the premises; or
- resides with an immediate family member who established residence in accordance with this subsection.

G.S. 14-208.16(d). An "immediate family member" means a child or sibling who is 18 years of age or older, or a parent, grandparent, legal guardian, or spouse of the registrant. *Id.*

This offense does not apply to individuals who established a residence before December 1, 2006. S.L. 2006-247, sec. 11(c).

Related Offenses Not in This Chapter

None

Working or Volunteering in Activities Involving Instruction, Supervision, or Care of Minors

Statute

See G.S. 14-208.17(a), reproduced above.

Elements

A person guilty of this offense

(1) is required to register as a sex offender *and*
(2) works or volunteers
(3) at any place where a minor is present *and*
(4) the person's responsibilities or activities include instruction, supervision, or care of a minor.

Punishment

Class F felony. G.S. 14-208.17(c).

Notes

Element (1). See the note entitled "Generally" and the note on Element (1) to "Failure to Register, etc. as a Sex Offender," above.

Element (3). Because the statute does not specify the minor's age, the general definition of "minor" in G.S. 48A-2 (a person under 18 years of age) probably applies to this offense.

Related Offenses Not in This Chapter

Prohibit baby sitting service by sex offender or in the home of sex offender. G.S. 14-321.1.

Caring for a Minor When a Sex Offender Resides in the Same Location

Statute

See G.S. 14-208.17(b), reproduced above.

Elements

A person guilty of this offense

(1) conducts any activity at his or her residence
(2) where the person accepts a minor into his or her care or custody
(3) knowing
(4) that a person required to register as a sex offender resides in the same location.

Punishment

Class F felony. G.S. 14-208.17(c)

Notes

Element (2). See the note on Element (3) to "Working or Volunteering in Activities Involving Instruction, Supervision, or Care of Minors," above.

Element (4). See the note entitled "Generally" and the note on Element (1) to "Failure to Register, etc. as a Sex Offender," above.

Related Offenses Not in This Chapter

Prohibit baby sitting service by sex offender or in the home of sex offender. G.S. 14-321.1.

Being Present at a Location Used by Minors

Statute

See G.S. 14-208.18, reproduced above.

Elements

A person guilty of this offense

(1) is required to register as a sex offender
(2) because of a conviction for any
  (a) rape, sexual offense, sexual battery, or related offense in G.S. Ch. 14 Art. 7A *or*
  (b) offense in which the victim was less than 16 years old *and*
(3) knowingly
(4) is present
  (a) on the premises of any place intended primarily for the use, care, or supervision of minors, including schools, children's museums, child care centers, nurseries, and playgrounds;
  (b) within 300 feet of any location intended primarily for the use, care, or supervision of minors when the place is located on premises that are not intended primarily for the use, care, or supervision of minors, including malls, shopping centers, or other property open to the general public; *or*
  (c) at any place where minors gather for regularly scheduled educational, recreational, or social programs.

Punishment

Class H felony. G.S. 14-208.18(h).

Notes

Element (1). See the note entitled "Generally" and the note on Element (1) to "Failure to Register, etc. as a Sex Offender," above.

Element (3). See "Knowingly" in Chapter 1 (States of Mind).

Element (4). The statute provides that the defendant may not "be" at the specified locations.

Exceptions. The statute contains explicit exceptions for when a person is present at a specified location related to medical treatment, voting, or school. G.S. 14-208.18(b), (d)–(g).

Related Offenses Not in This Chapter

None

Accessing a Social Networking Site

Statute

§14-202.5. Ban use of commercial social networking Web sites by sex offenders.

(a) Offense.—It is unlawful for a sex offender who is registered in accordance with Article 27A of Chapter 14 of the General Statutes to access a commercial social networking Web site where the sex offender knows that the site permits minor children to become members or to create or maintain personal Web pages on the commercial social networking Web site.

(b) For the purposes of this section, a "commercial social networking Web site" is an Internet Web site that meets all of the following requirements:

(1) Is operated by a person who derives revenue membership fees, advertising, or other sources related to the operation of the Web site.

(2) Facilitates the social introduction between two or more persons for the purposes of friendship, meeting other persons, or information exchanges.
(3) Allows users to create Web pages or personal profiles that contain information such as the name or nickname of the user, photographs placed on the personal Web page by the user, other personal information about the user, and links to other personal Web pages on the commercial social networking Web site of friends or associates of the user that may be accessed by other users or visitors to the Web site.
(4) Provides users or visitors to the commercial social networking Web site mechanisms to communicate with other users, such as a message board, chat room, electronic mail, or instant messenger.

(c) A commercial social networking Web site does not include an Internet Web site that either:

(1) Provides only one of the following discrete services: photo-sharing, electronic mail, instant messenger, or chat room or message board platform; or
(2) Has as its primary purpose the facilitation of commercial transactions involving goods or services between its members or visitors.

(d) Jurisdiction.—The offense is committed in the State for purposes of determining jurisdiction, if the transmission that constitutes the offense either originates in the State or is received in the State.

(e) Punishment.—A violation of this section is a Class I felony.

Elements

A person guilty of this offense

(1) is a sex offender who is required to register *and*
(2) accesses
(3) a commercial social networking website
(4) knowing that the site permits minors to become members or to create or maintain personal Web pages on the site.

Punishment

Class I felony. G.S. 14-202.5(e).

Notes

Element (1). See the note entitled "Generally" and the note on Element (1) to "Failure to Register, etc. as a Sex Offender," above.

Element (3). The term "commercial social networking Web site" is defined in G.S. 14-202.5(b). Exclusions are contained in G.S. 14-202.5(c).

Jurisdiction. The offense occurs in North Carolina if the transmission at issue either originates or is received in North Carolina. G.S. 14-202.5(d). See generally "Lack of Jurisdiction" in Chapter 2 (Bars and Defenses).

Related Offenses Not in This Chapter

None

Driving a Commercial Passenger Vehicle or School Bus Without P or S Endorsement

Statute

§20-27.1. Unlawful for sex offender to drive commercial passenger vehicle or school bus without appropriate commercial license or while disqualified.

A person who drives a commercial passenger vehicle or a school bus and who does not have a valid commercial drivers license with a P or S endorsement because the person was convicted of a violation that requires registration under Article 27A of Chapter 14 of the General Statutes is guilty of a Class F felony.

Elements

A person guilty of this offense

(1) drives
(2) (a) a commercial passenger vehicle *or*
 (b) a school bus *and*
(3) does not have a valid commercial drivers license with a P or S endorsement
(4) because the person was convicted of a violation that requires registration.

Punishment

Class F felony. G.S. 20-27.1.

Notes

Element (1). For the meaning of the term "drives," see the note on Element (1) to "Driving While License Revoked" in Chapter 28 (Motor Vehicle Offenses).

Element (2)(a). Although the terms "commercial motor vehicle" and "passenger vehicle" are defined in Chapter 20, *see* G.S. 20-4.01(3d) and (27), the term "commercial passenger vehicle" is not.

Element (2)(b). For the meaning of the term "school bus," see the note on Element (4) to "Passing or Failing to Stop for a Stopped School Bus" in Chapter 28 (Motor Vehicle Offenses).

Related Offenses Not in This Chapter

See the offenses in Chapter 28 (Motor Vehicle Offenses).
Knowingly falsely swear or affirm affidavit for DMV that affiant is not registered. G.S. 20-37.14A.

Failing to Enroll in a Satellite-Based Monitoring Program

Statute

See G.S. 14-208.44(a), reproduced above.

Elements

A person guilty of this offense

(1) is required to enroll in a satellite-based monitoring program *and*
(2) fails to enroll.

Punishment

Class F felony. G.S. 14-208.44(a).

Notes

Element (1). See G.S. 14-208.40 through 14-208.43 for enrollment and program requirements.

Element (2). "Enroll" includes appearing, as directed by the Department, to receive the necessary equipment. G.S. 14-208.44(d).

Related Offenses Not in This Chapter

Failing to provide information to or cooperate with the Department. G.S. 14-208.44(c).

Tampering with a Satellite-Based Monitoring Device

Statute

See G.S. 14-208.44(b), reproduced above.

Elements

A person guilty of this offense

(1) intentionally
(2) tampers with, removes, vandalizes, or otherwise interferes with the proper functioning of
(3) a device issued pursuant to a satellite-based monitoring program
(4) to a person duly enrolled in the program.

Punishment

Class E felony. G.S. 14-208.44(b).

Notes

Element (1). See "Intentionally" in Chapter 1 (States of Mind).

Elements (3) and (4). See the note on Elements (1) and (2) to "Failing to Enroll in a Satellite-Based Monitoring Program," above.

Related Offenses Not in This Chapter

Failing to provide information to or cooperate with the Department. G.S. 14-208.44(c).
Removing, destroying, etc., an electronic monitoring device. G.S. 14-226.3.

11

Crime against Nature, Incest, Indecent Exposure, and Related Offenses

11

Crime against Nature, Incest, Indecent Exposure, and Related Offenses

---

Crime against Nature

Statute

§14-177. Crime against nature.

If any person shall commit the crime against nature, with mankind or beast, he shall be punished as a Class I felon.

Elements

A person guilty of this offense

(1) commits a crime against nature.

Punishment

Class I felony. G.S. 14-177.

Notes

Element (1). Each of the following acts is an example of a crime against nature:

- the inserting, by a male, of his sexual organ into the mouth or anus of another male or a female, State v. Fenner, 166 N.C. 247 (1914); State v. Harward, 264 N.C. 746 (1965); State v. Copeland, 11 N.C. App. 516 (1971),
- the receiving, by a male or a female, of the sexual organ of a male into his or her mouth or anus, State v. Griffin, 175 N.C. 767 (1876); State v. Chance, 3 N.C. App. 459 (1969),
- fellatio (oral stimulation of the male sexual organ), State v. Poe, 40 N.C. App. 385 (1979),
- cunnilingus (penetration of the female sexual organ by the tongue), State v. Joyner, 295 N.C. 55 (1978),
- analingus (penetration of the anus by the tongue), and
- the inserting of an object into a person's genital opening, State v. Stiller, 162 N.C. App. 138 (2004).

While there are no North Carolina appellate cases on sexual acts with animals, the statute expressly includes "the crime against nature, with . . . [a] beast," which could be committed by a male or a female. G.S. 14-177.

Note that the penetration of the female sexual organ by the male sexual organ is not included, even though, depending on the facts, this act may violate other criminal offenses, such as rape or incest.

Constitutionality. In *Lawrence v. Texas,* 539 U.S. 558 (2003), the United States Supreme Court held that a state statute prohibiting people of the same sex from engaging in various sex acts violated the defendants' liberty interests protected by the Due Process Clause of the Fourteenth Amendment to the United States Constitution. The Court's ruling bars the State from prosecuting adults of the same or opposite sex for engaging in consensual sex acts in private. The ruling effectively overrules *Poe,* 40 N.C. App. 385 (constitutional right to privacy does not bar prosecution of unmarried people for crime against nature, consensual fellatio, done in private), and similar cases. However, the North Carolina courts have held that the crime against nature statute is not unconstitutional on its face under *Lawrence* and may be used to prosecute conduct involving a minor, nonconsensual or coercive sexual acts, conduct occurring in a public place, or conduct involving prostitution or solicitation. State v. Whiteley, 172 N.C. App. 772 (2005); State v. Pope, 168 N.C. App. 592 (2005).

Application of the crime against nature statute to a minor's consensual sexual activity with another minor does not violate the Due Process Clause of the Fourteenth Amendment to the United States Constitution. *In re* R.L.C., 361 N.C. 287 (2007).

Age. There is no age element for either the defendant or the victim. *See* State v. Griffin, 175 N.C. 767, 769 (1917) (the defendant was properly convicted despite his argument that the victim, a 9-year-old boy, had not attained the age of puberty so as to be capable of emission); *R.L.C.,* 361 N.C. 287 (the crime applies to consensual acts between minors, regardless of the age difference between the minors).

Consent. Some sexual offense crimes include force as an element. As such, the relevant conduct is never constitutionally protected. However, crime against nature does not include an element of force or lack of consent and thus can encompass constitutionally protected conduct. For example, if the relevant acts (fellatio, cunnilingus, etc.) occur between two consenting adults, in private and not for money, the conduct is constitutionally protected under *Lawrence v. Texas,* a case discussed in the note entitled "Constitutionality," above. As noted there, the crime against nature statute is not unconstitutional on its face under *Lawrence* and may be used to prosecute conduct involving a minor; nonconsensual or coercive sexual acts; conduct occurring in a public place; or conduct involving prostitution or solicitation. However, when the charge involves private conduct between adults not in public and not for money, *Lawrence* requires that the State prove lack of consent. State v. Hunt, ___ N.C. App. ___, 710 S.E.2d 339 (2011) (reversing the defendant's conviction for crime against nature based on private conduct with a 17-year-old female, not for money, the court concluded that there was insufficient evidence of lack of consent), *temp. stay allowed,* 708 S.E.2d 717 (2011).

Penetration required. Penetration of or by a sexual organ is required for this offense. State v. Whittemore, 255 N.C. 583 (1961); *In re* R.N., ___ N.C. App. ___, 696 S.E.2d 898 (2010). There was sufficient evidence of penetration when a 4-year-old victim licked an 11-year-old's penis. *In re* Heil, 145 N.C. App. 24 (2001). In contrast, evidence that a juvenile licked and put his mouth on the victim's private area and "touch[ed] . . . on her private parts" was insufficient to establish penetration, as was evidence that he forced the victim's head down to his privates and that she saw his private area. *R.N.,* ___ N.C. App. ___, 696 S.E.2d at 902.

Note that for first- or second-degree sexual offense, discussed in Chapter 10 (Sexual Assaults), based on the act of cunnilingus, penetration is not required; stimulation by tongue or lips of any part of the woman's genitalia is sufficient. State v. Ludlum, 303 N.C. 666 (1981).

Attempt. Previous law provided that an attempt to commit a crime against nature was punishable the same as if a defendant had actually committed the offense. State v. Spivey, 213 N.C. 45

(1938). However, under Structured Sentencing, an attempt to commit this offense is punished as a Class 1 misdemeanor. G.S. 14-2.5.

Greater and lesser-included offenses. As discussed in this note to "First-Degree Forcible Rape" in Chapter 10 (Sexual Assaults), crime against nature is not a lesser-included offense of forcible or statutory rape or sexual offense.

Crime against nature is not a lesser-included offense of "Sexual Activity by a Substitute Parent" or "Sexual Activity by a Custodian," both in Chapter 10 (Sexual Assaults). State v. Hoover, 89 N.C. App. 199 (1988).

Indecent liberties with a child is not a lesser-included offense of crime against nature. State v. Williams, 303 N.C. 507 (1981); State v. Etheridge, 319 N.C. 34 (1987).

Multiple convictions and punishments. Double jeopardy does not preclude simultaneous convictions for rape (forcible or statutory), sexual offense, indecent liberties with a child, crime against nature, and incest arising out of the same transaction. *Etheridge*, 319 N.C. 34; State v. Fletcher, 322 N.C. 415 (1988).

Relation to other offenses. Crime against nature differs from "Indecent Liberties with a Child," discussed in Chapter 10 (Sexual Assaults), in the following ways: (1) the age of the person upon or with whom the defendant commits this offense is irrelevant; for indecent liberties, the victim must be a child under 16 and the defendant must be at least 16 and at least five years older than the victim; (2) indecent liberties includes penetration of the female sexual organ by the male sexual organ, while crime against nature does not; (3) indecent liberties includes some sexual acts not included in crime against nature, such as various sexual acts that do not involve penetration of the mouth, anus, or female sexual organ—for example, rubbing private parts and fondling breasts.

Crime against nature differs from "Sexual Activity by a Substitute Parent," discussed in Chapter 10 (Sexual Assaults), in two ways: (1) penetration of or by the sexual organ is an essential element of crime against nature but not of sexual activity by a substitute parent; and (2) sexual activity by a substitute parent requires that the sexual act be performed by a person who has "assumed the role of parent" to the victim, which is not an element of crime against nature. *Hoover*, 89 N.C. App. 199.

Sex offender registration. This offense does not trigger the statutory requirements for registration as a sex offender.

Related Offenses Not in This Chapter

"Assault on a Female" (Chapter 7)
See child abuse (various offenses) in Chapter 9 (Abuse and Neglect).
See the offenses in Chapter 10 (Sexual Assaults).
See the offenses in Chapter 23 (Prostitution).
See the offenses in Chapter 24 (Obscenity, Exploitation of a Minor, and Adult Establishment Offenses).

Incest Offenses

Statute

§14-178. Incest.

(a) Offense.—A person commits the offense of incest if the person engages in carnal intercourse with the person's (i) grandparent or grandchild, (ii) parent or child or stepchild or legally adopted child, (iii) brother or sister of the half or whole blood, or (iv) uncle, aunt, nephew, or niece.

(b) Punishment and Sentencing.—

(1) A person is guilty of a Class B1 felony if either of the following occurs:

a. The person commits incest against a child under the age of 13 and the person is at least 12 years old and is at least four years older than the child when the incest occurred.

b. The person commits incest against a child who is 13, 14, or 15 years old and the person is at least six years older than the child when the incest occurred.

(2) A person is guilty of a Class C felony if the person commits incest against a child who is 13, 14, or 15 and the person is more than four but less than six years older than the child when the incest occurred.

(3) In all other cases of incest, the parties are guilty of a Class F felony.

(c) No Liability for Children Under 16.—No child under the age of 16 is liable under this section if the other person is at least four years older when the incest occurred.

Incest

Statute

See G.S. 14-178(a), reproduced above.

Elements

A person guilty of this offense

(1) has sexual intercourse with his or her
(2) (a) grandparent or grandchild,
(b) parent, child, stepchild, or legally adopted child,
(c) brother or sister of the half or whole blood, *or*
(d) uncle, aunt, nephew, or niece, *and*
(3) the person knows of that relationship.

Punishment

Class F felony. G.S. 14-178(b)(3).

Notes

Element (1). The statute describes the required act as "carnal intercourse." Courts have treated this term interchangeably with "sexual intercourse," State v. Collins, 44 N.C. App. 27 (1979), and have held that incest requires only the slightest penetration of the female sexual organ by the male sexual organ, State v. Bruce, 315 N.C. 273 (1985).

Element (2)(b). Case law interpreting an earlier version of this statute held that a "child" includes an illegitimate child, State v. Wood, 235 N.C. 636 (1952), and that uncorroborated testimony of the child alone can support conviction, State v. Vincent, 278 N.C. 63 (1971).

The evidence was sufficient to establish paternity when the victim testified that the defendant was her biological father and identified him in open court; the victim's birth certificate, clearly identifying the defendant as the victim's father, was admitted into evidence;

and the defendant testified that he sought to be a "cool dad" to the victim. State v. Ware, 188 N.C. App. 790 (2008).

Element (3). Cases decided under an earlier version of this statute required proof that the defendant knew of the relationship. *Vincent*, 278 N.C. 63; *Collins*, 44 N.C. App. 27.

Exceptions. A child under 16 years old is not guilty of incest if the other person involved was at least four years older than the child when the incest occurred. G.S. 14-178(c).

Greater and lesser-included offenses. Cases interpreting an earlier version of this statute held that "Indecent Liberties with a Child," discussed in Chapter 10 (Sexual Assaults), is not a lesser-included offense of incest. State v. Etheridge, 319 N.C. 34 (1987).

Multiple convictions and punishments. Multiple acts of incest support multiple convictions of incest. State v. Shelton, 167 N.C. App. 225 (2004).

Sex offender registration. This offense is a sexually violent offense triggering registration requirements under the sex offender registration statutes. G.S. 14-208.6(5).

Related Offenses Not in This Chapter

See the offenses listed under "Crime against Nature," above.

Incest with a Child under 13

Statute

See G.S. 14-178(a) and (b)(1)a, reproduced above.

Elements

A person guilty of this offense

(1) is at least 12 years old *and*
(2) commits incest with
(3) a child under 13 years old, *and*
(4) the person is at least four years older than the child.

Punishment

Class B1 felony. G.S. 14-178(b)(1). For special maximums that apply to defendants convicted of Class B1–E felonies that are reportable convictions under the sex offender registration program, see "Sex offenders" under "Special Provisions" in the discussion of felony sentencing in Chapter 4 (Punishment under Structured Sentencing).

Notes

Element (2). See "Incest," above.

Exceptions. See this note to "Incest," above.

Greater and lesser-included offenses. See this note to "Incest," above.

Multiple convictions and punishments. See this note to "Incest," above.

Relation to other offenses. Except for the required relationship between the perpetrator and the child and the fact that the perpetrator must know of that relationship, this offense is similar to "First-Degree Statutory Rape," discussed in Chapter 10 (Sexual Assaults).

Sex offender registration. This offense is a sexually violent offense triggering registration requirements under the sex offender registration statutes. G.S. 14-208.6(5).

Related Offenses Not in This Chapter

See the offenses listed under "Crime against Nature," above.

Incest with a Child Who Is 13, 14, or 15 Years Old by a Defendant Who Is at Least Six Years Older Than the Victim

Statute

See G.S. 14-178(a) and (b)(1)b, reproduced above.

Elements

A person guilty of this offense

(1) commits incest with
(2) a child who is 13, 14, or 15 years old *and*
(3) the person is at least six years older than the child.

Punishment

Class B1 felony. G.S. 14-178(b)(1).

Notes

Element (1). See "Incest," above.

Greater and lesser-included offenses. See this note to "Incest," above.

Multiple convictions and punishments. See this note to "Incest," above.

Relation to other offenses. Except for the required relationship between the perpetrator and the victim and the fact that the defendant must know of that relationship, this offense is similar to "Statutory Rape of a Person Who Is 13, 14, or 15 Years Old by a Defendant Who Is at Least Six Years Older Than the Victim," discussed in Chapter 10 (Sexual Assaults).

Sex offender registration. This offense is a sexually violent offense triggering registration requirements under the sex offender registration statutes. G.S. 14-208.6(5).

Related Offenses Not in This Chapter

See the offenses listed under "Crime against Nature," above.

Incest with a Child Who Is 13, 14, or 15 Years Old by a Defendant Who Is More Than Four but Less Than Six Years Older Than the Victim

Statute

See G.S. 14-178(a) and (b)(2), reproduced above.

Elements

A person guilty of this offense

(1) commits incest with
(2) a child who is 13, 14, or 15 years old *and*
(3) the person is more than four but less than six years older than the child.

Punishment

Class C felony. G.S. 14-178(b)(2). See the additional discussion in "Punishment" under "Incest with a Child under 13," above.

Notes

Element (1). See "Incest," above.

Greater and lesser-included offenses. See this note to "Incest," above.

Multiple convictions and punishments. See this note to "Incest," above.

Relation to other offenses. Except for the required relationship between the perpetrator and the victim and the fact that the defendant must know of that relationship, this offense is similar to "Statutory Rape of a Person Who Is 13, 14, or 15 Years Old by a Defendant Who Is More Than Four but Less Than Six Years Older Than the Victim," discussed in Chapter 10 (Sexual Assaults).

Sex offender registration. This offense is a sexually violent offense triggering registration requirements under the sex offender registration statutes. G.S. 14-208.6(5).

Related Offenses Not in This Chapter

See the offenses listed under "Crime against Nature," above.

Bigamy

Statute

§14-183. Bigamy.

If any person, being married, shall marry any other person during the life of the former husband or wife, every such offender, and every person counseling, aiding or abetting such offender, shall be punished as a Class I felon. Any such offense may be dealt with, tried, determined and punished in the county where the offender shall be apprehended, or be in custody, as if the offense had been actually committed in that county. If any person, being married, shall contract a marriage with any other person outside of this State, which marriage would be punishable as bigamous if contracted within this State, and shall thereafter cohabit with such person in this State, he shall be guilty of a felony and shall be punished as in cases of bigamy. Nothing contained in this section shall extend to any person marrying a second time, whose husband or wife shall have been continually absent from such person for the space of seven years then last past, and shall not have been known by such person to have been living within that time; nor to any person who at the time of such second marriage shall have been lawfully divorced from the bond of the first marriage; nor to any person whose former marriage shall have been declared void by the sentence of any court of competent jurisdiction.

Elements

A person guilty of this offense

(1) is a married person *and*

(2) (a) marries another person in this state *or*

(b) marries another person outside this state and thereafter cohabits with that person in this state.

Punishment

Class I felony. G.S. 14-183.

Notes

Element (1). The statute does not apply to someone (1) whose spouse has died or been absent and not known to be living for seven years; or (2) whose marriage has been dissolved by an annulment or a divorce. The defendant's belief that his or her divorce or annulment is valid is apparently no defense to this charge if the divorce was in fact invalid (for example, because the person who was granted the divorce was not a resident of the state in which it was obtained). State v. Williams, 224 N.C. 183 (1944).

Element (2). If a person who is already married "marries" again—that is, goes through a marriage ceremony with someone else—this second "marriage" is legally invalid. North Carolina law cannot forbid the second "marriage" if it takes place in another state, but bigamy is committed if the "married" couple thereafter cohabits (lives together as husband and wife) in North Carolina.

The validity of a marriage must be proved by the State and must be determined by the law of the state in which the ceremony was performed. A common law marriage is not valid in North Carolina. State v. Lynch, 301 N.C. 479 (1980). A ceremony solemnized by a Roman Catholic layman who bought for $10 a mail order certificate giving him ministerial status in the Universal Life Church was not a ceremony of marriage to be recognized in a bigamy prosecution. *Id.* A ceremony conducted by an assistant pastor who was not an ordained minister or a magistrate but who was authorized by his church to perform marriages was a ceremony of marriage to be recognized in a bigamy prosecution. State v. Woodruff, 99 N.C. App. 107 (1990).

Related Offenses Not in This Chapter

None

Fornication and Adultery

Statute

§14-184. Fornication and adultery.

If any man and woman, not being married to each other, shall lewdly and lasciviously associate, bed and cohabit together, they shall be guilty of a Class 2 misdemeanor: Provided, that the admissions or confessions of one shall not be received in evidence against the other.

Elements

A person guilty of this offense

(1) lewdly and lasciviously cohabits
(2) with a person to whom he or she is not married.

Punishment

Class 2 misdemeanor. G.S. 14-184.

Notes

Generally. This statute makes it a crime for a man and a woman, whether single or married, to cohabit if they are not married to each other. Each commits the offense. One party may be convicted even though the other is acquitted. State v. Cutshall, 109 N.C. 764 (1891).

Element (1). Cohabitation requires that the couple live together in the manner of husband and wife and have habitual sexual intercourse. A single act of intercourse is not enough to constitute this offense, State v. Davenport, 225 N.C. 13 (1945), but two weeks' cohabitation has been considered sufficient, State v. Kleiman, 241 N.C. 277 (1954).

Constitutionality. The North Carolina appellate courts have not yet considered the constitutionality of this statute in light of the United States Supreme Court's decision in *Lawrence v. Texas*, 539 U.S. 558 (2003). See "Constitutionality," under "Crime against Nature," above. At least one other state has held a fornication statute to be unconstitutional under *Lawrence*. Martin v. Ziherl, 607 S.E.2d 367 (Va. 2005).

Evidence issues. The statute provides "that the admissions or confessions of one [participant] shall not be received in evidence against the other." The courts have held that this language refers only to statements made out of court by either participant. State v. Davis, 229 N.C. 386 (1948). One participant may testify in court against the other, and statements made out of court by the participant then may be introduced to corroborate that participant's in-court testimony. Rarely is there any direct eyewitness testimony as to actual acts of intercourse, except by the participants themselves; a conviction of the offense can be supported entirely by circumstantial evidence. *Davenport*, 225 N.C. 13.

Related Offenses Not in This Chapter

Occupying hotel room for immoral purposes. G.S. 14-186.

Indecent Exposure

Statute

§14-190.9. Indecent exposure.

(a) Unless the conduct is punishable under subsection (a1) of this section, any person who shall willfully expose the private parts of his or her person in any public place and in the presence of any other person or persons, except for those places designated for a public purpose where the same sex exposure is incidental to a permitted activity, or aids or abets in any such act, or who procures another to perform such act; or any person, who as owner, manager, lessee, director, promoter or agent, or in any other capacity knowingly hires, leases or permits the land, building, or premises of which he is owner, lessee or tenant, or over which he has control, to be used for purposes of any such act, shall be guilty of a Class 2 misdemeanor.

(a1) Unless the conduct is prohibited by another law providing greater punishment, any person at least 18 years of age who shall willfully expose the private parts of his or her person in any public place in the presence of any other person less than 16 years of age for the purpose of arousing or gratifying sexual desire shall be guilty of a Class H felony. An offense committed under this subsection shall not be considered to be a lesser included offense under G.S. 14-202.1.

(b) Notwithstanding any other provision of law, a woman may breast feed in any public or private location where she is otherwise authorized to be, irrespective of whether the nipple of the mother's breast is uncovered during or incidental to the breast feeding.

(c) Notwithstanding any other provision of law, a local government may regulate the location and operation of sexually oriented businesses. Such local regulation may restrict or prohibit nude, seminude, or topless dancing to the extent consistent with the constitutional protection afforded free speech.

Misdemeanor Indecent Exposure

Statute

See G.S. 14-190.9(a), reproduced above.

Elements

A person guilty of this offense

(1) willfully
(2) (a) exposes, *or*
    (b) aids and abets or procures another to expose,

(3) his or her private parts
(4) in a public place *and*
(5) in the presence of another person.

Punishment

Class 2 misdemeanor. G.S. 14-190.9(a).

Notes

Element (1). See "Knowingly" in Chapter 1 (States of Mind).

Element (2)(a). The statute's specific mention of aiding and abetting seems unnecessary because aiders and abettors are always punished as if they were principals. See "Aiding and Abetting" in Chapter 3 (Participants in Crimes). When one "procures" another to commit a crime, he or she is generally understood to be an aider and abettor.

Element (3). Private parts include both the external organs of sex and of excretion—male and female genitalia and anus—but not buttocks. State v. Fly, 348 N.C. 556 (1998). The court of appeals has ruled that female breasts are not private parts. State v. Jones, 7 N.C. App. 166 (1970). *But see Fly*, 348 N.C. 556 (discussing *Jones*, 7 N.C. App. 166, but neither adopting nor rejecting that ruling). The statute provides that exposure of a woman's nipple during breast feeding is not a violation. G.S. 14-190.9(b).

Element (4). The statute specifically excludes from coverage "those places designated for a public purpose where the same sex exposure is incidental to a permitted activity." G.S. 14-190.9(a). Presumably such places would include locker rooms.

A public place is a place that is public as distinguished from private but not necessarily a place devoted to the uses of the public. State v. King, 268 N.C. 711 (1966); State v. Fusco, 136 N.C. App. 268 (1999). It is a place that is visited by many people and to which the public may have access. *King*, 268 N.C. 711; *Fusco*, 136 N.C. App. 268. A public place is also a place that is viewable from any location open to the view of the public at large. *Fusco*, 136 N.C. App. at 271. Exposing one's genitals to a person while lying on a creek embankment adjacent to a backyard was sufficient to support a conviction when evidence showed that the creek embankment was used by the public, nothing prevented anyone from walking through a private yard to get there, and "No Trespassing" signs were not posted anywhere along the creek. *Id.* Exposing one's genitals to a person while in a car in a shopping center parking lot or on a street is sufficient to support a conviction. State v. Lowery, 268 N.C. 162 (1966); *King*, 268 N.C. 711.

Element (5). It is not necessary that a person of the opposite sex actually see the defendant's private parts; it is sufficient if the private parts are exposed in the person's presence. State v. Fly, 348 N.C. 556, 561 (1998); *Fusco*, 136 N.C. App. 268.

Nude shows. Females who exhibited their private parts in a nightclub to males who paid a $5 admission charge and the nightclub operator who aided and abetted the women in doing this committed this offense. The exhibition need not be "obscene" within the meaning of G.S. 14-190.1(b) to violate this section. State v. King, 285 N.C. 305 (1974) (dicta).

Local regulation of sexually oriented businesses. A 1998 legislative amendment added subsection (c) to this statute so that local governments are not preempted by state law, *see, e.g.*, State v. Tenore, 280 N.C. 238 (1972), from regulating the local operation of sexually oriented businesses. Such regulation may restrict or prohibit nude, seminude, or topless dancing to the extent consistent with constitutional law protecting free speech.

Multiple convictions and punishments. A defendant may not be convicted of this offense and "Felony Indecent Exposure," discussed below. G.S. 14-190.9(a).

Sex offender registration. This offense does not trigger registration as a sex offender.

Related Offenses Not in This Chapter

"Stalking" (Chapter 8)
See the offenses in Chapter 10 (Sexual Assaults).
See the offenses in Chapter 23 (Prostitution).
See the offenses in Chapter 24 (Obscenity, Exploitation of a Minor, and Adult Establishment Offenses).

Use of Premises for Indecent Exposure

Statute

See G.S. 14-190.9(a), reproduced above.

Elements

A person guilty of this offense

(1) knowingly
(2) hires, leases, or permits
(3) land, building, or premises
(4) that the person owns, leases, or controls
(5) to be used for indecent exposure.

Punishment

Class 2 misdemeanor. G.S. 14-190.9(a).

Notes

Element (1). See "Knowingly" in Chapter 1 (States of Mind).

Element (5). See "Misdemeanor Indecent Exposure," above.

Related Offenses Not in This Chapter

See the offenses listed under "Misdemeanor Indecent Exposure," above.

Felony Indecent Exposure

Statute

See G.S. 14-190.9(a1), reproduced above.

Elements

A person guilty of this offense

(1) is at least 18 years of age *and*
(2) willfully
(3) exposes his or her private parts
(4) in a public place *and*
(5) in the presence of a person less than 16 years of age
(6) for the purpose of arousing or gratifying sexual desire.

Punishment

Class H felony. G.S. 14-190.9(a1).

Notes

Element (2). See "Willfully" in Chapter 1 (States of Mind).

Element (3). See this note to "Misdemeanor Indecent Exposure," above.

Element (4). See the note on Element (4) to "Misdemeanor Indecent Exposure," above.

Greater and lesser-included offenses. This offense is not a lesser-included offense of "Indecent Liberties with a Child," discussed in Chapter 10 (Sexual Assaults). G.S. 14-190.9(a1).

Multiple convictions and punishments. G.S. 14-190.9(a1) begins with the language, "Unless the conduct is prohibited by another law providing greater punishment." This language may mean that a defendant may not be convicted of this offense and another carrying a more serious punishment, based on the same act. See this note to "Assault Inflicting Serious Injury" in Chapter 7 (Assaults).

Sex offender registration. This offense is a sexually violent offense triggering registration requirements under the sex offender registration statutes. G.S. 14-208.6(5).

Related Offenses Not in This Chapter

See the offenses listed under "Misdemeanor Indecent Exposure," above.

Peeping

Statute

§14-202. Secretly peeping into room occupied by another person.

(a) Any person who shall peep secretly into any room occupied by another person shall be guilty of a Class 1 misdemeanor.

(a1) Unless covered by another provision of law providing greater punishment, any person who secretly or surreptitiously peeps underneath or through the clothing being worn by another person, through the use of a mirror or other device, for the purpose of viewing the body of, or the undergarments worn by, that other person without their consent shall be guilty of a Class 1 misdemeanor.

(b) For purposes of this section:

(1) The term "photographic image" means any photograph or photographic reproduction, still or moving, or any videotape, motion picture, or live television transmission, or any digital image of any individual.

(2) The term "room" shall include, but is not limited to, a bedroom, a rest room, a bathroom, a shower, and a dressing room.

(c) Unless covered by another provision of law providing greater punishment, any person who, while in possession of any device which may be used to create a photographic image, shall secretly peep into any room shall be guilty of a Class A1 misdemeanor.

(d) Unless covered by another provision of law providing greater punishment, any person who, while secretly peeping into any room, uses any device to create a photographic image of another person in that room for the purpose of arousing or gratifying the sexual desire of any person shall be guilty of a Class I felony.

(e) Any person who secretly or surreptitiously uses any device to create a photographic image of another person underneath or through the clothing being worn by that other person for the purpose of viewing the body of, or the undergarments worn by, that other person without their consent shall be guilty of a Class I felony.

(f) Any person who, for the purpose of arousing or gratifying the sexual desire of any person, secretly or surreptitiously uses or installs in a room any device that can be used to create a photographic image with the intent to capture the image of another without their consent shall be guilty of a Class I felony.

(g) Any person who knowingly possesses a photographic image that the person knows, or has reason to believe, was obtained in violation of this section shall be guilty of a Class I felony.

(h) Any person who disseminates or allows to be disseminated images that the person knows, or should have known, were obtained as a result of the violation of this section shall be guilty of a Class H felony if the dissemination is without the consent of the person in the photographic image.

(i) A second or subsequent felony conviction under this section shall be punished as though convicted of an offense one class higher. A second or subsequent conviction for a Class 1 misdemeanor shall be punished as a Class A1 misdemeanor. A second or subsequent conviction for a Class A1 misdemeanor shall be punished as a Class I felony.

(j) If the defendant is placed on probation as a result of violation of this section:

(1) For a first conviction under this section, the judge may impose a requirement that the defendant obtain a psychological evaluation and comply with any treatment recommended as a result of that evaluation.

(2) For a second or subsequent conviction under this section, the judge shall impose a requirement that the defendant obtain a psychological evaluation and comply with any treatment recommended as a result of that evaluation.

(k) Any person whose image is captured or disseminated in violation of this section has a civil cause of action against any person who captured or disseminated the image or procured any other person to capture or disseminate the image and is entitled to recover from those persons actual damages, punitive damages, reasonable attorneys' fees and other litigation costs reasonably incurred.

(l) When a person violates subsection (d), (e), (f), (g), or (h) of this section, or is convicted of a second or subsequent violation of subsection (a), (a1), or (c) of this section, the sentencing court shall consider whether the person is a danger to the community and whether requiring the person to register as a sex offender pursuant to Article 27A of this Chapter would further the purposes of that Article as stated in G.S. 14-208.5. If the sentencing court rules that the person is a danger to the community and that the person shall register, then an order shall be entered requiring the person to register.

(m) The provisions of subsections (a), (a1), (c), (e), (g), (h), and (k) of this section do not apply to:

(1) Law enforcement officers while discharging or attempting to discharge their official duties; or

(2) Personnel of the Department of Correction or of a local confinement facility for security purposes or during investigation of alleged misconduct by a person in the custody of the Department or the local confinement facility.

(n) This section does not affect the legal activities of those who are licensed pursuant to Chapter 74C, Private Protective Services, or Chapter 74D, Alarm Systems, of the General Statutes, who are legally engaged in the discharge of their official duties within their respective professions, and who are not engaging in activities for an improper purpose as described in this section.

Peeping into a Room Occupied by Another

Statute

See G.S. 14-202(a), reproduced above.

Elements

A person guilty of this offense

(1) peeps secretly
(2) into a room
(3) occupied by another person.

Punishment

Class 1 misdemeanor. G.S. 14-202(a). A second or subsequent conviction is punished as a Class A1 misdemeanor. G.S. 14-202(i). See G.S. 15A-928 for the rules regarding pleading and proving prior convictions.

Special sentencing provisions apply to peeping offenses. Under G.S. 14-202(j), if the defendant is placed on probation for a first conviction, the judge may impose a requirement that the defendant obtain a psychological evaluation and comply with any treatment recommended as a result of that evaluation. If the defendant is placed on probation for a second or subsequent conviction, the judge must impose a requirement that the defendant obtain a psychological evaluation and comply with any treatment recommended as a result of that evaluation.

Notes

Element (1). To "peep" means to "look cautiously or slyly—as if through a crevice—out from chinks and knotholes." In one case, looking through a window into a room occupied by a woman was held to be "peeping"; the venetian blind on the window (with its slats closed) was 6 to 10 inches short of the window sill and the defendant looked through this gap with his face pressing against the window screen. State v. Bivins, 262 N.C. 93 (1964). Peeping must be intentional and for the purpose of invading the privacy of the occupant of the room. *In re* Banks, 295 N.C. 236 (1978).

Element (2). A "room" includes, but is not limited to, a bedroom, a rest room, a bathroom, a shower, and a dressing room. G.S. 14-202(b)(2).

Charging issues. The person in the room must be identified by name in the charging instrument. State v. Banks, 263 N.C. 784 (1965).

Gender neutral. This offense may be committed by a male or a female.

Constitutionality. The prior version of this subsection was held not to be unconstitutionally vague. *In re* Banks, 295 N.C. 236.

Exceptions. Subsections (a), (a1), (c), (e), (g), (h), and (k) do not apply to certain law enforcement, corrections, and detention activities. G.S. 14-202(m). The entire section is inapplicable to the legal activities of certain licensed individuals. G.S. 14-202(n).

Sex offender registration. When a person violates subsection G.S. 14-202(d), (e), (f), (g), or (h) or is convicted of a second or subsequent violation of G.S. 14-202(a), (a1), or (c), the sentencing court must consider whether the person is a danger to the community and whether requiring the person to register as a sex offender pursuant to Article 27A of G.S. Chapter 14 would further the purposes of that Article as stated in G.S. 14-208.5. G.S. 14-202(l). If the sentencing court rules that the person is a danger to the community and that the person must register, then an order must be entered requiring the person to register. *Id.* If such an order is entered, the conviction of this offense is treated as a reportable conviction under the sex offender registration program. G.S. 14-208.6(4)d.

The portion of the statute requiring the court to consider whether the defendant must register as a sex offender is not constitutionally vague. State v. Pell, ___ N.C. App. ___, ___ S.E.2d ___ (Apr. 19, 2011). The court's determination must, however, be supported by competent evidence. *See id.* (court's findings not supported by record evidence when the defendant was deemed to have low to moderate risk of reoffending and testimony indicated that the defendant's depression, alcohol abuse, and paraphelia were in remission).

Civil cause of action. G.S. 14-202(f) provides for a civil cause of action for any person whose image is captured or disseminated in violation of the statute.

Related Offenses Not in This Chapter

See the offenses listed under "Misdemeanor Indecent Exposure," above.

Peeping underneath or through Clothing

Statute

See G.S. 14-202(a1), reproduced above.

Elements

A person guilty of this offense

(1) peeps secretly
(2) underneath or through clothing being worn by another
(3) using a mirror or other device
(4) for the purpose of viewing the other person's body or undergarments *and*
(5) without that person's consent.

Punishment

Class 1 misdemeanor. G.S. 14-202(a1). A second or subsequent conviction is punished as a Class A1 misdemeanor. G.S. 14-202(i). See G.S. 15A-928 for the rules regarding pleading and proving prior convictions. See the additional discussion of special sentencing provisions that apply to peeping offenses under this note to "Peeping into a Room Occupied by Another," above.

Notes

Element (1). See the note on Element (1) to "Peeping into a Room Occupied by Another," above.

Gender neutral. This offense may be committed by a male or a female.

Exceptions. See this note to "Peeping into a Room Occupied by Another," above.

Sex offender registration. See this note to "Peeping into a Room Occupied by Another," above.

Civil cause of action. See this note to "Peeping into a Room Occupied by Another," above.

Related Offenses Not in This Chapter

See the offenses listed under "Misdemeanor Indecent Exposure," above.

Peeping while Possessing a Device Capable of Creating a Photographic Image

Statute

See G.S. 14-202(c), reproduced above.

Elements

A person guilty of this offense

(1) peeps secretly
(2) into any room
(3) while in possession of any device which may be used to create a photographic image.

Punishment

Class A1 misdemeanor. G.S. 14-202(c). A second or subsequent conviction is punished as a Class I felony. G.S. 14-202(i). See G.S. 15A-928 for the rules regarding pleading and proving prior convictions. For special sentencing provisions that apply to peeping offenses, see "Punishment" under "Peeping into a Room Occupied by Another," above.

Notes

Elements (1) and (2). See these notes to "Peeping into a Room Occupied by Another," above.

Element (3). The term "photographic image" means any photograph or photographic reproduction, still or moving, or any videotape, motion picture, or live television transmission, or any digital image of any individual. G.S. 14-202(b)(1).

Gender neutral. This offense may be committed by a male or a female.

Exceptions. See this note to "Peeping into a Room Occupied by Another," above.

Multiple convictions and punishments. G.S. 14-202(c) begins with the language, "Unless covered by another provision of law providing greater punishment." This language may be interepreted to mean that a defendant may not be convicted of this offense and a more serious one, based on the same conduct. See this note to "Assault Inflicting Serious Injury" in Chapter 7 (Assaults).

Sex offender registration. See this note to "Peeping into a Room Occupied by Another," above.

Civil cause of action. See this note to "Peeping into a Room Occupied by Another," above.

Related Offenses Not in This Chapter

See the offenses listed under "Misdemeanor Indecent Exposure," above.

Peeping Using a Photographic Imaging Device

Statute

See G.S. 14-202(d), reproduced above.

Elements

A person guilty of this offense

(1) peeps secretly
(2) into any room
(3) while using any device to create a photographic image of another person in that room
(4) for the purpose of arousing or gratifying the sexual desire of any person.

Punishment

Class I felony. G.S. 14-202(d). A second or subsequent conviction is punished one class higher, G.S. 14-202(i). See G.S. 15A-928 for the rules regarding pleading and proving prior convictions. For special sentencing provisions that apply to peeping offenses, see "Punishment" under "Peeping into a Room Occupied by Another," above.

Notes

Element (1). See the note on Element (1) to "Peeping into a Room Occupied by Another," above.

Element (2). See the note on Element (2) to "Peeping into a Room Occupied by Another," above.

Element (3). See the note on Element (3) to "Peeping While Possessing a Device Capable of Creating a Photographic Image," above.

Gender neutral. This offense may be committed by a male or a female.

Exceptions. See this note to "Peeping into a Room Occupied by Another," above.

Multiple convictions and punishments. G.S. 14-202(d) begins with the language, "Unless covered by another provision of law providing greater punishment." This language may mean that a defendant may not be convicted of this offense and a more serious one, based on the same conduct. See this note to "Assault Inflicting Serious Injury" in Chapter 7 (Assaults).

Sex offender registration. See this note to "Peeping into a Room Occupied by Another," above.

Civil cause of action. See this note to "Peeping into a Room Occupied by Another," above.

Related Offenses Not in This Chapter

See the offenses listed under "Peeping into a Room Occupied by Another," above.

Secretly Using a Photographic Imaging Device to View Another's Body or Undergarments

Statute

See G.S. 14-202(e), reproduced above.

Elements

A person guilty of this offense

(1) secretly or surreptitiously
(2) uses any device
(3) to create a photographic image
(4) of another
(5) underneath or through the person's clothing
(6) for the purpose of viewing the person's body or undergarments *and*
(7) without the person's consent.

Punishment

Class I felony. G.S. 14-202(e). A second or subsequent conviction is punished one class higher, G.S. 14-202(i). See G.S. 15A-928 for the rules regarding pleading and proving prior convictions. For special sentencing provisions that apply to peeping offenses, see "Punishment" under "Peeping into a Room Occupied by Another," above.

Notes

Element (3). See the note on Element (3) to "Peeping While Possessing a Device Capable of Creating a Photographic Image," above.

Gender neutral. This offense may be committed by a male or a female.

Exceptions. See this note to "Peeping into a Room Occupied by Another," above.

Sex offender registration. See this note to "Peeping into a Room Occupied by Another," above.

Civil cause of action. See this note to "Peeping into a Room Occupied by Another," above.

Related Offenses Not in This Chapter

See the offenses listed under "Peeping into a Room Occupied by Another," above.

Secretly Using or Installing a Photographic Imaging Device to Arouse or Gratify Sexual Desire

Statute

See G.S. 14-202(f), reproduced above.

Elements

A person guilty of this offense

(1) secretly or surreptitiously *and*
(2) for the purpose of arousing the sexual desire of any person

(3) uses or installs
(4) in any room
(5) any device that can be used to create a photographic image
(6) with the intent to capture the image of another *and*
(7) without the person's consent.

Punishment

Class I felony. G.S. 14-202(f). A second or subsequent conviction is punished one class higher, G.S. 14-202(i). See G.S. 15A-928 for the rules regarding pleading and proving prior convictions. For special sentencing provisions that apply to peeping offenses, see "Punishment" under "Peeping into a Room Occupied by Another," above.

Notes

Element (5). See the note on Element (3) to "Peeping While Possessing a Device Capable of Creating a Photographic Image," above.

Gender neutral. This offense may be committed by a male or a female.

Exceptions. See this note to "Peeping into a Room Occupied by Another," above.

Sex offender registration. See this note to "Peeping into a Room Occupied by Another," above.

Civil cause of action. See this note to "Peeping into a Room Occupied by Another," above.

Related Offenses Not in This Chapter

See the offenses listed under "Peeping into a Room Occupied by Another," above.

Possessing a Photographic Image Obtained in Violation of the Peeping Statute

Statute

See G.S. 14-202(g), reproduced above.

Elements

A person guilty of this offense

(1) knowingly
(2) possesses
(3) a photographic image
(4) knowing or having reason to know
(5) that the image was obtained in violation G.S. 14-202.

Punishment

Class I felony. G.S. 14-202(g). A second or subsequent conviction is punished one class higher, G.S. 14-202(i). See G.S. 15A-928 for the rules regarding pleading and proving prior convictions. For special sentencing provisions that apply to peeping offenses, see "Punishment" under "Peeping into a Room Occupied by Another," above.

Notes

Element (3). See the note on Element (3) to "Peeping While Possessing a Device Capable of Creating a Photographic Image," above.

Element (5). See the peeping offenses discussed above and below.

Gender neutral. This offense may be committed by a male or a female.

Exceptions. See this note to "Peeping into a Room Occupied by Another," above.

Sex offender registration. See this note to "Peeping into a Room Occupied by Another," above.

Civil cause of action. See this note to "Peeping into a Room Occupied by Another," above.

Related Offenses Not in This Chapter

See the offenses listed under "Peeping into a Room Occupied by Another," above.

Disseminating Images Obtained in Violation of the Peeping Statute

Statute

See G.S. 14-202(h), reproduced above.

Elements

A person guilty of this offense

(1) disseminates or allows to be disseminated
(2) images
(3) that the person knows or should have known
(4) were obtained in violation of G.S. 14-202 *and*
(5) the dissemination is without the consent of the person in the image.

Punishment

Class H felony. G.S. 14-202(h). A second or subsequent conviction is punished one class higher, G.S. 14-202(i). See G.S. 15A-928 for the rules regarding pleading and proving prior convictions. For special sentencing provisions that apply to peeping offenses, see "Punishment" under "Peeping into a Room Occupied by Another," above.

Notes

Gender neutral. This offense may be committed by a male or a female.

Exceptions. See this note to "Peeping into a Room Occupied by Another," above.

Sex offender registration. See this note to "Peeping into a Room Occupied by Another," above.

Civil cause of action. See this note to "Peeping into a Room Occupied by Another," above.

Related Offenses Not in This Chapter

See the offenses listed under "Misdemeanor Indecent Exposure," above.

12

Kidnapping and Related Offenses

12
Kidnapping and Related Offenses

First-Degree Kidnapping

Statute

§14-39. Kidnapping.

(a) Any person who shall unlawfully confine, restrain, or remove from one place to another, any other person 16 years of age or over without the consent of such person, or any other person under the age of 16 years without the consent of a parent or legal custodian of such person, shall be guilty of kidnapping if such confinement, restraint or removal is for the purpose of:

(1) Holding such other person for a ransom or as a hostage or using such other person as a shield; or
(2) Facilitating the commission of any felony or facilitating flight of any person following the commission of a felony; or
(3) Doing serious bodily harm to or terrorizing the person so confined, restrained or removed or any other person; or
(4) Holding such other person in involuntary servitude in violation of G.S. 14-43.12.
(5) Trafficking another person with the intent that the other person be held in involuntary servitude or sexual servitude in violation of G.S. 14-43.11.
(6) Subjecting or maintaining such other person for sexual servitude in violation of G.S. 14-43.13.

(b) There shall be two degrees of kidnapping as defined by subsection (a). If the person kidnapped either was not released by the defendant in a safe place or had been seriously injured or sexually assaulted, the offense is kidnapping in the first degree and is punishable as a Class C felony. If the person kidnapped was released in a safe place by the defendant and had not been seriously injured or sexually assaulted, the offense is kidnapping in the second degree and is punishable as a Class E felony.

(c) Any firm or corporation convicted of kidnapping shall be punished by a fine of not less than five thousand dollars ($5,000) nor more than one hundred thousand dollars ($100,000), and its charter and right to do business in the State of North Carolina shall be forfeited.

Elements

A person guilty of this offense

(1) (a) confines,
(b) restrains, *or*
(c) removes from one place to another
(2) a person

(3) (a) without the person's consent *or,*
(b) if the person is under 16, without consent of the person's parent or guardian,
(4) for the purpose of
(a) holding the victim as hostage,
(b) holding the victim for ransom,
(c) using the victim as a shield,
(d) facilitating the commission of a felony,
(e) facilitating flight following the commission of a felony,
(f) doing serious bodily harm to the victim or any other person,
(g) terrorizing the victim or any other person,
(h) holding the victim in involuntary servitude in violation of G.S. 14-43.12,
(i) trafficking another person in violation of G.S. 14-43.11, *or*
(j) subjecting or maintaining the victim for sexual servitude in violation of G.S. 14-43.13 *and*
(5) (a) does not release the victim in a safe place,
(b) seriously injures the victim, *or*
(c) sexually assaults the victim.

Punishment

Class C felony. G.S. 14-39(b). Any firm or corporation convicted of kidnapping will be fined not less than $5,000 or more than $100,000 and will forfeit its charter and right to do business in North Carolina. G.S. 14-39(c).

For a discussion of special maximums that apply to defendants convicted of Class B1–E felonies that are reportable convictions under the sex offender registration program, see "Sex offenders" under "Special Provisions" in the discussion of felony sentencing in Chapter 4 (Punishment under Structured Sentencing). For a discussion of when this offense triggers sex offender reporting, see the note entitled "Sex offender registration," below.

Notes

Element (1) generally. Previous law required that the victim be moved from one place to another. State v. Fulcher, 294 N.C. 503 (1978). The current statute provides that restraint or confinement, without movement, also may constitute kidnapping. G.S. 14-39(a).

Element (1)(a). "Confinement" means some form of imprisonment within a given area, such as a room, house, or vehicle. State v. Gainey, 355 N.C. 73, 91 (2002) (quoting *Fulcher*, 294 N.C. at 523). There was sufficient evidence of confinement when (1) although the victim asked the defendant to leave her apartment, he stood by the door blocking the only exit and later admitted that he closed and locked the apartment door while the victim was inside, State v. Johnson, 183 N.C. App. 576, 581 (2007); and (2) the defendant entered a trailer, brandished a loaded shotgun, and ordered everyone inside to lie down; it was immaterial that the victim did not comply with the defendant's order, State v. Yarborough, 198 N.C. App. 22, 26 (2009).

Although confinement and restraint can occur simultaneously, *see, e.g.*, State v. Sapp, 190 N.C. App. 698, 708–09 (2008) (the evidence was sufficient to establish that the defendant restrained and confined young children when he and an accomplice entered the residence with a shotgun and isolated the children and two others in a bedroom away from the children's mother and her boyfriend; the defendant and his accomplice terrorized the mother and boyfriend, forced a woman in the room with the children to remove her clothes and refused to allow her to leave to use the bathroom, and directed racial slurs at a person in the room with the children), the terms are not synonymous. In *State v. Fulcher*, 294 N.C. 503, 523 (1978), the North Carolina Supreme Court recognized that while the term "restraint" is broad enough to include a restriction upon freedom of movement by confinement, it also includes a restriction, by force, threat, or fraud, without a confinement. *See also Gainey*, 355 N.C. at 95 (quoting *Fulcher*).

Element (1)(b). To "restrain" means to restrict by force, threat, or fraud, with or without confinement. *Fulcher*, 294 N.C. 503. A person is restrained, for example, when he or she is physically seized and held, when his or her hands or feet are bound, or when his or her freedom of movement is restricted by the threatened use of a deadly weapon. *Id.*; *see also* State v. Pigott, 331 N.C. 199 (1992); State v. Johnson, 337 N.C. 212 (1994); State v. Carrillo, 115 N.C. App. 674 (1994). The restraint does not have to last for a substantial period of time. *Fulcher*, 294 N.C. 503.

For a discussion of how restraint overlaps with and differs from confinement, see the note on Element (1)(a), immediately above.

There was sufficient evidence of restraint when the defendant pinned the victim on a bed by pushing his knee into her chest and grabbed her hair to prevent her from escaping. State v. Braxton, 183 N.C. App. 36, 40–41 (2007).

Element (1)(c). "Removal" contemplates some movement of the victim. The removal need not cover a substantial distance. State v. Silhan, 297 N.C. 660 (1979); *Fulcher*, 294 N.C. 503; State v. Pendergrass, 111 N.C. App. 310 (1993).

For a case in which there was insufficient evidence of removal, see *State v. Boyd*, ___ N.C. App. ___, 714 S.E.2d 466 (2011) (the crime occurred entirely in the victim's living room; the court stated that "where the victim was moved a short distance of several feet, and was not transported from one room to another, the victim was not 'removed' within the meaning of our kidnapping statute"), *temp. stay allowed* (N.C. Aug. 22, 2011).

Element (2). Kidnapping requires a live victim. State v. Keller, 198 N.C. App. 639, 644–46 (2009). Thus, if the defendant removes a dead body, no kidnapping has occurred.

Element (3) generally. "Without consent" can be accomplished by fraud. State v. Sexton, 336 N.C. 321 (1994); State v. Sturdivant, 304 N.C. 293 (1981); State v. Ingland, 278 N.C. 42 (1971); State v. Davis, 158 N.C. App. 1 (2003). For example, a removal was accomplished without consent when the defendant (1) persuaded a 15-year-old girl and her sister, who had advertised as babysitters, to accompany him in his car to allegedly babysit for him, when in fact he intended to assault them, State v. Gough, 257 N.C. 348 (1962); and (2) induced the victim to enter his car on the pretext of paying her in exchange for sex but his real intent was to assault her, State v. Williams, 201 N.C. App. 161, 171 (2009).

Element (3)(b). When the victim is a child under 16 years old, the State is not required to prove that the defendant knew the victim's age. State v. Bowman, 188 N.C. App. 635, 651–53 (2008).

In a multiple homicide case in which the defendant was also charged with kidnapping a minor victim, the court held that there was sufficient circumstantial evidence that the minor's parents did not consent to her kidnapping. State v. Phillips, 365 N.C. 103 (2011). Because the victim's parents did not testify, there was no direct evidence of lack of parental consent. *Id.* at 145. However, the State presented evidence that, having shot and repeatedly stabbed the victim while she was at the murder scene, the defendant and his accomplices found her after she crawled outside and removed her for the stated purpose of killing her. *Id.* They then loaded her into the bed of a truck and drove to a trash pile, only to abandon her there when they heard sirens. *Id.*

Element (4) generally. This element makes kidnapping a specific intent crime. State v. Washington, 157 N.C. App. 535, 537 (2003); see generally the note entitled "General intent and specific intent" under "Intentionally" in Chapter 1 (States of Mind).

For this element to be satisfied, the defendant need not actually carry out any of the acts listed in Elements (4)(a) through (4)(j) (hold the victim for ransom, commit another felony, do serious bodily harm to the victim, or terrorize the victim, etc.). Instead, this element is satisfied if the defendant has such a purpose in restraining, confining, or removing the victim, even if that purpose is not carried out. State v. Williams, 295 N.C. 655 (1978); State v. Moore, 315 N.C. 738 (1986); State v. Cole, 199 N.C. App. 151, 159–60 (2009); State v. Carrillo, 115 N.C. App.

674 (1994). Also, the defendant need not have had such an illegal purpose when the restraint, confinement, or removal began; it is sufficient if the defendant intended to carry out one of these purposes at any time during the confinement, restraint, or removal. *Moore*, 315 N.C. 738. Except as discussed below in the note on Elements (4)(d) and (e), there is insufficient evidence of kidnapping when the offense that was the alleged purpose of the unlawful restraint occurred before any unlawful restraint occurred; for example, if a defendant assaults a victim and then unlawfully restrains the victim, commission of the assault may not constitute the purpose of the unlawful restraint. State v. Brooks, 138 N.C. App. 185 (2000).

If there is sufficient evidence of a purpose listed in this element, it does not matter that the defendant had some other, additional purpose. State v. Harrison, 169 N.C. App. 257 (2005), *aff'd*, 360 N.C. 394 (2006) (per curiam) (equally divided court).

Element (4)(a). "Holding as hostage" means "the unlawful taking, restraining, or confining of a person with the intent that the person, or victim, be held as security for the performance or forbearance of some act by a third person." State v. Lee, 33 N.C. App. 162 (1977); State v. Bunch, 106 N.C. App. 128 (1992). When a defendant confined and restrained a law enforcement officer as security for preventing the defendant's arrest by other officers, this element was satisfied. *Bunch*, 106 N.C. App. 128.

Elements (4)(d) and (e). "Facilitating" means "to make easier." State v. Kyle, 333 N.C. 687 (1993). Again, it is only necessary that the kidnapping be for the purpose of facilitating a felony or flight following the felony. State v. Banks, 295 N.C. 399 (1978).

If a defendant is charged with confining, restraining, or removing the victim for the purpose of facilitating the commission of a felony, the kidnapping victim need not be the intended victim of the felony intended. For example, an infant was considered kidnapped when the defendant forced the child's mother to put the baby in a crib and then forced the mother into a dressing room where she was bound, gagged, and sexually assaulted; the removal of the infant facilitated the felony sexual assault on the mother. State v. Pendergrass, 111 N.C. App. 310, 319–20 (1993). A defendant cannot kidnap a person for the purpose of facilitating a felony murder; when a defendant is charged with kidnapping for the purpose of committing a murder, the State must prove that the defendant intended to commit a premeditated and deliberate murder. State v. Yarborough, 198 N.C. App. 22, 26–28 (2009) (insufficient evidence of an intent to commit such a murder).

For cases in which the evidence was sufficient to establish that the defendant confined, restrained, or removed the victim for the purpose of facilitating a felony or flight from a felony, see *State v. Shue*, 163 N.C. App. 58 (2004) (the defendant confined a child for the purpose of facilitating taking indecent liberties with the child when the defendant entered a bathroom stall occupied by the child and closed the door), and *State v. Scott*, 161 N.C. App. 104 (2003) (after assaulting the victim, the defendant removed the victim to facilitate his flight from the assault).

As a general rule, the evidence will be insufficient to show that the defendant confined, restrained, or removed the victim for the purpose of facilitating commission of another felony if the confinement, restraint, and/or removal occurred after the other felony was complete. State v. Jordan, 186 N.C. App. 576, 584–85 (2007) (burglary allegedly facilitated was completed when the kidnapping occurred); State v. Johnson, 183 N.C. App. 576, 584–85 (2007) (same). In this situation, the defendant's conduct might support a purpose of facilitating flight from a felony but, as a general rule, will not support a purpose of committing the other felony. State v. Morris, 147 N.C. App. 247 (2001) (when the defendant raped the victim in a house and then took her to an outside storage room and left her there, the evidence was insufficient to show that the defendant kidnapped the victim for the purpose of committing the rape because the rape had already occurred when he took her to the storage room; the court noted that these facts may have supported kidnapping for the purpose of facilitating flight after committing the rape, but this purpose was not alleged in the indictment). However, the courts have recognized exceptions to this general rule. For example, in *State v. Kyle*, 333 N.C. 687 (1993), the defendant broke into an occupied dwelling with the intent to commit murder (thereby committing burglary), restrained the victim, shot her, and then removed her from the dwelling and shot her again, killing her. The court held that the defendant's restraint of the victim in the dwelling and his subsequent removal of her from the home facilitated the burglary and the murder. *Id.* at 694–96 (rejecting the defendant's argument that the burglary was complete upon entry into the house and reasoning that restraining the victim "made the crime of burglary easier by enabling defendant to carry out his felonious intent"; also concluding that the confinement, restraint, and removal of the victim facilitated the commission of the murder).

Element (4)(f). "Serious bodily harm" means physical injury that causes great pain or suffering. State v. Bonilla, ___ N.C. App. ___, 706 S.E.2d 288, 295 (2011) (approving of jury instructions so defining serious bodily harm). It is irrelevant that the victim does not suffer serious bodily harm; the State is only required to prove that the defendant's purpose was to cause such harm. State v. Williams, 201 N.C. App. 161, 185–86 (2009) (kidnapping conviction based on the defendant's purpose of doing serious bodily harm to the victim was upheld even though the actual injury inflicted only rose to the level of serious injury); State v. Washington, 157 N.C. App. 535 (2003). For cases in which the evidence was sufficient to establish an intent to do serious bodily harm, see *Bonilla*, ___ N.C. App. ___, 706 S.E.2d 288 (the defendant beat and kicked victim Alvarez repeatedly, bound his hands and feet and placed a rag in his mouth, threatened to kill him, and pulled his pants down so an accomplice could force a bottle into his rectum; as to victim Cortes, the defendant and the accomplice knocked him to the floor, kicked him repeatedly, hog-tied him so severely that his spine was fractured, caused tissue paper to be in his mouth, and Cortes' cause of death was a combination of suffocation and strangulation, with a contributing factor being the fracture of the thoracic spine), *State v. Boozer*, ___ N.C. App. ___, 707 S.E.2d 756 (2011) (after severely beating the victim so that he stopped moving, the defendants first attempted to stuff him into a garbage can and then threw him into a 10- or 12-foot-deep ditch filled with rocks and water), and *Washington*, 157 N.C. App. 535 (the defendant initiated contact with the victim and attacked the victim intensely and continuously in an apparent rage).

Element (4)(g). "Terrorizing" means causing another person terror. Terror is not ordinary concern or fear but, rather, is some higher degree of fear, such as intense apprehension or fright. State v. Moore, 315 N.C. 738 (1986); *Bonilla*, ___ N.C. App. ___, 706 S.E.2d at 295 (approving of a jury instruction that "Terrorizing means more than just putting another in fear. It means putting that person in some high degree of fear, a state of intense fright or apprehension, or doing serious bodily injury to that person."). The test is not whether the victim was in fact terrorized but whether the defendant's purpose was to terrorize. State v. Baldwin, 141 N.C. App. 596 (2000); State v. Harrison, 169 N.C. App. 257 (2005), *aff'd*, 360 N.C. 394 (2006) (per curiam) (equally divided court). Nonetheless, the victim's subjective feeling of fear, while not determinative of the defendant's intent, is relevant. *Baldwin*, 141 N.C. App. 596.

Cases holding that the evidence was sufficient to establish a purpose of terrorizing a victim include *Bonilla*, ___ N.C. App. ___, 706 S.E.2d 288 (described in the note to Element (4)(f), above), *Boozer*, ___ N.C. App. ___, 707 S.E.2d 756 (2011) (reasonable inference that the defendants intended to terrorize the victim if, after severely beating him, they believed him to be conscious and aware of being stuffed into a garbage can and then flung into a deep, rocky, water-filled ditch), *State v. Rodriguez*, 192 N.C. App. 178, 188–89 (2008), *State v. Jacobs*, 172 N.C. App. 220, 225–27 (2005), and *State v. Washington*, 157 N.C. App. 535, 539 (2003).

Element (4)(h). See "Involuntary Servitude," below.

Element (4)(i). See "Human Trafficking," below.

Element (4)(j). See "Sexual Servitude," below.

Element (5) generally. The three factors in Element (5) elevate second-degree kidnapping to first-degree kidnapping and are essential elements of the first-degree offense. State v. Freeland, 316 N.C. 13, 20 (1986).

Element (5)(a). "Release" is more than mere "relinquishment of domain or control over a person." State v. Love, 177 N.C. App. 614, 626 (2006). Rather, a release of a victim in a safe place requires a defendant's conscious, willful action to assure the victim's release in a place of safety. State v. Jerrett, 309 N.C. 239 (1983); State v. Garner, 330 N.C. 273 (1991); State v. Raynor, 128 N.C. App. 244 (1998). The victim was not released in a safe place when:

- after being cornered and outnumbered by officers, the defendant released the victim into the focal point of the officers' weapons, State v. Heatwole, 333 N.C. 156 (1992); *see also* State v. Corbett, 168 N.C. App. 117 (2005);
- the victim was killed, State v. Roache, 358 N.C. 243 (2004); State v. Thomas, 350 N.C. 315, 352–53 (1999) (the victim was found stabbed to death in his own house, with his hands tied behind his back); State v. Bonilla, ___ N.C. App. ___, 706 S.E.2d 288, 296 (2011) (if the victim was killed, he was not released in a safe place; alternatively, if the victim was alive when left by the defendants, he was not left in a safe place given that he was bound so tightly that he suffered a fracture to his spine and ultimately suffocated);
- the victim was left bound, *Love*, 177 N.C. App. at 625–26 (the victims were bound and gagged); State v. Morgan, 183 N.C. App. 160, 166–67 (2007) (the victims were bound); State v. Ly, 189 N.C. App. 422, 428–29 (2008) (same but the victims also were blindfolded and without access to a telephone);
- the victim escaped, State v. Cole, 199 N.C. App. 151, 159 (2009); State v. Chambers, 92 N.C. App. 230 (1988);
- the defendants left the victim in an isolated location, State v. Burrell, 165 N.C. App. 134 (2004) (the defendants pushed the victim out of his vehicle onto the side of an interstate highway in an isolated, wooded area at 1:30 a.m.); State v. Sakobie, 157 N.C. App. 275 (2003) (the defendant released a child at night in a rural, isolated area unknown to the child and told the child to knock on a nearby trailer door);
- the defendant fled but continued to be constructively present, State v. Anderson, 181 N.C. App. 655, 659–60 (2007) (the defendant was constructively present because neither the victims nor officers were certain about whether he had actually relinquished the victims and vacated the premises);
- the defendant took no affirmative steps to release the victim from confinement, *id.* at 660 (the defendant left the child victims in an upstairs room where they had been confined while the defendant forced their mothers downstairs; the defendant did not engage in affirmative action to release the children); and
- the defendant turned the victim over to an accomplice from whom the victim later escaped, *id.* at 660–61.

In contrast, a defendant and his accomplice released the victim in a safe place when they gave her money to make a phone call and released her in a motel parking lot. State v. White, 127 N.C. App. 565 (1997).

When the State proceeds on an acting in concert theory and an accomplice, acting alone, releases the victim in a safe place, this does not mean that the defendant released the victim in a safe place. State v. Smith, 194 N.C. App. 120, 124–25 (2008).

Element (5)(b). For a discussion of the term "serious injury" in the assault context, see the note on Element (3) to "Assault Inflicting Serious Injury" in Chapter 7 (Assaults). For kidnapping cases in which the evidence was sufficient to show serious injury, see *State v. Johnson*, 320 N.C. 746, 751 (1987) (the victim was stabbed multiple times with a pair of scissors and a tip of the scissors was embedded in the victim's hand), and *State v. Wilson*, 322 N.C. 117, 139 (1988) (any one of the victim's thirty-nine stab wounds or ligature abrasions would constitute serious injury).

The trial court did not err by instructing the jury that serious injury is injury that causes great pain and suffering or mental injury that extends for some appreciable time beyond the crime; the court was not required to instruct that serious mental injury also must be beyond that normally experienced by victims of the type of crime charged. State v. Simpson, 187 N.C. App. 424, 428–29 (2007).

Element (5)(c). The "sexual assault" need not be rape, State v. Williams, 295 N.C. 655 (1978), but it probably must be the equivalent of one of the sexual assault offenses in Article 7A of G.S. Chapter 14 (see Chapter 10 (Sexual Assaults)) or crime against nature, G.S. 14-177, committed in a nonconsensual manner (see Chapter 11 (Crime against Nature, Incest, Indecent Exposure, and Related Offenses)).

Charging issues. For a discussion of charging issues that arise in connection with kidnapping and related offenses, see Jessica Smith, *The Criminal Indictment: Fatal Defect, Fatal Variance, and Amendment*, ADMIN. OF JUST. BULL. No. 2008/03 (UNC School of Government, July 2008) (online at www.sog.unc.edu/pubs/electronicversions/pdfs/aojb0803.pdf). For an additional case decided since that bulletin was published, see *State v. Yarborough*, 198 N.C. App. 22, 26–30 (2009) (although a kidnapping indictment need not allege the felony intended, if it does, the State is bound by that allegation; the indictment alleged confinement and restraint for the purpose of committing murder, but the evidence showed that the confinement or restraint was for the purpose of committing a robbery; the State was bound by the allegation and had to prove that the confinement and restraint was for the purposes of premeditated and deliberate murder (it could not rely on felony murder)).

Greater and lesser-included offenses. Second-degree kidnapping, felonious restraint, and false imprisonment are all lesser-included offenses of first-degree kidnapping. G.S. 14-43.3 (felonious restraint); State v. Boozer, ___ N.C. App. ___, 707 S.E.2d 756 (2011) (false imprisonment). However, a trial judge may not submit felonious restraint as a lesser-included offense of first- or second-degree kidnapping unless the kidnapping indictment alleges the elements of felonious restraint. State v. Wilson, 128 N.C. App. 688 (1998).

Multiple convictions and punishments. A defendant may be convicted of kidnapping and other crimes arising out of the same episode only when the other crimes are separate and distinct from the kidnapping and are not elements of the kidnapping offense. Recall that one of the factors in Element (5) that can elevate a kidnapping from second-degree to first-degree is that the defendant sexually assaulted the victim. The above-stated rule about multiple convictions means that a defendant may not be convicted of both first-degree kidnapping and rape if the rape is the factor in Element (5) that elevates the kidnapping from second-degree to first-degree. In such a situation, the first-degree kidnapping must be reduced to second-degree kidnapping; alternatively, the defendant could be convicted of first-degree kidnapping if judgment is arrested for the rape conviction. State v. Freeland, 316 N.C. 13, 20–24 (1986) (such multiple punishment would violate double jeopardy); State v. Mason, 317 N.C. 283, 292–93 (1986) (following *Freeland*); State v. Daniels, 189 N.C. App. 705, 709–10 (2008) (same). However, if the defendant is alleged to have committed a second sexual assault, such as a sexual offense, and the sexual offense is the sexual assault in Element (5) that elevates the kidnapping to first-degree, there is no bar to punishing the defendant for the kidnapping and the rape; in this instance, the sexual offense, not the rape, was an element of the kidnapping charge. State v. Belton, 318 N.C. 141, 162–65 (1986). A special verdict form may be required to ensure that no impermissible multiple punishment occurs. *Id.*; *Daniels*, 189 N.C. App. at 709–10. Similarly, convictions of both first-degree kidnapping and rape would be proper if the jury finds another factor in Element (5)—failure to release the victim in a safe place or infliction of serious injury on the victim—that would elevate the kidnapping to first-degree. State v. Williams, 201 N.C. App. 161, 181, 186 (2009) (convictions of first-degree sexual offense and kidnapping against victim A were proper where the jury was instructed that to convict the defendant of first-degree kidnapping, it was required to find that the victim was seriously injured; convictions for first-degree sexual offense and kidnapping against victim B were proper where the jury was instructed that to convict the defendant of first-degree kidnapping, it was required to find that the victim was seriously injured or not released in a safe place; neither instruction contained any mention of the sexual assault).

When serious injury is the factor in Element (5), a separate conviction for assault inflicting serious bodily injury has been upheld. Specifically, the North Carolina Court of Appeals has held that if a defendant is convicted of assault inflicting serious bodily injury and of first-degree kidnapping, elevated because of serious injury inflicted on the victim, there is no double jeopardy bar to punishing the defendant for both the felonious assault and the first-degree kidnapping. *Williams*, 201 N.C. App. at 181–82 (reasoning that the felonious assault conviction required proof of serious bodily injury, a greater level of injury than required for Element (5) of first-degree kidnapping).

When a defendant confines, restrains, or removes a person for the purpose of committing a felony, the intended felony is not an element of the kidnapping charge and the defendant may be convicted for both the kidnapping and the felony, if it was in fact completed. State v. Banks, 295 N.C. 399, 405–06 (1993) (the defendant was properly convicted of crime against nature, robbery, assault with the intent to commit rape, and kidnapping when the defendant's confinement and restraint of the victim was to facilitate the other felonies); *Williams*, 201 N.C. App. at 181 (a defendant may be convicted of assault inflicting serious bodily injury and a kidnapping predicated on the defendant's intent to abduct a victim for the purpose of doing her serious bodily injury).

Some felonies, such as armed robbery and forcible rape, involve some restraint of the victim. In this context, the rule is that a defendant may be convicted and punished for kidnapping and another felony arising out of the course of the same conduct if the confinement, restraint, or removal that is the basis of the kidnapping is a separate, complete act independent of, and not inherent in, the other felony; put another way, the cases require that the restraint for kidnapping expose the victim to a greater danger than that inherent in the other offenses. State v. Fulcher, 294 N.C. 503 (1978); State v. Johnson, 337 N.C. 212 (1994); State v. Beatty, 347 N.C. 555 (1998); State v. Thomas, 350 N.C. 315 (1999). If the confinement, restraint, or removal is inherent in the other felony, a defendant may not, based on the same confinement, restraint, or removal, be convicted of both that felony and kidnapping. *Fulcher*, 294 N.C. 503; State v. Irwin, 304 N.C. 93 (1981); *Beatty*, 347 N.C. 555; State v. Ross, 133 N.C. App. 310 (1999); State v. Weaver, 123 N.C. App. 276 (1996). If the other felony has not been charged, this issue is irrelevant. State v. Yarborough, 198 N.C. App. 22, 25 (2009) (rejecting the defendant's argument that he could not be convicted of kidnapping because any restraint or confinement of the victim was inherent in his attempted robbery; the court reasoned that because the defendant was not charged with or convicted of robbery, any relationship between the defendant's conduct "and a hypothetical robbery charge is irrelevant").

Cases upholding multiple convictions in this context include the following:

- There was sufficient evidence to support a conviction of kidnapping committed during an armed robbery when the defendant first robbed victim A of $50 and then forcibly restrained and moved him about the premises, using him as an interpreter to facilitate the robbery of other occupants. State v. McCree, 160 N.C. App. 19, 29–30 (2003). Other cases holding that the evidence supported kidnapping and robbery convictions include *State v. Boyce,* 361 N.C. 670, 673–75 (2007), *State v. Thomas,* 350 N.C. 315, 344–45 (1999), *State v. Johnson,* 337 N.C. 212, 221–22 (1994), *State v. Ly,* 189 N.C. App. 422, 427–28 (2008), *State v. Bagley,* 183 N.C. App. 514, 522–24 (2007), *State v. Morgan,* 183 N.C. App. 160, 166–67 (2007), *State v. Anderson,*

181 N.C. App. 655, 661–62 (2007), *State v. Roberts,* 176 N.C. App. 159 (2006), *State v. Hall,* 165 N.C. App. 658 (2004), *State v. Burrell,* 165 N.C. App. 134 (2004), *State v. Escoto,* 162 N.C. App. 419 (2004), and *State v. McNeil,* 155 N.C. App. 540 (2002).

- Evidence of confinement and restraint was separate and distinct from an attempted rape when the attempted rape conviction was supported by the fact that the defendant pulled a knife, threatened to rape the victim, and began to undress; additionally, he induced the victim into a bedroom, kept her from leaving, physically restrained her, and confined her again when he left the bedroom—this evidence of confinement and restraint was separate and apart from that required to prove attempted rape. State v. Robertson, 149 N.C. App. 563 (2002). Other cases holding that the evidence was sufficient to sustain kidnapping and sexual assault convictions include *State v. Thomas,* 196 N.C. App. 523, 533–35 (2009) (kidnapping and rape), *State v. Simpson,* 187 N.C. App. 424, 432 (2007) (kidnapping and attempted rape), and *Roberts,* 176 N.C. App. at 165–66 (kidnapping and sexual offense).
- The defendant's confinement of the victim was separate and apart from his killing of the victim. State v. Gainey, 355 N.C. 73, 90–91 (2002) (the defendant lured the victim to a location; when the victim arrived, the defendant put a gun to his head and forced him to drive his own car to another location; the victim was then taken to the woods and when he tried to escape, he was shot; the victim was alone when put in the trunk of a car, crying for help when the final and fatal shots were delivered).
- The defendant was properly convicted of both assault with a deadly weapon inflicting serious injury and kidnapping when the victim, after being assaulted by the defendant in her home, escaped outside and attempted to call for help; the defendant dragged her back inside, threatened her with a knife, and beat her with his belt and gun; the restraint and removal of the victim was separate and apart from the assault because the defendant could have assaulted her in the yard but instead dragged her inside to prevent others from witnessing the assault. State v. Romero, 164 N.C. App. 169 (2004). Other cases finding the evidence sufficient to support kidnapping and assault convictions include *State v. Braxton,* 183 N.C. App. 36, 41 (2007) (assault by strangulation), *State v. Gayton-Barbosa,* 197 N.C. App. 129, 140–41 (2009) (felonious assault), *State v. Washington,* 157 N.C. App. 535, 537–39 (2003) (simple assault), and *State v. Carrillo,* 115 N.C. App. 674, 677–78 (1994) (assault with a deadly weapon with intent to kill inflicting serious injury; noting that certain felonies—like forcible rape and robbery—involve some element of restraint but noting that the assault at issue "is not within that class of felonies" because it may be committed without any restraint or confinement of the victim).
- Convictions of kidnapping and crime against nature were proper when the restraint of the victims was separate and apart from and not an inherent incident of the crime against nature. State v. Fulcher, 294 N.C. 503 (1978).

Cases holding that the evidence could not support multiple convictions in this context include the following:

- The victim's restraint was an inherent and integral part of an armed robbery and was insufficient to support a kidnapping conviction when the defendant pointed a shotgun at the victim, demanded money, struck her in the back with the shotgun, and pushed her toward the cash register. State v. Stephens, 175 N.C. App. 328 (2006). Other cases holding that the evidence was insufficient to sustain kidnapping and robbery convictions include *State v. Cole,* 199 N.C. App. 151, 157–58 (2009) (the restraint of the victim did not go beyond that inherent in the accompanying robbery where the victim was not moved to another location and was held for only thirty minutes), *State v. Payton,* 198 N.C. App. 320, 325–28 (2009) (any removal and restraint was inherent in a robbery where the victims only were moved from a "bathroom area" to the bathroom and were asked to lie on the bathroom floor until the robbery was complete), *State v. Taylor*, 191 N.C. App. 561 (2008) (making restaurant patrons lie on the floor at gunpoint while the restaurant was robbed did not constitute confinement, restraint, or removal beyond that required for the robbery), and *State v. Cartwright*, 177 N.C. App. 531, 537 (2006) (mere asportation in connection with a robbery was insufficient evidence of confinement, restraint, or removal).

- The defendant's restraint of the victim was inherent in his rape of her when the rape began and ended in one room of the house. *Cartwright*, 177 N.C. App. at 537. Other cases holding that the evidence was insufficient to sustain kidnapping and sexual assault convictions include *State v. Simmons*, 191 N.C. App. 224, 231–32 (2008) (following *Cartwright*; the defendant raped the victim in a guest bedroom but there was no evidence of confinement, restraint, or removal other than that inherent in the rape), and *State v. Ackerman*, 144 N.C. App. 452, 457–59 (2001) (restraint was necessary to commission of the sexual offense).

When the evidence shows that the defendant confined the victim and the confinement was not inherent in any other charged felony, it is irrelevant whether the restraint involved with the kidnapping was inherent in another charged felony. State v. Johnson, 183 N.C. App. 576, 581 (2007) (kidnapping and attempted first-degree murder).

Constitutionality. The courts have held that a prior version of the statute was not unconstitutionally vague or overbroad. State v. Banks, 295 N.C. 399, 404–05 (1978).

Sex offender registration. If the victim is a minor and the person committing the offense is not the minor's parent, this offense is classified as an offense against a minor, triggering registration requirements under the sex offender registration statutes. G.S. 14-208.6(1m).

Related Offenses Not in This Chapter

See the various offenses in Chapter 7 (Assaults).
See the various offenses in Chapter 10 (Sexual Assaults).
"Crime against Nature" (Chapter 11)

Second-Degree Kidnapping

Statute

See G.S. 14-39, reproduced under "First-Degree Kidnapping," above.

Elements

A person guilty of this offense

(1) (a) confines,
 (b) restrains, *or*
 (c) removes from one place to another
(2) a person
(3) (a) without the person's consent *or*,
 (b) if the person is under 16, without consent of the person's parent or guardian,
(4) for the purpose of
 (a) holding the victim as hostage,
 (b) holding the victim for ransom,
 (c) using the victim as a shield,
 (d) facilitating the commission of a felony,

(e) facilitating flight following the commission of a felony,
(f) doing serious bodily harm to the victim or any other person,
(g) terrorizing the victim or any other person,
(h) holding the victim in involuntary servitude in violation of G.S. 14-43.12,
(i) trafficking another person in violation of G.S. 14-43.11, *or*
(j) subjecting or maintaining the victim for sexual servitude in violation of G.S. 14-43.13.

Punishment

Class E felony. G.S. 14-39(b). See the additional discussion in "Punishment" under "First-Degree Kidnapping," above.

Notes

Generally. Second-degree kidnapping is exactly the same as first-degree kidnapping except that second-degree kidnapping does not include Element (5) of first-degree kidnapping (fails to release in a safe place, seriously injures the victim, or sexually assaults the victim). Thus, the notes to first-degree kidnapping apply here as well.

Sex offender registration. If the victim is a minor and the person committing the offense is not the minor's parent, this offense is classified as an offense against a minor, triggering registration requirements under the sex offender registration statutes. G.S. 14-208.6(1m).

Related Offenses Not in This Chapter

See the offenses listed under "First-Degree Kidnapping," above.

Felonious Restraint

Statute

§14-43.3. Felonious restraint.

A person commits the offense of felonious restraint if he unlawfully restrains another person without that person's consent, or the consent of the person's parent or legal custodian if the person is less than 16 years old, and moves the person from the place of the initial restraint by transporting him in a motor vehicle or other conveyance. Violation of this section is a Class F felony. Felonious restraint is considered a lesser included offense of kidnapping.

Elements

A person guilty of this offense

(1) unlawfully restrains
(2) a person
(3) (a) without the person's consent *or*,
    (b) if the person is under 16, without consent of the person's parent or guardian, *and*
(4) transports the person by motor vehicle or other conveyance from the place of the initial restraint.

Punishment

Class F felony. G.S. 14-43.3.

Notes

Element (1). See the note on Element (1)(b) to "First-Degree Kidnapping," above.

Element (2). See the note on Element (2) to "First-Degree Kidnapping," above.

Element (3). See the notes on Element (3) and (3)(b) to "First-Degree Kidnapping," above.

Charging issues. See this note to "First-Degree Kidnapping," above.

Greater and lesser-included offenses. This offense is a lesser-included offense of kidnapping. G.S. 14-43.3. However, a trial judge may not submit felonious restraint as a lesser-included offense of first- or second-degree kidnapping unless the kidnapping indictment alleges the elements of felonious restraint. State v. Wilson, 128 N.C. App. 688 (1998).

Sex offender registration. If the victim is a minor and the person committing the offense is not the minor's parent, this offense is classified as an offense against a minor, triggering registration requirements under the sex offender registration statutes. G.S. 14-208.6(1m).

Related Offenses Not in This Chapter

See the offenses listed under "First-Degree Kidnapping," above.

False Imprisonment

Statute

This is a common law offense.

Elements

A person guilty of this offense

(1) intentionally and unlawfully
(2) (a) restrains *or*
(b) detains
(3) a person
(4) without the person's consent.

Punishment

Class 1 misdemeanor. G.S. 14-3(a).

Notes

Element (1). See "Intentionally" in Chapter 1 (States of Mind). The defendant is guilty only if the detention or restraint of the victim is unlawful. For example, a merchant may detain a person whom the merchant has probable cause to suspect is a shoplifter, provided that the detention is done in a reasonable manner and for a reasonable length of time. G.S. 14-72.1(c).

Element (2). For a discussion of the term "restrain," see the note on Element (1)(b) to "First-Degree Kidnapping," above.

Element (3). See the note on Element (2) to "First-Degree Kidnapping," above.

Element (4). To prove that the restraint was against the victim's will, the State must show that the defendant used actual force, threatened force, or fraud resulting in coerced consent. State v. Ingland, 278 N.C. 42 (1971); State v. Streath, 73 N.C. App. 546 (1985). For a more detailed discussion of this element, see the note on Element (3) to "First-Degree Kidnapping," above.

Charging issues. See this note to "First-Degree Kidnapping," above.

Greater and lesser-included offenses. See this note to "First-Degree Kidnapping," above.

Relation to other offenses. The main difference between kidnapping and false imprisonment is the defendant's purpose in restraining the victim. State v. Harrison, 169 N.C. App. 257, 265–66 (2005), *aff'd*, 360 N.C. 394 (2006) (per curiam) (equally divided court). If the purpose is one of the objectives listed under Element (4) to "First-Degree Kidnapping" and "Second-Degree Kidnapping," both above, then the offense is kidnapping; however, if the unlawful restraint occurs without any of the purposes specified in that element, the offense is false imprisonment. *Id.*; *see also* State v. Pigott, 331 N.C. 199, 210 (1992). Also, kidnapping covers confinement, restraint, and removal. False imprisonment, however, covers only restraining or detaining the victim.

Related Offenses Not in This Chapter

See the offenses listed under "First-Degree Kidnapping," above.

Abduction of a Child

Statute

§14-41. Abduction of children.

(a) Any person who, without legal justification or defense, abducts or induces any minor child who is at least four years younger than the person to leave any person, agency, or institution lawfully entitled to the child's custody, placement, or care shall be guilty of a Class F felony.

(b) The provisions of this section shall not apply to any public officer or employee in the performance of his or her duty.

Elements

A person guilty of this offense

(1) without legal justification or defense
(2) (a) abducts *or*
    (b) induces
(3) a minor child
(4) who is at least four years younger than the defendant
(5) to leave
(6) a person, agency, or institution lawfully entitled to the child's custody, placement, or care.

Punishment

Class F felony. G.S. 14-41.

Notes

Element (1). A noncustodial parent may be guilty of this offense when that parent abducts his or her child in violation of the terms of a child custody order and the other elements of this offense are satisfied.

Element (3). Although the term "minor child" is not defined in this statute, it would likely be defined as a person under 18 years of age. G.S. 48A-2.

Element (4). For a discussion about how a similar age difference is calculated in the context of sexual assaults, see the note on Element (3) to "First-Degree Statutory Rape" in Chapter 10 (Sexual Assaults).

Sex offender registration. If the victim is a minor and the person committing the offense is not the minor's parent, this offense is classified as an offense against a minor, triggering registration requirements under the sex offender registration statutes. G.S. 14-208.6(1m).

Related Offenses Not in This Chapter

See the offenses listed under "First-Degree Kidnapping," above.
See the various offenses, including sexual exploitation of a child, in Chapter 24 (Obscenity, Exploitation of a Minor, and Adult Establishment Offenses).
Enticing minor out of state for purpose of employment. G.S. 14-40.

Human Trafficking, Involuntary Servitude, and Sexual Servitude

Statute

§14-43.10. Definitions.

(a) Definitions.—The following definitions apply in this Article:

(1) Coercion.—The term includes all of the following:

a. Causing or threatening to cause bodily harm to any person, physically restraining or confining any person, or threatening to physically restrain or confine any person.

b. Exposing or threatening to expose any fact or information that if revealed would tend to subject a person to criminal or immigration proceedings, hatred, contempt, or ridicule.

c. Destroying, concealing, removing, confiscating, or possessing any actual or purported passport or other immigration document, or any other actual or purported government identification document, of any person.

d. Providing a controlled substance, as defined by G.S. 90-87, to a person.

(2) Deception.—The term includes all of the following:

a. Creating or confirming another's impression of an existing fact or past event that is false and which the accused knows or believes to be false.

b. Maintaining the status or condition of a person arising from a pledge by that person of his or her personal services as security for a debt, if the value of those services as reasonably assessed is not applied toward the liquidation of the debt or the length and nature of those services are not respectively limited and defined, or preventing a person from acquiring information pertinent to the disposition of such debt.

c. Promising benefits or the performance of services that the accused does not intend to deliver or perform or knows will not be delivered or performed.

(3) Involuntary servitude.—The term includes the following:

a. The performance of labor, whether or not for compensation, or whether or not for the satisfaction of a debt; and

b. By deception, coercion, or intimidation using violence or the threat of violence or by any other means of coercion or intimidation.

(4) Minor.—A person who is less than 18 years of age.

(5) Sexual servitude.—The term includes the following:

a. Any sexual activity as defined in G.S. 14-190.13 for which anything of value is directly or indirectly given, promised to, or received by any person, which conduct is induced or obtained by coercion or deception or which conduct is induced or obtained from a person under the age of 18 years; or

b. Any sexual activity as defined in G.S.14-190.13 that is performed or provided by any person, which conduct is induced or obtained by coercion or deception or which conduct is induced or obtained from a person under the age of 18 years.

§14-43.11. Human trafficking.

(a) A person commits the offense of human trafficking when that person knowingly recruits, entices, harbors, transports, provides, or obtains by any means another person with the intent that the other person be held in involuntary servitude or sexual servitude.

(b) A person who violates this section is guilty of a Class F felony if the victim of the offense is an adult. A person who violates this section is guilty of a Class C felony if the victim of the offense is a minor.

(c) Each violation of this section constitutes a separate offense and shall not merge with any other offense. Evidence of failure to deliver benefits or perform services standing alone shall not be sufficient to authorize a conviction under this section.

(d) A person who is not a legal resident of North Carolina, and would consequently be ineligible for State public benefits or services, shall be eligible for the public benefits and services of any State agency if the person is otherwise eligible for the public benefit and is a victim of an offense charged under this section. Eligibility for public benefits and services shall terminate at such time as the victim's eligibility to remain in the United States is terminated under federal law.

§14-43.12. Involuntary servitude.

(a) A person commits the offense of involuntary servitude when that person knowingly and willfully holds another in involuntary servitude.

(b) A person who violates this section is guilty of a Class F felony if the victim of the offense is an adult. A person who violates this section is guilty of a Class C felony if the victim of the offense is a minor.

(c) Each violation of this section constitutes a separate offense and shall not merge with any other offense. Evidence of failure to deliver benefits or perform services standing alone shall not be sufficient to authorize a conviction under this section.

(d) Nothing in this section shall be construed to affect the laws governing the relationship between an unemancipated minor and his or her parents or legal guardian.

(e) If any person reports a violation of this section, which violation arises out of any contract for labor, to any party to the contract, the party shall immediately report the violation to the sheriff of the county in which the violation is alleged to have occurred for appropriate action. A person violating this subsection shall be guilty of a Class 1 misdemeanor.

§14-43.13. Sexual servitude.

(a) A person commits the offense of sexual servitude when that person knowingly subjects or maintains another in sexual servitude.

(b) A person who violates this section is guilty of a Class F felony if the victim of the offense is an adult. A person who violates this section is guilty of a Class C felony if the victim of the offense is a minor.

(c) Each violation of this section constitutes a separate offense and shall not merge with any other offense. Evidence of failure to deliver benefits or perform services standing alone shall not be sufficient to authorize a conviction under this section.

Human Trafficking

Statute

See G.S. 14-43.11, reproduced above.

Elements

A person guilty of this offense

(1) knowingly
(2) recruits, entices, harbors, transports, provides, or obtains
(3) another person
(4) with the intent that the other person be held in involuntary or sexual servitude.

Punishment

Class F felony if the victim is an adult. G.S. 14-43.11(b). Class C felony if the victim is less than 18 years old. G.S. 14-43.11(b) and 14-43.10(a)(4). If the Class C version of this offense is charged, the relevant fact elevating punishment must be alleged in a charging instrument and proved at trial.

Notes

Element (1). See "Knowingly" in Chapter 1 (States of Mind).

Element (4). "Involuntary servitude" means the performance of labor by deception, coercion, or intimidation. G.S. 14-43.10(a)(3). "Sexual servitude" includes any "sexual activity" induced or obtained (1) by coercion or deception or (2) from a person less than 18 years old. G.S. 14-43.10(a)(5). The term includes sexual activity in exchange for something of value or in exchange for a promise of something of value. *Id.* The covered sexual activities are defined by G.S. 14-190.13 to include things such as masturbation; vaginal, anal, or oral intercourse with humans or animals; certain excretory functions; and other acts. G.S. 14-43.10(a)(5). "Deception" is defined in G.S. 14-43.10(a)(2); "coercion" is defined in G.S. 14-43.10(a)(1).

Multiple convictions and punishments. Each violation is a separate offense and does not merge with any other offense. G.S. 14-43.11(c).

Failure to deliver benefits or perform services. Evidence of failure to deliver benefits or perform services is, by itself, insufficient to support a conviction. G.S. 14-43.11(c).

Related Offenses Not in This Chapter

See the offenses listed under "First-Degree Kidnapping," above.

Involuntary Servitude

Statute

See G.S. 14-43.12, reproduced above.

Elements

A person guilty of this offense

(1) knowingly and willfully
(2) holds another
(3) in involuntary servitude.

Punishment

Class F felony if the victim is an adult. G.S. 14-43.12(b). Class C felony if the victim is under 18 years of age. G.S. 14-43.12(b) and 14-43.10(a)(4). If the Class C version of this offense is charged, the relevant fact elevating punishment must be alleged in a charging instrument and proved at trial.

Notes

Element (1). See "Knowingly" and "Willfully" in Chapter 1 (States of Mind).

Element (3). See the note on Element (4) to "Human Trafficking," above.

Multiple convictions and punishments. Each violation is a separate offense and does not merge with any other offense. G.S. 14-43.12(c).

Failure to deliver benefits or perform services. Evidence of failure to deliver benefits or perform services is, by itself, insufficient to support a conviction. G.S. 14-43.12(c).

Related Offenses Not in This Chapter

See the offenses listed under "First-Degree Kidnapping," above.
Failure to report involuntary servitude violation. G.S. 14-43.12(e).

Sexual Servitude

Statute

See G.S. 14-43.13, reproduced above.

Elements

A person guilty of this offense

(1) knowingly
(2) subjects or maintains another
(3) in sexual servitude.

Punishment

Class F felony if the victim of the offense is an adult. G.S. 14-43.13(b). Class C felony if the victim is less than 18 years old. G.S. 14-43.13(b) and 14-43.10(a)(4). If the Class C version of this offense is charged, the relevant fact elevating punishment must be alleged in a charging instrument and proved at trial. See "Sex offenders" under "Felonies," "Special Provisions," in Chapter 4 (Punishment under Structured Sentencing) for special maximums that apply to defendants convicted of class B1–E felonies that are reportable convictions under the sex offender registration program. For the sex offender registration requirements for this offense, see the note "Sex offender registration," below.

Notes

Element (1). See "Knowingly" in Chapter 1 (States of Mind).

Element (3). See the note on Element (4) to "Human Trafficking," above.

Multiple convictions and punishments. Each violation is a separate offense and does not merge with any other offense. G.S. 14-43.13(c).

Failure to deliver benefits or perform services. Evidence of failure to deliver benefits or perform services is, by itself, insufficient to support a conviction. G.S. 14-43.13(c).

Sex offender registration. Conviction of this offense triggers sex offender registration. G.S. 14-208.6(5).

Related Offenses Not in This Chapter

See the offenses listed under "First-Degree Kidnapping," above.
See the offenses in Chapter 23 (Prostitution).
See the offenses in Chapter 24 (Obscenity, Exploitation of a Minor, and Adult Establishment Offenses).

13

Larceny, Possession of Stolen Goods, Embezzlement, and Related Offenses

13

Larceny, Possession of Stolen Goods, Embezzlement, and Related Offenses

Larceny

Misdemeanor Larceny

Statute

§14-72. Larceny of property; receiving stolen goods or possessing stolen goods.

(a) Larceny of goods of the value of more than one thousand dollars ($1,000) is a Class H felony. The receiving or possessing of stolen goods of the value of more than one thousand dollars ($1,000) while knowing or having reasonable grounds to believe that the goods are stolen is a Class H felony. Larceny as provided in subsection (b) of this section is a Class H felony. Receiving or possession of stolen goods as provided in subsection (c) of this section is a Class H felony. Except as provided in subsections (b) and (c) of this section, larceny of property, or the receiving or possession of stolen goods knowing or having reasonable grounds to believe them to be stolen, where the value of the property or goods is not more than one thousand dollars ($1,000), is a Class 1 misdemeanor. In all cases of doubt, the jury shall, in the verdict, fix the value of the property stolen.

(b) The crime of larceny is a felony, without regard to the value of the property in question, if the larceny is any of the following:

(1) From the person.
(2) Committed pursuant to a violation of G.S. 14-51, 14-53, 14-54, 14-54.1, or 14-57.
(3) Of any explosive or incendiary device or substance. As used in this section, the phrase "explosive or incendiary device or substance" shall include any explosive or incendiary grenade or bomb; any dynamite, blasting powder, nitroglycerin, TNT, or other high explosive; or any device, ingredient for such device, or type or quantity of substance primarily useful for large-scale destruction of property by explosive or incendiary action or lethal injury to persons by explosive or incendiary action. This definition shall not include fireworks; or any form, type, or quantity of gasoline, butane gas, natural gas, or any other substance having explosive or incendiary properties but serving a legitimate nondestructive or nonlethal use in the form, type, or quantity stolen.

(4) Of any firearm. As used in this section, the term "firearm" shall include any instrument used in the propulsion of a shot, shell or bullet by the action of gunpowder or any other explosive substance within it. A "firearm," which at the time of theft is not capable of being fired, shall be included within this definition if it can be made to work. This definition shall not include air rifles or air pistols.

(5) Of any record or paper in the custody of the North Carolina State Archives as defined by G.S. 121-2(7) and G.S. 121-2(8).

(c) The crime of possessing stolen goods knowing or having reasonable grounds to believe them to be stolen in the circumstances described in subsection (b) is a felony or the crime of receiving stolen goods knowing or having reasonable grounds to believe them to be stolen in the circumstances described in subsection (b) is a felony, without regard to the value of the property in question.

(d) Where the larceny or receiving or possession of stolen goods as described in subsection (a) of this section involves the merchandise of any store, a merchant, a merchant's agent, a merchant's employee, or a peace officer who detains or causes the arrest of any person shall not be held civilly liable for detention, malicious prosecution, false imprisonment, or false arrest of the person detained or arrested, when such detention is upon the premises of the store or in a reasonable proximity thereto, is in a reasonable manner for a reasonable length of time, and, if in detaining or in causing the arrest of such person, the merchant, the merchant's agent, the merchant's employee, or the peace officer had, at the time of the detention or arrest, probable cause to believe that the person committed an offense under subsection (a) of this section. If the person being detained by the merchant, the merchant's agent, or the merchant's employee, is a minor under the age of 18 years, the merchant, the merchant's agent, or the merchant's employee, shall call or notify, or make a reasonable effort to call or notify the parent or guardian of the minor, during the period of detention. A merchant, a merchant's agent, or a merchant's employee, who makes a reasonable effort to call or notify the parent or guardian of the minor shall not be held civilly liable for failing to notify the parent or guardian of the minor.

Elements

A person guilty of the offense

(1) takes
(2) personal property
(3) in the possession of another *and*
(4) carries it away
(5) without the consent of the possessor *and*
(6) with the intent to deprive the possessor of its use permanently
(7) knowing that he or she was not entitled to it.

Punishment

Class 1 misdemeanor. G.S. 14-72(a).

Notes

Element (1). To constitute a taking, there must be a "severance of the goods from the possession of the owner." State v. Carswell, 296 N.C. 101, 104 (1978) (quoting State v. Roper, 14 N.C. 473, 474 (1832)). Put another way, the defendant must have the property in his or her possession, or under his or her control, even if only for an instant. *Id.* For example, when a defendant picked an air conditioner up from its stand and laid it on the floor, this was sufficient evidence of a taking; the air conditioner was briefly under the defendant's control and severed from the owner's possession. *Id.* The North Carolina Supreme Court has noted that in rare but amusing situations, there can be a carrying away, see the note on Element (4), without a taking. Specifically, the court described a scenario where a thief lifted an overcoat from a store mannequin and tried to walk away with it but then discovered that the overcoat was secured by a chain, which he was unable to break. In this instance, there was no larceny because the thief did not at any time have possession of the garment. *Id.* Of course, in these circumstances an attempted larceny occurred. See "Attempt" in Chapter 5 (General Crimes).

Element (2). G.S. 12-3(6) defines the term "personal property" as "moneys, goods, chattels, choses in action and evidences of debt, including all things capable of ownership, not descendable to heirs at law." For a discussion of the term "choses in action," and a specific felony that applies when that type of property is stolen, see "Larceny of a Chose in Action," below. Real property is not covered. State v. Jackson, 218 N.C. 373 (1940). However, personal property that has been affixed to real property may be the subject of a larceny. G.S. 14-83.1. Animals are personal property, G.S. 14-84, and as noted in the discussion of "Felony Larceny," below, larceny of certain animals is a felony. Contraband, such as illegal drugs, is personal property. State v. Oliver, 334 N.C. 513 (1993).

Element (3). The property may have been in the possession of another person or an entity capable of possessing the property, State v. Patterson, 194 N.C. App. 608, 613 (2009), such as a corporation. Because larceny requires that the property have been in the possession of another, it violates the right to possession, not the right to ownership. Thus, a property owner may be guilty of larceny if the owner steals his or her property when it is in another's lawful possession. 3 Charles E. Torcia, Wharton's Criminal Law 456 (15th ed. 1995).

When the defendant dug up another person's money buried on real property on which the defendant had a leasehold interest granting her lawful possession of the real property, the evidence was insufficient to establish larceny because no trespassory taking occurred. State v. Jones, 177 N.C. App. 269, 272 (2006).

Proof of mere ownership of the premises from which property was stolen does not by itself establish ownership, possession of, or interest in the stolen property. State v. Downing, 313 N.C. 164 (1985).

Element (4). "A bare removal from the place in which he [or she] found the goods, though the thief does not quite make off with them, is a sufficient asportation, or carrying away." State v. Carswell, 296 N.C. 101, 103 (1978). For example, a carrying away occurred when the defendant (1) unlocked his employer's safe and completely removed a drawer containing money but was stopped before any of the money was taken from the drawer; the defendant's actions were sufficient to constitute asportation of the money, *id.* (describing State v. Green, 81 N.C. 560 (1879)); (2) moved an air conditioner off its window base and four to six inches toward the door; this action constituted a bare removal from the place where the thief found the item, *id.* at 103–04; and (3) removed tires from cars parked at a car dealership and left them propped against the hubs, State v. Gray, 58 N.C. App. 102 (1982).

Element (5). This element may be satisfied by the possessor's testimony that he or she did not consent.

When consent is obtained by trick, the taking is deemed to be without consent. A larceny by trick occurred, for example, when the defendant obtained a vehicle by requesting and receiving consent to take it for a test drive, when his true intent was to keep it. State v. Barbour, 153 N.C. App. 500 (2002).

Element (6). A mere temporary taking under circumstances in which the possessor is likely to regain possession does not satisfy this element. An example of such a taking is when the defendant takes the victim's car to drive to a party and returns the car several hours later to the victim's driveway. However, a taking for temporary use can be sufficient if the property is abandoned under circumstances that both make it unlikely that the possessor will recover the property and show the taker's indifference to the possessor's rights. State v. Mann, 355 N.C. 294 (2002) (robbery case); State v. Kemmerlin, 356 N.C. 446 (2002) (same); State v. Hill, 139 N.C. App. 471 (2000).

For cases in which the evidence was sufficient to establish an intent to permanently deprive, see *State v. Allen*, 193 N.C. App. 375, 381 (2008) (the defendant took the victim's vehicle in North Carolina and abandoned it in Virginia; this act placed the vehicle beyond the defendant's power to return it and showed indifference to whether the victim ever recovered it), *State v. Sakobie*, 157 N.C. App. 275, 283–84 (2003) (the defendant stole the victim's car at 9 p.m. and drove it all night until she was stopped by the police early the next morning), and *State v. Simmons*, 167 N.C. App. 512, 521 (2004) (in a robbery case, there was sufficient evidence that the defendant intended to permanently deprive the victim of her phone when the defendant slapped the phone out of the victim's hand, said it was his, and began dialing on it immediately after exiting the home).

Element (7). A person who honestly believes he or she is entitled to taken property is not guilty of larceny, even if this belief is wrong. State v. Booker, 250 N.C. 272 (1959).

Charging issues. For a detailed discussion of charging issues in connection with larceny and related offenses, see Jessica Smith, *The Criminal Indictment: Fatal Defect, Fatal Variance, and Amendment*, ADMIN. OF JUST. BULL. No. 2008/03 (UNC School of Government, July 2008) (online at www.sog.unc.edu/pubs/electronicversions/pdfs/aojb0803.pdf). For cases decided after that paper was published, see *In re* D.B., ___ N.C. App. ___, ___ S.E.2d ___ (Aug. 16, 2011) (a juvenile petition alleging felony larceny was fatally defective because it contained no allegation that the alleged victim, the Crossings Golf Club, was a legal entity capable of owning property), *State v. McNeil*, ___ N.C. App. ___, 707 S.E.2d 674, 678–79 (2011) (an indictment for felonious larceny that failed to allege ownership in the stolen handgun was fatally defective), *State v. Patterson*, 194 N.C. App. 608, 612–15 (2009) (a larceny indictment alleging the victim's name as "First Baptist Church of Robbinsville" was fatally defective because it did not indicate that the church was a legal entity capable of owning property), and *State v. Gayton-Barbosa*, 197 N.C. App. 129, 137 (2009) (there was a fatal variance between a larceny indictment alleging that the stolen gun belonged to Minear and the evidence showing that it belonged to Leggett; Minear had no special property interest in the gun even though it was kept in a bedroom occupied by both Minear and Leggett).

Greater and lesser-included offenses. Depending on the evidence, unauthorized use of a motor-propelled conveyance can be a lesser-included offense of larceny of a vehicle. State v. Ross, 46 N.C. App. 338, 339 (1980) (so concluding as a matter of legislative intent); State v. Watson, 179 N.C. App. 228, 246 (2006) (citing *Ross*); N.C. PATTERN JURY INSTRUCTIONS—CRIM. 216.10 at n.6.

Because all of the elements of misdemeanor larceny are included in felony larceny, the former is a lesser-included offense of the latter. State v. Lawson, 105 N.C. App. 329, 330–31 (1992).

Multiple convictions and punishments. A defendant may be convicted for only one larceny if several pieces of property are taken during one continuous act or transaction. State v. Marr, 342 N.C. 607 (1996); State v. Adams, 331 N.C. 317 (1992); State v. Boykin, 78 N.C. App. 572 (1985). For example, only one larceny was committed when a defendant stole (1) a firearm and other property in a single breaking and entering, *Adams*, 331 N.C. 317; State v. Suggs, 130 N.C. App. 140 (1998); and (2) various items of personal property from several company vans during one continuous transaction. State v. Hargett, 157 N.C. App. 90 (2003).

A defendant may be convicted of multiple counts of larceny if the evidence shows separate incidents involving separate takings of property. State v. White, 322 N.C. 770 (1988); State v. Barton, 335 N.C. 741 (1994). For example, the evidence supported two convictions when the defendant stole a shotgun from a truck and then entered and stole another vehicle; the defendant's different purposes for taking the shotgun and the vehicle suggested that each taking was motivated by a unique criminal impulse or intent. State v. West, 180 N.C. App. 664, 666–67 (2006). When several items of property are stolen from different owners during the same continuous transaction, the courts are split nationally on whether one or multiple larcenies occurred, although a majority of jurisdictions would hold that only one taking occurred. 3 Torcia, cited in full *supra*, at 369–71 & nn.30–32.

Although larceny, possession of stolen goods, and receiving stolen goods are separate offenses for purposes of double jeopardy, the legislature did not intend that a defendant would be convicted of more than one of these offenses when charges are based on the same conduct. *See, e.g.*, State v. Perry, 305 N.C. 225, 231–37 (1982). Thus, while a defendant may be charged with and tried for larceny, receiving, and possession of the same property, he or she may be convicted of only one of those offenses when they are committed during a single transaction. *Id.* at 236–37; State v. Szucs, ___ N.C. App. ___, 701 S.E.2d 362, 368 (2010) (citing *Perry*).

Because larceny and "Obtaining Property by False Pretenses," discussed in Chapter 16 (Fraud, Forgery, False Pretenses, and Related Offenses), each contain an element not in the other, the offenses are not the same for purposes of double jeopardy, State v. Kelly, 75 N.C. App. 461, 463–64 (1985), and thus a defendant may be convicted of both based on the same conduct.

Relation to other offenses. Larceny differs from "Obtaining Property by False Pretenses," discussed in Chapter 16 (Fraud, Forgery, False Pretenses, and Related Offenses), in several ways. First, while larceny requires an intent to deprive the owner of property permanently, obtaining property by false pretenses does not. Second, while obtaining property by false pretenses requires that the defendant make a false representation to obtain property, larceny does not. And finally, larceny requires that the property be wrongfully taken without the owner's consent; by comparison, obtaining property by false pretenses frequently involves the initial consent of the property owner. *See generally Kelly*, 75 N.C. App. at 464 (discussing the second and third distinction).

Larceny differs from "Embezzlement" and "Embezzlement by Employee" because embezzlement requires that the defendant deprive an owner of property that has been entrusted to the defendant. With larceny, the defendant has not been entrusted with the property.

Larceny differs from "Shoplifting by Concealing Merchandise," below, in that it requires proof that the person intended to permanently deprive the lawful possessor of the property; shoplifting by concealing merchandise includes no such element. Also, shoplifting by concealing merchandise requires proof that the property was willfully concealed on the store's premises; larceny does not include this element. Although it is possible to charge a person with larceny if the person has been stopped on a store's premises with willfully concealed goods, the difficulty of proving an intent to permanently deprive under these circumstances makes shoplifting by concealing merchandise easier to prove. On the other hand, a person who willfully conceals goods on a store's premises and then leaves the store before being stopped is normally charged with larceny; in this case, an intent to permanently deprive is readily proved, and larceny is the more serious offense. It is unclear whether a person may be convicted and punished for both larceny and shoplifting by concealing merchandise based on the same incident.

Doctrine of recent possession. The doctrine of recent possession permits an inference of guilt based on a defendant's possession of stolen property recently after a larceny or breaking and entering. State v. Maines, 301 N.C. 669 (1981); State v. Gonzalez, 311 N.C. 80 (1984); State v. Ethridge, 168 N.C. App. 359 (2005); State v. McQueen, 165 N.C. App. 454 (2004); State v. Mitchell, 109 N.C. App. 222 (1993). In order for the inference to apply, the evidence must show that:

(1) the property was stolen,
(2) the stolen goods were found in the defendant's custody and subject to his or her control and disposition to the exclusion of others, and
(3) the defendant had possession of the property recently after it was stolen.

Maines, 301 N.C. 669; *Gonzalez*, 311 N.C. 80; *Ethridge*, 168 N.C. App. 359; *McQueen*, 165 N.C. App. 454; State v. Earwood, 155 N.C. App. 698 (2003).

The first prong of the test requires that the property be identified as stolen. State v. Carter, 122 N.C. App. 332 (1996). In one case, the doctrine was held not to apply when the owner could not positively identify the goods (tires) as the stolen items because they were mass produced and had no individual identifying characteristics. State v. Foster, 268 N.C. 480 (1966).

The second prong requires that the stolen property is found in the defendant's custody and possession or subject to his or her control and disposition. State v. Wilson, 313 N.C. 516 (1985); State v. Hamlet, 316 N.C. 41 (1986). Proof of either actual or constructive possession will suffice. *Maines*, 301 N.C. 669; *Wilson*, 313 N.C. 516; State v. Osborne, 149 N.C. App. 235 (2002). Actual possession could be, for example, the defendant having the items on his or her person. State v. Reid, 151 N.C. App. 379 (2002) (goods were in a briefcase carried by defendant). Constructive possession could be, for example, the defendant keeping the items in a locked facility. *Foster*, 268 N.C. 480; *Maines*, 301 N.C. 669. Joint possession can satisfy this prong of the doctrine. *Maines*, 301 N.C. 669. For the inference of guilt to arise in a case of joint possession, the possession must be to the exclusion of all persons not party to the crime. *Id.*; State v. Osborne, 149 N.C. App. 235 (2002); State v. Foster, 149 N.C. App. 206 (2002); State v. Sluka, 107 N.C. App. 200 (1992). Thus, the defendant possessed stolen property when the stolen items were found in a truck driven by the defendant and the two other passengers in the truck were parties to the crime. *Foster*, 149 N.C. App. 206 (2002). By contrast, the evidence was insufficient when the defendant was found, along with three other individuals, in a car containing stolen goods but no criminal conspiracy was shown among the four. *Maines*, 301 N.C. 669.

The third prong of the doctrine requires that the defendant had possession of the property recently after it was stolen. There are no firm rules about how soon the defendant must have come into possession of the property. State v. Wilson, 313 N.C. 516 (1985); State v. Patterson, 194 N.C. App. 608, 619 (2009) ("no bright line rule"). The general rule, however, is that the time between the theft and the possession must be close enough to make it unlikely that the possessor could have acquired the property honestly. State v. Jackson, 274 N.C. 594 (1968); State v. Hamlet, 316 N.C. 41 (1986); State v. Friend, 164 N.C. App. 430 (2004). Thus, for example, evidence supported application of the doctrine when (1) a video camera was found in the defendant's possession twenty-one days after a break-in, *Patterson*, 194 N.C. App. at 620–21; (2) the contents of a robbery victim's purse were found in the defendant's possession within twenty-four hours after the robbery, State v. Reid, 151 N.C. App. 379 (2002); (3) within several days of a number of larcenies from nearby houses, stolen articles were found in the defendants' home, State v. Eppley, 282 N.C. 249 (1972); and (4) the victim's stolen address book was seen in the defendant's car three days after the larceny, State v. Pickard, 143 N.C. App. 485 (2001).

If the stolen property is a type normally and commonly traded in lawful channels, a relatively brief time interval between the theft and the finding of an accused in possession is required. *Hamlet*, 316 N.C. 41; State v. McQueen, 165 N.C. App. 454 (2004). Thus, the doctrine was inapplicable when a defendant was found in possession of eight-track tapes nineteen days after they were stolen and a rifle thirty days after it was stolen and the State conceded that both items are frequently traded in normal channels. State v. Parker, 54 N.C. App. 522 (1981); *see also Hamlet*, 316 N.C. at 45–46 (possession after thirty days was insufficient to invoke doctrine given that the items were normally and frequently traded in lawful channels). When the item is not normally or commonly traded in lawful channels, the doctrine may apply after the passage of a longer period of time between the larceny and the defendant's possession. *Hamlet*, 316 N.C. 41; *McQueen*, 165 N.C. App. 454. For example, the doctrine applied when (1) the defendant possessed a unique tool not generally traded in his community twenty-seven days after it was stolen and fingerprint evidence tied the defendant to the theft, State v. Blackmon, 6 N.C. App. 66 (1969); (2) the defendant or his girlfriend possessed a stolen watch up to four weeks after it was stolen, State v. Wilson, 313 N.C. 516, 536–37 (1985); and (3) the defendant possessed commercial restaurant equipment eleven to twelve days after it had been stolen, State v. Callahan, 83 N.C. App. 323 (1986).

Lost property. A person who finds lost property and takes it for personal use is guilty of larceny if, at the time of finding it, the person knows who the owner is or has a reasonable means of ascertaining the owner—that is, if there is a clue as to the owner's identity. State v. Moore, 46 N.C. App. 259, 262 (1980). Thus, when three women divided and kept for their own use money in a deposit bag labeled "Bank of North Carolina" after one of them had found the bag on a sidewalk, the finder was guilty of larceny, and the defendant, who took a share of the money for her own use knowing how it had been obtained, was guilty of receiving stolen property. *Id.* at 262–64.

Payment of money under G.S. 1-538.2 does not bar prosecution. When a defendant made a payment of money to a business pursuant to a demand for payment under G.S. 1-538.2 (civil liability for larceny, shoplifting, etc.), double jeopardy did not bar a subsequent larceny prosecution. State v. Beckham, 148 N.C. App. 282 (2002).

Related Offenses Not in This Chapter

See the offenses in Chapter 14 (Robbery, Extortion, and Blackmail).
See the offenses in Chapter 15 (Burglary, Breaking or Entering, and Related Offenses).
Computer fraud (various offenses) (Chapter 16)
See electronic food and nutrition benefits fraud (various offenses) in Chapter 16 (Fraud, Forgery, False Pretenses and Related Offenses).
See exploitation of an elderly or disabled adult (various offenses) in Chapter 16 (Fraud, Forgery, False Pretenses and Related Offenses).
Medicaid fraud (various offenses) (Chapter 16)
"Obtaining Property by False Pretenses" (Chapter 16)
Welfare fraud (various offenses) (Chapter 16)
Removal of shopping cart from shopping premises. G.S. 14-72.3.
Unauthorized taking or sale of labeled dairy milk cases or milk crates bearing the name or label of owner. G.S. 14-72.4.
Larceny of motor fuel. G.S. 14-72.5.
Felonious larceny, possession, or receiving of stolen goods from a permitted construction site. G.S. 14-72.6.
Larceny of secret technical processes. G.S. 14-75.1.
Larceny, mutilation or destruction of public records and papers. G.S. 14-76.
Larceny, concealment or destruction of wills. G.S. 14-77.
Larceny of ungathered crops. G.S. 14-78.
Larceny of ginseng. G.S. 14-79.
Larceny of pine needles or pine straw. G.S. 14-79.1.
Taking horses, mules, or dogs for temporary purposes. G.S. 14-82.
Pursuing or injuring livestock with intent to steal. G.S. 14-85.
Larceny, destruction, defacement or vandalism of portable toilets or pumper trucks. G.S. 14-86.2.
Making, distributing, possessing, transferring or programming device for theft of telecommunication service. G.S. 14-113.5 and 14-113.6.
Defacing or desecrating grave sites. G.S. 14-148.
Interfering with electric, gas or water meters. G.S. 14-151.1.
Failure to return hired property. G.S. 14-167.
Looting; trespass during emergency. G.S. 14-288.6.
Unlawful operation of an audiovisual recording device. G.S. 14-440.1.
Protection of patient property. G.S. 108A-60.
Stealing political signs. G.S. 136-32(e).

Felony Larceny

Statute

See G.S. 14-72, reproduced under "Misdemeanor Larceny," above.

§14-81. Larceny of horses, mules, swine, cattle, or dogs.

(a) Larceny of horses, mules, swine, or cattle is a Class H felony.

(a1) Larceny of a dog is a Class I felony.

(b) In sentencing a person convicted of violating this section, the judge shall, as a minimum punishment, place a person on probation subject to the following conditions:

(1) A person must make restitution for the damage or loss caused by the larceny of the livestock or dogs, and

(2) A person must pay a fine of not less than the amount of the damages or loss caused by the larceny of the livestock or dogs.

(c) No provision in this section shall limit the authority of the judge to sentence the person convicted of violating this section to an active sentence.

Elements

A person guilty of this offense

(1) takes
(2) personal property
(3) in the possession of another *and*
(4) carries it away
(5) without the consent of the possessor *and*
(6) with the intent to deprive the possessor of its use permanently,
(7) knowing that he or she was not entitled to it, *and*
(8) the larceny was
  (a) of property worth more than $1,000,
  (b) from the person,
  (c) committed pursuant to burglary, breaking out of a dwelling, breaking or entering a building, breaking or entering a building that is a place of religious worship, or burglary with explosives,
  (d) of an explosive or incendiary device,
  (e) of a firearm,
  (f) of a record or paper in the custody of the North Carolina State Archives, *or*
  (g) of a horse, mule, swine, cattle, or dog.

Punishment

Class H felony, G.S. 14-72(a), except that larceny of a dog is a Class I felony. G.S. 14-81(a1). If the larceny was of a horse, mule, swine, cattle, or dog, the minimum sentence is probation subject to the conditions that the person must make restitution for the damage or loss caused by the larceny and pay a fine of not less than the amount of the damages or loss caused by the larceny. G.S. 14-81(b).

Notes

Generally. Felony larceny is the same as misdemeanor larceny except that felony larceny requires proof of Element (8). Put another way, Elements (8)(a) through (8)(g) are the factors that elevate a misdemeanor larceny to a felony larceny.

Elements (1) through (7). See the notes on elements (1) through (7) to "Misdemeanor Larceny," above.

Element (8) generally. Elements (8)(a) through (8)(g) are alternate ways of proving felonious larceny. Only one of these factors must be present to raise the larceny to a felony. For example, if the larceny was committed pursuant to a burglary under Element (8)(c), the value of the property taken under Element (8)(a) is irrelevant.

Element (8)(a). If a defendant steals several items in a single incident, their value can be added together to reach the $1,000 threshold.

In most cases, the value of stolen goods is determined by their fair market value at the time of the theft, not their replacement cost. State v. Morris, 318 N.C. 643 (1986); State v. Cook, 263 N.C. 730 (1965). Fair market value is the price that a willing buyer would pay a willing seller for the item in question on the open market. State v. Haire, 96 N.C. App. 209, 210 (1989). This might be shown by the price of an item of similar age and condition or the average purchase price of such an item on the open market.

If the stolen property is not commonly traded and has no ascertainable market value (for example, a pay telephone), a jury may determine the property's value from evidence of its replacement cost. State v. Helms, 107 N.C. App. 237 (1992).

The State is not required to produce direct evidence of value, but it must produce enough evidence so that the jury is not left to speculate about value. *Morris*, 318 N.C. 643; State v. Davis, 198 N.C. App. 146, 151–52 (2009) (although a stolen DVD player was missing a key component and was inoperable, evidence that it sold for more than $1,300 was sufficient); State v. Rahaman, ___ N.C. App. ___, 688 S.E.2d 58, 66–67 (2010) (there was sufficient evidence that a stolen truck was worth more than $1,000 where the owner purchased it new twenty years ago for $9,000; it was in "good shape," undamaged, had never been in an accident, and had been driven approximately 75,000 miles; the tires were in good condition and the radio and air conditioning worked; the owner later had an accident that resulted in a "total loss" for which he received $1,700 from insurance but would have received $2,100 had he given up title; and an officer testified that the vehicle had a value of approximately $3,000).

Element (8)(b). Larceny is "from the person" when the property is physically possessed by the person or when it is within the person's protection when it is stolen. State v. Buckom, 328 N.C. 313 (1991). This element was satisfied when (1) the defendant stole cash from an employee who was replenishing an automatic teller machine and the money was in a grocery cart by the employee's side, State v. Carter, 186 N.C. App. 259, 263-65 (2007); and (2) a convenience store employee opened a cash register to make change for the defendant, and the defendant reached into and took money from the register; the money was within the employee's protection when it was stolen, *Buckom*, 328 N.C. 313. This element was not satisfied when a defendant took a bank bag from a shopping mall kiosk when the kiosk employee was about twenty-five feet away; the bag was not in the immediate presence of and under the employee's protection or control when it was taken. State v. Barnes, 345 N.C. 146 (1996).

Element (8)(c). The statute specifies larceny "committed pursuant to a violation of G.S. 14-51, 14-53, 14-54, 14-54.1 or 14-57." It does not include larceny committed pursuant to breaking and entering a motor vehicle under G.S. 14-56; see "Breaking or Entering a Vehicle" in Chapter 15 (Burglary, Breaking or Entering, and Related Offenses). The breaking or entering or burglary that precedes the larceny need not have been committed by the defendant. State v. Pearcy, 50 N.C. App. 210 (1980) (after others broke into a store, the defendant acted in concert with them to steal the store's merchandise; on these facts the defendant could be found guilty of larceny after breaking or entering).

Element (8)(d). An "explosive or incendiary device or substance" includes any:

- explosive or incendiary grenade or bomb;
- dynamite, blasting powder, nitroglycerin, TNT, or other high explosive; and
- device, ingredient for such device, or type or quantity of substance primarily useful for large-scale destruction of property by explosive or incendiary action or lethal injury to persons by explosive or incendiary action.

G.S. 14-72(b)(3). It does not include:

- fireworks or
- any form, type, or quantity of gasoline, butane gas, natural gas, or any other substance having explosive or incendiary properties but serving a legitimate nondestructive or nonlethal use in the form, type, or quantity stolen.

Id.

Element (8)(e). Larceny of a firearm is a felony regardless of the value of the firearm. State v. Robinson, 51 N.C. App. 567, 568 (1981). The term "firearm" includes any instrument used in the propulsion of a shot, shell, or bullet by the action of gunpowder or any other explosive substance within it. G.S. 14-72(b)(4). A firearm that is not capable of being fired at the time of the theft is covered if it can be made to work. *Id.* Air rifles or air pistols are not included. *Id.*

Element (8)(f). This element covers any record or paper in the custody of the North Carolina State Archives. The "North Carolina State Archives" is defined in G.S. 121-2(7). The relevant papers are defined in G.S. 121-2(8) and include all documents, papers, letters, maps, books, photographs, films, sound recordings, magnetic or other tapes, electronic data processing records, artifacts, or other documentary material made or received pursuant to law or ordinance or in connection with the transaction of official business by any agency.

Element (8)(g). G.S. 14-81(a) provides that larceny of horses, mules, swine, or cattle is a Class H felony, regardless of the value of the animal taken. G.S. 14-81(a2) makes larceny of a dog a Class I felony, regardless of the value of the animal taken.

Charging issues. See this note to "Misdemeanor Larceny," above.

Greater and lesser-included offenses. See this note to "Misdemeanor Larceny," above.

Multiple convictions and punishments. See this note to "Misdemeanor Larceny," above.

Because the legislature intended that the crime of breaking or entering and the crime of felony larceny pursuant to that breaking or entering would be separately punished, a defendant may be punished for both crimes when the convictions are obtained in a single trial. State v. Gardner, 315 N.C. 444, 463 (1986). This rule likely applies to the other related offenses in Element (8)(c) as well (burglary, breaking out of a dwelling, breaking or entering a building that is a place of religious worship, and burglary with explosives).

Relation to other offenses. See this note to "Misdemeanor Larceny," above.

Verdict. A trial court may accept a guilty verdict of felonious larceny pursuant to a burglary or related crime and a not guilty verdict of the burglary or the related crime; although inconsistent, the verdicts are not mutually exclusive and thus are permissible. State v. Mumford, 364 N.C. 394, 402 (2010) (overruling contrary case law).

Doctrine of recent possession. See this note to "Misdemeanor Larceny," above.

Lost property. See this note to "Misdemeanor Larceny," above.

Payment of money under G.S. 1-538.2 does not bar prosecution. See this note to "Misdemeanor Larceny," above.

Forfeiture. G.S. 14-86.1 provides for the forfeiture of all conveyances (including vehicles, watercraft or aircraft) used

(1) to unlawfully conceal, convey, or transport property in violation of G.S. 14-71 (receiving stolen goods; receiving or possessing goods represented as stolen), 14-71.1 (possessing stolen goods), or 20-106 (receiving or transferring stolen vehicle),
(2) in the commission of a robbery,

(3) in violation of G.S. 14-72.7 (chop shop offenses), or
(4) in the commission of any larceny when the property taken is more than $2,000.

The statute provides for certain exceptions and for seizure of the conveyance subject to forfeiture. G.S. 14-86.1.

Related Offenses Not in This Chapter

See the offenses listed under "Misdemeanor Larceny," above.

Larceny of a Chose in Action

Statute

§14-75. Larceny of chose in action.

If any person shall feloniously steal, take and carry away, or take by robbery, any bank note, check or other order for the payment of money issued by or drawn on any bank or other society or corporation within this State or within any of the United States, or any treasury warrant, debenture, certificate of stock or other public security, or certificate of stock in any corporation, or any order, bill of exchange, bond, promissory note or other obligation, either for the payment of money or for the delivery of specific articles, being the property of any other person, or of any corporation (notwithstanding any of the said particulars may be termed in law a chose in action), that person is guilty of a Class H felony.

Elements

A person guilty of this offense

(1) (a) feloniously steals, takes, and carries away *or*
(b) takes by robbery
(2) a chose in action
(3) belonging to another.

Punishment

Class H felony. G.S. 14-75.

Notes

Element (1)(a). One reading of the statute is that the stealing, taking, and carrying away must be done feloniously. Under this reading, this element would appear to cover all felonious larcenies. See "Felony Larceny," above. It also would appear to cover any other felonious stealing, such as a felonious embezzlement, provided the felony involves a taking and carrying away. For an explanation of the terms "takes" and "carries away," see the notes on Elements (1) and (4) to "Misdemeanor Larceny," above. Another reading of the statute is that the word "feloniously" refers to the fact that the crime itself is a felony and does not require that the stealing, taking, and carrying away be felonious. However, such a reading does not give meaning to the term "feloniously," and as such it may be disfavored under traditional rules of statutory interpretation.

Element (1)(b). See "Common Law Robbery" and "Armed Robbery," both in Chapter 14 (Robbery, Extortion, and Blackmail).

Element (2). At common law, documents representing debts (known as choses in action), such as checks, were not recognized as property with the value of the debt. Therefore, a statute had to be enacted to cover the theft of these items. State v. Dill, 75 N.C. 257 (1876). The statute applies only to "any bank note, check or other order for the payment of money issued by or drawn on any bank or other society or corporation . . . , or any treasury warrant, debenture, certificate of stock or other public security, or certificate of stock in any corporation, or any order, bill of exchange, bond, promissory note or other obligation, either for the payment of money or for the delivery of specific articles." G.S. 14-75. A blank check does not appear to be a chose in action. Because a blank check has at least some value, however trivial, the theft of a blank check can be charged as misdemeanor larceny. *Cf.* State v. Murphy, 321 N.C. 738 (1988) (defendant was convicted of larceny of blank check and car keys).

Charging issues. See this note to "Misdemeanor Larceny," above.

Multiple convictions and punishments. See this note to "Misdemeanor Larceny," above.

Doctrine of recent possession. See this note to "Misdemeanor Larceny," above.

Related Offenses Not in This Chapter

See the offenses listed under "Misdemeanor Larceny," above.

Unauthorized Use of a Motor-Propelled Conveyance

Statute

§14-72.2. Unauthorized use of a motor-propelled conveyance.

(a) A person is guilty of an offense under this section if, without the express or implied consent of the owner or person in lawful possession, he takes or operates an aircraft, motorboat, motor vehicle, or other motor-propelled conveyance of another.

(b) Unauthorized use of an aircraft is a Class H felony. All other unauthorized use of a motor-propelled conveyance is a Class 1 misdemeanor.

(c) Unauthorized use of a motor-propelled conveyance shall be a lesser-included offense of unauthorized use of an aircraft.

(d) As used in this section, "owner" means any person with a property interest in the motor-propelled conveyance.

Elements

A person guilty of this offense

(1) willfully
(2) (a) takes *or*
    (b) operates
(3) a motor-propelled conveyance
(4) of another
(5) without the consent of
    (a) the owner *or*
    (b) other person in lawful possession.

Punishment

If the conveyance is an aircraft, the offense is a Class H felony. G.S. 14-72.2(b). For any other kind of motor-propelled conveyance, the offense is a Class 1 misdemeanor. *Id.* If the Class H version of this offense is charged, the relevant fact—that the conveyance was an aircraft—must be alleged in the indictment and proved to the jury.

Notes

Element (1). The taking or operating must be willful. State v. Milligan, 192 N.C. App. 677, 683 (2008). See "Willfully" in Chapter 1 (States of Mind).

Element (2) generally. Note that this element is satisfied by proof of taking *or* operating. Thus, a person lawfully may take a conveyance but later unlawfully be operating it beyond the scope of the owner's or possessor's consent.

Element (2)(a). See the note on Element (1) to "Misdemeanor Larceny," above.

Element (2)(b). For a discussion of the term "operating" in the context of motor vehicle offenses, see the note on Element (1) to "Driving While License Revoked" in Chapter 28 (Motor Vehicle Offenses).

Element (3). The statute covers aircrafts, motorboats, motor vehicles, and other motor-propelled conveyances. G.S. 14-72.2(a).

Element (5)(a). "Owner" means any person with a property interest in the motor-propelled conveyance. G.S. 14-72.2(d). The consent of one authorized to act for the owner also would be sufficient to grant lawful possession to the user (for example, a person who borrowed a vehicle). Evidence of tag letters and numbers along with a certified copy of the Division of Motor Vehicles registration or certificate of title is prima facie evidence of the ownership of a motor vehicle. G.S. 8-37.

Greater and lesser-included offenses. Unauthorized use of a motor-propelled conveyance is not a lesser-included offense of possession of stolen goods, discussed below. State v. Nickerson, ___ N.C. ___, 715 S.E.2d 845 (2011) (applying the definitional test and concluding that unauthorized use of a motor-propelled conveyance contains at least one element not present in possession of stolen goods); State v. Oliver, ___ N.C. App. ___, ___ S.E.2d ___ (Dec. 6, 2011) (following *Nickerson*).

Depending on the evidence, unauthorized use of a motor-propelled conveyance can be a lesser-included offense of larceny of a motor vehicle, discussed below. State v. Ross, 46 N.C. App. 338, 339 (1980) (so concluding as a matter of legislative intent); State v. Watson, 179 N.C. App. 228, 246 (2006) (citing *Ross*); N.C. PATTERN JURY INSTRUCTIONS—CRIM. 216.10 at n.6.

Unauthorized use of a motor-propelled conveyance is a lesser-included offense of unauthorized use of an aircraft. G.S. 14-72.2(c).

Relation to other offenses. This offense is used in cases of "joyriding," when a larceny charge is inappropriate because of the absence of an intent to deprive the owner of the vehicle's permanent use. See the note on Element (6) to "Misdemeanor Larceny," above.

Doctrine of recent possession. The doctrine of recent possession applies to this offense. State v. Frazier, 268 N.C. 249, 254 (1966). For a discussion of that doctrine, see this note to "Misdemeanor Larceny," above.

Related Offenses Not in This Chapter

Removing boats. G.S. 14-162.
Failure to return rented vehicle. G.S. 14-167.

Possession of Stolen Goods

Misdemeanor Possession of Stolen Goods

Statute

See G.S. 14-72, reproduced under "Misdemeanor Larceny," above.

Elements

A person guilty of this offense

(1) possesses
(2) stolen property
(3) knowing, or having reasonable grounds to believe, that it was stolen
(4) with a dishonest purpose.

Punishment

Class 1 misdemeanor. G.S. 14-72(a).

Notes

Generally. The prosecution typically prefers to charge possession of stolen goods rather than receiving stolen goods because the element of "possession" is likely easier to prove than the element of "receiving." Also, for the possession offense, it is not necessary to prove that someone other than the defendant stole the property, as long as circumstances would have led a reasonable person to believe it was stolen, State v. Perry, 305 N.C. 225 (1982); in contrast, proof that the property was stolen by another is required for receiving. For the elements of this offense, see *Perry*, 305 N.C. at 233.

Element (1). Possession may be actual or constructive. A defendant has actual possession of an item if it is on his or her person, the defendant is aware of its presence, and either alone or with others has the power and intent to control its disposition or use. Constructive possession exists when the defendant, while not having actual possession, has the intent and capability to maintain control or dominion over the item. State v. Szucs, ___ N.C. App. ___, 701 S.E.2d 362, 365–66 (2010) (possession of stolen goods may be actual or constructive); State v. Marshall, ___ N.C. App. ___, 696 S.E.2d 894, 897 (2010). When an item is found on premises under the defendant's exclusive control, this itself may be sufficient evidence of constructive possession. *See, e.g., Marshall*, 696 S.E.2d at 897. However, if the defendant does not have exclusive control over the premises, the State must show other incriminating circumstances before constructive possession may be inferred. *See id.*

The evidence established that the defendant possessed stolen tools found in a truck he was driving when the defendant had unrestricted access to the truck, gave permission for the tools to be placed in it, saw the tools placed in the truck, was given the tools by the passenger of the truck, and did not refuse the property. State v. Southards, 189 N.C. App. 152, 156–57 (2008). In a case involving felonious breaking or entering, larceny, and possession of stolen goods, there was sufficient evidence of possession when the defendant's truck was parked at the residence with its engine running; items found in the truck included electronic equipment from the residence; a man fitting the defendant's description was seen holding items later identified as stolen; items reported as missing included electronic equipment and a large quantity of loose change; the police dog's handler observed evidence that someone recently had been in a muddy area behind the residence; the side door of the residence showed pry marks; the defendant was found wearing muddy clothing and shoes and in possession of a Leatherman tool and a large quantity of loose change; the defendant had actual possession of the electronic equipment and the loose change and constructive possession of the items in the truck. *Szucs*, 701 S.E.2d at 365–66. In contrast, the trial court committed reversible error by instructing the jury on constructive possession when the property—a vehicle stolen from a gas station—was found parked on the street outside of the defendant's residence; the vehicle's location on a public street, the fact that it was not under the defendant's exclusive control, and the additional circumstances recounted by the State did not support an inference that defendant had "the intent and capability to maintain control and dominion over" the vehicle. *Marshall*, 696 S.E.2d at 896–98. For more detailed discussions of constructive possession as it applies to other crimes, see the note to Element (2) to "Possession of a Controlled Substance" in Chapter 27 (Drug Offenses) and the note on Element (2)(c) to "Possession of a Firearm by a Felon" in Chapter 22 (Weapons Offenses).

Element (2). It is not necessary to prove that someone else stole the property in order to convict a defendant for possession of stolen property. State v. Kelly, 39 N.C. App. 246, 248 (1978).

Element (3). Knowledge or reasonable grounds to believe that property was stolen can be inferred when a defendant-seller is willing to sell property at a fraction of its value or when a defendant-buyer purchases property at a fraction of its value. State v. Tanner, 193 N.C. App. 150, 155 (2008) (quoting *State v. Parker*, 316 N.C. 295, 304 (1986), and holding that there was sufficient evidence that the defendant knew that the property was stolen on this basis). For a case in which the evidence raised only a suspicion or conjecture that the defendant knew or should have known that the goods were stolen, and thus was insufficient, see *State v. Webb*, 192 N.C. App. 719, 721–24 (2008).

For a case holding that the evidence was sufficient to establish the defendant's knowledge that goods were stolen but insufficient to establish that the defendant knew that a gun was stolen, see *State v. Weakley*, 176 N.C. App. 642, 652–53 (2006). For another case in which the evidence was insufficient to show that the defendant knew that a gun was stolen, see *State v. Brown*, 182 N.C. App. 277, 281–82 (2007).

Whether the defendant knew or had reasonable grounds to believe that the property was stolen usually is proved through inferences from the evidence. *Weakley*, 176 N.C. App. at 652. When a defendant throws away a stolen weapon used in crime, it can be inferred that the defendant knew the weapon was stolen; however, that inference was inappropriate in a case where the defendant and an accomplice left the gun in the accomplice's mother's bedroom. State v. Wilson, ___ N.C. App. ___, 691 S.E.2d 734, 739–40 (2010).

The evidence was sufficient to establish that the defendant knew that tools had been stolen when (1) the tools were visible in the bed of a pickup driven by the defendant, both the tools and the truck were reported stolen hours before the defendant was stopped in the truck, and the defendant fled after being pulled over, State v. Marsh, 187 N.C. App. 235, 243 (2007); and (2) although the defendant only suspected that tools were stolen, he did not trust the person who gave him the tools and was not surprised that they were stolen, State v. Southards, 189 N.C. App. 152, 157–58 (2008).

For a case in which the evidence was insufficient to establish that the defendant knew that a four-wheeler was stolen, see *State v. Cannon*, ___ N.C. App. ___, ___ S.E.2d ___ (Nov. 1, 2011) (distinguishing *State v. Lofton*, 66 N.C. App. 79 (1984), the court noted, among other things, that the cosmetic changes to the four-wheeler were minimal, the defendant openly drove the four-wheeler and did not flee from the police, and there was no evidence regarding how the defendant obtained possession of the four-wheeler).

Element (4). This element requires some kind of illegal purpose, which may be inferred from the circumstances of the case, ROLLIN M. PERKINS & RONALD N. BOYCE, CRIMINAL LAW 404 (3d ed. 1982), such as evidence that the defendant intended to convert the property to his or her own use, N.C. PATTERN JURY INSTRUCTIONS—CRIM. 216.47. An illegal purpose may be shown with evidence that the defendant acted with intent to aid the thief, receiver, or possessor of stolen goods. State v. Parker, 316 N.C. 295, 305 (1986). It is not necessary that the defendant gain personally by his or her actions. *Id.* at 305–06; State v. Tanner, 193 N.C. App. 150, 155 (2008).

Evidence that a person received or possessed property with an innocent intent, such as an intent to return the property without reward to its owner, can disprove this element. PERKINS & BOYCE at 404.

A dishonest purpose was established when the defendant helped the thief carry items from the crime scene and later was found in possession of some of those items. *Tanner*, 193 N.C. App. at 155–56.

Charging issues. See this note to "Misdemeanor Larceny," above.

Greater and lesser-included offenses. Because each offense includes an element that is not in the other, possession of stolen goods is not a lesser-included offense of receiving stolen goods. State v. Davis, 302 N.C. 370, 373–74 (1981).

Unauthorized use of a motor-propelled conveyance, above, is not a lesser-included offense of possession of stolen goods. State v. Nickerson, ___ N.C. ___, 715 S.E.2d 845 (2011) (applying the definitional test and concluding that unauthorized use of a motor-propelled conveyance contains at least one element not present in possession of stolen goods); State v. Oliver, ___ N.C. App. ___, ___ S.E.2d ___ (Dec. 6, 2011) (following *Nickerson*).

Multiple convictions and punishments. If a defendant is found to possess more than one stolen item, the number of separate offenses of possession of stolen property for which the defendant may be convicted equals the number of times the defendant obtained possession of the property. Thus, if a defendant obtains ten stolen items during eight different times of receipt following break-ins over a six-week period, the defendant is guilty of eight separate offenses of possession of stolen goods. State v. White, 322 N.C. 770 (1988). However, when as part of one continuous transaction a defendant came into possession of several stolen items at the same time, only one conviction of possession of stolen goods was permitted. State v. Phillips, 172 N.C. App. 143 (2005).

Although larceny, possession of stolen goods, and receiving stolen goods are separate offenses for purposes of double jeopardy, the legislature did not intend that a defendant would be convicted of more than one of these offenses when charges are based on the same conduct. State v. Perry, 305 N.C. 225, 231–37 (1982). Thus, while a defendant may be charged with and tried for larceny, receiving, and possession of the same property, he or she may be convicted of only one of those offenses when they are committed during a single transaction. *Id.* at 236–37; State v. Szucs, ___ N.C. App. ___, 701 S.E.2d 362, 368 (2010) (citing *Perry*).

A defendant may not be sentenced for both robbery and possession of stolen property taken during the robbery. State v. Moses, ___ N.C. App. ___, 698 S.E.2d 688, 695–96 (2010) (coming to this conclusion as a matter of legislative intent).

Although a defendant may be indicted and tried for both possession of stolen goods under G.S. 14-71.1 and possession of a stolen vehicle under G.S. 20-106, a defendant may not be convicted of both offenses based on possession of the same motor vehicle. State v. Bailey, 157 N.C. App. 80, 85–87 (2003) (coming to this conclusion as a matter of legislative intent).

Doctrine of recent possession. The North Carolina Pattern Jury Instructions express doubt as to whether the doctrine of recent possession is applicable to possession offenses. N.C. PATTERN JURY INSTRUCTIONS—CRIM. 104.40 at n.1; see generally this note to "Misdemeanor Larceny" (describing the doctrine), above.

Lost property. See this note to "Misdemeanor Larceny," above.

Effect of acquittal of larceny and breaking or entering charges. A defendant acquitted of breaking or entering and larceny charges may be convicted of felonious possession of stolen goods. State v. Tanner, 364 N.C. 229, 232–33 (2010).

Related Offenses Not in This Chapter

See the offenses listed under "Misdemeanor Larceny," above.
"Accessory after the Fact to a Felony" (Chapter 5)
Criminal possession of financial transaction card forgery devices. G.S. 14-113.14.
Failure to follow record requirements for peddlers, itinerant merchants, and specialty market vendors. G.S. 66-257.
Failure to follow pawnbroker requirements. G.S. 91A-11.

Felony Possession of Stolen Goods

Statute

See G.S. 14-72, reproduced under "Misdemeanor Larceny," above.

> **§14-71.1. Possessing stolen goods.**
>
> If any person shall possess any chattel, property, money, valuable security or other thing whatsoever, the stealing or taking whereof amounts to larceny or a felony, either at common law or by virtue of any statute made or hereafter to be made, such person knowing or having reasonable grounds to believe the same to have been feloniously stolen or taken, he shall be guilty of a Class H felony, and may be indicted and convicted, whether the felon stealing and taking such chattels, property, money, valuable security or other thing shall or shall not have been previously convicted, or shall or shall not be amenable to justice; and any such possessor may be dealt with, indicted, tried and punished in any county in which he shall have, or shall have had, any such property in his possession or in any county in which the thief may be tried, in the same manner as such possessor may be dealt with, indicted, tried and punished in the county where he actually possessed such chattel, money, security, or other thing; and such possessor shall be punished as one convicted of larceny.

Elements

A person guilty of this offense

(1) possesses
(2) property
(3) stolen or taken feloniously
(4) knowing, or having reasonable grounds to believe, that the property was feloniously stolen or taken *and*
(5) with a dishonest purpose.

Punishment

Class H felony. G.S. 14-71.1.

Notes

Generally. See this note to "Misdemeanor Possession of Stolen Goods," above.

Element (1). See the note on Element (1) to "Misdemeanor Possession of Stolen Goods," above.

Element (2). The statute describes the covered property to include any "chattel, property, money, valuable security, or other thing whatsoever." G.S. 14-71.1.

Element (3). Pursuant to G.S. 14-71.1, possession of stolen goods is a Class H felony if the theft or taking was pursuant to a felony larceny or other felony (such as, for example, embezzlement). For a discussion of when a larceny is a felony, see the note on Element (8) to "Felony Larceny," above. Although G.S. 14-72(a) arguably could be read to limit felonious possession of stolen goods to the five circumstances specified in G.S. 14-72(b) that elevate a misdemeanor larceny to a felony larceny, it is not clear that such an interpretation is widely held, *see, e.g.,* N.C. Pattern Jury Instructions—Crim. 216.49A (providing a jury instruction for felonious possession when the goods were feloniously taken other than by larceny), or is appropriate given the express language of G.S. 14-71.1. Admittedly, however, the punishment provisions in G.S. 14-72(a) and 14-71.1 appear to be in conflict on this issue: while G.S. 14-72(a) suggests that the offense is only a felony in the five circumstances specified in G.S. 14-72(b) that elevate a misdemeanor larceny to a felony larceny, G.S. 14-71.1 suggests that the offense is a felony whenever the goods were taken pursuant to any felony larceny or any other felonious taking. This conflict came about with enactment of Structured Sentencing, when G.S. 14-71.1 was amended. S.L. 1993-539, sec. 1165. Prior to this change, G.S. 14-71.1 created the substantive offense and G.S. 14-72(a) specified punishment. When G.S. 14-71.1 was amended to specify Class H punishment, no corresponding clarifying change was made to G.S. 14-72. Ultimately, this issue will be one for the courts to resolve when faced with a defendant challenging the felony status of a conviction for possession of stolen goods when the underlying larceny was a felony not prescribed by G.S. 14-72(b) (for example, felony larceny of a dog under G.S. 14-84) or when the underlying taking was a non-larceny felony (such as embezzlement).

Element (4). See the note on Element (3) to "Misdemeanor Possession of Stolen Goods," above.

Element (5). This is equivalent to felonious intent. State v. Parker, 316 N.C. 295 (1986); State v. Withers, 111 N.C. App. 340 (1993). See the note on Element (3) to "Misdemeanor Possession of Stolen Goods," above.

Charging issues. See this note to "Misdemeanor Larceny," above.

Greater and lesser-included offenses. See this note to "Misdemeanor Possession of Stolen Goods," above.

Multiple convictions and punishments. See this note to "Misdemeanor Possession of Stolen Goods," above; *see also* State v. Surrett, ___ N.C. App. ___, ___ S.E.2d ___ (Nov. 15, 2011) (the trial court erred by convicting the defendant of two counts of possession of a stolen firearm under G.S. 14-71.1; "[w]hile defendant did possess the two separate stolen firearms, we hold that defendant may not be convicted on separate counts for each firearm possessed").

Doctrine of recent possession. See this note to "Misdemeanor Possession of Stolen Goods," above.

Lost property. See this note to "Misdemeanor Larceny," above.

Effect of acquittal of larceny and breaking or entering charges. See this note to "Misdemeanor Possession of Stolen Goods," above.

Impact of the thief's guilt. A person may be charged and convicted of this offense regardless of whether the felon who stole the property has or has not been convicted or is or is not amenable to justice. G.S. 14-71.1.

Jurisdiction and venue. A person may be tried in any county where he or she possessed the stolen item or where the theft occurred. G.S. 14-71.1; State v. Brown, 85 N.C. App. 583, 586–88 (1987). See generally "Lack of Jurisdiction" in Chapter 2 (Bars and Defenses).

Forfeiture. See this note to "Felony Larceny," above.

Related Offenses Not in This Chapter

See the offenses listed under "Misdemeanor Possession of Stolen Goods," above.

Possession of Goods Represented as Stolen

Statute

§14-71. Receiving stolen goods; receiving or possessing goods represented as stolen.

(a) If any person shall receive any chattel, property, money, valuable security or other thing whatsoever, the stealing or taking whereof amounts to larceny or a felony, either at common law or by virtue of any statute made or hereafter to be made, such person knowing or having reasonable grounds to believe the same to have been feloniously stolen or taken, he shall be guilty of a Class H felony, and may be indicted and convicted, whether the felon stealing and taking such chattels, property, money, valuable security or other thing, shall or shall not have been previously convicted, or shall or shall not be amenable to justice; and any such receiver may be dealt with, indicted, tried and punished in any county in which he shall have, or shall have had, any such property in his possession or in any county in which the thief may be tried, in the same manner as such receiver may be dealt with, indicted, tried and punished in the county where he actually received such chattel, money, security, or other thing; and such receiver shall be punished as one convicted of larceny.

(b) If a person knowingly receives or possesses property in the custody of a law enforcement agency that was explicitly represented to the person by an agent of the law enforcement agency or a person authorized to act on behalf of a law enforcement agency as stolen, the person is guilty of a Class H felony and may be indicted, tried, and punished in any county in which the person received or possessed the property.

Elements

A person guilty of this offense:

(1) knowingly
(2) possesses
(3) property
(4) in the custody of a law enforcement agency
(5) that was explicitly represented to the person to be stolen by
(6) (a) an agent of the law enforcement agency *or*
(b) a person authorized to act on behalf of a law enforcement agency.

Punishment

Class H felony. G.S. 14-71(b).

Notes

Element (1). See "Knowingly" in Chapter 1 (States of Mind).

Element (2). See the note on Element (1) to "Misdemeanor Possession of Stolen Goods," above.

Element (5). No specific words are required to be spoken to fulfill the "explicitly represented" element; rather, the statute "merely requires that a person knowingly receives or possesses property that was clearly expressed, either by words or conduct, as constituting stolen property." State v. Louali, ___ N.C. App. ___, ___ S.E.2d ___ (Aug. 16, 2011) (in a case involving receiving of stolen laptop computers, the evidence was sufficient when an undercover officer said that he was told that the business bought "stolen property, stolen laptops" and he twice reminded the defendant that "this stupid guy kept leaving the door open, [and] I kept running in the back of it and taking laptops;" after the exchange of money for the laptops, the officer told the defendant that he could get more laptops).

Jurisdiction and venue. A person may be charged, tried, and punished in any county in which he or she possessed the property. G.S. 14-71(b). See generally "Lack of Jurisdiction" in Chapter 2 (Bars and Defenses).

Forfeiture. See this note to "Felony Larceny," above.

Related Offenses Not in This Chapter

See the offenses listed under "Misdemeanor Possession of Stolen Goods," above.

Receiving Stolen Goods

Misdemeanor Receiving of Stolen Goods

Statute

See G.S. 14-72, reproduced under "Misdemeanor Larceny," above.

Elements

A person guilty of this offense

(1) (a) receives *or*
    (b) conceals
(2) property
(3) stolen by another
(4) knowing, or with reasonable grounds to believe, that it was stolen *and*
(5) with a dishonest purpose.

Punishment

Class 1 misdemeanor. G.S. 14-72(a).

Notes

Generally. See this note to "Misdemeanor Possession of Stolen Goods," above.

Element (1). Property may be constructively received to satisfy this element; that is, it is sufficient that property be delivered to the receiver's control, rather than into his or her physical possession. State v. Ellers, 234 N.C. 42 (1951); State v. Stroud, 95 N.C. 626 (1886); State v. Hart, 14 N.C. App. 120 (1972); See also the note on Element (1) to "Misdemeanor Possession of Stolen Goods," above. For a discussion of constructive possession in the context of drug offenses and weapons offenses, see the note on Element (2) to "Possession of a Controlled Substance" in Chapter 27 (Drug Offenses) and the note on Element (2)(c) to "Possession of a Firearm by a Felon" in Chapter 22 (Weapons Offenses).

Element (4). See the note on Element (3) to "Misdemeanor Possession of Stolen Goods," above.

Element (5). See the note on Element (4) to "Misdemeanor Possession of Stolen Goods," above.

Charging issues. See this note to "Misdemeanor Larceny," above.

Greater and lesser-included offenses. Because each offense includes an element that is not in the other, possession of stolen goods is not a lesser-included offense of receiving stolen goods. State v. Davis, 302 N.C. 370, 373–74 (1981).

Multiple convictions and punishments. Although larceny, possession of stolen goods, and receiving stolen goods are separate offenses for purposes of double jeopardy, the legislature did not intend that a defendant would be convicted of more than one of these offenses when charges are based on the same conduct. State v. Perry, 305 N.C. 225, 231–37 (1992). Thus, while a defendant may be charged with and tried for larceny, receiving, and possession of the same property, he or she may be convicted of only one of those offenses when they are committed during a single transaction. *Id.* at 236–37; State v. Szucs, ___ N.C. App. ___, 701 S.E.2d 362, 368 (2010) (citing *Perry*).

Doctrine of recent possession. The doctrine of possession of recently stolen property does not apply to receiving stolen goods. State v. Best, 202 N.C. 9 (1931); State v. Yow, 227 N.C. 585 (1947); *see also* N.C. Pattern Jury Instructions—Crim. 104.40; see generally this note to "Misdemeanor Larceny" (describing the doctrine), above.

Lost property. See this note to "Misdemeanor Larceny," above.

Related Offenses Not in This Chapter

See the offenses listed under "Misdemeanor Larceny," above.
"Accessory after the Fact to a Felony" (Chapter 5)
Criminal receipt of goods and services fraudulently obtained. G.S. 14-113.15.
Failure to follow pawnbroker requirements. G.S. 91A-11.

Felony Receiving Stolen Goods

Statute

See G.S. 14-71, reproduced under "Possession of Goods Represented as Stolen," and G.S. 14-72, reproduced under "Misdemeanor Larceny," both above.

Elements

A person guilty of this offense

(1) (a) receives *or*
    (b) conceals
(2) property
(3) stolen or taken feloniously
(4) by another
(5) knowing, or with reasonable grounds to believe, that the property was feloniously stolen or taken *and*
(6) with a dishonest purpose.

Punishment

Class H felony. G.S. 14-71(a).

Notes

Generally. See this note to "Misdemeanor Possession of Stolen Goods," above.

Element (1). See the note on Element (1) to "Misdemeanor Receiving of Stolen Goods," above.

Element (2). The statute specifies that the property at issue includes "chattel, property, money, valuable security or other thing whatsoever." G.S. 14-71(a).

Element (3). Pursuant to G.S. 14-71, receiving of stolen goods is a Class H felony if the theft or taking was pursuant to a felony larceny or other felony (such as, for example, embezzlement). For a discussion of when a larceny is a felony, see the notes on Element (8) to "Felony Larceny," above. Although G.S. 14-72(a) arguably could be read to limit felonious receiving of stolen goods to the five circumstances specified in G.S. 14-72(b) that elevate a misdemeanor larceny to a felony larceny, it is not clear that such an interpretation is widely held or appropriate given the express language of G.S. 14-71. Admittedly, however, the punishment provisions in G.S. 14-72(a) and 14-71 appear to be in conflict on this issue: while G.S. 14-72(a) suggests that the offense is only a felony in the five circumstances specified in G.S. 14-72(b) that elevate a misdemeanor larceny to a felony larceny, G.S. 14-71 suggests that the offense is a felony whenever the goods were taken pursuant to any felony larceny or any other felonious taking. This conflict came about with enactment of Structured Sentencing when G.S. 14-71 was amended. S.L. 1993-539, sec. 1164. Prior to this change, G.S. 14-71 created the substantive offense and G.S. 14-72(a) specified punishment. When G.S. 14-71 was amended to specify Class H punishment, no corresponding clarifying change was made to G.S. 14-72. Ultimately, this issue will be one for the courts to resolve when faced with a defendant challenging the felony status of a conviction for possession of stolen goods when the underlying larceny was a felony not prescribed by G.S. 14-72(b) (for example, felony larceny of a dog under G.S. 14-84) or when the underlying taking was a non-larceny felony (such as embezzlement).

Element (5). See the note on Element (3) to "Misdemeanor Possession of Stolen Goods," above.

Element (6). See the note on Element (4) to "Misdemeanor Possession of Stolen Goods," above.

Charging issues. See this note to "Misdemeanor Larceny," above.

Greater and lesser-included offenses. See this note to "Misdemeanor Receiving of Stolen Goods," above. Because all of the elements of misdemeanor receiving of stolen goods are included in this offense, the misdemeanor offense is a lesser-included offense of the felony version.

Doctrine of recent possession. See this note to "Misdemeanor Receiving of Stolen Goods," above.

Relation to other offenses. See this note to "Misdemeanor Larceny," above.

Lost property. See this note to "Misdemeanor Larceny," above.

Jurisdiction and venue. G.S. 14-71(a) provides that a person may be tried in the county where he or she received or possessed the property or where the thief may be tried. See generally "Lack of Jurisdiction" in Chapter 2 (Bars and Defenses).

Impact of the thief's guilt. A person may be indicted and convicted of this offense regardless of whether the felon stealing and taking the property has or has not been convicted or is or is not amenable to justice. G.S. 14-71(a).

Forfeiture. See this note to "Felony Larceny," above.

Related Offenses Not in This Chapter

See the offenses listed under "Misdemeanor Receiving of Stolen Goods," above.

Receiving Goods Represented as Stolen

Statute

See G.S. 14-71(b), reproduced under "Possession of Goods Represented as Stolen," above.

Elements

A person guilty of this offense:

(1) knowingly
(2) receives
(3) property
(4) in the custody of a law enforcement agency
(5) that was explicitly represented to the person to be stolen by
(6) (a) an agent of the law enforcement agency *or*
    (b) a person authorized to act on behalf of a law enforcement agency.

Punishment

Class H felony. G.S. 14-71(b).

Notes

Generally. This offense is exactly the same as "Possession of Goods Represented as Stolen," above, except that this offense involves receiving the goods and that one involved possessing them.

Element (1). See "Knowingly" in Chapter 1 (States of Mind).

Element (2). See the note on Element (1) to "Misdemeanor Receiving of Stolen Goods," above.

Related Offenses Not in This Chapter

See the offenses listed under "Misdemeanor Receiving of Stolen Goods," above.

Vehicle and Vehicle Part Offenses

Possession of a Stolen Vehicle

Statute

§20-106. Receiving or transferring stolen vehicles.

Any person who, with intent to procure or pass title to a vehicle which he knows or has reason to believe has been stolen or unlawfully taken, receives or transfers possession of the same from or to another, or who has in his possession any vehicle which he knows or has reason to believe has been stolen or unlawfully taken, and who is not an officer of the law engaged at the time in the performance of his duty as such officer shall be punished as a Class H felon.

Elements

A person guilty of this offense

(1) possesses
(2) a vehicle
(3) knowing, or with reasonable grounds to believe, that it was stolen or unlawfully taken.

Punishment

Class H felony. G.S. 20-106.

Notes

Element (1). See the note on Element (1) to "Misdemeanor Possession of Stolen Goods," above.

Element (2). For a definition of the term "vehicle," see the note on Element (2) to "Impaired Driving" in Chapter 28 (Motor Vehicle Offenses).

Element (3). For a discussion of actual and constructive possession, see the note on Element (3) to "Misdemeanor Possession of Stolen Goods," above.

Sufficient evidence supported a conviction when the defendant was found driving a vehicle several hours after it had been stolen, possessed the victim's keys, claimed the vehicle belonged to a "friend" but would not give the friend's name, and the victim testified that he had not given anyone permission to drive the vehicle. State v. Bailey, 157 N.C. App. 80 (2003).

Multiple convictions and punishments. When a defendant came into possession of five stolen vehicles during a continuous theft transaction, only one conviction of possession of stolen vehicles was permitted. State v. Phillips, 172 N.C. App. 143 (2005).

Although a defendant may be indicted and tried for both possession of stolen goods under G.S. 14-71.1 and possession of a stolen vehicle under G.S. 20-106, a defendant may not be convicted of both offenses based on possessing the same motor vehicle. *Bailey*, 157 N.C. App. 80.

Doctrine of recent possession. See this note to "Misdemeanor Larceny," above. At least one case has held that the doctrine of recent possession may provide a sufficient basis for concluding that a defendant who possesses a vehicle that has been recently stolen knows that the vehicle was stolen, unless there are circumstances tending to show that the person could have obtained the vehicle innocently. State v. Murchinson, 39 N.C. App. 163 (1978). However, the

North Carolina Pattern Jury Instructions express doubt as to whether the doctrine is applicable to possession offenses. N.C. PATTERN JURY INSTRUCTIONS—CRIM. 104.40 at n.1.

Exceptions. The statute exempts law enforcement officers engaged in their duties. G.S. 20-106. It is not necessary for the State to prove that the defendant was not such an officer because that provision of the statute is intended as an exemption to protect law enforcement officers and is not an element of the offense. *Murchinson*, 39 N.C. App. at 166–67.

Forfeiture. See this note to "Felony Possession of Stolen Goods," above.

Related Offenses Not in This Chapter

Failure to return hired property. G.S. 14-167.

Receiving or Transferring a Stolen Vehicle

Statute

See G.S. 20-106, reproduced under "Possession of a Stolen Vehicle," above.

Elements

A person guilty of this offense

(1) (a) receives *or*
    (b) transfers
(2) a vehicle
(3) knowing, or with reasonable grounds to believe, that it was stolen or unlawfully taken *and*
(4) with intent to procure or pass title to the vehicle.

Punishment

Class H felony. G.S. 20-106.

Notes

Generally. The prosecution generally would prefer a charge of "Possession of a Stolen Vehicle," above, to this crime because "possession" is likely easier to prove than "receiving" and because this crime requires proof of the intent to procure or pass title.

Element (1)(a). See the note on Element (1) to "Misdemeanor Receiving of Stolen Goods," above.

Element (2). For a definition of the term "vehicle," see the note on Element (2) to "Impaired Driving" in Chapter 28 (Motor Vehicle Offenses).

Element (3). See the note on Element (3) to "Misdemeanor Possession of Stolen Goods," above.

Element (4). This element makes this offense slightly different from receiving stolen goods. If someone receives stolen goods to help the thief, without intending to procure title (that is, legal ownership) of them, that person commits the offense of receiving stolen goods. To commit the offense of receiving or transferring a stolen vehicle, the defendant must have received the stolen vehicle intending to procure title or pass title to someone else.

Doctrine of recent possession. See this note to "Misdemeanor Larceny," above. At least one case has held that the doctrine of recent possession may provide a sufficient basis for concluding that a defendant who possesses a vehicle that has been recently stolen knows that the vehicle was stolen, unless there are circumstances tending to show that the person could have obtained the vehicle innocently. State v. Murchinson, 39 N.C. App. 163 (1978). However, the North Carolina Pattern Jury Instructions express doubt as to whether the doctrine is applicable to possession and receiving offenses. N.C. PATTERN JURY INSTRUCTIONS—CRIM. 104.40 at n.1.

Exceptions. See this note to "Possession of a Stolen Vehicle," above.

Forfeiture. See this note to "Felony Larceny," above.

Related Offenses Not in This Chapter

None

Altering, Destroying, etc. any Stolen Motor Vehicle or Part

Statute

§14-72.7. Chop shop activity.

(a) A person is guilty of a Class H felony if that person knowingly engages in any of the following activities, without regard to the value of the property in question:

(1) Altering, destroying, disassembling, dismantling, reassembling, or storing any motor vehicle or motor vehicle part the person knows to be illegally obtained by theft, fraud, or other illegal means.

(2) Permitting a place to be used for any activity prohibited by this section, where the person either owns or has legal possession of the place, and knows that the place is being used for any activity prohibited by this section.

(3) Purchasing, disposing of, selling, transferring, receiving, or possessing a motor vehicle or motor vehicle part with the knowledge that the vehicle identification number of the motor vehicle, or vehicle part identification number of the vehicle part, has been altered, counterfeited, defaced, destroyed, disguised, falsified, forged, obliterated, or removed.

(4) Purchasing, disposing of, selling, transferring, receiving, or possessing a motor vehicle or motor vehicle part to or from a person engaged in any activity prohibited by this section, knowing that the person is engaging in that activity.

(b) Innocent Activities. – The provisions of this section shall not apply to either of the following:

(1) Purchasing, disposing of, selling, transferring, receiving, possessing, crushing, or compacting a motor vehicle or motor vehicle part in good faith and without knowledge of previous illegal activity in regard to that vehicle or part, as long as the person engaging in the activity does not remove a vehicle identification number or vehicle part identification number before or during the activity.

(2) Purchasing, disposing of, selling, transferring, receiving, possessing, crushing, or compacting a motor vehicle or motor vehicle part after law enforcement proceedings are completed or as a part of law enforcement proceedings, as long as the activity is not in conflict with law enforcement proceedings.

(c) Civil Penalty. – Any court with jurisdiction of a criminal prosecution under this section may also assess a civil penalty. The clear proceeds of the civil penalties shall be remitted to the Civil Penalty and Forfeiture Fund in accordance with G.S. 115C-457.2. The civil penalty shall not exceed three times the assets obtained by the defendant as a result of violations of this section.

(d) Private Actions. – Any person aggrieved by a violation of this section may, in a civil action in any court of competent jurisdiction, obtain appropriate relief, including preliminary and other equitable or declaratory relief, compensatory and punitive damages, reasonable investigation expenses, costs of suit, and any attorneys' fees as may be provided by law.

(e) Seizure and Forfeiture. – Any instrumentality possessed or used to engage in the activities prohibited by this section are subject to the seizure and forfeiture provisions of

G.S. 14-86.1. The real property of a place used to engage in the activities prohibited by this section is subject to the abatement and forfeiture provisions of Chapter 19 of the General Statutes.

(f) Definitions. – For the purposes of this section, the following definitions apply:

(1) Instrumentality. – Motor vehicle, motor vehicle part, other conveyance, tool, implement, or equipment possessed or used in the activities prohibited under this section.

(2) Vehicle identification number. – A number, a letter, a character, a datum, a derivative, or a combination thereof, used by the manufacturer or the Division of Motor Vehicles for the purpose of uniquely identifying a motor vehicle.

(3) Vehicle part identification number. – A number, a letter, a character, a datum, a derivative, or a combination thereof, used by the manufacturer for the purpose of uniquely identifying a motor vehicle part.

Elements

A person guilty of this offense

(1) knowingly
(2) (a) alters,
 (b) destroys,
 (c) disassembles,
 (d) dismantles,
 (e) reassembles, *or*
 (f) stores
(3) any
 (a) motor vehicle *or*
 (b) motor vehicle part
(4) knowing the vehicle or part to be illegally obtained by theft, fraud, or other illegal means.

Punishment

Class H felony. G.S. 14-72.7(a).

Notes

Element (1). See "Knowingly" in Chapter 1 (States of Mind).

Element (3). For a definition of the term "motor vehicle" in the context of motor vehicle offenses, see the note on Element (2) to "Driving While License Revoked" in Chapter 28 (Motor Vehicle Offenses).

Element (4). This element requires actual knowledge; it does not cover a defendant who "should have known" the relevant fact. See "Objective knowledge" and "Subjective knowledge" in Chapter 1 (States of Mind).

Exceptions. G.S. 14-72.7(b) provides that the following activites are not covered by the statute:

- Purchasing, disposing of, selling, transferring, receiving, possessing, crushing, or compacting a motor vehicle or part in good faith and without knowledge of previous illegal activity, provided the person does not remove a vehicle identification number or part identification number before or during the activity. The terms "vehicle identification number" and "vehicle part identification number" are defined in G.S. 14-72.7(f)(2) and (3).
- Purchasing, disposing of, selling, transferring, receiving, possessing, crushing, or compacting a motor vehicle or part after law enforcement proceedings are completed or as a part of law enforcement proceedings, provided the activity is not in conflict with those proceedings.

Seizure and forfeiture. G.S. 14-72.7(e) provides that any instrumentality possessed or used to engage in the activities prohibited by this section are subject to seizure and forfeiture under G.S. 14-86.1. The real property of a place used to engage in the activities prohibited by this section is subject to the abatement and forfeiture provisions of Chapter 19 of the General Statutes. *Id.*

Related Offenses Not in This Chapter

None

Permitting a Place to Be Used to Violate the Chop Shop Laws

Statute

See G.S. 14-72.7(a)(2) reproduced under "Altering, Destroying, etc. Any Stolen Motor Vehicle or Part," above.

Elements

A person guilty of this offense

(1) knowingly
(2) permits
(3) a place that the person owns or has legal possession of
(4) to be used for any activity prohibited by G.S. 14-72.7.

Punishment

Class H felony. G.S. 14-72.7(a).

Notes

Element (1). See "Knowingly" in Chapter 1 (States of Mind).

Exceptions. See this note to "Altering, Destroying, etc. Any Stolen Motor Vehicle or Part," above.

Seizure and forfeiture. See this note to "Altering, Destroying, etc. Any Stolen Motor Vehicle or Part," above.

Related Offenses Not in This Chapter

None

Purchasing, Selling, etc. of a Motor Vehicle or Part with an Altered Identification Number

Statute

See G.S. 14-72.7(a)(3) reproduced under "Altering, Destroying, etc. Any Stolen Motor Vehicle or Part," above.

Elements

A person guilty of this offense

(1) knowingly
(2) (a) purchases,
  (b) disposes of,
  (c) sells,
  (d) transfers,
  (e) receives, *or*

(f) possesses
(3) (a) a motor vehicle *or*
(b) a motor vehicle part
(4) knowing that the vehicle identification number of the motor vehicle, or vehicle part identification number of the vehicle part, has been altered, counterfeited, defaced, destroyed, disguised, falsified, forged, obliterated, or removed.

Punishment

Class H felony. G.S. 14-72.7(a).

Notes

Element (1). See "Knowingly" in Chapter 1 (States of Mind).

Element (2)(c). For an explanation of the term "sells" in the context of drug offenses, see the note on Element (2)(a) to "Sale or Delivery of a Controlled Substance" in Chapter 27 (Drug Offenses).

Element (2)(e). For a discussion of the term "receives," see the note on Element (1) to "Misdemeanor Receiving of Stolen Goods," above.

Element (2)(f). For a discussion of the term "possesses," see the note on Element (1) to "Misdemeanor Possession of Stolen Goods," above.

Element (3). For a definition of the term "motor vehicle" as used in the context of motor vehicle offenses, see the note on Element (2) to "Driving While License Revoked" in Chapter 28 (Motor Vehicle Offenses).

Element (4). For definitions of the terms "vehicle identification number" and "vehicle part identification number," see G.S. 14-72.7(f)(2) and (3).

Exceptions. See this note to "Altering, Destroying, etc. Any Stolen Motor Vehicle or Part," above.

Seizure and forfeiture. See this note to "Altering, Destroying, etc. Any Stolen Motor Vehicle or Part," above.

Related Offenses Not in This Chapter

None

Purchasing, Disposing of, etc. a Motor Vehicle or Part in Connection with a Chop Shop Violation

Statute

See G.S. 14-72.7(a)(4) reproduced under "Altering, Destroying, etc. Any Stolen Motor Vehicle or Part," above.

Elements

A person guilty of this offense

(1) knowingly
(2) (a) purchases,
(b) disposes of,
(c) sells,
(d) transfers,
(e) receives, *or*
(f) possesses

(3) (a) a motor vehicle *or*
(b) a motor vehicle part
(4) to or from a person
(5) engaged in any activity prohibited by G.S. 14-72.7
(6) knowing that the person is engaging in that activity.

Punishment

Class H felony. G.S. 14-72.7(a).

Notes

Element (1). See "Knowingly" in Chapter 1 (States of Mind).

Element (2)(c). For an explanation of the term "sells" in the context of drug offenses, see the note on Element (2)(a) to "Sale or Delivery of a Controlled Substance" in Chapter 27 (Drug Offenses).

Element (2)(e). For a discussion of the term "receives," see the note on Element (1) to "Misdemeanor Receiving of Stolen Goods," above.

Element (2)(f). For a discussion of the term "possesses," see the note on Element (1) to "Misdemeanor Possession of Stolen Goods," above.

Element (3). For a definition of the term "motor vehicle" as used in the context of motor vehicle offenses, see the note on Element (2) to "Driving While License Revoked" in Chapter 28 (Motor Vehicle Offenses).

Element (6). This element requires actual knowledge; the fact that the defendant "should have known" does not satisfy this element. See "Subjective knowledge" and "Objective knowledge" in Chapter 1 (States of Mind).

Exceptions. See this note to "Altering, Destroying, etc. Any Stolen Motor Vehicle or Part," above.

Seizure and forfeiture. See this note to "Altering, Destroying, etc. Any Stolen Motor Vehicle or Part," above.

Related Offenses Not in This Chapter

None

Larceny of a Motor Vehicle Part

Statute

§14-72.8. Felony larceny of motor vehicle parts.

Unless the conduct is covered under some other provision of law providing greater punishment, larceny of a motor vehicle part is a Class I felony if the cost of repairing the motor vehicle is one thousand dollars ($1,000) or more.

For purposes of this section, the cost of repairing a motor vehicle means the cost of any replacement part and any additional costs necessary to install the replacement part in the motor vehicle.

Elements

A person guilty of this offense

(1) commits a larceny
(2) of a motor vehicle part *and*
(3) the cost of repairing the vehicle is $1,000 or more.

Punishment

Class I felony. G.S. 14-72.8.

Notes

Element (1). For the elements of larceny, see "Misdemeanor Larceny," above.

Element (2). For the definition of the term "motor vehicle" in the context of motor vehicle offenses, see the note on Element (2) to "Driving While License Revoked" in Chapter 28 (Motor Vehicle Offenses).

Element (3). The cost of repairing a motor vehicle means the cost of any replacement part and any additional costs necessary to install the replacement part in the motor vehicle. G.S. 14-72.8.

Multiple convictions and punishments. The statute begins with the following language: "Unless the conduct is covered under some other provision of law providing greater punishment." This language may be interpreted to mean that a defendant cannot be punished for this offense and another one providing a harsher punishment based on the same act. For a discussion of similar language in the assault context, see this note to "Assault Inflicting Serious Injury" in Chapter 7 (Assaults). Note that "Felony Larceny," above, is punished as a Class H felony.

Related Offenses Not in This Chapter

Larceny of motor fuel. G.S. 14-72.5.
Failure to return hired property. G.S. 14-167.

Stealing from Merchants and Retail Establishments

Larceny from a Merchant

Statute

§14-72.11. Larceny from a merchant.

A person is guilty of a Class H felony if the person commits larceny against a merchant under any of the following circumstances:

(1) If the property taken has a value of more than two hundred dollars ($200.00), by using an exit door erected and maintained to comply with the requirements of 29 C.F.R. §1910.36 and 29 C.F.R. §1910.37 upon which door has been placed a notice, sign, or poster providing information about the felony offense and punishment provided under this subsection, to exit the premises of a store.

(2) By removing, destroying, or deactivating a component of an antishoplifting or inventory control device to prevent the activation of any antishoplifting or inventory control device.

(3) By affixing a product code created for the purpose of fraudulently obtaining goods or merchandise from a merchant at less than its actual sale price.

(4) When the property is infant formula valued in excess of one hundred dollars ($100.00). As used in this subsection, the term "infant formula," has the same meaning as found in 21 U.S.C. §321(z).

Punishment

Class H felony. G.S. 14-72.11.

Elements

A person guilty of this offense

(1) commits a larceny
(2) against a merchant *and*
(3) (a) takes property valued at more than $200 using a specified exit door to leave the premises;
(b) removes, destroys, or deactivates a component of an anti-shoplifting or inventory control device to prevent the activation of any such device;
(c) affixes a product code created to fraudulently obtain goods or merchandise at less than actual sale price; *or*
(d) the property is infant formula valued at more than $100.

Notes

Element (1). For the elements of larceny, see "Misdemeanor Larceny," above.

Element (2). The statute does not define the term "merchant."

Element (3)(a). The exit door referenced in Element (3)(a) means an "exit door erected and maintained to comply with the requirements of 29 C.F.R. § 1910.36 and 29 C.F.R. § 1910.37, upon which door has been placed a notice, sign, or poster providing information about the felony offense and punishment provided under this subsection." G.S. 14-72.11(1). 29 C.F.R. § 1910.36 sets forth design and construction requirements for exit routes. 29 C.F.R. § 1910.37 sets forth maintenance requirements, safeguards, and operational features for exit routes.

Element (3)(d). The term "infant formula" is defined by a cross-reference to 21 U.S.C. § 321(z). G.S. 14-72.11(4).

Related Offenses Not in This Chapter

None

Conspiracy to Commit Retail Theft

Statute

§14-86.6. Organized retail theft.

(a) A person is guilty of a Class H felony if the person:

(1) Conspires with another person to commit theft of retail property from retail establishments, with a value exceeding one thousand five hundred dollars ($1,500) aggregated over a 90-day period, with the intent to sell that retail property for monetary or other gain, and who takes or causes that retail property to be placed in the control of a retail property fence or other person in exchange for consideration.

(2) Receives or possesses any retail property that has been taken or stolen in violation of subdivision (1) of this subsection while knowing or having reasonable grounds to believe the property is stolen.

(b) Any interest a person has acquired or maintained in violation of this section shall be subject to forfeiture pursuant to the procedures for forfeiture set out in G.S. 18B-504.

Elements

A person guilty of this offense

(1) conspires with another person
(2) to commit theft
(3) of retail property
(4) valued at more than $1,500 aggregated over a 90-day period
(5) from retail establishments

(6) with the intent to sell the property for gain *and*
(7) takes or causes the property to be placed in the control of a retail property fence or other person
(8) in exchange for consideration.

Punishment

Class H felony. G.S. 14-86.6(a).

Notes

Element (1). See "Conspiracy" in Chapter 5 (General Crimes).

Element (2). "Theft" is defined as follows: "[t]o take possession of, carry away, transfer, or cause to be carried away the retail property of another with the intent to steal the retail property." G.S. 14-86.5(3).

Element (3). "Retail property" is defined as "[a]ny new article, product, commodity, item, or component intended to be sold in retail commerce." G.S. 14-86.5(1).

Element (4). The value of an item is defined as the "retail value of an item as advertised by the affected retail establishment, to include all applicable taxes." G.S. 14-86.5(4).

Element (7). A "retail property fence" is "[a] person or business that buys retail property knowing or believing that retail property is stolen." G.S. 14-86.5(2).

Forfeiture. Any interest a person acquires or maintains in violation of G.S. 14-86.6 is subject to forfeiture under G.S. 18B-504. G.S. 14-86.6(b).

Related Offenses Not in This Chapter

"Conspiracy" (Chapter 5)

Receiving or Possessing Stolen Retail Property

Statute

See G.S. 86.6(a)(2), reproduced under "Conspiracy to Commit Retail Theft," above.

Elements

A person guilty of this offense

(1) (a) receives *or*
 (b) possesses
(2) retail property
(3) that has been taken or stolen in connection with a conspiracy to commit retail theft
(4) knowing or having reasonable grounds to believe that the property is stolen.

Punishment

Class H felony. G.S. 14-86.6(a).

Notes

Element (1)(a). For a discussion of the term "receives," see the note on Element (1)(a) to "Misdemeanor Receiving of Stolen Goods," above.

Element (1)(b). For a discussion of the term "possesses," see the note on Element (1) to "Misdemeanor Possession of Stolen Goods," above.

Element (2). See the note on Element (3) to "Conspiracy to Commit Retail Theft," above.

Element (3). See "Conspiracy to Commit Retail Theft," above.

Element (4). See the note on Element (3) to "Misdemeanor Possession of Stolen Goods," above.

Related Offenses Not in This Chapter

None

Shoplifting by Concealing Merchandise

Statute

§14-72.1. Concealment of merchandise in mercantile establishments.

(a) Whoever, without authority, willfully conceals the goods or merchandise of any store, not theretofore purchased by such person, while still upon the premises of such store, shall be guilty of a misdemeanor and, upon conviction, shall be punished as provided in subsection (e). Such goods or merchandise found concealed upon or about the person and which have not theretofore been purchased by such person shall be prima facie evidence of a willful concealment.

(b) Repealed by Session Laws 1985 (Regular Session, 1986), c. 841, s. 2.

(c) A merchant, or the merchant's agent or employee, or a peace officer who detains or causes the arrest of any person shall not be held civilly liable for detention, malicious prosecution, false imprisonment, or false arrest of the person detained or arrested, where such detention is upon the premises of the store or in a reasonable proximity thereto, is in a reasonable manner for a reasonable length of time, and, if in detaining or in causing the arrest of such person, the merchant, or the merchant's agent or employee, or the peace officer had at the time of the detention or arrest probable cause to believe that the person committed the offense created by this section. If the person being detained by the merchant, or the merchant's agent or employee, is a minor under the age of 18 years, the merchant or the merchant's agent or employee, shall call or notify, or make a reasonable effort to call or notify the parent or guardian of the minor, during the period of detention. A merchant, or the merchant's agent or employee, who makes a reasonable effort to call or notify the parent or guardian of the minor shall not be held civilly liable for failing to notify the parent or guardian of the minor.

(d) Whoever, without authority, willfully transfers any price tag from goods or merchandise to other goods or merchandise having a higher selling price or marks said goods at a lower price or substitutes or superimposes thereon a false price tag and then presents said goods or merchandise for purchase shall be guilty of a misdemeanor and, upon conviction, shall be punished as provided in subsection (e).

Nothing herein shall be construed to provide that the mere possession of goods or the production by shoppers of improperly priced merchandise for checkout shall constitute prima facie evidence of guilt.

(d1) Notwithstanding subsection (e) of this section, any person who violates subsection (a) of this section by using a lead-lined or aluminum-lined bag, a lead-lined or aluminum-lined article of clothing, or a similar device to prevent the activation of any antishoplifting or inventory control device is guilty of a Class H felony.

(e) Punishment.—For a first conviction under subsection (a) or (d), or for a subsequent conviction for which the punishment is not specified by this subsection, the defendant shall be guilty of a Class 3 misdemeanor. The term of imprisonment may be suspended only on condition that the defendant perform community service for a term of at least 24 hours. For a second offense committed within three years after the date the defendant was convicted of an offense under this section, the defendant shall be guilty of a Class 2 misdemeanor. The term of imprisonment may be suspended only on condition that the defendant be imprisoned for a term of at least 72 hours as a condition of special probation, perform community service for a term of at least 72 hours, or both. For a third or subsequent offense committed within five years after the date the defendant was convicted of two other offenses under this section, the defendant shall be guilty of a Class 1 misdemeanor. The term of imprisonment may be suspended only if a condition of special probation is imposed to require the defendant to serve a term of imprisonment of at least

11 days. However, if the sentencing judge finds that the defendant is unable, by reason of mental or physical infirmity, to perform the service required under this section, and the reasons for such findings are set forth in the judgment, the judge may pronounce such other sentence as the judge finds appropriate.

(f) Repealed by Session Laws 2009-372, s. 12, effective December 1, 2009, and applicable to offenses committed on or after that date.

(g) Limitations.—For active terms of imprisonment imposed under this section:

(1) The judge may not give credit to the defendant for the first 24 hours of time spent in incarceration pending trial;
(2) The defendant must serve the mandatory minimum period of imprisonment and good or gain time credit may not be used to reduce that mandatory minimum period; and
(3) The defendant may not be released or paroled unless he is otherwise eligible and has served the mandatory minimum period of imprisonment.

Elements

A person guilty of this offense

(1) willfully conceals
(2) goods or merchandise of a store
(3) without authority,
(4) without having purchased the goods or merchandise, *and*
(5) while still on the premises of the store.

Punishment

Class 3 misdemeanor. G.S. 14-72.1(e). The statute contains some limitation on when the sentence may be suspended and allows for deviation by the sentencing judge in specified circumstances. *Id.* G.S. 14-72.1(g) contains additional limitations on terms of active imprisonment.

Notes

Element (1). To convict a person of this offense, the State need not prove that he or she intended to remove the property from the premises. State v. Hales, 256 N.C. 27 (1961). This offense, unlike larceny, does not require proof of an intent to deprive the owner of possession of the property permanently. *Id.*

The concealment is willful when it is done on purpose. *Id.* Finding a person with concealed goods that have not been purchased is prima facie evidence of willful concealment. G.S. 14-72.1(a). See generally "Willfully" in Chapter 1 (States of Mind).

Element (2). The statute applies only when the goods or merchandise are from a store and not when they are from some other kind of premises, such as a residence. State v. Wooten, 18 N.C. App. 652 (1973).

Element (3). If the person has been authorized to conceal the merchandise, the offense has not been committed.

Element (4). Once the person has purchased the goods, he or she may conceal them without committing the offense.

Element (5). If the concealment occurs off the store's premises, this offense has not been committed, even if the goods have not been purchased.

Relation to other offenses. See this note to "Misdemeanor Larceny," above.

Related Offenses Not in This Chapter

None

Repeat Shoplifting by Concealing Merchandise

Statute

See G.S. 14-72.1 reproduced under "Shoplifting by Concealing Merchandise," above.

Elements

A person guilty of this offense

(1) willfully conceals
(2) goods or merchandise of a store
(3) without authority,
(4) without having purchased the goods or merchandise,
(5) while still on the premises of the store, *and*
(6) (a) the offense was committed within three years after a prior shoplifting conviction,
 (b) the offense is a third or subsequent shoplifting offense and was committed within five years after conviction of two other shoplifting offenses, *or*
 (c) the offense is a subsequent shoplifting conviction not falling into either Element (6)(a) or (b).

Punishment

When Element (6)(a) is established, the offense is punished as a Class 2 misdemeanor. G.S. 14-72.1(e). When Element (6)(b) is established, the offense is punished as a Class 1 misdemeanor. *Id.* When Element (6)(c) is at issue, the offense is a Class 3 misdemeanor. *Id.* The relevant fact elevating punishment must be alleged in a charging instrument and proved at trial. *See* G.S. 15A-928 (pleading and proving prior convictions). In all instances, the statute contains some restrictions on when the sentence may be suspended and allows deviation by the sentencing judge in specified circumstances. G.S. 14-72.1(e). G.S. 14-72.1(g) contains additional limitations on terms of active imprisonment.

Notes

Generally. The notes to "Shoplifting by Concealing Merchandise," above, apply here as well.

Related Offenses Not In This Chapter

None

Shoplifting by Concealing Merchandise Using a Lead- or Aluminum-Lined Bag

Statute

See G.S. 14-72.1, reproduced under "Shoplifting by Concealing Merchandise," above.

Elements

A person guilty of this offense

(1) willfully conceals
(2) goods or merchandise of a store
(3) without authority,
(4) without having purchased the goods or merchandise,
(5) while still on the premises of the store, *and*
(6) uses a lead-lined or aluminum-lined bag, article of clothing, or similar device
(7) to prevent the activation of any anti-shoplifting or inventory control device.

Punishment

Class H felony. G.S. 14-72.1(d1). G.S. 14-72.1(g) contains limitations on terms of active imprisonment.

Notes

Generally. The notes to "Shoplifting by Concealing Merchandise," above, apply here as well.

Related Offenses Not in This Chapter

None

Shoplifting by Substitution of Prices

Statute

See G.S. 14-72.1(d), reproduced under "Shoplifting by Concealing Merchandise," above.

Elements

A person guilty of this offense

(1) willfully
(2) (a) transfers a price tag from goods or merchandise to other goods or merchandise having a higher selling price,
 (b) marks goods or merchandise at a lower price, *or*
 (c) places a false price tag on goods or merchandise
(3) without authority *and*
(4) then presents the goods for purchase.

Punishment

Class 3 misdemeanor. G.S. 14-72.1(e). The statute contains some limitation on when the sentence may be suspended and allows for deviation by the sentencing judge in specified circumstances. *Id.* G.S. 14-72.1(g) contains additional limitations on terms of active imprisonment.

Notes

Element (1). See "Willfully" in Chapter 1 (States of Mind).

Element (3). If the person has been authorized to alter the price, then no offense has occurred.

Element (4). No offense occurs unless the person, in addition to altering the price, also presents the goods for purchase.

The statute provides that it is not to be construed to mean that mere possession of goods or production of improperly priced merchandise for checkout is prima facie evidence of guilt. G.S. 14-72.1(d).

Related Offenses Not in This Chapter

"Obtaining Property by False Pretenses" (Chapter 16)

Repeat Shoplifting by Substitution of Prices

Statute

See G.S. 14-72.1, reproduced under "Shoplifting by Concealing Merchandise," above.

Elements

A person guilty of this offense

(1) willfully
(2) (a) transfers a price tag from goods or merchandise to other goods or merchandise having a higher selling price,
 (b) marks goods or merchandise at a lower price, *or*

(c) places a false price tag on goods or merchandise
(3) without authority *and*
(4) then presents the goods for purchase *and*
(5) (a) the offense was committed within three years after a prior shoplifting conviction,
(b) the offense is a third or subsequent shoplifting offense and is committed within five years after conviction of two other shoplifting offenses, *or*
(c) the offense is a subsequent conviction not falling into either Element (5)(a) or (b).

Punishment

When Element (5)(a) is established, the offense is punished as a Class 2 misdemeanor. G.S. 14-72.1(e). When Element (5)(b) is established, the offense is punished as a Class 1 misdemeanor. *Id.* When Element (5)(c) is at issue, the offense is a Class 3 misdemeanor. *Id.* The relevant fact elevating punishment must be alleged in a charging instrument and proved at trial. *See* G.S. 15A-928 (pleading and proving prior convictions). In all instances, the statute contains some restrictions on when the sentence may be suspended and allows deviation by the sentencing judge in specified circumstances. G.S. 14-72.1(e). G.S. 14-72.1(g) contains additional limitations on terms of active imprisonment.

Notes

Generally. The notes to "Shoplifting by Substitution of Prices" apply here as well.

Related Offenses Not in This Chapter

See the offenses listed under "Shoplifting by Substitution of Prices," above.

Financial Transaction Card Theft

Statute

§14-113.9. Financial transaction card theft.

(a) A person is guilty of financial transaction card theft when the person does any of the following:

(1) Takes, obtains or withholds a financial transaction card from the person, possession, custody or control of another without the cardholder's consent and with the intent to use it; or who, with knowledge that it has been so taken, obtained or withheld, receives the financial transaction card with intent to use it or to sell it, or to transfer it to a person other than the issuer or the cardholder.

(2) Receives a financial transaction card that he knows to have been lost, mislaid, or delivered under a mistake as to the identity or address of the cardholder, and who retains possession with intent to use it or to sell it or to transfer it to a person other than the issuer or the cardholder.

(3) Not being the issuer, sells a financial transaction card or buys a financial transaction card from a person other than the issuer.

(4) Not being the issuer, during any 12-month period, receives financial transaction cards issued in the names of two or more persons which he has reason to know were taken or retained under circumstances which constitute a violation of G.S. 14-113.13(a)(3) and subdivision (3) of subsection (a) of this section.

(5) With the intent to defraud any person, either (i) uses a scanning device to access, read, obtain, memorize, or store, temporarily or permanently, information encoded on another person's financial transaction card, or (ii) receives the encoded information from another person's financial transaction card.

(b) Credit card theft is punishable as provided by G.S. 14-113.17(b).

Taking or Withholding a Card

Statute

See G.S. 14-113.9(a)(1), reproduced above.

Elements

A person guilty of this offense

(1) (a) takes,
    (b) obtains, *or*
    (c) withholds
(2) a financial transaction card
(3) from another
(4) without the cardholder's consent *and*
(5) with the intent to use it.

Punishment

Class I felony. G.S. 14-113.9(b) & 14-113.17(b).

Notes

Element (2). A "financial transaction card" is a credit card, bank services card, banking card, check guarantee card, debit card, or any other card that allows the cardholder to obtain goods, services, or money on credit; to guarantee a check to the person accepting it; or to deposit, withdraw, or transfer funds from an account. It does not include credit cards for telephone calls. G.S. 14-113.8(4) (note that the use of a false or counterfeit telephone credit card and the unauthorized use of a telephone credit card are prohibited by G.S. 14-113.1). Even when the cardholder has consented to the loan of the financial transaction card, this offense can occur if the defendant does not return the card, because the offense covers unauthorized withholding. The evidence was sufficient when it showed that the defendant obtained the cards without consent but not that the defendant stole the cards. State v. Fraley, 182 N.C. App. 683, 688–89 (2007).

Element (4). G.S. 14-113.8(2) defines "cardholder" as "the person or organization named on the face of a financial transaction card to whom or for whose benefit the financial transaction card is issued by an issuer."

Element (5). Conviction for this offense requires proof that the defendant intended to use the financial transaction card. However, it need not be established that he or she actually used the card. A defendant's intent, which is not always clear, may be shown by conduct, statements, and other circumstances.

Prima facie evidence. G.S. 14-113.10 provides that it is prima facie evidence of this or any other form of financial transaction card theft that "a person has in his possession or under his control financial transaction cards issued in the names of two or more other persons other than members of his immediate family." The jury must be instructed on the prima facie evidence rule if the evidence tends to establish the statutory requirements. State v. Springer, 283 N.C. 627 (1973).

Multiple convictions and punishments. The taking, obtaining, or withholding of two credit cards belonging to the same person are separate offenses under G.S. 14-113.9. State v. Rawlins, 166 N.C. App. 160, 165 (2004) (interpreting the statute, the court rejected the defendant's argument that the "single taking" rule in larceny cases applies to this crime).

Related Offenses Not in This Chapter

See offenses in Chapter 16 (Fraud, Forgery, and Related Offenses).
Possession of financial transaction card forgery devices. G.S. 14-113.14.
Receipt of goods and services fraudulently obtained. G.S. 14-113.15.

Receiving a Wrongfully Obtained Card

Statute

See G.S. 14-113.9(a)(1), reproduced above.

Elements

A person guilty of this offense

(1) receives
(2) a financial transaction card
(3) intending to use it, sell it, or transfer it to a person other than the issuer or cardholder *and*
(4) knowing that it was taken, obtained, or withheld in violation of "Taking or Withholding a Card," above.

Punishment

Class I felony. G.S. 14-113.9(b) & 14-113.17(b).

Notes

Element (1). G.S. 14-113.8(8) defines "receives" as "acquiring possession or control or accepting a financial transaction card as security for a loan."

Element (2). For the meaning of the term "financial transaction card," see the note on Element (2) to "Taking or Withholding a Card," above.

Element (3). G.S. 14-113.8(5) defines "issuer" as "the business organization or financial institution or its duly authorized agent which issues a financial transaction card." For the definition of "cardholder," see the note on Element (4) to "Taking or Withholding a Card," above.

Element (4). The defendant must know that the financial transaction card was taken, obtained, or withheld from the person, possession, custody, or control of another without the cardholder's consent and with the intent to use it. State v. Brunson, 51 N.C. App. 413 (1981).

Prima facie evidence. See this note to "Taking or Withholding a Card," above.

Related Offenses Not in This Chapter

See the offenses listed under "Taking or Withholding a Card," above.

Wrongful Retention of a Misplaced Card

Statute

See G.S. 14-113.9(a)(2), reproduced above.

Elements

A person guilty of this offense

(1) receives
(2) a financial transaction card
(3) that he or she knows to have been lost, mislaid, or delivered under a mistake as to the identity or address of the cardholder *and*
(4) retains possession intending to
  (a) use or sell it *or*
  (b) transfer it to someone other than the issuer or cardholder.

Punishment

Class I felony. G.S. 14-113.9(b) & 14-113.17(b).

Notes

Element (1). For the meaning of the term "receives," see the note on Element (1) to "Receiving a Wrongfully Obtained Card," above.

Element (2). For the meaning of the term "financial transaction card," see the note on Element (1) to "Taking or Withholding a Card," above.

Element (4). Note that this element is not satisfied if the person merely retains the card; the person must also intend to use it, sell it, or transfer it. For definitions of "issuer" and "cardholder," see the note on Element (3) to "Receiving a Wrongfully Obtained Card," above, and on Element (4) to "Taking or Withholding a Card," above.

Prima facie evidence. See this note to "Taking or Withholding a Card," above.

Related Offenses Not in This Chapter

See the offenses listed under "Taking or Withholding a Card," above.

Buying a Card

Statute

See G.S. 14-113.9(a)(3), reproduced above.

Elements

A person guilty of this offense

(1) is not the issuer *and*
(2) buys
(3) a financial transaction card
(4) from someone other than the issuer.

Punishment

Class I felony. G.S. 14-113.9(b) & 14-113.17(b).

Notes

Elements (1) and (4). For a definition of "issuer," see the note on Element (3) to "Receiving a Wrongfully Obtained Card," above.

Element (3). For the meaning of the term "financial transaction card," see the note on Element (2) to "Taking or Withholding a Card," above.

Prima facie evidence. See this note to "Taking or Withholding a Card," above.

Related Offenses Not in This Chapter

See the offenses listed under "Taking or Withholding a Card," above.

Selling a Card

Statute

See G.S. 14-113.9(a)(3), reproduced above.

Elements

A person guilty of this offense

(1) is not the issuer *and*

(2) sells
(3) a financial transaction card.

Punishment

Class I felony. G.S. 14-113.9(b) & 14-113.17(b).

Notes

Element (1). For a definition of "issuer," see the note on Element (3) to "Receiving a Wrongfully Obtained Card," above.

Element (3). "Financial transaction card" is defined in the note on Element (2) to "Taking or Withholding a Card," above.

Prima facie evidence. See this note to "Taking or Withholding a Card," above.

Related Offenses Not in This Chapter

See the offenses listed under "Taking or Withholding a Card," above.

Receiving Two Cards Issued to Different Names

Statute

See G.S. 14-113.9(a)(4), reproduced above.

Elements

A person guilty of this offense

(1) is not the issuer *and*
(2) receives
(3) during a twelve-month period
(4) financial transaction cards issued in the names of two or more persons
(5) which he or she has reason to know were taken or retained in violation of G.S. 14-113.9(a)(3) ("Buying a Card" and "Selling a Card") or G.S. 14-113.13(a)(3) (fraudulently taking financial transaction cards as security for debt).

Punishment

Class I felony. G.S. 14-113.9(b) & 14-113.17(b).

Notes

Element (1). For a definition of "issuer," see the note on Element (3) to "Receiving a Wrongfully Obtained Card," above.

Element (2). For the definition of "receives," see the note on Element (1) to "Receiving a Wrongfully Obtained Card," above.

Element (3). Note that this element is satisfied if the second card is received within twelve months of the first, even if the two are received in different calendar years. Note also that mere possession within the twelve months is insufficient to establish a violation; both cards must be received during that period.

Element (4). For the meaning of the term "financial transaction card," see the note on Element (2) to "Taking or Withholding a Card," above.

Element (5). For the law prohibiting buying and selling financial transaction cards, see "Buying a Card" and "Selling a Card," both above. For the law prohibiting fraudulently taking financial transaction cards as security for a debt, see "Obtaining a Card as Security for a Debt" in Chapter 16 (Fraud, Forgery, False Pretenses, and Related Offenses).

Prima facie evidence. See this note to "Taking or Withholding a Card," above.

Related Offenses Not in This Chapter

See the offenses listed under "Taking or Withholding a Card," above.

Obtaining or Receiving Encoded Information

Statute

See G.S. 14-113.9(a)(5), reproduced above.

Elements

A person guilty of this offense

(1) with the intent to defraud any person

(2) (a) uses a scanning device to access, read, obtain, memorize, or store, temporarily or permanently, information encoded on another person's financial transaction card *or*

(b) receives the encoded information from another person's financial transaction card.

Punishment

Class I felony. G.S. 14-113.9(b) & 14-113.17(b).

Notes

Element (2) generally. For a definition of "financial transaction card," see the note on Element (2) to "Taking or Withholding a Card," above.

Element (2)(a). G.S. 14-113.8(10) defines a "scanning device" as "a scanner, reader, or any other device that is used to access, read, scan, obtain, memorize, or store, temporarily or permanently, information encoded on a financial transaction card."

Element (2)(b). For a definition of "receives," see the note on Element (1) to "Receiving a Wrongfully Obtained Card," above.

Prima facie evidence. See this note to "Taking or Withholding a Card," above.

Related Offenses Not in This Chapter

See the offenses listed under "Taking or Withholding a Card," above.

Embezzlement Offenses

Embezzlement by Employee

Statute

§14-74. Larceny by servants and other employees.

If any servant or other employee, to whom any money, goods or other chattels, or any of the articles, securities or choses in action mentioned in G.S. 14-75, by his master shall be delivered safely to be kept to the use of his master, shall withdraw himself from his master and go away with such money, goods or other chattels, or any of the articles, securities or choses in action mentioned as aforesaid, or any part thereof, with intent to steal the same and defraud his master thereof, contrary to the trust and confidence in him reposed by his said master; or if any servant, being in the service of his master, without the assent of his master, shall embezzle such money, goods or other chattels, or any of the articles, securities or choses in action mentioned as aforesaid, or any part thereof, or otherwise convert the same to his own use, with like purpose to steal them, or to defraud his master thereof, the servant so offending shall be guilty of a felony: Provided, that nothing contained in this section shall extend to apprentices or servants within the age of 16 years. If the value of the money, goods, or other chattels, or any of the articles, securities, or choses in action mentioned in G.S. 14-75, is one hundred thousand dollars ($100,000) or more, the person is guilty of a Class C felony. If the value of the money, goods, or other chattels, or any of the articles, securities, or choses in action mentioned in G.S. 14-75, is less than one hundred thousand dollars ($100,000), the person is guilty of a Class H felony.

Elements

A person guilty of this offense

(1) is an employee *and*
(2) willfully
  (a) goes away with a thing of value *or*
  (b) embezzles or converts to his or her own use a thing of value
(3) entrusted to the employee
(4) with the intent to steal it and defraud the employer.

Punishment

Class H felony. G.S. 14-74. It is a Class C felony if the value of the property taken is $100,000 or more. *Id.* If the Class C felony version of this crime is charged, the value of the property must be alleged in the charging instrument and proved to the jury.

Notes

Generally. Although the statute refers to this offense as larceny by employee, it is more appropriately referred to as embezzlement by employee. See the note entitled "Relation to other offenses" below.

Element (1). A prisoner assigned to work in a prison canteen is not an employee for purposes of this offense. State v. Frazier, 142 N.C. App. 207 (2001).

Element (2). The statute specifies that the thing taken can be "money, goods or other chattels, or any of the articles, securities or choses in action mentioned in G.S. 14-75." G.S. 14-74. For the meaning of the term "choses in action," see the note on Element (2) to "Larceny of a Chose in Action," above.

Element (3). This offense is not committed when the defendant initially obtains possession of the property without consent or by tricking the employer. In that instance, larceny may be the proper charge. Examples of when this offense would apply include a foreman of a tire store who took tires from the store, *Babb*, 34 N.C. App. 336, a service station attendant who took money with which he had been entrusted, State v. Bullin, 34 N.C. App. 589 (1977), a drug store employee who was a section chief and took drugs from the store, State v. Hauser, 257 N.C. 158 (1962), a manager of a clothing store who took clothes, State v. Monk, 36 N.C. App. 337 (1978), and a farm foreman who took cattle, State v. Brown, 56 N.C. App. 228 (1982). On the other hand, a person hired by a grocery store to bag groceries and sweep up who took food from the store committed larceny, not embezzlement by employee, because the person had not been entrusted with the food. State v. Lovick, 42 N.C. App. 577 (1979).

Exceptions. This offense may not be charged if the employee is under 16 years old. G.S. 14-74.

Charging issues. See this note to "Misdemeanor Larceny," above.

Greater and lesser-included offenses. Larceny is not a lesser-included offense of this crime. State v. Daniels, 43 N.C. App. 556, 557–58 (1979).

Relation to other offenses. The statutory title of this offense is misleading because it is not an appropriate charge when the facts show that a common law larceny was committed. State v. Wilson, 101 N.C. 730 (1888); State v. Babb, 34 N.C. App. 336 (1977); *Bullin*, 34 N.C. App. 589; State v. Brown, 56 N.C. App. 228 (1982); State v. Lovick, 42 N.C. App. 577 (1979); *Daniels*, 43 N.C. App. 556. Common law larceny requires a taking from another's lawful possession, *Lovick*, 42 N.C. App. 577, whereas larceny by employee requires that an employee have lawful possession and then wrongfully take the property. This offense is similar to "Embezzlement," below, because it involves a taking of property in violation of a trust relationship between an employer and employee; in fact, the statute for this crime includes the term "embezzles."

Related Offenses Not in This Chapter

"Obtaining Property by False Pretenses" (Chapter 16)

Embezzlement

Statute

§14-90. Embezzlement of property received by virtue of office or employment.

(a) This section shall apply to any person:
(1) Exercising a public trust.
(2) Holding a public office.
(3) Who is a guardian, administrator, executor, trustee, or any receiver, or any other fiduciary, including, but not limited to, a settlement agent, as defined in G.S. 45A-3.
(4) Who is an officer or agent of a corporation, or any agent, consignee, clerk, bailee or servant, except persons under the age of 16 years, of any person.

(b) Any person who shall:
(1) Embezzle or fraudulently or knowingly and willfully misapply or convert to his own use, or
(2) Take, make away with or secrete, with intent to embezzle or fraudulently or knowingly and willfully misapply or convert to his own use, any money, goods or other chattels, bank note, check or order for the payment of money issued by or drawn on any bank or other corporation, or any treasury warrant, treasury note, bond or obligation for the payment of money issued by the United States or by any state, or any other valuable security whatsoever that (i) belongs to any other person or corporation, unincorporated association or organization or (ii) are closing funds as defined in G.S. 45A-3, which shall have come into his possession or under his care, shall be guilty of a felony.

(c) If the value of the property described in subsection (b) of this section is one hundred thousand dollars ($100,000) or more, the person is guilty of a Class C felony. If the value of the property is less than one hundred thousand dollars ($100,000), the person is guilty of a Class H felony.

Elements

A person guilty of this offense

(1) fraudulently or knowingly and willingly
(2) uses for a purpose other than that for which the defendant received it
(3) the property of another
(4) held by the defendant under his or her care.

Punishment

Class H felony. G.S. 14-90. It is a Class C felony if the value of the property embezzled is $100,000 or more. *Id.* If the Class C felony version of this offense is charged, the relevant sum of money must be alleged in the charging instrument and proved to a jury.

Notes

Element (1). When a defendant receives money under an agency relationship and does not transmit it to the party to whom it is due, this is circumstantial evidence of the requisite criminal intent. State v. Newell, 189 N.C. App. 138, 142 (2008). Evidence that the defendant was experiencing financial problems is also circumstantial evidence of intent. *Id.*

Element (2). To commit this offense, the person entrusted with the property need not convert it to his or her own use, State v. Foust, 114 N.C. 842 (1894); the offense can occur if the person converts it to someone else's use. It also occurs if a person secretes the property with the intent to misapply it, even though the person never actually uses it. State v. Smithey, 15 N.C. App. 427 (1972).

It is not a defense to a charge of embezzlement that the defendant intended and was willing to return the property later. State v. Agnew, 294 N.C. 382 (1978).

There was sufficient evidence to support a store employee's conviction of embezzlement for "underringing," "free bagging," and "markdown fraud" when the evidence showed that all store employees were entrusted with the store's merchandise. "Underringing" is when an employee receives merchandise from a customer for purchase, and the employee keys in a price on the cash register lower than the price on the price tag. "Free bagging" is when a customer presents multiple items for purchase at a cash register and the employee fails to ring up all of the items but places all of them in a bag for the customer to take from the store. "Markdown fraud" is when an employee takes an item from the sales floor to a markdown machine, creates a price tag for the item that is lower than the true price of the item, and then purchases the item at the lower price. State v. Robinson, 166 N.C. App. 654 (2004). It appears that the conduct covered by markdown fraud would also constitute shoplifting by substitution of prices. However, both the regular and repeat version of that offense carry a lower punishment than embezzlement. See "Shoplifting by Substitution of Prices" and "Repeat Shoplifting by Substitution of Prices," both above.

Element (3). The property can include money, goods or other chattels, bank notes, checks or orders for payment issued by or drawn on any bank or other corporation, treasury warrants, treasury notes, bonds or obligations for payment of money issued by the United States or by any State, or any other valuable securities, provided the items belong to any other person, corporation, or unincorporated association or organization or are closing funds defined by G.S. 45A-3. The statute does not cover services. A business partner cannot be guilty under G.S. 14-90 of embezzlement of partnership funds; instead, the partner may be prosecuted for appropriating partnership funds to personal use, which violates G.S. 14-97. State v. Brown, 81 N.C. App. 281 (1986).

Element (4). The statute applies only to one who exercises a public trust, holds a public office, or is a guardian, administrator, executor, trustee, receiver, fiduciary (including a settlement agent as defined in G.S. 45A-3), corporate officer or agent, consignee, clerk, bailee, or servant. G.S. 14-90(a)(1)–(4). This offense does not apply to a corporate officer, agent, consignee, clerk, bailee, or servant who is under the age of 16. *Id.* at 14-90(a)(4).

There was sufficient evidence of a fiduciary relationship when the defendant entered into contracts with vendors under which he promised to collect receipts on their behalf and remit the money less a commission, with an accounting each month, thus showing that the vendors owned the money at the time it came into the defendant's hands; the contracts referred to the defendant as a "service agent" and the parties' operating agreement, which was incorporated into the contracts, referred to the defendant as a "nonexclusive [marketing] agent." State v. Newell, 189 N.C. App. 138, 142 (2008). An attorney who forged a client's signature on a settlement check from an insurance agent for a car accident and then cashed the check was properly charged with embezzlement against his client; the defendant lawfully came into possession of the check from the insurer and was entrusted with care of the check by his client. State v. Johnson, 335 N.C. 509 (1994). Note that this defendant also may have been guilty of "Obtaining Property by False Pretenses," discussed in Chapter 16 (Fraud, Forgery, False Pretenses, and Related Offenses), for his actions against the insurance company. A "merchandise associate" who was a store employee selling merchandise was a "clerk" and thus could be convicted of embezzlement. State v. Robinson, 166 N.C. App. 654 (2004). It is not appropriate to charge embezzlement against one who does not fall into one of the specified categories; a debtor, for example, does not embezzle by leaving town without paying a debt.

To commit this offense, the defendant must have obtained the property by virtue of his or her position—put another way, the defendant must be entrusted with the property. State v. Griffin, 239 N.C. 41 (1953). An employee who takes property from a part of the store other than the part in which he or she works is guilty of larceny, not embezzlement, since the employee was not entrusted with that property. State v. Whitley, 208 N.C. 661 (1935); State v. Lovick, 42 N.C. App. 577 (1979). *But see Robinson*, 166 N.C. App. 654 (there was sufficient evidence to support a store employee's conviction of embezzlement when the evidence showed that all store employees were entrusted with the store's merchandise). Also, an employee who merely has access to his or her employer's property but is not entrusted with it commits larceny, not embezzlement, if the employee takes the property. Thus, defendants who had access to an entire plant as a troubleshooting team (one was an electrician and the other a mechanic) but did not have authority over machinery components were improperly convicted of embezzlement when they took machinery components; the proper charge was larceny. State v. Keyes, 64 N.C. App. 529 (1983). Similarly, there was insufficient evidence of embezzlement when (1) an employee had access to incoming checks but obtained them by misrepresentation and thus did not lawfully possess them and was not entrusted with them, State v. Palmer, 175 N.C. App. 208 (2005); and (2) an employee took a corporate signature stamp without permission and wrote unauthorized checks, thereby misappropriating funds; because the employee did not lawfully possess or control the misappropriated funds, the proper charge was larceny, not embezzlement, State v. Weaver, 359 N.C. 246 (2005).

Charging issues. See this note to "Misdemeanor Larceny," above.

Greater and lesser-included offenses. "Obtaining Property by False Pretenses," discussed in Chapter 16 (Fraud, Forgery, False Pretenses, and Related Offenses), is not a lesser-included offense of embezzlement. State v. Johnson, 108 N.C. App. 550, 554 (1993).

Multiple convictions and punishments. The State has the choice of charging one embezzlement or multiple embezzlements when a person is involved in a continuous course of conduct involving multiple takings of property. State v. Mullaney, 129 N.C. App. 506 (1998).

The State is not required to elect between embezzlement and "Obtaining Property by False Pretenses," discussed in Chapter 16 (Fraud, Forgery, False Pretenses, and Related Offenses), when there is substantial evidence tending to support both charges arising from the same transaction. When both charges are present in a single trial based on a single transaction, the trial court must instruct the jury that it may convict the defendant of only one offense or the other, not of both. State v. Speckman, 326 N.C. 576 (1990).

Relation to other offenses. Although embezzlement and malfeasance of corporation officers and agents, G.S. 14-254, may arise from the same conduct, there are significant differences between these offenses. First, to be convicted of embezzlement, a defendant must have received property in the course of employment, whereas to be convicted of malfeasance of corporation officers and agents, a defendant need only have taken or misapplied any property of the corporation for which he or she is an agent. Second, to be guilty of embezzlement, a defendant must have intended to defraud his or her principal, whereas the malfeasance offense covers intent to defraud any person.

And finally, to be guilty of embezzlement, a defendant need not be an agent or fiduciary of a corporation, whereas malfeasance of corporation officers and agents applies only to agents or fiduciaries of corporations. State v. Kornegay, 313 N.C. 1 (1985).

As stated in the note on Element (4), above, to commit embezzlement, a defendant must deprive an owner of property with which the defendant has been entrusted. Neither larceny, discussed above, nor "Obtaining Property by False Pretenses," discussed in Chapter 16 (Fraud, Forgery, False Pretenses, and Related Offenses), require that element.

Verdicts. Guilty verdicts of embezzlement and "Obtaining Property by False Pretenses," discussed in Chapter 16 (Fraud, Forgery, False Pretenses, and Related Offenses), are legally contradictory and cannot be accepted; property cannot be obtained simultaneously pursuant to both lawful and unlawful means. State v. Mumford, 364 N.C. 394 (2010).

Related Offenses Not in This Chapter

See exploitation of an elderly or disabled adult (various offenses) in Chapter 16 (Fraud, Forgery, False Pretenses, and Related Offenses).
"Obtaining Property by False Pretenses" (Chapter 16)
Embezzlement by treasurers of charitable and religious organizations. G.S. 14-93.
Embezzlement by officers of railroad companies. G.S. 14-94.
Appropriation of partnership funds by partner to personal use. G.S. 14-97.
Embezzlement by surviving partner. G.S. 14-98.
Embezzlement of taxes by officers. G.S. 14-99.
Failure to return hired property. G.S. 14-167.
Conversion by bailee, lessee, tenant or attorney-in-fact. G.S. 14-168.1.
Malfeasance of corporation officers and agents. G.S. 14-254.
Misapplication, embezzlement of funds, etc. (by officer or employee of bank). G.S. 53-129.
Embezzlement by insurance agents, brokers, or administrators. G.S. 58-2-162.
Trust funds to be kept separate. G.S. 128-11.

Embezzlement of State Property by Public Officers and Employees

Statute

§14-91. Embezzlement of State property by public officers and employees.

If any officer, agent, or employee of the State, or other person having or holding in trust for the same any bonds issued by the State, or any security, or other property and effects of the same, shall embezzle or knowingly and willfully misapply or convert the same to his own use, or otherwise willfully or corruptly abuse such trust, such offender and all persons knowingly and willfully aiding and abetting or otherwise assisting therein shall be guilty of a felony. If the value of the property is one hundred thousand dollars ($100,000) or more, a violation of this section is a Class C felony. If the value of the property is less than one hundred thousand dollars ($100,000), a violation of this section is a Class F felony.

Elements

A person guilty of this offense

(1) knowingly and willfully
(2) misapplies or converts to his or her own use
(3) property of the state
(4) held in trust by the defendant.

Punishment

Class F felony. G.S. 14-91. It is a Class C felony if the value of the property embezzled is $100,000 or more. *Id.* If the Class C version of the offense is charged, the relevant sum of money must be alleged in the charging instrument and proved to the jury.

Notes

Element (1). See "Knowingly" and "Willfully" in Chapter 1 (States of Mind).

Element (3). The statute identifies the covered property as "any bonds issued by the State, or any security, or other property and effects of the same." G.S. 14-91. The nature of the property is probably the same as that specified in G.S. 14-90 for "Embezzlement," above. The property is "of the [s]tate" whenever it is in the possession of the state, even if it is not owned by the state.

Element (4). The property must have been entrusted to the defendant. G.S. 14-91 (specifying that the offense applies to "any officer, agent, or employee of the State, or other person having or holding in trust for the same"). For example, a public employee who took a typewriter from a desk in another person's office at his or her place of work would not be guilty of this offense since the employee was never entrusted with the typewriter as a part of his or her work. In this case, the proper charge would be larceny.

A defendant's authority to hire school instructors as provided in the school's budget did not entrust him with the funds used to pay the instructors, and therefore he did not commit this offense when he embezzled those funds. State v. Bonner, 91 N.C. App. 424 (1988). However, because the employee obtained the funds by a deceptive scheme, he probably committed the offense of "Obtaining Property by False Pretenses," discussed in Chapter 16 (Fraud, Forgery, False Pretenses, and Related Offenses).

Related Offenses Not in This Chapter

See the offenses listed under "Embezzlement," above.
"Welfare Fraud" (Chapter 16)
Private use of publicly owned vehicle. G.S. 14-247.
Obtaining repairs and supplies for private vehicle at expense of state. G.S. 14-248.

Embezzlement by Officers, Agents, or Employees of Local Governments, Local Boards of Education, Penal, Charitable, Religious, or Educational Institutions

Statute

§14-92. Embezzlement of funds by public officers and trustees.

If an officer, agent, or employee of an entity listed below, or a person having or holding money or property in trust for one of the listed entities, shall embezzle or otherwise willfully and corruptly use or misapply the same for any purpose other than that for which such moneys or property is held, such person shall be guilty of a felony. If the value of the money or property is one hundred thousand dollars ($100,000) or more, the person is guilty of a Class C felony. If the value of the money or property is less than one hundred thousand dollars ($100,000), the person is guilty of a Class F felony. If any clerk of the superior court or any sheriff, treasurer, register of deeds or other public officer of any county, unit or agency of local government, or local board of education shall embezzle or wrongfully convert to his own use, or corruptly use, or shall misapply for any purpose other than that for which the same are held, or shall fail to pay over and deliver to the proper persons entitled to receive the same when lawfully required so to do, any moneys, funds, securities or other property which such officer shall have received by virtue or color of his office in trust for any person or corporation, such officer shall be guilty of a felony. If the value of the money, funds, securities, or other property is one hundred thousand dollars ($100,000) or more, the person is guilty of a Class C felony. If the value of the money, funds, securities, or other property is less than one hundred thousand dollars ($100,000), the person is guilty of a Class F felony. The provisions of this section shall apply to all persons who shall go out of office and fail or neglect to account to or deliver over to their successors in office or other persons lawfully entitled to receive the same all such moneys, funds and securities or property aforesaid. The following entities are protected by this section: a county, a city or other unit or agency of local government, a local board of education, and a penal, charitable, religious, or educational institution.

Elements

A person guilty of this offense

(1) is
 (a) an officer, agent, or employee of, *or*
 (b) a person having or holding money or property in trust for,
(2) a local government, local government agency, local board of education, or penal, charitable, religious, or educational institution *and*
(3) (a) embezzles *or*
 (b) willfully and corruptly uses or misapplies
(4) money or property
(5) of the entity
(6) held in trust by the defendant.

Punishment

Class F felony. G.S. 14-92. It is a Class C felony if the value of the property embezzled is $100,000 or more. *Id.* If the Class C version of the offense is charged, the relevant sum of money must be alleged in the charging instrument and proved to the jury.

Notes

Generally. The statute includes two offenses that are similar to "Embezzlement" and "Embezzlement of State Property by Public Officers and Employees," both above, but they are specifically aimed at local government officials and officials of quasi-public organizations (churches, charitable organizations, etc.). The two offenses overlap to some extent.

Element (2). Embezzlement under G.S. 14-92 does not apply to an employee of a city Alcoholic Beverage Control Board; the employee must be charged with embezzlement under G.S. 14-90. State v. Jones, 172 N.C. App. 161 (2005).

Element (3). This element basically means to act unlawfully and fraudulently. State v. Agnew, 294 N.C. 382 (1978). Generally, the basic criminal act is the same as that described under "Embezzlement" and "Embezzlement of State Property by Public Officers and Employees," both described above. See the notes on Element (2) to both of those offenses.

Element (4). See the discussion of similar elements to "Embezzlement" and "Embezzlement of State Property by Public Officers and Employees," both above, but remember that this offense applies to misappropriation of property from local governments and quasi-government organizations. A state official embezzling state property could not be prosecuted under this statute, nor could a fiduciary of a corporation embezzling from the corporation.

Failing to account. G.S. 14-92 provides that it also applies "to all persons who shall go out of office and fail or neglect to account to or deliver over to their successors in office or other persons lawfully entitled to receive the same all such money, funds and securities or property aforesaid."

Greater and lesser-included offenses. Violations of G.S. 159-8(a) and G.S. 159-181(a) are not lesser-included offenses of this crime. State v. James, 184 N.C. App. 149, 154–55 (2007).

Related Offenses Not in This Chapter

See the offenses listed under "Embezzlement" and "Embezzlement of State Property by Public Officers and Employees," both above.

Embezzlement by Clerks of Superior Court, Sheriffs, Treasurers, Registers of Deeds, or Officials of Boards of Education or Local Government

Statute

See G.S. 14-92, reproduced under "Embezzlement by Officers, Agents, or Employees of Local Governments, Local Boards of Education, Penal, Charitable, Religious, or Educational Institutions," above.

Elements

A person guilty of this offense

(1) is a clerk of superior court, sheriff, treasurer, register of deeds, or other public officer of any county unit or agency of local government or local board of education *and*
(2) (a) embezzles,
(b) wrongfully converts to his or her own use,
(c) corruptly uses,
(d) misapplies, *or*
(e) fails to pay over and deliver to the proper person entitled to receive when lawfully required to do so
(3) money, funds, securities, or other property
(4) held in trust by the defendant.

Punishment

Class F felony. G.S. 14-92. It is a Class C felony if the value of the property embezzled is $100,000 or more. *Id.* If the Class C version of the offense is charged, the relevant sum of money must be alleged in the charging instrument and proved to the jury.

Notes

Generally. See this note to "Embezzlement by Officers, Agents, or Employees of Local Governments, Local Boards of Education, Penal, Charitable, Religious, or Educational Institutions," above.

Element (2). See the note on Element (3) to "Embezzlement by Officers, Agents, or Employees of Local Governments, Local Boards of Education, Penal, Charitable, Religious, or Educational Institutions," above.

Element (3). See the note on Element (2) to "Embezzlement by Officers, Agents, or Employees of Local Governments, Local Boards of Education, Penal, Charitable, Religious, or Educational Institutions," above.

Failing to account. See this note to "Embezzlement by Officers, Agents, or Employees of Local Governments, Local Boards of Education, Penal, Charitable, Religious, or Educational Institutions," above.

Related Offenses Not in This Chapter

See the offenses listed under "Embezzlement" and "Embezzlement of State Property by Public Officers and Employees," both above.

Altered Serial Number Offenses

Statute

§14-160.1. Alteration, destruction or removal of permanent identification marks from personal property.

(a) It shall be unlawful for any person to alter, deface, destroy or remove the permanent serial number, manufacturer's identification plate or other permanent, distinguishing number or identification mark from any item of personal property with the intent thereby to conceal or misrepresent the identity of said item.

(b) It shall be unlawful for any person knowingly to sell, buy or be in possession of any item of personal property, not his own, on which the permanent serial number, manufacturer's identification plate or other permanent, distinguishing number or identification mark has been altered, defaced, destroyed or removed for the purpose of concealing or misrepresenting the identity of said item.

(c) Unless the conduct is covered under some other provision of law providing greater punishment, a violation of any of the provisions of this section shall be a Class 1 misdemeanor.

(d) This section shall not in any way affect the provisions of G.S. 20-108, 20-109(a) or 20-109(b).

Altering or Removing a Serial Number

Statute

See G.S. 14-160.1, reproduced above.

Elements

A person guilty of this offense

(1) (a) alters,
    (b) defaces,
    (c) destroys, *or*
    (d) removes
(2) (a) the permanent serial number,
    (b) manufacturer's identification plate, *or*
    (c) other permanent distinguishing number or mark
(3) from any item of personal property
(4) with the intent to conceal or misrepresent the identity of that property.

Punishment

Class 1 misdemeanor. G.S. 14-160.1(c).

Notes

Element (3). The statute does not specify that the property must belong to someone else in order for this offense to be charged.

G.S. 12-3(6) defines the term "personal property" as "moneys, goods, chattels, choses in action and evidences of debt, including all things capable of ownership, not descendable to heirs at law."

Element (4). Although the statute says that the defendant's intent must be to conceal or misrepresent the identity of the property, the statute probably also was intended to cover situations in which the intent is to conceal the true ownership of the property.

Multiple convictions and punishments. G.S. 14-160.1(c) begins with the language: "Unless the conduct is covered under some other provision of law providing greater punishment." This language may be interpreted to mean that a defendant may not be punished for this offense when he or she is punished, based on the same conduct, for an offense carrying a more severe punishment. For a discussion of this issue in the assault context, see this note to "Assault Inflicting Serious Injury" in Chapter 7 (Assaults).

Related Offenses Not in This Chapter

"Accessory after the Fact to a Felony" (Chapter 5)
See the offenses in Chapter 15 (Burglary, Breaking or Entering, and Related Offenses).
"Fraudulent Disposal of a Security" (Chapter 16)
"Obtaining Property by False Pretenses" (Chapter 16)
"Injury to Personal Property" (Chapter 18)
"Altering, etc. of a Firearm's Serial Number" (Chapter 22)
Injuring or tampering with vehicle. G.S. 20-107.
Vehicles or component parts of vehicles without manufacturer's numbers (buying, selling, or possessing such vehicle). G.S. 20-108.
Altering or changing engine or other numbers. G.S. 20-109.

Buying, Selling, or Possessing Property with an Altered Serial Number

Statute

See G.S. 14-160.1(b), reproduced above.

Elements

A person guilty of this offense

(1) knowingly
(2) (a) buys,
 (b) sells, *or*
 (c) possesses
(3) any item of personal property
(4) that is not his or her own *and*
(5) on which the permanent serial number, manufacturer's identification plate, or other permanent distinguishing number or mark has been altered, defaced, destroyed, or removed
(6) when the alteration, defacement, destruction, or removal was to conceal or misrepresent the identity of the property.

Punishment

Class 1 misdemeanor. G.S. 14-160.1(c).

Notes

Element (1). It is not clear what the word "knowingly" refers to—whether the defendant merely needs to know that the serial number has been altered or whether the defendant also needs to know that the alteration was for the purpose of concealing the identity of the property. See generally "Knowingly" in Chapter 1 (States of Mind).

Element (2). As with other possession offenses, the property could be constructively possessed—that is, considered in the defendant's possession, even though the defendant had not touched it, if it had been put in some place under the control of the defendant or the defendant's agent. See generally the note on Element (1) to "Misdemeanor Possession of Stolen Goods," above.

Element (3). G.S. 12-3(6) defines the term "personal property" as "moneys, goods, chattels, choses in action and evidences of debt, including all things capable of ownership, not descendable to heirs at law."

Element (4). This offense differs from altering or removing a serial number, above, in that the violation can occur only if the property involved belongs to someone other than the defendant.

Element (6). See the note on Element (4) to "Altering or Removing a Serial Number," above.

Multiple convictions and punishments. See this note to "Altering or Removing a Serial Number," above.

Related Offenses Not in This Chapter

See the offenses listed under "Altering or Removing a Serial Number," above.

14
Robbery, Extortion, and Blackmail

14

Robbery, Extortion, and Blackmail

Common Law Robbery

Statute

This is a common law offense.

Elements

A person guilty of this offense

(1) commits larceny
(2) from the person or from the person's presence
(3) by violence or intimidation.

Punishment

Class G felony. G.S. 14-87.1.

Notes

Generally. Elements (1) and (2) constitute a felonious larceny. See "Felony Larceny" in Chapter 13 (Larceny, Possession of Stolen Goods, Embezzlement, and Related Offenses). Thus, common law robbery is simply a felonious larceny (from the person or from the person's presence) committed by violence or intimidation.

Element (1). See the notes on Elements (1) through (7) to "Misdemeanor Larceny" in Chapter 13 (Larceny, Possession of Stolen Goods, Embezzlement, and Related Offenses). As discussed in those notes, a taking occurs when the defendant severs the property from the owner's possession. See the note on Element (1) to "Misdemeanor Larceny." The evidence was sufficient to show that a taking occurred in a robbery case when the defendant pressed a handgun to the victim's stomach, grabbed her purse from the seat of her car, and then threw it back on the seat when the victim said it contained very little money. State v. Patterson, 182 N.C. App. 102, 107 (2007) (the jury could reasonably find that the defendant exercised complete control over the purse, even if only for a brief moment).

Element (2). This element is similar to Element (8)(b) to "Felony Larceny," discussed in Chapter 13 (Larceny, Possession of Stolen Goods, Embezzlement, and Related Offenses). Examples of takings from the person in robbery cases include taking (1) a bag of groceries that the robber forced the victim to set down on the sidewalk, State v. Dunn, 26 N.C. App. 475 (1975); and (2) marijuana that the victim had placed in a vase on a porch for safekeeping, while the victim was being assaulted on the premises, State v. Shaw, 164 N.C. App. 723 (2004).

A homicide victim can be a person within the meaning of this offense, provided the death and the taking form a continuous chain of events. State v. Davis, 325 N.C. 607 (1989); State v. Earwood, 155 N.C. App. 698 (2003); *see also* State v. McHone, 174 N.C. App. 289 (2005).

A taking can be from the person even if the victim flees before the property is taken, provided that the use of force or intimidation and the taking are part of a continuous transaction. State v. Tuck, 173 N.C. App. 61, 66–68 (2005) (sustaining a conviction when the defendant took money from a store after pointing a gun at the employee, causing the employee to flee; discussing other cases on point); State v. Curry, ___ N.C. App. ___, 692 S.E.2d 129, 143 (2010) (citing *Tuck*).

Element (3). The State need not prove both violence and intimidation; either is sufficient. State v. Carter, 186 N.C. App. 259, 262 (2007). The violence or intimidation must induce the victim to part with his or her property. State v. Parker, 322 N.C. 559, 566–67 (1988) (element not satisfied); *Carter*, 186 N.C. App. at 263 (no robbery occurred when a battery did not induce the victim to part with the property; when the victim was sprayed with an unidentifiable substance, he felt the back of his head to see what it was and turned around to find the defendant running away with the money; "[c]ertainly, spraying someone with pepper spray, even on the back of the head, is a use of force, but in this instance that force did not instill the fear necessary such that defendant's obtaining the money could be considered common law robbery"). It includes injuring or immobilizing the victim so that the victim cannot protect his or her property. It also includes conduct that occurs after the larceny begins and when the victim resists. See the note entitled "Timing of elements" to "Armed Robbery," below. However, a robbery is not committed if the only force used is to obtain possession of the property, such as when a defendant snatches a purse from a person's shoulder. State v. Robertson, 138 N.C. App. 506 (2000). The purse snatching example contrasts with one where the defendant snatches a necklace that has been fastened around the victim's neck, causing the necklace to break in the process; in the necklace snatching situation there is sufficient actual force to constitute a robbery. State v. Harris, 186 N.C. App. 437, 440–42 (2007) (distinguishing *Robertson*).

Actual violence is not required if the victim is intimidated, that is, put in fear of some immediate injury and thereby induced to part with his or her property. *Robertson*, 138 N.C. App. at 508. The intimidation need not involve a great degree of terror provided that it makes the victim apprehensive about his or her own physical safety. The intimidation was sufficient when three sailors in a car were surrounded by five men, without weapons or actual violence, who told them "[t]his is a shakedown" and then took money from the sailors' pockets. State v. Sawyer, 224 N.C. 61 (1944). Intimidation also may occur when the robber asserts authority that he or she does not actually have, such as when the defendants, pretending to be police officers, "arrest" the victim, search the victim, and take the victim's money. ROLLIN M. PERKINS & RONALD N. BOYCE, CRIMINAL LAW 348 (3d ed. 1982) (citing an out-of-state case involving these facts).

The evidence was sufficient to establish that the defendant took money from a store clerk by means of violence or intimidation when the defendant hid his arm under his jacket in a manner suggesting that he had a gun and the clerk gave the defendant the money because he was afraid. State v. Elkins, ___ N.C. App. ___, 707 S.E.2d 744, 749–50 (2011) (distinguishing *Parker*, cited above, and finding the case analogous to *State v. White*, 142 N.C. App. 201 (2001) (the evidence was sufficient when the defendant handed a threatening note to store clerks implying that he had a gun, even though none of them saw a firearm)).

Timing of elements. See this note to "Armed Robbery," below.

Attempt. Attempted common law robbery is a Class H felony. G.S. 14-2.5. See Chapter 5 (General Crimes) for a discussion of attempt.

There was sufficient evidence of attempted common law robbery when a defendant entered a store, kept his right hand in his pocket as if he had a gun (although he did not), threatened to hurt the storekeeper unless she put her money in a bag and gave it to him, but was apprehended by a customer before he could take the bag and leave. State v. Bailey, 4 N.C. App. 407 (1969).

Charging issues. For a discussion of charging issues in connection with robbery offenses, see Jessica Smith, *The Criminal Indictment: Fatal Defect, Fatal Variance, and Amendment*, ADMIN. OF JUST. BULL. NO. 2008/03, UNC School of Government, July 2008) (online at www.sog.unc.edu/pubs/electronicversions/pdfs/aojb0803.pdf).

Doctrine of recent possession. The doctrine of recent possession applies in robbery cases. State v. Lee, ___ N.C. App. ___, 713 S.E.2d 174 (2011) (the trial judge properly instructed the jury in a robbery case on the doctrine of recent possession as to non-unique goods (cigarettes)). For a discussion of this doctrine, see this note to "Misdemeanor Larceny" in Chapter 13 (Larceny, Possession of Stolen Goods, Embezzlement, and Related Offenses).

Greater and lesser-included offenses. See this note to "Armed Robbery," below.

Multiple convictions and punishments. If a robber intimidates two victims and takes personal property from each of them, the robber commits two robberies. State v. Beaty, 306 N.C. 491 (1982). If the robber intimidates several people at the same time and takes only their employer's money from their control, only one robbery is committed. State v. Ballard, 280 N.C. 479 (1972); State v. Potter, 285 N.C. 238 (1974). Thus, for example, an armed robbery of a bank's money from two bank tellers supported only one armed robbery conviction. State v. Becton, 163 N.C. App. 592 (2004). If the robber intimidates only one employee and takes the money of that employee and the money of the employer, only one robbery is committed. *Beaty*, 306 N.C. 491; State v. Bellamy, 172 N.C. App. 649 (2005).

A defendant may not be sentenced for both robbery and possession of stolen property taken during the robbery. State v. Moses, ___ N.C. App. ___, 698 S.E.2d 688, 696 (2010) (so concluding as a matter of legislative intent).

Related Offenses Not in This Chapter

See the various offenses in Chapter 13 (Larceny, Possession of Stolen Goods, Embezzlement, and Related Offenses).

Train robbery. G.S. 14-88.

Armed Robbery

Statute

§14-87. Robbery with firearms or other dangerous weapons.

(a) Any person or persons who, having in possession or with the use or threatened use of any firearms or other dangerous weapon, implement or means, whereby the life of a person is endangered or threatened, unlawfully takes or attempts to take personal property from another or from any place of business, residence or banking institution or any other place where there is a person or persons in attendance, at any time, either day or night, or who aids or abets any such person or persons in the commission of such crime, shall be guilty of a Class D felony.

(b) Repealed by Session Laws 1979, c. 760, s. 5.

(c) Repealed by Session Laws 1979, c. 760, s. 5.

(d) Repealed by Session Laws 1993, c. 539, s. 1173.

Elements

A person guilty of this offense

(1) commits or attempts to commit larceny
(2) from the person or from the person's presence
(3) by the possession, use, or threatened use of a firearm or other dangerous weapon
(4) that endangers or threatens the life of a person.

Punishment

Class D felony. G.S. 14-87(a).

Notes

Generally. Elements (1) and (2) constitute a felonious larceny. See "Felony Larceny" in Chapter 13 (Larceny, Possession of Stolen Goods, Embezzlement, and Related Offenses). Thus, armed robbery is simply a felonious larceny (from the person or from the person's presence) committed by the possession, use, or threatened use of a firearm or dangerous weapon that endangers or threatens the life of a person.

Element (1). See the notes on Elements (1) through (7) to "Misdemeanor Larceny" in Chapter 13 (Larceny, Possession of Stolen Goods, Embezzlement, and Related Offenses).

Element (2). See the note on Element (2) to "Common Law Robbery," above.

Element (3). As with Element (3) of "Common Law Robbery" (violence or intimidation), discussed above, the use of the firearm or dangerous weapon must induce the victim to part with the property. State v. Richardson, 308 N.C. 470 (1983); State v. Dalton, 122 N.C. App. 666 (1996); see the note on Element (3) to "Common Law Robbery" (discussing this issue as to the violence and intimidation required for that crime), above.

As a general rule, a "dangerous weapon" is the same as a deadly weapon. State v. Mullen, 47 N.C. App. 667 (1980); State v. Smallwood, 78 N.C. App. 365 (1985); State v. Wiggins, 78 N.C. App. 405 (1985); See generally the note on Element (3) to "Assault with a Deadly Weapon" in Chapter 7 (Assaults). Thus, a stun gun has been found to be dangerous weapon for purposes of armed robbery, State v. Rivera, ___ N.C. App. ___, ___ S.E.2d ___ (Nov. 1, 2011) (reasoning that although the victim did not die or come close to death, she was seriously injured), as has a glass vase, when used to strike the victim's head, State v. Peacock, 313 N.C. 554 (1985). However, an exception to the general rule that a dangerous weapon is the same as a deadly weapon involves hands or feet. In the assault context, hands, fists, and feet may be considered deadly weapons, depending upon the manner in which they are used and the relative size and condition of the parties involved. See the note on Element (3) to "Assault with a Deadly Weapon" in Chapter 7 (Assaults). But a defendant's hands and feet are not dangerous weapons for purposes of the armed robbery statute. State v. Hinton, 361 N.C. 207 (2007).

Proof of use or threatened use of a dangerous weapon may be in many forms, including evidence of an actual weapon; victim or witness testimony about seeing or feeling a weapon; evidence of a victim's injuries, State v. Peacock, 313 N.C. 554 (1985); State v. Hines, 166 N.C. App. 202 (2004) (expert testified that victim's injury suggested massive trauma from a blunt force object, possibly a baton, crowbar, or similar object); State v. Singletary, 163 N.C. App. 449 (2004) (doctor testified that victim's head injuries were consistent with the use of a baseball bat, crowbar, baton, or similar instrument and not caused by a fall); a defendant's statement to the victim that he or she had a firearm, State v. Jarrett, 167 N.C. App. 336, 338–39 (2004) (sufficient evidence when the defendant told the victims that he had a gun and the victims reasonably believed this to be true, even though the defendant did not display a gun); State v. Lee, 128 N.C. App. 506, 510–11 (1998) (same when the defendant covered the victim's face and told her several times that he would shoot her if she resisted and at one point said, "Where did I drop my gun?"); and conduct suggesting that the defendant possessed such a weapon, State v. Bartley, 156 N.C. App. 490, 494–97 (2003) (the evidence was sufficient when the defendant acted as if he had a gun in his pocket and the victim reasonably believed that the defendant was armed).

The evidence was sufficient to establish this element when (1) the defendant used a firearm as a club to hit the victim on the head and then took the victim's property, State v. McNatt, 342 N.C. 173, 174–75 (1995); (2) the defendant placed a pellet gun against the victim's back and pointed it directly at her kidney, and there was evidence that a projectile from that gun was capable of penetrating a quarter-inch of plywood, State v. Westall, 116 N.C. App. 534

(1994); (3) the defendant placed a BB gun directly into the backs of two store clerks and pointed it at another victim's face, and there was testimony that the gun was capable of denting a quarter-inch piece of cedar plywood at distances of up to two feet, State v. Hall, 165 N.C. App. 658 (2004); (4) the victim testified that she was hit with a firm, rigid object that she did not believe to be a hand and the object loosened several teeth, drove her upper teeth through her lower lip, requiring twenty-five stitches, and forced her knees to buckle, causing her to fall to the ground, dazed, State v. Reid, 151 N.C. App. 379 (2002); (5) the defendant put his arm around the victim's neck and used a stun gun in an attempt to shock her, State v. Gay, 151 N.C. App. 530 (2002); (6) the victim was struck in the back of the head with a glass bottle, causing him to fall to the ground, State v. Moses, 154 N.C. App. 332 (2002); (7) the defendant waived a pocketknife at the victim, asking "you want a piece of this?", State v. Bellamy, 159 N.C. App. 143 (2003); and (8) the defendant tried to run over the victim with a car, State v. Hill, 182 N.C. App. 88, 91–92 (2007). By contrast, a BB gun was not a dangerous weapon when the State failed to prove that it was capable of causing serious injury or death. State v. Fleming, 148 N.C. App. 16 (2001).

When the evidence indicates that the defendant used a gun in an armed robbery and there is no evidence that the gun was inoperable, the State is not required to affirmatively demonstrate operability and the trial court is not required to instruct on common law robbery. State v. Bettis, ___ N.C. App. ___, 698 S.E.2d 507, 513 (2010); State v. Williamson, ___ N.C. App. ___, 698 S.E.2d 727, 730 (2010).

Element (4). Mere possession of a firearm or dangerous weapon does not satisfy the elements of this offense. The defendant must use the weapon in a way that threatens or endangers the victim's life. State v. Evans, 279 N.C. 447 (1971); State v. Gibbons, 303 N.C. 484 (1981); State v. Thomas, 85 N.C. App. 319 (1987). For example, in one case the defendant confronted the victim with a pocketknife, threatened to cut his head off if the victim did not give the defendant his billfold, and struck at the victim as he tried to escape. State v. Moore, 279 N.C. 455 (1971). In another case, the defendant attacked the victim, put him on his back, hit him on the head with a bottle, and later held an opened pocketknife in his hand and demanded the victim's wallet. State v. Norris, 264 N.C. 470 (1965). In both cases, the court found the pocketknife to be a dangerous weapon whereby the life of a person was endangered. For other cases in which the evidence was sufficient to establish that the dangerous weapon was used in a way that endangered or threatened a person's life, see *State v. Rivera*, ___ N.C. App. ___, ___ S.E.2d ___ (Nov. 1, 2011) (a stun gun endangered or threatened the victim's life when the victim was tased, suffered significant pain, fell, injured her rotator cuff, endured two surgeries and extensive physical therapy, and two years later still experienced pain and a limited range of motion in her arm), and *State v. Hill*, ___ N.C. ___, 715 S.E.2d 841 (2011) (so concluding based on the victim's injuries and report of being robbed by a man with a knife). On the other hand, when a defendant testified that he used the butt of a shotgun to break through a robbery victim's door and then rested the shotgun against a wall during the robbery, the court found insufficient evidence of this element. *Gibbons*, 303 N.C. 484.

To satisfy this element, it is not necessary to prove that the victim feared for his or her life; the relevant inquiry is simply whether the weapon endangered or threatened a person's life. State v. Joyner, 295 N.C. 55 (1978); State v. Hill, ___ N.C. ___, 715 S.E.2d 841 (2011) (rejecting the defendant's argument that the evidence failed to establish that the victim's life was endangered or threatened because the victim never indicated that he was afraid or felt threatened; the question is whether a person's life was in fact endangered or threatened, not whether the victim was scared or in fear for his or her life); State v. Johnson, 164 N.C. App. 1 (2004). Thus, there was sufficient evidence to support an armed robbery conviction when the victim testified that the defendant held an object that appeared to be a box cutter at his neck, even though the victim also testified that he did not feel that his life was threatened. State v. Pratt, 161 N.C. App. 161 (2003). Also, it need not be the victim's life that is threatened. In *State v. Corum*, 176

N.C. App. 150 (2006), for example, the evidence was sufficient when the defendant did not verbally threaten or wave a knife at the robbery victim but, rather, threatened the life of his accomplice who was posing as an innocent bystander, thus causing the victim to open a cash register.

Timing of elements. The elements may occur in any order, provided they are part of one continuous transaction. State v. Haselden, 357 N.C. 1 (2003); State v. Hope, 317 N.C. 302 (1986); State v. Bellamy, 159 N.C. App. 143 (2003). A common scenario to which this rule applies is when the defendant uses no violence or intimidation initially to obtain the item but then uses violence or intimidation to retain possession of it when confronted by the possessor. State v. Hurley, 180 N.C. App. 680, 681–83 (2006) (the defendant took a store item but did not brandish a weapon until confronted by a store employee in the parking lot); State v. Hill, 182 N.C. App. 88, 93–94 (2007) (the defendant and an accomplice took store merchandise without paying for it and were pursued by a store employee into the parking lot, where the defendant shoved the employee to the ground and the accomplice attempted to run over her with a vehicle); State v. Porter, 198 N.C. App. 183, 186–87 (2009) (in a common law robbery case, when the store manager confronted the defendant in the parking lot and attempted to retrieve the stolen property, the defendant struck the store manager). Likewise, there is sufficient evidence of armed robbery when property is taken from a dead victim, provided that the robbery and death occur in a single continuous transaction and the time between the two events is short. State v. Handy, 331 N.C. 515 (1992); State v. Fields, 315 N.C. 191 (1985); State v. Earwood, 155 N.C. App. 698 (2003). The evidence is also sufficient when the defendant's intent to steal is formed after the use or threat of force, provided that the theft and use or threat of force occur during a single continuous transaction. *Fields*, 315 N.C. 191; State v. Rasor, 319 N.C. 577 (1987); State v. Green, 321 N.C. 594 (1988). The defendant's rape of the victim, occurring after he attacked her but before he took her money, did not constitute a break in the continuous transaction between the attack and the taking of the money. State v. Blue, ___ N.C. App. ___, 699 S.E.2d 661, 666–68 (2010). If the events constitute a continuous transaction, a defendant may be convicted of armed robbery when a dangerous weapon taken during a robbery is also the weapon used to perpetrate the offense. State v. Maness, 363 N.C. 261, 282–83 (2009); State v. McMillan, ___ N.C. App. ___, ___ S.E.2d ___ (Aug. 2, 2011).

In contrast to these cases is *State v. Powell*, 299 N.C. 95 (1980), in which the defendant raped the victim, killed her, and then took her possessions, including her automobile. The court struck down the defendant's robbery conviction, finding that the evidence indicated only that the defendant took the objects as an afterthought after the victim was dead.

Attempt. The statute makes attempted armed robbery punishable as armed robbery. See "Attempt" in Chapter 5 (General Crimes) and the note on "Attempt" to "Common Law Robbery," above. Because this offense includes attempts, all of the elements of larceny need not have been completed for an armed robbery to have occurred. State v. Curry, ___ N.C. App. ___, 692 S.E.2d 129, 142–44 (2010) (even if the defendant did not carry away the items, the robbery was complete upon his attempt). When the defendant entered a house to rob two men, he shot the first man and took his wallet; the second man threw his wallet toward the defendant but the defendant left without taking it; on these facts the court held that the defendant committed attempted armed robbery against the second victim. State v. Blake, 326 N.C. 31 (1990). However, if the defendant assaults the victim but makes no attempt to take the victim's property, the evidence may be insufficient to establish an attempted armed robbery. State v. Johnson, ___ N.C. App. ___, 702 S.E.2d 547, 550 (2010) (the trial court erred by denying the defendant's motion to dismiss a charge of attempted robbery when there was no evidence that the defendant attempted to take the shooting victim's personal property).

Charging issues. See this note to "Common Law Robbery," above.

Doctrine of recent possession. See this note to "Common Law Robbery," above.

Greater and lesser-included offenses. Common law robbery is a lesser-included offense of armed robbery but not of attempted armed robbery. State v. White, 322 N.C. 506, 516 (1988). Attempted common law robbery is a lesser-included offense of attempted armed robbery. *Id.* Larceny is a lesser-included offense of both common law and armed robbery. *Id.* at 514–17 & n.1. Assault with a deadly weapon is a lesser-included offense of armed robbery. State v. Hinton, 361 N.C. 207, 210 (2007); State v. Richardson, 279 N.C. 621, 628 (1971).

Multiple convictions and punishments. See this note to "Common Law Robbery," above. Separate convictions for armed robbery and larceny are permitted if there are separate takings; separate convictions are not permitted if the takings occurred during one continuous transaction. *Compare* State v. Barton, 335 N.C. 741, 745–46 (1994) (the court upheld separate convictions for armed robbery and larceny of a firearm when the defendant and his accomplice shot the victim, took his wallet, fled in the victim's car, and later removed the victim's firearm from the victim's car), *and* State v. Robinson, 342 N.C. 74, 83–84 (1995) (convictions for both armed robbery and larceny were permitted when the defendant took the murder victim's wallet after shooting the victim and later returned to the murder scene and took the victim's car), *with* State v. Jaynes, 342 N.C. 249, 275–76 (1995) (convictions for both armed robbery and larceny were not permitted when the defendants took the murder victim's personal possessions and loaded them into the victim's two vehicles and drove away; the taking of the personal possessions and the vehicles occurred during one continuous transaction).

Because both assault with a deadly weapon inflicting serious injury and assault with a deadly weapon with intent to kill inflicting serious injury include an element not included in armed robbery, a defendant may be punished for either of those assaults and armed robbery, when based on the same conduct. *Richardson*, 279 N.C. at 628–33; State v. Stepney, 280 N.C. 306, 317–18 (1972). For the same reason, a defendant may be convicted of both armed robbery and aggravated assault on a handicapped person. State v. Hines, 166 N.C. App. 202, 208–09 (2004) (rejecting the defendant's argument that the language in the aggravated assault on a handicapped person statute providing that "[u]nless [defendant's] conduct is covered under some other provision of law providing greater punishment," barred double punishment). All of the assault crimes just mentioned are covered in Chapter 7 (Assaults).

"Presumption" of the use of a dangerous weapon. When the evidence shows that the victim thought that the robber used a firearm or other dangerous weapon and no evidence to the contrary is presented, there is a mandatory presumption that the robber used a firearm or dangerous weapon that threatened or endangered the victim's life (Elements (3) and (4), above) and the jury must so find. State v. Joyner, 312 N.C. 779, 782 (1985). In this circumstance, the judge is not required to instruct the jury on the lesser-included offense of common law robbery. *Id.* at 784; State v. Williams, 335 N.C. 518 (1994). If, however, there is any evidence tending to show that the weapon in question was not dangerous, the mandatory presumption disappears and is replaced by a permissive inference, *Joyner*, 312 N.C. at 783; *Williams*, 335 N.C. at 520–23 (citing *Joyner*); State v. Marshall, 188 N.C. App. 744, 753–54 (2008) (the defendant's testimony that he did not possess a dangerous weapon did not require dismissal of the armed robbery charge; the victim's testimony that she believed that the defendant had a gun created a mandatory presumption that a dangerous weapon was used; the defendant's testimony required that the mandatory presumption disappear and be replaced by a permissive inference; the permissive inference was enough to survive a motion to dismiss), and the trial court must submit the lesser-included offense of common law robbery to the jury. State v. Summey, 109 N.C. App. 518, 529 (1993).

Thus, if a victim testifies that he or she was robbed with what appeared to be a handgun, the jury must presume that a dangerous weapon threatening or endangering the victim's life was used. However, if the defendant presents evidence showing that the object used was a toy or otherwise not dangerous, the prosecution must prove that the object used was actually a handgun or other dangerous weapon and that the victim's life was endangered. State

v. Thompson, 297 N.C. 285 (1979); *Joyner*, 312 N.C. 779; State v. Everette, 111 N.C. App. 775 (1993).

Related Offenses Not in This Chapter

See the offenses in Chapter 13 (Larceny, Possession of Stolen Goods, Embezzlement, and Related Offenses).
See the various offenses involving deadly weapons in Chapter 7 (Assaults).
See the offenses in Chapter 22 (Weapons Offenses).
Train robbery. G.S. 14-88.

Extortion

Statute

§14-118.4. Extortion.

Any person who threatens or communicates a threat or threats to another with the intention thereby wrongfully to obtain anything of value or any acquittance, advantage, or immunity is guilty of extortion and such person shall be punished as a Class F felon.

Elements

A person guilty of this offense

(1) threatens or communicates a threat to another
(2) with the intent to obtain wrongfully
(3) anything of value, any acquittance, any advantage, or any immunity.

Punishment

Class F felony. G.S. 14-118.4.

Notes

Element (1). The statute applies both to the person who makes the threat and to any person who transmits the threat (a messenger, for example).

Element (2). It is not necessary that the defendant actually obtain any of the items listed in Element (3); the defendant must only make the threat with the intent to gain something listed. Perkins & Boyce, cited in full *supra*, at 449. Additionally, it is not necessary that the defendant seek one of the items for himself or herself.

Element (3). The threat or demand need not concern money. The terms "acquittance," "advantage," and "immunity" can be read to cover almost any action or inaction by the threatened individual that benefits the person who makes or communicates the threat. An offer to refrain from pressing criminal charges in exchange for money constituted threatening a criminal prosecution, satisfying this element. State v. Greenspan, 92 N.C. App. 563 (1989).

Relation to other offenses. Most, if not all, scenarios fitting the elements of the offense of blackmail, *see* G.S. 14-118, will also satisfy the elements of this offense. In fact, the North Carolina Court of Appeals has said that the offense of extortion has superseded the offense of blackmail. *Greenspan*, 92 N.C. App. at 567–68 (reasoning that by enacting a new extortion law in 1973 that covered all conduct previously covered by blackmail, there was evidence of legislative intent to repeal the prior offense of blackmail). Because extortion requires fewer elements of proof, in any case it is likely a preferable charge to blackmail. As a practical matter, the State may prefer charging extortion over blackmail because extortion is a Class F felony, while blackmail is a Class 1 misdemeanor.

Related Offenses Not in This Chapter

See the offenses in Chapter 8 (Threats, Harassment, Stalking, and Violation of Domestic Protective Orders).

Simulation of court process in connection with collection of claim, demand or account. G.S. 14-118.1.

15

Burglary, Breaking or Entering, and Related Offenses

15

Burglary, Breaking or Entering, and Related Offenses

First-Degree Burglary

Statute

Burglary is defined by common law. State v. Mumford, 227 N.C. 132, 133 (1947). G.S. 14-51, reproduced below, breaks the crime into degrees, and G.S. 14-52, also reproduced below, prescribes punishment for the two degrees of burglary.

> **§14-51. First and second degree burglary.**
>
> There shall be two degrees in the crime of burglary as defined at the common law. If the crime be committed in a dwelling house, or in a room used as a sleeping apartment in any building, and any person is in the actual occupation of any part of said dwelling house or sleeping apartment at the time of the commission of such crime, it shall be burglary in the first degree. If such crime be committed in a dwelling house or sleeping apartment not actually occupied by anyone at the time of the commission of the crime, or if it be committed in any house within the curtilage of a dwelling house or in any building not a dwelling house, but in which is a room used as a sleeping apartment and not actually occupied as such at the time of the commission of the crime, it shall be burglary in the second degree. For the purposes of defining the crime of burglary, larceny shall be deemed a felony without regard to the value of the property in question.
>
> **§14-52. Punishment for burglary.**
>
> Burglary in the first degree shall be punishable as a Class D felony, and burglary in the second degree shall be punishable as a Class G felony.

Elements

A person guilty of this offense

(1) breaks *and*
(2) enters
(3) without consent
(4) the dwelling house or sleeping apartment
(5) of another
(6) while it is actually occupied
(7) at night
(8) with the intent to commit any felony or larceny therein.

Punishment

Class D felony. G.S. 14-52. Pursuant to G.S. 14-2.5, attempted first-degree burglary is a Class E felony. This statute supersedes prior case law which held that attempted burglary was an infamous misdemeanor punishable under G.S. 14-3(b) as a Class H felony. State v. Surles, 230 N.C. 272 (1949); State v. Hageman, 307 N.C. 1 (1982). For a discussion of the status offense of habitual breaking and entering, see the note entitled "Habitual Breaking and Entering Status Offender" under "Special Provisions" in the discussion of felony sentencing in Chapter 4 (Punishment under Structured Sentencing).

Notes

Element (1). "Breaking" means the making of some kind of opening, however slight, in the building. State v. Shaw, 106 N.C. App. 433 (1992). It may be through a usual opening, such as a door, or an unusual opening, such as a chimney. State v. Willis, 52 N.C. 190 (1859) (the defendant removed boards covering a chimney and entered the house by descending the chimney to the fireplace). Merely going through an open door or window is not breaking. However, going through an open chimney constitutes a burglary. State v. Boon, 35 N.C. 244 (1852). The explanation for different treatment of chimneys is that a chimney, unlike a window or door, "is as much shut as the nature of the thing will admit." *Willis*, 52 N.C. at 191. Opening a door or window, even if unlocked, is breaking. State v. Simpson, 299 N.C. 335, 349 (1980); State v. Henderson, 285 N.C. 1, 22 (1974). A breaking does not require any destructive force. *Henderson*, 285 N.C. at 17. Thus, opening a partly opened door is a breaking, State v. Jaynes, 342 N.C. 249, 278 (1995), and as noted above, opening an unlocked door or window constitutes a breaking. Also, the breaking of an inner door of a house or apartment can satisfy this element. State v. Freeman, 313 N.C. 539, 549 (1985).

Breaking is sometimes shown by testimony that before the entry, all of the doors and windows were closed or that they were typically closed at the time the entry occurred. *See, e.g.*, State v. Howell, 335 N.C. 457, 473 (1994) ("While circumstantial evidence in burglary cases usually includes testimony that prior to entry all doors and windows were closed, evidence of habit or custom is also admissible to establish an essential element of the crime."); *Simpson*, 299 N.C. at 349 (the State's case included proof that it was the custom of the assistant supervisor to keep the windows closed as evidence that they were closed at the time in question).

A breaking may be actual or constructive. State v. Wilson, 289 N.C. 531, 539 (1976); State v. Thomas, 350 N.C. 315, 345 (1999). If the victim is induced to make the opening—by, for example, opening the front door—as a result of the defendant's fraud, trickery, force, or intimidation, this can constitute a "constructive breaking" and be sufficient to satisfy this element. State v. Ball, 344 N.C. 290, 306 (1996). A constructive breaking by threat occurs, for example, when the defendant threatens to set fire to the house unless the victim opens the door. *Wilson*, 289 N.C. at 539 (posing this example). A constructive breaking by fraud occurs, for example, when the defendant knocks on the door, pretending to need help, and thereby induces the victim to open the door. *Ball*, 344 N.C. at 306–07 (the defendant knocked on a reverend's door pretending to need to talk with the reverend); *Thomas*, 350 N.C. at 345–46 (the defendant knocked on the door pretending to need help because his car broke down). A constructive breaking by force occurs, for example, when the defendant forces the victim into a dwelling house or sleeping apartment at gunpoint, State v. Irons, 189 N.C. App. 201, 205 (2008), or when, after the victim voluntarily opens the door, the defendant pulls the victim out and then enters the house, State v. Goldsmith, 187 N.C. App. 162, 165 (2007) (a constructive breaking occurred on these facts); *see also* State v. Reid, 175 N.C. App. 613, 619–20 (2006) (a breaking occurred when the victim was grabbed and dragged outside by one or more individuals upon opening his front door, and then one or two of the assailants rushed past him and into his home). Similarly, if the door is opened by an accomplice or co-conspirator, a constructive breaking occurs. State v. Smith, 311 N.C. 145, 149–50 (1984).

Element (2). "Entering" does not require that the defendant put his or her whole body inside the premises. State v. Surcey, 139 N.C. App. 432, 435 (2000) (quoting State v. Gibbs, 297 N.C. 410, 428 (1979)). This element is satisfied "by inserting into the place broken the hand, the foot, or any instrument with which it is intended to commit a felony." *Id.* Thus, when the defendant put a shotgun through a window and fired the gun into the premises, there was sufficient evidence of this element. *Id.* at 435–36; *see also Gibbs*, 297 N.C. at 418–19 (the defendant stood at the window with his hand holding a small pistol extended into the victim's den). Inserting a tool into the building is not entering if the insertion is only for the purpose of breaking (for example, when a crowbar is shoved an inch or two into the building for the purpose of forcing a window open), but when the tool is inserted for the purpose of committing a felony (for example, when a hook for stealing something or the barrel of a gun for killing an occupant is thrust through a window opening), an entering occurs. ROLLIN M. PERKINS & RONALD N. BOYCE, CRIMINAL LAW 253 (3d ed. 1982); *see also Surcey*, 139 N.C. App. at 435–36 (shotgun put through a window to fire into the house).

Element (3). The breaking or entering must occur without the consent of the owner or some other person entitled to possession of the premises. State v. Upchurch, 332 N.C. 439 (1992); State v. Meadows, 306 N.C. 683 (1982); N.C. PATTERN JURY INSTRUCTIONS—CRIM. 214.10. If a person who is given a key and is authorized to enter the premises at any time uses the key to enter when the residents are away to steal items from the house, the entry is not without consent. 3 CHARLES E. TORCIA, WHARTON'S CRIMINAL LAW 231–36 (15th ed. 1995). However, if that person was only authorized to use the key at specified times and for specified purposes—such as from 9 am to 5 pm to clean the house—and he or she uses the key at a different time to steal, the entry is without consent. 3 *id.* at 236–38.

If a person consents to the defendant's entry as a result of fraud, trickery, coercion, threat, or conspiracy, not only does a constructive breaking occur, see the note on Element (1) above, but also the defendant's entry is deemed to be without consent. State v. Wheeler, 70 N.C. App. 191, 195–96 (1984) (same facts that supported the conclusion that there was a constructive breaking—pretending to need to call the hospital—made the entry without consent).

This element may be satisfied by the occupant's testimony that he or she did not consent to the entry or by other circumstantial evidence indicating lack of consent. State v. Williams, 330 N.C. 579 (1992). For example, evidence that the victim told the defendant that she did not want to talk with him, that she did not open a locked door, and that the defendant broke down the door to gain entry was sufficient evidence of the occupant's lack of consent. *Id.*

Permission to enter is valid only if given by the owner, occupant, or by some person authorized to give such permission. 3 TORCIA, cited in full *supra*, at 238. Occupants do not always have authority to consent to entry by others. For example, when a defendant and a juvenile resident of a house conspired to commit murder against the juvenile's parents who resided in the house and the defendant entered the house at night for that purpose while the juvenile was absent, the juvenile had no authority to give the defendant permission to enter the home in the middle of the night for the criminal purpose of committing murder. State v. Upchurch, 332 N.C. 439 (1992). Another case held that a minor had no authority to allow the defendant to enter her house for the purpose of committing statutory rape against her. State v. Brown, 176 N.C. App. 72 (2006).

Element (4). A "dwelling" is a structure regularly used by a person or persons for sleeping. State v. Foster, 129 N.C. 704 (1901). "Regularly used" means that use "occurs in ordinary practice or in the ordinary course of events." State v. Hobgood, 112 N.C. App. 262, 264 (1993). Homes owned by elderly people are dwellings, even though they live elsewhere because of health problems, when they intend to return to their homes when they are able to do so and their homes still contain their personal effects. State v. Smith, 121 N.C. App. 41, 44–47 (1995). A dwelling may be a house; an apartment; a room in a hotel, motel, or rooming house, State v. Nelson, 298 N.C. 573, 596–97 (1979) (motel room); State v. Clinton, 3 N.C. App. 571, 574

(1969) (room in a rooming house); or a condominium, *Hobgood*, 112 N.C. App. at 264–65. It also may be a house trailer or mobile home, State v. Taylor, 109 N.C. App. 692, 694–95 (1993) (rejecting the defendant's argument that the trailer's mobility and lack of permanence prevented it from being a dwelling).

Sometimes issues arise as to whether a particular space is part of the dwelling. For example, in *State v. Green*, 305 N.C. 463 (1982), the defendant argued that a storage room was not part of the dwelling but only in its curtilage (and thus that he could be convicted of only second-degree burglary). In that case, the storage room was at the back of the house, just behind a bedroom, and could be entered through an outside door or a window in the bedroom. *Id.* at 473. On these facts, the court rejected the defendant's argument that the storage room was not part of the dwelling, concluding that it was appurtenant to the main dwelling. *Id.* A similar issue arose in *State v. Merritt*, 120 N.C. App. 732 (1995), where the victims had an apartment in a sorority house. The court held there that the common areas of the sorority house appurtenant to the apartment were part of the victims' dwelling. *Id.* at 739.

Issues also can arise when the main premises serve a commercial or related purpose but also contain a regularly used sleeping apartment. When this is the case, the premises have been held to constitute a dwelling. State v. Williams, 90 N.C. 724 (1884) (the defendant broke and entered a storehouse in which the owner's clerk had a sleeping apartment, which he regularly used); State v. Brandon, 120 N.C. App. 815, 818 (1995) (the premises was a skaking rink, which contained a sleeping apartment frequently used by a rink employee).

A house used for only part of the year, such as a summer cottage or condominium, is a dwelling if the owner, members of the owner's household, or renters have at some time used it regularly for sleeping and intend to use it again. State v. Hobgood, 112 N.C. App. 262, 264–65 (1993). Even a condominium not rented on the night of a break-in qualifies as a dwelling if "in the ordinary course of events [it is] used as a dwelling or for sleeping by either the owner, [the owner's] family, or a renter" and it is "regularly available for rent." *Id.* However, if an owner moves out permanently with no intention of returning, and a new owner or renter has not begun to sleep in the house regularly, the house ceases to be a dwelling. PERKINS & BOYCE, cited in full *supra*, at 258.

Element (5). The phrase "of another" means that the property entered is legally possessed by a person other than the defendant, even though that person may not own the property. Even a defendant with an ownership interest in a house can be guilty of burglary if the house is legally and exclusively possessed by another person. State v. Harold, 312 N.C. 787 (1985); State v. Cox, 73 N.C. App. 432 (1985). A spouse may be convicted of burglary, or breaking or entering, for breaking into the other spouse's dwelling if the other spouse had exclusive possession of the dwelling. State v. Singletary, 344 N.C. 95 (1996); State v. Lindley, 81 N.C. App. 490 (1986); *Cox*, 73 N.C. App. 432. For example, if a defendant enters a spouse's residence after he or she has been expressly prohibited from so entering by a marital separation agreement, these offenses may be committed. When a building is rented to a tenant who regularly sleeps there, it becomes the tenant's dwelling, and the landlord who opens the door and enters without the tenant's agreement is breaking and entering the dwelling of another, PERKINS & BOYCE, cited in full *supra*, at 261, provided the lease does not authorize such entry.

Element (6). "Actually occupied" means that a person must be present somewhere inside the dwelling when the breaking and entering occurs. A motel room is not actually occupied if a defendant, who is standing outside the room, accomplishes a breaking and entering by pushing the victim into the room. State v. Jolly, 297 N.C. 121, 129–30 (1979).

This element is satisfied regardless of whether the offender knew the dwelling was occupied. State v. Tippett, 270 N.C. 588 (1967).

Element (7). "At night" is that time after sunset and before sunrise "when it is so dark that a man's face cannot be identified except by an artificial light or moonlight." State v. Frank, 284 N.C. 137 (1973); State v. Barnett, 113 N.C. App. 69 (1993). Evidence of nighttime may be by judicial notice of sunset and sunrise times for particular dates, as recorded in U.S. Naval Observatory Nautical Almanac reports, State v. Garrison, 294 N.C. 270 (1978); State v. Jordan, 186 N.C. App. 576, 583 (2007) (following *Garrison* and taking judicial notice of this fact), or in the official records of the National Climate Data Center, State v. Bowers, 135 N.C. App. 682 (1999).

Sufficient evidence was presented to establish that the burglary occurred at nighttime when (1) the victim's nude body was found near her nightclothes; evidence suggested that she was raped, beaten, and strangled in bed; the victim's electric blanket was on, suggesting she was using it at the time; and two witnesses testified that the defendant left their presence at night and returned later that night with possessions matching the description of items taken from the victim's dwelling, State v. Elliott, 360 N.C. 400 (2006); and (2) although the victim's testimony tended to show that the crime did not occur at night, the victim called 911 at 5:42 am; she told police the attack occurred between 5:00 and 5:30 am; a crime scene technician testified that "it was still pretty dark" when she arrived and that she used a flashlight to take photographs; and the defendant stipulated to a record from the U.S. Naval Observatory showing that on the relevant date the sun did not rise until 6:44 am, State v. Reavis, ___ N.C. App. ___, 700 S.E.2d 33, 40–41 (2010).

Element (8). This element requires that the defendant intend to commit a felony or larceny in the dwelling when the breaking and entering occurs. If the defendant does not form the requisite intent until after he or she breaks and enters, the offense is "Misdemeanor Breaking or Entering," discussed below, not burglary. State v. Peacock, 313 N.C. 554 (1985); State v. Goldsmith, 187 N.C. App. 162, 166 (2007). Note that the defendant must intend to commit the required crime inside the dwelling; if the defendant intends to commit the crime outside of the dwelling, this element is not satisfied. Thus, the evidence was insufficient when the defendant's act of pulling the victim outside of the house showed an intent to commit a robbery outside of the home. *Goldsmith,* 187 N.C. App. at 166 (reversing a burglary conviction on these facts).

Evidence will be considered sufficient to establish an intent to commit a particular felony alleged in an indictment even if it also supports an intent to commit a second unalleged felony. State v. Jordan, 186 N.C. App. 576, 581 (2007) (sufficient evidence of felonious assault, as alleged in the indictment, even though the evidence also supported an intent to commit the unalleged crime of murder).

The defendant must intend to commit any larceny or felony. For the purposes of burglary, any larceny, regardless of the value of the property taken, is a felony. G.S. 14-72; see "Felony Larceny" in Chapter 13 (Larceny, Possession of Stolen Goods, Embezzlement, and Related Offenses). When instructing the jury in such cases, the judge must define larceny. State v. Foust, 40 N.C. App. 71, 71 (1979). Of course, the intent to commit any felony, such as rape or murder, may satisfy this element as well.

The defendant need not be successful in committing the intended felony or larceny; the defendant merely has to intend to commit the crime when he or she breaks and enters. State v. Bell, 285 N.C. 746 (1974); State v. Brown, 308 N.C. 181 (1983); *Jordan,* 186 N.C. App. at 581. For example, if a defendant entered a building with intent to commit a felony but, once inside, was interrupted or frightened away before committing any felony, this element would still be satisfied. State v. Hedrick, 289 N.C. 232 (1976).

A defendant's intent typically is proved by circumstantial evidence. State v. Clagon, ___ N.C. App. ___, 700 S.E.2d 89, 92 (2010); State v. Goldsmith, 187 N.C. App. 162, 165–66 (2007). The fact that the intruder actually committed a felony inside would be strong evidence that he or she intended to do it before entering, *Clagon,* 700 S.E.2d at 92 (the evidence was sufficient to establish that the defendant intended to commit a felony assault inside the dwelling when the defendant entered the residence carrying an axe, asked where the victim was, and, upon locating her, assaulted her with the axe); State v. Williams, 330 N.C. 579 (1992); State v. Simpson, 299 N.C. 377 (1980), as would evidence that he or she attempted or prepared to commit a felony inside, State v. Tippett, 270 N.C. 588 (1967); State v. Ly, 189 N.C. App. 422, 431 (2008) (the evidence was sufficient to show an intent to commit an armed robbery when the defendants, armed with guns, entered the residence knowing that the residents soon would arrive; the defendants were not surprised by the arrival of the first family member and immediately bound and blindfolded him; and as each family member arrived, the defendants overcame them).

The fact that an intruder broke and entered a dwelling in the nighttime is sufficient, in the absence of contrary evidence, to support a finding that the intruder intended to steal. State v. Accor, 277 N.C. 65 (1970); State v. Cogdell, 165 N.C. App. 368 (2004); State v. King, 158 N.C. App. 60 (2003). However, the fact that at nighttime an intruder broke and entered a dwelling occupied by a woman is not sufficient to prove intent to rape. *In re* Owen, 207 N.C. 445 (1934); State v. Davis, 90 N.C. App. 185 (1988). Similarly, there was insufficient evidence of an intent to commit a sexual offense when the defendant reached inside an open window and grabbed the female above her elbows; the female had heard a noise in a room, found the screen missing and objects spilled onto the floor, and was trying to replace the screen when this occurred. State v. Cooper, 138 N.C. App. 495 (2000).

The defendant may offer evidence of his or her innocence by showing entry for some nonfelonious purpose. State v. Cook, 242 N.C. 700 (1955).

Charging issues. For charging issues in connection with burglary and breaking or entering crimes, see Jessica Smith, *The Criminal Indictment: Fatal Defect, Fatal Variance, and Amendment,* ADMIN. OF JUST. BULL. NO. 2008/03 (UNC School of Government, July 2008) (online at www.sogpubs.unc.edu/electronicversions/pdfs/aojb0803.pdf). For relevant cases decided after publication of that bulletin, see *State v. McCormick,* ___ N.C. App. ___, 693 S.E.2d 195, 199 (2010) (no fatal variance when a burglary indictment alleged that the defendant broke and entered "the dwelling house of Lisa McCormick located at 407 Ward's Branch Road, Sugar Grove Watauga County" but the evidence indicated that the house number was 317, not 407; the court also held that the burglary indictment was not defective on grounds that it failed to allege that the breaking and entering occurred without consent; the indictment language alleging that the defendant "unlawfully and willfully did feloniously break and enter" implied a lack of consent); *Chillo,* 705 S.E.2d at 396–98 (an indictment for breaking or entering a motor vehicle alleging that the vehicle was the personal property of "D.L. Peterson Trust" was not defective for failing to allege that the victim was a legal entity capable of owning property, given that a trust is a legal entity capable of owning property; also holding that because the State indicted the defendant for breaking or entering a motor vehicle with intent to commit larceny therein, it was bound by that allegation and had to prove that the defendant intended to commit larceny); *State v. Clagon,* ___ N.C. App. ___, 700 S.E.2d 89, 91 (2010) (a burglary indictment does not need to identify the felony that the defendant intended to commit inside the dwelling); *State v. Speight,* ___ N.C. App. ___, 711 S.E.2d 808 (2011) (a burglary indictment alleging that the defendant intended to commit "unlawful sex acts" was not defective); and *State v. Clark,* ___ N.C. App. ___, 702 S.E.2d 324, 326–27 (2010) (although the State is not required to allege the felony or larceny intended in an indictment charging breaking or entering a vehicle, if it does so, it will be bound by that allegation).

Doctrine of recent possession. Because the doctrine of recent possession applies to breaking and entering crimes, *see, e.g.,* State v. Patterson, 194 N.C. App 608, 617–18 (2009), it likely applies to burglary as well. For a discussion of the doctrine, see this note under "Misdemeanor Larceny" in Chapter 13 (Larceny, Possession of Stolen Goods, Embezzlement, and Related Offenses).

Greater and lesser-included offenses. Second-degree burglary, felony and misdemeanor breaking or entering, and first-degree trespass are lesser-included offenses of first-degree burglary. State v. Barnett, 113 N.C. App. 69 (1993); State v. Owens, ___ N.C. App. ___, 695 S.E.2d 823, 828 (2010) (trespass).

Multiple convictions and punishments. The North Carolina Supreme Court has held that because the legislature intended that the crime of breaking or entering and the crime of felony larceny pursuant to that breaking or entering would be separately punished, a defendant may be punished for both crimes when the convictions are obtained in a single trial. State v. Gardner, 315 N.C. 444, 463 (1986). That holding would likely apply to burglary as well.

Relation to other offenses. The main differences between first- and second-degree burglary are that (1) first-degree burglary requires that the dwelling actually be occupied when the breaking and entering occurs, whereas second-degree burglary does not; and (2) first-degree burglary is limited to a dwelling house or sleeping apartment, whereas second-degree burglary includes the breaking and entering of not only dwellings and sleeping apartments but also buildings within the curtilage of the dwelling.

First-degree burglary differs from felony breaking or entering in that (1) the breaking or entering crime requires only a breaking or entering, whereas burglary requires both; (2) the breaking or entering crime covers all buildings, unlike first-degree burglary, which is limited to dwelling houses and sleeping apartments; (3) the breaking or entering crime need not occur at night, whereas burglary must occur at night; and (4) the breaking or entering crime does not require the premises to be occupied, whereas first-degree burglary does.

Verdict. A trial court may accept a guilty verdict of felony larceny pursuant to a burglary or related crime and a not guilty verdict of the burglary or the related crime, even though the verdicts are inconsistent; because the verdicts are not mutually exclusive, they are permissible. State v. Mumford, 364 N.C. 394, 402 (2010).

Related Offenses Not in This Chapter

"Felony Larceny" (Chapter 13)
See the various trespass crimes and "Injury to Real Property" in Chapter 18 (Trespass, Property Damage, and Littering).
Breaking out of dwelling house burglary. G.S. 14-53.
Looting; trespass during emergency. G.S. 14-288.6.

Second-Degree Burglary

Statute

Burglary is defined by common law. State v. Mumford, 227 N.C. 132, 133 (1947). G.S. 14-51 breaks the crime into degrees and G.S. 14-52 prescribes punishment for the two degrees of burglary. See G.S. 14-51 and G.S. 14-52, reproduced under "First-Degree Burglary," above.

Elements

A person guilty of this offense

(1) breaks *and*
(2) enters
(3) without consent
(4) the dwelling house or sleeping apartment, or any building within the curtilage of the dwelling,
(5) of another
(6) at night
(7) with the intent to commit any felony or larceny therein.

Punishment

Class G felony. G.S. 14-52. Attempted second-degree burglary is a Class H felony, pursuant to G.S. 14-2.5. This statute supersedes prior case law, which held that attempted burglary was an infamous misdemeanor as defined in G.S. 14-3(b) and punishable as a Class H felony. State v. Surles, 230 N.C. 272 (1949); State v. Hageman, 307 N.C. 1 (1982). For a discussion of the status offense of habitual breaking and entering, see the note entitled "Habitual Breaking and Entering Status Offender" under "Special Provisions" in the discussion of felony sentencing in Chapter 4 (Punishment under Structured Sentencing).

Notes

Generally. Second-degree burglary is the same as first-degree burglary except that the second-degree offense (1) does not require the dwelling house or sleeping apartment to be occupied when the breaking and entering occurs; and (2) covers, in addition to dwelling houses and sleeping apartments, buildings within the curtilage of such premises. Otherwise, this offense is the same as "First-Degree Burglary," above, and the notes to that offense apply here.

Element (4). A building is "within the curtilage" if it is (1) close to the dwelling and (2) used as part of the dwelling. State v. Fields, 315 N.C. 191, 194–95 (1985). Whether a building is used as part of the dwelling turns on whether it serves the "comfort and convenience" of the dwelling. *Id.* at 194. Thus, it has been explained, separate kitchens, laundries, smokehouses, and dairies are considered to be used as part of dwellings because "they are all used as parts of one whole, each contributing in its way to the comfort and convenience of the place as a . . . dwelling." *Id.* at 195. As to the distance prong of the test, there are no bright line rules. *Id.* A good rule of thumb, however, is that a building is within the curtilage if it is in what we think of as the yard. A building is unlikely to be within the curtilage if it is across a public road from the dwelling. PERKINS & BOYCE, cited in full *supra*, at 259–60. An unoccupied tool shed located 45 feet from a dwelling is not within the curtilage. *Fields*, 315 N.C. at 196.

Related Offenses Not in This Chapter

See the offenses listed under "First-Degree Burglary," above.

Felony Breaking or Entering of a Building

Statute

§14-54. Breaking or entering buildings generally.

(a) Any person who breaks or enters any building with intent to commit any felony or larceny therein shall be punished as a Class H felon.

(b) Any person who wrongfully breaks or enters any building is guilty of a Class 1 misdemeanor.

(c) As used in this section, "building" shall be construed to include any dwelling, dwelling house, uninhabited house, building under construction, building within the curtilage of a dwelling house, and any other structure designed to house or secure within it any activity or property.

Elements

A person guilty of this offense

(1) breaks *or*
(2) enters
(3) without consent

(4) any building
(5) with the intent to commit any felony or larceny therein.

Punishment

Class H felony. G.S. 14-54(a). For a discussion of the status offense of habitual breaking and entering, see the note entitled "Habitual Breaking and Entering Status Offender" under "Special Provisions" in the discussion of felony sentencing in Chapter 4 (Punishment under Structured Sentencing).

Notes

Elements (1) and (2) generally. It is not necessary that there be both a "breaking" and an "entering" as in burglary; for this crime all that is required is a breaking or an entering. For example, it is sufficient simply to walk through an open door into a building with the intent to steal something inside; it is also sufficient when the intruder opens a closed door, intending to enter and steal, even if he or she is caught or forced to flee without being able to enter. State v. Nichols, 268 N.C. 152 (1966); State v. Burgess, 1 N.C. App. 104 (1968). For explanations of the terms "breaks" and "enters," see the notes on Elements (1) and (2) to "First-Degree Burglary," above.

Element (3). See the note on Element (3) to "First-Degree Burglary," above. A defendant who entered a clothing store during business hours and stole two sweaters did not commit this offense because he entered the store with the owner's consent. State v. Boone, 297 N.C. 652 (1979). But another defendant who entered a store during business hours, concealed himself in an area not open to the public, remained there until after the store closed, and then participated in a larceny was guilty of felonious entry of the store. State v. Speller, 44 N.C. App. 59, 60 (1979) (the defendant's acts "voided any consent to the entry").

Tricky issues about consent to enter can arise when some portions of the building are open to the public but others are not. Sometimes the courts analyze this issue by focusing on whether the defendant had consent to enter the particular portion of the premises. *In re* S.D.R., 191 N.C. App. 552, 558–59 (2008) (although the public had access to the building in question, it did not have full access to the private office at issue and thus there was no consent to enter this location); State v. Rawlinson, 198 N.C. App. 600, 609–10 (2009) (citing *S.D.R.* and holding that although a video store was open to the public, an office in the store was not, and thus the defendant did not have implied consent to enter the office). Alternatively, the courts analyze this issue by determining that any consent to enter was void ab initio because of the defendant's criminal intent. State v. Brooks, 178 N.C. App. 211, 214–15 (2006) (by entering a nonpublic area of a law firm to commit a theft and misinforming an employee as to his presence in the area, the initial consent to enter the firm was rendered void ab initio); State v. Perkins, 181 N.C. App. 209, 218 (2007) (following *Brooks*); *S.D.R.*, 191 N.C. App. at 559–60 (even if the defendant had implied consent to enter a private office in a public building, such consent was void ab initio when he entered the office with the intent to steal); *Rawlinson,* 198 N.C. App. at 609–10 (even if the defendant had implied consent to enter an office in a video store, his act of stealing the cash and checks inside a deposit bag located in the office rendered that implied consent void ab initio).

Element (4). Unlike burglary, felony breaking or entering of a building is not limited to dwellings, sleeping apartments, and buildings within the curtilage of a dwelling. The statute defines a "building" to include any dwelling, dwelling house, uninhabited house, building under construction, building within the curtilage of a dwelling house, and any other structure designed to house or secure within it any activity or property. G.S. 14-54(c). Thus, the term "building" covers dwellings, stores, State v. Brown, 266 N.C. 55 (1965), boiler rooms, shops, warehouses, banks, garages, mobile homes, State v. Douglas, 51 N.C. App. 594 (1981); State v. Douglas, 54 N.C. App. 85 (1981), trailers put up on blocks and used for storage of construction equipment, State v. Bost, 55 N.C. App. 612 (1982), and any other permanent structures with walls and a roof; none of these buildings need be occupied or inhabited.

Element (5). See the note on Element (8) to "First-Degree Burglary," above.

Charging issues. See this note to "First-Degree Burglary," above.

Doctrine of recent possession. See this note to "First-Degree Burglary," above.

Greater and lesser-included offenses. Misdemeanor breaking or entering and first- and second-degree trespass are lesser-included offenses of this offense. State v. Jones, 264 N.C. 134, 136–37 (1965) (misdemeanor breaking or entering); G.S. 14-159.14 (trespass).

Multiple convictions and punishments. Because the legislature intended that the crime of breaking or entering and the crime of felony larceny pursuant to that breaking or entering would be separately punished, a defendant may be punished for both crimes when the convictions are obtained in a single trial. State v. Gardner, 315 N.C. 444, 463 (1986).

Relation to other offenses. See this note to "First-Degree Burglary," above.

Verdict. See this note to "First-Degree Burglary," above.

Related Offenses Not in This Chapter

See the offenses listed under "First-Degree Burglary," above.

Misdemeanor Breaking or Entering of a Building

Statute

See G.S. 14-54(b) and (c), reproduced under "Felony Breaking or Entering of a Building," above.

Elements

A person guilty of this offense

(1) breaks *or*
(2) enters
(3) without consent
(4) any building.

Punishment

Class 1 misdemeanor. G.S. 14-54(b).

Notes

Generally. This offense is exactly the same as "Felony Breaking or Entering of a Building," above, except that for this offense there is no requirement of an intent to commit any felony of larceny when the breaking or entering occurs. State v. Dickens, 272 N.C. 515 (1968). Thus, the relevant notes to that offense apply here as well. An example of this offense is when the defendant breaks or enters a building to sleep inside. State v. Friend, 164 N.C. App. 430 (2004).

Related Offenses Not in This Chapter

See the offenses listed under "First-Degree Burglary," above.

Breaking or Entering a Place of Worship

Statute

§14-54.1. Breaking or entering a building that is a place of religious worship.

(a) Any person who wrongfully breaks or enters any building that is a place of religious worship with intent to commit any felony or larceny therein is guilty of a Class G felony.

(b) As used in this section, a "building that is a place of religious worship" shall be construed to include any church, chapel, meetinghouse, synagogue, temple, longhouse, or mosque, or other building that is regularly used, and clearly identifiable, as a place for religious worship.

Elements

A person guilty of this offense

(1) wrongfully breaks *or*
(2) enters
(3) without consent
(4) a building that is a place of religious worship
(5) with the intent to commit any felony or larceny therein.

Punishment

Class G felony. G.S. 14-54.1(a). For a discussion of the status offense of habitual breaking and entering, see the note entitled "Habitual Breaking and Entering Status Offender" under "Special Provisions" in the discussion of felony sentencing in Chapter 4 (Punishment under Structured Sentencing).

Notes

Generally. This offense is the same as "Felony Breaking or Entering of a Building," above, except that (1) felony breaking or entering of a building applies to any building and this offense applies only to a place of religious worship; and (2) felony breaking or entering of a building is a Class H felony and this offense is a Class G felony. Thus, the relevant notes to "Felony Breaking or Entering of a Building" apply here as well.

Element (4). G.S. 14-54.1(b) defines a "building that is a place of religious worship" to include any church, chapel, meetinghouse, synagogue, temple, longhouse, or mosque, or any other building that is regularly used and clearly identifiable as a place for religious worship.

Related Offenses Not in This Chapter

See the offenses listed under "First-Degree Burglary," above.
"Disorderly Conduct by Disrupting a Religious Service or Assembly" (Chapter 19)

Possession of Burglar's Tools

Statute

§14-55. Preparation to commit burglary or other housebreakings.

If any person shall be found armed with any dangerous or offensive weapon, with the intent to break or enter a dwelling, or other building whatsoever, and to commit any felony or larceny therein; or shall be found having in his possession, without lawful excuse, any picklock, key, bit, or other implement of housebreaking; or shall be found in any such building, with intent to commit any felony or larceny therein, such person shall be punished as a Class I felon.

Elements

A person guilty of this offense

(1) is found in possession of

(2) any picklock, key, bit, or other implement of housebreaking

(3) without lawful excuse.

Punishment

Class I felony. G.S. 14-55.

Notes

Generally. The statute proscribes two other crimes in addition to this one: being found in a building with intent to commit any felony or larceny and being found armed with intent to break or enter. However, since those offenses are rarely charged, they are not separately covered in this book.

Element (2). The statute refers to possession of "any picklock, key, bit, or other implement of housebreaking," but court decisions make it clear that the possession must be for the purpose of breaking in. The fact that the defendants were found with a picklock and homemade telephone box key—as well as hammers, chisels, other tools, and hundreds of coin wrappers—in their car was sufficient evidence that they possessed the tools for the purpose of breaking into buildings and stealing from pay telephone boxes. State v. Craddock, 272 N.C. 160 (1967). When the defendants were apprehended outside the rear of a drugstore with prescription drugs nearby, the front door having been pried open, a crowbar lying outside the back door, and a tire tool lying inside the building at the rear door, the tools were held to be implements of housebreaking. State v. Bagley, 300 N.C. 736 (1980). But in a case in which the defendants had a bolt cutter, a large screwdriver, and a brace and bit in their car, plus a pistol and blackjack they admitted carrying for protection while transporting illegal liquor, the evidence was insufficient because it failed to show they possessed the tools for the purpose of housebreaking. State v. Boyd, 223 N.C. 79 (1943).

Element (3). The State has the burden of proving that the defendant had no lawful excuse for possessing the tools. *Id.*; State v. Davis, 272 N.C. 469 (1968).

Charging issues. G.S. 14-55 creates three separate offenses, see the note "Generally," above, and the criminal pleading must clearly and individually identify the offense with which a defendant is charged. State v. Searcy, 37 N.C. App. 68 (1978).

Related Offenses Not in This Chapter

"Attempt" (Chapter 5)
Being found in a building with intent to commit any felony or larceny. G.S. 14-55.
Being found armed with intent to break or enter. G.S. 14-55.

Breaking or Entering a Vehicle

Statute

§14-56. Breaking or entering into or breaking out of railroad cars, motor vehicles, trailers, aircraft, boats, or other watercraft.

If any person, with intent to commit any felony or larceny therein, breaks or enters any railroad car, motor vehicle, trailer, aircraft, boat, or other watercraft of any kind, containing any goods, wares, freight, or other thing of value, or, after having committed any felony

> or larceny therein, breaks out of any railroad car, motor vehicle, trailer, aircraft, boat, or other watercraft of any kind containing any goods, wares, freight, or other thing of value, that person is guilty of a Class I felony. It is prima facie evidence that a person entered in violation of this section if he is found unlawfully in such a railroad car, motor vehicle, trailer, aircraft, boat, or other watercraft.

Elements

A person guilty of this offense

(1) breaks *or*
(2) enters
(3) without consent
(4) any railroad car, motor vehicle, trailer, aircraft, boat, or other watercraft
(5) containing goods, wares, freight, or anything of value
(6) with the intent to commit any felony or larceny therein.

Punishment

Class I felony. G.S. 14-56.

Notes

Generally. G.S. 14-56 also proscribes the separate offense of breaking out of a vehicle. However, because that offense is rarely charged, it is not separately covered in this book.

Element (1). See the note on Element (1) to "First-Degree Burglary," above.

Element (2). See the note on Element (2) to "First-Degree Burglary." This element was satisfied when (1) a defendant leaned the upper part of his body through an open van door while standing on the street, State v. Sneed, 38 N.C. App. 230 (1978); and (2) defendants opened and looked under an automobile hood even though a chain lock prevented the hood from being opened more than 18 inches, State v. Nealy, 64 N.C. App. 663 (1983).

Element (3). See the note on Element (3) to "First-Degree Burglary," above.

Element (5). This element requires proof that a vehicle contained personal property of some value, however trivial (such as a vehicle registration card, hubcap key, papers, cigarettes, or a shoe bag). State v. McLaughlin, 321 N.C. 267, 270–71 (1987) (insufficient evidence of this element). However, evidence of the vehicle's key, seats, carpeting, visors, handles, knobs, cigarette lighter, and radio did not satisfy this element; to satisfy this element, there must be proof of objects separate and distinct from the functioning vehicle. State v. Jackson, 162 N.C. App. 695, 698–99 (2004); State v. McDowell, ___ N.C. App. ___, ___ S.E.2d ___ (Dec. 20, 2011) (citing *Jackson* and holding that the evidence was insufficient where it failed to show that the vehicle contained any items of value apart from objects installed in the vehicle).

Element (6). See the note to Element (8) to "First-Degree Burglary," above. The evidence was insufficient to establish that the defendant intended to commit a larceny in a vehicle when it suggested that his only intent was to show another person how to break glass and the two left without taking anything once the glass was broken. State v. Chillo, ___ N.C. App. ___, 705 S.E.2d 394, 398–99 (2010).

The intended felony or larceny may be a theft of the motor vehicle that is the subject of the breaking or entering. State v. Clark, ___ N.C. App. ___, 702 S.E.2d 324, 326–29 (2010). The intended larceny may be a felony or a misdemeanor. State v. Kirkpatrick, 34 N.C. App. 452, 455–56 (1977). Note that a larceny pursuant to breaking into a vehicle is not necessarily a felony. A larceny committed pursuant to burglary, breaking out of a building, breaking or entering a building, breaking or entering a building that is a place of religious worship, or burglary by explosive is a felony regardless of the value of the property taken. See "Felony Larceny" in Chapter 13 (Larceny, Possession of Stolen Goods, Embezzlement, and Related Offenses).

However, larceny is not a felony simply because it was committed pursuant to breaking or entering a vehicle. If a larceny occurs in such a breaking, it is a felony only if one of the other factors making larceny a felony under G.S. 14-72 is present. For example, if the property taken from the vehicle was valued at more than $1,000 or if a firearm was stolen, then the larceny is a felony. See "Felony Larceny" in Chapter 13 (Larceny, Possession of Stolen Goods, Embezzlement, and Related Offenses).

Charging issues. See this note under "First-Degree Burglary," above.

Doctrine of recent possession. See this note under "First-Degree Burglary," above.

Prima facie case. Being found in a vehicle unlawfully creates a prima facie case that the person entered in violation of this statute. G.S. 14-56.

Greater and lesser-included offenses. Tampering with a motor vehicle under G.S. 20-107(a) or G.S. 20-107(b) are not lesser-included offenses of this crime. State v. Carver, 96 N.C. App. 230 (1989); *Jackson*, 162 N.C. App. 695. Trespass is a lesser-included offense of this crime. G.S. 14-159.14.

Relation to other offenses. If the vehicle that a defendant breaks or enters is a trailer serving as a dwelling, burglary or felonious breaking or entering may be charged, both of which carry higher penalties than this offense. As mentioned in the note entitled "Generally," above, the statute also covers breaking out of a vehicle after committing larceny or any other felony.

Related Offenses Not in This Chapter

See the offenses listed under "First-Degree Burglary," above.

Breaking out of railroad cars, motor vehicles, trailers, aircraft, boats, or other watercraft. G.S. 14-56.

Preparation to commit breaking or entering into motor vehicles. G.S. 14-56.4.

Injuring or tampering with vehicle. G.S. 20-107.

Breaking into a Coin- or Currency-Operated Machine

Statute

§14-56.1. Breaking into or forcibly opening coin- or currency-operated machines.

Any person who forcibly breaks into, or by the unauthorized use of a key or other instrument opens, any coin- or currency-operated machine with intent to steal any property or moneys therein shall be guilty of a Class 1 misdemeanor, but if such person has previously been convicted of violating this section, such person shall be punished as a Class I felon. The term "coin- or currency-operated machine" shall mean any coin- or currency-operated vending machine, pay telephone, telephone coin or currency receptacle, or other coin- or currency-activated machine or device.

There shall be posted on the machines referred to in G.S. 14-56.1 a decal stating that it is a crime to break into vending machines, and that a second offense is a felony. The absence of such a decal is not a defense to a prosecution for the crime described in this section.

Elements

A person guilty of this offense

(1) forcibly breaks into

(2) without consent

(3) a coin- or currency-operated machine
(4) with the intent to steal property or money therein.

Punishment

The first offense is a Class 1 misdemeanor. G.S. 14-56.1. A second or subsequent offense is a Class I felony. *Id.* If the felony version of this offense is charged, the prior conviction(s) must be properly pleaded and proved pursuant to G.S. 15A-928.

Notes

Generally. This offense also is committed by the unauthorized opening of the machine with a key or other instrument. G.S. 14-56.1.

Element (1). For a discussion of the term "breaks," see the note on Element (1) to "First-Degree Burglary," above. Note that unlike burglary, this statute specifies that the breaking be forcible. G.S. 14-56.1.

Element (2). This offense is not committed if an authorized person consents to the breaking. N.C. Pattern Jury Instructions—Crim. 214.55.

Element (3). A "coin- or currency-operated machine" is any coin- or currency-operated vending machine, pay telephone, telephone coin or currency receptacle, or other coin- or currency-activated machine or device. G.S. 14-56.1.

Notice of penalty. The coin- or currency-operated machine must be posted with a decal stating that breaking into the machine is a crime and that a second offense is a felony. *Id.* The absence of the required warning decal is not a defense to a prosecution. *Id.*

Charging issues. An allegation of ownership is not required for this offense. State v. Price, 170 N.C. App. 672, 675 (2005).

Related Offenses Not in This Chapter

"Felony Larceny" (Chapter 13)
"Misdemeanor Larceny" (Chapter 13)
"Injury to Personal Property" (Chapter 18)
Breaking into or forcibly opening coin- or currency-operated machines. G.S. 14-56.1.
Damaging or destroying coin- or currency-operated machines. G.S. 14-56.2.
Breaking into paper currency machines. G.S. 14-56.3.
Obtaining property or services from slot machines, etc., by false coins or tokens. G.S. 14-108.
Manufacture, sale, or gift of devices for cheating slot machines, etc. G.S. 14-109.

Burglary with Explosives

Statute

§14-57. Burglary with explosives.

Any person who, with intent to commit any felony or larceny therein, breaks and enters, either by day or by night, any building, whether inhabited or not, and opens or attempts to open any vault, safe, or other secure place by use of nitroglycerine, dynamite, gunpowder, or any other explosive, or acetylene torch, shall be deemed guilty of burglary with explosives. Any person convicted under this section shall be punished as a Class D felon.

Elements

A person guilty of this offense

(1) breaks *and*
(2) enters
(3) without consent
(4) any building
(5) with the intent to commit any felony or larceny therein *and*
(6) opens or attempts to open any vault, safe, or other secure place
(7) by use of nitroglycerine, dynamite, gunpowder, or any other explosive or acetylene torch.

Punishment

Class D felony. G.S. 14-57.

Notes

Elements (1) through (3). See the notes on these elements to "First-Degree Burglary," above.

Element (4). See the note on Element (4) to "Felony Breaking or Entering of a Building," above. The building need not be inhabited. G.S. 14-57.

Element (5). See the note on Element (8) to "First-Degree Burglary," above.

Attempt. Note that an attempt to open a vault, safe, or other secure place is punished like the completed crime, not one level lower, as is ordinarily the case for an attempt. See Element (6) above and "Attempt" in Chapter 5 (General Crimes).

Multiple convictions and punishments. The North Carolina Supreme Court has held that because the legislature intended that the crime of breaking or entering and the crime of felony larceny pursuant to that breaking or entering would be separately punished, a defendant may be punished for both crimes when the convictions are obtained in a single trial. State v. Gardner, 315 N.C. 444, 463 (1986). That holding would likely apply to burglary with explosives as well.

Relation to other offenses. If a defendant enters a building through a door standing open, without permission and with the intent to steal, and then forces open a vault or safe inside with dynamite, the defendant has not violated this statute because he or she did not break and enter the building. However the defendant has committed "Felony Breaking or Entering of a Building," above, because he or she entered the building with the intent to commit larceny, as well as "Safecracking," discussed below.

Related Offenses Not in This Chapter

See the offenses listed under "First-Degree Burglary" and "Breaking into a Coin- or Currency-Operated Machine," both above.

Safecracking

Statute

§14-89.1. Safecracking.

(a) A person is guilty of safecracking if he unlawfully opens, enters, or attempts to open or enter a safe or vault:

(1) By the use of explosives, drills, or tools; or
(2) Through the use of a stolen combination, key, electronic device, or other fraudulently acquired implement or means; or
(3) Through the use of a master key, duplicate key or device made or obtained in an unauthorized manner, stethoscope or other listening device, electronic device used for unauthorized entry in a safe or vault, or other surreptitious means; or
(4) By the use of any other safecracking implement or means.

(b) A person is also guilty of safecracking if he unlawfully removes from its premises a safe or vault for the purpose of stealing, tampering with, or ascertaining its contents.

(c) Safecracking shall be punishable as a Class I felony.

Elements

A person guilty of this offense

(1) unlawfully opens or attempts to open *or*
(2) enters or attempts to enter
(3) a safe or vault
(4) by any of the following means:
 (a) explosives,
 (b) drills,
 (c) tools,
 (d) a stolen combination,
 (e) a stolen key,
 (f) a stolen electronic device,
 (g) other fraudulently acquired implements or means,
 (h) a master key made or obtained in an unauthorized manner,
 (i) a duplicate key made or obtained in an unauthorized manner,
 (j) another device made or obtained in an unauthorized manner,
 (k) a stethoscope,
 (l) a listening device,
 (m) an electronic device,
 (n) other surreptitious means, *or*
 (o) any other safecracking implements or means.

Punishment

Class I felony. G.S. 14-89.1(c).

Notes

Element (3). It is not necessary that the safe or vault have a combination-type lock. State v. Pinyatello, 272 N.C. 312 (1968). Under a prior version of this statute, the safe had to be kept and customarily used for storing money or other valuables when the forcible opening occurred. Thus, when a defendant attempted to force open a safe that the owner had just acquired but had not yet begun using to store valuables, the defendant did not commit safecracking. State v. Hill, 272 N.C. 439 (1968). The present statute does not contain this requirement. A locked desk compartment is not a safe within the meaning of the statute. State v. Goodson, 178 N.C. App. 557 (2006).

Element (4)(c). "Tools" include acetylene torches, blowtorches, chisels, saws, sledgehammers, and the like. State v. Sanders, 280 N.C. 81 (1971); State v. Buie, 26 N.C. App. 151 (1975).

Attempt. Safecracking and attempted safecracking are punishable equally. G.S. 14-89.1. Thus, if an offender attempts to force open a safe, the offender commits safecracking even if he or she fails to open it. Mere preparation (such as obtaining the necessary tools) is not an attempt; for an attempt to be made, some step must be taken toward forcing the safe open, such as cutting off a dial, chiseling out part of the concrete base, or smudging the safe with a blowtorch. *Sanders*, 280 N.C. 81. For what constitutes an attempt, see "Attempt" in Chapter 5 (General Crimes).

Related Offenses Not in This Chapter

See the offenses listed under "First-Degree Burglary" and "Breaking into a Coin- or Currency-Operated Machine," both above.

Safecracking by Removing a Safe

Statute

See G.S. 14-89.1(b), reproduced under "Safecracking," above.

Elements

A person guilty of this offense

(1) unlawfully removes from its premises
(2) a safe or vault
(3) for the purpose of
  (a) stealing its contents,
  (b) tampering with its contents, *or*
  (c) ascertaining its contents.

Punishment

Class I felony. G.S. 14-89.1(c).

Notes

Element (2). A prior version of this statute required that the safe or vault be used for storing valuables, but that is no longer necessary for this offense to be charged. See the note on Element (3) to "Safecracking," above.

Element (3). It is not necessary that any one of these three purposes actually be accomplished; the defendant need only intend to commit one of these three acts when removing the safe.

Related Offenses Not in This Chapter

See the offenses listed under "First-Degree Burglary" and "Breaking into a Coin- or Currency-Operated Machine," both above.

16

Fraud, Forgery, False Pretenses, and Related Offenses

16

Fraud, Forgery, False Pretenses, and Related Offenses

Worthless Checks

Worthless Checks—Making or Uttering

Statute

§14-107. Worthless checks.

(a) It is unlawful for any person, firm or corporation, to draw, make, utter or issue and deliver to another, any check or draft on any bank or depository, for the payment of money or its equivalent, knowing at the time of the making, drawing, uttering, issuing and delivering the check or draft, that the maker or drawer of it has not sufficient funds on deposit in or credit with the bank or depository with which to pay the check or draft upon presentation.

(b) It is unlawful for any person, firm or corporation to solicit or to aid and abet any other person, firm or corporation to draw, make, utter or issue and deliver to any person, firm or corporation, any check or draft on any bank or depository for the payment of money or its equivalent, being informed, knowing or having reasonable grounds for believing at the time of the soliciting or the aiding and abetting that the maker or the drawer of the check or draft has not sufficient funds on deposit in, or credit with, the bank or depository with which to pay the check or draft upon presentation.

(c) The word "credit" as used in this section means an arrangement or understanding with the bank or depository for the payment of a check or draft.

(d) A violation of this section is a Class I felony if the amount of the check or draft is more than two thousand dollars ($2,000). If the amount of the check or draft is two thousand dollars ($2,000) or less, a violation of this section is a misdemeanor punishable as follows:

(1) Except as provided in subdivision (3) or (4) of this subsection, the person is guilty of a Class 2 misdemeanor. Provided, however, if the person has been convicted three times of violating this section, the person shall on the fourth and all subsequent convictions (i) be punished as for a Class 1 misdemeanor and (ii) be ordered, as a condition of probation, to refrain from maintaining a checking account or making or uttering a check for three years.

(2) Repealed by Session Laws 1999-408, s. 1.

(3) If the check or draft is drawn upon a nonexistent account, the person is guilty of a Class 1 misdemeanor.

(4) If the check or draft is drawn upon an account that has been closed by the drawer, or that the drawer knows to have been closed by the bank or

depository, prior to the time the check is drawn, the person is guilty of a Class 1 misdemeanor.

(e) In deciding to impose any sentence other than an active prison sentence, the sentencing judge shall consider and may require, in accordance with the provisions of G.S. 15A-1343, restitution to the victim for (i) the amount of the check or draft, (ii) any service charges imposed on the payee by a bank or depository for processing the dishonored check, and (iii) any processing fees imposed by the payee pursuant to G.S. 25-3-506, and each prosecuting witness (whether or not under subpoena) shall be entitled to a witness fee as provided by G.S. 7A-314 which shall be taxed as part of the cost and assessed to the defendant.

Elements

A person guilty of this offense

(1) (a) draws,
(b) makes,
(c) utters, *or*
(d) issues and delivers

(2) to another

(3) a check or draft

(4) knowing that there are insufficient funds or credit available for the payment.

Punishment

Class 2 misdemeanor if the check or draft is for $2,000 or less. G.S. 14-107(d)(1). A fourth or subsequent conviction is a Class 1 misdemeanor for which the sentencing judge must order as a condition of probation that the offender refrain from maintaining a checking account or making or uttering a check for three years. *Id.* If the check or draft is for more than $2,000, the offense is a Class I felony. G.S. 14-107(d). If the felony or Class 1 misdemeanor versions of the offense are charged, the relevant facts that elevate punishment must be alleged in a charging instrument and proved at trial. *See* G.S. 15A-928 (pleading and proving prior convictions). When deciding to impose any sentence other than active time, the judge must consider and may require restitution as provided in G.S. 14-107(e). Additionally, certain witness fees may be taxed to the defendant as costs. G.S. 14-107(e).

Notes

Element (1). The statute specifically requires that a person "draw, make, utter or issue and deliver" a worthless check. The exact meaning of this phrase is not entirely clear. One interpretation requires that the defendant both create the worthless check (by writing it, endorsing it, etc.) and deliver it to another person. State v. Yarboro, 194 N.C. 498 (1927); Gen. Tire & Rubber Co. v. Distribs., Inc., 253 N.C. 459 (1960); State v. Jackson, 243 N.C. 216 (1955); State v. Levy, 220 N.C. 812 (1942); State v. First Resort Props., 81 N.C. App. 499 (1986); N.C. PATTERN JURY INSTRUCTIONS—CRIM. 219.51A (defining the term "draw" to mean sign and deliver). However, some decisions emphasize the delivery of the bad check without mentioning its creation. *General Tire*, 253 N.C. 459. Other decisions interpret the term "issuing" as being synonymous with delivering or first delivering and "uttering" as being synonymous with putting forward or sending into circulation. State v. Beaver, 266 N.C. 115 (1965).

Black's Law Dictionary defines the term "draw" in the context of drawing a check to mean "to create and sign (a draft)," without emphasizing delivery. BLACK'S LAW DICTIONARY 568 (9th ed. 2009). It defines the term "make," in relevant part, as "[t]o legally perform, as by executing, signing, or delivering (a document)," *id.* at 1041, thus emphasizing both making and delivering. Black's defines the terms "utter" and "issue" similarly, stating that "utter" means, in part, "[t]o put or send (a document) into circulation; esp., to circulate (a forged note) as if genuine," *id.* at 1687, and that "issue" means, in part, "[t]o send out or distribute officially," *id.* at 908. The North Carolina Pattern Jury Instructions define the term "uttered" as "offered to another." N.C. PATTERN JURY INSTRUCTIONS—CRIM. 219.51A. Black's Law Dictionary defines "delivery" with respect to instruments as "the giving or yielding possession or control of something to another." BLACK'S LAW DICTIONARY, cited in full *supra*, at 494.

Element (3). The North Carolina Pattern Jury Instructions define a "check" as "a present unconditional order to a bank or financial institution to pay a certain sum of money to the order of a named person or to the bearer of the instrument. N.C. PATTERN JURY INSTRUCTIONS—CRIM. 219.51A, n.1; *see also* BLACK'S LAW DICTIONARY, cited in full *supra*, at 269 (defining the term as a draft signed by the maker or drawer, drawn on a bank, payable on demand, and unlimited in negotiability). A "draft," according to Black's, is an unconditional written order to a bank or financial institution to pay a certain sum of money to the order of a named person or to the bearer of the instrument. *Id.* at 566.

All checks and drafts on a bank or depository are covered by the statute, G.S. 14-107(a). However, postdated checks are not covered. State v. Crawford, 198 N.C. 522 (1930); State v. Byrd, 204 N.C. 162 (1933).

The North Carolina Supreme Court has issued conflicting rulings on whether this offense occurs when there is an agreement between the check writer and the recipient to hold a check written on an account with insufficient funds for later deposit. *Compare* State v. Levy, 220 N.C. 812 (1942) (evidence was sufficient), *with* State v. Tatum, 205 N.C. 784 (1932) (evidence was insufficient). Such an agreement is similar to when a person gives a postdated check to another; as noted above, postdated checks are not covered.

Element (4). The defendant must know that the funds on deposit are insufficient to cover the check. See generally "Knowingly" in Chapter 1 (States of Mind). The defendant only needs to know that the funds are insufficient, not that they are totally lacking.

"Credit" refers to an arrangement or understanding with the bank or depository for the payment of a check or draft. G.S. 14-107(c).

If the bank declines to honor the check for reasons other than insufficiency (for example, a "stop payment" on the check), the statute is not violated. State v. Coppley, 260 N.C. 542 (1963).

While G.S. 14-107.1 sets out methods by which prima facie evidence of other elements of this offense can be established, there is no such prima facie standard for proving knowledge that funds are insufficient. Semones v. S. Bell Tel. & Tel. Co., 106 N.C. App. 334 (1992). Return of a check due to insufficient funds or lack of credit does not constitute prima facie evidence that the person issuing the check knew at the time of issuance that there were insufficient funds or lack of credit to pay the check on presentation *Id.* However, knowledge that there were insufficient funds may be inferred from evidence that the defendant issued other worthless checks within the same time period as the check in question. State v. Mucci, 163 N.C. App. 615 (2004).

Evidence issues. G.S. 14-107.1 sets out special prima facie evidence rules that apply in worthless check cases.

Effect of federal bankruptcy. Filing a petition for bankruptcy in federal court under Chapter 7 of Title 11 of the United States Code does not bar a state from prosecuting a worthless check charge or ordering restitution upon conviction. Kelly v. Robinson, 479 U.S. 36 (1986).

Defenses. The fact that anyone, including the payee, consented to the making or uttering of a worthless check is not a defense to the charge. State v. Jackson, 243 N.C. 216 (1955).

Soliciting and aiding and abetting. The statute makes a person who solicits the writing of a bad check equally guilty with the check writer, G.S. 14-107(b), rather than classifying that person at a lower level, as is typically the case for a solicitation. See "Solicitation of Another to Commit a Felony" in Chapter 5 (General Crimes). The statute also makes an aider and abettor equally guilty of the main offense. However, this statutory language appears to be surplusage because aiders and abettors are always guilty as principals. See "Aiding and Abetting" in Chapter 5 (General Crimes).

Greater and lesser-included offenses. Uttering a worthless check is not a lesser-included offense of obtaining property by false pretenses, State v. Freeman, 308 N.C. 502, 514 (1983), or of uttering forged checks, State v. Turner, 330 N.C. 249, 258 (1991).

Relation to other offenses. For this offense to be committed, the defendant need not receive anything of value. Typically, however, the defendant does receive something of value in exchange for the worthless check. When this is the case, the defendant may be charged with "Obtaining Property for a Worthless Check" or "Obtaining Property by False Pretenses," both discussed below.

Related Offenses Not in This Chapter

See the various larceny and embezzlement offenses in Chapter 13 (Larceny, Possession of Stolen Goods, Embezzlement, and Related Offenses).

Worthless Check on a Nonexistent Account

Statute

See G.S. 14-107(a) and (d)(3), reproduced under "Worthless Checks—Making or Uttering," above.

Elements

A person guilty of this offense

(1) (a) draws,
(b) makes,
(c) utters, *or*
(d) issues and delivers
(2) to another
(3) a check or draft
(4) drawn on a nonexistent account
(5) knowing that the check was drawn on a nonexistent account.

Punishment

Class 1 misdemeanor. G.S. 14-107(d)(3). Class I felony if the amount of the check or draft is more than $2,000. G.S. 14-107(d). If the felony version of this offense is charged, the relevant fact elevating punishment must be alleged in the charging instrument and proved at trial. G.S. 15A-928. When deciding to impose any sentence other than active time, the judge must consider and may require restitution as provided in G.S. 14-107(e). Additionally, certain witness fees may be taxed to the defendant as costs. G.S. 14-107(e).

Notes

Elements (1) through (3). See the notes on these elements to "Worthless Checks—Making or Uttering," above.

Element (4). The State must prove that the person who made the check did not have a checking account with the institution at the time the check was drawn. N.C. PATTERN JURY INSTRUCTIONS—CRIM. 219.52. This charge probably would not be appropriate if the check was written on an account that simply had been closed, no matter how long it had been closed (although "Worthless Check on a Closed Account," below, might apply in these circumstances), or if the check was written on someone else's account with the institution. This charge would be appropriate, however, if the defendant had written a fictitious account number on a counter check.

Element (5). See the note on Element (4) to "Worthless Checks—Making or Uttering," above.

Evidence issues. See this note to "Worthless Checks—Making or Uttering," above.

Relation to other offenses. See this note to "Worthless Checks—Making or Uttering," above.

Related Offenses Not in This Chapter

See the offenses listed under "Worthless Checks—Making or Uttering," above.

Worthless Check on a Closed Account

Statute

See G.S. 14-107(a) and (d)(4), reproduced under "Worthless Checks—Making or Uttering," above.

Elements

A person guilty of this offense

(1) (a) draws,
 (b) makes,
 (c) utters, *or*
 (d) issues and delivers
(2) to another
(3) a check or draft
(4) drawn on an account that
 (a) had been closed by the drawer before the check or draft was drawn *or*
 (b) the drawer knew to have been closed by the bank or depository before the check or draft was drawn
(5) knowing that the check was drawn on such an account.

Punishment

Class 1 misdemeanor. G.S. 14-107(d)(4). Class I felony if the amount of the check or draft is more than $2,000. G.S. 14-107(d). If the felony version of this offense is charged, the relevant fact elevating punishment must be alleged in the charging instrument and proved at trial. G.S. 15A-928. When deciding to impose any sentence other than active time, the judge must consider and may require restitution as provided in G.S. 14-107(e). Additionally, certain witness fees may be taxed to the defendant as costs. G.S. 14-107(e).

Notes

Elements (1) through (3). See the notes to "Worthless Checks—Making or Uttering," above.

Element (4). For an explanation of the term "draw," see the note on Element (1) to "Worthless Checks—Making and Uttering," above. The drawer is the person who wrote the check. BLACK'S LAW DICTIONARY 568 (9th ed. 2009).

The person who wrote the check need not be the one who closed the account.

Under Element (4)(b), it is sufficient if the person who wrote the check knew that the account had been closed by the bank before the check was written.

Element (5). See the note on Element (4) to "Worthless Checks—Making or Uttering," above.

Evidence issues. See this note to "Worthless Checks—Making or Uttering," above.

Relation to other offenses. See this note to "Worthless Checks—Making or Uttering," above.

Related Offenses Not in This Chapter

See the offenses listed under "Worthless Checks—Making or Uttering," above.

Obtaining Property for a Worthless Check

Statute

§14-106. Obtaining property in return for worthless check, draft or order.

Every person who, with intent to cheat and defraud another, shall obtain money, credit, goods, wares or any other thing of value by means of a check, draft or order of any kind upon any bank, person, firm or corporation, not indebted to the drawer, or where he has not provided for the payment or acceptance of the same, and the same be not paid upon presentation, shall be guilty of a Class 2 misdemeanor. The giving of the aforesaid worthless check, draft, or order shall be prima facie evidence of an intent to cheat and defraud.

Elements

A person guilty of this offense

(1) with intent to cheat and defraud
(2) obtains money, credit, goods, wares, or anything of value
(3) by means of a check, draft, or order of any kind on any bank, person, firm, or corporation *and*
(4) (a) the bank, person, firm, or corporation was not indebted to the drawer *or*
    (b) the person did not provide for the payment or acceptance of the check, draft, or order *and*
(5) the check, draft, or order was not paid on presentment.

Punishment

Class 2 misdemeanor. G.S. 14-106.

Notes

Generally. Most of the conduct covered by this offense is also covered by "Worthless Checks—Making or Uttering," "Worthless Check on a Nonexistent Account," and "Worthless Check on a Closed Account," all above. Not only does the proof appear to be easier under those other offenses, but the prima facie evidence rule of G.S. 14-107.1 also applies to them, further facilitating the State's proof.

Element (2). G.S. 14-107(c), the statute proscribing the offenses discussed above, provides that "credit" refers to an arrangement or understanding with a bank or depository for the payment of a check of draft. The giving of a worthless check, draft, or order is prima facie evidence of an intent to cheat and defraud. G.S. 14-106.

Elements (3) through (5) generally. For a discussion of the meaning of the terms "check" and "draft," see the note on Element (3) to "Worthless Checks—Making or Uttering," above.

Element (4)(a). The drawer is the person who wrote the check. BLACK'S LAW DICTIONARY 568 (9th ed. 2009).

Element (4)(b). Even though a person has no money in an account, the person has not committed a crime if he or she has arranged for the bank to cover checks or to automatically make a loan to his or her account.

Related Offenses Not in This Chapter

See the offenses listed under "Worthless Checks—Making or Uttering," above.

Obtaining Property by False Pretenses

Statute

§14-100. Obtaining property by false pretenses.

(a) If any person shall knowingly and designedly by means of any kind of false pretense whatsoever, whether the false pretense is of a past or subsisting fact or of a future fulfillment or event, obtain or attempt to obtain from any person within this State any money, goods, property, services, chose in action, or other thing of value with intent to cheat or defraud any person of such money, goods, property, services, chose in action or other thing of value, such person shall be guilty of a felony: Provided, that if, on the trial of anyone indicted for such crime, it shall be proved that he obtained the property in such manner as to amount to larceny or embezzlement, the jury shall have submitted to them such other felony proved; and no person tried for such felony shall be liable to be afterwards prosecuted for larceny or embezzlement upon the same facts: Provided, further, that it shall be sufficient in any indictment for obtaining or attempting to obtain any such money, goods, property, services, chose in action, or other thing of value by false pretenses to allege that the party accused did the act with intent to defraud, without alleging an intent to defraud any particular person, and without alleging any ownership of the money, goods, property, services, chose in action or other thing of value; and upon the trial of any such indictment, it shall not be necessary to prove either an intent to defraud any particular person or that the person to whom the false pretense was made was the person defrauded, but it shall be sufficient to allege and prove that the party accused made the false pretense charged with an intent to defraud. If the value of the money, goods, property, services, chose in action, or other thing of value is one hundred thousand dollars ($100,000) or more, a violation of this section is a Class C felony. If the value of the money, goods, property, services, chose in action, or other thing of value is less than one hundred thousand dollars ($100,000), a violation of this section is a Class H felony.

(b) Evidence of nonfulfillment of a contract obligation standing alone shall not establish the essential element of intent to defraud.

(c) For purposes of this section, "person" means person, association, consortium, corporation, body politic, partnership, or other group, entity, or organization.

Elements

A person guilty of this offense

(1) makes a representation about a past or existing fact or a future event
(2) that is false and
(3) is calculated and intended to deceive, *and*
(4) the representation does in fact deceive another person, *and*
(5) the person thereby obtains, or attempts to obtain, money, goods, property, services, choses in action, or any other thing of value from that other person.

Punishment

Class H felony. G.S. 14-100(a). It is a Class C felony if the value of the property, etc. taken is $100,000 or more. *Id.* If the Class C felony version of this offense is charged, the relevant sum of money must be alleged in the charging instrument and proved at trial.

Notes

Generally. For case law stating the elements of this offense, see, for example, *State v. Parker*, 354 N.C. 268, 284 (2001).

Element (1). The representation may be of a past fact, an existing fact, a promise of future performance, or a statement that something will happen in the future. G.S. 14-100(a). The representation need not be oral or written; it can be communicated by action. *Parker*, 354 N.C. at 284. A false representation was communicated by action when a defendant used a credit card belonging to another person to obtain merchandise from a store; the false representation was that the defendant was authorized to use the card. State v. Perkins, 181 N.C. App. 209, 216–17 (2007).

Examples of false representations include:

- false statements that property pledged as security is free of liens, State v. Howley, 220 N.C. 113 (1941),
- false statements about the value of security given for a loan, State v. Cronin, 299 N.C. 229 (1980),
- false statements that a person is a broker who will invest money in stocks, State v. Clemmons, 111 N.C. App. 569 (1993),
- the creation of a false business for the purpose of writing worthless checks, State v. Bresse, 101 N.C. App. 519 (1991),
- false statements as to the defendant's identity, State v. Tesenair, 35 N.C. App. 531 (1978),
- the use of counterfeit money, State v. Mitchell, 35 N.C. App. 95 (1978),
- the presentation of a worthless check, State v. Rogers, 346 N.C. 262 (1997); State v. Cagle, 182 N.C. App. 71, 75 (2007),
- falsified invoices, State v. Grier, 35 N.C. App. 119 (1978), and
- false statements that the defendant had authority to lease a home, State v. Moore, ___ N.C. App. ___, 705 S.E.2d 797, 800 (2011).

The evidence was sufficient to support a conviction for aiding and abetting this crime when the defendant asked a county employee to fix an item in the defendant's home and the employee did so during the work day; the false pretense was the county employee's wrongfully obtaining public funds when he provided private services and later falsified time sheets. State v. Sink, 178 N.C. App. 217 (2006).

When the alleged false pretense is uttering a forged check, the evidence will be insufficient if the State fails to present evidence that the check was false—that it was not in fact a check from the issuer. State v. Brown, ___ N.C. App. ___, ___ S.E.2d ___ (Dec. 6, 2011) (so holding).

Element (2). The defendant's honest belief that the representation was true may be a valid defense to this offense. ROLLIN M. PERKINS & RONALD N. BOYCE, CRIMINAL LAW 379 (3d ed. 1982).

Element (3). The State does not need to prove an intent to defraud any particular person. G.S. 14-100(a); N.C. PATTERN JURY INSTRUCTIONS—CRIM. 219.10; State v. Cronin, 299 N.C. 229 (1980).

While a false promise to perform an act in the future may satisfy the requirement that a defendant made a false representation with an intent to defraud, proof that a defendant failed to fulfill a contractual duty through ineptness or lack of diligence is insufficient evidence. State v. Lang, 106 N.C. App. 695 (1992); State v. Compton, 90 N.C. App. 101 (1988). Evidence of nonfulfillment of a contract, standing alone, cannot establish intent to defraud. G.S. 14-100(b).

Element (4). "Person," in reference to either the defendant or victim, is broadly defined to include persons, associations, consortiums, corporations, bodies politic, partnerships, and other groups, entities, or organizations. G.S. 14-100(c). However, the victim must be a person "within this State." G.S. 14-100(a).

If an agent obtains something of value for a corporation by false pretenses, both the agent and the corporation may be charged. State v. Louchheim, 36 N.C. App. 271 (1978); *Lang*, 106 N.C. App. 695.

The person to whom the false pretense was made need not be the person defrauded. G.S. 14-100(a).

There was sufficient evidence that the victim, a pawnshop owner, was deceived by the defendant's false representation that he owned the cameras he sold to the victim; although the victim suspected that the cameras had been stolen, he did not know that to be the case. State v. Simpson, 159 N.C. App. 435 (2003).

Element (5). For an explanation of the term "chose in action" as it applies in the context of larceny, see the note on Element (2) to "Larceny of a Chose in Action" in Chapter 13 (Larceny, Possession of Stolen Goods, Embezzlement, and Related Offenses).

The defendant must gain possession of the property but need not gain title to or an ownership interest in it. State v. Kelly, 75 N.C. App. 461 (1985); State v. Walston, 67 N.C. App. 110 (1984). Thus, a defendant who rented a typewriter by falsely representing his identity and saying he would return the machine in one hour but who did not do so was properly convicted of this offense. *Walston*, 67 N.C. App. 110. Additionally, a defendant who told a car salesman that she wanted to test drive a car after falsely representing her identity was properly convicted of this offense after she drove away in the car and did not return it. *Kelly*, 75 N.C. App. 461.

Whether the defendant intends to pay for the property later is irrelevant; if the defendant intended to defraud the owner of the property to obtain it, this element is satisfied. State v. Tesenair, 35 N.C. App. 531 (1978).

If the defendant makes a false representation for some reason other than to obtain the property, this crime has not occurred.

Causation. There must be a causal relationship between the false representation and the obtaining of the property. State v. Cronin, 299 N.C. 229 (1980). For example, when a town official with the authority to write checks (1) wrote checks on the town's account to pay for train tickets for unauthorized private travel by herself and others; and (2) falsified check records to conceal the true purpose of the checks (thus making a false representation to the town), the required causal connection between the false representation (the falsified check records) and the obtaining of the town's money was absent (the official obtained the money/tickets by virtue of the already existing grant of check-writing authority, not because of her false representation), and the defendant was not guilty of this crime. State v. Davis, 48 N.C. App. 526 (1980). If this same defendant had been required to obtain another official's approval of the checks and vouchers before payment, and the defendant submitted a false voucher as described, then a prosecution for obtaining property by false pretenses would be proper. In this alternative scenario, the false statement would be causally related to obtaining the town's money. Likewise, if a person required to submit vouchers for reimbursement of work-related expenses makes a false statement on a voucher to receive payment to which the person is not entitled, obtaining property by false pretenses is a proper charge.

While the false representation must be a material factor in inducing the victim to part with property, it need not be the only inducement to the victim. State v. Howley, 220 N.C. 113 (1941).

Charging issues. For charging issues in connection with this offense and related ones covered in this chapter, see Jessica Smith, *The Criminal Indictment: Fatal Defect, Fatal Variance and Amendment*, ADMIN. OF JUST. BULL. No. 2008/03 (UNC School of Government, July 2008) (online at www.sogpubs.unc.edu/electronicversions/pdfs/aojb0803.pdf). For cases decided since publication of that bulletin, see *State v. Moore*, ___ N.C. App. ___, 705 S.E.2d 797, 801–02 (2011) (stating in dicta that under G.S. 14-100(a), an indictment alleging obtaining property by false pretenses need not identify a specific victim), and *State v. Guarascio*, ___ N.C. App. ___, 696 S.E.2d 704, 710–11 (2010) (no fatal variance between a forgery indictment and the evidence presented at trial; the indictment charged the defendant with forgery of "an order drawn on a government unit, STATE OF NORTH CAROLINA, which is described as follows: NORTH CAROLINA UNIFORM CITATION"; the evidence showed that the defendant, who was not a law enforcement officer, issued citations to several individuals; the court rejected the defendant's arguments that the citations were not "orders" and were not "drawn on a government unit" because he worked for a private police entity). *See also* G.S. 14-100(a) ("it shall be sufficient in any indictment . . . to allege that the party accused did the act with intent to defraud, without alleging an intent to defraud any particular person, and without alleging any ownership of the money, goods [etc.]").

Actual loss and absence of compensation not required. The person who gives up the property, etc. need not suffer economic loss. State v. Cagle, 182 N.C. App. 71, 77 (2007). Nor must it be proved that the defendant obtained the property, etc. without paying compensation. State v. Cronin, 299 N.C. 229, 240 (1980).

Attempt. The statute makes one who attempts to commit this offense guilty as if the offense was completed, G.S. 14-100(a); thus an attempt to commit this offense is not punished one level lower, as is typical for an attempt. See "Attempt" in Chapter 5 (General Crimes).

Jury instructions. G.S. 14-100(a) provides "that if, on the trial of anyone indicted for [obtaining property by false pretenses], it shall be proved that he obtained the property in such manner as to amount to larceny or embezzlement, the jury shall have submitted to them such other felony proved." However, if the evidence does not support an instruction on larceny or embezzlement, the statutory mandate does not apply. State v. Kelly, 75 N.C. App. 461, 465 (1985) ("The necessity for instructing the jury arises when and only when there is evidence from which the jury could find that the crime was committed.").

Verdict. Guilty verdicts of embezzlement and obtaining property by false pretenses are mutually exclusive and cannot be accepted; property cannot be obtained simultaneously pursuant to both lawful and unlawful means. State v. Mumford, 364 N.C. 394, 401 (2010) (discussing with approval State v. Speckman, 326 N.C. 576 (1990)).

Greater and lesser-included offenses. "Worthless Checks—Making or Uttering," "Worthless Check on a Nonexistent Account," "Worthless Check on a Closed Account," and "Obtaining Property for a Worthless Check," all above, are not lesser-included offenses of obtaining property by false pretenses. State v. Freeman, 308 N.C. 502 (1983).

Multiple convictions and punishments. Three separate purchases, separated by several minutes, in which different stolen credit cards were used supported three convictions of this offense. State v. Rawlins, 166 N.C. App. 160 (2004).

G.S. 14-100(a) provides that no person tried for obtaining property by false pretenses may be later prosecuted for larceny or embezzlement based on the same facts. But the reverse is not true; the statute does not bar the State from charging a defendant with obtaining property by false pretenses after a trial for larceny or embezzlement. State v. Kelly, 75 N.C. App. 461, 463–64 (1985) (larceny charge was dismissed in the first trial for insufficient evidence).

Relation to other offenses. There are three important differences between larceny and obtaining property by false pretenses: (1) obtaining property by false pretenses requires a false representation, while larceny does not (of course, a false representation may be the basis of larceny by trick; see "Larceny" (various offenses) in Chapter 13 (Larceny, Possession of Stolen Goods, Embezzlement, and Related Offenses)); (2) larceny generally requires that property be wrongfully taken without the owner's consent, while obtaining property by false pretenses frequently involves the initial consent of the property owner; and (3) larceny requires that the defendant intend to permanently deprive the property owner of his or her property, but obtaining property by false pretenses does not. Also, a defense to larceny might be that the defendant intended to return the property, but an intent to repay the victim is not a defense to obtaining property by false pretenses. State v. Martin, 105 N.C. App. 182, 188 (1992).

Embezzlement's most distinguishing feature is that it must be committed by a person who has been entrusted with the particular property. See the note on Element (4) to "Embezzlement" in Chapter 13 (Larceny, Possession of Stolen Goods, Embezzlement, and Related Offenses). However, a person who commits the crime of obtaining property by false pretenses wrongfully obtains the property from the start. State v. Speckman, 326 N.C. 576, 578 (1990) (drawing this distinction between the two crimes).

Because presentation of a worthless check constitutes a false pretense sufficient for this crime, see the note on Element (1) above, there is some overlap between this offense and the worthless check offenses discussed above.

Related Offenses Not in This Chapter

"Embezzlement" (Chapter 13)

See larceny (various offenses) in Chapter 13 (Larceny, Possession of Stolen Goods, Embezzlement, and Related Offenses)
"Creating a Counterfeit Controlled Substance" (Chapter 27)
"Obtaining a Controlled Substance by Fraud or Forgery" (Chapter 27)
"Possession of a Counterfeit Controlled Substance with Intent to Sell or Deliver" (Chapter 27)
"Sale or Delivery of a Counterfeit Controlled Substance" (Chapter 27)
Obtaining signatures by false pretenses. G.S. 14-101.
Obtaining property by false representation of pedigree of animals. G.S. 14-102.
Obtaining certificate of registration of animals by false representation. G.S. 14-103.
Obtaining advances under promise to work and pay for same. G.S. 14-104.
Obtaining property from slot machines, etc., by false coins or tokens. G.S. 14-108.
Obtaining ambulance services without intending to pay therefor. G.S. 14-111.1 and 14-111.2.
Obtaining merchandise on approval. G.S. 14-112.
Obtaining money by false representation of physical disability. G.S. 14-113.
Use of false or counterfeit credit device; unauthorized use of another's credit device; use after notice of revocation. G.S. 14-113.1.
Avoiding or attempting to avoid payment for telecommunication services. G.S. 14-113.4.
Prohibition of falsely obtaining, selling, or soliciting telephone records. G.S. 14-113.31.
Interfering with electric, gas or water meters; prima facie evidence of intent to alter, tamper with or bypass electric, gas or water meters; unlawful reconnection of electricity, gas, or water; civil liability. G.S. 14-151.1.
Opposite sexes occupying same bedroom at hotel for immoral purposes; falsely registering as husband and wife. G.S. 14-186.
Defrauding drug and alcohol screening tests. G.S. 14-401.20.
No docketing of lien unless authorized by statute. G.S. 44A-12.1.
Obtaining (marriage license) by false representation misdemeanor. G.S. 51-15.
Criminal use (and production) of counterfeit trademark. G.S. 80-11.1.
Falsely representing oneself as being licensed or registered to practice medicine or surgery. G.S. 90-18.
Improper receipt of decedent's retirement allowance. G.S. 135-18.11, 128-38.5, 135-75.2, and 120-4.34.
City ordinance violation: many ordinances prohibit obtaining taxi rides or meals in restaurants without paying

Exploitation of a Disabled or Elder Adult

Exploitation of a Disabled or Elder Adult through a Position of Trust or Business Relationship

Statute

§14-112.2. Exploitation of an elder adult or disabled adult.

(a) The following definitions apply in this section:

(1) Disabled adult.—A person 18 years of age or older or a lawfully emancipated minor who is present in the State of North Carolina and who is physically or mentally incapacitated as defined in G.S. 108A-101(d).

(2) Elder adult.—A person 60 years of age or older who is not able to provide for the social, medical, psychiatric, psychological, financial, or legal services necessary to safeguard the person's rights and resources and to maintain the person's physical and mental well-being.

(b) It is unlawful for a person: (i) who stands in a position of trust and confidence with an elder adult or disabled adult, or (ii) who has a business relationship with an elder adult or disabled adult to knowingly, by deception or intimidation, obtain or use, or endeavor to obtain or use, an elder adult's or disabled adult's funds, assets, or property with the intent to temporarily or permanently deprive the elder adult or disabled adult of the use, benefit, or possession of the funds, assets, or property, or to benefit someone other than the elder adult or disabled adult.

(c) It is unlawful for a person, who knows or reasonably should know that an elder adult or disabled adult lacks the capacity to consent, to obtain or use, endeavor to obtain or use, or conspire with another to obtain or use an elder adult's or disabled adult's funds, assets, or property with the intent to temporarily or permanently deprive the elder adult or disabled adult of the use, benefit, or possession of the funds, assets, or property, or benefit someone other than the elder adult or disabled adult. This subsection shall not apply to a person acting within the scope of that person's lawful authority as the agent for the elder adult or disabled adult.

(d) A violation of subsection (b) of this section is punishable as follows:

(1) If the funds, assets, or property involved in the exploitation of the elderly person or disabled adult is valued at one hundred thousand dollars ($100,000) or more, then the offense is a Class F felony.
(2) If the funds, assets, or property involved in the exploitation of the elderly person or disabled adult is valued at twenty thousand dollars ($20,000) or more but less than one hundred thousand dollars ($100,000), then the offense is a Class G felony.
(3) If the funds, assets, or property involved in the exploitation of the elderly person or disabled adult is valued at less than twenty thousand dollars ($20,000), then the offense is a Class H felony.

(e) A violation of subsection (c) of this section is punishable as follows:

(1) If the funds, assets, or property involved in the exploitation of the elderly person or disabled adult is valued at one hundred thousand dollars ($100,000) or more, then the offense is a Class G felony.
(2) If the funds, assets, or property involved in the exploitation of the elderly person or disabled adult is valued at twenty thousand dollars ($20,000) or more but less than one hundred thousand dollars ($100,000), then the offense is a Class H felony.
(3) If the funds, assets, or property involved in the exploitation of the elderly person or disabled adult is valued at less than twenty thousand dollars ($20,000), then the offense is a Class I felony.

Elements

A person guilty of this offense

(1) (a) stands in a position of trust and confidence *or*
    (b) has a business relationship
(2) with an elder or disabled adult *and*
(3) knowingly,
(4) by deception or intimidation,
(5) obtains, uses, or endeavors to obtain or use an elder or disabled adult's funds, assets, or property
(6) with the intent to
    (a) deprive temporarily or permanently the elder or disabled adult of the use, benefit, or possession of the funds, assets, or property *or*
    (b) benefit someone other than the elder or disabled adult.

Punishment

A violation is a Class F felony if the property is valued at $100,000 or more; a Class G felony if the property is valued at $20,000 or more but less than $100,000; and a Class H felony if the property is valued at less than $20,000. G.S. 14-112.2(d). If the Class F or G versions of this offense are charged, the value of the property must be alleged in the charging instrument and proved at trial.

Notes

Element (2). A "disabled adult" is a person 18 years of age or older or a lawfully emancipated minor who is present in the state and who is physically or mentally incapacitated as defined in G.S. 108A-101(d). G.S. 14-112.2(a)(1).

An "elder adult" is a person 60 years of age or older who is not able to provide for the social, medical, psychiatric, psychological, financial, or legal services necessary to safeguard the person's rights and resources and to maintain the person's physical and mental well-being. G.S. 14-112.2(a)(2). There was sufficient evidence that the victim was an elder adult when the victim was at least 99 years old and individuals helped him by paying his bills, providing transportation, bringing him meals and groceries, maintaining his vehicles, cashing his checks, helping him with personal hygiene, and making his medical appointments. State v. Forte, ___ N.C. App. ___, 698 S.E.2d 745, 750 (2010).

Element (3). See "Knowingly" in Chapter 1 (States of Mind).

Attempt. Because the statute covers one who "endeavor[s] to obtain or use," it appears to make an attempt to commit this offense punishable like the completed offense, not one class lower, as is typically the case for an attempt. See "Attempt" in Chapter 5 (General Crimes).

Related Offenses Not in This Chapter

"Embezzlement" (Chapter 13)

Exploitation of a Disabled or Elder Adult Lacking Capacity

Statute

See G.S. 14-112.2(c), reproduced under "Exploitation of a Disabled or Elder Adult through a Position of Trust or Business Relationship," above.

Elements

A person guilty of this offense

(1) knows or reasonably should know that
(2) an elder or disabled adult lacks the capacity to consent *and*
(3) obtains, uses, endeavors to obtain or use, or conspires with another to obtain or use an elder or disabled adult's funds, assets, or property
(4) with the intent to
  (a) deprive temporarily or permanently the elder or disabled adult of the use, benefit, or possession of the funds, assets, or property *or*
  (b) benefit someone other than the elder or disabled adult.

Punishment

A violation is a Class G felony if the property is valued at $100,000 or more; a Class H felony if the property is valued at $20,000 or more but less than $100,000; and a Class I felony if the property is valued at less than $20,000. G.S. 14-112.2(e). If the Class G or H versions of this offense are charged, the value of the property must be alleged in the charging instrument and proved to the jury.

Notes

Element (2). For definitions of "elder adult" and "disabled adult," see the note on Element (2) to "Exploitation of a Disabled or Elder Adult through a Position of Trust or Business Relationship," above.

Exceptions. This offense does not apply to a person acting within the scope of his or her lawful authority as the agent for the elder or disabled adult. G.S. 14-112.2(c).

Attempt. Because the statute covers one who "endeavor[s] to obtain use," it appears to make an attempt to commit this offense punishable like the completed offense, not one class lower, as is typically the case for an attempt. See "Attempt" in Chapter 5 (General Crimes).

Conspiracy. Note that Element (3) covers one who conspires to do the prohibited acts and punishes conspirators as if they had committed the completed crime, not one class lower, as is typically the case for conspiracies. See "Conspiracy" in Chapter 5 (General Crimes).

Related Offenses Not in This Chapter

See the offenses listed under "Exploitation of a Disabled or Elder Adult through a Position of Trust or Business Relationship," above.

Identity Theft and Frauds

Possession or Manufacture of Fraudulent Identification

Statute

§14-100.1. Possession or manufacture of certain fraudulent forms of identification.

(a) Except as otherwise made unlawful by G.S. 20-30, it shall be unlawful for any person to knowingly possess or manufacture a false or fraudulent form of identification as defined in this section for the purpose of deception, fraud, or other criminal conduct.

(b) Except as otherwise made unlawful by G.S. 20-30, it shall be unlawful for any person to knowingly obtain a form of identification by the use of false, fictitious, or fraudulent information.

(c) Possession of a form of identification obtained in violation of subsection (b) of this section shall constitute a violation of subsection (a) of this section.

(d) For purposes of this section, a "form of identification" means any of the following or any replica thereof:

(1) An identification card containing a picture, issued by any department, agency, or subdivision of the State of North Carolina, the federal government, or any other state.
(2) A military identification card containing a picture.
(3) A passport.
(4) An alien registration card containing a picture.

(e) A violation of this section shall be punished as a Class 1 misdemeanor.

Elements

A person guilty of this offense

(1) knowingly
(2) (a) possesses *or*
    (b) manufactures
(3) a false or fraudulent form of identification
(4) for the purpose of deception, fraud, or other criminal conduct.

Punishment

Class 1 misdemeanor. G.S. 14-100.1(e).

Notes

Element (1). See "Knowingly" in Chapter 1 (States of Mind).

Element (2)(a). In the criminal law generally, possession may be actual or constructive. For a discussion of these concepts, see the note on Element (2) to "Possession of a Controlled Substance" in Chapter 27 (Drug Offenses) and on Element (2)(c) to "Possession of a Firearm by a Felon" in Chapter 22 (Weapons Offenses).

Element (3). "Form of identification" includes

- a picture identification card issued by any department, agency, or subdivision of any state or the federal government;
- a picture military identification card;
- a passport;
- a picture alien registration card; and
- copies of any of these items.

G.S. 14-100.1(d).

Element (4). Possession of a form of identification that meets the elements of "Obtaining Identification by Fraud," below, constitutes this offense. G.S. 14-100.1(c).

Exceptions. This crime does not apply to violations of G.S. 20-30, which prohibits, among other things, possession of a fictitious license. G.S. 14-100.1(a), (b).

Related Offenses Not in This Chapter

Violations of license or learner's permit provisions. G.S. 20-30.

Obtaining Identification by Fraud

Statute

See G.S. 14-100.1(b), reproduced under "Possession or Manufacture of Fraudulent Identification," above.

Elements

A person guilty of this offense

(1) knowingly
(2) obtains
(3) a form of identification
(4) by the use of false, fictitious, or fraudulent information.

Punishment

Class 1 misdemeanor. G.S. 14-100.1(e).

Notes

Element (1). See "Knowingly" in Chapter 1 (States of Mind).

Element (3). See the note on Element (3) to "Possession or Manufacture of Fraudulent Identification," above.

Exceptions. See this note to "Possession or Manufacture of Fraudulent Identification," above.

Related Offenses Not in This Chapter

See the offenses listed under "Possession or Manufacture of Fraudulent Identification," above.

Identity Theft

Statute

§14-113.20. Identity Theft.

(a) A person who knowingly obtains, possesses, or uses identifying information of another person, living or dead, with the intent to fraudulently represent that the person is the other person for the purposes of making financial or credit transactions in the other person's name, to obtain anything of value, benefit, or advantage, or for the purpose of avoiding legal consequences is guilty of a felony punishable as provided in G.S. 14-113.22(a).

(b) The term "identifying information" as used in this Article includes the following:

(1) Social security or employer taxpayer identification numbers.
(2) Drivers license, State identification card, or passport numbers.
(3) Checking account numbers.
(4) Savings account numbers.
(5) Credit card numbers.
(6) Debit card numbers.
(7) Personal Identification (PIN) Code as defined in G.S. 14-113.8(6).
(8) Electronic identification numbers, electronic mail names or addresses, Internet account numbers, or Internet identification names.
(9) Digital signatures.
(10) Any other numbers or information that can be used to access a person's financial resources.
(11) Biometric data.
(12) Fingerprints.
(13) Passwords.
(14) Parent's legal surname prior to marriage.

(c) It shall not be a violation under this Article for a person to do any of the following:

(1) Lawfully obtain credit information in the course of a bona fide consumer or commercial transaction.
(2) Lawfully exercise, in good faith, a security interest or a right of offset by a creditor or financial institution.
(3) Lawfully comply, in good faith, with any warrant, court order, levy, garnishment, attachment, or other judicial or administrative order, decree, or directive, when any party is required to do so.

§14-113.22. Punishment and liability.

(a) A violation of G.S.14-113.20(a) is punishable as a Class G felony, except it is punishable as a Class F felony if: (i) the victim suffers arrest, detention, or conviction as a proximate result of the offense, or (ii) the person is in possession of the identifying information pertaining to three or more separate persons.

(a1) A violation of G.S. 14-113.20A is punishable as a Class E felony.

(a2) The court may order a person convicted under G.S. 14-113.20 or G.S. 14-113.20A to pay restitution pursuant to Article 81C of Chapter 15A of the General Statutes for financial loss caused by the violation to any person. Financial loss included under this subsection may include, in addition to actual losses, lost wages, attorneys' fees, and other costs incurred by the victim in correcting his or her credit history or credit rating, or in connection with any criminal, civil, or administrative proceeding brought against the victim resulting from the misappropriation of the victim's identifying information.

(b) Notwithstanding subsection (a), (a1), or (a2) of this section, any person who commits an act made unlawful by G.S. 14-113.20 or G.S. 14-113.20A may also be liable for damages under G.S. 1-539.2C.

(c) In any case in which a person obtains identifying information of another person in violation of this Article, uses that information to commit a crime in addition to a violation of this Article, and is convicted of that additional crime, the court records shall reflect that the person whose identity was falsely used to commit the crime did not commit the crime.

Elements

A person guilty of this offense

(1) knowingly
(2) (a) obtains,
    (b) possesses, *or*
    (c) uses
(3) identifying information of another person, living or dead,
(4) with the intent to fraudulently represent the person is the other person
(5) for the purpose of
    (a) making financial or credit transactions in the other person's name,
    (b) avoiding legal consequences, *or*
    (c) obtaining anything of value, benefit, or advantage.

Punishment

Class G felony, except it is punishable as a Class F felony if the victim suffers arrest, detention, or conviction as a proximate result of the offense or the person is in possession of identifying information pertaining to three or more separate persons. G.S. 14-113.20(a); G.S. 14-113.22(a). The applicable facts that elevate the punishment to a Class F felony must be alleged in the charging instrument and proved at trial. G.S. 14-113.22(a2) contains a special provision authorizing restitution.

Notes

Element (1). See "Knowingly" in Chapter 1 (States of Mind)"

Element (2)(b). See the note on Element (2)(a) to "Possession or Manufacture of Fraudulent Identification," above.

Element (2)(c). The defendant's active (and false) acknowledgment to an officer that the last four digits of his Social Security number were "2301" constituted the use of identifying information of another. State v. Barron, 202 N.C. App. 686 (2010).

Element (3). The term "identifying information" includes:

- Social Security or employer taxpayer identification numbers,
- drivers license, state identification card, or passport numbers,
- checking or savings account numbers,
- credit or debit card numbers,
- personal identification (PIN) codes as defined in G.S. 14-113.8(6),
- electronic identification numbers, electronic mail names or addresses, Internet account numbers, or Internet identification names,
- digital signatures,
- any other numbers or information that can be used to access a person's financial resources,
- biometric data,
- fingerprints,
- passwords, and
- parent's legal surname prior to marriage.

G.S. 14-113.20(b).

Element (5)(b). This offense primarily is aimed at the misuse of another person's identifying information for financial reasons. However, this element could be satisfied, for example, by evidence that a person gave a law enforcement officer another person's Social Security number to avoid the legal consequences of being issued a speeding ticket. *Barron*, 202 N.C. App. 686.

Charging issues. See this note to "Obtaining Property by False Pretenses," above.

Exceptions. This crime is not committed when a person lawfully

- obtains credit information in the course of a bona fide consumer or commercial transaction;
- exercises, in good faith, a security interest or a right of offset by a creditor or financial institution; or
- complies, in good faith, with any warrant, court order, levy, garnishment, attachment, or other judicial or administrative order, decree, or directive, when required to do so.

G.S. 14-113.20(c).

Venue. This crime is considered to be committed in the county where the victim resides, where the perpetrator resides, where any part of the crime took place, or in any other county instrumental to the completion of the crime, regardless of whether the defendant was ever actually present in that county. G.S. 14-113.21.

Civil damages. G.S. 14-113.22(b) provides for civil liability for damages as a result of this offense.

Related Offenses Not in This Chapter

"Obstruction of Justice" (Chapter 21)

Trafficking in Stolen Identities

Statute

§14-113.20A. Trafficking in stolen identities.

(a) It is unlawful for a person to sell, transfer, or purchase the identifying information of another person with the intent to commit identity theft, or to assist another person in committing identity theft, as set forth in G.S. 14-113.20.

(b) A violation of this section is a felony punishable as provided in G.S. 14-113.22(a1).

Elements

A person guilty of this offense

(1) (a) sells,
(b) transfers, *or*
(c) purchases
(2) identifying information of another person
(3) with the intent to
(a) commit identity theft *or*
(b) assist another person in committing identity theft.

Punishment

Class E felony. G.S. 14-113.20A(b); G.S. 14-113.22(a1). G.S. 14-113.22(a2) contains a special provision authorizing restitution.

Notes

Element (2). See the note on Element (3) to "Identity Theft," above.

Element (3). Identity theft, as used in this element, refers to a violation of G.S. 14-113.20, discussed above under "Identity Theft."

Civil damages. See this note to "Identity Theft," above.

Related Offenses Not in This Chapter

None

Defrauding an Innkeeper or Campground Owner

Statute

§14-110. Defrauding innkeeper or campground owner.

No person shall, with intent to defraud, obtain food, lodging, or other accommodations at a hotel, inn, boardinghouse, eating house, or campground. Whoever violates this section shall be guilty of a Class 2 misdemeanor. Obtaining such lodging, food, or other accommodation by false pretense, or by false or fictitious show of pretense of baggage or other property, or absconding without paying or offering to pay therefor, or surreptitiously removing or attempting to remove such baggage, shall be prima facie evidence of such fraudulent intent, but this section shall not apply where there has been an agreement in writing for delay in such payment.

Elements

A person guilty of this offense

(1) with intent to defraud
(2) obtains food, lodging, or other accommodations
(3) at a hotel, inn, boardinghouse, eating house, or campground
(4) when there is no written agreement to delay payment.

Punishment

Class 2 misdemeanor. G.S. 14-110.

Notes

Element (1). The statute provides that (1) obtaining food, lodging, or other accommodation by false pretense, see "Obtaining Property by False Pretenses," above, or by false or fictitious show of pretense of baggage or other property; (2) absconding without paying or offering to pay for food, lodging, or other accommodation; or (3) surreptitiously removing or attempting to remove false/fictitious baggage constitutes prima facie evidence of fraudulent intent. G.S. 14-110.

Element (2). The offense includes obtaining food, lodging, or other accommodation but not other items or services of value.

Element (3). A place is not a hotel, inn, boardinghouse, eating house, or campground unless it is licensed or held out to be such. A place is not necessarily a boardinghouse simply because the operator received payment for taking someone in. State v. McRae, 170 N.C. 712 (1915).

Element (4). The section does not apply when there is a written agreement to delay payment, even if the person never intended to pay. The statute does not clearly address the effect of payment of the bill by check or credit card, which naturally delays final receipt of cash by the innkeeper. It is also not clear whether the State must prove the absence of an agreement to delay payment unless the defendant claims that there was an agreement.

Related Offenses Not in This Chapter

Use of false or counterfeit credit device; unauthorized use of another's credit device; use after notice of revocation. G.S. 14-113.1.

Opposite sexes occupying same bedroom at hotel for immoral purposes; falsely registering as husband and wife. G.S. 14-186.

Crimes Involving Security Interests

Fraudulent Disposal of a Security

Statute

§14-114. Fraudulent disposal of personal property on which there is a security interest.

(a) If any person, after executing a security agreement on personal property for a lawful purpose, shall make any disposition of any property embraced in such security agreement, with intent to defeat the rights of the secured party, every person so offending and every person with a knowledge of the security interest buying any property embraced in which security agreement, and every person assisting, aiding or abetting the unlawful disposition of such property, with intent to defeat the rights of any secured party in such security agreement, shall be guilty of a Class 2 misdemeanor.

A person's refusal to turn over secured property to a secured party who is attempting to repossess the property without a judgment or order for possession shall not, by itself, be a violation of this section.

(b) Intent to commit the crime as set forth in subsection (a) may be presumed from proof of possession of the property embraced in such security agreement by the grantor thereof after execution of the security agreement, and while it is in force, the further proof of the fact that the sheriff or other officer charged with the execution of process cannot after due diligence find such property under process directed to him for its seizure, for the satisfaction of such security agreement. However, this presumption may be rebutted by evidence that the property has, through no fault of the defendant, been stolen, lost, damaged beyond repair, or otherwise disposed of by the defendant without intent to defeat the rights of the secured party.

Elements

A person guilty of this offense

(1) executes a security agreement on personal property for a lawful purpose *and*
(2) while the security agreement is in force, disposes of property embraced in the security agreement or assists, aids, or abets the disposition of such property
(3) with the intent to defeat the rights of the secured party.

Punishment

Class 2 misdemeanor. G.S. 14-114(a).

Notes

Element (1). The statute does not define the term "security agreement." However, that term is defined in G.S. 25-9-102(76) as "an agreement that creates and provides for a security interest." The term "security interest" is defined in G.S. 25-1-201(35) as "an interest in personal property or fixtures which secures payment or performance of an obligation." *See* N.C. Pattern Jury Instructions—Crim. 220.10 at n.2 (suggesting that these definitions apply). The statute also fails to define the term "personal property." However, G.S. 12-3(6) defines such property as "moneys, goods, chattels, choses in action and evidences of debt, including all things capable of ownership, not descendable [sic] to heirs at law." For an explanation of the term "choses in action" as that term applies in the context of larceny, see the note on Element (2) to "Larceny of a Chose in Action" in Chapter 13 (Larceny, Possession of Stolen Goods, Embezzlement, and Related Offenses).

Element (2). It is not necessary to prove the identity of the person to whom the property was conveyed.

Element (3). Intent to commit this crime may be inferred from "proof of possession of the property embraced in such security agreement by the grantor thereof after execution of the security agreement, and while it is in force, the further proof of the fact that the sheriff or other officer charged with execution of process cannot after due diligence find such property under the process directed to him for its seizure, for the satisfaction of such security agreement." G.S. 14-114(b). This inference "may be rebutted by evidence that the property has, through no fault of the defendant, been stolen, lost, damaged beyond repair, or otherwise disposed of by the defendant without [the] intent to defeat the rights of the secured party." *Id.*

Exceptions. A person's refusal to turn over secured property to a secured party who is attempting to repossess the property without a judgment or order for possession is not, by itself, a violation of the statute. G.S. 14-114(a).

Related Offenses Not in This Chapter

"Altering or Removing a Serial Number" (Chapter 13)

Obtaining advances under written promise to pay therefor out of designated property. G.S. 14-105.

Fraudulent Purchase of a Security

Statute

See G.S. 14-114(a), reproduced under "Fraudulent Disposal of a Security," above.

Elements

A person guilty of this offense

(1) buys personal property embraced in a security agreement
(2) knowing that the security agreement is in force
(3) with the intent to defeat the rights of the secured party.

Punishment

Class 2 misdemeanor. G.S. 14-114(a).

Notes

Generally. See the notes to "Fraudulent Disposal of a Security," above.

Related Offenses Not in This Chapter

Obtaining advances under written promise to pay therefor out of designated property. G.S. 14-105.

Fraudulent Filings

Statute

§14-401.19. Filing false security agreements.

It shall be unlawful for any person, firm, corporation, or any other association of persons in this State, under whatever name styled, to present a record for filing under the provisions of Article 9 of Chapter 25 of the General Statutes with knowledge that the record is not related to a valid security agreement or with the intention that the record be filed for an improper purpose, such as to hinder, harass, or otherwise wrongfully interfere with any person. A violation of this section shall be a Class 2 misdemeanor.

Elements

A person, firm, corporation, or association guilty of this offense

(1) presents a record for filing under the Uniform Commercial Code
(2) (a) knowing that the record is not related to a valid security agreement *or*
    (b) with the intent that the record be filed for an improper purpose, such as to hinder, harass, or otherwise wrongfully interfere with any person.

Punishment

Class 2 misdemeanor. G.S. 14-401.19.

Notes

Generally. The offense deals with fraudulent filings under the Uniform Commercial Code, G.S. Chapter 25, Article 9.

Element (2)(a). See the note on Element (1) to "Fraudulent Disposal of a Security," above.

Related Offenses Not in This Chapter

No docketing of lien unless authorized by statute. G.S. 44A-12.1.

Secreting Property to Hinder Enforcement of a Security Interest

Statute

§14-115. Secreting property to hinder enforcement of lien or security interest.

Any person who, with intent to prevent or hinder the enforcement of a lien or security interest after a judgment or order has been issued for possession for that personal property subject to said lien or security interest, either refuses to surrender such personal property in his possession to a law enforcement officer, or removes, or exchanges, or secretes such personal property, shall be guilty of a Class 2 misdemeanor.

Elements

A person guilty of this offense

(1) (a) removes, exchanges, or secretes personal property *or*
    (b) refuses to surrender to a law enforcement officer personal property in that person's possession
(2) on which a lien or security interest exists
(3) after a judgment or order for possession has been issued for possession for that personal property
(4) with the intent to prevent or hinder the enforcement of the lien or security interest.

Punishment

Class 2 misdemeanor. G.S. 14-115.

Notes

Generally. See the notes to "Fraudulent Disposal of a Security," above.

Elements (1) and (2). For this offense to be committed, it is not necessary that the property be sold or disposed of; it need only be hidden or otherwise removed from the one who has a lien on it. Apparently the defendant need not be a party to the security agreement.

Related Offenses Not in This Chapter

Obtaining advances under written promise to pay therefor out of designated property. G.S. 14-105.

Residential Mortgage Fraud

Statute

§14-118.11. Definitions.

Unless otherwise provided in this Article, the following definitions apply in this Article:

(1) Mortgage lending process. – The process through which a person seeks or obtains a mortgage loan including solicitation, application, origination, negotiation of terms, underwriting, signing, closing, and funding of a mortgage loan and services provided incident to a mortgage loan, including the appraisal of the residential real property. Documents involved in the mortgage lending process include (i) uniform residential loan applications or other loan applications, (ii) appraisal reports, (iii) settlement statements, (iv) supporting personal documentation for loan applications, including W-2 or other earnings or income statements, verifications of rent, income, and employment, bank statements, tax returns, and payroll stubs, and (v) any required mortgage-related disclosures.

(2) Mortgage loan. – A loan primarily secured by either (i) a mortgage or a deed of trust on residential real property or (ii) a security interest in a manufactured home (as defined by G.S. 143-145(7)) located or to be located on residential real property.

(3) Pattern of residential mortgage fraud. – Residential mortgage fraud that involves five or more mortgage loans, which have the same or similar intents, results, accomplices, victims, or methods of commission or otherwise are interrelated by distinguishing characteristics.

(4) Person. – An individual, partnership, limited liability company, limited partnership, corporation, association, or other entity, however organized.

(5) Residential real property. – Real property located in the State of North Carolina upon which there is located or is to be located a structure or structures designed principally for residential purposes, including, but not limited to, individual units of townhouses, condominiums, and cooperatives.

§14-118.12. Residential mortgage fraud.

(a) A person is guilty of residential mortgage fraud when, for financial gain and with the intent to defraud, that person does any of the following:

(1) Knowingly makes or attempts to make any material misstatement, misrepresentation, or omission within the mortgage lending process with the intention that a mortgage lender, mortgage broker, borrower, or any other person or entity that is involved in the mortgage lending process relies on it.

(2) Knowingly uses or facilitates or attempts to use or facilitate the use of any misstatement, misrepresentation, or omission within the mortgage lending process with the intention that a mortgage lender, borrower, or any other person or entity that is involved in the mortgage lending process relies on it.

(3) Receives or attempts to receive proceeds or any other funds in connection with a residential mortgage closing that the person knew, or should have known, resulted from a violation of subdivision (1) or (2) of this subsection.

(4) Conspires or solicits another to violate any of the provisions of subdivision (1), (2), or (3) of this subsection.

(b) It shall be sufficient in any prosecution under this Article for residential mortgage fraud to show that the party accused did the act with the intent to deceive or defraud. It shall be unnecessary to show that any particular person or entity was harmed financially in the transaction or that the person or entity to whom the deliberate misstatement, misrepresentation, or omission was made relied upon the misstatement, misrepresentation, or omission.

§14-118.15. Penalty for violation of Article.

(a) Unless the conduct is prohibited by some other provision of law providing for greater punishment, a violation of this Article involving a single mortgage loan is a Class H felony.

(b) Unless the conduct is prohibited by some other provision of law providing for greater punishment, a violation of this Article involving a pattern of residential mortgage fraud is a Class E felony.

Elements

A person guilty of this offense

(1) with the intent to defraud *and*
(2) for financial gain
(3) (a) knowingly makes or attempts to make any material misstatement, misrepresentation, or omission within the mortgage lending process with the intent that any person or entity involved in the mortgage lending process will rely on it,
(b) knowingly uses or facilitates or attempts to use or facilitate the use of any misstatement, misrepresentation, or omission within the mortgage lending process with the intent that any other person or entity involved in the mortgage lending process will rely on it, *or*
(c) receives or attempts to receive proceeds or funds in connection with a residential mortgage closing that the person knew, or should have known, resulted from the conduct described in (3)(a) or (3)(b).

Punishment

A violation involving a single mortgage loan is a Class H felony. G.S. 14-118.15(a). A violation involving a pattern of residential mortgage fraud is a Class E felony. G.S. 14-118.15(b). A pattern of residential mortgage fraud involves five or more mortgage loans that have the same or similar intents, results, accomplices, victims, or methods of commission or are otherwise interrelated. G.S. 14-118.11(a)(3). If the Class E version of this crime is charged, the relevant facts elevating punishment must be alleged in the charging instrument and proved at trial. The statute provides for forfeiture and for restitution. G.S. 14-118.16.

Notes

Element (3) generally. G.S. 14-118.11, reproduced above, defines the terms "mortgage lending process," "mortgage loan," "person," and "residential real property."

Element (3)(b). Unlike Element (3)(a), for this element the misstatement, misrepresentation, or omission apparently need not be material.

Financial harm or reliance not required. The State need not show that any person or entity was harmed financially or that any person or entity relied on the misstatement, misrepresentation, or omission. G.S. 14-118.12(b).

Attempt. All three grounds in Element (3) include attempts. Thus, an attempt to commit this offense is punished like the completed offense rather than one class lower, as is typically the case for an attempt. See "Attempt" in Chapter 5 (General Crimes).

Conspiracy or solicitation. Conspiracy or solicitation to do one of the prohibited acts is punished the same as the completed crime. G.S. 14-118.12(a)(4). See "Conspiracy" and "Solicitation," both in Chapter 5 (General Crimes).

Venue. Venue may be in the county where

- the residential real property for which a mortgage loan is being sought is located;
- any act was performed in furtherance of the violation;
- any person alleged to have violated the Article had control or possession of any proceeds of the violation;
- the closing occurred; or
- a document containing a deliberate misstatement, misrepresentation, or omission is filed with the official register of deeds or with the Division of Motor Vehicles.

G.S. 14-118.13.

Multiple convictions and punishments. Both subsections of the punishment provision for this offense begin with the following language: "Unless the conduct is prohibited by some other provision of law providing for greater punishment." G.S. 14-118.15(a) and (b). This language may mean that a defendant may not, based on the same conduct, be punished for this offense and another one carrying a more severe punishment. For a discussion of this issue in the assault context, see this note to "Assault Inflicting Serious Injury" in Chapter 7 (Assaults).

Authority to investigate and prosecute. G.S. 14-118.14 provides that on its own investigation or on referral by the Office of the Commissioner of Banks, the North Carolina Real Estate Commission, the Attorney General, the North Carolina Appraisal Board, or other parties, a district attorney may institute criminal proceedings for a violation of the residential mortgage fraud laws.

Liability for reporting suspected mortgage fraud. G.S. 14-118.17 provides that in the absence of fraud, bad faith, or malice, a person is not subject to civil liability for filing reports or furnishing other information to a regulatory or law enforcement agency regarding suspected residential mortgage fraud.

Related Offenses Not in This Chapter

None

Forgery and Related Offenses

Common Law Forgery

Statute

This is a common law offense.

Elements

A person guilty of this offense

(1) makes a false writing
(2) that is apparently capable of effecting a fraud
(3) with the intent to defraud.

Punishment

Class 1 misdemeanor.

Notes

Element (1). This element may be satisfied by

- making a false instrument, such as a railroad pass, State v. Weaver, 94 N.C. 836 (1886),
- signing a fictitious name to an instrument, State v. Phillips, 256 N.C. 445 (1962),
- signing a check with a name (fictitious or real) that is not on the signature card for the bank account, State v. Dunbar, 47 N.C. App. 623 (1980),
- altering an instrument so that it is different from what it originally was, State v. Coleman, 253 N.C. 799 (1961),
- signing a real name to an instrument intending that it be taken as the signature of someone with the same name, Peoples Bank & Trust Co. v. Fid. & Cas. Co., 231 N.C. 510 (1950), or
- signing someone else's name without authority, State v. Keller, 268 N.C. 522 (1966).

When a person signs someone else's name, the law presumes that he or she has the authority to do so, and thus the State must demonstrate the lack of such authority to prove forgery. *Phillips*, 256 N.C. 445; State v. Bean, 37 N.C. App. 40 (1978). This element was not satisfied when a defendant signed her real name under false authority as an agent. State v. King, 178 N.C. App. 122 (2006).

Evidence that a defendant uttered a forged instrument and attempted to obtain money from it or that he or she possessed a forged instrument supports an inference that the possessor either forged or consented to the forgery of the instrument, State v. Welch, 266 N.C. 291 (1966); that inference does not violate the defendant's rights to due process, State v. Roberts, 51 N.C. App. 221 (1981); State v. DeGina, 42 N.C. App. 156 (1979). A jury instruction was unconstitutional, however, when it stated that a person who possesses a forged instrument and endeavors to obtain money with it is *presumed* to have forged the instrument or consented to its forgery when the jury reasonably would have interpreted the presumption to be a conclusive or mandatory presumption; that presumption unconstitutionally shifted the burden of proof to the defendant. Reid v. Warden, Cent. Prison, 708 F. Supp. 730 (W.D.N.C. 1989). An instruction on a permissive presumption or inference, permitting the jury to accept or reject an inference of forgery, would be constitutional.

Element (2). The instrument must be of the kind that either has some legal effect, Barnes v. Crawford, 115 N.C. 76 (1894); ROLLIN M. PERKINS & RONALD N. BOYCE, CRIMINAL LAW 415 (3d ed. 1982), or can make the person who does the writing subject to legal liability, PERKINS & BOYCE at 416–17. This means, for example, that a painting, historical document, or letter of introduction could not be the subject of a forgery (although a copy of the painting, historical document, or letter of introduction, if used fraudulently to obtain property, can give rise to liability for obtaining property by false pretenses). *Id.* at 417.

For this element to be satisfied, the false writing must appear to be genuine. State v. Prince, 49 N.C. App. 145 (1980); N.C. PATTERN JURY INSTRUCTIONS—CRIM. 221.80. It must be enough like the real thing to mislead a reasonable person, State v. Covington, 94 N.C. 913 (1886), but it need not be a perfect copy. If the name of a person or corporation is misspelled, Peoples Bank & Trust Co. v. Fid. & Cas. Co., 231 N.C. 510 (1950); State v. Lane, 80 N.C. 407 (1879), or if the writing on the instrument is informal, *Covington*, 94 N.C. 913, the false writing is still a forgery.

Element (3). It is not necessary that a person actually be defrauded for this offense to have been committed. State v. Williams, 291 N.C. 442 (1976). The defendant need only intend that his or her false writing be used fraudulently. This element is satisfied even if no attempt is ever made to defraud anyone with the writing. State v. Keller, 268 N.C. 522 (1966).

Multiple convictions and punishments. A person can be convicted and punished for common law forgery and common law uttering of the same document; punishment for both offenses does not violate the defendant's double jeopardy rights. State v. DeGina, 42 N.C. App. 156, 160–61 (1979).

Relation to other offenses. When the forgery is of a check or security, the statutory offense of forgery of notes, checks, and other securities, discussed below, may be charged.

Related Offenses Not in This Chapter

"Obtaining a Controlled Substance by Fraud or Forgery" (Chapter 27)
Counterfeiting and Issuing Monetary Substitutes. G.S. 14-13 through -16.
Selling certain forged securities. G.S. 14-121.
Forgery of deeds, wills, and certain other instruments. G.S. 14-122.
Falsifying documents issued by a secondary school, postsecondary educational institution, or governmental agency. G.S. 14-122.1.
Forging names to petitions and uttering forged petitions. G.S. 14-123.
Forging certificate of corporate stock and uttering forged certificates. G.S. 14-124.

Forgery of bank notes and other instruments by connecting genuine parts. G.S. 14-125.
Altering or forging certificate of title, registration card or application, a felony; reproducing or possessing blank certificate of title. G.S. 20-71.
Violation of registration provisions. G.S. 20-111(2).
Criminal use of a counterfeit trademark. G.S. 80-11.1.
Certain violations of absentee ballot law made criminal offenses. G.S. 163-237(c).

Common Law Uttering of Forged Paper

Statute

This is a common law offense.

Elements

A person guilty of this offense

(1) utters as true
(2) a false writing
(3) that is apparently capable of effecting a fraud
(4) with the intent to defraud *and*
(5) knowing that the writing is false.

Punishment

Class 1 misdemeanor.

Notes

Element (1). For a discussion of the term "utters" in connection with worthless checks, see the note on Element (1) to "Worthless Checks—Making or Uttering," above.

Elements (2) through (4). See the notes on Elements (1) through (3) to "Common Law Forgery," above.

Related Offenses Not in This Chapter

See the offenses listed under "Common Law Forgery," above.

Forgery and Counterfeiting of Instruments

Statute

§14-119. Forgery of notes, checks, and other securities; counterfeiting instruments.

(a) It is unlawful for any person to forge or counterfeit any instrument, or possess any counterfeit instrument, with the intent to injure or defraud any person, financial institution, or governmental unit. Any person in violation of this subsection is guilty of a Class I felony.

(b) Any person who transports or possesses five or more counterfeit instruments with the intent to injure or defraud any person, financial institution, or governmental unit is guilty of a Class G felony.

(c) As used in this Article, the term:

(1) "Counterfeit" means to manufacture, copy, reproduce, or forge an instrument that purports to be genuine, but is not, because it has been falsely copied, reproduced, forged, manufactured, embossed, encoded, duplicated, or altered.
(2) "Financial institution" means any mutual fund, money market fund, credit union, savings and loan association, bank, or similar institution, either foreign or domestic.

(3) "Governmental unit" means the United States, any United States territory, any state of the United States, any political subdivision, agency, or instrumentality of any state, or any foreign jurisdiction.
(4) "Instrument" means (i) any currency, bill, note, warrant, check, order, or similar instrument of or on any financial institution or governmental unit, or any cashier or officer of the institution or unit; or (ii) any security issued by, or on behalf of, any corporation, financial institution, or governmental unit.

Elements

A person guilty of this offense

(1) (a) forges *or*
    (b) counterfeits
(2) an instrument
(3) with the intent to injure or defraud
(4) a person, financial institution, or governmental unit.

Punishment

Class I felony. G.S. 14-119(a).

Notes

Generally. This offense is a codified version of common law forgery, State v. Hall, 108 N.C. 776 (1891), except that it is limited to the specified kinds of written instruments and it is a felony. Forgery of instruments not covered by this statute may be charged under "Common Law Forgery," above.

Element (1)(a). There was sufficient evidence of forgery under G.S. 14-119 when the evidence showed that the defendant signed a law enforcement officer's name on five North Carolina Uniform Citations. State v. Guarascio, ___ N.C. App. ___, 696 S.E.2d 704, 711 (2010).

Element (1)(b). To "counterfeit" means to manufacture, copy, reproduce, or forge an instrument that purports to be genuine but is not because it has been falsely copied, reproduced, forged, manufactured, embossed, encoded, duplicated, or altered. G.S. 14-119(c)(1).

Element (2). "Instrument" means

- any currency, bill, note, warrant, check, order, or similar instrument of or on any financial institution or governmental unit or of or on any cashier or officer of the institution or unit; or
- any security issued by or on behalf of any corporation, financial institution, or governmental unit.

G.S. 14-119(c)(4). Counterfeiting United States currency violates this statute because the definition of instrument includes currency. North Carolina Uniform Citations are instruments within the meaning of this statute. *Guarascio*, ___ N.C. App. ___, 696 S.E.2d at 710–11.

Element (3). There was sufficient evidence of this element where the defendant signed an officer's name on five North Carolina Uniform Citations. *Id.* at 711.

Element (4). "Financial institution" means any mutual fund, money market fund, credit union, savings and loan association, bank, or similar institution, either foreign or domestic. G.S. 14-119(c)(2). "Governmental unit" means the United States; any United States territory; any state of the United States; any political subdivision, agency, or instrumentality of any state; or any foreign jurisdiction. G.S. 14-119(c)(3).

Charging issues. See this note to "Obtaining Property by False Pretenses," above.

Related Offenses Not in This Chapter

See the offenses listed under "Common Law Forgery," above.

Possessing and Transporting Counterfeit Instruments

Statute

See G.S. 14-119(a) and (b), reproduced under "Forgery and Counterfeiting of Instruments," above.

Elements

A person guilty of this offense

(1) (a) possesses a single *or*
 (b) possesses or transports five or more
(2) counterfeit instrument(s)
(3) with the intent to injure or defraud
(4) any person, financial institution, or governmental unit.

Punishment

If Element (1)(a) is present, the offense is a Class I felony. G.S. 14-119(a). If Element (1)(b) is present, the offense is a Class G felony. G.S. 14-119(b). If the Class G felony version is charged, the relevant facts elevating punishment must be alleged in the charging instrument and proved at trial.

Notes

Element (1)(a). In the criminal law generally, possession may be actual or constructive. For a discussion of those terms, see the note on Element (1) to "Possession of a Controlled Substance" in Chapter 27 (Drug Offenses) and the note on Element (2)(c) to "Possession of a Firearm by a Felon" in Chapter 22 (Weapons Offenses).

Element (2). The term "counterfeit" is defined in the note on Element (1)(b) to "Forgery and Counterfeiting of Instruments," above. The term "instrument" is defined in the note on Element (2) to that offense.

Element (4). See the note on Element (4) to "Forgery and Counterfeiting of Instruments," above.

Related Offenses Not in This Chapter

See the offenses listed under "Common Law Forgery," above.

Uttering Forged Instruments or Instruments with False Endorsements

Statute

§14-120. Uttering forged paper or instrument containing a forged endorsement.

If any person, directly or indirectly, whether for the sake of gain or with intent to defraud or injure any other person, shall utter or publish any such false, forged or counterfeited instrument as is mentioned in G.S. 14-119, or shall pass or deliver, or attempt to pass or deliver, any of them to another person (knowing the same to be falsely forged or counterfeited) the person so offending shall be punished as a Class I felon. If any person, directly or indirectly, whether for the sake of gain or with intent to defraud or injure any other person, shall falsely make, forge or counterfeit any endorsement on any instrument described in the preceding section, whether such instrument be genuine or false, or shall knowingly utter or publish any such instrument containing a false, forged or counterfeited endorsement or, knowing the same to be falsely endorsed, shall pass or deliver or attempt to pass or deliver any such instrument containing a forged endorsement to another person, the person so offending shall be guilty of a Class I felony.

Elements

A person guilty of this offense

(1) utters, publishes, passes, delivers, or attempts to pass or deliver
(2) an instrument
(3) (a) that is false, forged, or counterfeit *or*
 (b) that contains a false, forged, or counterfeit endorsement
(4) (a) for the sake of gain *or*
 (b) with the intent to defraud or injure another *and*
(5) knowing that
 (a) it was falsely forged or counterfeited *or*
 (b) falsely endorsed.

Punishment

Class I felony. G.S. 14-120.

Notes

Element (1). This element can be satisfied by putting the forged instrument in a place where it will be found, State v. White, 101 N.C. 770 (1888), *aff'd sub nom.* Cross v. North Carolina, 132 U.S. 131 (1889), or by delivering it to an agent to be passed, State v. Harris, 27 N.C. 287 (1844).

Element (2). See the note on Element (2) to "Forgery and Counterfeiting of Instruments," above. Uttering of other kinds of forged writings may constitute "Common Law Uttering of Forged Paper," above.

Element (3). If the charge is uttering a forged check, the "false writing must purport to be the writing of a party other than the one who makes it and it must indicate an attempted deception of similarity." State v. Brown, ___ N.C. App. ___, ___ S.E.2d ___ (Dec. 6, 2011) (evidence insufficient where the State presented no evidence that the check was not in fact a check from the issuer).

For the definition of the term "counterfeit," see the note on Element (1)(b) to "Forgery and Counterfeiting of Instruments," above.

Element (4)(b). See the note on Element (3) to "Common Law Forgery," above. The defendant need not have succeeded in defrauding anyone for this offense to have been committed. State v. Greenlee, 272 N.C. 651 (1968); State v. Seraphem, 90 N.C. App. 368 (1988).

Attempt. Element (1) includes attempts to pass and deliver, thus punishing an attempt the same as the completed crime, State v. Kirkpatrick, 343 N.C. 285, 287–88 (1996), rather than one level lower, as is typical for an attempt. See "Attempt" in Chapter 5 (General Crimes).

Related Offenses Not in This Chapter

See the offenses listed under "Common Law Forgery," above.

Forging an Endorsement on Checks and Securities

Statute

See G.S. 14-120, reproduced under "Uttering Forged Instruments or Instruments with False Endorsements," above.

Elements

A person guilty of this offense

(1) falsely makes, forges, or counterfeits
(2) an endorsement
(3) on an instrument

(4) (a) for the sake of gain *or*
(b) with the intent to defraud or injure another.

Punishment

Class I felony. G.S. 14-120.

Notes

Element (1). See the note on Element (1) to "Common Law Forgery," above, and on Element (1)(b) to "Forgery and Counterfeiting of Instruments," also above.

Element (2). This offense applies to a false endorsement made on an otherwise valid instrument or on a forged instrument. An "endorsement," also spelled "indorsement," is the signature by the holder of an instrument that transfers it to another person. BLACK'S LAW DICTIONARY 843 (9th ed. 2009).

Element (3). See the note on Element (2) to "Forgery and Counterfeiting of Instruments," above.

Element (4)(b). See the note on Element (3) to "Common Law Forgery," above.

Related Offenses Not in This Chapter

See the offenses listed under "Common Law Forgery," above.

Financial Transaction Card Crimes

Financial Transaction Card Forgery

Statute

§14-113.11. Forgery of financial transaction card.

(a) A person is guilty of financial transaction card forgery when:

(1) With intent to defraud a purported issuer, a person or organization providing money, goods, services or anything else of value, or any other person, he falsely makes or falsely embosses a purported financial transaction card or utters such a financial transaction card; or

(2) With intent to defraud a purported issuer, a person or organization providing money, goods, services or anything else of value, or any other person, he falsely encodes, duplicates or alters existing encoded information on a financial transaction card or utters such a financial transaction card; or

(3) He, not being the cardholder or a person authorized by him, with intent to defraud the issuer, or a person or organization providing money, goods, services or anything else of value, or any other person, signs a financial transaction card.

(b) A person falsely makes a financial transaction card when he makes or draws, in whole or in part, a device or instrument which purports to be the financial transaction card of a named issuer but which is not such a financial transaction card because the issuer did not authorize the making or drawing, or alters a financial transaction card which was validly issued.

(c) A person falsely embosses a financial transaction card when, without authorization of the named issuer, he completes a financial transaction card by adding any of the matter, other than the signature of the cardholder, which an issuer requires to appear on the financial transaction card before it can be used by a cardholder.

(d) A person falsely encodes a financial transaction card when, without authorization of the purported issuer, he records magnetically, electronically, electro-magnetically or by any other means whatsoever, information on a financial transaction card which will permit acceptance of that card by any automated banking device. Conviction of financial transaction card forgery shall be punishable as provided in G.S. 14-113.17(b).

Elements

A person guilty of this offense

(1) (a) falsely makes or embosses a purported financial transaction card or utters a falsely made or falsely embossed financial transaction card,
(b) falsely encodes, duplicates, or alters existing encoded information on a financial transaction card or utters a falsely encoded, duplicated, or altered card, *or*
(c) not being the cardholder or a person authorized by the cardholder, signs a financial transaction card

(2) with the intent to defraud.

Punishment

Class I felony. G.S. 14-113.11(d); G.S. 14-113.17(b).

Notes

Element (1) generally. A "financial transaction card" is a credit card, bank service card, bank card, check guarantee card, debit card, or any other card that allows the cardholder to obtain goods, services, or money on credit; to guarantee a check to the person who accepts it; or to deposit, withdraw, or transfer funds from an account. It does not include credit cards for telephone calls. G.S. 14-113.8(4).

Element (1)(a). A person falsely makes a financial transaction card when he or she (1) makes or draws, in whole or in part, a device or instrument which purports to be the financial transaction card of a named issuer but which is not such a financial transaction card because the issuer did not authorize the making or drawing; or (2) alters a financial transaction card which was validly issued. G.S. 14-113.11(b). The term "issuer" refers to the business or organization, or financial institution or its duly authorized agent, which issues a financial transaction card. G.S. 14-113.8(5). The term "cardholder" means "the person or organization named on the face of a financial transaction card to whom or for whose benefit the financial transaction card is issued." G.S. 14-113.8(2).

A person falsely embosses a financial transaction card when, without the authorization of the named issuer, he or she completes a financial transaction card by adding any of the matter, other than the signature of the cardholder, which an issuer requires to appear on the financial transaction card before it can be used by a cardholder. G.S. 14-113.11(c).

For a definition of the term "utters" in connection with worthless checks, see the note on Element (1) to "Worthless Checks—Making or Uttering," above.

Element (1)(b). A person falsely encodes a financial transaction card when, without the authorization of the purported issuer, he or she records magnetically, electronically, electromagnetically, or by any other means information on a financial transaction card which will permit acceptance of that card by any automated banking device. G.S. 14-113.11(d).

Element (2). For a discussion of the phrase "with intent to defraud," see the note on Element (3) to "Common Law Forgery," above. The statute specifies various types of persons and organizations that may be the object of the intent to defraud. Specifically, it lists "a purported issuer, a person or organization providing money, goods, services or anything else of value, or any other person." G.S. 14-113.11(a)(1). The list appears to include every possible victim.

Prima facie evidence. G.S. 14-113.12(a) provides that possession of two or more falsely made or falsely embossed financial transaction cards by someone other than the purported issuer is prima facie evidence that the cards were "obtained" in violation of the version of this offense involving Elements (1)(a) or (1)(b). Similarly, G.S. 14-113.12(b) provides that when a person other than the cardholder or a person authorized by the cardholder possesses two or more financial transaction cards which are signed, such possession is prima facie evidence that the cards were obtained in violation of the Element (1)(c) version of this offense.

Related Offenses Not in This Chapter

See financial transaction card theft (various offenses) in Chapter 13 (Larceny, Possession of Stolen Goods, Embezzlement, and Related Offenses).

Use of false or counterfeit credit device; unauthorized use of another's credit device; use after notice of revocation. G.S. 14-113.1.

Criminal possession of financial transaction card forgery devices. G.S. 14-113.14.

Criminal factoring of financial transaction card records. G.S. 14-113.15A.

Using an Illicit Card

Statute

§14-113.13. Financial transaction card fraud.

(a) A person is guilty of financial transaction card fraud when, with intent to defraud the issuer, a person or organization providing money, goods, services or anything else of value, or any other person, he

(1) Uses for the purpose of obtaining money, goods, services or anything else of value a financial transaction card obtained or retained, or which was received with knowledge that it was obtained or retained, in violation of G.S. 14-113.9 or 14-113.11 or a financial transaction card which he knows is forged, altered, expired, revoked or was obtained as a result of a fraudulent application in violation of G.S. 14-113.13(c); or

(2) Obtains money, goods, services, or anything else of value by:

a. Representing without the consent of the cardholder that he is the holder of a specified card; or

b. Presenting the financial transaction card without the authorization or permission of the cardholder; or

c. Representing that he is the holder of a card and such card has not in fact been issued; or

d. Using a financial transaction card to knowingly and willfully exceed:

1. The actual balance of a demand deposit account or time deposit account; or

2. An authorized credit line in an amount which exceeds such authorized credit line in the amount of five hundred dollars ($500.00), or fifty percent (50%) of such authorized credit line, whichever is greater; or

(3) Obtains control over a financial transaction card as security for debt; or

(4) Deposits into his account or any account, by means of an automated banking device, a false, fictitious, forged, altered or counterfeit check, draft, money order, or any other such document not his lawful or legal property; or

(5) Receives money, goods, services or anything else of value as a result of a false, fictitious, forged, altered, or counterfeit check, draft, money order or any other such document having been deposited into an account via an automated banking device, knowing at the time of receipt of the money, goods, services, or item of value that the document so deposited was false, fictitious, forged, altered or counterfeit or that the above deposited item was not his lawful or legal property.

(b) A person who is authorized by an issuer to furnish money, goods, services or anything else of value upon presentation of a financial transaction card by the cardholder, or any agent or employee of such person is guilty of a financial transaction card fraud when, with intent to defraud the issuer or the cardholder, he

(1) Furnishes money, goods, services or anything else of value upon presentation of a financial transaction card obtained or retained in violation of G.S. 14-113.9, or a financial transaction card which he knows is forged, expired or revoked; or

(2) Fails to furnish money, goods, services or anything else of value which he represents in writing to the issuer that he has furnished.

Conviction of financial transaction card fraud as provided in subsection (a) or (b) of this section is punishable as provided in G.S. 14-113.17(a) if the value of all money, goods, services and other things of value furnished in violation of this section, or if the difference between the value actually furnished and the value represented to the issuer to have been furnished in violation of this section, does not exceed five hundred dollars ($500.00) in any six-month period. Conviction of financial transaction card fraud as provided in subsection (a) or (b) of this section is punishable as provided in G.S. 14-113.17(b) if such value exceeds five hundred dollars ($500.00) in any six-month period.

(c) A person is guilty of financial transaction card fraud when, upon application for a financial transaction card to an issuer, he knowingly makes or causes to be made a false statement or report relative to his name, occupation, financial condition, assets, or liabilities; or willfully and substantially overvalues any assets, or willfully omits or substantially undervalues any indebtedness for the purpose of influencing the issuer to issue a financial transaction card.

Conviction of financial transaction card fraud as provided in this subsection is punishable as provided in G.S. 14-113.17(a).

(c1) A person authorized by an acquirer to furnish money, goods, services or anything else of value upon presentation of a financial transaction card or a financial transaction card account number by a cardholder, or any agent or employee of such person, who, with intent to defraud the issuer, acquirer, or cardholder, remits to an issuer or acquirer, for payment, a financial transaction card record of a sale, which sale was not made by such person, his agent or employee, is guilty of financial transaction card fraud.

Conviction of financial transaction card fraud as provided in this subsection is punishable as provided in G.S. 14-113.17(a).

(d) A cardholder is guilty of financial transaction card fraud when he willfully, knowingly, and with an intent to defraud the issuer, a person or organization providing money, goods, services, or anything else of value, or any other person, submits, verbally or in writing, to the issuer or any other person, any false notice or report of the theft, loss, disappearance, or nonreceipt of his financial transaction card.

Conviction of financial transaction card fraud as provided in this subsection is punishable as provided in G.S. 14-113.17(a).

(e) In any prosecution for violation of G.S. 14-113.13, the State is not required to establish and it is no defense that some of the acts constituting the crime did not occur in this State or within one city, county, or local jurisdiction.

(f) For purposes of this section, revocation shall be construed to include either notice given in person or notice given in writing to the person to whom the financial transaction card and/or personal identification code was issued. Notice of revocation shall be immediate when notice is given in person. The sending of a notice in writing by registered or certified mail in the United States mail, duly stamped and addressed to such person at his last address known to the issuer, shall be prima facie evidence that such notice was duly received after seven days from the date of the deposit in the mail. If the address is located outside the United States, Puerto Rico, the Virgin Islands, the Canal Zone and Canada, notice shall be presumed to have been received 10 days after mailing by registered or certified mail.

Elements

A person guilty of this offense

(1) with the intent to defraud

(2) uses a financial transaction card
(3) (a) obtained or retained, or received with knowledge that it was obtained or retained, in violation of G.S. 14-113.9 or G.S. 14-113.11,
   (b) that he or she knows is forged, expired, revoked, or altered, *or*
   (c) that he or she knows was obtained by a fraudulent application in violation of G.S. 14-113.13(c)
(4) for the purpose of obtaining money, goods, services, or anything else of value.

Punishment

If the value of all money, goods, services, and other things of value furnished in violation of G.S. 14-113.13 does not exceed $500 in any six-month period, or if the difference between the value actually furnished and the value represented to the issuer to have been furnished in violation of G.S. 14-113.13 does not go above this amount in that same span of time, the offense is punished as a Class 2 misdemeanor. G.S. 14-113.13(b); G.S. 14-113.17(a). If such value exceeds $500 in any six-month period, it is punished as a Class I felony. G.S. 14-113.13(b); G.S. 14-113.17(b). If the felony version of this offense is charged, the relevant facts elevating punishment must be alleged in the charging instrument and proved at trial.

Notes

Element (1). For a discussion of the phrase "intent to defraud," see the note on Element (3) to "Common Law Forgery," above. The statute specifies various types of persons and organizations that may be the object of the intent to defraud. Specifically, it lists "the issuer, a person or organization providing money, goods, services or anything else of value, or any other person." G.S. 14-113.13(a). The list appears to include every possible victim.

Element (2). See the note entitled "Element (1) generally" to "Financial Transaction Card Forgery," above, for a definition of "financial transaction card."

Element (3)(a). See "Financial Transaction Card Theft" in Chapter 13 (Larceny, Possession of Stolen Goods, Embezzlement, and Related Offenses) for when a card is obtained in violation of G.S. 14-113.9. See "Financial Transaction Card Forgery," above, for when a card is obtained in violation of G.S. 14-113.11. The terms "receives" and "receiving" mean "acquiring possession or control or accepting a financial transaction card as security for a loan." G.S. 14-113.8(8).

Element (3)(b). See "Financial Transaction Card Forgery," above, for when a card has been forged. This element also may be satisfied when a person uses a card originally issued to him or her that has expired or been revoked. An expired financial transaction card is "a financial transaction card which is no longer valid because the term shown on it has elapsed." G.S. 14-113.8(3). A revoked financial transaction card is "a financial transaction card which is no longer valid because permission to use it has been suspended or terminated by the issuer." G.S. 14-113.8(9). G.S. 14-113.13(f) provides further guidance on the meaning of the term "revoked," stating that revocation includes "notice given in person or . . . in writing to the person to whom the financial transaction card and/or personal identification code was issued" and provides rules for when such notice is effective.

Element (3)(c). See G.S. 14-113.13(c) for when a financial transaction card is obtained by a fraudulent application.

Jurisdiction. G.S. 14-113.13(e) provides that "the State is not required to establish and it is no defense that some of the acts constituting the crime did not occur in this State or within one city, county, or local jurisdiction." While the portion of this provision addressing the lack of a defense is clear, the portion stating that the State is not required to show that some of the acts did not occur in this State, etc. is difficult to understand. See generally "Lack of Jurisdiction" in Chapter 2 (Bars and Defenses).

Related Offenses Not in This Chapter

See financial transaction card theft (various offenses) in Chapter 13 (Larceny, Possession of Stolen Goods, Embezzlement, and Related Offenses).

Use of false or counterfeit credit device; unauthorized use of another's credit device; use after notice of revocation. G.S. 14-113.1.

Financial transaction card fraud (by employee). G.S. 14-113.13(b).

Financial transaction card fraud (false statement to obtain a financial transaction card). G.S. 14-113.13(c).

Financial transaction card fraud (submitting false credit card sales). G.S. 14-113.13(c1).

Financial transaction card fraud (filing false report of loss of financial transaction card). G.S. 14-113.13(d).

Criminal possession of financial transaction card forgery devices. G.S. 14-113.14.

Criminal receipt of goods and services fraudulently obtained (by financial transaction card fraud). G.S. 14-113.15.

Criminal factoring of financial transaction card records. G.S. 14-113.15A.

Obtaining a Thing of Value by Financial Transaction Card Fraud

Statute

See G.S. 14-113.13(a)(2), reproduced under "Using an Illicit Card," above.

Elements

A person guilty of this offense

(1) obtains money, goods, services, or anything else of value
(2) with the intent to defraud
(3) by
  (a) representing without the cardholder's consent that he or she is the holder of a financial transaction card,
  (b) presenting a financial transaction card without the cardholder's authorization or permission,
  (c) representing that he or she is the holder of a card when the card has not in fact been issued, *or*
  (d) using a financial transaction card to knowingly and willfully exceed the actual balance on a demand or time deposit or an authorized credit line.

Punishment

If the value of all money, goods, services, and other things of value furnished in violation of G.S. 14-113.13 does not exceed $500 in any six-month period, or if the difference between the value actually furnished and the value represented to the issuer to have been furnished in violation of G.S. 14-113.13 does not go above this amount in that same span of time, the offense is punished as a Class 2 misdemeanor. G.S. 14-113.13(b); G.S. 14-113.17(a). If such value exceeds $500 in any six-month period, it is punished as a Class I felony. G.S. 14-113.13(b); G.S. 14-113.17(b). If the felony version of this offense is charged, the relevant facts elevating punishment must be alleged in the charging instrument and proved at trial.

Notes

Element (2). See the note on Element (1) to "Using an Illicit Card," above.

Element (3) generally. See the note on Element (1) to "Financial Transaction Card Forgery," above, for a definition of "financial transaction card." A person can "represent" himself or herself to be the holder of a financial transaction card merely by presenting it to pay for something; he or she need not claim to be the cardholder.

Element (3)(a). This element involves representing oneself to be the holder of the card. It apparently covers not only situations in which the defendant falsely represents that he or she is the cardholder but also those in which the defendant falsely alleges authorization to make charges on someone else's card or implies such authorization by presenting the other person's card and signing his or her own name.

Element (3)(b). The term "presenting" is defined in G.S. 14-113.8(7) to include "those actions taken by a cardholder or any person to introduce a financial transaction card into an automated banking device, including utilization of a personal identification code, or merely displaying or showing a financial transaction card to the issuer, or to any person or organization providing money, goods, services, or anything else of value, or any other entity with intent to defraud."

Element (3)(d). See "Knowingly" and "Willfully" in Chapter 1 (States of Mind). With respect to exceeding a credit line, the statute specifies that the defendant must use the card to exceed an authorized credit line by 50 percent or $500, whichever is greater. G.S. 14-113.13(a)(2)d.1.

Jurisdiction. See this note to "Using an Illicit Card," above.

Related Offenses Not in This Chapter

See the offenses listed under "Using an Illicit Card," above.

Obtaining a Card as Security for a Debt

Statute

See G.S. 14-113.13(a)(3), reproduced under "Using an Illicit Card," above.

Elements

A person guilty of this offense

(1) obtains control over a financial transaction card as security for debt
(2) with the intent to defraud.

Punishment

If the value of all money, goods, services, and other things of value furnished in violation of G.S. 14-113.13 does not exceed $500 in any six-month period, or if the difference between the value actually furnished and the value represented to the issuer to have been furnished in violation of G.S. 14-113.13 does not go above this amount in that same span of time, the offense is punished as a Class 2 misdemeanor. G.S. 14-113.13(b); G.S. 14-113.17(a). If such value exceeds $500 in any six-month period, it is punished as a Class I felony. G.S. 14-113.13(b); G.S. 14-113.17(b). If the felony version of this offense is charged, the relevant facts elevating punishment must be alleged in the charging instrument and proved at trial.

Notes

Element (1). See note on Element (1) to "Financial Transaction Card Forgery," above, for a definition of "financial transaction card."

Element (2). See the note on Element (1) to "Using an Illicit Card," above.

Jurisdiction. See this note to "Using an Illicit Card," above.

Related Offenses Not in This Chapter

See the offenses listed under "Using an Illicit Card," above.

Fraudulent Deposits of Money

Statute

See G.S. 14-113.13(a)(4), reproduced under "Using an Illicit Card," above.

Elements

A person guilty of this offense

(1) with the intent to defraud
(2) deposits in an account
(3) using an automated banking device
(4) a false, fictitious, forged, altered, or counterfeit check, draft, money order, or other document
(5) that is not his or her property.

Punishment

If the value of all money, goods, services, and other things of value furnished in violation of G.S. 14-113.13 does not exceed $500 in any six-month period, or if the difference between the value actually furnished and the value represented to the issuer to have been furnished in violation of G.S. 14-113.13 does not go above this amount in that same span of time, the offense is punished as a Class 2 misdemeanor. G.S. 14-113.13(b); G.S. 14-113.17(a). If such value exceeds $500 in any six-month period, it is punished as a Class I felony. G.S. 14-113.13(b); G.S. 14-113.17(b). If the felony version of this offense is charged, the relevant facts elevating punishment must be alleged in the charging instrument and proved at trial.

Notes

Element (1). See the note on Element (1) to "Using an Illicit Card," above.

Element (3). The term "automated banking device" means "any machine which when properly activated by a financial transaction card and/or personal identification code may be used for any of the purposes for which a financial transaction card may be used." G.S. 14-113.8(1a).

Jurisdiction. See this note to "Using an Illicit Card," above.

Related Offenses Not in This Chapter

See the offenses listed under "Using an Illicit Card," above.

Receiving Money Improperly from a Bank Machine

Statute

See G.S. 14-113.13(a)(5), reproduced under "Using an Illicit Card," above.

Elements

A person guilty of this offense

(1) with the intent to defraud
(2) receives
(3) money, goods, services, or anything else of value

(4) as a result of having deposited a false, fictitious, forged, altered, or counterfeit check, draft, money order, or other document in an account
(5) using an automated banking device
(6) with knowledge
    (a) that the document was false, fictitious, forged, altered, or counterfeit *or*
    (b) that the deposited item was not his or her property.

Punishment

If the value of all money, goods, services, and other things of value furnished in violation of G.S. 14-113.13 does not exceed $500 in any six-month period, or if the difference between the value actually furnished and the value represented to the issuer to have been furnished in violation of G.S. 14-113.13 does not go above this amount in that same span of time, the offense is punished as a Class 2 misdemeanor. G.S. 14-113.13(b); G.S. 14-113.17(a). If such value exceeds $500 in any six-month period, it is punished as a Class I felony. G.S. 14-113.13(b); G.S. 14-113.17(b). If the felony version of this offense is charged, the relevant facts elevating punishment must be alleged in the charging instrument and proved at trial.

Notes

Element (1). See the note on Element (1) to "Using an Illicit Card," above.

Element (2). For the definition of the term "receives," see the note on Element (3)(a) to "Using an Illicit Card," above.

Element (5). For a definition of the term "automated banking device," see the note on Element (3) to "Fraudulent Deposits of Money," above.

Jurisdiction. See this note to "Using an Illicit Card," above.

Related Offenses Not in This Chapter

See the offenses listed under "Using an Illicit Card," above.

Medicaid Fraud

Fraudulent Application by a Provider

Statute

§108A-63. Medical assistance provider fraud.

(a) It shall be unlawful for any provider of medical assistance under this Part to knowingly and willfully make or cause to be made any false statement or representation of a material fact:

(1) In any application for payment under this Part, or for use in determining entitlement to such payment; or
(2) With respect to the conditions or operation of a provider or facility in order that such provider or facility may qualify or remain qualified to provide assistance under this Part.

(b) It shall be unlawful for any provider of medical assistance to knowingly and willfully conceal or fail to disclose any fact or event affecting:

(1) His initial or continued entitlement to payment under this Part; or
(2) The amount of payment to which such person is or may be entitled.

(c) Except as otherwise provided in subsection (e) of this section, any person who violates a provision of this section shall be guilty of a Class I felony.

(d) "Provider" shall include any person who provides goods or services under this Part and any other person acting as an employee, representative or agent of such person.

(e) In connection with the delivery of or payment for benefits, items, or services under this Part, it shall be unlawful for any provider of medical assistance under this Part to knowingly and willfully execute, or attempt to execute, a scheme or artifice to:

(1) Defraud the Medical Assistance Program.

(2) Obtain, by means of false or fraudulent pretenses, representations, or promises of material fact, any of the money or property owned by, or under the custody or control of, the Medical Assistance Program.

A violation of this subsection is a Class H felony. A conspiracy to violate this subsection is a Class I felony.

(f) It shall be unlawful for any provider, with the intent to obstruct, delay, or mislead an investigation of a violation of this section by the Attorney General's office, to knowingly and willfully make or cause to be made a false entry in, alter, destroy, or conceal, or make a false statement about a financial, medical, or other record related to the provision of a benefit, item, or service under this Part.

(g) It shall be unlawful for any person to knowingly and willfully solicit or receive any remuneration (including any kickback, bribe, or rebate) directly or indirectly, overtly or covertly, in cash or in-kind:

(1) In return for referring an individual to a person for the furnishing or arranging for the furnishing of any item or service for which payment may be made in whole or in part under this Part.

(2) In return for purchasing, leasing, ordering, or arranging for or recommending purchasing, leasing, or ordering any good, facility, service, or item for which payment may be made in whole or in part under this Part.

(h) It shall be unlawful for any person to knowingly and willfully offer or pay any remuneration (including any kickback, bribe, or rebate) directly or indirectly, overtly or covertly, in cash or in-kind to any person to induce such person:

(1) To refer an individual to a person for the furnishing or arranging for the furnishing of any item or service for which payment may be made in whole or in part under this Part.

(2) To purchase, lease, order, or arrange for or recommend purchasing, leasing, or ordering any good, facility, service, or item for which payment may be made in whole or in part under this Part.

(i) Subsections (g) and (h) of this section shall not apply to:

(1) Contracts between the State and a public or private agency where part of the agency's responsibility is referral of a person to a provider.

(2) Any conduct or activity that is specified in 42 U.S.C. §1320a-7b(b)(3), as amended, or any federal regulations adopted pursuant thereto.

(j) Nothing in subsections (g) and (h) of this section shall be interpreted or construed to conflict with 42 U.S.C. §1320a-7b(b), as amended, or with federal common law or federal agency interpretations of the statute.

Elements

A person guilty of this offense

(1) is a provider of medical assistance under the state Medical Assistance (Medicaid) Program *and*

(2) willfully and knowingly

(3) makes or causes to be made

(4) a false statement or a false representation of a material fact

(5) (a) in an application for payment or for use in determining entitlement to such payment *or*

(b) with respect to the conditions or operation of a provider or facility so that the provider or facility may qualify or remain qualified to provide assistance under the program.

Punishment

Class I felony. G.S. 108A-63(c).

Notes

Element (1). A "provider" is any person who provides goods or services in the program and any employee, representative, or agent of such a person. G.S. 108A-63(d). It includes a pharmacist who dispenses medicines to Medicaid patients. State v. Beatty, 64 N.C. App. 511 (1983).

Element (2). See "Knowingly" and "Willfully" in Chapter 1 (States of Mind).

Related Offenses Not in This Chapter

"Larceny" (various offenses) in Chapter 13 (Larceny, Possession of Stolen Goods, Embezzlement, and Related Offenses)
Medicaid assistance recipient fraud. G.S. 108A-64.
Medicaid conflict of interest. G.S. 108A-65.

Concealment of a Fact Affecting a Provider's Eligibility

Statute

See G.S. 108A-63(b), reproduced under "Fraudulent Application by a Provider," above.

Elements

A person guilty of this offense

(1) is a provider of medical assistance under the state Medical Assistance (Medicaid) Program *and*
(2) knowingly and willfully
(3) conceals or fails to disclose a fact or event
(4) that affects
  (a) his or her initial or continued entitlement to payment *or*
  (b) the amount of payment to which he or she is or may be entitled.

Punishment

Class I felony. G.S. 108A-63(c).

Notes

Element (1). See the note on Element (1) to "Fraudulent Application by a Provider," above.

Element (2). See "Knowingly" and "Willfully" in Chapter 1 (States of Mind).

Related Offenses Not in This Chapter

See the offenses listed under "Fraudulent Application by a Provider," above.

Fraud by Medical Assistance Provider

Statute

See G.S. 108A-63(e), reproduced under "Fraudulent Application by a Provider," above.

Elements

A person guilty of this offense

(1) is a provider of medical assistance under the state Medical Assistance (Medicaid) Program *and*

(2) knowingly and willfully
(3) executes or attempts to execute
(4) a scheme or artifice to
 (a) defraud the Program *or*
 (b) obtain, by means of false or fraudulent pretenses, representations, or promises of material fact, any of the money or property owned by or under the custody or control of the Program
(5) in connection with the delivery of or payment for benefits, items, or services under the Program.

Punishment

Class H felony. G.S. 108A-63(e).

Notes

Element (1). See the note on Element (1) to "Fraudulent Application by a Provider," above.

Element (2). See "Knowingly" and "Willfully" in Chapter 1 (States of Mind).

Attempt. An attempt to execute such a plan is punished just like the completed offense, see Element (3), as opposed to one level lower, as is typically the case for an attempt. See "Attempt" in Chapter 5 (General Crimes).

Conspiracy. A conspiracy to commit this offense is a Class I felony, G.S. 108A-63(e). See generally "Conspiracy" in Chapter 5 (General Crimes).

Related Offenses Not in This Chapter

See the offenses listed under "Fraudulent Application by a Provider," above.

Obstructing Investigation by Medical Assistance Provider

Statute

See G.S. 108A-63(f), reproduced under "Fraudulent Application by a Provider," above.

Elements

A person guilty of this offense

(1) is a provider *and*
(2) knowingly and willfully *and*
(3) with the intent to obstruct, delay, or mislead an investigation of a violation of G.S. 108A-63 by the Attorney General's office
(3) (a) makes or causes to be made a false entry in,
 (b) alters, destroys, or conceals, *or*
 (c) make a false statement about
(4) a financial, medical, or other record related to the provision of a benefit, item, or service under the state Medical Assistance Program.

Punishment

Class I felony. G.S. 108A-63(c).

Notes

Element (1). See the note on Element (1) to "Fraudulent Application by a Provider," above.

Element (2). See "Knowingly" and "Willfully" in Chapter 1 (States of Mind).

Element (3). G.S. 108A-63 includes all of the offenses listed in this book under "Medicaid Fraud."

Related Offenses Not in This Chapter

See the offenses listed under "Fraudulent Application by a Provider," above.
"Obstruction of Justice" (Chapter 21)

Soliciting or Receiving Kickbacks

Statute

See G.S. 108A-63(g), reproduced under "Fraudulent Application by a Provider," above.

Elements

A person guilty of this offense

(1) knowingly and willfully
(2) (a) solicits *or*
    (b) receives
(3) remuneration
(4) in return for
    (a) referring an individual to a person for the furnishing or arranging for the furnishing of any item or service for which payment may be made in whole or in part under the state Medical Assistance Program *or*
    (b) purchasing, leasing, or ordering, or arranging for or recommending purchasing, leasing, or ordering, any good, facility, service, or item for which payment may be made in whole or in part under the Program.

Punishment

Class I felony. G.S. 108A-63(c).

Notes

Element (1). See "Knowingly" and "Willfully" in Chapter 1 (States of Mind).

Element (2)(a). Because the crime covers solicitations for remuneration, the offense is complete once the solicitation for remuneration is made, even if it is rejected. See "Solicitation" in Chapter 5 (General Crimes).

Element (3). The statute specifies "any remuneration (including any kickback, bribe, or rebate) directly or indirectly, overtly or covertly, in cash or in-kind." G.S. 108A-63(g).

Solicitation. A solicitation of the prohibited remuneration is punished like the completed offense, not at a lower level, as is typically the case for a solicitation. See "Solicitation" in Chapter 5 (General Crimes).

Exceptions. This offense does not apply to (1) contracts between the State and a public or private agency where the agency's responsibilities include the referral of a person to a provider; (2) any conduct or activity specified in 42 U.S.C. § 1320a-7b(b)(3), as amended; or (3) any federal regulations adopted pursuant to 42 U.S.C. § 1320a-7b(b)(3), as amended. G.S. 108A-63(i).

Interpretation. G.S. 108A-63(j) provides that nothing in the statute may be interpreted or construed to conflict with 42 U.S.C. § 1320a-7b(b), as amended, or with federal common law or federal agency interpretations of the statute.

Related Offenses Not in This Chapter

See the offenses listed under "Fraudulent Application by a Provider," above.
"Solicitation" (Chapter 5)

Offering or Paying Kickbacks

Statute

See G.S. 108A-63(h), reproduced under "Fraudulent Application by a Provider," above.

Elements

A person guilty of this offense

(1) knowingly and willfully
(2) offers or pays
(3) remuneration
(4) to induce another to
  (a) refer an individual to a person for the furnishing of or arrange for the furnishing of any item or service for which payment may be made in whole or in part under the State Medical Assistance Program *or*
  (b) purchase, lease, order, or arrange for, or recommend the purchasing, leasing, or ordering of, any good, facility, service, or item for which payment may be made in whole or in part under the Program.

Punishment

Class I felony. G.S. 108A-63(c).

Notes

Element (1). See "Knowingly" and "Willfully" in Chapter 1 (States of Mind).

Element (2)(a). Because the statute covers offers to pay remuneration, the crime is complete if the offer is made with the requisite intent, regardless of whether it is accepted.

Element (3). The statute specifies "any remuneration (including any kickback, bribe, or rebate) directly or indirectly, overtly or covertly, in cash or in-kind." G.S. 108A-63(g).

Exceptions. See this note to "Soliciting or Receiving Kickbacks," above.

Interpretation. See this note to "Soliciting or Receiving Kickbacks," above.

Related Offenses Not in This Chapter

See the offenses listed under "Fraudulent Application by a Provider," above.

Welfare Fraud

Statute

§108A-39. Fraudulent misrepresentation.

(a) Any person whether provider or recipient, or person representing himself as such, who willfully and knowingly and with intent to deceive makes a false statement or representation or who fails to disclose a material fact and as a result of making a false statement or representation or failing to disclose a material fact obtains, for himself or another person, attempts to obtain for himself or another person, or continues to receive or enables another person to continue to receive public assistance in the amount of not more than four hundred dollars ($400.00) is guilty of a Class 1 misdemeanor.

(b) Any person, whether provider or recipient, or person representing himself as such who willfully and knowingly with the intent to deceive makes a false statement or representation or fails to disclose a material fact and as a result of making a false statement or representation or failing to disclose a material fact, obtains for himself or another person, attempts to obtain for himself or another person, or continues to receive or enables another person to continue to receive public assistance in an amount of more than four hundred dollars ($400.00) is guilty of a Class I felony.

(c) As used in this section the word "person" means person, association, consortium, corporation, body politic, partnership, or other group, entity, or organization.

Elements

A person guilty of this offense

(1) is a provider or recipient of public assistance or a person representing himself or herself as such *and*
(2) willfully and knowingly,
(3) with the intent to deceive,
(4) (a) makes a false statement or representation *or*
 (b) fails to disclose a material fact *and,*
(5) as a result
 (a) obtains or attempts to obtain public assistance for himself or herself or others *or*
 (b) continues to receive or enables another person to continue to receive public assistance.

Punishment

If the value of the public assistance wrongfully obtained exceeds $400, this offense is a Class I felony; otherwise, it is a Class 1 misdemeanor. G.S. 108A-39(a) and (b). If the felony version of this crime is charged, the relevant sum of money must be alleged in the charging instrument and proved at trial.

Notes

Element (1). A "person" is a "person, association, consortium, corporation, body politic, partnership, or other group, entity, or organization." G.S. 108A-39(c). G.S. 108A-24(5) defines recipient as "a person to whom, or on whose behalf, assistance is granted under this Article."

Element (2). See "Willfully" and "Knowingly" in Chapter 1 (States of Mind).

Element (5). G.S. 108A-39 does not define "public assistance," but a related statute in the same article, G.S. 108A-25, lists the following programs of public assistance: state-county special assistance, Food and Nutrition Services, foster care and adoption assistance payments, low-income energy assistance, the Work First program, and medical assistance.

Attempt. Note that Element (5)(a) covers an attempt to commit welfare fraud and makes it punishable like the completed offense, rather than one level lower, as is typically the case for an attempt. See "Attempt" in Chapter 5 (General Crimes).

Related Offenses Not in This Chapter

See larceny (various offenses) in Chapter 13 (Larceny, Possession of Stolen Goods, Embezzlement, and Related Offenses).

Electronic Food and Nutrition Benefits Fraud

Fraudulently Obtaining or Transferring Electronic Food and Nutrition Benefits

Statute

§108A-53. Fraudulent misrepresentation.

(a) Any person, whether provider or recipient or person representing himself as such, who knowingly obtains or attempts to obtain, or aids or abets any person to obtain by means of making a willfully false statement or representation or by impersonation or by failing to disclose material facts or in any manner not authorized by this Part or the regulations issued pursuant thereto, transfers with intent to defraud any electronic food and nutrition benefit to which that person is not entitled in the amount of four hundred dollars ($400.00) or less shall be guilty of a Class 1 misdemeanor. Whoever knowingly obtains or attempts to obtain, or aids or abets any person to obtain by means of making a willfully false statement or representation or by impersonation or by failing to disclose material facts or in any manner not authorized by this Part or the regulations issued pursuant thereto, transfers with intent to defraud any electronic food and nutrition benefit to which he is not entitled in an amount more than four hundred dollars ($400.00) shall be guilty of a Class I felony.

(b) Whoever presents, or causes to be presented, electronic food and nutrition benefits for payment or redemption, knowing the same to have been received, transferred, or used in any manner in violation of the provisions of this Part or the regulations issued pursuant to this Part shall be guilty of a Class 1 misdemeanor.

(c) Whoever receives any electronic food and nutrition benefits for any consumable item knowing that such benefits were procured fraudulently under subsections (a) and/or (b) of this section shall be guilty of a Class 1 misdemeanor.

(d) Whoever receives any electronic food and nutrition benefits for any consumable item whose exchange is prohibited by the United States Department of Agriculture shall be guilty of a Class 1 misdemeanor.

Elements

A person guilty of this offense

(1) is a provider or recipient of electronic food and nutrition benefits or a person representing himself or herself as such *and*
(2) knowingly
(3) (a) obtains, attempts to obtain, or aids and abets any person to obtain by means of making a willfully false statement or representation, by impersonation, by failing to disclose material facts, or by acting in any manner not authorized by the relevant statutes or regulations *or*
    (b) transfers with the intent to defraud
(4) electronic food and nutrition benefits
(5) to which the person is not entitled.

Punishment

If the value of the electronic food and nutrition benefits obtained or transferred exceeds $400, this offense is a Class I felony; otherwise, it is a Class 1 misdemeanor. G.S. 108A-53(a). If the felony version of the offense is charged, the relevant amount must be alleged in the charging instrument and proved at trial.

Notes

Element (2). See "Knowingly" in Chapter 1 (States of Mind).

Multiple convictions and punishments. When a person made false statements on nine separate occasions over a four-year period and received food stamps as a result of each misrepresentation, the successive acts of misrepresentation were a continuing act with the same criminal goal. Consequently, the value of the food stamps fraudulently received could be combined to reach the threshold for charging a felony offense under this section. State v. Williams, 101 N.C. App. 412 (1991).

Attempt. Note that Element (3)(a) covers an attempt to obtain benefits, thus punishing the attempt like the completed offense, not one class lower, as is typically the case for an attempt. See "Attempt" in Chapter 5 (General Crimes).

Related Offenses Not in This Chapter

See larceny (various offenses) in Chapter 13 (Larceny, Possession of Stolen Goods, Embezzlement, and Related Offenses).
Presenting fraudulently obtained electronic food and nutrition benefits. G.S. 108A-53(b).
Receiving fraudulently obtained electronic food and nutrition benefits. G.S. 108A-53(c).
Receiving electronic food and nutrition benefits for a nonexchangable item. G.S. 108A-53(d).

Illegally Buying, Selling, Distributing, or Possessing with Intent to Sell or Distribute Electronic Food and Nutrition Benefits

Statute

§108A-53.1. Illegal possession or use of electronic food and nutrition benefits.

(a) Any person who knowingly buys, sells, distributes, or possesses with the intent to sell, or distribute electronic food and nutrition benefits or access devices in any manner contrary to that authorized by this Part or the regulations issued pursuant thereto shall be guilty of a Class H felony.

(b) Any person who knowingly uses, transfers, acquires, alters, or possesses electronic food and nutrition benefits or access devices in any manner contrary to that authorized by this Part or the regulations issued pursuant thereto, other than as set forth in subsection (a) of this section, shall be guilty of a Class 1 misdemeanor if the value of such electronic food and nutrition benefits or access devices is less than one hundred dollars ($100.00), or a Class A1 misdemeanor if the value of such electronic food and nutrition benefits or access devices is equal to at least one hundred dollars ($100.00) but less than five hundred dollars ($500.00), or a Class I felony if the value of such electronic food and nutrition benefits or access devices is equal to at least five hundred dollars ($500.00) but less than one thousand dollars ($1,000), or a Class H felony if the value of such electronic food and nutrition benefits or access devices equals or exceeds one thousand dollars ($1,000).

Elements

A person guilty of this offense

(1) knowingly
(2) buys, sells, distributes, or possesses with the intent to sell or distribute
(3) electronic food and nutrition benefits or access devices
(4) in any manner not authorized by the food and nutrition benefit statutes (G.S. Ch. 108A, Art. 2, Part 5) and associated regulations.

Punishment

Class H felony. G.S. 108A-53.1(a).

Notes

Element (1). See "Knowingly" in Chapter 1 (States of Mind).

Related Offenses Not in This Chapter

None

Other Illegal Uses of Electronic Food and Nutrition Benefits

Statute

See G.S. 108A-53.1(b), reproduced under "Illegally Buying, Selling, Distributing, or Possessing with Intent to Sell or Distribute Electronic Food and Nutrition Benefits," above.

Elements

A person guilty of this offense

(1) knowingly
(2) uses, transfers, acquires, alters, or possesses
(3) electronic food and nutrition benefits or access devices
(4) in any manner not authorized by the food and nutrition benefit statutes (G.S. Ch. 108A, Art. 2, Part 5) and associated regulations.

Punishment

This offense is a Class 1 misdemeanor if the value of the electronic food and nutrition benefits or access devices is less than $100; a Class A1 misdemeanor if the value is at least $100 but less than $500; a Class I felony if the value is at least $500 but less than $1,000; a Class H felony if the value is at least or exceeds $1,000. G.S. 108A-53.1(b). If the Class A1 misdemeanor or Class I or H felony version of the offense is charged, the relevant value of benefits must be alleged in the charging instrument and proved at trial.

Notes

Element (1). See "Knowingly" in Chapter 1 (States of Mind).

Multiple convictions and punishments. The statute provides that this offense applies to unauthorized uses other than those covered by "Illegally Buying, Selling, Distributing, or Possessing with Intent to Sell or Distribute Electronic Food and Nutrition Benefits," above. G.S. 108A-53.1(b). This language likely means that a defendant cannot be convicted of that offense and this one based on the same conduct.

Related Offenses Not in This Chapter

None

False Statement to Procure Insurance Benefits

Statute

§58-2-161. False statement to procure or deny benefit of insurance policy or certificate.

(a) For the purposes of this section:

(1) "Insurer" has the same meaning as in G.S. 58-1-5(3) and also includes:

a. Any hull insurance and protection and indemnity club operating under Article 20 of this Chapter.
b. Any surplus lines insurer operating under Article 21 of this Chapter.
c. Any risk retention group or purchasing group operating under Article 22 of this Chapter.
d. Any local government risk pool operating under Article 23 of this Chapter.
e. Any risk-sharing plan operating under Article 42 of this Chapter.
f. The North Carolina Insurance Underwriting Association operating under Article 45 of this Chapter.
g. The North Carolina Joint Insurance Underwriting Association operating under Article 46 of this Chapter.

h. The North Carolina Insurance Guaranty Association operating under Article 48 of this Chapter.
i. Any multiple employer welfare arrangement operating under Article 49 of this Chapter.
j. The North Carolina Life and Health Insurance Guaranty Association operating under Article 62 of this Chapter.
k. Any service corporation operating under Article 65 of this Chapter.
l. Any health maintenance organization operating under Article 67 of this Chapter.
m. The State Health Plan for Teachers and State Employees and any optional plans or programs operating under Part 2 of Article 3 of Chapter 135 of the General Statutes.
n. A group of employers self-insuring their workers' compensation liabilities under Article 47 of this Chapter.
o. An employer self-insuring its workers' compensation liabilities under Article 5 of Chapter 97 of the General Statutes.
p. The North Carolina Self-Insurance Security Association under Article 4 of Chapter 97 of the General Statutes.
q. Any reinsurer licensed or accredited under this Chapter.

(2) "Statement" includes any application, notice, statement, proof of loss, bill of lading, receipt for payment, invoice, account, estimate of property damages, bill for services, diagnosis, prescription, hospital or doctor records, X rays, test result, or other evidence of loss, injury, or expense.

(b) Any person who, with the intent to injure, defraud, or deceive an insurer or insurance claimant:

(1) Presents or causes to be presented a written or oral statement, including computer-generated documents as part of, in support of, or in opposition to, a claim for payment or other benefit pursuant to an insurance policy, knowing that the statement contains false or misleading information concerning any fact or matter material to the claim, or

(2) Assists, abets, solicits, or conspires with another person to prepare or make any written or oral statement that is intended to be presented to an insurer or insurance claimant in connection with, in support of, or in opposition to, a claim for payment or other benefit pursuant to an insurance policy, knowing that the statement contains false or misleading information concerning a fact or matter material to the claim is guilty of a Class H felony. Each claim shall be considered a separate count. Upon conviction, if the court imposes probation, the court may order the defendant to pay restitution as a condition of probation. In determination of the amount of restitution pursuant to G.S. 15A-1343(d), the reasonable costs and attorneys' fees incurred by the victim in the investigation of, and efforts to recover damages arising from, the claim, may be considered part of the damage caused by the defendant arising out of the offense.

In a civil cause of action for recovery based upon a claim for which a defendant has been convicted under this section, the conviction may be entered into evidence against the defendant. The court may award the prevailing party compensatory damages, attorneys' fees, costs, and reasonable investigative costs. If the prevailing party can demonstrate that the defendant has engaged in a pattern of violations of this section, the court may award treble damages.

Elements

A person guilty of this offense

(1) with the intent to injure, defraud, or deceive
(2) an insurer or insurance claimant
(3) presents or causes to be presented a written or oral statement, including computer-generated documents,

(4) as part of, in support of, or in opposition to a claim for payment or other benefit under an insurance policy
(5) knowing
(6) that the statement contains false or misleading information concerning any fact or matter material to the claim.

Punishment

Class H felony. G.S. 58-2-161(b)(2). The statute contains specific provisions applicable to restitution. *Id.*

Notes

Element (2). The term "insurer" is broadly defined in G.S. 58-2-161(a)(1), reproduced above. It includes the specific kinds of insurers set out in subsections a through q. It also includes insurers defined in G.S. 58-1-5(3) as follows: "any corporation, association, partnership, society, order, individual or aggregation of individuals engaging or proposing or attempting to engage as principals in any kind of insurance business, including the exchanging of reciprocal or interinsurance contracts between individuals, partnerships and corporations"—but not "the State of North Carolina or any county, city, or other political subdivision of the State of North Carolina."

Elements (3) and (5). The term "statement" is defined in G.S. 58-2-161(a)(2), reproduced above. The predecessor statute for this offense was G.S. 14-214. It was later recodified and rewritten as the current statute, reproduced above. Examples of cases under G.S. 14-214 include *State v. Walker*, 22 N.C. App. 291 (1974) (the evidence was sufficient when the defendant fraudulently staged a car accident and filed an insurance claim); *State v. Moose*, 36 N.C. App. 202 (1978) (the evidence was sufficient when the defendant fraudulently reported in an insurance claim that a boat, motor, and trailer had been stolen); *State v. Carroll*, 101 N.C. App. 691 (1991) (the evidence was sufficient when the defendant fraudulently reported in an insurance claim more goods than were in fact stolen from a store break-in); *State v. Fraylon*, 240 N.C. 365 (1954) (the evidence was insufficient to establish that the defendant "willfully and knowingly" violated G.S. 14-214); and *State v. Stephenson*, 218 N.C. 258 (1940) (same).

Assisting, abetting, conspiring, and soliciting. Under G.S. 58-2-161(b)(2), the punishment for conspiracy and solicitation to commit this offense is the same as for the completed offense, rather than at a lower level, as is typically the case for conspiracy and solicitation. See "Conspiracy" and "Solicitation" in Chapter 5 (General Crimes). The statute also covers one who "[a]ssists" and "abets" the preparation or making of the statement. However, one who aids and abets is always punished as a principal. See "Aiding and Abetting" in Chapter 3 (Participants in Crimes). It is not clear whether the statutory term "[a]ssists" is meant to mean something different than aiding and abetting.

Multiple convictions and punishments. G.S. 58-2-161(b)(2) provides that each claim is a separate offense.

Related Offenses Not in This Chapter

Embezzlement by insurance agents, brokers or administrators. G.S. 58-2-162.
Motor vehicle insurance rate fraud. G.S. 58-2-164.
Refusal to exhibit or making false statements about insurance documents. G.S. 58-2-200.
False statements in applications for insurance. G.S. 58-33-105.

Computer Fraud

Accessing a Computer to Defraud or Obtain Property

Statute

§14-454. Accessing computers.

(a) It is unlawful to willfully, directly or indirectly, access or cause to be accessed any computer, computer program, computer system, computer network, or any part thereof, for the purpose of:

(1) Devising or executing any scheme or artifice to defraud, unless the object of the scheme or artifice is to obtain educational testing material, a false educational testing score, or a false academic or vocational grade, or

(2) Obtaining property or services other than educational testing material, a false educational testing score, or a false academic or vocational grade for a person, by means of false or fraudulent pretenses, representations or promises.

A violation of this subsection is a Class G felony if the fraudulent scheme or artifice results in damage of more than one thousand dollars ($1,000), or if the property or services obtained are worth more than one thousand dollars ($1,000). Any other violation of this subsection is a Class 1 misdemeanor.

(b) Any person who willfully and without authorization, directly or indirectly, accesses or causes to be accessed any computer, computer program, computer system, or computer network for any purpose other than those set forth in subsection (a) above, is guilty of a Class 1 misdemeanor.

(c) For the purpose of this section, the phrase "access or cause to be accessed" includes introducing, directly or indirectly, a computer program (including a self-replicating or a self-propagating computer program) into a computer, computer program, computer system, or computer network.

Elements

A person guilty of this offense

(1) willfully
(2) accesses or causes to be accessed
(3) a computer, computer program, computer system, computer network, or any part thereof
(4) for the purpose of
  (a) devising or executing a scheme or artifice to defraud *or*
  (b) obtaining property or services by means of false or fraudulent pretenses, representations, or promises.

Punishment

Class G felony if the fraud results in more than $1,000 in damage or if the property or services obtained are worth more than $1,000. G.S. 14-454(a). Otherwise, an offense is a Class 1 misdemeanor. G.S. 14-454(a). If the felony version of the offense is charged, the amount of damage or property or services obtained must be alleged in a charging instrument and proved at trial.

Notes

Element (1). See "Willfully" in Chapter 1 (States of Mind).

Element (2). "Access" means to instruct, communicate with, cause input, cause output, cause data processing, or otherwise make use of any resources of a computer, computer system, or computer network. G.S. 14-453(1). For the purposes of this offense, the term "access or cause to be accessed" also includes the introduction of a computer program, such as a virus, into a computer, computer system, or computer network. G.S. 14-454(c).

Element (3). A "computer" is an internally programmed, automatic device that performs data processing or telephone switching. G.S. 14-453(2). A "computer program" is an ordered set of data that are coded instructions or statements that, when executed by a computer, cause the computer to process data. G.S. 14-453(4). A "computer system" is at least one computer together with a set of related, connected, or unconnected peripheral devices. G.S. 14-453(6). A "computer network" is the interconnection of communication systems with a computer through remote terminals or a complex consisting of two or more connected computers or telephone switching equipment. G.S. 14-453(3).

Element (4)(b). "Property" includes financial instruments, information—including electronically processed or produced data—and computer software and computer programs in either machine or human readable form and any other tangible or intangible item of value. G.S. 14-453(8). "Services" include computer time, data processing, and storage functions. G.S. 14-453(9).

Exceptions. The statute excludes from coverage conduct targeted at obtaining educational testing material, a false education testing score, or a false academic or vocational grade. G.S. 14-454(a)(1) and (2). However, such conduct is covered by "Accessing a Computer without Authorization" and "Accessing Testing Material in a Government Computer," both below.

G.S. 14-453.1 provides that the computer-related offenses in G.S. Chapter 14, Article 60, do not apply to

- any terms or conditions in a contract or license related to a computer, computer network, software, computer system, database, or telecommunication device or
- any software or hardware designed to allow a computer, computer network, software, computer system, database, information, or telecommunication service to operate in the ordinary course of a lawful business or designed to allow an owner or authorized holder of information to protect data, information, or rights in it.

Jurisdiction. G.S. 14-453.2 provides that any computer-related offenses in G.S. Chapter 14, Article 60, committed by the use of electronic communication may be deemed to have been committed where the electronic communication was originally sent or where it was originally received in the state. "Electronic communication" means any transfer of signs, signals, writing, images, sounds, data, or intelligence of any nature, transmitted in whole or in part by a wire, radio, computer, electromagnetic, photoelectric, or photo-optical system. G.S. 14-453.2 and 14-196.3(a). See generally "Lack of Jurisdiction" in Chapter 2 (Bars and Defenses).

Related Offenses Not in This Chapter

"Cyberbullying" (Chapter 8)
See damage to computers (various offenses) in Chapter 18 (Trespass, Property Damage, and Littering).
Denial of computer services to an authorized user. G.S. 14-456.
Extortion by threatening computer damage. G.S. 14-457.

Accessing a Computer without Authorization

Statute

See G.S. 14-454(b), reproduced under "Accessing a Computer to Defraud or Obtain Property," above.

Elements

A person guilty of this offense
(1) willfully *and*
(2) without authorization
(3) accesses or causes to be accessed
(4) a computer, computer program, computer system, or computer network.

Punishment

Class 1 misdemeanor. G.S. 14-454(b).

Notes

Generally. This offense is the same as "Accessing a Computer to Defraud or Obtain Property," above, except as to the purpose for which the computer is illegally used. This offense covers unauthorized use for any purpose other than those covered by "Accessing a Computer to Defraud or Obtain Property," G.S. 14-454(b), including the educational-fraud purposes specifically exempted from prosecution under that offense. Thus, the relevant notes to "Accessing a Computer to Defraud or Obtain Property" apply here as well. Note, however, that if the educational testing materials are in a government computer, "Accessing Testing Material in a Government Computer," below, would apply.

Related Offenses Not in This Chapter

See the offenses listed under "Accessing a Computer to Defraud or Obtain Property," above.

Computer Trespass

Statute

§14-458. Computer trespass; penalty.

(a) Except as otherwise made unlawful by this Article, it shall be unlawful for any person to use a computer or computer network without authority and with the intent to do any of the following:

(1) Temporarily or permanently remove, halt, or otherwise disable any computer data, computer programs, or computer software from a computer or computer network.
(2) Cause a computer to malfunction, regardless of how long the malfunction persists.
(3) Alter or erase any computer data, computer programs, or computer software.
(4) Cause physical injury to the property of another.
(5) Make or cause to be made an unauthorized copy, in any form, including, but not limited to, any printed or electronic form of computer data, computer programs, or computer software residing in, communicated by, or produced by a computer or computer network.
(6) Falsely identify with the intent to deceive or defraud the recipient or forge commercial electronic mail transmission information or other routing information in any manner in connection with the transmission of unsolicited bulk commercial electronic mail through or into the computer network of an electronic mail service provider or its subscribers.

For purposes of this subsection, a person is "without authority" when (i) the person has no right or permission of the owner to use a computer, or the person uses a computer in a manner exceeding the right or permission, or (ii) the person uses a computer or computer network, or the computer services of an electronic mail service provider to transmit unsolicited bulk commercial electronic mail in contravention of the authority granted by or in violation of the policies set by the electronic mail service provider.

(b) Any person who violates this section shall be guilty of computer trespass, which offense shall be punishable as a Class 3 misdemeanor. If there is damage to the property of another and the damage is valued at less than two thousand five hundred dollars ($2,500) caused by the person's act in violation of this section, the offense shall be punished as a Class 1 misdemeanor. If there is damage to the property of another valued at two thousand five hundred dollars ($2,500) or more caused by the person's act in violation of this section, the offense shall be punished as a Class I felony.

(c) Any person whose property or person is injured by reason of a violation of this section may sue for and recover any damages sustained and the costs of the suit pursuant to G.S. 1-539.2A.

Elements

A person guilty of this offense

(1) uses a computer or computer network
(2) without authority *and*
(3) with the intent to
 (a) temporarily or permanently remove, halt, or otherwise disable any computer data, computer programs, or computer software from a computer or computer network,
 (b) cause a computer to malfunction,
 (c) alter or erase any computer data, computer programs, or computer software,
 (d) cause physical injury to the property of another,
 (e) make or cause to be made an unauthorized copy, in any form, including, but not limited to, any printed or electronic form of computer data, computer programs, or computer software residing in, communicated by, or produced by a computer or computer network, *or*
 (f) falsely identify, with the intent to deceive or defraud the recipient, or forge commercial electronic mail transmission information or other routing information in any manner in connection with the transmission of unsolicited bulk commercial electronic mail through or into the computer network of an electronic mail service provider or its subscribers.

Punishment

Class 3 misdemeanor. G.S. 14-458(b). However, if the violation causes damage to another's property and the damage is valued at less than $2,500, the offense is a Class 1 misdemeanor. *Id.* If the damage to another's property is $2,500 or more, the offense is a Class I felony. *Id.* If the felony or Class 1 misdemeanor version of this offense is charged, the relevant amount of damage must be alleged in a charging instrument and proved at trial.

Notes

Element (1). See the note on Element (3) to "Accessing a Computer to Defraud or Obtain Property," above.

Element (2). See the definition of "without authority" in G.S. 14-458(a), reproduced above.

Element (3)(f). "Electronic mail" is defined as "[t]he transmission of information or communication by the use of the Internet, a computer, a facsimile machine, a pager, a cellular telephone, a video recorder, or other electronic means sent to a person identified by a unique address or address number and received by that person." G.S. 14-453(6b) and 14-196.3(a)(2).

Exceptions. See this note to "Accessing a Computer to Defraud or Obtain Property," above.

Jurisdiction. See this note to "Accessing a Computer to Defraud or Obtain Property," above.

Multiple convictions and punishments. G.S. 14-458(a) begins with the following language: "Except as otherwise made unlawful by this Article, it shall be unlawful . . . ." It is not clear whether this language was meant to limit criminal liability for this offense when another offense in the same Article applies.

Civil damages. G.S. 14-458(c) provides for the recovery of civil damages.

Related Offenses Not in This Chapter

"Cyberbullying" (Chapter 8)

See damage to computers (various offenses) in Chapter 18 (Trespass, Property Damage, and Littering).

Accessing a Government Computer to Defraud or Obtain Property

Statute

§14-454.1. Accessing government computers.

(a) It is unlawful to willfully, directly or indirectly, access or cause to be accessed any government computer for the purpose of:

(1) Devising or executing any scheme or artifice to defraud, or

(2) Obtaining property or services by means of false or fraudulent pretenses, representations, or promises.

A violation of this subsection is a Class F felony.

(b) Any person who willfully and without authorization, directly or indirectly, accesses or causes to be accessed any government computer for any purpose other than those set forth in subsection (a) of this section is guilty of a Class H felony.

(c) Any person who willfully and without authorization, directly or indirectly, accesses or causes to be accessed any educational testing material or academic or vocational testing scores or grades that are in a government computer is guilty of a Class 1 misdemeanor.

(d) For the purpose of this section the phrase "access or cause to be accessed" includes introducing, directly or indirectly, a computer program (including a self-replicating or a self-propagating computer program) into a computer, computer program, computer system, or computer network.

Elements

A person guilty of this offense

(1) willfully
(2) accesses or causes to be accessed
(3) any government computer
(4) for the purpose of
   (a) devising or executing any scheme or artifice to defraud *or*
   (b) obtaining property or services by means of false or fraudulent pretenses, representations, or promises.

Punishment

Class F felony. G.S. 14-454.1(a).

Notes

Generally. This offense is the same as "Accessing a Computer to Defraud or Obtain Property," above, except that for this offense, the computer accessed is a government computer and this offense has a more severe punishment. Thus, the relevant notes to that offense apply here as well.

Element (1). See "Willfully" in Chapter 1 (States of Mind).

Element (2). For purposes of this section, the phrase "access or cause to be accessed" includes "introducing, directly or indirectly, a computer program (including a self-replicating or a self-propagating computer program) into a computer, computer program, computer system, or computer network." G.S. 14-454.1(d).

Element (3). A "government computer" means any computer, computer program, computer system, or computer network or any part thereof that is owned, operated, or used by any state or local governmental entity. G.S. 14-453(7a).

Related Offenses Not in This Chapter

See damage to computers (various offenses) in Chapter 18 (Trespass, Property Damage, and Littering).

Denial of government computer services to an authorized user. G.S. 14-456.1.

Accessing a Government Computer without Authorization

Statute

See G.S. 14-454.1(b), reproduced under "Accessing a Government Computer to Defraud or Obtain Property," above.

Elements

A person guilty of this offense

(1) willfully *and*
(2) without authorization
(3) accesses or causes to be accessed
(4) a government computer.

Punishment

Class H felony. G.S. 14-454.1(b).

Notes

Generally. This offense is the same as "Accessing a Computer without Authorization," above, except that for this offense, the computer accessed is a government computer and this offense has a more severe punishment. Thus, the relevant notes to that offense apply here as well. This offense also is the same as "Accessing a Government Computer to Defraud or Obtain Property," above, but for the defendant's purpose. For this offense, it must be for any purpose not covered by that other offense. G.S. 14-454.1(b).

Element (1). See "Willfully" in Chapter 1 (States of Mind).

Element (3). See the note on Element (2) to "Accessing a Government Computer to Defraud or Obtain Property," above.

Element (4). See the note on Element (3) to "Accessing a Government Computer to Defraud or Obtain Property," above.

Related Offenses Not in This Chapter

See damage to computers (various offenses) in Chapter 18 (Trespass, Property Damage, and Littering).

Accessing Testing Material in a Government Computer

Statute

See G.S. 14-454.1(c), reproduced under "Accessing a Government Computer to Defraud or Obtain Property," above.

Elements

A person guilty of this offense

(1) willfully *and*
(2) without authorization
(3) accesses or causes to be accessed
(4) any educational testing material or academic or vocational testing scores or grades
(5) in a government computer.

Punishment

Class 1 misdemeanor. G.S. 14-454.1(c).

Notes

Element (1). See "Willfully" in Chapter 1 (States of Mind).

Element (3). See the note on Element (2) to "Accessing a Computer to Defraud or Obtain Property," above.

Element (5). See the note on Element (3) to "Accessing a Government Computer to Defraud or Obtain Property," above.

Exceptions. See this note to "Accessing a Computer to Defraud or Obtain Property," above.

Jurisdiction. See this note to "Accessing a Computer to Defraud or Obtain Property," above.

Related Offenses Not in This Chapter

See the offenses listed under "Accessing a Government Computer to Defraud or Obtain Property," above.

Willful Failure to File a State Tax Return, Supply State Tax Information, or Pay State Tax

Statute

§105-236. Penalties; situs of violations; penalty disposition.

(a) Penalties. -- The following civil penalties and criminal offenses apply:

Subsections (1) through (8) are not reproduced here.

(9) Willful Failure to File Return, Supply Information, or Pay Tax. -- Any person required to pay any tax, to make a return, to keep any records, or to supply any information, who willfully fails to pay the tax, make the return, keep the records, or supply the information, at the time or times required by law, or rules issued pursuant thereto, shall, in addition to other penalties provided by law, be guilty of a Class 1 misdemeanor. Notwithstanding any other provision of law, no prosecution for a violation brought under this subdivision shall be barred before the expiration of six years after the date of the violation.

The remainder of the statute is not reproduced here.

Elements

A person guilty of this offense

(1) is required to
  (a) pay any tax,
  (b) make a return,
  (c) keep any records, *or*
  (d) supply any information *and*
(2) willfully
(3) fails to
  (a) pay such tax,
  (b) make such return,
  (c) keep such records, *or*
  (d) supply such information.

Punishment

Class 1 misdemeanor. G.S. 105-236(a)(9).

Notes

Generally. This offense applies to taxes levied under G.S. Chapter 105, Subchapters I, V, and VIII, and to inspection taxes levied under G.S. Chapter 119, Article 3. G.S. 105-228.90.

Element (2). See "Willfully" in Chapter 1 (States of Mind). In addressing this element, the North Carolina Court of Appeals said, "a good-faith misunderstanding of the law's requirements may negate willfulness, but a good-faith disagreement with the law does not." State v. Davis, 96 N.C. App. 545 (1989). Thus, disagreement with tax laws does not afford tax protesters a defense to this element.

Statute of limitations. Normally, the statute of limitations for misdemeanors is two years. See "Expiration of statute of limitations" in Chapter 2 (Bars and Defenses). However, for this offense, G.S. 105-236(a)(9) provides: "Notwithstanding any other provision of law, no prosecution for a violation brought under this subdivision shall be barred before the expiration of six years after the date of the violation."

Related Offenses Not in This Chapter

Attempt to evade or defeat tax. G.S. 105-236(a)(7).
Failure to collect, withhold, or pay over tax. G.S. 105-236(a)(8).
Aid, procure or advise preparation or filing of false tax documents. G.S. 105-236(a)(9a).
Misrepresentation concerning payment. G.S. 105-236(a)(10b).
Failing to remit taxpayer funds. G.S. 105-236.

17

Arson and Burning Offenses

17

Arson and Burning Offenses

Arson Offenses

First-Degree Arson

Statute

This is a common law offense. G.S. 14-58; State v. Vickers, 306 N.C. 90, 99 (1982). Punishment is provided for in G.S. 14-58, reproduced immediately below.

> **§14-58. Punishment for arson.**
> There shall be two degrees of arson as defined at the common law. If the dwelling burned was occupied at the time of the burning, the offense is arson in the first degree and is punishable as a Class D felony. If the dwelling burned was unoccupied at the time of the burning, the offense is arson in the second degree and is punishable as a Class G felony.

Elements

A person guilty of this offense

(1) willfully and maliciously
(2) burns
(3) the dwelling house or other buildings within the curtilage
(4) of another
(5) while someone is present inside the dwelling.

Punishment

Class D felony. G.S. 14-58.

Notes

Element (1). The burning must be done willfully and maliciously. State v. Long, 243 N.C. 393 (1956). To prove this element, the State must show (1) that the defendant intended to burn the dwelling or that the act committed would probably result in a burning of a dwelling; and (2) that the act was done "voluntarily and without excuse or justification and without any bona fide claim or right." State v. White, 288 N.C. 44 (1975). It is not necessary to prove that the defendant intended to injure a person; proof of intent to burn a particular house is sufficient. State v. McCarter, 98 N.C. 637 (1887). See generally, "Willfully" and "Maliciously" in Chapter 1 (States of Mind).

Element (2). The dwelling or buildings within the curtilage need not be destroyed; the evidence is sufficient if any part of the dwelling or building, however small, is consumed. Thus, for example, the evidence was sufficient when it showed that wallpaper was burned. State v. Oxendine, 305 N.C. 126, 130–31 (1982); State v. Shaw, 305 N.C. 327 (1982). To constitute a burning there must be actual charring rather than mere discoloration or scorching. Charring occurs when some part of the dwelling or buildings—for example, a piece of wood paneling—is reduced to coal and has its identity changed. *Oxendine*, 305 N.C. at 129. There was sufficient evidence of a burning of a mobile home when the vinyl exterior was melted by a fire. State v. Norris, 172 N.C. App. 722 (2005).

Arson has not been committed if only the contents of the dwelling or buildings are burned; some part of the structure itself must be burned. *Oxendine*, 305 N.C. at 129.

Element (3). To constitute a dwelling house for purposes of arson, the structure must be inhabited. State v. Long, 243 N.C. 393 (1956); State v. Vickers, 306 N.C. 90, 100 (1982). A dwelling is inhabited if someone uses it as a permanent, temporary, or seasonal residence. N.C. Pattern Jury Instructions—Crim. 215.11; *Vickers*, 306 N.C. at 100 (citing with approval an out-of-state case holding that a cabin was a dwelling house even though it was unoccupied at the time of the fire but was occupied by the owner at frequent intervals, particularly during hunting season, and was intended to serve as the owner's home following his retirement). However, "inhabited" does not mean occupied; a house can be inhabited and therefore a dwelling house even though the inhabitants are temporarily absent at the time of the burning. *Vickers*, 306 N.C. at 100.

When determining whether a structure is a dwelling house, its value is irrelevant; a shack, as well as a mansion, can be a dwelling house. Also, mobile homes, manufactured-type houses, and recreational trailer homes can be dwellings for purposes of this offense. G.S. 14-58.1; State v. Hodge, 121 N.C. App. 209 (1995).

The term "dwelling house," as used in the context of burglary offenses, includes all interconnecting portions of any building in which a person habitually sleeps, even if the building's main use is as a store. See the note on Element (4) to "First-Degree Burglary" in Chapter 15 (Burglary, Breaking or Entering, and Related Offenses). This interpretation is likely to apply for arson offenses as well.

Note that this offense covers burnings of not only the dwelling house but also buildings within the curtilage of the dwelling house. State v. Nipper, 177 N.C. App. 794, 796 (2006) (garage located thirty feet from a house was within the curtilage); *see also* State v. Cuthrell, 235 N.C. 173 (1952); State v. Thompson, 97 N.C. 496 (1887). Curtilage is defined as including "at least the yard around the dwelling house as well as the area occupied by barns, cribs, and other outbuildings." *Nipper*, 177 N.C. App. at 795 (quotation omitted). For a discussion of the term "curtilage" as it is used in the context of burglary offenses, see the note on Element (4) to "Second-Degree Burglary" in Chapter 15 (Burglary, Breaking or Entering, and Related Offenses).

Element (4). The house or dwelling must be possessed by someone other than or in addition to the defendant. State v. Shaw, 305 N.C. 327, 337–38 (1982); N.C. Pattern Jury Instructions—Crim. 215.11. A defendant who burned his own apartment in a building containing other inhabited apartments was convicted of arson (rather than of burning one's own dwelling house) because the entire building was considered the dwelling of the other tenants. State v. Jones, 296 N.C. 75 (1978); *see also* State v. Wyatt, 48 N.C. App. 709, 712 (1980) (citing *Jones*).

Possession, not legal ownership, is the key to this element. State v. Young, 187 N.C. 698 (1924). Thus, an owner can be guilty of arson for burning a dwelling rented to and possessed by someone else.

Element (5). For a burning to constitute first-degree arson, someone must physically be present in the dwelling when the burning occurs. State v. Barnes, 333 N.C. 666 (1993); N.C. Pattern Jury Instructions—Crim. 215.11. If no one is present, the crime is "Second-Degree Arson," discussed below. If a defendant burns one apartment in a multi-unit apartment building, the dwelling house is occupied if someone is present in another apartment, even if the other apartment is not burned. *Wyatt,* 48 N.C. App. at 711–12.

In a case involving arson and homicide, the arson can be a felony supporting a felony murder charge if the crimes are part of a continuous transaction. For a discussion of felony murder and the continuous transaction doctrine, see the note on Element (3)(c) to "First-Degree Murder" in Chapter 6 (Homicide). By the same token, if the homicide and arson are part of a continuous transaction, the dwelling house will be deemed to have been occupied for purposes of an arson charge even if the occupant was killed before the arson occurs. State v. Campbell, 332 N.C. 116, 121–23 (1992) (upholding a first-degree arson conviction in a case where the victim was dead when the defendant set the house on fire; the court held: "[I]f the murder and arson are so joined by time and circumstances as to be part of one continuous transaction, the temporal order of the murder and arson is immaterial. Stated differently, for purposes of the arson statute, a dwelling is 'occupied' if the interval between the mortal blow and the arson is short, and the murder and arson constitute parts of a continuous transaction." *Id.* at 122. This rule only applies when the arson and homicide are part of a continuous transaction. *Id.* at 122–23 (discussing *State v. Ward,* 93 N.C. App. 682 (1989), as a case where the continuous transaction doctrine did not apply; in *Ward,* the victim had been dead for several days and his body had been removed from the house and deposited in a trash dumpster when the fire was set).

Charging issues. For a discussion of charging issues in connection with arson offenses, see Jessica Smith, *The Criminal Indictment: Fatal Defect, Fatal Variance, and Amendment,* ADMIN. OF JUST. BULL. No. 2008/03 (UNC School of Government, July 2008) (online at www.sog.unc.edu/pubs/electronicversions/pdfs/aojb0803.pdf). The words "set fire to" should not be used in charging this offense because they are not the equivalent of the word "burn." State v. Hall, 93 N.C. 571 (1885). See the note on Element (2) to "Burning a Public Building," below, for a discussion of the phrase "set fire to."

Greater and lesser-includes offenses. "Burning an Uninhabited House, Factory, Store, etc.," below, is not a lesser-included offense of arson. State v. Britt, 132 N.C. App. 173, 178 (1999).

Relation to other offenses. G.S. 14-58.2 makes it a crime to willfully and maliciously burn a mobile home, manufactured-type house, or recreational trailer home that is a dwelling house of another while someone is present inside. That offense probably came about at a time when it was not clear that mobile homes were covered by the term "dwelling" as used in arson offenses. Since enactment of G.S. 14-58.2, however, the courts have recognized that structures such as mobile homes are dwellings. See the note on Element (3), above. In practice, the offense proscribed by G.S. 14-58.2 rarely is charged because first-degree arson (1) covers any act that would fall within this statute; (2) provides for the same punishment; and (3) has one less element and thus is easier to prove.

Related Offenses Not in This Chapter

"Attempt" (Chapter 5)
"Malicious Injury by Use of an Explosive or Incendiary" (Chapter 7)
See the offenses in Chapter 7 (Assaults).
See the offenses in Chapter 18 (Trespass, Property Damage, and Littering).
See malicious damage by use explosives or incendiaries (various offenses) in Chapter 20 (Bombing, Terrorism, and Related Offenses).
Burning of mobile home, manufactured-type house or recreational trailer. G.S. 14-58.2.
Burning of ginhouses and tobacco houses. G.S. 14-64.
Injuring houses, churches, fences, and walls. G.S. 14-144.
Injuring buildings or fences; taking possession of a house without consent. G.S. 14-159.
Exposing children to fire. G.S. 14-318.
Looting; trespass during an emergency. G.S. 14-288.6.

Second-Degree Arson

Statute

This offense is a common law offense. G.S. 14-58, reproduced under "First-Degree Arson," above, prescribes punishment.

Elements

A person guilty of this offense

(1) willfully and maliciously
(2) burns
(3) the dwelling house or other buildings within the curtilage
(4) of another.

Punishment

Class G felony. G.S. 14-58.

Notes

Generally. This offense is the same as first-degree arson except that this offense does not require that someone be present inside the dwelling when the burning occurs. Thus, the notes on first-degree arson apply here as well.

Related Offenses Not in This Chapter

See the offenses listed under "First-Degree Arson," above.

Burning Offenses

Burning a Public Building

Statute

§14-59. Burning of certain public buildings.

If any person shall wantonly and willfully set fire to or burn or cause to be burned or aid, counsel or procure the burning of, the State Capitol, the Legislative Building, the Justice Building or any building owned or occupied by the State or any of its agencies, institutions or subdivisions or by any county, incorporated city or town or other governmental or quasi-governmental entity, he shall be punished as a Class F felon.

Elements

A person guilty of this offense

(1) wantonly and willfully
(2) sets fire to, burns, causes to be burned, or aids, counsels, or procures the burning of
(3) the State Capitol, the Legislative Building, the Justice Building, or any other building owned or occupied by any agency or unit of state or local government or by any quasi-governmental entity.

Punishment

Class F felony. G.S. 14-59.

Notes

Element (1). See "Wantonly" and "Willfully" in Chapter 1 (States of Mind).

Element (2). The statute covers one who aids, counsels, or procures the burning and punishes such a person as if he or she had completed the crime. G.S. 14-59. This statutory language seems unnecessary because an aider and abettor is always punished like a principal. See "Aiding and Abetting" in Chapter 3 (Participants in Crimes).

This statute is broader than first- and second-degree arson. For arson offenses, there must be a burning. For this offense, a burning will suffice, but so, too, will the act of "set[ting] fire to" the building. One can set fire to a structure without causing a burning to occur. State v. Hall, 93 N.C. 571 (1885) (distinguishing between these terms). See the note on Element (2) to "First-Degree Arson," above, for a discussion of what constitutes a burning. For example, if the defendant sets fire to a public structure, causing the wood on the structure to become discolored but not sufficiently decomposed to be classified as burned, this crime has occurred.

A juvenile's act of setting off fireworks that ignited a flame approximately two to three feet high and caused markings on the floor and wall of a room constituted setting fire to a building. *In re* J.L.B.M., 176 N.C. App. 613 (2006).

In charging someone with procuring the burning of a building, the State is alleging actual complicity in the crime, not just solicitation. To convict, it must prove that the defendant instructed someone to burn the building and that the building was, in fact, burned. State v. Sargent, 22 N.C. App. 148, 150 (1974).

Element (3). G.S. 14-58.1 provides that for all the burning offenses, the term "building" includes mobile homes, manufactured-type houses, and recreational trailers. Thus, a trailer or mobile home used as an annex or temporary office by any governmental or quasi-governmental agency would be a public building covered by G.S. 14-59.

Charging issues. See this note to "First-Degree Arson," above.

Greater and lesser-included offenses. "Burning personal property," discussed below, is not a lesser-included offense of burning a public building. State v. Pierce, 208 N.C. 47 (1935).

Related Offenses Not in This Chapter

See the offenses listed under "First-Degree Arson," above.

Burning a Schoolhouse

Statute

§14-60. Burning of schoolhouses or buildings of educational institutions.

If any person shall wantonly and willfully set fire to or burn or cause to be burned or aid, counsel or procure the burning of, any schoolhouse or building owned, leased or used by any public or private school, college or educational institution, he shall be punished as a Class F felon.

Elements

A person guilty of this offense

(1) wantonly and willfully
(2) sets fire to, burns, causes to be burned, or aids, counsels, or procures the burning of
(3) any schoolhouse or building owned, used, or leased by an educational institution.

Punishment

Class F felony. G.S. 14-60.

Notes

Element (1). See "Wantonly" and "Willfully" in Chapter 1 (States of Mind).

Element (2). See the note on Element (2) to "Burning a Public Building," above.

Element (3). The statute covers "any schoolhouse or building owned, leased or used" by all types of educational institutions, both public and private. This language appears broad enough to cover buildings used for administrative, classroom, or recreational purposes. G.S. 14-58.1 provides that for all the burning offenses, mobile homes, manufactured-type houses, and recreational trailers are included within the term "building." Thus, a trailer or mobile home used or leased by an educational institution would be covered by G.S. 14-60.

Related Offenses Not in This Chapter

See the offenses listed under "First-Degree Arson," above.

Burning a Bridge, Fire Station, Rescue Squad Building, etc.

Statute

§14-61. Burning of certain bridges and buildings.

If any person shall wantonly and willfully set fire to or burn or cause to be burned, or aid, counsel or procure the burning of, any public bridge, or private toll bridge, or the bridge of any incorporated company, or any fire-engine house or rescue-squad building, or any house belonging to an incorporated company or unincorporated association and used in the business of such company or association, he shall be punished as a Class F felon.

Elements

A person guilty of this offense

(1) wantonly and willfully
(2) sets fire to, burns, causes to be burned, or aids, counsels, or procures the burning of
(3) a public, private toll, or corporation bridge, a fire engine house or rescue squad building, or a house owned and used by a corporation or unincorporated association in its business.

Punishment

Class F felony. G.S. 14-61.

Notes

Element (1). See "Wantonly" and "Willfully" in Chapter 1 (States of Mind).

Element (2). See the note on Element (2) to "Burning a Public Building," above.

Element (3). This statute apparently does not cover private non-toll bridges owned by individuals. However, the offense of "Burning a Structure Not Listed in Any Other Statute," discussed below, would cover such a bridge.

Related Offenses Not in This Chapter

See the offenses listed under "First-Degree Arson," above.
Injuring bridges. G.S. 14-146.

Burning an Uninhabited House, Factory, Store, etc.

Statute

§14-62. Burning certain buildings.

If any person shall wantonly and willfully set fire to or burn or cause to be burned, or aid, counsel or procure the burning of, any uninhabited house, or any stable, coach house, outhouse, warehouse, office, shop, mill, barn or granary, or any building, structure or erection used or intended to be used in carrying on any trade or manufacture, or any branch thereof, whether the same or any of them respectively shall then be in the possession of the offender, or in the possession of any other person, he shall be punished as a Class F felon.

Elements

A person guilty of this offense

(1) wantonly and willfully
(2) sets fire to, burns, causes to be burned, or aids, counsels, or procures the burning of
(3) an uninhabited house; coach house; outhouse; stable; warehouse; office; shop; mill; barn or granary; or any building, structure, or erection used or intended to be used in carrying on a trade or manufacture.

Punishment

Class F felony. G.S. 14-62.

Notes

Element (1). See "Wantonly" and "Willfully" in Chapter 1 (States of Mind).

Element (2). See the note on this Element to "Burning a Public Building," above.

Element (3). This offense covers setting fire to, etc. an uninhabited house. A house is not uninhabited if it is normally used as a residence, even if the tenants are absent at the time of the burning, State v. Gulley, 46 N.C. App. 822 (1980); the proper charge in such a case is second-degree arson.

"Building" means a structure or other erection built by humans that is designed to stand more or less permanently and can shelter humans or serve some other useful purpose. State v. Cuthrell, 235 N.C. 173 (1952). If a building is still under construction, "Burning a Building under Construction," discussed below, is the proper charge. For this offense, "outhouse" does not mean an outdoor toilet facility (which is more precisely called a "privy"); instead, it means a building within the curtilage of a dwelling that is used for storage or other purposes. Thus, all privies are outhouses, but all outhouses are not privies. State v. Woods, 109 N.C. App. 360 (1993).

A building, structure, or erection is "used in carrying on any trade or manufacture" when it is put to its intended purpose for any ordinary occupation or business, whether manual or mercantile, even if the building is used that way only once. *Cuthrell*, 235 N.C. 173. The use need not be habitual in order to satisfy Element (3). The statute also covers buildings intended for use in trade or manufacture and any farm buildings not covered by the arson statute, including tobacco barns. State v. Vickers, 306 N.C. 90 (1982).

Burning by possessor. The statute covers burnings by the possessor of the building or by someone else. G.S. 14-62.

Greater and lesser-included offenses. This offense is not a lesser-included offense of arson. State v. Britt, 132 N.C. App. 173 (1999).

Related Offenses Not in This Chapter

See the offenses listed under "First-Degree Arson," above.

Burning a Church or Other Religious Building

Statute

§14-62.2. Burning of churches and certain other religious buildings.

If any person shall wantonly and willfully set fire to or burn or cause to be burned, or aid, counsel or procure the burning of any church, chapel, or meetinghouse, the person shall be punished as a Class E felon.

Elements

A person guilty of this offense

(1) wantonly and willfully
(2) sets fire to, burns, causes to be burned, or aids, counsels, or procures the burning of
(3) a church, chapel, or meetinghouse.

Punishment

Class E felony. G.S. 14-62.2.

Notes

Element (1). See "Wantonly" and "Willfully" in Chapter 1 (States of Mind).

Element (2). See the note on Element (2) to "Burning a Public Building," above.

Related Offenses Not in This Chapter

See the offenses listed under "First-Degree Arson," above.
"Breaking or Entering a Place of Worship" (Chapter 15)

Burning a Building under Construction

Statute

§14-62.1. Burning of building or structure in process of construction.

If any person shall wantonly and willfully set fire to or burn or cause to be burned, or aid, counsel or procure the burning of, any building or structure in the process of construction for use or intended to be used as a dwelling house or in carrying on any trade or manufacture, or otherwise, whether the same or any of them respectively shall then be in the possession of the offender, or in the possession of any other person, he shall be punished as a Class H felon.

Elements

A person guilty of this offense

(1) wantonly and willfully
(2) sets fire to, burns, causes to be burned, or aids, counsels, or procures the burning of
(3) a building or structure in the process of construction
(4) that is intended for use as a dwelling house or in carrying on a trade or business.

Punishment

Class H felony. G.S. 14-62.1.

Notes

Element (1). See "Wantonly" and "Willfully" in Chapter 1 (States of Mind).

Element (2). See the note on Element (2) to "Burning a Public Building," above.

Element (3). This statute includes structures that would become buildings used as dwellings or for business but which are not yet completed. Note that G.S. 14-58.1 defines mobile homes, manufactured-type houses, and recreational trailers as buildings; burning one of those buildings while it is under construction apparently would violate this statute.

Element (4). See the discussion of the definition of "dwelling" in the note on Element (3) to "First-Degree Arson," above; see the discussion of building "used in any trade or manufacture" in the note on Element (3) to "Burning an Uninhabited House, Factory, Store, etc.," above.

Burning by possessor. The statute covers burnings by either the possessor of the building or someone else. G.S. 14-62.1.

Related Offenses Not in This Chapter

See the offenses listed under "First-Degree Arson," above.

Burning a Boat, Barge, Ferry, or Float

Statute

§14-63. Burning of boats and barges.

If any person shall wantonly and willfully set fire to or burn or cause to be burned or aid, counsel or procure the burning of, any boat, barge, ferry or float, without the consent of the owner thereof, he shall be punished as a Class H felon. In the event the consent of the owner is given for an unlawful or fraudulent purpose, however, the penalty provisions of this section shall remain in full force and effect.

Elements

A person guilty of this offense

(1) wantonly and willfully
(2) sets fire to, burns, causes to be burned, or aids, counsels, or procures the burning of
(3) any boat, barge, ferry, or float
(4) (a) without the owner's consent *or*
    (b) with the owner's consent and done for a fraudulent purpose.

Punishment

Class H felony. G.S. 14-63.

Notes

Element (1). See "Wantonly" and "Willfully" in Chapter 1 (States of Mind).

Element (2). See the note on this Element to "Burning a Public Building," above.

Element (4). The fraudulent purpose could, for example, be collection of insurance. See the note on Element (1) to "Burning One's Own Dwelling House," below.

Relation to other offenses. The willful and malicious burning of a houseboat of another person that is used as a dwelling probably would constitute arson.

Related Offenses Not in This Chapter

See the offenses listed under "First-Degree Arson," above.
"Obtaining Property by False Pretenses" (Chapter 16)
"False Statement to Procure Insurance Benefits" (Chapter 16)

Burning One's Own Dwelling House

Statute

§14-65. Fraudulently setting fire to dwelling houses.

If any person, being the occupant of any building used as a dwelling house, whether such person be the owner thereof or not, or, being the owner of any building designed or intended as a dwelling house, shall wantonly and willfully or for a fraudulent purpose set fire to or burn or cause to be burned, or aid, counsel or procure the burning of such building, he shall be punished as a Class H felon.

Elements

A person guilty of this offense

(1) (a) wantonly and willfully *or*
    (b) for a fraudulent purpose
(2) sets fire to, burns, causes to be burned, or aids, counsels, or procures the burning of
(3) (a) a dwelling house occupied by the defendant, whether as owner or not, *or*
    (b) a building designed or intended for use as a dwelling and owned by the defendant.

Punishment

Class H felony. G.S. 14-65.

Notes

Element (1)(a). See "Wantonly" and "Willfully" in Chapter 1 (States of Mind). A person who burns his or her own home in circumstances that do not create a danger of injury or loss to others does not act wantonly. State v. Brackett, 306 N.C. 138 (1982).

Element (1)(b). The phrase "for a fraudulent purpose" describes a mental state of having the desire for illegal monetary gain, usually at the expense of the property's insurer. State v. White, 288 N.C. 44 (1975). There was sufficient evidence of a fraudulent purpose when the defendant burned his dwelling to conceal evidence of another crime. State v. Lassiter, 160 N.C. App. 443 (2003).

Element (2). See the note on Element (2) to "Burning a Public Building," above.

Element (3). See the definition of "dwelling house" in the note on Element (3) to "First-Degree Arson," above. Note that G.S. 14-58.1 includes mobile homes, manufactured-type houses, and recreational trailers under the definitions of "houses" and "buildings."

Related Offenses Not in This Chapter

See the offenses listed under "First-Degree Arson," above.
"False Statement to Procure Insurance Benefits" (Chapter 16)
"Obtaining Property by False Pretenses" (Chapter 16)

Burning a Structure Not Listed in Any Other Statute

Statute

§14-67.1. Burning other buildings.

If any person shall wantonly and willfully set fire to or burn or cause to be burned or aid, counsel or procure the burning of any building or other structure of any type not otherwise covered by the provisions of this Article, he shall be punished as a Class H felon.

Elements

A person guilty of this offense

(1) wantonly and willfully
(2) sets fire to, burns, causes to be burned, or aids, counsels, or procures the burning of
(3) any structure of any type not otherwise covered in an offense already listed in this chapter.

Punishment

Class H felony. G.S. 14-67.1.

Notes

Element (1). See "Wantonly" and "Willfully" in Chapter 1 (States of Mind).

Element (2). See the note on Element (2) to "Burning a Public Building," above.

Element (3). This statute covers any structure not covered in the other burning offenses, such as an uninhabited storage building on a farm. State v. McWhorter, 34 N.C. App. 462 (1977).

Related Offenses Not in This Chapter

See the offenses listed under "First-Degree Arson," above.

Burning Personal Property

Statute

§14-66. Burning of personal property.

If any person shall wantonly and willfully set fire to or burn, or cause to be burned, or aid, counsel or procure the burning of, any goods, wares, merchandise or other chattels or personal property of any kind, whether or not the same shall at the time be insured by any person or corporation against loss or damage by fire, with intent to injure or prejudice the insurer, the creditor or the person owning the property, or any other person, whether the property is that of such person or another, he shall be punished as a Class H felon.

Elements

A person guilty of this offense

(1) wantonly and willfully
(2) sets fire to, burns, causes to be burned, or aids, counsels, or procures the burning of
(3) any goods, wares, or personal property of any kind
(4) with intent to injure or prejudice the insurer, creditor, owner, or any other person.

Punishment

Class H felony. G.S. 14-66.

Notes

Element (1). See "Wantonly" and "Willfully" in Chapter 1 (States of Mind).

Element (2). See the note on Element (2) to "Burning a Public Building," above.

Element (3). G.S. 12-3(6) defines the term "personal property" as "moneys, goods, chattels, choses in action and evidences of debt, including all things capable of ownership, not descendable to heirs at law."

The burned property need not be insured before this offense can occur, G.S. 14-66, but the question of whether it is insured might be relevant to the defendant's intent under Element (4).

Element (4). This offense can be committed when a person burns his or her own property with the specific intent to injure or prejudice another, such as a creditor or lien holder. This intent may be inferred from circumstances such as the nature of the act and how it was done. State v. Jordan, 59 N.C. App. 527 (1982). The injury may be physical or financial.

Relation to other offenses. Burning personal property is not a lesser-included offense of burning a public building. State v. Pierce, 208 N.C. 47 (1935).

Related Offenses Not in This Chapter

See the offenses listed under "First-Degree Arson," above.
"False Statement to Procure Insurance Benefits" (Chapter 16)
"Fraudulent Disposal of a Security" (Chapter 16)
"Obtaining Property by False Pretenses" (Chapter 16)

Arson or Burning Resulting in Serious Injury to a Firefighter or EMT

Statute

§14-69.3. Arson or other unlawful burning that results in serious injury to a firefighter or emergency medical technician.

A person is guilty of a Class E felony if the person commits a felony under Article 15 of Chapter 14 of the General Statutes and a firefighter or emergency medical technician suffers serious bodily injury while discharging or attempting to discharge the firefighter's or emergency medical technician's duties on the property, or proximate to the property, that is the subject of the firefighter's or emergency medical technician's discharge or attempt to discharge his or her respective duties. As used in this section, the term "emergency medical technician" includes an emergency medical technician, an emergency medical technician-intermediate, and an emergency medical technician-paramedic, as those terms are defined in G.S. 131E-155.

Elements

A person guilty of this offense

(1) commits a felony burning offense included in G.S. Chapter 14, Article 15, *and*
(2) a firefighter or emergency medical technician
(3) suffers serious bodily injury
(4) while discharging or attempting to discharge his or her duties
(5) on or proximate to the property involved in the felony burning offense.

Punishment

Class E felony. G.S. 14-69.3.

Notes

Element (1). Article 15 includes G.S. 14-58 through 14-69.3.

Element (2). The term "emergency medical technician" means an emergency medical technician, an emergency medical technician-intermediate, and an emergency medical technician-paramedic as those terms are defined in G.S. 131E-155. G.S. 14-69.3.

Element (3). The statute does not define "serious bodily injury." For a discussion of that term as it is used in the assault context, see the note on Element (3) to "Assault Inflicting Serious Bodily Injury" in Chapter 7 (Assaults).

Related Offenses Not in This Chapter

See the offenses in Chapter 7 (Assaults).

Setting Fire Offenses

Setting Fire to Woods and Fields

Statute

§14-137. Willfully or negligently setting fire to woods and fields.

If any person, firm or corporation shall willfully or negligently set on fire, or cause to be set on fire, any woods, lands or fields, whatsoever, every such offender shall be guilty of a Class 2 misdemeanor. This section shall apply only in those counties under the protection of the Department of Environment and Natural Resources in its work of forest fire control. It shall not apply in the case of a landowner firing, or causing to be fired, his own open, nonwooded lands, or fields in connection with farming or building operations at the time and in the manner now provided by law: Provided, he shall have confined the fire at his own expense to said open lands or fields.

Elements

A person guilty of this offense

(1) willfully or negligently
(2) sets on fire or causes to be set on fire
(3) any woods, land, or fields
(4) in any county that is under the protection of the Department of Environment and Natural Resources in its work of forest fire control.

Punishment

Class 2 misdemeanor. G.S. 14-137.

Notes

Element (1). See "Willfully" and "Negligently" in Chapter 1 (States of Mind).

Exceptions. This offense applies only in those counties under the protection of the Department of Environment and Natural Resources in its work of forest fire control. G.S. 14-137. Also, it does not apply to a landowner firing, or causing to be fired, his or her own open, nonwooded lands or fields in connection with farming or building operations, so long as the firing is done in compliance with other law and provided that the landowner has confined the fire at his or her own expense. *Id.*

Related Offenses Not in This Chapter

See the offenses in Chapter 18 (Trespass, Property Damage, and Littering).
"Malicious Damage by Use of Explosives or Incendiaries" (Chapter 20)
Cutting, injuring, or removing another's timber. G.S. 14-135.
Setting fire to grassland, brushland, or woodland. G.S. 14-138.1.
Certain fire to be guarded by watchman. G.S. 14-140.1.
Burning or otherwise destroying crops in the field. G.S. 14-141.

Intentionally Setting Fire to Grass, Brushlands, or Woodlands

Statute

§14-136. Setting fire to grass and brushlands and woodlands.

If any person shall intentionally set fire to grassland, brushland or woodland, except it be his own property, or in that case without first giving notice to all persons owning or in charge of lands adjoining the land intended to be fired, and without also taking care to watch such fire while burning and to extinguish it before it shall reach any lands near to or adjoining the lands so fired, he shall for every such offense be guilty of a Class 2 misdemeanor for the first offense, and for a second or any subsequent similar offense shall be guilty of a Class 1 misdemeanor. If intent to damage the property of another shall be shown, said person shall be punished as a Class I felon. This section shall not prevent an action for the damages sustained by the owner of any property from such fires. For the purposes of this section, the term "woodland" is to be taken to include all forest areas, both timber and cutover land, and all second-growth stands on areas that have at one time been cultivated. Any person who shall furnish to the State, evidence sufficient for the conviction of a violation of this section shall receive the sum of five hundred dollars ($500.00) to be paid from the State Fire Suppression Fund.

Elements

A person is guilty of this offense if he or she

(1) intentionally
(2) sets fire to
(3) any grassland, brushland, or woodland
(4) (a) of another *or*
  (b) owned by the person if the person fails to
    (i) notify adjacent property owners *or*
    (ii) watch the fire and ensure that it does not damage adjoining lands.

Punishment

The first offense is a Class 2 misdemeanor; a second or subsequent offense is a Class 1 misdemeanor. G.S. 14-136. If the Class 1 misdemeanor version is charged, the relevant fact elevating punishment must be alleged in a charging instrument and proved at trial. *See* G.S. 15A-928 (pleading and proving prior convictions).

Notes

Element (1). See "Intentionally" in Chapter 1 (States of Mind).

If the defendant burns his or her own land out of necessity (that is, to save a portion of the person's land from an approaching fire), the burning is not voluntary and thus does not constitute this offense. Tyson v. Rasberry, 8 N.C. 60 (1820). See generally "Necessity and Duress" in Chapter 2 (Bars and Defenses).

Element (2). For a discussion of the phrase "sets fire to," see the note on Element (2) to "Burning a Public Building," above.

Element (3). "Woodlands" means all forest areas, both timber and cutover areas, and all second-growth stands on previously cultivated areas. G.S. 14-136.

Element (4)(a). For a discussion of this phrase as used for arson, see the note on Element (4) to "First-Degree Arson," above.

Element (4)(b). An owner of property may be prosecuted under this statute for burning his or her own property if the owner (1) fails to notify adjoining landowners or those in charge of adjacent land about the burning; or (2) fails to watch the fire and extinguish it before it reaches the land of another. If the owner fails to do either of these things, he or she has violated this statute. Lamb v. Sloan, 94 N.C. 534 (1886).

Civil suits. Besides being tried under this statute, a defendant may be sued by a property owner whose land was damaged by the fire. G.S. 14-136.

Reward. The state gives a $500 reward to anyone who provides enough evidence to convict a defendant under this statute. G.S. 14-136.

Related Offenses Not in This Chapter

See the offenses listed under "Setting Fire to Woods and Fields," above.

Setting Fire to Grass, Brushlands, or Woodlands with Intent to Damage Property

Statute

See G.S. 14-136, reproduced under "Intentionally Setting Fire to Grass, Brushlands, or Woodlands," above.

Elements

A person guilty of this offense

(1) sets fire to
(2) the grassland, brushland, or woodland
(3) of another
(4) with willful or malicious intent
(5) to damage the property.

Punishment

Class I felony. G.S. 14-136.

Notes

Element (1). See the note on Element (2) to "Intentionally Setting Fire to Grass, Brushlands, or Woodlands," above.

Element (2). See the note on Element (3) to "Intentionally Setting Fire to Grass, Brushlands, or Woodlands," above.

Element (3). For a discussion of this phrase as used for arson, see the note on Element (4) to "First-Degree Arson," above.

Element (4). See "Willfully" and "Maliciously" in Chapter 1 (States of Mind).

Civil suits. See this note to "Intentionally Setting Fire to Grass, Brushlands, or Woodlands," above.

Reward. See this note to "Intentionally Setting Fire to Grass, Brushlands, or Woodlands," above.

Related Offenses Not in This Chapter

See the offenses listed under "Setting Fire to Woods and Fields," above.

18 Trespass, Property Damage, and Littering

18

Trespass, Property Damage, and Littering

Trespass Offenses

First-Degree Trespass

Statute

§14-159.12. First degree trespass.

(a) Offense.—A person commits the offense of first degree trespass if, without authorization, he enters or remains:

(1) On premises of another so enclosed or secured as to demonstrate clearly an intent to keep out intruders; or

(2) In a building of another.

(b) Classification.—First degree trespass is a Class 2 misdemeanor.

Elements

A person guilty of this offense

(1) without authorization
(2) (a) enters *or*
 (b) remains
(3) (a) on premises of another so enclosed or secured as to demonstrate clearly an intent to keep out intruders *or*
 (b) in a building of another.

Punishment

Class 2 misdemeanor. G.S. 14-159.12(b).

Notes

Element (1). "Without authorization" probably means the same as "without consent," the term used in breaking or entering offenses. See Element (3) to "Felony Breaking or Entering of a Building" in Chapter 15 (Burglary, Breaking or Entering, and Related Offenses). A person in lawful possession of premises or a building may exclude a person for any reason, State v. Clyburn, 247 N.C. 455, 458 (1958), except one that rests on a basis prohibited by law (such as race).

Unless a tenant's lease denies the tenant the authority to extend invitations, a guest who enters premises at the invitation of the tenant is not guilty of trespass, even if the landlord has told the guest not to enter. State v. Lawson, 101 N.C. 717 (1888).

Element (2). See the note on Element (2) to "First-Degree Burglary" in Chapter 15 (Burglary, Breaking or Entering, and Related Offenses) for the definition of "enters." To "remain" means to stay. WEBSTER'S II NEW COLLEGE DICTIONARY 937 (1999). If a homeowner tells a guest to leave the homeowner's residence and the guest refuses to do so, the guest has committed this offense by remaining in the residence without authorization.

Element (3)(a). The premises include the entire piece of real estate—not just the building but the land as well, provided it is so enclosed or secured as to clearly demonstrate an intent to keep intruders out. A locked six-foot-high chain link fence, for example, is likely to demonstrate such an intent.

Element (3)(b). G.S. 14-159.11 defines a "building" as "any structure or part of a structure, other than a conveyance, enclosed so as to permit reasonable entry only through a door and roofed to protect it from the elements." The building may be a residence, business, or have some other purpose, provided that it meets the definition in G.S. 14-159.11.

Defenses. It is an affirmative defense to trespass that a defendant entered with reasonable grounds to believe in a legal right to enter, even though the defendant did not actually have such a right. State v. Baker, 231 N.C. 136 (1949); State v. Faggart, 170 N.C. 737 (1915).

Spouse forbidding entry to spouse. Applying the law of trespass in domestic disputes can be difficult because of the problem of determining ownership or custody of the property. In these situations, the offense of "Domestic Criminal Trespass," discussed below, usually will be the more appropriate charge.

Free speech on shopping mall property. A defendant was properly convicted of trespass when he refused to leave the parking lot of a shopping mall after being asked to stop soliciting signatures against the draft. State v. Felmet, 302 N.C. 173 (1981). The mall parking lot was private property, and it had not been dedicated to public use in a way that would guarantee rights to free speech under federal or state constitutions. *Id.*

Greater and lesser-included offenses. G.S. 14-159.14 provides that first- and second-degree trespass are lesser-included offenses of the breaking or entering offenses set out in G.S. 14-54 and 14-56, discussed in Chapter 15 (Burglary, Breaking or Entering, and Related Offenses). *See also* State v. Owens, ___ N.C. App. ___, 695 S.E.2d 823, 828 (2010) (first-degree trespass is a lesser-included offense of felony breaking or entering).

Relation to other offenses. When a defendant commits this offense by entering without authorization, this offense overlaps with "Misdemeanor Breaking or Entering of a Building," discussed in Chapter 15 (Burglary, Breaking or Entering, and Related Offenses).

A handful of counties recognize the offense of third-degree trespass. A person commits this offense if, without authorization, the person enters or remains on the premises of another for the purpose of hunting, fishing, trapping, loitering, or operating an all-terrain vehicle. This offense is a Class 3 misdemeanor. The land need not be posted or securely enclosed for this offense to apply, nor does a person need to be warned to stay off the property. This offense is uncodified (that is, it has not been added to the General Statutes). See 1991 N.C. Sess. Laws 816 and 862 and 1993 N.C. Sess. Laws 593 and 659 for certain covered counties. The Class 2 misdemeanor of trespass for purposes of hunting, etc., is listed under "Related Offenses Not in This Chapter," immediately below.

Related Offenses Not in This Chapter

"Stalking" (Chapter 8)
"Misdemeanor Breaking or Entering of a Building" (Chapter 15)
"Picketing a Courthouse" (Chapter 21)
Being found in a building with intent to commit any felony or larceny. G.S. 14-55.

Taking, etc., of certain wild plants from land of another. G.S. 14-129.
Trespass on public lands. G.S. 14-130.
Trespass on land under option by the federal government. G.S. 14-131.
Willfully trespassing upon, damaging, or impeding the progress of a public school bus. G.S. 14-132.2.
Operating motor vehicle on utility easements after being forbidden to do so. G.S. 14-134.2.
Unlawful posting of advertisements. G.S. 14-145.
Injuring buildings or fences; taking possession of house without consent. G.S. 14-159.
Interference with animal research. G.S. 14-159.2.
Trespass to land on motorized all terrain vehicle. G.S. 14-159.3.
Trespassing for purposes of hunting, etc., without written consent a misdemeanor (including trespass to remove pine needles or straw). G.S. 14-159.6.
Obstruction of health care facilities. G.S. 14-277.4.
Trespassing on railroad right-of-way. G.S. 14-280.1.
Looting; trespass during an emergency. G.S. 14-288.6.
Disturbing human remains. G.S. 14-401.22.
Airport obstructions illegal. G.S. 63-37.1.
Violation of Department of Agriculture and Consumer Services rules regulating public use of lands and waters. G.S. 106-847.
Removing political signs. G.S. 136-32(e).

Second-Degree Trespass

Statute

§14-159.13. Second degree trespass.

(a) Offense.—A person commits the offense of second degree trespass if, without authorization, he enters or remains on premises of another:

(1) After he has been notified not to enter or remain there by the owner, by a person in charge of the premises, by a lawful occupant, or by another authorized person; or

(2) That are posted, in a manner reasonably likely to come to the attention of intruders, with notice not to enter the premises.

(b) Classification.—Second degree trespass is a Class 3 misdemeanor.

Elements

A person guilty of this offense

(1) without authorization
(2) (a) enters *or*
  (b) remains
(3) on premises of another
(4) (a) after having been notified not to enter or remain there by the owner, a person in charge of the premises, a lawful occupant, or another authorized person *or*
  (b) that are posted in a manner reasonably likely to come to the attention of intruders, with notice not to enter the premises.

Punishment

Class 3 misdemeanor. G.S. 14-159.13(b).

Notes

Generally. With the exception of the notes on Elements (3)(a) and (3)(b), all of the notes to "First-Degree Trespass," above, apply here as well.

Element (3). "Premises" include the entire piece of real estate—not just the building, but the land as well. With this offense, and unlike with first-degree trespass, the premises need not be enclosed so as to demonstrate an intent to keep intruders out. Thus, premises for this offense would include, for example, an unfenced front yard.

Element (4)(a). This element would be satisfied if a homeowner tells a defendant to leave the homeowner's front yard and the defendant refuses, or if a homeowner tells a defendant never to come back onto the homeowner's property but the defendant re-enters the property. However, if the unauthorized entering or remaining occurs in a building, first-degree trespass should be charged.

"Another authorized person" could include the owner's agent, such as a security guard.

The defendants committed trespass when they refused to leave the publicly accessible lobby of a private building after being ordered to leave and when they did not have a legitimate purpose to be there. State v. Marcoplos, 154 N.C. App. 581 (2002).

Element (4)(b). This element may be satisfied by posting "No trespassing" or similar signs in a manner reasonably likely to come to an intruder's attention. Proof that the intruder actually saw the signs is not required.

A sign reading "Girl's Locker Room" on a school locker room door was reasonably likely to give the male juvenile respondent notice that he was not authorized to be in the room. *In re* S.M.S., 196 N.C. App. 170, 172–73 (2009).

Related Offenses Not in This Chapter

See the related offenses under "First-Degree Trespass," above.

Domestic Criminal Trespass

Statute

§14-134.3. Domestic criminal trespass.

(a) Any person who enters after being forbidden to do so or remains after being ordered to leave by the lawful occupant, upon the premises occupied by a present or former spouse or by a person with whom the person charged has lived as if married, shall be guilty of a misdemeanor if the complainant and the person charged are living apart; provided, however, that no person shall be guilty if said person enters upon the premises pursuant to a judicial order or written separation agreement which gives the person the right to enter upon said premises for the purpose of visiting with minor children. Evidence that the parties are living apart shall include but is not necessarily limited to:

(1) A judicial order of separation;

(2) A court order directing the person charged to stay away from the premises occupied by the complainant;

(3) An agreement, whether verbal or written, between the complainant and the person charged that they shall live separate and apart, and such parties are in fact living separate and apart; or

(4) Separate places of residence for the complainant and the person charged.

Except as provided in subsection (b) of this section, upon conviction, said person is guilty of a Class 1 misdemeanor.

(b) A person convicted of a violation of this section is guilty of a Class G felony if the person is trespassing upon property operated as a safe house or haven for victims of domestic violence and the person is armed with a deadly weapon at the time of the offense.

Elements

A person guilty of this offense,

(1) (a) after having been forbidden to enter *or*

(b) after having been ordered to leave
(2) by a lawful occupant,
(3) (a) enters *or*
(b) refuses to leave
(4) the premises occupied by
(a) the charged person's present or former spouse *or*
(b) another person with whom the charged person has lived as if married
(5) at a time when the charged person and the present or former spouse or person with whom the charged person has lived as if married are living apart.

Punishment

Class 1 misdemeanor. G.S. 14-134.3(a). However, it is a Class G felony if the person trespassed on property operated as a safe house or haven for victims of domestic violence and the person was armed with a deadly weapon at the time of the offense. G.S. 14-134.3(b). If the felony version of this offense is charged, the relevant facts elevating punishment must be alleged in the charging instrument and proved at trial.

Notes

Element (2). The lawful occupant apparently may be someone other than the present or former spouse or person with whom the defendant has lived as if married; for example, the lawful occupant could be the new spouse or partner of the former spouse.

Element (4). The statute requires the premises to be "occupied" by the former or present spouse or person with whom the defendant has lived as if married.

Element (5). The following evidence may be used to prove that the parties are living apart:

- a judicial order of separation,
- a court order directing the defendant to stay away from the complainant's premises,
- an agreement (written or oral) between the parties that they will live apart, and
- the fact that the parties have separate residences.

G.S. 14-134.3(a).

Exceptions. A person who enters the premises pursuant to a judicial order or written separation agreement that allows the person entry to visit his or her children may not be convicted of this offense for that entry. G.S. 14-134.3(a). Presumably, if the person entered at a time not authorized by the order or agreement, he or she could commit this offense if all other elements are satisfied.

Relation to other offenses. In situations involving spouses, former spouses, and parties who have been living together as if married, it may be difficult to establish the accused trespasser's lack of legal authority to be present on the property—a necessary element of both first- and second-degree trespass. Consequently, this may be a more appropriate charge in such situations.

Related Offenses Not in This Chapter

"Simple Assault" (Chapter 7)
"Communicating Threats" (Chapter 8)
"Stalking" (Chapter 8)
See violation of a domestic violence protective order (various offenses) in Chapter 8 (Threats, Harassment, Stalking, and Violation of Domestic Protective Orders).
Purchase or possession of firearms by person subject to domestic violence order prohibited. G.S. 14-269.8.

Forcible Trespass

Statute

This is a common law offense. State v. Bates, 70 N.C. App. 477, 480 (1984); David J. Sharpe, *Forcible Trespass to Real Property*, 39 N.C. L. Rev. 121 (1960–61).

Elements

A person guilty of this offense

(1) (a) makes an unpermitted and unlawful entry on premises *or*
 (b) willfully refuses to leave the premises after being ordered to do so
(2) (a) using force against the occupant,
 (b) threatening to use force, *or*
 (c) appearing so as to inspire fear
(3) when the occupant is present on the premises *and*
(4) is in peaceful possession of the premises.

Punishment

Class 1 misdemeanor. G.S. 14-3(a). See the heading "Offense Class" under "Misdemeanors" in Chapter 4 (Punishment under Structured Sentencing).

Notes

Element (1)(b). Even if the defendant originally gains entry peaceably, he or she can commit this offense by later refusing to leave. State v. Wilson, 94 N.C. 839 (1886); State v. Buckner, 61 N.C. 558 (1868).

Element (2). Mere entry unaccompanied by a show of force normally does not satisfy this element. State v. Leary, 136 N.C. 578 (1904). Thus, the entry must be one that could or does cause a breach of the peace. State v. Blackmon, 36 N.C. App. 207 (1978). Appearing with weapons or a multitude of people may be sufficient to satisfy Element 2(b) or (c). State v. Covington, 70 N.C. 71 (1874). In one case it was held that the peaceful entry into property and staging of a sit-in by a multitude of people was sufficient to constitute the required force when the lawful occupant had to yield possession in order to avoid a breach of the peace. State v. Birkhead, 48 N.C. App. 575 (1980).

Element (3). If the premises are unoccupied when the trespass takes place, this element is not satisfied, State v. Laney, 87 N.C. 535 (1882), unless the occupant appears while the trespasser is still present, State v. Woodward, 119 N.C. 836 (1896).

Element (4). "Peaceful possession" means that the person present has occupied the premises for some time without the use of force; it does not require that the person must have title or a lease to the premises. State v. Fender, 125 N.C. 649 (1899).

Relation to other offenses. See this note under "First-Degree Trespass," above.

Related Offenses Not in This Chapter

See the offenses listed under "First-Degree Trespass," above.
"Simple Assault" (Chapter 7)
Assault on executive, legislative, or court officer (covering violent attacks on residence, office, means of transport, etc.). G.S. 14-16.6.

Injury to Property Offenses

Injury to Real Property

Statute

§14-127. Willful and wanton injury to real property.

If any person shall willfully and wantonly damage, injure or destroy any real property whatsoever, either of a public or private nature, he shall be guilty of a Class 1 misdemeanor.

Elements

A person guilty of this offense

(1) willfully and wantonly
(2) damages, injures, or destroys
(3) the real property of another.

Punishment

Class 1 misdemeanor. G.S. 14-127.

Notes

Element (1). See "Willfully" and "Wantonly" in Chapter 1 (States of Mind).

Element (3). G.S. 12-3(6) provides that the words "real property" are "coextensive with lands, tenements and hereditaments." For purposes of this statute, real property is land and anything affixed to it or a part of it, such as buildings, fences, water, growing things, and minerals in the ground. The real property may be publicly or privately owned. G.S. 14-127.

Charging issues. In *State v. Lilly*, 195 N.C. App. 697, 700–03 (2009), the court held that there was no fatal variance between an indictment charging injury to real property and the evidence at trial when the indictment incorrectly described the lessee of the real property as its owner; the indictment was sufficient because it identified the lawful possessor of the property.

Relation to other offenses. See this note to "First-Degree Trespass," above.

Related Offenses Not in This Chapter

"Ethnic Intimidation" (Chapter 7)
See the offenses in Chapter 17 (Arson and Burning Offenses).
"Picketing a Courthouse" (Chapter 21)
Assault on executive, legislative, or court officer (covering violent attacks on residence, office, means of transport, etc.). G.S. 14-16.6.
Larceny of ungathered crops. G.S. 14-78.
Larceny of ginseng. G.S. 14-79.
Larceny, destruction, defacement or vandalism of portable toilets or pumper trucks. G.S. 14-86.2.
Injury to trees, crops, lands, etc., of another. G.S. 14-128.
Taking, etc., of certain wild plants from land of another. G.S. 14-129.
Cutting, injuring, or removing another's timber. G.S. 14-135.
Setting fire to grassland, brushland, or woodland (without extinguishing). G.S. 14-138.1.
Certain fire to be guarded by watchman (failure to watch fire). G.S. 14-140.1.
Burning or otherwise destroying crops in the field. G.S. 14-141.
Injuries to dams and water channels of mills and factories. G.S. 14-142.
Injuring houses, churches, fences and walls. G.S. 14-144.
Injuring bridges. G.S. 14-146.
Removing, altering or defacing landmarks. G.S. 14-147.
Defacing or desecrating grave sites. G.S. 14-148.

Desecrating, plowing over or covering up graves; desecrating human remains. G.S. 14-149.
Interfering with electric, gas or water meters. G.S. 14-151.1.
Injuring fixtures and other property of gas companies. G.S. 14-152.
Injuring wires and fixtures of utility companies. G.S. 14-154, 14-156, and 14-158.
Injuring buildings or fences; taking possession of house without consent. G.S. 14-159.
Contaminating a public water system. G.S. 14-159.1.
Interference with animal research. G.S. 14-159.2.
Poisoning livestock. G.S. 14-163.
Willful injury to property of railroads. G.S. 14-278.
Unlawful injury to property of railroads. G.S. 14-279.
Looting; trespass during an emergency. G.S. 14-288.6.
Disturbing human remains. G.S. 14-401.22.
Robbing or injuring hatcheries and other aquaculture operations. G.S. 113-269.
Violation of Department of Agriculture and Consumer Services rules regarding public use of lands and waters. G.S. 106-847.

Defacing a Public Building, Statue, or Monument

Statute

§14-132. Disorderly conduct in and injuries to public buildings and facilities.

(a) It is a misdemeanor if any person shall:

(1) Make any rude or riotous noise, or be guilty of any disorderly conduct, in or near any public building or facility; or

(2) Unlawfully write or scribble on, mark, deface, besmear, or injure the walls of any public building or facility, or any statue or monument situated in any public place; or

(3) Commit any nuisance in or near any public building or facility.

(b) Any person in charge of any public building or facility owned or controlled by the State, any subdivision of the State, or any other public agency shall have authority to arrest summarily and without warrant for a violation of this section.

(c) The term "public building or facility" as used in this section includes any building or facility which is:

(1) One to which the public or a portion of the public has access and is owned or controlled by the State, any subdivision of the State, any other public agency, or any private institution or agency of a charitable, educational, or eleemosynary nature; or

(2) Dedicated to the use of the general public for a purpose which is primarily concerned with public recreation, cultural activities, and other events of a public nature or character.

(3) Designated by the Attorney General in accordance with G.S. 114-20.1.

The term "building or facility" as used in this section also includes the surrounding grounds and premises of any building or facility used in connection with the operation or functioning of such building or facility.

(d) Any person who violates any provision of this section is guilty of a Class 2 misdemeanor.

Elements

A person guilty of this offense

(1) writes on, marks, defaces, or injures

(2) the walls of any public building or facility or statue or monument in a public place.

Punishment

Class 2 misdemeanor. G.S. 14-132(d).

Notes

Element (2). The term "public building or facility" means a building or facility:

- to which the public or a portion of the public has access and that is owned or controlled by the state or its subdivisions, any other public agency, or any private institution or agency of a charitable, educational, or eleemosynary nature;
- that is dedicated to the use of the general public for a purpose primarily concerned with public recreation, cultural activities, and other events of a public nature or character; or
- that has been designated by the Attorney General in accordance with G.S. 114-20.1.

G.S. 14-132(c). The term also includes the surrounding grounds and premises of any building or facility used in connection with the operation or functioning of such building or facility. *Id.*

Arrest authority. G.S. 14-132(b) provides that anyone in charge of any public building or facility owned or controlled by the state or its subdivisions or any other public agency has authority to arrest summarily and without warrant for a violation of the statute.

Related Offenses Not in This Chapter

"Disorderly Conduct in a Public Building" (Chapter 19)
"Picketing a Courthouse" (Chapter 21)
Assault on executive, legislative, or court officer (covering violent attacks on residence, office, means of transport, etc.). G.S. 14-16.6.
Removing, altering, or defacing landmarks. G.S. 14-147.
Looting; trespass during emergency. G.S. 14-288.6.

Injury to Personal Property

Statute

§14-160. Willful and wanton injury to personal property; punishments.

(a) If any person shall wantonly and willfully injure the personal property of another he shall be guilty of a Class 2 misdemeanor.

(b) Notwithstanding the provisions of subsection (a), if any person shall wantonly and willfully injure the personal property of another, causing damage in an amount in excess of two hundred dollars ($200.00), he shall be guilty of a Class 1 misdemeanor.

(c) This section applies to injuries to personal property without regard to whether the property is destroyed or not.

Elements

A person guilty of this offense

(1) willfully and wantonly
(2) injures
(3) the personal property of another.

Punishment

If the damage is more than $200, the offense is a Class 1 misdemeanor. G.S. 14-160(b). If the damage is not more than $200, the offense is a Class 2 misdemeanor. G.S. 14-160(a). If the Class 1 misdemeanor version is charged, the relevant fact elevating punishment must be alleged in the charging instrument and proved at trial.

Notes

Element (1). See "Willfully" and "Wantonly" in Chapter 1 (States of Mind). It need not be proved that the defendant acted with malice. State v. Casey, 60 N.C. App. 414 (1983).

Element (2). Property need not be destroyed in order for a violation to occur. G.S. 14-160(c).

Element (3). The statute fails to define the term "personal property." However, G.S. 12-3(6) defines such property as "moneys, goods, chattels, choses in action and evidence of debt, including all things capable of ownership, not descendable [sic] to heirs at law." For an explanation of the term "choses in action" as that term applies in the context of larceny, see the note on Element (2) to "Larceny of a Chose in Action" in Chapter 13 (Larceny, Possession of Stolen Goods, Embezzlement, and Related Offenses).

Amount of damage. The extent of the damages is determined by the differential in market value just before and just after the injury. U.S. Fid. & Guar. Co. v. P. & F. Motor Express, 220 N.C. 721 (1942). In the absence of an established market value, the measure is the cost of repair. Carolina Power & Light Co. v. Paul, 261 N.C. 710 (1964).

Charging issues. For a discussion of charging issues in connection with this crime, see Jessica Smith, *The Criminal Indictment: Fatal Defect, Fatal Variance, and Amendment*, ADMIN. OF JUSTICE BULL. No. 2008/03 (UNC School of Government, July 2008) (online at www.sog.unc.edu/pubs/electronicversions/pdfs/aojb0803.pdf).

Related Offenses Not in This Chapter

See the offenses under "Injury to Real Property," above.
"Altering or Removing a Serial Number" (Chapter 13)
"Altering, etc. of a Firearm's Serial Number" and "Buying, Selling, or Possessing a Firearm with an Altered Serial Number" (Chapter 22)
Assault on executive, legislative, or court officer (covering violent attacks on residence, office, means of transport, etc.). G.S. 14-16.6.
Malicious or willful injury to hired personal property. G.S. 14-165.
Looting; trespass during an emergency. G.S. 14-288.6.
Defacing or vandalizing political signs. G.S. 136-32(e).

Damage to Computer Offenses

Statute

§14-455. Damaging computers, computer programs, computer systems, computer networks, and resources.

(a) It is unlawful to willfully and without authorization alter, damage, or destroy a computer, computer program, computer system, computer network, or any part thereof. A violation of this subsection is a Class G felony if the damage caused by the alteration, damage, or destruction is more than one thousand dollars ($1,000). Any other violation of this subsection is a Class 1 misdemeanor.

(a1) It is unlawful to willfully and without authorization alter, damage, or destroy a government computer. A violation of this subsection is a Class F felony.

(b) This section applies to alteration, damage, or destruction effectuated by introducing, directly or indirectly, a computer program (including a self-replicating or a self-propagating computer program) into a computer, computer program, computer system, or computer network.

Damaging a Non-Government Computer

Statute

See G.S. 14-455(a), reproduced above.

Elements

A person guilty of this offense

(1) willfully *and*
(2) without authorization
(3) alters, damages, or destroys
(4) a computer, computer program, computer system, computer network, or any part thereof.

Punishment

Class 1 misdemeanor. G.S. 14-455(a). If the damage caused by the alteration, damage, or destruction is more than $1,000, the offense is a Class G felony. *Id.* If the Class G felony version of this offense is charged, the relevant amount of damage must be alleged in the charging instrument and proved at trial.

Notes

Element (1). See "Willfully" in Chapter 1 (States of Mind).

Element (2). "Authorization" means having the consent or permission of the owner of, or the person licensed or authorized by the owner to grant consent or permission to access, a computer, computer system, or computer network in a manner not exceeding the consent or permission. G.S. 14-453(1a).

Element (3). This offense includes damage caused by the introduction of software computer viruses. G.S. 14-455(b).

Element (4). A "computer" is an internally programmed automatic device that performs data processing or telephone switching. G.S. 14-453(2). A "computer program" is an ordered set of data that is comprised of coded instructions or statements which, when executed by a computer, cause the computer to process data. G.S. 14-453(4). A "computer system" is at least one computer together with a set of related, connected, or unconnected peripheral devices. G.S. 14-453(6). A "computer network" is the interconnection of communication systems with a computer through remote terminals or a complex consisting of two or more connected computers or telephone switching equipment. G.S. 14-453(3). "Any part thereof" likely includes stored data. "Data" is broadly defined to include all information, facts, knowledge, concepts, or instructions intended for use on computers, computer systems, and computer networks; it may be embodied in printouts, magnetic storage media, internal hardware storage, punch cards, or any other form. G.S. 14-453(6a).

Related Offenses Not in This Chapter

See cyberstalking (various offenses) in Chapter 8 (Threats, Harassment, Stalking, and Violation of Domestic Protective Orders).
"Cyberbullying" (Chapter 8)
See computer fraud (various offenses) in Chapter 8 (Threats, Harassment, Stalking, and Violation of Domestic Protective Orders).

Damaging a Government Computer

Statute

See G.S. 14-455(a1), reproduced above.

Elements

A person guilty of this offense

(1) willfully *and*
(2) without authorization
(3) alters, damages, or destroys
(4) a government computer.

Punishment

Class F felony. G.S. 14-455(a1).

Notes

Generally. This offense is the same as "Damaging a Non-Government Computer," above, except that this offense involves a government computer and carries a more severe punishment. Thus, the notes to that offense apply here as well.

Element (4). The term "government computer" is defined by G.S. 14-453(7a) to include any computer, computer program, computer system, computer network, or any part thereof that is owned, operated, or used by any state or local governmental entity.

Related Offenses Not in This Chapter

See the offenses listed under "Damaging a Non-Government Computer," above.

Littering

Statute

§14-399. Littering.

(a) No person, including any firm, organization, private corporation, or governing body, agents or employees of any municipal corporation shall intentionally or recklessly throw, scatter, spill or place or intentionally or recklessly cause to be blown, scattered, spilled, thrown or placed or otherwise dispose of any litter upon any public property or private property not owned by the person within this State or in the waters of this State including any public highway, public park, lake, river, ocean, beach, campground, forestland, recreational area, trailer park, highway, road, street or alley except:

(1) When the property is designated by the State or political subdivision thereof for the disposal of garbage and refuse, and the person is authorized to use the property for this purpose; or
(2) Into a litter receptacle in a manner that the litter will be prevented from being carried away or deposited by the elements upon any part of the private or public property or waters.

(a1) No person, including any firm, organization, private corporation, or governing body, agents, or employees of any municipal corporation shall scatter, spill, or place or cause to be blown, scattered, spilled, or placed or otherwise dispose of any litter upon any public property or private property not owned by the person within this State or in the waters of this State including any public highway, public park, lake, river, ocean, beach, campground, forestland, recreational area, trailer park, highway, road, street, or alley except:

(1) When the property is designated by the State or political subdivision thereof for the disposal of garbage and refuse, and the person is authorized to use the property for this purpose; or

(2) Into a litter receptacle in a manner that the litter will be prevented from being carried away or deposited by the elements upon any part of the private or public property or waters.

(a2) Subsection (a1) of this section does not apply to the accidental blowing, scattering, or spilling of an insignificant amount of municipal solid waste, as defined in G.S. 130A-290(18a), during the automated loading of a vehicle designed and constructed to transport municipal solid waste if the vehicle is operated in a reasonable manner and according to manufacturer specifications.

(b) When litter is blown, scattered, spilled, thrown or placed from a vehicle or watercraft, the operator thereof shall be presumed to have committed the offense. This presumption, however, does not apply to a vehicle transporting nontoxic and biodegradable agricultural or garden products or supplies, including mulch, tree bark, wood chips, and raw logs.

(c) Any person who violates subsection (a) of this section in an amount not exceeding 15 pounds and not for commercial purposes is guilty of a Class 3 misdemeanor punishable by a fine of not less than two hundred fifty dollars ($250.00) nor more than one thousand dollars ($1,000) for the first offense. In addition, the court may require the violator to perform community service of not less than eight hours nor more than 24 hours. The community service required shall be to pick up litter if feasible, and if not feasible, to perform other labor commensurate with the offense committed. Any second or subsequent violation of subsection (a) of this section in an amount not exceeding 15 pounds and not for commercial purposes within three years after the date of a prior violation is a Class 3 misdemeanor punishable by a fine of not less than five hundred dollars ($500.00) nor more than two thousand dollars ($2,000). In addition, the court may require the violator to perform community service of not less than 16 hours nor more than 50 hours. The community service required shall be to pick up litter if feasible, and if not feasible, to perform other labor commensurate with the offense committed.

(c1) Any person who violates subsection (a1) of this section in an amount not exceeding 15 pounds is guilty of an infraction punishable by a fine of not more than one hundred dollars ($100.00). In addition, the court may require the violator to perform community service of not less than four hours nor more than 12 hours. The community service required shall be to pick up litter if feasible, and if not feasible, to perform other labor commensurate with the offense committed. Any second or subsequent violation of subsection (a1) of this section in an amount not exceeding 15 pounds within three years after the date of a prior violation is an infraction punishable by a fine of not more than two hundred dollars ($200.00). In addition, the court may require the violator to perform community service of not less than eight hours nor more than 24 hours. The community service required shall be to pick up litter if feasible, and if not feasible, to perform other labor commensurate with the offense committed. For purposes of this subsection, the term "litter" shall not include nontoxic and biodegradable agricultural or garden products or supplies, including mulch, tree bark, and wood chips.

(d) Any person who violates subsection (a) of this section in an amount exceeding 15 pounds but not exceeding 500 pounds and not for commercial purposes is guilty of a Class 3 misdemeanor punishable by a fine of not less than five hundred dollars ($500.00) nor more than two thousand dollars ($2,000). In addition, the court shall require the violator to perform community service of not less than 24 hours nor more than 100 hours. The community service required shall be to pick up litter if feasible, and if not feasible, to perform other community service commensurate with the offense committed.

(d1) Any person who violates subsection (a1) of this section in an amount exceeding 15 pounds but not exceeding 500 pounds is guilty of an infraction punishable by a fine of not more than two hundred dollars ($200.00). In addition, the court may require the violator to perform community service of not less than eight hours nor more than 24 hours. The community service required shall be to pick up litter if feasible, and if not feasible, to perform other labor commensurate with the offense committed.

(e) Any person who violates subsection (a) of this section in an amount exceeding 500 pounds or in any quantity for commercial purposes, or who discards litter that is a hazardous waste as defined in G.S. 130A-290 is guilty of a Class I felony.

(e1) Any person who violates subsection (a1) of this section in an amount exceeding 500 pounds is guilty of an infraction punishable by a fine of not more than three hundred dollars ($300.00). In addition, the court may require the violator to perform community service of not less than 16 hours nor more than 50 hours. The community service required shall be to pick up litter if feasible, and if not feasible, to perform other labor commensurate with the offense committed.

(e2) If any person violates subsection (a) or (a1) of this section in an amount exceeding 15 pounds or in any quantity for commercial purposes, or discards litter that is a hazardous waste as defined in G.S. 130A-290, the court shall order the violator to:

(1) Remove, or render harmless, the litter that he discarded in violation of this section;
(2) Repair or restore property damaged by, or pay damages for any damage arising out of, his discarding litter in violation of this section; or
(3) Perform community public service relating to the removal of litter discarded in violation of this section or to the restoration of an area polluted by litter discarded in violation of this section.

(f) A court may enjoin a violation of this section.

(f1) If a violation of subsection (a) of this section involves the operation of a motor vehicle, upon a finding of guilt, the court shall forward a record of the finding to the Department of Transportation, Division of Motor Vehicles, which shall record a penalty of one point on the violator's drivers license pursuant to the point system established by G.S. 20-16. There shall be no insurance premium surcharge or assessment of points under the classification plan adopted under G.S. 58-36-65 for a finding of guilt under this section.

(g) A motor vehicle, vessel, aircraft, container, crane, winch, or machine involved in the disposal of more than 500 pounds of litter in violation of subsection (a) of this section is declared contraband and is subject to seizure and summary forfeiture to the State.

(h) If a person sustains damages arising out of a violation of subsection (a) of this section that is punishable as a felony, a court, in a civil action for the damages, shall order the person to pay the injured party threefold the actual damages or two hundred dollars ($200.00), whichever amount is greater. In addition, the court shall order the person to pay the injured party's court costs and attorney's fees.

(i) For the purpose of the section, unless the context requires otherwise:

(1) "Aircraft" means a motor vehicle or other vehicle that is used or designed to fly, but does not include a parachute or any other device used primarily as safety equipment.
(2) Repealed by Session Laws 1999-454, s. 1.
(2a) "Commercial purposes" means litter discarded by a business, corporation, association, partnership, sole proprietorship, or any other entity conducting business for economic gain, or by an employee or agent of the entity.
(3) "Law enforcement officer" means any law enforcement officer sworn and certified pursuant to Chapter 17C or 17E of the General Statutes, except company police officers as defined in G.S. 74E-6(b)(3). In addition, and solely for the purposes of this section, "law enforcement officer" means any employee of a county or municipality designated by the county or municipality as a litter enforcement officer.
(4) "Litter" means any garbage, rubbish, trash, refuse, can, bottle, box, container, wrapper, paper, paper product, tire, appliance, mechanical equipment or part, building or construction material, tool, machinery, wood, motor vehicle or motor vehicle part, vessel, aircraft, farm machinery or equipment, sludge from a waste treatment facility, water supply treatment plant, or air pollution control facility, dead animal, or discarded material in any form resulting from domestic, industrial, commercial, mining, agricultural, or governmental operations. While being used for or distributed

in accordance with their intended uses, "litter" does not include political pamphlets, handbills, religious tracts, newspapers, and other similar printed materials the unsolicited distribution of which is protected by the Constitution of the United States or the Constitution of North Carolina.

(5) "Vehicle" has the same meaning as in G.S. 20-4.01(49).

(6) "Watercraft" means any boat or vessel used for transportation across the water.

(j) It shall be the duty of all law enforcement officers to enforce the provisions of this section.

(k) This section does not limit the authority of any State or local agency to enforce other laws, rules or ordinances relating to litter or solid waste management.

Elements

A person guilty of this offense

(1) intentionally or recklessly
(2) (a) throws, scatters, spills, or places *or*
    (b) causes to be blown, scattered, spilled, thrown, placed, or disposed of
(3) litter
(4) on property not owned by the person, *and*
(5) the litter was not placed into a litter receptacle so that it would be prevented from being carried away or deposited by the elements on any part of the public or private property or waters, *and*
(6) the property has not been designated for the disposal of garbage and refuse by the state or a political subdivision.

Punishment

If the amount of litter is fifteen pounds or less and the littering is not for a commercial purpose, the offense is a Class 3 misdemeanor punishable by a fine of not less than $250 or more than $1,000. G.S. 14-399(c). For a second or subsequent offense within three years after the date of a prior offense, it is a Class 3 misdemeanor punishable by a fine of not less than $500 or more than $2,000. *Id.* At both offense levels, community service may be imposed. *Id.* If the amount of litter is more than fifteen pounds but not more than 500 pounds and the littering is not for a commercial purpose, it is a Class 3 misdemeanor punishable by a fine of not less than $500 or more than $2,000. G.S. 14-399(d). Community service must be imposed in this situation. *Id.* If the amount of litter is more than 500 pounds, the littering is for commercial purposes, or the littering involves hazardous waste (defined by G.S. 130A-290), it is a Class I felony. G.S. 14-399(e). If an elevated version of this offense is charged, the relevant facts elevating punishment must be alleged in a charging instrument and proved at trial. *See* G.S. 15A-928 (charging and proving prior convictions). "Commercial purposes" is defined in G.S. 14-399(i)(2a) as "litter discarded by a business, corporation, association, partnership, sole proprietorship, or any other entity conducting business for economic gain, or by an employee or agent of the entity." See G.S. 14-399(e1), (f), and (g), reproduced above, for additional obligations or consequences of littering. See the note below entitled "Infractions" for littering infractions.

Notes

Element (1). See "Intentionally" in Chapter 1 (States of Mind). Although not defined in the statute or by case law concerning this offense, "recklessly" probably means being careless and indifferent to consequences.

Element (3). "Litter" is defined in G.S. 14-399(i)(4), reproduced above.

Element (4). Public and private property is covered. G.S. 14-399(a). Covered property includes that within the state or in its waters, including a public highway, public park, lake, river, ocean, beach, campground, forestland, recreational area, trailer park, highway, road, street, or alley.

This offense does not apply when a person disposes of litter on property that he or she owns. G.S. 14-399(a).

Element (5). A private dumpster is a litter receptacle. State v. Hinkle, 189 N.C. App. 762, 767 (2008).

The provision in G.S. 14-399(a)(2)—that the litter was not placed into a litter receptacle—is not an exception but, rather, is an element of the crime that must be proved by the State. *Id.* at 768–69.

Element (6). The *Hinkle* decision mentioned in the note on Element (5) did not address whether the provision in G.S. 14-399(a)(1)—disposal on property designated by the state or a political subdivision for the disposal of garbage and refuse by a person authorized to use the property for this purpose—is an exception or an element of the offense. However, because such a ruling appears likely, this provision is listed as Element (6).

If the property has been so designated, the defendant can be guilty of littering only if he or she is not authorized to use the property for that purpose. G.S. 14-399(a)(1).

Presumption relating to operator of vehicle or watercraft. G.S. 14-399(b) provides that when "litter is blown, scattered, spilled, thrown or placed from a vehicle or watercraft, the operator thereof shall be presumed to have committed the offense. This presumption, however, does not apply to a vehicle transporting nontoxic and biodegradable agricultural or garden products or supplies, including mulch, tree bark, wood chips, and raw logs." Because of constitutional problems with a mandatory presumption in criminal cases, it is likely that this provision will be treated as a permissive presumption or inference. *See generally* State v. White, 300 N.C. 494 (1980); Cnty. Court of Ulster Cnty. v. Allen, 442 U.S. 140 (1979).

Forfeiture. G.S. 14-399(g) provides that a motor vehicle, vessel, aircraft, container, crane, winch, or machine involved in the unlawful disposal of more than 500 pounds of litter may be seized and forfeited to the state.

Infractions. If the littering does not involve intentional or reckless conduct, it may be punished as an infraction. G.S. 14-399(a1), (c1), (d1), and (e1). Thus, a person who inadvertently spills or scatters litter is guilty of an infraction unless he or she comes within one of the statute's listed exceptions—for example, the accidental spilling of an insignificant amount of municipal solid waste during garbage pickup. G.S. 14-399(a1) and (a2).

Injunctions. A court may enjoin violations of the littering statute. G.S. 14-399(f).

Civil action. G.S. 14-399(h) provides for the payment of damages in a civil action.

Related Offenses Not in This Chapter

Certain plastic yoke and ring type holding devices prohibited. G.S. 14-399.2.
Various offenses in G.S. Chapter 130A, Article 9 (Solid Waste Management).
Various offenses in G.S. Chapter 143, Article 21 (Water and Air Resources), Article 21A (Oil Pollution and Hazardous Substances Control), and Article 21B (Air Pollution Control).

19

Disorderly Conduct, Riot, and Gang Offenses

19 Disorderly Conduct, Riot, and Gang Offenses

Drunk and Disruptive

Statute

§14-444. Intoxicated and disruptive in public.

(a) It shall be unlawful for any person in a public place to be intoxicated and disruptive in any of the following ways:

(1) Blocking or otherwise interfering with traffic on a highway or public vehicular area, or

(2) Blocking or lying across or otherwise preventing or interfering with access to or passage across a sidewalk or entrance to a building, or

(3) Grabbing, shoving, pushing or fighting others or challenging others to fight, or

(4) Cursing or shouting at or otherwise rudely insulting others, or

(5) Begging for money or other property.

(b) Any person who violates this section shall be guilty of a Class 3 misdemeanor. Notwithstanding the provisions of G.S. 7A-273(1), a magistrate is not empowered to accept a guilty plea and enter judgment for this offense.

Elements

A person guilty of this offense

(1) is intoxicated

(2) in a public place *and*

(3) is disruptive by

(a) interfering with traffic on a highway or public vehicular area,

(b) interfering with access to or passage across a sidewalk,

(c) interfering with an entrance to any building,

(d) grabbing, shoving, or pushing others,

(e) fighting or challenging others to fight,

(f) cursing, shouting at, or rudely insulting others, *or*

(g) begging.

Punishment

Class 3 misdemeanor. G.S. 14-444(b).

Notes

Element (1). "Intoxicated" means "the condition of a person whose mental or physical functioning is presently substantially impaired as a result of the use of alcohol." G.S. 14-443(2). The intoxication must be from alcohol; being impaired by drugs does not satisfy this element.

Element (2). A "public place" is one that is open to the public, whether publicly or privately owned. G.S. 14-443(3).

Element (3)(a). For a discussion of the meaning of the phrase "public vehicular area," as used in the context of motor vehicle offenses, see the note on Element (3) to "Impaired Driving" in Chapter 28 (Motor Vehicle Offenses). For a discussion of the term "highway" in the same context, see the note on Element (3) to "Driving While License Revoked," also in Chapter 28.

Guilty pleas. Magistrates may not accept guilty pleas to this offense; the defendant must appear in district court. G.S. 14-444(b).

Defenses. The fact that the defendant is an alcoholic is a complete defense to this crime. G.S. 14-445(a). "Alcoholism" is "the state of a person who habitually lacks self-control as to the use of alcoholic beverages, or uses alcoholic beverages to the extent that his health is substantially impaired or endangered or his social or economic function is substantially disrupted." G.S. 14-443(1). This defense must be considered by the judge even if not raised by the defendant. G.S. 14-445(b). However, a defendant found not guilty by reason of alcoholism is subject to possible civil commitment. G.S. 14-446.

Public intoxication. For this offense to be committed, the defendant must be both intoxicated *and* disruptive. Prosecutions for public intoxication are prohibited, G.S. 14-447(a); thus, a local ordinance creating such a crime would be invalid.

Assistance without arrest. G.S. 122C-301 authorizes officers to assist a person who is intoxicated in public without making an arrest. Depending on the person's condition, the assistance may be to take the person home, to a detoxification center, or to a hospital or other medical facility. G.S. 122C-303. In certain circumstances, the intoxicated person may be taken to jail. *Id.* If that occurs, the person must be released as soon as he or she is sober but not more than twenty-four hours later; the person also may be released from the jail at any time to a relative or other individual willing to be responsible for his or her care. *Id.*

Related Offenses Not in This Chapter

See the offenses listed under "Disorderly Conduct by Fighting," below.
See the offenses in Chapter 7 (Assaults).
"Indecent Exposure" (Chapter 11)
"First-Degree Trespass" (Chapter 18)
"Second-Degree Trespass" (Chapter 18)
"Resisting, Delaying, or Obstructing an Officer" (Chapter 21)

Disorderly Conduct

Statute

§14-288.4. Disorderly conduct.

(a) Disorderly conduct is a public disturbance intentionally caused by any person who does any of the following:

(1) Engages in fighting or other violent conduct or in conduct creating the threat of imminent fighting or other violence.

(2) Makes or uses any utterance, gesture, display or abusive language which is intended and plainly likely to provoke violent retaliation and thereby cause a breach of the peace.

(3) Takes possession of, exercises control over, or seizes any building or facility of any public or private educational institution without the specific authority of the chief administrative officer of the institution, or his authorized representative.

(4) Refuses to vacate any building or facility of any public or private educational institution in obedience to any of the following:

a. An order of the chief administrative officer of the institution, or the officer's representative, who shall include for colleges and universities the vice chancellor for student affairs or the vice chancellor's equivalent for the institution, the dean of students or the dean's equivalent for the institution, the director of the law enforcement or security department for the institution, and the chief of the law enforcement or security department for the institution.

b. An order given by any fireman or public health officer acting within the scope of the fireman's or officer's authority.

c. If a state of emergency is occurring or is imminent within the institution, an order given by any law-enforcement officer acting within the scope of the officer's authority.

(5) Shall, after being forbidden to do so by the chief administrative officer, or the officer's authorized representative, of any public or private educational institution:

a. Engage in any sitting, kneeling, lying down, or inclining so as to obstruct the ingress or egress of any person entitled to the use of any building or facility of the institution in its normal and intended use; or

b. Congregate, assemble, form groups or formations (whether organized or not), block, or in any manner otherwise interfere with the operation or functioning of any building or facility of the institution so as to interfere with the customary or normal use of the building or facility.

(6) Disrupts, disturbs or interferes with the teaching of students at any public or private educational institution or engages in conduct which disturbs the peace, order or discipline at any public or private educational institution or on the grounds adjacent thereto.

(6a) Engages in conduct which disturbs the peace, order, or discipline on any public school bus or public school activity bus.

(7) Except as provided in subdivision (8) of this subsection, disrupts, disturbs or interferes with a religious service or assembly or engages in conduct which disturbs the peace or order at any religious service or assembly.

(8) Engages in conduct with the intent to impede, disrupt, disturb, or interfere with the orderly administration of any funeral, memorial service, or family processional to the funeral or memorial service, including a military funeral, service, or family processional, or with the normal activities and functions occurring in the facilities or buildings where a funeral or memorial service, including a military funeral or memorial service, is taking place. Any of the following conduct that occurs within one hour preceding, during, or within one hour after a funeral or memorial service shall constitute disorderly conduct under this subdivision:

a. Displaying, within 300 feet of the ceremonial site, location being used for the funeral or memorial, or the family's processional route to the funeral or memorial service, any visual image that conveys fighting words or actual or imminent threats of harm directed to any person or property associated with the funeral, memorial service, or processional route.

b. Uttering, within 300 feet of the ceremonial site, location being used for the funeral or memorial service, or the family's processional route to the funeral or memorial service, loud, threatening, or abusive language or singing, chanting, whistling, or yelling with or without noise amplification in a manner that would tend to impede, disrupt, disturb, or interfere with a funeral, memorial service, or processional route.

c. Attempting to block or blocking pedestrian or vehicular access to the ceremonial site or location being used for a funeral or memorial.

As used in this section the term "building or facility" includes the surrounding grounds and premises of any building or facility used in connection with the operation or functioning of such building or facility.

(b) Except as provided in subsection (c) of this section, any person who willfully engages in disorderly conduct is guilty of a Class 2 misdemeanor.

(c) A person who commits a violation of subdivision (8) of subsection (a) of this section is guilty of:

(1) A Class 2 misdemeanor for a first offense.
(2) A Class 1 misdemeanor for a second offense.
(3) A Class I felony for a third or subsequent offense.

Disorderly Conduct by Fighting

Statute

See G.S. 14-288.4(a)(1), reproduced above.

Elements

A person guilty of this offense

(1) intentionally
(2) causes a public disturbance
(3) by
  (a) fighting,
  (b) other violent conduct, *or*
  (c) conduct creating an imminent threat of fighting or other violence.

Punishment

Class 2 misdemeanor. G.S. 14-288.4(b).

Notes

Element (1). See "Intentionally" in Chapter 1 (States of Mind).

Element (2). G.S. 14-288.1(8) defines a "public disturbance" as "any annoying, disturbing, or alarming act . . . exceeding the bounds of social toleration normal for the time and place in question." The disturbance must take place in a "public place," a phrase that includes but is not limited to "highways, transport facilities, schools, prisons, apartment houses, places of business or amusement, or any neighborhood." G.S. 14-288.1(8).

Related Offenses Not in This Chapter

See the offenses in Chapter 7 (Assaults).
"Communicating Threats" (Chapter 8)
"Misdemeanor Breaking or Entering of a Building" (Chapter 15)
"Defacing a Public Building, Statue, or Monument" (Chapter 18)
"First-Degree Trespass" (Chapter 18)
"Second-Degree Trespass" (Chapter 18)
"Injury to Personal Property" (Chapter 18)

"Injury to Real Property" (Chapter 18)
"Picketing a Courthouse" (Chapter 21)
"Resisting, Delaying, or Obstructing an Officer" (Chapter 21)
"Carrying a Concealed Weapon" (Chapter 22)
See possession of weapons on school grounds (various offenses) in Chapter 22 (Weapons Offenses).
Willfully trespassing upon, damaging, or impeding the progress of a public school bus. G.S. 14-132.2(b)–(c1).
Using profane or indecent language on public highways. G.S. 14-197.
Disorderly conduct at bus or railroad station or airport. G.S. 14-275.1.
Standing, sitting, or lying upon highways or streets prohibited. G.S. 20-174.1.
Violation of state of emergency ordinance. G.S. 14-288.12 through .15.
Governor's power to order evacuation of public building. G.S. 14-288.19.
Disruptions of official meetings. G.S. 143-318.17.
Going armed to the terror of the people (common law offense).

Disorderly Conduct by Abusive Language Provoking Retaliation

Statute

See G.S. 14-288.4(a)(2), reproduced above.

Elements

A person guilty of this offense

(1) intentionally
(2) causes a public disturbance
(3) by making or using any
  (a) utterance,
  (b) gesture,
  (c) display, *or*
  (d) abusive language
(4) that is intended to, and is plainly likely to, provoke violent retaliation and thereby cause a breach of the peace.

Punishment

Class 2 misdemeanor. G.S. 14-288.4(b).

Notes

Elements (1) and (2). See the notes on these Elements to "Disorderly Conduct by Fighting," above.

Element (3) generally. When the defendant, who was being given a traffic ticket, told the officer to "get his g.. d... ass out of the way" or the defendant would "run over (him)," his language was sufficient for conviction under this statute; those were plainly fighting words even though the officer was not likely to retaliate. State v. Cunningham, 34 N.C. App. 72 (1977). However, a later United States Supreme Court case suggests that when a defendant's words are directed at a law enforcement officer, the officer may be expected to exercise a higher degree of restraint than the average citizen, and thus be less likely to respond with a violent retaliation. City of Houston, Tex. v. Hill, 482 U.S. 451, 462 (1987).

Charging issues. To establish the provocative nature of the language used, the charging instrument should set out the exact words spoken.

Constitutionality. First Amendment free speech protections do not bar punishment for use of insulting or fighting words that are likely to cause an immediate breach of the peace. State v. Summrell, 282 N.C. 157 (1972). Although the issue has not yet been addressed in this jurisdiction, other jurisdictions have held that merely speaking profanity to a law enforcement officer is constitutionally protected and does not constitute the crime of disorderly conduct. Johnson v. Campbell, 332 F.3d 199 (3d Cir. 2003).

Related Offenses Not in This Chapter

See the offenses listed under "Disorderly Conduct by Fighting," above.

Disorderly Conduct by Seizing or Blocking a School Building

Statute

See G.S. 14-288.4(a)(3) through (5), reproduced above.

Elements

A person guilty of this offense

(1) intentionally
(2) causes a public disturbance
(3) by engaging in the following conduct in a building or facility of an educational institution:
(4) (a) seizing or otherwise taking control of the building or facility without specific authorization of the institution's chief administrative officer or his or her representative,
  (b) refusing to vacate the building or facility after being ordered to do so by
    (i) the institution's chief administrative officer or his or her representative,
    (ii) a firefighter or public health officer acting within the scope of his or her authority, *or*
    (iii) a law enforcement officer acting within the scope of his or her authority when a state of emergency is occurring or imminent, *or*
  (c) after having been forbidden to do so by the institution's chief administrative officer or his or her representative
    (i) obstructing entry to and exit from the building or facility by sitting, lying down, or inclining *or*
    (ii) interfering with the normal use of the building or facility by congregating, assembling, or forming groups or formations.

Punishment

Class 2 misdemeanor. G.S. 14-288.4(b).

Notes

Elements (1) and (2). See the notes on these Elements to "Disorderly Conduct by Fighting," above.

Element (3). Public and private educational institutions are covered. G.S. 14-288.4(a)(3). The term "building or facility" includes the surrounding grounds and premises used in connection with the operation or functioning of the building or facility. G.S. 14-288.4(a). The statute does not require that the building be used for classroom purposes.

Element (4). For colleges and universities, the representative of the institution's chief administrative officer may be the vice chancellor for student affairs or an equivalent officer, the dean of students or an equivalent officer, or the director or chief of the campus law enforcement or security department. G.S. 14-288.4(a)(4)a.

Related Offenses Not in This Chapter

See the offenses listed under "Disorderly Conduct by Fighting," above.

Disorderly Conduct by Disrupting Students

Statute

See G.S. 14-288.4(a)(6), reproduced above.

Elements

A person guilty of this offense

(1) intentionally
(2) causes a public disturbance
(3) by
  (a) disrupting, disturbing, or interfering with the teaching of students at an educational institution *or*
  (b) engaging in conduct that disturbs the peace, order, or discipline at an educational institution or on the adjacent grounds.

Punishment

Class 2 misdemeanor. G.S. 14-288.4(b).

Notes

Elements (1) and (2). See the notes on these Elements to "Disorderly Conduct by Fighting," above.

Element (3). Public and private institutions are covered. G.S. 14-288.4(a)(6).

The following evidence was insufficient to support adjudications of juvenile delinquency of this offense because the conduct did not substantially interfere with the operation of the school: (1) the juvenile and a friend were walking in the hall when they should have been in class; when asked to stop, they grinned, giggled, and ran away; the juvenile was stopped by a school resource officer after a brief chase; and a few students and teachers looked into the hall while the officer was escorting the juvenile to the school office, *In re* S.M., 190 N.C. App. 579 (2008); (2) during class a high school student loudly talked to another student and continued to do so after being reprimanded by the teacher; other students were distracted, and when the teacher again asked the student to stop talking, the student looked at her, made a face, and shrugged her shoulders, *In re* Grubb, 103 N.C. App. 452 (1991); (3) a juvenile made a move toward another student across an aisle, causing the other student to dodge; the teacher asked the juvenile to show her what was in her hand, and the juvenile willingly gave the teacher a carpenter's nail, *In re* Eller, 331 N.C. 714 (1992); (4) two high school students struck a radiator during class, producing a noise that caused other students to look toward the sound and the teacher to interrupt her teaching for fifteen to twenty seconds; with each noise, the teacher stared at the students and then continued her lecture, *id.*; and (5) the juvenile talked during a test, slammed a door, and begged the teacher in the hallway not to be sent to the principal's office, causing the class to be without a teacher for several minutes, *In re* Brown, 150 N.C. App. 127 (2002).

The following evidence was sufficient to support adjudications of juvenile delinquency of this offense: (1) the juvenile uttered an obscenity to another student, requiring the teacher to stop teaching and take the student to the principal's office, during which time the student twice uttered obscenities to the teacher; the teacher was required to stop teaching the class for at least several minutes, *In re* Pineault, 152 N.C. App. 196 (2002); (2) the juvenile uttered a profanity to another student and had to be detained in a first aid room to calm down, during which time he was belligerent, requiring restraint by the principal; the juvenile's behavior required the attention of several school officials, who were required to stop teaching and performing administrative duties, *id.*; and (3) a middle school student yelled "shut the fuck up" to a group of students in a hallway when classes were in session; a teacher who heard the juvenile's statement took the juvenile to the school's detention center and, as a result, was away from his assigned lunch duty in the cafeteria for at least several minutes, *In re* M.G., 156 N.C. App. 414 (2003).

Related Offenses Not in This Chapter

See the offenses listed under "Disorderly Conduct by Fighting," above.

Disorderly Conduct on a School Bus

Statute

See G.S. 14-288.4(a)(6a), reproduced above.

Elements

A person guilty of this offense

(1) intentionally
(2) causes a public disturbance
(3) by engaging in conduct that disturbs the peace, order, or discipline
(4) on a public school bus or public school activity bus.

Punishment

Class 2 misdemeanor. G.S. 14-288.4(b).

Notes

Elements (1) and (2). See the notes on these Elements to "Disorderly Conduct by Fighting," above.

Element (4). For definitions of the terms "school bus" and "school activity bus" as used in connection with motor vehicle offenses, see the note on Element (2) to "Operating a School Bus, School Activity Bus, or Child Care Vehicle after Consuming Alcohol" in Chapter 27 (Motor Vehicle Offenses).

Related Offenses Not in This Chapter

See the offenses listed under "Disorderly Conduct by Fighting," above.

Disorderly Conduct by Disrupting a Religious Service or Assembly

Statute

See G.S. 14-288.4(a)(7), reproduced above.

Elements

A person guilty of this offense

(1) intentionally
(2) causes a public disturbance

(3) by
  (a) disrupting, disturbing, or interfering with a religious service or assembly *or*
  (b) engaging in conduct that disturbs the peace at any religious service or assembly.

Punishment

Class 2 misdemeanor. G.S. 14-288.4(b).

Notes

Elements (1) and (2). See the notes on these Elements to "Disorderly Conduct by Fighting," above.

Multiple convictions and punishments. G.S. 14-288.4(a)(7), the subsection proscribing this offense, begins with the following language: "Except as provided in subdivision (8) . . ." Subsection (8) proscribes the offense of "Disorderly Conduct by Disrupting a Funeral," below. This language suggests that when a defendant is convicted of "Disorderly Conduct by Disrupting a Funeral" he or she may not also be convicted of this offense.

Related Offenses Not in This Chapter

See the offenses listed under "Disorderly Conduct by Fighting," above.

Disorderly Conduct by Disrupting a Funeral

Statute

See G.S. 14-288.4(a)(8), reproduced above.

Elements

A person guilty of this offense
  (1) intentionally
  (2) causes a public disturbance
  (3) by engaging in conduct with the intent to impede, disrupt, disturb, or interfere with
    (a) the orderly administration of any funeral or memorial service or family processional to such a service *or*
    (b) the normal activities and functions in the facilities or buildings where a funeral or memorial service is taking place.

Punishment

Class 2 misdemeanor for a first offense, Class 1 misdemeanor for a second offense, and Class I felony for a third or subsequent offense. G.S. 14-288.4(c). If an elevated version of this offense is charged, the fact elevating punishment must be alleged in a charging instrument and proved at trial. *See* G.S. 15A-928 (alleging and proving prior convictions).

Notes

Elements (1) and (2). See the notes on these Elements to "Disorderly Conduct by Fighting," above.

Element (3). The statute expressly includes military funerals and services. G.S. 14-288.4(a)(8). It also provides that any of the following conduct occurring within the time period beginning one hour before the service and ending one hour after the service constitutes disorderly conduct:

- displaying, within 300 feet of the ceremonial site or processional route, any visual image that conveys fighting words or actual or imminent threats of harm directed to any person or property associated with the event or processional route; and

- uttering, within 300 feet of the ceremonial site or processional route, loud, threatening, or abusive language or singing, chanting, whistling, or yelling with or without noise amplification in a manner that would tend to impede, disrupt, disturb, or interfere with a funeral, memorial service, or processional route; or
- attempting to block or blocking pedestrian or vehicular access to the ceremonial site or location being used for a funeral or memorial.

Id.

Constitutionality. In *Snyder v. Phelps*, 562 U.S. ___, 131 S. Ct. 1207 (2011), the United States Supreme Court held that the First Amendment shielded members of a church from tort liability for picketing near a soldier's funeral held in Maryland. A jury held members of the Westboro Baptist Church liable for millions of dollars in damages for picketing near a soldier's funeral service with signs that reflected the church's view that the United States is overly tolerant of sin and that God kills American soldiers as punishment. *Id.* at 1214. Although Maryland now has a criminal statute in effect restricting picketing at funerals, the statute was not in effect at the time of the picketing in *Snyder*. *Id.* at 1218. Noting that statute and pointing out that other jurisdictions have enacted similar provisions, the Court stated:

> To the extent these laws are content neutral, they raise very different questions from the tort verdict at issue in this case. Maryland's law, however, was not in effect at the time of the events at issue here, so we have no occasion to consider how it might apply to facts such as those before us, or whether it or other similar regulations are constitutional.

Id. In a prosecution for this offense, the issue that the Supreme Court did not have occasion to address in *Snyder* may be presented for decision.

Related Offenses Not in This Chapter

See the offenses listed under "Disorderly Conduct by Fighting," above.

Disorderly Conduct in a Public Building

Statute

§14-132. Disorderly conduct in and injuries to public buildings and facilities.

(a) It is a misdemeanor if any person shall:

(1) Make any rude or riotous noise, or be guilty of any disorderly conduct, in or near any public building or facility; or

(2) Unlawfully write or scribble on, mark, deface, besmear, or injure the walls of any public building or facility, or any statue or monument situated in any public place; or

(3) Commit any nuisance in or near any public building or facility.

(b) Any person in charge of any public building or facility owned or controlled by the State, any subdivision of the State, or any other public agency shall have authority to arrest summarily and without warrant for a violation of this section.

(c) The term "public building or facility" as used in this section includes any building or facility which is:

(1) One to which the public or a portion of the public has access and is owned or controlled by the State, any subdivision of the State, any other public agency, or any private institution or agency of a charitable, educational, or eleemosynary nature; or

(2) Dedicated to the use of the general public for a purpose which is primarily concerned with public recreation, cultural activities, and other events of a public nature or character.

(3) Designated by the Attorney General in accordance with G.S. 114-20.1.

The term "building or facility" as used in this section also includes the surrounding grounds and premises of any building or facility used in connection with the operation or functioning of such building or facility.

(d) Any person who violates any provision of this section is guilty of a Class 2 misdemeanor.

Elements

A person guilty of this offense

(1) (a) makes any rude or riotous noise,
(b) engages in disorderly conduct, *or*
(c) commits a nuisance
(2) in or near any public building or facility.

Punishment

Class 2 misdemeanor. G.S. 14-132(d).

Notes

Generally. Because the conduct prohibited by this statute is also prohibited by a more specific statute, G.S. 14-288.4, discussed above, law enforcement officers and prosecutors typically proceed under G.S. 14-288.4 rather than under this statute.

Element (2). The term "public building or facility" includes any building or facility

- to which the public or a portion of the public has access and which is owned or controlled by the State or one if its subdivisions, any other public agency, or any private institution or agency of a charitable, educational, or eleemosynary nature;
- dedicated to the general public's use for a purpose primarily concerned with public recreation, cultural activities, and other events of a public nature or character; or
- designated by the Attorney General in accordance with G.S. 114-20.1.

G.S. 14-132(c). The term also includes the surrounding grounds and premises of any building or facility used in connection with the operation or functioning of such building or facility. *Id.*

Related Offenses Not in This Chapter

See the offenses listed under "Disorderly Conduct by Fighting," above.

Throwing Objects at Sporting Events

Statute

§14-281.1. Throwing, dropping, etc., objects at sporting events.

It shall be unlawful for any person to throw, drop, pour, release, discharge, expose or place in an area where an athletic contest or sporting event is taking place any substance or object that shall be likely to cause injury to persons participating in or attending such contests or events or to cause damage to animals, vehicles, equipment, devices, or other things used in connection with such contests or events. Any person violating the provisions of this section shall be guilty of a Class 3 misdemeanor.

Elements

A person guilty of this offense

(1) throws, drops, pours, releases, discharges, exposes, or places
(2) any substance or object
(3) in an area where an athletic contest or sporting event is taking place

(4) in a manner likely to
  (a) injure participants in the contest or event,
  (b) injure spectators at the contest or event, *or*
  (c) damage animals, vehicles, equipment, devices, or other things used in connection with the contest or event.

Punishment

Class 3 misdemeanor. G.S. 14-281.1.

Notes

Element (3). The area in which the contest or event is taking place presumably includes the stands.

Element (4). The substance or object need not actually injure someone or damage equipment; it need only be likely to cause injury or damage.

Related Offenses Not in This Chapter

"Defacing a Public Building, Statue, or Monument" (Chapter 18)
"Injury to Personal Property" (Chapter 18)
"Injury to Real Property" (Chapter 18)
Injuring houses, churches, fences, and walls. G.S. 14-144.

Affray

Statute

§14-33. Misdemeanor assaults, batteries, and affrays, simple and aggravated; punishments.

(a) Any person who commits a simple assault or a simple assault and battery or participates in a simple affray is guilty of a Class 2 misdemeanor.

(b) Unless his conduct is covered under some other provision of law providing greater punishment, any person who commits any assault, assault and battery, or affray is guilty of a Class 1 misdemeanor if, in the course of the assault, assault and battery, or affray, he:

(1) through (3) Repealed by Session Laws 1995, c. 507, s. 19.5(b);
(4) through (7) Repealed by Session Laws 1991, c. 525, s. 1;
(8) Repealed by Session Laws 1995, c. 507, s. 19.5(b);
(9) Commits an assault and battery against a sports official when the sports official is discharging or attempting to discharge official duties at a sports event, or immediately after the sports event at which the sports official discharged official duties. A "sports official" is a person at a sports event who enforces the rules of the event, such as an umpire or referee, or a person who supervises the participants, such as a coach. A "sports event" includes any interscholastic or intramural athletic activity in a primary, middle, junior high, or high school, college, or university, any organized athletic activity sponsored by a community, business, or nonprofit organization, any athletic activity that is a professional or semiprofessional event, and any other organized athletic activity in the State.

(c) Unless the conduct is covered under some other provision of law providing greater punishment, any person who commits any assault, assault and battery, or affray is guilty of a Class A1 misdemeanor if, in the course of the assault, assault and battery, or affray, he or she:

(1) Inflicts serious injury upon another person or uses a deadly weapon;
(2) Assaults a female, he being a male person at least 18 years of age;

(3) Assaults a child under the age of 12 years;
(4) Assaults an officer or employee of the State or any political subdivision of the State, when the officer or employee is discharging or attempting to discharge his official duties;
(5) Repealed by Session Laws 1999-105, s. 1, effective December 1, 1999; or
(6) Assaults a school employee or school volunteer when the employee or volunteer is discharging or attempting to discharge his or her duties as an employee or volunteer, or assaults a school employee or school volunteer as a result of the discharge or attempt to discharge that individual's duties as a school employee or school volunteer. For purposes of this subdivision, the following definitions shall apply:
  a. "Duties" means:
    1. All activities on school property;
    2. All activities, wherever occurring, during a school authorized event or the accompanying of students to or from that event; and
    3. All activities relating to the operation of school transportation.
  b. "Employee" or "volunteer" means:
    1. An employee of a local board of education; or a charter school authorized under G.S. 115C-238.29D, or a nonpublic school which has filed intent to operate under Part 1 or Part 2 of Article 39 of Chapter 115C of the General Statutes;
    2. An independent contractor or an employee of an independent contractor of a local board of education, charter school authorized under G.S. 115C-238.29D, or a nonpublic school which has filed intent to operate under Part 1 or Part 2 of Article 39 of Chapter 115C of the General Statutes, if the independent contractor carries out duties customarily performed by employees of the school; and
    3. An adult who volunteers his or her services or presence at any school activity and is under the supervision of an individual listed in sub-sub-subdivision 1. or 2. of this sub-subdivision.
(7) Assaults a public transit operator, including a public employee or a private contractor employed as a public transit operator, when the operator is discharging or attempting to discharge his or her duties.
(8) Assaults a company police officer certified pursuant to the provisions of Chapter 74E of the General Statutes or a campus police officer certified pursuant to the provisions of Chapter 74G, Chapter 17C, or Chapter 116 of the General Statutes in the performance of that person's duties.

(d) Any person who, in the course of an assault, assault and battery, or affray, inflicts serious injury upon another person, or uses a deadly weapon, in violation of subdivision (c)(1) of this section, on a person with whom the person has a personal relationship, and in the presence of a minor, is guilty of a Class A1 misdemeanor. A person convicted under this subsection, who is sentenced to a community punishment, shall be placed on supervised probation in addition to any other punishment imposed by the court.

A person committing a second or subsequent violation of this subsection shall be sentenced to an active punishment of no less than 30 days in addition to any other punishment imposed by the court.

The following definitions apply to this subsection:
(1) "Personal relationship" is as defined in G.S. 50B-1(b).
(2) "In the presence of a minor" means that the minor was in a position to have observed the assault.
(3) "Minor" is any person under the age of 18 years who is residing with or is under the care and supervision of, and who has a personal relationship with, the person assaulted or the person committing the assault.

Simple Affray

Statute

The crime of affray is defined by the common law. *In re* May, 357 N.C. 423 (2003).
G.S. 14-33(a), reproduced above, sets out the punishment for simple affray and specifies when punishment is elevated.

Elements

A person guilty of this offense

(1) engages in a fight with at least one other person
(2) in a public place
(3) to the terror of the public.

Punishment

Class 2 misdemeanor. G.S. 14-33(a).

Notes

Element (1). A mere scuffle (friendly play, rather than "mad and fighting") does not satisfy this element. State v. Freeman, 127 N.C. 544 (1900). A person who has agreed to fight or brings on a fight by words or action but never lands a blow can be guilty of affray. State v. Gladden, 73 N.C. 150 (1875); State v. Fanning, 94 N.C. 940 (1886). The person must have engaged in the fighting willingly and without a lawful excuse. State v. Herrell, 107 N.C. 944 (1890).

To have a fight requires more than one person, so normally when one person is charged with affray, at least one other person also would be charged.

Element (2). Two types of locales qualify as "public places." *May*, 357 N.C. 423. One type includes places generally considered public by virtue of the nature of their use and intended use. *Id.* at 427. Parcels of land and places owned or maintained by a government entity or private business that are open to traffic fall into this category. *Id.* Examples include roads, sidewalks, shopping malls, apartment complexes, parks, and commons. *Id.* The other type of place that may be classified as "public" for purposes of Element (2) is private property situated near enough to public thoroughfares that people using such thoroughfares could see or hear the altercation on the private property. *Id.* In addition, proof of the third element (terror to people who qualify as members of the public) may in certain cases satisfy the element of public place. *Id.* at 428. For example, a fight that occurs on private property beyond the view or hearing of the general public may nevertheless be witnessed by members of the public who are on the property and are subject to the terror of the altercation. If this is the case, the establishment of the third element also satisfies the second element. *Id.* at 429–30.

Element (3). If members of the public experience fear, this element is satisfied. *In re* May, 357 N.C. 423, 428 (2003). When determining whether witnesses to a fight on private property are members of the public, the court will consider the associations between the combatants and the witnesses. *Id.* at 431. Although other state courts have held that this element may be presumed if the fight occurs in a public place even if no members of the public were present to witness the event, that issue has not been resolved in North Carolina. *Id.* at 428.

Relation to other offenses. In most affrays, the parties to the fight could be charged with assault. However, a person who provoked a fight but never got in or attempted a blow could properly be charged with affray, though not with assault.

Related Offenses Not in This Chapter

See the offenses in Chapter 7 (Assaults).
"Resisting, Delaying, or Obstructing an Officer" (Chapter 21)
Going armed to the terror of the people (common law offense)

Aggravated Misdemeanor Affray

Statute

See G.S. 14-33(b) and (c), reproduced above.

Elements

A person guilty of this offense

(1) engages in a fight with at least one other person
(2) in a public place
(3) to the terror of the public *and*
(4) (a) inflicts serious injury,
  (b) uses a deadly weapon,
  (c) is a male at least 18 years old who assaults a female,
  (d) assaults a child under the age of 12,
  (e) assaults an officer or employee of the state or any political subdivision of the state who is discharging or attempting to discharge official duties,
  (f) assaults a school employee or school volunteer who is discharging or attempting to discharge duties or assaults the employee or volunteer as a result of that individual's discharge or attempted discharge of duties,
  (g) assaults a public transit operator discharging or attempting to discharge his or her duties,
  (h) assaults a company or campus police officer in the performance of that person's duties,
  (i) commits an assault in the presence of a minor, *or*
  (j) commits an assault and battery against a sports official when the sports official is discharging or attempting to discharge official duties at a sports event or immediately after the sports event at which the sports official discharged official duties.

Punishment

An aggravated affray involving elements (4)(a) through (i) is a Class A1 misdemeanor. G.S. 14-33(c)–(d). A person convicted of an affray involving Element (4)(i) who is sentenced to a community punishment must be placed on supervised probation in addition to any other punishment imposed. G.S. 14-33(d). A second or subsequent violation involving Element (4)(i) requires an active punishment of no less than thirty days in addition to any other punishment imposed. *Id.* An aggravated affray involving Element (4)(j) is a Class 1 misdemeanor. G.S. 14-33(b)(9).

Notes

Elements (1) through (3). See the notes on Elements (1) through (3) to "Simple Affray," above.

Element (4). See "Simple Assault," "Assault Inflicting Serious Injury," "Assault with a Deadly Weapon," "Assault on a Female," "Assault on a Child under 12," "Assault on a Governmental Officer or Employee," "Assault on School Personnel," "Assault on a Public Transit Operator," "Assault on a Company or Campus Police Officer," "Assault in the Presence of a Minor," and "Assault and Battery on a Sports Official," all in Chapter 7 (Assaults).

Relation to other offenses. For a discussion of aggravated misdemeanor and felony affray involving firefighters and medical personnel under G.S. 14-34.6, see assaults on firefighters and emergency and medical personnel (various offenses) in Chapter 7 (Assaults).

Related Offenses Not in This Chapter

See the offenses listed under "Simple Affray," above.

Unlawful Assembly

Statute

This is a common law offense. State v. Brooks, 287 N.C. 392, 398 (1975).

Elements

A person guilty of this offense

(1) assembles with two or more other persons
(2) with the common intent to commit disorderly acts that will interfere with the rights of others *and*
(3) for the purpose of committing the acts in such a manner as would cause a firm person to apprehend a breach of peace.

Punishment

Class 1 misdemeanor. G.S. 14-3(a); see the section entitled "Offense Class" under "Misdemeanors" in Chapter 4 (Punishment under Structured Sentencing).

Notes

Generally. For the elements of this offense, see *Brooks,* 287 N.C. at 398. This offense has been recognized as a component of the crime of riot, both under the common law, State v. Cole, 249 N.C. 733 (1959), and under the 1969 Riot and Civil Disorder Act, G.S. 14-288.3; *Brooks,* 287 N.C. 392. G.S. 14-288.3 specifies that passage of the riot act was not intended to abolish this offense. Some of the notes under "Misdemeanor Riot," discussed below, apply to this offense as well.

Element (1). The prohibited assembly must have been for an unlawful purpose—that is, it was for the purpose of either doing an unlawful act or doing a lawful act in an unlawful manner; the purpose may be formed before or during the assembly; and the unlawful assembly may be created deliberately or by chance. *Cole,* 249 N.C. at 742. A Ku Klux Klan rally, even if organized for a lawful purpose, became an unlawful assembly when used to preach racial dissension and to intimidate and coerce other citizens. *Id.* at 743–44.

Constitutionality. Because of potential interference with First Amendment rights of free speech, officers generally avoid charging this offense and instead charge other offenses such as disorderly conduct, conspiracy, and riot, as the facts dictate.

Related Offenses Not in This Chapter

See the offenses listed under "Disorderly Conduct by Fighting," above.

Riot

Statute

§14-288.2. Riot; inciting to riot; punishment.

(a) A riot is a public disturbance involving an assemblage of three or more persons which by disorderly and violent conduct, or imminent threat of disorderly and violent conduct, results in injury or damage to persons or property or creates a clear and present danger of injury or damage to persons or property.

(b) Any person who willfully engages in a riot is guilty of a Class 1 misdemeanor.

(c) Any person who willfully engages in a riot is guilty of a Class H felony, if:

(1) In the course and as a result of the riot there is property damage in excess of fifteen hundred dollars ($1,500) or serious bodily injury; *or*

(2) Such participant in the riot has in his possession any dangerous weapon or substance.

(d) Any person who willfully incites or urges another to engage in a riot, so that as a result of such inciting or urging a riot occurs or a clear and present danger of a riot is created, is guilty of a Class 1 misdemeanor.

(e) Any person who willfully incites or urges another to engage in a riot, and such inciting or urging is a contributing cause of a riot in which there is property damage in excess of fifteen hundred dollars ($1,500) or serious bodily injury, shall be punished as a Class F felon.

Misdemeanor Riot

Statute

See G.S. 14-288.2(a) and (b), reproduced above.

Elements

A person guilty of this offense

(1) willfully assembles
(2) with two or more other persons *and*
(3) engages in a public disturbance
(4) that by
 (a) disorderly and violent conduct *or*
 (b) the imminent threat of disorderly and violent conduct
(5) (a) causes injury or damage to persons or property *or*
 (b) creates a clear and present danger of such injury or damage.

Punishment

Class 1 misdemeanor. G.S. 14-288.2(b).

Notes

Element (1). See "Willfully" in Chapter 1 (States of Mind).

For this element to be satisfied, the participants must have assembled for an unlawful purpose; the unlawful purpose can be formed either before or during the assembly. State v. Cole, 249 N.C. 733, 745–46 (1959); State v. Leary, 264 N.C. 51 (1965). A meeting of the Ku Klux Klan for purposes of intimidating and coercing other citizens is an unlawful assembly. *Cole,* 249 N.C. at 743–44.

Element (2). A defendant can be convicted even if other participants are not named, provided that the evidence establishes and the jury finds that there were two or more other participants. The parties need not have acted in concert so long as they all participated in the riot. *Leary,* 264 N.C. at 54.

Element (3). To "engage in" means to actively participate in the riotous activity. State v. Mitchell, 110 N.C. App. 250 (1993). Mere presence at the scene of a riot does not establish participation in the riot. State v. Riddle, 45 N.C. App. 34 (1980).

A "public disturbance" is "[a]ny annoying, disturbing, or alarming act or condition exceeding the bounds of social toleration normal for the time and place in question which occurs in a public place or which occurs in, affects persons in, or is likely to affect persons in a place to which the public or a substantial group has access." G.S. 14-288.1(8). The covered places include but are not limited to "highways, transport facilities, schools, prisons, apartment houses, places of business or amusement, or any neighborhood." *Id.*

Element (4). There must be both disorderly *and* violent conduct. See "Disorderly Conduct," above, for an explanation of what constitutes disorderly conduct; G.S. 14-288.1(4).

Element (5). The defendant need not have personally caused the injury or damage; a person can be convicted of riot as long as the injury or damage occurred or was threatened as part of the public disturbance in which he or she participated.

Constitutionality. This statute is not unconstitutionally vague and does not infringe on constitutionally protected free speech rights. State v. Brooks, 287 N.C. 392 (1975).

Related Offenses Not in This Chapter

See the offenses listed under "Disorderly Conduct by Fighting," above.

Felony Riot

Statute

See G.S. 14-288.2(a), (c), reproduced above.

Elements

A person guilty of this offense

(1) willfully assembles
(2) with two or more other persons *and*
(3) engages in a public disturbance
(4) that by disorderly and violent conduct
(5) (a) results in property damage in excess of $1,500,
  (b) results in serious bodily injury, *or*
  (c) (i) results in damage or injury to persons or property or creates a clear and present danger such of damage or injury, *and*
    (ii) the defendant possesses a dangerous weapon or substance.

Punishment

Class H felony. G.S. 14-288.4(2)(c).

Notes

Elements (1) through (4). See the notes on these elements to "Misdemeanor Riot, " above.

Element (5)(b). For a definition of the term "serious bodily injury" as used in the assault context, see "Assault Inflicting Serious Bodily Injury" in Chapter 7 (Assaults).

Element (5)(c). The defendant need not have personally caused the property damage or physical injury in Element (5)(a) or (b), but he or she must have had personal possession of the dangerous weapon or substance to be convicted of felony riot for that reason.

G.S. 14-288.1(2) defines "dangerous weapon or substance" to include

- any deadly weapon, ammunition, explosive, incendiary device, or radioactive material or device, as defined in G.S. 14-288.8(c)(5), or any instrument or substance designed for a use that carries a threat of serious bodily injury or destruction of property;
- any instrument or substance that is capable of being used to inflict serious bodily injury, when the circumstances indicate a probability that such instrument or substance will be so used; and
- any part or ingredient in any instrument or substance included above, when the circumstances indicate a probability that such part or ingredient will be so used.

Constitutionality. See this note to "Misdemeanor Riot," above.

Related Offenses Not in This Chapter

See the offenses listed under "Disorderly Conduct by Fighting," above.
"Assault Inflicting Serious Bodily Injury" (Chapter 7)

Misdemeanor Inciting to Riot

Statute

See G.S. 14-288.2(d), reproduced above.

Elements

A person guilty of this offense

(1) willfully
(2) incites or urges another
(3) to engage in a riot *and,*
(4) as a result, a riot occurs or a clear and present danger of a riot is created.

Punishment

Class 1 misdemeanor. G.S. 14-288.4(d).

Notes

Element (1). See "Willfully" in Chapter 1 (States of Mind).

Element (2). "Incite" means to arouse, stir up, urge, provoke, encourage, spur on, or goad. State v. Cole, 249 N.C. 733, 741 (1959). It includes using words, signs, or any other means that would naturally lead others to engage in conduct that would constitute a riot. *Id.* at 746. The defendant need not have participated in the riot itself to be guilty of this offense.

Element (3). See "Misdemeanor Riot," above, for the elements of the offense of riot.

Element (4). Under the common law crime of inciting to riot, it was necessary to prove that a riot actually had occurred. *Cole,* 249 N.C. at 744–45. The statute also allows a conviction for inciting even if the inciting merely creates a clear and present danger of a riot.

Constitutionality. See this note to "Misdemeanor Riot," above.

Related Offenses Not in This Chapter

See the offenses listed under "Disorderly Conduct by Fighting," above.

Felony Inciting to Riot

Statute

See G.S. 14-288.2(e), reproduced above.

Elements

A person guilty of this offense

(1) willfully
(2) incites or urges another
(3) to engage in a riot, *and*
(4) the inciting or urging is a contributing cause of a riot which
(5) results in
    (a) property damage of $1,500 or more *or*
    (b) serious bodily injury.

Punishment

Class F felony. G.S. 14-288.2(e).

Notes

Elements (1) through (3). See the notes on these elements to "Misdemeanor Inciting to Riot," above.

Element (4)(b). See the note on Element (5)(b) to "Felony Riot," above.

Constitutionality. See this note to "Misdemeanor Riot," above.

Related Offenses Not in This Chapter

See the offenses listed under "Disorderly Conduct by Fighting," above.
"Assault Inflicting Serious Bodily Injury" (Chapter 7)

Failure to Disperse on Command

Statute

§14-288.5. Failure to disperse when commanded a misdemeanor; prima facie evidence.

(a) Any law-enforcement officer or public official responsible for keeping the peace may issue a command to disperse in accordance with this section if he reasonably believes that a riot, or disorderly conduct by an assemblage of three or more persons, is occurring. The command to disperse shall be given in a manner reasonably calculated to be communicated to the assemblage.

(b) Any person who fails to comply with a lawful command to disperse is guilty of a Class 2 misdemeanor.

(c) If any person remains at the scene of any riot, or disorderly conduct by an assemblage of three or more persons, following a command to disperse and after a reasonable time for dispersal has elapsed, it is prima facie evidence that the person so remaining is willfully engaging in the riot or disorderly conduct, as the case may be.

Elements

A person guilty of this offense

(1) fails to comply with a command to disperse
(2) given in a manner reasonably calculated to be heard by those assembled
(3) by a law enforcement officer or public official responsible for keeping the peace
(4) when that officer reasonably believes that a riot or disorderly conduct by three or more persons is occurring.

Punishment

Class 2 misdemeanor. G.S. 14-288.5(b).

Notes

Element (3). G.S. 14-288.1(5) defines "law enforcement officer" as any officer with the power of arrest and any member of the armed forces or state militia called to duty in a state of emergency to preserve the peace.

Element (4). See "Misdemeanor Riot" and "Disorderly Conduct," both above, for definitions of "riot" and "disorderly conduct"; G.S. 14-288.1(4), (9).

The statute does not require that a person participate in the riot or disorderly conduct to be charged with this offense.

Evidence issues. G.S. 14-288.5(c) provides that failure by anyone to disperse after a reasonable time is prima facie evidence that the person is willfully participating in the riot or disorderly conduct.

Constitutionality. This statute is constitutional. State v. Brooks, 24 N.C. App. 338 (1975).

Related Offenses Not in This Chapter

See the offenses listed under "Disorderly Conduct by Fighting," above.
"Resisting, Delaying, or Obstructing an Officer" (Chapter 21)
Looting; trespass during emergency. G.S. 14-288.6.
Transporting dangerous weapon or substance during emergency; possession off premises. G.S. 14-288.7.

Gang-Related Crimes

Statute

§14-50.16. Pattern of criminal street gang activity.

(a) It is unlawful for any person employed by or associated with a criminal street gang to do either of the following:

(1) To conduct or participate in a pattern of criminal street gang activity.

(2) To acquire or maintain any interest in or control of any real or personal property through a pattern of criminal street gang activity.

A violation of this section is a Class H felony, except that a person who violates subdivision (a)(1) of this section, and is an organizer, supervisor, or acts in any other position of management with regard to the criminal street gang, shall be guilty of a Class F felony.

(b) As used in this Article, "criminal street gang" or "street gang" means any ongoing organization, association, or group of three or more persons, whether formal or informal, that:

(1) Has as one of its primary activities the commission of one or more felony offenses, or delinquent acts that would be felonies if committed by an adult;

(2) Has three or more members individually or collectively engaged in, or who have engaged in, criminal street gang activity; and

(3) May have a common name, common identifying sign or symbol.

(c) As used in this Article, "criminal street gang activity" means to commit, to attempt to commit, or to solicit, coerce, or intimidate another person to commit an act or acts, with the specific intent that such act or acts were intended or committed for the purpose, or in furtherance, of the person's involvement in a criminal street gang or street gang. An act or acts are included if accompanied by the necessary mens rea or criminal intent and would be chargeable by indictment under the following laws of this State:

(1) Any offense under Article 5 of Chapter 90 of the General Statutes (Controlled Substances Act).

(2) Any offense under Chapter 14 of the General Statutes except Articles 9, 22A, 40, 46, 47, 59 thereof; and further excepting G.S. 14-78.1, 14-82, 14-86, 14-145, 14-179, 14-183, 14-184, 14-186, 14-190.9, 14-195, 14-197, 14-201, 14-247, 14-248, 14-313 thereof.

(d) As used in this Article, "pattern of criminal street gang activity" means engaging in, and having a conviction for, at least two prior incidents of criminal street gang activity, that have the same or similar purposes, results, accomplices, victims, or methods of commission or otherwise are interrelated by common characteristics and are not isolated and unrelated incidents, provided that at least one of these offenses occurred after December 1, 2008, and the last of the offenses occurred within three years, excluding any periods of imprisonment, of prior criminal street gang activity. Any offenses committed by a defendant prior to indictment for an offense based upon a pattern of street gang activity shall not be used as the basis for any subsequent indictments for offenses involving a pattern of street gang activity.

Street Gang Activity

Statute

See G.S. 14-50.16(a), reproduced above.

Elements

A person guilty of this offense

(1) is employed by or associated with
(2) a criminal street gang *and*
(3) (a) conducts or participates in a pattern of criminal street gang activity *or*
 (b) acquires or maintains any interest in or control of any real or personal property through a pattern of criminal street gang activity.

Punishment

Class H felony. G.S. 14-50.16(a).

Notes

Element (2). The terms "criminal street gang" and "street gang" mean any ongoing organization, association, or group of three or more persons, formal or informal, that:

- has as one of its primary activities the commission of one or more felony offenses or delinquent acts that would be felonies if committed by an adult;
- has three or more members individually or collectively engaged in, or who have engaged in, criminal street gang activity; and
- may have a common name, common identifying sign, or symbol.

G.S. 14-50.16(b). The term "criminal street gang activity" is defined in the next note.

Element (3). To engage in "criminal street gang activity" means to commit, to attempt to commit, or to solicit, coerce, or intimidate another to commit an act or acts with the specific intent that such act or acts were intended or committed for the purpose of, or in furtherance of, the person's involvement in a criminal street gang or street gang. G.S. 14-50.16(c). An act or acts are covered by the offense if they are accompanied by the necessary mens rea or criminal intent and would be chargeable by indictment under Article 5 of G.S. Chapter 90 or an offense under G.S. Chapter 14, with certain exceptions. *Id.* The Chapter 14 exceptions include:

- offenses in Article 9 (Hazing);
- offenses in Article 22A (Trespassing upon "Posted" Property to Hunt, Fish, Trap, or Remove Pine Needles/Straw);
- offenses in Article 40 (Protection of the Family);
- offenses in Article 46 (Regulation of Landlord and Tenant);
- offenses in Article 47 (Cruelty to Animals);
- offenses in Article 59 (Public Intoxication);
- G.S. 14-82 (Taking horses, mules or dogs for temporary purposes);
- G.S. 14-145 (Unlawful posting of advertisements);
- G.S. 14-183 (Bigamy);
- G.S. 14-184 (Fornication and adultery);
- G.S. 14-186 (Opposite sexes occupying same bedroom at hotel for immoral purposes; falsely registering as husband and wife);

- G.S. 14-190.9 (Indecent exposure);
- G.S. 14-197 (Using profane or indecent language on public highways; counties exempt);
- G.S. 14-247 (Private use of publicly owned vehicle);
- G.S. 14-248 (Obtaining repairs and supplies for private vehicle at expense of State); and
- G.S. 14-313 (Youth access to tobacco products).

Id. The statute also excepts G.S. 14-78.1, G.S. 14-86, G.S. 14-179, G.S. 14-195, and G.S. 14-201, but these are repealed statutes.

The term "pattern of criminal street gang activity" means engaging in, and having a conviction for, at least two prior incidents of criminal street gang activity that have the same or similar purposes, results, accomplices, victims, or methods of commission or otherwise are interrelated by common characteristics and are not isolated and unrelated incidents, provided that at least one of these offenses occurred after December 1, 2008, and the last of the offenses occurred within three years, excluding any periods of imprisonment, of prior criminal street gang activity. G.S. 14-50.16(d). Any offenses committed by a defendant prior to indictment for an offense based upon a pattern of street gang activity may not be used as the basis for any subsequent indictments for offenses involving a pattern of street gang activity. *Id.*

Exceptions. This crime does not apply to a person under the age of 16. G.S. 14-50.28.

Multiple convictions and punishments. G.S. 14-50.21 provides that all of the gang-related offenses proscribed by G.S. 14-50.16 through 14-50.20 are separate offenses.

Forfeiture. G.S. 15-50.23 provides for seizure and forfeiture of property used or intended for use in, derived from, or realized through criminal street gang activity or a pattern of criminal street gang activity.

Real property declared a public nuisance. G.S. 14-50.24 provides that real property erected, established, maintained, owned, leased, or used by any criminal street gang to conduct criminal street gang activity shall constitute a public nuisance and may be abated as provided in the General Statutes.

Related Offenses Not in This Chapter

"Continuing Criminal Enterprise—Non-Drug Offenses" (Chapter 5)
"Continuing Criminal Enterprise—Drug Offenses" (Chapter 27)

Organizer of Street Gang Activity

Statute

See G.S. 14-50.16(a), reproduced above.

Elements

A person guilty of this offense

(1) is employed by or associated with
(2) a criminal street gang *and*
(3) is an organizer, supervisor, or acts in any other position of management with regard to the criminal street gang *and*
(4) (a) conducts or participates in a pattern of criminal street gang activity *or*
 (b) acquires or maintains any interest in or control of any real or personal property through a pattern of criminal street gang activity.

Punishment

Class F felony. G.S. 14-50.16(a).

Notes

Elements (1) and (3). For definitions of the terms "criminal street gang" and "street gang," see the note on Element (2) to "Street Gang Activity," above.

Element (4). For definitions of the terms "criminal street gang activity" and "pattern of criminal street gang activity," see the note on Element (3) to "Street Gang Activity," above.

Exceptions. See this note to "Street Gang Activity," above.

Multiple convictions and punishments. See this note to "Street Gang Activity," above.

Forfeiture. See this note to "Street Gang Activity," above.

Real property declared a public nuisance. See this note to "Street Gang Activity," above.

Related Offenses Not in This Chapter

See the offenses listed under "Street Gang Activity," above.
"Conspiracy" (Chapter 5)

Soliciting Participation in Street Gang Activity

Statute

§14-50.17. Soliciting; encouraging participation.

(a) It is unlawful for any person to cause, encourage, solicit, or coerce a person 16 years of age or older to participate in criminal street gang activity.

(b) A violation of this section is a Class H felony.

§14-50.18. Soliciting; encouraging participation; minor.

(a) It is unlawful for any person to cause, encourage, solicit, or coerce a person under 16 years of age to participate in criminal street gang activity.

(b) A violation of this section is a Class F felony.

(c) Nothing in this section shall preclude a person who commits a violation of this section from criminal culpability for the underlying offense committed by the minor under any other provision of law.

Elements

A person guilty of this offense

(1) causes, encourages, solicits, or coerces
(2) (a) a person 16 or older *or*
    (b) a person under 16
(3) to participate in criminal street gang activity.

Punishment

If Element (2)(a) is involved, the offense is a Class H felony. G.S. 14-50.17(b). If Element (2)(b) is involved, the offense is a Class F felony. G.S. 50.18(b).

Notes

Element (3). For the definition of the term "criminal street gang," see the note on Element (2) to "Street Gang Activity," above.

Exceptions. See this note to "Street Gang Activity," above.

Multiple convictions and punishments. See this note to "Street Gang Activity," above. G.S. 14-50.18(c) provides that "[n]othing in this section shall preclude a person who commits a violation of this section from criminal culpability for the underlying offense committed by the minor under any other provision of law."

Forfeiture. See this note to "Street Gang Activity," above.

Real property declared a public nuisance. See this note to "Street Gang Activity," above.

Related Offenses Not in This Chapter

See the offenses listed under "Street Gang Activity," above.
"Solicitation" (Chapter 5)
"Contributing to a Juvenile's Being Delinquent, Undisciplined, Abused, or Neglected" (Chapter 9)

Threat Regarding Gang Withdrawal

Statute

§14-50.19. Threats to deter from gang withdrawal.

(a) It is unlawful for any person to communicate a threat of injury to a person, or to damage the property of another, with the intent to deter a person from assisting another to withdraw from membership in a criminal street gang.

(b) A violation of this section is a Class H felony.

§14-50.20. Threats of punishment or retaliation.

(a) It is unlawful for any person to communicate a threat of injury to a person, or to damage the property of another, as punishment or retaliation against a person for having withdrawn from a criminal street gang.

(b) A violation of this section is a Class H felony.

Elements

A person guilty of this offense

(1) communicates
(2) a threat of injury to a person or of damage to the property of another
(3) (a) with the intent to deter a person from assisting another to withdraw from membership in a criminal street gang *or*
(b) as punishment or retaliation against a person for having withdrawn from a criminal street gang.

Punishment

Class H felony. G.S. 14-50.19(b) (Element (3)(a)); G.S. 14-50.20(b) (Element (3)(b)).

Notes

Element (3). For the definition of "criminal street gang," see the note on Element (2) to "Street Gang Activity," above.

Exceptions. See this note to "Street Gang Activity," above.

Multiple convictions and punishments. See this note to "Street Gang Activity," above.

Real property declared a public nuisance. See this note to "Street Gang Activity," above.

Related Offenses Not in This Chapter

See the offenses listed under "Street Gang Activity," above.

See various offenses in Chapter 8 (Threats, Harassment, Stalking, and Violation of Domestic Protective Orders).

Discharging a Firearm in Connection with a Pattern of Street Gang Activity

Statute

§14-34.9. Discharging a firearm from within an enclosure.

Unless covered under some other provision of law providing greater punishment, any person who willfully or wantonly discharges or attempts to discharge a firearm, as a part of a pattern of criminal street gang activity, from within any building, structure, motor vehicle, or other conveyance, erection, or enclosure toward a person or persons not within that enclosure shall be punished as a Class E felon.

Elements

A person guilty of this offense

(1) willfully or wantonly
(2) discharges or attempts to discharge
(3) a firearm
(4) from within any building, structure, motor vehicle, or other conveyance, erection, or enclosure
(5) toward a person or persons not within that enclosure *and*
(6) as a part of a pattern of criminal street gang activity.

Punishment

Class E felony. G.S. 14-34.9.

Notes

Element (1). See "Willfully" and "Wantonly" in Chapter 1 (States of Mind).

Element (3). For a discussion of the term "firearm" as used in connection with the offense of "Possession of a Firearm by a Felon," see the note on Element (3)(a) to that offense in Chapter 22 (Weapons Offenses). For a discussion of that term as used in the context of larceny, see the note on Element (8)(e) to "Felony Larceny" in Chapter 13 (Larceny, Possession of Stolen Goods, Embezzlement, and Related Offenses).

Element (6). The statute does not define "pattern of criminal street gang activity." For a definition of that term as used in a related statute, see the note on Element (3) to "Street Gang Activity," above.

Attempt. The offense covers both discharging a firearm and attempting to discharge one, thus punishing an attempt like the completed offense, not one class lower, as it typically the case for attempts. See "Attempt" in Chapter 5 (General Crimes).

Multiple convictions and punishments. The punishment provision for this offense begins with the language: "Unless covered under some other provision of law providing greater punishment." G.S. 14-34.9. This language may mean that a defendant may not, based on the same conduct, be convicted of this offense and another one carrying a more severe punishment. See this note to "Assault Inflicting Serious Injury" in Chapter 7 (Assaults).

Related Offenses Not in This Chapter

See the offenses listed under "Street Gang Activity," above.
"Discharging a Barreled Weapon or Firearm into Occupied Property" (Chapter 7)
"Discharging a Barreled Weapon or Firearm into an Occupied Dwelling or Conveyance in Operation" (Chapter 7)
"Discharging a Barreled Weapon or Firearm into Occupied Property Causing Serious Bodily Injury" (Chapter 7)
See various offenses in Chapter 22 (Weapons Offenses).

20

Bombing, Terrorism, and Related Offenses

20

Bombing, Terrorism, and Related Offenses

Malicious Damage by Use of Explosives or Incendiaries

Malicious Damage to Occupied Property by Use of an Explosive or Incendiary

Statute

§14-49.1. Malicious damage of occupied property by use of explosive or incendiary; punishment.
Any person who willfully and maliciously damages any real or personal property of any kind or nature, being at the time occupied by another, by the use of any explosive or incendiary device or material is guilty of a felony punishable as a Class D felony.

Elements

A person guilty of this offense

(1) willfully and maliciously
(2) damages
(3) real or personal property
(4) occupied by another
(5) by use of an explosive or incendiary device or material.

Punishment

Class D felony. G.S. 14-49.1.

Notes

Element (1). See "Willfully" and "Maliciously" in Chapter 1 (States of Mind).

Element (2). The State must prove "measurable damage" to satisfy this element. State v. Bennett, 132 N.C. App. 187 (1999). The defendant's burning of his blue jeans, which left only a slightly visible mark on a jail's floor after it was stripped and waxed, was insufficient to establish measurable damage. *Id.*

Element (3). G.S. 12-3(6) provides that the words "real property" are "coextensive with lands, tenements and hereditaments." G.S. 12-3(6) defines "personal property" as "moneys, goods, chattels, choses in action and evidences of debt, including all things capable of ownership, not descendable [sic] to heirs at law." For an explanation of the term "choses in action" as that term applies in the context of larceny, see the note on Element (2) to "Larceny of a Chose in Action" in Chapter 13 (Larceny, Possession of Stolen Goods, Embezzlement, and Related Offenses).

Element (4). The property must be occupied by another "at the time." G.S. 14-49.1. This suggests that someone must be present when the offense occurs. For the meaning of "actually occupied" in the burglary context, see the note on Element (6) to "First-Degree Burglary" in Chapter 15 (Burglary, Breaking or Entering, and Related Offenses).

Element (5). For the definition of the term "explosive or incendiary device or material," see the note on Element (3) to "Malicious Injury by Use of an Explosive or Incendiary" in Chapter 7 (Assaults).

Related Offenses Not in This Chapter

"Discharging a Barreled Weapon or Firearm into Occupied Property" (Chapter 7)
"Discharging a Barreled Weapon or Firearm into an Occupied Dwelling or Occupied Conveyance in Operation" (Chapter 7)
"Discharging a Barreled Weapon or Firearm into Occupied Property Causing Serious Bodily Injury" (Chapter 7)
"Malicious Injury by Use of an Explosive or Incendiary" (Chapter 7)
"Burglary with Explosives" (Chapter 15)
"Injury to Real Property" (Chapter 18)
See the offenses in Chapter 22 (Weapons Offenses).
Shooting or throwing at trains or passengers. G.S. 14-280.
Use of a laser device towards an aircraft. G.S. 14-280.2.
Exploding dynamite cartridges and bombs. G.S. 14-283.
Transporting dangerous weapon or substance during emergency; possessing off premises. G.S. 14-288.7.
Manufacture, sale and use of pyrotechnics prohibited; sale to persons under the age of 16 prohibited. G.S. 14-410.

Malicious Damage to Real or Personal Property by Use of an Explosive or Incendiary

Statute

§14-49. Malicious use of explosive or incendiary; punishment.

Subsection (a) is not reproduced here.

(b) Any person who willfully and maliciously damages any real or personal property of any kind or nature belonging to another by the use of any explosive or incendiary device or material is guilty of a Class G felony.

(b1) Any person who willfully and maliciously damages, aids, counsels, or procures the damaging of any church, chapel, synagogue, mosque, masjid, or other building of worship by the use of any explosive or incendiary device or material is guilty of a Class E felony.

(b2) Any person who willfully and maliciously damages, aids, counsels, or procures the damaging of the State Capitol, the Legislative Building, the Justice Building, or any building owned or occupied by the State or any of its agencies, institutions, or subdivisions or by any county, incorporated city or town, or other governmental entity by the use of any explosive or incendiary device or material is guilty of a Class E felony.

(c) Repealed by Session Laws 1993, c. 539, s. 1149, effective October 1, 1994.

Elements

A person guilty of this offense

(1) willfully and maliciously
(2) damages
(3) real or personal property of another
(4) by use of an explosive or incendiary device or material.

Punishment

Class G felony. G.S. 14-49(b).

Notes

Element (1). See "Willfully" and "Maliciously" in Chapter 1 (States of Mind).

Element (3). See the note on this Element to "Malicious Damage to Occupied Property by Use of an Explosive or Incendiary," above.

Element (4). For the definition of the term "explosive or incendiary device or material," see the note on Element (3) to "Malicious Injury by Use of an Explosive or Incendiary" in Chapter 7 (Assaults).

Multiple convictions and punishments. If a single explosion damages two or more pieces of property, even if one piece is real property and one personal, only one offense has occurred. State v. Conrad, 275 N.C. 342, 352–53 (1969).

Related Offenses Not in This Chapter

See the offenses listed under "Malicious Damage to Occupied Property by Use of an Explosive or Incendiary," above.

Malicious Damage to a Place of Religious Worship by Use of an Explosive or Incendiary

Statute

See G.S. 14-49(b1), reproduced under "Malicious Damage to Real or Personal Property by Use of an Explosive or Incendiary," above.

Elements

A person guilty of this offense

(1) willfully and maliciously
(2) damages, aids, counsels, or procures the damaging of
(3) a building of worship
(4) by use of an explosive or incendiary device or material.

Punishment

Class E felony. G.S. 14-49(b1).

Notes

Element (1). See "Willfully" and "Maliciously" in Chapter 1 (States of Mind).

Element (2). This offense covers damaging a building of worship. However, unlike "Malicious Damage to Real or Personal Property by Use of an Explosive or Incendiary," above, it also includes aiding, counseling, or procuring the damaging of a building of worship.

Element (3). The statute prohibits damage to a church, chapel, synagogue, mosque, masjid, or other building of worship. G.S. 14-49(b1).

Element (4). For the definition of the term "explosive or incendiary device or material," see the note on Element (3) to "Malicious Injury by Use of an Explosive or Incendiary" in Chapter 7 (Assaults).

Related Offenses Not in This Chapter

See the offenses listed under "Malicious Damage to Occupied Property by Use of an Explosive or Incendiary," above.
"Breaking or Entering a Place of Worship" (Chapter 15)

"Disorderly Conduct by Disrupting a Funeral" (Chapter 19)
"Disorderly Conduct by Disrupting a Religious Service or Assembly" (Chapter 19)

Malicious Damage to a Government Building by Use of an Explosive or Incendiary

Statute

See G.S. 14-49(b2), reproduced under "Malicious Damage to Real or Personal Property by Use of an Explosive or Incendiary," above.

Elements

A person guilty of this offense

(1) willfully and maliciously
(2) damages, aids, counsels, or procures the damaging of
(3) a government building
(4) by use of an explosive or incendiary device or material.

Punishment

Class E felony. G.S. 14-49(b2).

Notes

Element (1). See "Willfully" and "Maliciously" in Chapter 1 (States of Mind).

Element (2). This offense covers damaging a government building. However, unlike "Malicious Damage to Real or Personal Property by Use of an Explosive or Incendiary," above, it also includes aiding, counseling, or procuring the damaging of a government building.

Element (3). "Government buildings" include the State Capitol, the Legislative Building, the Justice Building, or any building owned or occupied by the state or any of its agencies, institutions, or subdivisions or by any county, incorporated city or town, or other governmental entity. G.S. 14-49(b2).

Element (4). For the definition of the term "explosive or incendiary device or material," see the note on Element (3) to "Malicious Injury by Use of an Explosive or Incendiary" in Chapter 7 (Assaults).

Related Offenses Not in This Chapter

See the offenses listed under "Malicious Damage to Occupied Property by Use of an Explosive or Incendiary," above.
"Defacing a Public Building, Statue, or Monument" (Chapter 18)
"Disorderly Conduct in a Public Building" (Chapter 19)

False Bomb Report Offenses

Statute

§14-69.1. Making a false report concerning destructive device.

(a) Except as provided in subsection (c) of this section, any person who, by any means of communication to any person or group of persons, makes a report, knowing or having reason to know the report is false, that there is located in or in sufficient proximity to cause damage to any building, house or other structure whatsoever or any vehicle, aircraft, vessel or boat any device designed to destroy or damage the building, house or structure or vehicle, aircraft, vessel or boat by explosion, blasting or burning, is guilty of a Class H felony.

(b) Repealed by S.L. 1997-443, s. 19.25(cc).

(c) Any person who, by any means of communication to any person or groups of persons, makes a report, knowing or having reason to know the report is false, that there is located in or in sufficient proximity to cause damage to any public building any device designed to destroy or damage the public building by explosion, blasting, or burning, is guilty of a Class H felony. Any person who receives a second conviction for a violation of this subsection within five years of the first conviction for violation of this subsection is guilty of a Class G felony. For purposes of this subsection, "public building" means educational property as defined in G.S. 14-269.2(a)(1), a hospital as defined in G.S. 131E-76(3), a building housing only State, federal, or local government offices, or the offices of State, federal, or local government located in a building that is not exclusively occupied by the State, federal, or local government.

(d) The court may order a person convicted under this section to pay restitution, including costs and consequential damages resulting from the disruption of the normal activity that would have otherwise occurred on the premises but for the false report, pursuant to Article 81C of Chapter 15A of the General Statutes.

(e) For purposes of this section, the term "report" shall include making accessible to another person by computer.

Making a False Bomb Report as to a Public Building

Statute

See G.S. 14-69.1(c), reproduced above.

Elements

A person guilty of this offense

(1) makes a report,
(2) knowing or having reason to know
(3) that the report is false,
(4) that there is located in or in sufficient proximity to cause damage to any public building
(5) any device designed to destroy or damage the public building
(6) by explosion, blasting, or burning.

Punishment

Class H felony. G.S. 14-69.1(c). A person who is convicted of this offense within five years of a first conviction is guilty of a Class G felony. *Id.* If the defendant is charged with the Class G version of this offense, the relevant fact elevating punishment must be alleged in a charging instrument and proved at trial. *See* G.S. 15A-928 (alleging and proving prior convictions). A defendant may be required to pay restitution, including costs and consequential damages resulting from the disruption of the normal activity that would have occurred but for the false report. G.S. 14-69.1(d).

Notes

Element (1). The report may be made by any means of communication, G.S. 14-69.1(c); the term "report" includes making accessible to another person by computer, G.S. 14-69.1(e). The report must be made to a person or group of persons. G.S. 14-69.1(c).

Element (4). "Public building" means educational property as defined in G.S. 14-269.2(a)(1), a hospital as defined in G.S. 131E-76(3), or a building housing state, federal, or local government offices. G.S. 14-69.1(c).

Relation to other offenses. A student who typed a message "Bomb at Lunch" on a school calculator while at school could have been charged under either G.S. 14-69.1(a) ("Making a False Bomb Report as to a Nonpublic Building or a Vehicle, Aircraft, Vessel, or Boat," discussed below) or G.S. 14-69.1(c) ("Making a False Bomb Report as to a Public Building" (the offense under discussion)); although the defendant could have been charged with making a false report about a bomb in a public building under G.S. 14-69.1(c), the conviction under G.S. 14-69.1(a) was proper because the school was a building covered by G.S. 14-69.1(a). *In re* B.D.N., 186 N.C. App. 108, 114–16 (2007).

Related Offenses Not in This Chapter

"Communicating Threats" (Chapter 8)
"False Report to Law Enforcement Agencies or Officers" (Chapter 21)

Making a False Bomb Report as to a Nonpublic Building or a Vehicle, Aircraft, Vessel, or Boat

Statute

See G.S. 14-69.1(a), reproduced above.

Elements

A person guilty of this offense

(1) makes a report,
(2) knowing or having reason to know
(3) that the report is false,
(4) that there is located in or in sufficient proximity to cause damage to any building, house, other structure, vehicle, aircraft, vessel, or boat
(5) any device designed to destroy or damage the building, house, other structure, vehicle, aircraft, vessel, or boat
(6) by explosion, blasting, or burning.

Punishment

Class H felony. G.S. 14-69.1(a). A defendant may be required to pay restitution, including costs and consequential damages resulting from the disruption of the normal activity that would have occurred but for the false report. G.S. 14-69.1(d).

Notes

Element (1). See this note to "Making a False Bomb Report as to a Public Building," above.

Relation to other offenses. See this note to "Making a False Bomb Report as to a Public Building," above.

Related Offenses Not in This Chapter

See the offenses listed under "Making a False Bomb Report as to a Public Building," above.

Perpetrating a Hoax by Use of a False Bomb or Other Device

Statute

§14-69.2. Perpetrating hoax by use of false bomb or other device.

(a) Except as provided in subsection (c) of this section, any person who, with intent to perpetrate a hoax, conceals, places, or displays any device, machine, instrument or artifact, so as to cause any person reasonably to believe the same to be a bomb or other device capable of causing injury to persons or property is guilty of a Class H felony.

(b) Repealed by S.L. 1997-443, s. 19.25(dd).

(c) Any person who, with intent to perpetrate a hoax, conceals, places, or displays in or at a public building any device, machine, instrument, or artifact, so as to cause any person reasonably to believe the same to be a bomb or other device capable of causing injury to persons or property is guilty of a Class H felony. Any person who receives a second conviction for a violation of this subsection within five years of the first conviction for violation of this subsection is guilty of a Class G felony. For purposes of this subsection "public building" means educational property as defined in G.S. 14-269.2(a)(1), a hospital as defined in G.S. 131E-76(3), a building housing only State, federal, or local government offices, or the offices of State, federal, or local government located in a building that is not exclusively occupied by the State, federal, or local government.

(d) The court may order a person convicted under this section to pay restitution, including costs and consequential damages resulting from the disruption of the normal activity that would have otherwise occurred on the premises but for the hoax, pursuant to Article 81C of Chapter 15A of the General Statutes.

Perpetrating a Hoax in or at a Public Building

Statute

See G.S. 14-69.2(c), reproduced above.

Elements

A person guilty of this offense

(1) with intent to perpetrate a hoax
(2) conceals, places, or displays
(3) in or at a public building
(4) any device, machine, instrument, or artifact
(5) so as to cause any person reasonably to believe the item to be a bomb or other device capable of causing injury to persons or property.

Punishment

Class H felony. G.S. 14-69.2(c). A second conviction within five years of the first conviction is punished as a Class G felony. *Id.* If the Class G version of this offense is charged, the fact elevating punishment must be alleged in a charging instrument and proved at trial. *See* G.S. 15A-928 (alleging and proving prior convictions). A defendant may be required to pay restitution, including costs and consequential damages resulting from the disruption of the normal activity interrupted by the hoax. G.S. 14-69.2(d).

Notes

Element (3). "Public building" means educational property as defined in G.S. 14-269.2(a)(1), a hospital as defined in G.S. 131E-76(3), or a building housing state, federal, or local government offices. G.S. 14-69.2(c).

Related Offenses Not in This Chapter

"Disorderly Conduct in a Public Building" (Chapter 19)

Perpetrating a Hoax in a Nonpublic Building or Other Location

Statute

See G.S. 14-69.2(a), reproduced above.

Elements

A person guilty of this offense

(1) with intent to perpetrate a hoax
(2) conceals, places, or displays
(3) any device, machine, instrument, or artifact
(4) so as to cause any person reasonably to believe the same to be a bomb or other device capable of causing injury to persons or property.

Punishment

Class H felony. G.S. 14-69.2(a). A defendant may be required to pay restitution, including costs and consequential damages resulting from the disruption of the normal activity interrupted by the hoax. G.S. 14-69.2(d).

Notes

Generally. This offense is the same as "Perpetrating a Hoax in or at a Public Building," above, except that for this offense the hoax need not occur in or at a public building. Also, it appears that this offense can be committed at any location and need not occur in a building.

Related Offenses Not in This Chapter

None

Making a False Report Concerning Mass Violence on Educational Property

Statute

§14-277.5. Making a false report concerning mass violence on educational property.

(a) The following definitions apply in this section:

(1) Educational property. – As defined in G.S. 14-269.2.
(2) Mass violence. – Physical injury that a reasonable person would conclude could lead to permanent injury (including mental or emotional injury) or death to two or more people.
(3) School. – As defined in G.S. 14-269.2.

(b) A person who, by any means of communication to any person or groups of persons, makes a report, knowing or having reason to know the report is false, that an act of mass violence is going to occur on educational property or at a curricular or extracurricular activity sponsored by a school, is guilty of a Class H felony.

(c) The court may order a person convicted under this section to pay restitution, including costs and consequential damages resulting from the disruption of the normal activity that would have otherwise occurred on the premises but for the false report, pursuant to Article 81C of Chapter 15A of the General Statutes.

Elements

A person guilty of this offense

(1) makes a report
(2) to any person or groups of persons
(3) that an act of mass violence

(4) is going to occur
(5) on educational property or at a school-sponsored activity
(6) knowing or having reason to know that the report is false.

Punishment

Class H felony. G.S. 14-277.5(b). The court may order restitution, including costs and consequential damages resulting from the disruption of the normal activity that would have otherwise occurred on the premises but for the false report. G.S. 14-277.5(c).

Notes

Element (1). The report may be made by any means of communication. G.S. 14-277.5(b).

Element (3). The term "mass violence" means "[p]hysical injury that a reasonable person would conclude could lead to permanent injury (including mental or emotional injury) or death to two or more people." G.S. 14-277.5(a)(2).

Element (5). The school-sponsored activity may be a curricular or extracurricular activity. G.S. 14-277.5(b).

The term "educational property" is defined by cross reference to G.S. 14-269.2 to include any school building, bus, campus, grounds, recreational area, athletic field, or other property owned, used, or operated by any board of education, school board of trustees, or directors for the administration of any school. G.S. 14-277.5(a)(1).

The term "school" is defined by cross-reference to G.S. 14-269.2 to mean any public or private school, community college, college, or university. G.S. 14-277.5(a)(3).

Related Offenses Not in This Chapter

"False Report to Law Enforcement Agencies or Officers" (Chapter 21)

Nuclear, Biological, or Chemical Weapon of Mass Destruction Offenses

Manufacture, Assembly, Possession, etc. of a Nuclear, Biological, or Chemical Weapon of Mass Destruction

Statute

§14-288.21. Unlawful manufacture, assembly, possession, storage, transportation, sale, purchase, delivery, or acquisition of a nuclear, biological, or chemical weapon of mass destruction; exceptions; punishment.

(a) Except as otherwise provided in this section, it is unlawful for any person to knowingly manufacture, assemble, possess, store, transport, sell, offer to sell, purchase, offer to purchase, deliver or give to another, or acquire a nuclear, biological, or chemical weapon of mass destruction.

(b) This section does not apply to:

(1) Persons listed in G.S. 14-269(b) with respect to any activities lawfully engaged in while carrying out their duties.

(2) Persons under contract with, or working under the direction of, the United States, the State of North Carolina, or any agency of either government, with respect to any activities lawfully engaged in under their contracts or pursuant to lawful direction.

(3) Persons lawfully engaged in the development, production, manufacture, assembly, possession, transport, sale, purchase, delivery or acquisition of any biological agent, disease organism, toxic or poisonous chemical, radioactive

substance or their immediate precursors, for preventive, protective, or other peaceful purposes.

(4) Persons lawfully engaged in accepted agricultural, horticultural, or forestry practices; aquatic weed control; or structural pest and rodent control, in a manner approved by the federal, State, county, or local agency charged with authority over such activities.

(c) The term "nuclear, biological, or chemical weapon of mass destruction", as used in this Article, means any of the following:

(1) Any weapon, device, or method that is designed or has the capability to cause death or serious injury through the release, dissemination, or impact of:
   a. Radiation or radioactivity;
   b. A disease organism; or
   c. Toxic or poisonous chemicals or their immediate precursors.

(2) Any substance that is designed or has the capability to cause death or serious injury and:
   a. Contains radiation or radioactivity;
   b. Is or contains toxic or poisonous chemicals or their immediate precursors; or
   c. Is or contains one or more of the following:
      1. Any select agent that is a microorganism, virus, bacterium, fungus, rickettsia, or toxin listed in Appendix A of Part 72 of Title 42 of the Code of Federal Regulations.
      2. Any genetically modified microorganisms or genetic elements from an organism on Appendix A of Part 72 of Title 42 of the Code of Federal Regulations, shown to produce or encode for a factor associated with a disease.
      3. Any genetically modified microorganisms or genetic elements that contain nucleic acid sequences coding for any of the toxins listed on Appendix A of Part 72 of Title 42 of the Code of Federal Regulations, or their toxic submits.

The term "nuclear, biological, or chemical weapon of mass destruction" also includes any combination of parts or substances either designed or intended for use in converting any device or substance into any nuclear, biological, or chemical weapon of mass destruction or from which a nuclear, biological, or chemical weapon of mass destruction may be readily assembled or created.

(d) Any person who violates any provision of this section is guilty of a Class B1 felony.

Elements

A person guilty of this offense

(1) knowingly
(2) (a) manufactures,
    (b) assembles,
    (c) possesses,
    (d) stores,
    (e) transports,
    (f) sells,
    (g) offers to sell,
    (h) purchases,
    (i) offers to purchase,
    (j) delivers,
    (k) gives to another, *or*
    (l) acquires
(3) a nuclear, biological, or chemical weapon of mass destruction.

Punishment

Class B1 felony. G.S. 14-288.21(d).

Notes

Element (3). The definition of "nuclear, biological, or chemical weapon of mass destruction" is set out in G.S. 14-288.21(c).

Exceptions. Certain persons listed in G.S. 14-288.21(b) are excepted from the statute.

Related Offenses Not in This Chapter

See the offenses in Chapter 22 (Weapons Offenses).

Injuring Another with a Nuclear, Biological, or Chemical Weapon of Mass Destruction

Statute

§14-288.22. Unlawful use of a nuclear, biological, or chemical weapon of mass destruction; punishment.

(a) Any person who unlawfully and willfully injures another by the use of a nuclear, biological, or chemical weapon of mass destruction is guilty of a Class A felony and shall be sentenced to life imprisonment without parole.

(b) Any person who attempts, solicits another, or conspires to injure another by the use of a nuclear, biological, or chemical weapon of mass destruction is guilty of a Class B1 felony.

(c) Any person who for the purpose of violating any provision of this Article, deposits for delivery or attempts to have delivered, a nuclear, biological, or chemical weapon of mass destruction by the United States Postal Service or other public or private business engaged in the delivery of mail, packages, or parcels is guilty of a Class B1 felony.

Elements

A person guilty of this offense

(1) unlawfully and willfully
(2) injures another
(3) by the use of a nuclear, biological, or chemical weapon of mass destruction.

Punishment

Class A felony requiring a sentence of life imprisonment without parole. G.S. 14-288.22(a).

Notes

Element (1). See "Willfully," in Chapter 1 (States of Mind).

Element (2). Unlike assault offenses that specify a particular type of injury, see for example, "Assault Inflicting Serious Injury" and "Assault Inflicting Serious Bodily Injury," both in Chapter 7 (Assaults), the term "injures" is not modified for this offense. Thus, it appears that any level of injury will satisfy this element. It is not clear whether the injury must be physical or whether mental injury will suffice.

Element (3). The definition of "nuclear, biological, or chemical weapon of mass destruction" is set out in G.S. 14-288.21(c), reproduced under "Manufacture, Assembly, Possession, etc. of a Nuclear, Biological, or Chemical Weapon of Mass Destruction," above.

Attempt, solicitation, or conspiracy. G.S. 14-288.22(b) provides that anyone who attempts, solicits another, or conspires to commit this crime is guilty of a Class B1 felony. See generally "Attempt," "Solicitation," and "Conspiracy," all in Chapter 5 (General Crimes).

Relationship to first-degree murder. If death results, the offense would be first-degree murder. See "First-Degree Murder" in Chapter 6 (Homicide).

Related Offenses Not in This Chapter

See the related offenses listed under "Malicious Damage to Occupied Property by Use of an Explosive or Incendiary," above.
"First-Degree Murder" (Chapter 6)
See the offenses in Chapter 7 (Assaults).

Delivery of a Nuclear, Biological, or Chemical Weapon of Mass Destruction by Mail or Other Carrier

Statute

See G.S. 14-288.22(c), reproduced under "Injuring Another with a Nuclear, Biological, or Chemical Weapon of Mass Destruction," above.

Elements

A person guilty of this offense

(1) (a) deposits for delivery *or*
    (b) attempts to have delivered
(2) (a) by the United States Postal Service *or*
    (b) other public or private business engaged in the delivery of mail, packages, or parcels
(3) a nuclear, biological, or chemical weapon of mass destruction
(4) for the purpose of violating any provision of G.S. Ch. 15, Article 36B.

Punishment

Class B1. G.S. 14-288.22(c).

Notes

Element (3). The definition of "nuclear, biological, or chemical weapon of mass destruction" is set out in G.S. 14-288.21(c), which is reproduced under "Manufacture, Assembly, Possession, etc. of a Nuclear, Biological, or Chemical Weapon of Mass Destruction," above.

Element (4). The offenses included in Article 36B include:

- "Manufacture, Assembly, Possession, etc. of a Nuclear, Biological, or Chemical Weapon of Mass Destruction" (discussed above);
- "Injuring Another with a Nuclear, Biological, or Chemical Weapon of Mass Destruction" (discussed above);
- "Making a False Report Concerning a Nuclear, Biological, or Chemical Weapon of Mass Destruction" (discussed below); and
- "Perpetrating a Hoax Concerning a Nuclear, Biological, or Chemical Weapon of Mass Destruction" (discussed below).

Attempt. The statute punishes an attempt to commit this offense like the completed offense, not one level lower, as is typically the case for an attempt. See "Attempt" in Chapter 5 (General Crimes).

Related Offenses Not in This Chapter

"Conspiracy" (Chapter 5)

Making a False Report Concerning a Nuclear, Biological, or Chemical Weapon of Mass Destruction

Statute

§14-288.23. Making a false report concerning a nuclear, biological, or chemical weapon of mass destruction; punishment; restitution.

(a) Any person who, by any means of communication to any person or group of persons, makes a report, knowing or having reason to know the report is false, that causes any person to reasonably believe that there is located at any place or structure whatsoever any nuclear, biological, or chemical weapon of mass destruction is guilty of a Class D felony.

(b) The court may order a person convicted under this section to pay restitution, including costs and consequential damages resulting from disruption of the normal activity that would have otherwise occurred but for the false report, pursuant to Article 81C of Chapter 15A of the General Statutes.

(c) For purposes of this section, the term "report" shall include making accessible to another person by computer.

Elements

A person guilty of this offense,

(1) by any means of communication,
(2) makes a report,
(3) knowing or having reason to know the report is false,
(4) that causes any person to reasonably believe
(5) that there is located in any place or structure
(6) a nuclear, biological, or chemical weapon of mass destruction.

Punishment

Class D felony. G.S. 14-288.23(a). A defendant may be ordered to pay restitution, including costs and consequential damages resulting from disruption of the normal activity by the false report. G.S. 14-288.23(b).

Notes

Element (2). The report must be made to a person or group of persons. G.S. 14-288.23(a). G.S. 14-288.23(c) provides that the term "report" includes making accessible to another person by computer.

Element (5). A threat to put a nuclear, biological, or chemical weapon of mass destruction in a place or structure does not satisfy this element—there must be a false report that such a weapon is at the place or structure. G.S. 14-288.23(a). The offense covers "any place or structure whatsoever" and is, therefore, very broad in coverage. *Id.*

Element (6). The definition of "nuclear, biological, or chemical weapon of mass destruction" is set out in G.S. 14-288.21(c), reproduced under "Manufacture, Assembly, Possession, etc. of a Nuclear, Biological, or Chemical Weapon of Mass Destruction," above.

Related Offenses Not in This Chapter

"Communicating Threats" (Chapter 8)
"False Report to Law Enforcement Agencies or Officers" (Chapter 21)

Perpetrating a Hoax Concerning a Nuclear, Biological, or Chemical Weapon of Mass Destruction

Statute

§14-288.24. Perpetrating hoax by use of false nuclear, biological, or chemical weapon of mass destruction; punishment; restitution.

(a) Any person who, with intent to perpetrate a hoax, conceals, places, or displays any device, object, machine, instrument, or artifact, so as to cause any person reasonably to believe the same to be a nuclear, biological, or chemical weapon of mass destruction is guilty of a Class D felony.

(b) The court may order a person convicted under this section to pay restitution, including costs and consequential damages resulting from disruption of the normal activity that would have otherwise occurred but for the hoax, pursuant to Article 81C of Chapter 15A of the General Statutes.

Elements

A person guilty of this offense,

(1) with the intent to perpetrate a hoax,
(2) conceals, places, or displays
(3) a device, object, machine, instrument, or artifact
(4) so as to cause a person reasonably to believe it is
(5) a nuclear, biological, or chemical weapon of mass destruction.

Punishment

Class D felony. G.S. 14-288.24(a). A defendant may be ordered to pay restitution, including costs and consequential damages resulting from disruption of the normal activity by the hoax. G.S. 14-288.24(b).

Notes

Element (6). The definition of "nuclear, biological, or chemical weapon of mass destruction" is set out in G.S. 14-288.21(c), reproduced under "Manufacture, Assembly, Possession, etc. of a Nuclear, Biological, or Chemical Weapon of Mass Destruction," above.

Related Offenses Not in This Chapter

None

Manufacture, Possession, etc. of a Machine Gun, Sawed-Off Shotgun, or Weapon of Mass Destruction

Statute

§14-288.8. Manufacture, assembly, possession, storage, transportation, sale, purchase, delivery, or acquisition of weapon of mass death and destruction; exceptions.

(a) Except as otherwise provided in this section, it is unlawful for any person to manufacture, assemble, possess, store, transport, sell, offer to sell, purchase, offer to purchase, deliver or give to another, or acquire any weapon of mass death and destruction.

(b) This section does not apply to any of the following:

(1) Persons exempted from the provisions of G.S. 14-269 with respect to any activities lawfully engaged in while carrying out their duties.
(2) Importers, manufacturers, dealers, and collectors of firearms, ammunition, or destructive devices validly licensed under the laws of the United States or

the State of North Carolina, while lawfully engaged in activities authorized under their licenses.

(3) Persons under contract with the United States, the State of North Carolina, or any agency of either government, with respect to any activities lawfully engaged in under their contracts.

(4) Inventors, designers, ordnance consultants and researchers, chemists, physicists, and other persons lawfully engaged in pursuits designed to enlarge knowledge or to facilitate the creation, development, or manufacture of weapons of mass death and destruction intended for use in a manner consistent with the laws of the United States and the State of North Carolina.

(5) Persons who lawfully possess or own a weapon as defined in subsection (c) of this section in compliance with 26 U.S.C. Chapter 53, §§ 5801-5871. Nothing in this subdivision shall limit the discretion of the sheriff in executing the paperwork required by the United States Bureau of Alcohol, Tobacco and Firearms for such person to obtain the weapon.

(c) The term "weapon of mass death and destruction" includes:

(1) Any explosive or incendiary:
   a. Bomb; or
   b. Grenade; or
   c. Rocket having a propellant charge of more than four ounces; or
   d. Missile having an explosive or incendiary charge of more than one-quarter ounce; or
   e. Mine; or
   f. Device similar to any of the devices described above; or

(2) Any type of weapon (other than a shotgun or a shotgun shell of a type particularly suitable for sporting purposes) which will, or which may be readily converted to, expel a projectile by the action of an explosive or other propellant, and which has any barrel with a bore of more than one-half inch in diameter; or

(3) Any firearm capable of fully automatic fire, any shotgun with a barrel or barrels of less than 18 inches in length or an overall length of less than 26 inches, any rifle with a barrel or barrels of less than 16 inches in length or an overall length of less than 26 inches, any muffler or silencer for any firearm, whether or not such firearm is included within this definition. For the purposes of this section, rifle is defined as a weapon designed or redesigned, made or remade, and intended to be fired from the shoulder; or

(4) Any combination of parts either designed or intended for use in converting any device into any weapon described above and from which a weapon of mass death and destruction may readily be assembled.

The term "weapon of mass death and destruction" does not include any device which is neither designed nor redesigned for use as a weapon; any device, although originally designed for use as a weapon, which is redesigned for use as a signaling, pyrotechnic, line-throwing, safety, or similar device; surplus ordnance sold, loaned, or given by the Secretary of the Army pursuant to the provisions of section 4684(2), 4685, or 4686 of Title 10 of the United States Code; or any other device which the Secretary of the Treasury finds is not likely to be used as a weapon, is an antique, or is a rifle which the owner intends to use solely for sporting purposes, in accordance with Chapter 44 of Title 18 of the United States Code.

(d) Any person who violates any provision of this section is guilty of a Class F felony.

Elements

A person guilty of this offense

(1) (a) manufactures,
    (b) assembles,
    (c) possesses,
    (d) stores,

(e) transports,
(f) sells,
(g) offers to sell,
(h) purchases,
(i) offers to purchase,
(j) delivers,
(k) gives to another, *or*
(l) acquires

(2) a weapon of mass death and destruction.

Punishment

Class F felony. G.S. 14-288.8(d).

Notes

Generally. Although this offense is included in the Riot and Civil Disorder Act, it also applies when no riot or state of emergency exists.

Element (1)(c). There was sufficient evidence to establish that the defendant constructively possessed a sawed-off shotgun when the evidence showed that the defendant owned the weapon. State v. Billinger, ___ N.C. App. ___, 714 S.E.2d 201 (2011) (following law from other jurisdictions, the court held that "constructive possession may be established by evidence showing the defendant's ownership of the contraband"). For a discussion of constructive possession as it applies with respect to other offenses, see the note on Element (2)(c) to "Posession of a Firearm by a Felon" in Chapter 22 (Weapons Offenses) and the note on Element (2) to "Possession of a Controlled Substance" in Chapter 27 (Drug Offenses).

Element (2). According to G.S. 14-288.8(c), the term "weapon of mass death and destruction" includes:

- any explosive or incendiary, including a bomb; grenade; rocket having a propellant charge of more than four ounces; missile having an explosive or incendiary charge of more than one-quarter ounce; mine; or any similar device;
- any type of weapon (other than a shotgun or a shotgun shell of a type particularly suitable for sporting purposes) that will or may be readily converted to expel a projectile by the action of an explosive or other propellant and which has any barrel with a bore of more than one-half inch in diameter;
- any firearm capable of fully automatic fire;
- any shotgun with a barrel or barrels of less than 18 inches in length or an overall length of less than 26 inches;
- any rifle with a barrel or barrels of less than 16 inches in length or an overall length of less than 26 inches;
- any muffler or silencer for any firearm, whether or not the firearm is itself a weapon of mass death and destruction; and
- any combination of parts either designed or intended for use in converting any device into any weapon described above and from which a weapon of mass death and destruction may readily be assembled.

G.S. 14-288.8(c). A rifle is a weapon designed or redesigned, made or remade, and intended to be fired from the shoulder. *Id.*

The State is not required to prove that the defendant knew of the physical characteristics of the weapon that made it unlawful under the statute. State v. Watterson, 198 N.C. App. 500 (2009).

Exceptions. G.S. 14-288.8(c) exempts the following weapons from coverage by the statute:

- a device neither designed nor redesigned for use as a weapon;
- a device, although originally designed for use as a weapon, redesigned for use as a signaling, pyrotechnic, line-throwing, safety, or similar device;
- surplus ordnance sold, loaned, or given by the Army; and
- any other device that the Secretary of the Treasury finds is not likely to be used as a weapon, is an antique, or is a rifle that the owner intends to use solely for sporting purposes.

G.S. 14-288.8(b) exempts certain persons from this offense.

Defenses. Whether a sawed-off shotgun fits the antique exception is an affirmative defense for which the defendant must present evidence. State v. Blackwell, 163 N.C. App. 12, 19 (2004).

Inoperability is generally not a defense to this offense, except that a defendant may prove that certain items seized were not designed or intended for use in converting any device into a weapon of mass death and destruction. State v. Jackson, 353 N.C. 495 (2001).

Multiple convictions and punishments. The evidence was sufficient to support multiple counts of possession of a weapon of mass death and destruction where the defendant used the same weapon during robberies that occurred on different days and in different locations. State v. Lee, ___ N.C. App. ___, 713 S.E.2d 174, 179 (2011) (reasoning that because "each possession of the weapon was separate in time and location, . . . the trial court did not err in denying defendant's motion to dismiss the multiple weapons possession charges").

Disposition of seized weapons. See the note on this topic under "Possession of a Firearm by a Felon" in Chapter 22 (Weapons Offenses).

Related Offenses Not in This Chapter

See the offenses in Chapter 22 (Weapons Offenses).

21
Perjury, Bribery, Obstruction, Resisting, and Related Crimes

21
Perjury, Bribery, Obstruction, Resisting, and Related Crimes

Obstruction of Justice

Statute

This is a common law offense. *In re* Kivett, 309 N.C. 635, 670 (1983).

Elements

A person guilty of this offense

(1) unlawfully and willfully
(2) obstructs justice.

Punishment

Class 1 misdemeanor. G.S. 14-3(a). If done with deceit and intent to defraud, the offense is a Class H felony. G.S. 14-3(b); State v. Clemmons, 100 N.C. App. 286, 292–93 (1990). See generally "Infamous or related misdemeanor enhancement" under "Misdemeanors" in Chapter 4 (Punishment under Structured Sentencing). If the Class H version is charged, the relevant fact elevating punishment must be alleged in a charging instrument and proved at trial.

Notes

Element (1). See "Willfully" in Chapter 1 (States of Mind); *see also* State v. Eastman, 113 N.C. App. 347 (1994).

Element (2). Obstructing justice consists of any act that prevents, obstructs, impedes, or hinders public or legal justice. The crime may take many forms. *Kivett*, 309 N.C. at 670. The following conduct has been implicitly or explicitly recognized as constituting this offense:

- attempting to prevent the convening of a grand jury, *id.*;
- supplying money to pay a fine and costs to a person who pled guilty to a criminal offense, knowing that the person pleading guilty was not the one actually charged with the offense, State v. Preston, 73 N.C. App. 174, 176 (1985);
- offering to pay money to a prosecuting witness in exchange for the witness requesting dismissal of a criminal charge, *Clemmons*, 100 N.C. App. at 290;
- interfering with police processing duties in connection with an impaired driving charge against a third person, State v. Taylor, ___ N.C. App. ___, 713 S.E.2d 82 (2011); and
- filing false campaign finance reports, State v. Wright, ___ N.C. App. ___, 696 S.E.2d 832, 835–36 (2010).

A judicial proceeding or investigation need not be ongoing for this offense to apply. *Wright*, ___ N.C. App. ___, 696 S.E.2d at 836 (the evidence was sufficient when the defendant knowingly filed with the State Board of Elections false campaign finance reports with the intent to mislead the board and the public even though no judicial proceeding or investigation was ongoing).

Relation to other offenses. "Intimidating a Witness," below, is limited to intimidating a person who is "summoned" or "acting as a witness," at least in those cases when the threat pertains to something other than the assertion or denial of parental rights. This offense, however, appears to cover all forms of witness intimidation, including intimidation of prospective witnesses not summoned or acting as witnesses.

The existence of a statutorily-defined criminal offense does not deprive the State of the ability to prosecute a defendant for common law obstruction of justice. *Taylor*, ___ N.C. App. ___, 713 S.E.2d 82 (2011) (by enacting G.S. 14-223 (proscribing resisting, delaying, or obstructing an officer), the General Assembly did not deprive the State of the ability to prosecute a defendant for common law obstruction of justice, even when the defendant's conduct could have been charged under G.S. 14-223).

Related Offenses Not in This Chapter

"Communicating Threats" (Chapter 8)
See cyberstalking (various offenses) in Chapter 8 (Threats, Harassment, Stalking, and Violation of Domestic Protective Orders).
See harassing telephone calls (various offenses) in Chapter 8 (Threats, Harassment, Stalking, and Violation of Domestic Protective Orders).
"Threat to Kill or Inflict Serious Injury on Executive, Legislative, or Court Officers" (Chapter 8)
"Extortion" (Chapter 14)
Bribery of jurors. G.S. 14-220.
Altering, destroying, or stealing evidence of criminal conduct. G.S. 14-221.1.
Altering court documents or entering unauthorized judgments. G.S. 14-221.2.
Harassment of and communication with jurors. G.S. 14-225.2.
Violating orders of court. G.S. 14-226.1.
Submitting false information in connection with petition for restoration of firearms rights. G.S. 14-415.4(l).
Interference with electronic monitoring devices. G.S. 14-226.3.
Concealment of death; disturbing human remains; dismembering human remains. G.S. 14-401.22.
Impersonation of a law-enforcement or other public officer. G.S. 14-277.
Destroying, altering, concealing, or tampering with biological evidence. G.S. 15A-268(i).
Omitting or misrepresenting evidence or information required to be disclosed under discovery laws. G.S. 15A-903(d).
Giving false information required in a report of a reportable accident. G.S. 20-279.31(b)(1).
Unauthorized practice of law. G.S. 84-4.

Interfering with Witnesses

Statute

§14-226. Intimidating or interfering with witnesses.

(a) If any person shall by threats, menaces or in any other manner intimidate or attempt to intimidate any person who is summoned or acting as a witness in any of the courts of this State, or prevent or deter, or attempt to prevent or deter any person summoned or acting as such witness from attendance upon such court, the person shall be guilty of a Class G felony.

(b) A defendant in a criminal proceeding who threatens a witness in the defendant's case with the assertion or denial of parental rights shall be in violation of this section.

Intimidating a Witness

Statute

See G.S. 14-226(a), reproduced above.

Elements

A person guilty of this offense

(1) threatens, menaces, or in any other manner

(2) (a) intimidates or attempts to intimidate a person who is summoned or acting as a witness in any North Carolina state court *or*

(b) prevents, deters, or attempts to prevent or deter a person who is summoned or acting as a witness from attendance in any North Carolina state court.

Punishment

Class G felony. G.S. 14-226(a).

Notes

Element (1). The words "menace" and "coerce" are synonymous with the word "threat." State v. Williams, 186 N.C. App. 233, 238 (2007).

The evidence was sufficient when (1) the defendant threatened to kill a witness's daughter if the witness did not "drop the charges" after the defendant's conviction in district court and appeal for trial de novo in superior court, State v. Isom, 52 N.C. App. 331 (1981); (2) a juvenile mouthed the words "I'm going to kick your ass" to another juvenile, B.T., after B.T. admitted that he and the juvenile had committed a crime and after B.T. agreed—in court and in the juvenile's presence—to be a witness for the State against the juvenile, *In re* R.D.R., 175 N.C. App. 397 (2006); and (3) the defendant left a voicemail message calling the victim a "stinking nasty bitch" and stating, "you've got me under a $5,000 bond. As soon as I make it, I'm going to give you a God damn taste of your own fucking medicine"; additionally the two had a volatile and violent relationship, State v. Braxton, 183 N.C. App. 36, 44 (2007).

For cases in which there was insufficient evidence of this offense, see *Williams*, 186 N.C. App. at 238–39 (insufficient evidence of alleged "menaces and coercive statements" when the defendant's letter did not hint at bodily harm or violence and contained no curses, vulgarity, or threatening language); and *Braxton*, 183 N.C. App. at 44–45 (the victim's testimony that the defendant told her not to testify was insufficient to establish that the defendant threatened the victim).

Element (2). The statute is limited to situations where the person has been "summoned" or is "acting as a witness."

A defendant was properly convicted of this offense when he threatened a witness after the witness had testified in district court and the defendant had appealed for trial de novo in superior court; the witness—although not under subpoena—was a prospective witness when the threats were made as a result of the defendant's appeal for trial de novo. State v. Neely, 4 N.C. App. 475, 476–77 (1969).

Attempt. Elements (2)(a) and (b) both cover attempts, thus punishing an attempt to commit this crime at the same level as the completed crime as opposed to one level lower, as it typical for an attempt. See "Attempt" in Chapter 5 (General Crimes).

A lawyer's inducement of a subpoenaed State's witness to leave the courthouse so the lawyer could attempt to obtain a dismissal of the charges against his client was sufficient evidence to support a conviction of an attempt to commit this offense. State v. Rogers, 68 N.C. App. 358 (1984).

Charging issues. If the State alleges that the defendant intimidated or attempted to intimidate the victim by "threats," it is bound by that allegation at trial and may not prove its case with evidence that the intimidation or attempted intimidation occurred by way of "menaces" or "any other manner." *Braxton*, 183 N.C. App. at 43–44.

Relation to other offenses. See this note to "Obstruction of Justice," above.

Related Offenses Not in This Chapter

See the offenses listed under "Obstruction of Justice," above.

Threatening a Witness Regarding Parental Rights

Statute

See G.S. 14-226(b), reproduced above.

Elements

A person guilty of this offense

(1) is a defendant in a criminal proceeding *and*
(2) threatens
(3) a witness in the defendant's case
(4) with the assertion or denial of parental rights.

Punishment

Class G felony. G.S. 14-226(a).

Notes

Element (2). See the note on Element (1) to "Intimidating a Witness," above.

Element (3). For the offense of "Intimidating a Witness," above, the statute specifies that the witness must be a person who is "summoned" or is "acting as a witness." G.S. 14-226(a). For this offense, by contrast, the statute says that the person must be "a witness in the defendant's criminal case." G.S. 14-226(b). The fact that the General Assembly used different words to describe the covered witnesses in these two subsections of the same statute suggests that different persons are covered. However, it is not clear how the scope of the subsections differ in terms of the witnesses that are covered.

Related Offenses Not in This Chapter

See the offenses listed under "Obstruction of Justice," above.

Picketing a Courthouse

Statute

§14-225.1. Picketing or parading.

Any person who, with intent to interfere with, obstruct, or impede the administration of justice, or with intent to influence any justice or judge of the General Court of Justice, juror, witness, district attorney, assistant district attorney, or court officer, in the discharge of his duty, pickets, parades, or uses any sound truck or similar device within 300 feet of an exit from any building housing any court of the General Court of Justice, or within 300 feet of any building or residence occupied or used by such justice, judge, juror, witness, district attorney, assistant district attorney, or court officer, shall upon plea or conviction be guilty of a Class 1 misdemeanor.

Elements

A person guilty of this offense

(1) (a) pickets,
 (b) parades, *or*
 (c) uses a sound truck or similar device
(2) within 300 feet of
(3) (a) any exit of any building that houses a North Carolina court *or*
 (b) any building or residence occupied or used by a North Carolina judge or justice, juror, witness, district attorney, assistant district attorney, or other court officer
(4) with the intent to
 (a) interfere with, obstruct, or impede the administration of justice *or*
 (b) influence a North Carolina judge or justice, juror, witness, district attorney, assistant district attorney, or other court officer in discharging his or her duty.

Punishment

Class 1 misdemeanor. G.S. 14-225.1.

Notes

Element (2). Apparently the offense is not committed if the picketing, parading, or use of sound truck occurs more than 300 feet from the courthouse, even though the demonstration might be heard from the courthouse, building, or residence.

Element (3)(a). To satisfy this element, a building need not be an actual courthouse; so long as court is held there, this will suffice.

Element (3)(b). The offense would be committed, for example, if the picketing, parading, or use of a sound truck took place within 300 feet of a motel housing a judge, jurors, witnesses, or other specified officials.

Constitutionality. Although this statute has been challenged on constitutional grounds, no published appellate cases have resolved the issue. *See, e.g.,* Crumpler v. Thornburg, 92 N.C. App. 719 (1989) (when a picketer challenged the statute as unconstitutional, the superior court entered summary judgment in favor of the picketer; the court of appeals held that the case was moot).

Related Offenses Not in This Chapter

"Communicating Threats" (Chapter 8)
See cyberstalking (various offenses) in Chapter 8 (Threats, Harassment, Stalking, and Violation of Domestic Protective Orders).
See harassing telephone calls (various offenses) in Chapter 8 (Threats, Harassment, Stalking, and Violation of Domestic Protective Orders).
"Threat to Kill or Inflict Serious Injury on Executive, Legislative, or Court Officers" (Chapter 8)
"Defacing a Public Building, Statue, or Monument" (Chapter 18)
"First-Degree Trespass" (Chapter 18)
"Second-Degree Trespass" (Chapter 18)
"Injury to Personal Property" (Chapter 18)
"Injury to Real Property" (Chapter 18)

See disorderly conduct (various offenses) in Chapter 19 (Disorderly Conduct, Riot, and Gang Offenses).
Trespass on public lands. G.S. 14-130.
Bribery of jurors. G.S. 14-220.
Harassment and communication with jurors. G.S. 14-225.2.

Perjury Offenses

Perjury

Statute

This offense is defined by the common law and by statute. State v. Denny, 361 N.C. 662, 665 (2007).

> **§14-209. Punishment for perjury.**
> If any person shall willfully and corruptly commit perjury, on his oath or affirmation, in any suit, controversy, matter or cause, depending in any of the courts of the State, or in any deposition or affidavit taken pursuant to law, or in any oath or affirmation duly administered of or concerning any matter or thing whereof such person is lawfully required to be sworn or affirmed, every person so offending shall be punished as a Class F felon.

Elements

A person guilty of this offense

(1) willfully and corruptly
(2) while under oath or affirmation
(3) gives testimony or makes a statement
(4) that is false *and*
(5) that is material.

Punishment

Class F felony. G.S. 14-209.

Notes

Generally. For the elements of this offense, see *Denny,* 361 N.C. at 665 and N.C. PATTERN JURY INSTRUCTIONS—CRIM. 228.10.

Element (1). The terms "willfully and corruptly" are understood to mean knowingly, purposefully, and designedly. N.C. PATTERN JURY INSTRUCTIONS—CRIM. 228.10.

To commit this offense, the defendant must know that the statement is false and must make it intentionally. State v. Smith, 230 N.C. 198 (1949); State v. Dowd, 201 N.C. 714 (1931); State v. Basden, 110 N.C. App. 449 (1993). For a case in which there was sufficient evidence of this element even though the defendant claimed that he did not intentionally misstate the facts regarding his ownership interest in real estate on an affidavit of indigency, see *Denny,* 361 N.C. at 665–67.

Element (2). The statement may be made "in any suit, controversy, matter or cause, depending in any of the courts of the State, or in any deposition or affidavit taken pursuant to law, or in any oath or affirmation duly administered of or concerning any matter or thing whereof such person is lawfully required to be sworn or affirmed." G.S. 14-209.

Element (3). Perjury can apply to both oral and written statements. Statements of qualification such as "I don't think so" or "I don't recall saying that" do not prevent testimony from being considered perjury. *Basden,* 110 N.C. App. at 454.

Element (5). To constitute perjury, the false statement must bear directly on a matter at issue in the proceedings; a false statement about something else is not perjury. State v. Smith, 230 N.C. 198 (1949); State v. Lucas, 247 N.C. 208 (1957); *Basden,* 110 N.C. App. at 454. The federal Constitution requires that the State prove the element of materiality to a jury beyond a reasonable doubt. United States v. Gaudin, 515 U.S. 506 (1995); State v. Linney, 138 N.C. App. 169, 176–77 (2000).

Charging issues. G.S. 15-145 provides the form for a bill of perjury.

Evidence issues. To establish perjury, the falsity of the statement must be proved by the testimony of two witnesses or by one witness and other corroborating testimony. State v. Allen, 260 N.C. 220 (1963); *Basden,* 110 N.C. App. at 453. For example, a doctor's opinion that a wound was inflicted by a sharp-edged instrument corroborated a witness's testimony that the defendant lied when he said he had not used an axe in a fight. State v. Hawkins, 115 N.C. 712 (1894).

Relation to other offenses. See *State v. Denny,* 361 N.C. 662 (2007), for a case in which a perjury conviction was upheld based on a false statement in an affidavit of indigency.

Related Offenses Not in This Chapter

"Obtaining Property by False Pretenses" (Chapter 16)
False statements regarding question of indigency. G.S. 7A-456.
Perjury before legislative committees. G.S. 14-211.
Altering court documents or entering unauthorized judgments. G.S. 14-221.2.
Swearing falsely to official reports. G.S. 14-232.
Providing materially false information regarding legality of firearm or ammunition transfer. G.S. 14-408.1.
Submitting false information in connection with a petition for restoration of firearms rights. G.S. 14-415.4(l).
Making false oath on matters required by Driver's License Act. G.S. 20-31.
Making false oath on matters required by Motor Vehicle Act of 1937. G.S. 20-112.
Giving false information required in a report of a reportable accident. G.S. 20-279.31(b)(1).
False swearing to creditor's oath. G.S. 23-9.
False taking of debtor's oath. G.S. 23-43.
False statement to procure or deny benefit of insurance policy or certificate. G.S. 58-2-161.
False statement to Commissioner of Insurance. G.S. 58-2-180.
False oath to certificate of mutual insurance company. G.S. 58-8-1.
False oath to statement required of fraternal benefit societies. G.S. 58-24-180.
False swearing in fire investigation by Attorney General. G.S. 58-79-10.
False complaint about failure of employer to use E-verify system. G.S. 64-28(b).
False swearing by person responding to investigation of trusts and monopolies. G.S. 75-12.
Swearing to false statement in hunting license application. G.S. 113-275.
Providing false information on an application for employment with a regional school. G.S. 115C-238.56N(h).
False certification that bids were submitted without collusion. G.S. 143-54.
False swearing before board of adjustment. G.S. 153A-345 and 160A-388.
False swearing before city council investigation. G.S. 160A-80.
False statement under oath to matter required for absentee ballot. G.S. 163-237.

Subornation of Perjury

Statute

§14-210. Subornation of perjury.

If any person shall, by any means, procure another person to commit such willful and corrupt perjury as is mentioned in G.S. 14-209, the person so offending shall be punished as a Class I felon.

Elements

A person guilty of this offense

(1) willfully
(2) procures or induces another to commit perjury, *and*
(3) the other person commits perjury.

Punishment

Class I felony. G.S. 14-210.

Notes

Generally. For the elements of this offense, see for example *State v. McBride*, 15 N.C. App. 742, 744 (1972), and *State v. Huff*, 56 N.C. App. 721, 723 (1982).

Element (1). See "Willfully" in Chapter 1 (States of Mind).

Element (3). To establish this offense, it must be proved that the person who testified actually committed perjury, satisfying each of the elements of the separate offense "Perjury," described above. State v. King, 267 N.C. 631 (1966); *Huff*, 56 N.C. App. 721.

If the person who testified did not commit perjury, the defendant still may be charged with solicitation to commit perjury. See "Solicitation" in Chapter 5 (General Crimes).

Charging issues. G.S. 15-146 provides the form for a bill of subornation of perjury.

Related Offenses Not in This Chapter

See the offenses listed under "Perjury," above.
"Solicitation" (Chapter 5)

Bribery Offenses

Taking or Agreeing to Take a Bribe

Statute

§14-217. Bribery of officials.

(a) If any person holding office, or who has filed notice of candidacy for or has been nominated for such office, under the laws of this State who, except in payment of his legal salary, fees or perquisites, shall receive, or consent to receive, directly or indirectly, anything of value or personal advantage, or the promise thereof, for performing or omitting to perform any official act, which lay within the scope of his official authority and was connected with the discharge of his official and legal duties, or with the express or implied understanding that his official action, or omission to act, is to be in any degree influenced thereby, he shall be punished as a Class F felon.

(b) Indictments issued under these provisions shall specify:

(1) The thing of value or personal advantage sought to be obtained; and

(2) The specific act or omission sought to be obtained; and
(3) That the act or omission sought to be obtained lay within the scope of the defendant's official authority and was connected with the discharge of his official and legal duties.

(c) Repealed by Session Laws 1993 (Reg. Sess., 1994), c. 539, s. 1207.

(d) For purposes of this section, a thing of value or personal advantage shall include a campaign contribution made or received under Article 22A of Chapter 163 of the General Statutes.

Elements

A person guilty of this offense,

(1) (a) holds an office under the laws of this state,
    (b) has filed notice of candidacy for such an office, *or*
    (c) has been nominated for such an office *and*
(2) (a) receives *or*
    (b) agrees to receive
(3) (a) something of value or personal advantage *or*
    (b) a promise of something of value or personal advantage,
(4) other than payment of his or her legal salary, fees, or perquisites,
(5) for performing or omitting to perform an official act
(6) in the scope of his or her official duties and authority and connected with the discharge of his or her official and legal duties,
(7) with the express or implied understanding
(8) that the person's official action or omission was to be influenced by the thing of value or personal advantage.

Punishment

Class F felony. G.S. 14-217(a).

Notes

Generally. This offense covers any official who takes or agrees to take a bribe. Individuals who offer bribes to officials are covered by "Offering a Bribe," discussed immediately below.

Element (1). Both law enforcement officers and county alcohol and beverage control (ABC) officers have been held to be office holders covered by the bribery statutes. State v. Stanley, 60 N.C. App. 568 (1983) (prosecution under G.S. 14-217; police officer); State v. Hair, 114 N.C. App. 464 (1994) (prosecution under G.S. 14-218; ABC officer).

Element (2). The statute covers direct and indirect receipts. G.S. 14-217.

Element (3). The term "anything of value or personal advantage" includes a campaign contribution made or received under G.S. Ch. 163, Art. 22A. G.S. 14-216(d).

Element (4). The term "perquisites" means fringe benefits or privileges—sometimes called "perks"—associated with an office or position, such as use of a vehicle. BLACK'S LAW DICTIONARY 1258 (9th ed. 2009).

Element (5). The act to be influenced must be within the scope of the officer's official authority, and it must be a legal duty and not just a moral one. State v. Greer, 238 N.C. 325 (1953). An example of an act within a law enforcement officer's duties and authority is conducting an arrest. State v. Stanley, 60 N.C. App. 568 (1983).

The evidence was sufficient to establish this offense when it showed that the defendant, a law enforcement officer, received a gun in exchange for dropping criminal charges. *Id.* at 570–71.

Charging issues. G.S. 14-217(b) specifies the contents of an indictment charging this offense.

Related Offenses Not in This Chapter

"Extortion" (Chapter 14)
Bribery of jurors. G.S. 14-220.
Buying and selling offices. G.S. 14-228.
Willfully failing to discharge duties. G.S. 14-230.
Bribery of players, managers, coaches, referees, umpires, and officials. G.S. 14-373.
Acceptance of bribes by players, managers, coaches, referees, umpires, and officials. G.S. 14-374.
Bribery of horse show judges or officials. G.S. 14-380.1.
Bribery of legislators. G.S. 120-86.
Bargains for office void. G.S. 128-3.
Receiving compensation of subordinates for appointment or retention; removal. G.S. 128-4.
Failure of building inspector to perform duties. G.S. 153A-356.

Offering a Bribe

Statute

The statute making it a Class F felony to offer a bribe does not set out the elements of the offense; the elements have been established by common law. State v. Hair, 114 N.C. App. 464, 467 (1994).

§14-218. Offering bribes.

If any person shall offer a bribe, whether it be accepted or not, he shall be punished as a Class F felon.

Elements

A person guilty of this offense

(1) offers something of value
(2) to a public official,
(3) knowing that person to be a public official,
(4) with the corrupt intent to influence the official in performing an official act.

Punishment

Class F felony. G.S. 14-218.

Notes

Generally. For the elements of this offense, see *State v. Weaver,* 160 N.C. App. 61, 67 (2003). Also see this note to "Taking or Agreeing to Take a Bribe," above.

Element (1). It is not necessary that the public official actually accept the offer. G.S. 14-218; *Weaver,* 160 N.C. App. at 67 (evidence was sufficient despite fact that police officer did not accept the bribe).

The evidence was sufficient to establish that the defendant offered money to a police officer to overlook drugs the officer found on an associate; the associate indicated that the defendant was coming into a $400,000 settlement and "would give [the officer] some money, just for free, to drop the charges"; when the associate asked the defendant, "How much money are you willing to give him to make this go away?" the defendant replied, "It doesn't matter to me, whatever it takes." *Weaver,* 160 N.C. App. at 63–64.

Element (2). Although the statute does not limit this offense to bribes to public officials, cases suggest that result. State v. Greer, 238 N.C. 325 (1953); *Weaver,* 160 N.C. App. at 67 (specifically using the term "public official").

Element (4). "Corrupt intent" means a wrongful design to acquire some pecuniary profit or other advantage. State v. Hair, 114 N.C. App. 464, 468 (1994). It does not necessarily mean requesting that an officer perform a duty in an illegal manner; this offense can be committed by offering a bribe to an officer to do something within the officer's legal authority.

The act to be influenced must be within the scope of the officer's official authority, and it must be a legal duty, not just a moral one, *Greer,* 238 N.C. at 328. "Duty" does not mean that an officer is required to perform the act; it simply means that the act is within the officer's authority. *Hair,* 114 N.C. App. at 467–68 (the evidence was sufficient when the officer was authorized but not required to perform the duty in question).

Charging issues. An indictment is sufficient if requisite knowledge can reasonably be inferred from the other allegations in the indictment. *Greer,* 238 N.C. at 331.

Related Offenses Not in This Chapter

See the offenses listed under "Taking or Agreeing to Take a Bribe," above.

Resisting, Delaying, or Obstructing an Officer

Statute

§14-223. Resisting officers.

If any person shall willfully and unlawfully resist, delay or obstruct a public officer in discharging or attempting to discharge a duty of his office, he shall be guilty of a Class 2 misdemeanor.

Elements

A person guilty of this offense

(1) willfully and unlawfully
(2) resists, delays, or obstructs
(3) a public officer
(4) knowing or having reasonable grounds to believe that the victim is a public officer *and*
(5) while the officer is discharging or attempting to discharge a duty of his or her office.

Punishment

Class 2 misdemeanor. G.S. 14-223.

Notes

Element (1). See "Willfully" in Chapter 1 (States of Mind).

A defendant does not act unlawfully if his or her action is legally permissible. For example, a defendant could not be convicted of this crime when he fled from an officer who stopped him without reasonable suspicion; since the encounter between the defendant and the officer was entirely consensual, the defendant had a right to disregard the police. State v. Sinclair, 191 N.C. App. 485, 490–91 (2008); *see also In re* A.J.M.-B., ___ N.C. App. ___, ___ S.E.2d ___ (June 21, 2011) (the trial court erred by denying the juvenile's motion to dismiss when no reasonable suspicion supported a stop of the juvenile, the activity that the juvenile allegedly resisted). By contrast, a conviction was upheld when the defendant fled during a lawful investigatory stop and after an officer had ordered him to stop. State v. Washington, 193 N.C. App. 670 (2008). For a related discussion, see the note on Element (5), below.

Element (2). Many people think of this offense as covering resisting an arrest. While this offense covers such conduct, it also covers any resistance, delay, or obstruction of an officer acting in the course of his or her duties, *id.* at 679, including, for example, the following duties:

- executing a search warrant,
- conducting an investigatory stop, *see, e.g.,* State v. Lynch, 94 N.C. App. 330 (1989), and
- investigating a crime, *see, e.g.,* State v. Leigh, 278 N.C. 243 (1971).

In all cases, the defendant's conduct must interfere with, hinder, or delay the officer's performance of the official duty. The officer need not have been permanently prevented from performing the duty for this offense to be established. State v. Burton, 108 N.C. App. 219, 225 (1992). Nor is force or violence by the defendant required. *Leigh*, 278 N.C. at 248 (citing cases). But the defendant must do something more than merely questioning or criticizing an officer. *Id.* at 251 ("merely remonstrating with an officer in behalf of another, or criticizing or questioning an officer while he is performing his duty, when done in an orderly manner, does not amount to obstructing or delaying an officer in the performance of his duties"); State v. Allen, 14 N.C. App. 485, 491 (1972) (same).

The evidence was sufficient to sustain a conviction when (1) a juvenile gave an officer a false name, *In re* J.L.B.M., 176 N.C. App. 613 (2006) (this delayed the officer's investigation, including any attempt to contact the juvenile's parent or guardian); (2) the defendant cursed and threatened an officer after receiving a parking ticket and had to be forcibly removed from his truck with mace and a blackjack so that he could be arrested for disorderly conduct, State v. Cunningham, 34 N.C. App. 72 (1977); (3) the defendant inserted herself into an investigation of a school fight, interfered with a school resource officer's attempts to secure a student in his patrol car, attempted to incite a crowd to interfere, and refused to cooperate with the officer, requiring the officer to halt his investigation and call for back-up and resulting in the student being left alone in the patrol car, State v. Bell, 164 N.C. App. 83 (2004); (4) responding to a reported assault, an officer found Blount, an individual he wished to question, sitting in the defendant's car; the defendant's actions and loud, raucous, and abusive language delayed and obstructed, for a period of several minutes, the officer's attempt to talk to Blount; additionally, when Blount left the defendant's vehicle and entered the officer's vehicle, the defendant followed, forcing the officer to leave the scene in order to talk to Blount, *Leigh*, 278 N.C. at 248–49; and (5) two defendants, despite being ordered to halt, approached within six feet of officers who were trying to arrest a man and began to shout; one defendant raised his fists into the air and shouted, "No, no, no, he ain't going nowhere," and the other yelled, "Stop it, he ain't going," State v. Singletary, 73 N.C. App. 612 (1985) (the defendants' conduct showed a determination to prevent the officers from arresting the man and caused the officers temporarily to lose control of that man).

In contrast, the conduct at issue did not constitute resisting when (1) the defendant refused to provide his Social Security number to officers during his arrest, Roberts v. Swain, 126 N.C. App 712, 724 (1997); and (2) the defendant argued with an officer and protested the officer's confiscation of his liquor while the officer was arresting a third person, State v. Allen, 14 N.C. App. 485, 491–92 (1972).

If an officer is engaged in or attempting to engage in a consensual encounter with a person (for example, if the officer wants to speak to the person but does not have probable cause for an arrest or reasonable suspicion for a stop), the person is free to walk away or even flee. Doing so does not constitute resisting an officer because the person had the right to decline the consensual encounter. State v. White, ___ N.C. App. ___, 712 S.E.2d 921 (2011) (the defendant's flight from a consensual encounter with the police did not constitute probable cause to arrest him for resisting an officer); State v. Joe, ___ N.C. App. ___, 711 S.E.2d 842 (2011) (there was insufficient evidence of resisting an officer when the defendant fled from a consensual encounter; when the officer approached an apartment complex on a rainy, chilly day, the defendant was standing outside, dressed appropriately in a jacket with the hood on his head; although the officer described the complex as a known drug area, he had no specific information about drug activity on that day; when the defendant saw the officer's van approach, "his eyes got big" and he walked behind the building; the officer followed to engage in a consensual conversation with him; when the officer rounded the corner, he saw the defendant run; the officer chased him, yelling several times that he was a police officer; the officer eventually found the defendant squatting beside an air conditioning unit and arrested him for resisting). If no reasonable suspicion exists for a stop, the encounter is deemed to be consensual, and any flight from the stop cannot constitute resisting an officer. *In re* A.J.M.-B., ___ N.C. App. ___, ___ S.E.2d ___ (June 21, 2011) (the trial court erred by denying the juvenile's motion to dismiss a charge of resisting a public officer when no reasonable suspicion supported a stop of the juvenile, the activity that the juvenile allegedly resisted; an anonymous caller reported to law enforcement "two juveniles in Charlie district . . . walking, supposedly with a shotgun or a rifle" in "an open field behind a residence"; a dispatcher relayed the information to Officer Price, who proceeded to an open field behind the residence, where he saw two juveniles "pop their heads out of the wood line" and look at him; neither was carrying firearms; when Price called out for them to stop, the juveniles ran around the residence and down the road). Similarly, a person who is present on property to be searched pursuant to a search warrant may under certain circumstances peacefully leave the premises; doing so does not constitute resisting. State v. Richardson, ___ N.C. App. ___, 689 S.E.2d 188, 192 (2010) (there was insufficient evidence of resisting an officer; the State argued that the defendant resisted by exiting a home through the back door after officers announced their presence with a search warrant; the court stated: "We find no authority for the State's presumption that a person whose property is not the subject of a search warrant may not peacefully leave the premises after the police knock and announce if the police have not asked him to stay.").

After the U.S. Supreme Court's decision in *Hiibel v. Sixth Judicial District Court of Nevada,* 542 U.S. 177 (2004), questions arose about whether a mere refusal to provide one's name to the police constituted this offense. In *Hiibel,* the Supreme Court upheld a conviction based on a Nevada law providing that a person who had been stopped based on reasonable suspicion of committing a crime must disclose his or her name to a law enforcement officer. Unlike Nevada, North Carolina does not require a person to disclose his or her name under similar circumstances. In the absence of such a statute, it appears that a person's mere refusal to disclose his or her name will be insufficient to support a charge under G.S. 14-223.

Element (3). By its terms, the statute is not limited to law enforcement officers but applies to all public officers. G.S. 14-223. One case held that campus police officers qualify as public officers for purposes of this statute. State v. Ferebee, 177 N.C. App. 785 (2006). The statute's broad language may prohibit resistance directed toward any public employee who is required to regulate the conduct of others, such as a firefighter or a building inspector.

Element (4). The defendant must know or have reasonable grounds to know that the victim was a public officer. State v. Washington, 193 N.C. App. 670, 679 (2008) (stating the elements of this offense).

Element (5). This element "presupposes lawful conduct of the officer in discharging or attempting to discharge a duty." State v. Sinclair, 191 N.C. App. 485, 489 (2008). If the officer is acting lawfully, as in making a lawful arrest, the person is required to submit peacefully. State v. Summrell, 13 N.C. App. 1, 8 (1971). Officers were acting lawfully when they stopped the defendant, mistakenly believing that he was a person with outstanding warrants for arrest; thus, the defendant's flight from the officers constituted this offense. State v. Lynch, 94 N.C. App. 330 (1989); *see also* State v. Truzy, 44 N.C. App. 53 (1979) (a person does not have a right to resist an arrest by an officer who, without illegal entry or use of excessive force, attempts to make an arrest pursuant to an arrest warrant that appears regular on its face but fails properly to state a crime).

If the officer was acting unlawfully, then there is insufficient evidence that the officer was discharging a duty of his or her office. *Sinclair,* 191 N.C. App. at 489–90 (so holding). Moreover, "[e]very person has the right to resist an unlawful arrest." State v. Mobley, 240 N.C. 476, 478 (1954) (conduct constituted legally resisting an illegal arrest); *see also* Roberts v. Swain, 126 N.C. App. 712, 723 (1997) (quoting *Mobley*).

Charging issues. For a discussion of charging issues that may arise in connection with this offense, see Jessica Smith, *The Criminal Indictment: Fatal Defect, Fatal Variance, and Amendment*, ADMIN. OF JUST. BULL. NO. 2008/03 (UNC School of Government, July 2008) (online at www.sogpubs.unc.edu/electronicversions/pdfs/aojb0803.pdf).

Multiple convictions and punishments. Even though this offense and "Assault on a Governmental Officer or Employee" in Chapter 7 (Assaults) each contain elements not in the other and are therefore not the "same" for purposes of double jeopardy, see "Double Jeopardy" in Chapter 2 (Bars and Defenses) (explaining when offenses are the "same" for purposes of double jeopardy), the North Carolina courts have held that double jeopardy prohibits a defendant from being convicted and punished, based on the same conduct, for both offenses. State v. Summrell, 282 N.C. 157, 173–74 (1972); State v. Hardy, 298 N.C. 191, 197–98 (1979) (citing *Summrell*); State v. Raynor, 33 N.C. App. 698, 700–01 (1977). These cases are not in accord with the great majority of double jeopardy decisions. *See, e.g.,* State v. Martin, 47 N.C. App. 223, 231 (1980) ("If . . . a single act constitutes an offense against two statutes and each statute requires proof of an additional fact which the other does not, the offenses are not the same in law and in fact and a defendant may be convicted and punished for both."); State v. Martin, 195 N.C. App. 43, 54–55 (2009) ("[D]ouble jeopardy is not violated merely because the same evidence is relevant to show both crimes." (quoting State v. Cumber, 32 N.C. App. 329, 337 (1977)); see also the notes entitled "Multiple convictions and punishments" throughout this book and "Double Jeopardy" in Chapter 2 (Bars and Defenses).

A defendant may be convicted of this offense and "Assault on a Governmental Officer or Employee" when different conduct supports each conviction, even if all of the conduct occurred during the same incident. State v. Newman, 186 N.C. App. 382, 386–89 (2007) (no double jeopardy violation when different conduct supported each charge).

Relation to other offenses. By enacting G.S. 14-223 (proscribing resisting, delaying, or obstructing an officer), the General Assembly did not deprive the State of the ability to prosecute a defendant for common law obstruction of justice, even when the defendant's conduct could have been charged under G.S. 14-223. State v. Taylor, ___ N.C. App. ___, 713 S.E.2d 82 (2011)

Constitutionality. This statute is not unconstitutionally vague. State v. Singletary, 73 N.C. App. 612 (1985).

Related Offenses Not in This Chapter

"Assault on a Company or Campus Police Officer" (Chapter 7)
See assaults on firefighters and emergency and medical personnel (various offenses) in Chapter 7 (Assaults).
"Assault on a Governmental Officer or Employee" (Chapter 7)
"Assault with a Firearm on a Law Enforcement Officer, Probation or Parole Officer, or Detention Facility Employee" (Chapter 7)
"Assault with a Firearm or Other Deadly Weapon on a Governmental Officer or Employee or Company or Campus Police Officer" (Chapter 7)
See failure to stop, move over, or slow down for an emergency vehicle (various offenses) in Chapter 28 (Motor Vehicle Offenses).
See speeding to elude arrest (various offenses) in Chapter 28 (Motor Vehicle Offenses).
Assaulting a law enforcement agency animal, an assistance animal, or a search and rescue animal. G.S. 14-163.1.
Violation of state of emergency ordinance. G.S. 14-288.12 through -288.14.
Violating a provision of a proclamation of the Governor in an emergency. G.S. 14-288.15.
Failure to evacuate on Governor's command. G.S. 14-288.19.
Failure to surrender license. G.S. 20-29.
Willful failure to obey law-enforcement or traffic-control officer. G.S. 20-114.1.
Willful interference with firemen. G.S. 58-82-1.

False Report to Law Enforcement Agencies or Officers

Statute

§14-225. False reports to law enforcement agencies or officers.

Any person who shall willfully make or cause to be made to a law enforcement agency or officer any false, misleading or unfounded report, for the purpose of interfering with the operation of a law enforcement agency, or to hinder or obstruct any law enforcement officer in the performance of his duty, shall be guilty of a Class 2 misdemeanor.

Elements

A person guilty of this offense

(1) willfully
(2) makes or causes to be made
(3) to a law enforcement agency or officer
(4) a false, misleading, or unfounded report
(5) for the purpose of
   (a) interfering with the operation of a law enforcement agency *or*
   (b) hindering or obstructing any law enforcement officer in performing official duties.

Punishment

Class 2 misdemeanor. G.S. 14-225.

Notes

Element (1). See "Willfully" in Chapter 1 (States of Mind).

Element (5). It is not enough that the false report had the effect of interfering with the operation of a law enforcement officer; the State must show that the defendant committed the act with one of the statutory purposes in mind. State v. Dietze, 190 N.C. App. 198, 200–02 (2008).

Related Offenses Not in This Chapter

See the various false report and hoax offenses in Chapter 20 (Bombing, Terrorism, and Related Offenses).
Misuse of 911 system. G.S. 14-111.4.
False fire alarms. G.S. 14-286.
Making false ambulance request. G.S. 14-286.1.

Interfering with an Emergency Communication

Statute

§14-286.2. Interfering with emergency communication.

(a) Offense.—A person who intentionally interferes with an emergency communication, knowing that the communication is an emergency communication, and who is not making an emergency communication himself, is guilty of a Class A1 misdemeanor. In addition, a person who interferes with a communications instrument or other emergency equipment with the intent to prevent an emergency communication is guilty of a Class A1 misdemeanor.

(b) Repealed by Session Laws 2001-148, s. 1.

(b1) Definitions.—The following definitions apply in this section:

(1) Emergency communication.—The term includes communications to law enforcement agencies or other emergency personnel, or other individuals,

relating or intending to relate that an individual is or is reasonably believed to be, or reasonably believes himself or another person to be, in imminent danger of bodily injury, or that an individual reasonably believes that his property or the property of another is in imminent danger of substantial damage, injury, or theft.

(2) Intentional interference.—The term includes forcefully removing a communications instrument or other emergency equipment from the possession of another, hiding a communications instrument or other emergency equipment from another, or otherwise making a communications instrument or other emergency equipment unavailable to another, disconnecting a communications instrument or other emergency equipment, removing a communications instrument from its connection to communications lines or wavelengths, damaging or otherwise interfering with communications equipment or connections between a communications instrument and communications lines or wavelengths, disabling a theft-prevention alarm system, providing false information to cancel an earlier call or otherwise falsely indicating that emergency assistance is no longer needed when it is, and any other type of interference that makes it difficult or impossible to make an emergency communication or that conveys a false impression that emergency assistance is unnecessary when it is needed.

Elements

A person guilty of this offense

(1) (a) intentionally interferes
  (i) with an emergency communication,
  (ii) knowing that the communication is an emergency communication *and*
  (iii) while not making an emergency communication himself or herself, *or*
(b) interferes
  (i) with a communications instrument or other emergency equipment
  (ii) with the intent to prevent an emergency communication.

Punishment

Class A1 misdemeanor. G.S. 14-286.2(a).

Notes

Element (1) generally. The term "emergency communication" includes communications to law enforcement agencies, other emergency personnel, or other individuals "relating or intending to relate that an individual is or is reasonably believed to be, or reasonably believes himself or another person to be, in imminent danger of bodily injury, or that an individual reasonably believes that his property or the property of another is in imminent danger of substantial damage, injury, or theft." G.S. 14-286.2(b1)(1). Thus, it appears to cover emergency communications to private persons.

Element (1)(a). G.S. 14-286.2(b1)(2) defines the term "intentional interference" as including:

- forcefully removing, hiding, or making unavailable a communications instrument or other emergency equipment,
- disconnecting such an instrument or equipment,
- removing a covered instrument or equipment from its connection to communications lines or wavelengths,
- damaging or otherwise interfering with communications equipment or connections between a communications instrument and communications lines or wavelengths,
- disabling a theft-prevention alarm system,
- providing false information to cancel an earlier call or otherwise falsely indicating that emergency assistance is no longer needed, and

- any other type of interference that makes it difficult or impossible to make an emergency communication or that conveys a false impression that emergency assistance is unnecessary when it is in fact needed.

Related Offenses Not in This Chapter

See violation of a domestic violence protective order (various offenses) in Chapter 8 (Threats, Harassment, Stalking, and Violation of Domestic Protective Orders).

See the offenses in Chapter 15 (Burglary, Breaking or Entering, and Related Offenses).

Misuse of 911 system. G.S. 14-111.4.

Injuring wires and fixtures of utility companies. G.S. 14-154, 14-156, and 14-158.

Concealing a Death

Statute

§14-401.22. Concealment of death.

(a) Any person who, with the intent to conceal the death of a person, fails to notify a law enforcement authority of the death or secretly buries or otherwise secretly disposes of a dead human body is guilty of a Class I felony.

(b) Any person who aids, counsels, or abets any other person in concealing the death of a person is guilty of a Class A1 misdemeanor.

Elements

A person guilty of this offense

(1) with the intent to conceal the death of a person

(2) (a) fails to notify a law enforcement authority of the death *or*

(b) secretly buries or disposes of a dead human body.

Punishment

Class I felony. G.S. 14-401.22.

Notes

Aiding, abetting, or counseling. The statute provides that any person who aids, abets, or counsels any other person in committing this crime is guilty of a Class A1 misdemeanor. G.S. 14-401.22(b). This is a departure from the general rule that aiders and abettors are punished like the principal. See "Aiding and Abetting" in Chapter 3 (Participants in Crimes).

Related Offenses Not in This Chapter

See the offenses in Chapter 6 (Homicide).

Defacing or desecrating grave sites. G.S. 14-148.

Desecrating, plowing over or covering up graves; desecrating human remains. G.S. 14-149.

Prison and Other Escapes

Prison Breach and Escape from County or Municipal Confinement Facilities or Officers

Statute

§14-256. Prison breach and escape from county or municipal confinement facilities or officers.
If any person shall break any prison, jail or lockup maintained by any county or municipality in North Carolina, being lawfully confined therein, or shall escape from the lawful custody of any superintendent, guard or officer of such prison, jail or lockup, he shall be guilty of a Class 1 misdemeanor, except that the person is guilty of a Class H felony if:

(1) He has been convicted of a felony and has been committed to the facility pending transfer to the State prison system; or

(2) He is serving a sentence imposed upon conviction of a felony.

Elements

A person guilty of this offense

(1) escapes from

(2) (a) lawful confinement in a prison, jail, or lockup maintained by a county or municipality *or*

(b) lawful custody of any superintendent, guard, or officer of a prison, jail, or lockup maintained by a county or municipality.

Punishment

Class 1 misdemeanor. G.S. 14-256. Class H felony if the defendant (1) has been convicted of a felony and has been committed to the facility pending transfer to the state prison system; or (2) is serving a sentence imposed on conviction of a felony. *Id.* The facts elevating the offense to a felony must be alleged in a charging instrument and proved at trial.

Notes

Element (2). The statute does not apply if a person escapes from an officer before being confined to jail. State v. Brown, 82 N.C. 585 (1880). The statute did not apply when Orange County deputy sheriffs took the defendant into custody at the Durham County Jail to transport him to Orange County for trial, and while traveling in a vehicle, the defendant obtained control of a weapon and forced the deputies to drive him elsewhere; the court held that the evidence showed only that the defendant escaped from Orange County deputies and not from the Durham County Jail or from the lawful custody of any superintendent, guard, or officer of such jail. State v. Brame, 71 N.C. App. 270 (1984). By contrast, a conviction was proper when a deputy picked up the defendant from Raleigh's Central Prison and transported him to Alamance County for a court appearance; before the hearing the defendant was placed in a holding cell; after the hearing, the deputy again placed the defendant in a holding cell while he took a break; after this, the deputy began driving the defendant back to Central Prison and, during this time, the defendant dove through a broken window; the court reasoned that because the deputy placed the defendant in the Alamance jail both before and after the hearing, the deputy was an officer of "such jail" within the meaning of G.S. 14-256. State v. Farrar, 178 N.C. App. 231 (2006).

Defenses. For a discussion of the defense of duress as it applies to escape from prison or jail, see "Necessity and Duress" in Chapter 2 (Bars and Defenses).

Related Offenses Not in This Chapter

"Malicious Conduct by a Prisoner" (Chapter 7)

"Possession of a Controlled Substance on Premises of a Prison or Local Confinement Facility" (Chapter 27)

Allowing prisoners to escape. G.S. 14-239.
Escape of working prisoners from custody. G.S. 14-255.
Escape from private correctional facility. G.S. 14-256.1.
Conveying messages and weapons to or trading with convicts and other prisoners. G.S. 14-258.
Furnishing poison, controlled substances, deadly weapons, cartridges, ammunition, or alcoholic beverages to inmates of charitable, mental or penal institutions or local confinement facilities; furnishing tobacco or mobile phones to inmates. G.S. 14-258.1.
Taking of hostage, etc., by prisoner. G.S. 14-258.3.
Harboring or aiding certain persons. G.S. 14-259.

Escape from the State Prison System

Statute

§148-45. Escaping or attempting escape from State prison system; failure of conditionally and temporarily released prisoners and certain youthful offenders to return to custody of Department of Correction.

(a) Any person in the custody of the Department of Correction in any of the classifications hereinafter set forth who shall escape from the State prison system, shall for the first such offense, except as provided in subsection (g) of this section, be guilty of a Class 1 misdemeanor:

(1) A prisoner serving a sentence imposed upon conviction of a misdemeanor;
(2) A person who has been charged with a misdemeanor and who has been committed to the custody of the Department of Correction under the provisions of G.S. 162-39;
(3) Repealed by Session Laws 1985, c. 226, s. 4.
(4) A person who shall have been convicted of a misdemeanor and who shall have been committed to the Department of Correction for presentence diagnostic study under the provisions of G.S. 15A-1332(c).

(b) Any person in the custody of the Department of Correction, in any of the classifications hereinafter set forth, who shall escape from the State prison system, shall, except as provided in subsection (g) of this section, be punished as a Class H felon.

(1) A prisoner serving a sentence imposed upon conviction of a felony;
(2) A person who has been charged with a felony and who has been committed to the custody of the Department of Correction under the provisions of G.S. 162-39;
(3) Repealed by Session Laws 1985, c. 226, s. 5.
(4) A person who shall have been convicted of a felony and who shall have been committed to the Department of Correction for presentence diagnostic study under the provisions of G.S. 15A-1332(c); or
(5) Any person previously convicted of escaping or attempting to escape from the State prison system.

(c) Repealed by Session Laws 1979, c. 760, s. 5.

(d) Any person who aids or assists other persons to escape or attempt to escape from the State prison system shall be guilty of a Class 1 misdemeanor.

(e) Repealed by Session Laws 1983, c. 465, s. 5.

(f) Any person convicted of an escape or attempt to escape classified as a felony by this section shall be immediately classified and treated as a convicted felon even if such person has time remaining to be served in the State prison system on a sentence or sentences imposed upon conviction of a misdemeanor or misdemeanors.

(g) (1) Any person convicted and in the custody of the North Carolina Department of Correction and ordered or otherwise assigned to work under the work-release program, G.S. 148-33.1, or any convicted person in the custody of the North Carolina Department of Correction and temporarily allowed to leave a place of confinement by the Secretary of Correction or his designee or other authority of law, who shall fail to return to custody of the North Carolina Department of Correction, shall be guilty of the crime of escape and subject to the applicable provisions of this section and shall be deemed an escapee. For the purpose of this subsection, escape is defined to include, but is not restricted to, willful failure to return to an appointed place and at an appointed time as ordered.

(2) If a person, who would otherwise be guilty of a first violation of G.S. 148-45(g)(1), voluntarily returns to his place of confinement within 24 hours of the time at which he was ordered to return, such person shall not be charged with an escape as provided in this section but shall be subject to such administrative action as may be deemed appropriate for an escapee by the Department of Correction; said escapee shall not be allowed to be placed on work release for a four-month period or for the balance of his term if less than four months; provided, however, that if such person commits a subsequent violation of this section then such person shall be charged with that offense and, if convicted, punished under the provisions of this section.

Elements

A person guilty of this offense

(1) escapes
(2) from the custody of the Department of Correction.

Punishment

For an escapee who was in the Department of Correction's custody because of a misdemeanor conviction, or while charged with a misdemeanor, this offense is a Class 1 misdemeanor. G.S. 148-48(a). For a person in custody because of a felony conviction, in custody while charged with a felony, or previously convicted of this offense, the offense is a Class H felony. G.S. 148-45(b). If the Class H felony version of this offense is charged, the relevant facts elevating punishment must be alleged in a charging instrument and proved at trial.

Notes

Element (1). "Escape" is not limited to breaking free of confinement from a state prison facility. It includes failure to return to the Department of Correction's custody at the appropriate time by persons on work release or temporary parole. It also includes failure to return to custody after having been temporarily released by the Secretary of Correction under G.S. 148-4. For example, a prisoner's failure to return after having been instructed to clean a chapel located just beyond the prison fence was an offense under this statute. State v. Eppley, 30 N.C. App. 217 (1976). A person "on escape" from work release, early parole, or temporary release may avoid being charged with escape by returning to confinement within twenty-four hours of the time at which he or she was ordered to report. G.S. 148-45(g)(2). While returning within twenty-four hours will not be treated as an escape for purposes of this offense, the person so returning may be subject to administrative action by the department. *Id.* If a person fails to return more than once, a subsequent non-return is an escape even if the person eventually returns within twenty-four hours. *Id.*

Element (2). The statute applies to all prisoners in the department's custody, for example, those

- serving a sentence for a conviction;
- being held by the department for a local confinement facility because of overcrowding or for safekeeping, G.S. 162-39;
- being held by the department pending appeal, G.S. 15A-1353(a); and
- being held by the department for presentence diagnostic study.

Aiders and assisters. People who aid and assist inmates to escape are guilty of a Class 1 misdemeanor. G.S. 148-45(d). This offense would apply both to other inmates and people outside the prison system who help the inmate escape. If the assistance is furnishing deadly weapons, cartridges, or ammunition to prisoners, the aider might also violate G.S. 14-258.1 (furnishing poison, controlled substances, deadly weapons, cartridges, ammunition, or alcoholic beverages to inmates of charitable, mental, or penal institutions or local confinement facilities; furnishing tobacco products or mobile phones to inmates) and G.S. 14-258 (conveying messages and weapons to or trading with convicts and other prisoners).

Defenses. For a discussion of the defense of duress as it applies to escape from prison or jail, see "Necessity and Duress" in Chapter 2 (Bars and Defenses).

Related Offenses Not in This Chapter

See the offenses listed under "Prison Breach and Escape from County or Municipal Confinement Facilities or Officers," above.

Failure to Appear

Statute

§15A-543. Penalties for failure to appear.

(a) In addition to forfeiture imposed under Part 2 of this Article, any person released pursuant to this Article who willfully fails to appear before any court or judicial official as required is subject to the criminal penalties set out in this section.

(b) A violation of this section is a Class I felony if:

(1) The violator was released in connection with a felony charge against him; or

(2) The violator was released under the provisions of G.S. 15A-536.

(c) If, except as provided in subsection (b) above, a violator was released in connection with a misdemeanor charge against him, a violation of this section is a Class 2 misdemeanor.

Elements

A person guilty of this offense

(1) is released pursuant to G.S. Chapter 15, Article 26 (Bail), *and*
(2) willfully
(3) fails to appear before any court or judicial official as required.

Punishment

Class I felony if the violator was released in connection with a felony charge or under G.S. 15A-536 (release after conviction in superior court). G.S. 15A-543(b). If the violator was released in connection with a misdemeanor (and the release was not under G.S. 15A-536), a violation is punished as a Class 2 misdemeanor. G.S. 15A-543(c). A defendant who failed to appear on felony charges was not entitled to an instruction on misdemeanor failure to appear even though the felony charges ultimately resulted in misdemeanor convictions. State v. Goble, ___ N.C. App. ___, 695 S.E.2d 152 (2010). If the felony version of this offense is charged, the relevant fact elevating punishment must be alleged in a charging instrument and proved at trial.

Notes

Generally. Failure to appear is a substantive offense. State v. Dammons, 159 N.C. App. 284 (2003). The failure to appear alternatively could be punished as contempt. *Id.*

Element (2). See "Willfully" in Chapter 1 (States of Mind).

Element (3). A release order signed by the defendant in the presence of a magistrate and read to him by his bondsman was sufficient evidence to establish that the defendant was ordered to appear in court. *Id.* at 289–90. The evidence was sufficient when the defendant signed an Appearance Bond for Pretrial Release and then subsequently failed to appear, even though he did not also sign the Conditions of Release and Release Order. *Goble*, ___ N.C. App. ___, 695 S.E.2d 152.

Related Offenses Not in This Chapter

"Failure to Appear after an Implied Consent Offense Charge" (Chapter 28)

22
Weapons Offenses

22
Weapons Offenses

Possession of a Firearm by a Felon

Statute

§14-415.1. Possession of firearms, etc., by felon prohibited.

(a) It shall be unlawful for any person who has been convicted of a felony to purchase, own, possess, or have in his custody, care, or control any firearm or any weapon of mass death and destruction as defined in G.S. 14-288.8(c). For the purposes of this section, a firearm is (i) any weapon, including a starter gun, which will or is designed to or may readily be converted to expel a projectile by the action of an explosive, or its frame or receiver, or (ii) any firearm muffler or firearm silencer. This section does not apply to an antique firearm, as defined in G.S. 14-409.11.

Every person violating the provisions of this section shall be punished as a Class G felon.

(b) Prior convictions which cause disentitlement under this section shall only include:

(1) Felony convictions in North Carolina that occur before, on, or after December 1, 1995; and

(2) Repealed by Session Laws 1995, c. 487, s. 3, effective December 1, 1995.

(3) Violations of criminal laws of other states or of the United States that occur before, on, or after December 1, 1995, and that are substantially similar to the crimes covered in subdivision (1) which are punishable where committed by imprisonment for a term exceeding one year.

When a person is charged under this section, records of prior convictions of any offense, whether in the courts of this State, or in the courts of any other state or of the United States, shall be admissible in evidence for the purpose of proving a violation of this section. The term "conviction" is defined as a final judgment in any case in which felony punishment, or imprisonment for a term exceeding one year, as the case may be, is authorized, without regard to the plea entered or to the sentence imposed. A judgment of a conviction of the defendant or a plea of guilty by the defendant to such an offense certified to a superior court of this State from the custodian of records of any state or federal court shall be prima facie evidence of the facts so certified.

(c) The indictment charging the defendant under the terms of this section shall be separate from any indictment charging him with other offenses related to or giving rise to a charge under this section. An indictment which charges the person with violation of this section must set forth the date that the prior offense was committed, the type of offense and the penalty therefor, and the date that the defendant was convicted or plead guilty to such offense, the identity of the court in which the conviction or plea of guilty took place and the verdict and judgment rendered therein.

(d) This section does not apply to a person who, pursuant to the law of the jurisdiction in which the conviction occurred, has been pardoned or has had his or her firearms rights restored if such restoration of rights could also be granted under North Carolina law.

(e) This section does not apply and there is no disentitlement under this section if the felony conviction is a violation under the laws of North Carolina, another state, or the United States that pertains to antitrust violations, unfair trade practices, or restraints of trade.

Elements

A person guilty of this offense

(1) has previously been convicted of
  (a) a felony in North Carolina *or*
  (b) a violation of the criminal law of another state or the United States for an offense substantially similar to one in Element (1)(a) and carrying a punishment of more than one year imprisonment *and*
(2) (a) purchases,
  (b) owns,
  (c) possesses, *or*
  (d) has in his or her custody, care, or control
(3) (a) a firearm *or*
  (b) a weapon of mass death and destruction.

Punishment

Class G felony. G.S. 14-415.1(a).

Notes

Generally. Prior to 1995, the weapons ban in this section lasted five years after the person completed his or her sentence, including probation or parole, and allowed felons to possess weapons in their homes or places of business. In 1995, the statue was amended to impose a lifetime ban on the possession of handguns by convicted felons outside their homes or businesses. In 2004, the statute was amended again, this time to extend the ban to all firearms, regardless of type or length and regardless of where possessed. Thus, the statute now contains a lifetime ban that applies to all property, including the defendant's home and place of business. Moreover, this offense applies regardless of whether the weapon was concealed or not.

Element (1). The statute applies regardless of when the prior conviction occurred. G.S. 14-415.1(b).

Element (2)(c). Possession may be actual or constructive. State v. Glasco, 160 N.C. App. 150 (2003); State v. Clark, 159 N.C. App. 520 (2003); State v. Boyd, 154 N.C. App. 302 (2002). Actual possession requires that a person have physical or personal custody of the item, *Clark*, 159 N.C. App. at 525, such as when the defendant holds the gun in his or her hand. Like any issue of fact, actual possession may be proved by circumstantial evidence. There was sufficient evidence to establish actual possession when (1) on a cool day, a warm, dry handgun was found in wet grass six inches from the defendant's hand after he was tackled by officers and the defendant was reaching for the gun; this constituted circumstantial evidence suggesting that the defendant possessed the gun before he was tackled, State v. Barksdale, 181 N.C. App. 302, 305–06 (2007); and (2) an officer saw an object coming out of a van controlled solely by the defendant, sparks flew when the object hit the ground, and a firearm was recovered from a nearby roadside within minutes, State v. Leach, 166 N.C. App. 711, 717 (2004). For a case in which there was insufficient evidence to establish actual possession of a firearm, see *State v. Pierce*, ___ N.C. App. ___, ___ S.E.2d ___ (Oct. 18, 2011) (a firearm was found along the route of the defendant's flight by vehicle from an officer who was attempting to make a lawful stop, the officer did not see a firearm thrown from the defendant's vehicle, the firearm was found several hours after the chase, the firearm was traced to a dealer in Winston-Salem, where the other two occupants of the defendant's vehicle lived, and during the investigation a detective came to believe that one of the vehicle's other occupants owned the firearm).

Constructive possession is when the item is not in the person's physical custody but he or she has the power and intent to control its disposition. *Glasco,* 160 N.C. App. at 156; *Clark,* 159 N.C. App. at 525; *Boyd,* 154 N.C. App. 302. The requirements of power and intent imply that the defendant must be aware of the firearm's presence. State v. McNeil, ___ N.C. App. ___, 707 S.E.2d 674, 682 (2011). When the defendant does not have exclusive control of the location where the firearm is found (for example, when the defendant shares the bedroom where the gun was found with two other people), constructive possession may not be inferred without other incriminating circumstances, *Clark,* 159 N.C. App. at 525, such as suspicious behavior by the defendant or the fact that the firearm was found among other items belonging to the defendant. Constructive possession depends on the totality of the circumstances. *McNeil,* ___ N.C. App. ___, 707 S.E.2d at 681. However, to establish constructive possession, there must be more than mere association or presence linking the defendant to the item. *Id.* at 682. Thus, the mere fact that the defendant was in a location where a gun was found—e.g., in a car—is insufficient evidence of constructive possession. *Clark,* 159 N.C. App. at 525. There was insufficient evidence of constructive possession when the firearm was located on the console between the driver's and front passenger's seats of a car when the defendant was sitting in the front passenger seat, his wife was driving, the car was registered to the defendant's brother, and the firearm was purchased by and registered to the defendant's wife, State v. Alston, 131 N.C. App. 514 (1998).

By contrast, constructive possession was established when (1) a firearm was found under the driver's seat of a vehicle that the defendant jointly owned with his girlfriend, only the defendant had driven the vehicle that day, and the gun could readily be seen when the driver's door was opened, *Clark,* 159 N.C. App. at 525–26; (2) a gun was found in a vehicle, under the defendant's seat, officers saw the defendant reach under the seat, the vehicle's driver did not own the gun, and the gun previously had been seen at the home of the defendant's mother, State v. Boyd, 154 N.C. App. 302 (2002); (3) the defendant acted in concert with three other men to commit burglary and armed robbery and a gun found in a car used by the men matched the description of the gun used by a co-defendant during the crimes, State v. Walker, 154 N.C. App. 645 (2002); (4) the weapon was found wrapped in a man's jacket in the cargo area of a vehicle owned and driven by the defendant, the defendant had exclusive control of the vehicle, the cargo area contained other objects owned by the defendant and the defendant said that everything in the cargo area belonged to him, State v. Smith, 192 N.C. App. 690, 695 (2008); (5) a frisk of the defendant after he fled from a probation officer revealed spent .45 caliber shells that smelled like they had been recently fired; the defendant told the officer that he had been shooting and showed the officer additional ammunition of the same type found during the frisk; and a search revealed a .45 caliber handgun near where the defendant had fled, State v. Taylor, ___ N.C. App. ___, 691 S.E.2d 755, 764–65 (2010); (6) the defendant was identified as having broken into a house from which a gun was stolen; the gun was found in a clothes hamper at the home of the defendant's ex-girlfriend's mother; the defendant arrived at the home shortly after the breaking and entering, entering through the back door and walking past the hamper; and when the defendant was told that police were at the house, he fled to the porch, State v. McNeil, ___ N.C. App. ___, 707 S.E.2d 674 (2011); (7) the defendant ran through a field in a high-traffic area, appeared to have something heavy in his pocket and to make throwing motions from that pocket, and a clean, dry gun was found on the wet grass, State v. Mewborn, 200 N.C. App. 731, 737–38 (2009); and (8) the handgun was found under a mattress, the defendant's shoes were near the bed, and there was evidence that the defendant resided at the premises, State v. Fuller, 196 N.C. App. 412, 423 (2009).

Element (3)(a). A "firearm" is "(i) any weapon, including a starter gun, which will or is designed to or may readily be converted to expel a projectile by the action of an explosive, or its frame or receiver, or (ii) any firearm muffler or firearm silencer." G.S. 14-415.1(a).

Element (3)(b). A "weapon of mass destruction" is defined by cross-reference to G.S. 14-288.8(c), reproduced under "Manufacture, Possession, etc. of a Machine Gun, Sawed-Off Shotgun, or Weapon of Mass Destruction" in Chapter 20 (Bombing, Terrorism, and Related Offenses). G.S. 14-415.1(a).

Substantive offense. G.S. 14-415.1 creates a substantive offense and is not merely a recidivist statute. State v. Coltrane, 188 N.C. App. 498, 503–04 (2008).

Exceptions. The statute does not apply to a person (1) who, pursuant to the law of the jurisdiction in which the conviction occurred, has been pardoned or has had his or her firearms rights restored if such restoration of rights could also be granted under North Carolina law; or (2) whose prior felony conviction pertains to antitrust violations, unfair trade practices, or restraints of trade. G.S. 14-415.1(d), (e).

Also, the firearms ban does not apply to antique firearms. G.S. 14-415.1(a). "Antique firearms" include (1) any firearm (including any firearm with a matchlock, flintlock, percussion cap, or similar ignition system) manufactured on or before 1898; (2) any replica of such a firearm if it is not designed or redesigned for using rimfire or conventional centerfire fixed ammunition; and (3) any muzzle loading rifle, shotgun, or pistol designed to use black powder substitute and which cannot use fixed ammunition. G.S. 14-409.11(a). The term "antique firearm" does not include any weapon that (1) incorporates a firearm frame or receiver; (2) is converted into a muzzle loading weapon; or (3) is a muzzle loading weapon that can be readily converted to fire fixed ammunition by replacing the barrel, bolt, and/or breechblock. G.S. 14-409.11(b).

Constitutionality. Numerous constitutional challenges have been asserted against the felon in possession statute. Cases have held that a prior version of the statute was not unconstitutionally vague and that it did not deny equal protection of the laws. State v. Tanner, 39 N.C. App. 668 (1979). The statute also has been upheld in the face of ex post facto, unconstitutional bill of attainder, and double jeopardy challenges. United States v. Farrow, 364 F.3d 551, 554–55 (4th Cir. 2004) (the 1995 statutory revision replacing a five-year weapons ban with a permanent one did not violate the Ex Post Facto Clause); State v. Whitaker, 364 N.C. 404 (2010) (not an ex post facto law or unconstitutional bill of atttainder); State v. Johnson, 169 N.C. App. 301, 303–10 (2005) (same); State v. Coltrane, 188 N.C. App. 498, 504–05 (2008) (does not violate double jeopardy); State v. Wood, 185 N.C. App. 227, 237 (2007) (same).

However, the North Carolina Supreme Court held, in *Britt v. North Carolina*, 363 N.C. 546 (2009), that G.S. 14-415.1 as applied to the plaintiff violated his state constitutional right to bear and keep arms. In *Britt*, the plaintiff pleaded guilty in 1979 to a drug crime that was nonviolent and did not involve a firearm. He completed his sentence and in 1987 his civil rights were fully restored, including his right to possess a firearm. At the time, the statute did not completely prohibit him from possessing firearms. However, 2004 amendments to G.S. 14-415.1 made criminal any possession of a firearm by the plaintiff. Following passage of the 2004 amendments, the plaintiff spoke with the local sheriff to determine whether his possession of firearms would be illegal. Because the sheriff concluded that the plaintiff could no longer possess firearms at all, the plaintiff divested himself of all of his firearms and then brought suit challenging the statute. In the thirty years between his initial drug conviction and when he filed his lawsuit, the plaintiff had not been charged with any crime. The *Britt* court held that as applied, G.S. 14-451.1 was not a reasonable regulation, stating that

> Plaintiff, through his uncontested lifelong nonviolence towards other citizens, his thirty years of law-abiding conduct since his crime, his seventeen years of responsible, lawful firearm possession between 1987 and 2004, and his assiduous and proactive compliance with the 2004 amendment, has affirmatively demonstrated that he is not among the class of citizens who pose a threat to public peace and safety.

Id. at 550. The court concluded: "[I]t is unreasonable to assert that a nonviolent citizen who has responsibly, safely, and legally owned and used firearms for seventeen years is in reality so dangerous that any possession at all of a firearm would pose a significant threat to public safety." *Id.* Post-*Britt* North Carolina Court of Appeals cases have come out both ways on the as applied challenge. *Compare* State v. Whitaker, 201 N.C. App. 190, 202–07 (2009) (distinguishing *Britt* and rejecting an as applied challenge to the statute), *aff'd*, 364 N.C. 404 (2010), *with* Baysden v. North Carolina, ___ N.C. App. ___, ___ S.E.2d ___ (Nov. 15, 2011) (over a dissent the court held that the statute was unconstitutional as applied to the plaintiff).

In *McDonald v. City of Chicago*, 130 S. Ct. 3020 (2010), the United States Supreme Court held that the Second Amendment right to keep and bear arms applies to the states. However, the Court clarified that its ruling should not be read to foreclose all restrictions on gun possession, particularly restrictions on gun possession by convicted felons. *Id.* at 3047. Thus, while *McDonald* may have little impact on North Carolina law criminalizing felon in possession, it may ultimately impact other restrictions on gun ownership and use.

Charging issues. G.S. 14-415.1(c) sets forth rules for the form and content of an indictment charging this offense. For a discussion of charging issues in connection with this offense, see Jessica Smith, *The Criminal Indictment: Fatal Defect, Fatal Variance, and Amendment*, ADMIN. OF JUST. BULL. No. 2008/03 (UNC School of Government, July 2008) (online at www.sog.unc.edu/pubs/electronicversions/pdfs/aojb0803.pdf). For a case decided since publication of that bulletin, see *State v. Taylor*, ___ N.C. App. ___, 691 S.E.2d 755, 760–62 (2010) (felon in possession indictment alleging the wrong date for the prior felony conviction (it alleged December 8, 1992, but the judgment was dated December 18, 1992) was not defective, nor was there a fatal variance on this basis).

Evidence issues. G.S. 14-415.1(b) provides for the admissibility of records of prior convictions.

At trial the defense may seek to limit the prejudicial effect of evidence related to a prior conviction by offering to stipulate to its existence and asking the trial judge to preclude the State from introducing evidence of the crime. The primary case supporting such a procedure is *Old Chief v. United States*, 519 U.S. 172 (1997) (interpreting federal evidence rule 403 and holding that because the nature of the prior offense raised a risk of a verdict tainted by improper considerations, and as the evidence was admitted solely to prove the fact of the prior conviction, the trial court abused its discretion by admitting the record of the defendant's prior conviction where an admission was available as an alternative form of proof). Noting that *Old Chief* was decided under federal evidence rule 403, several North Carolina Court of Appeals decisions have concluded that the case is not binding on North Carolina courts interpreting state evidence rule 403. State v. Little, 191 N.C. App. 655 (2008); State v. Jackson, 139 N.C. App. 721 (2000); State v. Faison, 128 N.C. App. 745 (1998). However, the North Carolina Court of Appeals has declined to reject *Old Chief* outright, opting instead to distinguish it from the facts presented. *Jackson*, 139 N.C. App. at 731–32 (at the defendant's trial for carrying a concealed weapon, possession of a firearm by a felon, and resisting an officer, the State offered evidence of the defendant's prior voluntary manslaughter conviction and the defendant offered to stipulate to having a prior felony conviction; the defendant was not "charged with any attendant offenses similar to his prior conviction of voluntary manslaughter, thus reducing the potential of prejudice in comparison to *Old Chief*"); *Little*, 191 N.C. App. at 661–62 (the defendant was charged with felon in possession, attempted first-degree murder, assault with a deadly weapon with intent to kill inflicting serious injury, and discharging a firearm into occupied property; the defendant offered to stipulate to the existence of a prior felony conviction; distinguishing *Old Chief*, the court concluded that given the charged crimes, "we cannot say admission of the record evidence of [the] defendant's prior involuntary manslaughter conviction in lieu of [the] defendant's stipulation . . . so risked unfair prejudice that it substantially outweighed the discounted probative value of the record of conviction"); State v. Fortney, ___ N.C. App. ___, 687 S.E.2d 518 (2010) (no abuse of discretion by allowing the State to introduce evidence of the defendant's prior rape conviction, notwithstanding the defendant's offer to stipulate to a prior felony conviction; the prior conviction was not substantially similar to the offenses being tried: drug possession, possession of a firearm by a felon, and carrying a concealed weapon).

Defenses. The North Carolina appellate courts have not ruled on whether justification is a defense to this crime. Assuming without deciding that such a defense exists, several cases have ruled that it was unavailable when the defendant was not under a present or imminent threat of death or injury. State v. McNeil, 196 N.C. App. 394, 405–06 (2009); State v. Craig, 167 N.C. App. 793 (2005); State v. Boston, 165 N.C. App. 214 (2004); State v. Napier, 149 N.C. App. 462 (2002).

The inoperability of the firearm is not a defense to this crime. State v. Jackson, 353 N.C. 495, 498–504 (2001); State v. McCree, 160 N.C. App. 200, 205 (2003) (citing *Jackson*).

Multiple convictions and punishments. A defendant may be convicted and sentenced only once for simultaneous possession of more than one firearm. State v. Wiggins, ___ N.C. App. ___, 707 S.E.2d 664, 668–72 (2011) (the statute does not authorize multiple convictions and sentences predicated on evidence that the defendant simultaneously obtained and possessed one or more firearms used during multiple substantive criminal offenses during the course of the same transaction or series of transactions; the extent to which a defendant is guilty of single or multiple offenses hinges upon the extent to which the weapons were acquired and possessed at different times; in the case at hand, the weapons came into the defendant's possession simultaneously and were used over a two-hour period, within a relatively limited part of town, and in connection with the commision of a series of similar offenses); State v. Whitaker, ___ N.C. App. ___, 689 S.E.2d 395, 405–06 (2009); State v. Garris, 191 N.C. App. 276 (2008).

The evidence was sufficient to support multiple counts of possession of a firearm by a felon when the defendant used the same weapon in multiple robberies that occurred on different days and in different locations. State v. Lee, ___ N.C. App. ___, 713 S.E.2d 174 (2011) (concluding that because each possession was separate in time and location, the trial court did not err by denying the defendant's motion to dismiss the multiple weapons possession charges).

Disposition of weapons. G.S. 14-269.1 and G.S. 15-11.1 govern disposition of seized weapons. G.S. 14-269.1 applies to disposition of deadly weapons after conviction. G.S. 15-11.1 applies to disposition of other kinds of seized property, including nondeadly weapons. However, G.S. 15-11.1(b1) also provides a disposition procedure for firearms. These statutes overlap in applying to firearms that may be deadly weapons within the meaning of G.S. 14-269.1. How they should be applied together is not completely clear.

Ban for those acquitted by reason of insanity or determined to lack capacity to stand trial. G.S. 14-415.3 makes it a Class H felony for a particular class of people to purchase, own, possess, or have in the person's custody, care, or control any firearm or any weapon of mass death and destruction as defined by G.S. 14-288.8(c). This prohibition applies to (1) any person who has been acquitted by reason of insanity for certain specified offenses; and (2) any person who has been determined to lack capacity to proceed as a criminal defendant in a criminal prosecution by the procedure provided in G.S. 15A-1002 for certain specified offenses. This prohibition applies to a broader set of criminal offenses than possession of firearm by felon, including some misdemeanors. G.S. 14-415.3 specifies that weapons confiscated in relation to a violation of this prohibition must be disposed of in accordance with G.S. 15-11.1.

Federal law. The federal firearms statute, at 18 U.S.C. § 922(g), further restricts a felon's ability to possess a firearm.

Related Offenses Not in This Chapter

See the various offenses involving weapons in Chapter 7 (Assaults).

"Manufacture, Possession, etc. of a Machine Gun, Sawed-Off Shotgun, or Weapon of Mass Destruction" (Chapter 20)

Conveying messages and weapons to or trading with convicts and other prisoners. G.S. 14-258.

Furnishing poison, controlled substances, deadly weapons, cartridges, ammunition or alcoholic beverages to inmates of charitable, mental or penal institutions or local confinement facilities; furnishing tobacco products or mobile phones to inmates. G.S. 14-258.1.

Possession of dangerous weapon in prison. G.S. 14-258.2.

Weapons on certain State property and in courthouses. G.S. 14-269.4.

Purchase or possession of firearms by person subject to domestic violence order prohibited. G.S. 14-269.8.

Transporting dangerous weapon or substance during emergency. G.S. 14-288.7

Selling or giving weapons to minors. G.S. 14-315.

Permitting young children to use dangerous firearms. G.S. 14-316.

Sale of certain weapons without permit forbidden. G.S. 14-402.

Solicit unlawful purchase of firearm; unlawful to provide materially false information regarding legality of firearm or ammunition transfer. G.S. 14-408.1.

Machine guns and other like weapons (possession of). G.S. 14-409.

Purchase of rifles and shotguns out of State. G.S. 14-409.10.

Carrying a Concealed Weapon

Statute

§14-269. Carrying concealed weapons.

(a) It shall be unlawful for any person willfully and intentionally to carry concealed about his person any bowie knife, dirk, dagger, slung shot, loaded cane, metallic knuckles, razor, shurikin, stun gun, or other deadly weapon of like kind, except when the person is on the person's own premises.

(a1) It shall be unlawful for any person willfully and intentionally to carry concealed about his person any pistol or gun except in the following circumstances:

(1) The person is on the person's own premises.

(2) The deadly weapon is a handgun, the person has a concealed handgun permit issued in accordance with Article 54B of this Chapter or considered valid under G.S. 14-415.24, and the person is carrying the concealed handgun in accordance with the scope of the concealed handgun permit as set out in G.S. 14-415.11(c).

(3) The deadly weapon is a handgun and the person is a military permittee as defined under G.S. 14-415.10(2a) who provides to the law enforcement officer proof of deployment as required under G.S. 14-415.11(a).

(b) This prohibition shall not apply to the following persons:

(1) Officers and enlisted personnel of the armed forces of the United States when in discharge of their official duties as such and acting under orders requiring them to carry arms and weapons;

(2) Civil and law enforcement officers of the United States;

(3) Officers and soldiers of the militia and the national guard when called into actual service;

(4) Officers of the State, or of any county, city, or town, or company police agency charged with the execution of the laws of the State, when acting in the discharge of their official duties;

(4a) Any person who is a district attorney, an assistant district attorney, or an investigator employed by the office of a district attorney and who has a concealed handgun permit issued in accordance with Article 54B of this Chapter or considered valid under G.S. 14-415.24; provided that the person shall not carry a concealed weapon at any time while in a courtroom or while consuming alcohol or an unlawful controlled substance or while alcohol or an unlawful controlled substance remains in the person's body. The district attorney, assistant district attorney, or investigator shall secure the weapon in a locked compartment when the weapon is not on the person of the district attorney, assistant district attorney, or investigator;

(4b) Any person who meets all of the following conditions:
  a. Is a qualified retired law enforcement officer as defined in G.S. 14-415.10.
  b. Is the holder of a concealed handgun permit in accordance with Article 54B of this Chapter.
  c. Is certified by the North Carolina Criminal Justice Education and Training Standards Commission pursuant to G.S. 14-415.26.

(4c) Detention personnel or correctional officers employed by the State or a unit of local government who park a vehicle in a space that is authorized for their use in the course of their duties may transport a firearm to the parking space and store that firearm in the vehicle parked in the parking space, provided that: (i) the firearm is in a closed compartment or container within the locked vehicle, or (ii) the firearm is in a locked container securely affixed to the vehicle.

(5) Sworn law-enforcement officers, when off-duty, provided that an officer does not carry a concealed weapon while consuming alcohol or an unlawful controlled substance or while alcohol or an unlawful controlled substance remains in the officer's body.

(6) State probation or parole certified officers, when off-duty, provided that an officer does not carry a concealed weapon while consuming alcohol or an unlawful controlled substance or while alcohol or an unlawful controlled substance remains in the officer's body.

(b1) It is a defense to a prosecution under this section that:
  (1) The weapon was not a firearm;
  (2) The defendant was engaged in, or on the way to or from, an activity in which he legitimately used the weapon;
  (3) The defendant possessed the weapon for that legitimate use; and
  (4) The defendant did not use or attempt to use the weapon for an illegal purpose.

The burden of proving this defense is on the defendant.

(b2) It is a defense to a prosecution under this section that:
  (1) The deadly weapon is a handgun;
  (2) The defendant is a military permittee as defined under G.S.14-415.10(2a); and
  (3) The defendant provides to the court proof of deployment as defined under G.S. 14-415.10(3a).

(c) Any person violating the provisions of subsection (a) of this section shall be guilty of a Class 2 misdemeanor. Any person violating the provisions of subsection (a1) of this section shall be guilty of a Class 2 misdemeanor for the first offense. A second or subsequent offense is punishable as a Class I felony.

(d) This section does not apply to an ordinary pocket knife carried in a closed position. As used in this section, "ordinary pocket knife" means a small knife, designed for carrying in a pocket or purse, that has its cutting edge and point entirely enclosed by its handle, and that may not be opened by a throwing, explosive, or spring action.

Carrying a Concealed Pistol or Gun

Statute

See G.S. 14-269(a1), reproduced above.

Elements

A person guilty of this offense

(1) (a) willfully *and*
 (b) intentionally
(2) carries
(3) concealed about his or her person
(4) (a) a pistol *or*
 (b) a gun
(5) (a) while off his or her own premises *and,*
 (b) if the weapon is a handgun, the person does not have a concealed handgun permit or is not carrying the handgun in accordance with a valid concealed handgun permit *and*
 (c) if the weapon is a handgun, the person is not allowed to carry a handgun as a military permittee.

Punishment

First offense is a Class 2 misdemeanor. G.S. 14-269(c). A second or subsequent offense is a Class I felony. *Id.* If the felony version of this offense is charged, the fact elevating punishment must be alleged in a charging instrument and proved at trial. G.S. 15A-928 (pleading and proving prior convictions).

Notes

Element (1). See "Willfully" and "Intentionally" in Chapter 1 (States of Mind). It is not necessary to show any intent to use the weapon. State v. Reams, 121 N.C. 556 (1897).

Element (3). The weapon must be concealed, State v. Lilly, 116 N.C. 1049 (1895); State v. Soles, 191 N.C. App. 241, 243 (2008); if it is carried openly, the statute is not violated, State v. Mangum, 187 N.C. 477 (1924); State v. Brown, 125 N.C. 704 (1899). A weapon probably is not concealed if it is partly exposed to view. *Reams,* 121 N.C. 556. *But see Mangum,* 187 N.C. 477 (conviction upheld when the pistol was sticking out of the defendant's pocket). Whether the weapon was concealed is a factual question for the jury. *Reams,* 121 N.C. 556.

The concealment need not be on the person but may be "about" the person, in a position providing ready access. State v. Gainey, 273 N.C. 620 (1968); *Soles,* 191 N.C. App at 244. Cases indicate that this means the weapon must be within the reach and control of the person charged. *Id.* The evidence was sufficient when an officer found a gun under the driver's seat of a car driven by the defendant; after an accident, the defendant was seen reaching under the seat as though placing something there. State v. Jordan, 75 N.C. App. 637 (1985). By contrast, the evidence was insufficient when (1) the defendant was in the driver's seat of a car and a gun was found under the back seat, *Gainey,* 273 N.C. 620; and (2) a gun was found in a backpack in a van driven by the defendant but there was no evidence regarding the backpack's location in the van or its proximity to the defendant, *Soles,* 191 N.C. App. at 245–46.

Element (4). G.S. 14-269 does not define the terms "pistol" or "gun." For definitions of the related terms "firearm" and "handgun," see the note on Element (3)(a) to "Possession of a Firearm by a Felon," above, and the note on Element (4) to "Possession of a Handgun by a Minor," below.

Element (5) generally. One area of uncertainty is whether the provisions in G.S. 14-269(a1)(1) through (3) are elements or defenses. Subsection (a1)(1) applies when the person is on his or her own premises; (a1)(2) applies when the weapon is a handgun and the person has an appropriate permit and is a carrying the handgun in accordance with the permit; and (a1)(3) applies when the weapon is a handgun and the person is a specified military permittee.

Notably, other sections of the statute specifically identify two defenses. The first expressly stated defense applies when the weapon is not a firearm; the defendant was engaged in, or on the way to or from, an activity in which he or she legitimately used the weapon; the defendant possessed the weapon for that legitimate use; and the defendant did not use or attempt to use the weapon for an illegal purpose. G.S. 14-269(b1). The statute expressly provides that the defendant bears the burden of proving this defense. *Id.* The second statutory defense tracks the exception in G.S. 14-269(a1)(3) and provides that it is a defense that the weapon is a handgun, the defendant is a military permittee, and the defendant provides proof of deployment. G.S. 14-269(b2). It could be argued that because the General Assembly clearly delineated these situations as defenses and did not do so for the exceptions in subsection (a1)—at least those other than military permittee—the (a1) exceptions are not defenses but, rather, elements. This argument finds support in the case law interpreting an earlier version of G.S. 14-269 and suggesting that the premises exception is an element of the offense. State v. Williamson, 238 N.C. 652 (1953); State v. Stanfield, 19 N.C. App. 622 (1973).

If the provisions in subsection (a1) are in fact elements, a further issue arises: Will the State be required to prove these elements, absent any evidence from the defendant that they apply? The North Carolina Pattern Jury Instructions Committee answered this question in the negative, providing that the State need not prove this issue unless there is an issue as to this element. N.C. PATTERN JURY INSTRUCTIONS—CRIM. 235.12. This approach is consistent with case law construing a now-deleted "premises" exception in an older version of the possession of firearm by felon statute. That case law held that a defendant who sought to utilize the old premises exception to that offense had the burden of producing evidence of the exception before the State would be required to prove that it did not apply. State v. Bishop, 119 N.C. App. 695 (1995). As a practical matter, if the State is required to prove the lack of a permit in every concealed weapon case regardless of whether the defendant has put the matter at issue, the State will have the difficult task of proving an absence of a permit from every North Carolina county or from every jurisdiction to which North Carolina grants reciprocity.

Element (5)(a). A private security guard is considered to be on his or her own premises and exempt from the statute when on premises that he or she has been employed to watch. State v. Anderson, 129 N.C. 521 (1901). A person is not on his or her own premises for purposes of the statute while in his or her car on a public highway. State v. Gainey, 273 N.C. 620 (1968).

Element (5)(b). G.S. 14-269(a1)(2) provides that the ban on carrying a concealed pistol or gun does not apply if (1) the weapon is a handgun and the person has a concealed handgun permit issued in accordance with G.S. Chapter 14, Article 54B, or considered valid under G.S. 14-415.24; and (2) the person is carrying the concealed handgun in accordance with the scope of the permit as set out in G.S. 14-415.11(c). Note, however, that under G.S. 14-415.27, district attorneys and related individuals are exempted from the limitations in G.S. 14-415.11(c), provided the exemption is consistent with federal law.

If a person has been issued a permit for carrying a concealed handgun but carries the concealed handgun without the permit in his or her possession, he or she is guilty of an infraction. G.S. 14-415.21(a). A second offense is a Class 2 misdemeanor. G.S. 14-415.21(b).

Restrictions apply to a person carrying a concealed handgun with a permit. *See* G.S. 14-415.11(c). *But see* G.S. 14-415.27 (exempting district attorneys and related individuals from the limitations in G.S. 14-145.11(c), provided the exemption is consistent with federal law). For example, "Possession of Weapons on School Grounds," "Carrying a Gun into an Assembly or Establishment Where Alcoholic Beverages Are Sold and Consumed," and "Weapons at Parades, etc. Prohibited," all discussed below, prohibit a person with a handgun permit from carrying that weapon in certain places. Additionally, G.S. 14-269.4, which prohibits possession of deadly weapons on some state property and in courthouses, applies to such a person. Other federal and state laws also may restrict the rights of a person carrying a concealed weapon with a proper permit.

Element 5(c). G.S. 14-269(a1)(3) provides that the ban on carrying a concealed pistol or gun does not apply when the weapon is a handgun and the person is a military permittee, as defined under G.S. 14-415.10(2a), who provides to the law enforcement officer proof of deployment as required under G.S. 14-415.11(a).

Constitutionality. As indicated in this note to "Possession of a Firearm by a Felon," above, in *McDonald v. City of Chicago,* 130 S. Ct. 3020 (2010), the United States Supreme Court held that the Second Amendment right to keep and bear arms applies to the states. *McDonald's* impact on this statute is unclear.

Defenses. G.S. 14-269(b2) provides that it is a defense to prosecution that: (1) the deadly weapon is a handgun; (2) the defendant is a military permittee under G.S. 14-415.10(2a); and (3) the defendant provides proof of deployment. G.S. 14-269(b2).

G.S. 14-269(b1) provides that it is a defense to a prosecution that (1) the weapon was not a firearm; (2) the defendant was engaged in, or on the way to or from, an activity in which he or she legitimately used the weapon; (3) he or she possessed the weapon for that legitimate use; and (4) he or she did not use or attempt to use the weapon for an illegal purpose. The burden of proving this defense is on the defendant.

Exceptions. The statute does not apply to

- military officers and enlisted personnel who are discharging official duties and acting under orders requiring them to carry arms and weapons;
- federal civil and law enforcement officers;
- militia and National Guard officers and soldiers when called into service;
- officers of the State, a local government, or a company police agency charged with the execution of the laws of the State who are discharging official duties;
- individuals who are district attorneys, assistant district attorneys, and investigators employed by the district attorney who have concealed handgun permits issued under G.S. Ch. 14 Art. 54B or valid under G.S. 14-415.24, provided any such person does not carry concealed in a courtroom, while consuming alcohol or an unlawful controlled substance, or while alcohol or an unlawful controlled substance remains in the person's body;
- qualified retired law enforcement officers, as defined by G.S. 14-415.10, who hold concealed handgun permits in accordance with G.S. Ch. 14 Art. 54B and who are certified by the N.C. Criminal Justice Education and Training Standards Commission pursuant to G.S. 14-415.26;
- detention personnel or correctional officers employed by the State or by a local government who park a vehicle in a space authorized for their use and who in the course of their duties transport a firearm to the parking space and store it in the vehicle, provided that the firearm is in a closed compartment or container within the locked vehicle or is in a locked container securely affixed to the vehicle; or
- off duty sworn law enforcement officers and off-duty State probation or parole certified officers, provided they do not carry a concealed weapon while consuming alcohol or an unlawful controlled substance or while alcohol or an unlawful controlled substance remains in the officer's body.

G.S. 14-269(b).

Federal law. Federal law permits qualified active and retired law enforcement officers to carry concealed weapons throughout the United States, with some exceptions. 18 U.S.C. §§ 926B, 926C.

Disposition of weapons. See this note to "Possession of a Firearm by a Felon," above.

Related Offenses Not in This Chapter

See the offenses listed under "Possession of a Firearm by a Felon," above.
Possession and sale of spring-loaded projectile knives prohibited. G.S. 14-269.6.

Carrying a Concealed Weapon Other Than a Pistol or Gun

Statute

See G.S. 14-269(a), reproduced above.

Elements

A person guilty of this offense

- (1) (a) willfully *and*
  - (b) intentionally
- (2) carries
- (3) concealed about his or her person
- (4) a
  - (a) bowie knife,
  - (b) dirk,
  - (c) dagger,
  - (d) slung shot,
  - (e) loaded cane,
  - (f) metallic knuckles,
  - (g) razor,
  - (h) shurikin,
  - (i) stun gun, *or*
  - (j) other deadly weapon of like kind
- (5) while off his or her own premises.

Punishment

Class 2 misdemeanor. G.S. 14-269(c).

Notes

Element (1). See the note on Element (1) to "Carrying a Concealed Pistol or Gun," above.

Element (3). See the note on Element (3) to "Carrying a Concealed Pistol or Gun," above.

Element (4)(b). A "dirk" is a short, straight dagger.

Element (4)(d). A "slung shot" is a flexible weapon, loaded at one end, to be swung at another, such as a sock with a heavy paperweight in the toe.

Element (4)(h). A "shurikin" is a star-shaped martial arts throwing weapon.

Element (4)(j). In the assault context, cases hold that a weapon may be deadly either because of its character (for example, a large knife) or because of the way it is used (for example, a brass lamp used to strike the victim's head). See the note on Element (3) to "Assault with a Deadly Weapon" in Chapter 7 (Assaults). A butcher's knife is a "deadly weapon of the like kind." State v. Erwin, 91 N.C. 545 (1884).

Element (5) generally. See the note on Element (5)(a) to "Carrying a Concealed Pistol or Gun," above.

Defenses. See this note to "Carrying a Concealed Pistol or Gun," above.

Exceptions. See this note to "Carrying a Concealed Pistol or Gun," above.

This offense does not apply to an ordinary pocket knife carried in a closed position. G.S. 14-269(d). An "ordinary pocket knife" is a small knife, designed for carrying in a pocket or purse, that has its cutting edge and point entirely enclosed by its handle and which may not be opened by throwing, explosive, or spring action. *Id.* "Small" has not been precisely defined by the North Carolina appellate courts or legislature, but a pocket knife that was 4.5 inches when folded was held to be an "ordinary pocket knife." *In re* Dale B., 96 N.C. App. 375 (1989).

Federal law. See this note to "Carrying a Concealed Pistol or Gun," above.

Charging issues. There was no fatal variance when the indictment identified the weapon as "a Metallic set of Knuckles" but the trial court instructed the jury concerning "one or more knives." State v. Bollinger, 192 N.C. App. 241, 244–46 (2008) (language in indictment was surplusage).

Disposition of weapons. See this note to "Possession of a Firearm by a Felon," above.

Related Offenses Not in This Chapter

See the offenses listed under "Carrying a Concealed Pistol or Gun," above.

Possession of a Handgun by a Minor

Statute

§14-269.7. Prohibition on handguns for minors.

(a) Any minor who willfully and intentionally possesses or carries a handgun is guilty of a Class 1 misdemeanor.

(b) This section does not apply:

(1) To officers and enlisted personnel of the armed forces of the United States when in discharge of their official duties or acting under orders requiring them to carry handguns.

(2) To a minor who possesses a handgun for educational or recreational purposes while the minor is supervised by an adult who is present.

(3) To an emancipated minor who possesses such handgun inside his or her residence.

(4) To a minor who possesses a handgun while hunting or trapping outside the limits of an incorporated municipality if he has on his person written permission from a parent, guardian, or other person standing in loco parentis.

(c) The following definitions apply in this section:

(1) Handgun.—A firearm that has a short stock and is designed to be fired by the use of a single hand, or any combination of parts from which such a firearm can be assembled.

(2) Minor.—Any person under 18 years of age.

Elements

A person guilty of this offense

(1) is a minor *and*
(2) willfully and intentionally
(3) possesses or carries
(4) a handgun.

Punishment

Class 1 misdemeanor. G.S. 14-269.7(a).

Notes

Element (1). A "minor" is a person under the age of 18. G.S. 14-269.7(c)(2).

Element (2). See "Willfully" and "Intentionally" in Chapter 1 (States of Mind).

Element (4). A "handgun" is a firearm with a short stock designed to be fired by the use of a single hand, or any combination of parts from which such a firearm can be assembled. G.S. 14-269.7(c)(1). Pistols and revolvers fit this definition, but it may also include weapons modified to be fired with a single hand.

Constitutionality. See this note to"Carrying a Concealed Pistol or Gun," above.

Exceptions. G.S. 14-269.7(b) provides a number of exceptions to this prohibition, including:

- a minor in the United States armed forces carrying out official duties,
- a minor possessing such a weapon for educational or recreation purposes while supervised by an adult,
- an emancipated minor possessing such a weapon inside his or her residence, and
- a minor hunting or trapping outside the limits of an incorporated municipality while in possession of written permission from a parent or guardian authorizing possession of the weapon.

Disposition of weapons. See this note to "Possession of a Firearm by a Felon," above.

Federal law. Federal law also prohibits a juvenile from knowingly possessing a handgun, 18 U.S.C. § 922(x)(2), and prohibits anyone from transferring a handgun to someone he or she knows or has reasonable cause to believe is a juvenile, 18 U.S.C. § 922(x)(1), although some exceptions apply.

Related Offenses Not in This Chapter

See the offenses listed under "Possession of a Firearm by a Felon," above.

Possession of Weapons on School Grounds

Statute

§14-269.2. Weapons on campus or other educational property.

(a) The following definitions apply to this section:

(1) Educational property.—Any school building or bus, school campus, grounds, recreational area, athletic field, or other property owned, used, or operated by any board of education or school board of trustees, or directors for the administration of any school.

(1a) Employee.—A person employed by a local board of education or school whether the person is an adult or a minor.

(1b) School.—A public or private school, community college, college, or university.

(2) Student.—A person enrolled in a school or a person who has been suspended or expelled within the last five years from a school, whether the person is an adult or a minor.

(3) Switchblade knife.—A knife containing a blade that opens automatically by the release of a spring or a similar contrivance.

(4) Weapon.—Any device enumerated in subsection (b), (b1), or (d) of this section.

(b) It shall be a Class I felony for any person knowingly to possess or carry, whether openly or concealed, any gun, rifle, pistol, or other firearm of any kind on educational property or to a curricular or extracurricular activity sponsored by a school. Unless the conduct is covered under some other provision of law providing greater punishment, any person who willfully discharges a firearm of any kind on educational property is guilty of a Class F felony. However, this subsection does not apply to a BB gun, stun gun, air rifle, or air pistol.

(b1) It shall be a Class G felony for any person to possess or carry, whether openly or concealed, any dynamite cartridge, bomb, grenade, mine, or powerful explosive as defined in G.S. 14-284.1, on educational property or to a curricular or extracurricular activity sponsored by a school. This subsection shall not apply to fireworks.

(c) It shall be a Class I felony for any person to cause, encourage, or aid a minor who is less than 18 years old to possess or carry, whether openly or concealed, any gun, rifle, pistol, or other firearm of any kind on educational property. However, this subsection does not apply to a BB gun, stun gun, air rifle, or air pistol.

(c1) It shall be a Class G felony for any person to cause, encourage, or aid a minor who is less than 18 years old to possess or carry, whether openly or concealed, any dynamite cartridge, bomb, grenade, mine, or powerful explosive as defined in G.S. 14-284.1 on educational property. This subsection shall not apply to fireworks.

(d) It shall be a Class 1 misdemeanor for any person to possess or carry, whether openly or concealed, any BB gun, stun gun, air rifle, air pistol, bowie knife, dirk, dagger, slungshot, leaded cane, switchblade knife, blackjack, metallic knuckles, razors and razor blades (except solely for personal shaving), firework, or any sharp-pointed or edged instrument except instructional supplies, unaltered nail files and clips and tools used solely for preparation of food, instruction, and maintenance, on educational property.

(e) It shall be a Class 1 misdemeanor for any person to cause, encourage, or aid a minor who is less than 18 years old to possess or carry, whether openly or concealed, any BB gun, stun gun, air rifle, air pistol, bowie knife, dirk, dagger, slung shot, leaded cane, switchblade knife, blackjack, metallic knuckles, razors and razor blades (except solely for personal shaving), firework, or any sharp-pointed or edged instrument except instructional supplies, unaltered nail files and clips and tools used solely for preparation of food, instruction, and maintenance, on educational property.

(f) Notwithstanding subsection (b) of this section it shall be a Class 1 misdemeanor rather than a Class I felony for any person to possess or carry, whether openly or concealed, any gun, rifle, pistol, or other firearm of any kind, on educational property or to a curricular or extracurricular activity sponsored by a school if:

(1) The person is not a student attending school on the educational property or an employee employed by the school working on the educational property; and

(1a) The person is not a student attending a curricular or extracurricular activity sponsored by the school at which the student is enrolled or an employee attending a curricular or extracurricular activity sponsored by the school at which the employee is employed; and

(2) Repealed by Session Laws 1999-211, s. 1, effective December 1, 1999, and applicable to offenses committed on or after that date.

(3) The firearm is not loaded, is in a motor vehicle, and is in a locked container or a locked firearm rack.

(4) Repealed by Session Laws 1999-211, s. 1, effective December 1, 1999, and applicable to offenses committed on or after that date.

(g) This section shall not apply to any of the following:

(1) A weapon used solely for educational or school-sanctioned ceremonial purposes, or used in a school-approved program conducted under the supervision of an adult whose supervision has been approved by the school authority.

(1a) A person exempted by the provisions of G.S. 14-269(b).

(2) Firefighters, emergency service personnel, and North Carolina Forest Service personnel, and any private police employed by a school, when acting in the discharge of their official duties.

(3) Home schools as defined in G.S. 115C-563(a).

(4) Weapons used for hunting purposes on the Howell Woods Nature Center property in Johnston County owned by Johnston Community College when used with the written permission of Johnston Community College or for hunting purposes on other educational property when used with the written permission of the governing body of the school that controls the educational property.

(5) A person registered under Chapter 74C of the General Statutes as an armed armored car service guard or an armed courier service guard when acting in the discharge of the guard's duties and with the permission of the college or university.

(6) A person registered under Chapter 74C of the General Statutes as an armed security guard while on the premises of a hospital or health care facility located on educational property when acting in the discharge of the guard's duties with the permission of the college or university.

(h) No person shall be guilty of a criminal violation of this section with regard to the possession or carrying of a weapon so long as both of the following apply:

(1) The person comes into possession of a weapon by taking or receiving the weapon from another person or by finding the weapon.

(2) The person delivers the weapon, directly or indirectly, as soon as practical to law enforcement authorities.

Possession of Firearms on School Grounds

Statute

See G.S. 14-269.2(b), reproduced above.

Elements

A person guilty of this offense

(1) knowingly
(2) possesses or carries
(3) a gun, rifle, pistol, or other firearm
(4) (a) on educational property *or*
    (b) to a school-sponsored activity.

Punishment

Class I felony. G.S. 14-269.2(b). However, it is a Class 1 misdemeanor if (1) the person is not a student attending school on the educational property or an employee employed by the school working on the educational property; (2) the person is not a student attending a curricular or extracurricular activity sponsored by the school at which the student is enrolled or an employee attending a curricular or extracurricular activity sponsored by the school at which the employee is employed; and (3) the firearm is not loaded, is in a motor vehicle, and is in a locked container or a locked firearm rack. G.S. 14-269.2(f). The term "employee" is defined in G.S. 14-269.2(a)(1a). The term "student" is defined in G.S. 14-269.2(a)(2).

Notes

Generally. This offense is committed regardless of whether or not the weapon was concealed. G.S. 14-269.2(b).

Element (1). See "Knowingly" in Chapter 1 (States of Mind).

Element (2). See the note on Element (2)(c) to "Possession of a Firearm by a Felon," above.

Element (3). The statute does not define the terms "gun," "rifle," "pistol," or "firearm." For the definition of the term "firearm" as used in another weapons offense, see the note on

Element (3)(a) to "Possession of a Firearm by a Felon," above. For the definition the term "handgun" as used in another weapons offense, see the note on Element (4) to "Possession of a Handgun by a Minor," above.

A gun need not be operable to satisfy this element. *In re* Cowley, 120 N.C. App. 274 (1995).

Element (4)(a). G.S. 14-269.2(a)(1) defines "educational property" to mean a school building or bus, school campus, grounds, recreational area, athletic field, or other property owned, used, or operated by any board of education, school board of trustees, or directors for the administration of any school. The term "school" means a public or private school, community college, college, or university. G.S. 14-269.2(a)(1b).

Element (4)(b). Curricular and extracurricular activities are covered. G.S. 14-269.2(b). This element could be satisfied, for example, if a person took a gun to a school-sponsored prom held at a hotel.

Constitutionality. See this note to "Carrying a Concealed Pistol or Gun," above.

No criminal intent required. The State is not required to prove mens rea or criminal intent. State v. Haskins, 160 N.C. App. 349 (2003).

Aiding minor to commit offense. G.S. 14-269.2(c) makes it a Class I felony for a person to cause, encourage, or aid a minor less than 18 years old to commit this offense on educational property.

Exceptions. BB guns, stun guns, air rifles, and air pistols are excluded from coverage of the statute. G.S. 14-269.2(b). However, those items are covered by "Possession of Weapons Other Than Firearms and Explosives on School Grounds," below. Additionally, the offense does not apply to:

- a weapon used solely for educational or school-sanctioned ceremonial purposes or one used in a school-approved program conducted under adult supervision approved by the school authority;
- a person exempted by G.S. 14-269(b) (see "Carrying a Concealed Weapon," above);
- firefighters, emergency service personnel, N.C. Forest Service personnel, and any private police employed by a school who are discharging official duties;
- home schools;
- weapons used for hunting purposes on the Howell Woods Nature Center property or other educational property, under certain conditions;
- a person registered as an armed armored car or armed courier service guard who is discharging his or her duties and acting with the permission of the college or university; or
- a person registered as an armed security guard while on the premises of a hospital or health care facility located on educational property who is discharging his or her guard duties with the permission of the college or university.

G.S. 14-269.2(g).

A bail bondsman is not an officer of the state and thus is not exempt from prosecution for this offense, *Haskins,* 160 N.C. App. 349.

G.S. 14-269.2(h) further provides that this offense is not committed if a person (1) comes into possession of a weapon by taking or receiving the weapon from another person or by finding the weapon and (2) delivers the weapon, directly or indirectly, as soon as practicable to law enforcement authorities.

Disposition of weapons. See this note to "Possession of a Firearm by a Felon," above.

Federal law. Subject to some exceptions, federal law prohibits a person from knowingly possessing a firearm that has moved in or affects interstate or foreign commerce at a place the person knows or has reasonable cause to believe is a school zone. 18 U.S.C. § 922(q)(2).

Related Offenses Not in This Chapter

See the offenses listed under "Possession of a Firearm by a Felon," above.

Possession of Explosives on School Grounds

Statute

See G.S. 14-269.2(b1), reproduced above.

Elements

A person guilty of this offense

(1) possesses or carries
(2) a
  (a) dynamite cartridge,
  (b) bomb,
  (c) grenade,
  (d) mine, *or*
  (e) powerful explosive as defined in G.S. 14-284.1
(3) (a) on educational property *or*
  (b) to a school-sponsored activity.

Punishment

Class G felony. G.S. 14-269.2(b1).

Notes

Generally. The offense applies regardless of whether or not the item is concealed. G.S. 14-269.2(b1).

Elements (3)(a) and (b). See the notes on Elements (4)(a) and (b) to "Possession of Firearms on School Grounds," above.

Aiding minor to commit offense. G.S. 14-269.2(c1) makes it a Class G felony for a person to cause, encourage, or aid a minor less than 18 years old to commit this offense on educational property.

Exceptions. See this note to "Possession of Firearms on School Grounds," above.
G.S. 14-269.2(b1) excludes fireworks from this offense. Possessing or carrying fireworks is, however, covered under "Possession of Weapons Other Than Firearms and Explosives on School Grounds," below.

Disposition of weapons. See this note to "Possession of a Firearm by a Felon," above.

Related Offenses Not in This Chapter

See the offenses in Chapter 20 (Bombing, Terrorism, and Related Offenses).
Exploding dynamite cartridges and bombs. G.S. 14-283.

Possession of Weapons Other Than Firearms and Explosives on School Grounds

Statute

See G.S. 14-269.2(d), reproduced above.

Elements

A person guilty of this offense

(1) possesses or carries
(2) a
  (a) BB gun,
  (b) stun gun,
  (c) air rifle,
  (d) air pistol,
  (e) bowie knife,
  (f) dirk,
  (g) dagger,
  (h) slung shot,
  (i) leaded cane,
  (j) switchblade knife,
  (k) blackjack,
  (l) metallic knuckles,
  (m) razors,
  (n) razor blades,
  (o) firework, *or*
  (p) any sharp-pointed or edged instrument
(3) on educational property.

Punishment

Class 1 misdemeanor. G.S. 14-269.2(d).

Notes

Element (1). This offense applies regardless of whether or not the item was concealed. G.S. 14-269.2(d).

For a discussion of actual and constructive possession, see the note on Element (2)(c) to "Possession of a Firearm by a Felon," above. There was sufficient evidence to prove a student's constructive possession of a pellet gun when the gun was found in the student's book bag. *In re* Murray, 136 N.C. App. 648 (2000).

Element (2)(f). See the note on Element (4)(b) to "Carrying a Concealed Weapon Other Than a Pistol or Gun," above.

Element (2)(h). See the note on Element (4)(d) to "Carrying a Concealed Weapon Other Than a Pistol or Gun," above.

Element (2)(l). The evidence was sufficient to support a juvenile delinquency adjudication when the juvenile possessed a 3/8-inch-thick steel bar forming a C-shaped "link" about 3 inches long and weighing at least 1 pound; several fingers could be put through the link so that it could be held securely across the knuckles. *In re* J.C., ___ N.C. App. ___, 695 S.E.2d 168, 170–71 (2010).

Element (2)(j). A "switchblade knife" is defined in G.S. 14-269.2(a)(3) as a knife containing a blade that opens automatically by the release of a spring or a similar contrivance.

Elements (2)(m) and (n). A razor or razor blade used solely for personal shaving is not covered. G.S. 14-269.2(d).

Element (2)(p). If the sharp-pointed or -edged instrument is an instructional item; unaltered nail file or clip; or tool used solely for the preparation of food, instruction, or maintenance, it is not covered. G.S. 14-269.2(d).

A closed pocket knife with a 2-1/2-inch blade is covered by the statute. *In re* B.N.S., 182 N.C. App. 155 (2007).

Element (3). See the note on Element (4)(a) to "Possession of Firearms on School Grounds," above.

Aiding minor to commit offense. G.S. 14-269.2(e) makes it a Class 1 misdemeanor for a person to cause, encourage, or aid a minor less than 18 years old to commit this offense on educational property.

Exceptions. See this note to "Possession of Firearms on School Grounds," above.

Charging issues. A juvenile petition sufficiently alleged that the juvenile was delinquent for possession of a weapon on school grounds when it alleged that the juvenile possessed an "other weapon" but the evidence revealed the item to be equivalent to metallic knuckles. *J.C.*, ___ N.C. App. at ___, 695 S.E.2d at 171.

Disposition of weapons. See this note to "Possession of a Firearm by a Felon," above.

Related Offenses Not in This Chapter

None

Discharging a Firearm on School Grounds

Statute

See G.S. 14-269.2(b), reproduced above.

Elements

A person guilty of this offense

(1) willfully
(2) discharges
(3) a firearm
(4) on educational property.

Punishment

Class F felony. G.S. 14-269.2(b).

Notes

Element (1). See "Willfully" in Chapter 1 (States of Mind).

Element (3). The statute does not define the term "firearm." For a definition of that term as it is used in another weapons offense, see the note on Element (3)(a) to "Possession of a Firearm by a Felon," above.

Element (4). See the note on Element (4)(a) to "Possession of Firearms on School Grounds," above.

Exceptions. See this note to "Possession of Firearms on School Grounds," above.

Multiple convictions and punishments. The subsection proscribing this offense begins with the language: "Unless the conduct is covered under some other provision of law providing greater punishment." G.S. 14-269.2(b). This language may be interpreted to mean that a defendant cannot be punished for this offense when he or she is punished for another offense carrying a more severe punishment that is based on the same conduct. See this note to "Assault Inflicting Serious Injury" in Chapter 7 (Assaults).

Disposition of weapons. See this note to "Possession of a Firearm by a Felon," above.

Federal law. Subject to some exceptions, federal law prohibits a person from knowingly or with reckless disregard discharging or attempting to discharge a firearm that has moved in or affects interstate or foreign commerce in a place the person knows to be a school zone. 18 U.S.C. § 922(q)(3).

Related Offenses Not in This Chapter

See the "Discharging Barreled Weapons and Firearms" offenses in Chapter 7 (Assaults).

Storing a Firearm in a Manner Accessible to a Minor

Statute

§14-315.1. Storage of firearms to protect minors.

(a) Any person who resides in the same premises as a minor, owns or possesses a firearm, and stores or leaves the firearm (i) in a condition that the firearm can be discharged and (ii) in a manner that the person knew or should have known that an unsupervised minor would be able to gain access to the firearm, is guilty of a Class 1 misdemeanor if a minor gains access to the firearm without the lawful permission of the minor's parents or a person having charge of the minor and the minor:

(1) Possesses it in violation of G.S. 14-269.2(b);
(2) Exhibits it in a public place in a careless, angry, or threatening manner;
(3) Causes personal injury or death with it not in self defense; or
(4) Uses it in the commission of a crime.

(b) Nothing in this section shall prohibit a person from carrying a firearm on his or her body, or placed in such close proximity that it can be used as easily and quickly as if carried on the body.

(c) This section shall not apply if the minor obtained the firearm as a result of an unlawful entry by any person.

(d) "Minor" as used in this section means a person under 18 years of age who is not emancipated.

Elements

A person guilty of this offense

(1) resides in the same premises as a minor, *and*
(2) owns or possesses
(3) a firearm, *and*
(4) stores or leaves the firearm
(5) (a) in a condition that the firearm can be discharged *and*
    (b) in a manner in which the person knew or should have known that an unsupervised minor would be able to gain access to it, *and*
(6) a minor
    (a) gains access to the firearm without the lawful permission of his or her parents or the person having charge of the minor, *and*
    (b) (i) illegally possesses the firearm on school grounds in violation of G.S. 14-269.2(b),
        (ii) exhibits the firearm in a public place in a careless, angry, or threatening manner,

(iii) causes personal injury or death with the firearm not in self-defense, *or*
(iv) uses it in the commission of a crime.

Punishment

Class 1 misdemeanor. G.S. 14-315.1(a).

Notes

Generally. A minor is a person under 18 years of age who has not been emancipated. G.S. 14-315.1(d).

Element (3). The statute does not define the term "firearm." For a definition of that term as used in another weapons offense, see the note on Element (3)(a) to "Possession of a Firearm by a Felon," above.

Exceptions. This offense does not apply if a minor obtains the firearm as a result of an unlawful entry by any person. G.S. 14-315.1(c). For example, if an adult has improperly stored a firearm and a minor obtains the firearm by breaking into the adult's home, the adult may not be charged with this offense. Similarly, if the minor obtains the firearm from another person who broke in and stole the weapon, the adult may not be charged with this offense. Additionally, G.S. 14-315.1(b) provides that the statute does not prohibit a person from carrying a firearm on his or her body or placed in such close proximity that it can be used as easily and quickly as if carried on the body.

Disposition of weapons. See this note to "Possession of a Firearm by a Felon," above.

Related Offenses Not in This Chapter

See the offenses listed under "Possession of a Firearm by a Felon," above.
See the various child abuse offenses in Chapter 9 (Abuse and Neglect).
Failure to deliver notice of or post warning sign about firearm storage requirements by retailers or transferrors of firearms. G.S. 14-315.2.

Carrying a Gun into an Assembly or Establishment Where Alcoholic Beverages Are Sold and Consumed

Statute

§14-269.3. Carrying weapons into assemblies and establishments where alcoholic beverages are sold and consumed.

(a) It shall be unlawful for any person to carry any gun, rifle, or pistol into any assembly where a fee has been charged for admission thereto, or into any establishment in which alcoholic beverages are sold and consumed. Any person violating the provisions of this section shall be guilty of a Class 1 misdemeanor.

(b) This section shall not apply to the following:

(1) A person exempted from the provisions of G.S. 14-269;
(2) The owner or lessee of the premises or business establishment;
(3) A person participating in the event, if he is carrying a gun, rifle, or pistol with the permission of the owner, lessee, or person or organization sponsoring the event; and
(4) A person registered or hired as a security guard by the owner, lessee, or person or organization sponsoring the event.

Elements

A person guilty of this offense

(1) carries into
(2) any
  (a) assembly where an admission fee has been charged *or*
  (b) establishment in which alcoholic beverages are sold and consumed
(3) a gun, rifle, or pistol.

Punishment

Class 1 misdemeanor. G.S. 14-269.3(a).

Notes

Element (1). The statute apparently does not apply to a person who simply has possession of a gun, rifle, or pistol in one of the named establishments; there must be proof by direct or circumstantial evidence that the person carried the weapon into the place.

Element (2)(a). Examples of such assemblies are athletic events with admission fees, stock car races, concerts, movie theaters, dances, and fairs.

Element (2)(b). "Alcoholic beverage" includes any beverage with at least 0.5 percent alcohol by volume, including malt beverages, fortified and unfortified wine, spirituous liquor, and mixed beverages. G.S. 18B-101(4). Note that the establishment must be licensed for both the sale and consumption of alcoholic beverages. Therefore, neither a store with only an off-premises beer permit nor an Alcoholic Beverage Control (ABC) store would be covered by the statute. A restaurant with a brown-bagging permit (which authorizes only consumption, not sale) would be covered only if it also had a permit allowing the sale of some kind of alcoholic beverage, such as beer or wine. It is not clear whether the statute is limited to establishments that are legally permitted to sell alcoholic beverages for consumption on their premises.

Element (3). The statute does not define the terms "gun," "rifle," or "pistol." For the definition of the related term "firearm" as used in another weapons offense, see the note on Element (3)(a) to "Possession of a Firearm by a Felon," above. For the definition the related term "handgun" as used in another weapons offense, see the note on Element (4) to "Possession of a Handgun by a Minor," above.

Constitutionality. See this note to "Carrying a Concealed Pistol or Gun," above.

Exceptions. This offense does not apply to:

- a person exempted from the provisions of G.S. 14-269 ("Carrying a Concealed Weapon," above);
- the owner or lessee of the premises or business establishment;
- a person participating in a particular event, if he or she is carrying a gun, rifle, or pistol with the permission of the owner, lessee, or person or organization sponsoring the event; or
- a person registered or hired as a security guard by the owner, lessee, or person or organization sponsoring the event.

Relation to other offenses. Although this statute concerns only guns, rifles, and pistols, in some situations the same conduct that gives rise to this charge would justify a charge of "Carrying a Concealed Weapon" or "Possession of Weapons on School Grounds," both above.

Related Offenses Not in This Chapter

See the offenses listed under "Possession of a Firearm by a Felon," above.

Weapons at Parades, etc.

Statute

§14-277.2. Weapons at parades, etc., prohibited.

(a) It shall be unlawful for any person participating in, affiliated with, or present as a spectator at any parade, funeral procession, picket line, or demonstration upon any private health care facility or upon any public place owned or under the control of the State or any of its political subdivisions to willfully or intentionally possess or have immediate access to any dangerous weapon. Violation of this subsection shall be a Class 1 misdemeanor. It shall be presumed that any rifle or gun carried on a rack in a pickup truck at a holiday parade or in a funeral procession does not violate the terms of this act.

(b) For the purposes of this section the term "dangerous weapon" shall include those weapons specified in G.S. 14-269, 14-269.2, 14-284.1, or 14-288.8 or any other object capable of inflicting serious bodily injury or death when used as a weapon.

(c) The provisions of this section shall not apply to a person exempted by the provisions of G.S. 14-269(b) or to persons authorized by State or federal law to carry dangerous weapons in the performance of their duties or to any person who obtains a permit to carry a dangerous weapon at a parade, funeral procession, picket line, or demonstration from the sheriff or police chief, whichever is appropriate, of the locality where such parade, funeral procession, picket line, or demonstration is to take place.

Elements

A person guilty of this offense

(1) willfully or intentionally
(2) possesses or has immediate access to
(3) any dangerous weapon
(4) while participating in, affiliated with, or present as a spectator at any
  (a) parade,
  (b) funeral procession,
  (c) picket line,
  (d) demonstration at any private health care facility, *or*
  (e) demonstration in a public place owned or controlled by the state or a local government.

Punishment

Class 1 misdemeanor. G.S. 14-277.2(a).

Notes

Element (1). See "Willfully" and "Intentionally" in Chapter 1 (States of Mind).

Element (3). G.S. 14-277.2(b) defines "dangerous weapon" to include weapons specified by G.S. 14-269, 14-269.2, 14-284.1, and 14-288.8 and any other object capable of causing serious bodily injury or death when used as a weapon. For a more complete discussion of what constitutes a dangerous weapon, see the note on Element (3) to "Armed Robbery" in Chapter 14 (Robbery, Extortion, and Blackmail).

Element (4)(d). A "health care facility" is defined in G.S. 14-277.4(f) to include any hospital, clinic, or other facility licensed to administer medical treatment or any such facility that provides, as its primary function, medical treatment in this State.

Constitutionality. See this note to "Carrying a Concealed Pistol or Gun," above.

Exceptions. The statute does not apply to any person:

- exempted under G.S. 14-269(b) (see "Carrying a Concealed Weapon," above);
- authorized by state or federal law to carry a dangerous weapon in performing his or her duties; or

- who obtains a permit to carry a dangerous weapon during a particular event from the sheriff or police chief of the jurisdiction in which the event will occur. G.S. 14-277.2(c).

The statute provides that "[i]t shall be presumed" that a rifle or gun carried in a gun rack in a pickup truck at a holiday parade or in a funeral procession does not violate the statute. G.S. 14-277.2(a).

Disposition of weapons. See this note to "Possession of a Firearm by a Felon," above.

Related Offenses Not in This Chapter

See the offenses listed under "Possession of a Firearm by a Felon," above.

See disorderly conduct (various offenses) in Chapter 19 (Disorderly Conduct, Riot, and Gang Offenses).

"Picketing a Courthouse" (Chapter 21)

Altered Firearm Serial Number Offenses

Statute

§14-160.2. Alteration, destruction, or removal of serial number from firearm; possession of firearm with serial number removed.

(a) It shall be unlawful for any person to alter, deface, destroy, or remove the permanent serial number, manufacturer's identification plate, or other permanent distinguishing number or identification mark from any firearm with the intent thereby to conceal or misrepresent the identity of the firearm.

(b) It shall be unlawful for any person knowingly to sell, buy, or be in possession of any firearm on which the permanent serial number, manufacturer's identification plate, or other permanent distinguishing number or identification mark has been altered, defaced, destroyed, or removed for the purpose of concealing or misrepresenting the identity of the firearm.

(c) A violation of any of the provisions of this section shall be a Class H felony.

Altering, etc. of a Firearm's Serial Number

Statute

See G.S. 14-160.2(a), reproduced above.

Elements

A person guilty of this offense

(1) (a) alters,
(b) defaces,
(c) destroys, *or*
(d) removes
(2) (a) the permanent serial number,
(b) manufacturer's identification plate, *or*
(c) other permanent distinguishing number or identification mark
(3) from any firearm
(4) with the intent to conceal or misrepresent the identity of the firearm.

Punishment

Class H felony. G.S. 14-160.2(c).

Notes

Element (3). The statute does not define the term "firearm." For a discussion of that term as used in another weapons offense, see the note on Element (3)(a) to "Possession of a Firearm by a Felon," above.

Related Offenses Not in This Chapter

See the "Altered Serial Number Offenses" in Chapter 13 (Larceny, Possession of Stolen Goods, Embezzlement, and Related Offenses).

Buying, Selling, or Possessing a Firearm with an Altered Serial Number

Statute

See G.S. 14-160.2(b), reproduced above.

Elements

A person guilty of this offense

(1) knowingly
(2) (a) sells,
  (b) buys, *or*
  (c) possesses
(3) a firearm
(4) on which the permanent serial number, manufacturer's identification plate, or other permanent distinguishing number or identification mark has been altered, defaced, destroyed, or removed for the purpose of concealing or misrepresenting the identity of the firearm.

Punishment

Class H felony. G.S. 14-160.2(c).

Notes

Element (1). See "Knowingly" in Chapter 1 (States of Mind).

Element (3). See this note to "Altering, etc. of a Firearm's Serial Number," above.

Related Offenses Not In This Chapter

See the altered serial number offenses (various offenses) in Chapter 13 (Larceny, Possession of Stolen Goods, Embezzlement, and Related Offenses).

23

Prostitution

23
Prostitution

Engaging in Prostitution

Statute

§14-203. Definition of terms.

The term "prostitution" shall be construed to include the offering or receiving of the body for sexual intercourse for hire, and shall also be construed to include the offering or receiving of the body for indiscriminate sexual intercourse without hire. The term "assignation" shall be construed to include the making of any appointment or engagement for prostitution or any act in furtherance of such appointment or engagement.

§14-204. Prostitution and various acts abetting prostitution unlawful.

It shall be unlawful:

(1) To keep, set up, maintain, or operate any place, structure, building or conveyance for the purpose of prostitution or assignation.

(2) To occupy any place, structure, building, or conveyance for the purpose of prostitution or assignation; or for any person to permit any place, structure, building or conveyance owned by him or under his control to be used for the purpose of prostitution or assignation, with knowledge or reasonable cause to know that the same is, or is to be, used for such purpose.

(3) To receive, or to offer or agree to receive any person into any place, structure, building, or conveyance for the purpose of prostitution or assignation, or to permit any person to remain there for such purpose.

(4) To direct, take, or transport, or to offer or agree to take or transport, any person to any place, structure, or building or to any other person, with knowledge or reasonable cause to know that the purpose of such directing, taking, or transporting is prostitution or assignation.

(5) To procure, or to solicit, or to offer to procure or solicit for the purpose of prostitution or assignation.

(6) To reside in, enter, or remain in any place, structure, or building, or to enter or remain in any conveyance, for the purpose of prostitution or assignation.

(7) To engage in prostitution or assignation, or to aid or abet prostitution or assignation by any means whatsoever.

Elements

A person guilty of this offense

(1) engages in

(2) (a) prostitution *or*

(b) assignation.

Punishment

Class 1 misdemeanor. G.S. 14-208. The court may order a convicted defendant to be examined for venereal disease and, if the defendant has such a disease, the court must order such terms and conditions of probation that will provide for medical treatment and prevent the spread of the disease. *Id.* No female may be placed on probation in the care of any person other than a female probation officer. *Id.* Although G.S. 14-207 divides prostitution into two degrees, the distinction no longer appears to have significance. *See* JOHN RUBIN, BEN F. LOEB JR., & JAMES C. DRENNAN, PUNISHMENTS FOR NORTH CAROLINA CRIMES AND MOTOR VEHICLE OFFENSES 45 (UNC School of Government, 3d ed. 2005).

Notes

Element (1). The statute also covers those who aid and abet prostitution or assignation. This statutory language appears to be unnecessary because aiders and abettors are always punished like principals. See "Aiding and Abetting" in Chapter 3 (Participants in Crimes).

Element (2)(a). "Prostitution" is "the offering or receiving of the body for sexual intercourse for hire . . . [or] for indiscriminate sexual intercourse without hire." G.S. 14-203. Prostitution does not include masturbation, sodomy, fellatio, or cunnilingus for hire, State v. Richardson, 307 N.C. 692 (1983), although those acts could be charged as "Crime against Nature," which is discussed in Chapter 11 (Crime against Nature, Incest, Indecent Exposure, and Related Offenses). Under this definition, a person of either sex and either the "seller" or the "buyer" can be guilty of this crime.

Element (2)(b). "Assignation" includes "the making of any appointment or engagement for prostitution or any act in furtherance of such appointment or engagement." G.S. 14-203. Under this definition, a person of either sex and either the "seller" or the "buyer" can be guilty of engaging this act.

Evidence issues. G.S. 14-206 provides that "testimony of a prior conviction, or testimony concerning the reputation of any place, structure, or building, and of the person or persons who reside in or frequent the same, and of the defendant" is admissible to prove this offense.

For an example of circumstantial evidence establishing the purpose of prostitution, see *State v. Willis*, 220 N.C. 712 (1942).

Constitutionality. The statute has been held not to be unconstitutionally vague or overbroad. State v. Demott, 26 N.C. App. 14, 17–18 (1975).

It would be unconstitutional to prosecute consenting adults who engaged in private sexual intercourse not for hire. Lawrence v. Texas, 539 U.S. 558 (2003).

Defenses. Entrapment is sometimes raised as a defense to this crime. *See, e.g., Demott*, 26 N.C. App. at 18–19 (the defendant asserted entrapment). For more detail on that defense, see JOHN RUBIN, THE ENTRAPMENT DEFENSE IN NORTH CAROLINA (UNC School of Government, 2001).

Multiple convictions and punishments. When a person is charged with several violations of G.S. 14-204 that arise out of the same transaction (for example, entering a place for prostitution, G.S. 14-204(6), receiving a person into a place for prostitution, G.S. 14-204(3), and "Occupying or Permitting Use of a Place for Prostitution," below), he or she may be convicted and punished for only one violation. *Demott*, 26 N.C. App. at 19–20 (rejecting a double jeopardy challenge asserted on this ground but so concluding as a matter of legislative intent).

Related Offenses Not in This Chapter

"Crime against Nature" (Chapter 11)
"Fornication and Adultery" (Chapter 11)

Opposite sexes occupying same bedroom at hotel for immoral purposes; falsely registering as husband and wife. G.S. 14-186.
Keeping bawdy house. G.S. 14-188.
Receiving a person into a place or allowing a person to remain in a place for prostitution. G.S. 14-204(3).
Arranging transportation for prostitution. G.S. 14-204(4).
Residing, entering, or remaining in a place for the purpose of prostitution. G.S. 14-204(6).

Procuring for Prostitution

Statute

See G.S. 14-204(5), reproduced under "Engaging in Prostitution or Assignation," above.

Elements

A person guilty of this offense

(1) procures, solicits, or offers to procure or solicit
(2) for the purpose of
  (a) prostitution *or*
  (b) assignation.

Punishment

Class 1 misdemeanor. G.S. 14-208. The court may order a convicted defendant to be examined for venereal disease and, if the defendant has such a disease, the court must order such terms and conditions of probation that will provide for medical treatment and prevent the spread of the disease. *Id.* No female may be placed on probation in the care of any person other than a female probation officer. *Id.* Although G.S. 14-207 divides prostitution into two degrees, the distinction no longer appears to have significance. *See* JOHN RUBIN, BEN F. LOEB JR., & JAMES C. DRENNAN, PUNISHMENTS FOR NORTH CAROLINA CRIMES AND MOTOR VEHICLE OFFENSES 45 (UNC School of Government, 3d ed. 2005).

Notes

Element (1). No particular words need to be spoken for a solicitation to occur. The fact of solicitation is proved by the circumstances, giving everyday meanings to the words used by the parties. State v. Haggard, 59 N.C. App. 727 (1982). See "Solicitation" in Chapter 5 (General Crimes). Although solicitation to commit a misdemeanor normally is punished as a Class 3 misdemeanor, see "Punishment" under "Solicitation" in Chapter 5 (General Crimes), this statute specifies punishment at a higher level.

Elements (2)(a) and (b). See the notes on these elements to "Engaging in Prostitution," above.

Evidence issues. See this note to "Engaging in Prostitution," above.

Constitutionality. See this note to "Engaging in Prostitution," above.

Defenses. See this note to "Engaging in Prostitution," above.

Multiple convictions and punishments. See this note to "Engaging in Prostitution," above.

Related Offenses Not in This Chapter

See the offenses listed under "Engaging in Prostitution," above.

Maintaining a Place for Prostitution

Statute

See G.S. 14-204(1), reproduced under "Engaging in Prostitution," above.

Elements

A person guilty of this offense

(1) keeps, sets up, maintains, or operates
(2) any place, structure, building, or conveyance
(3) for the purpose of
  (a) prostitution *or*
  (b) assignation.

Punishment

Class 1 misdemeanor. G.S. 14-208. The court may order a convicted defendant to be examined for venereal disease and, if the defendant has such a disease, the court must order such terms and conditions of probation that will provide for medical treatment and prevent the spread of the disease. *Id.* No female may be placed on probation in the care of any person other than a female probation officer. *Id.* Although G.S. 14-207 divides prostitution into two degrees, the distinction no longer appears to have significance. *See* JOHN RUBIN, BEN F. LOEB JR., & JAMES C. DRENNAN, PUNISHMENTS FOR NORTH CAROLINA CRIMES AND MOTOR VEHICLE OFFENSES 45 (UNC School of Government, 3d ed. 2005).

Notes

Element 1. For an explanation of the term "maintains" in an analogous drug offense, see the note on Element (2) to "Maintaining a Store, Dwelling, Vehicle, Boat, or Other Place for Use, Storage, or Sale of Controlled Substances" in Chapter 27 (Drug Offenses).

Elements (3)(a) and (b). See the notes on Elements (2)(a) and (b) to "Engaging in Prostitution," above.

Evidence issues. See this note to "Engaging in Prostitution," above.

Constitutionality. See this note to "Engaging in Prostitution," above.

Defenses. See this note to "Engaging in Prostitution," above.

Multiple convictions and punishments. See this note to "Engaging in Prostitution," above.

Related Offenses Not in This Chapter

See the offenses listed under "Engaging in Prostitution," above.

Occupying or Permitting Use of a Place for Prostitution

Statute

See G.S. 14-204(2), reproduced under "Engaging in Prostitution," above.

Elements

A person guilty of this offense

(1) occupies or permits use of
(2) a place, structure, building, or conveyance

(3) for the purpose of
  (a) prostitution *or*
  (b) assignation
(4) knowing or having reasonable cause to know of that use.

Punishment

Class 1 misdemeanor. G.S. 14-208. The court may order a convicted defendant to be examined for venereal disease and, if the defendant has such a disease, the court must order such terms and conditions of probation that will provide for medical treatment and prevent the spread of the disease. *Id.* No female may be placed on probation in the care of any person other than a female probation officer. *Id.* Although G.S. 14-207 divides prostitution into two degrees, the distinction no longer appears to have significance. *See* JOHN RUBIN, BEN F. LOEB JR., & JAMES C. DRENNAN, PUNISHMENTS FOR NORTH CAROLINA CRIMES AND MOTOR VEHICLE OFFENSES 45 (UNC School of Government, 3d ed. 2005).

Notes

Element (1). This element is satisfied if the defendant merely allows the use of a place, even if he or she makes no money from the operation or does not otherwise participate. State v. Herndon, 223 N.C. 208 (1943).

Element (2). If the charge is based on permitting use of a place for prostitution or assignation, the defendant must own the place or it must be under his or her control. G.S. 14-204(2).

Elements (3)(a) and (b). See the notes on Elements (2)(a) and (b) to "Engaging in Prostitution," above.

Element (4). This offense has occurred only if the defendant knew of the use or if circumstances were such that the defendant should have known of it. This element may be proved by showing facts about the use without showing the defendant's actual knowledge. State v. Boyd, 175 N.C. 791 (1918); *Herndon,* 223 N.C. 208. See generally "Objective Knowledge" and "Subjective Knowledge" in Chapter 1 (States of Mind).

Evidence issues. See this note to "Engaging in Prostitution," above.

Constitutionality. See this note to "Engaging in Prostitution," above.

Defenses. See this note to "Engaging in Prostitution," above.

Multiple convictions and punishments. See this note to "Engaging in Prostitution," above.

Related Offenses Not in This Chapter

See the offenses listed under "Engaging in Prostitution," above.

Loitering for Prostitution

Statute

§14-204.1. Loitering for the purpose of engaging in prostitution offense.

(a) For the purposes of this section, "public place" means any street, sidewalk, bridge, alley or alleyway, plaza, park, driveway, parking lot or transportation facility, or the doorways and entrance ways to any building which fronts on any of those places, or a motor vehicle in or on any of those places.

(b) If a person remains or wanders about in a public place and

(1) Repeatedly beckons to, stops, or attempts to stop passers-by, or repeatedly attempts to engage passers-by in conversation; or
(2) Repeatedly stops or attempts to stop motor vehicles; or
(3) Repeatedly interferes with the free passage of other persons for the purpose of violating any subdivision of G.S. 14-204 or 14-177, that person is guilty of a Class 1 misdemeanor.

Elements

A person guilty of this offense

(1) repeatedly
 (a) beckons to, stops, or attempts to stop passers-by or engage them in conversation,
 (b) stops or attempts to stop motor vehicles, *or*
 (c) interferes with the free passage of other persons
(2) in a public place
(3) for the purpose violating G.S. 14-204 or G.S. 14-177.

Punishment

Class 1 misdemeanor. G.S. 14-204.1(b).

Notes

Element (2). "Public place" means any "street, sidewalk, bridge, alley or alleyway, plaza, park, driveway, parking lot or transportation facility, or the doorways and entrance ways to any building which fronts on any of those places, or a motor vehicle in or on any of those places." G.S. 14-204.1(a).

Element (3). G.S. 14-204 prohibits prostitution, assignation, and related offenses (see "Engaging in Prostitution," "Procuring for Prostitution," "Maintaining a Place for Prostitution," and "Occupying or Permitting Use of a Place for Prostitution," all above). G.S. 14-177 criminalizes crime against nature. See "Crime against Nature" in Chapter 11 (Crime against Nature, Incest, Indecent Exposure, and Related Offenses).

Constitutionality. This statute is not unconstitutionally vague. State v. Evans, 73 N.C. App. 214 (1985). It would be unconstitutional to prosecute an individual who committed the relevant acts for the purpose of engaging in private consensual sexual acts with another adult, not for hire. Lawrence v. Texas, 539 U.S. 558 (2003).

Related Offenses Not in This Chapter

See the offenses listed under "Engaging in Prostitution," above.

Prostitution Offenses Involving Minors

Facilitating a Minor's Prostitution

Statute

§14-190.13. Definitions for certain offenses concerning minors.

The following definitions apply to G.S. 14-190.14, displaying material harmful to minors; G.S. 14-190.15, disseminating or exhibiting to minors harmful material or performances; G.S. 14-190.16, first degree sexual exploitation of a minor; G.S. 14-190.17, second degree sexual exploitation of a minor; G.S. 14-190.17A, third degree sexual exploitation of a minor; G.S. 14-190.18, promoting prostitution of a minor; G.S. 14-190.19, participating in prostitution of a minor.

Subsections (1) and (2) are not reproduced here.

(3) Minor.—An individual who is less than 18 years old and is not married or judicially emancipated.
(4) Prostitution.—Engaging or offering to engage in sexual activity with or for another in exchange for anything of value.
(5) Sexual Activity.—Any of the following acts:
   a. Masturbation, whether done alone or with another human or an animal.
   b. Vaginal, anal, or oral intercourse, whether done with another human or with an animal.
   c. Touching, in an act of apparent sexual stimulation or sexual abuse, of the clothed or unclothed genitals, pubic area, or buttocks of another person or the clothed or unclothed breasts of a human female.
   d. An act or condition that depicts torture, physical restraint by being fettered or bound, or flagellation of or by a person clad in undergarments or in revealing or bizarre costume.
   e. Excretory functions; provided, however, that this sub-division shall not apply to G.S. 14-190.17A.
   f. The insertion of any part of a person's body, other than the male sexual organ, or of any object into another person's anus or vagina, except when done as part of a recognized medical procedure.
   g. The lascivious exhibition of the genitals or pubic area of any person.

Subsection (6) is not reproduced here.

§14-190.18. Promoting prostitution of a minor.

(a) Offense.—A person commits the offense of promoting prostitution of a minor if he knowingly:

(1) Entices, forces, encourages, or otherwise facilitates a minor to participate in prostitution; or
(2) Supervises, supports, advises, or protects the prostitution of or by a minor.

(b) Mistake of Age.—Mistake of age is not a defense to a prosecution under this section.

(c) Punishment and Sentencing.—Violation of this section is a Class C felony.

Elements

A person guilty of this offense

(1) knowingly
(2) entices, forces, encourages, or otherwise facilitates
(3) a minor
(4) to participate in prostitution.

Punishment

Class C felony. G.S. 14-190.18(c). For special maximum sentences that apply to offenders convicted of Class B1–E felonies that are reportable convictions under the sex offender registration program, see "Sex offenders" under "Special Provisions" in the discussion of felony sentencing in Chapter 4 (Punishment under Structured Sentencing).

Notes

Element (1). See "Knowingly" in Chapter 1 (States of Mind).

Element (3). A minor is a person less than 18 years old who is not married or judicially emancipated. G.S. 14-190.13(3).

Element (4). "Prostitution" means "engaging or offering to engage in sexual activity with or for another in exchange for anything of value." G.S. 14-190.13(4). "Sexual activity" in turn includes:

- masturbation, alone or with another human or an animal;
- vaginal, anal, or oral intercourse, with another human or an animal;
- touching, in an act of apparent sexual stimulation or sexual abuse, another's clothed or unclothed genitals, pubic area, buttocks, or breasts;
- an act or condition that depicts torture, physical restraint by being fettered or bound, or flagellation of or by a person clad in undergarments or in revealing or bizarre costume;
- excretory functions;
- the insertion of any part of a person's body, other than the male sexual organ, or of any object into another person's anus or vagina, except when done as part of a recognized medical procedure; and
- the lascivious exhibition of the genitals or pubic area of any person.

G.S. 14-190.13(5).

This broad definition of sexual activity means that prostitution of a minor will cover many more acts than the sexual intercourse required for the prostitution offenses discussed above. Sexual activity performed for another also is included in this definition. Thus, a voyeur who pays a minor to masturbate or commit some other act constituting sexual activity would be participating in prostitution. Under Element (2), anyone who facilitates this arrangement also would be guilty of this offense.

As noted, "prostitution" means "engaging or offering to engage in sexual activity with or for another in exchange for anything of value." Thus, a person who agrees to give a minor a marijuana cigarette in exchange for conduct constituting sexual activity commits this offense. Under Element (2), anyone who facilitates this arrangement also would be guilty of this offense.

A person may be guilty of this offense even if the minor does not actually commit an act of prostitution; the mere attempt to corrupt a minor by knowingly promoting prostitution satisfies the elements of the offense. State v. Morris, 87 N.C. App. 499 (1987).

Defenses. Mistake as to the age of a minor is not a defense to a prosecution. G.S. 14-190.18(b).

Relation to other offenses. The differences between this offense and "Supervising, Supporting, or Protecting a Minor's Prostitution," below, are not clear. This offense may be aimed more at the pimp or other person who directly deals with the prostitute, whereas the offense below may be aimed more at the organizer of the prostitution business who mainly deals indirectly with the prostitute and whose activities of supervision, support, and protection are given to persons in the network rather than to the prostitute personally. This also may explain the words used in G.S. 14-190.18(a)(2) to set out the offense of protecting a minor's prostitution. The "prostitution of . . . a minor" could refer to the minor's status as a prostitute rather than to specific acts of prostitution; the phrase "prostitution . . . by a minor" would cover the latter situation. The distinctions are not clear-cut and the subdivisions overlap. Most conceivable acts of promoting prostitution of a minor could be charged under either offense.

Sex offender registration. This offense is a sexually violent offense triggering registration requirements under the sex offender registration statutes. G.S. 14-208.6(5).

Related Offenses Not in This Chapter

See the offenses listed under "Engaging in Prostitution," above.

See the various offenses involving minors in Chapter 7 (Assaults).

See the various child abuse offenses in Chapter 9 (Abuse and Neglect).

See the various offenses involving children in Chapter 10 (Sexual Assaults).

See the offenses in Chapter 11 (Crime against Nature, Incest, Indecent Exposure, and Related Offenses).

See the offenses involving minors in Chapter 24 (Obscenity, Exploitation of a Minor, and Adult Establishment Offenses).

Supervising, Supporting, or Protecting a Minor's Prostitution

Statute

See G.S. 14-190.18(a)(2), reproduced under "Facilitating a Minor's Prostitution," above.

Elements

A person guilty of this offense

(1) knowingly
(2) supervises, supports, advises, or protects
(3) the prostitution
(4) of a minor or by a minor.

Punishment

Class C felony. G.S. 14-190.18(c). For special maximum sentences that apply to offenders convicted of Class B1–E felonies that are reportable convictions under the sex offender registration program, see "Sex offenders" under "Special Provisions" in the discussion of felony sentencing in Chapter 4 (Punishment under Structured Sentencing).

Notes

Element (1). See "Knowingly" in Chapter 1 (States of Mind).

Element (3). See the note on Element (4) to "Facilitating a Minor's Prostitution," above.

Element (4). See the note on Element (3) to "Facilitating a Minor's Prostitution," above.

Defenses. See this note to "Facilitating a Minor's Prostitution," above.

Relation to other offenses. See this note to "Facilitating a Minor's Prostitution," above.

Sex offender registration. This offense is a sexually violent offense triggering registration requirements under the sex offender registration statutes. G.S. 14-208.6(5).

Related Offenses Not in This Chapter

See the offenses listed under "Facilitating a Minor's Prostitution," above.

Participating in Prostitution of a Minor

Statute

See G.S. 14-190.13, reproduced under "Facilitating a Minor's Prostitution," above.

§14-190.19. Participating in prostitution of a minor.

(a) Offense.—A person commits the offense of participating in the prostitution of a minor if he is not a minor and he patronizes a minor prostitute. As used in this section, "patronizing a minor prostitute" means:

(1) Soliciting or requesting a minor to participate in prostitution;
(2) Paying or agreeing to pay a minor, either directly or through the minor's agent, to participate in prostitution; or

(3) Paying a minor, or the minor's agent, for having participated in prostitution, pursuant to a prior agreement.

(b) Mistake of Age.—Mistake of age is not a defense to a prosecution under this section.

(c) Punishment and Sentencing.—Violation of this section is a Class F felony.

Elements

A person guilty of this offense

(1) is not a minor *and*

(2) (a) solicits or requests a minor to participate in prostitution,

(b) pays or agrees to pay a minor to participate in prostitution, *or*

(c) pays a minor or the minor's agent for having participated in prostitution pursuant to a prior agreement.

Punishment

Class F felony. G.S. 14-190.19(c).

Notes

Element (1). This section applies to adults who patronize minor prostitutes; the minor is not subject to prosecution under this section. G.S. 14-190.19(a). A minor is a person less than 18 years old who is not married or judicially emancipated. G.S. 14-190.13(3).

Element (2) generally. For a discussion of the meaning of the term "prostitution" as used in this statute, see the note on Element (4) to "Facilitating a Minor's Prostitution," above.

Elements (2)(b) (covering payment to, or an agreement to pay, a minor to participate in prostitution) and (c) (covering payment to a minor or the minor's agent for having participated in prostitution pursuant to a prior agreement) overlap to some extent.

Element (2)(b). The payment or agreement to pay may be made with the minor directly or through the minor's agent. G.S. 14-190.19(a)(2).

Relation to other offenses. While this offense does not punish activity by a participating minor, prostitution and assignation applies to sexual intercourse for hire on the part of both the supplier of the service and the recipient and thus would criminalize the minor's actions if sexual intercourse occurred.

Defenses. Mistake as to the age of a minor is not a defense to this offense. G.S. 14-190.19(b).

Sex offender registration. This offense is a sexually violent offense triggering registration requirements under the sex offender registration statutes. G.S. 14-208.6(5).

Related Offenses Not in This Chapter

See the offenses listed under "Facilitating a Minor's Prostitution," above.

24

Obscenity, Exploitation of a Minor, and Adult Establishment Offenses

24

Obscenity, Exploitation of a Minor, and Adult Establishment Offenses

Obscenity Offenses

Disseminating Obscenity

Statute

§14-190.1. Obscene literature and exhibitions.

(a) It shall be unlawful for any person, firm or corporation to intentionally disseminate obscenity. A person, firm or corporation disseminates obscenity within the meaning of this Article if he or it:

(1) Sells, delivers or provides or offers or agrees to sell, deliver or provide any obscene writing, picture, record or other representation or embodiment of the obscene; or

(2) Presents or directs an obscene play, dance or other performance or participates directly in that portion thereof which makes it obscene; or

(3) Publishes, exhibits or otherwise makes available anything obscene; or

(4) Exhibits, presents, rents, sells, delivers or provides; or offers or agrees to exhibit, present, rent or to provide: any obscene still or motion picture, film, filmstrip, or projection slide, or sound recording, sound tape, or sound track, or any matter or material of whatever form which is a representation, embodiment, performance, or publication of the obscene.

(b) For purposes of this Article any material is obscene if:

(1) The material depicts or describes in a patently offensive way sexual conduct specifically defined by subsection (c) of this section; and

(2) The average person applying contemporary community standards relating to the depiction or description of sexual matters would find that the material taken as a whole appeals to the prurient interest in sex; and

(3) The material lacks serious literary, artistic, political, or scientific value; and

(4) The material as used is not protected or privileged under the Constitution of the United States or the Constitution of North Carolina.

(c) As used in this Article, "sexual conduct" means:

(1) Vaginal, anal, or oral intercourse, whether actual or simulated, normal or perverted; or

(2) Masturbation, excretory functions, or lewd exhibition of uncovered genitals; or

(3) An act or condition that depicts torture, physical restraint by being fettered or bound, or flagellation of or by a nude person or a person clad in undergarments or in revealing or bizarre costume.

(d) Obscenity shall be judged with reference to ordinary adults except that it shall be judged with reference to children or other especially susceptible audiences if it appears from the character of the material or the circumstances of its dissemination to be especially designed for or directed to such children or audiences.

(e) It shall be unlawful for any person, firm or corporation to knowingly and intentionally create, buy, procure or possess obscene material with the purpose and intent of disseminating it unlawfully.

(f) It shall be unlawful for a person, firm or corporation to advertise or otherwise promote the sale of material represented or held out by said person, firm or corporation as obscene.

(g) Violation of this section is a Class I felony.

(h) Obscene material disseminated, procured, or promoted in violation of this section is contraband.

(i) Nothing in this section shall be deemed to preempt local government regulation of the location or operation of sexually oriented businesses to the extent consistent with the constitutional protection afforded free speech.

Elements

A person guilty of this offense

(1) intentionally
(2) disseminates
(3) obscenity.

Punishment

Class I felony. G.S. 14-190.1(g).

Notes

Generally. The statute applies to any person, firm, or corporation that does the prohibited acts. G.S. 14-190.1(a). The statutory language regarding corporations appears to be unnecessary given that the term "person" as used in the General Statutes always is interpreted to include corporations. See " 'Person' includes corporation" in the Introduction to this book.

Element (1). See "Intentionally" in Chapter 1 (States of Mind). The defendant must know the character or content of the material or performance disseminated. Smith v. California, 361 U.S. 147 (1959); State v. Anderson, 322 N.C. 22 (1988); State v. Watson, 88 N.C. App. 624 (1988); State v. Von Wilds, 88 N.C. App. 69 (1987); State v. Smith, 87 N.C. App. 217 (1987); Cinema I Video, Inc. v. Thornburg, 83 N.C. App. 544 (1986).

Element (2). Dissemination occurs if the defendant:

- sells, delivers, provides, or offers, or agrees to sell, deliver, or provide, any obscene writing, picture, record, or other representation or embodiment of the obscene;
- presents or directs an obscene performance or participates directly in the portion of the performance that makes it obscene;
- publishes, exhibits, or makes available anything obscene; or
- exhibits, presents, rents, sells, delivers, provides, or offers or agrees to exhibit, present, rent, or provide, any obscene still or motion picture, film, filmstrip, projection slide, sound recording, sound tape, sound track, or any matter or material of whatever form which is a representation, embodiment, performance, or publication of the obscene.

G.S. 14-190.1(a)(1)–(4).

Element (3). The product of dissemination can be either material or a performance. G.S. 14-190.1(a).

Under G.S. 14-190.1(b), material is obscene if all four of the following criteria apply:

1. *The material depicts or describes sexual conduct in a patently offensive way.* No matter how offensive the material may be, unless it involves sexual conduct, it is not obscene. "Sexual conduct" includes:
   - vaginal, anal, or oral intercourse, actual or simulated, normal or perverted;
   - masturbation, excretory functions, or lewd exhibition of uncovered genitals (although "simulated" is not repeated here, the statutory definition of obscene material covers material that "depicts or describes" sexual conduct); and
   - an act or condition that depicts torture, physical restraint by being fettered or bound, or flagellation of or by a nude person or a person clad in undergarments or in revealing or bizarre costume.

   G.S. 14-190.1(c).

   Whether the material is patently offensive is a jury question and is to be judged by contemporary community standards. State v. Anderson, 322 N.C. 22 (1988); State v. Watson, 88 N.C. App. 624 (1988). The statute does not specify the geographical limits of the relevant community; a trial judge may permit jurors to apply the standards of their local communities. State v. Mayes, 323 N.C. 159 (1988); *Anderson,* 322 N.C. 22.
2. *The average person applying contemporary community standards relating to the depiction or description of sexual matters would find that the material taken as a whole appeals to the prurient interest in sex.* In making this determination, a trial judge may permit jurors to apply the standards of their local communities. *Mayes,* 323 N.C. 159, *Anderson,* 322 N.C. 22. The State is not required to present evidence of what constitutes contemporary community standards. State v. Johnston, 123 N.C. App. 292 (1996). A "prurient" interest in sex means a shameful or morbid interest, as opposed to a normal, healthy interest. Brockett v. Spokane Arcades, Inc., 472 U.S. 491 (1985); *Johnston,* 123 N.C. App. 292.
3. *The material lacks serious literary, artistic, political, or scientific value.* The value of material must be decided with reference to the work as a whole. Miller v. California, 413 U.S. 15 (1973); State v. Smith, 89 N.C. App. 19 (1988); *Watson,* 88 N.C. App. 624. Also, in contrast to the criteria of patent offensiveness and appeal to the prurient interest in sex discussed above, the criterion of value must be assessed by reference to a "reasonable person" standard and not by community standards. Pope v. Illinois, 481 U.S. 497 (1987); *Anderson,* 322 N.C. 22; *Smith,* 89 N.C. App. 19; *Watson,* 88 N.C. App. 624; State v. Roland, 88 N.C. App. 19 (1987); State v. Smith, 87 N.C. App. 217 (1987).
4. *The material as used is not protected or privileged under the U.S. or N.C. Constitutions.* Note that possession of obscene material in one's own home is constitutionally protected. Cinema I Video, Inc. v. Thornburg, 83 N.C. App. 544 (1986); *Smith,* 89 N.C. App. 19.

Obscenity is judged with reference to ordinary adults, except that it is judged with reference to children or other especially susceptible audiences if its dissemination is designed for or directed toward children or such audiences. G.S. 14-190.1(d).

A witness's testimony describing the material alleged to be obscene was sufficient to sustain a conviction without introduction of the material itself. State v. Mueller, 184 N.C. App. 553, 564–67 (2007) ("[n]othing in section 14-190.1 requires the State to produce the precise material alleged to be obscene").

Search warrant and criminal process. Violations of G.S. 14-190.1 through 14-190.5 are subject to G.S. 14-190.20, which provides that a search warrant or criminal process for these offenses may be issued only on the request of a prosecutor.

In 1985, the General Assembly repealed the statutory requirement that material be declared obscene in a civil adversary hearing before a person may be prosecuted for its dissemination. The repeal of that requirement has been upheld as constitutional, *Cinema I Video,* 83 N.C. App. 544; *Smith,* 87 N.C. App. 217, though a defendant has a constitutional right under the First and Fourteenth Amendments to a prompt, post-seizure adversary hearing on the obscenity of seized material pending trial. The burden is on the person seeking return of the material to request a hearing. *Cinema I Video,* 83 N.C. App. 544.

Constitutionality. The statute is not unconstitutionally vague or overbroad. *Id.*; State v. Cinema Blue of Charlotte, Inc., 98 N.C. App. 628 (1990).

Multiple convictions and punishments. When a person disseminates several obscene items during a single transaction, only one offense is committed. State v. Smith, 323 N.C. 439 (1988).

Material contraband. G.S. 14-190.1(h) provides that obscene material disseminated, procured, or promoted in violation of the statute is contraband. The statute sets out no disposition procedure for contraband obscene material, and therefore a court order should be obtained to dispose of it.

Related Offenses Not in This Chapter

See the offenses in Chapter 10 (Sexual Assaults).
See the offenses in Chapter 11 (Crime against Nature, Incest, Indecent Exposure, and Related Offenses).
See the offenses in Chapter 23 (Prostitution).
Coercing acceptance of obscene articles or publications. G.S. 14-190.4.
Preparation of obscene photographs, slides and motion pictures. G.S. 14-190.5.

Creating, Buying, Procuring, or Possessing Obscenity with Intent to Distribute

Statute

See G.S. 14-190.1(e), reproduced under "Disseminating Obscenity," above.

Elements

A person guilty of this offense

(1) knowingly and intentionally
(2) (a) creates,
  (b) buys,
  (c) procures, *or*
  (d) possesses
(3) obscene material
(4) with the purpose and intent of disseminating it unlawfully.

Punishment

Class I felony. G.S. 14-190.1(g).

Notes

Generally. See this note to "Disseminating Obscenity," above.

Element (1). See "Knowingly" and "Intentionally" in Chapter 1 (States of Mind).

Element (2)(d). As a general rule, possession may be actual or constructive. For a discussion of actual and constructive possession as those terms apply with regard to other offenses, see the note on Element (2) to "Possession of a Controlled Substance" in Chapter 27 (Drug Offenses) and the note on Element (2)(c) to "Possession of a Firearm by a Felon" in Chapter 22 (Weapons Offenses).

Element (3). See the note on Element (3) to "Disseminating Obscenity," above, for a definition of obscenity.

Element (4). For the meaning of the term "disseminates," see the note on Element (2) to "Disseminating Obscenity," above. Intent typically is determined by circumstantial evidence.

Search warrant and criminal process. See this note to "Disseminating Obscenity," above.

Material contraband. See this note to "Disseminating Obscenity," above.

Related Offenses Not in This Chapter

See the offenses listed under "Disseminating Obscenity," above.

Advertising or Promoting the Sale of Obscene Material

Statute

See G.S. 14-190.1(f), reproduced under "Disseminating Obscenity," above.

Elements

A person guilty of this offense

(1) (a) advertises *or*
    (b) otherwise promotes the sale of
(2) material
(3) that the person represents or holds out
(4) as obscene.

Punishment

Class I felony. G.S. 14-190.1(g).

Notes

Generally. See this note to "Disseminating Obscenity," above.

Element (3). This offense does not require proof that the material was in fact obscene; it is sufficient if the material is represented or held out to be obscene.

Element 4. See the note on Element (3) to "Disseminating Obscenity," above, for a discussion of the meaning of the term "obscene."

Search warrant and criminal process. See this note to "Disseminating Obscenity," above.

Material contraband. See this note to "Disseminating Obscenity," above. Because a conviction for this offense may be obtained without proving that the advertised or promoted material was obscene in fact, it will be necessary to establish as a matter of record that the material is obscene before it is deemed contraband.

Related Offenses Not in This Chapter

See the offenses listed under "Disseminating Obscenity," above.

Using a Minor to Assist in an Obscenity Offense

Statute

§14-190.6. Employing or permitting minor to assist in offense under Article.

Every person 18 years of age or older who intentionally, in any manner, hires, employs, uses or permits any minor under the age of 16 years to do or assist in doing any act or thing constituting an offense under this Article and involving any material, act or thing he knows or reasonably should know to be obscene within the meaning of G.S. 14-190.1, shall be guilty of a Class I felony.

Elements

A person guilty of this offense

(1) is 18 years of age or older *and*
(2) intentionally
(3) hires, employs, uses, or permits
(4) a minor under the age of 16
(5) to do or assist in doing
(6) any act or thing constituting an offense under Article 26 of G.S. Chapter 14
(7) involving any obscene material, act, or thing
(8) that the person knows or reasonably should know
(9) is obscene.

Punishment

Class I felony. G.S. 14-190.6.

Notes

Element (2). See "Intentionally" in Chapter 1 (States of Mind).

Element (6). Article 26 includes all of the offenses covered in this chapter of this book plus a variety of other offenses, including "Indecent Liberties with Children," discussed in Chapter 10 (Sexual Assaults), "Crime against Nature" and "Incest," both addressed in Chapter 11 (Crime against Nature, Incest, Indecent Exposure, and Related Offenses), and "Cyberstalking," covered in Chapter 8 (Threats, Harrassment, Stalking, and Violation of Domestic Protective Orders), to name a few. The North Carolina Pattern Jury Instructions Committee interpreted the statute as requiring that the defendant hire, employ, use, or permit the minor to do anything constituting an obscenity offense. N.C. PATTERN JURY INSTRUCTIONS—CRIM. 238.14. However, the statute prohibits hiring, employing, using, or permitting the minor "to do or assist in doing any act or thing constituting an offense under this Article and involving any material, act or thing he knows or reasonably should know to be obscene." G.S. 14-190.6. Based on a plain reading of the statute, the defendant's acts would appear to be covered if he or she engaged in, for example, crime against nature (an offense "under this Article") with the minor and obscenity was "involved" but no obscenity offense was committed. Put another way, the North Carolina Pattern Jury Instructions Committee may have been overly narrow in its reading of the statute. *See* State v. Martin, 195 N.C. App. 43, 55 (2009) (stating the elements of the offense as set forth above and not as requiring an obscenity offense).

Elements (7) and (9). See the note on Element (3) to "Disseminating Obscenity," above, for a discussion of the meaning of the term "obscene."

Defenses. The question of whether a mistake of age would be a defense remains unsettled.

Multiple convictions and punishments. Because each offense includes an element not in the other, no double jeopardy violation occurred when a defendant was convicted and punished for indecent liberties and using a minor in obscenity based on the same photograph. State v. Martin, 195 N.C. App. 43, 54–55 (2009).

Relation to other offenses. "First-Degree Sexual Exploitation of a Minor," below, may be charged in almost every instance in which this offense applies. That offense is punished more heavily and provides that mistake of age is no defense.

Sex offender registration. This offense is a sexually violent offense triggering registration requirements under the sex offender registration statutes. G.S. 14-208.6(5).

Related Offenses Not in This Chapter

See the offenses involving minors in Chapter 7 (Assaults).
See the various child abuse offenses in Chapter 9 (Abuse and Neglect).
See the various offenses involving minors in Chapter 10 (Sexual Assaults).
See the offenses in Chapter 11 (Crime against Nature, Incest, Indecent Exposure, and Related Offenses).
See the offenses involving minors in Chapter 23 (Prostitution).

Disseminating Obscene Material to a Minor under 16

Statute

§14-190.7. Dissemination to minors under the age of 16 years.

Every person 18 years of age or older who knowingly disseminates to any minor under the age of 16 years any material which he knows or reasonably should know to be obscene within the meaning of G.S. 14-190.1 shall be guilty of a Class I felony.

Elements

A person guilty of this offense

(1) is 18 years of age or older *and*
(2) knowingly
(3) disseminates
(4) to a minor under the age of 16 years
(5) obscene material
(6) that the person knows or reasonably should know
(7) is obscene.

Punishment

Class I felony. G.S. 14-190.7

Notes

Element (2). See "Knowingly" in Chapter 1 (States of Mind).

Element (3). For a discussion of the term "disseminates" as it applies in another obscenity offense, see the note on Element (2) to "Disseminating Obscenity," above.

Elements (5) and (7). See the note on Element (3) to "Disseminating Obscenity," above, for a discussion of the meaning of the term "obscenity."

Defenses. The question of whether a mistake of age would be a defense remains unsettled.

Related Offenses Not in This Chapter

See the offenses listed under "Using a Minor to Assist in an Obscenity Offense," above.

Disseminating Obscene Material to a Minor under 13

Statute

§14-190.8. Dissemination to minors under the age of 13 years.

Every person 18 years of age or older who knowingly disseminates to any minor under the age of 13 years any material which he knows or reasonably should know to be obscene within the meaning of G.S. 14-190.1 shall be punished as a Class I felon.

Elements

A person guilty of this offense

(1) is 18 years of age or older *and*
(2) knowingly
(3) disseminates
(4) to a minor under the age of 13 years
(5) obscene material
(6) that the person knows or reasonably should know
(7) is obscene.

Punishment

Class I felony. G.S. 14-190.8.

Notes

Generally. This offense is identical to "Disseminating Obscene Material to a Minor under 16," above, except that this offense covers younger victims. Thus, the notes to that offense apply here as well.

Related Offenses Not in This Chapter

See the offenses listed under "Using a Minor to Assist in an Obscenity Offense," above.

Disseminating and Exhibiting Material Harmful to Minors

Displaying Material Harmful to Minors

Statute

§14-190.13. Definitions for certain offenses concerning minors.

The following definitions apply to G.S. 14-190.14, displaying material harmful to minors; G.S. 14-190.15, disseminating or exhibiting to minors harmful material or performances to minors; G.S. 14-190.16, first degree sexual exploitation of a minor; G.S. 14-190.17, second degree sexual exploitation of a minor; G.S. 14-190.17A, third degree sexual exploitation of a minor; G.S. 14-190.18, promoting prostitution of a minor; and G.S. 14-190.19, participating in prostitution of a minor.

(1) Harmful to Minors.—That quality of any material or performance that depicts sexually explicit nudity or sexual activity and that, taken as a whole, has the following characteristics:

a. The average adult person applying contemporary community standards would find that the material or performance has a predominant tendency to appeal to a prurient interest of minors in sex; and

b. The average adult person applying contemporary community standards would find that the depiction of sexually explicit nudity or sexual activity in the material or performance is patently offensive to prevailing standards in the adult community concerning what is suitable for minors; and

c. The material or performance lacks serious literary, artistic, political, or scientific value for minors.

(2) Material.—Pictures, drawings, video recordings, films or other visual depictions or representations but not material consisting entirely of written words.

(3) Minor.—An individual who is less than 18 years old and is not married or judicially emancipated.

(4) Prostitution.—Engaging or offering to engage in sexual activity with or for another in exchange for anything of value.

(5) Sexual Activity.—Any of the following acts:

a. Masturbation, whether done alone or with another human or an animal.

b. Vaginal, anal, or oral intercourse, whether done with another human or with an animal.

c. Touching, in an act of apparent sexual stimulation or sexual abuse, of the clothed or unclothed genitals, pubic area, or buttocks of another person or the clothed or unclothed breasts of a human female.

d. An act or condition that depicts torture, physical restraint by being fettered or bound, or flagellation of or by a person clad in undergarments or in revealing or bizarre costume.

e. Excretory functions; provided, however, that this sub-division shall not apply to G.S. 14-190.17A.

f. The insertion of any part of a person's body, other than the male sexual organ, or of any object into another person's anus or vagina, except when done as part of a recognized medical procedure.

g. The lascivious exhibition of the genitals or pubic area of any person.

(6) Sexually Explicit Nudity.—The showing of:

a. Uncovered, or less than opaquely covered, human genitals, pubic area, or buttocks, or the nipple or any portion of the areola of the human female breast, except as provided in G.S. 14-190.9(b); or

b. Covered human male genitals in a discernibly turgid state.

§14-190.14. Displaying material harmful to minors.

(a) Offense.—A person commits the offense of displaying material that is harmful to minors if, having custody, control, or supervision of a commercial establishment and knowing the character or content of the material, he displays material that is harmful to minors at that establishment so that it is open to view by minors as part of the invited general public. Material is not considered displayed under this section if the material is placed behind "blinder racks" that cover the lower two thirds of the material, is wrapped, is placed behind the counter, or is otherwise covered or located so that the portion that is harmful to minors is not open to the view of minors.

(b) Punishment.—Violation of this section is a Class 2 misdemeanor. Each day's violation of this section is a separate offense.

Elements

A person guilty of this offense

(1) displays
(2) material
(3) that is harmful to minors
(4) at a commercial establishment
(5) so that it is open to view by minors as part of the invited general public *and*
(6) has custody, control, or supervision
(7) of the commercial establishment *and*
(8) knows the material's character or content.

Punishment

Class 2 misdemeanor. G.S. 14-190.14(b).

Notes

Element (1). Material is not considered to be "displayed" if it is:

- placed behind "blinder racks" that cover the lower two thirds of the material,
- wrapped,
- placed behind the counter, or
- otherwise covered or located so that the portion that is harmful to minors is not open to the view of minors.

G.S. 14-190.14(a).

Element (2). "Material" means "pictures, drawings, video recordings, films or other visual depictions or representations but not material consisting entirely of written words." G.S. 14-190.13(2).

Element (3). A "minor" is an individual who is less than 18 years old and is not married or judicially emancipated. G.S. 14-190.13(3).

The term "harmful to minors" means that quality of any material or performance that depicts "sexually explicit nudity" or "sexual activity" and that, taken as a whole, has the following characteristics:

- the average adult applying contemporary community standards would find that the material or performance has a predominant tendency to appeal to a prurient interest of minors in sex;
- the average adult applying contemporary community standards would find that the depiction of sexually explicit nudity or sexual activity in the material or performance is patently offensive to prevailing standards in the adult community concerning what is suitable for minors; and
- the material or performance lacks serious literary, artistic, political, or scientific value for minors.

G.S. 14-190.13(1).

"Sexually explicit nudity" involves the showing of: uncovered, or less than opaquely covered, human genitals, pubic area, or buttocks, or the nipple or areola of the female breast, except during breastfeeding; or "covered human male genitals in a discernibly turgid state." G.S. 14-190.13(6).

"Sexual activity" includes:

- masturbation, alone or with another human or an animal;
- vaginal, anal, or oral intercourse, with another human or an animal;
- touching, in an act of apparent sexual stimulation or sexual abuse, of the clothed or unclothed genitals, pubic area, buttocks, or breasts of another person;
- an act or condition that depicts torture, physical restraint by being fettered or bound, or flagellation of or by a person clad in undergarments or in revealing or bizarre costume;
- excretory functions;
- the insertion of any part of a person's body, other than the male sexual organ, or of any object, into another person's anus or vagina, except when done as part of a recognized medical procedure; and
- the lascivious exhibition of the genitals or pubic area of any person.

G.S. 14-190.13(5).

Noting that the statute does not define the term "masturbation," the North Carolina Court of Appeals applied a dictionary definition, interpreting that term to mean "[e]xcitation of the genital organs, usually to orgasm, by manual contact or means other than sexual intercourse." State v. Ligon, ___ N.C. App. ___, 697 S.E.2d 481, 489 (2010) (a sexual exploitation of a minor case in which the G.S. 14-190.13(5) definition of "sexual activity" applied).

Element (5). This element requires proof that the commercial establishment welcomed the general public and made no attempt to exclude minors from the area of the establishment in which material harmful to minors was open to view.

Multiple convictions and punishments. Each day's violation is a separate offense. G.S. 14-190.14(b).

Related Offenses Not in This Chapter

See the offenses listed under "Using a Minor to Assist in an Obscenity Offense," above.

Disseminating Material Harmful to Minors

Statute

See G.S. 14-190.13, reproduced under "Displaying Material Harmful to Minors," above.

§14-190.15. Disseminating harmful material to minors; exhibiting harmful performances to minors.

(a) Disseminating Harmful Material.—A person commits the offense of disseminating harmful material to minors if, with or without consideration and knowing the character or content of the material, he:

(1) Sells, furnishes, presents, or distributes to a minor material that is harmful to minors; or

(2) Allows a minor to review or peruse material that is harmful to minors.

(b) Exhibiting Harmful Performance.—A person commits the offense of exhibiting a harmful performance to a minor if, with or without consideration and knowing the character or content of the performance, he allows a minor to view a live performance that is harmful to minors.

(c) Defenses.—Except as provided in subdivision (3), a mistake of age is not a defense to a prosecution under this section. It is an affirmative defense to a prosecution under this section that:

(1) The defendant was a parent or legal guardian of the minor.

(2) The defendant was a school, church, museum, public library, governmental agency, medical clinic, or hospital carrying out its legitimate function; or an employee or agent of such an organization acting in that capacity and carrying out a legitimate duty of his employment.

(3) Before disseminating or exhibiting the harmful material or performance, the defendant requested and received a driver's license, student identification card, or other official governmental or educational identification card or paper indicating that the minor to whom the material or performance was disseminated or exhibited was at least 18 years old, and the defendant reasonably believed the minor was at least 18 years old.

(4) The dissemination was made with the prior consent of a parent or guardian of the recipient.

(d) Punishment.—Violation of this section is a Class 1 misdemeanor.

Elements

A person guilty of this offense

(1) (a) sells, furnishes, presents, or distributes to a minor *or*
(b) allows a minor to review or peruse

(2) material

(3) that is harmful to minors

(4) knowing the material's character or content.

Punishment

Class 1 misdemeanor. G.S. 14-190.15(d).

Notes

Element (1). The offense occurs if the defendant engages in these acts either with or without consideration. G.S. 14-190.15(a).

For a definition of the term "minor," see the note on Element (3) to "Displaying Material Harmful to Minors," above.

Element (2). See the note on this Element to "Displaying Material Harmful to Minors," above.

Element (3). See the note on this Element to "Displaying Material Harmful to Minors," above.

Relation to other offenses. Whereas "Displaying Material Harmful to Minors," above, is limited to commercial establishments, this offense applies everywhere and is not limited to such establishments.

Defenses. Mistake of age is not a defense to a prosecution for this crime, except as discussed immediately below. G.S. 14-190.15(c). G.S. 14-190.15(c) sets out the following affirmative defenses to this offense. They include proof that:

(1) The defendant was the minor's parent or legal guardian.
(2) The defendant was a school, church, museum, public library, governmental agency, medical clinic, or hospital carrying out its legitimate function or was an employee or agent of such an organization acting in that capacity and carrying out a legitimate duty of his or her employment.
(3) Before disseminating or exhibiting the harmful material or performance, the defendant requested and received a driver's license, student identification card, or other official governmental or educational identification card or paper indicating that the minor to whom the material or performance was disseminated or exhibited was at least 18 years old, and the defendant reasonably believed the minor was at least 18 years old.
(4) The dissemination was made with the prior consent of a parent or guardian of the recipient.

Related Offenses Not in This Chapter

See the offenses listed under "Using a Minor to Assist in an Obscenity Offense," above.

Exhibiting a Performance Harmful to Minors

Statute

See G.S. 14-190.13, reproduced under "Displaying Material Harmful to Minors," above.
See G.S. 14-190.15(b), reproduced under "Disseminating Material Harmful to Minors," above.

Elements

A person guilty of this offense

(1) allows
(2) a minor
(3) to view
(4) a live performance
(5) that is harmful to minors
(6) knowing the performance's character or content.

Punishment

Class 1 misdemeanor. G.S. 14-190.15(d).

Notes

Element (1). The offense occurs if the defendant engages in the relevant conduct either with or without consideration. G.S. 14-190.15(b).

Element (2). For the meaning of the term "minor," see the note on Element (3) to "Displaying Material Harmful to Minors," above.

Element (5). See the note on Element (3) to "Displaying Material Harmful to Minors," above.

Defenses. See this note to "Disseminating Material Harmful to Minors," above.

Related Offenses Not in This Chapter

See the offenses listed under "Using a Minor to Assist in an Obscenity Offense," above.

Sexual Exploitation of a Minor

First-Degree Sexual Exploitation of a Minor

Statute

See G.S. 14-190.13, reproduced under "Displaying Material Harmful to Minors," above.

§14-190.16. First degree sexual exploitation of a minor.

(a) Offense.—A person commits the offense of first degree sexual exploitation of a minor if, knowing the character or content of the material or performance, he:

(1) Uses, employs, induces, coerces, encourages, or facilitates a minor to engage in or assist others to engage in sexual activity for a live performance or for the purpose of producing material that contains a visual representation depicting this activity; or

(2) Permits a minor under his custody or control to engage in sexual activity for a live performance or for the purpose of producing material that contains a visual representation depicting this activity; or

(3) Transports or finances the transportation of a minor through or across this State with the intent that the minor engage in sexual activity for a live performance or for the purpose of producing material that contains a visual representation depicting this activity; or

(4) Records, photographs, films, develops, or duplicates for sale or pecuniary gain material that contains a visual representation depicting a minor engaged in sexual activity.

(b) Inference.—In a prosecution under this section, the trier of fact may infer that a participant in sexual activity whom material through its title, text, visual representations, or otherwise represents or depicts as a minor is a minor.

(c) Mistake of Age.—Mistake of age is not a defense to a prosecution under this section.

(d) Punishment and Sentencing.—Violation of this section is a Class C felony.

Elements

A person guilty of this offense

(1) knowing the character or content of the material or performance

(2) (a) (i) uses, employs, induces, coerces, encourages, or facilitates

(ii) a minor

(iii) to engage in or assist others to engage in sexual activity for a live performance or for the purpose of producing material that contains a visual representation depicting this activity;

(b) (i) permits
(ii) a minor
(iii) under his or her custody or control
(iv) to engage in sexual activity for a live performance or for the purpose of producing material that contains a visual representation depicting this activity;

(c) (i) transports or finances the transportation of
(ii) a minor
(iii) through or across the state
(iv) with the intent that the minor engage in sexual activity for a live performance or for the purpose of producing material that contains a visual representation depicting this activity; *or*

(d) (i) records, photographs, films, develops, or duplicates
(ii) for sale or pecuniary gain
(iii) material containing a visual representation depicting a minor engaged in sexual activity.

Punishment

Class C felony. G.S. 14-190.16(d). For special maximum sentences that apply to offenders who commit Class B1–E felonies that are reportable convictions under the sex offender registration program, see "Sex offenders" under "Special Provisions" in the discussion of felony sentencing in Chapter 4 (Punishment under Structured Sentencing).

Notes

Element (2). For the definition of the term "material," see the note on Element (2) to "Displaying Material Harmful to Minors," above. For a definition of the terms "minor" and "sexual activity," see the note on Element (3) to that offense. For a case in which the evidence was insufficient to establish that the photographs at issue depicted sexual activity, see *State v. Ligon*, ___ N.C. App. ___, 697 S.E.2d 481, 488–90 (2010) (the court rejected the State's arguments that a picture depicting the child pulling up the leg of her shorts while her fingers were in her pubic area depicted masturbation; it also rejected the State's argument that the picture, along with other evidence, supported an inference that the defendant coerced or encouraged the child to touch herself for the purpose of producing a photograph depicting masturbation; finally, the court rejected the State's argument that a photograph of the defendant pulling aside the child's shorts depicted prohibited touching).

The "visual representation" must be tied to the actual exposure of a minor to sexual activity. Cinema I Video, Inc. v. Thornburg, 83 N.C. App. 544 (1986). This interpretation avoids having the sexual exploitation statutes run afoul of the United States Supreme Court's decision in *Ashcroft v. Free Speech Coalition*, 535 U.S. 234 (2002) (holding that the federal Child Pornography Prevention Act of 1996 (CPPA) was unconstitutionally overbroad because it proscribed "virtual" child pornography, as well as movies where adult actors play minor children, both of which depict minors but are produced without using real children). State v. Howell, 169 N.C. App. 58, 64–67 (2005) (third-degree exploitation case; citing *Cinema I Video* and concluding: "The crucial distinction between the CPAA [sic] and the North Carolina statutes is that the CPAA [sic] prohibits images in which the person only *appears* to be a minor, whereas our statutes prohibit only depictions which use an *actual* minor in their production.") (emphasis in original).

Evidence issues. A defendant's offer to stipulate that the material contains images of child pornography does not bar the State from presenting evidence as to the material's content. State v. Riffe, 191 N.C. App. 86, 94–95 (2008) (third-degree exploitation case). For a discussion of a potential limitation of this rule, see this note to "Felon in Possession of a Firearm" in Chapter 22 (Weapons Offenses) (discussing the United States Supreme Court's decision in *Old Chief v. United States*, 519 U.S. 172 (1997), and the evidence rule 403 analysis when a defendant charged with possession of a firearm by a felon offers to stipulate to the prior felony conviction).

Under G.S. 14-190.16(b), the trier of fact may infer that a participant in sexual activity whom material through its title, text, visual representations, or otherwise represents or depicts as a minor is in fact a minor. The constitutionality of this inference has been upheld. *Cinema I Video*, 83 N.C. App. 544.

Jurisdiction. The First Amendment does not bar the State from prohibiting the distribution of unprotected materials produced outside the state. New York v. Ferber, 458 U.S. 747 (1982). See generally "Lack of Jurisdiction" in Chapter 2 (Bars and Defenses).

Defenses. Mistake of age is not a defense to a prosecution for this offense. G.S. 14-190.16(c).

Sex offender registration. This offense is a sexually violent offense triggering registration requirements under the sex offender registration statutes. G.S. 14-208.6(5).

Related Offenses Not in This Chapter

See the offenses listed under "Using a Minor to Assist in an Obscenity Offense," above.

Second-Degree Sexual Exploitation of a Minor

Statute

See G.S. 14-190.13, reproduced under "Displaying Material Harmful to Minors," above.

§14-190.17. Second degree sexual exploitation of a minor.

(a) Offense.—A person commits the offense of second degree sexual exploitation of a minor if, knowing the character or content of the material, he:

(1) Records, photographs, films, develops, or duplicates material that contains a visual representation of a minor engaged in sexual activity; or

(2) Distributes, transports, exhibits, receives, sells, purchases, exchanges, or solicits material that contains a visual representation of a minor engaged in sexual activity.

(b) Inference.—In a prosecution under this section, the trier of fact may infer that a participant in sexual activity whom material through its title, text, visual representations or otherwise represents or depicts as a minor is a minor.

(c) Mistake of Age.—Mistake of age is not a defense to a prosecution under this section.

(d) Punishment and Sentencing.—Violation of this section is a Class E felony.

Elements

A person guilty of this offense

(1) knowing the material's character or content

(2) (a) records, photographs, films, develops, or duplicates *or*

(b) distributes, transports, exhibits, receives, sells, purchases, exchanges, or solicits

(3) material

(4) containing a visual representation of a minor engaged in sexual activity.

Punishment

Class E felony. G.S. 14-190.17(d). For special maximum sentences that apply to offenders who commit Class B1–E felonies that are reportable convictions under the sex offender registration program, see "Sex offenders" under "Special Provisions" in the discussion of felony sentencing in Chapter 4 (Punishment under Structured Sentencing).

Notes

Element (3). For a definition of the term "material," see the note on Element (2) to "Displaying Material Harmful to Minors," above.

Element (4). For a definition of the terms "minor" and "sexual activity," see the note on Element (3) to "Displaying Material Harmful to Minors," above.

Evidence issues. The statute contains a provision allowing for an inference that a model or actor is a minor, G.S. 14-190.17(b), that is identical to the inference that applies in prosecutions for first-degree sexual exploitation of a minor. For details, see this note to "First-Degree Sexual Exploitation of a Minor," above.

Jurisdiction. See this note to "First-Degree Sexual Exploitation of a Minor," above.

Defenses. G.S. 14-190.17(c) provides that mistake of age is not a defense to this offense.

Relation to other offenses. The Element (2)(a) version of this offense is aimed at noncommercial production of child pornography; it is identical to the Element (2)(d) version of "First-Degree Sexual Exploitation of a Minor," above, except that the first-degree offense adds the element "for sale or pecuniary gain." The Element (2)(b) version of this offense is aimed at circulation of the child pornography—whether done commercially or noncommercially.

Multiple convictions and punishments. There is no double jeopardy violation when a defendant is convicted and punished for second-degree sexual exploitation of a minor based on receipt of images of minors and for third-degree sexual exploitation of a minor based on possession of those same images. State v. Anderson, 362 N.C. 90 (2008).

Sex offender registration. This offense is a sexually violent offense triggering registration requirements under the sex offender registration statutes. G.S. 14-208.6(5).

Related Offenses Not in This Chapter

See the related offenses under "Using a Minor to Assist in an Obscenity Offense," above.

Third-Degree Sexual Exploitation of a Minor

Statute

See G.S. 14-190.13, reproduced under "Displaying Material Harmful to Minors," above.

> **§14-190.17A. Third degree sexual exploitation of a minor.**
>
> (a) Offense.—A person commits the offense of third degree sexual exploitation of a minor if, knowing the character or content of the material, he possesses material that contains a visual representation of a minor engaging in sexual activity.
>
> (b) Inference.—In a prosecution under this section, the trier of fact may infer that a participant in sexual activity whom material through its title, text, visual representations or otherwise represents or depicts as a minor is a minor.
>
> (c) Mistake of Age.—Mistake of age is not a defense to a prosecution under this section.
>
> (d) Punishment and Sentencing.—Violation of this section is a Class H felony.

Elements

A person guilty of this offense

(1) knowing the material's character or content
(2) possesses
(3) material containing a visual representation of a minor engaged in sexual activity.

Punishment

Class H felony. G.S. 14-190.17A(d).

Notes

Element (1). Sufficient evidence was presented as to this element when the defendant conceded that his computer contained images of a minor engaging in sexual activity, a State Bureau of Investigation agent testified that he found twelve saved files with names indicating that they contained child pornography (e.g., "Child Porn, Very Illegal"), a computer forensic analysis revealed that the pornography was stored on the device's hard drive, and the jury reviewed the files to determine whether their names reflected their content. State v. Riffe, 191 N.C. App. 86, 90–91 (2008).

Element (2). Although cases have stated that there is no requirement of knowing possession, *Riffe*, 191 N.C. App. at 89–90, 92; State v. Dexter, 186 N.C. App. 587, 595 (2007), they also have stated that a defendant is in possession of child pornography when he or she has the power and intent to control the disposition of the images. *Riffe*, 191 N.C. App. at 92. This element is satisfied when the State establishes that a computer belongs to the defendant and that the images have been opened and saved on that computer. *Id.* (the evidence established possession under this standard). For another case in which there was sufficient evidence that the defendant was in possession of computer images in violation of the statute, see *Dexter*, 186 N.C. App. at 595–96.

Element (3). For a definition of the term "material," see the note on Element (2) to Displaying Material Harmful to Minors," above. For a definition of the terms "minor" and "sexual activity," see the note on Element (3) to that same offense. Note that sexual activity for purposes of this offense is distinguishable from first-degree and second-degree sexual exploitation of a minor in that G.S. 14-190.13(5)(e) explicitly states that "excretory functions" do not constitute sexual activity covered by this offense.

Evidence issues. The statute contains a provision allowing for an inference that a model or actor is a minor, G.S. 14-190.17A(b), that is identical to the inference that applies in prosecutions for first-degree sexual exploitation of a minor. For details, see this note to "First-Degree Sexual Exploitation of a Minor," above.

Defenses. G.S. 14-190.17A(c) provides that mistake of age is not a defense to this offense.

Multiple convictions and punishments. Forty-three convictions were permitted for forty-three child pornography photographs on the defendant's home computer. State v. Howell, 169 N.C. App. 58 (2005).

There is no double jeopardy violation when a defendant is convicted and punished for second-degree sexual exploitation of a minor based on receipt of images of minors and for third-degree sexual exploitation of a minor based on possession of those same images. State v. Anderson, 362 N.C. 90 (2008).

Constitutionality. This offense is not constitutionally overbroad. *Howell*, 169 N.C. App. 58.

Sex offender registration. This offense is a sexually violent offense triggering registration requirements under the sex offender registration statutes. G.S. 14-208.6(5).

Related Offenses Not in This Chapter

See the related offenses under "Using a Minor to Assist in an Obscenity Offense," above.

Adult Establishment Offenses

Statute

§14-202.10. Definitions.

As used in this Article:

(1) "Adult bookstore" means a bookstore:

a. Which receives a majority of its gross income during any calendar month from the sale or rental of publications (including books, magazines, other periodicals, videotapes, compact discs, other photographic, electronic, magnetic, digital, or other imaging medium) which are distinguished or characterized by their emphasis on matter depicting, describing, or relating to specified sexual activities or specified anatomical areas, as defined in this section; or

b. Having as a preponderance (either in terms of the weight and importance of the material or in terms of greater volume of materials) of its publications (including books, magazines, other periodicals, videotapes, compact discs, other photographic, electronic, magnetic, digital, or other imaging medium) which are distinguished or characterized by their emphasis on matter depicting, describing, or relating to specified sexual activities or specified anatomical areas, as defined in this section.

(2) "Adult establishment" means an adult bookstore, adult motion picture theatre, adult mini motion picture theatre, adult live entertainment business, or massage business as defined in this section.

(3) "Adult live entertainment" means any performance of or involving the actual presence of real people which exhibits specified sexual activities or specified anatomical areas, as defined in this section.

(4) "Adult live entertainment business" means any establishment or business wherein adult live entertainment is shown for observation by patrons.

(5) "Adult motion picture theatre" means an enclosed building or premises used for presenting motion pictures, a preponderance of which are distinguished or characterized by an emphasis on matter depicting, describing, or relating to specified sexual activities or specified anatomical areas, as defined in this section, for observation by patrons therein. "Adult motion picture theatre" does not include any adult mini motion picture theatre as defined in this section.

(6) "Adult mini motion picture theatre" means an enclosed building with viewing booths designed to hold patrons which is used for presenting motion pictures, a preponderance of which are distinguished or characterized by an emphasis on matter depicting, describing or relating to specified sexual activities or specified anatomical areas as defined in this section, for observation by patrons therein.

(7) "Massage" means the manipulation of body muscle or tissue by rubbing, stroking, kneading, or tapping, by hand or mechanical device.

(8) "Massage business" means any establishment or business wherein massage is practiced, including establishments commonly known as health clubs, physical culture studios, massage studios, or massage parlors.

(9) "Sexually oriented devices" means without limitation any artificial or simulated specified anatomical area or other device or paraphernalia that is designed principally for specified sexual activities but shall not mean any contraceptive device.

(10) "Specified anatomical areas" means:

a. Less than completely and opaquely covered: (i) human genitals, pubic region, (ii) buttock, or (iii) female breast below a point immediately above the top of the areola; or

b. Human male genitals in a discernibly turgid state, even if completely and opaquely covered.

(11) "Specified sexual activities" means:
a. Human genitals in a state of sexual stimulation or arousal;
b. Acts of human masturbation, sexual intercourse or sodomy; or
c. Fondling or other erotic touchings of human genitals, pubic regions, buttocks or female breasts.

§14-202.11. Restrictions as to adult establishments.

(a) No person shall permit any building, premises, structure, or other facility that contains any adult establishment to contain any other kind of adult establishment. No person shall permit any building, premises, structure, or other facility in which sexually oriented devices are sold, distributed, exhibited, or contained to contain any adult establishment.

(b) No person shall permit any viewing booth in an adult mini motion picture theatre to be occupied by more than one person at any time.

(c) Nothing in this section shall be deemed to preempt local government regulation of the location or operation of adult establishments or other sexually oriented businesses to the extent consistent with the constitutional protection afforded free speech.

§14-202.12. Violations; penalties.

Any person who violates G.S. 14-202.11 shall be guilty of a Class 3 misdemeanor. Any person who has been previously convicted of a violation of G.S. 14-202.11, upon conviction for a second or subsequent violation of G.S. 14-202.11, shall be guilty of a Class 2 misdemeanor.

As used herein, "person" shall include:

(1) The agent in charge of the building, premises, structure or facility; or
(2) The owner of the building, premises, structure or facility when such owner knew or reasonably should have known the nature of the business located therein, and such owner refused to cooperate with the public officials in reasonable measures designed to terminate the proscribed use; provided, however, that if there is an agent in charge, and if the owner did not have actual knowledge, the owner shall not be prosecuted; or
(3) The owner of the business; or
(4) The manager of the business.

Permitting a Facility to Contain Multiple Adult Establishments

Statute

See G.S. 14-202.11(a), reproduced above.

Elements

A person guilty of this offense

(1) permits
(2) any building, premises, structure, or other facility
(3) that contains any adult establishment
(4) to contain any other kind of adult establishment.

Punishment

Class 3 misdemeanor. G.S. 14-202.12. A second or subsequent conviction is punished as a Class 2 misdemeanor. *Id.* If the Class 2 misdemeanor version of this offense is charged, the facts elevating punishment must be alleged in a charging instrument and proved at trial. *See* G.S. 15A-928 (pleading and proving prior convictions).

Notes

Generally. G.S. 14-202.12 defines a "person" who can be guilty of this offense as:

- the agent in charge of the building, premises, structure, or facility;
- the owner of the building, premises, structure, or facility if the owner knew or reasonably should have known the nature of the business and refused to cooperate with public officials in reasonable measures designed to terminate the prohibited use;
- the owner of the business; or
- the manager of the business. However, if there is an agent in charge and the owner did not have actual knowledge, the owner may not be prosecuted.

G.S. 14-202.12.

Element (3). G.S. 14-202.10(2) defines "adult establishment" as an adult bookstore, an adult motion picture theatre, an adult mini–motion picture theatre, an adult live entertainment business, or a massage business. G.S. 14-202.10 sets out detailed definitions for each of these kinds of adult establishments. The term "preponderance" used in the definition of "adult mini motion picture theatre" in G.S. 14-202.10(6) is not unconstitutionally vague. Hart Book Stores, Inc. v. Edmisten, 612 F.2d 821 (4th Cir. 1979); Fantasy World, Inc. v. Greensboro Bd. of Adjustment, 128 N.C. App. 703 (1998); S. Blvd. Video & News, Inc. v. Charlotte Zoning Bd. of Adjustment, 129 N.C. App. 282 (1998).

Related Offenses Not in This Chapter

See the offenses listed under "Disseminating Obscenity," above.

Permitting an Adult Establishment in a Facility Where Sexually Oriented Devices Are Contained

Statute

See G.S. 14-202.11(a), reproduced above.

Elements

A person guilty of this offense

(1) permits
(2) any building, premises, structure, or other facility
(3) in which sexually oriented devices are sold or distributed or exhibited or contained
(4) to contain any adult establishment.

Punishment

Class 3 misdemeanor. G.S. 14-202.12. A second and subsequent conviction is punished as a Class 2 misdemeanor. *Id.* If the Class 2 misdemeanor version of this offense is charged, the facts elevating punishment must be alleged in a charging instrument and proved at trial. *See* G.S. 15A-928 (pleading and proving prior convictions).

Notes

Generally. See this note under "Permitting a Facility to Contain Multiple Adult Establishments," above.

Element (3). G.S. 14-202.10(9) defines "sexually oriented devices" to mean "without limitation any artificial or simulated specified anatomical area or other device or paraphernalia that is designed principally for specified sexual activities but shall not mean any contraceptive device."

Element (4). See the note on Element (3) under "Permitting a Facility to Contain Multiple Adult Establishments," above.

Related Offenses Not in This Chapter

See the offenses listed under "Disseminating Obscenity," above.

Permitting Multiple Occupancy in a Viewing Booth

Statute

See G.S. 14-202.11(b), reproduced above.

Elements

A person guilty of this offense

(1) permits
(2) any viewing booth
(3) in an adult mini–motion picture theater
(4) to be occupied by more than one person at any time.

Punishment

Class 3 misdemeanor. G.S. 14-202.12. A second or subsequent offense is punished as a Class 2 misdemeanor. *Id.* If the Class 2 misdemeanor version of this offense is charged, the facts elevating punishment must be alleged in a charging instrument and proved at trial. *See* G.S. 15A-928 (pleading and proving prior convictions).

Notes

Generally. See this note under "Permitting a Facility to Contain Multiple Adult Establishments," above.

Element (3). An "adult mini motion picture theatre" is an enclosed building with viewing booths designed to hold patrons and used for presenting motion pictures, a preponderance of which are distinguished or characterized by an emphasis on matter depicting, describing or relating to "specified sexual activities" or "specified anatomical areas." G.S. 14-202.10(6). The term "preponderance" in this definition is not unconstitutionally vague. Hart Book Stores, Inc. v. Edmisten, 612 F.2d 821 (4th Cir. 1979); Fantasy World, Inc. v. Greensboro Bd. of Adjustment, 128 N.C. App. 703 (1998); S. Blvd. Video & News, Inc. v. Charlotte Zoning Bd. of Adjustment, 129 N.C. App. 282 (1998). The definition of "specified anatomical areas" includes less than completely and opaquely covered human genitals, pubic region, buttock, or female breast below a point immediately above the top of the areola, as well as human male genitals in a discernibly turgid state, even if completely and opaquely covered. G.S. 14-202.10(10). "Specified sexual activities" means human genitals in a state of sexual stimulation or arousal; acts of human masturbation, sexual intercourse, or sodomy; or fondling or other erotic touchings of human genitals, pubic regions, buttocks, or female breasts. G.S. 14-202.10(11).

Related Offenses Not in This Chapter

See the offenses listed under "Disseminating Obscenity," above.

25

Lotteries, Gambling, and Related Offenses

25

Lotteries, Gambling, and Related Offenses

Lottery Offenses

Advertising a Lottery

Statute

§14-289. Advertising lotteries.

Except as provided in Chapter 18C of the General Statutes or in connection with a lawful raffle as provided in Part 2 of this Article, if anyone by writing or printing or by circular or letter or in any other way, advertises or publishes an account of a lottery, whether within or without this State, stating how, when or where the same is to be or has been drawn, or what are the prizes therein or any of them, or the price of a ticket or any share or interest therein, or where or how it may be obtained, he shall be guilty of a Class 2 misdemeanor. News medium as defined in G.S. 8-53.11 shall be exempt from this section provided the publishing is in connection with a lawful activity of the news medium.

Elements

A person guilty of this offense

(1) advertises or publishes an account
(2) of a lottery
(3) stating
  (a) how, when, or where the lottery will be or has been drawn,
  (b) the prizes in the lottery,
  (c) the price of a lottery ticket, *or*
  (d) where or how to obtain entry in the lottery.

Punishment

Class 2 misdemeanor. G.S. 14-289.

Notes

Element (1). This element is satisfied if the advertising or publishing is done "by writing or printing or by circular or letter or in any other way," inside or outside the state. G.S. 14-289.

Element (2). A "lottery" is any scheme by which a person gives some benefit in order to be considered for winning a prize and the selection of the prize winner is predominantly by chance. State v. Lipkin, 169 N.C. 265 (1915); State v. Simmons, 59 N.C. App. 287 (1982).

Element (3)(c). The advertised price may be of "a ticket or any share or interest therein." G.S. 14-289.

Exceptions. A news medium defined by G.S. 8-53.11 is exempt from prosecution for an offense under G.S. 14-289, provided the publishing at issue is in connection with lawful activity of the news medium. G.S. 14-289.

The North Carolina state-run lottery is excluded from the coverage of this offense. G.S. 14-289 ("Except as provided in Chapter 18C"). A lawful raffle also is excluded from coverage. *Id.* Lawful raffles are described in G.S. 14-309.15.

Seizure of illegal gaming items. Subject to certain procedural protections, G.S. 14-298 provides for the seizure of:

- gaming tables prohibited by G.S. 14-289 through -300,
- illegal punchboard or illegal slot machines,
- video game machines prohibited by G.S. 14-306 or -306.1A,
- game terminals described in G.S. 14-306.3(b), and
- electronic machines or devices using an entertaining display in violation of G.S. 14-306.4.

Related Offenses Not in This Chapter

Pyramid and chain schemes prohibited. G.S. 14-291.2.
Allowing gambling in houses of public entertainment. G.S. 14-293.
Gambling with faro banks and tables. G.S. 14-294.
Keeping gaming tables, illegal punchboards or slot machines, or betting thereat. G.S. 14-295.
Allowing gaming tables, illegal punchboards or slot machines on premises. G.S. 14-297.
Opposing destruction of gaming tables and seizure of property. G.S. 14-300.
Operation or possession of slot machine. G.S. 14-301.
Punchboards, vending machines, and other gambling devices. G.S. 14-302.
Agreements with reference to slot machines or devices made unlawful. G.S. 14-305.
Warehousing a video gaming machine. G.S. 14-306.1A(d).
Unlawful bingo. G.S. 14-309.5; 14-309.12.
Conducting a raffle in violation of law. G.S. 14-309.15(a).
Entering into or aiding contract for "futures" illegal. G.S. 16-4.
Opening office for sales of "futures" misdemeanor. G.S. 16-5.
Sales and sale price of tickets and shares; sales to minors prohibited. G.S. 18C-131(d).

Operating a Lottery

Statute

§14-290. Dealing in lotteries.

Except as provided in Chapter 18C of the General Statutes or in connection with a lawful raffle as provided in Part 2 of this Article, if any person shall open, set on foot, carry on, promote, make or draw, publicly or privately, a lottery, by whatever name, style or title the same may be denominated or known; or if any person shall, by such way and means, expose or set to sale any house, real estate, goods, chattels, cash, written evidence of debt, certificates of claims or any other thing of value whatsoever, every person so offending shall be guilty of a Class 2 misdemeanor which may include a fine not to exceed two thousand dollars ($2,000). Any person who engages in disposing of any species of property whatsoever, including money and evidences of debt, or in any manner distributes gifts or prizes upon tickets, bottle crowns, bottle caps, seals on containers, other devices or certificates sold for that purpose, shall be held liable to prosecution under this section. Any person who shall have in his possession any tickets, certificates or orders used in the operation of any lottery shall be held liable under this section, and the mere possession of such tickets shall be prima facie evidence of the violation of this section. This section shall not apply to the possession of a lottery ticket or share for a lottery game being lawfully conducted in another state.

Elements

A person guilty of this offense

(1) operates
(2) a lottery.

Punishment

Class 2 misdemeanor, which may include a fine not to exceed $2,000. G.S. 14-290.

Notes

Element (1). The statute prohibits other activity in connection with a lottery, but operating a lottery is the offense most commonly charged.

Element (2). See the note on Element (2) to "Advertising a Lottery," above.

Exceptions. The North Carolina state-run lottery and lawful raffles are excluded from coverage of this offense. G.S. 14-290. Lawful raffles are described in G.S. 14-309.15.

Seizure of illegal gaming items. See this note to "Advertising a Lottery," above.

Related Offenses Not in This Chapter

See the offenses listed under "Advertising a Lottery," above.

Possession of Lottery Tickets

Statute

See G.S. 14-290, reproduced under "Operating a Lottery," above.

Elements

A person guilty of this offense

(1) knowingly
(2) possesses
(3) lottery tickets, certificates, or orders
(4) used in the operation of any lottery.

Punishment

Class 2 misdemeanor, which may include a fine not to exceed $2,000. G.S. 14-290.

Notes

Element (1). See "Knowingly" in Chapter 1 (States of Mind). See also the note on Element (1)(b) to "Selling or Possessing Numbers Tickets," below, and N.C. PATTERN JURY INSTRUCTIONS—CRIM. 237.20.

Element (2). To satisfy this element, the defendant need not have immediate personal possession of the tickets; it is sufficient if the tickets are in the defendant's place of business under his or her control. State v. Jones, 213 N.C. 640 (1938). This is consistent with the general rule that possession may be actual or constructive. For an explanation of those terms as they apply to other offenses, see the note on Element (2)(c) to "Possession of a Firearm by a Felon" in Chapter 22 (Weapons Offenses) and the note on Element (2) to "Possession of a Controlled Substance" in Chapter 27 (Drug Offenses).

Element (3). See the note on Element (2) to "Advertising a Lottery," above, for the meaning of the term "lottery."

Evidence issues. Mere possession of a lottery ticket, certificate, or order constitutes prima facie evidence of a violation. G.S. 14-290.

Exceptions. This offense does not apply to possession of a lottery ticket or share for a lottery game being lawfully conducted in another state. G.S. 14-290. For other exceptions, see this note to "Operating a Lottery," above.

Seizure of illegal gaming items. See this note to "Advertising a Lottery," above.

Related Offenses Not in This Chapter

See the offenses listed under "Advertising a Lottery," above.

Selling Lottery Tickets

Statute

§14-291. Selling lottery tickets and acting as agent for lotteries.

Except as provided in Chapter 18C of the General Statutes or in connection with a lawful raffle as provided in Part 2 of this Article, if any person shall sell, barter or otherwise dispose of any lottery ticket or order for any number of shares in any lottery, or shall in anywise be concerned in such lottery, by acting as agent in the State for or on behalf of any such lottery, to be drawn or paid either out of or within the State, such person shall be guilty of a Class 2 misdemeanor.

Elements

A person guilty of this offense

(1) sells, barters, or disposes of
(2) a lottery ticket or order for any number of shares in a lottery.

Punishment

Class 2 misdemeanor. G.S. 14-291.

Notes

Element (2). See the note on Element (2) to "Advertising a Lottery," above, for a definition of the term "lottery."

Exceptions. The North Carolina state-run lottery and lawful raffles are excluded from coverage of this offense. G.S. 14-291. Lawful raffles are described in G.S. 14-309.15.

Seizure of illegal gaming items. See this note to "Advertising a Lottery," above.

Related Offenses Not in This Chapter

See the offenses listed under "Advertising a Lottery," above.

Acting as an Agent for a Lottery

Statute

See G.S. 14-291, reproduced under "Selling Lottery Tickets," above.

Elements

A person guilty of this offense

(1) acts as agent in this state
(2) for a lottery.

Punishment

Class 2 misdemeanor. G.S. 14-291.

Notes

Element (1). In a civil case that likely would apply to this offense, the state supreme court held that an "agent" is not "a subordinate employee without discretion"; to be an agent, a person must have "some charge or measure of control over the business entrusted to him, or of some feature of it." Whitehurst v. Kerr, 153 N.C. 76 (1910).

Element (2). See the note on Element (2) to "Advertising a Lottery," above. The statute covers lotteries drawn or paid either within or outside the state. G.S. 14-291.

Exceptions. See this note to "Selling Lottery Tickets," above.

Seizure of illegal gaming items. See this note to "Advertising a Lottery," above.

Related Offenses Not in This Chapter

See the offenses listed under "Advertising a Lottery," above.

Selling or Possessing Numbers Tickets

Statute

§14-291.1. Selling "numbers" tickets; possession prima facie evidence of violation.

Except as provided in Chapter 18C of the General Statutes, in connection with a lawful lottery conducted in another state, or in connection with a lawful raffle as provided in Part 2 of this Article, if any person shall sell, barter or cause to be sold or bartered, any ticket, token, certificate or order for any number or shares in any lottery, commonly known as the numbers or butter and egg lottery, or lotteries of similar character, to be drawn or paid within or without the State, such person shall be guilty of Class 2 misdemeanor. Any person who shall have in his possession any tickets, tokens, certificates or orders used in the operation of any such lottery shall be guilty under this section, and the possession of such tickets shall be prima facie evidence of the violation of this section.

Elements

A person guilty of this offense

(1) (a) sells, barters, or causes to be sold or bartered *or*
 (b) knowingly possesses
(2) a ticket, token, certificate, or order for shares
(3) used in a "numbers" or "butter and egg" lottery or a lottery of similar character.

Punishment

Class 2 misdemeanor. G.S. 14-291.1.

Notes

Element (1)(a). The offense may be committed by obtaining either money (sale) or goods (barter) for the tickets. G.S. 14-291.1; State v. Albarty, 238 N.C. 130 (1953).

Element (1)(b). The defendant must know that the items possessed are numbers tickets, certificates, or orders used in a lottery. State v. Mayo, 27 N.C. App. 336 (1975). See "Knowingly" in Chapter 1 (States of Mind).

As a general rule, possession may be actual or constructive. For an explanation of those terms as they apply to other offenses, see the note on Element (2)(c) to "Possession of a Firearm by a Felon" in Chapter 22 (Weapons Offenses) and the note on Element (2) to "Possession of a Controlled Substance" in Chapter 27 (Drug Offenses).

Element (3). For a discussion of the term "lottery" in general, see the note on Element (2) to "Advertising a Lottery," above. This statute apparently does not apply to all lotteries; it applies only to numbers or butter and egg lotteries and lotteries of a similar character. A "butter and egg" lottery is one in which the winning numbers are determined by closing prices in the commodities markets. In a "numbers" lottery, the winning numbers may be determined from a variety of sources, such as the number of shares traded on the New York Stock Exchange. The statute specifies that it applies whether the lottery is drawn or paid within or outside the state. G.S. 14-291.1.

Evidence issues. Possession of lottery tickets constitutes prima facie evidence of a violation under Element (1)(b). G.S. 14-291.1.

Exceptions. This offense does not apply to activities in connection with a lawful lottery conducted in another state. G.S. 14-291.1. Also excluded from coverage are the North Carolina state-run lottery and lawful raffles. Lawful raffles are described in G.S. 14-309.15.

Seizure of illegal gaming items. See this note to "Advertising a Lottery," above.

Related Offenses Not in This Chapter

See the offenses listed under "Advertising a Lottery," above.

Gambling

Statute

§14-292. Gambling.

Except as provided in Chapter 18C of the General Statutes or in Part 2 of this Article, any person or organization that operates any game of chance or any person who plays at or bets on any game of chance at which any money, property or other thing of value is bet, whether the same be in stake or not, shall be guilty of a Class 2 misdemeanor. This section shall not apply to a person who plays at or bets on any lottery game being lawfully conducted in any state.

Elements

A person guilty of this offense

(1) operates, plays at, or bets on
(2) a game of chance
(3) at which any money, property, or other thing of value is bet.

Punishment

Class 2 misdemeanor. G.S. 14-292.

Notes

Element (1). The statute specifically covers any person "or organization" that operates a game of chance. G.S. 14-292. Although the term "person" normally is construed to include corporations, see "'Person' includes corporations" in the Introduction to this book, because the gambling statute uses the term "organization," it appears to have broader reach than just to individuals and corporations.

Element (2). In a "game of chance," the element of chance determines the outcome of the game, dominating the element of skill. State v. Stroupe, 238 N.C. 34 (1953). It has been suggested that all card games are games of chance. State v. Taylor, 111 N.C. 680 (1892). Poker is a game of chance, Joker Club, L.L.C. v. Hardin, 183 N.C. App. 92, 99 (2007), as is blackjack, State v. Eisen, 16 N.C. App. 532, 535–36 (1972). The fact that the money used to place bets is converted into a prize for the winner does not change the character of the game. State v. De Boy, 117 N.C. 702 (1895). Even if the game involves skill on the part of the participants, it may be a game of chance as to those who bet on the game; thus betting on a horse race violates the statute. State v. Brown, 221 N.C. 301 (1942).

Dice games are considered to be games of chance, but shuffleboard and tenpins are not. State v. Stroupe, 238 N.C. 34, 37 (1953). Video poker is a game of chance. Collins Coin Music Co. of N.C., Inc. v. N.C. Alcoholic Beverage Control Comm'n, 117 N.C. App. 405 (1994). However, video gaming machines may be lawfully used under certain circumstances. See the note entitled "Exceptions" to "Operation, etc. of a Video Gaming Machine," below.

Exceptions. The statute does not apply to a person who plays at or bets on a lottery being lawfully conducted in any state. G.S. 14-292. Nor does it apply to the North Carolina state-run lottery. *Id.* This offense also does not apply to activities permitted by Chapter 14 of the North Carolina General Statutes, Article 37, Part 2. G.S. 14-292. Part 2 provides for lawful bingo and raffles. Lawful raffles are described in G.S. 14-309.15; lawful bingo is described in G.S. 14-309.5 through -309.14.

Seizure of illegal gaming items. See this note to "Advertising a Lottery," above.

Related Offenses Not in This Chapter

See the offenses listed under "Advertising a Lottery," above.
Betting on a prearranged race. G.S. 20-141.3(c).

Possession of a Slot Machine

Statute

§14-304. Manufacture, sale, etc., of slot machines and devices.

It shall be unlawful to manufacture, own, store, keep, possess, sell, rent, lease, let on shares, lend or give away, transport, or expose for sale or lease, or to offer to sell, rent, lease, let on shares, lend or give away, or to permit the operation of, or for any person to permit to be placed, maintained, used or kept in any room, space or building owned, leased or occupied by him or under his management or control, any slot machine or device where the user may become entitled to receive any money, credit, allowance, or any thing of value, as defined in G.S. 14-306.

§14-306. Slot machine or device defined.

(a) Any machine, apparatus or device is a slot machine or device within the provisions of G.S. 14-296 through 14-309, if it is one that is adapted, or may be readily converted into one that is adapted, for use in such a way that, as a result of the payment of any piece of money or coin or token or any credit card, debit card, prepaid card, or any other method that requires payment to activate play, whether directly into the slot machine or device or resulting in remote activation, such machine or device is caused to operate or may be operated in such manner that the user may receive or become entitled to receive any piece of money, credit, allowance or thing of value, or any check, slug, token or memorandum, whether of value or otherwise, or which may be exchanged for any money, credit, allowance or any thing of value, or which may be given in trade, or the user may secure additional chances or rights to use such machine, apparatus or device; or any other machine or device designed and manufactured primarily for use in connection with gambling and which machine or device is classified by the United States as requiring a federal gaming device tax stamp under applicable provisions of the Internal Revenue Code. This definition is intended to embrace all slot machines and similar devices except slot machines in which is kept any article to be purchased by depositing any coin or thing of value, and for which may be had any article of merchandise which makes the same return or returns of equal value each and every time it is operated, or any machine wherein may be seen any pictures or heard any music by depositing therein any coin or thing of value, or any slot weighing machine or any machine for making stencils by the use of contrivances operated by depositing in the machine any coin or thing of value, or any lock operated by slot wherein money or thing of value is to be deposited, where such slot machines make the same return or returns of equal value each and every time the same is operated and does not at any time it is operated offer the user or operator any additional money, credit, allowance, or thing of value, or check, slug, token or memorandum, whether of value or otherwise, which may be exchanged for money, credit, allowance or thing of value or which may be given in trade or by which the user may secure additional chances or rights to use such machine, apparatus, or device, or in the playing of which the operator does not have a chance to make varying scores or tallies.

(b) The definition contained in subsection (a) of this section and G.S. 14-296, 14-301, 14-302, and 14-305 does not include coin-operated machines, video games, pinball machines, and other computer, electronic or mechanical devices that are operated and played for amusement, that involve the use of skill or dexterity to solve problems or tasks or to make varying scores or tallies and that:

(1) Do not emit, issue, display, print out, or otherwise record any receipt, paper, coupon, token, or other form of record which is capable of being redeemed, exchanged, or repurchased for cash, cash equivalent, or prizes, or award free replays; or
(2) In actual operation, limit to eight the number of accumulated credits or replays that may be played at one time and which may award free replays or paper coupons that may be exchanged for prizes or merchandise with a value not exceeding ten dollars ($10.00), but may not be exchanged or converted to money.

(c) Any video machine, the operation of which is made lawful by subsection (b)(2) of this section, shall have affixed to it in view of the player a sticker informing that person that it is a criminal offense with the potential of imprisonment to pay more than that which is allowed by law. In addition, if the machine has an attract chip which allows programming, the static display shall contain the same message.

(d) The exception in subsection (b)(2) of this section does not apply to any machine that pays off in cash. The exemption in subsection (b)(2) of this section does not apply where the prizes, merchandise, credits, or replays are (i) repurchased for cash or rewarded by cash, (ii) exchanged for merchandise of a value of more than ten dollars ($10.00), or (iii) where there is a cash payout of any kind, by the person operating or managing the machine or the premises, or any agent or employee of that person. It is also a criminal offense, punishable under G.S. 14-309, for the person making the unlawful payout to the player of the machine to violate this section, in addition to any other person whose conduct may be unlawful.

Elements

A person guilty of this offense

(1) possesses
(2) a slot machine.

Punishment

Class 1 misdemeanor for first conviction, Class H felony for second conviction, and Class G felony for third or subsequent convictions. G.S. 14-309. If the felony version of this offense is charged, the relevant fact elevating punishment must be alleged in a charging instrument and proved at trial. G.S. 15A-928 (pleading and proving prior convictions).

Notes

Element (1). As a general rule, possession may be actual or constructive. For an explanation of those terms as they apply to other offenses, see the note on Element (2)(c) to "Possession of a Firearm by a Felon" in Chapter 22 (Weapons Offenses) and the note on Element (2) to "Possession of a Controlled Substance" in Chapter 27 (Drug Offenses).

Element (2). G.S. 14-306(a), reproduced above, defines "slot machine." In general, a slot machine is a device that allows a user, by inserting money or tokens, to receive something of value in return, including chances to continue playing. G.S. 14-306(a); *see also* State v. Abbott, 218 N.C. 470 (1940).

Constitutionality. G.S. 14-304 has been held to be constitutional. Calcutt v. McGeachy, 213 N.C. 1 (1938). The definition of a slot machine is not unconstitutionally vague. State v. Crabtree, 126 N.C. App. 729 (1997).

Other activities prohibited. G.S. 14-304 also prohibits almost any other kind of activity that uses a slot machine, including, among other things, manufacture, sale, leasing, and allowing operation.

Exceptions. The statute specifically exempts from the definition of slot machine vending machines in which the same amounts of goods are sold to all purchasers. G.S. 14-306(a). Other machines are excepted in G.S. 14-306(b), subject to the provisions of G.S. 14-306(c) and (d).

Defenses. In a prosecution for possession of a slot machine, it is a defense that the machine was not intended to be used in the operation or promotion of an unlawful gambling activity or enterprise and that the slot machine is an antique. G.S. 14-309.1.

Multiple convictions and punishments. Because each offense contains an element not in the other, there is no double jeopardy bar to convicting a defendant under both G.S. 14-301 (operation or possession of slot machine) and G.S. 14-304 (manufacture, sale, etc. of slot machines and devices) for the same act. State v. Calcutt, 219 N.C. 545 (1941).

Relation to other offenses. Simple possession is sufficient for conviction under this (G.S. 14-304) statute. For a conviction under G.S. 14-301, mentioned just above, it is necessary to show that the defendant possessed the slot machine for purposes of operation. The punishment for a first conviction of either offense is the same, but charges under G.S. 14-304 would be easier to prove.

Possession of revenue license. The statutes requiring revenue licenses for slot machines do not make possession lawful. State v. Abbott, 218 N.C. 470 (1940); State v. May, 188 N.C. 470 (1924).

Seizure of illegal gaming items. See this note to "Advertising a Lottery," above.

Related Offenses Not in This Chapter

See the offenses listed under "Advertising a Lottery," above.

Operation, etc. of a Video Gaming Machine

Statute

§14-306.1A. Types of machines and devices prohibited by law; penalties.

(a) Ban on Machines.—It shall be unlawful for any person to operate, allow to be operated, place into operation, or keep in that person's possession for the purpose of operation any video gaming machine as defined in subsection (b) of this section, except for the exemption for a federally recognized Indian tribe under subsection (e) of this section for whom it shall be lawful to operate and possess machines as listed in subsection (b) of this section if conducted in accordance with an approved Class III Tribal-State Compact applicable to that tribe, as provided in G.S. 147-12(14) and G.S. 71A-8.

(b) Definitions. – As used in this section, a video gaming machine means a slot machine as defined in G.S. 14-306(a) and other forms of electrical, mechanical, or computer games such as, by way of illustration and not exclusion:

(1) A video poker game or any other kind of video playing card game.
(2) A video bingo game.
(3) A video craps game.
(4) A video keno game.
(5) A video lotto game.
(6) Eight liner.
(7) Pot-of-gold.
(8) A video game based on or involving the random or chance matching of different pictures, words, numbers, or symbols not dependent on the skill or dexterity of the player.
(9) Any other video game not dependent on skill or dexterity that is played while revealing a prize as the result of an entry into a sweepstakes.

For the purpose of this section, a video gaming machine is a video machine which requires deposit of any coin or token, or use of any credit card, debit card, prepaid card, or any other method that requires payment, whether directly into the video gaming machine or resulting in remote activation, to activate play of any of the games listed in this subsection.

For the purpose of this section, a video gaming machine includes those that are within the scope of the exclusion provided in G.S. 14-306(b)(2) unless conducted in accordance with an approved Class III Tribal-State Compact applicable to that tribe as provided in G.S. 147-12(14) and G.S. 71A-8. For the purpose of this section, a video gaming machine does not include those that are within the scope of the exclusion provided in G.S. 14-306(b)(1).

(c) Exemption for Certain Machines.—This section shall not apply to:

(1) Assemblers, repairers, manufacturers, sellers, lessors, or transporters of video gaming machines who assemble, repair, manufacture, sell, lease, or transport them for use out-of-state, or
(2) Assemblers, repairers, manufacturers, sellers, lessors, or transporters of video gaming machines who assemble, repair, manufacture, sell, or lease video gaming machines for use only by a federally recognized Indian tribe if such machines may be lawfully used on Indian land under the Indian Gaming Regulatory Act.

To qualify for an exemption under this subsection, the machines must be disabled and not operable, unless the machines are located on Indian land where they may be lawfully operated under a Tribal-State Compact.

(d) Ban on Warehousing.—It is unlawful to warehouse any video gaming machine except in conjunction with the activities permitted under subsection (c) of this section.

(e) Exemption for Activities Under IGRA.—Notwithstanding any other prohibitions in State law, the form of Class III gaming otherwise prohibited by subsections (a) through (d) of this section may be legally conducted on Indian lands which are held in trust by the United States government for and on behalf of federally recognized Indian tribes if conducted in accordance with an approved Class III Tribal-State Gaming Compact applicable to that tribe as provided in G.S. 147-12(14) and G.S. 71A-8.

(f) Machines described in G.S. 14-306(b)(1) are excluded from this section.

Elements

A person guilty of this offense

(1) (a) operates,
(b) allows to be operated,
(c) places into operation, *or*
(d) keeps in that person's possession for the purpose of operation
(2) any video gaming machine.

Punishment

First offense is a Class 1 misdemeanor, second offense is a Class H felony, and third or subsequent offense is a Class G felony. G.S. 14-309(a). Operation of five or more machines is a Class G felony. G.S. 14-309(b). If the felony versions of this offense are charged, the relevant facts elevating punishment must be alleged in a charging instrument and proved at trial. *See* G.S. 15A-928 (pleading and proving prior convictions).

Notes

Element (2). "Video gaming machines" are defined in G.S. 14-306.1A(b).

Exceptions. The statute exempts operation, etc. by a federally recognized Indian tribe. G.S. 14-306.1A(a), (e). Granting the Eastern Band of Cherokee Indians of North Carolina exclusive rights to conduct certain gaming on tribal land while prohibiting such gaming throughout the rest of the State does not violate federal Indian gaming law. McCracken v. Perdue, 201 N.C. App. 480 (2009).

Additional exemptions for certain assemblers, repairers, manufacturers, and others are provided in G.S. 14-306.1A(c). Machines described in G.S. 14-306(b)(1) also are excluded from coverage. G.S. 14-306.1A(b), (f).

Related Offenses Not in This Chapter

See the offenses listed under "Advertising a Lottery," above.

Server-Based Electronic Game Offenses

Promoting, Operating, or Conducting a Server-Based Electronic Game Promotion

Statute

§14-306.3. Certain game promotions unlawful.

(a) It is unlawful to promote, operate, or conduct a server-based electronic game promotion.

(b) It is unlawful for any person to possess any game terminal with a display that simulates a game ordinarily played on a slot machine regulated under G.S. 14-306 or a video gaming machine regulated under G.S. 14-306.1A for the purpose of promoting, operating, or conducting a server-based electronic game promotion.

(c) As used in this section, "server-based electronic game promotion" means a system that meets all of the following criteria:

(1) A database contains a pool of entries with each entry associated with a prize value.
(2) Participants purchase, or otherwise obtain by any means, a prepaid card.
(3) With each prepaid card purchased or obtained, the participant also obtains one or more entries.

(4) Entries may be revealed in any of the following ways:
  a. At a point-of-sale terminal at the time of purchase or later.
  b. At a game terminal with a display that simulates a game ordinarily played on a slot machine regulated under G.S. 14-306 or a video gaming machine regulated under G.S. 14-306.1A.

(d) Upon conviction or plea of guilty, all of the following held by the person shall be automatically revoked:
(1) A permit issued under Chapter 18B of the General Statutes.
(2) A contract to sell tickets or shares under Article 5 of Chapter 18C of the General Statutes.

(e) Nothing in this section shall apply to the form of Class III gaming legally conducted on Indian lands which are held in trust by the United States government for and on behalf of federally recognized Indian tribes if conducted in accordance with an approved Class III Tribal-State Gaming Compact applicable to that tribe as provided in G.S. 147-12(14) and G.S. 71A-8.

Elements

A person guilty of this offense
(1) promotes, operates, or conducts
(2) a server-based electronic game promotion.

Punishment

Class 1 misdemeanor for a first offense, Class H felony for a second offense, and Class G felony for a third or subsequent offense. G.S. 14-309(a). If the felony version of this offense is charged, the relevant fact elevating punishment must be alleged in a charging instrument and proved at trial. *See* G.S. 15A-928 (pleading and proving prior convictions).

Notes

Element (2). The term "server-based electronic game promotion" is defined in G.S. 14-306.3(c), reproduced above.

Exceptions. G.S. 14-306.3(e) exempts certain gaming on Indian lands.

Revocations. G.S. 14-306.3(d) provides for automatic revocation, after a conviction or guilty plea for this offense, of any alcoholic beverage and control permit under G.S. Chapter 18B and any contract to sell lottery tickets under Article 5 of G.S. Chapter 18C.

Seizure of illegal gaming items. See this note under "Advertising a Lottery," above.

Related Offenses Not in This Chapter

See the offenses listed under "Advertising a Lottery," above.

Possession of a Server-Based Electronic Game Terminal

Statute

See G.S. 14-306.3(b), reproduced under "Promoting, Operating, or Conducting a Server-Based Electronic Game Promotion," above.

Elements

A person guilty of this offense
(1) possesses
(2) any game terminal with a display that simulates a game ordinarily played on a slot machine regulated under G.S. 14-306 or a video gaming machine regulated under G.S. 14-306.1A

(3) for the purpose of promoting, operating, or conducting a server-based electronic game promotion.

Punishment

Class 1 misdemeanor for a first offense, Class H felony for a second offense, and Class G felony for a third or subsequent offense or when the person possesses five or more machines. G.S. 14-309(a), (c). If a felony version of this offense is charged, the relevant fact elevating punishment must be alleged in a charging instrument and proved at trial. *See* G.S. 15A-928 (pleading and proving prior convictions).

Notes

Element (1). As a general rule, possession may be actual or constructive. For an explanation of those terms as they apply to other offenses, see the note on Element (2)(c) to "Possession of a Firearm by a Felon" in Chapter 22 (Weapons Offenses) and the note on Element (2) to "Possession of a Controlled Substance" in Chapter 27 (Drug Offenses).

Element (3). The term "server-based electronic game promotion" is defined in G.S. 14-306.3(c), reproduced under "Promoting, Operating, or Conducting a Server-Based Electronic Game Promotion," above.

Exceptions. See this note to "Promoting, Operating, or Conducting a Server-Based Electronic Game Promotion," above.

Revocations. See this note to "Promoting, Operating, or Conducting a Server-Based Electronic Game Promotion," above.

Seizure of illegal gaming items. See this note to "Advertising a Lottery," above.

Related Offenses Not in This Chapter

See the offenses listed under "Advertising a Lottery," above.

Electronic Sweepstakes

Statute

§14-306.4. Electronic machines and devices for sweepstakes prohibited.

(a) Definitions.—For the purposes of this section, the following definitions apply:

(1) "Electronic machine or device" means a mechanically, electrically or electronically operated machine or device, that is owned, leased or otherwise possessed by a sweepstakes sponsor or promoter, or any of the sweepstakes sponsor's or promoter's partners, affiliates, subsidiaries or contractors, that is intended to be used by a sweepstakes entrant, that uses energy, and that is capable of displaying information on a screen or other mechanism. This section is applicable to an electronic machine or device whether or not:

a. It is server-based.

b. It uses a simulated game terminal as a representation of the prizes associated with the results of the sweepstakes entries.

c. It utilizes software such that the simulated game influences or determines the winning or value of the prize.

d. It selects prizes from a predetermined finite pool of entries.

e. It utilizes a mechanism that reveals the content of a predetermined sweepstakes entry.

f. It predetermines the prize results and stores those results for delivery at the time the sweepstakes entry results are revealed.

g. It utilizes software to create a game result.
h. It requires deposit of any money, coin, or token, or the use of any credit card, debit card, prepaid card, or any other method of payment to activate the electronic machine or device.
i. It requires direct payment into the electronic machine or device, or remote activation of the electronic machine or device.
j. It requires purchase of a related product.
k. The related product, if any, has legitimate value.
l. It reveals the prize incrementally, even though it may not influence if a prize is awarded or the value of any prize awarded.
m. It determines and associates the prize with an entry or entries at the time the sweepstakes is entered.
n. It is a slot machine or other form of electrical, mechanical, or computer game.

(2) "Enter" or "entry" means the act or process by which a person becomes eligible to receive any prize offered in a sweepstakes.
(3) "Entertaining display" means visual information, capable of being seen by a sweepstakes entrant, that takes the form of actual game play, or simulated game play, such as, by way of illustration and not exclusion:
a. A video poker game or any other kind of video playing card game.
b. A video bingo game.
c. A video craps game.
d. A video keno game.
e. A video lotto game.
f. Eight liner.
g. Pot-of-gold.
h. A video game based on or involving the random or chance matching of different pictures, words, numbers, or symbols not dependent on the skill or dexterity of the player.
i. Any other video game not dependent on skill or dexterity that is played while revealing a prize as the result of an entry into a sweepstakes.

(4) "Prize" means any gift, award, gratuity, good, service, credit, or anything else of value, which may be transferred to a person, whether possession of the prize is actually transferred, or placed on an account or other record as evidence of the intent to transfer the prize.
(5) "Sweepstakes" means any game, advertising scheme or plan, or other promotion, which, with or without payment of any consideration, a person may enter to win or become eligible to receive any prize, the determination of which is based upon chance.

(b) Notwithstanding any other provision of this Part, it shall be unlawful for any person to operate, or place into operation, an electronic machine or device to do either of the following:

(1) Conduct a sweepstakes through the use of an entertaining display, including the entry process or the reveal of a prize.
(2) Promote a sweepstakes that is conducted through the use of an entertaining display, including the entry process or the reveal of a prize.

(c) It is the intent of this section to prohibit any mechanism that seeks to avoid application of this section through the use of any subterfuge or pretense whatsoever.

(d) Nothing in this section shall be construed to make illegal any activity which is lawfully conducted on Indian lands pursuant to, and in accordance with, an approved Tribal-State Gaming Compact applicable to that Tribe as provided in G.S. 147-12(14) and G.S. 71A-8.

(e) Each violation of this section shall be considered a separate offense.

(f) Any person who violates this section is guilty of a Class 1 misdemeanor for the first offense and is guilty of a Class H felony for a second offense and a Class G felony for a third or subsequent offense.

Elements

A person guilty of this offense

(1) operates or places into operation
(2) an electronic machine or device
(3) (a) to conduct a sweepstakes through the use of an entertaining display, including the entry process or the reveal of a prize, *or*
(b) to promote a sweepstakes conducted through the use of an entertaining display, including the entry process or the reveal of a prize.

Punishment

First offense is a Class 1 misdemeanor, second offense is a Class H felony, and third or subsequent offense is a Class G felony. G.S. 14-306.4(f). If a felony version of this offense is charged, the relevant fact elevating punishment must be alleged in a charging instrument and proved at trial. *See* G.S. 15A-928 (pleading and proving prior convictions).

Notes

Generally. G.S. 14-306.4(c) sets forth the legislative intent "to prohibit any mechanism that seeks to avoid application of this section through the use of any subterfuge or pretense whatsoever."

Element (2). The term "electronic machine or device" is defined in G.S. 14-306.4(a)(1).

Element (3). The terms "enter" and "entry" are defined in G.S. 14-306.4(a)(2). The term "entertaining display" is defined in G.S. 14-306.4(a)(3). The term "prize" is defined in G.S. 14-306.4(a)(4). The term "sweepstakes" is defined in G.S. 14-306.4(a)(5).

Exceptions. The statute provides that it may not be construed to make illegal any activity lawfully conducted on Indian lands pursuant to, and in accordance with, an approved Tribal-State Gaming Compact applicable to that tribe as provided in G.S. 147-12(14) and G.S. 71A-8. G.S. 14-306.4(d).

Multiple convictions and punishments. Each violation is a separate offense. G.S. 14-306.4(e).

Seizure of illegal gaming items. See this note under "Advertising a Lottery," above.

Related Offenses Not in This Chapter

None

26
Abandonment and Nonsupport

26
Abandonment and Nonsupport

Abandonment and Nonsupport—Spouses

Statute

§14-322. Abandonment and failure to support spouse and children.

(a) For purposes of this Article:

(1) "Supporting spouse" means a spouse, whether husband or wife, upon whom the other spouse is actually substantially dependent or from whom such other spouse is substantially in need of maintenance and support.

(2) "Dependent spouse" means a spouse, whether husband or wife, who is actually substantially dependent upon the other spouse for his or her maintenance and support or is substantially in need of maintenance and support from the other spouse.

(b) Any supporting spouse who shall willfully abandon a dependent spouse without providing that spouse with adequate support shall be guilty of a Class 1 or 2 misdemeanor and upon conviction shall be punished according to subsection (f).

(c) Any supporting spouse who, while living with a dependent spouse, shall willfully neglect to provide adequate support for that dependent spouse shall be guilty of a misdemeanor and upon conviction shall be punished according to subsection (f).

(d) Any parent who shall willfully neglect or refuse to provide adequate support for that parent's child, whether natural or adopted, and whether or not the parent abandons the child, shall be guilty of a misdemeanor and upon conviction shall be punished according to subsection (f). Willful neglect or refusal to provide adequate support of a child shall constitute a continuing offense and shall not be barred by any statute of limitations until the youngest living child of the parent shall reach the age of 18 years.

(e) Upon conviction for an offense under this section, the court may make such order as will best provide for the support, as far as may be necessary, of the abandoned spouse or child, or both, from the property or labor of the defendant. If the court requires the payment of child support, the amount of the payments shall be determined as provided in G.S. 50-13.4(c). For child support orders initially entered on or after January 1, 1994, the immediate income withholding provisions of G.S. 110-136.5(c1) shall apply.

(f) A first offense under this section is a Class 2 misdemeanor. A second or subsequent offense is a Class 1 misdemeanor.

Abandonment and Nonsupport of a Spouse

Elements

A person guilty of this offense

(1) is a supporting spouse *and*
(2) willfully
(3) abandons his or her dependent spouse
(4) without providing that spouse with adequate support.

Punishment

The first offense is a Class 2 misdemeanor. G.S. 14-322(b) & (f). A second or subsequent offense is a Class 1 misdemeanor. *Id.* If the Class 1 misdemeanor version is charged, the relevant fact elevating punishment must be alleged in a charging instrument and proved at trial. *See* G.S. 15A-928 (alleging and proving prior connections).

Notes

Element (1). A supporting spouse is "a spouse . . . upon whom the other spouse is actually substantially dependent or from whom such other spouse is substantially in need of maintenance and support." G.S. 14-322(a)(1).

Element (2). As used in this offense, the term "willful" means that both the abandonment and the nonsupport are intentional and without excuse or justification. N.C. PATTERN JURY INSTRUCTIONS—CRIM. 240.05; State v. Lucas, 242 N.C. 84 (1955); State v. Smith, 164 N.C. 475 (1913). See "Willfully" in Chapter 1 (States of Mind).

Element (3). The defendant abandoned his wife when he left the marital residence taking some of his belongings and then returned the next day to gather his remaining things. State v. Talbot, 123 N.C. App. 698, 700 (1996). A defendant's acts of cruelty toward a spouse may constitute constructive abandonment. *Id.* (so concluding based on the defendant's physical abuse of his wife).

The term "dependent spouse" means a "spouse . . . who is actually substantially dependent upon the other spouse for his or her maintenance and support or is substantially in need of maintenance and support from the other spouse." G.S. 14-322(a)(2).

Element (4). A person has not committed this offense if he or she abandons a spouse but continues to provide support. State v. Carson, 228 N.C. 151 (1947); *Lucas*, 242 N.C. 84. The support required is clothing, food, lodging, medical attention, and other necessities for a person of the dependent spouse's social position and circumstances and commensurate with the supporting spouse's ability to provide. State v. Clark, 234 N.C. 192 (1951); *see also* N.C. PATTERN JURY INSTRUCTIONS—CRIM. 240.05.

Statute gender neutral. A husband or a wife may commit this offense. G.S. 14-322(a)(1).

Defenses. A defendant's inability to provide support is a defense, though the defendant may not be excused if he or she is able to work and simply refuses to do so. State v. Green, 55 N.C. App. 255 (1981); ROLLIN M. PERKINS & RONALD N. BOYCE, CRIMINAL LAW 673 (3d ed. 1982).

If a husband and wife consent to separate, neither may be charged with this crime. State v. Smith, 164 N.C. 475 (1913). Once a couple divorces they are no longer spouses, and thus this offense is unlikely to apply. PERKINS & BOYCE at 676.

Adultery by the dependent spouse is a defense to this offense. State v. Johnson, 194 N.C. 378 (1927).

Multiple convictions and punishments. If the defendant cohabits with the dependent spouse after having been convicted of this offense, the defendant may be charged again under this offense if he or she again willfully abandons and fails to support the dependent spouse. State v. Beam, 181 N.C. 597 (1921).

Venue and jurisdiction. Even if the defendant is out of state, the crime occurs in North Carolina if the abandonment occurs here and the dependent spouse continues to live in the state. State v. Beam, 181 N.C. 597 (1921). See generally "Lack of Jurisdiction" in Chapter 2 (Bars and Defenses).

Order for support. On conviction, the court may order the defendant to provide for the necessary support of the dependent spouse from the defendant's income or property. G.S. 14-322(e); State v. Vickers, 196 N.C. 239 (1928).

Related Offenses Not in This Chapter

None

Failure to Support a Spouse While Living Together

Statute

See G.S. 14-322(c), reproduced under "Abandonment and Nonsupport—Spouses," above.

Elements

A person guilty of this offense

(1) is a supporting spouse *and,*
(2) while living with a dependent spouse,
(3) willfully
(4) neglects to provide adequate support for that spouse.

Punishment

The first offense is a Class 2 misdemeanor. G.S. 14-322(c) & (f). A second or subsequent offense is a Class 1 misdemeanor. *Id.* If the Class 1 misdemeanor version is charged, the relevant fact elevating punishment must be alleged in a charging instrument and proved at trial. *See* G.S. 15A-928 (alleging and proving prior convictions).

Notes

Element (1). See the note on Element (1) to "Abandonment and Nonsupport of a Spouse," above.

Element (2). This crime covers nonsupport when the defendant continues to live with his or her spouse; if the defendant abandons his or her spouse, the crime is "Abandonment and Nonsupport of a Spouse," above.

Element (3). See the note on Element (2) to "Abandonment and Nonsupport of a Spouse," above.

Element (4). See the note on Element (4) to "Abandonment and Nonsupport of a Spouse," above.

Statute gender neutral. See this note to "Abandonment and Nonsupport of a Spouse," above.

Order for support. See this note to "Abandonment and Nonsupport of a Spouse," above.

Related Offenses Not in This Chapter

None

Abandonment and Nonsupport—Children

Nonsupport of a Child

Statute

See G.S. 14-322(d), reproduced under "Abandonment and Nonsupport—Spouses," above.

Elements

A parent guilty of this offense

(1) willfully
(2) (a) neglects *or*
(b) refuses
(3) to support adequately
(4) his or her child.

Punishment

The first offense is a Class 2 misdemeanor. G.S. 14-322(d) & (f). A second or subsequent offense is a Class 1 misdemeanor. *Id.* If the Class 1 misdemeanor version is charged, the relevant fact elevating punishment must be alleged in a charging instrument and proved at trial. *See* G.S. 15A-928 (alleging and proving prior convictions).

Notes

Generally. Abandonment is not an element of this offense. G.S. 14-322(d); N.C. PATTERN JURY INSTRUCTIONS—CRIM. 240.06 n.2.

Elements (1) and (2). See the note on Element (2) to "Abandonment and Nonsupport of a Spouse," above, and the notes on Elements (2) and (3) to "Nonsupport of an Illegitimate Child," below.

Element (3). To "provide adequate support" means to provide such things as food, clothing, a place to live, and reasonably required medical attention; what is adequate support depends on the defendant's property, earnings, and ability to earn. N.C. PATTERN JURY INSTRUCTIONS—CRIM. 240.06.

The duty to support continues even though others, such as grandparents, might be providing for the child. ROLLIN M. PERKINS & RONALD N. BOYCE, CRIMINAL LAW 675 (3d ed. 1982). The parent may not relieve himself or herself of the obligation to support by contract. Goodyear v. Goodyear, 257 N.C. 374, 377 (1962).

Element (4). The statute applies to both natural and adopted children, G.S. 14-322(d), but does not apply to illegitimate children, State v. Gardner, 219 N.C. 331 (1941). However, nonsupport of an illegitimate child is a separate offense (covered immediately below). It appears that a "child" is one who is less than 18 years of age. G.S. 14-322(d) (a prosecution for the offense is not barred by any statute of limitations "until the youngest living child of the parent shall reach the age of 18 years").

Evidence issues. When a child is born during a marriage, it is presumed to be the child of the mother's husband. State v. White, 300 N.C. 494, 508–09 (1980). The presumption is rebutted if the defendant offers some evidence sufficient to raise a factual issue as to paternity. *Id.* at 509. The rebutting evidence must at least show that the defendant could not have been the father because, for example, he did not have sex with his wife at the time of conception, or that even if he could be the father, some other man could have fathered the child because the other man also had sex with the defendant's wife at the time when conception could have occurred. *Id.* In the face of such rebuttal evidence, the presumption of paternity disappears and the State must prove paternity from all of the facts and circumstances of the case. *Id.*

Blood tests to prove or disprove parentage, including the statistical likelihood of the alleged parent's parentage, are admissible in a criminal action. G.S. 8-50.1.

Statute gender neutral. A father or mother may commit this offense. G.S. 14-322(d) ("any parent").

Exceptions. A parent may not be prosecuted for nonsupport of a child when the parent abandons an infant less than seven days of age by voluntarily delivering the infant in compliance with the provisions of G.S. 7B-500(b) or -500(d) and does not express an intent to return for the infant. G.S. 14-322.3.

Statute of limitations. Generally a two-year statute of limitations applies to misdemeanors. See "Expiration of Statute of Limitations" in Chapter 2 (Bars and Defenses). For this offense, a prosecution "shall not be barred by any statute of limitations until the youngest living child of the parent shall reach the age of 18 years." G.S. 14-322(d).

Multiple convictions and punishments. This is a continuing offense. G.S. 14-322(d). As such, if a parent is convicted of this offense and then again fails to support his or her child, the parent may again be convicted of this offense. State v. Hinson, 209 N.C. 187 (1936).

Effect of divorce. The duty to support a child continues even after a divorce of the parents, State v. Bell, 184 N.C. 701 (1922), and even if the other parent has custody, PERKINS & BOYCE, cited in full *supra*, at 676.

Order for support. Upon conviction, the court may order support of the child. G.S. 14-322(e). If child support is ordered, the amount of payments must be determined as provided in G.S. 50-13.4(c), and the income withholding provision of G.S. 110-136.5(c1) applies. *Id.*

Venue and jurisdiction. G.S. 14-325.1 provides that a parent commits this offense if the child resides in North Carolina, regardless of where the parent resides. See generally "Lack of Jurisdiction" in Chapter 2 (Bars and Defenses).

Related Offenses Not in This Chapter

"Contributing to a Juvenile's Being Delinquent, Undisciplined, Abused, or Neglected" (Chapter 9)
Unlawful payments related to adoption. G.S. 48-10-102.

Nonsupport of an Illegitimate Child

Statute

§49-2. Nonsupport of illegitimate child by parents made misdemeanor.

Any parent who willfully neglects or who refuses to provide adequate support and maintain his or her illegitimate child shall be guilty of a Class 2 misdemeanor. A child within the meaning of this Article shall be any person less than 18 years of age and any person whom either parent might be required under the laws of North Carolina to support and maintain if such child were the legitimate child of such parent.

Elements

A person guilty of this offense

(1) is a parent *and*
(2) willfully
(3) (a) neglects *or*
    (b) refuses
(4) to support adequately
(5) his or her illegitimate child.

Punishment

Class 2 misdemeanor. G.S. 49-2.

Notes

Generally. It is not a crime to father or give birth to an illegitimate child, but failure to support the child is a crime. State v. Ellis, 262 N.C. 446 (1964); State v. Tyson, 208 N.C. 231 (1935).

Element (1). Proof that the defendant is the parent is essential to a conviction for this offense. State *ex rel.* Lewis v. Lewis, 311 N.C. 727 (1984); State v. Spillman, 210 N.C. 271 (1936).

Elements (2) and (3). "Willful" as used in this offense refers to the "intentional neglect or refusal to support the illegitimate child," State v. McDay, 232 N.C. 388 (1950), "without any lawful justification, reason or excuse," State v. Stiles, 228 N.C. 137 (1947). See the note on Element (2) to "Abandonment and Nonsupport of a Spouse," above. A refusal to support an illegitimate child is not willful unless the parent has first refused a demand for support of the child. State v. Perry, 241 N.C. 119 (1954); *Ellis*, 262 N.C. 446.

Element (4). To "provide adequate support" means to provide food, clothing, and other necessities, including medical care. State v. Love, 238 N.C. 283 (1953). This offense does not cover the failure to provide either medical care for the mother during pregnancy or the expenses of birth, but a judge may require the defendant to pay those expenses as a part of a judgment. *Stiles*, 228 N.C. 137.

Element (5). A "child" is "any person less than 18 years of age and any person whom either parent might be required under the laws of North Carolina to support and maintain as if such child were the legitimate child of such parent." G.S. 49-2. Where the child was born is irrelevant; the only requirement is that the child now reside in North Carolina. G.S. 49-3; State v. Tickle, 238 N.C. 206 (1953).

An illegitimate child is one born out of wedlock. G.S. 49-1.

Evidence issues. The results of a blood test are admissible in evidence in cases in which paternity is disputed; a test that excludes the defendant as a father is conclusive evidence if the jury believes that it was administered properly; and if the test result does not exclude the defendant, the statistical probability that the defendant could have been the parent is admissible. G.S. 8-50.1 and 49-7.

Statute gender neutral. Mothers as well as fathers may be prosecuted for this offense. G.S. 49-4 ("any parent").

Defenses. G.S. 49-4 creates a statute of limitations for this offense. It provides that a reputed father may be prosecuted within, but not after, any of the following time periods:

- within three years of the child's birth;
- at any time before the child attains the age of 18 years, if paternity was judicially determined within three years of birth; or
- if the father acknowledged paternity by making support payments within three years of birth, three years from the date of the last payment, so long as the action is instituted before the child reaches 18 years of age.

A mother of an illegitimate child may be prosecuted at any time before the child attains the age of 18 years. G.S. 49-4.

Multiple convictions and punishments. If a person again does not support his or her illegitimate child after being released from prison or probation for a previous conviction of this offense, the person may be prosecuted again for the same offense. State v. Johnson, 212 N.C. 566 (1937).

Relation to other offenses. Failure to support a legitimate child is punishable under "Nonsupport of a Child," above.

Procedures. G.S. 49-5 specifies who may bring prosecutions under this section, where such prosecutions may be brought, and other procedural matters.

Order for support. Upon finding that the defendant is a parent of the child for whom the proceeding has been initiated and that the defendant has neglected or refused to provide adequate support for that child, the court is required to order future support as specified in G.S. 49-7.

Related Offenses Not in This Chapter

See the offenses listed under "Nonsupport of a Child," above.

Abandonment of a Child for Six Months

Statute

> **§14-322.1. Abandonment of child or children for six months.**
>
> Any man or woman who, without just cause or provocation, willfully abandons his or her child or children for six months and who willfully fails or refuses to provide adequate means of support for his or her child or children during the six months' period, and who attempts to conceal his or her whereabouts from his or her child or children with the intent of escaping his lawful obligation for the support of said child or children, shall be punished as a Class I felon.

Elements

A person guilty of this offense

(1) willfully
(2) abandons
(3) his or her child,
(4) willfully fails or refuses to provide adequate support for that child
(5) for six months, *and*
(6) attempts to conceal his or her whereabouts from the child
(7) with the intent to escape the obligation to support.

Punishment

Class I felony. G.S. 14-322.1.

Notes

Element (1). See the note on Element (2) to "Abandonment and Nonsupport of a Spouse," above.

Element (4). See the note on Element (3) to "Nonsupport of a Child," above.

Statute gender neutral. A father or mother may commit this offense. G.S. 14-322.1 ("a man or woman").

Exceptions. A parent may not be prosecuted for nonsupport of a child when the parent abandons an infant less than seven days of age by voluntarily delivering the infant in compliance with the provisions of G.S. 7B-500(b) or -500(d) and does not express an intent to return for the infant. G.S. 14-322.3.

Order for support. While child support orders and income withholding are authorized upon conviction of nonsupport of a child as well as conviction of abandonment and failure to support a spouse, there is no clear statutory authority for such remedies upon conviction of this offense.

Related Offenses Not in This Chapter

See the offenses listed under "Nonsupport of a Child," above.

Failure to Support a Parent

Statute

§14-326.1. Parents; failure to support.

If any person being of full age, and having sufficient income after reasonably providing for his or her own immediate family shall, without reasonable cause, neglect to maintain and support his or her parent or parents, if such parent or parents be sick or not able to work and have not sufficient means or ability to maintain or support themselves, such person shall be deemed guilty of a Class 2 misdemeanor; upon conviction of a second or subsequent offense such person shall be guilty of a Class 1 misdemeanor.

If there be more than one person bound under the provisions of the next preceding paragraph to support the same parent or parents, they shall share equitably in the discharge of such duty.

Elements

A person guilty of this offense

(1) is 18 years of age or more *and*
(2) has sufficient income after providing for his or her immediate family *and*
(3) without reasonable cause
(4) neglects to support his or her parent
(5) when the parent is sick or unable to work and support himself or herself.

Punishment

The first offense is a Class 2 misdemeanor. G.S. 14-326.1. A second or subsequent offense is a Class 1 misdemeanor. *Id.* If the Class 1 version of this offense is charged, the relevant fact elevating punishment must be alleged in a charging instrument and proved at trial. *See* G.S. 15A-928 (alleging and proving prior convictions).

Notes

Element (4). The definition of "support" is probably similar to that set out under "Nonsupport of a Child" and "Abandonment and Nonsupport of a Spouse," both above.

Statute gender neutral. A son or daughter may commit this offense. G.S. 14-326.1 ("any person").

Children share costs equitably. If more than one child is at fault, they must share the financial cost of parental support equitably. G.S. 14-326.1.

Venue and jurisdiction. Both statutory and case law expressly provide that the defendant's state of residence is irrelevant to the commission of the offense of nonsupport of a child; for this offense, there is no such provision. However, G.S. 15A-134, which permits prosecution of a person for an offense that occurs only partly in North Carolina, should permit prosecution of a nonresident for failure to support a parent who resides in North Carolina. See generally "Lack of Jurisdiction" in Chapter 2 (Bars and Defenses).

Related Offenses Not in This Chapter

"Abuse or Neglect of a Disabled or Elder Adult" (Chapter 9)

27

Drug Offenses

27
Drug Offenses

Statute

§90-87. Definitions.

As used in this Article:

(1) "Administer" means the direct application of a controlled substance, whether by injection, inhalation, ingestion, or any other means to the body of a patient or research subject by:
   a. A practitioner (or, in his presence, by his authorized agent), or
   b. The patient or research subject at the direction and in the presence of the practitioner.

(2) "Agent" means an authorized person who acts on behalf of or at the direction of a manufacturer, distributor, or dispenser but does not include a common or contract carrier, public warehouseman, or employee thereof.

(3) "Bureau" means the Bureau of Narcotics and Dangerous Drugs, United States Department of Justice or its successor agency.

(3a) "Commission" means the Commission for Mental Health, Developmental Disabilities, and Substance Abuse Services established under Part 4 of Article 3 of Chapter 143B of the General Statutes.

(4) "Control" means to add, remove, or change the placement of a drug, substance, or immediate precursor included in Schedules I through VI of this Article.

(5) "Controlled substance" means a drug, substance, or immediate precursor included in Schedules I through VI of this Article.

(5a) "Controlled substance analogue" means a substance (i) the chemical structure of which is substantially similar to the chemical structure of a controlled substance in Schedule I or II; (ii) which has a stimulant, depressant, or hallucinogenic effect on the central nervous system that is substantially similar to or greater than the stimulant, depressant, or hallucinogenic effect on the central nervous system of a controlled substance in Schedule I or II; or (iii) with respect to a particular person, which such person represents or intends to have a stimulant, depressant, or hallucinogenic effect on the central nervous system that is substantially similar to or greater than the stimulant, depressant, or hallucinogenic effect on the central nervous system of a controlled substance in Schedule I or II; and does not include (i) a controlled substance; (ii) any substance for which there is an approved new drug application; (iii) with respect to a particular person any substance, if an exemption is in effect for investigational use, for that person, under § 355 of Title 21 of the United States Code to the extent conduct with respect to such substance is pursuant to such exemption; or (iv) any substance to the extent not intended for human consumption before such an exemption takes effect with respect to that substance. The designation of gamma butyrolactone or any other chemical as a listed chemical pursuant to subdivision 802(34) or 802(35) of Title 21 of the United States Code does not preclude a finding pursuant to this subdivision that the chemical is a controlled substance analogue.

(6) "Counterfeit controlled substance" means:
   a. A controlled substance which, or the container or labeling of which, without authorization, bears the trademark, trade name, or other identifying mark, imprint, number, or device, or any likeness thereof, of a manufacturer, distributor, or dispenser other than the person or persons who in fact manufactured, distributed, or dispensed such substance and which thereby falsely purports, or is represented to be the product of, or to have been distributed by, such other manufacturer, distributor, or dispenser; or
   b. Any substance which is by any means intentionally represented as a controlled substance. It is evidence that the substance has been intentionally misrepresented as a controlled substance if the following factors are established:
      1. The substance was packaged or delivered in a manner normally used for the illegal delivery of controlled substances.
      2. Money or other valuable property has been exchanged or requested for the substance, and the amount of that consideration was substantially in excess of the reasonable value of the substance.
      3. The physical appearance of the tablets, capsules or other finished product containing the substance is substantially identical to a specified controlled substance.

(7) "Deliver" or "delivery" means the actual constructive, or attempted transfer from one person to another of a controlled substance, whether or not there is an agency relationship.

(8) "Dispense" means to deliver a controlled substance to an ultimate user or research subject by or pursuant to the lawful order of a practitioner, including the prescribing, administering, packaging, labeling, or compounding necessary to prepare the substance for that delivery.

(9) "Dispenser" means a practitioner who dispenses.

(10) "Distribute" means to deliver other than by administering or dispensing a controlled substance.

(11) "Distributor" means a person who distributes.

(12) "Drug" means a. substances recognized in the official United States Pharmacopoeia, official Homeopathic Pharmacopoeia of the United States, or official National Formulary, or any supplement to any of them; b. substances intended for use in the diagnosis, cure, mitigation, treatment, or prevention of disease in man or other animals; c. substances (other than food) intended to affect the structure or any function of the body of man or other animals; and d. substances intended for use as a component of any article specified in a, b, or c of this subdivision; but does not include devices or their components, parts, or accessories.

(13) "Drug dependent person" means a person who is using a controlled substance and who is in a state of psychic or physical dependence, or both, arising from use of that controlled substance on a continuous basis. Drug dependence is characterized by behavioral and other responses which include a strong compulsion to take the substance on a continuous basis in order to experience its psychic effects, or to avoid the discomfort of its absence.

(14) "Immediate precursor" means a substance which the Commission has found to be and by regulation designates as being the principal compound commonly used or produced primarily for use, and which is an immediate chemical intermediary used or likely to be used in the manufacture of a controlled substance, the control of which is necessary to prevent, curtail, or limit such manufacture.

(14a) The term "isomer" means, except as used in G.S. 90-87(17)(d), G.S. 90-89(c), G.S. 90-90(1)d., and G.S. 90-95(h)(3), the optical isomer. As used in

G.S. 90-89(c) the term "isomer" means the optical, position, or geometric isomer. As used in G.S. 90-87(17)(d), G.S. 90-90(1)d., and G.S. 90-95(h)(3) the term "isomer" means the optical isomer or diastereoisomer.

(15) "Manufacture" means the production, preparation, propagation, compounding, conversion, or processing of a controlled substance by any means, whether directly or indirectly, artificially or naturally, or by extraction from substances of a natural origin, or independently by means of chemical synthesis, or by a combination of extraction and chemical synthesis; and "manufacture" further includes any packaging or repackaging of the substance or labeling or relabeling of its container except that this term does not include the preparation or compounding of a controlled substance by an individual for his own use or the preparation, compounding, packaging, or labeling of a controlled substance:
- a. By a practitioner as an incident to his administering or dispensing of a controlled substance in the course of his professional practice, or
- b. By a practitioner, or by his authorized agent under his supervision, for the purpose of, or as an incident to research, teaching, or chemical analysis and not for sale.

(16) "Marijuana" means all parts of the plant of the genus Cannabis, whether growing or not; the seeds thereof; the resin extracted from any part of such plant; and every compound, manufacture, salt, derivative, mixture, or preparation of such plant, its seeds or resin, but shall not include the mature stalks of such plant, fiber produced from such stalks, oil, or cake made from the seeds of such plant, any other compound, manufacture, salt, derivative, mixture, or preparation of such mature stalks (except the resin extracted therefrom), fiber, oil, or cake, or the sterilized seed of such plant which is incapable of germination.

(17) "Narcotic drug" means any of the following, whether produced directly or indirectly by extraction from substances of vegetable origin, or independently by means of chemical synthesis, or by a combination of extraction and chemical synthesis:
- a. Opium and opiate, and any salt, compound, derivative, or preparation of opium or opiate.
- b. Any salt, compound, isomer, derivative, or preparation thereof which is chemically equivalent or identical with any of the substances referred to in clause a, but not including the isoquinoline alkaloids of opium.
- c. Opium poppy and poppy straw.
- d. Cocaine and any salt, isomer, salts of isomers, compound, derivative, or preparation thereof, or coca leaves and any salt, isomer, salts of isomers, compound, derivative or preparation of coca leaves, or any salt, isomer, salts of isomers, compound, derivative, or preparation thereof which is chemically equivalent or identical with any of these substances, except that the substances shall not include decocanized coca leaves or extraction of coca leaves, which extractions do not contain cocaine or ecgonine.

(18) "Opiate" means any substance having an addiction-forming or addiction-sustaining liability similar to morphine or being capable of conversion into a drug having addiction-forming or addiction-sustaining liability. It does not include, unless specifically designated as controlled under G.S. 90-88, the dextrorotatory isomer of 3-methoxy-n-methyl-morphinan and its salts (dextromethorphan). It does include its racemic and levorotatory forms.

(19) "Opium poppy" means the plant of the species Papaver somniferum L., except its seeds.

(20) "Person" means individual, corporation, government or governmental subdivision or agency, business trust, estate, trust, partnership or association, or any other legal entity.

(21) "Poppy straw" means all parts, except the seeds, of the opium poppy, after mowing.

(22) "Practitioner" means:

a. A physician, dentist, optometrist, veterinarian, scientific investigator, or other person licensed, registered or otherwise permitted to distribute, dispense, conduct research with respect to or to administer a controlled substance so long as such activity is within the normal course of professional practice or research in this State.

b. A pharmacy, hospital or other institution licensed, registered, or otherwise permitted to distribute, dispense, conduct research with respect to or to administer a controlled substance so long as such activity is within the normal course of professional practice or research in this State.

(23) "Prescription" means:

a. A written order or other order which is promptly reduced to writing for a controlled substance as defined in this Article, or for a preparation, combination, or mixture thereof, issued by a practitioner who is licensed in this State to administer or prescribe drugs in the course of his professional practice; or issued by a practitioner serving on active duty with the armed forces of the United States or the United States Veterans Administration who is licensed in this or another state or Puerto Rico, provided the order is written for the benefit of eligible beneficiaries of armed services medical care; a prescription does not include an order entered in a chart or other medical record of a patient by a practitioner for the administration of a drug; or

b. A drug or preparation, or combination, or mixture thereof furnished pursuant to a prescription order.

(24) "Production" includes the manufacture, planting, cultivation, growing, or harvesting of a controlled substance.

(25) "Registrant" means a person registered by the Commission to manufacture, distribute, or dispense any controlled substance as required by this Article.

(26) "State" means the State of North Carolina.

(27) "Ultimate user" means a person who lawfully possesses a controlled substance for his own use, or for the use of a member of his household, or for administration to an animal owned by him or by a member of his household.

G.S. 90-88 is not reproduced here.

§90-89. Schedule I controlled substances.

This schedule includes the controlled substances listed or to be listed by whatever official name, common or usual name, chemical name, or trade name designated. In determining that a substance comes within this schedule, the Commission shall find: a high potential for abuse, no currently accepted medical use in the United States, or a lack of accepted safety for use in treatment under medical supervision. The following controlled substances are included in this schedule:

(1) Any of the following opiates, including the isomers, esters, ethers, salts and salts of isomers, esters, and ethers, unless specifically excepted, or listed in another schedule, whenever the existence of such isomers, esters, ethers, and salts is possible within the specific chemical designation:

a. Acetyl-alpha-methylfentanyl (N[1-(1-methyl-2-phenethyl)-4-piperidinyl]-N-phenylacetamide).

b. Acetylmethadol.

c. Repealed by Session Laws 1987, c. 412, s. 2.

d. Alpha-methylthiofentanyl N-[1-methyl-2-(2-thienyl) ethyl-4-piperidinyl]-N-phenylpropanamide).

e. Allylprodine.

f. Alphacetylmethadol.

g. Alphameprodine.

h. Alphamethadol.
i. Alpha-methylfentanyl (N-(1-(alpha-methyl-beta-phenyl) ethyl-4-piperidyl) propionalilide; 1(1-methyl-2-phenyl-ethyl)-4-(N-propanilido) piperidine).
j. Benzethidine.
k. Betacetylmethadol.
l. Beta-hydroxfentanyl (N-[1-(2-hydroxy-2-phenethyl)-4-piperidinyl]-N-phenylpropanamide).
m. Beta-hydroxy-3-methylfentanyl (N-[1-(2-hydroxy-2-phenethyl)-3-methyl-4-piperidinyl]-N-phenylpropanamide).
n. Betameprodine.
o. Betamethadol.
p. Betaprodine.
q. Clonitazene.
r. Dextromoramide.
s. Diampromide.
t. Diethylthiambutene.
u. Difenoxin.
v. Dimenoxadol.
w. Dimepheptanol.
x. Dimethylthiambutene.
y. Dioxaphetyl butyrate.
z. Dipipanone.
aa. Ethylmethylthiambutene.
bb. Etonitazene.
cc. Etoxeridine.
dd. Furethidine.
ee. Hydroxypethidine.
ff. Ketobemidone.
gg. Levomoramide.
hh. Levophenacylmorphan.
ii. 1-methyl-4-phenyl-4-propionox ypiperidine (MPPP).
jj. 3-Methylfentanyl (N-[3-methyl-1-(2-Phenylethyl)-4-Pi-peridyl]-N-Phenylpropanamide).
kk. 3-Methylthiofentanyl (N-[(3-methyl-1-(2-thienyl) ethyl-4-piperidinyl]-N-phenylpropa namide).
ll. Morpheridine.
mm. Noracymethadol.
nn. Norlevorphanol.
oo. Normethadone.
pp. Norpipanone.
qq. Para-fluorofentanyl (N-(4-fluorophenyl)-N-[1-(2-phen-ethyl)-4-piperidinyl]-propanamide.
rr. Phenadoxone.
ss. Phenampromide.
tt. 1-(2-phenethyl)-4-phenyl-4-acetoxypiperidine (PEPAP).
uu. Phenomorphan.
vv. Phenoperidine.
ww. Piritramide.
xx. Proheptazine.
yy. Properidine.
zz. Propiram.
aaa. Racemoramide.
bbb. Thiofentanyl (N-phenyl-N-[1-(2-thienyl)ethyl-4-piperidinyl]-propanamide.
ccc. Tilidine.
ddd. Trimeperidine.

(2) Any of the following opium derivatives, including their salts, isomers, and salts of isomers, unless specifically excepted, or listed in another schedule, whenever the existence of such salts, isomers, and salts of isomers is possible within the specific chemical designation:
a. Acetorphine.
b. Acetyldihydrocodeine.
c. Benzylmorphine.
d. Codeine methylbromide.
e. Codeine-N-Oxide.
f. Cyprenorphine.
g. Desomorphine.
h. Dihydromorphine.
i. Etorphine (except hydrochloride salt).
j. Heroin.
k. Hydromorphinol.
l. Methyldesorphine.
m. Methyldihydromorphine.
n. Morphine methylbromide.
o. Morphine methylsulfonate.
p. Morphine-N-Oxide.
q. Myrophine.
r. Nicocodeine.
s. Nicomorphine.
t. Normorphine.
u. Pholcodine.
v. Thebacon.
w. Drotebanol.

(3) Any material, compound, mixture, or preparation which contains any quantity of the following hallucinogenic substances, including their salts, isomers, and salts of isomers, unless specifically excepted, or listed in another schedule, whenever the existence of such salts, isomers, and salts of isomers is possible within the specific chemical designation:
a. 3, 4-methylenedioxyamphetamine.
b. 5-methoxy-3, 4-methylenedioxyamphetamine.
c. 3, 4-Methylenedioxymethamphetamine (MDMA).
d. 3,4-methylenedioxy-N-ethylamphetamine (also known as N-ethyl-alpha-methyl-3,4-(methylenedioxy)phenethylamine, N-ethyl MDA, MDE, and MDEA).
dd. Alpha-Methyltryptamine.
e. N-hydroxy-3,4-methylenedioxyamphetamine (also known as N-hydroxy-alpha-methyl-3,4-(methylenedioxy)phenethylamine, and N-hydroxy MDA).
ee. 5-Methoxy-n-diisopropyltryptamine.
f. 3, 4, 5-trimethoxyamphetamine.
g. Alpha-ethyltryptamine. Some trade or other names: etryptamine, Monase, alpha-ethyl-1H-indole-3-ethanamine, 3-(2-aminobutyl) indole, alpha-ET, and AET.
h. Bufotenine.
i. Diethyltryptamine.
j. Dimethyltryptamine.
k. 4-methyl-2, 5-dimethoxyamphetamine.
l. Ibogaine.
m. Lysergic acid diethylamide.
n. Mescaline.
o. Peyote, meaning all parts of the plant presently classified botanically as Lophophora Williamsii Lemaire, whether growing or not; the seeds thereof; any extract from any part of such plant; and every compound,

manufacture, salt, derivative, mixture or preparation of such plant, its seed or extracts.

p. N-ethyl-3-piperidyl benzilate.
q. N-methyl-3-piperidyl benzilate.
r. Psilocybin.
s. Psilocin.
t. 2, 5-dimethoxyamphetamine.
u. 2, 5-dimethoxy-4-ethylamphetamine. Some trade or other names: DOET.
v. 4-bromo-2, 5-dimethoxyamphetamine.
w. 4-methoxyamphetamine.
x. Ethylamine analog of phencyclidine. Some trade or other names: N-ethyl-1-phenylcyclohexylamine, (1-phenylcyclohexyl) ethylamine, N-(1-phenylcyclohexyl) ethylamine, cyclohexamine, PCE.
y. Pyrrolidine analog of phencyclidine. Some trade or other names: 1-(1-phenylcyclohexyl)-pyrrol idine, PCPy, PHP.
z. Thiophene analog of phencyclidine. Some trade or other names: 1-[1-(2-thienyl)-cyclohexyl]-piperidine, 2-thienyl analog of phencyclidine, TPCP, TCP.
aa. 1-[1-(2-thienyl)cyclohexyl]pyrrolidine; Some other names: TCPy.
bb. Parahexyl.
cc. 4-Bromo-2, 5-Dimethoxyphenethylamine.

(4) Any material compound, mixture, or preparation which contains any quantity of the following substances having a depressant effect on the central nervous system, including its salts, isomers, and salts of isomers whenever the existence of such salts, isomers, and salts of isomers is possible within the specific chemical designation, unless specifically excepted or unless listed in another schedule:
a. Mecloqualone.
b. Methaqualone.
c. Gamma hydroxybutyric acid; Some other names: GHB, gamma-hydroxybutyrate, 4-hydroxybutyrate, 4-hydroxybutanoic acid; sodium oxybate; sodium oxybutyrate.

(5) Stimulants.—Unless specifically excepted or unless listed in another schedule, any material, compound, mixture, or preparation that contains any quantity of the following substances having a stimulant effect on the central nervous system, including its salts, isomers, and salts of isomers:
a. Aminorex. Some trade or other names: aminoxaphen; 2-amino-5-phenyl-2-oxazoline; or 4,5-dihydro-5-phenly-2-oxazolamine.
b. Cathinone. Some trade or other names: 2-amino-1-phenyl-1-propanone, alpha-aminopropiophenone, 2-aminopropiophenone, and norephedrone.
c. Fenethylline.
d. Methcathinone. Some trade or other names: 2-(methylamino)propiophenone, alpha-(methylamino)propiophenone, 2-(methylamino)-1-phenylpropan-1-one, alpha-N-methylaminopropiophenone, monomethylproprion, ephedrone, N-methylcathinone, methylcathinone, AL- 464, AL-422, AL-463, and UR1432.
e. (+/-)cis-4-methylaminorex [(+/-)cis-4,5-dihydro-4-methyl-5-phenyl-2-oxazolamine] (also known as 2-amino-4-methyl-5-phenyl-2-oxazoline).
f. N,N-dimethylamphetamine. Some other names: N,N,alpha-trimethyl-benzeneethaneamine; N,N,alpha-trimethylphenethylamine.
g. N-ethylamphetamine.
h. 4-methylmethcathinone (also known as mephedrone).
i. 3,4-Methylenedioxypyrovalerone (also known as MDPV).

j. A compound, other than buproprion, that is structurally derived from 2-amino-1-phenyl-1-propanone by modification in any of the following ways: (i) by substitution in the phenyl ring to any extent with alkyl, alkoxy, alkylenedioxy, haloalkyl, or halide substituents, whether or not further substituted in the phenyl ring by one or more other univalent substituents; (ii) by substitution at the 3-position with an alkyl substituent; or (iii) by substitution at the nitrogen atom with alkyl or diakyl groups or by inclusion of the nitrogen atom in a cyclic structure.

Note: The 2011 technical corrections bill, S.L. 2011-326, also added subsections (5)(h) and (5)(i) as follows:

h. N-Benzylpiperazine.

i. 2,5-Dimethoxy-4-(n)-propylthiophenethylamine.

However, an earlier 2011 session law, S.L. 2011-12, had already added different controlled substances in new subsections (h) and (i) as reflected above. The revisor of statutes has informed the author that subsections (5)(h) and (5)(i), as added by the technical corrections bill, will be denominated subsections (5)(k) and (5)(l) in the codified statutes.

§90-89.1. Treatment of controlled substance analogues.

A controlled substance analogue shall, to the extent intended for human consumption, be treated for the purposes of any State law as a controlled substance in Schedule I.

§90-90. Schedule II controlled substances.

This schedule includes the controlled substances listed or to be listed by whatever official name, common or usual name, chemical name, or trade name designated. In determining that a substance comes within this schedule, the Commission shall find: a high potential for abuse; currently accepted medical use in the United States, or currently accepted medical use with severe restrictions; and the abuse of the substance may lead to severe psychic or physical dependence. The following controlled substances are included in this schedule:

(1) Any of the following substances whether produced directly or indirectly by extraction from substances of vegetable origin, or independently by means of chemical synthesis, or by a combination of extraction and chemical synthesis, unless specifically excepted or unless listed in another schedule:

a. Opium and opiate, and any salt, compound, derivative, or preparation of opium and opiate, excluding apomorphine, nalbuphine, dextrorphan, naloxone, naltrexone and nalmefene, and their respective salts, but including the following:

1. Raw opium.
2. Opium extracts.
3. Opium fluid extracts.
4. Powdered opium.
5. Granulated opium.
6. Tincture of opium.
7. Codeine.
8. Ethylmorphine.
9. Etorphine hydrochloride.
10. Hydrocodone.
11. Hydromorphone.
12. Metopon.
13. Morphine.
14. Oxycodone.
15. Oxymorphone.

16. Thebaine.
17. Dihydroetorphine.

b. Any salt, compound, derivative, or preparation thereof which is chemically equivalent or identical with any of the substances referred to in paragraph 1 of this subdivision, except that these substances shall not include the isoquinoline alkaloids of opium.
c. Opium poppy and poppy straw.
d. Cocaine and any salt, isomer, salts of isomers, compound, derivative, or preparation thereof, or coca leaves and any salt, isomer, salts of isomers, compound, derivative, or preparation of coca leaves, or any salt, isomer, salts of isomers, compound, derivative, or preparation thereof which is chemically equivalent or identical with any of these substances, except that the substances shall not include decocanized coca leaves or extraction of coca leaves, which extractions do not contain cocaine or ecgonine.
e. Concentrate of poppy straw (the crude extract of poppy straw in either liquid, solid or powder form which contains the phenanthrine alkaloids of the opium poppy).

(2) Any of the following opiates, including their isomers, esters, ethers, salts, and salts of isomers, whenever the existence of such isomers, esters, ethers, and salts is possible within the specific chemical designation unless specifically exempted or listed in other schedules:

a. Alfentanil.
aa. Tapentatol.
b. Alphaprodine.
c. Anileridine.
d. Bezitramide.
e. Carfentanil.
f. Dihydrocodeine.
g. Diphenoxylate.
h. Fentanyl.
i. Isomethadone.
j. Levo-alphacetylmethadol. Some trade or other names: levo-alpha-acetylmethadol, levomethadyl acetate, or LAAM.
k. Levomethorphan.
l. Levorphanol.
m. Metazocine.
n. Methadone.
o. Methadone—Intermediate, 4-cyano-2-dimethylamino-4, 4- diphenyl butane.
p. Moramide—Intermediate, 2-methyl-3-morpholino-1, 1-diphenyl-propane-carboxylic acid.
q. Pethidine.
r. Pethidine—Intermediate – A, 4-cyano-1-methyl-4-phenylpiperidine.
s. Pethidine—Intermediate – B, ethyl-4-phenylpiperidine-4-carboxylate.
t. Pethidine—Intermediate – C, 1-methyl-4-phenylpiperidine-4-carboxylic acid.
u. Phenazocine.
v. Piminodine.
w. Racemethorphan.
x. Racemorphan.
y. Remifentanil.
z. Sufentanil.

(3) Any material, compound, mixture, or preparation which contains any quantity of the following substances having a potential for abuse associated

with a stimulant effect on the central nervous system unless specifically exempted or listed in another schedule:
a. Amphetamine, its salts, optical isomers, and salts of its optical isomers.
b. Phenmetrazine and its salts.
c. Methamphetamine, including its salts, isomers, and salts of isomers.
d. Methylphenidate.
e. Phenylacetone. Some trade or other names: Phenyl-2-propanone; P2P; benzyl methyl ketone; methyl benzyl ketone.
f. Lisdexamfetamine, including its salts, isomers, and salts of isomers.

(4) Any material, compound, mixture, or preparation which contains any quantity of the following substances having a depressant effect on the central nervous system, including its salts, isomers, and salts of isomers whenever the existence of such salts, isomers, and salts of isomers is possible within the specific chemical designation, unless specifically exempted by the Commission or listed in another schedule:
a. Amobarbital
b. Glutethimide
c. Repealed by Session Laws 1983, c. 695, s. 2.
d. Pentobarbital
e. Phencyclidine
f. Phencyclidine immediate precursors:
  1. 1-Phenylcyclohexylamine
  2. 1-Piperidinocyclohexanecarbonitrile (PCC)
g. Secobarbital.

(5) Any material, compound, mixture, or preparation which contains any quantity of the following hallucinogenic substances, including their salts, isomers, and salts of isomers, unless specifically excepted, or listed in another schedule, whenever the existence of such salts, isomers, and salts of isomers is possible within the specific chemical designation:
a. Repealed by Session Laws 2001-233, s. 2(a).
b. Nabilone [Another name for nabilone: (+/-)-trans-3-(1,1-dimethylheptyl) -6,6a,7,8,10,10a-hexahyd ro-1-hydroxy-6,6-dimethyl-9H-dibenzo[b,d] pyran-9-one].

§90-91. Schedule III controlled substances.

This schedule includes the controlled substances listed or to be listed by whatever official name, common or usual name, chemical name, or trade name designated. In determining that a substance comes within this schedule, the Commission shall find: a potential for abuse less than the substances listed in Schedules I and II; currently accepted medical use in the United States; and abuse may lead to moderate or low physical dependence or high pyschological dependence. The following controlled substances are included in this schedule:

(a) Repealed by Session Laws 1973, c. 540, s. 5.

(b) Any material, compound, mixture, or preparation which contains any quantity of the following substances having a depressant effect on the central nervous system unless specifically exempted or listed in another schedule:

1. Any substance which contains any quantity of a derivative of barbituric acid, or any salt of a derivative of barbituric acid.
2. Chlorhexadol.
3. Repealed by Session Laws 1993, c. 319, s. 5.
4. Lysergic acid.
5. Lysergic acid amide.
6. Methyprylon.
7. Sulfondiethylmethane.
8. Sulfonethylmethane.
9. Sulfonmethane.

9a. Tiletamine and zolazepam or any salt thereof. Some trade or other names for tiletamine-zolazepam combination product: Telazol. Some trade or other names for tiletamine:
2-(ethylamino)-2-(2-thienyl)-cyclohexanone. Some trade or other names for zolazepam: 4-(2-fluorophenyl)-6,8-dihydro-1,3,8-trimethylpyrazolo-[3,4-e] [1,4]-diazepin-7(1H)-one. flupyrazapon.

10. Any compound, mixture or preparation containing
    (i) Amobarbital.
    (ii) Secobarbital.
    (iii) Pentobarbital.
    or any salt thereof and one or more active ingredients which are not included in any other schedule.

11. Any suppository dosage form containing
    (i) Amobarbital.
    (ii) Secobarbital.
    (iii) Pentobarbital.
    or any salt of any of these drugs and approved by the federal Food and Drug Administration for marketing as a suppository.

12. Ketamine.

(c) Nalorphine.

(d) Any material, compound, mixture, or preparation containing limited quantities of any of the following narcotic drugs, or any salts thereof unless specifically exempted or listed in another schedule:

1. Not more than 1.80 grams of codeine per 100 milliliters or not more than 90 milligrams per dosage unit with an equal or greater quantity of an isoquinoline alkaloid of opium.
2. Not more than 1.80 grams of codeine per 100 milliliters or not more than 90 milligrams per dosage unit, with one or more active, nonnarcotic ingredients in recognized therapeutic amounts.
3. Not more than 300 milligrams of dihydrocodeinone per 100 milliliters or not more than 15 milligrams per dosage unit with a four-fold or greater quantity of an isoquinoline alkaloid of opium.
4. Not more than 300 milligrams of dihydrocodeinone per 100 milliliters or not more than 15 milligrams per dosage unit, with one or more active, nonnarcotic ingredients in recognized therapeutic amounts.
5. Not more than 1.80 grams of dihydrocodeine per 100 milliliters or not more than 90 milligrams per dosage unit, with one or more active, nonnarcotic ingredients in recognized therapeutic amounts.
6. Not more than 300 milligrams of ethylmorphine per 100 milliliters or not more than 15 milligrams per dosage unit, with one or more active, nonnarcotic ingredients in recognized therapeutic amounts.
7. Not more than 500 milligrams of opium per 100 milliliters or per 100 grams, or not more than 25 milligrams per dosage unit, with one or more active, nonnarcotic ingredients in recognized therapeutic amounts.
8. Not more than 50 milligrams of morphine per 100 milliliters or per 100 grams with one or more active, nonnarcotic ingredients in recognized therapeutic amounts.

(e) Any compound, mixture or preparation containing limited quantities of the following narcotic drugs, which shall include one or more active, nonnarcotic, medicinal ingredients in sufficient proportion to confer upon the compound, mixture, or preparation, valuable medicinal qualities other than those possessed by the narcotic drug alone:

1. Paregoric, U.S.P.; provided, that no person shall purchase or receive by any means whatsoever more than one fluid ounce of paregoric within a consecutive 24-hour period, except on prescription issued by a duly licensed physician.

(f) Paregoric, U.S.P., may be dispensed at retail as permitted by federal law or administrative regulation without a prescription only by a registered pharmacist and no other person, agency or employee may dispense paregoric, U.S.P., even if under the direct supervision of a pharmacist.

(g) Notwithstanding the provisions of G.S. 90-91(f), after the pharmacist has fulfilled his professional responsibilities and legal responsibilities required of him in this Article, the actual cash transaction, credit transaction, or delivery of paregoric, U.S.P., may be completed by a nonpharmacist. A pharmacist may refuse to dispense a paregoric, U.S.P., substance until he is satisfied that the product is being obtained for medicinal purposes only.

(h) Paregoric, U.S.P., may only be sold at retail without a prescription to a person at least 18 years of age. A pharmacist must require every retail purchaser of a paregoric, U.S.P., substance to furnish suitable identification, including proof of age when appropriate, in order to purchase paregoric, U.S.P. The name and address obtained from such identification shall be entered in the record of disposition to consumers.

(i) The Commission may by regulation except any compound, mixture, or preparation containing any stimulant or depressant substance listed in paragraphs (a)1 and (a)2 of this schedule from the application of all or any part of this Article if the compound, mixture, or preparation contains one or more active medicinal ingredients not having a stimulant or depressant effect on the central nervous system; and if the ingredients are included therein in such combinations, quantity, proportion, or concentration that vitiate the potential for abuse of the substances which have a stimulant or depressant effect on the central nervous system.

(j) Any material, compound, mixture, or preparation which contains any quantity of the following substances having a stimulant effect on the central nervous system, including its salts, isomers, and salts of said isomers whenever the existence of such salts, isomers, and salts of isomers is possible within the specific chemical designation, unless specifically excluded or listed in some other schedule.

1. Benzphetamine.
2. Chlorphentermine.
3. Clortermine.
4. Repealed by Session Laws 1987, c. 412, s. 10.
5. Phendimetrazine.

(k) Anabolic steroids. The term "anabolic steroid" means any drug or hormonal substance, chemically and pharmacologically related to testosterone (other than estrogens, progestins, and corticosteroids) that promotes muscle growth, including, but not limited to, the following:

1. Methandrostenolone,
2. Stanozolol,
3. Ethylestrenol,
4. Nandrolone phenpropionate,
5. Nandrolone decanoate,
6. Testosterone propionate,
7. Chorionic gonadotropin,
8. Boldenone,
9. Chlorotestosterone (4-chlorotestosterone),
10. Clostebol,
11. Dehydrochlormethyltestosterone,
12. Dibydrostestosterone (4-dihydrotestosterone),
13. Drostanolone,
14. Fluoxymesterone,
15. Formebulone (formebolone),
16. Mesterolene,
17. Methandienone,
18. Methandranone,
19. Methandriol,
20. Methenolene,

21. Methyltestosterone,
22. Mibolerone,
23. Nandrolene,
24. Norethandrolene,
25. Oxandrolone,
26. Oxymesterone,
27. Oxymetholone,
28. Stanolone,
29. Testolactone,
30. Testosterone,
31. Trenbolone, and
32. Any salt, ester, or isomer of a drug or substance described or listed in this subsection, if that salt, ester, or isomer promotes muscle growth. Except such term does not include an anabolic steroid which is expressly intended for administration through implants to cattle or other nonhuman species and which has been approved by the Secretary of Health and Human Services for such administration. If any person prescribes, dispenses, or distributes such steroid for human use, such person shall be considered to have prescribed, dispensed, or distributed an anabolic steroid within the meaning of this subsection.

(l) Repealed by Session Laws 2001-233, s. 3(a).

(m) Any drug product containing gamma hydroxybutyric acid, including its salts, isomers, and salts of isomers, for which an application is approved under section 505 of the Federal Food, Drug, and Cosmetic Act.

(n) Dronabinol (synthetic) in sesame oil and encapsulated in a soft gelatin capsule in a U.S. Food and Drug Administration approved drug product. [Some other names: (6aR-trans), -6a,7,8,10a-tetrahydro-6,6,9-trimethyl-3-pentyl-6H-dibenzo [b,d]pyran-1-o1 or (-)-delta-9-(trans)-tetrahydrocannabinol].

§90-92. Schedule IV controlled substances.

(a) This schedule includes the controlled substances listed or to be listed by whatever official name, common or usual name, chemical name, or trade name designated. In determining that a substance comes within this schedule, the Commission shall find: a low potential for abuse relative to the substances listed in Schedule III of this Article; currently accepted medical use in the United States; and limited physical or pyschological dependence relative to the substances listed in Schedule III of this Article. The following controlled substances are included in this schedule:

(1) Depressants.—Unless specifically excepted or unless listed in another schedule, any material, compound, mixture, or preparation which contains any quantity of the following substances, including its salts, isomers, and salts of isomers whenever the existence of such salts, isomers, and salts of isomers is possible within the specific chemical designation:

a. Alprazolam.
b. Barbital.
c. Bromazepam.
d. Camazepam.
e. Chloral betaine.
f. Chloral hydrate.
g. Chlordiazepoxide.
h. Clobazam.
i. Clonazepam.
j. Clorazepate.
k. Clotiazepam.
l. Cloxazolam.
m. Delorazepam.
n. Diazepam.

o. Estazolam.
p. Ethchlorvynol.
q. Ethinamate.
r. Ethyl loflazepate.
s. Fludiazepam.
t. Flunitrazepam.
u. Flurazepam.
v. Repealed by Session Laws 2000, c. 140, s. 92.2(c).
w. Halazepam.
x. Haloxazolam.
y. Ketazolam.
z. Loprazolam.
aa. Lorazepam.
bb. Lormetazepam.
cc. Mebutamate.
dd. Medazepam.
ee. Meprobamate.
ff. Methohexital.
gg. Methylphenobarbital (mephobarbital).
hh. Midazolam.
ii. Nimetazepam.
jj. Nitrazepam.
kk. Nordiazepam.
ll. Oxazepam.
mm. Oxazolam.
nn. Paraldehyde.
oo. Petrichloral.
pp. Phenobarbital.
qq. Pinazepam.
rr. Prazepam.
ss. Quazepam.
tt. Temazepam.
uu. Tetrazepam.
vv. Triazolam.
ww. Zolpidem.
xx. Zaleplon.

(2) Any material, compound, mixture, or preparation which contains any of the following substances, including its salts, or isomers and salts of such isomers, whenever the existence of such salts, isomers, and salts of isomers is possible:
a. Fenfluramine.
b. Pentazocine.

(3) Stimulants.—Unless specifically excepted or unless listed in another schedule, any material, compound, mixture, or preparation which contains any quantity of the following substances having a stimulant effect on the central nervous system, including its salts, isomers (whether optical, position, or geometric), and salts of such isomers whenever the existence of such salts, isomers, and salts of isomers is possible within the specific chemical designation:
a. Diethylpropion.
b. Mazindol.
c. Pemoline (including organometallic complexes and chelates thereof).
d. Phentermine.
e. Cathine.
f. Fencamfamin.
g. Fenproporex.

h. Mefenorex.
i. Sibutramine.
j. Modafinil.

(4) Other Substances.—Unless specifically excepted or unless listed in another schedule, any material, compound, mixture or preparation which contains any quantity of the following substances, including its salts:
a. Dextropropoxyphene (Alpha-(plus)-4-dimethylamino-1, 2-diphenyl-3-methyl-2-propionoxybutane).
b. Pipradrol.
c. SPA ((-)-1-dimethylamino-1, 2-diphenylethane).
d. Butorphanol.

(5) Narcotic Drugs.—Unless specifically excepted or unless listed in another schedule, any material, compound, mixture, or preparation containing limited quantities of any of the following narcotic drugs, or any salts thereof:
a. Not more than 1 milligram of difenoxin and not less than 25 micrograms of atropine sulfate per dosage unit.
b. Buprenorphine.

(b) The Commission may by regulation except any compound, mixture, or preparation containing any stimulant or depressant substance listed in this schedule from the application of all or any part of this Article if the compound, mixture, or preparation contains one or more active, nonnarcotic, medicinal ingredients not having a stimulant or depressant effect on the central nervous system; provided, that such admixtures shall be included therein in such combinations, quantity, proportion, or concentration as to vitiate the potential for abuse of the substances which do have a stimulant or depressant effect on the central nervous system.

§90-93. Schedule V controlled substances.

(a) This schedule includes the controlled substances listed or to be listed by whatever official name, common or usual name, chemical name, or trade name designated. In determining that a substance comes within this schedule, the Commission shall find: a low potential for abuse relative to the substances listed in Schedule IV of this Article; currently accepted medical use in the United States; and limited physical or psychological dependence relative to the substances listed in Schedule IV of this Article. The following controlled substances are included in this schedule:

(1) Any compound, mixture or preparation containing any of the following limited quantities of narcotic drugs or salts thereof, which shall include one or more nonnarcotic active medicinal ingredients in sufficient proportion to confer upon the compound, mixture, or preparation valuable medicinal qualities other than those possessed by the narcotic alone:
a. Not more than 200 milligrams of codeine or any of its salts per 100 milliliters or per 100 grams.
b. Not more than 100 milligrams of dihydrocodeine or any of its salts per 100 milliliters or per 100 grams.
c. Not more than 100 milligrams of ethylmorphine or any of its salts per 100 milliliters or per 100 grams.
d. Not more than 2.5 milligrams of diphenoxylate and not less than 25 micrograms of atropine sulfate per dosage unit.
e. Not more than 100 milligrams of opium per 100 milliliters or per 100 grams.
f. Not more than 0.5 milligram of difenoxin and not less than 25 micrograms of atropine sulfate per dosage unit.

(2) Repealed by Session Laws 1985, c. 172, s. 9.

(3) Stimulants.—Unless specifically exempted or excluded or unless listed in another schedule, any material, compound, mixture, or preparation which contains any quantity of the following substances having a stimulant effect

on the central nervous system, including its salts, isomers and salts of isomers:

a. Repealed by Session Laws 1993, c. 319, s. 7.

b. Pyrovalerone.

(b) A Schedule V substance may be sold at retail without a prescription only by a registered pharmacist and no other person, agent or employee may sell a Schedule V substance even if under the direct supervision of a pharmacist.

(c) Notwithstanding the provisions of G.S. 90-93(b), after the pharmacist has fulfilled the responsibilities required of him in this Article, the actual cash transaction, credit transaction, or delivery of a Schedule V substance, may be completed by a nonpharmacist. A pharmacist may refuse to sell a Schedule V substance until he is satisfied that the product is being obtained for medicinal purposes only.

(d) A Schedule V substance may be sold at retail without a prescription only to a person at least 18 years of age. The pharmacist must require every retail purchaser of a Schedule V substance to furnish suitable identification, including proof of age when appropriate, in order to purchase a Schedule V substance. The name and address obtained from such identification shall be entered in the record of disposition to consumers.

§90-94. Schedule VI controlled substances.

This schedule includes the controlled substances listed or to be listed by whatever official name, common or usual name, chemical name, or trade name designated. In determining that such substance comes within this schedule, the Commission shall find: no currently accepted medical use in the United States, or a relatively low potential for abuse in terms of risk to public health and potential to produce psychic or physiological dependence liability based upon present medical knowledge, or a need for further and continuing study to develop scientific evidence of its pharmacological effects.

The following controlled substances are included in this schedule:

(1) Marijuana.

(2) Tetrahydrocannabinols.

(3) Synthetic cannabinoids. – Any material, compound, mixture, or preparation that is not listed as a controlled substance in Schedule I through V, is not an FDA-approved drug, and contains any quantity of the following substances, their salts, isomers (whether optical, positional, or geometric), homologues, and salts of isomers and homologues, unless specifically excepted, whenever the existence of these salts, isomers, homologues, and salts of isomers and homologues is possible within the specific chemical designation:

a. Naphthoylindoles. Any compound containing a 3-(1-naphthoyl)indole structure with substitution at the nitrogen atom of the indole ring by an alkyl, haloalkyl, alkenyl, cycloalkylmethyl, cycloalkylethyl, 1-(N-methyl-2-piperidinyl)methyl, or 2-(4-morpholinyl)ethyl group, whether or not further substituted in the indole ring to any extent and whether or not substituted in the naphthyl ring to any extent. Some trade or other names: JWH-015, JWH-018, JWH-019, JWH-073, JWH-081, JWH-122, JWH-200, JWH-210, JWH-398, AM-2201, WIN 55-212.

b. Naphthylmethylindoles. Any compound containing a 1H-indol-3-yl-(1-naphthyl)methane structure with substitution at the nitrogen atom of the indole ring by an alkyl, haloalkyl, alkenyl, cycloalkylmethyl, cycloalkylethyl, 1-(N-methyl-2-piperidinyl)methyl, or 2-(4-morpholinyl) ethyl group, whether or not further substituted in the indole ring to any extent and whether or not substituted in the naphthyl ring to any extent.

c. Naphthoylpyrroles. Any compound containing a 3-(1-naphthoyl) pyrrole structure with substitution at the nitrogen atom of the pyrrole ring by an alkyl, haloalkyl, alkenyl, cycloalkylmethyl, cycloalkylethyl, 1-(N-methyl-2-piperidinyl)methyl, or 2-(4-morpholinyl)ethyl group, whether or not further substituted in the pyrrole ring to any extent and whether or not substituted in the naphthyl ring to any extent. Another name: JWH-307.

d. Naphthylmethylindenes. Any compound containing a naphthylideneindene structure with substitution at the 3-position of the indene ring by an alkyl, haloalkyl, alkenyl, cycloalkylmethyl, cycloalkylethyl, 1-(N-methyl-2-piperidinyl)methyl, or 2-(4-morpholinyl)ethyl group, whether or not further substituted in the indene ring to any extent and whether or not substituted in the naphthyl ring to any extent.

e. Phenylacetylindoles. Any compound containing a 3-phenylacetylindole structure with substitution at the nitrogen atom of the indole ring by an alkyl, haloalkyl, alkenyl, cycloalkylmethyl, cycloalkylethyl, 1-(N-methyl-2-piperidinyl)methyl, or 2-(4-morpholinyl)ethyl group, whether or not further substituted in the indole ring to any extent and whether or not substituted in the phenyl ring to any extent. Some trade or other names: SR-18, RCS-8, JWH-250, JWH-203.

f. Cyclohexylphenols. Any compound containing a 2-(3-hydroxycyclohexyl)phenol structure with substitution at the 5-position of the phenolic ring by an alkyl, haloalkyl, alkenyl, cycloalkylmethyl, cycloalkylethyl, 1-(N-methyl-2-piperidinyl)methyl, or 2-(4-morpholinyl)ethyl group, whether or not substituted in the cyclohexyl ring to any extent. Some trade or other names: CP 47,497 (and homologues), cannabicyclohexanol.

g. Benzoylindoles. Any compound containing a 3-(benzoyl)indole structure with substitution at the nitrogen atom of the indole ring by an alkyl, haloalkyl, alkenyl, cycloalkylmethyl, cycloalkylethyl, 1-(N-methyl-2-piperidinyl)methyl, or 2-(4-morpholinyl)ethyl group, whether or not further substituted in the indole ring to any extent and whether or not substituted in the phenyl ring to any extent. Some trade or other names: AM-694, Pravadoline (WIN 48,098), RCS-4.

h. 2,3-Dihydro-5-methyl-3-(4-morpholinylmethyl)pyrrolo[1,2,3-de]-1,4-benzoxazin-6-yl]-1-napthalenylmethanone. Some trade or other names: WIN 55,212-2.

i. (6aR,10aR)-9-(hydroxymethyl)-6, 6-dimethyl-3-(2-methyloctan-2-yl) – 6a,7,10,10a-tetrahydrobenzo[c]chromen-1-ol 7370. Some trade or other names: HU-210.

§90-95. Violations; penalties.

(a) Except as authorized by this Article, it is unlawful for any person:

(1) To manufacture, sell or deliver, or possess with intent to manufacture, sell or deliver, a controlled substance;

(2) To create, sell or deliver, or possess with intent to sell or deliver, a counterfeit controlled substance;

(3) To possess a controlled substance.

(b) Except as provided in subsections (h) and (i) of this section, any person who violates G.S. 90-95(a)(1) with respect to:

(1) A controlled substance classified in Schedule I or II shall be punished as a Class H felon, except as follows: (i) the sale of a controlled substance classified in Schedule I or II shall be punished as a Class G felony, and (ii) the manufacture of methamphetamine shall be punished as provided by subdivision (1a) of this subsection.

(1a) The manufacture of methamphetamine shall be punished as a Class C felony unless the offense was one of the following: packaging or repackaging methamphetamine, or labeling or relabeling the methamphetamine container. The offense of packaging or repackaging methamphetamine, or labeling or relabeling the methamphetamine container shall be punished as a Class H felony.

(2) A controlled substance classified in Schedule III, IV, V, or VI shall be punished as a Class I felon, except that the sale of a controlled substance classified in Schedule III, IV, V, or VI shall be punished as a Class H felon. The transfer of less than 5 grams of marijuana or less than 2.5 grams of a synthetic cannabinoid or any mixture containing such substance for no remuneration shall not constitute a delivery in violation of G.S. 90-95(a)(1).

(c) Any person who violates G.S. 90-95(a)(2) shall be punished as a Class I felon.

(d) Except as provided in subsections (h) and (i) of this section, any person who violates G.S. 90-95(a)(3) with respect to:

(1) A controlled substance classified in Schedule I shall be punished as a Class I felon. However, if the controlled substance is MDPV and the quantity of the MDPV is 1 gram or less, the violation shall be punishable as a Class 1 misdemeanor.

(2) A controlled substance classified in Schedule II, III, or IV shall be guilty of a Class 1 misdemeanor. If the controlled substance exceeds four tablets, capsules, or other dosage units or equivalent quantity of hydromorphone or if the quantity of the controlled substance, or combination of the controlled substances, exceeds one hundred tablets, capsules or other dosage units, or equivalent quantity, the violation shall be punishable as a Class I felony. If the controlled substance is methamphetamine, amphetamine, phencyclidine, or cocaine and any salt, isomer, salts of isomers, compound, derivative, or preparation thereof, or coca leaves and any salt, isomer, salts of isomers, compound, derivative, or preparation of coca leaves, or any salt, isomer, salts of isomers, compound, derivative or preparation thereof which is chemically equivalent or identical with any of these substances (except decocanized coca leaves or any extraction of coca leaves which does not contain cocaine or ecgonine), the violation shall be punishable as a Class I felony.

(3) A controlled substance classified in Schedule V shall be guilty of a Class 2 misdemeanor;

(4) A controlled substance classified in Schedule VI shall be guilty of a Class 3 misdemeanor, but any sentence of imprisonment imposed must be suspended and the judge may not require at the time of sentencing that the defendant serve a period of imprisonment as a special condition of probation. If the quantity of the controlled substance exceeds one-half of an ounce (avoirdupois) of marijuana, 7 grams of a synthetic cannabinoid or any mixture containing such substance, or one-twentieth of an ounce (avoirdupois) of the extracted resin of marijuana, commonly known as hashish, the violation shall be punishable as a Class 1 misdemeanor. If the quantity of the controlled substance exceeds one and one-half ounces (avoirdupois) of marijuana, 21 grams of a synthetic cannabinoid or any mixture containing such substance, or three-twentieths of an ounce (avoirdupois) of the extracted resin of marijuana, commonly known as hashish, or if the controlled substance consists of any quantity of synthetic tetrahydrocannabinols or tetrahydrocannabinols isolated from the resin of marijuana, the violation shall be punishable as a Class I felony.

(d1) (1) Except as authorized by this Article, it is unlawful for any person to:

a. Possess an immediate precursor chemical with intent to manufacture a controlled substance; or

b. Possess or distribute an immediate precursor chemical knowing, or having reasonable cause to believe, that the immediate precursor chemical will be used to manufacture a controlled substance.

Any person who violates this subsection shall be punished as a Class H felon, unless the immediate precursor is one that can be used to manufacture methamphetamine.

(2) Except as authorized by this Article, it is unlawful for any person to:

a. Possess an immediate precursor chemical with intent to manufacture methamphetamine; or

b. Possess or distribute an immediate precursor chemical knowing, or having reasonable cause to believe, that the immediate precursor chemical will be used to manufacture methamphetamine.

Any person who violates this subsection shall be punished as a Class F felon.

(d2) The immediate precursor chemicals to which subsection (d1) and (d1a) of this section applies are those immediate precursor chemicals designated by the Commission pursuant to its authority under G.S. 90-88, and the following (until otherwise specified by the Commission):

(1) Acetic anhydride.
(2) Acetone.
(3) Anhydrous ammonia.
(4) Anthranilic acid.
(5) Benzyl chloride.
(6) Benzyl cyanide.
(7) 2-Butanone (Methyl Ethyl Ketone).
(8) Chloroephedrine.
(9) Chloropseudoephedrine.
(10) D-lysergic acid.
(11) Ephedrine.
(12) Ergonovine maleate.
(13) Ergotamine tartrate.
(14) Ethyl ether.
(15) Ethyl Malonate.
(16) Ethylamine.
(17) Gamma-butyrolactone.
(18) Hydrochloric Acid.
(19) Iodine.
(20) Isosafrole.
(21) Lithium.
(22) Malonic acid.
(23) Methylamine.
(24) Methyl Isobutyl Ketone.
(25) N-acetylanthranilic acid.
(26) N-ethylephedrine.
(27) N-ethylepseudoephedrine.
(28) N-methylephedrine.
(29) N-methylpseudoephedrine.
(30) Norpseudoephedrine.
(31) Phenyl-2-propane.
(32) Phenylacetic acid.
(33) Phenylpropanolamine.
(34) Piperidine.
(35) Piperonal.
(36) Propionic anhydride.
(37) Pseudoephedrine.
(38) Pyrrolidine.
(39) Red phosphorous.
(40) Safrole.
(41) Sodium.
(42) Sulfuric Acid.
(43) Tetrachloroethylene.
(44) Thionylchloride.
(45) Toluene.

(e) The prescribed punishment and degree of any offense under this Article shall be subject to the following conditions, but the punishment for an offense may be increased only by the maximum authorized under any one of the applicable conditions:

(1), (2) Repealed by Session Laws 1979, c. 760, s. 5.

(3) If any person commits a Class 1 misdemeanor under this Article and if he has previously been convicted for one or more offenses under any law of North Carolina or any law of the United States or any other state, which offenses are punishable under any provision of this Article, he shall be punished as a Class I felon. The prior conviction used to raise the current offense to a Class I felony shall not be used to calculate the prior record level;

(4) If any person commits a Class 2 misdemeanor, and if he has previously been convicted for one or more offenses under any law of North Carolina or any law of the United States or any other state, which offenses are punishable under any provision of this Article, he shall be guilty of a Class 1 misdemeanor. The prior conviction used to raise the current offense to a Class 1 misdemeanor shall not be used to calculate the prior conviction level;

(5) Any person 18 years of age or over who violates G.S. 90-95(a)(1) by selling or delivering a controlled substance to a person under 16 years of age but more than 13 years of age or a pregnant female shall be punished as a Class D felon. Any person 18 years of age or over who violates G.S. 90-95(a)(1) by selling or delivering a controlled substance to a person who is 13 years of age or younger shall be punished as a Class C felon. Mistake of age is not a defense to a prosecution under this section. It shall not be a defense that the defendant did not know that the recipient was pregnant.

(6) For the purpose of increasing punishment under G.S. 90-95(e)(3) and (e)(4), previous convictions for offenses shall be counted by the number of separate trials at which final convictions were obtained and not by the number of charges at a single trial;

(7) If any person commits an offense under this Article for which the prescribed punishment requires that any sentence of imprisonment be suspended, and if he has previously been convicted for one or more offenses under any law of North Carolina or any law of the United States or any other state, which offenses are punishable under any provision of this Article, he shall be guilty of a Class 2 misdemeanor;

(8) Any person 21 years of age or older who commits an offense under G.S. 90-95(a)(1) on property used for a child care center, or for an elementary or secondary school or within 1,000 feet of the boundary of real property used for a child care center, or for an elementary or secondary school shall be punished as a Class E felon. For purposes of this subdivision, the transfer of less than five grams of marijuana for no remuneration shall not constitute a delivery in violation of G.S. 90-95(a)(1). For purposes of this subdivision, a child care center is as defined in G.S. 110-86(3)a., and that is licensed by the Secretary of the Department of Health and Human Services.

(9) Any person who violates G.S. 90-95(a)(3) on the premises of a penal institution or local confinement facility shall be guilty of a Class H felony.

(10) Any person 21 years of age or older who commits an offense under G.S. 90-95(a)(1) on property that is a public park or within 1,000 feet of the boundary of real property that is a public park shall be punished as a Class E felon. For purposes of this subdivision, the transfer of less than five grams of marijuana for no remuneration shall not constitute a delivery in violation of G.S. 90-95(a)(1).

(f) Any person convicted of an offense or offenses under this Article who is sentenced to an active term of imprisonment that is less than the maximum active term that could have been imposed may, in addition, be sentenced to a term of special probation. Except as indicated in this subsection, the administration of special probation shall be the same as probation. The conditions of special probation shall be fixed in the same manner as probation, and the conditions may include requirements for rehabilitation treatment. Special probation shall follow the active sentence. No term of special probation shall exceed five years. Special probation may be revoked in the same manner as probation; upon revocation, the original term of imprisonment may be increased by no more than the difference between the active term of imprisonment actually served and the maximum active term that could have been imposed at trial for the offense or offenses for which the person was convicted, and the resulting term of imprisonment need not be diminished by the time spent on special probation.

(g) Whenever matter is submitted to the North Carolina State Bureau of Investigation Laboratory, the Charlotte, North Carolina, Police Department Laboratory or to the Toxicology Laboratory, Reynolds Health Center, Winston-Salem for chemical analysis to determine if the matter is or contains a controlled substance, the report of that analysis certified to upon a form approved by the Attorney General by the person performing the analysis shall be admissible without further authentication and without the testimony of the analyst in all proceedings in the district court and superior court divisions of the General Court of Justice as evidence of the identity, nature, and quantity of the matter analyzed. Provided, however, the provisions of this subsection may be utilized by the State only if:

(1) The State notifies the defendant at least 15 days before the proceeding at which the report would be used of its intention to introduce the report into evidence under this subsection and provides a copy of the report to the defendant, and

(2) The defendant fails to file a written objection with the court, with a copy to the State, at least five days before the proceeding that the defendant objects to the introduction of the report into evidence.

If the defendant's attorney of record, or the defendant if that person has no attorney, fails to file a written objection as provided in this subsection, then the report may be admitted into evidence without the testimony of the analyst. Upon filing a timely objection, the admissibility of the report shall be determined and governed by the appropriate rules of evidence.

Nothing in this subsection precludes the right of any party to call any witness or to introduce any evidence supporting or contradicting the evidence contained in the report.

(g1) Procedure for establishing chain of custody without calling unnecessary witnesses.—

(1) For the purpose of establishing the chain of physical custody or control of evidence consisting of or containing a substance tested or analyzed to determine whether it is a controlled substance, a statement signed by each successive person in the chain of custody that the person delivered it to the other person indicated on or about the date stated is prima facie evidence that the person had custody and made the delivery as stated, without the necessity of a personal appearance in court by the person signing the statement.

(2) The statement shall contain a sufficient description of the material or its container so as to distinguish it as the particular item in question and shall state that the material was delivered in essentially the same condition as received. The statement may be placed on the same document as the report provided for in subsection (g) of this section.

(3) The provisions of this subsection may be utilized by the State only if:
   a. The State notifies the defendant at least 15 days before trial of its intention to introduce the statement into evidence under this subsection and provides the defendant with a copy of the statement, and
   b. The defendant fails to notify the State at least five days before trial that the defendant objects to the introduction of the statement into evidence.

(4) Nothing in this subsection precludes the right of any party to call any witness or to introduce any evidence supporting or contradicting the evidence contained in the statement

Subsections (h) and (i) are not reproduced here but are reproduced under "Trafficking," below.

Sale or Delivery and Related Offenses

Sale or Delivery of a Controlled Substance

Statute

See G.S. 90-95(a)(1), reproduced above.

Elements

A person guilty of this offense

(1) knowingly
(2) (a) sells *or*
    (b) delivers
(3) a controlled substance
(4) to another person.

Punishment

For the sale of a Schedule I or II substance, the crime is a Class G felony. G.S. 90-95(b)(1).

For the delivery of a Schedule I or II substance, the crime is a Class H felony. *Id.*

For the sale or delivery of a Schedule III, IV, V, or VI substance, the crime is a Class H felony. G.S. 90-95(b)(2).

If the defendant is sentenced to an active term less than the maximum term that could have been imposed, special probation may be imposed as specified in G.S. 90-95(f).

Notes

Element (1). For a general discussion of the term "knowingly," see "Knowingly" in Chapter 1 (States of Mind). The knowledge required for the various drug crimes included in this chapter is that the defendant knew that the activity the defendant was engaged in was manufacturing, possessing, selling, etc. a controlled substance. Thus, if the defendant knowingly accepts custody of a piece of luggage but, unknown to him or her, the luggage contains a controlled substance, this element is not satisfied because the defendant did not knowingly possess the controlled substance. State v. Boone, 310 N.C. 284 (1984). The State must prove knowledge only if evidence of lack of knowledge is produced at trial. State v. Perez, 55 N.C. App. 92 (1981); State v. Gleason, 24 N.C. App. 732 (1975).

Element (2)(a). To "sell" means to transfer for remuneration (that is, compensation). State v. Moore, 327 N.C. 378 (1990). The remuneration may be cash or non-monetary items such as clothing, video games, State v. Carr, 145 N.C. App. 335 (2001), or services, State v. Yelton, 175 N.C. App. 349 (2006).

Element (2)(b). To "deliver" means actual or constructive transfer to another person and includes attempts to transfer. G.S. 90-87(7); *see also* State v. Beam, ___ N.C. App. ___, 688 S.E.2d 40 (2010) (applying this definition in a trafficking by delivery case). It is not a delivery to transfer for no remuneration less than 5 grams of marijuana or less than 2.5 grams of a synthetic cannabinoid or any mixture containing cannabinoids, G.S. 90-95(b)(2); such activity could be punished only as possession of a controlled substance.

Element (3). A "controlled substance" means any drug, substance, or immediate precursor included in Schedules I through VI, reproduced above, G.S. 90-87(5); G.S. 90-89 through -94, or added to the schedules by the Commission for Mental Health, Developmental Disabilities, and Substance Abuse Services, G.S. 90-88(a). The drugs added to each schedule by the Commission appear at 10A N.C.A.C. 26F.0102 *et seq.*

A controlled substance analogue, if intended for human consumption, is treated as a controlled substance in Schedule I. G.S. 90-89.1. "Controlled substance analogue" is defined in G.S. 90-87(5a).

Note that Oxycodone (Oxycontin) is an opium derivative and thus is covered in Schedule II.

Attempt and conspiracy. G.S. 90-98 provides that, except as otherwise provided in another statute, a person who attempts or conspires to commit a drug offense will be punished as if he or she committed the offense that was the object of the attempt or conspiracy, rather than at a lower classification, as is typically the case for an attempt and for conspiracy. See "Attempt" and "Conspiracy," both in Chapter 5 (General Crimes). Note that special rules apply for attempted drug trafficking and conspiracy to traffic (see the note entitled "Attempt and conspiracy" under "Trafficking in Marijuana," below).

Note also that the definition of "deliver" or "delivery" in G.S. 90-87(7) includes an attempt to transfer a controlled substance. Thus, an element that includes deliver or delivery also includes an attempt to deliver.

Charging issues. For a discussion of charging issues related to this offense, see Jessica Smith, *The Criminal Indictment: Fatal Defect, Fatal Variance, and Amendment*, ADMIN. OF JUST. BULL. NO. 2008/03 (UNC School of Government, July 2008) (online at www.sog.unc.edu/pubs/electronicversions/pdfs/aojb0803.pdf). For controlled substance cases decided after publication of that bulletin, see *State v. LePage*, ___ N.C. App. ___, 693 S.E.2d 157 (2010) (indictments identifying the controlled substance as "BENZODIAZEPINES, which is included in Schedule IV of the North Carolina Controlled Substances Act" were defective; the word "benzodiazepines" is not listed in Schedule IV and actually describes a category of drugs, some of which are listed individually in Schedule IV, some of which are not), and *State v. Johnson*, ___ N.C. App. ___, 690 S.E.2d 707 (2010) (no fatal variance where an indictment charging sale and delivery of a controlled substance alleged that the sale was made to "Detective Dunabro"; the evidence at trial showed that the detective had since gotten married and was known as Amy Gaulden; because Detective Dunabro and Amy Gaulden were the same person, known by both her married and her maiden name, the indictment sufficiently identified the purchaser; "[w]here different names are alleged to relate to the same person, the question is one of identity and is exclusively for the jury to decide").

In criminal pleadings for drug offenses, it is not necessary to negate any exemption or exception in G.S. Chapter 90 Article 5 (the N.C. Controlled Substances Act). G.S. 90-113.1.

Evidence issues. G.S. 90-95(g) contains a notice and demand statute pertaining to the admissibility of forensic reports identifying a substance as a controlled substance. G.S. 90-95(g1) does the same for chain of custody information. G.S. 90-95(g) has been held constitutional. State v. Steele, 201 N.C. App. 689 (2010).

Defenses. A defendant has the burden of proving that he or she was authorized by G.S. Chapter 90 Article 5 (the N.C. Controlled Substances Act) to possess, deliver, manufacture, etc. a controlled substance. G.S. 90-113.1; State v. McNeil, 47 N.C. App. 30 (1980). See G.S. 90-101 for descriptions of persons authorized to engage in those activities.

Greater and lesser-included offenses. Possession of a controlled substance (or possession with intent to manufacture, sell, or deliver) is not a lesser-included offense of sale of the controlled substance, since possession is not necessary to a sale; a defendant may be convicted and punished for both offenses. State v. Cameron, 283 N.C. 191 (1973); State v. Stoner, 59 N.C. App. 656 (1982). Although the North Carolina Court of Appeals has ruled that possession of a controlled substance is a lesser-included offense of delivery of the controlled substance, State v. Clark, 71 N.C. App. 55 (1984), that opinion has been disapproved of in significant respects, State v. Moore, 327 N.C. 378 (1990).

Multiple convictions and punishments. A defendant may not be separately convicted of both the sale and delivery of a controlled substance arising from a single transaction; in such a situation there can be only one conviction. *Moore*, 327 N.C. 378 (explaining that the gist of the offense is a transfer of a controlled substance, whether accomplished by sale or delivery); State v. Rogers, 186 N.C. App. 676 (2007) (citing *Moore*).

Even when based on the same substance, a defendant may be convicted and punished for both "Sale or Delivery of a Controlled Substance" (this offense) and "Possession of a Controlled Substance with Intent to Manufacture, Sell, or Deliver" (discussed below). *Stoner*, 59 N.C. App. 656; State v. Dickerson, 152 N.C. App. 714 (2002).

As stated immediately above, a defendant may be convicted of possession of a controlled substance (or possession with intent to manufacture, sell, or deliver) and sale of the controlled substance.

For purposes of double jeopardy, a second-degree murder conviction based on unlawful distribution of and ingestion of a controlled substance is not the same offense as sale or delivery of a controlled substance to a juvenile or possession with intent to sell or deliver a controlled substance, and thus a defendant may be convicted of both offenses. State v. Parlee, ___ N.C. App. ___, 703 S.E.2d 866 (2011).

Relation to other offenses. A physician who writes a prescription for a controlled substance outside the normal course of professional practice does not violate this statute but may be charged under G.S. 90-108(a)(2) (unlawful distribution of controlled substance by registrant or practitioner). State v. Best, 292 N.C. 294 (1977).

Restitution for drug purchases and other costs. G.S. 90-95.3(a) allows a court to order a convicted defendant to make restitution to a law enforcement agency for reasonable expenditures made in purchasing controlled substances from the defendant or his or her agent as part of an investigation leading to the defendant's conviction. *See* State v. Stallings, 316 N.C. 535 (1986) (money paid by State Bureau of Investigation (SBI) in connection with the purchase of cocaine was the proper subject of restitution). G.S. 7A-304(a)(7) provides for costs to be assessed against a convicted defendant in connection with SBI analysis of controlled substances.

Related Offenses Not in This Chapter

Unlawful manufacture, sale, delivery, or possession of Salvia divinorum (or Salvinorin A). G.S. 14-401.23.

Distributing or dispensing by a registrant or practitioner in violation of G.S. 90-105 or 90-106. G.S. 90-108(a)(2).

Registrant's manufacturing, distributing, or dispensing of a controlled substance not authorized by registration. G.S. 90-108(a)(3).

Distribution by registrant or practitioner of Schedule I or II substance without an order form. G.S. 90-108(a)(8).

Use of fictitious, etc. registration number in the course of manufacture or distribution of a controlled substance. G.S. 90-108(a)(9).

Sale or Delivery of a Controlled Substance to a Pregnant Female

Statute

See G.S. 90-95(e)(5), reproduced above.

Elements

A person guilty of this offense

(1) is 18 years old or older *and*
(2) knowingly

(3) (a) sells *or*
(b) delivers
(4) a controlled substance to
(5) a pregnant female.

Punishment

Class D felony. G.S. 90-95(e)(5). If the defendant is sentenced to an active term less than the maximum term that could have been imposed, special probation may be imposed as specified in G.S. 90-95(f).

Notes

Generally. This offense is the same as "Sale or Delivery of a Controlled Substance," above, except that for this offense (1) the defendant must be 18 years old or older; and (2) the sale or delivery must be to a pregnant female. Thus, the notes on that offense apply here as well.

Element (5). It is no defense that the person who sold or delivered a controlled substance did not know that the recipient was pregnant. G.S. 90-95(e)(5).

Related Offenses Not in This Chapter

"Murder of an Unborn Child" (Chapter 6)
"Voluntary Manslaughter of an Unborn Child" (Chapter 6)
"Involuntary Manslaughter of an Unborn Child" (Chapter 6)
"Battery on an Unborn Child" (Chapter 7)
"Assault Inflicting Serious Injury on an Unborn Child" (Chapter 7)
See the various child abuse offenses in Chapter 9 (Abuse and Neglect).

Furnishing a Controlled Substance to an Inmate

Statute

§14-258.1. Furnishing poison, controlled substances, deadly weapons, cartridges, ammunition or alcoholic beverages to inmates of charitable, mental or penal institutions or local confinement facilities; furnishing tobacco products or mobile phones to inmates.

(a) If any person shall give or sell to any inmate of any charitable, mental or penal institution, or local confinement facility, or if any person shall combine, confederate, conspire, aid, abet, solicit, urge, investigate, counsel, advise, encourage, attempt to procure, or procure another or others to give or sell to any inmate of any charitable, mental or penal institution, or local confinement facility, any deadly weapon, or any cartridge or ammunition for firearms of any kind, or any controlled substances included in Schedules I through VI contained in Article 5 of Chapter 90 of the General Statutes except under the general supervision of a practitioner, poison or poisonous substance, except upon the prescription of a physician, he shall be punished as a Class H felon; and if he be an officer or employee of any institution of the State, or of any local confinement facility, he shall be dismissed from his position or office.

Subsections (b) through (e) are not reproduced here.

Elements

A person guilty of this offense

(1) (a) gives *or*
(b) sells
(2) a controlled substance
(3) to an inmate
(4) of any charitable, mental, or penal institution or local confinement facility.

Punishment

Class H felony. G.S. 14-258.1(a). If the defendant is an officer or employee of any state institution or local confinement facility, he or she must be dismissed from employment. *Id.*
The provision pertaining to special probation noted in this section under "Sale or Delivery of a Controlled Substance," above, does not apply to this offense because this offense is not in Article 5 of G.S. Chapter 90.

Notes

Element (1)(b). For a discussion of the meaning of the term "sells," see the note on Element (2)(a) to "Sale or Delivery of a Controlled Substance," above.

Element (2). The statute specifically covers any substance in Schedules I through VI, reproduced above. The amount given or sold is irrelevant.

Element (4). The term "local confinement facility" includes "a county or city jail, a local lockup, a regional or district jail, a juvenile detention facility, a detention facility operated for adults operated by a local government, and any other facility operated by a local government for confinement of persons awaiting trial or serving sentences." State v. Moncree, 188 N.C. App. 221, 228 (2008) (quoting G.S. 153A-217).

Conspiring, aiding and abetting, etc. The statute specifies that the offense covers any person who "shall combine, confederate, conspire, aid, abet, solicit, urge, investigate, counsel, advise, encourage, attempt to procure, or procure another or others to give or sell to any inmate" a controlled substance. G.S. 14-258.1(a). Thus, while some of these acts would normally lead to lower punishment, see generally Chapter 5 (General Crimes), for this offense they carry the same punishment as the completed offense.

Evidence issues. See this note to "Sale or Delivery of a Controlled Substance," above.

Exception. This offense is not committed when the substance is given under the supervision of a practitioner. G.S. 14-258.1(a).

Related Offenses Not in This Chapter

Conveying messages and weapons to or trading with convicts and other prisoners. G.S. 14-258.
Furnishing poison or a poisonous substance to an inmate. G.S. 14-258.1(a).
Furnishing alcoholic beverages, tobacco products, or cell phones to an inmate. G.S. 14-258.1(b)–(d).
Inmate's possession of a tobacco product or a cell phone. G.S. 14-258.1(e).

Manufacture of a Controlled Substance

Statute

See G.S. 90-95(a)(1), reproduced above.

Elements

A person guilty of this offense

(1) knowingly
(2) manufactures
(3) a controlled substance *and,*
(4) if the manufacturing involves preparing or compounding, the person acts with an intent to distribute.

Punishment

For a Schedule I or II substance, the crime is a Class H felony. G.S. 90-95(b)(1).

For a Schedule III, IV, V, or VI substance, the crime is a Class I felony. G.S. 90-95(b)(2).

The manufacture of methamphetamine is a Class C felony, except that packaging or repackaging methamphetamine or labeling or relabeling the methamphetamine container is punished as a Class H felony. G.S. 90-95(b)(1a). For the special felony sentencing enhancement that can apply in manufacturing of methamphetamine cases, see "Methamphetamine enhancement" under "Special Provisions" in the discussion of felony sentencing in Chapter 4 (Punishment under Structured Sentencing).

If the defendant is sentenced to an active term that is less than the maximum term that could have been imposed, special probation may be imposed as specified in G.S. 90-95(f).

Notes

Element (1). See the note on Element (1) to "Sale or Delivery of a Controlled Substance," above.

Element (2). The term "manufacture" means:

- production, preparation, propagation, compounding, conversion, or processing of a controlled substance by any means, directly or indirectly, artificially or naturally, or by extraction from substances of a natural origin, or independently by means of chemical synthesis, or by a combination of extraction and chemical synthesis; and
- any packaging or repackaging of the substance or labeling or relabeling of its container.

G.S. 90-87(15). Excluded from the meaning of the term is:

- preparation or compounding of a controlled substance by an individual for his or her own use;
- preparation, compounding, packaging, or labeling of a controlled substance by a practitioner as an incident to administering or dispensing a controlled substance in the course of professional practice, and
- preparation, compounding, packaging, or labeling of a controlled substance by a practitioner, or by an authorized agent under the practitioner's supervision, for the purpose of, or as an incident to, research, teaching, or chemical analysis and not for sale.

Id.

The evidence was sufficient to establish manufacturing when the defendant possessed plastic bag corners, two sets of scales, and Ziploc bags with marijuana. State v. Roseboro, 55 N.C. App. 205 (1981).

The defendant need not be in actual possession of the controlled substance and/or drug paraphernalia used in the manufacturing; the fact that the defendant was in constructive possession of the items is sufficient to sustain a conviction. State v. Brown, 310 N.C. 563, 568–70 (1984) (evidence sufficient to establish manufacturing by constructive possession of drugs and paraphernalia); State v. Owen, 51 N.C. App. 429, 431–32 (1981) (evidence was sufficient to establish that the defendant had constructive possession of a patch of marijuana plants near his trailer). For a discussion of constructive possession of controlled substances, see the note on Element (2) to "Possession of a Controlled Substance," below.

Element (3). See the note on Element (3) to "Sale or Delivery of a Controlled Substance," above.

Element (4). Because the statute provides that preparation and compounding for one's own use is not manufacturing, see the note on Element (2) above, when the charge is preparing or compounding, the State must prove an intent to distribute. *Brown*, 310 N.C. at 567–68. When the manufacturing is accomplished in any other manner, the State need not prove such an intent. State v. Hinson, ___ N.C. App. ___, 691 S.E.2d 63, 72–73 (2010) (the State was not required to prove an intent to distribute when the defendant was charged with manufacturing by chemically synthesizing precursor chemicals to create methamphetamine and not preparing or compounding).

Attempt and conspiracy. See this note to "Sale or Delivery of a Controlled Substance," above.

Charging issues. See this note to "Sale or Delivery of a Controlled Substance," above. *See also* State v. Hinson, 364 N.C. 414 (2010) (for the reasons stated in the dissenting opinion below, the court reversed *State v. Hinson*, ___ N.C. App. ___, 691 S.E.2d 63 (2010); the defendant was indicted for manufacturing methamphetamine by "chemically combining and synthesizing precursor chemicals to create methamphetamine"; however, the trial judge instructed the jury that it could find the defendant guilty if it found that he produced, prepared, propagated, compounded, converted, or processed methamphetamine, either by extraction from substances of natural origin or by chemical synthesis; the court of appeals held, over a dissent, that this was plain error as it allowed the jury to convict on theories not charged in the indictment; the dissenting judge concluded that while the trial court's instructions used slightly different words than the indictment, the import of the indictment and the charge were the same; the dissent reasoned that the manufacture of methamphetamine is accomplished by the chemical combination of precursor elements to create methamphetamine and that the charge to the jury, construed contextually as a whole, was correct).

Evidence issues. See this note to "Sale or Delivery of a Controlled Substance," above.

Defenses. See this note to "Sale or Delivery of a Controlled Substance," above.

Greater and lesser-included offenses. Possession of a controlled substance is not a lesser-included offense of manufacture of a controlled substance. State v. Jenkins, 74 N.C. App. 295, 299–300 (1985).

Restitution for cleanup of drug manufacturing laboratory. G.S. 90-95.3(c) provides that when a defendant is convicted of an offense involving the manufacturing of controlled substances, the court must order the defendant to make restitution to the law enforcement agency that cleaned up any clandestine laboratory used to manufacture the controlled substances for the actual cost of cleanup, including personnel overtime, equipment, and supplies.

Related Offenses Not in This Chapter

Contaminate food or drink to render one mentally incapacitated or physically helpless. G.S. 14-401.16.
Unlawful manufacture, sale, delivery, or possession of Salvia divinorum (or Salvinorin A). G.S. 14-401.23.
Unlawful manufacturing of a controlled substance by registrant. G.S. 90-108(a)(3).
Use of fictitious registration number in manufacturing. G.S. 90-108(a)(9).

Possession Offenses

Possession of a Controlled Substance

Statute

See G.S. 90-95(a)(3), reproduced above.

Elements

A person guilty of this offense

(1) knowingly
(2) possesses
(3) a controlled substance.

Punishment

For a Schedule I substance, the crime is a Class I felony. G.S. 90-95(d)(1). However, if the controlled substance is 3,4-Methylenedioxypyrovalerone (MDPV) and the quantity of the MDPV is 1 gram or less, the crime is a Class 1 misdemeanor. *Id.*

For a Schedule II, III, or IV substance, the crime is a Class I felony if the amount possessed is

- more than 100 tablets, capsules, dosage units, or equivalent quantity;
- more than four tablets, capsules, or dosage units of hydromorphone; or
- any amount of methamphetamine, amphetamine, phencyclidine, cocaine, and any salt, isomer, salts of isomers, compound, derivative, or preparation thereof; or cocoa leaves and any salt, isomer, salts of isomers, compound, derivative, or preparation thereof which is chemically equivalent or identical with any of these substances (except decocanized cocoa leaves or any extraction of cocoa leaves which does not contain cocaine or ecgonine).

G.S. 90-95(d)(2); *see* State v. Jones, 358 N.C. 473 (2004) (possession of cocaine is a felony). Otherwise, possession of a Schedule II, III, or IV substance is a Class 1 misdemeanor. G.S. 90-95(d)(2).

For a Schedule V substance, the crime is a Class 2 misdemeanor. G.S. 90-95(d)(3).

Except as discussed immediately below, for a Schedule VI controlled substance, the offense is a Class 3 misdemeanor for which a sentence of imprisonment must be suspended and the judge may not require that the defendant serve a period of imprisonment as a special condition of probation. G.S. 90-95(d)(4). There are two exceptions to this punishment level for Schedule VI controlled substances. First, if the defendant possessed

- more than ½ ounce of marijuana and up to 1½ ounces of marijuana,
- more than 7 and up to 21 grams of a synthetic cannabinoid or any mixture containing such substance, or
- more than 1/20 of an ounce and up to 3/20 of an ounce of hashish,

the offense is a Class 1 misdemeanor. Second, if the defendant possessed

- more than 1½ ounces of marijuana,
- more than 21 grams of a synthetic cannabinoid or any mixture containing such substance, or
- more than 3/20 of an ounce of hashish or any amount of synthetic tetrahydrocannabinols or tetrahydrocannabinols isolated from marijuana resin,

the offense is a Class I felony. G.S. 90-95(d)(4).

Note that for all misdemeanor controlled substance offenses, several provisions elevate punishment based on the defendant's prior conviction record. These include:

- G.S. 90-95(e)(3): For any person who commits a Class 1 misdemeanor under the N.C. Controlled Substances Act (CSA) with at least one prior conviction (in this state, in any other state, or under federal law) for conduct punishable under the CSA, the offense is a Class I felony.

- G.S. 90-95(e)(4): For any person who commits a Class 2 misdemeanor with at least one prior conviction (in this state, in any other state, or under federal law) for conduct punishable under the CSA, the offense is a Class 1 misdemeanor.
- G.S. 90-95(e)(7): For any person who commits an offense under the CSA for which the prescribed punishment requires that any sentence of imprisonment be suspended and who has at least one prior conviction (in this state, in any other state, or under federal law) for conduct punishable under the CSA, the offense is a Class 2 misdemeanor.

For purposes of increasing punishment under G.S. 90-95(e)(3) and (4), previous convictions for offenses must be counted by the number of separate trials at which final convictions were obtained and not by the number of charges at a single trial, G.S. 90-95(e)(6), and no prior conviction used to increase punishment may be used to calculate prior conviction level for the new offense, G.S. 90-95(e)(3) & (4).

Any fact that elevates punishment must be alleged in a charging instrument and proved at trial. *See* G.S. 15A-928 (pleading and proving prior convictions).

If the defendant is sentenced to an active term that is less than the maximum term that could have been imposed, special probation may be imposed as specified in G.S. 90-95(f).

Notes

Element (1). See the note on Element (1) to "Sale or Delivery of a Controlled Substance," above. The fact that a controlled substance was found on premises controlled by the defendant permits an inference that the defendant knowingly possessed the substance. State v. Harvey, 281 N.C. 1, 13 (1972). Evidence of track marks on the defendant's arms was relevant to show prior knowledge. State v. Thomas, 20 N.C. App. 255 (1973). For cases in which the evidence was sufficient to establish knowing possession, see *State v. Nunez*, ___ N.C. App. ___, 693 S.E.2d 223, 226 (2010) (among other things, the defendant accepted delivery of packages containing drugs that were addressed to a person no longer living at the address); and *State v. Robledo*, 193 N.C. App. 521, 525–28 (2008) (among other things, the defendant signed for and collected a UPS package containing drugs).

A positive urinalysis for marijuana metabolites is insufficient, without other evidence, to prove that the defendant knowingly possessed marijuana. State v. Harris, 361 N.C. 400 (2007).

Element (2). Possession may be actual or constructive. A defendant has actual possession of contraband if it is on his or her person, the defendant is aware of its presence, and either alone or with others the defendant has the power and intent to control its disposition or use. State v. Loftis, 185 N.C. App. 190 (2007); State v. Reid, 151 N.C. App. 420 (2002).

Constructive possession exists when the defendant, while not having actual possession, has the intent and capability to maintain control and dominion over the contraband. State v. Miller, 363 N.C. 96 (2009); State v. Matias, 354 N.C. 549 (2001). The defendant may have the power to control either alone or jointly with others. *Miller*, 363 N.C. 96. Exclusive possession by the defendant of the place where an item containing contraband is found, such as a home or a vehicle, ordinarily is sufficient to establish the requisite intent and capability to maintain control and dominion over the contraband required for constructive possession. State v. Butler, 356 N.C. 141 (2002); *Matias*, 354 N.C. 549. Thus, if drugs are found in a closet in the defendant's home and the defendant is the sole resident of the home, the evidence of constructive possession is sufficient to take the issue to the jury.

Often, however, contraband is found in a place over which the defendant does not have exclusive possession. For example, drugs may be found in a vehicle driven by one person and carrying several others as passengers. To establish constructive possession, it is not necessary to show that a defendant has exclusive control of the premises. State v. McLaurin, 320 N.C. 143 (1987). However, when the defendant does not have exclusive possession of the place where, or of the item in which, the contraband is found, the State must show other incriminating circumstances to establish sufficient evidence of constructive possession. State v. Miller, 363 N.C. 96 (2009) (other incriminating circumstances shown); *Butler*, 356 N.C. 141 (same); *Matias*,

354 N.C. 549 (same); *McLaurin*, 320 N.C. 143 (insufficient evidence of constructive possession when drug paraphernalia was found in a house over which the defendant had non-exclusive possession and the State offered no incriminating evidence linking her to the paraphernalia).

The determination of whether sufficient incriminating circumstances exist to support a finding of constructive possession is fact-specific. *Miller*, 363 N.C. 96. The courts consider the totality of the circumstances and no one factor controls, State v. McBride, 173 N.C. App. 101 (2005); the following factors are among those taken into consideration:

The defendant's proximity or lack of proximity to the contraband. Compare Miller, 363 N.C. 96 (evidence was sufficient to establish constructive possession when, among other things, cocaine was found within the defendant's reach), *with* State v. Slaughter, ___ N.C. ___, ___ S.E.2d ___ (Dec. 9, 2011) (for the reasons stated in the dissenting opinion below, the court reversed the court of appeals and held that the evidence was insufficient in part because of the lack of evidence regarding proximity), State v. Barron, 202 N.C. App. 686 (2010) (evidence was insufficient with respect to drugs found at a home in which the defendant did not reside; an officer saw plastic baggies—later determined to contain marijuana and cocaine—on a couch about three feet away from where the defendant was standing at the front door; when executing a search warrant, officers found a crack pipe approximately two-and-one-half feet away from where the defendant had been standing and a push rod (sometimes used to clean or pack crack pipes) and piece of Chore Boy (a brand of scouring pad sometimes used by individuals smoking crack to retain cocaine vapors) approximately ten to twelve feet from where he had been standing), *and* State v. Autry, 101 N.C. App. 245 (1991) (evidence was insufficient when the defendant was found upstairs in a small hallway or landing in the premises but the drugs were found in an upstairs bedroom, with two other people present). However, mere presence at a location where drugs are found does not create an inference of constructive possession. State v. Slaughter, ___ N.C. ___, ___ S.E.2d ___ (Dec. 9, 2011) (for the reasons stated in the dissenting opinion below, the court reversed the court of appeals and held that the evidence was insufficient to show constructive possession; in the opinion below, the dissenting judge had noted that mere presence in a room where contraband is located does not itself support an inference of constructive possession); State v. Minor, 290 N.C. 68, 75 (1976) ("The most the State has shown is that defendant had been in an area where he could have committed the crimes charged. Beyond that we must sail in a sea of conjecture and surmise. This we are not permitted to do."); State v. Ferguson, ___ N.C. App. ___, 694 S.E.2d 470 (2010) (mere presence is insufficient); *Autry*, 101 N.C. App. 245 (same).

Whether or not the defendant owned or occupied the location where, or had control of the item in which, the contraband was found. Compare State v. Terry, ___ N.C. App. ___, 699 S.E.2d 671 (2010) (there was sufficient evidence of constructive possession of drugs found in a house when the defendant lived at and held a possessory interest in the house; he shared the master bedroom where the majority of the marijuana and drug paraphernalia was found; and he demonstrated actual control over the premises by demanding a search warrant), State v. Fortney, 201 N.C. App. 662 (2010) (evidence was sufficient with respect to drugs found in a motorcycle carry bag when, among other things, the defendant borrowed the motorcycle from the owner and was driving it), State v. Wiggins, 185 N.C. App. 376 (2007) (evidence was sufficient when, among other things, cocaine was found in the fender well of a vehicle registered to and driven by the defendant), State v. Loftis, 185 N.C. App. 190 (2007) (evidence was sufficient when, among other things, the defendant was found alone in a shed where contraband was located; the shed door was locked from the inside and the defendant left the premises only after being confronted by the owner), State v. Weakley, 176 N.C. App. 642 (2006) (evidence was sufficient when the defendant leased and resided in a house where controlled substances and drug paraphernalia were found, even though another man also lived there and another person stayed there a couple of nights a week), *and* State v. Nettles, 170 N.C. App. 100 (2005) (evidence was sufficient with respect to contraband found in a vehicle when, although the vehicle's title was in another's name, the defendant had a key to the vehicle, registration forms and an auto insurance policy listed the defendant as owner, and the defendant placed a license plate on the vehicle that was from his previous vehicle), *with* State v. Finney, 290 N.C. 755 (1976) (evidence was insufficient when, among other things, although the defendant leased an apartment where marijuana was found, he had not been in the apartment for forty-four days, there was evidence that he had sublet it to another person who was living there, and that person admitted sole possession of the marijuana), State v. Minor, 290 N.C. 68 (1976) (evidence was insufficient when the defendant had been a visitor at an abandoned house leased or controlled by a co-defendant; a marijuana field was 100 feet away from the house, obscured by a wooded area, and accessible by several routes; and on the date of the defendant's arrest, he was a front-seat passenger in a vehicle owned and operated by a co-defendant in which officers found wilted marijuana leaves on the left rear floorboard and a marijuana leaf in the trunk), State v. Barron, 202 N.C. App. 686, (2010) (evidence was insufficient when the defendant did not have exclusive possession of the premises where the drugs were found; the evidence showed only that he was present, with others, in the room where the drugs were found); State v. Ferguson, ___ N.C. App. ___, 694 S.E.2d 470 (2010) (evidence was insufficient when, among other things, the defendant was not the owner or driver of the vehicle in which drugs were found), State v. Richardson, 202 N.C. App. 570 (2010) (evidence was insufficient when, among other things, the defendant did not rent the premises in question and there was no evidence that he slept or lived there), State v. Givens, 95 N.C. App. 72 (1989) (evidence was insufficient when, although there was evidence that the defendant knew there was cocaine inside the premises, others were present when cocaine was found in the building and the defendant did not exercise ownership or possession of the building), *and* State v. Balsom, 17 N.C. App. 655 (1973) (the mere fact that the defendants were transient visitors at a residence where drugs were found was insufficient to establish constructive possession).

The defendant's opportunity, or lack thereof, to dispose of or place the contraband in the location where it was found. Compare State v. Butler, 356 N.C. 141 (2002) (evidence was sufficient when, among other things, the defendant was the only person in a position to place a package containing drugs under the driver's seat of a cab), State v. Matias, 354 N.C. 549 (2001) (evidence was sufficient when, among other things, the defendant was the only person in the car who could have put the cocaine into the crease of the car seat), State v. Sinclair, 191 N.C. App. 485 (2008) (evidence was sufficient when, among other things, contraband was found on the route the defendant took when fleeing), *and* State v. Loftis, 185 N.C. App. 190 (2007) (evidence was sufficient when, among other things, the defendant was found alone in a shed where contraband later was seized), *with* State v. Acolatse, 158 N.C. App. 485 (2003) (evidence was insufficient when, among other things, the defendant, while being chased by detectives, made a throwing motion toward some bushes; cocaine was found on the roof of a detached garage but not in the bushes).

Whether or not the defendant's personal items were found in the same location as the contraband. Compare State v. Miller, 363 N.C. 96 (2009) (evidence was sufficient when, among other things, the defendant's birth certificate and state-issued identification card were found in the bedroom where cocaine was discovered), State v. Hough, 202 N.C. App. 674 (2010) (evidence was sufficient when, among other things, the defendant's luggage, mail, and cellular telephone were found at the residence and his car was parked in the driveway), *Loftis*, 185 N.C. App. 190 (evidence was sufficient when, among other things, investigators found an envelope addressed to the defendant and containing the defendant's tax document in a shed where contraband was located), *and* State v. Balsom, 17 N.C. App. 655 (1973) (evidence was sufficient when, among other things, drugs were found in a drawer with a wallet containing the defendant's identification and in a closet containing his clothes), *with* State v. Richardson, 202 N.C. App. 570 (2010) (evidence was insufficient when, among other things, no documents bearing the defendant's name were found in the residence in question), *and* State v. Moore, 162 N.C. App. 268 (2007) (evidence was insufficient when, among other things, five individuals, including the defendant, were found in or near a mobile home containing drugs; the home was owned by someone else; and officers did not find any documents or other items linking the defendant to the residence).

Whether or not the defendant fled or engaged in other suspicious behavior. Compare State v. Butler, 356 N.C. 141 (2002) (evidence was sufficient when, among other things, after making eye contact with officers, the defendant walked briskly away, repeatedly glancing back at the officers; the defendant hurried into a cab, slammed the door, and urged the driver to leave immediately; the defendant appeared nervous and fidgety when officers approached the cab and asked him to step out with his bag; and the defendant was slow to exit the cab and before exiting, bent over and reached toward the driver's seat, where cocaine later was discovered), State v. Hudson, ___ N.C. App. ___, 696 S.E.2d 577 (2010) (evidence was sufficient when, among other things, the defendant acted suspiciously when his truck was stopped by an officer; he exited with his back to the officer and his hands up, unusual activity under the circumstances; his hand shook when he handed over information requested by the officer; he was sweating despite cold weather; and an officer could see his carotid artery pulsing), State v. Hough, 202 N.C. App. 674 (2010) (evidence was sufficient when the defendant was found pushing a trash can that contained the bulk of the marijuana seized, acted suspiciously when approached by officers, and ran when an officer attempted to lift the lid of the can), State v. Fortney, 201 N.C. App. 662 (2010) (evidence was sufficient with respect to drugs found in a motorcycle carry bag when, among other things, the defendant evaded an impaired driving checkpoint by turning into a closed business, obscured his motorcycle's rear reflector, and pushed the motorcycle into the lower portion of the parking lot; the police found the defendant crouched behind two parked cars a few feet away from the motorcycle; and the defendant was evasive when asked about who owned the motorcycle and the license plate was fictitious), State v. Sinclair, 191 N.C. App. 485 (2008) (evidence was sufficient when, among other things, the defendant fled when he learned that officers wanted to search him), *and* State v. McBride, 173 N.C. App. 101 (2005) (evidence was sufficient when, among other things, the defendant tried to get into a motel room when he saw officers approaching and then scuffled with an officer), *with* State v. Ferguson, ___ N.C. App. ___, 694 S.E.2d 470 (2010) (evidence was insufficient when, among other things, it did not show that the defendant behaved suspiciously), State v. Barron, 202 N.C. App. 686 (2010) (evidence was insufficient to establish that the defendant possessed items found in a house in which he did not reside; the State had argued in part that the defendant acted suspiciously by standing behind an open front door and by lying about his identity), *and* State v. Acolatse, 158 N.C. App. 485 (2003) (evidence was insufficient even though the defendant fled from approaching officers).

Whether or not the defendant engaged in drug activity or was impaired by drugs. Compare McBride, 173 N.C. App. 101 (evidence was sufficient when, among other things, officers who responded to a call about drug activity approached the motel in question and observed an apparent drug transaction between the defendant and another person; the transaction occurred outside of the motel room in question; the defendant smelled of crack cocaine and had the characteristics of someone under the influence of the drug), *with* State v. Balsom, 17 N.C. App. 655 (1973) (evidence was insufficient when, among other things, there was no evidence that the defendants were under the influence or were users of narcotics).

Element (3). See the note on Element (3) to "Sale or Delivery of a Controlled Substance," above. No minimum amount of a controlled substance is required; possession of residue of crack cocaine in a crack pipe has been held sufficient to support a conviction of possession of cocaine. State v. Williams, 149 N.C. App. 795 (2002).

Attempt or conspiracy. See this note to "Sale or Delivery of a Controlled Substance," above. The evidence was sufficient to show an attempt to possess cocaine when the defendant intended to possess cocaine, drove to an area known for drug sales, approached people believed to be cocaine dealers, and exchanged money for what the defendant thought was cocaine but in fact was pieces of Brazil nut represented to be rock cocaine. State v. Gunnings, 122 N.C. App. 294, 296 (1996).

Charging issues. See this note to "Sale or Delivery of a Controlled Substance," above.

Evidence issues. See this note to "Sale or Delivery of a Controlled Substance," above.

Defenses. G.S. 90-113.1(a) provides that the defendant bears the burden of establishing that an exemption or exception from prosecution applies. *See also* State v. Beam, 201 N.C. App. 643 (2010) (trafficking by possession case holding that the defendant bears the burden of showing a valid prescription). *But see* State v. Tuggle, 109 N.C. App. 235, 240–41 (1993) (the State failed to present substantial evidence that the defendant possessed diazepam unlawfully when there was no evidence that the drugs were not issued pursuant to a prescription or that the quantity possessed was larger than amounts normally prescribed).

See also this note to "Sale or Delivery of a Controlled Substance," above.

Greater and lesser-included offenses. Possession of a controlled substance is not a lesser-included offense of sale of that substance because possession is not necessary for a sale to be made; a defendant may be tried and sentenced for both. State v. Cameron, 283 N.C. 191 (1973). Although the North Carolina Court of Appeals has ruled that possession of a controlled substance is a lesser-included offense of delivery of the substance, State v. Clark, 71 N.C. App. 55 (1984), that opinion has been disapproved of in significant respects, State v. Moore, 327 N.C. 378 (1990).

Possession of a controlled substance is a lesser-included offense of possession with intent to manufacture, sell, or deliver, except as discussed below; a defendant may be sentenced for one or the other, but not both. State v. Aiken, 286 N.C. 202 (1974). Possession of more than ½ ounce of marijuana (Class 1 misdemeanor) or 1½ ounces of marijuana (Class I felony) are not lesser-included offenses of possession with intent to sell or deliver because these possession offenses (unlike simple misdemeanor possession, a Class 3 misdemeanor) require additional proof that the amount possessed was more than ½ ounce or 1½ ounces, as the case may be. This same principle applies to other controlled substances when the classification of the possession offense depends on the amount of the substance possessed. However, if the criminal pleading charging possession with intent to manufacture, sell, or deliver ("Possession of a Controlled Substance with Intent to Manufacture, Sell, or Deliver" is discussed below) alleges the amount possessed, the jury may be instructed on the offenses of felony and misdemeanor possession even though these offenses may not be lesser-included offenses. State v. Perry, 84 N.C. App. 309 (1987).

Multiple convictions and punishments. In order for the State to obtain multiple convictions for possession of a controlled substance, the State must show distinct acts of possession separated in time and space. State v. Moncree, 188 N.C. App. 221, 231 (2008). The defendant could be convicted of only one offense where, on the same day, law enforcement officers found marijuana in the defendant's automobile and later found marijuana in his shoe; there was no evidence that the defendant possessed the marijuana for two distinct purposes or that the possession was simultaneous. *Id.* at 231–32. In contrast, a defendant could be separately punished for felonious possession of cocaine sold to police (a large amount of cocaine was sold) and misdemeanor possession of trace amounts of cocaine in vials for personal use found during a search incident to arrest on the same day. State v. Rozier, 69 N.C. App. 38, 54–56 (1984). The court in that case noted that there was no evidence that the defendant filled the vials out of the larger amount or that the defendant had done so and then used the cocaine; there also was no evidence that the defendant intended to sell the residual cocaine. *Id.* at 55.

A defendant may be convicted and sentenced for both possession of ecstasy and possession of ketamine when both controlled substances are contained in a single pill. State v. Hall, ___ N.C. App. ___, 692 S.E.2d 446, 450–51 (2010).

As a general rule, a person may not be convicted of possession of a controlled substance and posession with intent to manufacture, sell, or deliver that substance. State v. Aiken, 286 N.C. 202 (1974). However, a defendant may, based on the same contraband, be convicted and punished for both felony possession of marijuana (which requires possession of more than 1½ ounces of marijuana, see "Punishment," above) and felony possession of marijuana with intent to manufacture, sell, or deliver. State v. Springs, 200 N.C. App. 288, 294–95 (2009); State v. Spencer, 192 N.C. App. 143, 149 (2008). "Possession of a Controlled Substance with Intent to Manufacture, Sell, or Deliver" is discussed below. The same principle would apply to other possession offenses that receive elevated punishment because of the quantity of controlled substance possessed.

A person may be convicted and punished for both possession of a controlled substance under G.S. 90-95(a)(3) and trafficking by possessing a controlled substance even though the offenses are based on the same controlled substance. State v. Pipkins, 337 N.C. 431 (1994).

A defendant may be convicted of both possession of cocaine and possession of drug paraphernalia even though the cocaine was found in the drug paraphernalia. State v. Williams, 149 N.C. App. 795 (2002).

No double jeopardy bar to prosecuting drug offense after imposition of drug tax. There is no double jeopardy bar to prosecuting a drug offense after a defendant has been assessed and paid a drug tax under Chapter 105 of the General Statutes. State v. Adams, 132 N.C. App. 819 (1999).

Related Offenses Not in This Chapter

None

Possession of a Controlled Substance at a Prison or Local Confinement Facility

Statute

See G.S. 90-95(e)(9), reproduced above.

Elements

A person guilty of this offense

(1) knowingly
(2) possesses
(3) a controlled substance
(4) on the premises of a penal institution or local confinement facility.

Punishment

Class H felony. G.S. 90-95(e)(9). If the defendant is sentenced to an active term that is less than the maximum term that could have been imposed, special probation may be imposed as specified in G.S. 90-95(f).

Notes

Generally. This offense is the same as "Possession of a Controlled Substance," above, except that for this offense, the possession must occur on the premises of a penal institution or local confinement facility. Thus, the notes on that offense apply equally here.

This offense applies to any person, not just an inmate.

Element (4). The term "local confinement facility" includes "a county or city jail, a local lockup, a regional or district jail, a juvenile detention facility, a detention facility operated for adults operated by a local government, and any other facility operated by a local government for confinement of persons awaiting trial or serving sentences." State v. Moncree, 188 N.C. App. 221, 228 (2008) (quoting G.S. 153A-217). This offense may occur not just in confinement areas but anywhere on the property of a prison, jail, or other kind of confinement facility. The premises of a local confinement facility include the secured area in the facility where officers detain and search arrestees before they are taken before a magistrate. State v. Dent, 174 N.C. App. 459 (2005). However, the State is not required to show that the defendant was in a secured area accessible only to officers and their detainees. *Moncree*, 188 N.C. App. at 228–29.

Charging issues. See this note to "Sale or Delivery of a Controlled Substance," above.

Multiple convictions and punishments. A defendant may not be convicted of possession of a controlled substance and this offense based on the same incident. *Moncree*, 188 N.C. App. at 230.

Related Offenses Not in This Chapter

None

Possession of a Controlled Substance with Intent to Manufacture, Sell, or Deliver

Statute

See G.S. 90-95(a)(1), reproduced above.

Elements

A person guilty of this offense

(1) knowingly
(2) possesses
(3) a controlled substance
(4) with the intent to manufacture, sell, or deliver it.

Punishment

For a Schedule I or II substance, the crime is a Class H felony. G.S. 90-95(b)(1).

For a Schedule III, IV, V, or VI substance, the crime is a Class I felony. G.S. 90-95(b)(2).

If the defendant is sentenced for less than the maximum term that could have been imposed, special probation may be imposed as specified in G.S. 90-95(f).

Notes

Element (1). See the note on Element (1) to "Sale or Delivery of a Controlled Substance," above.

Element (2). See the note on Element (2) to "Possession of a Controlled Substance," above.

Element (3). See the note on Element (3) to "Sale or Delivery of a Controlled Substance," above.

Element (4). For the meaning of the term "manufacture," see the note on Element (2) to "Manufacture of a Controlled Substance," above. For the meaning of the terms "sell" and "deliver," see the notes on Elements (2)(a) and (b) to "Sale or Delivery of a Controlled Substance," above.

Evidence will be considered sufficient to establish an intent to sell, regardless of the amount possessed, when the State introduces evidence of an actual sale. State v. Neal, 196 N.C. App. 100, 103 (2009).

There is no specific amount that automatically proves that a person possesses a controlled substance with the intent to manufacture, sell, or deliver, although quantity alone may sometimes be sufficient. State v. Morgan, 329 N.C. 654 (1991). Aside from the quantity of controlled substance possessed, the requisite intent may be inferred from:

- the packaging of the controlled substance,
- the labeling of the controlled substance,
- the storage of the controlled substance,
- the defendant's activities,
- the presence of cash, and
- the presence of drug paraphernalia.

State v. Wilkins, ___ N.C. App. ___, 703 S.E.2d 807, 809–10 (2010); *In re* I.R.T., 184 N.C. App. 579, 588 (2007). For example, the required intent was inferred from the amount of marijuana found (219 grams), the manner in which it was packaged (in sixteen separate envelopes), and the presence of other packaging materials (another twenty-eight empty envelopes, tape, and cigarette papers). State v. Baxter, 285 N.C. 735 (1974). Other cases in which the evidence was sufficient to show the required intent include those where the defendant possessed (1) 2.7 grams of heroin, drug paraphernalia, and ten to fifteen tinfoil squares, State v. Williams, 307 N.C. 452 (1983); (2) 3/4 of an ounce of cocaine and there was evidence of prior purchases, *Morgan,* 329 N.C. 654; (3) 4.27 grams of cocaine packaged in twenty separate envelopes and a large amount of cash, State v. Alston, 91 N.C. App. 707 (1988); (4) 20 grams of cocaine, packaged separately and in close proximity to money, State v. Davis, 160 N.C. App. 693 (2003); (5) 5.5 grams of crack cocaine individually wrapped in twenty-two pieces and placed in the corner of a paper bag, State v. McNeil, 165 N.C. App. 777 (2004); and (6) 414.5 grams of marijuana, as well as surveillance equipment, guns, and a bag with what appeared to be a cutting agent for cocaine, State v. Baldwin, 161 N.C. App. 382 (2003).

In contrast, the evidence was insufficient to establish an intent to manufacture, sell, or deliver when (1) the defendant possessed 215.5 grams of marijuana, State v. Wiggins, 33 N.C. App. 291 (1977); (2) the defendant possessed seventy phenobarbital tablets, State v. King, 42 N.C. App. 210 (1979); (3) the defendant possessed 1.9 grams of compressed powder cocaine but no drug implements or paraphernalia, State v. Battle, 167 N.C. App. 730 (2005); (4) the defendant possessed approximately ten rocks of crack cocaine but no incriminating statements were made by the defendant and there was no behavior or other circumstances associated with drug transactions, State v. Turner, 168 N.C. App. 152 (2005); (5) the defendant possessed four to five crack cocaine rocks weighing 1.2 grams, State v. Nettles, 170 N.C. App. 100 (2005); (6) the defendant possessed thirty diazepam pills, State v. Sanders, 171 N.C. App. 46 (2005); (7) the defendant possessed 1.89 grams of marijuana separated into three smaller packages, worth about $30 in total, and $1,264 in cash, State v. Wilkins, ___ N.C. App. ___, 703 S.E.2d 807, 810 (2010); and (8) the juvenile was found with a single rock of crack cocaine wrapped in cellophane and $271 in cash, *In re* I.R.T., 184 N.C. App. 579, 588–89 (2007).

Attempt or conspiracy. See this note to "Sale or Delivery of a Controlled Substance," above.

Charging issues. See this note to "Sale or Delivery of a Controlled Substance," above.

Evidence issues. See this note to "Sale or Delivery of a Controlled Substance," above.

Defenses. See this note to "Sale or Delivery of a Controlled Substance," above.

Greater and lesser-included offenses. As a general rule, possession of a controlled substance is a lesser-included offense of possession with intent to manufacture, sell, or deliver the same substance. *I.R.T.,* 184 N.C. App. at 589. However, possession of more than ½ ounce of marijuana (Class 1 misdemeanor) or 1½ ounces of marijuana (Class I felony) are not lesser-included offenses of possession with intent to manufacture, sell, or deliver, since these possession offenses (unlike simple misdemeanor possession, a Class 3 misdemeanor) require additional proof that the amount possessed was more than ½ ounce or 1½ ounces, as the case may be.

This same principle applies to other controlled substances when the classification of the possession offense depends on the amount of the substance possessed. However, if a criminal pleading charging possession with intent to manufacture, sell, or deliver alleges the amount possessed, the jury may be instructed on the offenses of felony and misdemeanor possession even though these offenses may not be lesser-included offenses. State v. Perry, 84 N.C. App. 309 (1987).

Possession with intent to manufacture, sell, or deliver is not a lesser-included offense of trafficking by possession. State v. McCain, ___ N.C. App. ___, 713 S.E.2d 21, 24–25 (2011) (the trial court erred by submitting to the jury the charge of possession with intent to manufacture cocaine because it is not a lesser-included offense of the charged crime of trafficking by possession of cocaine).

Multiple convictions and punishments. Based on the same controlled substance, a defendant may be convicted and punished for possession with intent to manufacture, sell, or deliver and:

- felony possession of marijuana, State v. Springs, 200 N.C. App. 288, 294–95 (2009) (explaining that felony possession of marijuana requires proof that the defendant possessed more than 1½ ounces of marijuana, an element not required for the crime of possession with intent); State v. Spencer, 192 N.C. App. 143, 149–50 (2008) (same);
- sale or delivery, State v. Stoner, 59 N.C. App. 656 (1982); State v. Dickerson, 152 N.C. App. 714 (2002); or
- trafficking by possession, State v. Doe, 190 N.C. App. 723, 732 (2008).

A verdict finding a defendant guilty of possession of a controlled substance with intent to sell or deliver was not fatally ambiguous since possession with intent to sell or deliver is only one offense. State v. Creason, 313 N.C. 122 (1985); State v. McLamb, 313 N.C. 572 (1985).

Related Offenses Not in This Chapter

Unlawful manufacture, sale, delivery, or possession of Salvia divinorum (or Salvinorin A). G.S. 14-401.23.

Possession of an Immediate Precursor with Intent to Manufacture a Controlled Substance

Statute

See G.S. 90-95(d1)(1)a. and (d2), reproduced above.

Elements

A person guilty of this offense

(1) knowingly
(2) possesses
(3) an immediate precursor chemical
(4) with intent to manufacture
(5) a controlled substance.

Punishment

Class H felony. G.S. 90-95(d1)(1). However, it is a Class F felony if the immediate precursor chemical is to be used to manufacture methamphetamine. G.S. 90-95(d1)(2). If the Class F felony version of this offense is charged, the relevant fact elevating punishment must be alleged in the charging instrument and proved at trial.

If the defendant is sentenced for less than the maximum term that could have been imposed, special probation may be imposed as specified in G.S. 90-95(f).

Notes

Element (1). See the note on Element (1) to "Sale or Delivery of a Controlled Substance," above.

Element (2). See the note on Element (2) to "Possession of a Controlled Substance," above.

Element (3). "Immediate precursor" is defined in G.S. 90-87(14) as a substance which the Commission for Mental Health, Developmental Disabilities, and Substance Abuse Services "has found to be and by regulation designates as being the principal compound commonly used or produced primarily for use, and which is an immediate chemical intermediary used or likely to be used in the manufacture of a controlled substance, the control of which is necessary to prevent, curtail, or limit such manufacture." In addition, G.S. 90-95(d2), reproduced above, lists specific chemicals as immediate precursor chemicals.

Element (4). See the note on Element (2) to "Manufacture of a Controlled Substance," above, for the definition of "manufacture."

Element (5). See the note on Element (3) to "Sale or Delivery of a Controlled Substance," above.

Attempt or conspiracy. See this note to "Sale or Delivery of a Controlled Substance," above.

Charging issues. See this note to "Sale or Delivery of a Controlled Substance," above.

Evidence issues. See this note to "Sale or Delivery of a Controlled Substance," above.

Defenses. See this note to "Sale or Delivery of a Controlled Substance," above.

Related Offenses Not in This Chapter

Unlawful for certain merchants to sell pseudoephedrine. G.S. 66-254.1.
Possessing or distributing an immediate precursor knowing it will be used to manufacture a controlled substance. G.S. 90-95(d1)(1)b.
Possessing or distributing an immediate precursor knowing it will be used to manufacture methamphetamine. G.S. 90-95(d1)(2)b.
Pseudoephedrine: restrictions on sales. G.S. 90-113.52.
Violation of recordkeeping and stop sale requirements for pseudoephedrine sales. G.S. 90-113.52A.
Pseudoephedrine transaction limits. G.S. 90-113.53.

Counterfeit Controlled Substance Offenses

Creating a Counterfeit Controlled Substance

Statute

See G.S. 90-95(a)(2), reproduced above.

Elements

A person guilty of this offense

(1) knowingly
(2) creates
(3) a counterfeit controlled substance.

Punishment

Class I felony. G.S. 90-95(c).

If the defendant is sentenced for less than the maximum term that could have been imposed, special probation may be imposed as specified in G.S. 90-95(f).

Notes

Element (1). See "Knowingly" in Chapter 1 (States of Mind).

The statute does not require that a defendant knowingly misrepresent a counterfeit controlled substance as an actual controlled substance. State v. Bivens, ___ N.C. App. ___, 693 S.E.2d 378, 382 (2010) (rejecting the defendant's argument that he was an unwitting middleman who believed that he was selling real crack cocaine and concluding that a defendant need not have specific knowledge that the substance is counterfeit to be found to have intentionally represented the substance as a controlled substance); State v. Mobley, ___ N.C. App. ___, 696 S.E.2d 862, 866–67 (2010) (citing *Bivens;* same).

Element (2). The term "create" is not defined by statute; according to WEBSTER'S COLLEGE DICTIONARY (Random House, 2d ed. 1997), the term means "to cause to come into being."

Element (3). G.S. 90-87(6) defines a counterfeit controlled substance as:

(1) a controlled substance, or the container or labeling of such substance, which, without authorization, bears the trademark, trade name, or other identifying mark, imprint, number, or device, or any likeness thereof, of a manufacturer, distributor, or dispenser other than the person or persons who in fact manufactured, distributed, or dispensed such substance and which thereby falsely purports to be the product of or to have been distributed by, or is represented to be the product of or to have been distributed by, such other manufacturer, distributor, or dispenser; or

(2) any substance which is by any means intentionally represented as a controlled substance.

The first category includes controlled substances that are labeled or otherwise marked to indicate that they are manufactured, distributed, or dispensed by someone (usually a company) other than the actual manufacturer, distributor, or dispenser.

The second category includes substances that are intentionally represented as a controlled substances even though they are not. This category applies, for example, when a person puts oregano into a plastic bag and asserts that it is marijuana or puts flour in tin foil and asserts that it is heroin. As to this category, the statute provides that it is evidence that the substance has been intentionally misrepresented as a controlled substance if the following factors are established:

- the substance was packaged or delivered in a manner normally used for the illegal delivery of controlled substances;
- money or other valuable property has been exchanged or requested for the substance and the amount of that consideration was substantially in excess of the reasonable value of the substance; or
- the physical appearance of the tablets, capsules, or other finished product containing the substance is substantially identical to a specified controlled substance.

G.S. 90-87(6)b. The State need not prove all of these factors to prove that the substance was intentionally misrepresented. *Bivens,* ___ N.C. App. ___, 693 S.E.2d at 381.

The evidence was sufficient to establish that the defendant represented the substance as a controlled substance when (1) the defendant approached a vehicle, asked its occupants what they were looking for, departed to fill their request for "a 20," and handed the occupants a little baggie containing a white rock-like substance that was calcium carbonate, *Bivens,* ___ N.C. App. ___, 693 S.E.2d 378; and (2) in response to an undercover officer's request for a "40" ($40 worth of crack cocaine), an accomplice produced a hard, white substance packaged in two small corner baggies, which the officers believed to be crack cocaine but which in fact was not crack cocaine, *Mobley*, ___ N.C. App. ___, 696 S.E.2d 862.

Attempt or conspiracy. See this note to "Sale or Delivery of a Controlled Substance," above.

Charging issues. See this note to "Sale or Delivery of a Controlled Substance," above.

Evidence issues. See this note to "Sale or Delivery of a Controlled Substance," above.

Related Offenses Not in This Chapter

"Obtaining Property by False Pretenses" (Chapter 16)

Sale or Delivery of a Counterfeit Controlled Substance

Statute

See G.S. 90-95(a)(2), reproduced above.

Elements

A person guilty of this offense

(1) knowingly
(2) (a) sells *or*
    (b) delivers
(3) a counterfeit controlled substance
(4) to another person.

Punishment

Class I felony. G.S. 90-95(c).

If the defendant is sentenced for less than the maximum term that could have been imposed, special probation may be imposed as specified in G.S. 90-95(f).

Notes

Element (1). See the note on Element (1) to "Creating a Counterfeit Controlled Substance," above.

Elements (2)(a) and (b). See the notes on Elements (2)(a) and (b) to "Sale or Delivery of a Controlled Substance," above.

Element (3). See the note on Element (3) to "Creating a Counterfeit Controlled Substance," above.

Attempt or conspiracy. See this note to "Sale or Delivery of a Controlled Substance," above.

Charging issues. See this note to "Sale or Delivery of a Controlled Substance," above.

Evidence issues. See this note to "Sale or Delivery of a Controlled Substance," above.

Related Offenses Not in This Chapter

"Obtaining Property by False Pretenses" (Chapter 16)

Possession of a Counterfeit Controlled Substance with Intent to Sell or Deliver

Statute

See G.S. 90-95(a)(2), reproduced above.

Elements

A person guilty of this offense

(1) knowingly
(2) possesses
(3) a counterfeit controlled substance
(4) with the intent to sell or deliver it.

Punishment

Class I felony. G.S. 90-95(c).

If the defendant is sentenced for less than the maximum term that could have been imposed, special probation may be imposed as specified in G.S. 90-95(f).

Notes

Element (1). See the note on Element (1) to "Creating a Counterfeit Controlled Substance," above.

Element (2). See the note on Element (2) to "Possession of a Controlled Substance," above.

Element (3). See the note on Element (3) to "Creating a Counterfeit Controlled Substance," above.

Element (4). See the note on Element (4) to "Possession of a Controlled Substance with Intent to Manufacture, Sell, or Deliver," above.

Attempt or conspiracy. See this note to "Sale or Delivery of a Controlled Substance," above.

Charging issues. See this note to "Sale or Delivery of a Controlled Substance," above.

Evidence issues. See this note to "Sale or Delivery of a Controlled Substance," above.

Related Offenses Not in This Chapter

"Obtaining Property by False Pretenses" (Chapter 16)

Drug Offenses Involving Minors

Sale or Delivery of a Controlled Substance to a Person under 16

Statute

See G.S. 90-95(e)(5), reproduced above.

Elements

A person guilty of this offense

(1) is 18 years old or older *and*
(2) knowingly
(3) (a) sells *or*
    (b) delivers

(4) a controlled substance to
(5) a person who is under age 16 but over age 13.

Punishment

Class D felony. G.S. 90-95(e)(5).

If the defendant is sentenced for less than the maximum term that could have been imposed, special probation may be imposed as specified in G.S. 90-95(f).

Notes

Generally. This offense is exactly the same as "Sale or Delivery of a Controlled Substance," above, except that for this offense, there are age requirements for both the defendant and the buyer or recipient of the controlled substance and this offense carries a more severe punishment. Thus, the notes to "Sale or Delivery of a Controlled Substance" apply here as well.

Defenses. The statute provides that mistake of age is not a defense to this offense. G.S. 90-95(e)(5).

Related Offenses Not in This Chapter

"Contributing to a Juvenile's Being Delinquent, Undisciplined, Abused, or Neglected" (Chapter 9)

Sale or Delivery of a Controlled Substance to a Person under 13

Statute

See G.S. 90-95(e)(5), reproduced above.

Elements

A person guilty of this offense

(1) is 18 years old or older *and*
(2) knowingly
(3) (a) sells *or*
    (b) delivers
(4) a controlled substance to
(5) a person 13 years old or younger.

Punishment

Class C felony. G.S. 90-95(e)(5).

If the defendant is sentenced for less than the maximum term that could have been imposed, special probation may be imposed as specified in G.S. 90-95(f).

Notes

Generally. This offense is the same as "Sale or Delivery of a Controlled Substance to a Person under 16," immediately above, except that for this offense, the victim must be 13 years old or younger. Thus, the notes to that other offense apply equally here.

Related Offenses Not in This Chapter

"Contributing to a Juvenile's Being Delinquent, Undisciplined, Abused, or Neglected" (Chapter 9)

Employing or Intentionally Using a Minor to Commit a Controlled Substance Offense

Statute

§90-95.4. Employing or intentionally using minor to commit a drug law violation.

(a) A person who is at least 18 years old but less than 21 years old who hires or intentionally uses a minor to violate G.S. 90-95(a)(1) shall be guilty of a felony. An offense under this subsection shall be punishable as follows:

(1) If the minor was more than 13 years of age, then as a felony that is one class more severe than the violation of G.S. 90-95(a)(1) for which the minor was hired or intentionally used.

(2) If the minor was 13 years of age or younger, then as a felony that is two classes more severe than the violation of G.S. 90-95(a)(1) for which the minor was hired or intentionally used.

(b) A person 21 years of age or older who hires or intentionally uses a minor to violate G.S. 90-95(a)(1) shall be guilty of a felony. An offense under this subsection shall be punishable as follows:

(1) If the minor was more than 13 years of age, then as a felony that is three classes more severe than the violation of G.S. 90-95(a)(1) for which the minor was hired or intentionally used.

(2) If the minor was 13 years of age or younger, then as a felony that is four classes more severe than the violation of G.S. 90-95(a)(1) for which the minor was hired or intentionally used.

(c) Mistake of Age.—Mistake of age is not a defense to a prosecution under this section.

(d) The term "minor" as used in this section is defined as an individual who is less than 18 years of age.

Elements

A person guilty of this offense

(1) (a) is 21 years old or older *or*
(b) is at least 18 but less than 21 years old *and*
(2) (a) hires *or*
(b) intentionally uses
(3) (a) a minor who is more than 13 years old *or*
(b) a minor who is 13 years old or younger
(4) to violate G.S. 90-95(a)(1) by
(a) selling or delivering a controlled substance,
(b) manufacturing a controlled substance, *or*
(c) possessing a controlled substance with the intent to manufacture, sell, or deliver.

Punishment

For an offense including Elements (1)(a) and (3)(a), the punishment is three classes more severe than the violation of G.S. 90-95(a)(1) for which the minor was hired or intentionally used. For example, a Class H felony becomes a Class E felony. G.S. 90-95.4(b)(1).

For an offense including Elements (1)(a) and (3)(b), the punishment is four classes more severe than the violation of G.S. 90-95(a)(1) for which the minor was hired or intentionally used. For example, a Class H felony becomes a Class D felony. G.S. 90-95.4(b)(2).

For an offense including Elements (1)(b) and (3)(a), the punishment is one class more severe than the violation of G.S. 90-95(a)(1) for which the minor was hired or intentionally used. For example, a Class H felony becomes a Class G felony. G.S. 90-95.4(a)(1).

For an offense including Elements (1)(b) and (3)(b), the punishment is two classes more severe than the violation of G.S. 90-95(a)(1) for which the minor was hired or intentionally used. For example, a Class H felony becomes a Class F felony. G.S. 90-95.4(a)(2).

If the defendant is sentenced for less than the maximum term that could have been imposed, special probation may be imposed as specified in G.S. 90-95(f).

Notes

Element (2)(a). The term "hires" means pays someone to do something; the payment can be in the form of money or other things of value.

Element (2)(b). The term "intentionally uses" would not require payment.

Element (3). A "minor" is a person under 18 years old. G.S. 90-95.4(d).

Element (4)(a). See "Sale or Delivery of a Controlled Substance, above.

Element (4)(b). See "Manufacture of a Controlled Substance," above.

Element (4)(c). See "Possession of a Controlled Substance with Intent to Manufacture, Sell, or Deliver," above.

Attempt or conspiracy. See this note to "Sale or Delivery of a Controlled Substance," above.

Charging issues. See this note to "Sale or Delivery of a Controlled Substance," above.

Evidence issues. See this note to "Sale or Delivery of a Controlled Substance," above.

Defenses. Mistake of age is not a defense to this crime. G.S. 90-95.4(c). See this note to "Sale or Delivery of a Controlled Substance," above.

Related Offenses Not in This Chapter

"Contributing to a Juvenile's Being Delinquent, Undisciplined, Abused, or Neglected" (Chapter 9)

Promoting Drug Sales by a Minor

Statute

§90-95.6. Promoting drug sales by a minor.

(a) A person who is 21 years of age or older is guilty of promoting drug sales by a minor if the person knowingly:

(1) Entices, forces, encourages, or otherwisé facilitates a minor in violating G.S. 90-95(a)(1).

(2) Supervises, supports, advises, or protects the minor in violating G.S. 90-95(a)(1).

(b) Mistake of age is not a defense to a prosecution under this section.

(c) A violation of this section is a Class D felony.

Elements

A person guilty of this offense

(1) is 21 years old or older *and*
(2) knowingly
(3) entices, forces, encourages, or otherwise facilitates
(4) a minor
(5) in violating G.S. 90-95(a)(1) by
  (a) selling or delivering a controlled substance,
  (b) manufacturing a controlled substance, *or*
  (c) possessing a controlled substance with the intent to manufacture, sell, or deliver *and*
(6) supervises, supports, advises, or protects
(7) the minor
(8) in violating G.S. 90-95(a)(1) by
  (a) selling or delivering a controlled substance,

(b) manufacturing a controlled substance, *or*
(c) possessing a controlled substance with the intent to manufacture, sell, deliver.

Punishment

Class D felony. G.S. 90-95.6(c).

If the defendant is sentenced for less than the maximum term that could have been imposed, special probation may be imposed as specified in G.S. 90-95(f).

Notes

Element (2). See "Knowingly" in Chapter 1 (States of Mind).

Elements (3) through (8). Because the statute does not include the word "and" or "or" between subdivision (a)(1) (requiring that a person entice, force, encourage, or otherwise facilitate a minor in violating G.S. 90-95(a)(1)—Elements (3) through (5) above) and subdivision (a)(2) (requiring that the person supervise, support, advise, or protect the minor in violating G.S. 90-95(a)(1)—Elements (6) through (8) above), it is not clear whether the State must prove both subdivisions or whether a conviction can be based on proof of only one subdivision. On the one hand, if proof of only one subdivision was required, the listed acts (enticing, supervising, and so on) could have been set out in a single clause. Further, subdivision (a)(1) refers to "a" minor and subdivision (a)(2) refers to "the" minor, suggesting that a defendant must enlist a minor's assistance and then oversee that minor's activities. Finally, the punishment for this offense is potentially greater than the punishment for "Employing or Intentionally Using a Minor to Commit a Controlled Substance Offense" under G.S. 90-95.4, discussed earlier in this chapter, suggesting that more is required for conviction than the acts listed in subdivision (a)(1) alone. On the other hand, the North Carolina Pattern Jury Commission appears to have concluded that proof of either subdivision will suffice to sustain a conviction. N.C. PATTERN JURY INSTRUCTION—CRIM. 260.41. Additionally, no "and" or "or" separates the provisions of G.S. 90-95(a)(1) through (3), and these provisions are recognized as creating separate offenses. This book lists both subdivisions as elements because that seemed to be the most conservative approach, but the issue is an open one.

Element (4). Because the statute does not specify the minor's age, the general definition of "minor" in G.S. 48A-2 (a person under 18 years of age) probably applies to this offense. See G.S. 90-95.4 (so defining a minor for the offense set out in that section).

Elements (5) and (8). See "Sale or Delivery of a Controlled Substance," "Manufacture of a Controlled Substance," and "Possession of a Controlled Substance with Intent to Manufacture, Sell, or Deliver," all above.

Attempt or conspiracy. See this note to "Sale or Delivery of a Controlled Substance," above.

Charging issues. See this note to "Sale or Delivery of a Controlled Substance," above.

Evidence issues. See this note to "Sale or Delivery of a Controlled Substance," above.

Defenses. Mistake of age is not a defense to this offense. G.S. 90-95.6(b). See this note to "Sale or Delivery of a Controlled Substance," above.

Related Offenses Not in This Chapter

"Contributing to a Juvenile's Being Delinquent, Undisciplined, Abused, or Neglected" (Chapter 9)

Participating in Drug Violations by a Minor

Statute

§90-95.7. Participating in a drug violation by a minor.

(a) A person 21 years of age or older who purchases or receives a controlled substance from a minor 13 years of age or younger who possesses, sells, or delivers the controlled substance in violation of G.S. 90-95(a)(1) is guilty of participating in a drug violation of a minor.

(b) Mistake of age is not a defense to a prosecution under this section.

(c) A violation of this section is a Class G felony.

Elements

A person guilty of this offense

(1) is 21 years old or older *and*
(2) purchases or receives
(3) a controlled substance
(4) from a minor 13 years old or younger
(5) who sells, delivers, or possesses the controlled substance with intent to manufacture, sell, or deliver the controlled substance in violation of G.S. 90-95(a)(1).

Punishment

Class G felony. G.S. 90-95.7(c).

If the defendant is sentenced for less than the maximum term that could have been imposed, special probation may be imposed as specified in G.S. 90-95(f).

Notes

Element (5). Although the statute uses the word "possesses," its linkage to a violation of G.S. 90-95(a)(1) requires that the defendant possess the controlled substance with the intent to sell, deliver, or manufacture. Of course, if the person who is 21 years old or older purchases or receives the controlled substance from the minor, the minor always will have possessed the controlled substance with the intent to sell or deliver.

Attempt or conspiracy. See this note to "Sale or Delivery of a Controlled Substance," above.

Charging issues. See this note to "Sale or Delivery of a Controlled Substance," above.

Evidence issues. See this note to "Sale or Delivery of a Controlled Substance," above.

Defenses. Mistake of age is no defense to this crime. G.S. 90-95.7(b). See this note to "Sale or Delivery of a Controlled Substance," above.

Related Offenses Not in This Chapter

"Contributing to a Juvenile's Being Delinquent, Undisciplined, Abused, or Neglected" (Chapter 9)

Manufacture, Sale, Delivery, or Possession of a Controlled Substance with Intent to Manufacture, Sell, or Deliver at or Near a School, Child Care Center, or Public Park

Statute

See G.S. 90-95(e)(8) and (10), reproduced above.

Elements

A person guilty of this offense

(1) is 21 years old or older *and*

(2) knowingly
(3) (a) manufactures,
    (b) sells or delivers, *or*
    (c) possesses with intent to manufacture, sell, or deliver
(4) a controlled substance
(5) on property used for, or within 1,000 feet of the boundary of real property used for,
    (a) an elementary or secondary school,
    (b) a child care center, *or*
    (c) a public park.

Punishment

Class E felony. G.S. 90-95(e)(8) and (10).

If the defendant is sentenced for less than the maximum term that could have been imposed, special probation may be imposed as specified in G.S. 90-95(f).

Notes

Element (2). See the note on Element (1) to "Sale or Delivery of a Controlled Substance," above.

Element (3)(a). See the note on Element (2) to "Manufacture of a Controlled Substance," above.

Element (3)(b). See the notes on Elements (2)(a) and (b) to "Sale or Delivery of a Controlled Substance," above. The statute provides that the transfer of less than 5 grams of marijuana for no remuneration does not constitute a delivery. G.S. 90-95(e)(8); (e)(10). Note that G.S. 90-95(b)(2) was amended to provide that the transfer of less than 2.5 grams of synthetic cannabinoid or any mixture containing such a substance for no remuneration shall not constitute a delivery in violation of G.S. 90-95(a)(1). However, no parallel amendment was made to G.S. 90-95(e)(8) and (10), and thus transfers of 2.5 grams of synthetic cannabinoid or any mixture containing such a substance for no remuneration are not excluded from the coverage of the term "delivery" for purposes of this offense.

Element (3)(c). See the notes on Element (2) to "Possession of a Controlled Substance" and Element (4) to "Possession of a Controlled Substance with Intent to Manufacture, Sell, or Deliver," both above.

Element (4). See the note on Element (3) to "Sale or Delivery of a Controlled Substance," above.

Element (5). Evidence was sufficient to prove that the distance was within the requisite range (then 300 feet), based on the testimony of school employees. State v. Alston, 111 N.C. App. 416 (1993); State v. Ussery, 106 N.C. App. 371 (1992).

Element (5)(a). This statute includes both private and public elementary and secondary schools, kindergarten through twelfth grade. The drug transaction likely does not have to involve school students or personnel.

Element (5)(b). The term "child care center" is a facility defined in G.S. 110-86(3)a and licensed by the Secretary of the Department of Health and Human Services. G.S. 90-95(e)(8).

Attempt or conspiracy. See this note to "Sale or Delivery of a Controlled Substance," above.

Charging issues. See this note to "Sale or Delivery of a Controlled Substance," above.

Evidence issues. See this note to "Sale or Delivery of a Controlled Substance," above.

Defenses. See this note to "Sale or Delivery of a Controlled Substance," above.

Related Offenses Not in This Chapter

None

Trafficking

Statute

§90-95. Violations; penalties

Subsections (a) through (g1) are not reproduced here but are reproduced above.

(h) Notwithstanding any other provision of law, the following provisions apply except as otherwise provided in this Article.

(1) Any person who sells, manufactures, delivers, transports, or possesses in excess of 10 pounds (avoirdupois) of marijuana shall be guilty of a felony which felony shall be known as "trafficking in marijuana" and if the quantity of such substance involved:

a. Is in excess of 10 pounds, but less than 50 pounds, such person shall be punished as a Class H felon and shall be sentenced to a minimum term of 25 months and a maximum term of 30 months in the State's prison and shall be fined not less than five thousand dollars ($5,000);

b. Is 50 pounds or more, but less than 2,000 pounds, such person shall be punished as a Class G felon and shall be sentenced to a minimum term of 35 months and a maximum term of 42 months in the State's prison and shall be fined not less than twenty-five thousand dollars ($25,000);

c. Is 2,000 pounds or more, but less than 10,000 pounds, such person shall be punished as a Class F felon and shall be sentenced to a minimum term of 70 months and a maximum term of 84 months in the State's prison and shall be fined not less than fifty thousand dollars ($50,000);

d. Is 10,000 pounds or more, such person shall be punished as a Class D felon and shall be sentenced to a minimum term of 175 months and a maximum term of 219 months in the State's prison and shall be fined not less than two hundred thousand dollars ($200,000).

(1a) For the purpose of this subsection, a "dosage unit" shall consist of 3 grams of synthetic cannabinoid or any mixture containing such substance. Any person who sells, manufactures, delivers, transports, or possesses in excess of 50 dosage units of a synthetic cannabinoid or any mixture containing such substance, shall be guilty of a felony, which felony shall be known as "trafficking in synthetic cannabinoids," and if the quantity of such substance involved:

a. Is in excess of 50 dosage units, but less than 250 dosage units, such person shall be punished as a Class H felon and shall be sentenced to a minimum term of 25 months and a maximum term of 30 months in the State's prison and shall be fined not less than five thousand dollars ($5,000);

b. Is 250 dosage units or more, but less than 1250 dosage units, such person shall be punished as a Class G felon and shall be sentenced to a minimum term of 35 months and a maximum term of 42 months in the State's prison and shall be fined not less than twenty-five thousand dollars ($25,000);

c. Is 1250 dosage units or more, but less than 3750 dosage units, such person shall be punished as a Class F felon and shall be sentenced to a minimum term of 70 months and a maximum term of 84 months in the State's prison and shall be fined not less than fifty thousand dollars ($50,000);

d. Is 3750 dosage units or more, such person shall be punished as a Class D felon and shall be sentenced to a minimum term of 175 months and a maximum term of 219 months in the State's prison and shall be fined not less than two hundred thousand dollars ($200,000).

(2) Any person who sells, manufactures, delivers, transports, or possesses 1,000 tablets, capsules or other dosage units, or the equivalent quantity, or more of methaqualone, or any mixture containing such substance, shall be guilty of a felony which felony shall be known as "trafficking in methaqualone" and if the quantity of such substance or mixture involved:
 a. Is 1,000 or more dosage units, or equivalent quantity, but less than 5,000 dosage units, or equivalent quantity, such person shall be punished as a Class G felon and shall be sentenced to a minimum term of 35 months and a maximum term of 42 months in the State's prison and shall be fined not less than twenty-five thousand dollars ($25,000);
 b. Is 5,000 or more dosage units, or equivalent quantity, but less than 10,000 dosage units, or equivalent quantity, such person shall be punished as a Class F felon and shall be sentenced to a minimum term of 70 months and a maximum term of 84 months in the State's prison and shall be fined not less than fifty thousand dollars ($50,000);
 c. Is 10,000 or more dosage units, or equivalent quantity, such person shall be punished as a Class D felon and shall be sentenced to a minimum term of 175 months and a maximum term of 219 months in the State's prison and shall be fined not less than two hundred thousand dollars ($200,000).

(3) Any person who sells, manufactures, delivers, transports, or possesses 28 grams or more of cocaine and any salt, isomer, salts of isomers, compound, derivative, or preparation thereof, or any coca leaves and any salt, isomer, salts of isomers, compound, derivative, or preparation of coca leaves, and any salt, isomer, salts of isomers, compound, derivative or preparation thereof which is chemically equivalent or identical with any of these substances (except decocainized coca leaves or any extraction of coca leaves which does not contain cocaine) or any mixture containing such substances, shall be guilty of a felony, which felony shall be known as "trafficking in cocaine" and if the quantity of such substance or mixture involved:
 a. Is 28 grams or more, but less than 200 grams, such person shall be punished as a Class G felon and shall be sentenced to a minimum term of 35 months and a maximum term of 42 months in the State's prison and shall be fined not less than fifty thousand dollars ($50,000);
 b. Is 200 grams or more, but less than 400 grams, such person shall be punished as a Class F felon and shall be sentenced to a minimum term of 70 months and a maximum term of 84 months in the State's prison and shall be fined not less than one hundred thousand dollars ($100,000);
 c. Is 400 grams or more, such person shall be punished as a Class D felon and shall be sentenced to a minimum term of 175 months and a maximum term of 219 months in the State's prison and shall be fined at least two hundred fifty thousand dollars ($250,000).

(3a) Repealed by Session Laws 1999-370, s. 1, effective December 1, 1999.

(3b) Any person who sells, manufactures, delivers, transports, or possesses 28 grams or more of methamphetamine or any mixture containing such substance shall be guilty of a felony which felony shall be known as "trafficking in methamphetamine" and if the quantity of such substance or mixture involved:
 a. Is 28 grams or more, but less than 200 grams, such person shall be punished as a Class F felon and shall be sentenced to a minimum term of 70 months and a maximum term of 84 months in the State's prison and shall be fined not less than fifty thousand dollars ($50,000);
 b. Is 200 grams or more, but less than 400 grams, such person shall be punished as a Class E felon and shall be sentenced to a minimum term of 90 months and a maximum term of 117 months in the State's

prison and shall be fined not less than one hundred thousand dollars ($100,000);

c. Is 400 grams or more, such person shall be punished as a Class C felon and shall be sentenced to a minimum term of 225 months and a maximum term of 279 months in the State's prison and shall be fined at least two hundred fifty thousand dollars ($250,000).

(3c) Any person who sells, manufactures, delivers, transports, or possesses 28 grams or more of amphetamine or any mixture containing such substance shall be guilty of a felony, which felony shall be known as "trafficking in amphetamine", and if the quantity of such substance or mixture involved:

a. Is 28 grams or more, but less than 200 grams, such person shall be punished as a Class H felon and shall be sentenced to a minimum term of 25 months and a maximum term of 30 months in the State's prison and shall be fined not less than five thousand dollars ($5,000);

b. Is 200 grams or more, but less than 400 grams, such person shall be punished as a Class G felon and shall be sentenced to a minimum term of 35 months and a maximum term of 42 months in the State's prison and shall be fined not less than twenty-five thousand dollars ($25,000);

c. Is 400 grams or more, such person shall be punished as a Class E felon and shall be sentenced to a minimum term of 90 months and a maximum term of 117 months in the State's prison and shall be fined at least one hundred thousand dollars ($100,000).

(3d) Any person who sells, manufactures, delivers, transports, or possesses 28 grams or more of MDPV or any mixture containing such substance shall be guilty of a felony, which felony shall be known as "trafficking in MDPV," and if the quantity of such substance or mixture involved:

a. Is 28 grams or more, but less than 200 grams, such person shall be punished as a Class F felon and shall be sentenced to a minimum term of 70 months and a maximum term of 84 months in the State's prison and shall be fined not less than fifty thousand dollars ($50,000);

b. Is 200 grams or more, but less than 400 grams, such person shall be punished as a Class E felon and shall be sentenced to a minimum term of 90 months and a maximum term of 117 months in the State's prison and shall be fined not less than one hundred thousand dollars ($100,000);

c. Is 400 grams or more, such person shall be punished as a Class C felon and shall be sentenced to a minimum term of 225 months and a maximum term of 279 months in the State's prison and shall be fined at least two hundred fifty thousand dollars ($250,000).

(3e) Any person who sells, manufactures, delivers, transports, or possesses 28 grams or more of mephedrone or any mixture containing such substance shall be guilty of a felony, which felony shall be known as "trafficking in mephedrone," and if the quantity of such substance or mixture involved:

a. Is 28 grams or more, but less than 200 grams, such person shall be punished as a Class F felon and shall be sentenced to a minimum term of 70 months and a maximum term of 84 months in the State's prison and shall be fined not less than fifty thousand dollars ($50,000);

b. Is 200 grams or more, but less than 400 grams, such person shall be punished as a Class E felon and shall be sentenced to a minimum term of 90 months and a maximum term of 117 months in the State's prison and shall be fined not less than one hundred thousand dollars ($100,000);

c. Is 400 grams or more, such person shall be punished as a Class C felon and shall be sentenced to a minimum term of 225 months and a maximum term of 279 months in the State's prison and shall be fined at least two hundred fifty thousand dollars ($250,000).

(4) Any person who sells, manufactures, delivers, transports, or possesses four grams or more of opium or opiate, or any salt, compound, derivative, or preparation of opium or opiate (except apomorphine, nalbuphine, analoxone and naltrexone and their respective salts), including heroin, or any mixture containing such substance, shall be guilty of a felony which felony shall be known as "trafficking in opium or heroin" and if the quantity of such controlled substance or mixture involved:
   a. Is four grams or more, but less than 14 grams, such person shall be punished as a Class F felon and shall be sentenced to a minimum term of 70 months and a maximum term of 84 months in the State's prison and shall be fined not less than fifty thousand dollars ($50,000);
   b. Is 14 grams or more, but less than 28 grams, such person shall be punished as a Class E felon and shall be sentenced to a minimum term of 90 months and a maximum term of 117 months in the State's prison and shall be fined not less than one hundred thousand dollars ($100,000);
   c. Is 28 grams or more, such person shall be punished as a Class C felon and shall be sentenced to a minimum term of 225 months and a maximum term of 279 months in the State's prison and shall be fined not less than five hundred thousand dollars ($500,000).

(4a) Any person who sells, manufactures, delivers, transports, or possesses 100 tablets, capsules, or other dosage units, or the equivalent quantity, or more, of Lysergic Acid Diethylamide, or any mixture containing such substance, shall be guilty of a felony, which felony shall be known as "trafficking in Lysergic Acid Diethylamide". If the quantity of such substance or mixture involved:
   a. Is 100 or more dosage units, or equivalent quantity, but less than 500 dosage units, or equivalent quantity, such person shall be punished as a Class G felon and shall be sentenced to a minimum term of 35 months and a maximum term of 42 months in the State's prison and shall be fined not less than twenty-five thousand dollars ($25,000);
   b. Is 500 or more dosage units, or equivalent quantity, but less than 1,000 dosage units, or equivalent quantity, such person shall be punished as a Class F felon and shall be sentenced to a minimum term of 70 months and a maximum term of 84 months in the State's prison and shall be fined not less than fifty thousand dollars ($50,000);
   c. Is 1,000 or more dosage units, or equivalent quantity, such person shall be punished as a Class D felon and shall be sentenced to a minimum term of 175 months and a maximum term of 219 months in the State's prison and shall be fined not less than two hundred thousand dollars ($200,000).

(4b) Any person who sells, manufactures, delivers, transports, or possesses 100 or more tablets, capsules, or other dosage units, or 28 grams or more of 3,4-methylenedioxyamphetamine (MDA), including its salts, isomers, and salts of isomers, or 3,4-methylenedioxymethamphetamine (MDMA), including its salts, isomers, and salts of isomers, or any mixture containing such substances, shall be guilty of a felony, which felony shall be known as "trafficking in MDADMA." If the quantity of the substance or mixture involved:
   a. Is 100 or more tablets, capsules, or other dosage units, but less than 500 tablets, capsules, or other dosage units, or 28 grams or more, but less than 200 grams, the person shall be punished as a Class G felon and shall be sentenced to a minimum term of 35 months and a maximum term of 42 months in the State's prison and shall be fined not less than twenty-five thousand dollars ($25,000);
   b. Is 500 or more tablets, capsules, or other dosage units, but less than 1,000 tablets, capsules, or other dosage units, or 200 grams or more, but less than 400 grams, the person shall be punished as a Class F felon

and shall be sentenced to a minimum term of 70 months and a maximum term of 84 months in the State's prison and shall be fined not less than fifty thousand dollars ($50,000);

c. Is 1,000 or more tablets, capsules, or other dosage units, or 400 grams or more, the person shall be punished as a Class D felon and shall be sentenced to a minimum term of 175 months and a maximum term of 219 months in the State's prison and shall be fined not less than two hundred fifty thousand dollars ($250,000).

(5) Except as provided in this subdivision, a person being sentenced under this subsection may not receive a suspended sentence or be placed on probation. The sentencing judge may reduce the fine, or impose a prison term less than the applicable minimum prison term provided by this subsection, or suspend the prison term imposed and place a person on probation when such person has, to the best of his knowledge, provided substantial assistance in the identification, arrest, or conviction of any accomplices, accessories, co-conspirators, or principals if the sentencing judge enters in the record a finding that the person to be sentenced has rendered such substantial assistance.

(6) Sentences imposed pursuant to this subsection shall run consecutively with and shall commence at the expiration of any sentence being served by the person sentenced hereunder.

(i) The penalties provided in subsection (h) of this section shall also apply to any person who is convicted of conspiracy to commit any of the offenses described in subsection (h) of this section.

Trafficking in Marijuana

Statute

See G.S. 90-95(h)(1) and (i), reproduced above.

Elements

A person guilty of this offense

(1) knowingly
(2) (a) manufactures, sells, delivers, transports, or possesses *or*
    (b) conspires to manufacture, sell, deliver, transport, or possess
(3) marijuana
(4) to another person (if the person sells or delivers), *and*
(5) the quantity of marijuana is
    (a) in excess of 10 pounds but less than 50 pounds,
    (b) 50 pounds or more but less than 2,000 pounds,
    (c) 2,000 pounds or more but less than 10,000 pounds, *or*
    (d) 10,000 pounds or more.

Punishment

For the amount in Element (5)(a), the crime is a Class H felony punishable by a mandatory minimum imprisonment of 25 months, a mandatory maximum imprisonment of 30 months, and a mandatory minimum fine of $5,000. G.S. 90-95(h)(1)a. For the amount in Element (5)(b), the crime is a Class G felony punishable by a mandatory minimum imprisonment of 35 months, a mandatory maximum imprisonment of 42 months, and a mandatory minimum fine of $25,000. *Id.* at (h)(1)b. For the amount in Element (5)(c), the crime is a Class F felony punishable by a mandatory minimum imprisonment of 70 months, a mandatory maximum imprisonment of 84 months, and a mandatory minimum fine of $50,000. *Id.* at (h)(1)c. For the amount in Element (5)(d), the crime is a Class D felony punishable by a mandatory minimum imprisonment of 175 months, a mandatory maximum imprisonment of 219 months, and a mandatory minimum fine of $200,000. *Id.* at (h)(1)d. Sentences must run consecutively to any sentence being served at the time of sentencing. G.S. 90-95(h)(6). However, G.S. 90-95(h) does not require consecutive sentences for offenses disposed of in the same sentencing hearing. State v. Walston, 193 N.C. App. 134, 141–42 (2008).

The punishment for this offense under Structured Sentencing is exactly as set out above and is not affected by a defendant's prior record level or aggravating and mitigating factors. However, a sentencing judge may impose a lesser sentence under G.S. 90-95(h)(5) if the defendant has provided substantial assistance in the identification, arrest, or conviction of any accomplices, accessories, co-conspirators, or principals involved in controlled substances offenses. *See generally* State v. Wells, 104 N.C. App. 274 (1991).

Notes

Element (1). See the note on Element (1) to "Sale or Delivery of a Controlled Substance," above. The offense of trafficking by possession includes an element of knowing possession. State v. Robledo, 193 N.C. App. 521, 525 (2008); State v. Doe, 190 N.C. App. 723, 730 (2008). Knowing possession may be established by evidence that (1) the defendant had actual possession, (2) the defendant had constructive possession, or (3) the defendant acted in concert with another to commit the crime. *Robledo,* 193 N.C. App. at 525–26 (sufficient evidence of knowing possession).

In a trafficking case, the State needs to prove only that the defendant knowingly sold, manufactured, delivered, transported, or possessed the controlled substance; the State need not prove that the defendant knowingly sold, manufactured, delivered, transported, or possessed a specific amount or weight of the controlled substance. State v. Shelman, 159 N.C. App. 300 (2003); State v. Cardenas, 169 N.C. App. 404 (2005).

Element (2)(a). For a discussion of the term "manufacture," see the note on Element (2) to "Manufacture of a Controlled Substance," above. There was sufficient evidence of trafficking in marijuana by manufacture when police found a large plastic trash bag containing 1,000 to 2,000 plastic "dime bags" near marijuana in the garage of the defendants' house and found a scale and a vacuum sealer in the kitchen. State v. Harrington, 171 N.C. App. 17 (2005).

For a discussion of the term "possesses," see the note on Element (2) to "Possession of a Controlled Substance," above.

For a discussion of the terms "sells" and "delivers," see the notes on Elements (2)(a) and (b) to "Sale or Delivery of a Controlled Substance," above.

"Transportation" means the "real carrying about or movement from one place to another." *See Harrington,* 171 N.C. App. 17; State v. Carmon, 156 N.C. App. 235 (2003). This element is satisfied if there is evidence that the defendant moved the controlled substance just a short distance. State v. Sares, 182 N.C. App. 762, 764 (2007). There was sufficient evidence of transportation when (1) although the defendant argued that there was no evidence that he personally transported the marijuana because someone else drove the vehicle in question, which the defendant did not own, the court relied on the fact that the defendant supplied the marijuana that was in the vehicle and did not contest that he had possession of the marijuana at the time, *Sares,* 182 N.C. App. 762, 764; (2) a witness testified that he and the defendant drove to the location where the drug transaction was to occur with cocaine in the vehicle, State v. Doe, 190 N.C. App. 723, 730–31 (2008); (3) the defendant removed drugs from a dwelling and brought them to an undercover agent in a car, State v. McRae, 110 N.C. App. 643 (1993); (4) when officers surrounded a house, the defendant zipped up a bag containing cocaine and tossed it in the yard next door, State v. Greenidge, 102 N.C. App. 447 (1991); (5) the defendant carried cocaine from his house to his truck, which was in his driveway, and began to back out of the driveway, State v. Outlaw, 96 N.C. App. 192 (1989); (6) the defendant threw a package of cocaine from a car into some bushes to avoid being caught by law enforcement officers and so that he could retrieve the cocaine later, State v. Wilder, 124 N.C. App. 136 (1996); and (7) the defendant ran away from officers while possessing cocaine, State v. Manning, 139 N.C. App. 454 (2000). By contrast, there was insufficient evidence of transportation in the following cases: (1) recognizing that the State may prove this element by demonstrating that a defendant acted in concert with another person to move the controlled substances from one place to another, the court held that such a theory could not apply when there was no evidence that the defendant was actually or constructively present when the drugs were transported, State v. Zamora-Ramos, 190 N.C. App. 420, 425–26 (2008); (2) the defendants stored marijuana in a house and used an apartment for distribution but no evidence showed that they actively moved or carried the marijuana, State v. Harrington, 171 N.C. App. 17 (2005); and (3) drugs were found in a vehicle that remained stationary during the course of the law enforcement operation and there was no evidence as to when or how the drugs were placed in the vehicle, State v. Williams, 177 N.C. App. 725 (2006).

Element (2)(b). See "Conspiracy" in Chapter 5 (General Crimes).

Element (3). "Marijuana" is defined in G.S. 90-87(16) to mean "all parts of the plant of the genus Cannabis, whether growing or not; the seeds thereof; the resin extracted from any part of such plant; and every compound, manufacture, salt, derivative, mixture, or preparation of such plant, its seeds or resin, but shall not include the mature stalks of such plant, fiber produced from such stalks, oil, or cake made from the seeds of such plant, any other compound, manufacture, salt, derivative, mixture, or preparation of such mature stalks (except the resin extracted therefrom), fiber, oil, or cake, or the sterilized seed of such plant which is incapable of germination."

Element (4). See the note on Element (4) to "Sale or Delivery of a Controlled Substance," above.

Element (5). To prove the weight of the marijuana, the State must either offer evidence of its actual measured weight or demonstrate that the quantity of marijuana is so large as to permit a reasonable inference that its weight satisfied this element. State v. Manning, 184 N.C. App. 130, 137–38 (2007). The weight of marijuana is determined at the time of seizure and includes moisture naturally contained within the marijuana; the weight need not be determined when the marijuana is later usable or suitable for consumption. State v. Gonzales, 164 N.C. App. 512 (2004). However, those parts of the plant not included in the statutory definition of marijuana, see the note on Element (3), above, are not included when determining its weight. *Manning*, 184 N.C. App. at 138. Once the State introduces evidence as to the weight of the marijuana, the defendant must make an affirmative showing that the weight improperly included excludable material, such as mature stalks. *Id.* at 138–39. The issue of weight, however, always is a factual question for the jury.

The evidence was sufficient to prove that the amount of marijuana was over 10,000 pounds when one load seized from a field, wet and including dirt and mature stalks, excludable under G.S. 90-87(16), weighed 16,620 pounds, and another pickup truckload had not been weighed because it had been plowed under. State v. Simmons, 66 N.C. App. 402 (1984).

Attempt and conspiracy. G.S. 90-98 states that except as otherwise provided, a person who attempts or conspires to commit any of the offenses in Article 5 of G.S. Chapter 90, the North Carolina Controlled Substances Act, is guilty of an offense that is the same class of crime as the object of the attempt or conspiracy and is punished accordingly. This statute overrides the provisions in G.S. 14-2.4 and 14-2.5 that set lower classifications for attempts and conspiracies than for the completed offenses themselves. See "Attempt" and "Conspiracy" in Chapter 5 (General Crimes). A drug trafficking conspiracy is the same class of offense and is punished the same as a completed trafficking offense, with its special mandatory minimum provisions, because that result is specifically required by G.S. 90-95(i). However, an attempt to commit a drug trafficking offense, although in the same class of offense as a completed trafficking offense, G.S. 90-98, is not punished with the trafficking mandatory minimum provisions because there is no statutory provision to require that result; instead, the punishment is determined under standard grid-based Structured Sentencing provisions, State v. Clark, 137 N.C. App. 90, 97 (2000); see Chapter 4 (Punishment under Structured Sentencing) (discussing Structured Sentencing).

A drug trafficking conspiracy includes the cumulative amount of controlled substances sold during the course of an open-ended conspiracy, even though the conspirators' agreement was silent about the exact quantity. State v. Williamson, 110 N.C. App. 626, 628–31 (1993) (evidence was sufficient to show one master agreement that extended over a three-and-one-half-year period).

When a defendant intends to commit a trafficking offense and performs an overt act beyond mere preparation towards committing the crime, he or she may be guilty of attempted trafficking. State v. Shook, 155 N.C. App. 183, 187 (2002). This fact pattern can arise, for example, when the defendant thinks that he or she is selling, delivering, etc. a trafficking amount but for some reason the quantity of actual controlled substances involved falls short of a trafficking amount. *Clark,* 137 N.C. App. at 93–95 (the evidence was insufficient to prove that the defendant possessed a trafficking amount of marijuana when an officer intercepted a package containing a trafficking amount of marijuana, removed most of the marijuana so that there was no longer a trafficking amount, and then delivered the package of marijuana to the defendant; instead, the defendant was guilty of attempted trafficking by possession); *Shook,* 155 N.C. App. at 187–88 (there was sufficient evidence to support four convictions of attempted trafficking in 28 or more grams of cocaine when the defendant accepted the purchaser's order for one ounce (28.35 grams) and possessed, transported, delivered, and sold slightly less than 28 grams; the sole reason that the defendant did not deliver the amount ordered was that the defendant "shorted" the purchaser, an undercover law enforcement officer).

Charging issues. See this note to "Sale or Delivery of a Controlled Substance," above. *See also* State v. Outlaw, 159 N.C. App. 423, 427–28 (2003) (an indictment alleging conspiracy to traffic in cocaine by possession was invalid because it failed to allege the weight of the cocaine that was the object of the conspiracy to possess cocaine); State v. Cobos, ___ N.C. App. ___, 711 S.E.2d 464, 467–69 (2011) (the trial court committed reversible error by allowing the State to amend an indictment charging conspiracy to engage in "trafficking to deliver Cocaine" to add the following language: "to deliver 28 grams or more but less than 200 grams of cocaine"; an indictment for conspiracy to traffic in cocaine must allege that the defendant facilitated the transfer of 28 grams or more of cocaine.

Evidence issues. See this note to "Sale or Delivery of a Controlled Substance," above.

The State established an adequate foundation that a scale used to weigh marijuana was properly functioning when it showed that ordinary scales, common procedures, and reasonable steps to ensure accuracy were used. State v. Manning, 184 N.C. App. 130, 134–36 (2007).

Defenses. See this note to "Sale or Delivery of a Controlled Substance," above.

Greater and lesser-included offenses. Possession with intent to manufacture is not a lesser-included offense of trafficking by possession but possession of a controlled substance is. State v. McCain, ___ N.C. App. ___, 713 S.E.2d 21, 23–25 (2011).

Multiple convictions and punishments. Trafficking by sale, manufacture, delivery, transportation, and possession are separate offenses for which a defendant may be separately convicted and punished. State v. Lyons, 330 N.C. 298 (1991); State v. Perry, 316 N.C. 87 (1986).

When only one agreement encompasses a conspiracy to sell, deliver, manufacture, transport, and possess, only one trafficking conspiracy may be charged and punished. State v. Worthington, 84 N.C. App. 150, 163–64 (1987).

A person may be convicted and punished for both possession of a controlled substance under G.S. 90-95(a)(3) and trafficking by possessing a controlled substance, even though the offenses are based on the same controlled substance, State v. Pipkins, 337 N.C. 431 (1994); this principle also would apply to convictions for sale, delivery, and manufacture under G.S. 90-95(a)(1) and to the corresponding trafficking offenses of sale, delivery, and manufacture.

A defendant may be convicted of possession with intent to manufacture, sell, or deliver and trafficking by possession based on the same cocaine. State v. Doe, 190 N.C. App. 723, 732 (2008).

Relation to other offenses. "[T]he controlled substance schedule to which a particular opiate derivative is assigned has nothing to do with the extent to which activities involving that substance are subject to punishment under the trafficking statutes." State v. Ellison, ___ N.C. App. ___, 713 S.E.2d 228, 244 (2011).

Related Offenses Not in This Chapter

None

Trafficking in Synthetic Cannabinoids

Statute

See G.S. 90-95(h)(1a) and (i), reproduced above.

Elements

A person guilty of this offense

(1) knowingly
(2) (a) sells, manufactures, delivers, transports, or possesses *or*
    (b) conspires to sell, manufacture, deliver, transport, or possess
(3) dosage units of a synthetic cannabinoid or any mixture containing such a substance
(4) to another person (if the person sells or delivers) *and*
(5) the quantity of synthetic cannabinoid or any mixture containing such a substance is
    (a) more than 50 dosage units but less than 250 dosage units,
    (b) 250 dosage units or more but less than 1,250 dosage units,
    (c) 1,250 dosage units or more but less than 3,750 dosage units, *or*
    (d) 3,750 dosage units or more.

Punishment

For the amount in Element (5)(a), the crime is a Class H felony punishable by a mandatory minimum imprisonment of 25 months, a mandatory maximum imprisonment of 30 months, and a mandatory minimum fine of $5,000. G.S. 90-95(h)(1a)a. For the amount in Element (5)(b), the crime is a Class G felony punishable by a mandatory minimum imprisonment of 35 months, a mandatory maximum imprisonment of 42 months, and a mandatory minimum fine of $25,000. *Id.* at (h)(1a)b. For the amount in Element (5)(c), the crime is a Class F felony punishable by a mandatory minimum imprisonment of 70 months, a mandatory maximum imprisonment of 84 months, and a mandatory minimum fine of $50,000. *Id.* at (h)(1a)c. For the amount in Element (5)(d), the crime is a Class D felony punishable by a mandatory minimum imprisonment of 175 months, a mandatory maximum imprisonment of 219 months, and a mandatory minimum fine of $200,000. *Id.* at (h)(1a)d. Sentences must run consecutively to any sentence being served at the time of sentencing. G.S. 90-95(h)(6). However, G.S. 90-95(h) does not require consecutive sentences for offenses disposed of in the same sentencing hearing. State v. Walston, 193 N.C. App. 134, 141–42 (2008).

The punishment for this offense under Structured Sentencing is exactly as set out above and is not affected by a defendant's prior record level or aggravating and mitigating factors. However, a sentencing judge may impose a lesser sentence under G.S. 90-95(h)(5) if the defendant has provided substantial assistance in the identification, arrest, or conviction of any accomplices, accessories, co-conspirators, or principals involved in controlled substances offenses. *See generally* State v. Wells, 104 N.C. App. 274 (1991).

Notes

Generally. This offense is the same as "Trafficking in Marijuana," above, except that this offense involves a different controlled substance and different quantities. Thus, many of the notes to that offense apply here as well.

Element (5). A "dosage unit" consists of 3 grams of synthetic cannabinoid or any mixture containing such a substance. G.S. 90-95(h)(1a).

Related Offenses Not in This Chapter

None

Trafficking in Methaqualone

Statute

See G.S. 90-95(h)(2) and (i), reproduced above.

Elements

A person guilty of this offense

(1) knowingly
(2) (a) sells, manufactures, delivers, transports, or possesses *or*
 (b) conspires to sell, manufacture, deliver, transport, or possess
(3) tablets, capsules, or other dosage units, or the equivalent quantity, or methaqualone, or any mixture containing methaqualone
(4) to another person (if the person sells or delivers) *and*
(5) the quantity of methaqualone or mixture containing methaqualone is
 (a) 1,000 or more dosage units or equivalent quantity but less than 5,000,
 (b) 5,000 or more dosage units or equivalent quantity but less than 10,000, *or*
 (c) 10,000 or more dosage units or equivalent quantity.

Punishment

For the amount in Element (5)(a), the crime is a Class G felony punishable by a mandatory minimum imprisonment of 35 months, a mandatory maximum imprisonment of 42 months, and a mandatory minimum fine of $25,000. G.S. 90-95(h)(2)a. For the amount in Element (5)(b), the crime is a Class F felony punishable by a mandatory minimum imprisonment of 70 months, a mandatory maximum imprisonment of 84 months, and a mandatory minimum fine of $50,000. *Id.* at (h)(2)b. For the amount in Element (5)(c), the crime is a Class D felony punishable by a mandatory minimum imprisonment of 175 months, a mandatory maximum imprisonment of 219 months, and a mandatory minimum fine of $200,000. *Id.* at (h)(2)c. Sentences must run consecutively to any sentence being served at the time of sentencing. G.S. 90-95(h)(6). However, G.S. 90-95(h) does not require consecutive sentences for offenses disposed of in the same sentencing hearing. State v. Walston, 193 N.C. App. 134, 141–42 (2008).

The punishment for this offense under Structured Sentencing is exactly as set out above and is not affected by a defendant's prior record level or aggravating and mitigating factors.

However, a sentencing judge may impose a lesser sentence under G.S. 90-95(h)(5) if the defendant has provided substantial assistance in the identification, arrest, or conviction of any accomplices, accessories, co-conspirators, or principals involved in controlled substances offenses. *See generally* State v. Wells, 104 N.C. App. 274 (1991).

Notes

Generally. This offense is the same as "Trafficking in Marijuana," above, except that this offense involves a different controlled substance and different quantities. Thus, many of the notes on that offense apply here as well.

Element (3). This element is satisfied if the tablet, capsule, other dosage unit, or equivalent quantity has any mixture containing methaqualone; the dosage unit need not contain pure methaqualone. For similar rulings involving heroin, see *State v. Agubata*, 92 N.C. App. 651 (1989), and *State v. Horton*, 75 N.C. App. 632 (1985).

Related Offenses Not in This Chapter

None

Trafficking in Cocaine

Statute

See G.S. 90-95(h)(3) and (i), reproduced above.

Elements

A person guilty of this offense

(1) knowingly
(2) (a) sells, manufactures, delivers, transports, or possesses *or*
 (b) conspires to sell, manufacture, deliver, transport, or possess
(3) cocaine or any mixture containing cocaine
(4) to another person (if the person sells or delivers) *and*
(5) the quantity of cocaine or mixture containing cocaine is
 (a) 28 grams or more but less than 200 grams,
 (b) 200 grams or more but less than 400 grams, *or*
 (c) 400 grams or more.

Punishment

For the amount in Element (5)(a), the crime is a Class G felony punishable by a mandatory minimum imprisonment of 35 months, a mandatory maximum imprisonment of 42 months, and a mandatory minimum fine of $50,000. G.S. 90-95(h)(3)a. For the amount in Element (5)(b), the crime is a Class F felony punishable by a mandatory minimum imprisonment of 70 months, a mandatory maximum imprisonment of 84 months, and a mandatory minimum fine of $100,000. *Id.* at (h)(3)b. For the amount in Element (5)(c), the crime is a Class D felony punishable by a mandatory minimum imprisonment of 175 months, a mandatory maximum imprisonment of 219 months, and a mandatory minimum fine of $250,000. *Id.* at (h)(3)c. Sentences must run consecutively to any sentence being served at the time of sentencing. G.S. 90-95(h)(6). However, G.S. 90-95(h) does not require consecutive sentences for offenses disposed of in the same sentencing hearing. State v. Walston, 193 N.C. App. 134, 141–42 (2008).

The punishment for this offense under Structured Sentencing is exactly as set out above and is not affected by a defendant's prior record level or aggravating and mitigating factors. However, a sentencing judge may impose a lesser sentence under G.S. 90-95(h)(5) if the defendant has provided substantial assistance in the identification, arrest, or conviction of any accomplices, accessories, co-conspirators, or principals involved in controlled substances offenses. *See generally* State v. Wells, 104 N.C. App. 274 (1991).

Notes

Generally. This offense is the same as "Trafficking in Marijuana," above, except that this offense involves a different controlled substance and different quantities. Thus, many of the notes on that offense apply here as well.

Element (3). The statute prohibits trafficking in the following substances: "cocaine and any salt, isomer, salts of isomers, compound, derivative, or preparation thereof, or any coca leaves and any salt, isomer, salts of isomers, compound, derivative, or preparation of coca leaves, and any salt, isomer, salts of isomers, compound, derivative or preparation thereof which is chemically equivalent or identical with any of these substances (except decocainized coca leaves or any extraction of coca leaves which does not contain cocaine) or any mixture containing such substances." G.S. 90-95(h)(3).

This element is satisfied if any mixture contains a prohibited substance. Thus, a defendant who sold an undercover agent a powdery mixture weighing 37.1 grams, of which only 5.565 grams were cocaine, was properly convicted of trafficking in cocaine by delivering over 28 grams of cocaine. State v. Tyndall, 55 N.C. App. 57 (1981).

Related Offenses Not in This Chapter

None

Trafficking in Methamphetamine

Statute

See G.S. 90-95(h)(3b) and (i), reproduced above.

Elements

A person guilty of this offense

(1) knowingly
(2) (a) sells, manufactures, delivers, transports, or possesses *or*
    (b) conspires to sell, manufacture, deliver, transport, or possess
(3) methamphetamine or any mixture containing such substance
(4) to another person (if the person sells or delivers) *and*
(5) the quantity of methamphetamine or mixture containing such substance is
    (a) 28 grams or more but less than 200 grams,
    (b) 200 grams or more but less than 400 grams, *or*
    (c) 400 grams or more.

Punishment

For the amount in Element (5)(a), the crime is a Class F felony punishable by a mandatory minimum imprisonment of 70 months, a maximum term of 84 months, and a mandatory minimum fine of $50,000. G.S. 90-95(h)(3b)a. For the amount in Element (5)(b), the crime is a Class E felony punishable by a mandatory minimum imprisonment of 90 months, a maximum term of 117 months, and a mandatory minimum fine of $100,000. *Id.* at (h)(3b)b. For the amount in Element (5)(c), the crime is a Class C felony punishable by a mandatory minimum imprisonment of 225 months, a maximum term of 279 months, and a mandatory minimum fine of $250,000. *Id.* at (h)(3b)c. Sentences must run consecutively to any sentence being served at the time of sentencing. G.S. 90-95(h)(6). However, G.S. 90-95(h) does not require consecutive sentences for offenses disposed of in the same sentencing hearing. State v. Walston, 193 N.C. App. 134, 141–42 (2008).

The punishment for this offense under Structured Sentencing is exactly as set out above and is not affected by a defendant's prior record level or aggravating and mitigating factors. However, a sentencing judge may impose a lesser sentence under G.S. 90-95(h)(5) if the defendant has provided substantial assistance in the identification, arrest, or conviction of any accomplices, accessories, co-conspirators, or principals involved in controlled substances offenses. *See generally* State v. Wells, 104 N.C. App. 274 (1991).

Notes

Generally. This offense is the same as "Trafficking in Marijuana," above, except that this offense involves a different controlled substance and different quantities. Thus, many of the notes on that offense apply here as well.

Element (3). The statute prohibits trafficking in methamphetamine or any mixture containing methamphetamine. When a mixture containing methamphetamine is involved, it is the weight of the mixture, not the methamphetamine alone, that determines whether this element is satisfied. See the note on Element (3) to "Trafficking in Opium or Heroin," below.

Related Offenses Not in This Chapter

None

Trafficking in Amphetamine

Statute

See G.S. 90-95(h)(3c) and (i), reproduced above.

Elements

A person guilty of this offense

(1) knowingly
(2) (a) sells, manufactures, delivers, transports, or possesses *or*
    (b) conspires to sell, manufacture, deliver, transport, or possess
(3) amphetamine or any mixture containing such substance
(4) to another person (if the person sells or delivers) *and*
(5) the quantity of amphetamine or mixture containing such substance is
    (a) 28 grams or more but less than 200 grams,
    (b) 200 grams or more but less than 400 grams, *or*
    (c) 400 grams or more.

Punishment

For the amount in Element (5)(a), the crime is a Class H felony punishable by a mandatory minimum imprisonment of 25 months, a maximum term of 30 months, and a mandatory minimum fine of $5,000. G.S. 90-95(h)(3c)a. For the amount in Element (5)(b), the crime is a Class G felony punishable by a mandatory minimum imprisonment of 35 months, a maximum term of 42 months, and a mandatory minimum fine of $25,000. *Id.* at (h)(3c)b. For the amount in Element (5)(c), the crime is a Class E felony punishable by a mandatory minimum imprisonment of 90 months, a maximum term of 117 months, and a mandatory minimum fine of $100,000. *Id.* at (h)(3c)c. Sentences must run consecutively to any sentence being served at the time of sentencing. G.S. 90-95(h)(6). However, G.S. 90-95(h) does not require consecutive sentences for offenses disposed of in the same sentencing hearing. State v. Walston, 193 N.C. App. 134, 141–42 (2008).

The punishment for this offense under Structured Sentencing is exactly as set out above and is not affected by a defendant's prior record level or aggravating and mitigating factors. However, a sentencing judge may impose a lesser sentence under G.S. 90-95(h)(5) if the defendant has provided substantial assistance in the identification, arrest, or conviction of any accomplices, accessories, co-conspirators, or principals involved in controlled substances offenses. *See generally* State v. Wells, 104 N.C. App. 274 (1991).

Notes

Generally. This offense is the same as "Trafficking in Marijuana," above, except that this offense involves a different controlled substance and different quantities. Thus, many of the notes on that offense apply here as well.

Element (3). The statute prohibits trafficking in amphetamine or any mixture containing amphetamine. When a mixture containing amphetamine is involved, it is the weight of the mixture, not the amphetamine alone, that determines whether this element is satisfied. See the note on Element (3) to "Trafficking in Opium or Heroin," below.

Related Offenses Not in This Chapter

None

Trafficking in MDPV

Statute

See G.S. 90-95(h)(3d) and 90-95(i), reproduced above.

Elements

A person guilty of this offense

(1) knowingly
(2) (a) sells, manufactures, delivers, transports, or possesses *or*
    (b) conspires to sell, manufacture, deliver, transport, or possess
(3) 3,4-Methylenedioxypyrovalerone (MDPV) or any mixture containing MDPV
(4) to another person (if the person sells or delivers) *and*
(5) the quantity of MDPV or any mixture containing MDPV is
    (a) 28 grams or more but less than 200 grams,
    (b) 200 grams or more but less than 400 grams, *or*
    (c) 400 grams or more.

Punishment

For the amount in Element (5)(a), the crime is a Class F felony punishable by a minimum term of imprisonment of 70 months, a maximum term of 84 months, and a mandatory minimum fine of $50,000. G.S. 90-95(h)(3d)a. For the amount in Element (5)(b), the crime is a Class E felony punishable by a minimum term of imprisonment of 90 months, a maximum term of 117 months, and a mandatory minimum fine of $100,000. *Id.* at (h)(3d)b. For the amount in Element (5)(c), the crime is a Class C felony punishable by a minimum term of imprisonment of 225 months, a maximum term of 279 months, and a mandatory minimum fine of $250,000. *Id.* at (h)(3d)c. Sentences must run consecutively to any sentence being served at the time of sentencing. G.S. 90-95(h)(6). However, G.S. 90-95(h) does not require consecutive sentences for offenses disposed of in the same sentencing hearing. State v. Walston, 193 N.C. App. 134, 141–42 (2008).

The punishment for this offense under Structured Sentencing is exactly as set out above and is not affected by a defendant's prior record level or aggravating and mitigating factors. However, a sentencing judge may impose a lesser sentence under G.S. 90-95(h)(5) if the defendant has provided substantial assistance in the identification, arrest, or conviction of any accomplices, accessories, co-conspirators, or principals involved in controlled substances offenses. *See generally* State v. Wells, 104 N.C. App. 274 (1991).

Notes

Generally. This offense is the same as "Trafficking in Marijuana," above, except that this offense involves a different controlled substance and different quantities. Thus, many of the notes on that offense apply here as well.

Related Offenses Not in This Chapter

None

Trafficking in Mephedrone

Statute

See G.S. 90-95(h)(3e) and 90-95(i), reproduced above.

Elements

A person guilty of this offense

(1) knowingly
(2) (a) sells, manufactures, delivers, transports, or possesses *or*
    (b) conspires to sell, manufacture, deliver, transport, or possess
(3) mephedrone or any mixture containing mephedrone
(4) to another person (if the person sells or delivers) *and*
(5) the quantity of mephedrone or any mixture containing mephedrone is
    (a) 28 grams or more but less than 200 grams,
    (b) 200 grams or more but less than 400 grams, *or*
    (c) 400 grams or more.

Punishment

For the amount in Element (5)(a), the crime is a Class F felony punishable by a minimum term of imprisonment of 70 months, a maximum term of 84 months, and a mandatory minimum fine of $50,000. G.S. 90-95(h)(3e)a. For the amount in Element (5)(b), the crime is a Class E felony punishable by a minimum term of imprisonment of 90 months, a maximum term of 117 months, and a mandatory minimum fine of $100,000. *Id.* at (h)(3e)b. For the amount in Element (5)(c), the crime is a Class C felony punishable by a minimum term of imprisonment of 225 months, a maximum term of 279 months, and a mandatory minimum fine of $250,000. *Id.* at (h)(3e)c. Sentences must run consecutively to any sentence being served at the time of sentencing. G.S. 90-95(h)(6). However, G.S. 90-95(h) does not require consecutive sentences for offenses disposed of in the same sentencing hearing. State v. Walston, 193 N.C. App. 134, 141–42 (2008).

The punishment for this offense under Structured Sentencing is exactly as set out above and is not affected by a defendant's prior record level or aggravating and mitigating factors. However, a sentencing judge may impose a lesser sentence under G.S. 90-95(h)(5) if the defendant has provided substantial assistance in the identification, arrest, or conviction of any accomplices, accessories, co-conspirators, or principals involved in controlled substances offenses. *See generally* State v. Wells, 104 N.C. App. 274 (1991).

Notes

Generally. This offense is the same as "Trafficking in Marijuana," above, except that this offense involves a different controlled substance and different quantities. Thus, many of the notes on that offense apply here as well.

Related Offenses Not in This Chapter

None

Trafficking in Opium or Heroin

Statute

See G.S. 90-95(h)(4) and (i), reproduced above.

Elements

A person guilty of this offense

(1) knowingly
(2) (a) sells, manufactures, delivers, transports, or possesses *or*
 (b) conspires to sell, manufacture, deliver, transport, or possess
(3) opium, including heroin, or any mixture containing opium or heroin
(4) to another person (if the person sells or delivers) *and*
(5) the quantity of opium, including heroin, or any mixture containing opium or heroin is
 (a) 4 grams or more but less than 14 grams,
 (b) 14 grams or more but less than 28 grams, *or*
 (c) 28 grams or more.

Punishment

For the amount in Element (5)(a), the crime is a Class F felony punishable by a mandatory minimum imprisonment of 70 months, a mandatory maximum imprisonment of 84 months, and a mandatory minimum fine of $50,000. G.S. 90-95(h)(4)a. For the amount in Element (5)(b), the crime is a Class E felony punishable by a mandatory minimum imprisonment of 90 months, a mandatory maximum imprisonment of 117 months, and a mandatory minimum fine of $100,000. *Id.* at (h)(4)b. For the amount in Element (5)(c), the crime is a Class C felony punishable by a mandatory minimum imprisonment of 225 months, a mandatory maximum imprisonment of 279 months, and a mandatory minimum fine of $500,000. *Id.* at (h)(4)c. Sentences must run consecutively to any sentence being served at the time of sentencing. G.S. 90-95(h)(6). However, G.S. 90-95(h) does not require consecutive sentences for offenses disposed of in the same sentencing hearing. State v. Walston, 193 N.C. App. 134, 141–42 (2008).

The punishment for this offense under Structured Sentencing is exactly as set out above and is not affected by a defendant's prior record level or aggravating and mitigating factors. However, a sentencing judge may impose a lesser sentence under G.S. 90-95(h)(5) if the defendant has provided substantial assistance in the identification, arrest, or conviction of any accomplices, accessories, co-conspirators, or principals involved in controlled substances offenses. *See generally* State v. Wells, 104 N.C. App. 274 (1991).

Notes

Generally. This offense is the same as "Trafficking in Marijuana," above, except that this offense involves a different controlled substance and different quantities. Thus, many of the notes on that offense apply here as well.

Element (3). The statute prohibits trafficking in the following substances: "opium or opiate, or any salt, compound, derivative, or preparation of opium or opiate (except apomorphine, nalbuphine, analoxone and naltrexone and their respective salts), including heroin, or any mixture containing such substance." G.S. 90-95(h)(4).

This element is satisfied if the mixture contains any amount of a prohibited substance. It is the weight of the entire mixture, not the weight of the controlled substance in the mixture, that determines liability and punishment under this statute. Thus, a white powder that weighed 13.2 grams but contained only 30 percent pure heroin was sufficient to prove trafficking by possessing at least 4 grams, since the weight of the entire mixture was at least 4 grams. State v. Willis, 61 N.C. App. 23 (1983); for similar rulings see *State v. Agubata*, 94 N.C. App. 710 (1989); *State v. Agubata*, 92 N.C. App. 651 (1989); and *State v. Horton*, 75 N.C. App. 632 (1985). The entire weight (5.4 grams) of Oxycontin tablets was properly admitted to prove a drug trafficking amount, even though the tablets contained only 1.6 grams of the controlled substance oxycodone (a derivative of opium), because a tablet is a "mixture" under G.S. 90-95(h)(4). State v. McCracken, 157 N.C. App. 524 (2003).

Related Offenses Not in This Chapter

None

Trafficking in LSD

Statute

See G.S. 90-95(h)(4a) and (i), reproduced above.

Elements

A person guilty of this offense

(1) knowingly
(2) (a) sells, manufactures, delivers, transports, or possesses *or*
    (b) conspires to sell, manufacture, deliver, transport, or possess
(3) tablets, capsules, or other dosage units, or the equivalent quantity, of lysergic acid diethylamide (LSD) or any mixture containing such substance
(4) to another person (if the person sells or delivers) *and*
(5) the quantity of LSD or any mixture containing such substance is
    (a) 100 or more dosage units, or equivalent quantity, but less than 500 dosage units, or equivalent quantity,
    (b) 500 or more dosage units, or equivalent quantity, but less than 1,000 dosage units, or equivalent quantity, *or*
    (c) 1,000 or more dosage units, or equivalent quantity.

Punishment

For the amount in Element (5)(a), the crime is a Class G felony punishable by a mandatory minimum imprisonment of 35 months, a mandatory maximum imprisonment of 42 months, and a mandatory minimum fine of $25,000. G.S. 90-95(h)(4a)a. For the amount in Element (5)(b), the crime is a Class F felony with a mandatory minimum imprisonment of 70 months, a mandatory maximum imprisonment of 84 months, and a mandatory minimum fine of $50,000. *Id.* at (h)(4a)b. For the amount in Element (5)(c), the crime is a Class D felony with a mandatory minimum imprisonment of 175 months, a mandatory maximum imprisonment of 219 months, and a mandatory minimum fine of $200,000. *Id.* at (h)(4a)c. Sentences must run consecutively to any sentence being served at the time of sentencing. G.S. 90-95(h)(6). However, G.S. 90-95(h) does not require consecutive sentences for offenses disposed of in the same sentencing hearing. State v. Walston, 193 N.C. App. 134, 141–42 (2008).

The punishment for this offense under Structured Sentencing is exactly as set out above and is not affected by a defendant's prior record level or aggravating and mitigating factors.

However, a sentencing judge may impose a lesser sentence under G.S. 90-95(h)(5) if the defendant has provided substantial assistance in the identification, arrest, or conviction of any accomplices, accessories, co-conspirators, or principals involved in controlled substances offenses. *See generally* State v. Wells, 104 N.C. App. 274 (1991).

Notes

Generally. This offense is the same as "Trafficking in Marijuana," above, except that this offense involves a different controlled substance and different quantities. Thus, many of the notes on that offense apply here as well.

Element (3). This element is satisfied if the tablet, capsule, other dosage unit, or equivalent quantity has any mixture containing LSD. The dosage unit need not contain pure LSD. See the note on Element (3) to "Trafficking in Opium or Heroin," above.

Related Offenses Not in This Chapter

None

Trafficking in MDA and MDMA

Statute

See G.S. 90-95(h)(4b) and (i), reproduced above.

Elements

A person guilty of this offense

(1) knowingly
(2) (a) sells, manufactures, delivers, transports, or possesses *or*
    (b) conspires to sell, manufacture, deliver, transport, or possess
(3) grams, tablets, capsules, or other dosage units of 3,4-methylenedioxyamphetamine (MDA) or 3,4-methylenedioxymethamphetamine (MDMA), including its salts, isomers, and salts of isomers, or any mixture containing such substances,
(4) to another person (if the person sells or delivers) *and*
(5) the weight or quantity of MDA or MDMA, including its salts, isomers, and salts of isomers, or any mixture containing such substances, is
    (a) 100 or more tablets, capsules, or other dosage units but less than 500 tablets, capsules, or other dosage units, or 28 grams or more but less than 200 grams,
    (b) 500 or more tablets, capsules, or other dosage units but less than 1,000 tablets, capsules, or other dosage units, or 200 grams or more but less than 400 grams, *or*
    (c) 1,000 or more tablets, capsules, or other dosage units, or 400 grams or more.

Punishment

For the amount in Element (5)(a), the crime is a Class G felony punishable by a mandatory minimum imprisonment of 35 months, a maximum term of 42 months, and a mandatory minimum fine of $25,000. G.S. 90-95(h)(4b)a. For the amount in Element (5)(b), the crime is a Class F felony punishable by a mandatory minimum imprisonment of 70 months, a maximum term of 84 months, and a mandatory minimum fine of $50,000. *Id.* at (h)(4b)b. For the amount in Element (5)(c), the crime is a Class D felony punishable by a mandatory minimum imprisonment of 175 months, a maximum term of 219 months, and a mandatory minimum fine of $250,000. *Id.* at (h)(4b)c. Sentences must run consecutively to any sentence being served at the time of sentencing. G.S. 90-95(h)(6). However, G.S. 90-95(h) does not require consecutive sentences for offenses disposed of in the same sentencing hearing. State v. Walston, 193 N.C. App. 134, 141–42 (2008).

The punishment for this offense under Structured Sentencing is exactly as set out above and is not affected by a defendant's prior record level or aggravating and mitigating factors. However, a sentencing judge may impose a lesser sentence under G.S. 90-95(h)(5) if the defendant has provided substantial assistance in the identification, arrest, or conviction of any accomplices, accessories, co-conspirators, or principals involved in controlled substances offenses. *See generally* State v. Wells, 104 N.C. App. 274 (1991).

Notes

Generally. This offense is the same as "Trafficking in Marijuana," above, except that this offense involves a different controlled substance and different quantities. Thus, many of the notes on that offense apply here as well.

Element (3). This element is satisfied if the grams, tablet, capsule, other dosage unit, or equivalent quantity has any mixture containing MDA or MDMA. The dosage unit need not contain pure MDA or MDMA. See the note on Element (3) to "Trafficking in Opium or Heroin," above.

Related Offenses Not in This Chapter

None

Continuing Criminal Enterprise—Drug Offenses

Statute

§90-95.1. Continuing criminal enterprise.

(a) Any person who engages in a continuing criminal enterprise shall be punished as a Class C felon and in addition shall be subject to the forfeiture prescribed in subsection (b) of this section.

(b) Any person who is convicted under subsection (a) of engaging in a continuing criminal enterprise shall forfeit to the State of North Carolina:

(1) The profits obtained by him in such enterprise, and

(2) Any of his interest in, claim against, or property or contractual rights of any kind affording a source of influence over, such enterprise.

(c) For purposes of this section, a person is engaged in a continuing criminal enterprise if:

(1) He violates any provision of this Article, the punishment of which is a felony; and

(2) Such violation is a part of a continuing series of violations of this Article;

a. Which are undertaken by such person in concert with five or more other persons with respect to whom such person occupies a position of organizer, a supervisory position, or any other position of management; and

b. From which such person obtains substantial income or resources.

(d) Repealed by Session Laws 1979, c. 760, s. 5.

Elements

A person guilty of this offense

(1) commits any felony under Article 5 of G.S. Chapter 90 (North Carolina Controlled Substances Act)

(2) that is part of a continuing series of violations of Article 5 *and*

(3) that are undertaken in concert with five or more other persons

(4) over whom the person occupies a position of organizer, supervisor, or other position of management *and*
(5) the person obtains substantial income or other resources from the continuing violations.

Punishment

Class C felony. G.S. 90-95.1(a). In addition, property set out in G.S. 90-95.1(b) must be forfeited.

Notes

Elements (1) and (2). Article 5 of the North Carolina Controlled Substances Act encompasses sections 90-86 through 90-113.8.

Attempt or conspiracy. See this note to "Sale or Delivery of a Controlled Substance," above.

Defenses. See this note to "Sale or Delivery of a Controlled Substance," above.

Related Offenses Not in This Chapter

Continuing criminal enterprise (non-drug offenses). G.S. 14-7.20.

Controlled Substance Offenses Involving Fraud, Misrepresentation, or Similar Activities

Obtaining a Controlled Substance by Misrepresenting Oneself as a Licensed Practitioner

Statute

§90-108. Prohibited acts; penalties.

(a) It shall be unlawful for any person:

(1) Other than practitioners licensed under Articles 1, 2, 4, 6, 11, 12A of this Chapter to represent to any registrant or practitioner who manufactures, distributes, or dispenses a controlled substance under the provision of this Article that he is a licensed practitioner in order to secure or attempt to secure any controlled substance as defined in this Article or to in any way impersonate a practitioner for the purpose of securing or attempting to secure any drug requiring a prescription from a practitioner as listed above and who is licensed by this State;
(2) Who is subject to the requirements of G.S. 90-101 or a practitioner to distribute or dispense a controlled substance in violation of G.S. 90-105 or 90-106;
(3) Who is a registrant to manufacture, distribute, or dispense a controlled substance not authorized by his registration to another registrant or other authorized person;
(4) To omit, remove, alter, or obliterate a symbol required by the Federal Controlled Substances Act or its successor;
(5) To refuse or fail to make, keep, or furnish any record, notification, order form, statement, invoice or information required under this Article;
(6) To refuse any entry into any premises or inspection authorized by this Article;
(7) To knowingly keep or maintain any store, shop, warehouse, dwelling house, building, vehicle, boat, aircraft, or any place whatever, which is resorted to by persons using controlled substances in violation of this Article for the

purpose of using such substances, or which is used for the keeping or selling of the same in violation of this Article;

(8) Who is a registrant or a practitioner to distribute a controlled substance included in Schedule I or II of this Article in the course of his legitimate business, except pursuant to an order form as required by G.S. 90-105;

(9) To use in the course of the manufacture or distribution of a controlled substance a registration number which is fictitious, revoked, suspended, or issued to another person;

(10) To acquire or obtain possession of a controlled substance by misrepresentation, fraud, forgery, deception, or subterfuge;

(11) To furnish false or fraudulent material information in, or omit any material information from, any application, report, or other document required to be kept or filed under this Article, or any record required to be kept by this Article;

(12) To make, distribute, or possess any punch, die, plate, stone, or other thing designed to print, imprint, or reproduce the trademark, trade name, or other identifying mark, imprint, or device of another or any likeness of any of the foregoing upon any drug or container or labeling thereof so as to render such drug a counterfeit controlled substance;

(13) To obtain controlled substances through the use of legal prescriptions which have been obtained by the knowing and willful misrepresentation to or by the intentional withholding of information from one or more practitioners;

(14) Who is an employee of a registrant or practitioner and who is authorized to possess controlled substances or has access to controlled substances by virtue of his employment, to embezzle or fraudulently or knowingly and willfully misapply or divert to his own use or other unauthorized or illegal use or to take, make away with or secrete, with intent to embezzle or fraudulently or knowingly and willfully misapply or divert to his own use or other unauthorized or illegal use any controlled substance which shall have come into his possession or under his care.

(b) Any person who violates this section shall be guilty of a Class 1 misdemeanor. Provided, that if the criminal pleading alleges that the violation was committed intentionally, and upon trial it is specifically found that the violation was committed intentionally, such violations shall be a Class I felony. A person who violates subdivision (7) of subsection (a) of this section and also fortifies the structure, with the intent to impede law enforcement entry, (by barricading windows and doors) shall be punished as a Class I felon.

Elements

A person guilty of this offense

(1) is not a practitioner licensed under G.S. Ch. 90 Art. 1 (Practice of Medicine), 2 (Dentistry), 4 (Pharmacy), 6 (Optometry), 11 (Veterinarians), or 12A (Podiatrists) *and*

(2) (a) (i) represents to any registrant or practitioner
(ii) who manufactures, distributes, or dispenses
(iii) a controlled substance under G.S. Ch. 90 Art. 5
(iv) that he or she is a licensed practitioner
(v) in order to secure or attempt to secure any controlled substance *or*

(b) (i) impersonates a practitioner
(ii) for the purpose of securing or attempting to secure
(iii) any drug requiring a prescription
(iv) from a practitioner listed in Element (1) who is licensed by the State.

Punishment

Class 1 misdemeanor. G.S. 90-108(b). If the act was committed intentionally, the offense is a Class I felony. *Id.* If the felony version of this offense is charged, a charging instrument must allege the relevant fact elevating punishment and the State must prove that fact at trial.

For a discussion of other circumstances when punishment may be higher than a Class 1 misdemeanor because of prior convictions, see "Punishment" under "Possession of a Controlled Substance," above.

Notes

Attempt or conspiracy. The statute expressly covers attempts to secure controlled substances or prescription drugs. G.S. 90-108(a). See this note to "Sale or Delivery of a Controlled Substance," above.

Charging issues. See this note to "Sale or Delivery of a Controlled Substance," above.

Related Offenses Not in This Chapter

"Obtaining Property by False Pretenses" (Chapter 16)

Non-pharmacist's compounding or dispensing prescription drug. G.S. 90-85.40(c).

Unlawful distributing or dispensing by a registrant or practitioner in violation of G.S. 90-105 or 90-106. G.S. 90-108(a)(2).

Registrant's manufacturing, distributing or dispensing of a controlled substance not authorized by registration. G.S. 90-108(a)(3).

Omitting, removing, altering, or obliterating symbol required by Federal Controlled Substances Act. G.S. 90-108(a)(4).

Refusing or failing to make, keep, or furnish any required record, order form, etc. G.S. 90-108(a)(5).

Refusing entry or inspection authorized by Controlled Substances Act. G.S. 90-108(a)(6).

Distribution by registrant or practitioner of Schedule I or II controlled substance without an order form. G.S. 90-108(a)(8).

Use of fictitious, etc. registration number in the course of manufacturing or distributing a controlled substance. G.S. 90-108(a)(9).

Furnishing false information or omitting material information in application or records required by Controlled Substances Act. G.S. 90-108(a)(11).

Making, distributing, or possessing punch, die, plate, etc. for printing trademark or other mark on drug or container so as to make it a counterfeit controlled substance. G.S. 90-108(a)(12).

Obtaining controlled substances by using legal prescriptions that have been obtained by the knowing and willful misrepresentation to, or by the intentional withholding of, information from a practitioner. G.S. 90-108(a)(13).

Employee of registrant or practitioner who embezzles a controlled substance that has come into one's possession or under one's care. G.S. 90-108(a)(14).

Drugs deemed misbranded. G.S. 106-134; 106-124.

Obtaining a Controlled Substance by Fraud or Forgery

Statute

See G.S. 90-108(a)(10), reproduced under "Obtaining a Controlled Substance by Misrepresenting Oneself as a Licensed Practitioner," above.

Elements

A person guilty of this offense

(1) obtains possession
(2) of a controlled substance
(3) by misrepresentation, fraud, forgery, deception, or subterfuge.

Punishment

Class I felony. G.S. 90-108(b). By definition, the conduct prohibited by this subdivision—a specific intention to deceive—can only be done intentionally; therefore a violation of this provision can only be a felony. State v. Church, 73 N.C. App. 645 (1985).

Notes

Element (1). See the note on Element (2) to "Possession of a Controlled Substance," above.

Element (3). This statute is most often violated by the use of a forged prescription. A defendant who forges a prescription would be guilty of this offense by forgery; someone who copies a legitimate prescription or uses one forged by someone else would be guilty by misrepresentation, fraud, deception, or subterfuge. When the defendant possesses a forged prescription, a jury may infer that the defendant either forged it or knew that it was forged. State v. Fleming, 52 N.C. App. 563 (1981).

Relation to other offenses. If fraud or forgery is used to obtain a prescription drug that is not a controlled substance, the proper charge is under G.S. 106-122(19) (obtaining or attempting to obtain prescription drug by fraud, forgery, misrepresentation, etc.).

Attempt or conspiracy. See this note to "Sale or Delivery of a Controlled Substance," above.

Charging issues. See this note to "Sale or Delivery of a Controlled Substance," above.

Defenses. See this note to "Sale or Delivery of a Controlled Substance," above.

Related Offenses Not in This Chapter

"Common Law Forgery" (Chapter 16)
"Obtaining Property by False Pretenses" (Chapter 16)

Maintaining a Store, Dwelling, Vehicle, Boat, or Other Place for Use, Storage, or Sale of Controlled Substances

Statute

See G.S. 90-108(a)(7), reproduced under "Obtaining a Controlled Substance by Misrepresenting Oneself as a Licensed Practitioner," above.

Elements

A person guilty of this offense

(1) knowingly
(2) keeps or maintains
(3) a store, shop, warehouse, dwelling house, building, vehicle, boat, aircraft, or other place
(4) (a) being resorted to by persons unlawfully using controlled substances *or*
    (b) being used for unlawfully keeping or selling controlled substances.

Punishment

Class 1 misdemeanor. G.S. 90-108(b). If the act was committed intentionally, the offense is a Class I felony. *Id.;* State v. Bright, 78 N.C. App. 239 (1985). Additionally, if a person commits this offense and fortifies the structure with the intent to impede law enforcement entry by barricading windows and doors, the offense is a Class I felony. G.S. 90-108(b). If the Class I felony version of this offense is charged, the relevant fact elevating punishment must be alleged in a charging instrument and proved at trial.

For a discussion of other circumstances when punishment may be higher than a Class 1 misdemeanor because of prior convictions, see "Punishment" under "Possession of a Controlled Substance," above.

Notes

Element (1). See "Knowingly" in Chapter 1 (States of Mind).

Element (2). In determining whether a person keeps or maintains property, the courts have considered whether the defendant

- had title to or owned the property, State v. Spencer, 192 N.C. App. 143, 148 (2008); State v. Bowens, 140 N.C. App. 217, 221 (2000); State v. Allen, 102 N.C. App. 598, 608–09 (1991);
- paid taxes on the property, *Spencer*, 192 N.C. App. at 148; *Bowens*, 140 N.C. App. at 221;
- paid for repairs to or maintenance of the property, *Spencer*, 192 N.C. App. at 148; State v. Frazier, 142 N.C. App. 361, 365 (2001); *Bowens*, 140 N.C. App. at 221;
- paid rent on the property; *Spencer*, 192 N.C. App. at 148; State v. Hart, 179 N.C. App. 30, 41–42 (2006); *Frazier*, 142 N.C. App. at 365; *Bowens*, 140 N.C. App. at 221; State v. Alston, 91 N.C. App. 707, 711 (1988);
- paid the property's utility bills or contributed to expenses associated with the property, State v. Fuller, 196 N.C. App. 412, 424 (2009); *Spencer*, 192 N.C. App. at 148; State v. Moore, 188 N.C. App. 416, 424 (2008) (household expenses); *Hart*, 179 N.C. App. at 42 (utility bills); *Frazier*, 142 N.C. App. at 365; *Bowens*, 140 N.C. App. at 221; *Allen*, 102 N.C. App. at 609;
- resided at the property, *Moore*, 188 N.C. App. at 424; State v. Baldwin, 161 N.C. App. 382, 393 (2003) (the defendant received mail at the address for one year, his driver's license showed the address as his home address, and his car was registered there);
- occupied the property, *Spencer*, 192 N.C. App. at 148; State v. Shine, 173 N.C. App. 699, 704–05 (2005); *Frazier*, 142 N.C. App. at 365; *Bowens*, 140 N.C. App. at 221;
- possessed the property over a duration of time, *Frazier*, 142 N.C. App. at 365; and
- had a key to the property, *Frazier*, 142 N.C. App. at 365; State v. Alston, 91 N.C. App. 707, 711 (1988).

Although occupancy (presence and/or use of the premises) is a relevant factor, evidence of occupancy, without more, will not support this element. State v. Cowan, 194 N.C. App. 330, 337 (2008); *Spencer,* 192 N.C. App. at 148. However, evidence of residency (living there), standing alone, is sufficient evidence to establish this element. *Cowan*, 194 N.C. App. at 337 (the evidence was sufficient when the defendant told police that he resided at the premises); *Spencer*, 192 N.C. App. at 148 (same).

Except as discussed immediately above, when determining whether a person keeps or maintains property, the courts look to the totality of the circumstances. State v. Fuller, 196 N.C. App. 412, 424 (2009); *Hart*, 179 N.C. App. at 41. For examples of cases in which the evidence was held to be insufficient to establish this element, see *Fuller,* 196 N.C. App at 424–25 (the evidence was insufficient when it showed only that the defendant discussed with the mobile home's actual tenant taking over the rent payments for the mobile home but never reached an agreement to do so, a black Charger, similar to the defendant's, was regularly parked outside the trailer even after the tenant vacated the trailer, and the defendant's shoes and some of his personal papers were found in the mobile home; there was no evidence that the defendant paid the rent, the utilities, or for any repairs or that he made any repairs or otherwise took responsibility for the mobile home; at most the evidence suggested that the defendant occupied the mobile home trailer for approximately two months); *State v. Toney*, 187 N.C. App. 465, 471 (2007) (the evidence was insufficient when, although the defendant occupied a hotel room one night and was present during a police search of it, there was no proof that he paid for the room or was a registered guest; it would be speculation to say that the defendant, as opposed to his wife, maintained or kept the room); *State v. Carter*, 184 N.C. App. 706, 710 (2007) (the defendant was the sole occupant of a residence when a search of it was conducted, three photographs found in a bedroom showed the defendant in various places in the house, and the defendant's identification and other papers were found there but none listed the residence as his home address; the State presented no evidence showing that the defendant owned the property or took any other responsibility for it, and, in fact, a utility bill was found in the name of the defendant's brother); *State v. Harris*, 157 N.C. App. 647, 651–53 (2003) (the evidence was insufficient when the defendant was seen at the house in question several times and some of his personal property was found in a bedroom but none of his papers listed the house as his address); *State v. Kraus*, 147 N.C. App. 766, 768–69 (2001) (the evidence was insufficient when the defendant had access to a key, spent the previous night in the motel room at issue, and was present when contraband was found, but there was no evidence that she paid for or maintained the motel room and she had occupied it for less than twenty-four hours when law enforcement officers arrived); *State v. Hamilton*, 145 N.C. App. 152, 153–54 (2001) (the evidence was insufficient when the defendant visited an apartment leased to his girlfriend and regularly used her vehicles parked there); and *State v. Bowens*, 140 N.C. App. 217, 221–22 (2000) (the evidence was insufficient when the defendant was seen in and out of a certain dwelling eight to ten times over the course of two to three days, nobody else was seen entering the premises during this period of time, and men's clothing was found in a closet in the dwelling; there was no evidence that the defendant owned or leased the dwelling or that he had any responsibility for the payment of the utilities or the general upkeep of the dwelling; furthermore, although men's clothing was found in the dwelling, there is no evidence that the clothes belonged to the defendant).

Element (4)(b). Element (2) requires that the defendant keep or maintain the property. Element (4)(b), however, requires that the property be used for unlawfully keeping or selling controlled substances. The statute's use of the word "keep" in Element (2) and the related term "keeping" in Element (4)(b) has created some confusion, particularly because those terms mean different things in each element. In Element (2) the word "keep" refers to the defendant's control and authority over the premises, vehicle, etc. See the note on Element (2), above. In Element (4)(b), the word "keeping" refers to possession of controlled substances on or in the property.

As used in Element (4)(b), the term "keeping" "denotes not just possession, but possession that occurs over a duration of time." State v. Dickerson, 152 N.C. App. 714, 716 (2002) (quoting State v. Mitchell, 336 N.C. 22, 32 (1994)). Thus, one isolated instance of possession on the property is insufficient evidence that the property is used for keeping controlled substances. *Compare* State v. Craven, ___ N.C. App. ___, 696 S.E.2d 750, 756 (sufficient evidence when the defendant possessed cocaine in a vehicle over a duration of time and/or on more than one occasion), *temp. stay allowed*, 364 N.C. 327 (2010), *with* State v. Thompson, 188 N.C. App. 102, 105 (2008) (insufficient evidence when the defendant possessed 2.1 grams of cocaine but there was no evidence that he used the premises to keep cocaine over a duration of time), *and* State v. Lane, 163 N.C. App. 495, 499–500 (2004) (insufficient evidence when drugs were found in the defendant's vehicle on only one occasion and the evidence did not indicate possession over a duration of time). Similarly, when the allegation is that the property is being used for the selling of controlled substances, evidence of more than one sale is required. *Compare* State v. Moore, 188 N.C. App. 416, 424-25 (2008) (evidence was sufficient when it showed two sales), *and* State v. Calvino, 179 N.C. App. 219, 222–23 (2006) (same), *with* State v. Dickerson, 152 N.C. App. 714, 716–17 (2002) (the fact that the defendant was in his vehicle on one occasion when he sold a controlled substance did not demonstrate that the vehicle was used for the keeping or selling of controlled substances); State v. Lane, 163 N.C. App. 495, 499–500 (2004) (following *Dickerson*).

As a general matter, when determining whether property is being used for keeping or selling controlled substances, the courts consider the totality of the circumstances. *See, e.g.*, State v. Mitchell, 336 N.C. 22, 34 (1994); *Moore*, 188 N.C. App. at 424. Factors relevant to the determination include:

- the amount of controlled substances found, State v. Doe, 190 N.C. App. 723, 731 (2008) (insufficient evidence when 6.5 grams of cocaine was found); State v. Thompson, 188 N.C. App. 102, 106–07 (2008) (insufficient evidence when 2.1 grams of cocaine was found); State v. Battle, 167 N.C. App. 730, 734–35 (2005) (listing this as a relevant factor; insufficient evidence when the defendant possessed 1.9 grams of compressed cocaine powder); State v. Frazier, 142 N.C App. 361, 366 (2001) (evidence sufficient when five rocks of crack cocaine were found in ceiling tiles to which the defendant had access);
- whether a large amount of cash was found, *Doe*, 190 N.C. App. at 731 (listing this as a relevant factor); *Thompson*, 188 N.C. App. at 106–07 (no bright line test as to how much money is enough; $345 in cash insufficient here); *Frazier*, 142 N.C. App. at 366 (listing this as a relevant factor; evidence sufficient when a wallet contained $1,493 in cash);
- whether drug paraphernalia was found, *Thompson*, 188 N.C. App. at 106–08 (listing this as a relevant factor; evidence insufficient when no paraphernalia was found); *Doe*, 190 N.C. App. at 731 (same); *Battle*, 167 N.C. App. at 734 (same); State v. Shine, 173 N.C. App. 699, 707–08 (2005) (evidence sufficient when police found a set of digital scales which police officer testified were the type frequently used to weigh controlled substances for sale);
- whether firearms were found, State v. Cowan, 194 N.C. App. 330, 337 (2008) (sufficient evidence when firearms were found);
- whether multiple cellular phones or pagers were found, *Thompson*, 188 N.C. App. at 106 (listing this as a relevant factor); *Frazier*, 142 N.C. App. at 366 (evidence sufficient when a number of pagers were found);
- whether there were other indicia of drug dealing, *Shine*, 173 N.C. App. at 708 (evidence sufficient when, among other things, three pieces of scrap paper were found listing initials and corresponding dollar amounts, which the jury could infer was a list of customers and their orders or debts);
- whether the defendant admitted selling controlled substances at the premises, *Thompson*, 188 N.C. App. at 107–08 (evidence insufficient when, among other things, the defendant did not admit to selling drugs); *Doe*, 190 N.C. App. at 731 (listing this as a relevant factor); *Frazier*, 142 N.C. App. at 366 (evidence sufficient when defendant neither confirmed nor denied selling drugs from hotel room);
- whether there is witness testimony that drug sales occurred at the property, State v. Calvino, 179 N.C. App. 219, 222–23 (2006) (evidence sufficient when a witness so testified); and
- whether large numbers of people have been observed coming and going from the premises, *Thompson*, 188 N.C. App. at 107 (evidence insufficient when there was no evidence that people "were coming and going from his home in a manner to suggest they were buying drugs").

Attempt or conspiracy. See this note to "Sale or Delivery of a Controlled Substance," above.

Charging issues. See this note to "Sale or Delivery of a Controlled Substance," above. *See also* State v. Garnett, ___ N.C. App. ___, 706 S.E.2d 280, 286–87 (2011) (the theories included in the trial judge's jury instructions were supported by the indictment; the indictment charged the defendant with maintaining a dwelling "for keeping and selling a controlled substance." The trial court instructed the jury on maintaining a dwelling "for keeping or selling marijuana;" the use of the conjunctive "and" in the indictment did not require the State to prove both theories alleged).

Multiple convictions and punishment. Multiple convictions of this offense were not permitted when the evidence showed that the defendant continuously maintained the dwelling for using a controlled substance; that is, there was no evidence indicating a termination and later resumption of drug trafficking at the dwelling that might otherwise permit multiple convictions. State v. Grady, 136 N.C. App. 394 (2000); *see also Calvino*, 179 N.C. App. at 223.

Related Offenses Not in This Chapter

None

Possession of Drug Paraphernalia

Statute

§90-113.21. General provisions.

(a) As used in this Article, "drug paraphernalia" means all equipment, products and materials of any kind that are used to facilitate, or intended or designed to facilitate, violations of the Controlled Substances Act, including planting, propagating, cultivating, growing, harvesting, manufacturing, compounding, converting, producing, processing, preparing, testing, analyzing, packaging, repackaging, storing, containing, and concealing controlled substances and injecting, ingesting, inhaling, or otherwise introducing controlled substances into the human body. "Drug paraphernalia" includes, but is not limited to, the following:

(1) Kits for planting, propagating, cultivating, growing, or harvesting any species of plant which is a controlled substance or from which a controlled substance can be derived;

(2) Kits for manufacturing, compounding, converting, producing, processing, or preparing controlled substances;

(3) Isomerization devices for increasing the potency of any species of plant which is a controlled substance;

(4) Testing equipment for identifying, or analyzing the strength, effectiveness, or purity of controlled substances;

(5) Scales and balances for weighing or measuring controlled substances;

(6) Diluents and adulterants, such as quinine, hydrochloride, mannitol, mannite, dextrose, and lactose for mixing with controlled substances;

(7) Separation gins and sifters for removing twigs and seeds from, or otherwise cleaning or refining, marijuana;

(8) Blenders, bowls, containers, spoons, and mixing devices for compounding controlled substances;

(9) Capsules, balloons, envelopes and other containers for packaging small quantities of controlled substances;

(10) Containers and other objects for storing or concealing controlled substances;

(11) Hypodermic syringes, needles, and other objects for parenterally injecting controlled substances into the body;

(12) Objects for ingesting, inhaling, or otherwise introducing marijuana, cocaine, hashish, or hashish oil into the body, such as:

a. Metal, wooden, acrylic, glass, stone, plastic, or ceramic pipes with or without screens, permanent screens, hashish heads, or punctured metal bowls;

b. Water pipes;

c. Carburetion tubes and devices;

d. Smoking and carburetion masks;

e. Objects, commonly called roach clips, for holding burning material, such as a marijuana cigarette, that has become too small or too short to be held in the hand;
f. Miniature cocaine spoons and cocaine vials;
g. Chamber pipes;
h. Carburetor pipes;
i. Electric pipes;
j. Air-driven pipes;
k. Chillums;
l. Bongs;
m. Ice pipes or chillers.

(b) The following, along with all other relevant evidence, may be considered in determining whether an object is drug paraphernalia:

(1) Statements by the owner or anyone in control of the object concerning its use;
(2) Prior convictions of the owner or other person in control of the object for violations of controlled substances law;
(3) The proximity of the object to a violation of the Controlled Substances Act;
(4) The proximity of the object to a controlled substance;
(5) The existence of any residue of a controlled substance on the object;
(6) The proximity of the object to other drug paraphernalia;
(7) Instructions provided with the object concerning its use;
(8) Descriptive materials accompanying the object explaining or depicting its use;
(9) Advertising concerning its use;
(10) The manner in which the object is displayed for sale;
(11) Whether the owner, or anyone in control of the object, is a legitimate supplier of like or related items to the community, such as a seller of tobacco products or agricultural supplies;
(12) Possible legitimate uses of the object in the community;
(13) Expert testimony concerning its use;
(14) The intent of the owner or other person in control of the object to deliver it to persons whom he knows or reasonably should know intend to use the object to facilitate violations of the Controlled Substances Act.

§90-113.22. Possession of drug paraphernalia.

(a) It is unlawful for any person to knowingly use, or to possess with intent to use, drug paraphernalia to plant, propagate, cultivate, grow, harvest, manufacture, compound, convert, produce, process, prepare, test, analyze, package, repackage, store, contain, or conceal a controlled substance which it would be unlawful to possess, or to inject, ingest, inhale, or otherwise introduce into the body a controlled substance which it would be unlawful to possess.

(b) Violation of this section is a Class 1 misdemeanor.

Elements

A person guilty of this offense

(1) knowingly
(2) uses or possesses with the intent to use
(3) drug paraphernalia
(4) for any of the following purposes:
  (a) to plant, propagate, cultivate, grow, harvest, manufacture, compound, convert, produce, process, prepare, test, analyze, package, repackage, store, contain, or conceal *or*
  (b) to inject, ingest, inhale, or otherwise introduce into the body
(5) a controlled substance that is unlawful to possess.

Punishment

Class 1 misdemeanor. G.S. 90-113.22(b). G.S. 90-95(e)(3), which elevates a Class 1 misdemeanor under Article 5 of Chapter 90 to a Class I felony if a defendant has a prior drug conviction, does not apply to possession of drug paraphernalia, which is a Class 1 misdemeanor under Article 5B of Chapter 90. State v. Stevens, 151 N.C. App. 561 (2002).

Notes

Element (1). See "Knowingly" in Chapter 1 (States of Mind).

Element (3). "Drug paraphernalia" is defined in G.S. 90-113.21(a), reproduced above. G.S. 90-113.21(b) provides examples of evidence relevant to determining whether an object is drug paraphernalia, such as the proximity of the object to a controlled substance.

Triple-beam weighing scales found in a car's trunk in a box next to a suitcase containing cocaine constituted sufficient evidence of drug paraphernalia. State v. Jones, 96 N.C. App. 389 (1989).

Charging issues. See this note to "Sale and Delivery of a Controlled Substance," above.

Multiple convictions and punishments. A defendant may be convicted of both possession of cocaine and possession of drug paraphernalia even though the cocaine was found in the drug paraphernalia. State v. Williams, 149 N.C. App. 795 (2002).

Related Offenses Not in This Chapter

Knowingly manufacture, sell, give, deliver, possess, or use an alcohol vaporizing device. G.S. 90-113.10A.
Manufacture or delivery of drug paraphernalia. G.S. 90-113.23.
Advertisement of drug paraphernalia. G.S. 90-113.24.
Glass tubes or splitters; restrictions on sales. G.S. 90-113.82.

Toxic Fume Offenses

Inhaling Toxic Fumes

Statute

§90-113.10. Inhaling fumes for purpose of causing intoxication.

It is unlawful for any person to knowingly breathe or inhale any compound, liquid, or chemical containing toluol, hexane, trichloroethane, isopropanol, methyl isobutyl ketone, methyl cellosolve acetate, cyclohexanone, ethyl alcohol, or any other substance for the purpose of inducing a condition of intoxication. This section does not apply to any person using as an inhalant any chemical substance pursuant to the direction of a licensed medical provider authorized by law to prescribe the inhalant or chemical substance possessed.

Elements

A person guilty of this offense

(1) knowingly
(2) breathes or inhales
(3) any compound, liquid, or chemical containing
 (a) toluol,
 (b) hexane,
 (c) trichloroethane,

(d) isopropanol,
(e) methyl isobutyl ketone,
(f) methyl cellosolve acetate,
(g) cyclohexanone,
(h) ethyl alcohol, *or*
(i) any other substance
(4) to induce intoxication.

Punishment

Class 1 misdemeanor. G.S. 90-113.13.

Notes

Element (3)(i). Although the statute refers to "any other substance," it is likely that the other substance would have to be of the same general character as the ones listed. The kinds of products likely to contain these substances include fast-drying glues and cements, many paints, lacquers and varnishes, thinners and removers, gasoline, kerosene, lighter and dry-cleaning fluid, fingernail polish remover, and various aerosol products.

Element (4). G.S. 90-113.9 defines "intoxication" as "drunkenness, stupefaction, depression, giddiness, paralysis, irrational behavior, or other change, distortion, or disturbance of the auditory, visual or mental processes."

Exceptions. This offense does not apply "to any person using as an inhalant any chemical substance pursuant to the direction of a licensed medical provider authorized by law to prescribe the inhalant or chemical substance possessed." G.S. 90-113.10.

Related Offenses Not in This Chapter

Knowingly manufacture, sell, give, deliver, possess, or use an alcohol vaporizing device. G.S. 90-113.10A.

Glass tubes and splitters; restrictions on sales. G.S. 90-113.82.

Possession of a Toxic Substance

Statute

§90-113.11. Possession of substances.

It is unlawful for any person to possess any compound, liquid, or chemical containing toluol, hexane, trichloroethane, isopropanol, methyl isobutyl ketone, methyl cellosolve acetate, cyclohexanone, ethyl alcohol, or any other substance which will induce a condition of intoxication through inhalation for the purpose of violating G.S. 90-113.10.

Elements

A person guilty of this offense

(1) possesses
(2) any compound, liquid, or chemical containing
(a) toluol,
(b) hexane,
(c) trichloroethane,
(d) isopropanol,
(e) methyl isobutyl ketone,
(f) methyl cellosolve acetate,
(g) cyclohexanone,
(h) ethyl alcohol, *or*
(i) any other substance

(3) for the purpose of violating G.S. 90-113.10.

Punishment

Class 1 misdemeanor. G.S. 90-113.13.

Notes

Element (1). Presumably "possession" for this statute would be the same as possession for the North Carolina Controlled Substances Act, which means that the possession may be either actual or constructive. See the note on Element (2) to "Possession of a Controlled Substance," above, for a discussion of the term "possesses" as it applies to controlled substances offenses.

Element (2). See the note on Element (3) to "Inhaling Toxic Fumes," above.

Element (3). The reference to G.S. 90-113.10 means that the possession must be for purposes of committing the offense of "Inhaling Toxic Fumes," above.

Related Offenses Not in This Chapter

See the offenses listed under "Inhaling Toxic Fumes", above.

Sale, etc. of a Toxic Substance

Statute

§90-113.12. Sale of substance.

It is unlawful for any person to sell, offer to sell, deliver, give, or possess with the intent to sell, deliver, or give any other person any compound, liquid, or chemical containing toluol, hexane, trichloroethane, isopropanol, methyl isobutyl ketone, methyl cellosolve acetate, cyclohexanone, ethyl alcohol, or any other substance which will induce a condition of intoxication through inhalation if he has reasonable cause to suspect that the product sold, offered for sale, given, delivered, or possessed with the intent to sell, give, or deliver, will be used for the purpose of violating G.S. 90-113.10.

Elements

A person guilty of this offense

(1) sells, offers to sell, delivers, or gives
(2) a compound, liquid, or chemical containing
  (a) toluol,
  (b) hexane,
  (c) trichloroethane,
  (d) isopropanol,
  (e) methyl isobutyl ketone,
  (f) methyl cellosolve acetate,
  (g) cyclohexanone,
  (h) ethyl alcohol, *or*
  (i) any other substance
(3) to another person,
(4) having reasonable grounds to believe that it will be used in violation of G.S. 90-113.10.

Punishment

Class 1 misdemeanor. G.S. 90-113.13.

Notes

Element (1). For a discussion of the terms "sells" and "delivers" as used in controlled substances offenses, see the notes on Elements (2)(a) and (b) to "Sale or Delivery of a Controlled Substance," above.

Element (2). See the note on Element (3) to "Inhaling Toxic Fumes", above.

Element (4). The reference to G.S. 90-113.10 means that the defendant must have reason to believe that the person to whom he or she sells or gives the toxic substance will commit the offense of "Inhaling Toxic Fumes," above.

Related Offenses Not in This Chapter

See the offenses listed under "Inhaling Toxic Fumes," above.

Possession of a Toxic Substance with Intent to Sell, etc.

Statute

See G.S. 90-113.12, reproduced under "Sale, etc. of a Toxic Substance," above.

Elements

A person guilty of this offense

(1) possesses
(2) a compound, liquid, or chemical containing
  (a) tuluol,
  (b) hexane,
  (c) trichloroethane,
  (d) isopropanol,
  (e) methyl isobutyl ketone,
  (f) methyl cellosolve acetate,
  (g) cyclohexanone,
  (h) ethyl alcohol, *or*
  (i) a similar substance
(3) with the intent to sell, deliver, or give that substance
(4) to another person,
(5) having reasonable grounds to believe that the other person will use it in violation of G.S. 90-113.10.

Punishment

Class 1 misdemeanor. G.S. 90-113.13.

Notes

Element (1). For a discussion of the term "possesses," as used in controlled substances offenses, see the note on Element (2) to "Possession of a Controlled Substance," above.

Element (2). See the note on Element (3) to "Inhaling Toxic Fumes," above.

Element (3). The intent might be shown by the amount of the toxic substance possessed or the circumstances under which it is possessed, such as being hidden or being near paraphernalia that might indicate illegal use. On this subject, see the note on Element (4) to "Possession of a Controlled Substance with Intent to Manufacture, Sell, or Deliver," above.

Element (5). The reference to G.S. 90-113.10 means that the defendant who possesses the toxic substance must have some reason to believe that the person to whom the defendant intends to give or sell the substance will commit the offense of "Inhaling Toxic Fumes," above.

Related Offenses Not in This Chapter

See the offenses listed under "Inhaling Toxic Fumes," above.

28 Motor Vehicle Offenses

28
Motor Vehicle Offenses

Driving While License Revoked or Disqualified

Statute

§20-28. Unlawful to drive while license revoked, after notification, or while disqualified.

(a) Driving While License Revoked.—Except as provided in subsection (a1) of this section, any person whose drivers license has been revoked who drives any motor vehicle upon the highways of the State while the license is revoked is guilty of a Class 1 misdemeanor. Upon conviction, the person's license shall be revoked for an additional period of one year for the first offense, two years for the second offense, and permanently for a third or subsequent offense.

The restoree of a revoked drivers license who operates a motor vehicle upon the highways of the State without maintaining financial responsibility as provided by law shall be punished as for driving without a license.

(a1) Driving Without Reclaiming License.—A person convicted under subsection (a) shall be punished as if the person had been convicted of driving without a license under G.S. 20-35 if the person demonstrates to the court that either subdivisions (1) and (2), or subdivision (3) of this subsection is true:

(1) At the time of the offense, the person's license was revoked solely under G.S. 20-16.5; and

(2) a. The offense occurred more than 45 days after the effective date of a revocation order issued under G.S. 20-16.5(f) and the period of revocation was 45 days as provided under subdivision (3) of that subsection; or

b. The offense occurred more than 30 days after the effective date of the revocation order issued under any other provision of G.S. 20-16.5; or

(3) At the time of the offense the person had met the requirements of G.S. 50-13.12, or G.S. 110-142.2 and was eligible for reinstatement of the person's drivers license privilege as provided therein.

In addition, a person punished under this subsection shall be treated for drivers license and insurance rating purposes as if the person had been convicted of driving without a license under G.S. 20-35, and the conviction report sent to the Division must indicate that the person is to be so treated.

(a2) Driving After Notification or Failure to Appear.—A person shall be guilty of a Class 1 misdemeanor if:

(1) The person operates a motor vehicle upon a highway while that person's license is revoked for an impaired drivers license revocation after the Division has sent notification in accordance with G.S. 20-48; or

(2) The person fails to appear for two years from the date of the charge after being charged with an implied-consent offense.

Upon conviction, the person's drivers license shall be revoked for an additional period of one year for the first offense, two years for the second offense, and permanently for a third or subsequent offense. The restoree of a revoked drivers license who operates a motor vehicle upon the highways of the State without maintaining financial responsibility as provided by law shall be punished as for driving without a license.

(b) Repealed by Session Laws 1993 (Reg. Sess. 1994), c. 761, s. 3.

Subsections (c), (c1), (c2), (c3), (c4), and (c5) are not reproduced here.

(d) Driving While Disqualified.—A person who was convicted of a violation that disqualified the person and required the person's drivers license to be revoked who drives a motor vehicle during the revocation period is punishable as provided in the other subsections of this section. A person who has been disqualified who drives a commercial motor vehicle during the disqualification period is guilty of a Class 1 misdemeanor and is disqualified for an additional period as follows:

(1) For a first offense of driving while disqualified, a person is disqualified for a period equal to the period for which the person was disqualified when the offense occurred.

(2) For a second offense of driving while disqualified, a person is disqualified for a period equal to two times the period for which the person was disqualified when the offense occurred.

(3) For a third offense of driving while disqualified, a person is disqualified for life.

The Division may reduce a disqualification for life under this subsection to 10 years in accordance with the guidelines adopted under G.S. 20-17.4(b). A person who drives a commercial motor vehicle while the person is disqualified and the person's drivers license is revoked is punishable for both driving while the person's license was revoked and driving while disqualified.

Driving While License Revoked

Statute

See G.S. 20-28(a), reproduced above.

Elements

A person guilty of this offense

(1) drives
(2) a motor vehicle
(3) on a highway
(4) knowing
(5) that his or her driver's license is revoked.

Punishment

Class 1 misdemeanor. G.S. 20-28(a). In two instances, punishment is reduced to that applicable to driving without a license, G.S. 20-7 (proscribing that crime), an offense punished under G.S. 20-35 as a Class 2 misdemeanor. G.S. 20-28(a) and (a1). The first instance is when a person drives while his or her license is revoked solely under G.S. 20-16.5 (the pretrial revocation that applies to implied consent offenses) and either (1) the offense occurred more than forty-five days after the effective date of a G.S. 20-16.5(f) revocation that lasted for forty-five days; or (2) it occurred more than thirty days after the effective date of a revocation order issued under any other provision of G.S. 20-16.5. G.S. 20-28(a1)(1)–(2). The second instance when punishment is reduced to a Class 2 misdemeanor is when a person has met the requirements of G.S. 50-13.12 (forfeiture of licensing privileges for failure to pay child support or failure to comply with subpoena issued pursuant to child support or paternity establishment proceedings) or G.S. 110-142.2 (suspension, revocation, restriction of license to operate a motor vehicle or hunting, fishing, or trapping licenses; refusal of registration of motor vehicle) and the person was eligible for reinstatement of his or her driver's license when charged with this offense. G.S. 20-28(a1)(3).

Notes

Element (1). A person "drives" when he or she is "in actual physical control of a vehicle which is in motion or which has the engine running." G.S. 20-4.01(7) and (25). The terms "driving" and "operating" are synonymous. G.S. 20-4.01(7); State v. Coker, 312 N.C. 432 (1984).

Element (2). The term "motor vehicle" includes "[e]very vehicle which is self-propelled and every vehicle designed to run upon the highways which is pulled by a self-propelled vehicle." G.S. 20-4.01(23). Mopeds, however, are not motor vehicles. *Id.* To qualify as a moped, the vehicle must have two or three wheels, no external shifting device, and a motor that does not exceed 50 cubic centimeters piston displacement and cannot propel the vehicle at a speed greater than 30 mph on a level surface. G.S. 20-4.01(27)(d1); G.S. 105-164.3(22).

Element (3). A "highway" is "[t]he entire width between property or right-of-way lines of every way or place of whatever nature, when any part thereof is open to the use of the public as a matter of right for the purposes of vehicular traffic." G.S. 20-4.01(13). The terms "street" and "highway" are synonymous. *Id.*; G.S. 20-4.01(46). For this offense to apply, the driving must occur on a highway; other types of public vehicular areas are not covered. See the note on Element (3) to "Impaired Driving," below, for a discussion of the term "public vehicular area."

Element (4). The State must prove that the defendant had actual or constructive knowledge of the revocation. State v. Atwood, 290 N.C. 266, 271 (1976); State v. Cruz, 173 N.C. App. 689, 697 (2005). Proof by the State that it complied with the notice requirements of G.S. 20-48 creates a rebuttable presumption that the defendant had the requisite knowledge. *Atwood*, 290 N.C. at 271; *Cruz*, 173 N.C. App. at 697.

G.S. 20-48 permits the Department of Motor Vehicles (DMV) to provide notice by personal delivery or by United States mail to a person's address as listed in DMV records. Notice provided by mail is considered complete four days after the mailing. G.S. 20-48(a). Before it was amended in 2006, G.S. 20-48 provided that proof of the giving of notice could be made by a certificate from a DMV employee or another adult naming the person to whom notice was given and specifying the time, place, and manner in which notice was provided. Such a certificate, when combined with a copy of the notice, established a prima facie case of knowledge. *Cruz*, 173 N.C. App. 689. G.S. 20-48 now provides that proof of notice may be made by a notation in DMV records that the notice has been sent and dispenses with the requirement that the actual notice be produced. G.S. 20-48(a). Because, however, DMV has not altered its record-keeping practices to implement this change, the State still must establish constructive notice under G.S. 20-48 by producing the actual notice and a certificate describing the time, place, and manner of notice.

In a case in which the 2006 amendments to G.S. 20-48 did not apply, adequate proof of notice was established when the State introduced a signed certificate of a DMV employee stating that the employee deposited notice of the defendant's license suspension in the mail in a postage-paid envelope addressed to the defendant's address as shown in DMV records. State v. Coltrane, 184 N.C. App. 140 (2007). The State's evidence that it sent notice to the defendant at his address as listed in DMV records created a "prima facie presumption of receipt," notwithstanding the defendant's argument that DMV records reflected an incorrect address; since the defendant presented no evidence, the presumption was not rebutted. *Id.* at 143.

Element (5). G.S. 20-4.01(36) defines the term "revocation" as "[t]ermination of a licensee's or permittee's privilege to drive or termination of the registration of a vehicle for a period of time stated in an order of revocation or suspension." The terms "revocation" and "suspension" are synonymous. *Id.*; G.S. 20-4.01(47).

G.S. 20-4.01(17) defines "license" as "[a]ny driver's license or any other license or permit to operate a motor vehicle issued under or granted by the laws of this State," including:

- any temporary license or learner's permit,
- the privilege to drive a motor vehicle whether or not the person holds a valid license, and
- any nonresident's operating privilege.

Thus, a nonresident or unlicensed resident who is convicted of a motor vehicle offense and has his or her driving privilege revoked in this state as a result of the conviction may be charged with this offense even though he or she has never been issued a North Carolina driver's license.

Charging issues. For a discussion of charging issues in connection with this offense, see Jessica Smith, *The Criminal Indictment: Fatal Defect, Fatal Variance, and Amendment*, ADMIN. OF JUST. BULL. No. 2008/03 (UNC School of Government, July 2008) (online at www.sog.unc.edu/pubs/electronicversions/pdfs/aojb0803.pdf).

Multiple convictions and punishments. A person who drives a commercial motor vehicle while he or she is disqualified from doing so and while his or her driver's license is revoked may be punished for both this offense and "Driving While Commercial Driver's License Disqualified," below. G.S. 20-28(d).

License revocations and disqualifications. For a discussion of the license revocation and disqualification consequences of conviction of a motor vehicle offense, see JOHN RUBIN & SHEA RIGGSBEE DENNING, PUNISHMENTS FOR NORTH CAROLINA CRIMES AND MOTOR VEHICLE OFFENSES: 2008 CUMULATIVE SUPPLEMENT (UNC School of Government, 2009) (online at http://sogpubs.unc.edu/electronicversions/pdfs/punchtsuppl08.pdf).

Related Offenses Not in This Chapter

Driving without a license. G.S. 20-7.

Restoree of a revoked license operating a motor vehicle without maintaining financial responsibility. G.S. 20-28(a); (a2).

Driving While License Revoked for an Impaired Driving Revocation

Statute

See G.S. 20-28(a2)(1), reproduced above.

Elements

A person guilty of this offense

(1) drives
(2) on a highway
(3) while his or her license is revoked for an impaired driver's license revocation
(4) after notification has been sent in accordance with G.S. 20-48.

Punishment

Class 1 misdemeanor. G.S. 20-28(a2).

Notes

Generally. The main differences between this offense and "Driving While License Revoked," above, are:

- this offense applies only to impaired driving revocations while "Driving While License Revoked" applies to all revocations;
- this offense is punished as a Class 1 misdemeanor, with no special punishment provisions, whereas "Driving While License Revoked" is subject to reduced punishment in certain circumstances; and
- for this offense, knowledge of the revocation does not appear to be required—the State need only show that notice was given pursuant to G.S. 20-48; for "Driving While License Revoked," however, the State must prove that the person had knowledge of the revocation.

Element (1). The statute uses the term "operates," which is synonymous with the term "drives." G.S. 20-4.01(7); State v. Coker, 312 N.C. 432 (1984). See the note on Element (1) to "Driving While License Revoked," above, for an explanation of the term "drives." The statute does not specify the type of conveyance that the person must be driving.

Element (2). For an explanation of the term "highway," see the note on Element (3) to "Driving While License Revoked," above.

Element (3). While "Driving While License Revoked," above, applies to any revocation, this offense applies only to an impaired driving revocation under G.S. 20-28.2(a).

Element (4). G.S. 20-48 specifies how the Division of Motor Vehicles should give notice, when notice is complete, and what is required for proof of notice. See the note on Element (4) to "Driving While License Revoked," above, for details.

License revocations and disqualifications. See this note to "Driving While License Revoked," above.

Related Offenses Not in This Chapter

See the offenses listed under "Driving While License Revoked," above.

Driving While Commercial Driver's License Disqualified

Statute

See G.S. 20-28(d), reproduced above.

Elements

A person guilty of this offense

(1) drives
(2) a commercial motor vehicle
(3) on a highway
(4) while his or her commercial driver's license is disqualified.

Punishment

Class 1 misdemeanor. G.S. 20-28(d).

Notes

Element (1). For an explanation of the term "drives," see the note on Element (1) to "Driving While License Revoked," above.

Element (2). G.S. 20-4.01(3d) defines "commercial motor vehicle" as any of the following motor vehicles that are designed or used to transport passengers or property:

- a Class A motor vehicle that has a combined Gross Vehicle Weight Rating (GVWR) of at least 26,001 pounds and includes as a part of the combination a towed unit that has a GVWR of at least 10,001 pounds;
- a Class B motor vehicle; or
- a Class C motor vehicle that is designed to transport sixteen or more passengers, including the driver, or that is transporting hazardous materials and is required to be placarded in accordance with 49 C.F.R. part 172, subpart F.

G.S. 20-4.01(2a), (2b), and (2c) define Class A, Class B, and Class C motor vehicles, respectively. G.S. 20-4.01(12e) defines GVWR.

Element (3). G.S. 20-28(d) does not explicitly require that this offense occur on a highway. However, a person is not required to have a commercial driver's license to operate a commercial vehicle in areas that are not included in the definition of highway. G.S. 20-37.12. Therefore, it seems implicit that this offense must occur on a highway. For the meaning of the term "highway," see the note on Element (3) to "Driving While License Revoked," above.

Element (4). A commercial driver's license authorizes a person to drive a particular class of commercial motor vehicle. G.S. 20-4.01(3c). Disqualification means that a person may not legally drive a commercial vehicle. However, the person may drive a noncommercial vehicle if his or her license to drive the noncommercial vehicle is not otherwise revoked. G.S. 20-4.01(5a) and 20-17.5.

Multiple convictions and punishments. A person who drives a commercial motor vehicle while he or she is disqualified from doing so and while his or her driver's license is revoked may be punished for both this offense and "Driving While License Revoked," above. G.S. 20-28(d).

License revocations and disqualifications. See this note to "Driving While License Revoked," above.

Related Offenses Not in This Chapter

See the offenses listed under "Driving While License Revoked," above.
Possession of driver's license in addition to commercial driver's license. G.S. 20-30(8).

Failure to Appear after an Implied Consent Offense Charge

Statute

See G.S. 20-28(a2), reproduced above.

Elements

A person guilty of this offense

(1) fails to appear
(2) for two years
(3) from the date he or she was charged with an implied consent offense.

Punishment

Class 1 misdemeanor. G.S. 20-28(a2).

Notes

Element (1). Although the statute does not say, presumably the term "fails to appear" means to "fail[] to appear before any court or judicial official as required" in connection with the charged implied consent offense. *See* G.S. 15A-543.

Element (2). It is not clear whether a person who appeared one time but then failed to appear for a subsequent court date could be charged with this offense.

Element (3). G.S. 20-16.2(a1) provides that the term "implied-consent offense" includes

- an "offense involving impaired driving,"
- misdemeanor death by vehicle in violation of G.S. 20-141.4(a2) (but only if the offense is committed on or after December 1, 2011), and
- an alcohol-related offense made subject to G.S. 20-16.2.

Additionally, G.S. 20-138.2A(b) provides that operating a commercial vehicle after consuming alcohol is an implied consent offense.

As noted above, implied consent offenses include any "offense involving impaired driving." G.S. 20-4.01(24a) identifies the following offenses as "offenses involving impaired driving":

- impaired driving,
- habitual impaired driving,
- impaired driving in commercial vehicle,
- death or serious injury by vehicle under G.S. 20-141.4 based on impaired driving,
- first- or second-degree murder under G.S. 14-17 based on impaired driving,
- involuntary manslaughter under G.S. 14-18 based on impaired driving,
- a repealed or superseded offense substantially similar to impaired driving, and
- substantially similar offenses committed in another state or jurisdiction.

Also as noted above, the term "implied consent offense" includes alcohol-related offenses made subject to G.S. 20-16.2. Alcohol-related offenses made subject to that provision include

- driving by a person under 21 years of age after consuming alcohol or drugs, G.S. 20-138.3(b),
- operating a school bus, school activity bus, or child care vehicle after consuming alcohol, G.S. 20-138.2B(b),
- impaired supervision or instruction, G.S. 20-12.1(b),
- transporting an open container of alcoholic beverage, G.S. 20-138.7(b), and
- violation of a limited driving privilege, G.S. 20-179.3(j).

License revocations and disqualifications. See this note to "Driving While License Revoked," above.

Related Offenses Not in This Chapter

See the offenses listed under "Driving While License Revoked," above.
"Failure to Appear" (Chapter 21)

Impaired Driving and Related Offenses

Impaired Driving

Statute

§20-138.1. Impaired driving.

(a) Offense.—A person commits the offense of impaired driving if he drives any vehicle upon any highway, any street, or any public vehicular area within this State:

(1) While under the influence of an impairing substance; or

(2) After having consumed sufficient alcohol that he has, at any relevant time after the driving, an alcohol concentration of 0.08 or more. The results of a chemical analysis shall be deemed sufficient evidence to prove a person's alcohol concentration; or

(3) With any amount of a Schedule I controlled substance, as listed in G.S. 90-89, or its metabolites in his blood or urine.

(a1) A person who has submitted to a chemical analysis of a blood sample, pursuant to G.S. 20-139.1(d), may use the result in rebuttal as evidence that the person did not have, at a relevant time after driving, an alcohol concentration of 0.08 or more.

(b) Defense Precluded.—The fact that a person charged with violating this section is or has been legally entitled to use alcohol or a drug is not a defense to a charge under this section.

(b1) Defense Allowed.—Nothing in this section shall preclude a person from asserting that a chemical analysis result is inadmissible pursuant to G.S. 20-139.1(b2).

(c) Pleading.—In any prosecution for impaired driving, the pleading is sufficient if it states the time and place of the alleged offense in the usual form and charges that the defendant drove a vehicle on a highway or public vehicular area while subject to an impairing substance.

(d) Sentencing Hearing and Punishment.—Impaired driving as defined in this section is a misdemeanor. Upon conviction of a defendant of impaired driving, the presiding judge shall hold a sentencing hearing and impose punishment in accordance with G.S. 20-179.

(e) Exception.—Notwithstanding the definition of "vehicle" pursuant to G.S. 20-4.01(49), for purposes of this section the word "vehicle" does not include a horse.

Elements

A person guilty of this offense

(1) drives

(2) a vehicle

(3) on a street, highway, or public vehicular area

(4) (a) while under the influence of an impairing substance,

(b) after consuming a sufficient quantity of alcohol that the person has an alcohol concentration of 0.08 or more at any relevant time after the driving, *or*

(c) with any amount of a Schedule I controlled substance or its metabolites in his or her blood or urine.

Punishment

This offense is a misdemeanor, G.S. 20-138.1(d), to which the Structured Sentencing laws do not apply. See generally Chapter 4 (Punishment under Structured Sentencing). Rather, punishment is prescribed by G.S. 20-179. *Id.* For offenses committed before December 1, 2011, there are five different levels of punishment. A defendant is assigned to a particular punishment level based on the presence of and weight assigned to certain aggravating and mitigating factors found by the court. Punishment for each level is as follows:

Level One: Minimum imprisonment of thirty days, maximum imprisonment of two years, and a maximum fine of $4,000. G.S. 20-179(g). The term of imprisonment may be suspended in specified circumstances. *Id.* The judge may impose as a probation condition that the defendant abstain from alcohol consumption for a minimum of thirty days to a maximum of sixty days, as verified by a continuous alcohol monitoring system (CAM). G.S. 20-179(h1).

Level Two: Minimum imprisonment of seven days, maximum imprisonment of one year, and a maximum fine of $2,000. G.S. 20-179(h). The term of imprisonment may be suspended in specified circumstances. *Id.* The judge may impose as a probation condition that the defendant abstain from alcohol consumption for a minimum of thirty days to a maximum of sixty days, as verified by a CAM. G.S. 20-179(h1).

Level Three: Minimum imprisonment of seventy-two hours, maximum imprisonment of six months, and a maximum fine of $1,000. G.S. 20-179(i). The term of imprisonment may be suspended on the condition that the defendant meet at least one of the following two conditions: at least seventy-two hours of community service or imprisonment for at least seventy-two hours. *Id.*

Level Four: Minimum imprisonment of forty-eight hours, maximum imprisonment of 120 days, and a maximum fine of $500. G.S. 20-179(j). The term of imprisonment may be suspended on the condition that the defendant meet at least one of the following two conditions: forty-eight hours of community service or imprisonment for forty-eight hours. *Id.*

Level Five: Minimum imprisonment of twenty-four hours, maximum imprisonment of sixty days, and a maximum fine of $200. G.S. 20-179(k). The term of imprisonment may be suspended on the condition that the defendant meet at least one of the following two conditions: twenty-four hours of community service or imprisonment for twenty-four hours. *Id.*

For each of the above punishment levels, special probation may be imposed in which a person serves a term of imprisonment equal to that level's minimum imprisonment period. Also, under G.S. 20-179(k1), inpatient treatment at a facility operated or licensed by the state for the treatment of alcoholism or substance abuse may substitute for jail time if the treatment occurs after the commission of the offense for which the defendant is being sentenced. If a defendant is placed on probation in any level, the sentencing judge must impose a requirement that the defendant obtain a substance abuse assessment and the education or treatment required by G.S. 20-17.6 for license restoration. G.S. 20-179(g)–(k).

For offenses committed on or after December 1, 2011, there is an additional punishment level for impairing driving offenses. Specifically, S.L. 2011-191 creates a new Aggravated Level One punishment (Level A1) when at least three grossly aggravating factors are present. A conviction punished at Level A1 requires a minimum term of twelve months imprisonment up to a maximum term of thirty-six months. The maximum fine is $10,000. The court can suspend the sentence only if a condition of special probation is imposed requiring the defendant to serve a term of imprisonment of at least 120 days. If a defendant convicted of a Level A1 offense is placed on probation, the judge must require the defendant to abstain from alcohol for at least 120 days up to the entire term of probation, as verified by a CAM. As is the case for probationary sentences imposed for other levels of impaired driving, the judge must require as a condition of probation for a Level A1 sentence that the defendant obtain a substance abuse assessment and the education or treatment required by G.S. 20-17.6. A defendant sentenced for a Level A1 offense is not eligible for parole. Level A1 defendants must, however, be released from imprisonment four months before the end of the "maximum imposed term of imprisonment" and must be placed on post-release supervision with a requirement that they abstain from alcohol during this four-month period, as verified by a CAM.

S.L. 2011-191 affects other types of impaired driving sentencing as well. Amended G.S. 20-179(h1) increases from sixty days to the term of probation the maximum period for which abstinence from alcohol consumption and monitoring (CAM) may be required of defendants sentenced for Level One or Two offenses. It also eliminates the provision in G.S. 20-179(h1) that formerly capped a defendant's total CAM costs at $1,000 and repeals G.S. 20-179(h2), which had prohibited a court from requiring CAM if it determined that the defendant "should not be required to pay the costs" of CAM and the local government entity responsible for the defendant's incarceration was unwilling to pay for CAM.

A separate piece of 2011 legislation, S.L. 2011-329, also impacts sentencing under G.S. 20-179. That legislation amends G.S. 20-179 to require, effective for offenses committed on or after December 1, 2011, that persons convicted of covered impaired driving offenses be sentenced to Level One punishment if the grossly aggravating factor in G.S. 20-179(c)(4) exists. The act also amends the grossly aggravating factor in G.S. 20-179(c)(4), making it apply when the defendant drives while impaired with a passenger who is:

- a child under the age of 18,
- a person with the mental development of a child under the age of 18, or
- a person with a physical disability that prevents the person from getting out of the vehicle without assistance.

A judge is not authorized to enter a prayer for judgment continued for an impaired driving offense; the judge must enter a sentence pursuant to G.S. 20-179. *In re* Tucker, 348 N.C. 677 (1998).

Finally, impaired driving convictions may not be consolidated with each other for judgment. G.S. 20-179(f2).

Notes

Element (1). For a discussion of the term "drives," see the note on Element (1) to "Driving While License Revoked," above.

The evidence was sufficient to establish that the defendant was driving the vehicle in question when (1) there was blood on the driver's side airbag and blood on the defendant but no blood on the passenger side; the driver's seat was pushed too far back for the only other person involved to have been driving; and the other person experienced a fabric burn consistent with a passenger-side seatbelt injury, State v. Hernandez, 188 N.C. App. 193, 200 (2008); (2) a law enforcement officer found a motionless vehicle in the road with the defendant behind the wheel and the vehicle's owner on the passenger side; both claimed that the owner had been driving, that he stopped the vehicle so that they could use the bathroom, and that the defendant got back into the driver's seat and turned the car on because he was cold, State v. Fields, 77 N.C. App. 404 (1985); (3) after seeing tire marks on the road, dust in the air, and a car, with its headlights on, lying upside down in a field near the highway, another driver found the defendant in the overturned car, the doors of which were closed and the windows rolled up; no one else was in the area; the tire marks on the road lead to the overturned car; and an officer could not open the car doors, State v. Dula, 77 N.C. App. 473 (1985); (4) the defendant was seen getting out of the car immediately after the collision and no one else was seen in or near the car; the defendant claimed that his friend had been driving but that he fled; the defendant claimed that his friend left through the driver's side door, but an officer was unable to open that door because of collision damage; and when a wrecker driver arrived, the defendant pulled the car keys out of his pocket and handed them to the wrecker driver, State v. Riddle, 56 N.C. App. 701 (1982); and (5) a witness testified about her observations of the car, which continued from her first sighting of it until the car stopped in the median and the police arrived; the witness did not observe the driver or anyone else exit the car and the car did not move; an officer testified that when she arrived at the scene shortly after the call went out, another officer was already talking to the driver who was still seated in the car, State v. Clowers, ___ N.C. App. ___, ___ S.E.2d ___ (Dec. 20, 2011).

By contrast, the evidence was insufficient to establish that the defendant was driving when an officer found the defendant sitting "approximately halfway in the front seat, between the driver and passenger area in the front seat"; the officer noticed that the defendant smelled of alcohol and had a gash above his nose but no evidence suggested that the defendant had been driving. State v. Ray, 54 N.C. App. 473, 475 (1981).

Element (2). G.S. 20-4.01(49) defines a "vehicle" as "[e]very device in, upon, or by which any person or property is or may be transported or drawn upon a highway, excepting devices moved by human power or used exclusively upon fixed rails or tracks." However, bicycles are vehicles despite being moved by human power. G.S. 20-4.01(49). Certain devices used as transportation by a person with a mobility impairment are excluded from the definition of the term "vehicle." *Id.* Horses are not vehicles for purposes of the impaired driving offense only. G.S. 20-138.1(e). Mopeds are vehicles but are not motor vehicles. G.S. 20-4.01(21a), (23), and (27d1).

A motorized scooter having two wheels approximately 6–8 inches in diameter arranged in tandem is a vehicle for purposes of impaired driving. State v. Crow, 175 N.C. App. 119 (2005).

Element (3). For an explanation of the terms "street" and "highway," see the note on Element (3) to "Driving While License Revoked," above.

G.S. 20-4.01(32) defines "public vehicular area" as any area that falls in one or more of four categories. The first category includes areas used by the public for vehicular traffic at any time. G.S. 20-4.01(32)(a). Examples include a drive, driveway, road, roadway, street, alley, or parking lot on the grounds of

- any public or private hospital, college, university, school, orphanage, church, or any institution, park, or other facility maintained and supported by the State or its subdivisions;
- any service station, drive-in theater, supermarket, store, restaurant, or office building, or any other business, residential, or municipal establishment providing parking space whether the business or establishment is open or closed; and
- property owned by the United States and subject to the State's jurisdiction.

Id. The second category includes beach areas used by the public for vehicular traffic. G.S. 20-4.01(32)(b). The third category of public vehicular areas includes roads used by vehicular traffic within or leading to gated or nongated subdivisions or communities, whether or not the subdivision or community roads have been offered for dedication to the public. G.S. 20-4.01(32)(c). The fourth category includes any portion of private property used by vehicular traffic and designated by the private property owner as a public vehicular area in accordance with G.S. 20-219.4. G.S. 20-4.01(32)(d).

Courts have held each of the following types of property to be a public vehicular area:

- a privately owned mobile home park in which the streets are marked and open for the use of residents and visitors, State v. Turner, 117 N.C. App. 457 (1994); and
- a private nightclub's parking lot when the lot could generally be used as a thoroughfare by the general public to access the club or an adjacent motel, State v. Snyder, 343 N.C. 61 (1996).

Both *Turner* and *Snyder* interpreted now-repealed language in G.S. 20-4.01(32) stating that a public vehicular area included property "generally open to and used by the public for vehicular traffic." However, both cases would likely come out the same based on the current definition of that term.

Element (4) generally. Elements (4)(a) through (c) are alternate ways of establishing impairment; all that is required for conviction is proof of either Element (4)(a), (4)(b), or (4)(c).

Element (4)(a). G.S. 20-4.01(14a) defines "impairing substance" as including "[a]lcohol, controlled substance under Chapter 90 of the General Statutes, any other drug or psychoactive substance capable of impairing a person's physical or mental faculties, or any combination of these substances." For a description of substances that constitute controlled substances, see the note on Element (3) to "Sale or Delivery of a Controlled Substance" in Chapter 27 (Drug Offenses).

G.S. 20-4.01(48b) defines "under the influence of an impairing substance" to mean "[t]he state of a person having his physical or mental faculties, or both, appreciably impaired by an impairing substance."

If the State presents evidence that the defendant has been drinking and that the defendant engaged in faulty driving, this constitutes a prima facie showing of impairment. State v. Coffey, 189 N.C. App. 382, 387 (2008) (quoting Atkins v. Moye, 277 N.C. 179, 185 (1970)); State v. Norton, ___ N.C. App. ___, 712 S.E.2d 387, 390 (2011) (quoting *Coffey*).

There was sufficient evidence to support an impaired driving conviction when (1) the defendant's alcohol concentration was 0.07, she admitted consuming alcohol before driving, there was an open half-filled bottle of vodka in the passenger area of her car, and an officer smelled alcohol and thought that the defendant's faculties were appreciably impaired, State v. Wood, 174 N.C. App. 790 (2005); (2) the defendant was driving over 60 mph, he did not immediately stop for the officer, and when he did stop, he blocked an intersection; the officer smelled a strong odor of alcohol and observed an open container of beer in the vehicle; and the defendant's coat appeared wet from beer waste, his speech was slurred, and he refused to take Alco-Sensor and Intoxilyzer tests, State v. Scott, 356 N.C. 591 (2002); (3) the responding officer believed that the defendant was impaired and smelled a strong odor of alcohol about him; the defendant drove across the center line of the road on which he was traveling, was sleepy, and had difficulty walking and speaking clearly; and the defendant refused to take the Intoxilyzer test, State v. Allen, 164 N.C. App. 665 (2004); (4) the defendant drank at a party, drove 92 mph in a 45 mph speed zone, and ran off the road; the defendant's eyes were red and glassy and he had trouble maintaining his balance, *Coffey*, 189 N.C. App. at 387; and (5) the defendant had a "wild look" and appeared to be in a rage, drove recklessly without regard for human life, drove in circles on a busy street and on a golf course, twice collided with other motorists, drove at speeds varying between 45 and 100 mph; he drove with the car door open and with his leg and both hands hanging out and struck a patrol vehicle; and blood tests established the defendant's alcohol and cocaine use, and a witness smelled alcohol on the defendant, *Norton*, ___ N.C. App. at ___, 712 S.E.2d at 390–91.

By contrast, the evidence was insufficient to establish that the defendant was impaired when although it showed that the defendant had been drinking before driving, the accident occurred when the defendant collided with someone or something extending over the double yellow line and into the defendant's lane of traffic; the fact of the collision itself did not establish faulty or irregular driving indicating impairment. State v. Davis, ___ N.C. App. ___, 702 S.E.2d 507, 516 (2010) (addressing impairment as it related to reckless driving and assault with a deadly weapon inflicting serious injury).

Element (4)(b). "Alcohol" is "any substance containing any form of alcohol, including ethanol, methanol, propanol, and isopropanol." G.S. 20-4.01(1a). "Alcohol concentration" is "[t]he concentration of alcohol in a person, expressed either as grams of alcohol per 100 milliliters of blood or grams of alcohol per 210 liters of breath." G.S. 20-4.01(1b). G.S. 20-4.01(33a) defines "relevant time after the driving" as "[a]ny time after the driving in which the driver still has in his body alcohol consumed before or during the driving." The practical effect of these definitions is that the State proves this element if it shows that the defendant had an alcohol concentration of 0.08 or more when the chemical analysis was made, as long as the alcohol was in the defendant's body when the driving stopped. The alcohol concentration at the time of the driving is not required to prove this element.

The results of a chemical analysis are sufficient evidence to prove a person's alcohol concentration. G.S. 20-138.1(a)(2). The evidence was sufficient to show that an Intoxilyzer test was administered on the defendant when a technician testified that he administered the test to the defendant. State v. Clowers, ___ N.C. App. ___, ___ S.E.2d ___ (Dec. 20, 2011) (although the technician did not directly identify the defendant as the person to whom he administered the test, an officer identified the defendant in the courtroom as the person who was arrested and transported to the jail to submit to the test). A person who has submitted to a chemical analysis of a blood sample pursuant to G.S. 20-139.1(d) may use the result in rebuttal as evidence that he or she did not have, at a relevant time after driving, the required alcohol concentration. G.S. 20-138.1(a1).

The evidence was sufficient to sustain a conviction for impaired driving when there were two Intoxilyzer 0.08 readings; the court rejected the defendant's argument that the evidence was insufficient because the blood alcohol reading was the lowest for which he could be convicted under the statute. State v. Arrington, ___ N.C. App. ___, 714 S.E.2d 777 (2011).

Even if a defendant's blood alcohol concentration at a relevant time after driving is less than 0.08, the defendant still may be convicted of impaired driving under Element (4)(a), an alternative way to establish impairment.

Element (4)(c). For a list of Schedule I controlled substances, see G.S. 90-89, reproduced in Chapter 27 (Drug Offenses).

Constitutionality. This statute is not unconstitutionally vague. State v. Rose, 312 N.C. 441 (1984).

Charging issues. See this note to "Driving While License Revoked," above.

Aiders and abettors. Aiders and abettors to impaired driving are punished at Level Five. G.S. 20-179(f1). See "Punishment," above, for a description of Level Five punishment. This is an exception to the general rule that aiders and abettors are punished as if they were principals. See "Aiding and Abetting" in Chapter 3 (Participants in Crimes).

Double jeopardy issues. Neither imposition of a thirty-day pretrial license revocation under G.S. 20-16.5, State v. Hinchman, 192 N.C. App. 657 (2008); State v. Evans, 145 N.C. App. 324 (2001), nor seizure of the defendant's out-of-state driver's license in conjunction with a pretrial revocation, State v. Streckfuss, 171 N.C. App. 81 (2005), constitute punishment under the Double Jeopardy Clause, and thus neither action bars a later prosecution for impaired driving.

Defenses. The fact that a person is legally entitled to use alcohol or a drug is not a defense to this offense. G.S. 20-138.1(b). G.S. 20-138.1(b1) provides that nothing precludes a person from asserting that a chemical analysis result is inadmissible pursuant to G.S. 20-139.1(b2).

Verdict. Because a not guilty verdict of impaired driving and a guilty verdict of "Felony Serious Injury by a Vehicle," below, are merely inconsistent and not legally contradictory, a trial court does not err by accepting the verdict if it is supported by sufficient evidence. State v. Mumford, 364 N.C. 394, 401 (2010).

Greater and lesser-included offenses. Impaired driving is a lesser-included offense of "Felony Death by Vehicle," in Chapter 6 (Homicide). State v. Davis, 198 N.C. App. 443, 452–53 (2009). Reckless driving is not a lesser-included offense of impaired driving. *In re* Brown, 351 N.C. 601 (2000).

G.S. 20-138.2B provides that "Operating a School Bus, School Activity Bus, or Child Care Vehicle after Consuming Alcohol," below, is a lesser-included offense of impaired driving in a commercial vehicle under G.S. 20-138.1. This provision is confusing because G.S. 20-138.1 proscribes the offense of impaired driving, while G.S. 20-138.2 proscribes the offense of impaired driving in a commercial vehicle.

Multiple convictions and punishments. A defendant may be convicted of impaired driving and second-degree murder when the evidence of malice supporting the murder charge is that the defendant drove while impaired and had prior impaired driving convictions. State v. McAllister, 138 N.C. App. 252, 256–57 (2000); State v. Armstrong, ___ N.C. App. ___, 691 S.E.2d 433, 438 (2010) (citing *McAllister*). A defendant also may be convicted of impaired driving and involuntary manslaughter arising out of the same incident. State v. Davis, 198 N.C. App. 443,

453 (2009). However, because impaired driving is a lesser-included offense of felony death by vehicle, a defendant may not be sentenced for both felony death by vehicle and impaired driving arising out of the same incident. *Id.*

License revocations. See this note to "Driving While License Revoked," above.

Related Offenses Not in This Chapter

See murder (various offenses) in Chapter 6 (Homicide).
See manslaughter (various offenses) in Chapter 6 (Homicide).
See death by vehicle (various offenses) in Chapter 6 (Homicide).
Transporting open container of fortified wine or spirituous liquor. G.S. 18B-401.
Driving motor vehicle while consuming malt beverage or unfortified wine. *Id.*
Impaired supervision or instruction. G.S. 20-12.1.
Tampering with, circumventing, or attempting to circumvent an ignition interlock system. G.S. 20-17.8A
Possession of alcoholic beverages while operating a commercial motor vehicle. G.S. 20-138.2C.
Transporting an open container of alcoholic beverage. G.S. 20-138.7.

Impaired Driving in a Commercial Vehicle

Statute

§20-138.2. Impaired driving in commercial vehicle.

(a) Offense.—A person commits the offense of impaired driving in a commercial vehicle if he drives a commercial motor vehicle upon any highway, any street, or any public vehicular area within the State:

(1) While under the influence of an impairing substance; or
(2) After having consumed sufficient alcohol that he has, at any relevant time after the driving, an alcohol concentration of 0.04 or more. The results of a chemical analysis shall be deemed sufficient evidence to prove a person's alcohol concentration; or
(3) With any amount of a Schedule I controlled substance, as listed in G.S. 90-89, or its metabolites in his blood or urine.

(a1) A person who has submitted to a chemical analysis of a blood sample, pursuant to G.S. 20-139.1(d), may use the result in rebuttal as evidence that the person did not have, at a relevant time after driving, an alcohol concentration of 0.04 or more.

(a2) In order to prove the gross vehicle weight rating of a vehicle as defined in G.S. 20-4.01(12e), the opinion of a person who observed the vehicle as to the weight, the testimony of the gross vehicle weight rating affixed to the vehicle, the registered or declared weight shown on the Division's records pursuant to G.S. 20-26(b1), the gross vehicle weight rating as determined from the vehicle identification number, the listed gross weight publications from the manufacturer of the vehicle, or any other description or evidence shall be admissible.

(b) Defense Precluded.—The fact that a person charged with violating this section is or has been legally entitled to use alcohol or a drug is not a defense to a charge under this section.

(b1) Defense Allowed.—Nothing in this section shall preclude a person from asserting that a chemical analysis result is inadmissible pursuant to G.S. 20-139.1(b2).

(c) Pleading.—To charge a violation of this section, the pleading is sufficient if it states the time and place of the alleged offense in the usual form and charges the defendant drove a commercial motor vehicle on a highway, street, or public vehicular area while subject to an impairing substance.

(d) Implied Consent Offense.—An offense under this section is an implied consent offense subject to the provisions of G.S. 20-16.2.

(e) Punishment.—The offense in this section is a misdemeanor and any defendant convicted under this section shall be sentenced under G.S. 20-179. This offense is not a lesser included offense of impaired driving under G.S. 20-138.1, and if a person is convicted under this section and of an offense involving impaired driving under G.S. 20-138.1 arising out of the same transaction, the aggregate punishment imposed by the Court may not exceed the maximum punishment applicable to the offense involving impaired driving under G.S. 20-138.1.

(f) Repealed by Sessions Laws 1991, c. 726, s. 19.

(g) Chemical Analysis Provisions.—The provisions of G.S. 20-139.1 shall apply to the offense of impaired driving in a commercial vehicle.

Elements

A person guilty of this offense

(1) drives
(2) a commercial motor vehicle
(3) on a highway, street, or public vehicular area
(4) (a) while under the influence of an impairing substance,
 (b) after consuming a sufficient quantity of alcohol that the person has an alcohol concentration of 0.04 or more at any relevant time after the driving, *or*
 (c) with any amount of a Schedule I controlled substance or its metabolites in his or her blood or urine.

Punishment

This offense is a misdemeanor and is punished the same as impaired driving. G.S. 20-138.2(e). For a discussion of the punishment scheme for impaired driving, see "Punishment" under "Impaired Driving," above.

Notes

Generally. This offense is the same as "Impaired Driving," above, except that

- "Impaired Driving" applies when the person drives any vehicle and this offense applies only when the person drives a commercial motor vehicle, and
- "Impaired Driving" requires an alcohol concentration of 0.08 and this offense requires a lower concentration of 0.04.

Thus, the notes on the identical elements to that offense apply here as well.

Element (2). For an explanation of the term "commercial motor vehicle," see the note on Element (2) to "Driving While Commercial Driver's License Disqualified," above.

The tractor portion of a tractor-trailer is a commercial motor vehicle. State v. Jones, 140 N.C. App. 691 (2000).

Element (4)(b). The results of a chemical analysis are sufficient evidence to prove a person's alcohol concentration. G.S. 20-138.2(a)(2).

Charging issues. See this note to "Driving While License Revoked," above.

Evidence issues. In order to prove the gross vehicle weight rating (GVWR) of a vehicle, the following types of evidence are admissible:

- the opinion of a person who observed the vehicle as to the weight;
- the testimony of the gross vehicle weight rating affixed to the vehicle;
- the registered or declared weight shown on Division of Motor Vehicle records pursuant to G.S. 20-26(b1);
- the GVWR as determined from the vehicle identification number;

- the listed gross weight publications from the manufacturer of the vehicle; and
- any other description or evidence.

G.S. 20-138.2(a2).

Defenses. The statute for this offense contains the same provisions regarding defenses as the impaired driving statute. For a discussion of those defenses, see this note to "Impaired Driving," above. *See also* G.S. 20-138.2(b) & (b1).

Greater and lesser-included offenses. Impaired driving in a commercial vehicle is not a lesser-included offense of "Impaired Driving," above. G.S. 20-138.2(e). However, "Operating a Commercial Vehicle after Consuming Alcohol," below, is a lesser-included offense of this offense. G.S. 20-138.2A(c).

Multiple convictions and punishments. If a person is convicted of this offense and "Impaired Driving" arising out of the same incident, a court may not impose an aggregate punishment greater than the maximum punishment applicable to the impaired driving offense. G.S. 20-138.2(e).

License revocations and disqualifications. See this note to "Driving While License Revoked," above.

Related Offenses Not in This Chapter

See the offenses listed under "Impaired Driving," above.

Operating a Commercial Vehicle after Consuming Alcohol

Statute

§20-138.2A. Operating a commercial vehicle after consuming alcohol.

(a) Offense.—A person commits the offense of operating a commercial motor vehicle after consuming alcohol if the person drives a commercial motor vehicle, as defined in G.S. 20-4.01(3d)a. and b., upon any highway, any street, or any public vehicular area within the State while consuming alcohol or while alcohol remains in the person's body.

(b) Implied-Consent Offense.—An offense under this section is an implied-consent offense subject to the provisions of G.S. 20-16.2. The provisions of G.S. 20-139.1 shall apply to an offense committed under this section.

(b1) Odor Insufficient.—The odor of an alcoholic beverage on the breath of the driver is insufficient evidence by itself to prove beyond a reasonable doubt that alcohol was remaining in the driver's body in violation of this section unless the driver was offered an alcohol screening test or chemical analysis and refused to provide all required samples of breath or blood for analysis.

(b2) Alcohol Screening Test.—Notwithstanding any other provision of law, an alcohol screening test may be administered to a driver suspected of violation of subsection (a) of this section, and the results of an alcohol screening test or the driver's refusal to submit may be used by a law enforcement officer, a court, or an administrative agency in determining if alcohol was present in the driver's body. No alcohol screening tests are valid under this section unless the device used is one approved by the Department of Health and Human Services, and the screening test is conducted in accordance with the applicable regulations of the Department as to its manner and use.

(c) Punishment.—Except as otherwise provided in this subsection, a violation of the offense described in subsection (a) of this section is a Class 3 misdemeanor and, notwithstanding G.S. 15A-1340.23, is punishable by a penalty of one hundred dollars ($100.00). A second or subsequent violation of this section is a misdemeanor punishable under G.S. 20-179. This offense is a lesser included offense of impaired driving of a commercial vehicle under G.S. 20-138.2.

(d) Second or Subsequent Conviction Defined.—A conviction for violating this offense is a second or subsequent conviction if at the time of the current offense the person has a previous conviction under this section, and the previous conviction occurred in the seven years immediately preceding the date of the current offense. This definition of second or subsequent conviction also applies to G.S. 20-17(a)(13) and G.S. 20-17.4(a)(6).

Elements

A person guilty of this offense

(1) drives
(2) a commercial motor vehicle
(3) on a highway, street, or public vehicular area
(4) while consuming alcohol or while alcohol remains in his or her body.

Punishment

Class 3 misdemeanor, but apparently the only authorized punishment is a $100 fine. G.S. 20-138.2A(c). Second and subsequent convictions are misdemeanors punishable under G.S. 20-179 in the same manner as "Impaired Driving." G.S. 20-138.2A(c) and 20-179(a). For a discussion of punishment for impaired driving, see "Punishment" under "Impaired Driving," above. A conviction is a second or subsequent conviction if the person has a previous conviction in the seven years preceding the date of the current offense. G.S. 20-138.2A(d).

Notes

Element (1). For the meaning of the term "drives," see the note on Element (1) to "Driving While License Revoked," above.

Element (2). For a discussion of the term "commercial motor vehicle," see the note on Element (2) to "Driving While Commercial Driver's License Disqualified," above. However, this offense excludes a commercial motor vehicle defined in G.S. 20-4.01(3d)c. G.S. 20-138.2A(a). That provision identifies a Class C motor vehicle as a motor vehicle that is designed to transport sixteen or more passengers, including the driver, or that is transporting hazardous materials and is required to be placarded in accordance with 49 C.F.R. Part 172, Subpart F.

Element (3). For a discussion of the terms "street," "highway," and "public vehicular area," see the notes on Element (3) to "Driving While License Revoked" and "Impaired Driving," both above.

Element (4). For a definition of the term "alcohol," see the note on Element (4)(b) to "Impaired Driving," above. The result of an alcohol screening test (or the driver's refusal to submit to such a test) may be used to prove this element if the test complies with statutory requirements. G.S. 20-138.2A(b2). The odor of an alcoholic beverage on the driver's breath is insufficient by itself to prove that alcohol was remaining in the driver's body, unless the driver was offered an alcohol screening test or chemical analysis and refused to provide the appropriate samples. G.S. 20-138.2A(b1).

Charging issues. See this note to "Driving While License Revoked," above.

Greater and lesser-included offenses. This offense is a lesser-included offense of "Impaired Driving in a Commercial Vehicle," above. G.S. 20-138.2A(c).

License revocations and disqualifications. See this note to "Driving While License Revoked," above.

Related Offenses Not in This Chapter

See the offenses listed under "Impaired Driving," above.

Operating a School Bus, School Activity Bus, or Child Care Vehicle after Consuming Alcohol

Statute

§20-138.2B. Operating a school bus, school activity bus, or child care vehicle after consuming alcohol.

(a) Offense.—A person commits the offense of operating a school bus, school activity bus, or child care vehicle after consuming alcohol if the person drives a school bus, school activity bus, or child care vehicle upon any highway, any street, or any public vehicular area within the State while consuming alcohol or while alcohol remains in the person's body.

(b) Implied-Consent Offense.—An offense under this section is an implied-consent offense subject to the provisions of G.S. 20-16.2. The provisions of G.S. 20-139.1 shall apply to an offense committed under this section.

(b1) Odor Insufficient.—The odor of an alcoholic beverage on the breath of the driver is insufficient evidence by itself to prove beyond a reasonable doubt that alcohol was remaining in the driver's body in violation of this section unless the driver was offered an alcohol screening test or chemical analysis and refused to provide all required samples of breath or blood for analysis.

(b2) Alcohol Screening Test.—Notwithstanding any other provision of law, an alcohol screening test may be administered to a driver suspected of violation of subsection (a) of this section, and the results of an alcohol screening test or the driver's refusal to submit may be used by a law enforcement officer, a court, or an administrative agency in determining if alcohol was present in the driver's body. No alcohol screening tests are valid under this section unless the device used is one approved by the Department of Health and Human Services, and the screening test is conducted in accordance with the applicable regulations of the Department as to its manner and use.

(c) Punishment.—Except as otherwise provided in this subsection, a violation of the offense described in subsection (a) of this section is a Class 3 misdemeanor and, notwithstanding G.S. 15A-1340.23, is punishable by a penalty of one hundred dollars ($100.00). A second or subsequent violation of this section is a misdemeanor punishable under G.S. 20-179. This offense is a lesser included offense of impaired driving of a commercial vehicle under G.S. 20-138.1.

(d) Second or Subsequent Conviction Defined.—A conviction for violating this offense is a second or subsequent conviction if at the time of the current offense the person has a previous conviction under this section, and the previous conviction occurred in the seven years immediately preceding the date of the current offense. This definition of second or subsequent conviction also applies to G.S. 20-19(c2).

Elements

A person guilty of this offense

(1) drives
(2) a school bus, school activity bus, or child care vehicle
(3) on a street, highway, or public vehicular area
(4) while consuming alcohol or while alcohol remains in his or her body.

Punishment

Class 3 misdemeanor, but the only authorized punishment is a $100 fine. G.S. 20-138.2B(c). Second and subsequent convictions are misdemeanors punishable under G.S. 20-179 in the same manner as "Impaired Driving" convictions. G.S. 20-138.2B(c). For a discussion of sentencing for impaired driving offenses, see "Punishment" under "Impaired Driving," above. A conviction is a second or subsequent conviction if the person has a previous conviction in the seven years preceding the current offense. G.S. 20-138.2B(d).

Notes

Element (1). For a discussion of the term "drives," see the note on Element (1) to "Driving While License Revoked," above.

Element (2). A "school bus" is a vehicle with a primary purpose of transporting students over an established route to and from a public, private, or parochial school for the regularly scheduled school day. G.S. 20-4.01(27)(d4).

A "school activity bus" is a vehicle with a primary purpose of transporting public, private, or parochial students and others to or from a place for participation in an event other than regular classroom work. G.S. 20-4.01(27)(d3).

A "child care vehicle" is a vehicle under the direction and control of a child care facility, as defined in G.S. 110-86(3), and driven by an owner, employee, or agent of the facility for the primary purpose of transporting children to and from the facility or to and from an event or activity in connection with the facility. G.S. 20-4.01(27)(c1).

Element (3). For an explanation of the terms "street," "highway," and "public vehicular area", see the notes on Element (3) to "Driving While License Revoked" and "Impaired Driving," both above.

Element (4). For a definition of the term "alcohol," see the note on Element (4)(b) to "Impaired Driving," above. The result of an alcohol screening test (or the driver's refusal to submit to such a test) may be used to prove this element if the test complies with statutory requirements. G.S. 20-138.2B(b2). The odor of an alcoholic beverage on the driver's breath is insufficient by itself to prove that alcohol was remaining in the driver's body, unless the driver was offered an alcohol screening test or chemical analysis and refused to provide the appropriate samples. G.S. 20-138.2B(b1).

Greater and lesser-included offenses. G.S. 20-138.2B(c) provides that "[t]his offense is a lesser included offense of impaired driving of a commercial vehicle under G.S. 20-138.1." This provision is somewhat confusing because G.S. 20-138.1 proscribes the offense of impaired driving, while G.S. 20-138.2 proscribes the offense of impaired driving in a commercial vehicle.

License revocations and disqualification. See this note to "Driving While License Revoked," above.

Related Offenses Not in This Chapter

See the offenses listed under "Impaired Driving," above.

Habitual Impaired Driving

Statute

§20-138.5. Habitual impaired driving.

(a) A person commits the offense of habitual impaired driving if he drives while impaired as defined in G.S. 20-138.1 and has been convicted of three or more offenses involving impaired driving as defined in G.S. 20-4.01(24a) within ten years of the date of this offense.

(b) A person convicted of violating this section shall be punished as a Class F felon and shall be sentenced to a minimum active term of not less than 12 months of imprisonment, which shall not be suspended. Sentences imposed under this subsection shall run consecutively with and shall commence at the expiration of any sentence being served.

(c) An offense under this section is an implied consent offense subject to the provisions of G.S. 20-16.2. The provisions of G.S. 20-139.1 shall apply to an offense committed under this section.

(d) A person convicted under this section shall have his license permanently revoked.

(e) If a person is convicted under this section, the motor vehicle that was driven by the defendant at the time the defendant committed the offense of impaired driving becomes property subject to forfeiture in accordance with the procedure set out in G.S. 20-28.2. In applying the procedure set out in that statute, an owner or a holder of a security interest is considered an innocent party with respect to a motor vehicle subject to forfeiture under this subsection if any of the following applies:

(1) The owner or holder of the security interest did not know and had no reason to know that the defendant had been convicted within the previous seven years of three or more offenses involving impaired driving.

(2) The defendant drove the motor vehicle without the consent of the owner or the holder of the security interest.

Elements

A person guilty of this offense

(1) drives
(2) a vehicle
(3) on a street, highway, or public vehicular area
(4) (a) while under the influence of an impairing substance,
    (b) after consuming a sufficient quantity of alcohol so that the person has an alcohol concentration of 0.08 or more at any relevant time after the driving, *or*
    (c) with any amount of a Schedule I controlled substance or its metabolites in his or her blood or urine *and*
(5) within ten years of the date of this offense, the person has had convictions of three or more offenses involving impaired driving.

Punishment

Class F felony. G.S. 20-138.5(b). A minimum sentence of twelve months imprisonment must be imposed, which may not be suspended. *Id.* This latter provision overrides the Structured Sentencing Act, which sometimes allows a suspended sentence for a Class F felony. The sentence must commence at the expiration of any sentence being served. *Id.*

Notes

Generally. This offense is the same as "Impaired Driving," above, except that this offense has an additional element—Element (5). Thus, the notes on Elements (1) through (4) to "Impaired Driving" apply here as well.

Element (5). G.S. 20-4.01(24a) defines offenses involving impaired driving as including

- impaired driving;
- habitual impaired driving;
- impaired driving in commercial vehicle;
- death or serious injury by vehicle under G.S. 20-141.4 based on impaired driving;
- first- or second-degree murder under G.S. 14-17 based on impaired driving;
- involuntary manslaughter under G.S. 14-18 based on impaired driving;
- a repealed or superseded offense substantially similar to impaired driving; and
- substantially similar offenses committed in another state or jurisdiction.

The statute does not specify whether or not the prior convictions must have occurred before the present offense. There is, however, some support for the argument that such a timing rule applies. State v. Bradley, 181 N.C. App. 557, 559 (2007) ("[t]he habitual impaired driving statute is intended to provide an increased sentence for someone convicted of a fourth impaired driving offense, with the previous three offenses occurring within seven years of the fourth offense"; note that this case construed an earlier version of the statute that had a seven-year look-back period); State v. Vardiman, 146 N.C. App. 381, 385 (2001) ("[p]rior convictions of driving while impaired are the elements of the offense of habitual impaired driving, but the statute 'does not impose punishment for [these] previous crimes, [it] imposes an enhanced punishment' for the latest offense") (internal citation omitted); State v. Smith, 139 N.C. App. 209, 213 (2000) ("[b]oth the habitual misdemeanor assault statute and the habitual impaired driving statute declare that a person 'commits the offense' if that person currently commits specified acts and has been convicted of a specified number of similar offenses in the past").

The impaired driving convictions within ten years do not need to occur consecutive to each other as under the habitual felon statute, G.S. 14-7.1; thus, convictions that occurred on the same date can be used, State v. Baldwin, 117 N.C. App. 713 (1995). Also, two impaired driving convictions consolidated for judgment count as two convictions for habitual impaired driving. State v. Allen, 164 N.C. App. 665 (2004).

Constitutionality. The habitual impaired driving statute does not violate double jeopardy, even when prior convictions used to support one habitual impaired driving conviction later are used to support a second such conviction. *Vardiman*, 146 N.C. App. 381; State v. Johnson, 187 N.C. App. 190, 192 (2007). *Blakely v. Washington*, 542 U.S. 296 (2004), does not change this holding. State v. Bradley, 181 N.C. App. 557, 559–60 (2007).

Substantive offense. The habitual impaired driving statute creates a substantive felony offense. State v. Priddy, 115 N.C. App. 547 (1994); State v. Bowden, 177 N.C. App. 718 (2006).

Charging issues. See this note to "Driving While License Revoked," above. For an additional case decided since publication of the bulletin cited in that note, see *State v. White*, ___ N.C. App. ___, 689 S.E.2d 595, 596–99 (2010) (the trial court did not err by allowing the State to amend a habitual impaired driving indictment that mistakenly alleged the old seven-year look-back period instead of the current ten-year look-back; all of the prior convictions alleged in the indictment fell within the ten-year period; the language regarding the seven-year look-back was surplusage).

License revocations and disqualifications. See this note to "Driving While License Revoked," above.

Related Offenses Not in This Chapter

See the offenses listed under "Impaired Driving," above.

Driving by a Person under 21 after Consuming Alcohol or Drugs

Statute

§20-138.3. Driving by person less than 21 years old after consuming alcohol or drugs.

(a) Offense.—It is unlawful for a person less than 21 years old to drive a motor vehicle on a highway or public vehicular area while consuming alcohol or at any time while he has remaining in his body any alcohol or controlled substance previously consumed, but a person less than 21 years old does not violate this section if he drives with a controlled substance in his body which was lawfully obtained and taken in therapeutically appropriate amounts.

(b) Subject to Implied-Consent Law.—An offense under this section is an alcohol-related offense subject to the implied-consent provisions of G.S. 20-16.2.

(b1) Odor Insufficient.—The odor of an alcoholic beverage on the breath of the driver is insufficient evidence by itself to prove beyond a reasonable doubt that alcohol was remaining in the driver's body in violation of this section unless the driver was offered an alcohol screening test or chemical analysis and refused to provide all required samples of breath or blood for analysis.

(b2) Alcohol Screening Test.—Notwithstanding any other provision of law, an alcohol screening test may be administered to a driver suspected of violation of subsection (a) of this section, and the results of an alcohol screening test or the driver's refusal to submit may be used by a law enforcement officer, a court, or an administrative agency in determining if alcohol was present in the driver's body. No alcohol screening tests are valid under this section unless the device used is one approved by the Department of Health and Human Services, and the screening test is conducted in accordance with the applicable regulations of the Department as to its manner and use.

(c) Punishment; Effect When Impaired Driving Offense Also Charged.—The offense in this section is a Class 2 misdemeanor. It is not, in any circumstances, a lesser included offense of impaired driving under G.S. 20-138.1, but if a person is convicted under this section and of an offense involving impaired driving arising out of the same transaction, the aggregate punishment imposed by the court may not exceed the maximum applicable to the offense involving impaired driving, and any minimum punishment applicable shall be imposed.

(d) Limited Driving Privilege.—A person who is convicted of violating subsection (a) of this section and whose drivers license is revoked solely based on that conviction may apply for a limited driving privilege as provided in G.S. 20-179.3. This subsection shall apply only if the person meets both of the following requirements:

(1) Is 18, 19, or 20 years old on the date of the offense.
(2) Has not previously been convicted of a violation of this section.

The judge may issue the limited driving privilege only if the person meets the eligibility requirements of G.S. 20-179.3, other than the requirement in G.S. 20-179.3(b)(1)c. G.S. 20-179.3(e) shall not apply. All other terms, conditions, and restrictions provided for in G.S. 20-179.3 shall apply. G.S. 20-179.3, rather than this subsection, governs the issuance of a limited driving privilege to a person who is convicted of violating subsection (a) of this section and of driving while impaired as a result of the same transaction.

Elements

A person guilty of this offense

(1) is less than 21 years old *and*
(2) drives
(3) a motor vehicle
(4) on a highway or public vehicular area
(5) (a) while the person is consuming alcohol,
(b) while the person has remaining in his or her body any alcohol, *or*
(c) while the person has remaining in his or her body any controlled substance.

Punishment

Class 2 misdemeanor. G.S. 20-138.3(c).

Notes

Element (1). This element requires proof of the defendant's age at the time of the offense; his or her age when the trial takes place is irrelevant.

Element (2). For a discussion of the term "drives," see the note on Element (1) to "Driving While License Revoked," above.

Element (3). For a discussion of the term "motor vehicle," see the note on Element (2) to "Driving While License Revoked," above.

Element (4). For a discussion of the terms "highway" and "public vehicular area," see the notes on Element (3) to "Driving While License Revoked" and "Impaired Driving," both above.

Element (5). For a definition of the term "alcohol," see the note on Element (4)(b) to "Impaired Driving," above. Any amount of alcohol satisfies this element. The result of an alcohol screening test (or the driver's refusal to submit to such a test) may be used to prove whether alcohol was present in the driver's body if the test is conducted in compliance with statutory requirements. G.S. 20-138.3(b2). The odor of an alcoholic beverage on the driver's breath is insufficient by itself to prove that alcohol was remaining in the driver's body, unless the driver was offered an alcohol screening test or chemical analysis and refused to provide the appropriate samples. G.S. 20-138.3(b1).

Exceptions. This offense does not apply to a person who drives with a controlled substance in his or her body if the controlled substance was lawfully obtained and taken in therapeutically appropriate amounts. G.S. 20-138.3(a).

Greater and lesser-included offenses. G.S. 20-138.3(c) provides that this offense is not a lesser-included offense of impaired driving under G.S. 20-138.1. However, if a person is convicted of this offense and impaired driving arising out of the same transaction, the total punishment imposed may not exceed the maximum applicable to the impaired driving conviction, and any applicable minimum must be imposed. *Id.*

License revocations and disqualifications. See this note to "Driving While License Revoked," above.

Related Offenses Not in This Chapter

Selling alcohol to underage person. G.S. 18B-302(a).
Giving alcohol to underage person. G.S. 18B-302(a1).
Purchase, possession, or consumption of alcohol by underage person. G.S. 18B-302(b).
Impaired supervision or instruction. G.S. 20-12.1.
Transporting an open container of alcoholic beverage. G.S. 20-138.7.

Serious Injury by a Vehicle

Statute

§20-141.4. Felony and misdemeanor death by vehicle; felony serious injury by vehicle; aggravated offenses; repeat felony death by vehicle.

(a) Repealed by Session Laws 1983, c. 435, s. 27.

Subsections (a1) and (a2) are not reproduced here.

(a3) Felony Serious Injury by Vehicle.—A person commits the offense of felony serious injury by vehicle if:

(1) The person unintentionally causes serious injury to another person,
(2) The person was engaged in the offense of impaired driving under G.S. 20-138.1 or G.S. 20-138.2, and
(3) The commission of the offense in subdivision (2) of this subsection is the proximate cause of the serious injury.

(a4) Aggravated Felony Serious Injury by Vehicle.—A person commits the offense of aggravated felony serious injury by vehicle if:

(1) The person unintentionally causes serious injury to another person,
(2) The person was engaged in the offense of impaired driving under G.S. 20-138.1 or G.S. 20-138.2,
(3) The commission of the offense in subdivision (2) of this subsection is the proximate cause of the serious injury, and
(4) The person has a previous conviction involving impaired driving, as defined in G.S. 20-4.01(24a), within seven years of the date of the offense.

Subsections (a5) and (a6) are not reproduced here.

(b) Punishments.—Unless the conduct is covered under some other provision of law providing greater punishment, the following classifications apply to the offenses set forth in this section:

(1) Aggravated felony death by vehicle is a Class D felony.
(2) Felony death by vehicle is a Class E felony.
(3) Aggravated felony serious injury by vehicle is a Class E felony.
(4) Felony serious injury by vehicle is a Class F felony.
(5) Misdemeanor death by vehicle is a Class 1 misdemeanor.

Subsection (c) is not reproduced here.

Felony Serious Injury by a Vehicle

Statute

See G.S. 20-141.4(a3), reproduced above.

Elements

A person guilty of this offense

(1) unintentionally
(2) causes
(3) serious injury
(4) to another person
(5) while engaged in the offense of
  (a) "Impaired Driving" *or*
  (b) "Impaired Driving in a Commercial Vehicle" *and*
(6) the commission of that offense is the proximate cause of the injury.

Punishment

Class F felony. G.S. 20-141.4(b)(4).

Notes

Element (3). The statute does not define the term "serious injury." For a definition of that term as used in the assault context, see the note on Element (3) to "Assault Inflicting Serious Injury" in Chapter 7 (Assaults).

Element (5)(a). See "Impaired Driving," above.

Element (5)(b). See "Impaired Driving in a Commercial Vehicle," above.

Element (6). The impaired driving offense under G.S. 20-138.1 or G.S. 20-138.2 must be the proximate cause of the injury. G.S. 20-141.4(a3)(3). The evidence was sufficient to establish this element notwithstanding the defendant's argument that his willful action in attempting to elude arrest was the proximate cause of the victim's injuries, not his impaired driving; the court rejected this argument, concluding that even if the defendant's willful attempt to elude arrest was a cause of the injuries, his driving under the influence could also have been a proximate cause. State v. Leonard, ___ N.C. App. ___, 711 S.E.2d 867, 871 (2011). For a discussion of proximate cause generally, see the note entitled "Proximate cause" to "First-Degree Murder" in Chapter 6 (Homicide).

Verdict. See this note to "Impaired Driving," above.

Multiple convictions and punishments. G.S. 20-141.4(b), the punishment provision for the injury by vehicle offenses, provides, in part, that "[u]nless the conduct is covered under some other provision of law providing greater punishment," aggravated felony serious injury by a vehicle is a Class E felony and felony serious injury by a vehicle is a Class F felony. This language means that a defendant may not be punished for a serious injury by vehicle offense if the defendant has been convicted of an offense carrying a greater punishment when both offenses arise from the same conduct. State v. Davis, 364 N.C. 297, 302–05 (2010) (the trial court erred by imposing punishment for felony serious injury by a vehicle, a Class F felony, and assault with a deadly weapon inflicting serious injury, a Class E felony).

License revocations and disqualifications. See this note to "Driving While License Revoked," above.

Related Offenses Not in This Chapter

See death by vehicle (various offenses) in Chapter 6 (Homicide).
"Assault Inflicting Serious Injury" (Chapter 7)
"Assault with a Deadly Weapon" (Chapter 7)

Aggravated Felony Serious Injury by a Vehicle

Statute

See G.S. 20-141.4(a4), reproduced above.

Elements

A person guilty of this offense

(1) unintentionally
(2) causes
(3) serious injury
(4) to another person
(5) while engaged in the offense of
  (a) "Impaired Driving" *or*
  (b) "Impaired Driving in a Commercial Vehicle" *and*
(6) the commission of that offense is the proximate cause of the injury *and*
(7) within seven years of the present offense, the person has a previous conviction involving impaired driving.

Punishment

Class E felony. G.S. 20-141.4(b)(3).

Notes

Generally. This offense is the same as "Felony Serious Injury by a Vehicle," above, except that this offense has an additional element—Element (7)—involving the prior conviction. Thus, the relevant notes to that offense apply here as well.

Element (7). See the note on Element (5) to "Habitual Impaired Driving," above, but note that for this offense there is a seven-year "look back" period.

Related Offenses Not in This Chapter

See the offenses listed under "Felony Serious Injury by a Vehicle," above.

Aggressive Driving

Statute

§20-141.6. Aggressive Driving.

(a) Any person who operates a motor vehicle on a street, highway, or public vehicular area is guilty of aggressive driving if the person:

(1) Violates either G.S. 20-141 or G.S. 20-141.1, and
(2) Drives carelessly and heedlessly in willful or wanton disregard of the rights or safety of others.

(b) For the purposes of this section only, in order to prove a violation of subsection (a)(2), the State must show that the person committed two or more of the below specified offenses while in violation of subsection (a)(1):

(1) Running through a red light in violation of G.S. 20-158(b)(2) or (b)(3), or G.S. 20-158(c)(2) or (c)(3).
(2) Running through a stop sign in violation of G.S. 20-158(b)(1) or (c)(1).
(3) Illegal passing in violation of G.S. 20-149 or G.S. 20-150.
(4) Failing to yield right-of-way in violation of G.S. 20-155, 20-156, 20-158(b)(4) or (c)(4) or 20-158.1.
(5) Following too closely in violation of G.S. 20-152.

(c) A person convicted of aggressive driving is guilty of a Class 1 misdemeanor.

(d) The offense of reckless driving under G.S. 20-140 is a lesser-included offense of the offense set forth in this section.

Elements

A person guilty of this offense

(1) operates
(2) a motor vehicle
(3) on a street, highway, or public vehicular area *and*
(4) speeds in violation of G.S. 20-141 or 20-141.1 *and*
(5) drives carelessly and heedlessly in willful or wanton disregard of the rights or safety of others.

Punishment

Class 1 misdemeanor. G.S. 20-141.6(c).

Notes

Element (1). See the note on Element (1) to "Driving While License Revoked," above.

Element (2). See the note on Element (2) to "Driving While License Revoked," above.

Element (3). See the note on Element (3) to "Impaired Driving," above.

Element (4). G.S. 20-141 sets out speed restrictions generally. G.S. 20-141.1 sets out speed limits in school zones.

Element (5). To satisfy this element, the person must have committed at least two of the following offenses while speeding:

- running a red light in violation of G.S. 20-158(b)(2)–(3) or (c)(2)–(3);
- running a stop sign in violation of G.S. 20-158(b)(1) or (c)(1);
- illegal passing in violation of G.S. 20-149 or 20-150;
- failing to yield right-of-way in violation of G.S. 20-155, 20-156, 20-158(b)(4) or (c)(4), or 20-158.1; or
- following too closely in violation of G.S. 20-152.

G.S. 20-141.6(b).

Greater and lesser-included offenses. "Reckless Driving," below, is a lesser-included offense of "Aggressive Driving." G.S. 20-141.6(d).

Related Offenses Not in This Chapter

None

Reckless Driving

Statute

§20-140. Reckless driving.

(a) Any person who drives any vehicle upon a highway or any public vehicular area carelessly or heedlessly in willful or wanton disregard of the rights or safety of others shall be guilty of reckless driving.

(b) Any person who drives any vehicle upon a highway or any public vehicular area without due caution and circumspection and at a speed or in a manner so as to endanger or be likely to endanger any person or property shall be guilty of reckless driving.

(c) Repealed by Session Laws 1983, c. 435, s. 23.

(d) Reckless driving as defined in subsections (a) and (b) is a Class 2 misdemeanor.

(e) Repealed by Session Laws 1983, c. 435, s. 23.

(f) A person is guilty of the Class 2 misdemeanor of reckless driving if the person drives a commercial motor vehicle carrying a load that is subject to the permit requirements of G.S. 20-119 upon a highway or any public vehicular area either:

(1) Carelessly and heedlessly in willful or wanton disregard of the rights or safety of others; or

(2) Without due caution and circumspection and at a speed or in a manner so as to endanger or be likely to endanger any person or property.

Reckless Driving: Carelessly and Heedlessly

Statute

See G.S. 20-140(a), reproduced above.

Elements

A person guilty of this offense

(1) drives
(2) a vehicle
(3) on a highway or public vehicular area
(4) carelessly and heedlessly *and*
(5) in willful or wanton disregard
(6) of the rights and safety of others.

Punishment

Class 2 misdemeanor. G.S. 20-140(d).

Notes

Element (1). For a discussion of the term "drives," see the note on Element (1) to "Driving While License Revoked," above.

Element (2). For a discussion of the term "vehicle," see the note on Element (2) to "Impaired Driving," above.

Element (3). For a discussion of the terms "highway" and "public vehicular area," see the notes on Element (3) to "Driving While License Revoked" and "Impaired Driving," both above.

Elements (4) through (6). In discussing reckless driving, the courts rarely address these elements individually. Instead, the issue is usually whether the defendant committed an act of criminal negligence. For a detailed discussion of that concept, see "Criminal Negligence" in Chapter 1 (States of Mind).

The evidence was sufficient to prove reckless driving when (1) the defendant drove at night on a highway at 70 mph in a 60 mph zone and, in attempting to elude a law enforcement officer, traveled down a dirt road at 45 mph with the vehicle lights off and then skidded to a stop, State v. Lewis, 256 N.C. 430 (1962); (2) the defendant drove 70 mph in a 45 mph zone in a residential area, suddenly applied brakes, came down the road sideways with the car's back end coming across the road, slowed down to 5 mph, and then accelerated and swerved left and right three times, State v. Floyd, 15 N.C. App. 438 (1972); and (3) in a 25 mph zone, the defendant drove his vehicle into the rear of a truck, which was propelled 125 feet by the collision, and a tire mark made by one of the defendant's rear wheels extended back twenty feet from the point of impact, indicating that the vehicle slid on one wheel for that distance, State v. Steelman, 228 N.C. 634 (1948); *see also* State v. Wilson, 218 N.C. 769 (1941) (the evidence was sufficient where witnesses testified that the defendant was driving approximately 60 mph when he struck the rear of another vehicle that was driving approximately 20–25 mph; upon impact the other vehicle turned over then came to rest in a ditch facing in the opposite direction).

The evidence was insufficient to prove reckless driving when the defendant's vehicle was on the left of the center line in the direction in which it was traveling when it collided with another vehicle, but there was no evidence that the defendant's vehicle was being operated at a dangerous speed or in a perilous manner. State v. Dupree, 264 N.C. 463 (1965).

Greater and lesser-included offenses. This offense is a lesser-included offense of "Aggressive Driving," above. G.S. 20-141.6(d).

Multiple convictions and punishments. Although there are two kinds of reckless driving, a person may be convicted of only one for each occasion on which the person drives recklessly, even if his or her behavior meets both descriptions of reckless driving. *Lewis*, 256 N.C. 430.

Related Offenses Not in This Chapter

Reckless driving in a commercial vehicle. G.S. 20-140(f).

Reckless Driving: Endangering Persons or Property

Statute

See G.S. 20-140(b), reproduced above.

Elements

A person guilty of this offense

(1) drives
(2) a vehicle
(3) on a highway or public vehicular area
(4) without due caution and circumspection *and*
(5) at a speed or in a manner
(6) that endangers or is likely to endanger any person or property.

Punishment

Class 2 misdemeanor. G.S. 20-140(d).

Notes

Elements (1) through (3). See the notes on these elements to "Reckless Driving: Carelessly and Heedlessly," above.

Element (5). A person can commit this offense even though he or she does not speed, if he or she drives in a manner that endangers or is likely to endanger others. Primm v. King, 249 N.C. 228 (1958); State v. Mills, 181 N.C. 530 (1921). A person can violate the speeding statute, G.S. 20-141, and not be guilty of reckless driving, State v. Weston, 273 N.C. 275 (1968).

Element (6). This element, unlike Element (5) of "Reckless Driving: Carelessly and Heedlessly," above, does not depend on the driver's intent. Instead, if the driver actually endangers persons or property or is likely to endanger persons or property, the driver can be guilty of this offense, even with innocent intentions.

There was sufficient evidence to support a conviction when (1) the defendant drove a motorcycle over 100 mph in a 45 mph zone, followed an unmarked police car from a distance of two to three feet, attempted to pass on a double yellow line and on the shoulder, crossed a double yellow center line two to three times, and came into contact with the white line two or three times, State v. Teel, 180 N.C. App. 446 (2006); and (2) the defendant was impaired and drove 92 mph in a 45 mph zone, State v. Coffey, 189 N.C. App. 382, 387–88 (2008).

Greater and lesser-included offenses. This offense is a lesser-included offense of "Aggressive Driving," above. G.S. 20-141.6(d).

Multiple convictions and punishments. See this note to "Reckless Driving: Carelessly and Heedlessly," above.

Related Offenses Not in This Chapter

Reckless driving in a commercial vehicle. G.S. 20-140(f).

Racing Offenses

Statute

§20-141.3. Unlawful racing on streets and highways.

(a) It shall be unlawful for any person to operate a motor vehicle on a street or highway willfully in prearranged speed competition with another motor vehicle. Any person violating the provisions of this subsection shall be guilty of a Class 1 misdemeanor.

(b) It shall be unlawful for any person to operate a motor vehicle on a street or highway willfully in speed competition with another motor vehicle. Any person willfully violating the provisions of this subsection shall be guilty of a Class 2 misdemeanor.

Subsections (c) through (g) are not reproduced here.

Willful Racing

Statute

See G.S. 20-141.3(b), reproduced above.

Elements

A person guilty of this offense

(1) operates
(2) a motor vehicle
(3) on a street or highway
(4) willfully
(5) in speed competition with another motor vehicle.

Punishment

Class 2 misdemeanor. G.S. 20-141.3(b).

Notes

Element (1). For an explanation of the term "operates," see the note on Element (1) to "Driving While License Revoked," above.

Element (2). For an explanation of the term "motor vehicle," see the note on Element (2) to "Driving While License Revoked," above.

Element (3). For an explanation of the terms "street" and "highway," see the note on Element (3) to "Driving While License Revoked," above.

Element (4). See "Willfully" in Chapter 1 (States of Mind).

License revocations and disqualifications. See this note to "Driving While License Revoked," above.

Related Offenses Not in This Chapter

Permitting use of a vehicle for prearranged racing. G.S. 20-141.3(c).
Betting on a prearranged race. G.S. 20-141.3(c).

Prearranged Racing

Statute

See G.S. 20-141.3(a), reproduced above.

Elements

A person guilty of this offense

(1) operates
(2) a motor vehicle
(3) on a street or highway
(4) willfully
(5) in prearranged speed competition with another motor vehicle.

Punishment

Class 1 misdemeanor. G.S. 20-141.3(a).

Notes

Elements (1) through (4). See the notes on Elements (1) through (4) to "Willful Racing," above.

Element (5). This offense is different from "Willful Racing," above, only in its requirement that the race be prearranged.

License revocations and disqualifications. See this note to "Driving While License Revoked," above.

Related Offenses Not in This Chapter

See the offenses listed under "Willful Racing," above.

Hit and Run and Related Offenses

Driver's Failure to Stop or Remain at the Scene When Serious Bodily Injury or Death Occurs

Statute

§20-166. Duty to stop in event of a crash; furnishing information or assistance to injured person, etc.; persons assisting exempt from civil liability.

(a) The driver of any vehicle who knows or reasonably should know:

(1) That the vehicle which he or she is operating is involved in a crash; and

(2) That the crash has resulted in serious bodily injury, as defined in G.S. 14-32.4, or death to any person;

shall immediately stop his or her vehicle at the scene of the crash. The driver shall remain with the vehicle at the scene of the crash until a law-enforcement officer completes the investigation of the crash or authorizes the driver to leave and the vehicle to be removed, unless remaining at the scene places the driver or others at significant risk of injury.

Prior to the completion of the investigation of the crash by a law enforcement officer, or the consent of the officer to leave, the driver may not facilitate, allow, or agree to the removal of the vehicle from the scene for any purpose other than to call for a law enforcement officer, to call for medical assistance or medical treatment as set forth in subsection (b) of this section, or to remove oneself or others from significant risk of injury. If the driver does leave for a reason permitted by this subsection, then the driver must return with the vehicle to the accident scene within a reasonable period of time, unless otherwise instructed by a law enforcement officer. A willful violation of this subsection shall be punished as a Class F felony.

(a1) The driver of any vehicle who knows or reasonably should know:

(1) That the vehicle which he or she is operating is involved in a crash; and

(2) That the crash has resulted in injury;

shall immediately stop his or her vehicle at the scene of the crash. The driver shall remain with the vehicle at the scene of the crash until a law enforcement officer completes the investigation of the crash or authorizes the driver to leave and the vehicle to be removed, unless remaining at the scene places the driver or others at significant risk of injury.

Prior to the completion of the investigation of the crash by a law enforcement officer, or the consent of the officer to leave, the driver may not facilitate, allow, or agree to the removal of the vehicle from the scene for any purpose other than to call for a law enforcement officer, to call for medical assistance or medical treatment as set forth in subsection (b) of this section, or to remove oneself or others from significant risk of injury. If the driver does leave for a reason permitted by this subsection, then the driver must return with the vehicle to the crash scene within a reasonable period of time, unless otherwise instructed by a law enforcement officer. A willful violation of this subsection shall be punished as a Class H felony.

(b) In addition to complying with the requirements of subsections (a) and (a1) of this section, the driver as set forth in subsections (a) and (a1) shall give his or her name, address, driver's license number and the license plate number of the vehicle to the person struck or the driver or occupants of any vehicle collided with, provided that the person or persons are physically and mentally capable of receiving such information, and shall render to any person injured in such crash reasonable assistance, including the calling for medical assistance if it is apparent that such assistance is necessary or is requested by the injured person. A violation of this subsection is a Class 1 misdemeanor.

(c) The driver of any vehicle, when the driver knows or reasonably should know that the vehicle which the driver is operating is involved in a crash which results:

(1) Only in damage to property; or

(2) In injury or death to any person, but only if the operator of the vehicle did not know and did not have reason to know of the death or injury;

shall immediately stop the vehicle at the scene of the crash. If the crash is a reportable crash, the driver shall remain with the vehicle at the scene of the crash until a law enforcement officer completes the investigation of the crash or authorizes the driver to leave and the vehicle to be removed, unless remaining at the scene places the driver or others at significant risk of injury.

Prior to the completion of the investigation of the crash by a law enforcement officer, or the consent of the officer to leave, the driver may not facilitate, allow, or agree to the removal of the vehicle from the scene, for any purpose other than to call for a law enforcement officer, to call for medical assistance or medical treatment, or to remove oneself or others from significant risk of injury. If the driver does leave for a reason permitted by this subsection, then the driver must return with the vehicle to the accident scene within a reasonable period of time, unless otherwise instructed by a law enforcement officer. A willful violation of this subsection is a Class 1 misdemeanor.

(c1) In addition to complying with the requirement of subsection (c) of this section, the driver as set forth in subsection (c) shall give his or her name, address, driver's license number and the license plate number of his vehicle to the driver or occupants of any other vehicle involved in the crash or to any person whose property is damaged in the crash. If the damaged property is a parked and unattended vehicle and the name and location of the owner is not known to or readily ascertainable by the driver of the responsible vehicle, the driver shall furnish the information required by this subsection to the nearest available peace officer, or, in the alternative, and provided the driver thereafter within 48 hours fully complies with G.S. 20-166.1(c), shall immediately place a paper-writing containing the information in a conspicuous place upon or in the damaged vehicle. If the damaged property is a guardrail, utility pole, or other fixed object owned by the Department of Transportation, a public utility, or other public service corporation to which report cannot readily be made at the scene, it shall be sufficient if the responsible driver shall furnish the information required to the nearest peace officer or make written report thereof containing the information by U.S. certified mail, return receipt requested, to the North Carolina Division of Motor Vehicles within five days following the collision. A violation of this subsection is a Class 1 misdemeanor.

(c2) Notwithstanding subsections (a), (a1), and (c) of this section, if a crash occurs on a main lane, ramp, shoulder, median, or adjacent area of a highway, each vehicle shall be moved as soon as possible out of the travel lane and onto the shoulder or to a designated accident investigation site to complete the requirements of this section and minimize interference with traffic if all of the following apply:

(1) The crash has not resulted in injury or death to any person or the drivers did not know or have reason to know of any injury or death.

(2) Each vehicle can be normally and safely driven. For purposes of this subsection, a vehicle can be normally and safely driven if it does not require towing and can be operated under its own power and in its usual manner, without additional damage or hazard to the vehicle, other traffic, or the roadway.

(d) Any person who renders first aid or emergency assistance at the scene of a motor vehicle crash on any street or highway to any person injured as a result of the accident, shall not be liable in civil damages for any acts or omissions relating to the services rendered, unless the acts or omissions amount to wanton conduct or intentional wrongdoing.

(e) The Division of Motor Vehicles shall revoke the drivers license of a person convicted of violating subsection (a) or (a1) of this section for a period of one year, unless the court makes a finding that a longer period of revocation is appropriate under the circumstances of the case. If the court makes this finding, the Division of Motor Vehicles shall revoke that person's drivers license for two years. Upon a first conviction only for a violation of subsection (a1) of this section, a trial judge may allow limited driving privileges in the manner set forth in G.S. 20-179.3(b)(2) during any period of time during which the drivers license is revoked.

Elements

A person guilty of this offense

(1) drives
(2) a vehicle that is
(3) involved in a crash,
(4) causing serious bodily injury or death to any person, *and*
(5) the person driving knows or reasonably should know that the vehicle is involved in a crash that has caused serious bodily injury or death to any person *and*
(6) willfully
  (a) fails to immediately stop at the scene of the crash,
  (b) fails to remain with the vehicle at the scene until a law enforcement officer completes an investigation of the crash or authorizes the person to leave and the vehicle to be removed, *or*
  (c) facilitates, allows, or agrees to the removal of the vehicle before the completion of an investigation of the crash by a law enforcement officer or before receiving consent by the officer to leave.

Punishment

Class F felony. G.S. 20-166(a).

Notes

Element (1). For a discussion of the term "drives," see the note on Element (1) to "Driving While License Revoked," above.

Element (2). For a discussion of the term "vehicle," see the note on Element (2) to "Impaired Driving," above.

Element (3). G.S. 20-4.01(4b) defines the term "crash" as "[a]ny event that results in injury or property damage attributable directly to the motion of a motor vehicle or its load." It further provides that "[t]he terms collision, accident, and crash and their cognates are synonymous." G.S. 20-4.01(4b).

Element (4). The statute defines the term "serious bodily injury" by cross-referencing G.S. 14-32.4, G.S. 20-166(a), the provision proscribing the crime of "Assault Inflicting Serious Bodily Injury," discussed in Chapter 7 (Assaults). For a discussion of the meaning of the term "serious bodily injury" as it applies in the assault context, see the note on Element (3) to that offense.

Element (6). See "Willfully" in Chapter 1 (States of Mind).

Exceptions. The statute provides an exception to Element (6)(b) for instances when remaining at the scene places the driver or others at significant risk of injury. G.S. 20-166(a).

The statute provides an exception to Element (6)(c), authorizing a driver to facilitate, allow, or agree to the removal of the vehicle to

- call for a law enforcement officer,
- call for medical assistance or treatment if it is apparent that such assistance is necessary or requested by the injured person, or
- remove him or herself or others from significant risk of injury.

G.S. 20-166(a)–(b). If the driver leaves for one of these reasons, he or she must return to the scene with the vehicle within a reasonable period of time, unless otherwise instructed by a law enforcement officer. G.S. 20-166(a).

Finally, the statute allows a vehicle to be moved out of a main lane, ramp, shoulder, median, or adjacent area of a highway in certain circumstances. G.S. 20-166(c2).

Multiple convictions and punishments. Interpreting an earlier version of the statute, one case held that failure to do any of the three actions listed under Element (6) satisfies that element, but if a person fails to do all three in the same accident, he or she may be convicted of only one offense. State v. Lucas, 58 N.C. App. 141 (1982).

Application to accidents off public highways. This statute is not restricted to public highways. Thus, it covers accidents that occur, for example, on public vehicular areas and private roads. State v. Smith, 264 N.C. 575 (1965). See the note on Element (3) to "Impaired Driving," above, for the definition of the term "public vehicular area."

Fault not relevant. The driver's duties under this statute exist whether or not he or she is at fault in the accident. *Smith*, 264 N.C. 575.

License revocations and disqualifications. See this note to "Driving While License Revoked," above.

Related Offenses Not in This Chapter

See various offenses in Chapter 6 (Homicide).
"Assault with a Deadly Weapon" (Chapter 7)

Driver's Failure to Stop or Remain at the Scene When Injury Occurs

Statute

See G.S. 20-166(a1), reproduced above.

Elements

A person guilty of this offense

(1) drives
(2) a vehicle that is
(3) involved in a crash,
(4) causing injury, *and*
(5) the person driving knows or reasonably should know that the vehicle is involved in a crash that has caused injury *and*
(6) willfully
  (a) fails to immediately stop at the scene of the crash,
  (b) fails to remain with the vehicle at the scene until a law enforcement officer completes an investigation of the crash or authorizes the person to leave and the vehicle to be removed, *or*
  (c) facilitates, allows, or agrees to the removal of the vehicle before the completion of an investigation of the accident by a law enforcement officer or before receiving consent by the officer to leave.

Punishment

Class H felony. G.S. 20-166(a1).

Notes

Generally. This offense is the same as "Driver's Failure to Stop or Remain at the Scene When Serious Bodily Injury or Death Occurs," above, except that for this offense only injury is required; for the previous offense, serious bodily injury or death is required. Thus, the relevant notes to that offense apply here as well.

Element (4). The statute does not define the term "injury."

Related Offenses Not in This Chapter

See the offenses listed under "Driver's Failure to Stop or Remain at the Scene When Serious Bodily Injury or Death Occurs," above.

Driver's Failure to Give Information or Assistance When Injury, Serious Bodily Injury, or Death Occurs

Statute

See G.S. 20-166(b), reproduced under "Failure to Stop or Remain at the Scene When Serious Bodily Injury or Death Occurs," above.

Elements

A person guilty of this offense

(1) drives
(2) a vehicle that is
(3) involved in a crash,
(4) causing injury, serious bodily injury, or death to any person, *and*
(5) the person driving knows or reasonably should know that the vehicle is involved in a crash that has caused injury, serious bodily injury, or death to any person *and*
(6) the person driving fails to
  (a) give his or her name, address, and driver's license and license plate numbers to any person struck or to the driver or occupants of any vehicle collided with *or*
  (b) render reasonable assistance to any person injured in the crash.

Punishment

Class 1 misdemeanor. G.S. 20-166(b).

Notes

Elements (1) through (3). See the notes on these Elements to "Driver's Failure to Stop or Remain at the Scene When Serious Bodily Injury or Death Occurs," above.

Element (4). See the notes on this Element to "Driver's Failure to Stop or Remain at the Scene When Serious Bodily Injury or Death Occurs" and "Driver's Failure to Stop or Remain at the Scene When Injury Occurs," both above.

Element (6)(a). The duty to give information applies only if the person to receive the information is mentally and physically able to receive it. G.S. 20-166(b).

Element (6)(b). The driver must render medical assistance as well as any other type of reasonable assistance. That duty includes calling for medical assistance if it is apparent that such aid is necessary or if the injured party requests it. *Id.*

Application to accidents off public highways. See this note to "Driver's Failure to Stop or Remain at the Scene When Serious Bodily Injury or Death Occurs," above.

Related Offenses Not in This Chapter

See the offenses listed under "Driver's Failure to Stop or Remain at the Scene When Serious Bodily Injury or Death Occurs," above.

Driver's Failure to Stop or Give Information When Injury or Death Is Not Apparent or Only Property Damage Occurs

Statute

See G.S. 20-166(c) and (c1), reproduced under "Driver's Failure to Stop or Remain at the Scene When Serious Bodily Injury or Death Occurs," above.

Elements

A person guilty of this offense

(1) drives
(2) a vehicle that is
(3) involved in a crash, causing
(4) (a) only property damage *or*
  (b) injury or death to any person that is not apparent, *and*
(5) the person driving knows or reasonably should know that the vehicle was involved in a crash *and*
(6) (a) willfully fails to immediately stop at the scene of the crash,
  (b) willfully fails to remain with the vehicle at the scene of a reportable crash until a law enforcement officer completes an investigation or authorizes the driver to leave and the vehicle to be removed,
  (c) willfully facilitates, allows, or agrees to the removal of the vehicle before completion of an investigation by a law enforcement officer or before receiving consent from the officer, *or*
  (d) fails to give his or her name, address, and driver's license and license plate number to the driver or occupant of any other vehicle involved in the crash or to any person whose property is damaged in the crash.

Punishment

Class 1 misdemeanor. G.S. 20-166(c), (c1).

Notes

Elements (1) through (3). See the notes on these elements to "Driver's Failure to Stop or Remain at the Scene When Serious Bodily Injury or Death Occurs," above.

Element (4)(b). The statute speaks in terms of injury or death to any person when the operator of the vehicle did not know and did not have reason to know of the injury or death. G.S. 20-166(c)(2).

Elements (6)(a)–(c) generally. See "Willfully" in Chapter 1 (States of Mind).

Element (6)(b). A "reportable crash" is a crash involving a motor vehicle that results in

- death or injury of a human being,
- total property damage of $1,000 or more, or
- property damage in any amount to a vehicle seized under G.S. 20-28.3 (impaired driving seizures).

G.S. 20-4.01(33b). For the meaning of the term "crash," see the note on Element (3) to "Driver's Failure to Stop or Remain at the Scene When Serious Bodily Injury or Death Occurs," above.

Element (6)(d). If the damaged property is a parked and unattended vehicle and the name and location of the owner is not known or readily ascertainable, the driver has two choices:

- provide the required information to the nearest available officer or
- immediately place a written note containing the information in a conspicuous place on or in the damaged vehicle.

G.S. 20-166(c1). If the driver opts for the second option, he or she must also comply with G.S. 20-166.1(c) (reporting of accidents) within forty-eight hours. *Id.*

If the damaged property is a guardrail, utility pole, or other fixed object owned by the Department of Transportation, a public utility, or other public service corporation to which report cannot readily be made at the scene, the driver again has two options:

- furnish the information required to the nearest officer or
- make a written report containing the information by U.S. certified mail, return receipt requested, to the Department of Motor Vehicles within five days following the collision.

Id.

Exceptions. The statute creates an exception to Element (6)(b) that applies when remaining at the scene places the driver or others at significant risk of injury. G.S. 20-166(c).

The statute creates exceptions to Element (6)(c) authorizing the driver to facilitate, allow, or agree to the removal of the vehicle to

- call a law enforcement officer,
- call for medical assistance or treatment, or
- remove him or herself or others from significant risk of injury.

G.S. 20-166(c). If the driver leaves for one of these authorized reasons, he or she must return the vehicle within a reasonable period of time, unless otherwise instructed by a law enforcement officer. *Id.*

Finally, the statute allows a vehicle to be moved out of a main lane, ramp, shoulder, median, or adjacent area of a highway in certain circumstances. G.S. 20-166(c2).

Related Offenses Not in This Chapter

"Injury to Personal Property" (Chapter 18)

Passenger's Failure to Remain at the Scene or Unauthorized Removal of a Vehicle When Serious Bodily Injury or Death Occurs

Statute

§20-166.2. Duty of passenger to remain at the scene of an accident.

(a) The passenger of any vehicle who knows or reasonably should know that the vehicle in which he or she is a passenger is involved in an accident or collision shall not willfully leave the scene of the accident by acting as the driver of a vehicle involved in the accident until a law enforcement officer completes the investigation of the accident or collision or authorizes the passenger to leave, unless remaining at the scene places the passenger or others at significant risk of injury.

Prior to the completion of the investigation of the accident by a law enforcement officer, or the consent of the officer to leave, the passenger may not facilitate, allow, or agree to the removal of the vehicle from the scene, for any purpose other than to call for a law enforcement officer, to call for medical assistance or medical treatment as set forth in subsection (b) of this section, or to remove oneself or others from a significant risk of injury. If the passenger does leave the scene of an accident by driving a vehicle involved in the accident for a reason permitted by this subsection, the passenger must return with the vehicle to the accident scene within a reasonable period of time, unless otherwise instructed by a law enforcement officer. A willful violation of this subsection is a Class H felony if the accident or collision is described in G.S. 20-166(a). A willful violation of this subsection is a Class 1 misdemeanor if the accident or collision is a reportable accident described in G.S. 20-166(c).

(b) In addition to complying with the requirement of subsection (a) of this section, the passenger shall give the passenger's name, address, drivers license number, and the license plate number of the vehicle in which the passenger was riding, if possible, to the person struck or the driver or occupants of any vehicle collided with, provided that the person or persons are physically and mentally capable of receiving the information, and shall render to any person injured in the accident or collision reasonable assistance, including the calling for medical assistance if it is apparent that such assistance is necessary or is requested by the injured person. A violation of this subsection is a Class 1 misdemeanor.

Elements

A person guilty of this offense

(1) is a passenger
(2) in a vehicle that is
(3) involved in an accident or collision
(4) causing serious bodily injury or death to any person *and*
(5) the passenger knows or reasonably should know that the vehicle is involved in an accident or collision that has caused serious bodily injury or death to any person *and*
(6) willfully
  (a) leaves the scene by acting as the driver of a vehicle involved in the accident before a law enforcement officer completes an investigation or authorizes the passenger to leave *or*
  (b) facilitates, allows, or agrees to the removal of the vehicle before a law enforcement officer completes an investigation or before receiving consent from the officer to leave.

Punishment

Class H felony. G.S. 20-166.2(a).

Notes

Element (2). See the note on Element (2) to "Driver's Failure to Stop or Remain at the Scene When Serious Bodily Injury or Death Occurs," above.

Element (3). Although a 2008 legislative amendment, S.L. 2008-28, changed the term "accident or collision" to "crash" in G.S. 20-166, a parallel change was not made to this statute. However, G.S. 20-4.01(4b) provides that "[t]he terms collision, accident, and crash and their cognates are synonymous." It further defines the term "crash" to mean "[a]ny event that results in injury or property damage attributable directly to the motion of a motor vehicle or its load." G.S. 20-4.01(4b).

Element (6). See "Willfully" in Chapter 1 (States of Mind).

Exceptions. The statute creates an exception to Element (6)(a), authorizing a passenger to leave if remaining at the scene places the passenger or others at significant risk of injury. G.S. 20-166.2(a).

The statute also creates exceptions to Element (6)(b), authorizing the passenger to facilitate, allow, or agree to the removal of the vehicle to

- call for law enforcement,
- call for medical assistance or treatment if it is apparent that such assistance is necessary or is requested by the injured person, or
- remove him or herself or others from significant risk of injury.

G.S. 20-166.2(a) and (b). If the passenger leaves the scene by driving an involved vehicle for any of these authorized purposes, he or she must return within a reasonable period of time, unless otherwise instructed by a law enforcement officer. G.S. 20-166.2(a).

Related Offenses Not in This Chapter

None

Passenger's Failure to Remain at the Scene or Unauthorized Removal of a Vehicle When Serious Bodily Injury or Death Is Not Apparent or Only Property Damage Occurs

Statute

See G.S. 20-166.2(a), reproduced above under "Passenger's Failure to Remain at the Scene or Unauthorized Removal of a Vehicle When Serious Bodily Injury or Death Occurs," above.

Elements

A person guilty of this offense

(1) is a passenger
(2) in a vehicle that is
(3) involved in a reportable accident causing
(4) (a) only property damage *or*
    (b) injury or death that is not apparent *and*
(5) the passenger knows or reasonably should know that the vehicle is involved in an accident or collision *and*
(6) willfully
    (a) leaves the scene by acting as the driver of a vehicle involved in the accident before a law enforcement officer completes an investigation or authorizes the passenger to leave *or*
    (b) facilitates, allows, or agrees to the removal of the vehicle before a law enforcement officer completes an investigation or before receiving consent from the officer.

Punishment

Class 1 misdemeanor. G.S. 20-166.2(a).

Notes

Generally. This offense is the same as "Passenger's Failure to Remain at the Scene or Unauthorized Removal of a Vehicle When Serious Bodily Injury or Death Occurs," above, with the following exceptions:

- the other offense involves an accident that causes serious bodily injury or death to any person, while this offense involves an accident that causes only property damage or injury or death that is not apparent, and
- this offense requires a "reportable accident," while the other offense does not.

Thus, the relevant notes to "Passenger's Failure to Remain at the Scene or Unauthorized Removal of a Vehicle When Serious Bodily Injury or Death Occurs" apply here as well.

Element (3). Although a 2008 legislative amendment, S.L. 2008-128, amended G.S. 20-166 to replace the term "reportable accident" with "reportable crash," a parallel change was not made to this statute. For the meaning of the term "reportable crash," see the note on Element (6)(b) to "Driver's Failure to Stop or Give Information When Injury or Death Is Not Apparent or Only Property Damage Occurs," above. Because the terms "accident" and "crash" are synonymous, G.S. 20-4.01(4b), the same definition would likely apply to this offense.

Related Offenses Not in This Chapter

None

Passenger's Failure to Give Information or Assistance

Statute

See G.S. 20-166.2(b), reproduced under "Passenger's Failure to Remain at the Scene or Unauthorized Removal of a Vehicle When Serious Bodily Injury or Death Occurs," above.

Elements

A person guilty of this offense

(1) is a passenger
(2) in a vehicle that is
(3) involved in an accident or collision *and*
(4) the passenger knows or reasonably should know that the vehicle is involved in an accident or collision *and*
(5) (a) fails to give his or her name, address, driver's license number, and the license plate number of the vehicle in which he or she was riding to the person struck or the driver or occupants of any other vehicle collided with *or*
    (b) fails to provide reasonable assistance to any person injured in the accident or collision.

Punishment

Class 1 misdemeanor. G.S. 20-166.2(b).

Notes

Element (2). See the note on Element (2) to "Driver's Failure to Stop or Remain at the Scene When Serious Bodily Injury or Death Occurs," above.

Element (5)(a). The statute states that the passenger must provide the information "if possible" and if the other person or persons are physically and mentally capable of receiving the information. G.S. 20-166.2(b).

Element (5)(b). Reasonable assistance includes calling for medical assistance if it is apparent that such assistance is necessary or requested by the injured person. G.S. 20-166(b).

Related Offenses Not in This Chapter

None

Failure to Notify Authorities

Statute

§20-166.1. Reports and investigations required in event of accident.

(a) Notice of Accident.—The driver of a vehicle involved in a reportable accident must immediately, by the quickest means of communication, notify the appropriate law enforcement agency of the accident. If the accident occurred in a city or town, the appropriate agency is the police department of the city or town. If the accident occurred outside a city or town, the appropriate agency is the State Highway Patrol or the sheriff's office or other qualified rural police of the county where the accident occurred.

(b) Insurance Verification.—When requested to do so by the Division, the driver of a vehicle involved in a reportable accident must furnish proof of financial responsibility.

(c) Parked Vehicle.—The driver of a motor vehicle that collides with another motor vehicle left parked or unattended on a highway of this State must report the collision to the owner of the parked or unattended motor vehicle. This requirement applies to an accident that is not a reportable accident as well as to one that is a reportable accident. The report may be made orally or in writing, must be made within 48 hours of the accident, and must include the following:

(1) The time, date, and place of the accident.
(2) The driver's name, address, and drivers license number.
(3) The registration plate number of the vehicle being operated by the driver at the time of the accident.

If the driver makes a written report to the owner of the parked or unattended vehicle and the report is not given to the owner at the scene of the accident, the report must be sent to the owner by certified mail, return receipt requested, and a copy of the report must be sent to the Division.

(d) Repealed by Session Laws 1995, c. 191, s. 2.

Subsections (e) through (j) are not reproduced here.

(k) Punishment.—A violation of any provision of this section is a misdemeanor of the Class set in G.S. 20-176.

Elements

A person guilty of this offense

(1) drives
(2) a vehicle that is
(3) involved in a reportable accident *and*
(4) fails to immediately notify the appropriate law enforcement agency
(5) by the quickest means of communication.

Punishment

Class 2 misdemeanor. G.S. 20-166.1(k) and 20-176.

Notes

Element (1). For an explanation of the term "drives," see the note on Element (1) to "Driving While License Revoked," above.

Element (2). For an explanation of the term "vehicle," see the note on Element (2) to "Impaired Driving," above.

Element (3). See the note on Element (3) to "Passenger's Failure to Remain at the Scene or Unauthorized Removal of Vehicle When Injury or Death Is Not Apparent or Only Property Damage Occurs," above.

Element (4). If the accident or collision occurs within a municipality, the driver must notify the police department. G.S. 20-166.1(a). If it occurs outside a municipality, the State Highway Patrol, the local sheriff, or county police must be notified. *Id.*

Defenses. Although there are no cases on point, it is likely that not knowing that an accident or collision occurred is a defense. *See* State v. Ray, 229 N.C. 40 (1948).

Related Offenses Not in This Chapter

"Injury to Personal Property" (Chapter 18)
Failure to report collision with parked vehicle. G.S. 20-166.1(c).
Providing false information in accident report. G.S. 20-279.31(b).

School Bus Offenses

Statute

§20-217. Motor vehicles to stop for properly marked and designated school buses in certain instances; evidence of identity of driver.

(a) When a school bus is displaying its mechanical stop signal or flashing red lights and the bus is stopped for the purpose of receiving or discharging passengers, the driver of any other vehicle that approaches the school bus from any direction on the same street, highway, or public vehicular area shall bring that other vehicle to a full stop and shall remain stopped. The driver of the other vehicle shall not proceed to move, pass, or attempt to pass the school bus until after the mechanical stop signal has been withdrawn, the flashing red stoplights have been turned off, and the bus has started to move.

(b) For the purpose of this section, a school bus includes a public school bus transporting children or school personnel, a public school bus transporting senior citizens under G.S. 115C-243, or a privately owned bus transporting children. This section applies only in the event the school bus bears upon the front and rear a plainly visible sign containing the words "school bus."

(c) Notwithstanding subsection (a) of this section, the driver of a vehicle traveling in the opposite direction from the school bus, upon any road, highway or city street that has been divided into two roadways, so constructed as to separate vehicular traffic between the two roadways by an intervening space (including a center lane for left turns if the roadway consists of at least four more lanes) or by a physical barrier, need not stop upon meeting and passing any school bus that has stopped in the roadway across the dividing space or physical barrier.

(d) It shall be unlawful for any school bus driver to stop and receive or discharge passengers or for any principal or superintendent of any school, routing a school bus, to authorize the driver of any school bus to stop and receive or discharge passengers upon any roadway described by subsection (c) of this section where passengers would be required to cross the roadway to reach their destination or to board the bus; provided, that passengers may be discharged or received at points where pedestrians and vehicular traffic are controlled by adequate stop-and-go traffic signals.

(e) Except as provided in subsection (g) of this section, any person violating this section shall be guilty of a Class 1 misdemeanor. A person who violates subsection (a) of this section shall not receive a prayer for judgment continued under any circumstances.

(f) Expired.

(g) Any person who willfully violates subsection (a) of this section and strikes any person shall be guilty of a Class I felony. Any person who willfully violates subsection (a) of this section and strikes any person, resulting in the death of that person, shall be guilty of a Class H felony.

(h) Automated camera and video recording systems may be used to detect and prosecute violations of this section. Any photograph or video recorded by a camera or video recording system shall, if consistent with the North Carolina Rules of Evidence, be admissible as evidence in any proceeding alleging a violation of subsection (a) of this section.

Passing or Failing to Stop for a Stopped School Bus

Statute

See G.S. 20-217(a), reproduced above.

Elements

A person guilty of this offense

(1) drives
(2) a vehicle *and*

(3) approaches, from any direction, on the same street, highway, or public vehicular area,
(4) a school bus
(5) that is
  (a) displaying its mechanical stop signal or flashing red lights *and*
  (b) is stopped for the purpose of receiving or discharging passengers *and*
(6) (a) passes or attempts to pass the school bus *or*
  (b) fails to bring the vehicle to a full stop and remain stopped
(7) before the bus's mechanical stop signal has been withdrawn, the flashing red stoplights have been turned off, and the bus has started to move.

Punishment

Class 1 misdemeanor. G.S. 20-217(e). A defendant may not receive a prayer for judgment continued for this offense. *Id.*

Notes

Element (1). For an explanation of the term "drives," see the note on Element (1) to "Driving While License Revoked," above.

Element (2). For an explanation of the term "vehicle," see the note on Element (2) to "Impaired Driving," above.

Element (3). For an explanation of the terms "street," "highway," and "public vehicular area," see the notes on Element (3) to "Driving While License Revoked" and "Impaired Driving," both above. This statute does not apply if the vehicle is on the opposite side of a divided highway. G.S. 20-217(c).

Element (4). A school bus includes a public school bus transporting children or school personnel, a public school bus transporting senior citizens under G.S. 115C-243, or a privately owned bus transporting children. G.S. 20-217(b). Additionally, to qualify for coverage under the statute, the school bus must have plainly visible front and rear signs containing the words "school bus." *Id.*

Element (6). The statute provides that the driver must bring the vehicle to a stop, must remain stopped, and may not proceed to move, pass, or attempt to pass the school bus until the events in Element (7) occur. G.S. 20-217(a).

Related Offenses Not in This Chapter

Improper discharging or receiving of passengers. G.S. 20-217(d).

Felony Passing or Failing to Stop for a School Bus

Statute

See G.S. 20-217(a) and (g), reproduced above.

Elements

A person guilty of this offense

(1) willfully
(2) commits the offense of "Passing or Failing to Stop for a Stopped School Bus" *and*
(3) (a) strikes any person *or*
  (b) strikes any person resulting in that person's death.

Punishment

If Element (3)(a) is present, the offense is a Class I felony. G.S. 20-217(g). If Element (3)(b) is present, the offense is a Class H felony. *Id.* If the Class H felony version is charged, the relevant fact elevating punishment must be alleged in a charging instrument and proved at trial.

Notes

Element (1). See "Willfully" in Chapter 1 (States of Mind).

Element (2). See "Passing or Failing to Stop for a Stopped School Bus," above.

Element (3). The statute does not require that the person struck be entering or leaving the bus.

Evidence issues. G.S. 20-217(h) provides that any photograph or video recorded by a camera or video recording system, if consistent with the rules of evidence, is admissible as evidence in any prosecution of this crime.

Related Offenses Not in This Chapter

See the offenses in Chapter 6 (Homicide).
See the offenses in Chapter 7 (Assaults).

Using a Cell Phone When Operating a School Bus

Statute

§20-137.4. Unlawful use of a mobile phone.

(a) Definitions. – For purposes of this section, the following terms shall mean:

(1) Additional technology. – As defined in G.S. 20-137.3(a)(1).

(2) Emergency situation. – Circumstances such as medical concerns, unsafe road conditions, matters of public safety, or mechanical problems that create a risk of harm for the operator or passengers of a school bus.

(3) Mobile telephone. – As defined in G.S. 20-137.3(a)(2).

(4) School bus. – As defined in G.S. 20-4.01(27)d4. The term also includes any school activity bus as defined in G.S. 20-4.01(27)d3. and any vehicle transporting public, private, or parochial school students for compensation.

(b) Offense. – Except as otherwise provided in this section, no person shall operate a school bus on a public street or highway or public vehicular area while using a mobile telephone or any additional technology associated with a mobile telephone while the school bus is in motion. This prohibition shall not apply to the use of a mobile telephone or additional technology associated with a mobile telephone in a stationary school bus.

(c) Seizure. – The provisions of this section shall not be construed as authorizing the seizure or forfeiture of a mobile telephone or additional technology, unless otherwise provided by law.

(d) Exceptions. – The provisions of subsection (b) of this section shall not apply to the use of a mobile telephone or additional technology associated with a mobile telephone for the sole purpose of communicating in an emergency situation.

(e) Local Ordinances. – No local government may pass any ordinance regulating the use of mobile telephones or additional technology associated with a mobile telephone by operators of school buses.

(f) Penalty. – A violation of this section shall be a Class 2 misdemeanor and shall be punishable by a fine of not less than one hundred dollars ($100.00). No drivers license points or insurance surcharge shall be assessed as a result of a violation of this section. Failure to comply with the provisions of this section shall not constitute negligence per se or contributory negligence by the operator in any action for the recovery of damages arising out of the operation, ownership, or maintenance of a school bus.

Elements

A person guilty of this offense

(1) operates
(2) a school bus
(3) on a public street, highway, or public vehicular area *and*
(4) uses a mobile telephone
(5) while the school bus is in motion.

Punishment

Class 2 misdemeanor, punishable by a fine of not less than $100. G.S. 20-137.4(f).

Notes

Element (1). For a discussion of the term "operates," see the note on Element (1) to "Driving While License Revoked," above.

Element (2). The term "school bus" is defined by cross reference to G.S. 20-4.01(27)(d4), except that it also includes any school activity bus defined in G.S. 20-4.01(27)(d3) and any vehicle transporting public, private, or parochial school students for compensation. G.S. 20-137.4(a)(4).

Element (3). For a discussion of the terms "street," "highway," or "public vehicular area," see the notes on Element (3) to "Driving While License Revoked" and "Impaired Driving," both above.

Element (4). The term "mobile telephone" is defined in G.S. 20-137.3(a)(2). The statute also covers use of "any additional technology associated with a mobile phone." G.S. 20-137.4(b). The term "additional technology" is defined by cross-reference to G.S. 20-137.3(a)(1). G.S. 20-137.4(a)(1).

Element (5). The offense does not apply if the bus is stationary. G.S. 20-137.4(b).

Exceptions. G.S. 20-137.4(d) provides that the offense does not apply to the use of a mobile telephone or additional technology associated with a mobile telephone for the sole purpose of communicating in an emergency situation. "Emergency situation" is defined in G.S. 20-137.4(a)(2), reproduced above.

Related Offenses Not in This Chapter

None

Texting While Operating a School Bus

Statute

§20-137.4A. Unlawful use of mobile telephone for text messaging or electronic mail.

(a) Offense. – It shall be unlawful for any person to operate a vehicle on a public street or highway or public vehicular area while using a mobile telephone to:

(1) Manually enter multiple letters or text in the device as a means of communicating with another person; or
(2) Read any electronic mail or text message transmitted to the device or stored within the device, provided that this prohibition shall not apply to any name or number stored in the device nor to any caller identification information.

(b) Exceptions. – The provisions of this section shall not apply to:

(1) The operator of a vehicle that is lawfully parked or stopped.
(2) Any of the following while in the performance of their official duties: a law enforcement officer; a member of a fire department; or the operator of a public or private ambulance.

(3) The use of factory-installed or aftermarket global positioning systems (GPS) or wireless communications devices used to transmit or receive data as part of a digital dispatch system.

(4) The use of voice operated technology.

(c) Penalty. – A violation of this section while operating a school bus, as defined in G.S. 20-137.4(a)(4), shall be a Class 2 misdemeanor and shall be punishable by a fine of not less than one hundred dollars ($100.00). Any other violation of this section shall be an infraction and shall be punishable by a fine of one hundred dollars ($100.00) and the costs of court.

No drivers license points or insurance surcharge shall be assessed as a result of a violation of this section. Failure to comply with the provisions of this section shall not constitute negligence per se or contributory negligence per se by the operator in any action for the recovery of damages arising out of the operation, ownership, or maintenance of a vehicle.

Elements

A person guilty of this offense

(1) operates
(2) a school bus
(3) on a public street, highway, or public vehicular area
(4) while using a mobile telephone to
(5) (a) manually enter multiple letters or text in the device as a means of communicating with another person *or*
  (b) read any electronic mail or text message transmitted to the device or stored within the device.

Punishment.

Class 2 misdemeanor punishable by a fine of not less than one hundred dollars. G.S. 20-137.4A(c).

Notes

Element (1). For a discussion of the term "operates," see the note on Element (1) to "Driving While License Revoked," above.

Element (2). The term "school bus" is defined by cross-reference to G.S. 20-137.4(a)(4). G.S. 20-137.4A(c). For a discussion of that provision, see the note on Element (2) to "Use of Cell Phone When Operating a School Bus," above.

Element (3). For a discussion of the terms "street," "highway," and "public vehicular area," see the notes on Element (3) to "Driving While License Revoked" and "Impaired Driving," both above.

Exceptions. The statute provides that the prohibition on reading any electronic mail or text message transmitted to the device or stored within the device does not apply to any name or number stored in the device nor to any caller identification information. G.S. 20-137.4A(a)(2). G.S. 20-137.4A(b) further provides that the offense does not apply to

- the operator of a vehicle that is lawfully parked or stopped;
- a law enforcement officer, member of a fire department, or operator of a public or private ambulance while in the performance of official duties;
- the use of factory-installed or aftermarket global positioning systems or wireless communications devices used to transmit or receive data as part of a digital dispatch system; or
- the use of voice operated technology.

Related infraction. If a vehicle other than a school bus is involved, violation of the statute is an infraction. G.S. 20-137.4A(c). If a person under the age of 18 engages in this conduct while using a mobile telephone or any additional technology associated with a mobile telephone while the vehicle is in motion, it is an infraction under G.S. 20-137.3.

Related Offenses Not in This Chapter

None

Failure to Stop, Move Over, or Slow Down for an Emergency Vehicle

Statute

§20-157. Approach of law enforcement, fire department or rescue squad vehicles or ambulances; driving over fire hose or blocking fire-fighting equipment; parking, etc., near law enforcement, fire department, or rescue squad vehicle or ambulance.

(a) Upon the approach of any law enforcement or fire department vehicle or public or private ambulance or rescue squad emergency service vehicle giving warning signal by appropriate light and by audible bell, siren or exhaust whistle, audible under normal conditions from a distance not less than 1000 feet, the driver of every other vehicle shall immediately drive the same to a position as near as possible and parallel to the right-hand edge or curb, clear of any intersection of streets or highways, and shall stop and remain in such position unless otherwise directed by a law enforcement or traffic officer until law enforcement or fire department vehicle or public or private ambulance or rescue squad emergency service vehicle shall have passed. Provided, however, this subsection shall not apply to vehicles traveling in the opposite direction of the vehicles herein enumerated when traveling on a four-lane limited access highway with a median divider dividing the highway for vehicles traveling in opposite directions, and provided further that the violation of this subsection shall be negligence per se. Violation of this subsection is a Class 2 misdemeanor.

(b) It shall be unlawful for the driver of any vehicle other than one on official business to follow any fire apparatus traveling in response to a fire alarm closer than one block or to drive into or park such vehicle within one block where fire apparatus has stopped in answer to a fire alarm.

(c) Outside of the corporate limits of any city or town it shall be unlawful for the driver of any vehicle other than one on official business to follow any fire apparatus traveling in response to a fire alarm closer than 400 feet or to drive into or park such vehicle within a space of 400 feet from where fire apparatus has stopped in answer to a fire alarm.

(d) It shall be unlawful to drive a motor vehicle over a fire hose or any other equipment that is being used at a fire at any time, or to block a fire-fighting apparatus or any other equipment from its source of supply regardless of its distance from the fire.

(e) It shall be unlawful for the driver of a vehicle, other than one on official business, to park and leave standing such vehicle within 100 feet of law enforcement or fire department vehicles, public or private ambulances, or rescue squad emergency service vehicles which are engaged in the investigation of an accident or engaged in rendering assistance to victims of such accident.

(f) When an authorized emergency vehicle as described in subsection (a) of this section or any public service vehicle is parked or standing within 12 feet of a roadway and is giving a warning signal by appropriate light, the driver of every other approaching vehicle shall, as soon as it is safe and when not otherwise directed by an individual lawfully directing traffic, do one of the following:

(1) Move the vehicle into a lane that is not the lane nearest the parked or standing authorized emergency vehicle or public service vehicle and continue traveling in that lane until safely clear of the authorized emergency vehicle. This paragraph applies only if the roadway has at least two lanes for traffic

proceeding in the direction of the approaching vehicle and if the approaching vehicle may change lanes safely and without interfering with any vehicular traffic.

(2) Slow the vehicle, maintaining a safe speed for traffic conditions, and operate the vehicle at a reduced speed and be prepared to stop until completely past the authorized emergency vehicle or public service vehicle. This paragraph applies only if the roadway has only one lane for traffic proceeding in the direction of the approaching vehicle or if the approaching vehicle may not change lanes safely and without interfering with any vehicular traffic.

For purposes of this section, "public service vehicle" means a vehicle that is being used to assist motorists or law enforcement officers with wrecked or disabled vehicles, or is a vehicle being used to restore electric utility service due to an unplanned event, and is operating an amber-colored flashing light authorized by G.S. 20-130.2. Violation of this subsection shall be negligence per se.

(g) Except as provided in subsections (a), (h), and (i) of this section, violation of this section shall be an infraction punishable by a fine of two hundred fifty dollars ($250.00).

(h) A person who violates this section and causes damage to property in the immediate area of the authorized emergency vehicle or public service vehicle in excess of five hundred dollars ($500.00), or causes injury to a law enforcement officer, a firefighter, an emergency vehicle operator, an Incident Management Assistance Patrol member, a public service vehicle operator, or any other emergency response person in the immediate area of the authorized emergency vehicle or public service vehicle is guilty of a Class 1 misdemeanor.

(i) A person who violates this section and causes serious injury or death to a law enforcement officer, a firefighter, an emergency vehicle operator, an Incident Management Assistance Patrol member, a public service vehicle operator, or any other emergency response person in the immediate area of the authorized emergency vehicle or public service vehicle is guilty of a Class I felony. The Division may suspend, for up to six months, the drivers license of any person convicted under this subsection. If the Division suspends a person's license under this subsection, a judge may allow the licensee a limited driving privilege for a period not to exceed the period of suspension, provided the person's license has not also been revoked or suspended under any other provision of law. The limited driving privilege shall be issued in the same manner and under the terms and conditions prescribed in G.S. 20-16.1(b).

Failure to Stop for an Emergency Vehicle

Statute

See G.S. 20-157(a), reproduced above.

Elements

A person guilty of this offense

(1) drives
(2) a vehicle *and*,
(3) upon the approach of a law enforcement or fire department vehicle, ambulance, or rescue squad vehicle
(4) that is giving a warning signal by appropriate light and bell, siren, or exhaust whistle that is audible under normal conditions from a distance of not less than 1,000 feet,
(5) (a) fails to immediately drive his or her vehicle to the right-hand edge or curb and stop *or*
    (b) fails to remain stopped until the emergency vehicle has passed or until otherwise directed by a law enforcement or traffic officer.

Punishment

Class 2 misdemeanor. G.S. 20-157(a).

Notes

Element (1). For a discussion of the term "drives," see the note on Element (1) to "Driving While License Revoked," above.

Element (2). For a discussion of the term "vehicle," see the note on Element (2) to "Impaired Driving," above.

Element (5). The driver must drive to a position as near as possible and parallel to the right-hand edge or curb, clear of any intersection of streets or highways. G.S. 20-157(a).

Exceptions. If the emergency vehicle is traveling on a four-lane, limited-access highway with a median dividing the highway, drivers traveling in the opposite direction need not stop. *Id.*

Related Offenses Not in This Chapter

"Resisting, Delaying, or Obstructing an Officer" (Chapter 21)

Aggravated Failure to Stop for an Emergency Vehicle

Statute

See G.S. 20-157(a), (h) and (i), reproduced above.

Elements

A person guilty of this offense

(1) drives
(2) a vehicle *and,*
(3) upon the approach of a law enforcement or fire department vehicle, ambulance, or rescue squad vehicle
(4) that is giving a warning signal by appropriate light and bell, siren, or exhaust whistle,
(5) (a) fails to immediately drive his or her vehicle to the right-hand edge or curb and stop *or*
  (b) fails to remain stopped until the emergency vehicle has passed or until otherwise directed by a law enforcement or traffic officer *and*
(6) (a) causes damage to property in the immediate area of the emergency vehicle or public service vehicle in excess of $500,
  (b) causes injury to a law enforcement officer, a firefighter, an emergency vehicle operator, an Incident Management Assistance Patrol member, a public service vehicle operator, or any other emergency response person in the immediate area of the emergency vehicle or public service vehicle, *or*
  (c) causes serious injury or death to a law enforcement officer, a firefighter, an emergency vehicle operator, an Incident Management Assistance Patrol member, a public service vehicle operator, or any other emergency response person in the immediate area of the emergency vehicle or public service vehicle.

Punishment

A violation involving Element (6)(a) or (6)(b) is a Class 1 misdemeanor. G.S. 20-157(h). A violation involving Element (6)(c) is a Class I felony. G.S. 20-157(i). If the felony version of this offense is charged, the relevant facts elevating punishment must be alleged in a charging instrument and proved at trial.

Notes

Generally. This offense is the same as "Failure to Stop for an Emergency Vehicle," above, except that this offense contains an additional Element (6). Thus, the relevant notes on "Failure to Stop for an Emergency Vehicle" apply to this offense as well.

Element (6). The statute does not define the terms "injury" or "serious injury." For a definition of serious injury in the assault context, see the note on Element (3) to "Assault Inflicting Serious Injury" in Chapter 7 (Assaults).

The term "public service vehicle" means "a vehicle that is being used to assist motorists or law enforcement officers with wrecked or disabled vehicles, or is a vehicle being used to restore electric utility service due to an unplanned event, and is operating an amber-colored flashing light authorized by G.S. 20-130.2." G.S. 20-157(f).

Relation to other offenses. G.S. 20-157 prohibits other acts, such as driving over a fire hose, leaving a vehicle standing within 100 feet of official vehicles engaged in the investigation of an accident or rendering assistance to victims, etc. These acts appear to be infractions unless the factors in Element (6) exist, in which case they would be criminal offenses. G.S. 20-157(g).

License revocations and disqualifications. See this note to "Driving While License Revoked," above.

Related Offenses Not in This Chapter

See the offenses in Chapter 6 (Homicide).
See the offenses in Chapter 7 (Assaults).
"Resisting, Delaying, or Obstructing an Officer" (Chapter 21)

Failure to Move Over or Slow Down for a Stopped Emergency or Public Service Vehicle

Statute

See G.S. 20-157(f), reproduced above.

Elements

A person guilty of this offense

(1) drives
(2) a vehicle *and*
(3) approaches
(4) (a) a law enforcement or fire department vehicle, ambulance, rescue squad vehicle, or public service vehicle
  (b) that is parked or standing within twelve feet of a roadway *and*
  (c) is giving a warning signal by appropriate light *and*
(5) the driver fails to
  (a) move over *or*
  (b) slow down *and*
(6) (a) causes damage to property in the immediate area of the emergency vehicle or public service vehicle in excess of $500,
  (b) causes injury to a law enforcement officer, a firefighter, an emergency vehicle operator, an Incident Management Assistance Patrol member, a public service vehicle operator, or any other emergency response person in the immediate area of the emergency vehicle or public service vehicle, *or*
  (c) causes serious injury or death to a law enforcement officer, a firefighter, an emergency vehicle operator, an Incident Management Assistance Patrol member, a

public service vehicle operator, or any other emergency response person in the immediate area of the emergency vehicle or public service vehicle.

Punishment

A violation involving Element (6)(a) or (6)(b) is a Class 1 misdemeanor. G.S. 20-157(h). A violation involving Element (6)(c) is a Class I felony. G.S. 20-157(i). If the felony version of this offense is charged, the relevant facts elevating punishment must be alleged in a charging instrument and proved at trial.

Notes

Element (1). For an explanation of the term "drives," see the note on Element (1) to "Driving While License Revoked," above.

Element (2). For an explanation of the term "vehicle," see the note on Element (2) to "Impaired Driving," above.

Element (4)(a). For the meaning of the term "public service vehicle," see the note on Element (6) to "Aggravated Failure to Stop for an Emergency Vehicle," above.

Element (5) generally. These actions must be taken as soon as it is safe, unless the driver is otherwise directed by an individual lawfully directing traffic. G.S. 20-157(f).

Element (5)(a). The driver must move his or her vehicle into a lane that is not the lane nearest the parked or standing emergency vehicle and continue traveling in that lane until safely clear of the emergency or public service vehicle. G.S. 20-157(f)(1). This requirement only applies if the roadway has at least two lanes for traffic proceeding in the direction of the approaching vehicle and if the approaching vehicle may change lanes safely and without interfering with any vehicular traffic. *Id.*

Element (5)(b). The statute requires that the driver slow the vehicle, maintaining a safe speed for traffic conditions, and operate the vehicle at a reduced speed until completely past the emergency or public service vehicle. G.S. 20-157(f)(2). This requirement applies only if the roadway has just one lane for traffic proceeding in the direction of the approaching vehicle or if the approaching vehicle may not change lanes safely and without interfering with any vehicular traffic. *Id.*

Element (6). See the note on this Element to "Aggravated Failure to Stop for an Emergency Vehicle," above.

License revocations and disqualifications. See this note to "Driving While License Revoked," above.

Relation to other offenses. See this note to "Aggravated Failure to Stop for an Emergency Vehicle," above.

Related Offenses Not in This Chapter

See the offenses in Chapter 6 (Homicide).
See the offenses in Chapter 7 (Assaults).
"Resisting, Delaying, or Obstructing an Officer" (Chapter 21)

Speeding to Elude Arrest

Statute

§20-141.5. Speeding to elude arrest.

(a) It shall be unlawful for any person to operate a motor vehicle on a street, highway, or public vehicular area while fleeing or attempting to elude a law enforcement officer who is in the lawful performance of his duties. Except as provided in subsection (b) of this section, violation of this section shall be a Class 1 misdemeanor.

(b) If two or more of the following aggravating factors are present at the time the violation occurs, violation of this section shall be a Class H felony.

(1) Speeding in excess of 15 miles per hour over the legal speed limit.
(2) Gross impairment of the person's faculties while driving due to:
a. Consumption of an impairing substance; or
b. A blood alcohol concentration of 0.14 or more within a relevant time after the driving.
(3) Reckless driving as proscribed by G.S. 20-140.
(4) Negligent driving leading to an accident causing:
a. Property damage in excess of one thousand dollars ($1,000); or
b. Personal injury.
(5) Driving when the person's drivers license is revoked.
(6) Driving in excess of the posted speed limit, during the days and hours when the posted limit is in effect, on school property or in an area designated as a school zone pursuant to G.S. 20-141.1, or in a highway work zone as defined in G.S. 20-141(j2).
(7) Passing a stopped school bus as proscribed by G.S. 20-217.
(8) Driving with a child under 12 years of age in the vehicle.

(b1) When a violation of subsection (a) of this section is the proximate cause of the death of any person, the person violating subsection (a) of this section shall be guilty of a Class H felony. When a violation of subsection (b) of this section is the proximate cause of the death of any person, the person violating subsection (b) of this section shall be guilty of a Class E felony.

(c) Whenever evidence is presented in any court or administrative hearing of the fact that a vehicle was operated in violation of this section, it shall be prima facie evidence that the vehicle was operated by the person in whose name the vehicle was registered at the time of the violation, according to the Division's records. If the vehicle is rented, then proof of that rental shall be prima facie evidence that the vehicle was operated by the renter of the vehicle at the time of the violation.

Subsections (d) through (j) are not reproduced here.

Felony Speeding to Elude Arrest

Statute

See G.S. 20-141.5(a) and (b), reproduced above.

Elements

A person guilty of this offense

(1) operates
(2) a motor vehicle
(3) on a street, highway, or public vehicular area
(4) while fleeing or attempting to elude
(5) a law enforcement officer
(6) who is lawfully performing his or her duties *and*

(7) two or more of the following aggravating factors are present when the violation occurs:
   (a) speeding in excess of 15 miles per hour over the legal speed limit;
   (b) gross impairment of the person's faculties while driving due to consumption of an impairing substance or a blood alcohol concentration of 0.14 or more within a relevant time after the driving;
   (c) reckless driving as proscribed by G.S. 20-140;
   (d) negligent driving leading to an accident causing property damage in excess of one thousand dollars ($1,000) or personal injury;
   (e) driving when the person's driver's license is revoked;
   (f) driving in excess of the posted speed limit, during the days and hours when the posted limit is in effect, on school property or in an area designated as a school zone pursuant to G.S. 20-141.1, or in a highway work zone as defined in G.S. 20-141(j2);
   (g) passing a stopped school bus as proscribed by G.S. 20-217; *or*
   (h) driving with a child under the age of 12 in the vehicle.

Punishment

Class H felony. G.S. 20-141.5(b).

Notes

Element (1). For a discussion of the term "operates," see the note on Element (1) to "Driving While License Revoked," above.

Element (2). For a discussion of the term "motor vehicle," see the note on Element (2) to "Driving While License Revoked," above.

Element (3). For a discussion of the terms "street," "highway," and "public vehicular area," see the notes on Element (3) to "Driving While License Revoked" and "Impaired Driving," both above.

Element (4). Although the statutory title of this offense includes the word "speeding," proof of speeding is not necessary to satisfy this element. State v. Stokes, 174 N.C. App. 447 (2005).

Element (5). See the note on Element (3)(a) to "Assault with a Firearm on a Law Enforcement Officer, Probation or Parole Officer, or Detention Facility Employee" in Chapter 7 (Assaults).

Element (6). See the note on Element (4) to "Assault with a Firearm or Other Deadly Weapon on a Governmental Officer or Employee or Company or Campus Police Officer" in Chapter 7 (Assaults).

Element (7)(b). There was sufficient evidence to support the "gross impairment" aggravating factor when the defendant had a strong odor of alcohol about him; his eyes were very red, glazed, and glassy; his speech was "mush mouthed" and very hard to understand; he repeatedly used profanity and told one officer that he was "going to die"; he drove his vehicle one-half mile with a law enforcement officer hanging out of the window; he had to be forcibly removed from the vehicle; and he admitted to consuming six to seven beers and that he was under the influence of alcohol. *Stokes*, 174 N.C. App. 447.

Element (7)(c). See "Reckless Driving," above. There was sufficient evidence that the defendant drove recklessly when an officer testified that he drove 82 mph in a 55 mph zone and that he was weaving around traffic; also a jury could infer from the officer's testimony that the defendant crossed the solid double yellow line. State v. Jackson, ___ N.C. App. ___, 710 S.E.2d 414, 419–20 (2011).

Element (7)(e). See "Driving While License Revoked," above. Although the offense of driving while license revoked under G.S. 20-28 requires that the defendant drive on a highway, driving while license revoked can serve as an aggravating factor for felony speeding to elude arrest even if it occurs on a public vehicular area. State v. Dewalt, ___ N.C. App. ___, 703 S.E.2d 872, 875–76 (2011).

Element (7)(g). See "Passing or Failing to Stop for a Stopped School Bus" and "Felony Passing or Failing to Stop for a School Bus," both above.

Charging issues. See this note to "Driving While License Revoked," above. For an additional case decided since publication of the bulletin cited in that note, see *State v. Leonard*, ___ N.C. App. ___, 711 S.E.2d 867 (2011) (an indictment charging felonious speeding to elude arrest and alleging an aggravating factor of reckless driving was not required to specify the manner in which the defendant drove recklessly).

Evidence issues. G.S. 20-141.5(c) provides that it is prima facie evidence that a person is an operator of a vehicle under the statute when the vehicle was operated by the person in whose name it was registered with the Department of Motor Vehicles at the time of the violation. If the vehicle was rented, then proof of that rental is prima facie evidence that the vehicle was operated by the renter of the vehicle at the time of the violation. G.S. 20-141.5(c).

Defenses. It is a defense to this charge that a defendant did not know that he or she was being chased by a law enforcement officer and was afraid to stop the vehicle because the defendant did not know who was in pursuit. State v. Borland, 21 N.C. App. 559 (1974).

Jury instructions. In a felony speeding to elude case, the trial court did not err by giving an instruction that allowed the jury to convict the defendant if it found at least two of three aggravating factors submitted; the defendant had argued that the trial court should have required the jury to be unanimous as to which aggravating factors it found. State v. Banks, ___ N.C. App. ___, 713 S.E.2d 754 (2011). The trial judge did not commit plain error by failing to define the aggravating factor of reckless driving in felony speeding to elude jury instructions; the defendant had argued that the trial court was obligated to include the statutory definition of reckless driving in G.S. 20-140. *Id.*

License revocations and disqualifications. See this note to "Driving While License Revoked," above.

Related Offenses Not in This Chapter

"Resisting, Delaying, or Obstructing an Officer" (Chapter 21)

Aggravated Felony Speeding to Elude Arrest

Statute

See G.S. 20-141.5(a) through (b1), reproduced above.

Elements

A person guilty of this offense

(1) operates
(2) a motor vehicle
(3) on a street, highway, or public vehicular area
(4) while fleeing or attempting to elude
(5) a law enforcement officer
(6) who is lawfully performing his or her duties *and*

(7) two or more of the following aggravating factors are present when the violation occurs:
   (a) speeding in excess of 15 miles per hour over the legal speed limit;
   (b) gross impairment of the person's faculties while driving due to consumption of an impairing substance or a blood alcohol concentration of 0.14 or more within a relevant time after the driving;
   (c) reckless driving as proscribed by G.S. 20-140;
   (d) negligent driving leading to an accident causing property damage in excess of one thousand dollars ($1,000) or personal injury;
   (e) driving when the person's driver's license is revoked;
   (f) driving in excess of the posted speed limit, during the days and hours when the posted limit is in effect, on school property or in an area designated as a school zone pursuant to G.S. 20-141.1, or in a highway work zone as defined in G.S. 20-141(j2);
   (g) passing a stopped school bus as proscribed by G.S. 20-217; *or*
   (h) driving with a child under the age of 12 in the vehicle *and*

(8) the conduct is the proximate cause of the death of any person.

Punishment

Class E felony. G.S. 20-141.5(b1).

Notes

Generally. This offense is the same as "Felony Speeding to Elude Arrest," above, except that for this offense, the felony speeding to elude arrest must be the proximate cause of death of any person. Thus, the notes to "Felony Speeding to Elude Arrest" apply to this offense as well.

Element (8). See the note on "Proximate cause" to "First-Degree Murder" in Chapter 6 (Homicide).

Related Offenses Not in This Chapter

See death by vehicle (various offenses) in Chapter 6 (Homicide).
"Second-Degree Murder" (Chapter 6)
"Resisting, Delaying, or Obstructing an Officer" (Chapter 21)

Misdemeanor Speeding to Elude Arrest

Statute

See G.S. 20-141.5(a), reproduced above.

Elements

A person guilty of this offense

(1) operates
(2) a motor vehicle
(3) on a street, highway, or public vehicular area
(4) while fleeing or attempting to elude
(5) a law enforcement officer
(6) who is lawfully performing his or her duties.

Punishment

Class 1 misdemeanor. G.S. 20-141.5(a).

Notes

Generally. This offense is the same as “Felony Speeding to Elude Arrest,” above, except that this offense does not require the aggravating factors found in Element (7) of the other offense. Thus, the relevant notes on that offense apply here as well.

Related Offenses Not in This Chapter

“Resisting, Delaying, or Obstructing an Officer” (Chapter 21)

Aggravated Misdemeanor Speeding to Elude Arrest

Statute

See G.S. 20-141.5(a) and (b1), reproduced above.

Elements

A person guilty of this offense

(1) operates
(2) a motor vehicle
(3) on a street, highway, or public vehicular area
(4) while fleeing or attempting to elude
(5) a law enforcement officer
(6) who is lawfully performing his or her duties *and*
(7) the operator’s conduct is the proximate cause of death of any person.

Punishment

Class H felony. G.S. 20-141.5(b1).

Notes

Generally. This offense is the same as “Misdemeanor Speeding to Elude Arrest,” above, except that for this offense, the conduct must be the proximate cause of death of any person. Thus, the notes on that offense apply here as well.

Element (7). See the note on “Proximate cause” to “First-Degree Murder” in Chapter 6 (Homicide).

Related Offenses Not in This Chapter

See the offenses listed under “Death by Vehicle” in Chapter 6 (Homicide).
“Second-Degree Murder” (Chapter 6)
“Resisting, Delaying, or Obstructing an Officer” (Chapter 21)

Indexes

Case Index

[Different cases of the same name have been distinguished by the addition of a parenthetical containing the court and year of decision; same-name cases decided by the same court in the same year are further delineated by the addition of a bracketed citation]

A

B

C

D

E

F

G

H

L

M

N

O

P

R

S

T

U

V

W

Y

Z

Table of Statutes

[References are to page numbers and, where applicable, to footnotes]

NORTH CAROLINA

North Carolina General Statutes

North Carolina Session Laws

Yr.-No. **Page**

North Carolina Administrative Code

Tit./No. **Page**

FEDERAL STATUTES AND REGULATIONS

United States Code

Tit./Sec. **Page**

Code of Federal Regulations

Tit./Sec. **Page**

Subject Index

[References are to page numbers; numbers in italics indicate tables]

B

C

D

E

F

G

H

I

J

K

L

M

N

O

P

R

T